A COMMENTARY ON H

Herodotus, the first and greatest of western prose authors, set out in the late fifth century BC to describe the world as he knew it—its peoples and their achievements, together with the causes and course of the great wars that brought the Greek cities into conflict with the empires of the Near East. Each subsequent generation of historians has sought to use his text and to measure their knowledge of these cultures against his words.

This commentary by leading Western scholars, originally published in Italian under the auspices of the Fondazione Lorenzo Valla, has been fully revised by the original authors and has now been edited for the English-speaking world. It is designed for use alongside the Oxford Classical Text of Herodotus, and will replace the century-old historical commentary of How and Wells (1912) as the most authoritative account of modern scholarship on Herodotus.

Books I–IV cover the history and cultures of Lydia, Egypt, Persia, and the nomads of Scythia and North Africa, in their contacts with the Greeks from mythical times to the start of the fifth century BC; these themes, with many digressions, are woven into an account of the expansion of the Persian Empire and its contacts with the Greeks.

The Late *David Asheri was formerly Professor of Ancient History at The Hebrew University of Jerusalem.*

Alan Lloyd is Emeritus Professor of Ancient History at the University of Wales.

Aldo Corcella is Professor of Classical Philology at the University of Basilicata.

Oswyn Murray is Emeritus Fellow of Balliol College, Oxford.

Alfonso Moreno is Fellow of Magdalen College, Oxford.

Maria Brosius is Reader in Ancient History at the University of Newcastle upon Tyne.

A COMMENTARY ON HERODOTUS

BOOKS I–IV

DAVID ASHERI
ALAN LLOYD
ALDO CORCELLA

Edited by
OSWYN MURRAY
and
ALFONSO MORENO

with a Contribution by
MARIA BROSIUS

Translated by
BARBARA GRAZIOSI, MATTEO ROSSETTI,
CARLOTTA DUS, *and* VANESSA CAZZATO

OXFORD
UNIVERSITY PRESS

OXFORD

UNIVERSITY PRESS

Great Clarendon Street, Oxford OX2 6DP

Oxford University Press is a department of the University of Oxford.
It furthers the University's objective of excellence in research, scholarship,
and education by publishing worldwide in

Oxford New York

Auckland Cape Town Dar es Salaam Hong Kong Karachi
Kuala Lumpur Madrid Melbourne Mexico City Nairobi
New Delhi Shanghai Taipei Toronto

With offices in

Argentina Austria Brazil Chile Czech Republic France Greece
Guatemala Hungary Italy Japan Poland Portugal Singapore
South Korea Switzerland Thailand Turkey Ukraine Vietnam

Oxford is a registered trade mark of Oxford University Press
in the UK and in certain other countries

Published in the United States
by Oxford University Press Inc., New York

This English edition has been translated from the original
Italian publication *Erodoto: Le Storie* å Fondazione Lorenzo Valla

English edition å Oxford University Press 2007

British Library Cataloguing in Publication Data
Data available

Library of Congress Cataloging in Publication Data
Data available

Typeset by SPI Publisher Services, Pondicherry, India
Printed and bound by
CPI Group (UK) Ltd, Croydon, CRO 4YY

ISBN 978–0–19–814956–9 (Hbk)
ISBN 978–0–19–963936–6 (Pbk)

David Asheri
Florence 1. 11. 1925–Jerusalem 3. 2. 2000

Editorial Preface

The idea of publishing in English a revised translation of the great nine-volume Italian Valla commentary on Herodotus was suggested to the Oxford University Press in 1993, when the first four volumes of the original became available; for various reasons work began seriously in 1996. It was decided to follow the principles adopted in the English translation of the Valla *Odyssey* commentary, that is, to produce a two-volume commentary based on the original nine-volume edition (which also contains text, translation, and additional critical material).

It proved impossible to find a single person capable of translating such a complex work, and we decided to produce a first draft of the translation by engaging a team of young graduate and undergraduate students in Classics who were bilingual in Italian and English. The primary responsibilities were as follows: the General Introduction and Book I were prepared by Barbara Graziosi (Corpus Christi College), Book III by Matteo Rossetti (Balliol College), Book IV by Barbara Graziosi, Carlotta Dus (Balliol College), and Vanessa Cazzato (Trinity College, Dublin). The team was overseen and their work was extensively revised by myself and by my colleague and former graduate student, Alfonso Moreno (Balliol and Magdalen Colleges).

The three authors of the different volumes were consulted at all stages. Lloyd independently prepared a new edition of his commentary on Book II. Corcella revised and updated the translation of his commentary on Book IV. Asheri checked and revised his commentary on Book III, and virtually rewrote the General Introduction and his commentary on Book I; he and his partner Dwora Gilula have revised the translation of these two books. Asheri willingly agreed to my suggestion that we should ask Maria Brosius to provide the English translation of the Bisitun inscription, which appears in place of his Italian translation as an appendix to Book III; this is taken with permission from her sourcebook, *The Persian Empire from Cyrus II to Artaxerxes I* (LACTOR 16, 2000), published by the London Association of Classical Teachers: we thank the Association, who hold the copyright.

The result is a new English edition, completely updated to the date of Asheri's death in February 2000. At an early stage the editors took the decision that we should not interfere in any way with the views of the original authors, or seek to add anything to their commentaries; we have, however, rationalized maps and bibliography.

In preparing the commentary we have followed the practice of the English translation of the *Odyssey* commentary referred to above. The text of our lemmata is that of the Oxford Classical Text edition of C. Hude (1906; third edition 1927), which is still that most commonly in use; we have adapted comments on textual problems to take account of the information supplied by

Hude in his *apparatus criticus*. The numeration of chapters and paragraphs is the standard system adopted by Hude. These decisions were made for reasons of convenience, and do not preclude using the commentary with any other of the available modern texts.

We thank Hilary O'Shea of Oxford University Press for her unfailing support, and Jeff New who was responsible for reducing the multi-authored commentary to a coherent copy-edited text. Thanks also go to Kathleen McLaughlin, Jenny Wagstaffe, Dorothy McCarthy, and Maggie Shade who comprised this volume's editorial team, to cartographer Paul Simmons for creating its many detailed maps, and to the Jowett Copyright Trust for making a generous donation towards their cost.

The work of our team is dedicated to the memory of the greatest Herodotus scholar of his generation, who oversaw the whole, and wrote almost half, of the original Italian edition, and who helped the editors at all stages; our only sadness is that we were unable to present him with the English version of the book that will establish his reputation for all time.

Oswyn Murray

Holywell Manor
August 2004

Contents

David Asheri

Oswyn Murray

For fifteen years David Asheri worked on his Herodotus commentaries. He began in 1984; Book I was published in 1988, Book III in 1990. On his death, in 2000, he had revised the English translations of these two books and had finished Books VIII and IX for the Italian edition. He did many other things, but the Herodotus commentary is his greatest achievement, and represents his scholarship at the height of its power: in these last years he became the greatest living Herodotus scholar, though he would have denied such a verdict as likely to bring down the Herodotean thunderbolt of Zeus on those who stand too tall. He had the ideal talents for writing such a commentary—a consistency of purpose and a love of detailed work, an immense knowledge of the scholarly literature, a sense of reality, and a natural modesty and balance of judgement, a variety of approach and a generosity towards the achievements of others; yet he was also decisive and clear in the expression of his opinions. He set the standard for the other authors in the series of commentaries on Herodotus, and himself contributed both the masterly General Introduction and commentaries on four out of the nine books—almost half the work. It is for this reason that we have decided to dedicate to his memory the English edition of the commentary that essentially he created.

David Asheri was born in Florence in 1925; his family was Sephardic and perhaps originally from Spain, but it had been established in Tuscany since before the Napoleonic period; the family name, Bonaventura, is probably an Italian translation of a Hebrew name, such as Ben-Ashur, Meushar, or the like; Asheri is in turn a translation of Bonaventura. David's grandfather, after whom a street is named in Livorno, was a musicologist and a librarian at the Vatican; he was born in 1862, and belonged to the age of assimilation to the secular values of the Risorgimento; he lived to the age of 90. His father returned to a form of 'integral Judaism'; he was a professor of psychology at the university of Florence; there were three boys in the family. Asheri himself described the family as middle class, completely assimilated, and politically anti-fascist. After a Jewish elementary school, David had a normal Italian education for two years at the famous public gymnasium, the Michelangelo. He studied Latin, and Greek literature in translation, but hated history because it was 'presented in a demagogic way'. Though exempt from religious lessons, he was required to study 'cultura fascista' and undertake weapons practice; he also had to belong to a fascist youth movement. In September 1938 the racial laws were passed, and his third year was spent at a gymnasium organized by the Jewish community for the children expelled from the state schools; nevertheless he recalled taking the normal state oral examinations in an atmosphere whose friendliness showed the real opinions of the professors about the racial laws.

His father had lost his post immediately in 1938, and the family decided to emigrate. After a year of investigation, his father was offered a post at the Hebrew University, and the rest of the family left for Palestine from Trieste in September 1939, a few days after the German invasion of Poland and the British and French declarations of war. As David said, 'for our survival I have to thank the Hebrew University'; his aunt was murdered in Auschwitz.

In British Palestine David learned Hebrew and continued his education in a modern religious school; he spent a year in a college of education, since he wanted to become a teacher. The war of independence and a brief sojourn in a kibbutz interrupted his studies until 1952, when he was already 27 years old. He had been interested in mathematics but decided that he was too old to pursue such a career, and chose history as a major, with philosophy and Greek as minor subjects. He began to take an additional seminar in ancient history, which was taught by V. Tcherikover, and after his death by Ch. Wirszubski and A. Fuks. After graduating he found a post in the university library (1954–62) and studied for a doctorate on land distribution in ancient Greece under Fuks, during which period he spent eighteen months in Rome. He completed his doctorate in 1962 and became an assistant in the Classics department at Jerusalem; in 1965 he was given tenure, with the grade of senior lecturer.

Asheri's initial research had centred on the legal and social aspects of land tenure in ancient Greece, and questions of the law of property and inheritance, especially in Athens. He approached agrarian history from this point of view, and became interested in colonization and urbanism as a result of seeing the aerial photographs of planned landscapes from the Black Sea and south Italy. Here he saw the practical implications of equality in colonial urbanism, which led him to a renewed interest in Greek utopian thought.

Then, in the mid sixties, I met a man to whom I owe one of the most important turns in my intellectual development, Arnaldo Momigliano... He came to Israel invited by Wirszubski, who had studied with him when working on his Ph.D. Thanks to Momigliano, with whom I had close ties for more than twenty years, from that time until his death (1964–1987), I became interested in historiography, and understood that we are only very seldom able to know exactly what happened in history, the sources being as they are. But the image, how people saw and understood what happened, people who came later and wrote about it, this is something that can be known and can be based on sources. That is, we cannot know exactly how the battles between the Persians and the Greeks were conducted, in the way that it is possible to reconstruct the battle of Trafalgar today, because we do not know how the ships manoeuvred and because there are no archival documents; but we can know how people saw the events one generation later, through the historians of the fifth century; and we can follow the image generation after generation through the historiography. This is, as a matter of fact, almost the only thing possible in all areas of ancient history with a few exceptions. Therefore I became more and more sceptical about the possibilities, and I am regarded as a hypercritical historian in this field of the research of the history of things as they really were, the *res gestae*.

The last resort is the history of historiography. I owe this direction to Momigliano. In the nineteenth century, scholars used historiography as a source for learning what really happened. The aim was not to discover how the historian saw what happened, but to discover what happened: if they thought that the historian lied, they simply said, 'he lied.' It is a question of how you look at it, whether the aim of studying historiography is the historian and his world, or what he wrote in its relation to historical reality. I started to study the historians themselves, in order to understand them. If they falsified events, why did they falsify them? Of course one has to know what happened in order to know that it was falsified; but the focus of interest is on the man, on a group of historians, on a school, rather than on what actually happened. In a sense this is the *histoire des mentalités*: it is more important to understand the mentality of human beings, how they see things, than to know how things really happened.

The study of historiography brings us *ad absurdum* to the study of the historiography of what did not happen, the study of myths. The Trojan War is one of the subjects I work on now (1993)—the war of Troy in ancient Greek historiography. For them it was history. Today nobody knows whether such a war took place; everything is open, there is no proof. No archaeological finds have proved anything to this day: it has been proved that Troy existed, that Mycenae existed; but no-one can prove by excavations or by documents that such a war took place. But the ancient historians, writing hundreds of years later, were certain that it had taken place. They established causes and consequences, the people that took part in it, an exact chronology, and so on. This interests me because it is an example of something that did not happen, and yet had influence. One of the subjects that has interested me recently is the chronology of myths. The Greeks had their ways to establish a date that they believed in. This research can be done for other myths, for example Biblical mythology: it is not important whether there was or was not a crossing of the Red Sea, what is important is that generations believed that it had actually occurred and fixed a date for it, with causes and consequences, and put it into a historical context: from this aspect the question is important. This is not a new philosophy, only an application of an existing view in the research of ancient historiography.

Asheri spent a lifetime teaching in Jerusalem, and participated in the usual administrative tasks, as head of the Institute of History (1971), Dean of Humanities (1972–5), and head of the School of Graduate Studies (1986–8). He was made a professor in 1978 and elected to the Israel Academy of Sciences and Humanities in 1991. But from 1984 (after his first major heart attack), his life was centred on his research. Every year in July he would leave for Oxford, where he would spend the next three months working in the Ashmolean Library: 'I spend my sabbaticals in Oxford because the libraries there are the best. It is very difficult to work in Italy.' For his Oxford friends it was a sign that summer had really arrived, the day that David and Dwora were first seen walking towards the Ashmolean Library shortly before nine o'clock, down the Woodstock Road from the flat in a student block that they rented each year; their departure in late September presaged the start of a new university year. Yet despite this almost annual visitation for fifteen years, David never asked for anything from Oxford: he never sought to involve himself in Oxford life, to give lectures or attend seminars, or to intrude on the sacred research time of others. He was there to work: any social events would be at your insistence, and at lunchtime or in the evenings. He loved the anonymity of Oxford in the summer.

David was physically small and always enjoyed avoiding notice. In later life he had an ironic and sceptical air; his manner was deliberate and thoughtful: he said only what was necessary, and spent much time smiling at the follies of others. He was a man of very high standards in scholarship, and he lived in a circle of a few friends to whom he remained committed, even when they were scarcely on speaking terms with each other: in friendship as in youth he practised the virtues of loyalty and absolute discretion. That is perhaps illustrated by the fact that his closest friends included Arnaldo Momigliano, Emilio Gabba, Luciano Canfora, and myself.

David and I had known each other earlier through Momigliano, but when he began to visit Oxford he came deliberately to offer me the hand of personal friendship. In the course of these years we explored our common love of Herodotus and our common debt to Momigliano's approach to history. In September 1999 we said goodbye over a meal at his favourite restaurant, the Elizabeth, knowing that in all probability we would not meet again. He was a great scholar and a man of absolute integrity. He died in Jerusalem on 3 February 2000.

This brief memoir is based on a recording made by David Asheri for the Israel Academy of Sciences in September 1993; I am grateful to Dwora Gilula for providing me with a translated transcript, and for her comments on an earlier draft. As far as I am aware the passage quoted above from this recording represents one of the few theoretical statements he ever made.

Bibliographical Abbreviations

Editions

The principal editions of Herodotus are the following:

Aldus Manutius	Ἡροδότου λόγοι ἐννέα, οἵπερ ἐπικαλοῦνται Μοῦσαι, *Herodoti libri novem, quibus Musarum indita sunt nomina,* Venice 1502 (editio princeps)
Stephanus	*Herodoti Halicarnassensis Historia,* ed. H. Estienne, Geneva 1570
G. Jungermann	Frankfurt 1608 (first division into chapters)
T. Gale	London 1679
J. Gronovius	Leiden 1715
P. Wesseling	Amsterdam 1763 (and L. C. Valckenaer)
F. V. Reiz	Leipzig 1778
G. H. Schaefer	Leipzig 1800–3
J. Schweighäuser	Strasburg 1806
T. Gaisford	Oxford 1824
J. C. F. Baehr	Leipzig 1830–5
G. Dindorf	Paris 1844
J. Bekker	Berlin 1845[2]
B. H. Lhardy	Leipzig 1850–2
K. W. Krueger	Berlin 1855–6
K. Abicht	Leipzig 1861
H. Stein	*Herodoti Historiae,* I–II (editio maior), Berlin 1869–71; editiones minores 1856–61, etc.
H. R. Dietsch	*Herodoti Historiarum Libri IX,* 2 vols., revised H. Kallenberg, Leipzig 1884–5 (1924–33[2])
H. van Herwerden	Utrecht 1885
C. Hude	*Herodoti Historiae* I–II, Oxford 1908; 1927[3]
Ph.-E. Legrand	*Hérodote, Histoires.* Texte établi et traduit par..., I–X, XI (Index analytique), Paris 1932–54
H. B. Rosén	*Herodotus, Historiae,* Stuttgart–Leipzig, I 1987; II 1997

Latin Translations

L. Valla, Venice 1474.
J. Gronovius, Leiden 1715.
F. V. Reiz (continuavit G. G. Schaefer), I–III, Leipzig 1778–1813.
J. Schweighäuser (ad ed. Reizii et Schaferi emendata), I–III, Oxford 1820.
G. Dindorf, Paris 1844.

Overviews of Herodotean Studies

L. Bergson, 'Herodot 1937–1960', *Lustrum*, XI (1966), 71–138 (with list of previous overviews).
G. T. Griffith, in M. Platnauer (ed.), *Fifty Years (and Twelve) of Classical Scholarship*, Oxford 1968, pp. 182–241 (for the years 1906–68).
W. Krause, 'Herodot', *Anzeiger für die Altertumswissenschaft*, XIV (1961), 25–58 (for the years 1950–60).
P. MacKendrick, 'Herodotus: The Making of a World Historian', *CW* XLVII (1954), 145–52 (for the years 1944–53)
'Herodotus 1954–1961', *CW* LVI (1963), 269–75.
H. Verdin, 'Hérodote historien? Quelques interprétations récentes', *AC* XLIV (1975), 668–85 (for the years 1970–5).
F. Bubel, *Herodot-Bibliographie 1980–1988*, Hildesheim 1991.
See also the compilation in W. Marg (ed.), *Herodot. Eine Auswahl aus der neueren Forschung, Wege der Forschung* XXVI, Darmstadt 1982², with copious bibliography. References to older work will be found in W. Schmid, *Geschichte der griechischen Literatur*, I2, Munich 1934, p. 673.

Abbreviations

Abicht	K. Abicht, *Curae Herodoteae*, Lüneburg 1862.
Adams	W. Y. Adams, *Nubia, Corridor to Africa*, London 1977.
Adkins	A. W. H. Adkins, *Moral Values and Political Behaviour in Ancient Greece from Homer to the End of the Fifth Century*, London 1972.
Albaum–Brentjes	Lj. Albaum and B. Brentjes, *Wächter des Goldes. Zur Geschichte und Kultur mittelasiatischer Völker vor dem Islam*, Berlin 1972.

Alföldi	A. Alföldi, *Die Struktur des voretruskischen Römerstaates*, Heidelberg 1974.
Alliot	M. Alliot, *Le Culte d'Horus à Edfou au temps des Ptolémées*, I, Cairo 1949; II, Cairo 1954.
Altheim–Stiehl, *Die aramäische Sprache*	F. Altheim and R. Stiehl, *Die aramäische Sprache unter den Achaimeniden*, I–III, Frankfurt am Main 1960.
Altheim–Stiehl, *Geschichte*	F. Altheim and R. Stiehl, *Geschichte Mittelasiens im Altertum*, Berlin 1970.
Aly	W. Aly, *Volksmärchen, Sage und Novelle bei Herodot und seinen Zeitgenossen*, Göttingen 1921 (1969²).
Amandry	P. Amandry, *La Mantique apollinienne à Delphes. Essai sur le fonctionnement de l'Oracle*, Paris 1950.
Ampolo	*Plutarco. Le Vite di Teseo e di Romolo*, ed. C. Ampolo and M. Manfredini, Milan 1988.
Anderson, *Zoology: Mammalia*	J. Anderson, *Zoology of Egypt. Mammalia*, rev. W. E. de Winton, London 1902.
Anderson, *Zoology: Reptilia*	J. Anderson, *Zoology of Egypt. 1. Reptilia and Batrachia*, London 1898.
Andrewes	A. Andrewes, *The Greek Tyrants*, London 1977.
ANET	*Ancient Near Eastern Texts Relating to the Old Testament*, ed. J. B. Pritchard, Princeton 1955²; Princeton 1969³.
ANW	*Aufstieg und Niedergang der römischen Welt*, ed. W. Haase and H. Temporini, Berlin–New York 1971 ff.
Apffel	H. Apffel, 'Die Verfassungsdebatte bei Herodot (3, 80–82)', Diss. Erlangen 1957.
Applebaum	S. Applebaum, *Jews and Greeks in Ancient Cyrene*, Leiden 1979.
Archeologija SSSR IX	*Archeologija SSSR*, tom IX: *Antičnye gosudarstva Severnogo Pričernomor'ja*, ed. G. A. Košelenko and V. Dolgorukov, Moscow 1984.
Arkell	A. J. Arkell, *A History of the Sudan from the Earliest Times to 1821*, London 1955.
Arieti	A. J. Arieti, *Discourses on the First Book of Herodotus*, Lanham, Md. 1995.
Armayor	O. K. Armayor, *Herodotus' Autopsy of the Fayoum: Lake Moeris and the Labyrinth of Egypt*, Amsterdam 1985.

Artamonov, *Etnogeografija*	M. I. Artamonov, *Etnogeografija Skifii*, Moscow 1949.
Artamonov, *Kimmerijcy*	M. I. Artamonov, *Kimmerijcy i Skify*, Leningrad 1974.
Artemis Lexikon	*Artemis Lexikon*, Zurich and Stuttgart 1965
Austin	M. M. Austin, *Greece and Egypt in the Archaic Age, Proceedings of the Cambridge Philological Society*, Suppl. II, Cambridge 1970.
Bäbler	B. Bäbler, *Fleissige Thrakerinnen und wehrhafte Skythen*, Stuttgart–Leipzig 1998.
Baedeker, *Egypt*	K. Baedeker, *Egypt and the Sûdân*, London 1914[7].
Bähr	*Herodoti Halicarnassensis Musae*, comm. J. C. F. Baehr, I–IV, Lipsiae 1856–61[2].
Bakker	E. J. Bakker, I. J. F. De Jong, and H. Van Wees (eds.), *Brill's Companion to Herodotus*, Leiden 2002.
Balcer	J. M. Balcer, *Herodotus and Bisitun: Problems in Ancient Persian Historiography*, Historia Einzelschriften, XLIX, Stuttgart 1987.
Balcer, *Prosopographical Study*	J. M. Balcer, *A Prosopographical Study of the Ancient Persians Royal and Noble c. 550–450 B.C.*, Lewiston–Queenston–Lampeter 1993.
Ball, *A Description*	J. Ball, *A Description of the First or Aswan Cataract of the Nile*, Cairo 1907.
Ball, *Contributions*	J. Ball, *Contributions to the Geography of Egypt*, Cairo 1939.
Ball, *Egypt*	J. Ball, *Egypt in the Classical Geographers*, Cairo 1942.
BAR	J. H. Breasted, *Ancient Records of Egypt: Historical Documents from the Earliest Times to the Persian Conquest*, I–V, Chicago 1906–7.
Barth, 'Einwirkungen'	H. Barth, 'Einwirkungen der vorsokratischen Philosophie auf die Herausbildung der historiographischen Methoden Herodots', in *Neue Beiträge zur Geschichte der Alten Welt. Zweite Internationale Tagung der Fachgruppe Alte Geschichte der Deutschen Historiker Gesellschaft vom 4. bis 8. September 1962 in Stralsund*, I, Berlin 1964, pp. 173 ff.
Barth, *Methodologische*	H. Barth, 'Methodologische und Historiographische Probleme der Geschichtsschreibung bei Herodot', Diss. Halle 1963.
Bates	O. Bates, *The Eastern Libyans: An Essay*, London 1914.

Beaulieu   P. A. Beaulieu, *The Reign of Nabonidus, King of Babylon 556–539 B.C.*, New Haven–London 1989.

Beck   Beck, *Die Ringkomposition bei Herodot und ihre Bedeutung für die Beweistechnik, Spudasmata*, XXV, Hildesheim–New York 1971.

Beloch   K. J. Beloch, *Griechische Geschichte*, I–IV, Strasburg–Berlin 1912–27².

Beltrametti   A. Beltrametti, *Erodoto. Una storia governata dal discorso. Il racconto morale come forma della memoria*, Florence 1986.

Benardete   S. Benardete, *Herodotean Inquiries*, The Hague 1969.

Bengtson   H. Bengtson et al., *The Greeks and the Persians: From the Sixth to the Fourth Centuries*, London–New York 1969.

Berger   H. Berger, *Geschichte der wissenschaftlichen Erdkunde der Griechen*, Leipzig 1903.

Bernand   A. Bernand, *Le Delta égyptien d'après les textes grecs, MIFAO* XCI, Cairo 1970

Bernal   M. Bernal, *Black Athena: The Afroasiatic Roots of Classical Civilization*, I, London 1987.

Berve   H. Berve, *Die Tyrannis bei den Griechen*, I–II, Munich 1967.

Bessonova   S. S. Bessonova, *Religioznye predstavlenija skifov*, Kiev 1983.

BGU   *Berliner Griechische Urkunden*

BHT   S. Smith, *Babylonian Historical Texts Relating to the Capture and Downfall of Babylon*, London 1924.

Bichler   R. Bichler, *Herodots Welt. Der Aufbau der Historie am Bild der fremden Länder und Völker, ihrer Zivilisation und ihrer Geschichte*, Berlin 2000.

Bichler–Rollinger   R. Bichler and R. Rollinger, *Herodot*, Darmstadt 2000.

Bickerman   E. J. Bickerman, *Chronology of the Ancient World*, London–Southampton 1968.

Bischoff   H. Bischoff, 'Der Warner bei Herodot', Diss. Marburg 1932.

Blavatskij   V. D. Blavatskij, *Zemledelie v antičnych gosudarstvach Severnogo Pričernomor'ja*, Moscow 1953.

Blom   J. W. S. Blom, *De typische Getallen bij Homeros en Herodotos. I, Triaden, Hebdomaden en Enneaden*, Nijmegen 1936.

Blösel   W. Blösel, *Themistokles bei Herodot: Spiegel Athens im fünften Jahrhundert. Studien zur Geschichte und historiographischen Konstruktion des griechischen Freiheitskampfes 480 v. Chr.*, Stuttgart 2004.

Boardman, *Greeks
Overseas*   J. Boardman, *The Greeks Overseas: Their Early Colonies and Trade*, London 1999⁴.

Boedeker–Sider   *The New Simonides: Contexts of Praise and Desire*, ed.
D. Boedeker and D. Sider, Oxford 2001.

Bolton   J. D. P. Bolton, *Aristeas of Proconnesus*, Oxford 1962.

Bonacasa–Ensoli   N. Bonacasa and S. Ensoli (eds.), *Cirene*, Milan 2000.

Bonneau, *La Crue* D. Bonneau, *La Crue du Nil*, Paris 1964.

Bonnet, *RÄRG*   H. Bonnet, *Reallexikon der ägyptischen Religions-
geschichte*, Berlin 1952.

Borchardt   L. Borchardt, *Die Entstehung der Pyramide. Beiträge
zur ägyptischen Bauforschung und Altertumskunde*,
I, Cairo 1937.

Bornitz   H. F. Bornitz, *Herodot-Studien. Beiträge zum Ver-
ständnis der Einheit des Geschichtswerks*, Berlin 1968.

Bosworth   A. B. Bosworth, *A Historical Commentary on Arrian's
History of Alexander*, I. *Commentary on Books I–III*,
Oxford 1980.

Bottini   A. Bottini, *Archeologia della salvezza. L'escatologia
greca nelle testimonianze archeologiche*, Milan 1992.

Boulenger   G. Boulenger, *Zoology of Egypt: The Fishes of the Nile*,
London 1907.

Bowden   H. Bowden, 'Herodotos and Greek Sanctuaries', Diss.
Oxford 1991.

Braswell   B. K. Braswell, *A Commentary on the Fourth Pythian
Ode of Pindar*, Berlin–New York 1988.

Braun   M. Braun, *History and Romance in Graeco-Oriental
Literature*, Oxford 1938.

Braund   D. Braund, *Georgia in Antiquity: A History of Colchis
and Transcaucasian Iberia, 550 BC–AD 562*, Oxford
1994

Bredow   F. I. C. Bredovius, *Quaestionum criticarum de dialecto
Herodotea libri IV*, Lipsiae 1846.

Briant, *État et
pasteurs*   P. Briant, *État et pasteurs au Moyen-Orient ancien*,
Cambridge–Paris 1982.

Briant, *Histoire* P. Briant, *Histoire de l'empire perse. De Cyrus à Alexandre*, Paris 1996 (*From Cyrus to Alexander: A His-
tory of the Persian Empire*, trans. P. D. Daniels,
Winona Lake, Ind. 2002).

Brouwer   S. Brouwer, *Een Studie over enige archaische Elemen-
ten in de Stijl van Herodotus*, Meppel 1975.

Brugsch   H. K. Brugsch, *Dictionnaire géographique de l'ancienne Egypte*, Leipzig 1877–80.

Bruneau–Ducat   Ph. Bruneau and J. Ducat, *Guide de Délos*, Paris 1983.

Brunner-Traut	E. Brunner-Traut, *Altägyptische Tiergeschichte und Fabel*, Darmstadt 1968.
BTCGI	G. Nenci (ed.), *Bibliografia topografica della colonizzazione greca in Italia e nelle isole tirreniche*, Pisa–Rome 1977–2001.
Budge	E. A. W. Budge, *The Mummy*, London 1925.
Bunbury	E. Bunbury, *A History of Ancient Geography*, I–II, London 1883².
Burguière	P. Burguière, *Histoire de l'infinitif en grec*, Paris 1960.
Burkert	W. Burkert, *Lore and Science in Ancient Pythagoreanism*, Cambridge, Mass. 1972.
Burkert, *Homo Necans*	W. Burkert, *Homo Necans: The Anthropology of Ancient Greek Sacrificial Ritual and Myths*, Berkeley 1983.
Burn	A. R. Burn, *Persia and the Greeks: The Defence of the West 546–478 B.C.*, London 1962.
Bury	J. B. Bury, *The Ancient Greek Historians*, New York.
Butzer	K. W. Butzer, *Early Hydraulic Civilization in Egypt: A Study in Cultural Ecology*, Chicago–London 1976.
CAH	*Cambridge Ancient History*, I–XII, ed. J. Bury *et al.*, Cambridge 1923–39.
CAH²	*The Cambridge Ancient History*, III–IV, ed. J. Boardman *et al.*, Cambridge 1982–8.
CAH³	*The Cambridge Ancient History*, I–II, ed. I. E. S. Edwards *et al.*, Cambridge 1970–7.
Camerer	L. Camerer, *Praktische Klugheit bei Herodot. Untersuchungen zu den Begriffen* μηχανή, τέχνη, σοφία, *Tübingen 1965*.
Camps, *Aux origines*	G. Camps, *Aux origines de la berbérie. Monuments et rites funéraires protohistoriques*, Paris 1961.
Camps, *Berbères*	G. Camps, *Berbères. Aux marges de l'histoire*, Toulouse 1982.
Cartledge	P. Cartledge, *Sparta and Lakonia: A Regional History 1300–362 B.C.*, London 1979 (2002²).
Casevitz	M. Casevitz, *Le Vocabulaire de la colonisation en grec ancien*, Paris 1985.
Casson	L. Casson, *Ships and Seamanship in the Ancient World*, Princeton 1971.
Cawkwell	G. L. Cawkwell, *The Greek Wars: The Failure of Persia*, Oxford 2005.
Černenko	E. V. Černenko, *Skifo-persidskaja vojna*, Kiev 1984.
CGC	Catalogue Général des Antiquités égyptiennes du Musée du Caire.

CHA — The Cambridge History of Africa, I–II, ed. J. D. Fage and R. Oliver, Cambridge 1978–82.

Chamoux — F. Chamoux, *Cyrène sous la monarchie des Battiades*, Paris 1953.

Chantraine, *Grammaire* — P. Chantraine, *Grammaire homérique*, I–II, Paris 1942–53.

Chassinat, *Dendera* — E. Chassinat, *Le Temple de Dendera*, I–V, Cairo 1934–52.

Chassinat, *Edfou* — E. Chassinat, *Le Temple d'Edfou*, Mémoires publiés par les membres de la Mission Archéologique Française au Caire, I–XIV, Paris–Cairo 1892–1934.

Chassinat, *Le Mystère* — E. Chassinat, *Le Mystère d'Osiris au mois de Khoiak*, I–II, Cairo 1966–8.

Chatelet — F. Chatelet, *La Naissance de l'histoire*, Paris 1962.

Chazanov — A. M. Chazanov, *Social'naja istorija skifov. Osnovnye problemy razvitija drevnich kočevnikov evrazijskich stepej*, Moscow 1975.

CHI — The Cambridge History of Iran, II. *The Median and Achaemenian Periods*, ed. I. Gershevitch, Cambridge 1985.

CHJud — The Cambridge History of Judaism, I, ed. W. D. Davies and L. Finkelstein, Cambridge 1984.

CIL — Corpus Inscriptionum Latinarum, Berolini 1863 ff.

Cirene. Storia — Cirene. Storia, mito, letteratura, ed. B. Gentili, Urbino 1990.

Clark — R. T. Rundle Clark, *Myth and Symbol in Ancient Egypt*, London 1959.

Cobet — J. Cobet, *Herodots Exkurse und die Frage der Einheit seines Werkes*, Historia Einzelschriften, XVII, Wiesbaden 1971.

Colin — F. Colin, *Les Peuples libyens de la Cyrénaïque à l'Egypte d'après les sources de l'antiquité classique*, Brussels 2000.

Cook — J. M. Cook, *The Persian Empire*, London 1983.

Coppola — A. Coppola, in *Erodoto e l'Occidente*, Rome 1999 (*Kokalos* Suppl. XV).

Corcella — A. Corcella, *Erodoto e l'analogia*, Palermo 1984.

Costanzi — Erodoto. Il primo libro delle Storie, commentato da V. Costanzi, Turin 1924².

Cowley — A. E. Cowley, *Aramaic Papyri of the Fifth Century B.C.*, Oxford 1923.

Cozzoli — U. Cozzoli, *I Cimmeri*, Rome 1968.

Crahay — R. Crahay, *La Littérature oraculaire chez Hérodote*, Paris 1956.

Cyrenaica   *Cyrenaica in Antiquity*, ed. G. Barker, J. Lloyd, and J. Reynolds, Oxford 1985.

Dandamaev   M. A. Dandamaev, *Persien unter den ersten Achämeniden*, Wiesbaden 1976.

Dandamaev–Lukonin   M. A. Dandamaev and V. G. Lukonin, *The Culture and Social Institutions of Ancient Iran*, Eng edn. ed. P. L. Kohl and D. J. Dadson, Cambridge 1989.

Daniëls   G. C. J. Daniëls, *Religieus-historische Studie over Herodotus*, Antwerp–Nijmegen 1946.

Danov   Ch. M. Danov, *Altthrakien*, Berlin 1976.

Davies   J. K. Davies, *Athenian Propertied Families, 600–300 B.C.*, Oxford 1971.

Decker   W. Decker, *Die physische Leistung Pharaos. Untersuchungen zu Heldentum, Jagd und Leibesübungen der ägyptischen Könige*, Cologne 1971.

Decret–Fantar   F. Decret and M. Fantar, *L'Afrique du nord dans l'antiquité*, Paris 1981.

Deffner   A. Deffner, 'Die Rede bei Herodot und ihre Weiterbildung bei Thukydides', Diss. Munich 1933.

Defradas   J. Defradas, *Les Thèmes de la propagande delphique*, Paris 1954.

Delcourt   M. Delcourt, *Oedipe ou la légende du conquérant*, Paris 1981.

Demand   N. H. Demand, *Urban Relocation in Archaic and Classical Greece: Flight and Consolidation*, Norman, Okla. 1990.

de Meulenaere   H. de Meulenaere, *Herodotos over de 26ste Dynastie, Bibliothèque du Muséon*, XXVII, Leuven 1951.

Demografičeskaja situacija   *Demografičeskaja situacija v Pričernomor'e v period velikoj grečeskoj kolonizacii*, Tbilisi 1980.

Denniston, *Greek Particles*   J. D. Denniston, *The Greek Particles*, Oxford 1966².

Derow–Parker   P. Derow and R. Parker (eds.), *Herodotus and his World*, Oxford 2003.

Desanges, *Catalogue*   J. Desanges, *Catalogue des tribus africaines de l'antiquité classique à l'ouest du Nil*, Dakar 1962.

Desanges, *Pline*   *Pline l'Ancien, Histoire naturelle, livre V 1–46. L'Afrique du Nord*, texte établi, traduit et commenté par J. Desanges, Paris 1980.

Desanges, *Recherches*   J. Desanges, *Recherches sur l'activité des Méditeranéens aux confins de l'Afrique (VIᵉ siècle avant J.C.–IVᵉ siècle après J.C.)*, Rome 1978.

De Siena   A. De Siena, in *Siritide e Metapontino. Storie di due territori coloniali*, Naples–Paestum 1998.

Dewald–Marincola   C. Dewald and J. Marincola, 'A Selective Introduction to Herodotean Studies', *Arethusa* XX (1987), 9–40.

Dickey   E. Dickey, *Greek Forms of Address from Homer to Lucian*, Oxford 1996.

Diller   H. Diller, *Wanderarzt und Aitiologe*, Leipzig 1934.

Dindorf   L. Dindorf, *Historici Graeci Minores*, I–II, Leipzig 1870–1.

Dion   R. Dion, *Aspects politiques de la géographie antique*, Paris 1977.

Di Tillio   Z. Di Tillio, *Personalità e stile di Erodoto*, Naples 1967.

DK   H. Diels and W. Kranz (eds.), *Die Fragmente der Vorsokratiker*, I–III, Berlin 1951–2⁶.

DNP   *Der Neue Pauly-Encyclopädie der Antike*, ed. H. Cancik and H. Schneider, Stuttgart–Weimar, 1996–2003.

Dobias-Lalou   C. Dobias-Lalou, *Le Dialecte des inscriptions grecques de Cyrène*, Paris 2000 (*Karthago*, XXV).

Dobree   P. P. Dobree, *Adversaria*, ed. G. Wagner, Berlin 1874.

Dodds   E. R. Dodds, *The Greeks and the Irrational*, Berkeley–Los Angeles–London 1973.

Dombrowki   B. W. W. Dombrowki, *Der Name Europas auf seinen griechischen und altsyrischen Hintergrund*, Amsterdam, 1984.

Dorati   M. Dorati, *Le Storie di Erodoto: etnografia e racconto*, Pisa–Rome 2000.

Drevnosti   *Drevnosti severo-zapadnogo pričernomor'ja*, Kiev 1981.

Drevnosti stepnoi   *Drevnosti stepnoj Skifii*, Kiev 1982.

Drews   R. Drews, *The Greek Accounts of Eastern History*, Washington, DC 1973.

Drexler   H. Drexler, *Herodot-Studien*, Hildesheim–New York 1972.

Drioton–Vandier   E. Drioton and J. Vandier, *L'Égypte*, Paris 1962⁴.

Dumézil, *La Courtisane*   G. Dumézil, *La Courtisane et les seigneurs colorés et autres essais*, Paris 1983.

Dumézil, *Le Livre*   G. Dumézil, *Le Livre des héros. Légendes sur les Nartes*, Paris 1965.

Dumézil, *Mythe*   G. Dumézil, *Mythe et épopée*, I, Paris 1986.

Dumézil, *Romans*   G. Dumézil, *Romans de Scythie et d'alentour*, Paris 1978.

EAA   *Enciclopedia dell'arte antica, classica e orientale*, I–VII, Rome 1958–66.

Ebert   M. Ebert, *Südrussland im Altertum*, Bonn–Leipzig 1921.

Edwards	I. E. S. Edwards, *The Pyramids of Egypt*, Harmondsworth 1985.
EGF	G. Kinkel, *Epicorum Graecorum Fragmenta*, Leipzig 1877.
Ehrhardt	N. Ehrhardt, *Milet und seine Kolonien. Vergleichende Untersuchungen der kultischen und politischen Einrichtungen*, Frankfurt a.M.–Berlin–New York 1983.
Eliade, *Shamanism*	M. Eliade, *Shamanism: Archaic Techniques of Ecstasy*, London 1989.
Eliade, *Zalmoxis*	M. Eliade, *De Zalmoxis à Gengis-Khan*, Paris 1970.
Eltz	G. J. Eltz, *Quaestiones Herodoteae*, Lipsiae 1841.
Emery	W. B. Emery, *Archaic Egypt*, Harmondsworth 1961.
Erbse	H. Erbse, *Ausgewählte Schriften zur Klassischen Philologie*, Berlin–New York 1979.
Erbse, *Studien*	H. Erbse, *Studien zur Verständnis Herodots*, Berlin 1992.
Erman	A. Erman, *Die Religion der Ägypter*, Berlin 1934.
Erman–Grapow	A. Erman and H. Grapow, *Wörterbuch der ägyptischen Sprache*, I–VII, Leipzig 1926–63.
Erman–Ranke	A. Erman and H. Ranke, *Ägypten und ägyptisches Leben im Altertum*, Tübingen 1923.
Etnogenez	*Etnogenez narodov Balkan i severnogo Pričernomor'ja. Lingvistika istorija archeologija*, Moscow 1984.
Evans	J. A. S. Evans, *Herodotus*, Boston 1982.
Evans, *Explorer*	J. A. S. Evans, *Herodotus, Explorer of the Past: Three Essays*, Princeton 1991.
Fahr	H. Fahr, 'Kambyses. Ein Beitrag zur Herodotsinterpretation', Diss. Hamburg 1959.
Farnell	L. Farnell, *The Cults of the Greek States*, I–V, Oxford 1896–1909.
Faulkner	R. O. Faulkner, *The Ancient Egyptian Pyramid Texts*, I–II, Oxford 1969.
Fehling	D. Fehling, *Herodotus and his 'Sources': Citation, Invention and Narrative Art*, trans. J. G. Howie, Leeds 1989.
FGrHist	F. Jacoby, *Die Fragmente der griechischen Historiker*, I–XIII, Berlin–Leiden 1923–58.
FHG	B. Müller and T. Müller, *Fragmenta Historicorum Graecorum*, I–V, Paris 1841–73.
Figueira	T. J. Figueira (ed.), *Spartan Society*, Swansea 2004.
Flory	S. Flory, *The Archaic Smile of Herodotus*, Detroit 1987.
Flower–Marincola	*Herodotus, Histories Book IX*, ed. M. A. Flower and J. Marincola, Cambridge 2002.
Focke	F. Focke, *Herodot als Historiker*, Stuttgart 1927.

Fohl
H. Fohl, 'Tragische Kunst bei Herodot', Diss. Rostock 1913.

Fontenrose
J. Fontenrose, *The Delphic Oracle: Its Responses and Operations*, Berkeley 1978.

Forbes
R. J. Forbes, *Studies in Ancient Technology*, I–IX, Leiden 1955–64; IV–IX, Leiden 1964–72³.

Fornara
C. W. Fornara, *Herodotus: An Interpretative Essay*, Oxford 1971.

François
G. François, *Le Polythéisme et l'emploi au singulier des mots* θεός, δαίμων, *dans la littérature grecque d'Homère* à *Platon*, Paris 1957.

Frankfort, *Kingship*
H. Frankfort, *Kingship and the Gods*, Chicago 1948.

Frankfort, *Religion*
H. Frankfort, *Ancient Egyptian Religion*, New York 1948.

Frau
S. Frau, *Le Colonne d'Ercole. Un'inchiesta*, Rome 2002.

Frisch
P. Frisch, *Die Träume bei Herodot*, Beiträge zur klass. Philol., XXVII, Meisenheim am Glan 1968.

v. Fritz
K. von Fritz, *Die griechische Geschichtsschreibung*, I–II, Berlin 1967.

Froidefond
C. Froidefond, *Le Mirage égyptien dans la littérature grecque d'Homère à Aristote*, Publications Universitaires des Lettres et Sciences Humaines d'Aix-en-Provence, 1971.

Frye
R. N. Frye, *The History of Ancient Iran, Handbuch der Altertumswissenschaft*, III 7, Munich 1983.

Gabain
A. von Gabain, *Einführung in die Zentralasienkunde*, Darmstadt 1979.

Gaillard–Daressy, *La Faune momifiée*
C. Gaillard and G. Daressy, *La Faune momifiée de l'antique Égypte*, CGC, Cairo 1905.

Gajdukevič
V. T. Gajdukevič, *Das Bosporanische Reich*, Berlin–Amsterdam 1971.

Gallotta
B. Gallotta, *Dario e l'occidente prima delle guerre persiane*, Milan 1980.

Gardiner, *AEO*
A. H. Gardiner, *Ancient Egyptian Onomastica*, I–III, Oxford 1947.

Gardiner, *Egypt*
A. H. Gardiner, *Egypt of the Pharaohs*, Oxford 1961.

Gardiner, *Egyptian Grammar*
A. H. Gardiner, *Egyptian Grammar*, London 1957³.

Garstang
J. Garstang, *The Burial Customs of Ancient Egypt as Illustrated by Tombs of the Middle Kingdom*, London 1907.

Gauthier, *DG*	H. Gauthier, *Dictionnaire des noms géographiques contenus dans les textes hiéroglyphiques*, I–VII, Cairo 1925–31.
Gauthier, *Le Livre*	H. Gauthier, *Le Livre des Rois d'Égypte*, I–V, *MIFAO* XVII–XXI, Cairo 1907–17.
Gauthier, *Les Nomes*	H. Gauthier, *Les Nomes d'Égypte depuis Hérodote jusqu' à la conquête arabe*, *MIE* XXV, Cairo 1935.
Gebhardt	G. A. Gebhardt, *Emendationum Herodotearum*, Pars I, Curiae Regnitianae 1857; Pars V, 1864.
Gentili	B. Gentili, *Anacreon*, Rome 1958.
GGM	C. Müller, *Geographi Graeci Minores* I–III, Paris 1855–61.
GHA	*General History of Africa*, II. *Ancient Civilizations of Africa*, ed. G. Mokhtar, Berkeley–Los Angeles 1981.
Ghirshman	R. Ghirshman, *Iran*, Harmondsworth 1954.
Gigante	M. Gigante, Νόμος βασιλεύς, Naples 1956.
Giraudeau	M. Giraudeau, *Les Notions juridiques et sociales chez Hérodote. Études sur le vocabulaire*, Paris 1984.
GL	D. A. Campbell (ed.), *Greek Lyric*, I–V, Cambridge, Mass.–London 1982–93.
Godley	A. D. Godley, *Herodotus*, London–New York 1920–4.
Gold der Skythen	*Gold der Skythen aus der Leningrader Eremitage*, Munich 1984.
Gold der Steppe	*Gold der Steppe. Archäologie der Ukraine*, Neumünster 1991.
Gomme	A. W. Gomme, A. Andrewes, and K. J. Dover, *A Historical Commentary on Thucydides*, I–V, Oxford 1944–81.
Gomme, *Greek Attitude*	A. W. Gomme, *The Greek Attitude to Poetry and History*, Berkeley–Los Angeles 1954.
Gomperz	T. Gomperz, *Herodoteische Studien*, II, Vienna 1883.
Goodchild	R. G. Goodchild, *Kyrene und Apollonia*, Zurich 1971.
Goodwin, *Moods and Tenses*	W. W. Goodwin, *Syntax of the Moods and Tenses of the Greek Verb*, rev. edn., London 1912.
Gottlieb	G. Gottlieb, 'Das Verhältnis der ausserherodotischen Ueberlieferung zu Herodot', Diss. Bonn 1963.
Gould	J. Gould, *Herodotus*, London 1990.
Goyon	G. Goyon, *Rituels funéraires de l'ancienne Égypte*, Paris 1972.
Graham	A. J. Graham, *Colony and Mother City in Ancient Greece*, New York 1971.

Grakow   B. N. Grakow, *Die Skythen*, Berlin 1980².
Grassl   A. Grassl, 'Herodot als Ethnologe', Diss. Munich–
                         Salzbach 1904.
Graziosi   P. Graziosi, *L'arte rupestre della Libia*, Naples 1942.
Griechenland. Lexikon *Griechenland. Lexikon der historischen Stätten. Von
                         den Anfängen bis zu Gegenwart*, ed. S. Lauffer, Mun-
                         ich 1989.
Griffith, *Catalogue*   F. Ll. Griffith, *Catalogue of the Demotic Papyri in the
                         John Rylands Library Manchester*, I–III, Manchester
                         1909.
Griffith, *Stories*   F. Ll. Griffith, *Stories of the High Priests of Memphis*,
                         Oxford 1900.
Griffiths, *The Conflict* J. Gwyn Griffiths, *The Conflict of Horus and Seth*,
                         Liverpool 1960.
Griffiths, *The Origins* J. Gwyn Griffiths, *The Origins of Osiris*, MÄS IX,
                         Berlin 1966.
Griffiths, *Plutarch*   J. Gwyn Griffiths, *Plutarch, De Iside et Osiride*, Aber-
                         ystwyth 1970.
v. Groningen   B. A. van Groningen, *Herodotus' Historiën*, I–III,
                         Leiden 1959–63².
Grottanelli–Milano   C. Grottanelli and L. Milano (eds.), *Food and Iden-
                         tity*, Padua 2003.
Gsell, *Hérodote*   S. Gsell, *Hérodote. Textes relatifs à l'histoire de l'Afri-
                         que du Nord*, Paris–Algiers 1916.
Gsell, *Histoire*   S. Gsell, *Histoire ancienne de l'Afrique du Nord*,
                         I–VIII, Paris 1913–28.
Guthrie   W. Guthrie, *The Greeks and their Gods*, London 1950.
Gyles   M. F. Gyles, *Pharaonic Policies and Administration
                         663 to 323 B.C.*, James Sprunt Studies in History
                         and Political Science, XLI, Chapel Hill, Nebr. 1959.
Haider   P. W. Haider, *Griechenland–Nordafrika. Ihre Bezie-
                         hungen zwischen 1500 und 600 v. Chr.*, Darmstadt
                         1988.
Halliday   W. R. Halliday, *Indo-European Folk-tales and Greek
                         Legend*, Cambridge 1933.
Hamdi Sayar   M. Hamdi Sayar, *Perinthos-Herakleia (Marmara Ere-
                         glisi) und Umgebung. Geschichte, Testimonien, grie-
                         chische und lateinische Inschriften*, Vienna 1998.
Harmatta, *Quellenstudien* J. Harmatta, *Quellenstudien zu den Skythika des Hero-
                         dot*, Budapest 1941.
Harmatta, *Studies*   J. Harmatta, *Studies in the History and Language of
                         the Sarmatians*, Szeged 1970.
Harrison   T. Harrison, *Divinity and History: The Religion of
                         Herodotus*, Oxford 2000.

Harrison, *Emptiness*   T. Harrison, *The Emptiness of Asia: Aeschylus' Persians and the History of the Fifth Century*, London 2000.

Harrison, *Greeks and Barbarians*   T. Harrison (ed.), *Greeks and Barbarians*, Edinburgh 2002.

Hart   J. Hart, *Herodotus and Greek History*, London 1982.

Hartmann   F. Hartmann. *L'Agriculture dans l'ancienne Égypte*, Paris 1923.

Hartog   F. Hartog, *Le Miroir d'Hérodote: Essai sur la représentation de l'autre*, Paris 1980 (= *The Mirror of Herodotus: The Representation of the Other in the Writing of History*, trans. J. Lloyd, Berkeley–London 1988).

Haussig, *Archäologie*   H. W. Haussig, *Archäologie und Kunst der Seidenstrasse*, Darmstadt 1992.

Haussig, *Die Geschichte islamischer Zeit*   H. W. Haussig, *Die Geschichte Zentralasiens und der Seidenstrasse in islamischer Zeit*, Darmstadt 1983.

Haussig, *Die Geschichte vorislamischer Zeit*   H. W. Haussig, *Die Geschichte Zentralasiens und der Seidenstrasse in vorislamischer Zeit*, Darmstadt 1983.

Hauvette   A. Hauvette, *Hérodote: historien des guerres médiques*, Paris 1894.

Head   B. V. Head, *Historia Numorum. A Manual of Greek Numismatics*, Oxford 1911² (rev. edn. London 1963).

Heidel   W. A. Heidel, *The Frame of the Ancient Greek Maps*, New York 1937.

Heilmann   L. Heilmann, 'De infinitivi syntaxi Herodotea', Diss. Gissae 1879.

Heinen   H. Heinin, *Antike am Rande der Steppen. Der nördliche Schwarzmeerraum als Forschungsaufgabe*, Mainz-Stuttgart 2006.

Helck, *Wirtschaftsgeschichte*   W. Helck, *Wirtschaftsgeschichte des alten Ägypten im 3. und 2. Jahrtausend vor Chr.*, Handbuch der Orientalistik, I 1,5, Leiden–Cologne 1975.

Helck, *Zur Verwaltung*   W. Helck, *Zur Verwaltung des Mittleren und Neuen Reichs. Probleme der Ägyptologie*, III, Leiden–Cologne 1975.

Hellmann   F. Hellmann, *Herodots Kroisos-Logos*, Berlin 1934.

Hemmerdinger   B. Hemmerdinger, *Les Manuscrits d'Hérodote et la critique verbale*, Genoa 1981.

Heni   R. Heni, 'Die Gespräche bei Herodot', Diss. Heidelberg 1976.

HERE   *Hastings Encyclopedia of Religion and Ethics*, I–XII, Edinburgh–New York 1908–21.

Herminghausen   D. Herminghausen, 'Herodots Angaben über Äthiopien', Diss. Hamburg 1964.

Hérodote et les peuples non grecs   *Hérodote et les peuples non grecs, Entretiens Hardt,* XXXV, Vandoeuvres–Geneva 1990.

Herold   G. Herold, *Emendationum Herodotearum specimen,* Norimbergae 1850; *Emendationes Herodoteae,* Pars I, 1853.

Herzfeld   E. Herzfeld, *The Persian Empire: Studies in Geography and Ethnography of the Ancient Near East,* ed. G. Walser, Wiesbaden 1968.

Heubeck   A. Heubeck, 'Das Nationalbewusstsein des Herodot', Diss. Erlangen 1936.

HGM   L. Dindorf, *Historici Graeci Minores,* I–II, Leipzig 1870–1.

Hiller von Gärtringen   F. Hiller von Gärtringen, *Thera,* I–IV, Berlin 1899–1909.

Hinz   W. Hinz, *Darius und die Perser,* I–II, Baden-Baden 1976–9.

Hofmann–Vorbichler   I. Hofmann and A. Vorbichler, *Der Äthiopenlogos bei Herodot, Beiträge zur Afrikanistik,* III, Vienna 1979.

Hofstetter   J. Hofstetter *Die Griechen in Persien, AMI* Ergänzungsband, V, Berlin 1978.

Hohti   P. Hohti, *The Interrelation of Speech and Action in the Histories of Herodotus,* Helsinki 1976.

Hölscher   W. Hölscher, *Libyer und Ägypter,* Glückstadt–Hamburg–New York 1937.

Hommel   F. Hommel, *Ethnologie und Geographie des alten Orients,* Munich 1926.

Hopfner, *Fontes*   T. Hopfner, *Fontes Historiae Religionis Aegyptiacae,* I–IV, Bonn 1922–5.

Hopfner, *Tierkult*   T. Hopfner, *Der Tierkult der alten Ägypter, Denkschriften Wien,* LVII 2, Vienna 1913.

How–Wells   W. W. How and J. Wells, *A Commentary on Herodotus,* I–II, Oxford 1912.

Huber   L. Huber, 'Religiöse und politische Beweggründe des Handels in der Geschichtsschreibung des Herodot', Diss. Tübingen 1965.

Hunter   V. Hunter, *Past and Process in Herodotus and Thucydides,* Princeton 1982.

Hurst, *The Nile*   H. E. Hurst, *The Nile,* London 1952.

Huxley   G. L. Huxley, *The Early Ionians,* London 1966.

IC   *Inscriptiones Creticae,* I–IV, curavit M. Guarducci, Rome 1935–50.

IEG   M. L. West, *Iambi et Elegi Graeci ante Alexandrum Cantati,* I, Oxford 1971 (1989²); II, Oxford 1972 (1992²).

IG	*Inscriptiones Graecae*, consilio et auctoritate Academiae litterarum regiae Borussicae editae, Berolini 1873 ff.
IGDoP	Laurent Dubois (ed.), *Inscriptions grecques dialectales d'Olbia du Pont*, Geneva 1996.
I Greci	S. Settis (ed.), *I Greci. Storia cultura arte società*, I–IV, Turin 1996–2002.
Il'inskaja–Terenožkin	V. A. Il'inskaja and A. I. Terenožkin, *Skifija VII–IV vv. do n.e.*, Kiev 1983.
Immerwahr	H. R. Immerwahr, *Form and Thought in Herodotus*, *Phil. Monographs*, XXIII, Cleveland 1966 (rev. edn. Atlanta 1986).
IOSPE	*Inscriptiones antiquae orae septentrionalis Ponti Euxini Graecae et Latinae*, I–II, IV, ed. B. Latyschev, Petropoli 1885–91; I 1916².
Isaac	B. H. Isaac, *The Greek Settlements in Thrace until the Macedonian Conquest*, Leiden 1986.
Ivantchik	A. M. Ivantchik, in V. Fromentin and S. Gotteland (ed.), *Origines gentium*, Bordeaux 2001.
Jacenko	I. V. Jacenko, *Skifija VII–V vv. do n.e.*, Moscow 1959.
Jacoby	F. Jacoby, *Herodotos*, *RE* Suppl. II, 1913, coll. 205–520 (= *Griechische Historiker*, Stuttgart 1956, pp. 7–164).
Jacoby, *Apollodors Chronik*	F. Jacoby, *Apollodors Chronik: eine Sammlung der Fragmente*, repr. of 1902 edn., New York 1973.
Jacoby, *Das Marmor*	F. Jacoby, *Das Marmor Parium*, Berlin 1904.
Jacquemin	A. Jacquemin, *Offrandes monumentales à Delphes*, Paris 1999.
Jaeger	W. Jaeger, *The Theology of the Early Greek Philosophers*, London–Oxford–New York 1967.
Janni	P. Janni, *La mappa e il periplo*, Rome 1984.
Jeffery	L. H. Jeffery, *The Local Scripts of Archaic Greece*, Oxford 1961.
Jeffery, *Archaic Greece*	L. H. Jeffery, *Archaic Greece: The City States c.700–500 B.C.*, London–Tonbridge 1976.
Jéquier, *Considérations*	G. Jéquier, *Considérations sur les religions égyptiennes*, Neuchatel 1946.
Jéquier, *Manuel*	G. Jéquier, *Manuel d'archéologie égyptienne. Les éléments de l'architecture*, Paris 1924.
Jettmar	K. Jettmar, *Art of the Steppes: The Eurasian Animal Style* (trans. A. E. Keep), London 1967.
Jonckheere	F. Jonckheere, *Les Médecins de l'Égypte pharaonique*, Brussels 1958.
Junge	J. Junge, *Saka-Studien*, Leipzig 1939.
Justi	F. Justi, *Iranisches Namenbuch*, Marburg 1895.

Karageorghis–Taifacos   V. Karageorghis and I. Taifacos (eds.), *The World of Herodotus: Proceedings of an International Conference held at the Foundation A.G. Leventis, Nicosia, September 18–21, 2003*, Nicosia 2004.

Karetsou *et al.*   A. Karetsou, M. Andreadaki-Vlazaki, and N. Papadakis, *Crete–Egypt: Three Thousand Years of Cultural Links*, Heraklion–Cairo 2001.

Kearns   E. Kearns, *Heroes of Attica*, BICS Suppl. LVII, London 1989.

Kees, *Ägypten*   H. Kees, *Ägypten, Kulturgeschichte des alten Orients*, III 1, Munich 1933.

Kees, *Ancient Egypt*   H. Kees, *Ancient Egypt: A Cultural Topography*, London 1961.

Kees, *Götterglaube*   H. Kees, *Der Götterglaube im alten Ägypten*, Berlin 1956.

Kees, *Totenglauben*   H. Kees, *Totenglauben und Jenseitsvorstellungen der alten Ägypter*, Berlin 1956².

Kenrick, *Egypt*   J. Kenrick, *The Egypt of Herodotus*, London 1841.

Kent   R. G. Kent, *Old Persian: Grammar, Texts, Lexicon*, New Haven 1953².

Kiechle   F. Kiechle, *Lakonien und Sparta*, Munich 1963.

Kienitz   F. K. Kienitz, *Die politische Geschichte Ägyptens vom 7. bis zum 4. Jahrhundert vor der Zeitwende*, Berlin 1953.

Kindstrand   F. Kindstrand, *Anacharsis: The Legend and the Apophthegmata*, Uppsala 1981.

Kirchberg   J. Kirchberg, *Die Funktion der Orakel im Werke Herodots, Hypomnemata*, XI, Göttingen 1965.

Kitchen   K. A. Kitchen, *The Third Intermediate Period in Egypt (1100–650 B.C.)*, Warminster 1973.

Klebs, *AR*   L. Klebs, *Die Reliefs des alten Reiches*, Heidelberg 1915.

Klebs, *MR*   L. Klebs, *Die Reliefs und Malereien des mittleren Reiches*, Heidelberg 1922.

Klebs, *NR*   L. Klebs, *Die Reliefs und Malereien des neuen Reiches*, I, Heidelberg 1934.

Klees   H. Klees, *Die Eigenart des griechischen Glaubens an Orakel und Seher, Tübinger Beiträge zur Altertumswissenschaft*, XLIII, Stuttgart 1965.

Kleingünther   A. Kleingünther, πρῶτος εὑρετής, *Philologus* Suppl., XXVI 1, Leipzig 1933.

Kocybala   A. X. Kocybala, 'Greek Colonization on the North Shore of the Black Sea in the Archaic Period', Diss. Pennsylvania 1978.

König   F. W. König, *Der falsche Bardija. Dareios der Grosse und die Lügenkönige, Klotho,* IV, Vienna 1938.

KP   K. Ziegler and W. Sontheimer, *Der Kleine Pauly,* I–V, Stuttgart 1964–75.

KR   G. S. Kirk and J. E. Raven, *The Presocratic Philosophers,* Cambridge 1962.

KR²   G. S. Kirk and J. E. Raven, *The Presocratic Philosophers,* rev. M. Schofield, Cambridge 1983².

Krause   F. Krause, *ΑΛΛΟΤΕ ΑΛΛΟΣ. Untersuchungen zum Motiv des Schicksalswechsels in der griechischen Dichtung bis Euripides,* Tuduv Studien. Reihe Kulturwissenschaften, IV, Munich 1976.

Kühner–Gerth,
Gr. Grammatik   R. Kühner and B. Gerth, *Ausführliche Grammatik der griechischen Sprache,* II. Satzlehre 1–2, Hanover–Leipzig 1898–1904.

Kuklina   I. V. Kuklina, *Etnogeografija Skifii po antičnym istočnikam,* Leningrad 1985.

Lacey   W. K. Lacey, *The Family in Classical Greece,* London–Southampton 1968.

Lachenaud   G. Lachenaud, *Mythologies, religion et philosophie de l'histoire dans Hérodote,* Lille–Paris 1978.

L'Africa Romana   *L'Africa Romana X,* Sassari 1992.

Lamberts   E. Lamberts, *Studien zur Parataxe bei Herodot,* Vienna 1970.

Lane   E. Lane, *The Manners and Customs of the Modern Egyptians,* Everyman edn., London 1966.

Lang   M. L. Lang, *Herodotean Narrative and Discourse,* Cambridge, Mass.–London 1984.

Lange   K. Lange, *Sesostris: ein ägyptischer König in Mythos, Geschichte und Kunst,* Munich 1954.

Laronde   A. Laronde, *Cyrène et la Libye hellénistique,* Paris 1987.

Lateiner   D. Lateiner, *The Historical Method of Herodotus,* Phoenix Suppl., XXIII, Toronto 1989.

Lauer, *Le Problème*   J.-P. Lauer, *Le Problème des pyramides d'Égypte,* Paris 1948.

Lauer, *Observations*   J.-P. Lauer, *Observations sur les pyramides,* MIFAO XXX, Cairo 1960.

Lawrence   A. W. Lawrence, *The History of Herodotus of Halicarnassus,* London 1935.

LdÄ   *Lexikon der Ägyptologie,* I–VI, ed. W. Helck *et al.,* Wiesbaden 1975–86.

Leahy   A. Leahy (ed.), *Libya and Egypt* c. 1300–750, London
                         1990.
Lebedynsky   L. Lebedynsky, *Les Scythes. La Civilisation nomade des*
                         steppes, VIIe–IIIe siècle av J.-C., Paris 2001.
Leclant   J. Leclant, 'Les Relations entre l'Égypte et la Phénicie
                         du voyage d'Ounamon à l'expédition d'Alexandre', in
                         W. A. Ward, *The Role of the Phoenicians in the Inter-*
                         action of Mediterranean Civilisations. Papers Pre-
                         sented to the Archaeological Symposium at the
                         American University of Beirut. March 1967, Beirut
                         1968, pp. 9 ff.
Lefebvre   G. Lefebvre, *Le Tombeau de Petosiris*, I–III, Cairo
                         1923–4.
Legrand, *Hérodote,*
Histoires   Ph.-E. Legrand, *Hérodote, Histoires* I–XI, Paris
                         1932–54.
Legrand, *Introduction* Ph.-E. Legrand, *Hérodote; Introduction*, Paris 1955².
Lepsius, *Denkmäler*   K. R. Lepsius, *Denkmäler aus Ägypten und Äthiopien*,
                         I–XII, Berlin 1849–58.
Leuze   O. Leuze, *Die Satrapieneinteilung in Syrien und*
                         Zweiströmlande von 520–320, Schriften der Königs-
                         berger Gelehrten Gesellschaft, XI, Halle 1935.
Levi   M. A. Levi, *I nomadi alla frontiera*, Rome 1989.
Lewis   D. M. Lewis, *Sparta and Persia, Cincinnati Classical*
                         Studies, NS I, Leiden 1977.
LGPN   *A Lexicon of Greek Personal Names*, ed. P. M. Fraser
                         and E. Matthews, Oxford 1987 ff.
Lhardy   B. H. Lhardy, *Quaestionum de dialecto Herodotea*
                         caput I, Berolini 1844.
Lhote   H. Lhote, *The Search for the Tassili Frescoes: The Story*
                         of the Prehistoric Rock-paintings of the Sahara (trans.
                         A. H. Brodrick) London 1959 (1973²).
Lichtheim, *Late Period* M. Lichtheim, *Ancient Egyptian Literature*, III. *The*
                         Late Period, Berkeley–Los Angeles 1980.
Lichtheim, *Old and*
Middle Kingdoms   M. Lichtheim, *Ancient Egyptian Literature*, I. *The Old*
                         and Middle Kingdoms, Berkeley–Los Angeles 1975.
Lichtheim, *New Kingdom* M. Lichtheim, *Ancient Egyptian Literature*, II. *The*
                         New Kingdom, Berkeley–Los Angeles–London 1976.
Lie   A. G. Lie, *The Inscriptions of Sargon II King of Assyria*,
                         I. *The Annals*, Paris 1929.
LIMC   *Lexicon Iconographicum Mythologiae Classicae*,
                         Zurich–Munich 1984 ff.

Lindegger	P. Lindegger, *Griechische und römische Quellen zum peripheren Tibet*, I. *Frühe Zeugnisse bis Herodot (Der fernere skythische Nordosten)*, Zurich 1979.
Linforth	I. M. Linforth, *Greek Gods and Foreign Gods in Herodotus*, UCPCPh IX 1, Berkeley 1926.
Lloyd, *Commentary 1–98*	Alan B. Lloyd, *Herodotus Book II. Commentary 1–98*, EPRO 43, Leiden 1976.
Lloyd, *Commentary 99–182*	Alan B. Lloyd, *Herodotus Book II. Commentary 99–182*, EPRO 43, Leiden–New York–Copenhagen–Cologne 1988.
Lloyd, *Introduction*	Alan B. Lloyd, *Herodotus Book II. Introduction*, EPRO 43, Leiden 1975.
Long	T. Long, *Repetition and Variation in the Short Stories of Herodotus*, Frankfurt 1987.
Lortet–Gaillard, *La Faune momifiée*	L. Lortet and C. Gaillard, *La Faune momifiée de l'ancienne Égypte*, Lyon 1905–7.
LSJ	H. G. Liddell and R. Scott, A *Greek–English Lexicon*, rev. H. Jones, Oxford 1966⁹.
Lucas–Harris, *AEMI*	A. Lucas, *Ancient Egyptian Materials and Industries*, rev. J. R. Harris, London 1962⁴.
Luckenbill	D. D. Luckenbill, *Ancient Records of Assyria and Babylonia*, II, Chicago 1927.
Lüddeckens	E. Lüddeckens, 'Herodot und Ägypten', ZDMG CIV (1954), 330 ff. = *Herodot*, ed. W. Marg, *Wege der Forschung*, XXVI, Darmstadt 1965, pp. 434 ff.
Luni	Mario Luni (ed.), *Cirene 'Atene d'Africa'*, Monografie di archeologia libica, XXVIII, Rome 2006.
Luraghi	N. Luraghi (ed.), *The Historian's Craft in the Age of Herodotus*, Oxford 2001.
LXX	The Septuagint
Macan	*Herodotus, The Fourth, Fifth, and Sixth Book*, with introduction, notes, appendices, indices, maps, by R. W. Macan, London–New York 1895.
MacDowell	D. M. MacDowell, *The Law in Classical Athens*, London 1978.
Maddalena	A. Maddalena, *Interpretazioni erodotee*, Padua 1942.
Madvig	J. N. Madvig, *Adversaria critica ad scriptores graecos et latinos*, I–III, Hauniae 1871–84.
Magie	D. Magie, *Roman Rule in Asia Minor*, I–II, Princeton 1950.
Malkin	I. Malkin, *Religion and Colonization in Ancient Greece*, Leiden 1987.
Malten	L. Malten, *Kyrene*, Berlin 1911.

Marg   W. Marg (ed.), *Herodot: eine Auswahl aus der neueren Forschung*, Darmstadt, 1962.

Marincola   J. Marincola, *Authority and Tradition in Ancient Historiography*, Cambridge 1997.

Marquart   J. Marquart, *Untersuchungen zur Geschichte von Eran*, I, Göttingen 1896; II, *Philologus* Suppl., X 1, Leipzig 1905.

Martynov–Alekseev   A. I. Martynov and V. P. Alekseev, *Istorija i paleoantropologija skifo-sibirskogo mira. Učebnoe posobie*, Kemerovo 1986.

Masaracchia   A. Masaracchia, *Studi erodotei*, Biblioteca di Helikon, *Testi e studi*, X, Rome 1976.

Masson–Yoyotte   O. Masson and J. Yoyotte, *Objets pharaoniques à inscription carienne*, XV, Cairo 1956.

Mayrhofer   M. Mayrhofer, *Onomastica Persepolitana. Das altiranische Namengut der Persepolis-Täfelchen*, Vienna 1973.

Mazzarino   S. Mazzarino, *Fra oriente e occidente*, Florence 1947.

Mazzarino, *Il pensiero* S. Mazzarino, *Il pensiero storico classico*, I, Rome–Bari 1965.

Meiggs   R. Meiggs, *The Athenian Empire*, Oxford 1972 (rev. edn. 1975).

Meinertzhagen   R. Meinertzhagen, *Nicoll's Birds of Egypt*, I–II, London 1930.

Mele   A. Mele, *Il commercio greco arcaico. Prexis ed emporie*, Naples 1979.

Meljukova, *Skifija*   A. I. Meljukova, *Skifija i frakijskij mir*, Moscow 1979.
Meljukova, *Vooruženie*   A. I. Meljukova, *Vooruženie Skifov*, Moscow 1964.
Meulenaere   H. de Meulenaere, *Herodotos over de 26ste Dynastie*, Leuven, 1951.

Meyer, *Forschungen*   Ed. Meyer, *Forschungen zur alten Geschichte*, I, Halle 1892; II, Halle 1899.

Meyer, *Geschichte*   Ed. Meyer, *Geschichte des Altertums*, Stuttgart–Berlin 1926[5].

Miller   M. Miller, *The Thalassocracies*, Albany, NY 1971.
Minns   E. H. Minns, *Scythians and Greeks: A Survey of Ancient History and Archaeology on the North Coast of the Euxine from the Danube to the Caucasus*, Cambridge 1913.

ML   R. Meiggs and D. M. Lewis, *A Selection of Greek Historical Inscriptions*, Oxford 1969 (1989[2]).

Moggi   M. Moggi, *I sinecismi interstatali greci*, I, Pisa 1976.
Mongol Mission   *The Mongol Mission: Narratives and Letters of the Franciscan Missionaries in Mongolia and China in*

	the Thirteenth and Fourteenth Centuries, ed. C. Dawson, London 1955.
Montet, *Everyday Life*	P. Montet, *Everyday Life in Egypt in the Days of Ramesses the Great*, London 1962.
Montet, *Géographie*	P. Montet, *Géographie de l'Égypte ancienne*, I–II, Paris 1957–61.
Montet, *Les Scènes*	P. Montet, *Les Scènes de la vie privée dans les tombeaux égyptiens de l'ancien Empire*, Strasbourg 1925.
Montgomery	H. Montgomery, *Gedanke und Tat. Zur Erzählungstechnik bei Herodot, Thukydides, Xenophon und Arrian*, Lund 1965.
Moorhouse	A. C. Moorhouse, *The Syntax of Sophocles*, Leiden 1982.
Mora	F. Mora, *Religione e religioni nelle Storie di Erodoto*, Milan 1986.
Morenz, *Ägyptische Religion*	S. Morenz, *Ägyptische Religion*, Stuttgart 1960.
Morenz, *Die Begegnung*	S. Morenz, *Die Begegnung Europas mit Ägypten*, Berlin 1968.
Moret	A. Moret, *Le Rituel du culte divin journalier en Égypte*, Paris 1902.
Moretti	L. Moretti, *Olympionikai*, *MAL* VIII 8, Rome 1957.
Morrison	J. S. Morrison, J. F. Coates, and N. B. Rankov, *The Athenian Trireme: The History and Reconstruction of an Ancient Greek Warship*, Cambridge 1986; 2000[2].
Müller	D. Müller, *Topographischer Bildkommentar zu den Historien Herodots*, I. *Griechenland*, Tübingen 1987; II, *Kleinasien und angrenzende Gebiete mit Südostthrakien und Zypern*, Tübingen 1997.
Müller, *Geschichte*	K. E. Müller, *Geschichte der antiken Ethnographie und ethnologischen Theoriebildung, Studien zur Kulturkunde XXIX*, I, Wiesbaden 1972.
Musti–Beschi	*Pausania, Guida della Grecia. Libro I. L'Attica*, ed. D. Musti and L. Beschi, Milan 1986.
Musti–Torelli	*Pausania, Guida della Grecia. Libro III. La Laconia*, ed. D. Musti and M. Torelli, Milan 1991.
Myres	J. L. Myres, *Herodotus Father of History*, Oxford 1953.
Nafissi	M. Nafissi, *La nascita del 'kosmos'. Studi sulla storia e societa di Sparta*, Naples 1991.
Narody	A. I. Dovatur, D. P. Kallistov, and I. A. Šišova, *Narody našej strany v 'istorii' Gerodota. Teksty, perevod, kommentarij*, Moscow 1982.
Nejchardt	A. A. Nejchardt, *Skifskij rasskaz Gerodota v otečestvennoj istoriografii*, Leningrad 1982.

Nelson, *Medinet Habu*   H. H. Nelson (ed.), *Medinet Habu*, I–VIII, Chicago 1930 ff.

Nenci   G. Nenci, *Introduzione alle guerre persiane*, Pisa 1958.

Nestle   W. Nestle, *Herodots Verhältnis zur Philosophie und Sophistik*, Stuttgart 1908.

Neumann, *Die Hellenen*   K. Neumann, *Die Hellenen im Skythenland*, I, Berlin 1855.

Neumann, *Nordafrika*   C. W. R. Neumann, *Nordafrika (mit Ausschluss des Nilgebietes) nach Herodot*, Leipzig 1891.

Nicolai   W. Nicolai, *Versuch über Herodots Geschichtsphilosophie*, Bibliothek der klassischen Altertumswissenschaften, NF II 77, Heidelberg 1986.

Nicoll   M. J. Nicoll, *Handlist of the Birds of Egypt*, Cairo 1919.

Nielsen   T. M. Nielsen (ed.), *Yet More Studies in the Ancient Greek Polis*, Stuttgart 1997.

Nilsson, *Feste*   M. P. Nilsson, *Griechische Feste*, Leipzig 1906.

Nilsson, *GgrR*   M. P. Nilsson, *Geschichte der griechischen Religion*, I, Munich 1967³; II, Munich 1950.

Nomodeiktes   R. Rosen and J. Farrell (eds.), *Nomodeiktes: Greek Studies in Honor of Martin Ostwald*, Ann Arbor 1993.

Norden   E. Norden, *Die germanische Urgeschichte in Tacitus' 'Germania'*, Darmstadt 1959⁴.

Noshy   I. Noshy, 'Arcesilaus III', in *Libya in History*, Benghazi–Beyrouth 1971, pp. 53–79.

OCD³   *The Oxford Classical Dictionary*, ed. S. Hornblower and A. Spawforth, 3rd edn. revised, Oxford 2003.

Oertel   F. Oertel, *Herodots ägyptischer Logos und die Glaubwürdigkeit Herodots*, Bonn 1970.

Olmstead   A. T. Olmstead, *The History of the Persian Empire*, Chicago–London 1959.

Le origini dei Greci   *Le origini dei Greci. Dori e mondo egeo*, Rome–Bari 1986.

Ottone   G. Ottone, *Libyka. Testimonianze e frammenti*, Rome 2002.

Paap   A. H. R. E. Paap, *De Herodoti reliquiis in papyris et membranis Aegyptiis servatis*, Papyrologica Lugduno-Batava, IV, Leiden 1948.

Pagel   K. A. Pagel, 'Die Bedeutung des aitiologisches Momentes für Herodots Geschichtsschreibung', Diss. Berlin 1927.

Panitz   H. Panitz, *Mythos und Orakel bei Herodot*, Greifswalder Beiträge, II, Greifswald 1935.

Parke, *Greek Oracles*   H. W. Parke, *Greek Oracles*, London 1967

Parke, *Oracles of Zeus*   H. W. Parke, *The Oracles of Zeus*, Oxford 1967.

Parker	R. A. Parker, *The Calendars of Ancient Egypt*, Chicago 1950.
Parker, *AR*	R. Parker, *Athenian Religion: A History*, Oxford 1996.
Parker, *Polytheism*	R. Parker, *Polytheism and Society at Athens*, Oxford 2005.
Parker–Dubberstein	R. A. Parker and W. H. Dubberstein, *Babylonian Chronology 626 B.C–A.D. 75, Brown University Studies*, XIX, Providence 1956 (rev. edn. 1971).
Pasquali, *Scritti*	G. Pasquali, *Scritti Filologici*, I, Florence 1986.
Pasquali, *Storia*	G. Pasquali, *Storia della tradizione e critica del testo*, Florence 1962².
Payen	P. Payen, *Les Îles nomades. Conquérir et résister dans l'enquête d'Hérodote*, Paris 1997.
PCG	*Poetae Comici Graeci*, ed. C. Austin and R. Kassel, Berlin–New York 1983 ff.
PE	*Poetae Elegiaci. Testimonia et fragmenta*, II. Ed. B. Gentili and C. Prato, Munich/Leipzig 2002².
Pearson	L. Pearson, *The Early Ionian Historians*, Oxford 1939.
PECS	*The Princeton Encyclopedia of Classical Sites*, ed. R. Stillwell, W. L. MacDonald, and M. H. McAllister, Princeton 1976.
Pedley	J. G. Pedley, *Ancient Literary Sources on Sardis*, Cambridge, Mass. 1972.
PEG	*Poetarum Epicorum Graecorum Testimonia et Fragmenta*, I, ed. A. Bernabé, Leipzig 1987.
Peradotto–Boedeken	J. Peradotto and D. Boedeker (eds.), *Herodotus and the Invention of History, Arethusa*, XX 1–2, New York 1987.
Peretti	A. Peretti, *Il Periplo di Scilace. Studio sul primo portolano del Mediterraneo*, Pisa 1979.
PFT	R. T. Hallock, *Persepolis Fortification Tablets*, Chicago 1969.
Philippson	A. Philippson, *Die griechischen Landschaften*, I–IV, Frankfurt am Main 1950–9.
Picard	G. Ch. Picard, *Les Religions de l'Afrique antique*, Paris 1954.
Piccirilli	L. Piccirilli, *Gli arbitrati interstatali greci*, I, Pisa 1973.
Pippidi	D. M. Pippidi, *I Greci nel basso Danubio*, Milan 1971.
Pirro	A. Pirro, *Studi erodotei*, Pisa 1894.
PLF	E. Lobel and D. Page, *Poetarum Lesbiorum Fragmenta*, Oxford 1955.
PM	B. Porter and R. L. B. Moss, *Topographical Bibliography of Ancient Egyptian Hieroglyphic Texts, Reliefs, and Paintings*, I–II, Oxford 1960–72²; III, rev. and augm. J. Malek, Oxford 1974 ff.; IV–VII, Oxford 1962 ff.

PMG   D. L. Page, *Poetae Melici Graeci*, Oxford 1961 (rev.
                        edn. 1983).

Pohlenz   M. Pohlenz, *Herodot, der erste Geschichtsschreiber des
                        Abendlandes, Neue Wege zur Antike*, II 7/8, Leipzig
                        1937.

Posener   G. Posener, *La Première domination perse en Égypte*,
                        Bibliothèque d'étude, XI, Cairo 1936.

Potratz   J. A. H. Potratz, *Die Skythen in Südrussland*, Basel
                        1963.

Powell, *Lexicon*   J. E. Powell, *A Lexicon to Herodotus*, Cambridge 1938.

Powell, *The History*   J. E. Powell, *The History of Herodotus*, Cambridge
                        1939.

Powell–Hodkinson   A. Powell and S. Hodkinson (eds.), *Sparta Beyond the
                        Mirage*, London–Swansea 2002.

Prášek   J. V. Prášek, *Kambyses, Der Alte Orient*, XIV 2, Leipzig
                        1913.

Pritchett   W. K. Pritchett, *Studies in Ancient Greek Topography*,
                        IV, Berkeley 1982.

Problemi   *Problemi della 'chora' coloniale dall'Occidente al Mar
                        Nero. Atti del XL Convegno di studi sulla Magna
                        Grecia, Taranto, 29 settembre–3 ottobre 2000*, Taranto
                        2001.

Problemy   *Problemy antičnogo istočnikovedenija*, Moscow-
                        Leningrad 1986.

P–W   H. W. Parke and D. E. W. Wormell, *The Delphic
                        Oracle*, I–II, Oxford 1956.

Raaflaub   K. Raaflaub, *The Discovery of Freedom in Ancient
                        Greece*, Chicago 2004 (rev. English edn. of *Die
                        Entdeckung der Freiheit. Zur historischen Semantik
                        und Gesellschaftsgeschichte eines politischen Grund-
                        begriffes der Griechen*, Munich 1985).

RAC   *Reallexikon für Antike und Christentum*, ed.
                        F. J. Dölger *et al.*, Stuttgart 1950 ff.

Raevskij   D. S. Raevskij, *Očerki ideologii Skifo-Sakskich plemën
                        (opyt rekonstrukcii skifskoj ideologii)*, Moscow 1977.

Raevskij, *Model' mira* D. S. Raevskij, *Model' mira skifskoj kul'tury*, Moscow
                        1985.

Ranke   H. Ranke, *Die ägyptischen Personennamen*, I–II,
                        Glückstadt 1935–52.

Rasch   I. Rasch, *Sophocles quid debeat Herodoto in rebus ad
                        fabulas exornandas adhibitis*, Leipzig 1913.

Ravn   O. E. Ravn, *Herodotus' Description of Babylon*,
                        Copenhagen 1942.

Rawlinson   G. Rawlinson (with notes by Sir J. Gardner
                        Wilkinson), *History of Herodotus*, London 1880⁴.

RE	*Real-Encyclopädie der classischen Altertumswissenschaft*, ed. G. Wissowa, W. Kroll, K. Mittelhaus, and K. Ziegler, Stuttgart 1893 ff.
Reeder	E. D. Reeder (ed.), *Scythian Gold*, New York 1999.
Reese	W. Reese, *Die griechische Nachrichten für Indien bis zum Feldzuge Alexanders des Grossen. Eine Sammlung der Berichte und ihre Untersuchung*, Leipzig 1914.
Reiske	J. J. Reiske, *Animadversionum ad Graecos auctores libri III*, Lipsiae 1761.
Rennell	J. Rennell, *The Geographical System of Herodotus*, I–II, London 1830².
Rhodes	P. J. Rhodes, *A Commentary on the Aristotelian Athenaion Politeia*, Oxford 1981.
Riemann	K. Riemann, 'Das herodotische Geschichtswerk in der Antike', Diss. Munich 1967.
RLA	*Reallexikon der Assyriologie*, Berlin 1931 ff.
Rohde	E. Rohde, *Psyche: The Cult of Souls and Belief in Immortality Among the Greeks*, London 1925.
Rolle, *Scythians*	R. Rolle, *The World of the Scythians* (trans. G. Walls), London 1989.
Rolle, *Totenkult*	R. Rolle, *Totenkult der Skythen*, I. *Das Steppengebiet*, 1–2, Berlin–New York 1979.
Romm	J. S. Romm, *The Edges of the Earth in Ancient Thought: Geography, Exploration and Fiction*, Princeton 1992.
Romm, *Herodotus*	J. S. Romm, *Herodotus*, New Haven–London 1998
Roscher, *AGWL*	W. H. Roscher, *Die Sieben- und Neunzahl in kultus und Mythus des Griechen...*, *Abhandlung der Philologisch-Historischen Klasse der Königlichen Sächsischen Gesellschaft der wiss. in Leipzig*, XXIV, Leipzig 1904.
Roscher, *Lexikon*	W. H. Roscher (ed.), *Ausführliches Lexikon der griechischen und römischen Mythologie*, I–VI, Leipzig–Berlin 1884–1937.
Rose, *Handbook Greek Literature*	H. J. Rose, *A Handbook of Greek Literature*, London 1951⁴.
Rose, *Handbook Greek Mythology*	H. J. Rose, *A Handbook of Greek Mythology*, Oxford 1964⁶.
Rosén, *Sprachform*	H. B. Rosén, *Eine Laut- und Formenlehre der herodotischen Sprache*, Heidelberg 1962.
Rostovtzeff	M. Rostovtzeff, *Iranians and Greeks in South Russia*, Oxford 1922.

Rostowzew   M. Rostowzew, *Skythien und der Bosporus*, I. *Kritische Übersicht der schriftlichen und archäologischen Quellen*, Berlin 1931.

Rudenko   S. I. Rudenko, *Frozen Tombs of Siberia*, London 1970.

Rusjaeva   A. S. Rusjaeva, *Zemledel'českie kul'ty v Ol'vii dogetskogo perioda*, Kiev 1979.

Rybakov   B. A. Rybakov, *Gerodotova Skifija. Istoriko-geografičeskij analiz*, Moscow 1979.

Sabri Kolta   K. Sabri Kolta, 'Die Gleichsetzung ägyptischer und griechischer Götter bei Herodot', Diss. Tübingen 1968.

Salmon   P. Salmon, *La Politique égyptienne d'Athènes (VIe et Ve siècles avant J.-C.)*, Brussels 1965.

Sancisi-Weerdenburg   H. Sancisi-Weerdenburg, 'Yaunā en Persai. Grieken en Perzen in een ander perspectief', Diss. Leiden 1980.

Sauneron   S. Sauneron *et al.*, *Les Songes et leur interprétation*, Sources Orientales, II, Paris 1959.

Sayce   A. H. Sayce, *The Ancient Empires of the East: Herodotus I–III*, London 1883.

Schaefer   H. Schaefer, *Probleme der alten Geschichte*, Göttingen 1963.

v. Scheliha   R. von Scheliha, *Die Wassergrenze im Altertum*, Historische Untersuchungen, VIII, Breslau 1931.

Schepens   G. Schepens, *L'Autopsie' dans la méthode des historiens grecs du Ve siècle avant J.-C.*, Brussels 1980.

Schlatter   F. W. Schlatter, 'Salamis and Plataea in the Tradition of the Attic Orator', Diss. Princeton 1960.

Schlott   A. Schlott, 'Die Ausmaße Ägyptens nach altägyptischen Texten', Diss. Tübingen 1969.

Schmitt   R. Schmitt, *Compendium Linguarum Iranicarum*, Wiesbaden 1989.

Schnebel   M. Schnebel, *Die Landwirtschaft im hellenistischen Ägypten*, I, Munich 1925.

Schramm   G. Schramm, *Nordpontische Ströme. Namenphilologische Zugänge zur Frühzeit des europäischen Ostens*, Göttingen 1973.

Schulte   E. H. Schulte, 'Herodots Darstellung der grossen griechischen Feldherrn', Diss. Marburg 1966.

Schulte-Atedorneburg   J. Schulte-Atedorneburg, *Geschichtliches Handeln und tragisches Scheitern. Herodots Konzept historiographischer Mimesis*, Frankfurt–Berlin–Bern 2001.

Schulz   E. Schulz, 'Die Reden im Herodot', Diss. Greifswald 1933.

Schwarz   E. Schwarz, *Quaestiones Herodoteae*, Rostock 1890.

Schwyzer, *Gr. Grammatik*   E. Schwyzer, A. Debrunner, and D. J. Georgacas, *Griechische Grammatik*, I–III, Munich 1934–53.

SEG   *Supplementum Epigraphicum Graecum*, Lugduni Batavorum 1923 ff.

Seibert   J. Seibert, *Metropolis und Apoikie*, Würzburg 1963.

Seidl   E. Seidl, *Ägyptische Rechtsgeschichte der Saiten- und Perserzeit*, *Ägyptologische Forschungen*, XX, Glückstadt 1968².

de Selincourt   A. de Selincourt, *The World of Herodotus*, London 1962.

Šelov   D. B. Šelov, 'Der nördliche Schwarzmeerraum in der Antike', in H. Heinen (ed.), *Geschichte des Altertums im Spiegel der sowietischen Forschung*, Darmstadt 1980, pp. 341–409.

Sethe, *Ägyptische*   K. Sethe, *Ägyptische Lesestücke: Texte des Mittleren Reiches*, Leipzig 1924.

Sethe, *Sesostris*   K. Sethe, *Sesostris, Untersuchungen*, II 1, Leipzig 1900.

SGDI   H. Collitz and F. Bechtel, *Sammlung der griechischen Dialekt-Inschriften*, I–IV, Göttingen 1885–1910.

Shimron   B. Shimron, *Politics and Belief in Herodotus*, Historia Einzelschriften, LVIII, Wiesbaden 1989.

Shipley   G. Shipley, *A History of Samos 800–188 BC*, Oxford 1987.

Sieberer   W. Sieberer, *Das Bild Europas in den Historien. Studien zu Herodots Geographie und Ethnographie Europas und seiner Schilderung der persischen Feldzüge*, Innsbruck 1995.

Sigerist   H. Sigerist, *A History of Medicine*, I–II, New York 1951–61.

Singer *et al.*   C. Singer, E. J. Holmyard, and H. R. Hall, *History of Technology*, I–V, Oxford 1954–8.

Skifskij mir   *Skifskij mir*, Kiev 1975.

Skify i Sarmaty   *Skify i Sarmaty*, Kiev 1977.

Skify severnogo   *Skify severnogo pričernomor'ja*, Kiev 1987.

Slovo o pŭlku Igorevě   *The Song of Igor's Campaign: An Epic of the Twelfth Century*, trans. Vladimir Nabokov, London 1960.

Smirnov   K. F. Smirnov, *Savromaty*, Moscow 1964.

Smith–Dawson   G. E. Smith and W. R. Dawson, *Egyptian Mummies*, London 1924.

Smith   W. S. Smith, *The Art and Architecture of Ancient Egypt*, rev. with additions by W. Kelly Simpson, Harmondsworth 1981.

Solovyov   S. L. Solovyov, *Ancient Berezan: The Architecture, History and Culture of the First Greek Colony in the Northern Black Sea*, Leiden–Boston–Cologne 1999.

Sourdille, *Hérodote*   C. Sourdille, *Hérodote et la religion de l'Égypte*, Paris
                               1910.

Sourdille, *La Durée*   C. Sourdille, *La Durée et l'étendue du voyage d'Hér-
                               odote en Égypte*, Paris 1910.

Spath   T. Spath, 'Das Motiv der doppelten Beleuchtung bei
                               Herodot', Diss. Vienna 1968.

Spencer   A. J. Spencer, *Death in Ancient Egypt*, Harmonds-
                               worth 1982.

Spiegelberg, *Demotische*
Chronik   W. Spiegelberg, *Die sogenannte Demotische Chronik
                               des Pap. 215 der Bibliothèque Nationale zu Paris*,
                               Demotische Studien, VII, Leipzig 1914.

Spiegelberg,
Glaubwürdigkeit   W. Spiegelberg, *Die Glaubwürdigkeit von Herodots
                               Bericht über Ägypten im Lichte der ägyptischen Denk-
                               mäler*, *Orient und Antike*, III, Heidelberg 1926.

Šramko   B. A. Šramko, *Bel'skoe gorodišče skifskoj epochi (gorod
                               Gelon)*, Kiev 1987.

Stahlenbrecher   W. Stahlenbrecher, 'Die Motivation des Handelns bei
                               Herodot', Diss. Hamburg 1963.

Steinger   G. Steinger, 'Epische Elemente im Redenstil
                               Herodots', Diss. Kiel 1957.

Stepi   *Stepi evropejskoj časti SSSR v skifo-sarmatskoe vremia*,
                               ed. A. I. Meljukova, Moscow 1989.

Stern   M. Stern, *Greek and Latin Authors on Jews and Juda-
                               ism*, I–III, Jerusalem 1974–84.

Stibbe   C. M. Stibbe, *Lakonische Vasenmaler des sechsten
                               Jahrhunderts v. Chr.*, Amsterdam–London 1972.

Strasburger   H. Strasburger, 'Herodots Zeitrechnung', *Historia*, V
                               (1956), 129 ff.; rev. in *Herodot*, ed. W. Marg, *Wege der
                               Forschung*, XXVI, Darmstadt 1965, pp. 677 ff.

Stucchi   S. Stucchi, *Architettura cirenaica*, Rome 1975.

Studniczka   F. Studniczka, *Kyrene, eine altgriechische Göttin*,
                               Leipzig 1890.

StV   H. Bengtson, *Die Staatsverträge des Altertums*, II,
                               Munich 1962.

Sulimirski, *Prehistoric*
Russia   T. Sulimirski, *Prehistoric Russia*, London 1970.

Sulimirski, *Sarmatians*   T. Sulimirski, *The Sarmatians*, London 1970.

Syll.   W. Dittenberger, *Sylloge Inscriptionum Graecarum*,
                               I–IV, Leipzig 1915–21³.

Szemerényi   O. Szemerényi, *Four Old Iranian Ethnic Names:
                               Scythian–Skudra–Sogdian–Saka*, Vienna 1980.

Täckholm–Drar   V. and G. Täckholm, and M. Drar, *Flora of Egypt*,
                               I–III, Cairo 1941–54.

Talamo	C. Talamo, *La Lidia arcaica*, Bologna 1979.
Talbot Rice	T. Talbot Rice, *The Scythians*, London 1957.
Terenožkin	A. I. Terenožkin, *Kimmerijcy*, Kiev 1976.
Testi dello sciamanesimo	*Testi dello sciamanesimo siberiano e centroasiatico*, ed. U. Marazzi, Turin 1984.
TGF	A. Nauck and B. Snell, *Tragicorum Graecorum Fragmenta* (new edn.), Hildesheim 1964.
Thomas, *Herodotus*	R. Thomas, *Herodotus in Context: Ethnography, Science and the Art of Persuasion*, Cambridge 2000
Thomas, *Oral Tradition*	R. Thomas, *Oral Tradition and Written Record in Classical Athens*, Cambridge 1989.
Thompson, *Greek Birds*	D. W. Thompson, *A Glossary of Greek Birds*, Oxford 1936².
Thompson, *Greek Fishes*	D. W. Thompson, *A Glossary of Greek Fishes*, Oxford 1947.
Thompson, *Folktale*	S. Thompson, *The Folktale*, Berkeley–Los Angeles–London 1977.
Thompson, *Motif-Index*	S. Thompson, *Motif-Index of Folk Literature*, I–VI, Copenhagen 1955–8.
Thomson	J. O. Thomson, *History of Ancient Geography*, Cambridge 1948.
Tod	M. N. Tod, *A Selection of Greek Historical Inscriptions*, I–II, Oxford 1946²–8.
Tölle-Kastenbein	R. Tölle-Kastenbein, *Herodot und Samos*, Bochum 1976.
Toynbee	A. J. Toynbee, *A Study of History*, VII, Oxford 1954.
Traill	J. S. Traill, *Persons of Ancient Athens*, I ff., Toronto 1994 ff.
Travlos	J. Travlos, *Bildlexicon zur Topographie des antiken Attika*, Tübingen 1988.
Trigger	B. G. Trigger *et al.*, *Ancient Egypt: A Social History*, Cambridge 1983.
Trüdinger	K. Trüdinger, *Studien zur Geschichte der griechisch-römischen Ethnographie*, Basel 1918.
Tsetskhladze, *Ancient Greeks*	G. R. Tsetskhladze (ed.), *Ancient Greeks East and West*, Leiden–Boston–Cologne 1999.
Tsetskhladze, *North Pontic Archaeology*	G. R. Tsetskhladze (ed.), *North Pontic Archaeology: Recent Discoveries and Studies*, Leiden–Boston–Cologne 1999.
Tsetskhladze–De Angelis	G. R. Tsetskhladze and F. De Angelis (eds.), *The Archaeology of Greek Colonisation: Essays Dedicated to Sir John Boardman*, Oxford 1994.

Tsetskhladze–Snodgrass   G. R. Tsetskhladze and A. M. Snodgrass (eds.), *Greek Settlements in the East Mediterranean and the Black Sea*, Oxford 2002 (BAR Int. Series 1062).

Tyrrell   W. B. Tyrrell, *Amazons: A Study in Athenian Mythmaking*, Baltimore 1984.

Ubsdell   S. Ubsdell, 'Herodotus on Human Nature', Diss. Oxford 1983.

Urk.   K. Sethe *et al.*, *Urkunden des aegyptischen Altertums*, I–VIII, Leipzig–Berlin 1904–57.

Vandier, *La Religion*   J. Vandier, *La Religion égyptienne*, Paris 1949².

Vandier, *Manuel*   J. Vandier, *Manuel d'archéologie égyptienne*, I–VI, Paris 1952–78.

Vanhaegendoren   K. Vanhaegendoren, *Das Afrikanische Volk der Ataranten: zur ethnographischen Tradition der Antike*, Münster 1998.

Van Wees   H. van Wees (ed.), *War and Violence in Ancient Greece*, London–Swansea 2000.

Van Wees, *Greek Warfare*   H. van Wees, *Greek Warfare: Myths and Realities*, London 2004.

Vasmer   M. Vasmer, *Untersuchungen über die älteste Wohnsitze der Slaven*, I. *Die Iranier in Südrussland*, Leipzig 1923.

Verdin   H. Verdin, *De historisch-kritische Methode van Herodotus*, Brussels 1971.

Vignolo Munson   R. Vignolo Munson, *Telling Wonders: Ethnographic and Political Discourse in the Work of Herodotus*, Ann Arbor 2001.

Vinogradov, *Olbia*   Ju. G. Vinogradov, *Olbia. Geschichte einer altgriechischen Stadt am Schwarzen Meer*, Konstanz 1981.

Vinogradov, *Političeskaja*   Ju. G. Vinogradov, *Političeskaja istorija Ol'vijskogo polisa VII–I vv. do n.e. Istoriko-epigrafičeskoe issledovanie*, Moscow 1989.

Vinogradov–Kryžickij   Jurij G. Vinogradov and Sergei D. Kryžickij, *Olbia: eine altgriechische Stadt in nordwestlichen Schwarzmeerraum*, *Mnemosyne* Suppl. *CXLIX*, Leiden–New York 1995.

Virgilio   B. Virgilio, *Commento storico al quinto libro delle 'Storie' di Erodoto*, Pisa 1975.

Vittmann   G. Vittmann, *Ägypten und die Fremden im ersten vorchristlichen Jahrtausend*, Mainz 2003.

Vogt   J. Vogt, 'Herodot in Ägypten', in *Genethliakon Wilhelm Schmid, Tübinger Beiträge zur Altertumswissenschaft*, V, Stuttgart 1929, pp. 95 ff. = *Herodot*, ed. W. Marg, *Wege der Forschung*, XXVI, Darmstadt 1965, pp. 412 ff.

Voigtlander	E. N. Von Voigtlander, *The Bisitun Inscription of Darius the Great. Babylonian Version*, Corpus Inscriptionum Iranicarum, I 2, London 1978.
Volten	A. Volten, *Die demotische Traumdeutung*, Analecta Aegyptiaca, III, Copenhagen 1942.
Vos	M. F. Vos, *Scythian Archers in Archaic Attic Vasepainting*, Groningen 1963.
Waddell	W. G. Waddell, *Herodotus II*, London 1939.
Walbank	F. W. Walbank, A *Historical Commentary on Polybius*, I–III, Oxford 1957-79.
Wallinga	H. T. Wallinga, *Xerxes' Greek Adventure: The Naval Perspective*, Leiden–Boston 2005.
Walser, *Beiträge*	G. Walser (ed.), *Beiträge zur Achämeniden Geschichte*, *Historia* Einzelschriften, XVIII, Wiesbaden 1972.
Walser, *Völkerschaften*	G. Walser, *Die Völkerschaften auf den Reliefs von Persepolis*, Berlin 1966.
Wąsowicz	A. Wąsowicz, *Olbia pontique et son territoire: L'aménagement de l'espace*, Paris 1975.
Waters	K. H. Waters, *Herodotos on Tyrants and Despots. A Study in Objectivity*, *Historia* Einzelschriften XV, Wiesbaden 1971.
Waters, *Herodotus the Historian*	K. H. Waters, *Herodotus the Historian: His Problems, Methods and Originality*, London–Sidney 1985.
Wb.	A. Erman and H. Grapow, *Wörterbuch der ägyptischen Sprache*, I–VII, Leipzig 1926–63.
Weber	H. A. Weber, *Herodots Verständnis von Historie: Untersuchungen zur Methodologie und Argumentationsweise Herodots*, Bern–Frankfurt am Main-Munich 1976.
Wehrli	F. Wehrli (ed.), *Die Schule des Aristoteles. Texte und Kommentar*, I–X, Basel–Stuttgart 1967–9².
Wells	J. Wells, *Studies in Herodotus*, Oxford 1923.
Wheeler	J. Talboys Wheeler, *The Geography of Herodotus*, London 1854.
Wiesehöfer	J. Wiesehöfer, 'Der Aufstand Gaumatas und die Anfänge Dareios I', Diss. Bonn 1978.
Wilcken, *Chrestomathie*	U. Wilcken, in L. Mitteis and U. Wilcken, *Grundzüge und Chrestomathie der Papyruskunde*, I–II, Leipzig–Berlin 1912.
Wilkinson–Birch	J. Gardner Wilkinson and S. Birch, *The Manners and Customs of the Ancient Egyptians*, I–III, London 1878.
Wilson	J. A. Wilson, *Herodotus in Egypt*, Scholae Adriani de Buck Memoriae Dicatae, V, Leiden 1970.

Windberg	F. C. Windberg, 'De Herodoti Scythiae et Libyae descriptione', Diss. Göttingen 1913.
Wiseman	D. J. Wiseman, *Chronicles of Chaldaean Kings (626–556 B.C.) in the British Museum*, London 1961.
Wood	H. Wood, *The Histories of Herodotus: An Analysis of the Formal Structure*, The Hague–Paris 1972.
Wörterbuch der Myth.	*Wörterbuch der Mythologie*, ed. H. W. Haussig, Stuttgart 1965 ff.
Wreszinski	W. Wreszinski, *Atlas zur altägyptischen Kulturgeschichte*, I–III, Leipzig 1923–38.
Wüst	K. Wüst, 'Politisches Denken bei Herodot', Diss. Munich 1935.
Yoyotte	J. Yoyotte *et al.*, *Les Pèlerinages, Sources Orientales*, III, Paris 1960.
Zgusta	L. Zgusta, *Die Personennamen griechischer Städte der nördlichen Schwarzmeerküste*, Prague 1955.
Zimmerman	K. Zimmerman, *Libyen: Das Land südlich des Mittelmeers im Weltbild der Griechen*, Munich 1999.

Journals

AA	*Archäologischer Anzeiger*
A&A	*Antike und Abendland*
AAntHung	*Acta Antiqua Academiae Scientiarum Hungaricae*
AAT	*Atti della Accademia delle Scienze di Torino*
AAWW	*Anzeiger der Österreichischen Akademie der Wissenschaften in Wien, Phil.-Hist. Klasse*
ABSA	*Annual of the British School at Athens*
AC	*L'Antiquité Classique*
ACD	*Acta Classica Universitatis Scientiarum Debrecensis*
AE	*Archaiologiké Ephemeris*
AFLPer	*Annali della Facoltà di Lettere e Filosofia. Università degli Studi di Perugia*
AH	*Achaemenid History*
AI	*Acta Iranica*
AIIN	*Annali dell'Instituto Italiano di Numismatica*
AION	*Annali dell'Instituto Orientale di Napoli*
AJA	*American Journal of Archaeology*
AJAH	*American Journal of Ancient History*
AJPh	*American Journal of Philology*
AJSL	*American Journal of Semitic Languages and Literatures*
AMI	*Archäologische Mitteilungen aus Iran*
Anc. Soc.	*Ancient Society*

AncW	The Ancient World
AntAfr	Antiquités Africaines
AO	Archiv Orientální
APF	Archiv für Papyrusforschung
A&R	Atene e Roma
AS	Anatolian Studies
ASAE	Annales du Service des Antiquités d'Égypte
ASGE	Archeologičeskij Sbornik Gosudarstvennogo Ermitaža
ASNP	Annali della Scuola Normale Superiore di Pisa
AUB	Annales Universitatis Budapestinensis
AW	Antik Welt
BABesch	Bulletin Antieke Beschaving
BACPS	Bulletin of the Center of Papyrological Studies Cairo
BAB	Bulletin de la Classe des Lettres et des Sciences morales et politiques de l'Académie Royale de Belgique
BAGB	Bulletin de l'Association G. Budé
BASOR	Bulletin of the American Schools of Oriental Research
BCH	Bulletin de Correspondance Hellénique
BdE	Bibliothèque d'Étude
BHM	Bulletin of the History of Medicine
BICS	Bulletin of the Institute of Classical Studies
BIE	Bulletin de l'Institut d'Égypte
BIFAN	Bulletin de l'Institut Français d'Afrique Noire
BIFAO	Bulletin de l'Institut Français d'Archéologie Orientale
BNJ	Byzantinische-Neugriechische Jahrbücher
Boll.Class.	Bollettino dei classici, a cura del Comitato per la preparazione dell'Edizione nazionale dei Classici greci e latini
BSL	Bulletin de la Société de Linguistique de Paris
Burs Jb	Bursians Jahresbericht
BzN	Beiträge zur Namenforschung
CdE	Chronique d'Égypte
CISA	Contributi dell'Instituto di Storia antica dell'Università del Sacro Cuore Milano
CJ	The Classical Journal
ClassAnt	Classical Antiquity
CPh	Classical Philology
CQ	Classical Quarterly
CR	Classical Review
CRAI	Comptes rendus de l'Académie des Inscriptions et Belles-Lettres
CRDAC	Centro ricerche e documentazione sull'antichità classica
CSCA	California Studies in Classical Antiquity
CW	The Classical World
DHA	Dialogues d'Histoire Ancienne
EAZ	Ethnographisch-archäologische Zeitschrift
EC	Études Classiques

EEAth	Ἐπιστημονικὴ Ἐπετηρὶς τῆς Φιλοσοφικῆς Σχολῆς τοῦ Πανεπιστημίου Ἀθηνῶν
EMC	Echos du Monde Classique. Classical News and Views
GM	Göttinger Miszellen
G&R	Greece and Rome
GRBS	Greek, Roman and Byzantine Studies
HSCPh	Harvard Studies in Classical Philology
HThR	Harvard Theological Review
IA	Iranica Antiqua
ICS	Illinois Classical Studies
JA	Journal Asiatique
JAOS	Journal of the American Oriental Society
JARCE	Journal of the American Research Center in Egypt
JBL	Journal of Biblical Literature
JDAI	Jahrbuch des Deutschen Archäologischen Instituts
JEA	Journal of Egyptian Archaeology
JESHO	Journal of the Economic and Social History of the Orient
JHS	Journal of Hellenic Studies
JNES	Journal of Near Eastern Studies
JRAS	Journal of the Royal Asiatic Society
JRGZ	Jahrbuch des Römisch-Germanischen Zentralmuseums Mainz
JSOR	Journal of the Society of Oriental Research
JVEG	Jaarbericht van het Vooraziatisch-Egyptisch Genootschap 'Ex Oriente Lux'
JWI	Journal of the Warburg and Courtauld Institute
KSIA	Kratkie Soobščenija Instituta Archeologii Akademii Nauk SSSR
KSIIMK	Kratkie Soobščenija Instituta Istorii Material'noj Kultury
LAAA	Liverpool Annals of Archaeology and Anthropology
LCM	Liverpool Classical Monthly
LibStud	Libyan Studies
MAL	Memorie della Classe di Scienze morali e storiche dell'Accademia dei Lincei
MÄS	Münchner ägyptologische Studien
MASP	Materialy po Archeologii Severnogo Pričernomor'ja
MDAI(A)	Mitteilungen des Deutschen Archäologischen Instituts (Abt. Athens)
MDAI(K)	Mitteilungen des Deutschen Archäologischen Instituts (Abt. Kairo)
MDAI(M)	Mitteilungen des Deutschen Archäologischen Instituts (Abt. Madrid)
MEFRA	Mélanges de l'École Française de Rome, Antiquité
MGR	Miscellanea greca e romana
MH	Museum Helveticum
MIA	Materialy i Issledovanija po Archeologii SSSR
MIE	Mémoires de l'Institut d'Égypte
MIFAO	Mémoires publiés par les membres de l'Institut Français d'Archéologie orientale du Caire

MMF	*Mémoires publiés par les membres de la Mission archéologique française au Caire*
MMS	*Metropolitan Museum Studies*
MSS	*Münchener Studien zur Sprachwissenschaft*
NAWG	*Nachrichten der Akademie der Wissenschaften in Göttingen. Phil.-Hist. Klasse*
NC	*Numismatic Chronicle*
NJPh	*Neue Jahrbücher für Philologie und Paedagogik*
OA	*Opuscula Atheniensia*
OLZ	*Orientalistische Literaturzeitung*
PCPhS	*Proceedings of the Cambridge Philological Society*
PhW	*Philologische Wochenschrift*
PP	*La Parola del Passato*
PRIA	*Proceedings of the Royal Irish Academy*
QAL	*Quaderni di Archeologia della Libya*
QS	*Quaderni di Storia*
QUCC	*Quaderni Urbinati di Cultura Classica*
RA	*Revue Archéologique*
RAL	*Rendiconti della Classe di Scienze morali, storiche e filologiche dell'Accademia dei Lincei*
RAss	*Revue d'Assyriologie*
RB	*Revue Biblique*
RBPh	*Revue Belge de Philologie et d'Histoire*
REA	*Revue des Études Anciennes*
REG	*Revue des Études Grecques*
RFIC	*Rivista di Filologia e di Istruzione Classica*
RHA	*Revue Hittite et Asianique*
RHDFE	*Revue Historique de Droit Français et Étranger*
RhM	*Rheinisches Museum*
RHR	*Revue de l'Histoire des Religions*
RIDA	*Revue Internationale des Droits de l'Antiquité*
RIL	*Rendiconti dell'Istituto Lombardo*
RIO	*Revue Internationale d'Onomastique*
RPh	*Revue de Philologie*
RSI	*Rivista Storica Italiana*
RSO	*Rivista degli Studi Orientali*
SA	*Sovetskaja Archeologija*
SAK	*Studien zur altägyptischen Kultur*
SAWW	*Sitzungsberichte der Österreichischen Akademie der Wissenschaften in Wien*
SBAW	*Sitzungsberichte der Bayerischen Akademie der Wissenschaften Phil.-hist. Klasse*
SCO	*Studi Classici e Orientali*
SIFC	*Studi Italiani di Filologia Classica*
SMSR	*Studi e materiali di storia delle religioni*

SO	*Symbolae Osloenses*
StClas	*Studii Clasice*
StudPap	*Studia Papyrologica*
TAPhA	*Transactions and Proceedings of the American Philological Association*
UCPCPh	*University of California Publications in Classical Philology*
VDI	*Vestnik Drevnej Istorii*
VopJaz	*Voprosy Jazykoznanija*
WS	*Wiener Studien*
YCS	*Yale Classical Studies*
ZArch	*Zeitschrift für Archäologie*
ZÄS	*Zeitschrift für Ägyptische Sprache und Altertumskunde*
ZAss	*Zeitschrift für Assyriologie*
ZDMG	*Zeitschrift der Deutschen Morgenländischen Gesellschaft*
ZDPV	*Zeitschrift des Deutschen Palästina-Vereins*
ZII	*Zeitschrift für Indologie und Iranistik*
ZPE	*Zeitschrift für Papyrologie und Epigraphik*

List of Maps and Plans

Maps have been redrawn from the originals listed below.

List of Figures

MAPS

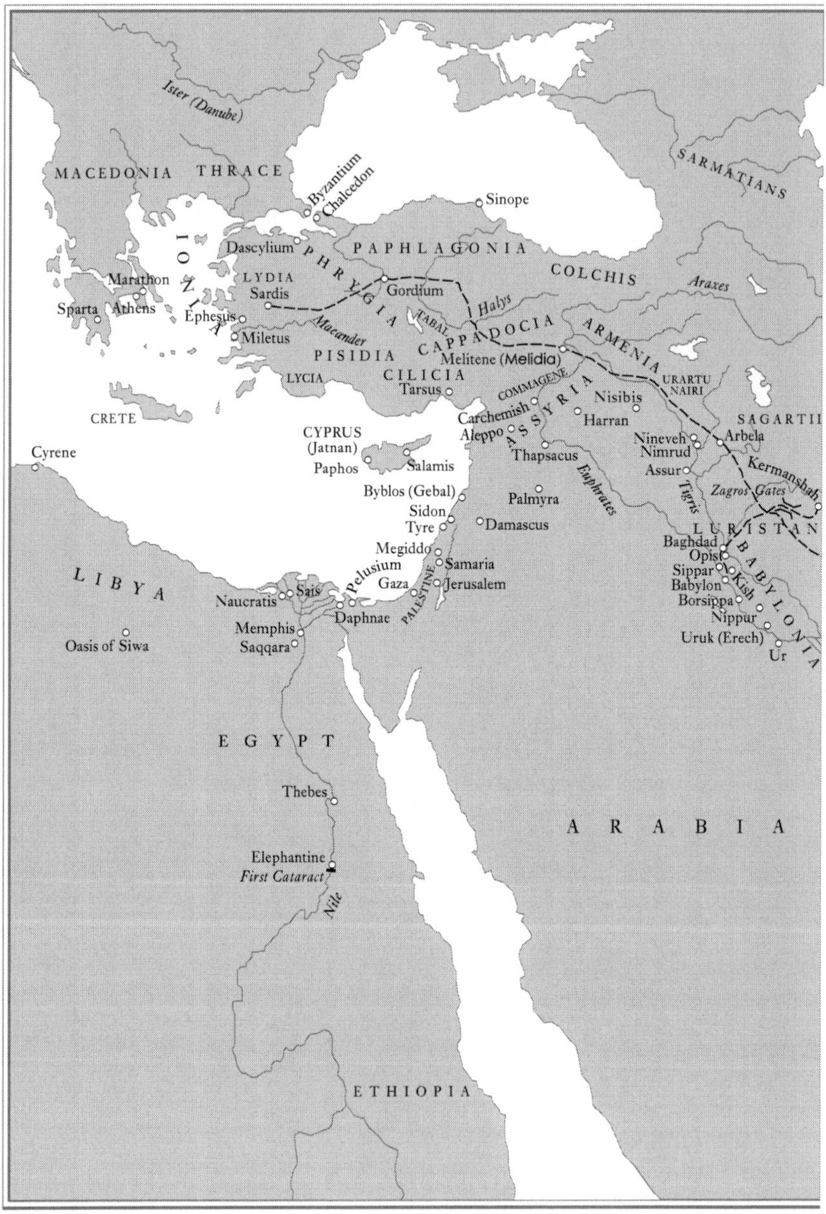

Map 1. The Empires of the Assyrians, Medes and Persians

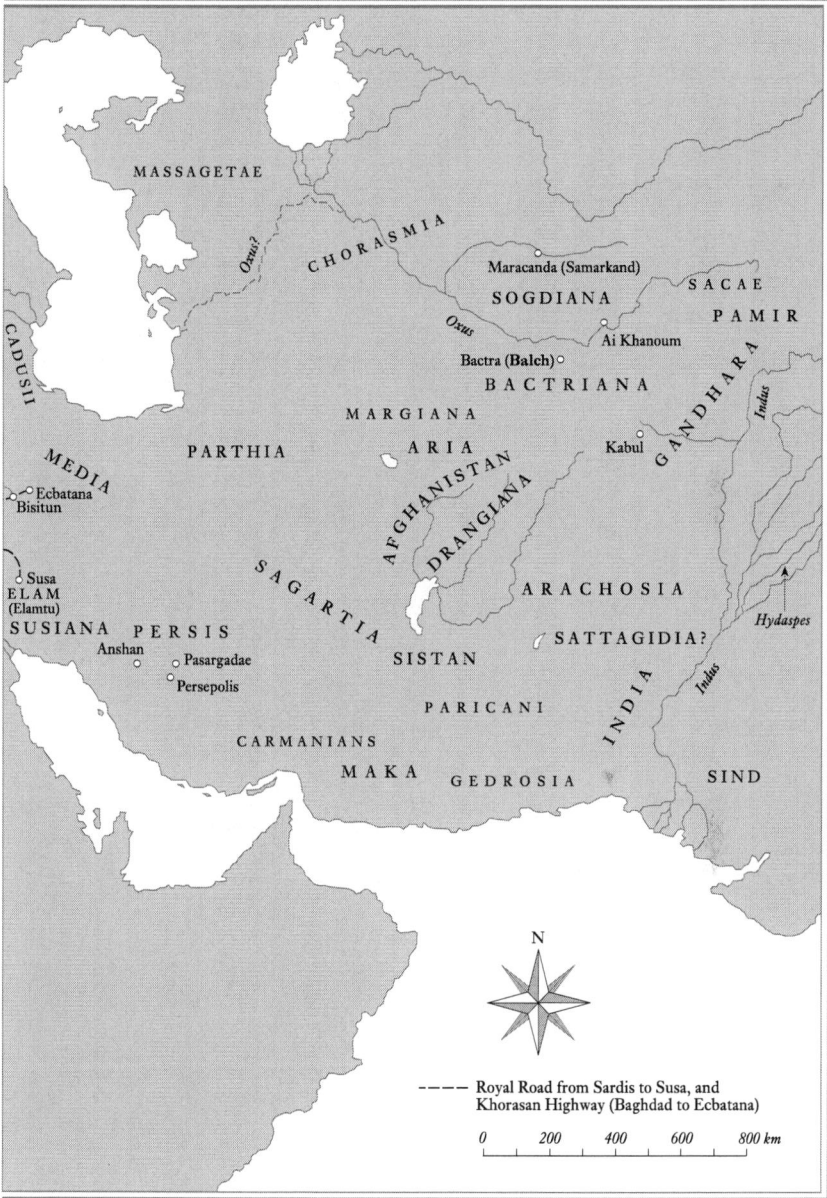

MASSAGETAE

CHORASMIA

Oxus?

SOGDIANA

Maracanda (Samarkand)

SACAE

PAMIR

Oxus

Ai Khanoum

Bactra (**Balch**)○

BACTRIANA

GANDHARA

CADUSII

MEDIA

PARTHIA

MARGIANA

ARIA

AFGHANISTAN

DRANGIANA

Kabul○

Indus

○ Ecbatana
Bisitun

○ Susa
ELAM
(Elamtu)

SUSIANA   PERSIS

Anshan
○

○ Pasargadae
○ Persepolis

S A G A R T I A

SISTAN

ARACHOSIA

SATTAGIDIA?

INDIA

Hydaspes

Indus

PARICANI

CARMANIANS

M A K A   GEDROSIA

SIND

N

- - - - Royal Road from Sardis to Susa, and
Khorasan Highway (Baghdad to Ecbatana)

0   200   400   600   800 km

Rome

CAMPANIA

APULIA

CALABRIA

ILLYRIA

Epidamnus

VESUVIUS

Cumae
Pithecusae
Neapolis (Naples)

(Brindisi)

Apollonia

Taras
(Tarentum)

EPIRUS

Posidonia (Paestum)

LUCANIA

Heraclea
Siris

Dodona

Elea (Velia)

Sybaris/Thurii

Corcyra

Croton

LEUCAS

Hipponium

Zancle (Messana)

Medma

CEPHALLENIA

Panormus
(Palermo)

Mylae

Caulonia

BRUTTIUM

Eryx

Locri

Rhegium

Solus
Himera
(Soluntum)

Tyndaris

Egesta
(Segesta)

ETNA

Tauromenium
Naxos

Selinus

Heraclea Minoa

SICILY

Catane

Acragas
(Agrigentum)

Leontini

Gela

Megara Hyblaea
Syracuse

Camarina

N

0   100   200   300 miles

Map 2. The Greek Cities

THRACE

Byzantium
Chalcedon

MACEDONIA

Abdera

Thasos
Pella
Samothrace
CHALCIDICE
Cyzicus
Sestos
Abydos
PHRYGIA
Pydna
Olynthus
MT ATHOS
Troy (Ilium)
Potidaea
MT IDA
MYSIA
LEMNOS
Assos
MT.
OLYMPUS
AEOLIS
Pergamum
Larissa
Mytilene
Hermus
EPIRUS
Achelous
Smyrna
LYDIA
THESSALY
LESBOS
Cyme
Sardis
Ambracia
Phocaea
Scyros
Chios
Lamia
ACARNANIA
PARNASSUS
EUBOEA
Clazomene
Maeander
AETOLIA
Orchomenos
Chalcis
CHIOS
Teos
Ephesus
Thermum
Delphi
PHOCIS
Eretria
SAMOS
Priene
ITHACA
Patrae
Thebes
Rhamnous
Heraion
Myous
BOEOTIA
Eleusis
ICARIA
Miletus
Aegae
ATTICA
Andros
ACHAEA
Sicyon
Athens
CEOS
IONIA
CARIA
Elis
Corinth
Aegina
Tenos
Halicarnassus
Nemea
Mycenae
ARGOLIS
Myconos
Olympia
ARCADIA
Epidaurus
Sunium
Delos
Cos
Tegea
Argos
Troezen
CYCLADES
ZACYNTHUS
PELOPONNESE
Tiryns
Paros
Naxos
Pylos
Messene
Siphnos
Cnidos
Rhodes
MESSENIA
Sparta
Melos
Ialysos
LACONIA
RHODES
Lindos
Thera

CYTHERA

Cnossos
Gortyn
Phaestos
CRETE

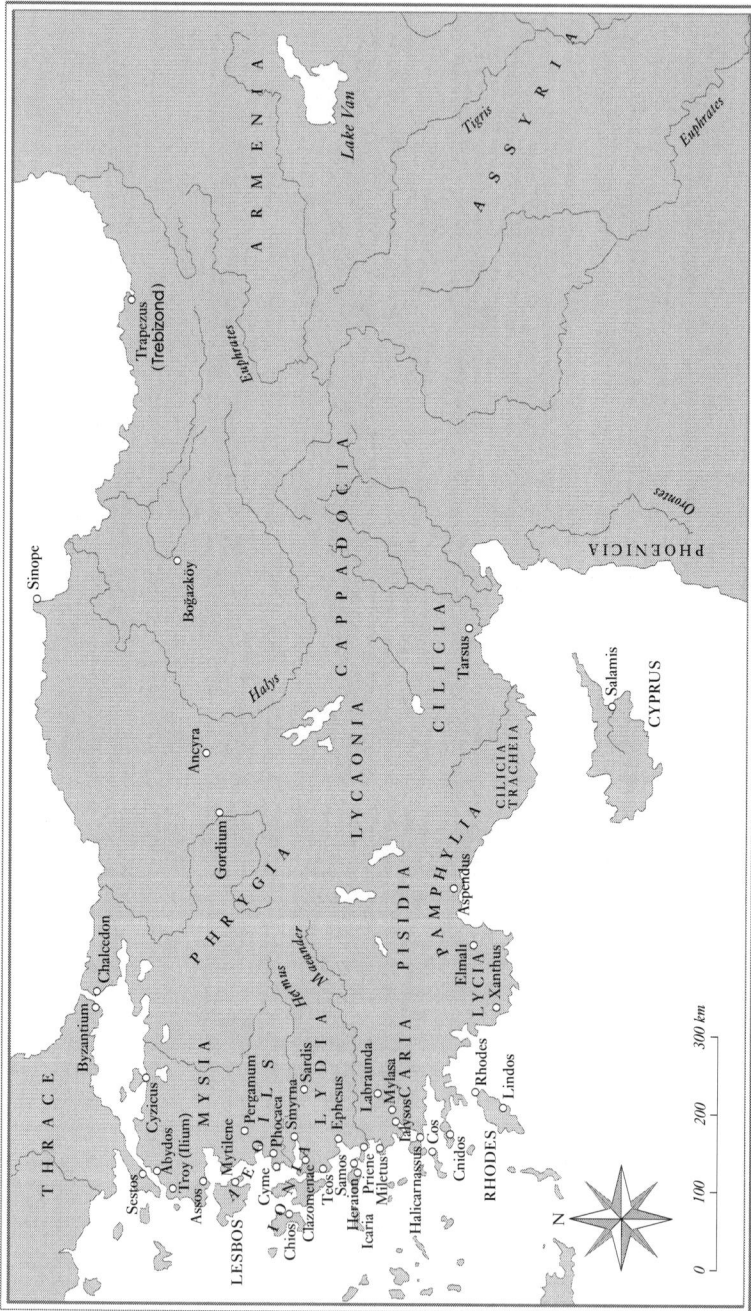

Map 3. Asia Minor

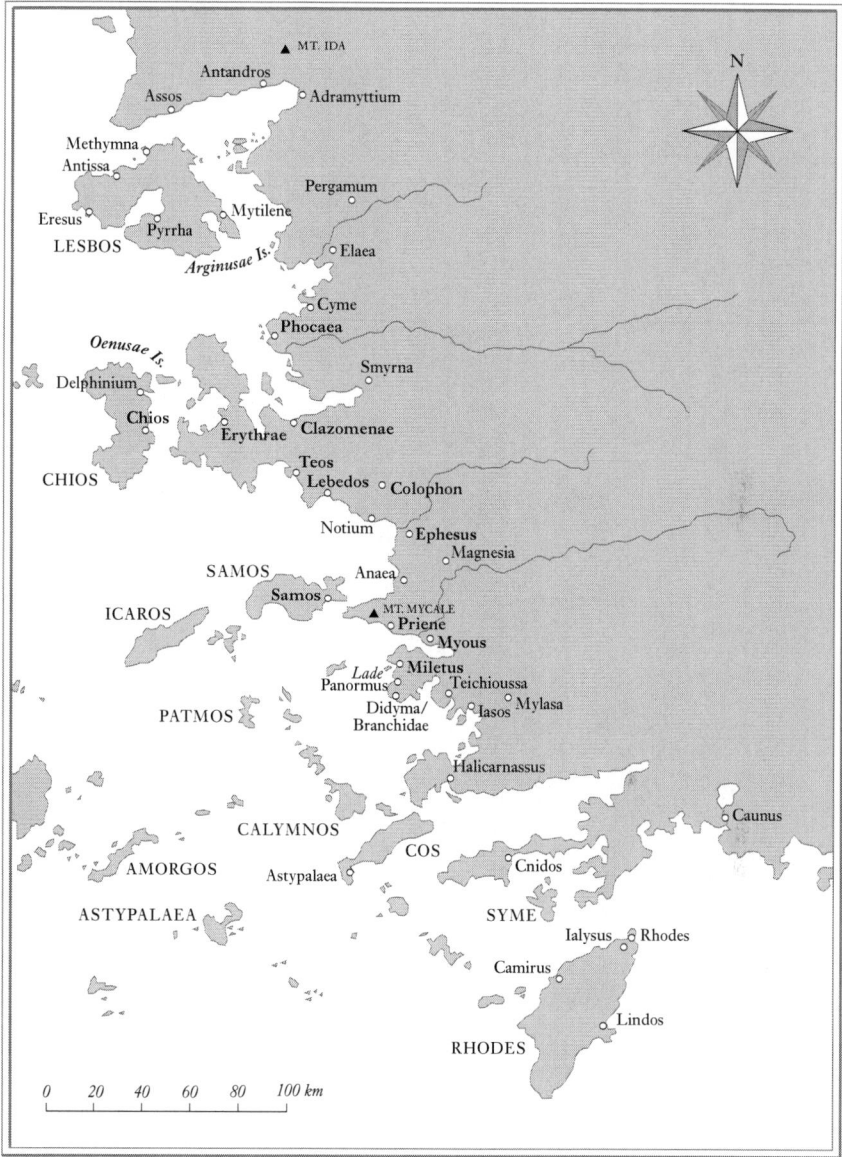

Map 4. Ionia

Map 5. The Peloponnese

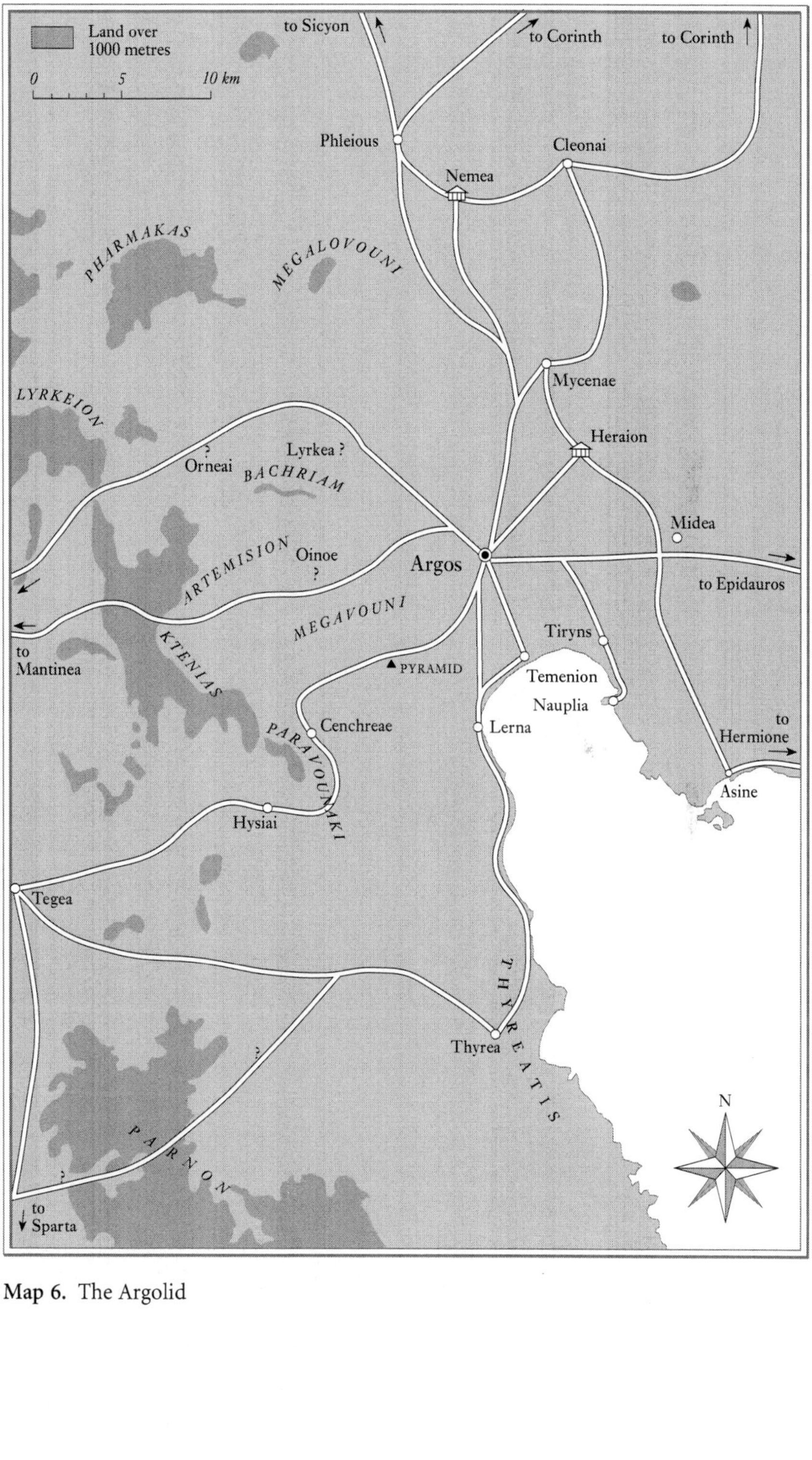

Map 6. The Argolid

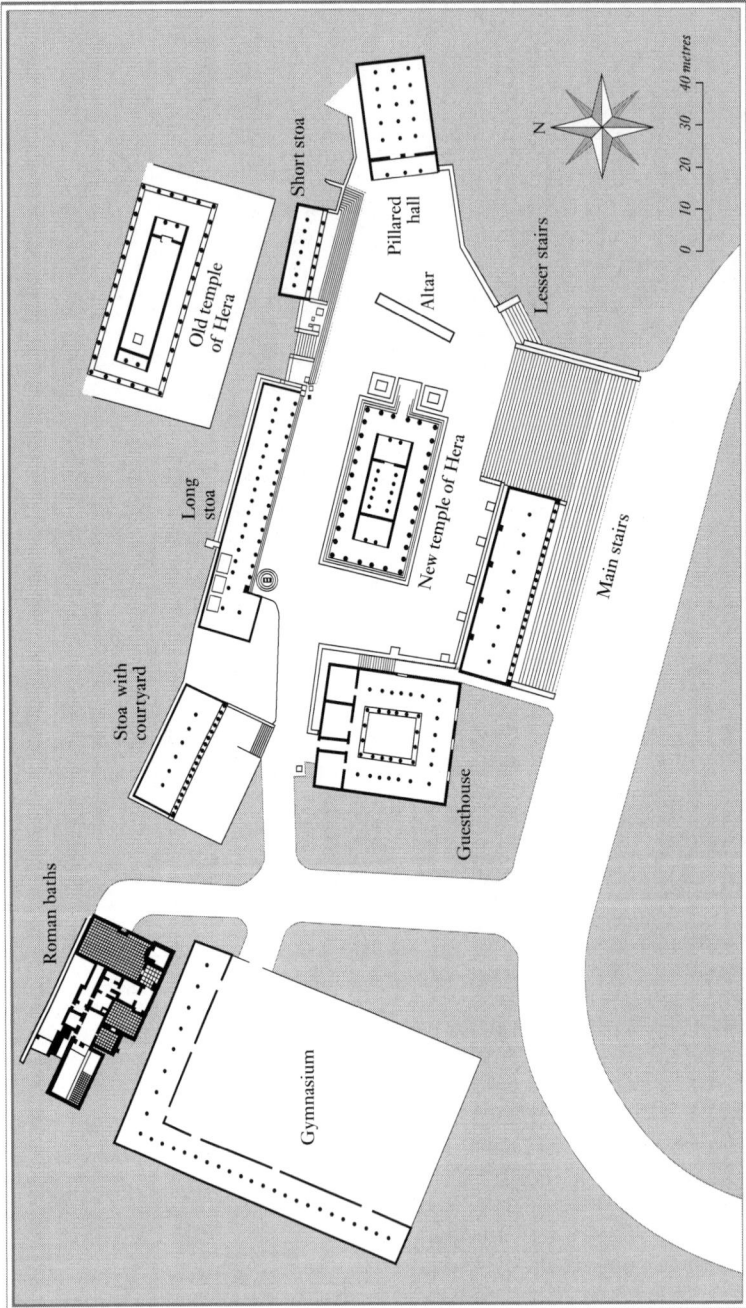

Map 7. The Argive Heraion

Roman baths

Gymnasium

Stoa with
courtyard

Long
stoa

Old temple
of Hera

Short stoa

Pillared
hall

Altar

Lesser stairs

New temple of Hera

Guesthouse

Main stairs

N

0   10   20   30   40 metres

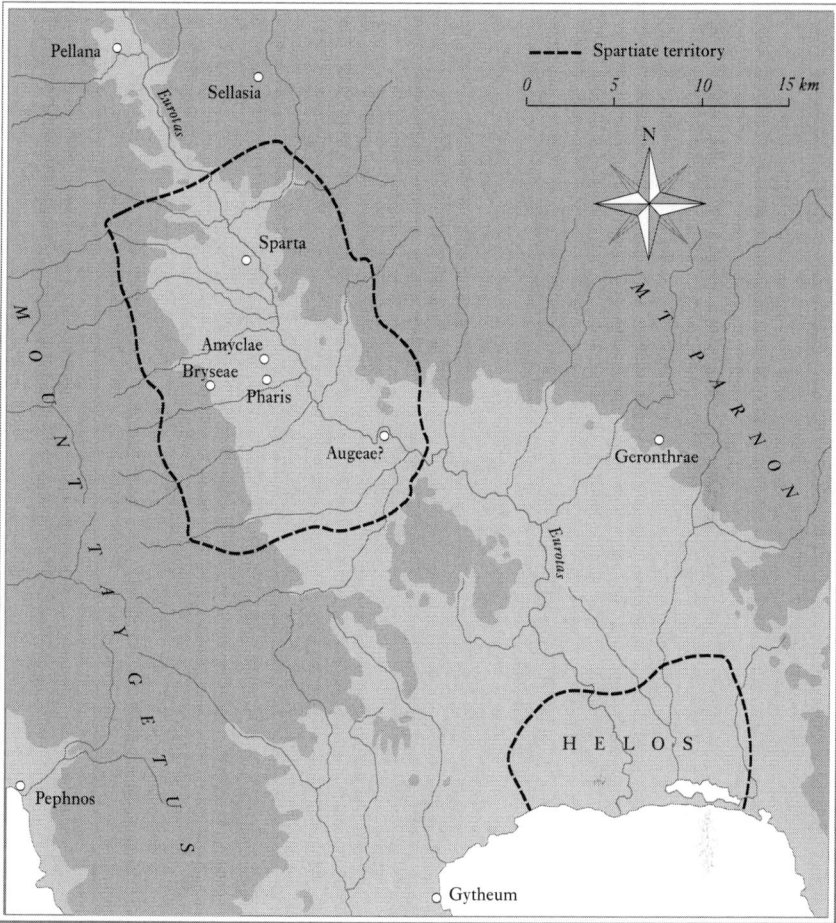

Map 8. Sparta and Laconia

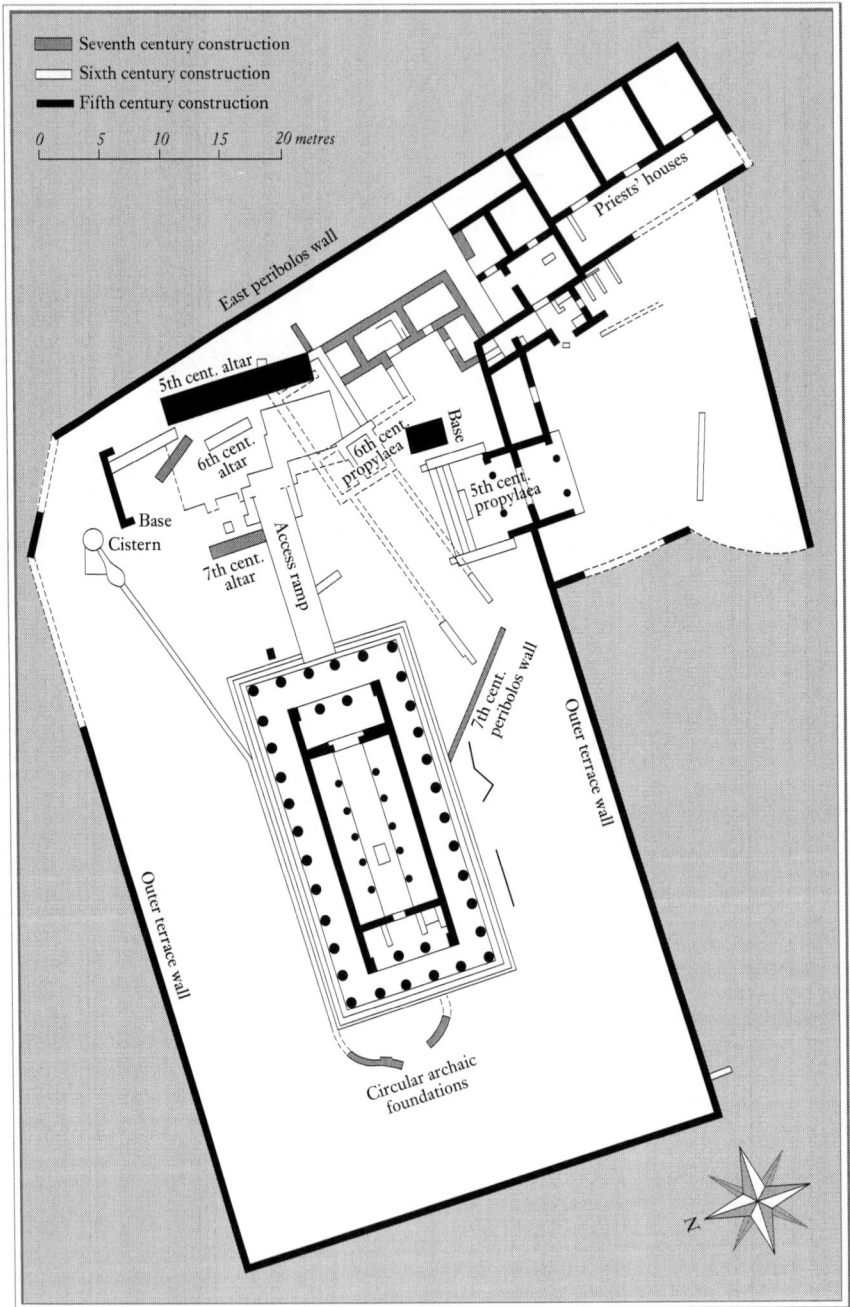

Map 9. Aegina: temple of Aphaia

Seventh century construction
Sixth century construction
Fifth century construction

0   5   10   15   20 metres

East peribolos wall

5th cent. altar

6th cent. altar

6th cent. propylaea

Base

5th cent. propylaea

Priests' houses

Base
Cistern

7th cent. altar

Access ramp

7th cent. peribolos wall

Outer terrace wall

Outer terrace wall

Circular archaic foundations

Z

Inset map (top left)

o Laciadae

0   250   500 metres

Sacred Way

?Butadae

Cerameis

Oion
Cerameicon?

Ceiriadae

Coele

Melite

Acropolis

Collytus

■ Hephaestus temple

● **Scambonidae**

● **Cydathenaeon**

Olympieium

Upper
Ancyle

Upper
Agryle

Lower
Ancyle

Diomeia

Daedalidae Lower
Agryle

Lower

Long walls

Phalerum wall

Long walls

Ilissus

Alopece

Main map

N

Land elevations
Over 400 metres
Over 200 metres
Over 100 metres
Sea level to 100 metres

0   50   100   150 km

OROPIA

Oropus

Delphinium

EPACRIA

Aphidna   Eitea
             ?Semachidae

Temple of ● **Rhamnus**
Nemesis

Panactum

Oenoe

Cephisus

PARNES MT.

Decelea

Phyle

Oeon
Deceleicon?

Plotheia

Genoe   Tricorynthus

Hecale

PLAIN OF MARATHON

PENTELICUS MT.

Marathon   Pr. Cynosoura

Peleces?

Cholleidae?

Trinemeia?

Pentele

Icarium

?Probalinthus

Cothocidae?

Upper Pergase?

THRIASIAN PLAIN   Oe **Acharnae** Lower
Pergase?

Cropidae?

Cephisia   Colonae?

Phegaea?

KERATA MT.

Temple of Coprus? **Thria**
Demeter

Sypalettus

Iphistiadae **Athmonon**

Iomdae?   Araphen?

Eleusis
Bay of Eleusis

Pharmacussae
Lerus

?**Cholargus**

Hermus

Leuconoeon?

Lusia

Phlya

Gargettus **Teithras**

?Cydantidae

Perithpedae?

Colonus

Ptelea Eiresidae?

Epicephisia?

Upper
Potamus

Upper
Pallene

Pallene

Mastiaea?

Halae Araphenides

Boudoron

Thymaetadae

Bate?

Athens

Xypete

Lower
Potamus

Oa

Erchia

Salamis

Pr.
Cynosoura ACTE

Phalerum

Lower
Paeanea

Upper
Paeanea

Lower
Paeania ?Conthyle

Temple of
Artemis

SALAMIS

Halimus

?Themacus

Peiraeus

Cephisus

Euonymon

Cicynna?

Sphettus

Philaidae Brauron

Angele ?Cytherus

o Eleusa

Saronic

Pr. Colias

Upper
Lamptrae **Myrrhinus** ?Stiria Pr. Coroneia

Hagnus

?Prasiae

Gulf

Aexone

Lower
Lamptrae Prospalta

Halae Aexonides **Anagyrus**

Cephale Deiradiotae?

Pr. Zoster

Thorae

?Potamus
Deiradiotes

Phrearrhii

LAUREION

Thoricus

Phabra

Aegilia

Besa

Anaphlystus

Aegina

Temple of
Aphaia

Elaeousa Atene

Sunium

AEGINA

Patroclus   Pr. Sunium

Temple of
Poseidon

Legend

● Large deme
○ Small deme
◉ Other settlement (non-constitutional deme)
□ Important fort
△ Temple
ACTE Regional name
═══ Sacred way
─── Ancient wall
◉? Approximate location; few remains
Oe? Deme-site; name uncertain
Stiria?

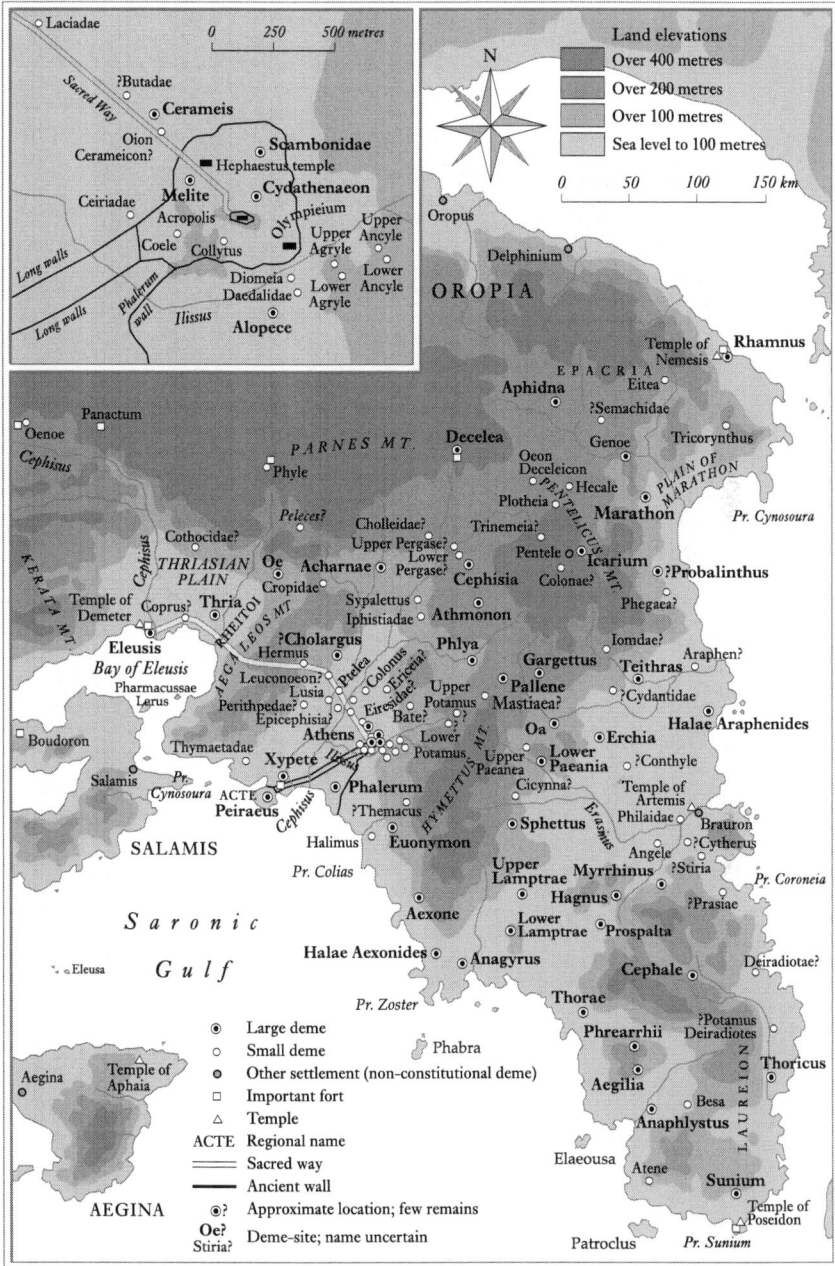

Map 10. Athens and Attica

Map 11. Magna Graecia and Sicily

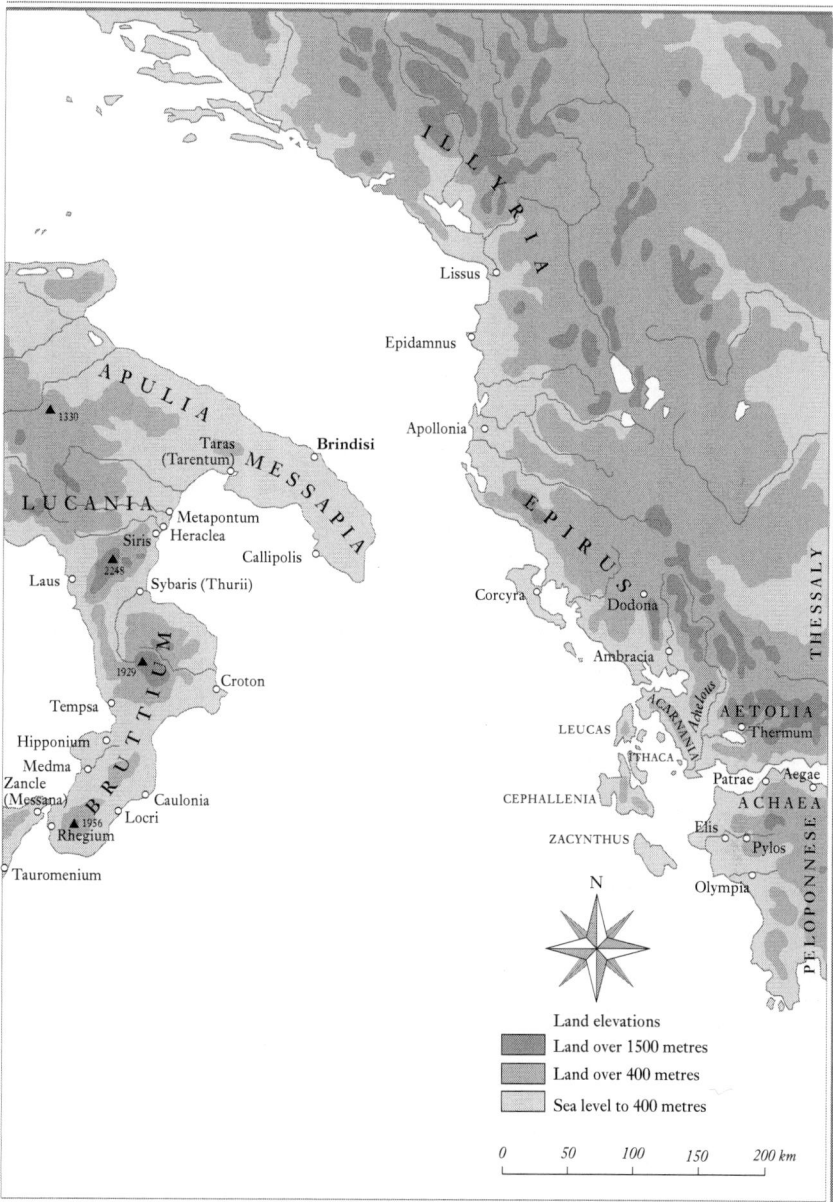

ILLYRIA

Lissus

Epidamnus

Apollonia

APULIA

▲ 1330

Taras
(Tarentum)   MESSAPIA

Brindisi

LUCANIA

Metapontum
Siris   Heraclea
▲ 2248
Callipolis

Laus   Sybaris (Thurii)

EPIRUS

Corcyra

Dodona

Ambracia

BRUTTIUM
▲ 1929
Croton

THESSALY

Tempsa

Hipponium

Medma

Zancle
(Messana)
Caulonia
Locri
▲ 1956
Rhegium

Tauromenium

ACARNANIA   AETOLIA
Achelous
Thermum

LEUCAS

ITHACA

CEPHALLENIA   Patrae   Aegae

ACHAEA

Elis

ZACYNTHUS   Pylos

N

Olympia

PELOPONNESE

Land elevations

Land over 1500 metres

Land over 400 metres

Sea level to 400 metres

0   50   100   150   200 km

GENERAL INTRODUCTION

David Asheri

I

'This is the exposition of the enquiries made by Herodotus of Halicarnassus': Herodotus' first book begins with these famous words. There is no absolute certainty that they are authentic. A writer of the first century AD, Ptolemy Hephaistion or Chennos ('quail'), attributed them to a certain Plesirrhous, a Thessalian hymnographer who was said to be Herodotus' lover and his heir.[1] Nobody has paid any attention to this testimony, which has been dismissed as *Schwindelphilologie* ('deceitful philology'). However, since there are not a few, even in recent times, who would include Herodotus' own work within this category, the notion of *Schwindlerei* in connection with Greek literature has become relative. It is possible that the authenticity of the first sentence was debated already in antiquity and that Ptolemy proposed an alluring solution. Whatever the case may be, the opening sentence clearly functions as a title. It probably appeared at the beginning and at the end of the work, as in the copy owned by Dionysius of Halicarnassus;[2] or on the *sillybos* or *index* attached to the scrolls in the libraries of Alexandria and Pergamon. Whether authentic or not, this famous sentence tells us almost nothing about the personality of our author: we are just told his name and place of origin. It is rather more informative about the theme and aim of his work; but this will be discussed later.

A guiding rule should be to look for biographical information about an ancient author in his own work, rather than relying on apocryphal reconstructions. Unfortunately, except for his travels, Herodotus tells us very little about himself. Greek historiography inherited a convention of archaic epic: the author should not mention himself unless the topic required it. Despite this, Herodotus' presence can be felt throughout: to read his work is like hearing him talk. References to himself such as 'I', 'me', 'mine', 'to me', 'we' (*pluralis maiestatis*) are frequent. Herodotus often shares his thoughts with us: he tells us what he has seen or heard; announces what he intends to say; reports with whom he has talked; expresses his doubts, thoughts, and opinions; he even invokes the gods.[3] And yet he gives us

---

[1] Photius, *Bibliotheca* 190; see A. Dihle, *Hermes*, LXXXV (1957), 314 f. and *RE* XXIII 2 1959, col. 1862 (with coll. 1859–60); K. H. Tomberg, 'Die Kaine Historia des Ptolemaios Chennos', Diss. Bonn 1967, p. 153, n. 56. See note on I 1,1.

[2] *Ad Pompeium* III 2; cf. Dio Chrysostom, *Or.* LIII 9.

[3] See C. Darbo-Peschansky, *Le Discours du particulier: Essai sur l'enquête hérodotienne*, Paris 1987, esp. pp. 107–63.

very little factual information about himself. He tells us that he has been to Egypt, Tyre, and Arabia; claims that he has talked with an agent of a Scythian king and suggests—unless he is being ironic—that his family possessed an illustrious genealogy (II 143,1), though not perhaps a divine origin. This latter detail may indicate that Herodotus was not an aristocrat. The last events recorded by Herodotus refer to the first two years of the Peloponnesian war (431/30 BC):[4] hence it seems plausible to conclude that his activity as a writer ended shortly after those events. This is all that can be inferred about Herodotus' life from his own work. Some further indirect evidence may be provided by his occasional comparisons with Attic, Delian, Ionian, or South Italian features:[5] these give us a clue as to the different audiences by whom he wanted to be understood in various regions of the Greek world.

For further biographical information we must turn to other sources from very different times and cultures. The short biography found under the heading *Herodotus* in the Byzantine Suidas lexicon runs as follows:

Herodotus: son of Lyxes and Dryo, from Halicarnassus, one of the renowned [local citizens]. He had a brother: Theodorus. He moved to Samos due to Lygdamis, third tyrant of Halicarnassus after Artemisia [...] In Samos he became acquainted with the Ionian dialect and wrote a history in nine books, beginning with Cyrus and Candaules, king of the Lydians. He subsequently returned to Halicarnassus and expelled the tyrant, later he found himself hated by the citizens and voluntarily left for Thurii, which was then being colonized by the Athenians. He died there and was buried in the agora. Others, however, say that he died at Pella.

To this report we may add the information found in the same lexicon under other entries: Herodotus was a nephew or a cousin of the poet and seer Panyassis, who was put to death by the tyrant Lygdamis (s.v. *Πανύασσις*); he stayed at the Macedonian court at Pella together with the historian Hellanicus of Lesbos (s.v. *Ἑλλάνικος*); after a public declamation of the Histories, during which the boy Thucydides shed many tears, he comforted Thucydides' father, Olorus (s.v. *Θουκυδίδης*).[6]

The Suidas lexicographer is not basing this account on Herodotus' work; he does not even use some information that could have been found in it: he does not mention his travels to the East, but rather claims that after his exile in Samos he went directly to Thurii. Suidas' entire report seems to be based on sources extraneous to the text; although we must take into consideration the possibility that the biographer, or one of his sources, tried to give an aetiological explanation of the origin of two textual variants found in ancient manuscripts. The opening of the first book actually presented two variant readings: 'Herodotus of Halicarnassus' and 'Herodotus of Thurii'. Ancient sources agree almost unanimously

---

[4] The most recent event (VII 137,1–3) is dated by Thucydides to the late summer 430 BC (II 67, 1–4). The absence of later events does not prove anything: cf. F. Jacoby, *RE* Suppl. II, 1913, coll. 230–3.

[5] See e.g. I 192,3; II 7,1–2; 10,1; IV 99,4–5. See Powell, *History*, pp. 36 ff.

[6] For the sources and variants of this famous anecdote see L. Piccirilli, *Storie dello storico Tucidide*, Genova 1985, pp. 158–61.

that his place of origin was Halicarnassus.[7] There are, however, a few exceptions: Aristotle, apparently quoting from memory, gives the Thurian variant of the opening sentence (*Rhet.* 1409a27); the Lydian Chronicle (99 BC), probably drawing on a fourth-century BC historian, quotes 'Herodotus the Thurian' as a source (*FGrHist* 532 F 1 (C29)); Avienus (fl. *c.* AD 350) may have found the same formula in a fourth-century BC *periplus* (*Ora maritima* 40); the historian Duris of Samos, out of patriotism or because he knew of Herodotus' exile in Samos, claimed as his compatriots Panyassis, and also it seems Herodotus; and the emperor Julian called Herodotus the 'λογοποιός from Thurii' (*Epistulae* 22), presumably relying on the opening of the manuscript in his possession. That Herodotus came from Halicarnassus cannot be doubted, since a local mid-fifth-century inscription (*Syll.*³ 46) shows that the Carian names of his father Lyxes and of Panyassis, as well as the Greek name of his brother Theodorus, appear also in other Carian-Greek families from Halicarnassus.[8] It cannot be excluded that these and other family names appeared in epigraphic lists of exiles or in records of confiscated property at Halicarnassus known to ancient historians and biographers, and that these lists provided the basis for inferences and interpretations that eventually ended up, through intermediary sources, in the Suidas lexicon. To believe this a good dose of optimism is needed, but Lygdamis is indeed a historical figure, attested also in a reliable epigraphic source (ML 32). There is likewise no reason to doubt that the stories about the exile and return of Herodotus' wealthy family contain a kernel of truth. That they chose to take refuge in Samos, an autonomous member of the Delian league since 478 BC, should not be taken as evidence that the exiles were pro-Athenian or anti-Persian, let alone that they were democrats. Besides, we should not think that Herodotus needed to go to Samos to familiarize himself with the Ionic dialect. Halicarnassus was originally a Carian-Doric city, but Ionic was by now also used there even for official purposes, and had been recognized as a literary dialect ever since Homer. The Samian chapter in Herodotus' biography should not take us beyond 454 BC, when free Halicarnassus became a member of the Delian league. Yet, Herodotus' stay in Samos remains an important formative period of his life: its importance can be traced in his sentiments and attachment to the island where he had found political asylum.[9]

Herodotus certainly spent some time in Athens. Eusebius knew that the Athenians rewarded him for his public readings in 445/4 BC. It is likely that

[7] Hellenistic inscriptions: *Die Inschriften von Pergamon*, ed. M. Fränkel, I, Berlin 1890, no. 199; *IG* XII 1,145 = *SEG* XXVIII, 1978, no. 842. (A partial translation into English can be found in O. Murray *CQ* XXII (1972), 204.) For the literary sources, see Jacoby, *RE* Suppl. II, coll. 213–14, and the bibliography quoted on I 1,1.

[8] See *FGrHist* 76 F 64 = Suidas s.v. Πανύασσις 248 Adler: Δοῦρις δὲ Διοκλέους τε παῖδα ἀνέγραψε (*scil.* τὸν Πανύασσιν) καὶ Σάμιον· ὁμοίως δὲ καὶ Ἡρόδοτος Θούριον (codd., Ἡρόδοτον Wesseling, Okin, Ἡροδοτον <τὸν> Θούριον Krausse, Jacoby). Cf. the bibliography quoted on I 1,1.

[9] For Herodotus and Samos, see E. E. Cole, *The Samos of Herodotus*, New Haven 1912; B. M. Mitchell, *JHS* XCV (1975), 79–91; Tölle-Kastenbein; T. S. Brown, *AncW* XVII (1988), 3–15; M. Ameruoso, *MGR* XVI (1991), 85–132.

Diyllus of Athens, writing about a century-and-a-half after Herodotus, refers to the same circumstances in his *Greek History*: he says that a certain Anytus (?)—homonymous with the more famous prosecutor of Socrates—proposed to offer Herodotus the exorbitant sum of ten talents.[10] An old tradition may have been used later for hostile purposes; yet public readings are a well-known and important aspect of the predominantly oral culture of fifth-century Greece: Thucydides' famous allusive remark against those who write history as 'display pieces for instant listening' (I 22,4) seems to be directed in particular against Herodotus' public recitations in Athens. While in Athens, Herodotus must have been in contact with the intellectual circles of the time. A friendship with Sophocles may be alluded to in the story that, on reaching the age of 55 (i.e at around 442 BC), he composed a short epigram for Herodotus (Plutarch, *Mor.* 785b). However, since 'Herodotus' was a common name in Ionia and the islands,[11] it is no longer certain that the Herodotus of the poem is Herodotus the historian. Be this as it may, it is not to be denied that Herodotus' public readings were renowned in intellectual circles at Athens and that Sophocles in particular was impressed by his views on the barbarians as well as by his ethical and religious ideas. Ancient sources do not mention any contact with Pericles: Herodotus' 'philopericleanism' is a modern construction (see below p. 46). It remains true, however, that Herodotus' Athens was also Pericles' Athens, as well as the Athens of Sophocles, Euripides, and Protagoras. This is what matters, rather than personal meetings reported or invented by ancient sources, which conventionally expressed in biographical terms abstract ideas about cultural affiliations and influences.

Delphi was certainly one of the places Herodotus came to know best. He also went to Sparta, where he met a certain Archias (III 55,2). In Boeotia he talked with Thersander of Orchomenus (IX 16,1 and 5). According to malicious rumours, Herodotus wrote harshly of the Corinthians and the Thebans because they had refused to pay him for his public readings; it is even said that the Theban authorities opposed Herodotus' attempt to speak with the local youth.[12] Such anecdotes testify to the success of hostility against Herodotus, which had begun already in the early fourth century. As has been suggested, the story about Herodotus' emigration to Thurii may well have been a learned conjecture based on the textual variants of the opening sentence; but ancient scholars believed, on the contrary, that the textual variant was based on the biographical fact of his emigration: Herodotus' emigration must therefore have been known from other sources. Herodotus never mentions Thurii, whereas he refers to Sybaris and the Sybarites more than once.[13] It is in any case certain that Herodotus stayed in

[10] *FGrHist* 73 F 3, quoted maliciously by Plutarch, *Mor.* 862b. Ἀνύτου is a correction by A. Turnebus for ἀντὶ τοῦ of the codices. For a possible epigraphic source see W. Aly, *RhM* LXIV (1909), 637. On the problem of Herodotus' public lectures see Erbse, pp. 139–46.

[11] The same arguments apply also to the inscription ʽΗ[ρο]δότου found on vases from Naucratis: see D. G. Hogarth, *JHS* XXV (1905), 116; D. W. J. Gill, *JHS* CVI (1986), 184–7.

[12] Aristophanes of Boeotia (early 4th cent.), *FGrHist* 379 F 5; Dio Chrysostom, *Or.* XXXVII, 7; Plutarch, *Mor.* 864d ff.

[13] Cf. Jacoby, *RE* Suppl. II, col. 245.

Magna Graecia and composed parts of his work there: this is shown by a well-known passage where an ethnic and geographical problem is explained by referring to distances familiar to a Western audience which is presumed not to know the terms current in Attica (IV 99,5). Herodotus' emigration to Thurii may thus be a true biographical episode. Chronologically, it is entirely possible that Herodotus, after staying in Athens, joined for a while the new Panhellenic colony of Thurii, founded in 444/3 BC, as did other contemporary intellectuals, such as Protagoras and Hippodamus of Miletus. For a while, Thurii became Herodotus' adopted fatherland and competed for this honour with Halicarnassus.

As a rule, ancient biographers had no knowledge of their characters' dates of birth and death. In Herodotus' case they probably did not even know the dates of Lygdamis' tyranny. The only chronological peg they could take hold of must have been the foundation of Thurii. The choice of this date as marking Herodotus' ἀκμή (which, by convention, was defined as one's fortieth birthday), is the source of the calculation of the fictional date of his birth in 484/3 BC. A similar date is assumed, for example, by Pamphila of Epidaurus, a contemporary of Nero: following Apollodorus of Athens (second century BC), she claims that Herodotus was 53 when the Peloponnesian war broke out (431 + 53 = 484 BC).[14] Similarly, Cornelius Nepos, followed by Pliny (*NH* XII 18), believed that Herodotus began to write the *Histories* in Thurii in 444 BC, clearly when he was already a middle-aged man. Though he is less precise, Dionysius of Halicarnassus follows the same approach when he dates the birth of his fellow-citizen to just before 'the Persian wars', meaning 480 BC, and claims that he lived up to the Peloponnesian war (*De Thucydide* 5). A different chronological school wrongly dated Herodotus' active life to the reign of Xerxes,[15] thereby making the historian an eyewitness of the most important events told in his work, just as some ancient biographers took Homer to have lived at the time of the Trojan war.[16] Dating Herodotus' birth to the eighties need not be wrong. Clearly, Herodotus had no personal memories of the events of 480/79 BC: he recorded the accounts of older witnesses who were still alive. When he left Halicarnassus for good he was about 30; he then began to travel: he went to Egypt, Phoenicia, and Mesopotamia between 448 and 446, to Athens in 445/4, and then to Thurii. It is impossible to establish whether he died at Thurii, as the biography in the Suidas claims, or whether he went back to Athens. We cannot even establish the year of his death: we can only fix a *terminus ante quem non*: 430 BC.[17]

---

[14] *FGrHist* 244 F 7, quoted by Aulus Gellius XV 23. According to A. A. Mosshammer, *GRBS* XVI (1973), 5–13, the calculation is based on the honorary decree accorded by the Athenians in 445/4.

[15] Diodorus II 32,3 γεγονώς was taken by Photius (*Bibliotheca* 60, p. 19b Henry) to mean 'lived' rather than 'was born'.

[16] A third school dated Herodotus' ἀκμή to 468/7, the year of Simonides' death (*Marmor Parium*, *FGrHist* 239 A 57) and of Panyassis' ἀκμή, which was sometimes made to coincide with that of Herodotus. Some believe that 468/7 was the year of Herodotus' exile from Halicarnassus (e.g. Hauvette, pp. 12 ff.).

[17] See Marcellinus, *Vita Thucydidis* 17, with Piccirilli, *Storie* (n. 6), pp. 91 f. For the tradition according to which Herodotus was still alive at the end of the Peloponnesian war, see e.g. E. Rohde, *RhM* XXXIII (1878), 169, n. 4. For modern datings of the 'publication' of Herodotus' work, see p. 51, n. 125.

In order to understand Herodotus' intellectual formation and the composition of his work, the most significant event of his life is precisely the one that his ancient biographers never mention: his travels. It is Herodotus himself who gives for these travels direct and explicit evidence: 'I went and I saw' ($\alpha\mathring{v}\tau\acute{o}\pi\tau\eta\varsigma$ $\grave{\epsilon}\lambda\theta\acute{\omega}\nu$) the course of the Nile up to Elephantine (II 29,1); 'I learned things at Memphis'; 'I went also to Thebes and Heliopolis' (II 3,1); the Theban priests 'took me into a big hall' (II 143,1–4); 'we saw in person the high chambers' of the labyrinth at lake Moeris (II 148,1 and 5–6); 'I saw' the bones of the dead on the battlefields of Pelusium and Papremis (III 12,1 and 4); 'I went to a place' opposite Buto in Arabia (II 75,1); 'I sailed also to Tyre' (II 44, 1–4); in the temple of Babylon 'I have not seen' the statue removed by Xerxes (I 183,3); 'I went to Thasos' (II 44,4); 'I have myself seen' the mines in Thasos (VI 47,1); 'I was shown' a crater in Exampaeus (IV 81,2); 'I myself saw' the Cadmean letters in Thebes (V, 59). There are those who attribute all these claims to direct knowledge, others who believe a certain portion of them, and others still who believe none at all. We shall return to this fundamental question below (pp. 15, 54f.). It should be pointed out, as a preliminary remark, that rather than generalize, these declarations ought more properly to be evaluated case by case. Clearly, we should not assume first-hand knowledge in the case of indirect expressions regarding, for example, monuments 'which still existed in my time', or which are described in the present tense (e.g. I 98,4–6). However, on the basis of most of Herodotus' explicit declarations, it seems justified to infer with sufficient certainty that he went to Egypt, Phoenicia, Babylon, the coast of Pontus from Byzantium to Olbia, the Thracian coast and the neighbouring islands; it is also evident that he was personally familiar with Ionia, Caria, Lydia, and Lycia and the major islands of the Eastern Aegean (Samos, Lesbos); within mainland Greece he knew well Delphi, Sparta, Boeotia. There are no claims to direct knowledge of Athens, nor does he mention Pericles' newly built acropolis among the major buildings of Greece, as the Artemision at Ephesus and the Heraion at Samos (cf. II 148,2). But it would obviously be ridiculous to doubt the historicity of his stay in Athens on the basis of these observations.[18] There is also no evidence that the historian of the Persian wars ever systematically visited the main battlefields of 480/79 BC, although his topographical knowledge of the area is usually good. One notorious exception may be his faulty orientation of the pass of Thermopylae as running apparently from north to south (VII 176,3).[19] Likewise, we cannot estimate the extent to which he had direct knowledge of the West (Magna Graecia, Sicily, Etruria).

The dates and circumstances which modern scholars propose for Herodotus' travels are often hypothetical or pure fantasy.[20] As far as dates are concerned,

---

[18] See, however, A. J. Podlecki, in *Greece and the Eastern Mediterranean: Studies Presented to F. Schachermeyr* (ed. K. H. Kinzl), Berlin 1977, pp. 246–55.

[19] See How–Wells, ad loc.; C. Hignett, *Xerxes' Invasion of Greece*, Oxford 1963, p. 358; Waters, *Herodotus the Historian*, p. 158.

[20] See T. S. Brown, *AncW* XVII (1988), 67–75, who follows Jacoby, 'Herodotus', *RE*, col. 253. On the length and itinerary of Herodotus' journey in Egypt see C. Sourdille, *La Durée*, which is still fundamental.

the only certainty is that his travels in the East and in the areas of Pontus and Thrace pre-date his stay in Athens. However, the arguments in favour of a hypothetical order or a hypothetical itinerary for his travels are far from compelling. Everyone knows and repeats that Herodotus' book is not a travel diary. The consequence is a weakening of the assumption that comparisons with things already known to the traveller necessarily indicate previous stages in his journey. For example, it is dangerous to conclude that Herodotus went first to Cyrene and then to Egypt because he compares the Egyptian acacia to the Cyrenaean lotus and not vice versa (II 96,1), or that when he stressed the exceptional sexual purity of the Egyptians (II 64,1) he had not yet acquainted himself with Babylonian practices (I 198). In accord with this criterion, it should be inferred that Herodotus visited Egypt before Scythia, since he compares the Borysthenes to the Nile (IV 53,1) and not the other way around. But something more positive and significant can be said about the aim of Herodotus' travels. He never stepped outside the Graeco–Persian *oikoumene*. In the cities which he chose as his bases—Memphis, Babylon, or Olbia—he was sure to find guides and Greek or bilingual interpreters. Hence his aim was not to explore unknown geographic areas (as Scylax of Caryanda and the Achaemenid Sataspes set out to do: IV 43–4). On the other hand, the evidence for first-hand knowledge is particularly copious for areas marginal to the main theatre of the Graeco–Persian wars: Egypt, Mesopotamia, the coast of Pontus; for example, no direct knowledge is attested on Persia nor on the main stopping places of Xerxes during his march. This means that when Herodotus began his travels he did not as yet have specific aims of historical research. We are thus left with the more general aim of θεωρίη or ἱστορίη, terms which Herodotus himself uses in relation to his own travels or those of others:[21] curiosity and the search for solutions to the problems which present themselves each time to the traveller on the road. Herodotus goes to Tyre in order to solve a problem which he encountered in Egypt; for the same reason he travels to Thasos; he goes to Thebes and Heliopolis to check some information gathered at Memphis. It seems just to conclude that at the beginning of his travels the historian had no precise aim, but rather that the journeys themselves created various aims from time to time in their course. It is important to bear this in mind in order to understand exactly the author's intellectual development and the composition of his work.

II

Let us return to the opening sentence of the first book: 'This is the exposition of the enquiries made by Herodotus of Halicarnassus, in order that the accomplishments of men may not perish in time, nor the great and wondrous deeds of Greeks and barbarians lack renown, and especially the reason why they fought one another.' As was said before, this is a descriptive title that also endeavours rhetorically to allude to the subject and the general aim of the work. The models

---

[21] II 29, 1; 44,4; Solon: I 29,1; 30,1–2; the Greeks in Egypt: III 139,1; Anacharsis: IV 76,2; Darius: IV 85,1; Xerxes: VII 43,1; 128,1.

available to Herodotus, or his editor, were not only the so-called epic 'proems' with their traditional invocation to the Muse, which is here absent; but also the openings of earlier works in prose, historical, geographic, mythographic, or of other types. We know the opening of a work by Hecataeus of Miletus (*FGrHist* 1 F 1): as does our opening, it includes the name and place of origin of the author, but also a statement of belief concerning his critical methodology, which is here missing. Herodotus' beginning is therefore different from that of his models; hence it may be concluded that, when Herodotus composed his proem, the conventional structure of historical proems had not yet reached its final and crystallized form. Herodotus' proem seems to have been written straight off, freely and without preconceived formal concepts.[22]

'Exposition of the enquiries (ἱστορίη)' would, strictly speaking, be the title of the work. In view of that, Herodotus' book came to be called *History* or *Histories* in late antiquity and modern times. In fact, however, as we all know, ἱστορίη means enquiry, study, research, independently of the actual object of the research. Only in the fourth century BC did the scope of ἱστορίη begin to be restricted to the field of the human past, as it is also used today. In Herodotus, as far as we know, the term ἱστορίη occurs for the first time. He uses it four times, apart from the opening. In two related passages (II 118,1 and 119,3), ἱστορίῃσι are the enquiries about Helen carried out by the Egyptians. In a third and important passage Herodotus mentions ἱστορίη, together with first-hand knowledge (ὄψις) and reasoning or opinion (γνώμη), among the tools of his own methodology, which he considers far superior to a mere collection of 'hearsay' (τὰ λεγόμενα), for which he takes no responsibility (II 99,1). In a fourth and last passage, Herodotus points out that certain information is not relevant to 'the account of the ἱστορίη' (VII 96,1).[23] The verb ἱστορέω is used seventeen times, once in the composite form ἐξιστορέω: it almost invariably means to ask, to enquire orally; τὰ ἱστορημένα (II 44,5) are the results of the enquiry. Thus, in the first place, the opening of our book aims to inform the reader that the roll he is holding in his hands is the 'exposition of the enquiry' carried out by Herodotus of Halicarnassus.[24]

What follows is a subordinate final clause where the purpose of the enquiry is specified: to save human events and works, whether Greek or barbarian, from oblivion. The apparent opposition between 'events' (τὰ γενόμενα ἐξ ἀνθρώπων) and 'deeds' (ἔργα) used to be interpreted as a sharp and intentional distinction between historical events, such as wars, and permanent accomplishments, such as monuments, a distinction supposedly parallel to the two main disciplines intertwined in Herodotus' work: a history of political/military events and a long-term *Kulturgeschichte*; in other words 'kinetic' and 'static' history. Recent

---

[22] On 'formal introductions' in ancient historiography see Marincola, pp. 271–5.

[23] For a different interpretation of this passage see How–Wells, ad loc. The Homeric predecessor, ἵστωρ, never appears in Herodotus. It implies the notion of arbitration or judgement between contrasting evidences or opinions; see W. R. Connor, in *Nomodeiktes*, pp. 3–15.

[24] The expression ἀπόδεξις does not imply oral delivery: it alludes here to the written work in the reader's hands. For ἀποδείκνυμι and its cognates in Herodotus see Drexler, pp. 11–4. See n. 22 and the commentary, ad loc.

research, however, has shown that this reading of the text, though rich in ideas, has no basis in Herodotus' usage of the terms. Ἔργον in Herodotus can actually refer to actions and accomplishments of all sorts: to wars, acts of exceptional valour, great monuments, original ideas, technical inventions, *et cetera*.[25] Therefore the initial sentence should also be understood to refer to all human events deserving to be remembered, and especially those which, due to their greatness or excellence, inspire admiration or curiosity and have left visible or memorable traces. The qualification that the deeds recorded may be Greek or barbarian is a pledge of impartiality; and suggests that, in comparison with human greatness and the admiration it inspires, differences between peoples, states, and cultures become irrelevant. The ἔργον entails fame (κλέος) that must be preserved, and it is the fame which in its turn justifies the toil of enquiry. It is easy to recognize in such assumptions a mixture of epic reminiscences (e.g. Homer, *Il.* IX 189; *Od.* I 338) with the pragmatic attitudes of a traveller (choice of sites or monuments worth seeing, etc.), this aptly reflecting the blend of epic narrative and scientific observation which generally well characterizes Herodotus' work. The final clause of the proem is followed by a short phrase, a sort of appendix, which directly introduces the reader to the first digression (I 1–5) dedicated to the 'cause' of the wars between Greeks and barbarians. This scarcely allusive reference to the Graeco–Persian conflict already shows that the main topic of the work—as conceived by Herodotus or the editor when writing the proem—cannot be the conflict itself. At the least, it may be deduced that the opening would suggest that the 'cause' of this conflict is one of the main subjects of the work.

Actually, the 'cause' is the subject of the first digression, which deals with the Persian and Phoenician accounts of the origin of the conflict between Greeks and barbarians, or rather between Europe and Asia. Herodotus brushes off these accounts as mythical. The origin of the historical conflict should be ascribed to Croesus, the last king of Lydia (560–46 BC), to whom he dedicates the first *logos* (I 6–94): the history of his kingdom up to the Persian conquest of Sardis.[26] The narrative then shifts to Persia. Cyrus, the conqueror of Sardis, is also the founder of the Persian empire: his life, his reign (559–30 BC), and his main campaigns are the core of the second *logos* in the first book. The story of Cambyses, Cyrus' son and successor to the throne, ruling from 530 to 522 BC, and of the Persian conquest of Egypt, start at the beginning of the second book and continue until chapter 38 of the third book. But, apart from the brief first chapter, the entire second book is an independent *logos* devoted to the geography, religion, customs, and ancient history of Egypt. To the kingdom of Darius, the third Achaemenid king (522–486 BC), more than three books (III 60–VII 4) are dedicated: the main narrative starts with the dynastic crisis of 522 BC and Darius' rise to power (III 61–88); and then focuses on his military campaigns: the conquest of Samos

[25] Cf. Bischoff, pp. 5–6; Focke, pp. 1 ff.; H. R. Immerwahr, *AJPh* LXXXI (1960), esp. pp. 262 f.; H. Barth, *Klio* L (1968), 93 ff., with a review of previous discussions. Erbse, *Studien*, pp. 146–56; W. Hendrick Jr., in *Nomodeiktes*, pp. 25–6; R. Oswald, *GB* XXI 1995, pp. 47 ff. For human thought as ἔργον cf. also Montgomery; Hohti.

[26] See the Introduction to Book I. For the detailed structure of the entire work, see Jacoby, *RE* Suppl. II, coll. 283–326.

(III 120–49), the repression of the Babylonian revolt in 521–19 BC (III 150–60), the expeditions in Scythia (*c.*514/3 BC) and against Cyrene (IV 83–98; 200–5), the conquest of Thrace (V 1–27), the Ionian revolt and its repression (between *c.*500 and 494 BC: V 28–126; IV 1–47), the expedition of Datis and Artaphrenes against Athens and Eretria in 490 BC (VI 95–140), and the battle of Marathon (VI 102–17), the first of the six great campaigns for the independence of Greece. To this main narrative are linked a number of ethnographic and historical digressions; particularly worthy of note are the story of Polycrates, tyrant of Samos (III 39–60; 120–49), the description of the tributes and satrapies of the Persian empire (III 89–96), the long *logos* devoted to Scythia (IV 1–144), the *logos* about Cyrene and Libya (IV 145–99), the chapters devoted to Sparta at the time of King Cleomenes (V 39–48) and to Athens in the last decade of the sixth century (V 55–96). Herodotus' last three books (VII 4–IX 122) deal with the first seven years of Xerxes' reign (485–79 BC) and the history of the 'Persian wars' (τὰ Μηδικά) in the strict sense (480–79), that is, Xerxes' great invasion with its five famous battles: Thermopylae, Artemisium, Salamis (480 BC), Plataea, and Mycale (479 BC). The main narrative dominates these three books and is developed symmetrically: Persian attack and Greek movements, land front and sea front. Here too there is no dearth of digressions: for example, the didactic speeches at Xerxes' court (VII 5–21), the dialogues between Xerxes and Artabanus (VII 44–53), and between Xerxes and Demaratus (VII 101–5), the review of the Persian troops (VII 59–100), the digression on the history of Sicily (VII 153–67) and the Macedonian kings (VIII 137–9), and the tale about Xerxes and Masistes' wife (IX 108–13). In the last chapters of the last book (IX 114–21) the Greek naval expedition to the Hellespont after the battle of Mycale is recounted, and the Athenian occupation of Sestos in the autumn of 479 BC—the last recorded episode of the Persian wars. The torture of the satrap Artaÿctes, imprisoned at Sestos, introduces the last anecdotic digression about a homonymous ancestor of Artaÿctes. Herodotus' book ends with a didactic maxim delivered by Cyrus the Great (IX 122).

Ends, or rather breaks off. At least an epilogue is missing. A work of this scope could not end with an incidental anecdote, inspired in turn by another anecdote about a minor character. Herodotus is perfectly able, when he so wishes, to write introductions and epilogues. Cyrus' last maxim is not a didactic 'message' which can serve to conclude and unify the entire work, nor does the episode at Sestos endeavour to symbolize the re-establishment of the natural boundaries between Europe and Asia, which Darius and Xerxes had attempted to obliterate. Nothing in Herodotus' words suggests such a design, nor did his readers actually decipher such hidden meanings until the end of the nineteenth century.[27] Since, as we have

[27] See Jacoby, *RE* Suppl. II, cols. 372–9; cf. P. Cartledge, *EMC* XXXIV (1990), 40; C. Dewald, in D. M. Roberts *et al.* (eds.), *Classical Closures: Reading the End in Greek and Latin Literature*, Princeton 1997, ch. 4 (pp. 62–82). For the Sestos episode see H. R. Immerwahr, *TAPhA* LXXXV (1954), 16 ff. For our view on the ending, cf. v. Fritz, pp. 274 ff.; S. Cagnazzi, *Hermes*, CIII (1975), 406 ff.; and A. Masaracchia, *Erodoto. La battaglia di Salamina. Libro VIII delle Storie*, Milan 1977, pp. xxx–xxxiii. For closing sentences in Bk. I see note on 92,1.

seen, an epilogue is certainly missing, Herodotus' work is technically unfinished; it is, moreover, possible that a number of digressive chapters are also missing. The main narrative concerning the events of 479 BC ends at chapter 121 with the clearly concluding phrase 'and nothing else happened that year'. On the other hand, there is no sufficient reason to assume that Herodotus intended to continue his history beyond this year, and to relate the events of the πεντηκονταετία (478–31 BC), possibly up to a significant date in the Graeco-Persian conflict, such as the battle at Eurymedon (*c.*467 BC) or the so-called 'peace of Callias' (449/8 BC); nor to continue writing with no date limit, until death will knock the pen out of his hand. After all, the occupation of Sestos could appear sufficiently significant as a conclusion to the two years of 'Persian wars'. For this reason Herodotus' work was considered complete in antiquity, and Thucydides began his work precisely where Herodotus had ended his.[28] Thus, though technically unfinished, we may also consider Herodotus' work complete.[29]

In the medieval manuscript tradition, Herodotus' work is divided into nine books named after the nine Muses, in the canonical order found in Hesiod (*Theog.* 77). The division is attested for the first time in the first century BC, and should be attributed to the Alexandrian librarians of the third and second centuries BC; the names of the Muses are not attested as titles of Herodotus' books before the second century AD.[30] It is not always easy to grasp the criteria for this book division. The content is not always respected; the length of the books varies, and it cannot therefore correspond to a standard length for a papyrus roll. The books do not correspond to the *logoi* that Herodotus himself mentions when he refers the reader to other sections of his work ('in the first *logos*', 'in this *logos*', 'in another *logos*', 'in the Assyrian *logoi*', 'in the Libyan *logoi*', etc.), or when he resumes the main narrative ('I return to the previous *logos*').[31] It is, however, possible that each of Books I, II, and IV is originally composed of a pair of *logoi* of varying lengths.[32] The attempts at reconstructing a hypothetical original division, though sometimes very ingenious,[33] do not so far seem very helpful. It seems just as pointless to regard the nine traditional books as basic units for further partitions into three triads, or into two or six parts,[34] though such partitions may be useful for practical purposes.

---

[28] Thucydides I 97,2 clearly includes Herodotus among those who wrote about the Persian wars but not about the πεντηκονταετία.

[29] Unfulfilled promises (I 184 and 106,2 with notes; VII 213,3) are irrelevant to the question of completeness.

[30] For other authors, the Muses' names are attested as titles already in the 1st cent. BC: see W. Aly *RhM* LXIV (1909), 593–4 and n. 2; Legrand, *Hérodote, Histoires* I, p. 225 n. 2. The hypothesis that the division and the titles should be attributed to Herodotus himself must be rejected: B. Baldwin, *QUCC* XLV (1984), 31–4.

[31] For a list of cross-references, see Powell, *History,* app. II.

[32] I 6–94; 95–216; II 1–98; 99–182; IV 1–144; 145–205.

[33] See Cagnazzi, *Hermes,* CIII (1975), 385–423; Hemmerdinger, p. 26, cf. *SIFC* XXV (1951), 84.

[34] The triads supposedly are I–III, IV–VI, VII–IX; the two halves are I–VI, VII–IX: see D. Hagel, 'Das zweite Prooimion des herodoteischen Geschichtswerk (Zu Hdt. 7, 8–18)', Diss. Erlangen–Nürnberg 1968.

As must by now be clear, Herodotus' work is an extremely complex composition. A thread of main narrative runs all the way through from beginning to end, but it is constantly interrupted by excursuses of various lengths, from a brief subordinate or parenthetical clause to a number of chapters or even an entire book. Such digressive excursuses branch out from the main story as from the trunk of a tree, giving rise sometimes to digressions within digressions. Herodotus is aware of his way of writing: he confesses that 'from the start my *logos* sought out digressions (προσθήκας)' (IV 30,1).[35] In the first six books the ramifications increase to such an extent that even a careful reader may easily lose the thread of the story and wonder what is the subject and purpose of the book. The main narrative follows a chronological order and well-defined events. It comprises approximately eighty years of history: from Croesus' and Cyrus' rise to power to the battle at Mycale and the occupation of Sestos, from 560/59 BC to 479 BC. The pillars on which this story rests are the reigns of the first four Achaemenids, from Cyrus to Xerxes. The subject at the centre of the narrative is the military campaigns of the four kings against neighbouring or rebellious peoples: the Medes, Lydians, Ionians, Carians, Lycians, Babylonians, and Massagetae (Cyrus); the Egyptians and Ethiopians (Cambyses); the Samians, Babylonians, Scythians, Cyreneans, Thracians, and Ionians (Darius); and the Greeks (Xerxes). The result is a political and military history of Persian expansionism during these reigns, interspersed with digressive geo-ethnographic *logoi* on the countries, peoples, and states attacked or conquered in the process. If one were to give a title to a work of this kind, one would perhaps at first opt for Περσικά, 'things Persian'; but the space devoted to the Greeks in the main narrative of Books V–IX exceeds the conventional terms of reference of *Persika*. In the first four books, the Greeks are discussed in digressive *logoi*, just as other peoples. From Book V onwards, however, they infiltrate the main narrative until they dominate it. The Ionian revolt, the battle of Marathon, and the 'Persian wars' of 480/79 BC are no digressive ramification branching off from the main narrative of Persian history—they are integral parts of that very history. One might say that, due to necessity or to a shift of interest or orientation, the developing Greek subject transformed what was meant to be a historical-ethnographic treatise of Περσικά into a history of the Persian wars. But the transformation is incomplete: traces of this evolution in two main stages are clearly preserved in the work as we have it.

This does not at all mean that at the beginning of his literary activity Herodotus had conceived any sort of unifying plan. On the contrary, the first six books create the impression that a number of pre-existing ethnographic, geographical, historical, and constitutional *logoi* were later integrated into the

---

[35] Cf. VII 171,1 (παρενθήκη in the sense of 'digression'); for the same term in the sense of 'second(ary) section', 'accessory addition', see VI 19,1 (in an oracle) and VII 5,3 (in a speech). The two terms cannot be clearly distinguished in Herodotus: see H. Erbse, *Gymnasium*, LXVIII (1961), 243 ff. On the excursuses and the relationship between main narrative and digressions see esp. Cobet; E. Lanzillotta, in M. Sordi (ed.), *Geografia e storiografia nel mondo classico*, Milan 1988 (CISA 14), pp. 24–7; Erbse, *Studien*, pp. 119–21; Payen, pp. 95–130.

work: independent *logoi*, so it seems, originally conceived of as short monographs on the Lydians, the Persians, Babylon, Egypt, and so on. The transformation of independent *logoi* into digressions dependent upon a unified narrative must have required a considerable amount of effort in the reworking and integrating into one whole of the contents, thought, and style, obliterating in the process traces of the separate compositions. In Herodotus' work this process of reworking is incomplete. Transitions from the main narrative to a digressing *logos* are often abrupt, and the traces of tacking and patching seem provisional. The examples in the first book are described in the Introduction to that book (pp. 62 f.). For the other books, we may note, in the first place, the double Egyptian *logos* (II 1–98; 99–182), linked artificially to Cambyses' story by a brief introductory remark (II 1,2) and a concluding linking phrase on Amasis, the last king against whom Cambyses fought (III 1,1). The Samian *logos* ends up being 'too long', not because it is relevant to the history of the Persian empire, but because, as Herodotus himself explains, the city's three main monuments deserve it (III 60,1). The Scythian *logos* is artificially attached to the account of Darius' expedition by a couple of allusive references (IV 1,1; 83,1). This is true also of the tenuous link between the *excursus* on Cyrene and Libya and the narrative about the Persian campaign in Africa, and of a number of other *logoi*, some in the wrong place, others disproportionately long in relation to the organization of the whole work. Recurrent formulae of ring composition, unfulfilled promises, references to recent events added during a later reworking of the text, as well as some contradictions and imprecisions of detail[36] are other signs of imperfect editing. The hypothetical connections that some 'unitarian' scholars have sought to uncover, in their attempts artificially to incorporate the ethnographic, historic, or constitutional digressions in the main narrative, usually escape the notice of intelligent readers. Whenever Herodotus wants to establish a link, he does not conceal it: one only needs to see how he connects the Spartans' military success to Lycurgus' reform (I 66,1), or the rise of Athens to its liberation from tyranny (V 78). Links of this kind, however, are rare. Essentially the writer's and the reader's interest are captured by physical and human nature, topography, rivers, vegetation, animal life, population, economy, tribal organization, customs, cults and religious beliefs, wonders, local history, and myth, quite independently of the main narrative concerning the history of the Persian empire and the Graeco-Persian conflict.[37] In sum, Herodotus began by writing separate monographs on various, independent topics, following the fashion of the first Greek prose writers. Hellanicus of Lesbos can serve as an example of such prose: he wrote some thirty separate monographs on local history, genealogy, ethnography, and other topics. Eventually, however, Herodotus abandoned the conventional canons, and in two stages shifted towards a new genre to whose creation he himself contributed, that of 'great historiography'. This intellectual process is also incomplete, since it left

---

[36] See e.g. I 175 and VIII 104.
[37] See v. Fritz, pp. 144 ff. For Herodotus' interest in geography and ethnography see Müller, *Geschichte* I, pp. 101–31.

traces of its various stages in the final work. It is precisely thanks to such imperfections that we are able to reconstruct today, albeit tentatively and without absolute certainty, the progessive stages of Herodotus' thought throughout his long journey from ethnography to history.

III

Throughout his ἱστορίη, we can follow Herodotus not only in his travels but also in his intellectual adventure. We see him enter temples, observe, hold conversations with priests, question and listen, think, compare, raise issues, argue, and sometimes even draw conclusions.[38] His natural curiosity is the driving force of the adventure. He shares this gift with many Greeks since the late eighth century, when new horizons in the Mediterranean and in the Pontus opened to travellers, tradesmen, mercenaries, and colonists. Herodotus is the heir of those intellectual attitudes which inspired the archaic adventure epic (the *Odyssey*, the *Herakleiai*, the *Argonautika*, the *Arimaspeia*) and the first prose works on geography (the Περίοδος γῆς, attributed to Hesiod, and those by Hecataeus and Scylax). The shift from geographical curiosity ('where are the sources of the Nile?') to enquiring about history and chronology ('how did the Persians come to rule over Asia?') is logical and easy. Here also Herodotus has predecessors: for example, the *Theogonies* and *Genealogies* of Hesiod, Acusilaus, and Pherecydes.

Herodotus' curiosity is boundless. He wants to know what the shape of the earth is and whether the continents are really surrounded by the Ocean, as some say. He wants to be acquainted with the customs of all the peoples in the world, and in particular with their food, clothes, sexual and funerary habits, religious beliefs and cults, their myths about origins, and their connections with other peoples. He wants to discover things unknown to others and verify what others have said, more in the hope of refuting than confirming their reports. Above all, he is fascinated by 'wonders' (θώματα): he divides the world into countries which have many natural marvels or human inventions, such as Egypt and Babylon, and nations which have few or none, such as Lydia and Scythia. He is full of admiration for the pyramids, the labyrinth of Moeris, the temple of Bubastis, the walls of Babylon, as well as for enormous artistic craters, massive gold statues, exotic animals, ingenious techniques. He finds wonderful everything unusual or strange, or exceptional from his point of view, which is that of a Greek from Asia Minor. He reacts like a peasant on his first visit to a big city, perhaps also like a journalist intending to astonish his public on his return. It is understandable that Herodotus' marvels should be found mainly in the East: Egypt, in particular, seems to him a land where everything is upside-down. The marvels include also supernatural phenomena: miracles, fulfilled dreams, portents and prophecies, extraordinary adventures, sudden reversals of situations, moral virtues of the good old days, heroism on the battlefield, gruesome tortures,

---

[38] On Herodotus' personal presence in his research, see Darbo-Peschanski, loc. cit. (n. 3).

stratagems, trickeries, witticisms: in short, the products of the irrational and of intelligence.[39] All that is unconventional poses problems, inspires credulity or scepticism: this is the starting point. 'I was curious ($\pi\rho\delta\theta\nu\mu\sigma$) to know' why the Nile rises at the summer solstice and ebbs after a hundred days: 'wanting to know, I asked' ($\beta\sigma\nu\lambda\delta\mu\epsilon\nu\sigma$ $\epsilon i\delta\epsilon\nu\alpha\iota$, $i\sigma\tau\delta\rho\epsilon\sigma\nu$, II 19,2). 'Wanting to know clearly' the origins of Heracles, 'I set out for Tyre' (II 44,1). When the resemblance between Colchians and Egyptians 'presented itself to my attention', 'I asked them both' (II, 104,1; cf. 150,2). With these non-technical, colloquial expressions Herodotus introduces problems as he encounters them each time; then he starts the enquiry proper, which consists essentially in what we would call today the collection of evidence.

His sources are mainly of two types: first-hand knowledge ($\check{o}\psi\iota\varsigma$) and oral testimony ($\dot{\alpha}\kappa\sigma\dot{\eta}$).[40] He considers direct knowledge more reliable, because it creates a direct relationship with reality and does not depend upon others. When Herodotus' visual descriptions can still be verified, they often turn out to be accurate and precise; but in other cases they are entirely inaccurate or even fanciful, or reveal very strange omissions. This has created the view that some of the descriptions are not first-hand, but based on the reports of others, whether heard or read. A notorious example is in the gross omissions and errors in his description of the sites of Upper Egypt (between lake Moeris and Elephantine), that have caused some scholars to deny credibility to Herodotus' direct knowledge in general. However, the problem of Upper Egypt is much disputed, and should not be used as a pretext for generalizations.[41] Herodotus used direct knowledge also to check some Ionian scientific theories. Although he considers sight and hearing as the main means to knowledge, he too sometimes does not refrain from a priori theorizing, nor does he reach purely subjective conclusions: he somehow follows a middle path between Ionian epistemology and the Sophists.[42]

Direct knowledge has its limits: it is useful for objects that can be seen, but not for places that cannot be reached, such as Ethiopia or northern Europe, or for

---

[39] On the 'marvellous' and the origin of the enquiry see B. Uhde, *Tijdschrift voor Filosofie*, XXXIII (1971), 559–71; W. M. Bloomer, *ClassAnt* XII (1993), 30–50. For virtue and intelligence, stratagems and trickster-figures, see M. Detienne and J.-P. Vernant, *Les Ruses de l'intelligence: la mètis de Grecs*, Paris 1974 = *Cunning Intelligence in Greek Culture and Society* (trans. J. Lloyd), Hassocks 1978; see S. Saïd, *Anc. Soc.* XI–XII (1980–1), 83–117; and M. Giraudoux, *BAGB* (1984), 4–13; C. Dewald, in *The Greek Historians: Literature and History. Papers Presented to A. E. Raubitschek*, Saratoga 1985, pp. 47–63; M. Dorati, *QS* XXXVIII (1993), 65–84.

[40] On first-hand knowledge, see Schepens, *L'Autopsie* (with extensive bibliography). The terms $\dot{\alpha}\kappa\sigma\dot{\eta}$, $\dot{\alpha}\kappa\sigma\dot{\upsilon}\omega$, etc. sometimes indicate 'hearsay' of little value (e.g. at II 99,1). See Hartog, pp. 260–309 = ET pp. 248–302.

[41] Apart from Sayce, see Fehling, and O. K. Armayor, *JARCE* XV (1978), 59–73; id., *Herodotus' Autopsy of the Fayoum*. For some recent reactions to this hypercritical trend see W. K. Pritchett, *The Liar School of Herodotus*, Amsterdam 1993; G. S. Shrimpton, *History and Memory in Ancient Greece. With an Appendix on Herodotus' Source Citation*, Montreal–Kingston 1997; K. J. Dover, in *Modus operandi: Essays in Honour of G. Rickman*, London 1998, pp. 219–25. For bibliography on Herodotus and Egypt see Lloyd, *Introduction*, and Schepens.

[42] Cf. Müller, 'Herodot', pp. 299–318.

historical events, except such that are indirectly based on archaeological evidence. The shift of Herodotus from ethnography to history corresponds to the shift from first-hand knowledge to oral research. Ἰστορίη proper is oral enquiry (cf. e.g. II 29,1 and 113,1). Herodotus' work is historiography based mainly on oral traditions. It displays many characteristics of this type of historiography (aetiological and etymological exegesis, typical numbers, stories based on proverbs, etc.), its faults and originality. At this point we encounter a problem: who were Herodotus' oral informants? Only rarely will he have met direct witnesses of geographal sites or historical events: more often, indeed always in the case of remote historical events, he will have had to content himself with the last links in a chain of a more or less long oral transmission. As is well known, oral traditions are kept at a local or tribal level for practical purposes, such as legitimization or cultural and other types of aetiology. Even if they are considered 'official' and are regularly checked, and even if they are entrusted to professional 'memorizers' (this is the original meaning of the term μνήμονες), in the course of three or four generations they undergo considerable changes due to mnemonic or technical reasons, to various interests, tendentiousness, and manipulations of all sorts.[43] Herodotus must have been partially aware of the problem, just as he was aware of being at times the first to record in writing oral traditions. Perhaps also his informants were conscious of this, since their decision to entrust their oral heritage to the written page was sometimes an act of acculturation, which in itself may have influenced the form and content of their testimonies. All this explains well the origins of Herodotus' scepticism and reservations towards ἀκοή, though he valued oral traditions so much that he sometimes presented as oral items information that he actually read in written sources or completely invented.

Ancient Greece and the ancient Eastern civilizations were not oral societies like those studied by modern anthropologists or Africanists. Writing had been known for hundreds and perhaps thousands of years. There was no dearth of experts and educated men able to consult and even translate written documents.

---

[43] On Herodotus' informants see C. Darbo-Peschanski, *QS* XXII (1985), 105–28. On the theory and practice of oral enquiry see J. Vansina, *Oral Tradition as History*, Madison 1985; R. H. Finnegan, *Oral Literature in Africa*, Oxford 1970; D. P. Henige, *The Chronology of Oral Tradition*, Oxford 1974; id., *Oral Historiography*, London 1982. On these problems in ancient historiography see A. Momigliano, in *Studies in Historiography*, London 1966, pp. 211–20; V. Rotolo, in *Studi classici in onore di Q. Cataudella*. I, Catania 1972, pp. 395–414; J. Cobet, in J. von Ungern-Sternberg and H. Reinau (eds.), *Vergangenheit in mündlichen Überlieferung*, Stuttgart 1988, pp. 226–33, 235–44; B. Rochette, *REG* CIX (1996), 325–47; Thomas, *Oral Tradition*; id., in N. Kullmann and J. Althoff (eds.), *Vermittlung und Tradierung von Wissen in der griechischen Kultur*, Tübingen 1993; B. Gentili and G. Cerri, *Il Verri* (June 1973), 53–78. For these issues in Herodotus see M. Lang, *Proc. of the American Philos. Ass.*, CXXVII (1984), 93–103; and O. Murray, 'Herodotus and oral history' (1987), repr. in Luraghi, pp. 16–44. Evans, *Explorer*, pp. 89–146. For Greek views on human memory see M. Simondon, *La Mémoire et l'oubli dans la pensée grecque jusqu'à la fin du Ve siècle avant J.C.*, Paris 1982. On orality in Greek culture see E. A. Havelock, *Preface to Plato*, Cambridge, Mass. 1963; id., *The Literate Revolution in Greece and its Cultural Consequences*, Princeton 1982.

However, it seems that Herodotus only rarely succeeded in meeting such people: the staff of the Babylonian satrap Tritantaechmes, the agent Tymnes at Olbia, Archias of Sparta, Tersander of Orchomenos.[44] That at Dascyleum he had contact with satraps descended from Artabazus; at Athens met Pericles, the Alcmaeonids, the Cimonids, the descendants of Sophanes of Decelea and of Zopyrus the younger; at Croton, the descendants of Callias of Elea and of the physician Democedes—these are modern hypotheses of varying plausibility, often suggested by the political or historical tendentiousness of the passages in question. The Egyptian 'priests' and the Babylonian Chaldaeans, whose testimonies Herodotus believes with great respect (though not always), were actually low-ranking ministers with limited learning, restricted to religious practices and beliefs pertaining to their temples and objects of cult. To this category of people also belongs the 'treasurer' of Athena at Sais; Herodotus, in any case, thought that the information he obtained from him about the sources of the Nile was hardly serious (II 28,1–2). Whoever tries today to ask questions about history, theology, or geography of contemporary monks in Egyptian monasteries, surely knows what type of information he is likely to get, even about the history of their own monastery. The Persian, Egyptian, and Scythian 'learned people' (λόγιοι: see note on I 1,1) are either purely fictional figures or informants of this kind. Usually, Herodotus had to rely on hired guides, Greek or bilingual, such as the interpreter whose translation of the hieroglyphics on Cheops' pyramid he could not verify (II, 125,6). Whenever Herodotus vaguely quotes what the 'locals' (ἐπιχώριοι) told him, for instance Babylonians, Phoenicians, or Siceliots,[45] his sources are either fictional or real but ordinary people, whom he met in the street and who, in any case, spoke Greek.[46] Add to this the linguistic barrier in the Eastern countries, the total dependence upon interpreters and guides, the limitations encountered by a foreigner who has no access to sacred places and religious rites, and Herodotus' instinctive tendency, as well as that of his guides, to interpret foreign gods, institutions, and customs in Greek terms. Herodotus' scepticism towards most of his oral sources is entirely understandable, as is modern scepticism towards the reliability of Herodotus himself, at least as far as non-Greek cultures are concerned.[47] However, it cannot be excluded that Herodotus sometimes managed, perhaps in spite of his ignorance, to collect reliable sources even in the East. Six out of the seven names of the conspirators against the false Smerdis (III 70,1–3) are confirmed by Darius' inscription at Bisitun. Herodotus' catalogues of tributes, satrapies, and army contingents in the Persian empire, and of the stations and distances along the 'Royal Road', are ultimately based upon written documents, although they may be badly translated, misinterpreted,

---

[44] I 192,2; IV 76,6; III 55,2; IX 16,1–5.

[45] For lists of epichoric sources see e.g. Pirro, pp. 71–99; and Jacoby, *RE* Suppl. II, coll. 398–9; cf. note on I 1,1. On translation and interpreters in Herodotus see Hartog, pp. 237–48; T. Harrison, *Histos*, II (1998) (on-line).

[46] Cf. Thucydides' objections to the use of information 'randomly acquired' (I 20,3; 22,2).

[47] On Herodotus' conception of foreign languages see T. Harrison, art. cit. For the improbable theory that Herodotus knew Aramaic see S. Mandell, *AncW* XXI (1990), 103–8.

and placed in wrong historical contexts. They are not purely artistic creations, modelled on the Homeric catalogues, nor should they be compared to the list of Persian generals in Aeschylus' *Persae,* or the armed units in Xenophon's *Cyropaedia.* The tablets at Persepolis now allow us to give more credit also to Herodotus' Persian onomastics.[48] Of course, Herodotus was unable to consult the original texts, or the Elamite, Accadian, Aramaic, and other translations of official documents which circulated in the empire, 'in every state according to its script and to each people according to its language', as the Book of Esther repeatedly tells us.[49] He may have consulted Greek translations, if there were any for the benefit of the Greeks in Asia Minor. It is more probable, however, that he asked his bilingual informers to dictate names and lists to him. Some have postulated the existence of collections of Persian stories as an (intermediary) source for such famous court tales of a typically oriental type as the legend of Cyrus' birth and upbringing, the last events of Cambyses' life, the conspiracy of the seven Persians, Zopyrus' adventures, and the tale of Xerxes and Masistes' wife. These stories must have been given a Greek flavour already by Herodotus' informants. One has only to remember the famous Persian debate about different forms of government (III 80–3): in its Herodotean form it looks like a purely Greek, sophistic debate; but this may ultimately have replaced a piece of Achaemenid propaganda legitimizing the kingdom, or a charter of Persian privileges.[50]

That historians necessarily use written sources is a modern assumption: Herodotus and Thucydides preferred oral ones without reflection. By written sources I do not mean the twenty-four or so inscriptions quoted or mentioned by Herodotus,[51] since the reading of the twelve Greek inscriptions constitutes first-hand knowledge, while the reading of the many oriental inscriptions (in Lydian, Babylonian, hieroglyphic Egyptian, Persian) is part of the oral enquiry from bilingual interpreters.[52] Herodotus' true written sources are, in the first place, the works of the Greek poets from Homer to Aeschylus: he cites about fifteen poets, among them two tragedians (Phrynichus and Aeschylus), and sometimes uses them as historical sources.[53] Among prose writers, Herodotus certainly read attentively Hecataeus, his great predecessor, whom he mentions several

---

[48] Cf. D. M. Lewis' correct assessment in *The Greek Historians* (n. 39), pp. 101–17, criticizing O. K. Armayor, *TAPhA* CVIII (1978), 1–9. For Persian personal names, cf. note on I 139,2.

[49] Esther 1: 22; 3: 12; 8: 9.

[50] Cf. note on III 80–2.

[51] Cf. the bibliography quoted at I 51,15; see also A. Martorelli, *RIL* CXI (1977), 115–25.

[52] The same applies also to the theogonic incantation of the Magi (see note on I 132,3) and the list of Egyptian kings (II 100,1). Herodotus distinguished between the two Egyptian scripts (II 36,4) but not between Persian and Aramaic.

[53] For Herodotus' poetic sources see Pirro, pp. 57–71. For Archilochus see note on I 12,2. On Pindar and the Greek historical spirit see Ch. G. Starr, *Hermes,* XCV (1967), 393–403. Herodotus does not quote Sophocles (cf. above p. 4) or Choerilus of Samos (see *FGrHist* 696 F 33–4; D. Mulder, *Klio,* VII (1907), 29–44), or Panyassis. He quotes the *Arimaspaea* by the Proconnesian Aristeas: IV 14,3; the Hymns of Olen: IV 35,3–4; the oracles of Bacis and Musaeus: VIII 20,1–2; 77,1–2; 96,2; IX 43,1–2. Aeschylus is quoted maliciously (II 156,6). For a general discussion see H. Verdin, in *Historiographia antiqua (Festschrift W. Peremans),* Leuven 1977, pp. 53–76.

times and makes much use of. He mentions no other prose writer; perhaps in his time it was not yet usual to mention predecessors. As for other possible works such as the *Persika* of Dionysius of Miletus, the *Indika* of Scylax of Caryanda, the *Lydiaka* of Xanthus of Sardis, or the various works of Charon of Lampsacus, let alone the hypothetical memoirs of the Athenian exile Dicaeus or the Spartan exile Demaratus (VIII 65,6), we are in the realm of pure hypothesis.[54] It is uncertain whether Herodotus knew Hellanicus' first works when he collected his material. He certainly consulted various collections of Delphic and other oracles, such as those attributed to Musaeus and Bacis (cf. note 53). Some ethnographic chapters, for example those about India (III 98–116) and about African tribes (IV 168–99), seem to be based on written sources. Porphyry asserts that Herodotus copied from Hecataeus word for word with few changes the passages describing the hunt of the crocodile, the hippopotamus, and the phoenix (II 70–3; cf. *FGrHist* 1 T 22 and F 324a–b).[55] Some inadmissible epichoric testimonies ('as the Ammonians themselves say' at III 26,3; or the Issedones and the Phalacrians at IV 25, 1–2; 27) were probably found in the works of an ethnographer or a poet (Aristeas?). However, the tendency of some modern scholars to overestimate the importance of written sources, and even regularly to attribute almost all oral testimonies to written texts,[56] does not agree with our general knowledge of the abilities and methods of early Greek ethnographers and historians. In the fifth century it was not yet possible to consult archives and libraries; even if a document was technically accessible, its reading and interpretation posed enormous problems. Overestimating the importance of written sources ultimately leads to assuming the existence of other Herodotuses before Herodotus, and to regarding his work as an eclectic compilation written in a library, a *Sekundärarbeit* rather than a *Primärforschung*, in Strasburger's terms.[57] Herodotus would thus be placed at the end of a mature tradition of scholarship, rather than at the beginning of the rising science of history and ethnography. The little we know about the work of Herodotus' predecessors and his contemporaries, and about the prevalent oral character of Greek culture in the fifth century, does not support such an evaluation of the place due to Herodotus in the history of ancient historiography. Obviously Herodotus was not always the first to write down oral material which was unknown to others or to insert it for the first time in the context in which we now find it. Sometimes Herodotus found his material already elaborated, interpreted, and integrated within a solid system of traditions: this must be the case,

[54] For Herodotus' polemics with his predecessors see Lateiner, pp. 91–108 (including an 'Inventory of Herodotean Polemic', pp. 104–8); Marincola, pp. 225–6. Scylax is not quoted as a writer (IV 44,1). Dionysius of Miletus: *FGrHist* 687; Xanthos: *FGrHist* 765; see P. Tozzi, *RIL* XCIX (1965), 175–84. For Greek texts about Persia and the East in general see Drews, ch. 3; C. Masetti, *Helikon*, XI-XII (1971–2), 279–88.

[55] For Herodotus and Hecataeus see H. Diels, *Hermes*, XXII (1887), 411–47; S. Lilja, *Arctos*, V (1967), 85–96; Schepens, pp. 37 f. and n. 18, with bibliography; Mora, pp. 249–256.

[56] The 'things already said by others' at VI 55 are an exception. See Jacoby's assessment in *RE* Suppl. II, col. 403.

[57] *Die Wesensbestimmung der Geschichte durch die antike Geschichtsschreibung*, Wiesbaden 1966.

for example, with the Greek traditions on the events of 480–79 BC. Herodotus did not create his history out of nothing; perhaps he did for historical traditions what Homer had done, centuries earlier, for epic ones.

Despite appearances to the contrary, Herodotus does not usually quote his sources: he tells the story that he considers true. In Herodotus' work we usually read the final results of the enquiry. Only in exceptional cases does Herodotus quote one or more sources and make us participate in the enquiry, though he does so more often than other ancient historians. It is worth asking ourselves why he quotes these sources.[58] Sometimes it seems that he wants to lend authority to the version he relates. In Book II, for example, the Egyptian priests are often quoted as the ultimate authority, especially on questions of religion, culture, and geography. In other cases it seems that quotations serve an opposite function: to insinuate doubts or reservations concerning accounts for which the enquirer himself does not wish to assume responsibility. This often happens when implausible 'marvels' are reported: the phoenix arrives every 500 years, 'according to what the Heliopolitans say' (II 73,1), a legend about which Herodotus is clearly sceptical. In numerous cases two or more different and opposing versions are given: for example, the Spartan and Samian accounts of the crater sent to Croesus (I 70,2–3); the Ionian version and the Egyptian one of the origins of the Delta (II 15–16); the three theories ($\tau\rho\iota\phi\alpha\sigma\iota\alpha\varsigma$ $\delta\delta\sigma\dot{\upsilon}\varsigma$) about the flooding of the Nile (II 20–3); 'the double story' ($\delta\iota\xi\dot{\sigma}\varsigma$ $\lambda\dot{\sigma}\gamma\sigma\varsigma$), Greek and Egyptian, about Cambyses' wife/sister's death (III 32,1–4); 'the double cause' ($\alpha\dot{\iota}\tau\dot{\iota}\alpha\iota$ $\delta\iota\phi\dot{\alpha}\sigma\iota\alpha\iota$) of Polycrates' death (III 120–2); the Athenian and Aeginetan versions of the conflict between the two cities (V 85–6); the accounts of Sybaris and Croton, both supported by evidence, of Dorieus' intervention in Magna Graecia (V 44–5); the Spartan account of the mythical conqueror of Laconia, which contradicts all the poets (VI 52,1); the Argive and Spartan accounts of Cleomenes' madness (VI 84,1–3); Hecataeus' version and that of the Athenians on the expulsion of the Pelasgians from Attica (VI 137,1–4); the Argive version and that of the rest of Greece on the policy of Argos in 480 BC (VII 148–52); the Sicilian and the Phoenician versions of the death of Hamilcar (VII 166–7); the Athenian and the Aeginetan accounts of the start of the battle of Salamis (VIII 84,2); 'the double story' ($\delta\iota\xi\sigma\dot{\upsilon}\varsigma$ $\lambda\dot{\sigma}\gamma\sigma\upsilon\varsigma$) about the deeds of Sophanes of Decelea at the battle of Plataea, 'of which the second contradicts the first' (IX 74,2). Herodotus feels under a moral obligation to report all the versions collected, even if they are not trustworthy: 'My duty is to report what is said ($\lambda\dot{\epsilon}\gamma\epsilon\iota\nu$ $\tau\dot{\alpha}$ $\lambda\epsilon\gamma\dot{\sigma}\mu\epsilon\nu\alpha$), but it is not my duty to believe it all alike. May this rule govern my entire work' (VII 152,3). 'Those who believe in such things may well rely on what the Egyptians say; as for myself I record what everybody says just as I hear it related—that is the basis of my work' (II 123,1); 'Whether this is true or not, I do not know: I write down what is said' (IV 195,2); 'This is the more credible of the two versions, but there is also another less credible one that should be reported, because it too is told' (III 9,2). Thus for

---

[58] Cf. F. J. Groten Jr., *Phoenix*, XVII (1963), 79–89.

Herodotus it is important to record what is being said, whether credible or not, in order to save from oblivion and all-erasing time traditions that survive orally. In this respect too, Herodotus is the true heir of epic poetry. He is inspired by a profound respect for what is known, said, or remembered, that is, for the sources, though he often voluntarily leaves the task of evaluating and judging to the reader, or to posterity. His frame of mind is characteristic of people aware of the fleetingness of human memory and in contact with a largely oral society, whose traditions are in constant peril of being altered or extinguished. In some respects, the situation of a modern anthropologist is analogous: he may some-times prefer to record the evidence of a dying ethnic group or generation, and not waste time in studying the material. Herodotus also often prefers to give up what should be the main task of the ἵστωρ, the witness who not only 'sees' but also 'judges'.[59] In many cases, his enquiry consists in the exposition of testimonies; if they are not satisfactory, the enquiry continues through additional evaluation and verification, but it does not always lead to a conclusion.

It is, however, easy to infer, from the way that Herodotus presents his testi-monies, that he is not impartial. Sometimes it is possible to see that he leans towards one version. In some cases he quotes two perfectly consistent or support-ing and complementary accounts: 'The Corinthians say this (and the Lesbians confirm it)' (I 23; 24,8); 'The Arabs say this ... and the Egyptians agree' (II 74,4); 'This story is admitted by Greeks and barbarians alike' (IV 12,3); 'I know that this is what happened because I heard it in Delphi; the Milesians add the following' (I 20); 'Up to this point the Spartans and the Theraeans tell the same story; from here onwards only the Theraeans tell what happened' (IV 150,1). Herodotus thus tries to create an impression of over-carefulness and credibility in respect of confirmed or uncontested versions. For similar purposes he sometimes declares that he cannot say something with certainty (ἀτρεκέως), or was unable to check something else, or was unable to see this or that, despite his efforts: he could not interview a direct witness or obtain oral reports, or else 'no one knows anything';[60] he could not visit the underground chambers of the labyrinth of Moeris (II 148,5), or see the statue at Babylon because it had been removed by Xerxes (I 183,3); he only saw a painting of the phoenix (II 73,1). In other cases, he claims to know certain things or the names of persons or gods, but chooses not to mention them for various reasons: they are not worthy of being remem-bered;[61] they are, but it is preferable not to mention them (I 51,4 with note *ad loc.*); they would seem incredible (I 193,4) or have been discussed by others (VI 55); it would be irreverent and out of place to discuss religious matters if

---

[59] Cf. above, p. 8, n. 23.

[60] See e.g. II 19,1; 28,1; 126,1; III 155,1–2; IV 16,1; 23,5; 81,1; V 66,1; VI 82,1; 118,1; VII 26,2; 60,1; 152,1; VIII 128,1; 133; IX 84,1–2. In geographic and ethnographic sections the 'isolation' of certain areas serves to excuse lack of knowledge or uncertainty, see H. Edelmann, *Klio*, LII (1970), 79–86. Argumentation about truth, certainty, reliability, etc. are mostly related to geographic and ethno-graphic issues; see J. R. Grant, *Phoenix*, XXXVII (1983), 283–98.

[61] See e.g. I 14,4; 177; V 57,2; VII 96,1; VIII 85,2–3.

not 'necessary'.[62] By these means, Herodotus attempts to establish his prestige as an authoritative, responsible, careful, and honest expert, who expresses himself with cautiousness about things he knows perfectly well, and who knows more than he says. With this typical attitude Herodotus has created a characteristic style, which can be easily parodied, as Lucian does in the *De dea Syria*. Some have wanted to detect in this the tricks of *Lügenliteratur*, mendacious literature; these are certainly not absent from Herodotus' work, but have not always been successful, as ancient and modern critics of his proverbial 'malice' demonstrate. It is possible, although it cannot be proven, that Herodotus sometimes deliberately fails to mark the end of a testimony and the beginning of his personal views; or that he sometimes invents certain 'sources' in order to introduce, in sophistic fashion, two logical or legitimate alternatives on a given issue. After all, as Artabanus tells Xerxes, only when two opposite views are put forward is it possible to make a choice (VII 10*a*,1). Though generalizations should be resisted and each case should be considered individually, we may say here that for Herodotus the most important thing is not always to corroborate his reports, but rather to present different moral and political points of view. The real problem, therefore, is not Herodotus' 'honesty', but the literary conventions of the new historiographical genre, in which Herodotus is involved as both creator and representative. One cannot accuse an ancient historian of dishonesty for having freely composed speeches or dialogues that were not actually delivered. Even Thucydides acknowledges having done this sometimes.

Although for Herodotus respect for tradition is perhaps more important than criticism, this does not mean that a critical process is not intrinsic to the very nature of his ἱστορίη. As we have seen, Herodotus usually makes choices: for example, he states that he has chosen, from the four alternatives known to him, the more 'truthful' version of Cyrus' story, since the other three seemed to him tendentious (I 95,1). This is a choice between what is more and less plausible, not between true and false accounts in absolute terms: in this respect Herodotus proves to be the true heir of Hecataeus.[63] Among the numerous versions circulating on Cyrus' death he chose 'the most plausible' (ὁ πιθανώτατος: I 214,5). In a number of cases he rejects a given account because it is 'not credible' (οὐ πιθανός, or similar expressions) or 'incorrect' (οὐκ ὀρθῶς λέγοντες) or 'it resembles falsehood' (ψευδέσι ἴκελα) or is 'implausible' (οὐδὲ λόγος αἱρέει, οὔ νύν τοι ἀεικὲς οὐδέν); sometimes he adds a proof (μαρτύριον, τεκμήριον), or a logical argument, or an interpretation, to justify his judgement and formulate a final 'opinion' (γνώμη, δοκέειν ἐμοί, and similar expressions). In these highly interesting

[62] This rule is expressed in general terms (II 65,2), but in practice it applies only to Egyptian religion (II 3,2; 46,2; 47,2; 61,1; 62,2; 86,2; 132,2; 170,1; 171,1). On Herodotus' silences and reserves, esp. on religious issues, see Mora, pp. 136–9; Lateiner, pp. 64–7; J. Gould, in S. Hornblower (ed.), *Greek Historiography*, Oxford 1994, pp. 91–7; on Herodotus' style to this purpose see G. L. Cooper III, *TAPhA* CIV (1974), 23–76.

[63] Cf. *FGrHist* 1 F 1. On Herodotus and truth see the brief summary of two unpublished theses (F. Haible, Tübingen 1963, and H. Barth, Halle 1968) in Schepens, pp. 43 ff. For Sophistic justifications of lying see III 72,4–5.

instances, there predominate arguments based on common sense (κατὰ τὸ εἰκός), plausibility of the testimonies, proofs or lack of proofs, the weight of direct knowledge, the intrinsic inconsistency of some stories or the mythical and political falsification of others.[64] Sometimes Herodotus creates hypotheses or establishes analogies based on oral testimonies, which he then tries to verify through other testimonies. He is fully aware that some of his ideas are controversial. He sometimes proudly declares that he reached a certain γνώμη before even knowing the evidence, which he then quotes to support his opinion (II 18,1; 104,1).

Refusing to believe blindly all that is told is the first step towards a critical attitude. Herodotus does not believe fantastic tales about the existence of headless men or men with dogs' heads, an eye in their chest (IV 194,4), goats' feet, or people sleeping through six months of the year (IV 25,1); nor does he believe the legends of the phoenix (II 73), the feather rain (IV 7,3; 31,1–2), the floating island of Chemmis (II 156,1–2), or the story of the Neuri becoming wolves once a year (IV 105,2). But he also refuses to believe that in circumnavigating Africa at a certain point the sun can be seen 'to one's right' (IV 42,4). He does, however, believe the 'absolutely marvellous story' of Arion and the dolphin (I 23,4) and the tale of Rhampsinitus and the thieves, except for one 'unbelievable' detail (II 121). He rationalizes the myths about Cyrus' bitch, the doves at Dodona, Skyllias' underwater swimming, the synchronism of the battles of Plataea and Mycale. He prefers a rational explanation of Cambyses' madness (III 33), while he himself proposes an irrational one of the madness of Cleomenes (VI 84,3). He is acquainted with the rationalistic school of dream interpretation (VII 16 β–γ), but believes in their divine origin. He also believes in the miracles which saved Delphi from the Persian attack (VIII 37–9) and asks the gods and the heroes forgiveness for his excessive critical spirit (II 45,3); he tries to find explanations and seeks compromises in order to solve chronological problems concerning gods (II 142–6); and he is able to prefer a clear archaeological proof to an aetiological legend (II 131,2–3). This fascinating mixture of credulity and scepticism on the part of a curious, restless, and exceptionally intelligent man eventually created a rudimentary set of analytical procedures, which never developed into a true, coherent, technical 'method', yet stand for what can be seen as the proto-historical phase of historical critical thought.

IV

A direct relationship between Herodotus' methods of historical research and his spatial and chronological frames emerges clearly. The enquiry poses the problem of plausibility, which in turn inspires questions about the spatial and

[64] On ἄπιστος, etc. in Herodotus and other Greek historians see Z. M. Packman, *Hermes*, CXIX (1991), 399–414. For a typology of Herodotean arguments see Lloyd, below pp. 288 ff. On the so-called 'empirical element' in Herodotus' method of enquiry see D. Muller in *Gnomosyne. Festschrift W. Marg*, Munich 1981, pp. 299–318; D. Lateiner, *Antichthon*, XX (1986), 1–20, and Lateiner, pp. 94, 201–2. On 'proof' in Greek historiography see P. Butti de Lima, *L'inchiesta e la prova*, Turin 1996.

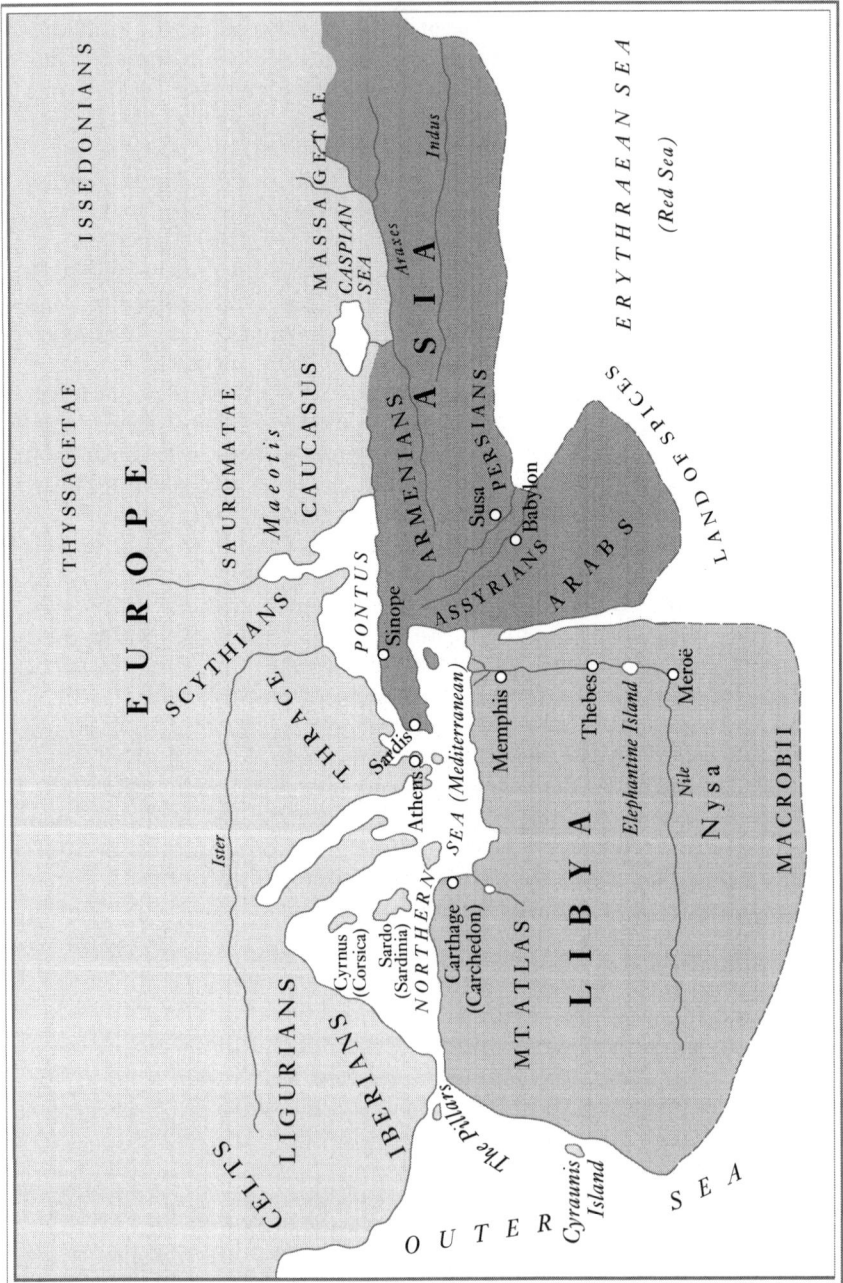

Map 12. The world of Herodotus according to Niebuhr

temporal limits of the enquiry itself: beyond certain geographical or chronological boundaries one can at best engage in theoretical speculations, lacking empirical basis (a thing which can 'be said', λόγῳ, but cannot be proved 'in practice', ἔργῳ: IV 8,2). He sets off on his journeys well equipped with epic and Ionian presuppositions and beliefs concerning the shape of the earth, but at the same time quite ready to expose the ignorance and foolishness of his countrymen and colleagues, to criticize and correct them, even to demolish their theories through personal exploration and alternative evidence gathered in the East. The result is a mass of geographical digressions,[65] many of them revealing a typical mixture of ethnographical observation, evidence obtained from other inform- ants, utopian fantasies of upside-down worlds, admiration, scepticism, pedes- trian acceptance of widespread commonplaces, and aprioristic models, side by side with inferences from empirical observation and experiment.[66] As Solon before him, Herodotus sailed to the East under the pretence of 'seeing' the world, that is, as an intelligent voyager, tourist, or explorer. He was a great admirer of exploration, in itself a product of human curiosity. Pharaoh Nechos is given credit for organizing a successful circumnavigation of Africa by Phoen- ician ships (IV 42,2 ff.), and Darius for the discovery of the greatest part of Asia, especially thanks to Scylax's expedition to the Indus and his circumnavigation of the Arabian peninsula (IV 44,1–3).[67] Even Cambyses is granted a measure of curiosity with regard to the 'Table of the Sun' in Ethiopia (III, 17), and Xerxes is said to have tried a circumnavigation of Africa (IV 43,1–7). The Phoenicians, the Samians, the Phocaeans are all credited with venturing on long voyages that eventually brought them to the western end of the Mediterranean, thus making the Greeks acquainted with the Adriatic, Tyrrhenia, Corsica, Sardinia, Iberia, and Tartessus (I 1,1;163, 1–2; IV 152, 1–5). About unexplored lands and seas he feels unable to say anything certain (see e.g. III 115,1) and prefers to leave the questions open. He deems it worthwhile to mention what he has learnt from hearsay (ἀκοῇ) only if it results from the most exact enquiries (IV 161–2).

Since no one at this time assumed that the earth is a globe, Herodotus should not be expected to think otherwise. But he rejected the commonly accepted view that the Ocean is a river surrounding the flat earth, because of lack of proof.[68] The Mediterranean, the Atlantic, and the Red Sea (see note to I 1,1) 'are all one and the same sea' (I 20,4), that is interconnected; but since the boundaries of Europe were quite unknown, and there was no one who knew with certainty whether it was surrounded by water, in the north or in the east (IV 45,1), his map of the world has the sea only on two sides, west and south, while the other two have no

---

[65] For a collection see E. Lanzillotta, *CISA* XIV (1988), 19–31.

[66] On Herodotus' geography see J. L. Myres, *Geographical J.*, VI (Dec. 1896), 606–631; Myres, pp. 32–46; Waters, *Herodotus the Historian*, pp. 6, 88, 158–60; Hartog, ch. 1 (pp. 31–51 = ET pp. 12–33); Gould, ch. 5 (pp. 86–109); C. Jacob, *Géographie et ethnographie en Grèce ancienne*, Paris 1991, pp. 47–72; F. Cordano, *La geografia degli antichi*, Bari 1993², pp. 53–62.

[67] See J. F. Salles, in *L'Arabie et ses mers bordières*, I, Lyon 1988, pp. 79–86.

[68] II 21; 23; III 115,1–2; IV 8,2; 45,1.

Map 13. The travels of Herodotus (ca. 450–430 B. C.)

Map showing the ancient Near East with labelled regions and places: Tanais, Lake Maeotis, SEA, Sinope, PONTUS, Themiscyra, CAPPADOCIA, ARMENIA, Araxes, CASPIAN SEA, PARTHIA, ASSYRIA, Nineveh, Arbela, Assur, Tigris, Ecbatana, MEDIA, Thapsacus, ARABIA, Chaaspes, Ardericca?, Babylon, BABYLONIA, Euphrates, SUSIANA, Susa, Eulaeus, PERSIA, Pasargadae, Persepolis, Tyre, Damascus, Jerusalem, Dead Sea, RED SEA.

known borders. Apart from some vague notions about the amber and tin routes connecting the Adriatic to the Baltic and 'coming to us from the ends of the earth' (III 115,1–2, and notes), he viewed the entire *terra incognita* of northern and eastern Eurasia as stretching out interminably.[69] Herodotus apparently accepted the bronze map of the world brought by Aristagoras of Miletus to Sparta about 500 BC and said to have included the 'chart of the entire earth' (γῆς ἁπάσης περίοδος), the 'whole sea' and 'all the rivers' (IV 49,1). It was a Milesian map, one of the very first Greek attempts at cartography, probably drawn originally by Anaximander but later updated by Hecataeus to make it useful in the new world of the Persian empire. He also endorsed Ionian descriptions of the Royal Road from Sardis to Susa (V 52–3; VIII 98) and, in general, the Ionian view of the Persian empire (III 89–96 and note). But he had some harsh words to say about the accepted basic division of the earth into three continents, though he was ready to use it as sanctioned by custom (IV 45,5). 'For my part I cannot conceive why three names, and women's names especially, should ever have been given to a tract (γῆ) which is in reality one, or why the Egyptian Nile and the Colchian Phasis— or, according to others, the Maeotic Tanais and the Cimmerian ferry—should have been fixed upon for boundary lines; nor can I say who gave the three tracts their names, or whence they took their epithets' (IV 45,2).[70] Moreover, 'I cannot but laugh when I see numbers of persons drawing maps of the world without having any reason to guide them: making, as they do, the Ocean-stream run all around the earth, and the earth itself to be an exact circle, as if described by a pair of compasses, with Europe and Asia just of the same size' (IV 36,2).[71] According to Herodotus, on the contrary, the three continents are exceedingly unequal in size, Europe extending in length as far as both Asia and Libya (IV 42,1; 45,1); and since the Nile separates Asia from Libya, the Ionians and the Greeks in general ought to add a fourth continent, namely the Delta of the Nile, being as they say the 'gift of the Nile' (II 5,1; 10,1; 15–16). This looks like a piece of polemical sophistry. The Ionians, of course, were absurdly mistaken in their limited view of 'Egypt' (II 16,1), and Herodotus' definition of 'Egypt' as the entire country inhabited by the Egyptians, just as Cilicia is the country occupied by the Cilicians and Assyria by the Assyrians (II 17,1), is, no doubt, much more open-minded. But it is the point of view of an ethnographer, or of a cultural historian, and leaves open the problem as to which of the two neighbouring continents Egypt ought to be assigned: it is indeed an old Greek dilemma, arising out of an ethno-cultural, not a physical-geographical approach. Egyptian civilization and history, as we all know, gravitated much more to the Middle East than to the rest of Africa. And Herodotus himself, like most ancient geographers, was more interested in ethnography and cultural history than in physical geography, in spite of his own keen interest in the geomorphology of the 'gift of the Nile' (II 11).

[69] See map of Herodotus' world, p. 24.
[70] Rawlinson's translation.
[71] Rawlinson's translation.

For all his criticism, Herodotus felt the need to offer his audience an alternative description of the earth. Yet, what he in fact offers us is a shadowy human geography of four tracts of the Persian empire: one between the Euxine and the Persian Gulf; another Asia Minor; a third what is today called Transeuphratene, with Egypt and Libya adjoining Phoenicia and Arabia; and the fourth the area between the Caspian and the Red Seas, east of Persia and up to India (IV 37–41). Europe, Greece included, is missing from this map (in spite of what we read at IV 36,2): it is not a περίοδος γῆς in the traditional sense of Ionian science. It must have been derived from a Persian source, putting Persia at the centre and the four cardinal points as seen from that centre. A compass-card from the Pontus to Egypt and from the Hellespont to India echoes, in fact, the well-known Achaemenid formula, 'from the Scythians who are beyond Sogdiana and thence to Ethiopia, from India and thence to Sardis',[72] and would better find its place in a treatise of *Persika*.

As a matter of fact, Herodotus' earth is only relatively less geometricized than the Ionian one he so criticizes, and contains many fallacies which he inherited from the same school. His earth is cut latitudinally by two parallel rivers, both having their sources somewhere in the unknown far west and both inclining at their eastern end towards each other: the Ister (Danube) in Europe and the Nile in Libya and Egypt (II 32–3; IV 47–9). His Egypt lies almost exactly opposite the imaginary line Cilicia–Sinope–delta of the Ister (II 34,1–2)—an amazing statement, generated by an entirely distorted view of the longitude of the Euxine and of the course of the Ister.[73] His Scythia is square in shape, two of its sides reaching down to the sea and extending inland to the same distance that it stretches along the coast, 'being thus equal every way' (IV 101,1–3).[74] Herodotus' a priori assumption that if there are men beyond the north wind ('Hyperboreans') there must also be men beyond the south wind ('Hypernotians') comes immediately before his already mentioned sarcastic comment on the Ionian geometricization of the earth (IV 36,1–2). His water-springs dot the western Libyan desert at precise intervals of a ten-days' journey (IV 181,2); and finally, the earth has a centre, Greece of course, which enjoys the best temperate climate, and a periphery, namely the extreme regions of the earth, blessed by nature with the most excellent resources, like tin, amber, and gold, with strange trees and fabulous animals and human beings (III 106,1; 116,3).[75] In short, symmetry, geometry, and parallelism are the main fallacies vitiating Herodotus' view of the world, as they distort the Ionian one. His 'empiricist' explorations emerge therefore seriously impaired by his a priori cultural preconditions. His fondness for long distances does not match his accuracy (with few exceptions). He did not

---

[72] See *DPh* and *DH* Kent.

[73] Surprisingly enough, Herodotus measurements of the Euxine (IV 85,2) are grossly miscalculated, while those of the Caspian seem reasonably precise (I 203,1 and note).

[74] See map in Hartog, p. 351 = ET map no. 2, p. 347.

[75] The two doves and the foundation of the two oracles at Dodona and Sîwa (II 54–7) is another example of geographic parallelism. But the connection between the Scythian and Libyan *logoi* is due to the synchronism of Darius' campaigns in both continents (IV 145).

possess, of course, any adequate instruments to calculate distances: most of them are in fact just guesses, sometimes gross mistakes and at their best quite approximate estimates. Besides, in many cases his distances are almost impossible to evaluate with any degree of precision, owing to our uncertainties as to his units of measure and to his meaning of a 'travel-day' of a light-travelling man, or of a ship as a measure of length.[76] Such inaccuracies continued to be typical of most ancient geographers in the following centuries, even of the great Ptolemy, most of them criticizing inaccuracies of their predecessors. In spite of all this, there are here and there in Herodotus some sound conclusions, with which he can be credited even though they were reached by others before him: his assertion that Africa is washed by the sea on all its sides except the part that borders on Asia (IV 42), his polemical declaration that the Caspian is not a gulf in the north-eastern Ocean but an inland lake (I 203,1 and note), and his observations on the stilling action of rivers (II 10–12), are permanent acquisitions of ancient geography.

Also in his explorations of past times, Herodotus' starting point was the epic tradition and Ionian rationalistic reconstructions of mythical chronology. Herodotus was acquainted with the myths concerning the origins of the conflict between Asia and Europe. At the beginning of the first book he relates several stories about mutual abductions of women leading to the Trojan war (I 1–5); but he clarifies immediately that he does not pass judgement on the truth of such stories, and wants to start his narrative with the historical person he 'knows' to have been the first barbarian king to attack the Greeks: Croesus. He 'knows' that, 'leaving aside Minos of Cnossos and whoever else may have dominated the sea before him', the first Greek to aspire to thalassocracy was Polycrates of Samos: he is the first thalassocrat in the so-called 'human generation' (III 122,2); he also 'knows' that Xerxes' expedition was greater than those of his predecessors, including the expedition which 'they say' the Atreidai led against Troy (VII 20,2). Herodotus is not interested in the generations of gods and demigods, but in the 'human generation', a term which corresponds to Varro's *tertium tempus … quod dicitur* ἱστορικόν, *quia res in eo gestae veris historiis continentur*.[77] Mythical times must be left out because they cannot be verified by methods available to the enquiry. In this respect, Herodotus sets himself apart from both mythographers and genealogists of the old school and from contemporary local historians, who begin their works with the legends of the foundation or origin of a city or a people, telling the story from ancient up to very recent times without making any break or distinction between myth and 'true' history. Hellanicus in his *Atthis*, for example, presented a continuous history of Athens from Cecrops and the Flood up to the last years of the Peloponnesian war. Herodotus explicitly refuses to place on the same level of historicity the stories of Io and Croesus, Minos and Polycrates, Agamemnon and Xerxes. The need to know the recent past, that immediately precedes the present and explains its origins, is a requirement of

---

[76] See I 72; 105.

[77] Cf. Censorinus *De Die Natali* 21,1–2. For myth and history in Greek historiography see M. I. Finley, *The Use and Abuse of History*, London 1975, ch. 1; Marincola, pp. 117–27.

the typical methodological approach present for the first time in Herodotus; it gave a new direction to Greek historiography from Thucydides onwards: the study of contemporary history. Indifference towards myth should not be taken as equivalent to a firm denial of the historicity of the main characters and events of traditional epic poetry. For Herodotus the Trojan war, Priam and Helen, are historical persons and events with their own chronology. However, he thinks that the poets, guided by artistic requirements rather than truth, freely and consciously distorted the facts. He is sure that Homer was familiar with the 'true' story of Helen, but preferred to tell a false one because the true account was 'not suitable ($\epsilon \dot{v} \pi \rho \epsilon \pi \dot{\eta} s$) for epic poetry' (II 116,1). In this masterly example of Homeric higher criticism, Herodotus contrasts the poets, and his own predecessors who used them as a historical source, with written documents and the reliable memory of the Egyptians.

Yet Herodotus felt the need of placing his eighty years of recent, and verifiable, history within a chronological framework of universal history. Such a framework already existed: it had been drawn up by mythographers and genealogists following the lead of Hesiod, who thus contributed their share to the historicization of myth, which by now already formed a part of traditional Greek culture. Herodotus accepts it, adapts its reckoning to his own time, takes it to be a piece of public knowledge, and makes use of it for his own polemical purposes.[78] The result is a universal synchronous system based on genealogical calculations, and therefore approximate by definition; any attempt to translate it into absolute dates becomes even more approximate, since it depends on the different units of time (33, 40, etc.) used for a 'generation'. Leaving aside the myths of Decaulion, Io, Cecrops, and Erechtheus, with which Herodotus was familiar, but where we are unable to guess the chronological order into which he put them, his earliest character of *Sagenchronologie* is Cadmus, the mythical king of Tyre and the founder of the royal dynasty at Thebes. Herodotus imagined that he lived around 1500 BC, since his grandchild Dionysus lived about '1000 years before me' (II 145,4),[79] that is, around 1450–40 BC. A century after Dionysus, there flourished Heracles, 'about 900 years before me'; a couple of generations later the Trojan war was fought: it should then be dated to around 1280–70 BC. Heracles heads the chronological axis adopted by Herodotus. Related to him as founder are seven dynasties of 'Heraclids': in Greece, the two ruling families at Sparta (Agiads: VII 204; Eurypontids: VIII 131),

---

[78] For Herodotus' chronology, H. Strasburger, *Historia*, V (1956), pp. 129–61 is fundamental. See also Lloyd, *Introduction*, pp. 171–94; W. Den Boer, *Mnemosyne*, XX (1976), 30–60; v. Fritz, pp. 364 ff. and D. Fehling, *Die Sieben Weisen und die frühgriechische Chronologie*, Bern 1985, pp. 79–97. Ed. Meyer's thesis that the chronology found in Herodotus is Hecataeus' work remains unproven. Cf. P. Vannicelli, *Erodoto e la storia dell' alto e medio arcaismo*, Rome 1993, pp. 9–18; W. Burkert, in J. B. Carter and S. P. Morris (eds.), *The Ages of Homer: A Tribute to E. T. Vermeule*, Austin, Tex. 1995, pp. 139–48. For an amusing examination of Herodotus' and archaic chronology in general see S. K. Heidrich, *Olympia's Uhren gingen falsch. Die revidierte Geschichte der griechisch-archaischen Zeit*, Berlin 1987.

[79] $\kappa a \tau \grave{a} \chi i \lambda \iota a$ [$\dot{\epsilon} \xi a \kappa \acute{o} \sigma \iota a$], according to the emendation of Wilamowitz, Hude, and others. The conjecture is based on the generally accepted genealogy of Cadmus (V 59–61): Dionysus is a contemporary of Labdacus, grandfather of Oedipus.

Fig. 1. Chronological Table

Date	EGYPT	ASSYRIA/BABYLON	LYDIA	PERSIA	MEDIA	ARGOS/MACEDONIA	SPARTA	THEBES	CRETE/THERA/CYRENE	ATHENS
	Min									
	330 kings =11340 years							Agenor		
	Nitocris							CADMUS — Polydorus	EUROPA — Sarpedon / Minos	
1500								Labdacus		CECROPS — Aglaurus
	MOERIS			Amphitryon = Alcmene				Laius		
1350	Sesostris			HERACLES				OEDIPUS		Erechtheus
	Pheros			CEPHEUS				POLYNICES / ETEOCLES		Pandion
	PROTEUS	NINUS		Danae / Andromeda = Perseus			Hyllus	Thersandrus / Laodamas		Orithyia / Lycus
1270	Rhampsinitus	Sardanapallus	AGRON	Perses			Cleodaeus	Tisamenus		Aegeus / THESEUS (Menestheus) Melanthus
	Cheops	Assyrian kings for 520 years	22 Lydian kings for 505 years				Aristomachus	Autesion		
	Chephren						ARISTODEMUS = Argeia	Theras	(Thera)	CODRUS
	Mycerinus		Myrsus			Temenus	Eurysthenes / Procles	Oeolycus		Neleus (Miletus)
	Asychis		Candaules	ACHAEMENES			Agis / Eurypon			
	Anysis			Teispes			Echestratus / Prytanis			
	Sabacus						Leobotes / Polydectes			
700	Amysis	Sanacheribus	GYGES	Ariaramnes / Arsames	DEIOCES	PERDICCAS	Doryssus / Eunomus		Aesanias	
	Sethus		Ardys		Phraortes	Argaeus	Agesilaus / Charilaus			
650	Dodecarchia	Semiramis	Sadyattes		Cyaxares	Philippus	Archelaus / Nicandrus		Grinnus / Polymnestus	
600	Psammetichus		Alyattes	Hystaspes	ASTYAGES = Mandane	Aeropus	Teleclus / Theopompus		BATTUS I	
	Necus					Alcetas	Alcamenes / Anaxandrides	Hegesicles (Agis)	Arcesilaus I	
550	Psammis	Nitocris	CROESUS	Cyrus I / Cambyses I = Mandane		Amyntas	Polydorus / Archidamus	Menares	Battus II	
	Apries			CYRUS II			Eurycrates / Anaxilaus		Arcesilaus II	
525	AMASIS	LABYNETUS		CAMBYSES II / Smerdis			Anaxandrus / Leotychides		Battus III	
	Psammenitus						Eurycratides / Hippocratides		Arcesilaus III	
500				DARIUS			Leon / Agasicles		(Battus IV)	
480				XERXES		ALEXANDER	Anaxandrides / Ariston			
							CLEOMENES / LEONIDAS — DEMARATUS / LEOTYCHIDES			
Main Passages	II 99–182; III 10	174,77,95, 184–8; II 140,150	17,14, 15,25, 86	II 144; III 66; V 99; VI 53; VII 4,11,20, 61,150; VIII 51	196–106, 130	VIII 137–9	IV 147; V 41; VI 52; VII 204; VIII 131	V 60–1; IV 147, 149	IV 145–67; VII 171	I 147, 173; V 65, 82; VII 92, 161, 189; VIII 44, 53; IX 73, 97

and the Temenids of Argos and Macedon (VI 52,1; VIII 137–9); in the Pontic region, the Scythian kings (according to a local Greek tradition which did not convince Herodotus: IV 8–10);[80] in Asia Minor, the Lydian kings from Agron to Candaules (I 7 and note on I 7,1); in Mesopotamia, the Assyrian kings, beginning with Ninus, the eponym of Niniveh and a great grandson of Heracles (I 7,2); in Iran, the Persian kings, who descend from the eponymous Perses, son of Perseus and of Andromeda, who was an offspring of Heracles (VII 61). Three more dynasties are synchronically adjusted to the axis of Heracles: in Greece, Cadmus' Theban dynasty (Oedipus is a contemporary of Heracles) with its branch in Cyrene (IV 147,1–2; 159–63); in the East, the Median kings, called after the eponymous Medea (VII 62,1), who is a contemporary of the Argonauts and Heracles, and the Egyptian kings beginning with Moeris, who lived in Egypt 900 years before Herodotus' visit (II 13,1), that is, in Heracles' time (Moeris' third successor, Proteus, was a contemporary of the Trojan war; II 112 ff.). This systematic 'Heraclization' of Greek and barbarian dynasties conforms to the epic tradition that tended to consider all civilized people as descendants of gods and demigods.

Heracles' dates (fl. 1350–40 BC) were obtained by someone who reckoned that twenty-one generations of forty years each separated him from the Spartan kings Leonidas and Leotychidas, who died in 480 and 469 BC respectively.[81] The chronology of the Lydian Heraclid kings (cf. note on I 7,1) and the Assyrian kings (cf. note on I 95,6) leads to the same date, whereas the chronology of the Egyptian kings does not fit this scheme (the eleven kings from Moeris to Sethos would have to occupy an impossibly long span of time—650 years). Herodotus is thus consciously in favour of dating the beginning of universal history, or the origins of the states and empires of his time, to the middle of the fourteenth century BC, only 900 years before his time. However, the greater part of this history belongs to an inscrutable and unverifiable mythical era. Events become clearer at the time of Gyges, the first Mermnad king of Lydia, Deïoces, the founder of the kingdom of the Medes, Perdiccas, the first Macedonian king, Achaemenes, founder of the Persian dynasty, and Psammetichus, that is, between the late eighth and the early seventh centuries. Herodotus points out that from Psammetichus onwards 'we know with certainty (ἀτρεκέως) all that happened in Egypt, thanks to the Greek settlements' (II 154,4). However, Herodotus does not begin his main narrative from 700, but from 560 BC. Thus we have a tripartite division of time, according to the degree of verifiability: modern and contemporary history (from 560 onwards); a middle period of a century-and-a-half (710/700–560 BC); and a μακρὸς χρόνος when anything could have happened, but nothing can be said about it with certainty (V 9,3). Egypt perhaps escapes this tripartite division, although it has an acceptable chronological structure based on

[80] For the 'millennium' in Scythian tradition see IV 7,1.
[81] On Heracles in Herodotus see Mora, pp. 208–12. The 40-year unit known from the Old Testament must have been introduced into Greek historiography by genealogists before Herodotus: Herodotus reckoned three generations per century (II 142,2). See also note on 7,1.

dynastic succession, and an ancient age of about six to eight centuries (from 1500–1350 to 700 BC) of totally unverifiable mythical history or proto-history.[82] The limits of Herodotus' perception of time being what they are, it is as if history began for us in the eighteenth century, and we only had documentary evidence about it from 1870 onwards.

Herodotus' recent chronology also lacks a firm basis. Not even sixth-century events are placed in a clear and fixed chronological order, perhaps because Olympic or eponymic lists were as yet unavailable. As a result, his dates are quite vague ('not much later', and similar expressions), or rounded off (see note on I 30,1); his synchronisms are imprecise ('when Cambyses was fighting against Egypt, the Spartans launched a campaign against Samos', III 39,1), when not simply invented for literary or didactic purposes, as, for example, the meeting of Solon and Croesus (see notes on I 27,2 and 29–33). Usually Herodotus' dates are relative. For example, the chronology of the Persian kings (as that of other dynasties) is composed of the lengths of their reigns; in this case, however, it is possible to translate them into precise dates, starting from the sixth year of Xerxes' reign (VII 20), the year of the Persian invasion of Attica, which Herodotus quite exceptionally marks with the name of the Athenian archon Calliades (VIII 51,1), who is known from late sources to have held office in 480/79 BC. Finally, dates of fundamental historical events are missing in Herodotus, such as the Persian conquests of Babylon and Egypt, Darius' Scythian campaign, the battle of Marathon—a sign that, although he felt the need for some chronological points of reference, Herodotus valued chronology less than other aspects of the events he was discussing.

In Egypt the conception of time is completely different, and of immense dimensions compared to that of the Greeks: according to the Egyptians, Dionysus was born over 15,000 years before Amasis' reign and Heracles over 17,000 (II 145,2; 43,4). The Egyptians think of time in terms of *temps des dieux*, to use an apt expression coined by Vidal-Naquet:[83] in comparison, Greek history is very recent indeed (II 53,1). The 'human generation' exemplified by Hecataeus' family tree that began only 600 years before him (II 143,1) lasted in Egypt more than 11,000 years (II 142,3). Egyptian and Greek gods thus belong to completely different eras; so it follows that either they are not the same, though they are called by the same names, or they are the same, but they arrived in Greece thousands of years after their Egyptian period. Herodotus realized at once that this discrepancy posed a serious problem: there was a danger that, alongside the traditional

[82] Shimron's tripartite division (*Eranos*, LXXI (1973), 45–51) is preferable to V. Hunter's bipartite one (Hunter, pp. 87 f. and n. 52). It should be noted that Varro's tripartite division (quoted above p. 30) is very different from Herodotus' three eras in its absolute length (the mythical period lasts 1,600 years, whereas the historical period begins with the first Olympiad = 776 BC). The two more recent Herodotean periods (c. 700–480 BC) together fill the span of historical times normal in all oral traditions (see bibliography at p. 16, n. 43), cf. the 220 years that Dionysius of Halicarnassus calculates for Herodotus' history, in *De Thucydide* 5 and in *ad Pompeium* 3. For the conception of the historical past in Hecataeus, Herodotus, and Thucydides, see Hunter, and W. von Leyden, *Durham Univ. J.*, XLII (1949–50), 89–104.

[83] P. Vidal-Naquet, *Le Chasseur noir*, Paris 1981, pp. 69–94 = *The Black Hunter* (trans. A. Szegedy-Maszak), Baltimore 1986, pp. 36–60.

chronology based on Heracles, the whole Greek conception of the past would collapse, as well as the entire Greek mythological system with its gods and heroes. He was startled by the Egyptian dates, but his reaction was typical: he made enquiries and settled for a number of compromises; the Egyptian Heracles, a very ancient god, is different from the mortal Greek hero of the same name (II 43–4); Pan and Dionysus, very ancient Egyptian gods as well, became known to the Greeks in a much later period (II 146,2).[84] In this way, he saved the authority of the Egyptian dynastic lists (II 145,3), without shaking the foundations of Greek tradition. How much the 'Egyptian time' was irrelevant for Herodotus' practical purposes can be gathered from the absence of its impact outside the Egyptian book: it is limited to the Egyptian experience, and is meaningful only in relation to the controversy about the priority of Egyptian culture over the Greek.[85]

Post hoc ergo propter hoc: Egypt's chronological priority became for Herodotus also a priority in the evolutionary process. Herodotus is a great admirer of human inventions. His idealized Egyptians, who are as old as the beginning of humanity, are the 'first inventors' of the twelve gods, with their cults, altars, statues, temples, oracles, divination, and processions, together with the doctrine of metempsychosis, the lunisolar calendar, and land surveying. As chronology clearly shows, these inventions were exported from Egypt to Greece and not the other way round:

Whence the gods severally sprang, whether or not they had all existed from eternity, and what forms they bore—these are questions of which (the Greeks) knew nothing until the other day, so to speak. For I think that Hesiod and Homer are about 400 years older than me, not more, and they created the theogony for the Greeks and gave epithets to the gods, ascribed to them honours and abilities, and described their form. (II 53,1–2)[86]

What Herodotus says is that the Egyptians were the 'first inventors' of the universal polytheistic system, which was then adopted by other peoples, with appropriate epithets and forms. In Greece the 'first inventors' of these national variations were Homer and Hesiod.[87] Thus, creativity and diffusion are not mutually exclusive; there is space for creativity also in the process of diffusion.[88] However, fundamental to the Herodotean theory of the cultural priority of the

[84] The compromise of the two Heracles is based on an interpretation of the Greek double cult of Heracles, Olympic and heroic: II 44,5; cf. Paus. V 25,12. Herodotus did not split Perseus (II 91,2–6; VI 53,1–2; VII 61,3), perhaps because he lacked a comparable double cult: cf. Mazzarino, *Il pensiero*, pp. 156 ff., 566 ff. and n. 148.

[85] Book II is a digression, completely isolated from the rest of Herodotus' work. Cf. Polybius' Book VI, whose cyclic theory of constitutions has no bearing on the linear conception found in the rest of the work; see A. Momigliano, *Essays in Ancient and Modern Historiography*, Oxford 1977, pp. 179–204.

[86] Rawlinson's translation.

[87] On the concept of the 'first inventor' see A. Kleingünther; K. Thraede, *RhM* CV (1962), 158–86. In Herodotus, persons rather than mythical characters are 'first inventors'. On the invention of gods and names see W. Burkert *MH* XLII (1985), 121–32; on the invention of coinage see note on I. 94,1. On diffusionism and cultural receptivity as interpretive categories in Herodotus see Mora, pp. 225 ff.; for the so-called 'ancient model' of diffusionism see Bernal (on Herodotus: pp. 98–101).

[88] See e.g. V 58,1: the invention and the adoption of the alphabet in Greece.

Egyptians over the Greeks are his polemics against the prejudices of the Greeks,
his predecessors, and in particular the Ionians, who believe on the one hand the
inventions of the poets, and on the other say stupid things about Egypt. In
the field of ideas, one result of this polemical attitude was the discovery or the
invention of universal historical space and a first attempt at reappraising the role
of Hellenic culture within the larger outline of human history. At a personal level,
it resulted in Herodotus being accused of 'philo-barbarism'.

Universal history in Herodotus is linear: it is represented graphically by parallel
genealogical lists connecting the mythical era with the historical present. But at
the level of local or biographical history of a city, a people, or rulers, history seems
to be cyclical or semi-cyclical ('pedimental', to use a term introduced by Myres,
shaped like an arc with two end-points). The tripartite notion of rise, acme, and
decadence of a city or an empire is well known to Herodotus: he is aware that
some great cities of the past have become small (I 5,4), that those who were brave
in ancient times may have grown cowardly since, and those who were cowardly
then may now be braver (IX 27,4). A similar notion shapes the narrative structure
of the history of kingdoms and rulers: the Lydian kingdom from Gyges to Croesus
to the fall of Sardis; the kingdom of the Medes, from Deïoces to Cyaxares to
Cyrus' insurrection; the Persian empire, from Cyrus to Darius to Xerxes' defeat;
the biographical and historical careers of Apries, Polycrates, Croesus, and the
Persian kings follow a similar course. In these *logoi*, the narrative does not follow
the straight and uniform line of a chronicle, but rather rises to a climax, and then
descends. It is a narrative that wants to make sense of historical events or reveal
their direction. On the banks of the Araxes, Croesus tells Cyrus: 'In the first place
learn this: there is a cycle (κύκλος) of human affairs, and by its revolving, it
prevents the same people from being always fortunate' (I 207,2). In Herodotus,
the great tragic figures of kings and tyrants stand out against the background
of a cyclic vision of human life. This conception, however, does not become
a universal philosophical or historical doctrine: the theory of the 'Four Monarchies' had not yet been invented. In Herodotus, history repeats itself in the
sense that, behind variable and changeable single events that never repeat themselves, there are exemplary patterns which persistently keep recurring, and that
can be detected if one is perceptive to analogy: 'I know how terrible an evil
excessive craving is, since I remember how Cyrus' expedition against the Massagetae ended, or Cambyses' campaign against the Ethiopians; and I myself took
part in Darius' campaign against the Scythians. Knowing all this, I have reached
the conclusion that you (Xerxes) would be the happiest of men, if you remained
here in peace' (VII 18,2–3). Artabanus, or rather Herodotus, wants to say that
behind the single Persian expeditions, though individual in detail, in that they
are led by different kings against different nations, there looms a recurrent
'model' of failed expansionism. If the individual detail has a curiosity interest,
it is the symptomatic and paradigmatic phenomenon that acquires historical
significance. That does not mean that Herodotus falsifies details in order to make
them conform to a model, but paradigmatic history necessarily implies a selection of human actions. In a sense, Herodotus is more of a philosopher than a

historian, if 'philosophy', in the Ionian sense of the word, is primarily the search for Being in Becoming. Moreover, he is more of a poet than a historian, even though he wrote prose, because he is interested more in what can happen than in what really happened, less in 'what Alcibiades did and suffered' than in the paradigmatic example.[89]

Like Attic tragedy, the cycle of events in Herodotus is generated by the unconscious cooperation of gods and men. Herodotus is convinced that in the end all that takes place happens according to the plan of divine providence (τοῦ θείου ἡ προνοίη, III 108,2), personified ever since Homer in the figures of the three Moirai, whose decisions even a god cannot escape (I 91,1). Candaules, Apries, Scyles, Miltiades, Artaÿnte 'must' (χρῆν, ἔδεε) have met a bad end,[90] as Demaratus 'had' to lose his throne (VI 64); Egypt 'must' have suffered for 150 years (II 133,3); Darius' conquest of Babylon was 'fated' (μόρσιμον εἶναι, III 154,1); Attica 'had' to fall into Persian hands (VIII 53,1); whereas the Naxians 'were not to' be destroyed by Aristagoras (V 33,2). Before the battle of Plataea, a Persian noble tells the Boeotian Thersander: 'A man cannot avert what must happen according to the will of the gods. No one wants to listen, not even to someone who says sound things. Although we Persians are many who know this, we follow him, prisoners of necessity. And this is the greatest pain for human beings: to have much knowledge and no power' (IX 16,4–6). Yet, Herodotus' fatalism is not a dogmatic principle but an attitude which comes and goes. People usually act in the belief that they are free to do what is most convenient for them. Herodotus grants human beings a certain degree of free will, which, though unable to influence the predestined course of history, may influence its time and manner. Artabanus will be punished because he unsuccessfully attempted to 'avert what had to happen' (VII 17,2), but Croesus' gifts to Delphi were worth three more years of rule to the Lydian king (I 91,2–3). Free will, in sum, does exist; but since fate must be accomplished, men are driven by the gods to choose the course of action most conducive to the realization of that fate. For three days and two nights Xerxes is torn between his personal desire to fight the Greeks and the wise advice of his counsellor Artabanus. In the end, with the aid of dreams, divine will prevails and drives the king to his final decision (VII 8–19).

The end of Croesus' kingdom was predicted more than 150 years before the last king of Lydia sat on his throne. Regardless of his political and ethical choices, Croesus paid the penalty (τίσις) for the sin committed by his forefather Gyges (I 13,2; 91,1). Croesus also was a sinner, but he was not punished for his own transgressions. Herodotus' gods sometimes need an 'excuse' (πρόφασις, see II

---

[89] Herodotus and Thucydides are not good examples for the theory that history is 'less philosophical' than poetry (Aristotle, *Poet.* 1451b1). Cf. H. Schwabl, *Gymnasium*, LXXVI (1969), pp. 253–72; Arieti (1995), pp. 2–3 and CMJ. Sicking, *Distant Companions. Selected Papers*, Leiden 1998, pp. 147–157. Waters, *Herodotos on Tyrants and Despots*, minimizes the paradigmatic impact of Herodotus' work and denies its tragic temper.

[90] I 8,2; II 161,3; IV 79,1; VI 135,3; IX 109,2. The verb μέλλω, usually used to denote free human 'intention' or 'purpose', implies in some cases the opposite notion of 'necessity': see e.g. in Book I, 45,2; 108,2; 175; 210,1.

161,3) to justify their actions; and human beings provide them in abundance. The most common pretext is the notorious *hybris*, the typical reaction of man at the peak of his power.[91] The prototypes are Croesus, guilty of believing that he was the happiest human being in the world (I 34,1); Apries, convinced that no god would end his reign (II 169,2); the tyrant Polycrates, guilty of excessive prosperity (III 40–3); Xerxes, who truly personifies *hybris*, and becomes in Herodotus the prototype of the arrogant king who competes with the gods. Xerxes wishes Persia to have no other boundary but Zeus' ether, and 'the sun not to see another land bordering on ours', and both guilty and innocent to be subjected to Persian rule (VII 8γ,1–3). He violates nature by linking Asia to Europe with a bridge, whipping the rebellious sea, and digging a canal through Mount Athos (VII 22–4; 33–6).[92] Perhaps Herodotus found an earlier version of the events of 480/79 already interpreted in terms of *hybris*, possibly echoing the moral message that in 472 BC Aeschylus had communicated to the Athenians in the *Persae*.[93] Herodotus' last three books are dominated by the tragic figure of Xerxes. *Hybris* is evil not so much in that it inspires hatred in other human beings, but in that it provokes the 'jealousy of the gods' (φθόνος θεῶν).[94] The gods are by nature 'jealous and troublesome' (I 32,1), they cannot bear exceedingly successful human beings, their self-confidence, boundless power, arrogance and, worst of all, their inborn tendency to transgress the limits imposed on them by nature or law. Transgression of natural boundaries, as bridging a strait or crossing a river with an army for aggressive purposes, is a symptom of *hybris*, punished sooner or later by the gods.[95] Themistocles comments maliciously that it was the gods and the heroes who defeated Xerxes: 'they did not want a single man to rule over Asia and Europe' (VIII 109,3). The Persian retreat to Asia assumes, therefore, theological dimensions. Artabanus warns:

Look at how the god strikes down the most imposing animals and cannot stand their vanity, whereas he is not at all irritated by the small ones. Mark how the highest buildings and trees are struck down by his lightning. God delights in humiliating everything that looks proud. A big army can be defeated by a small one, if the jealous god throws against it panic or lightning to inflict on it a humiliating defeat. He cannot stand the presence of other arrogant beings. (VII 10ε)

[91] For a comprehensive discussion of *hybris* see N. R. E. Fisher, *Hybris: A Study in the Values of Honour and Shame in Ancient Greece*, Warminster 1992 (on Herodotus: ch. 9, pp. 343–85).

[92] Cf. Masaracchia, pp. 47 ff.

[93] See, J. Jouanna, *Ktema*, VI (1981), pp. 3–15.

[94] See P. Walcot, *Envy and the Greeks: A Study of Human Behaviour*, Warminster 1978, chs. 3–4. On Herodotus' views on reciprocity see D. Braund, in C. Gill *et al.* (eds.), *Reciprocity in Ancient Greece*, Oxford 1998, pp. 159–80.

[95] See Lateiner, ch. 6 (pp. 126–44); Payen, pp. 133–62. For this motif in the histories of Alexander and the Alexander romance see Chr. Jacob, *QS* XXXIV (1991), 5–40; J. L. Desnier, *De Cyrus le Grand à Julien l'Apostat 'Le passage du fleuve' Essai sur la legitimité du souverain*, Paris 1995; F. de Polignac, in *I Greci* II 3 1998, pp. 282 ff.

Polycrates' excessive prosperity worries his ally Amasis, who thinks that 'the divinity is jealous' and that those who have most success meet a bad end (III 40,2–3). The gods, then, are not driven by moral principles: quite the contrary, they are driven by envy, self-esteem, and self-love, and the desire to avenge and persecute. They are the enemies of humankind: human beings should beware them, placate them, but they cannot love them. Divine jealousy may seem like a reaction to human *hybris*, but that *hybris* is sometimes provoked by the divinity itself in accordance with the famous maxim *quos deus vult perdere dementat prius*. The catastrophes which befall Croesus, Cambyses, and Xerxes are interpreted in this tragic way. Herodotus' extremely negative conception of the gods' behaviour is not a new invention: its roots can be found in the pessimism of archaic Greek thought. In expressing the fear that a superior person may rise too high, the theory of *hybris* seems to be in tune with the egalitarian world of the archaic hoplite *polis*, on guard at all times against the danger of tyranny. But this is a *forma mentis* rather than a dogma or a theological doctrine. Herodotus leaves room for hope as well as for free will. His anthropomorphic gods or his collective, abstract 'god' do not mingle with human beings on earth, as in Homeric epic, but interfere in human affairs from afar in order to punish, save, and influence the course of history. God destroyed in a storm a certain number of Persian ships so that the two fleets might become equal (VIII 13); it was the gods who saved Delphi from the Persian attack (VIII 36–9); the Potidaeans rightly believe that it was Poseidon who destroyed Artabanus' troops to punish sacrilegious acts (VIII 129,2); it was Demeter who prevented the Persians from entering her sanctuary at Plataea because they had burned her temple at Eleusis (IX 65,2). In such cases it seems that Herodotus' pessimism is balanced by the belief that nemesis (I 34,1) sometimes also fulfils the function of retributive justice and therefore also of a power that safeguards cosmic balance and order. Just like human kings, the gods too behave sometimes as arbitrary tyrants, sometimes as wise and just rulers.

Human reactions to the tragic side of life are different, but also typical. Artabanus is the heroic type, who chooses to struggle and actively to intervene in the preordained course of historical events, convinced that the validity of his choice does not depend upon the whims of fortune (VII 10δ,2). Amasis is fatalistic: he capitulates and abandons his ally, since 'it would be impossible for a human being' to save a man from his fate (III 43). Mycerinus is the pious man who has been disappointed, and turns into an epicure who devotes the last years of his life to revelry, and to the demonstration of the deceptiveness of oracles (II 133,1–5). Adrastus is the victim of fate: he succumbs to despair and commits suicide (I 45). Xerxes is the pragmatic type who tries not to think too much about existential problems (VII 47,1). Finally, Themistocles is the astute statesman who can manipulate the gods towards his own ends, and believes, or declares himself to believe, that they only help those who have reasonable plans (VIII 60γ; 109,3–5). Herodotus was impressed by the variety of human reactions, just as much as by different human customs and beliefs; and he knew how to turn them into exemplary types, skilfully personify them, and suitably place them in his great paradigmatic history.

V

Together with the possibility of choice (παρεόν σφι τούτων τὰ ἕτερα ποιέειν, VII 229,1) comes responsibility: αἰτίη. Herodotus was interested in the problem of who was the 'first responsible', or the culprit, for the conflict between Asia and Europe, just as he was interested in the 'first inventors' of all things. He wants to know for what reason and in what ways one is driven to act, what desires and considerations precede decisions. Usually, Herodotus' αἰτίη is a personal responsibility or guilt of varying degree:[96] an offence, a murder, a cruel act, lack of gratitude; hatred, remembrance of offences inflicted, the desire for retribution or revenge, or for territorial expansion or defence of one's country; the trust in oracles, dreams, or prophecies; the wish to accomplish a great ἔργον worthy of memory or to demonstrate one's superiority over nature; the influence of powerful women or good and bad counsellors; miscalculations and folly. Such types of causation are more evident in oriental kingdoms or the world of Greek tyrannies, where at first sight everything seems to be decided within the palace. That does not mean that Herodotus was not aware of political and social causes which do not depend upon individuals: he knows very well that expansionism is intrinsic to ἀρχή, that is, to power or empire; that less civilized people love liberty more; that tyranny is born from chaos and illegality; that revolts and military support of revolts cause repression and punitive expeditions; he sees a link between population growth and territorial expansion, between poverty and emigration, between colonization and acculturation; he has his own ideas about the influence of climate and customs upon the character of different peoples; on the other hand, he does not deny the influence of unpredictable chance (τύχη). In general, Herodotus is conscious of a relationship between culture and political history; but he is apparently convinced that even impersonal causes, though invisible, need real personalities to embrace them and translate them into action. Personal histories interest him (and his public) much more than abstract analysis of economic and social developments. Consequently, the process of acculturation is personified and dramatized: one only needs to think of the amusing description of the love affairs between the Scythians and the Amazons (IV 111–7)[97] or of Scyles' adventures at Olbia (IV 78–80). Therefore a traditional schema based on aetiology and eponyms prevails over possible im-

---

[96] On causality in Herodotus see H. R. Immerwahr, *TAPhA* LXXXVII (1965), 241–80. For the usages of the term αἰτίη see Bornitz, pp. 139–63; Evans, *Explorer*, pp. 15–23, 29–33; C. Darbo-Peschanski, in *I Greci* II 2 1997, pp. 1063–84 (esp. pp. 1063–5). On πρόφασις see the bibliography at I 29,6. The study by J. de Romilly, *REG* LXXXIV (1971), 314–37 is important. For the causes of wars see A. Momigliano, *Secondo contributo alla storia degli studi classici*, Rome 1960, pp. 13–27; see also J. Cobet, in I. S. Moxon *et al.* (eds.), *Past Perspectives*, Cambridge 1986, pp. 1–18; for irrational and political motives see Huber; J. A. Arieti, in D. V. Stump *et al.* (eds.), *Hamartia: The Concept of Error in the Western Tradition: Essays in Honor of J. M. Crossett*, New York–Toronto 1983, pp. 1–25.

[97] See T. Cole, *Democritus and the Sources of Greek Anthropology*, American Philological Assoc. Monograph, XXV, Western Reserve Univ. 1967, pp. 143 ff.

personal interpretations.[98] For the same reason, a great political and social development, such as the evolution of tyranny in Athens, or the events leading to the Ionian revolt, is reduced to a series of anecdotes and gossip. Herodotus' history often tends to become 'biographical' around the main characters—he does not feel the need to create a precise aetiological terminology of the Hippocratic or Thucydidean type.

His aetiology consists then, in the first place, in the analysis of the thought which precedes action:[99] consultation of oracles and seers, political speeches, counsels, debates. The materials recorded in these decision-making sessions are of course not derived from written or oral sources: they are mainly Herodotus' own literary reconstructions, serving purely didactic functions. The aetiological chapters devoted to the 'causes' of Xerxes' great expedition against Greece include a number of different motivations: the desire for revenge, the Persian ideology of expansionism, the influence of Mardonius and Artabanus, considerations of the wealth of Europe, Persian claims upon the Peloponnese, the incitement of Greek political exiles, the crucial importance of the gods' will revealed in dreams (VII 5–18).[100] No one published the minutes of Xerxes' council: Herodotus skilfully created it in order to express his own views about the motives of the Great King and his most famous ministers.

'It so happens that there is a warning (προσημαίνειν) every time a great catastrophe is about to bring down a city or a people' (VI 27,1). In Herodotus' aetiology, signs of warning occupy a privileged space: oracles, dreams, portents, prophecies. These 'great signs' (σημήια μεγάλα) with which the divinity warns men (cf. VI 98,1) are of course literary means which the author uses to prepare the reader for an impending catastrophe and its moral. Herodotus' book contains a vast collection of oracles, mainly Delphic ones.[101] Whether they are authentic or not, the texts were not composed by Herodotus: he read, selected, and inserted them at the appropriate place in his work. Usually, oracles have a precise function in Herodotus' narrative: they are used to explain and justify the origins of certain actions or historical, political, and military events, and in cultic or expiatory procedures. The choice of texts, which are quoted verbatim, seems to be determined by literary or intellectual considerations. The proverbial ambiguity and the enigmatic nature of the most famous oracular responses are perfect vehicles for arousing the reader's curiosity. Herodotus does not expect us to trust oracles blindly: he himself stresses their differences. 'I cannot talk against

---

[98] See e.g. the eponyms Lycus (I 173,3) and Dorus (I 56,3); impersonal aetiologies about the origins of the Ionians (I 7–8) and the Scythians (IV 11).

[99] Cf. Montgomery; Huber; Hohti. For the organization of biographical material see H. Homeyer, *Philologus*, CVI (1962), 75–85, and A. Momigliano, *The Development of Greek Biography*, Cambridge, Mass. 1971, ch. 2. On individuals in Herodotus see Waters, *Herodotus the Historian*, pp. 136–51; Evans, *Explorer*, pp. 41–88.

[100] See F. Solmsen, *Two Crucial Decisions in Herodotus*, Amsterdam–London 1974, pp. 7 ff.

[101] See Panitz; Crahay; Kirchberg; Defradas; Fontenrose; D. Asheri, *CISA* XIX (1993), 63–76; cf. Ph.-E. Legrand, in *Mélanges offerts à A.-M. Desrousseaux*, Paris 1937, pp. 275–84. For Herodotus' oracular terminology see L. Bernabò, *Boll. dell'Ist. di Filologia greca*, IV, Padua 1977–8, pp. 157–74.

oracles and say that they are not true, nor do I want to try to discredit those which speak clearly (ἐναργέως λέγοντας)', as, for example, Bacis' prophecies; 'I do not dare to speak about the contradictory nature of oracles, nor do I consent to anyone else doing so' (VIII 77,1–2). But it is also risky to trust all oracles indiscriminately: some are false or deceptive (see note on I 66,3), others uttered by a corrupted Pythia;[102] still others are pure and simple pro-Persian defeatist propaganda, and it is to the credit of the Athenians that they ignored them (VII 139,6) or gave them an interpretation favourable to Greek resistance (as in the case of the famous oracle of the 'wooden wall', VII 141–3). Herodotus loves to relate, with a grain of humour and frivolity, stories of oracles, in which the ambiguity of the response, the cunning of the enquirer, and the problems of interpretation inspire not just curiosity and amusement, but also scepticism and irreverence. Among the most famous examples, we may cite the tests of oracles carried out by Croesus (I 48–9), by Mardonius (VIII 133), Aristodicus of Cyme (I 158–9), and Amasis (II 174); Mycerinus' criticism (II 133), and the irreverent request of the Spartan Glaucus (VI 86). In his attitude towards oracles, Herodotus therefore steers a middle course between the extremes current at his time: credulity and scepticism, conventional morality and ironic frivolity, archaic traditionalism and sophistic criticism. Views of Herodotus as a 'most religious man' or as a 'freethinker' are equally wrong.[103]

Dreams and portents serve the same functions and fascinate the historian for similar reasons.[104] Herodotean dreamers are mostly non-Greeks, typically oriental kings, whose dreams usually predict deaths and births, or the fate of dynasties and reigns. Sometimes they contain orders, threats, or symbolic figures. Herodotus is familiar with rationalistic theories of dreams (VII 16 γ,1) and does not condemn them.[105] Portents (τέρατα) are exceptional phenomena, but they need not be supernatural: rain in Egyptian Thebes (III 10,3), winter thunders in Scythia (IV 28,3), summer storms (VII 188–9; VII 12–13), eclipses (cf. note on I 74,7–8), earthquakes (VI 98), various disasters (VI 27), strange diseases (I 167,1–2; 174,4–6), infestations of mice (II 141,5–6), unusual encounters and fights between animals (I 78,1–3; III 76,3). Herodotus does not always believe true and proper supernatural phenomena, such as a mule giving birth (III 153; VII 57,2), a mare giving birth to a hare (VII 57,1), cauldrons boiling without fire (I 59,1), the beard of the priestess at Pedasa (I 175; VIII 104), salt fish jumping in the fire (IX 120). Appearance of a portent before or during a historical event, such

[102] V 63,1; 66,1; VI 123,2.

[103] Cf. the testing of the dream at VII 15–17. Aristodicus and Glaucus invalidate the theory that only barbarian kings test oracles (the main thesis of Klees, *Die Eigenart der griechischen Glaubens an Orakel und Seher*). On Herodotus and the Sophists see A. Dihle, *Gymnasium*, LXIX (1962), 22–32, and *Philologus*, CVI (1962), 207–20; S. Ubsdell I, pp. 339–99.

[104] Cf. the bibliography quoted on I 34,3 and the collections of studies on dreams in ancient societies in *Ktema*, VII (1982) and VIII (1983); A. Missiou, *Ariadne*, VI (1993), 89–107. Significant exceptions are the dreams of the Athenian Hipparchus (V 55–6) and Agariste (VI 131,2).

[105] Cf. H. A. Gärtner, *Ktema*, VIII (1983), 11–18, with bibliography.

as a military march, is usually interpreted by specialists (prophets, seers, the Magi) either as a sign of divine intention or as a forewarning. Sometimes the portent is interpreted as a punishment for a sin which must be expiated according to specific precepts (I 167,1–2; 174,4–5, etc.). Ignoring portents, as for example Xerxes did during the great invasion (VII 57,1), is a symptom of *hybris* and impiety.

The advice of court counsellors is intellectually superior to the interpretation of portents, but serves the same literary and didactic functions. The 'wise counsellor' in the court of an oriental king is a typically Herodotean figure (see note on I 27,2). In the court of Croesus, this role is given to one of the 'Seven Sages' of archaic Greece: Bias or Pittacus, Solon and Thales; at the Achaemenid court, to one of the Median or Persian noblemen, such as Harpagus and Artaÿctes the advisers of Cyrus, Zopyrus, Gobryas, and Megabazus the advisers of Darius, Artabanus and Mardonius the advisers of Xerxes, or sometimes to a foreign wise man, who is occasionally included in the entourage of the Persian king: Croesus, who had ignored the advice of Solon and Sandanis, becomes in captivity the counsellor of Cyrus and then of Cambyses; Coes of Mytilene offers his services to Darius, Demaratus of Sparta and the Carian queen Artemisia offer theirs to Xerxes. These persons are historical, but the historicity of their role at the Persian court remains unproved, and the thoughts they express are those Herodotus puts in their mouths for his own didactic and literary purposes. Apart from Solon's lecture on human happiness for the benefit of Croesus (I 29–32), a programmatic exposition of ethical and religious ideas which pervade the entire work, all the other dialogues and speeches of warning pertain to strategic and military issues, even in such cases as the dialogues of Croesus and Cyrus, or Artabanus and Xerxes, when practical issues give rise to moral considerations. In the most significant dialogues of this kind, the counsellor cautions the king against the risks of a war of expansion that the king is preparing and about which he sought his advice. The war in question is to be waged against savage people, not yet enfeebled by the luxuries of civilization, still accustomed to simple traditions of tribal life, proud and freedom-loving.[106] These wars should be considered unjust, motivated as they are by the sheer desire to conquer, not the need for redress of former injustice (IV 118,4; VII 8 γ,3; 9,2), even if reparation for damages is advanced by an aggressive king as a pretext for war, as, for example, the wars against the Scythians or the Greeks. This is the meaning of Sandanis' advice to Croesus (I 71,2–4 and note on 71,2) concerning the war planned against the Persians, still savage in Cyrus' times (cf. IX 122,2–4) in comparison to the effeminate Lydians; of Croesus' suggested stratagem during the campaign against the Massagetae (I 207,6–7); of Artabanus' warning against the Scythian campaign (IV 83; VII 10a,2), of the advice of Coes (IV 97,2–6) and Gobryas in Scythia (IV

---

[106] On imperialism and expansionism in Herodotus see Evans, *Explorer,* pp. 9–40; on Herodotus and Achaemenid expansionism: H. Verdin, in *Studia P. Naster oblata, II Orientalia antiqua,* Louvain 1982, pp. 327–336. On Herodotus' ideas on 'just' and 'unjust' wars see S. Clavadetscher-Thürlemann, Πόλεμος δίκαιος *und Bellum justum. Versuch einer Ideengeschichte,* Zurich 1985, *passim.*

134,2–3). Rulers of countries attacked express similar views: the queen of the Massagetae, Tomyris (I 206), the king of the Ethiopians (III 21), and the Scythian king Idanthyrsus (IV 127), who fiercely warn the aggressors against violating borders and desiring other people's lands. Resembling such discourses are also the words describing the Spartans which the Greek Demaratus addresses to Xerxes: they are few but free, they obey only one 'despot', the law that forbids them to flee the battlefield (VII 104,4–5). In the case of the Ethiopians, the description of their customs and their mentality is intentionally connected to the main narrative of Cambyses' campaign; in other cases the connection is not as clear.[107] The Greeks are, of course, a case apart, but they share with the barbarians we have mentioned, and with the Persians themselves who rebelled against the Medes and were later attacked by Croesus, an uncompromising love of freedom. The roots of this common cult of freedom, however, are different: uncouth tribal pride on the one hand, civic structure of the *polis* on the other.

Herodotus never divided humanity into born slaves and born master peoples, and he had no Hellenic superiority-complex in respect of the barbarians. He was well aware that every nation believes in its own superiority;[108] but thanks to travel and research he freed himself from prejudices of this kind. He acknowledges the merits of Greek culture: wisdom, moderation, respect for the law, simplicity of customs; but it does not prevent him from admiring the great oriental civilizations and respecting their exotic customs, which he partly approves and partly criticizes. He is fully aware that laws and costumes are diverse and relative, and that each people instinctively prefers its own institutions.[109] The Persians are capable of great deeds and have their moral principles, such as love of truth, justice, generosity (of which even Xerxes is capable: VII 135–6). That in 480–79 BC the Persians were the 'national' enemy of the Greeks, or rather, of those Greeks who had chosen to resist them, does not prevent Herodotus from moral evaluation of their virtues or from calm and objective assessment of their civilization, devoid of 'chauvinistic' passions and of racial hatred. In this respect too, Herodotus shows himself a fine disciple of Homer and Aeschylus. Also in this attitude it is clear how he could easily be branded as *philobarbaros*, as committing an act of political and cultural betrayal. In fact, Herodotus never hides the traditional Greek views prevailing in his times concerning the social, political, and ideological contrast between Greeks and Persians during the period of the great confrontation: on the one hand a poor country, a gallant army consisting of a few brave individuals ruled by strict laws defending their freedom; on the other, a fabulously rich empire, a huge, amorphous mass of soldiers, counted roughly as cattle, and whipped by commanders to force them to fight (VII 60; 101–4). In order to emphasize this contrast, Herodotus fantastically exaggerates the number

---

[107] See Cobet, who tends to generalize. P. Payen, *REG* CVIII (1995), 308–38; id., *Les Îles nomades*. For the idealized presentation of the 'noble savage', which does not always apply to the Ethiopians or to some Scythian techniques, see Hunter, p. 177 and n. 5; on the Scythians see Mazzarino, *Il pensiero*, p. 148; Hartog; E. Lévy, *Ktema*, VI (1981), 57–68, with bibliography.

[108] See e.g. I 60,3 (the Athenians); I 134,2–3 (the Persians); II 121ζ,2 (the Egyptians).

[109] See III 38 and note; cf. Gigante, pp. 109 ff., 114 ff. On the tyranny of the law, cf. VII 102,1 and 104,4.

of Xerxes' soldiers, while he states that he knows the names of all the 300 valiant soldiers who were killed at Thermopylae with Leonidas (VII 224,1).

It has been claimed that in Herodotus' eyes the conflict between Asia and Europe is a conflict between despotism and freedom.[110] This interpretation schematizes the more complex ideas of Herodotus in order to fit them into certain modern ideologies prevalent before and after the Second World War. Herodotus was well aware that despotism was also a Greek phenomenon and that love of freedom could also be found among barbarians. Medes, Persians, Babylonians, Egyptians, Ethiopians, Scythians, Massagetae all fought for freedom (ἐλευθερίη), in the sense of 'independence from foreign rule'. Among the Greeks there were some who preferred the Persian rule to any form of 'freedom', or even to a temporary Spartan leadership.[111] 'Freedom' in the sense of republican regime as opposed to monarchy (βασιληίη) or tyranny (τυραννίς) is a different matter.[112] Herodotus believes that in the Greek cities free regimes are superior to tyrannies: tyranny binds and weakens the people, whereas liberty releases their energy and prepares the rise of a state to hegemony. This is what happened to Athens after the expulsion of the Peisistratids (I 65,1; V 78). In Egypt or Media, on the other hand, free regimes are brief intervals between periods of despotism, degenerating quickly into anarchy and facilitating the rise of a new monarchy (I 95–6; II 147; 151–3). Herodotus considers monarchy a stable, traditional, and very efficient regime for the large oriental states (cf., for the Thracians, V 3,1), without denying the short-lived manifestations of other political aspirations. He insists on the historicity of the famous constitutional debate held by the Persian conspirators (III 80,1 and note); and he does not wonder that Otanes could speak in favour of democracy, because it was a Persian satrap who established this regime in the Ionian cities after the revolt (VI 43,3).

Between despotism and freedom in the Greek cities, Herodotus certainly chooses freedom, but is not dogmatic also in this respect. He does not hide his negative view of Pisistratus' tyranny, but he acknowledges his initial good rule and respect for the laws (I 59,6; 64). The harsh criticism of Cypselus' tyranny is attributed to a Corinthian speaker (V 92), and may not represent Herodotus' own view. Hippias and the exiled Pisistratids do not evoke sympathy, but here perhaps Herodotus is following traditional Athenian stereotypes. On the other hand, Herodotus is not upset by the cunning and the methods of government of certain Greek tyrants, such as Thrasybulus of Miletus and Polycrates of Samos; and he finds ways of praising Syloson for having tried to save his country from the worst catastrophe (III 140,5). All in all, Herodotus' criticism of tyranny is negative, albeit impartial and complex, resembling in fact the general historic evaluation by Greeks of archaic tyrannies.[113]

[110] See Pohlenz, and Gigante, pp. 123 ff.; for a different view see Heubeck. Cf. the reaction of B. Laurot, *Ktema*, VI (1981), 39–48. For the Graeco-barbarian conflict see the large collection of papers, in four parts and seven volumes, by A. M. Babi, *Les grecs et les barbares*, I–IV, Lausanne 1963–75.

[111] See v. Fritz, pp. 256 ff.; id., *WS* LXXVIII (1965), 5–31.

[112] For the usage of the terms βασιλεύς and τύραννος in Herodotus see notes on I 6,1 and III 42, 2.

[113] On Herodotus and tyranny see G. M. Hirst, *Collected Classical Papers*, Oxford 1938, pp. 97–100; H. J. Diesner, *Forschungen und Fortschritte*, XXXIV (1960), 270–2; Waters, *Herodotos on Tyrants*, and in

It is almost impossible to establish what form of 'free' government Herodotus preferred, democracy or oligarchy. The old thesis that he was a convinced democrat of the Periclean school and a follower of the Alcmaeonid tradition has no basis. Agariste dreamed of a lion and gave birth to Pericles (VI 131,2): from that one cannot deduce sympathy or admiration either for the man or his regime, especially since another lion in Herodotus predicts the birth of a tyrant (V 92β,3).[114] Otanes' speech in favour of democracy does not represent Herodotus' thought any more than Megabyzus' speech in favour of oligarchy or Darius' praise of monarchy. 'It seems easier to fool many men than one' (V 97,2), says Herodotus, describing how Aristagoras was unable to persuade the king of Sparta, but succeeded in convincing 30,000 Athenians. Herodotus found the paradox to his liking, though it was rather uncomplimentary to democracy, all the more so because the assembly vote was 'the origin of evils' for Greeks and barbarians. Great energies were released at Athens with the advent of ἰσηγορίη, 'an excellent thing', according to Herodotus (V 78), but certainly not equivalent to democracy.[115] Great energies were released at Sparta as well with the advent of Lycurgus' εὐνομίη (I 66,1): a 'free' government in as much as it was entirely opposite to tyranny, but also opposite to democracy. Herodotus finds a way to express great respect for the Spartans: they are the bravest of all Greeks (IX 48,1), their way of life is simple and their regime is good. For these reasons Sparta, not Athens, is chosen to represent the direct contrast with Persia (IX 82), a contrast that, in the famous dialogue between Xerxes and Demaratus, is not so much between despotism and freedom, but rather between the personal despotism of an arbitrary king and the impersonal and objective despotism of the law. But Herodotus does not also conceal the faults of the Spartan form of government: on the one hand it is extremely meticulous, formal, strongly attached to traditional laws and customs, and slow to act; on the other, it does not have the constitutional means to control the manoeuvres of a narrow-minded and unbalanced king such as Cleomenes. In turn, Cleisthenes' democratic reforms in Athens are presented as a copy of the reforms introduced by his homonymous grandfather at Sicyon, who was a tyrant, and the only positive aspect of the reform that Herodotus found was the anti-Ionian bias of the new tribal organization (V 69,1–2). Cleisthenes' father, Megacles, emerges as a politically ambiguous figure, since he is responsible for Pisistratus' restoration to power as well as for

---

G&R XIX (1972), 136–50; P. Barceló, *Basileia, Monarchia, Tyrannis. Untersuchungen zu Entwicklung und Beurteilung von Alleinherrschaft im vorhellenistischen Griechenland*, Stuttgart 1993, pp. 149–77. Cf. p. 46, n. 111.

[114] This old thesis of Ed. Meyer and Jacoby was refuted years ago by Strasburger, *Historia*, IV (1955), 1–25. It was based on the questionable assumption that Herodotus was wholly dependent on Alcmaeonid sources; see P. Develin's criticism of this approach in J. W. Eadie and J. Ober (eds.), *The Craft of the Historian: Essays in Honour of Chester G. Starr*, Lanham–New York–London 1985, pp. 125–39. On Herodotus and the Alcmaeonids see Thomas, *Oral Tradition*, pp. 247–82. On Pericles as a lion-cub see B. McNellen, *ICS* XXII (1997), 11–23.

[115] This 'equality of speech', or of laws, is essentially seen as a source of imperial power; cf. V 93,1 and VII 162,1.

his expulsion (I 60). Herodotus considers the Alcmeonidai the 'real liberators' of Athens, and defends them from the accusation of collaboration with the Persians after Marathon (VI 115; 121–4). He does not, however, hide the rumours which circulated in Athens of their dubious scheming at Delphi during their exile (V 62–3; VI 123). Herodotus' political preference for one or other of the rival Athenian factions remains entirely elusive, as does his preference for democracy or oligarchy.

In a famous chapter (VII 139), Herodotus openly maintains that Athens saved Greece in 480 BC, though he knows that for the majority such a view is 'abominable'. He speaks or writes for a non-Athenian public in a period of general hostility against Athens, perhaps on the brink of the Peloponnesian war. His historic evaluation of the Athenian role in 480 has created the impression, already in antiquity and especially in modern times, that he was a doctrinaire and consistent supporter of Athens.[116] However, the recognition of Athens' role in 480 is not a sign of sympathy with all that Athens did or stood for in other historical periods, nor its form of government, nor its ruthless imperialism in Pericles' time and afterwards. Undoubtedly nothing favours the hypothesis that Herodotus was on Athens' side and against Sparta when the Peloponnesian war broke out. Various considerations were the source of a contrary hypothesis, namely that he belonged to a group of moderate intellectuals who looked back with yearning to the years of the hegemonic 'dualism' of Athens and Sparta (478–61 BC), and preferred the difficult alliance born out of common victory against the Persians to a fratricidal war between the two major Greek cities.[117] In addition to his general aversion to wars (I 87,4), Herodotus also does not conceal the dangers of internal divisions between the Greeks. Mardonius tells Xerxes: 'As far as I know, the Greeks often fight wars against one another foolishly. Since they speak the same language, they should use heralds and ambassadors to solve their controversies by any other means than war' (VII 9β, 1–2). He also proclaims that 'an internal conflict is worse than a war conducted in unity in the same proportion as war is worse than peace' (VIII 3,1), referring certainly to the problem of Greek unity. The Panhellenic ideal is certainly not alien to Herodotus. In a famous passage the Athenians, when put to the test by Alexander of Macedon, declare themselves enemies of Persia in the name of 'Greekness' (τὸ Ἑλληνικόν), of 'the community of blood and language of the Greeks', 'the common sanctuaries to the gods', 'the common cults and customs and the similar institutions' (VIII 144,2). His praise of Athens should of course be reappraised if it is held that Herodotus

---

[116] On the so-called 'counterfactual conditional causal argument' used in this chapter and elsewhere by Herodotus (cf. II 26,2; III 49,1 and note; IV 140,2; VIII 30,2), see N. Demand, *AJPh* CVIII (1987), 746–58. For Herodotus and Athens see, among other publications, J. A. S. Evans, *AC* XLVIII (1979), 112–18, and W. G. Forrest, *Phoenix*, XXXVIII (1984), 1–11; M. Ostwald, *ICS* XVI (1991),137–49.

[117] Nissen, *Historische Zeitschrift*, LXIII (1889), 419 ff. already expressed this sort of view; cf. Heubeck, pp. 54 ff. For Herodotus and 'dualism' see Forrest, art. cit., pp. 1 ff.; for Athens and Greek unity see K. v. Fritz, *WS* LXXVIII (1965), 5 ff; for the *Histories* as a 'monumental demonstration of Athenian failure' see J. D. Smart, *Phoenix*, XXXI (1977), 251–2.

believed that the Spartan opposition to Persia was more obvious and natural than that of Athens. Actually, he does not exclude the possibility that Athens might have chosen to take sides with the Medes in view of the impending danger, whereas he believes that Sparta would have fought till the end and chosen to surrender only as an *ultima ratio* (VII 139; cf. 102,2–3). The purest patriotic sacrifice is that of the Spartans at Thermopylae, the greatest victory is that of Plataea. A Spartan remains patriotic even in exile: after all, Demaratus unsuccessfully tries to dissuade Xerxes' from his plans, whereas the Athenian exiles encourage him to pursue them. The 'actuality' of Herodotus' *Histories* consists precisely in raising the Panhellenic banner in an era of ruthless 'dualism', openly opposing the stream and the mood of his time. Yet, it is uncertain whether in all that a message of national unity is implied. He is not explicit nor does he write propaganda; he often repeats, and with great clarity, an ethical and religious view of a historical or philosophical order, but never a political view on current affairs. It was certainly not Panhellenic pride that had driven him to commemorate in his own way the great events of 480–79: the ancients, anyway, suspected him of 'malice' towards the Greeks and admiration for the barbarians. Only in recent times has he become a writer of Panhellenic propaganda in a Cimonian vein. Herodotus related what actually happened in those two years: examples of almost superhuman patriotic sacrifice next to examples of treachery; acts of disunion next to acts of subordination to the supreme command. There emerges the depiction of a great historical moment, when Athens and Sparta managed, though with difficulty and mutual threats, to overcome their rivalry, and lead to resistance and to victory some of the other Greek cities, though few and disunited. Only those who want to may assume that Herodotus' description of this historical moment was intentionally contrasted with the Peloponnesian war. The present influenced Herodotus, as indeed it influences any historian, but he never idealized the past, as is very clear when one reads the last three books.

Partiality or impartiality never hinder his praise and criticism. Herodotus' resentment of the Ionians is well known: the very name 'Ionian' has become an insult, a symbol of effeminacy, servile behaviour, and unjustified arrogance. And yet, Herodotus found a way to underline also the love of freedom of the Ionian cities, whether those who chose armed resistance to the Persian rule, or those who preferred emigration *en masse* to slavery. The famous chapter on the Theban desertion at Thermopylae (VII 233) is certainly not impartial, and in fact shocked the Boeotian Plutarch; yet at Plataea the Thebans on the Persian side fought valiantly (IX 67–8). In another famous chapter (VII 152) Herodotus abstains from harsh criticism of the cities that sided with the Medes in 480. In his treatment of the great Greek generals also, Herodotus manages to avoid eulogy as well as insults. He admires Themistocles' shrewdness, his power of persuasion, his bravery and fierce patriotism; he fully recognizes his decisive role in the development of the Athenian fleet and during the battle of Salamis: he is the Odysseus of the Persian wars, and yet Herodotus does not hide his greed and ruthlessness, nor his plan of deserting the Greek cause and siding with the Persians (VIII 109,5). Pausanias is the hero of Plataea *sans peur et sans reproche*, a symbol of Spartan frugality contrasted to Persian luxury; but his *hybris* was known to all, and there were rumours, 'perhaps true', that he counted on Persian support to become 'tyrant of Greece', and that is why he married the daughter of an Achaemenid (V 32). Herodotus could also have told, in a digression, the less edifying events in the later lives of the two main heroes of the Persian wars. He did not; perhaps he might have done so, if and when he had reached the narration of events after 479/8 BC. Obviously these persons interested him not only for their role on the battlefield, but also for their characters, their morality and their amorality, the aspects which in fact fascinated him above all.

VI

In simple terms, Herodotus' personality emerges from a reading of his work with two aspects, those of the storyteller and the man of science. His work is incomprehensible unless it is read against the double cultural background of epic tradition and Ionian science. This too, however, is a simplification, because the influence of poetry is not only restricted to epic, but includes lyric poetry and tragedy, whereas the scientific background is not exclusively Ionian, but includes also the teaching of the Sophists and the science of Hippocratic medicine.

Herodotus was called 'most Homeric' (μόνος Ἡρόδοτος Ὁμηρικώτατος ἐγένετο;) by the author of the treatise *On the Sublime* (13,3), mainly in relation to characteristics of style and language. It is actually not difficult to discern other Homeric elements in Herodotus' literary technique, such as the alternation between narrative and speech; the digressions on mythological themes; the dialogues and debates with which he dramatizes a situation, defines characters, examines the causes of human action, and expresses a didactic messages;[118] the successful mixture of irony and macabre detail;[119] the geographical descriptions of the settings of historical events; the recurrent use of typical numbers. Even the enumeration of Xerxes' army units could have been inspired by the Homeric Catalogue of Ships. Herodotus' flowing style, continuously varied, that invites the reader to change topic from one moment to the next—from a strange tale to a critical argument on a geographical problem, from the description of a battle to a dynastic genealogy, from a didactic speech to a series of scenes dramatized in dialogue, from a moralizing story on human fate to a playful anecdote about cunning resourcefulness,[120] from the description of a miraculous dream to a political debate—this constitutes his characteristic 'variety' (ποικιλίη) which enlivens the narrative, avoiding tediousness, monotony, and severeness: 'he wanted to vary his writing, emulating Homer' (Dionysius of Halicarnassus, *Ad Pompeium* III 11). Herodotus fascinated

---

[118] For speeches and dialogues in Herodotus see Deffner; Steinger; Heni; Lang. On the 'historical' function of speeches see K. H. Waters, *Historia*, XV (1966), 157–71. On Herodotus' Homeric model see Erbse, *Studien*, pp. 122–32.

[119] See e.g. II 111; VIII 25,1–2; 107,2; 111,2–3; IX 11; 84–5.

[120] On the variety of Herodotus' storytelling, see H. Erbse, in *Gnomosyne. Festschrift W. Marg*, Munich 1981, pp. 251–69.

even a hostile critic such as Plutarch, who was aware of the dangerous power of 'someone who knows how to write', and of a 'pleasing story' full of grace, skill and elegance (*Mor.* 874b). It is a book written to delight, as well as for moral edification: Gibbon aptly said that Herodotus 'sometimes writes for children and sometimes for philosophers'. But from this colourful diversity of themes and genres there emerges clearly a full command of the material, the art of its collection and organization, and a unity of thought. This can be seen both in individual sections and in the work as a whole. Thus the first great work of artistic prose was born, to set the standards for subsequent prose writing in Greek literature, and to establish for prose a post of honour hitherto unknown.

Ancient readers, on the whole, generally liked Herodotus' archaic language and style. Aristotle found 'archaic' his 'continuous' style (λέξις εἰρωμένη) made up of paratactic clauses coming to a halt only with the completion of the sense (*Rhet.* 1409a30). Demetrius, who defined this style as 'disconnected' (λέξις διῃρημένη), deemed it typical of Hecataeus and of the 'greater part' of Herodotus (*De Elocutione* 12). He meant the plain and continuous style with parenthetic clauses, especially typical of the geographical and ethnographic digressions; certainly there is no lack of relative clauses, complex periods, and passages in indirect speech, but in spite of them the impression of 'fluidity' prevails: Cicero claimed that Herodotus *sine ullis salebris quasi sedatus amnis fluit* (*Orat.* 39). Delight, grace, sweetness, gentleness, gaiety, naturalness, calm: such are the terms most commonly used in antiquity to describe Herodotus' prose (sometimes contrasted with the 'terror' inspired by Thucydides' style), which seemed full of poetic nuances, and therefore better suited for an entertaining tale than for history.

According to the rhetor Hermogenes of Tarsus (*c.* AD 200), Herodotus' Ionic dialect is 'mixed' (μεμιγμένη, ποικίλη) rather than 'pure' like that of Hecataeus (περὶ ἰδεῶν II 12).[121] Photius, on the other hand, thought that Herodotus had fixed the 'canon' of the Ionic dialect exactly as Thucydides did for the Attic, and that Herodotus, unlike Ctesias, was consistent in his usage of Ionic forms.[122] These are extremely interesting appraisals from late antiquity and the Byzantine period, which we have no reason to doubt as far as the manuscripts available to Hermogenes and Photius are concerned; but at the same time we are totally unable to evaluate them with respect to the original text. The tendency of ancient editors and scribes to adapt Herodotus' language to the tastes and requirements of their time—whether by introducing archaisms, or hyper-Ionic and epic forms, or on the contrary by making Herodotus' language conform to the vulgar Attic *koiné*, in order to make it easier to read—must have significantly corrupted the original text. The language of our best medieval manuscripts is certainly mixed: Ionic and Attic forms alternate (λεώς—λαός), as do open and contracted ones (θωῦμα—θῶμα, οὖρος—ὄρος). To reconstruct the original text under such circumstances is an impossible undertaking. Herodotus himself knew four variants

---

[121] On ποικιλίη and the rhythmical or sung reading of the text see Hemmerdinger, pp. 170 ff.

[122] *Bibliotheca* 60, p. 19a; 72, p. 45b Henry. According to Dionysius of Halicarnassus (*Ad Pompeium* III 3), Herodotus' dialect is standard Ionic. On Ctesias' language see D. Del Corno, *Athenaeum*, XL (1962), 126–41, and M. Gigante, *RFIC* XL (1962), 249–72.

of the Ionic dialect (see note on I 142,3); today, we cannot know which one he preferred, especially since he considered all of them 'departures' from a model canon of perfection. The linguistic evidence of the few fifth-century Ionian inscriptions is too scanty to allow satisfactory comparisons.[123]

In antiquity Herodotus was almost unanimously admired for the art of telling a story, due to which he became a 'classic' in the schools of rhetoric, often compared with Thucydides. Much more critical and complex was the evaluation of his merits as a historian.[124] It is probable that substantial parts of his book were known to educated Athenian circles after 430 BC, and perhaps even before, if there is a grain of truth in the reports of Herodotus' public readings (cf. above p. 3 f.). But it is far from certain that verses by Sophocles, Euripides, or Aristophanes allude to, recall, or parody Herodotus, like the famous verses of *Acharnians* (523–9), assumed to parody the proem of the *Histories*. It is therefore impossible to date the so-called 'publication' of the work on the basis of such questionable evidence,[125] as it is likewise impossible to tell whether the 'publication' was a great success, as some suppose, or a great failure, as others claim. We can only assume that in the last decades of the fifth century the Athenian literary *elite* knew Herodotus' book in whole or in part.

Thucydides certainly began his history of the πεντηκονταετία with the last event mentioned in Herodotus' work, the Athenian capture of Sestos, thereby inaugurating the 'cycle' or chain tradition linking together the great works of Greek and Roman historiography, whereby an author begins his story where his chosen predecessor left off. Without mentioning Herodotus by name, Thucydides probably criticizes his great predecessor for preferring 'pleasure' over 'truth' and usefulness; and he probably also corrects some factual details. He may, after all, have come across Herodotus twice, first as a 'lecturer' in an oral society, and then as a 'writer' in a literate one.[126] Ctesias opened the list of Greek historians who, for one reason or another, were happy, or thought it right, to slander Herodotus, to denounce his lies, his unreliability, sometimes even his plagiarism.[127] Ctesias, second to none in deceit and unreliability, also had political reasons in his pro-Spartan orientation to oppose the supposedly pro-Athenian historian (see, particularly, *FGrHist* 688 T 7–8). Herodotus became the 'father of lies' long before

---

[123] Cf. C. Favre, *Thesaurus verborum quae in titulis ionicis leguntur cum Herodoteo sermone comparatus*, Heidelberg 1914. On all aspects of Herodotus' dialect see Rosén, *Sprachform*; cf. C. Schick, *Mon. Acc. Lincei*, VIII 7 (1956).

[124] On Herodotus' reception in antiquity see Riemann. Cf. also J. A. S. Evans, *CJ* LXIV (1968), 11–7.

[125] Among other publications see C. W. Fornara, *JHS* XCI (1971), 25–34; J. Cobet, *Hermes*, CV (1977), 2–27; *Athenaeum* LXV (1987), 508–11; J. A. S. Evans, *Athenaeum*, LVIII (1979), 145–9; S. Flory, *AJPh* CI (1980), 12–28; D. M. MacDowell, *G&R* XXX (1983), 151; R. Meridor, *Eranos*, LXXXI (1983), 13–20; D. Sansone, *ICS* X (1985), 1–9; U. Bernini, *MGR* XVII (1992), 45–64.

[126] Thuc. I 89,2 and 97,2. On the 'historical cycle' see bibliography quoted in Piccirilli (op. cit., n. 6), pp. 160–1, esp. the works of L. Canfora quoted there; W. Rösler, *Philologus*, CXXXV (1991), 215–20; Marincola, pp. 237–41 and 289–292. For possible linguistic parodies in Thucydides see Beltrametti, pp. 32 ff. On Thucydides' indirect criticism of Herodotus see *Schol. Thuc.* I 22,4. For a full discussion of Thucydides' use of Herodotus see S. Hornblower, *A Commentary on Thucydides*, II, Oxford 1996, pp. 122–45.

[127] See D. Lenfant, *REG* CIX (1996), 348–80.

becoming the 'father of history'. No other ancient historian was censured with such violence; but he was never ignored. Ephorus took his work for granted and used it, Theopompus epitomized it in two books, and many local historians of the fourth century rectified his presumed faults perhaps for reasons of local patriotism. Aristotle calls him μυθολόγος in his *De Generatione Animalium* (756b5), whereas in the famous chapter 9 of the *Poetica* (1451b1) he considers him a typical 'historian' (ἰστορικός), that is, astonishingly, less philosophical than the poets. He also uses him, together with local histories of Attica, for his *Athenaion Politeia* (14,4), and records his opening sentence.[128] In the Hellenistic period, owing to the climate of revived interest in geography, ethnography, and paradoxography of the Orient following upon Alexander's conquest, Herodotus continued to be criticized as a historian, but also to be widely read and to influence the views of these very critics.[129] In the fourth and third centuries BC, whether they were following or criticizing him, Callisthenes, Nearchus, Timaeus, Hecataeus of Abdera, Manetho (who may have written a *Contra Herodotum*, probably criticizing the Egyptian book), Megasthenes, and Eratosthenes all expected their readers to know him. In the third/second century BC, Aristarchus commented on his work, but whether he also edited the text is uncertain. In all events Herodotus' work belonged to the classical canon of the libraries at Alexandria and Pergamon. This does not mean that ancient philologists concerned themselves with the composition of the work: in antiquity 'the most Homeric' Herodotus had only unitarian critics. Nymphodorus of Syracuse knew him and Agatharchides of Cnidus' judgement of him was favourable. Polybius surprisingly does not refer to him at all. In the first century BC Cicero christened him once and for all 'the father of history', *pater historiae* (*Leg.* I 5), for he was the *princeps* who *genus hoc* (= history) *ornavit* (*De Orat.* II 55); but he was also convinced that his work contained numberless *fabulae*, and he doubted the authenticity of the Delphic oracle delivered to Croesus.[130] Diodorus and Strabo usually quoted him in order to criticize him,[131] whereas his fellow-countryman Dionysius of Halicarnassus, without expressing an opinion on the problem of reliability, admired his style, writing in a sententious manner that *ethos* characterizes Herodotus, as *pathos* characterizes Thucydides.[132] Nicolaus of Damascus preferred Xanthus for the history of Lydia, Ctesias for that of Persia, and probably Hellanicus for Greek history.[133] Reading the Greek historians, Josephus records the impression that 'all agree on Herodotus' mendacity' (*Contra Apionem* I 16). Plutarch, hurt in his Boeotian pride by Herodotus, dedicated to the Herodotean 'malice' his famous pamphlet that was

---

[128] On Aristotle's criticism of Herodotus see N. Thompson, *Herodotus and the Origins of the Political Community*, New Haven–London 1996, pp. 7–27.

[129] See O. Murray, *CQ* XXII (1972), 200–13.

[130] Cf. note on I 53, 3; see H. Schönberger, *Blätter für Bayer. Gymnasalschulwesen*, LI (1915), 13 ff.

[131] Diod. I 69,7; for Strabo see W. Althaus, 'Die Herodotzitate in Strabons Geographie', Diss. Freiburg 1941. L. Prandi, *CISA* XIV (1988), 52–72.

[132] *Ad Pompeium* III 3; for ethical and stylistic influence see S. Ek, *Herodotismen in der Archäologie des Dionys von Halicarnass*, Lund 1942.

[133] Cf. B. Z. Wacholder, *Nicolaus of Damascus*, Berkeley–Los Angeles 1962, pp. 66 ff.

intended only in part to criticize the historian's falsehoods and argumentations: for a man like Plutarch, who thought that history should be encomiastic, 'malice' implies a bias towards the barbarians or the Athenians at the expense of other Greek cities such as Thebes or Corinth, as well as disengaged impartiality, an interest in scandals and insinuations, and a pessimistic tendency to focus on the more unedifying and unflattering accounts of events and human motives.[134] With the revival of an erudite and archaizing interest in ancient literature written in dialect, the philologist Alexander of Cotyaeion, in Phrygia, studied various textual problems in Herodotus;[135] Lucian parodied his language and style in *De dea Syria*;[136] Arrian and other historians of the second and third centuries AD imitated him; and a *Vita Homeri*, composed by someone who knew Herodotus well, was attributed to him. In his Egyptian oration (*Or.* 48), the rhetor Aelius Aristides was the first to raise doubts about the reality of Herodotus' visit to Elephantine and about his knowledge of Upper Egypt (vol. II, pp. 458–9 Dindorf). Study and criticism of Herodotus continued in the late Roman empire: lexica were compiled, *excerpta* collected, a number of commentaries and pamphlets on his lies and plagiarisms appeared.[137] Photius' absurdly short summary of Herodotus does not suggest much interest for the most ancient author in his collection: in very conventional fashion he praises his style but criticizes the digressions, which in his view distort the truth. In the tenth century, when the most ancient and important of Herodotus' medieval manuscripts (A) was produced, the biography of the historian was also written or compiled for the Suidas lexicon (cf. above, p. 2 f.).

Herodotus was known to fourteenth-century Italian humanists, including Petrarch.[138] In the fifteenth century, when the first manuscripts bought in Greece appeared in Western Europe, there appeared the first translations into Latin: that of Lorenzo Valla, begun in Rome in 1452 on the initiative of of Pope Nicholas V, and based on codices of the 'Roman family', was published posthumously in Venice in 1474.[139] Debates about Herodotus' reliability were

---

[134] For a recent English translation and commentary see *Plutarch, The Malice of Herodotus* (*De Malignitate Herodoti*), trans. with an introduction and commentary by Anthony Bowen, Warminster 1992. See H. Homeyer, *Klio*, XLIX (1967), 181–7; J. M. Marincola, *AncW* XXV (1994), 191–203. Plutarch is not always wrong: see Ph.-E. Legrand, in *Mélanges Gustave Glotz*, II, Paris 1932, pp. 535–47.

[135] Porphyry, *Quaest. Hom.* II, p. 288 Schrader. From this passage it does not follow that Alexander edited the text.

[136] Cf. J. Bompaire, *Lucien écrivain. Imitation et création*, Paris 1958, pp. 646 ff., 652 f., with bibliography. For Herodotus the storyteller see Lucian, *Philopseudes*; for Herodotus and Ctesias as writers of lies: *Vera Historia* II 31.

[137] For the lexica see the *editio maior* of Stein, II, pp. 443 ff.; for the commentaries, Jacoby *RE* Suppl. II, col. 514.

[138] For a complete discussion see Momigliano, *Secondo contributo*, pp. 29–44 and 46–56; cf. Virgilio, pp. 36–8. Petrarch calls Herodotus 'di greca historia padre', whereas his Byzantine contemporary Nicephorus Gregoras surprisingly refers to him as ὁ τὰ Περσικὰ συγγραψάμενος (῾Ρωμαικὴ ἱστορία II 4γ). For Herodotus in the middle ages see E. Hermes, *Neue Sammlung*, II (1962), 554–72.

[139] See Alber, *Maia*, XI (1959), 315–19 ff., and *Boll Class* VII (1959), 65–84. On other partial Latin translations see Hemmerdinger, p. 48. On Guarino da Verona see R. Sabbadini, *Giornale storico della letteratura italiana*, XLII (1904), 251. Among Herodotus' Byzantine imitators in the 15th century we should mention Laonicus Chalcondyles, for whom see H. Ditten, *Klio*, XLIII–XLV, (1965), 185–246.

soon enough revived. Unsurprisingly, the Spanish moralist Juan Luis Vives (1492–1540) called him *mendaciorum pater*. On the other hand, the interest in geography and ethnography aroused by the discovery of America was favourable to Herodotus the ethnographer. Various 'apologies' for Herodotus appeared; the most famous is that of the great philologist Henri Estienne (Stephanus), who openly declared that Herodotus' descriptions of the customs of ancient peoples are reliable, arguing that, when compared to modern ones, they are not at all incredible; besides, Herodotus, a religious man, could not have lied.[140] With this treatise Estienne initiated the comparative ethnography of ancient and modern customs, a new discipline which flourished in Europe in the sixteenth and seventeenth centuries. Herodotus started to be regularly quoted as an authoritative source for information. Rabelais was extremely interested in Herodotus' descriptions of customs and monuments; and he may have edited a partial Latin translation, which has not survived.[141] Loys le Roy (Ludovicus Regius) also believed unconditionally Herodotus' descriptions of Babylon, Egypt, Persia, and Greece; while the great Scaliger declared that Herodotus was indispensable for the truly learned but inadvisable for the half-educated. In the eighteenth century the need was still felt for a *Défense d'Hérodote*, a work by the Abbé Geinoz (1753–6), and a *Disputatio Historica de Fide Herodoti Recte Estimanda* by C. W. Rhoer (Haarlem, 1781), published in Latin and Dutch. The Jesuit J.-F. Lafitau, who was a missionary in America, developed Estienne's approach, and in 1724 published the *Moeurs des sauvages amériquains*,[142] where the customs of the Indians are compared with those described in the Bible and in classical sources: Herodotus is one of the most quoted authors. Generally speaking, Herodotus was often set against the Bible, either to discredit his reliability or to reassert it as against *historia sacra*.[143]

The nineteenth century, from Ranke onwards, declared that Thucydides was the greatest historian of all time: clearly the new political, diplomatic, and military historiography could not find its model in Herodotus. The comparison with Thucydides was once again damaging for Herodotus, reborn again in a new incarnation of 'the father of lies', a dishonest narrator who invented travels, visits, and sources in order to deceive his readers. His work came to be regarded as belonging not to historiography, but to the so-called 'swindle-literature'. The most famous exponent of these views was Sayce.[144] Alongside the problem of

[140] See the edition, with German translation, by J. Kramer, Meisenheim am Glan 1980.

[141] Cf. H. H. Glidden, *ICS* IX (1984), 197–214. For references to Herodotus in the *Essais* by Montaigne see Giraudeau, p. 179; for the commentary to Herodotus by David Chytraeus (1531–1600) see H. Barth, *Antiquitas graeco-romana*, Prague 1968, pp. 381–9.

[142] See the English translation by W. N. Fenton and E. L. Moore (Toronto 1974), with a long introduction; see also the anthology compiled by E. H. Lemay (Paris 1983). On 16th- and 17th-century comparisons of Herodotus and the Bible see C. Grell, *QS* XX (1984), 111–56 (on Cyrus the Great). For Herodotus in English literature see Wells, pp. 205–28. For Herodotean elements in the humoristic writings of Jean Paul (1763–1825) see P. Sprengel, *Jhrb. d. Jean Paul Gesellschaft*, X (1975), 213–48.

[143] See C. Grell, *SS* VII (1985), 60–91.

[144] For other representatives of this school in the 19th century see Jacoby, *RE* Suppl. II, col 251. Particularly interesting is G. F. Grotefend (1775–1853), who found in Herodotus inspiration for his research on the Orient: see Doblhofer, *Gymnasium*, LXXI (1964), 434–41.

Herodotus' credibility arose that of the composition of his work, destined to become the origin of the prolonged debate between 'unitarians' and 'separatists', which has not yet exhausted itself.[145] In the twentieth century, among the 'unitarians' a group tried to redefine Herodotus as the 'father of history', with the addition of the title of 'First Historian of the West'. Along with much rhetoric, he was presented as a great historian who from the very beginning allegedly conceived a grand unifying theme of universal history, with the epic of the Persian wars at its centre, interpreted as an example of the eternal conflict between Asia and Europe, despotism and freedom, barbarism and civilization. Indeed, ever since the sixteenth century Herodotus' reception has had its highs and lows in response to contemporary ideologies about race, slavery, and imperialism.[146] The unitarian school has had the merit of underlining the fundamental unity of Herodotus' thought. At the same time, Herodotus the storyteller, with his dialogues, speeches, style, and language, continues to fascinate. The comparative approach of social anthropology and the new conception of 'total' history have certainly contributed to the appreciation of Herodotus as the 'father of ethnography and *Kulturgeschichte*'. It is not by chance that a learned journal devoted to geography and geopolitics is called *Hérodote*. However, this modern enthusiasm is sometimes spoiled by some *enfants terribles* who, following Sayce, still claim that Herodotus based his work on written sources, and raise again the question of his reliability, if not his honesty.[147] These excessively critical studies, often vitiated by theoretical and unjustified generalizations, nevertheless have the merit of counteracting excessive enthusiasm. Nineteenth-century scepticism is not yet dead. Anthropological interest in oral cultures and, in particular, a series of African studies (see above, p. 16, n. 43) are responsible for the topical conception of Herodotus as the first writer to record oral traditions. Finally, modern psycho-philosophical concern with the personal and collective perception of time have reopened the problem of the origins and nature of the archaic historical consciousness from Homer to Herodotus.

Herodotus taught the historians of all times a series of things unknown or only confusedly known before him. He taught that, to solve a problem, research needs to be carried out; that research must be based on evidence; that the evidence must be reliable; and that direct observation is superior to oral information; that there is no need to believe blindly all that the sources say, but that sources deserve to be respected, collected, and presented faithfully, even if unreliable, so that one may study, compare, and eventually assess them; and that ascertained facts must be convincingly explained. For all his debt to Hecataeus and other precursors, Herodotus is for us the true 'first inventor' of the critical method. But his contribution is not limited to methodology in the strict sense of the word. He

---

[145] See the reviews by Fornara, and Cobet, pp. 188 ff.; as well as the Doxographie by Drexler, pp. 187–227; cf. also H. Hommel, in *Gnomosyne, Festschrift W. Marg*, Munich 1981, pp. 271 ff.

[146] Cf. D. S. Wiesen, *AncW* III (1980), 3–16.

[147] The major representative of this school is D. Fehling; for a polemical criticism of such views see W. K. Pritchett, *The Liar School of Herodotus*, Amsterdam 1993.

chose to restrict his research to the recent past. This choice became a rigorous principle in Thucydides and a characteristic sign distinguishing the historians from 'archaeologists' or antiquarians, for whom ancient historians never had much respect. Within the chronological limits of the research, the subject must be selected according to its importance: it must deserve to be told, remembered, or at least mentioned. 'Important' is what the historian and his public recognize as such: for example, a great war, like that sung by Homer. Herodotus, at the end of his long journey, became convinced that the ἔργον which most deserves to be studied is a great war. In the course of time this view became one of the most widespread principles of ancient historiography: Tacitus was ashamed of being forced to deal with a period of peace.[148]

Last but not least, in the true spirit of Homeric epic and Ionian science, Herodotus taught all historians a fundamental principle: the real aim of historical research is not an accurate collection of facts, important though they may be, but the discovery of what is universal—human passions, the rules that govern humanity, or as we would say, the search for meaning, a 'model' or the direction of the course of historical events. As we have seen, what matters to Herodotus is to emphasize the ethical, historical, and philosophical universal significance of what he tells, not just recording events whose only merit is to arouse curiosity. Coming from a Greek colony with no fatherland, he heads a long list of ancient historians in exile who, as Plutarch remarks, knew how to draw profit from their situation. Life in exile broadens horizons, limits parochialism, furthers scepticism and impartiality. Herodotus, then, had something to say also to future generations, besides amusing his contemporary public. He too knew the difference between what is pleasing and what is true (VII 101,3). In the end Herodotus too produced a 'possession for all time', a κτῆμα εἰς ἀεί.

[148] See Marincola, pp. 34–43.

BOOK I
David Asheri

The first book of the *Histories* foreshadows the entire work and, in a sense, constitutes its quintessence. All the characteristic features of the work's content and form, thought, and style immediately present themselves to the reader with great clarity. The universal panorama of Herodotus' history opens immediately before our eyes: the world of the sixth century, East and West, cultures and conflicts, continuity and change, nations and great protagonists. The curtain rises at Sardis, Miletus, and Ephesus in western Asia Minor, with shifts to Greece: to Corinth, Delphi, Athens, and Sparta; then we move to Media, from Ecbatana and Niniveh to the Caucasus; to Philistia and Persia; then back to Asia Minor, Lydia, Ionia, and the islands, and to Caria and Lycia with occasional visits to the West: Corsica, Etruria, Lucania; the scene then moves to Babylon and ends in the land of the Massagetae, east of the Caspian Sea. It is a tour of the archaic world in 216 chapters, as well as an introduction to the main settings where the historical drama of the following books will be played out: Persia, Ionia, Athens, Sparta. Chronologically, the nucleus of the main narrative is the thirty years between Croesus' rise to power and the death of Cyrus the Great (560–530 BC), with digressions into the remote past of the Lydians and the Assyrians from the thirteenth century BC, of the Medes from the eighth century, and of the Athenians and the Spartans from the early sixth century. The entire structure of the book is organized around the two main characters, Croesus and Cyrus, foreshadowing in this respect too the rest of the work, which is constructed around the dynastic succession of the Achaemenid kings from Cyrus to Xerxes.[1]

Apart from the introductory chapters (1–5), the first book can be easily divided into two main *logoi*: the *logos* of Croesus (6–94) and the *logos* of Cyrus (95–216). The hypothesis that it was originally composed of three *logoi* (1–94; 95–140; 141–216), corresponding to three papyrus rolls, is undermined by the banal difficulty that these three *logoi* are very different in length, whereas the papyrus roll should be understood as a unit of length. There is, however, no objection to the hypothesis that the first book originally occupied two papyrus rolls each about 7 metres long, corresponding roughly to the two aforementioned main *logoi*.[2] The 'first *logos*', as Herodotus himself calls it at V 36,4, is dedicated to Lydia, with the last king at its centre.[3] In a few introductory sentences (ch. 6),

---

[1] Cf. General Introduction, pp. 36 ff. Herodotus' tendency to organize his historical material along dynastic successions is found in the first book also in the prologue to Lydian history (13–22; 25) and in the history of the Medes (96–130). For an unusual, but useful, reading of Book I see Arieti.

[2] *Logoi* and papyrus rolls rarely correspond. For the division of Herodotus' work into *logoi*, see General Introduction, pp. 11 ff.

[3] On the *logos* of Croesus see, above all, Hellmann, *passim*, with a review of previous discussions; F. Stoessl, *Gymnasium*, LXVI (1959), 477–90; Huber, pp. 122–4; Wood, pp. 21–33; A. Heuss, *Hermes*, CI (1973), 385–419; A. C. Sheffield, 'Herodotus' Portrayal of Croesus', Diss. Stanford 1973; H. P. Stahl *YCS* XXIV (1975), 1–36; Erbse, pp. 180–202; Evans, *Explorer*, pp. 44–51; H. I. Flower, in M. A. Flower and M. Toher (eds.), *Georgica: Greek Studies in Honour of George Cawkwell* (*BICS* Suppl. 58), London 1991, pp. 57–77; Erbse, *Studien*, pp. 10–30.

Herodotus summarizes the essential information about Croesus, 'whom I know to have been the first to wrong the Greeks' (5,3), in order to justify the starting point of his enquiry: the cause (αἰτίη) of the war between Greeks and barbarians is after all an intention deliberately expressed by the author in the proem. He then passes on to a brief prologue on the Lydian kings preceding Croesus: the autochthonous kings and the Heraclid dynasty up to Candaules, and the first four Mermnadae (three of whom were the first to have hostile relations with the Greeks in Asia Minor, chs. 7–22). The fifth king is Croesus, whose reign ends with Cyrus' capture of Sardis (546 BC). In this prologue, that essentially presents a chronological list of reigns, some episodes of war embellished with anecdotes, and a report on the first Lydian offerings to the temple at Delphi, two famous tales stand out: the story of Candaules and Gyges (8–12) and the tale of Arion (24–5). From ch. 26 to ch. 94 the main subject is the reign of Croesus. Formally faithful to his declared intention, Herodotus starts with a brief account of Croesus' hostility and plans of expansion towards the Ionian coast and the nearby islands (26–8). Later on, however, this hostile relationship is no longer mentioned, and the Lydian king is presented on the contrary as a philhellene benefactor in friendly relations with Delphi, and seeking an alliance with the Greeks against the Persian menace. There is an obvious discrepancy between the proem and the first *logos*. Before passing on to the historical events of the conflict between Lydians and Persians, Herodotus inserts two other famous literary pieces: the dialogue between Croesus and Solon about human happiness (29–33), with its equally well-known tales about the Athenian Tellus (30) and the Argives Cleobis and Biton (31), and the tragic story of Atys and Adrastus (34–45). The moral of these stories is clearly premonitory and serves to outline the tragic figure of Croesus, whose unjustified arrogance changes into perplexity and suffering. The narrative then moves to the main theme: the Persian threat and Croesus' appeal to the Greeks and their oracles, handsomely rewarded with lavish offerings (46–55), and to their armies. Croesus seeks to secure the support of the two most important city-states, Athens and Sparta. This justifies the insertion of two pairs of digressions: one, very brief on the descent of the Athenians from the Pelasgians and the descent of the Peloponnesian Dorians from Hellen (56–8); and the second on Athens at the time of Pisistratus (59–64) and on Sparta in the mid-sixth century (65–8). At that time, only Sparta was able to promise the requested support (69–70). Thus reassured by the Delphic oracle and Sparta's promises, Croesus crosses with his troops the river Halys and invades Cappadocia. After an inconclusive battle, Croesus withdraws (71–8) and Cyrus invades Lydia, routs Croesus' army on the Hermus plain, and conquers Sardis (79–81). Croesus then asks the Spartans for the help they had promised; but precisely at that time the Spartans are engaged in a war with Argos over Thyrea (82–3). Sardis falls into Persian hands after only fourteen days of siege, and Croesus is made prisoner (84–5), placed on the pyre, and then pardoned, beginning his career as counsellor to the Persian king (89–91). With additional information on Croesus' offerings to the Greek oracles (92), and two chapters on the history and ethnography of Lydia (93–4), Herodotus' 'first *logos*' comes to an end.[4]

The second half of Book I (95–216) contains the *logos* of Cyrus' life, from birth to death, according to the plan briefly presented in the second proem.[5] This section can easily be subdivided into four quite separate *logoi*, each with its own digressions: the Medo-Persian *logos* (95–140), with a historical introduction on the kingdom of the Medes (95–106), the story of Cyrus' birth and childhood until his rise to power (107–30) and an ethnographic addendum on the religion and customs of the Persians (131–40). The second or 'Ionian' *logos* (141–76) picks up the thread of the main narrative of the Croesus *logos*,[6] and relates the history of the Persians' systematic subjection of Ionia, Caria, and Lycia; among its most important digressions are those concerning the Ionians, Aeolians, and Dorians in Asia Minor (142–51), the Phocaeans in the West (163–7), and the origins and customs of the Carians, Caunians, and Lycians (171–3). Then comes the Babylonian *logos* (177–200), with the account of the Persian conquest of Babylon (188–91) at its centre, inserted between a historical and topographical description of the city (177–87) and a section on the geography and ethnography of the city and district of Babylon (192–200). The book ends with the *logos* of the Massagetae (201–16); the story of Cyrus' last campaign and death (204–14) is also inserted between two geographical and ethnographic digressions. Chronologically, the first of the four *logoi* starts with the reign of Deïoces, founder of the kingdom of the Medes (dated by Herodotus to about 700 BC), and ends with Cyrus' deposition of the last king, Astyages, in 550 BC. The Ionian *logos* refers to the capture of Sardis (546 BC) and narrates the events of the following years. The Babylonian *logos* relates the city's capture in 539 BC, and the *logos* on the Massagetae extends to the death of Cyrus in the summer of 530 BC.

The history of the events in the thirty years between 560 and 530 BC occupies barely one-fifth of the book: the remainder is a mass of introductions or prologues, appendices, tales, didactic dialogues, digressions on constitutional history, on ethnography, and so on. This collection of material, at first sight accessory, is in fact the most characteristic and significant part of the book.[7] One cannot escape the impression that these numerous digressions on diverse topics and of varying length had already been collected by Herodotus in some form, before they were attached to the final version of the book. Some digressions are

[4] The second *logos* begins with τὸ ἐνθεῦτεν (95,1). Ch. 75,1 refers to 107 ff. which is said to belong to the τοῖσι ὀπίσω λόγοισι, i.e. to the *logos* of Cyrus. On the formal break between chs. 94 and 95, see S. Cagnazzi, *Hermes*, CIII (1975), 385 ff.

[5] On the *logos* about Cyrus see esp. R. Schubert, *Herodots Darstellung der Cyrussage*, Breslau 1900; H. C. Avery, *AJPh* XCIII (1972), 529–46; Wood, pp. 33–57; A. Cizek, *AC* XLIV (1975), 531–52; S. Accame, *MGR* VIII (1982), 1–43; Evans, *Explorer*, pp. 51–6; Erbse, *Studien*, pp. 31–44.

[6] ἄνειμι δὲ ἐπὶ τὸν πρότερον λόγον (140,3) takes us back to the beginning (a good example of *Ringkomposition*: see Beck) and introduces the Ionian *logos*: see Cagnazzi, *Hermes*, CIII (1975), 385 ff. and Powell, *History*, pp. 9 f.

[7] See R. V. Munson, 'Transitions in Herodotus: An Analysis Based Principally on the First Book', Diss. Penn., Philadelphia 1983.

independent *logoi*, artificially attached to other digressions or to the main
narrative by brief connective clauses. For example, the tale of Arion and the
dolphin, introduced by association through the passing mention of Periander of
Corinth; the dialogue of Croesus and Solon, closely linked to the dramatic story
of Atys and Adrastus, but with no serious ties to the main narrative; the digressions on the Pelasgians and the Dorians, on the tyrannies of Pisistratus, and on
Sparta's wars against Tegea; the account of Lydian antiquities, which seems to be
composed of spare material that Herodotus did not want to waste; the chapter on
Persian tribes, that abruptly and unjustifiably interrupts the story of Cyrus.
Sometimes the digressive material is better integrated into the main narrative,
as with the ethnographic chapters on the Carians and the Lycians, the topography
of Babylon, the ethnography of the Massagetae. But in these cases too the
integration is not complete. A particularly obvious case is the famous *aporia*
arising between chs. 5–6 and ch. 14. At 5,3 and 6,2–3 we are told that Croesus was
the first Asian king to harm the Greeks and make them subject; but at 14,4 we
read that Gyges too (καὶ οὗτος), and subsequently Ardys (15) and Alyattes
(16–22), had attacked, besieged, and occupied many Ionian cities. On this *aporia*
depends the entire relationship between chs. 1–5 and the *logos* of Croesus
(cf. General Introduction, pp. 13 f.). Various attempts have been made to solve
the problem, either by distinguishing between occasional plunderings with brief
occupations and permanent, tributary subjection, or by arguing that the verbal
forms οἶδα and ἴδμεν (5,3; 6,2) indicate verified knowledge based on evidence
that Herodotus claims to possess about Croesus' offences, but not about those of
his predecessors.[8] The problem, however, cannot be reduced to this: it is the
figure of Croesus himself which undergoes a transformation, without any explanation, from the hostile despot into a king devoted to Delphi, who converses
with Greek sages, becomes an ally of Sparta, and is preferred by the Greeks of Asia
Minor to the Persian conquerors. This contradiction, deriving from different
views of the facts held by Herodotus at different stages of the composition of the
book, has not been eliminated in its final version.[9] According to Herodotus' plan,
the *logos* of Croesus was supposed to have been the history of the 'first subjection'
of the Ionians to a barbarian king (92,1), and the *logos* of Cyrus the history of the
'second subjection' (169,2); actually, in both *logoi* the conflict between Greeks and
barbarians remains a side issue. The first book was not written all at once: it
resembles a colourful patchwork held together from beginning to end by a single

[8] See, above all, Focke, pp. 8 ff., Hellmann, pp. 25 ff., G. de Sanctis, *Scritti minori*, V, Rome 1983,
pp. 333–51; Maddalena, pp. 1–16; A. E. Wardman, *AJPh* LXXXII (1961), 133–50; Immerwahr,
pp. 17 ff.; M. E. White, *Phoenix*, XXIII (1969), 39–48; B. Shimron, *Eranos* LXXI (1973), 45–51; V. La
Bua, *MGR* V (1977), 18–22; Erbse, pp. 180–202; M. Lloyd, *LCM* IX 1 (1984), 11; H. I. Flower (see n. 3),
pp. 59–61; Arieti, pp. 12–14; G. B. Lanfranchi, in A. Aloni and L. De Finis (eds.), *Dall' Indo a Thule: i
Greci, i Romani, gli altri*, Trento 1996, pp. 89–94.

[9] Other signs of imperfect editing in Book I: 157,3, where the meaning of 'Branchidae' is explained,
although they have already been mentioned at 46,2 and 92,2; 162,1, where we are told that Harpagus,
the main character already known from 107–30, is a Mede.

thread. The real unity of the first book does not reside in its compilation, but in the ethical, historical, and philosophical spirit that pervades it.

The ἱστορίη reveals all its characteristic elements in the first book.[10] The most obvious is the quotation of sources, sometimes as a genuine need on the part of the enquirer, in other cases a mere literary convention of the genre of historiography. The importance that Herodotus attributes to personal observation accounts for the detailed descriptions of objects, monuments, and techniques, with accurate data concerning their material, measurements, and weight: Croesus' offerings at Delphi,[11] the furniture of the temple at Babylon (183,1–3), the tombs of Alyattes (93,2–3) and Nitocris (187,1–5), the walls and palaces of Ecbatana (98,3–6) and Babylon (178–83), hydraulic works (184–6), and the boats on the Euphrates (194). Of the three epigraphic texts mentioned in Book I (all seen by Herodotus), one is in Greek but a fake (51,3–4), and the other two are written in foreign languages for whose interpretation Herodotus depended on local guides (93,3; 187,1–5). Among written literary sources are the numerous oracular responses, in which the remarkable collection related to the story of Croesus stands out.[12] A poet, Archilochus of Paros, is apparently quoted in this book, if the passage is not an interpolation (12,2). Many ethnic and local oral sources are quoted: 'As they say'—the Corinthians, the Lesbians, the Lydians, the Spartans, the Phoenicians, the Persian λόγιοι, the Chaldaeans. Another typical characteristic of ἱστορίη is the citation of various accounts of the same event or problem, with or without preference: the Persian and the Phoenician version of the abduction of Io (2,1; 5,1–2); the choice of the least flattering version of Cyrus' birth and upbringing from among four known ones (95,1), and the 'most credible' account of Cyrus' death among the many that circulated (214,3); two versions of the origins of the form of government instituted by Lycurgus in Sparta (65,4); a Spartan and a Samian account of the fate of the crater sent to Croesus (70,2–3). Herodotus wants to protect his credibility and abstains from telling incredible stories (193,4). Some characteristic expressions (such as ὡς πυνθάνομαι, 22,2) imply reservations of the author concerning the reliability of the quoted source; in other places he distinguishes between things he 'knows for certain' and things about which he has no knowledge or for which he assumes no responsibility (140,1; 160,2; 172,1). In some cases, sources are explicitly criticized: Herodotus declares false the inscription on the sprinkler of Croesus (51,3–4), and refuses to accept the story about the canalization of the Halys (75,6); he likewise doubts the report of the Chaldaeans about what happens in the temple of Babylon (182,1). He shows little regard, if not true scepticism, concerning certain myths (5,3), which sometimes seem to him acceptable only in a rationalized

---

[10] In Book I the verb ἱστορέω is used in the general sense of 'to ask' (24,7; 122,1), 'make an enquiry' (56,1; 2,6; 61,2); εὑρίσκω means 'finding' the answer or the solution to the enquiry (56,2; 105,3; 139; etc.).

[11] See 50,2–51,5; 92,1; for offerings to other oracles, see 52; 92,1–2; offerings of Gyges and Midas, see 14,1–3; of Alyattes, see 25,2. For the Spartan crater, see 70,1.

[12] Verbatim quotations: 47,1; 55,1; 65,2; 66,1; 67,3; 85,1.

version (122,3). Other signs of ἱστορίη are the researches undertaken on his own initiative in order to resolve controversial problems such as the relative antiquity of the temples of Aphrodite at Ascalon, Cyprus, and Cythera (105,3), or whether the Carian tribute to Minos is a historical fact (171,2); logical arguments aimed at solving such debated questions as the canalization of the Halys (75,6), the language of the Pelasgians (57–8), the absence of Persian temples (131,1), the ethnic purity of the Ionians (146,1–3); the enquiry into the causes and the responsibility for the conflict between Asia and Europe (1–5), for the wars between Croesus and Cyrus (46,1; 73,1), between Sparta and Tegea (66,1), or the campaign against the Massagetae (204,2); the tendency to make ethnological comparisons: the sacred marriages at Babylon, Thebes, and Patara (182,1–2); the hydraulic works of the Babylonians and the Egyptians (193,1–2); the wedding customs of the Babylonians, the Enetans, and the Egyptians (196,1; 198); sacred prostitution at Babylon and Cyprus (199,5); the formulation of linguistic rules (139; 148,2); the moral or practical evaluation of certain exotic customs (137; 196–9); or advice given by 'wise counsellors' (170,1 and 3), and the naivety of the Athenians in archaic times (60,3).

These are all typical characteristics of Herodotus the researcher. Herodotus the storyteller offers in the first book five superb examples of his art.[13] They are all enjoyable tales with a didactic purpose, self-contained and complete, though different in structure and form of expression. The first example is the story of Gyges and Candaules (8–12), which some scholars have described as a three-character play in five scenes. The comic situation, the witty dialogues, the moral dilemma, and the tragic development of the events are fascinating. The tale of Arion (23–4) is centred both on the 'absolutely extraordinary event' of a dolphin rescuing the singer on its back, and on the sailors' discomfiture. The story of Cleobis and Biton (31) illustrates the ethical and religious idea of the greatest happiness of a painless death, attained by those who have performed a pious and admirable deed: it is their own mother who, in her gratitude and unawareness, paradoxically prays for 'the greatest happiness' for her sons. The parable of Atys and Adrastus (34–45) is composed of a series of interconnected dramatic dialogues illustrating the notion of νέμεσις, the retributive power that punishes excessive happiness and arrogance, and irrevocably creates a tragic situation in which Croesus unwittingly causes the death of his favourite son. Finally, the popular saga of Cyrus' birth (107–20), with its typically oriental flavour, and the continuous change of scene from palace to village, the rescue of the baby, the dramatic sequence of dialogues, and the recognition scenes, displays once again in this book Herodotus' narrative taste, his fascination for the miraculous, his curiosity before the unexpected, and his ethical and religious preoccupations.

To the storytelling part belong anecdotes about oracles, dreams and portents, and didactic dialogues. Oracular literature is well represented in the first book

---

[13] See Erbse, *Studien*, pp. 133–45.

with fourteen Delphic responses, of which six are quoted verbatim;[14] one Theban oracle of Amphiaraus (49) and three oracles of the Branchidae at Miletus (157,3–158,1; 159,1–4). Prominent in this type of literature are the collections of the oracular responses for Croesus (five) and for Sparta (four). They are almost always clearly composed *ex eventu*; even in the few cases where some lines may pre-date the events told, their adaptation to the historical context of Croesus or Sparta is clearly a historiographical construct, which should perhaps be attributed to Herodotus himself. The predominance of Delphic oracles may create the impression that Herodotus also had propagandistic aims in favour of the greatest oracular centre of the Hellenic world. But, apart from the fact that Amphiaraus' oracle also turned out to be true (49), it is most probably the choice of sources, rather than Herodotus' personal intention, which arouses suspicions of this sort. Herodotus himself, though he believed in oracles, took pleasure in telling stories about fallacious or controversial responses, wrong interpretations, and apologetic corrections on the part of the oracles themselves (91; 159,4); he also enjoyed various other anecdotes, such as Croesus' famous testing of the Greek oracles (46–9), or the clever plan carried out by Aristodicus of Cyme (159). The effect of these stories on the beliefs of the ordinary man may in fact have been deleterious, regardless of the piety of Herodotus and his personal intentions. The function of dream-stories is similar: in the first book they predict the future of three great dynasties, those of Croesus (34,1–2), Astyages (107,1; 108,1), and Cyrus (209,1). Portents too have a similar role: one predicts the birth of a tyrant (59,1–3)—a type of event predicted elsewhere by oracles (e.g. at V 92β,2–3) or by dreams (e.g. VI 131,2); other portents predict misfortune (175), or reveal the gods' anger for some human wrong-doing, and invariably lead to the consultation of oracles (167,1–2; 175,4–5).

The didactic dialogues and speeches are on a higher intellectual level;[15] for example, the dialogues of Croesus and Solon (29–33), Croesus and Sandanis (71), Croesus and Cyrus after the pyre episode (86–90), and before the crossing of the Araxes (207). They all present the role of the 'wise counsellor' in the practical as well as the didactic sense of the term (see note on 27,2). The theological basis of these dialogues is that, within the limits of preordained fate, human beings do have a certain measure (though more illusory than real) of free will, thanks to which in some cases certain marginal aspects of the preordained course of historical events can eventually be affected. Hence moral advice, and sometimes even practical advice (which is not necessarily always right: see e.g. 207,5), may be of relative use. In such dialogues Herodotus summarizes his theological principles and his philosophical and historical reflections, the very elements which unify the first book and the work as a whole—above all the tragic conception of life and history. Everything is predestined (see especially 91,1–3) and man's life is pure chance (32,4); in a world ruled by 'jealous and troublesome' gods, today's apparent

---

[14] For the oracles in the first book see Crahay, pp. 182–208; Defradas, pp. 208–28; Kirchberg, pp. 11–33 and *passim*; J. Elayi, *IA* XIII (1978), 93–118.

[15] See Deffner, Heni, Hohti, and Lang.

happiness can easily become the extreme misery of tomorrow. Thus everything in human affairs is relative, transient, and unstable. Transitory 'good luck' must therefore be distinguished from true and proper definitive 'happiness'. The 'lucky' man ($\epsilon\vec{v}\tau v\chi\acute{\eta}s$) can become 'happy' ($\check{o}\lambda\beta\iota os$) even if he is not rich, provided he reaches the end of his life without attracting the gods' attention and provoking their envy, conserving to the maximum the material and social advantages and satisfactions which are within human reach (32). To achieve this, men possess on the one hand the intellectual ability to investigate the will of the gods and decode their signs (oracles, dreams, portents), on the other the moral strength to refrain from *hybris*, from the excessive confidence in one's own happiness and success; and from the temptation to transgress the limits imposed by fate.[16]

The relativity of the human condition—a tenet of Delphic theology, but also a notion of 'secular' archaic wisdom—is expressed, in the field of historical and philosophical thought, through a cyclical tripartite conception of the history of individuals and states: rise, climax, and decline. These three stages correspond to a certain extent, though not exactly, to the tragic triad $\check{v}\beta\rho\iota s$—$\kappa\acute{o}\rho os$—$\check{a}\tau\eta$. Herodotus declares at the beginning of the book (5,3–4) that he wishes to treat in the same way the history of cities great and small, since each has had, has, or will have its moment of prosperity and decline. For Herodotus, the history of a people, such as the Medes, begins with their gaining of independence and ends with the loss of that same independence. Croesus instructs Cyrus to beware 'the cycle of human affairs' which, by its revolving, prevents the same people being always fortunate (207,2; cf. General Introduction, p. 37). It is chiefly in this light that Croesus and Cyrus become two great paradigmatic figures: one foreshadows the other and both foreshadow the later great Persian kings and other minor Greek and Eastern despots.[17] The story of Croesus and Cyrus becomes a parable: Herodotus uses it to illustrate the meaning of universal history envisaged as the continuous repetition of human and political situations, which are morally analogous and uniformly governed by an internal cyclical mechanism. On this reading the first book gives the impression that Herodotus was not originally interested in the conflict between the Greeks and the barbarians and its causes (despite the opening sentence and the first five chapters), but rather in the rise, climax, and decline of the great oriental monarchies, Assyria and Babylon, Lydia, Media, and Persia. In particular, Herodotus wants to expound 'how the Persians came to dominate Asia' (95,1). Persia is actually the superpower of his time, the one the Greeks had to face and fight in the period which is the heart of his work. The historian takes the occasion to note the first signs of its decadence. In the first book there is an undeniable link between the cyclic thought, the choice of historical material, and the structure of the main narrative. Herodotus relates Croesus' initial great conquests in Asia Minor, sets him up against Solon at the climax of his success, and, after recording his premonitory personal misfortune, concludes with his military defeat and the end of his reign. Regarding Cyrus, he tells the story of his birth and upbringing till his rise to power; the culmination of his success is the

---

[16] For $\mu o\hat{\iota}\rho a$ in the sense of 'fate', see note on 91,3.   [17] See Wood, pp. 21 ff., 25 ff.

conquest of Babylon, the richest and most wonderful city; his decline is the mistaken campaign against the Massagetae and the events leading to his death.

It is not difficult to understand why the territorial expansionism of a state posed for Herodotus an ethical problem, and provoked historical and philosophical questions. First, expansionism implies violation of natural and universally respected boundaries between peoples and countries: Croesus crosses the Halys and invades Cappadocia, Cyrus crosses the Araxes and invades the country of the Massagetae. In this respect too, the two main protagonists of the first book foreshadow those who will come after them: Darius crossing the Danube, Xerxes the Hellespont, Mardonius the Asopus.[18] These are all acts of *hybris*, in the sense of transgression and offence against nature and international law, and their function is to prepare the reader for the impending catastrophe. Secondly, excessive territorial expansionism and accumulation of great riches give rise to luxury and effeminacy; hence the risks for peoples softened by luxury in waging war against uncouth, primitive peoples like Cyrus' Persians, when compared to Croesus' Lydians and Nabonidus' Babylonians; or the Massagetae, the Ethiopians, the Scythians, and the Greeks (cf. note on 71,2) in comparison to the Persians themselves. It is worth pointing out that the contrast between decadent and primitive peoples in Herodotus has nothing to do with the anti-thesis between East and West or between despotism and freedom. Croesus and Cyrus are oriental despots who attack other Eastern peoples. The assaulted or conquered peoples offer resistance, rebel, hasten to strike agreements, or emigrate, or commit collective suicide, always in order to safeguard or achieve some form of 'freedom' (ἐλευθερίη), in the sense of full or partial political independence from foreign rule. The examples are the Medes, Persians, Ionians, Milesians, Phocaeans, Xanthians, and Massagetae.[19] Herodotus makes no distinction here between the behaviour of Greeks and barbarians: it is the human responses which interest him. He thinks, however, that Pisistratus' tyranny is the cause of Athens' weakness (59,1; 64,3; cf. V 66,1; 78), whereas in Deïoces' tyranny he perceives the origin of the Medes' universal supremacy (95–101). One may suspect that Herodotus judged the historical function of tyranny in Greece and the East by different criteria. The Medes initially chose 'freedom' in the sense of political independence from Assyrian rule and also in the sense of a wholly non-tyrannical form of government. However, in order to overcome the anarchy (ἀνομίη) that followed, they elected a king (95,2 ff.), as if soon becoming convinced that it was impossible to govern the country without a king, whether local or foreign.[20] In Greece a 'good' (εὐνομίη at Sparta: 65,2) or 'free' (ἐλευθερίη at Athens: 62,1) regime is possible and is actually necessary if the Greek city is to become a hegemonic power; on the contrary, in Asia, or among the barbarians at large, such regimes are unstable, and in order to

---

[18] Ibid., pp. 25 ff.

[19] Medes: 95,2; Persians: 126,6 and 210,2; Ionians: 6,3 and 170,2; Milesians: 141,4; Phocaeans: 164,2; Xanthians: 176,1–2; Massagetae: 206,1–3.

[20] Cf. what Herodotus says about the Egyptians at II 147,2.

achieve hegemony what a state needs is a national, unitary monarchy (cf., with respect to the Thracians, V 3,1).

Herodotus' theology clearly influenced the final version of the first book. The principle of predestination creates an explicit link between Gyges' usurpation of power and the fate of his descendant in the fifth generation, Croesus, who pays the penalty for Gyges' crime (13,2; 91,1–3). The moral link between ὕβρις and ἄτη connects the dialogue of Croesus and Solon to the drama of Atys and Adrastus, as well as to Croesus' words on the pyre and afterwards, and to his last dialogue with Cyrus on the banks of the Araxes (207). These are premeditated editorial connections. Admittedly, they do not succeed in disguising the various phases in Herodotus' work, of the collection of material, the composition of independent *logoi*, and the final editing; but they do convey a clear sense of unity in the book at the level of historical and philosophical thought, permit a glimpse of Herodotus at work, and emphasize the characteristic features of his creative talent.

The problem of the reliability and the historical value of the first book belongs to the more complex issue of 'Herodotus the historian' (see General Introduction, pp. 14 ff.). Once again, it is important to make a clear distinction between the sources that Herodotus actually uses and those he quotes, which are sometimes fictitious. It would be absurd to dismiss Herodotus' direct observations as a traveller and 'tourist' as a source for his detailed descriptions mentioned above; but direct observation is often coupled with oral information obtained from incompetent guides. For obvious reasons, the information he collected in Ionia, Delphi, Athens, and Sparta seems more reliable than what he was told in Babylon. In a few precise cases it has been possible to identify Herodotus' oral sources: for example, the Harpagids at Xanthus are supposed to have been the source for the story about Harpagus and Cyrus and the Persian conquest of Asia Minor; officials at the satrap Tritantaichmes' court apparently provided some current information about the resources of mid-fifth-century Babylon under Persian rule; local informants in South Italy, at Velia, Posidonia, Rhegium, could have told Herodotus the stories about the Phocaeans in the West. Other types of local source could have been used for the ethnographies of Lydia and Persia. On the other hand, a few tales seem to be taken from oriental popular sagas, readapted and rationalized either by Herodotus himself or by a learned Greek predecessor. To Herodotus' written sources belong the oracles, the Greek poets, and eventually authors of Περσικά and Σκυθικά (Hecataeus, Dionysius of Miletus, Xanthus of Lydia, Hellanicus of Lesbos). When compared with Eastern written sources—Assyrian, Babylonian, Persian, or biblical—or with archaeological data, or with other Greek sources (in the first place Xanthus' Λυδιακά and Ctesias' Περσικά), Herodotus' credibility emerges almost undamaged. From many aspects, his version is the best we have and has resisted respectably the attacks of its critics; some obvious mistakes can be attributed to his informers or to misunderstandings. Herodotus' Achaemenid genealogy corresponds to that of Persian inscriptions. The chronologies of the Mermnads and Median kings extend far beyond the declared limits of Herodotus' planned *spatium historicum* but are, nevertheless, not at all fantastic and can be made to correspond, although with

some serious difficulties and some amendments, to the chronological grid reconstructed from Assyian and Babylonian sources. Nothing of the sort would be
thinkable for the chronologies of a Ctesias. There are no signs of bad faith in
Herodotus' first book, except for the conventional fabrication of some fictional
sources (e.g. the Persian λόγιοι at 1,1, and the Corinthian and Lesbian versions
about Arion at 23,1), that, as has already been noted, were not aimed at deceiving
the public.[21] The most essential fact is that without Herodotus, we would lack a
historical frame into which we could fit the isolated pieces of information that
can be obtained from Sargon's annals, the oracular consultations of Esarhaddon,
the chronicles of Nabopolassar and Nabonidus, the cylinders of Sippar and of
Cyrus. Whether true or *ben trovato*, the material that Herodotus assembles,
organizes, and presents in the first book is the most ancient extant attempt to
write a 'history', in the modern sense of the term, of the great oriental monarchies
of the sixth century BC.

Summary of Book I

1–5	Proem: the author, the contents, and the aims of the work.
1–5,2	Mythical stories about the origins of the conflict between Asia and Europe (the rapes of Io, Europa, Medea, and Helen).
5,3	The author declares that he wants to begin his history with the first historical person to have wronged the Greeks (Croesus).
6–94	*The 'first logos'* (or the Lydian *logos*, or the *logos* of Croesus)
6	Introduction to Croesus and his relations with the Greeks.
7–25	The Lydian kings before Croesus.
7	The Lydian dynasty descending from Heracles.
8–13	Story of Gyges and Candaules; Gyges usurps power, but obtains recognition of his rule from Delphi; end of the dynasty descending from Heracles.
14–22	The Mermnadae and their relations with the Greek cities of Asia Minor; Gyges (14), Ardys (15), Sadyattes (16), Alyattes and the war against Miletus (16–22).
23–4	Digression: the tale of Arion and the dophin.
25	End of the reign of Alyattes; the king's offerings to Delphi.
26–8	Beginning of the reign of Croesus, the last king of the Mermnadae; war against Ephesus, plan to invade the Greek islands in the eastern Aegean, subjection of all the people in Asia Minor west of the river Halys.
29–33	Dialogue of Croesus and Solon on the problem of human happiness.
34–45	The story of Atys, son of Croesus, who was accidentally killed by Adrastus, a Phrygian guest; Croesus mourns his son for two years.
46–70	Croesus plans the war against Cyrus, who has become king of Persia and has put an end to the empire of the Medes.
46–9	Croesus tests several Greek oracles and the Libyan oracle of Ammon; the Delphic oracle and the oracle of Amphiaraus turn out to be true.

---

[21] See General Introduction, pp. 20 ff.

COMMENTARY

Proem. In the strict sense of the word, this comprises only the opening sentence; in a wider sense it includes also chs. 1–5. On the proem and the problem of the work's composition see Introduction, pp. 1 and 7 ff. For discussion of the opening sentence see G. Nagy, *Arethusa*, XX (1987), 175–84, with bibl., and *Pindar's Homer: The Lyric Possessions of an Epic Past*, Baltimore–London 1990, chs. 8–11 (esp. pp. 217–49); Lateiner, pp. 6–17; J. Herington, *Arion*, III 1 (1991), 5–16; R. Oswald, *GB* XXI (1995), 47–59.

1. Ἡροδότου...: Herodotus formally introduces himself by stating his name and country. This form of introduction is already attested in archaic literature: see 'Theognis of Megara', 22–3 Young; 'Alcmaeon of Croton', 24 B 1 DK; possibly 'Heracleitos of Ephesus', 22 B 1 DK; and, of course, 'Hecataeus of Miletus', *FGrHist* 1 F 1. After Herodotus, it was used by 'Thucydides of Athens' (I 1,1); and in Roman times by Herodotus' fellow countryman 'Dionysius of Halicarnassus' (*Ant. Rom.* I 8,4), 'Josephus of Jerusalem' (*Bell. Iud.* I 3), and 'Appian of Alexandria' (*Praef.* 15). Some Greek historians were reluctant to reveal their name and country on the ground that Homer had not revealed his, and Roman historians usually did not introduce themselves formally at all. See Marincola, pp. 271–5. Archaic poets like Phocylides and Demodocus introduce themselves without an ethnic. For an appealing explanation of the origin of such conventions see L. Koenen, *ZPE* XCVII (1993), 95–6. On proems in ancient historiography see L. Porciani, *La forma proemiale. Storiographia e pubblico nel mondo antico*, Pisa 1997 (with bibl.).   Ἁλικαρνησσέος: this is the unanimous reading of the manuscript tradition and the original one according to Plutarch, though in his time many already 'changed' it to Θουρίου (*Mor.* 604f; see also *Mor.* 868a; and Photius, *Bibliotheca* 190, 148b Henry). The reading Θουρίου was in fact already known in the 4th cent. BC (Arist. *Rhet.* 1409a34), while Ἁλικαρνησσέος, with phonetic variations, prevailed only in the 1st cent. BC (Strabo, Dionysius of Halicarnassus). That Θουρίου was the original reading is a famous thesis of Jacoby (coll. 205 ff.), accepted by Pasquali (pp. 312 f.) and others, and Legrand went as far as accepting it for his edition of the text, thus originating a controversy: see L. Th. Lefort, *AC* III (1934), 203–8 (with reply by Legrand, *REA* XXXVI (1934), 407–10; cf. A. Colonna, *Athenaeum*, XXVIII (1940), 11–25). I unhesitatingly prefer over indirect testimonies the reading which prevailed in antiquity and was unanimously accepted in the middle ages. See, among other discussions, Erbse, pp. 146–53; V. J. Matthews, *Panyassis of Halicarnassus*, Leiden 1974, pp. 7 f.; L. A. Okin, *EMC* XXVI (1982), 21–33; T. S. Brown, *EMC* XXVII (1983), 5 f.; J. Dillery, *CQ* XLII (1992), 525–8. For Herodotus' biography see Introduction, pp. 1 ff.   ἱστορίης: see Introduction, pp. 8 ff.   ἀπόδεξις: from ἀποδείκνυμι = to point out, demonstrate, perform, etc.; here, the sense is 'publication' (oral publication? see Hunter, p. 227 and n. 1), or 'performance' (cf. ἔργα... ἀποδεχθέντα in this proem, and I 207,7; II 101,1; 148,2) rather than 'witness,' 'proof' (VIII 101,2; C. W. Hedrick, in *Nomodeiktes*, pp. 23 ff.) or 'demonstration' (Lateiner, p. 10). A derivation from ἀποδέκομαι = 'receive' has been suggested by H. B. Rosén (*Glotta*, LXXI (1993), 146–53; see H. Erbse's objections ibid. LXXIII (1995/6), 64–7); for the usage of ἀποδείκνυμι, etc., see Drexler, pp. 11–14; cf. I 16,2; 59,4; 174,1; 176,1.   τὰ γενόμενα...: see Introduction, pp. 8 ff. The main idea of the sentence is clear: Herodotus wants to save from oblivion or from all-devouring time what deserves to be remembered; in a still predominantly oral culture this task mainly consists in writing down memories and testimonies.   ἐξίτηλα: cf. V 39,2 (in the genealogical sense of becoming extinct; see H. Pelliccia, *YCS* XXIX (1992), 74–80). The adjective is first attested in Aeschylus' *Niobe* (fr. 162 Radt). The meaning here is 'fading away,' 'evanescent'; cf. e.g. Xen. *Oec.* 10,3; Paus. X 38,9; Nagy, op. cit., p. 225.   μεγάλα τε καὶ θωμαστά: The 'greatness of the subject' became a *topos* in Greek historiography; cf. Marincola, pp. 34–43, and see VII 20,2, on Xerxes' invasion greater than all the previous ones. Not only buildings and constructions are worthy of admiration (A. Raubitschek, *REA* XLI (1939), 217–22), but also great battles, conquests, legislations, etc. Herodotus is the 'prototype of the historian who always marvels' (A. Momigliano, *Alien Wisdom*, Cambridge 1975, p. 25). In addition to the bibl. quoted in the Introduction, p. 15, n. 39, see H. Barth, *Klio*, L (1968), 93–110; Hartog, pp. 243–9 = ET pp. 230–7.   τὰ μὲν...: the intention of impartiality towards the ἔργα of all peoples is implied. On Herodotus' 'philobarbarism' see Introduction, pp. 44 ff.   ἀκλεᾶ: 'fame' or 'glory' is the aim of Homeric epic (see e.g. *Il.* IX 189; *Od.* I 338): in this respect the historian is the heir of the bard: see Introduction, p. 9.   τά τε ἄλλα: 'apart from all this, and in particular', see Drexler, pp. 9 ff.; cf. I 174,4; 193,5. For the tedious controversy on the meaning of this expression see F. Stoessl, *Gymnasium*, LVI (1959), 489; F. Bömer, ibid. LVII (1960), 202.   αἰτίην: here in the meaning of blame, offence, responsibility, etc; of a king who, with his actions, provokes reactions, retaliations (or retributions), revenge, etc. For Herodotus, Croesus is the first offender (5,3), for he began, in recent times, the series of historical conflicts between Asia and Europe. δι' ἣν αἰτίην also introduces the first digression (1–5; see 1,1–2) dedicated to mutual accusations of responsibility. With that the problem of causality in Herodotus, which is far more complex, is not exhausted, see Introduction, pp. 40 ff.; cf. I 73,1 and 204,2 with note on 73,1–2. On this passage see, in particular, Pagel (with Maddalena, pp. 56 ff.); H. R. Immerwahr, *TAPhA* LXXXVII (1956), 247–51; Bornitz, pp. 139–63; Huber, pp. 75–9; P. Hohti, *Arctos*, X (1976), 37–48; Arieti, pp. 1–7. See also the bibl. quoted at 29,1.

1–5. This first digression deals with the so-called Persian (1–4) and Phoenician (5) accounts of the mythical origins of the conflict between Asia and Europe, these continents being represented in the 5th cent. by the Persians and the Greeks respectively. Herodotus ends this section with a clarification of the purpose and method of his work. The main theme is 'blame' (αἰτίη), or 'offence' (ἀδικίη), and

retribution (τίσις): see preceding note. The Phoenicians' abduction of Io is
avenged by the Greeks' abduction of Europa, after which the two sides are
equal. With the third abduction, that of Medea, the Greeks become once more
the offenders, while the fourth, that of Helen, is supposed to be its justified Asian
'retribution'. With the last episode in the series, the Trojan war, responsibility
definitely rests on the Greeks, since they overreacted with a military invasion of
Asia (this is the first 'historical' act of transgression, by which the natural
or divinely sanctioned borders between the two continents are violated: the
'retribution' will be Xerxes' invasion). All the elements in this series of events
are drawn from Greek mythology; but whereas in the original versions of
the myths the responsibility ultimately rests with the gods, this version is rationalized and politicized, and could serve as the narrative or probatory part of
a Greek 'sophistic' apologetic speech composed in favour of Asia and based
on the legal criteria of Greek international law or customs of retribution
(cf. H. J. Rose, *CQ* XXXIV (1940), 79; on the rape-motif in Greek mythology
see M. L. Lang, *PAPhS* CXVI (1972), 410–14; on rape in Herodotus see
T. Harrison, in S. Deacy and K. F. Pierce (eds.), *Rape in Antiquity*, London
1997, pp. 185–208). The supposed Persian and Phoenician 'sources' which
Herodotus quotes in these chapters are thus pure invention and a literary
convention (cf. Fehling, pp. 50–7; Verdin, pp. 93–5). The widespread view that
Aristophanes parodies these chapters in the *Acharnians* (524 ff.) lacks a serious
basis: see Introduction, p. 51. On women and their influence in history in
Herodotus see A. Tourraix *DHA* II (1976), 369–90; Lateiner, pp. 135–40 and
the bibl. on p. 264, n. 25.

1,1. οἱ λόγιοι: 'experts of *logoi*', 'learned'. In Herodotus, and in later authors, the
term regularly indicates barbarian wise men (II 3,1 and 77,1; IV 46,1). Pindar
distinguishes between 'wise men' and 'bards' (*Pyth.* 1,183) although both have in
common the task of glorifying great deeds; see Nagy, op. cit., pp. 221–4; Evans,
Explorer, pp. 95–9. This is the first instance of Herodotus, quoting an 'epichoric'
(native or national) source; among many examples in Book I, see e.g. 5,2
(Phoenicians), 23 (Corinthians and Lesbians), 87,1 (Lydians), 105,4 (Scythians),
171,5 (Cretans and Carians), 174,5 (Cnidians), 181,5 (Chaldeans). For a full list
of passages in the *Histories* see Jacoby, pp. 397–9; on the term οἱ ἐπιχώριοι see
78,3 and note. Thucydides doubted the validity of native sources (I 20,1),
usually highly appreciated by later Greek historians; see Fehling, pp. 162–4;
Marincola, pp. 283–5. The Persian and Phoenician 'sources' quoted in this
chapter are a pure narrative invention of Herodotus himself or his source; see
Fehling, pp. 50–9. For the hypothesis that the source was Phrynichus' *Phoenician
Women* see A. E. Raubitschek, *Tyche*, VIII (1993), 143–4.   **Φοίνικας:** Herodotus believed that the Phoenicians originally came from the coast of the Red Sea
(the Indian Ocean; more specifically the Arabic coasts, the Persian Gulf and the
Suez Gulf: see L. Casson, *The Periplus Maris Erythraei*, Princeton 1989;
A. B. Bosworth, *Alexander and the East*, Oxford 1996, pp. 66–70), whence they
supposedly emigrated to settle on the Phoenician coast (cf. VII 89,2), where they

had founded Tyre '2,300 years ago' (II 44,2), i.e. around 2750 BC. Herodotus' contemporary Dionysius of Miletus also knew of a region on the Red Sea called Φοινίκη (*FGrHist* 687 F 4). According to a historian of Alexander the Great (Androsthenes of Thasos: *FGrHist* 711 F 2), Tyre and Aradus were 'colonies', 'foundations' of two cities with the same name in the Persian Gulf; see also Justin XVIII 3,1–5. Modern scholars regard this theory with extreme scepticism. Phoenician civilization did not develop before 1000 BC: see J. O. Thompson, *CR* XLI (1927), 57; R. Dussaud, *RHR* CVIII (1933), 5–49; J. D. Muhly, *Berytus*, XIX (1970), 24 ff.; B. Couroyer, *Revue biblique*, LXXX (1973), 264–76. On the Phoenicians in Herodotus see S. F. Bondì, in *Hérodote et les peuples non-Grecs*, pp. 255–300. On Phoenicia and the Phoenicians in the West see M. E. Aubet, *The Phoenicians in the West: Politics, Colonies, and Trade*, Cambridge 2001². For ancient Phoenicians and modern ideologies see Bernal, ch. 8.   ἐπὶ τήνδε τὴν θάλασσαν: the Mediterranean, also called 'this sea' (IV 39,2; 41; V 49,6). Historic Phoenicia was called Canaan in the local language; the biblical ethnic name and toponym were known to Hecataeus (Χνᾶ): cf. *FGrHist* 1 F 21 and 272. It extended along the coast of Lebanon and Palestine between Aradus (Arvad) in the North and Dora, beyond Mt Carmel, in the South. In Herodotus' time Phoenicia, together with Syria-Palestine and Cyprus, belonged to the fifth Persian satrapy (III 91,1 and note). Herodotus knew its main cities: Sidon, Tyre, Aradus.   αὐτίκα…: in fact, Phoenician expansion into the Mediterranean did not begin much earlier than 1000 BC. Phoenician trade, well known to the Greeks already in Homer's time, is mentioned by Herodotus also elsewhere (III 6,1; 107,2; 111,2). Herodotus is familiar with their bold sea journeys (for the circumnavigation of Africa, cf. IV 42,2–4) and their war fleet, which participated actively in the repression of the Ionian revolt and the expedition of Xerxes.   ναυτιλίῃσι μακρῇσι: cf. 161,1 (on the Phocaeans).

2. Ἄργος: Herodotus believed that the Phoenicians had settled in various areas of Greece in mythical times (Cadmus and the Gephyraei in Boeotia: II 49,3; V 57,1–2; other descendants of Cadmus at Thera: IV 147,4–5), and that they left traces of their presence in some temples (in Cythera: I 105,3 and see note on 105,9; in Thasos: II 44,4 and VI 47,1–2). These connected them with the introduction to Greece of various crafts and the art of writing (V 58,1). Modern scholarship has usually denied, though not always on purely scientific grounds, the historicity of permanent Phoenician settlements in Greece and the Aegean (see the bibl. quoted above); the problem surfaced again in 1964 when a storage of Babylonian seals was found in Thebes. The existence of trading and cultural connections since the early 1st millenium BC has always been admitted: see T. F. R. G. Brown, *CAH*² III 3, pp. 5–7. The image of a Phoenician ship selling goods on the Argive coast reflects the actual barter trade still continuing in other areas even in historical times (IV 196). Homer's usage of the term Ἀργεῖοι as well as Ἀχαιοί, for 'Greeks', and the presentation of Agamemnon as the ruler of 'the whole of Argos', may have easily suggested that, in ancient times, the Argolid was the most important district of Greece. Herodotus, who knew nothing of 'Mycenaean civilization' as we understand it today, rather displays here his

Homeric erudition.   πέμπτῃ δὲ ἢ ἔκτῃ ἡμέρῃ: on 'typical numbers' in Herodotus' narrative art see Fehling, pp. 216–39.
3. ᾽Ιοῦν: for the myth of Io see K. Dowden, *Death and the Maiden*, London 1989,
ch. 6; N. Yalouris, *LIMC* V 1 1990, pp. 661–78; M. Davidson, in D. C. Pozzi and
J. M. Wickersham (eds.), *Myth and the Polis*, Ithaca–London 1991, pp. 49–63. The
myth which Herodotus rationalizes is differently treated in the Epic Cycle, in
Aeschylus, and in a dithyramb of Bacchylides; see the criticism of Plutarch, *Mor.*
856d–e. On Io in Herodotus cf. II 41,2. In the chronology of Greek myth, Io
belongs to the first generation of Zeus' rule, i.e. centuries earlier than the heroic
age and the historical travels of the Phoenicians.

2,1. οὐκ ὡς Ἕλληνες: in the original version Io, turned by Hera into a white cow,
fleeing a gadfly, finally arrived in Egypt, where she regained her human shape and
gave birth to Epaphus, whom Herodotus and others identified with Apis (II 153;
III 27,1). Lycophron (*Alexandra* 1291 ff.) follows Herodotus: see S. West, *JEA* LXX
(1984), 151 ff. and the bibl. quoted above.   οὐ γὰρ ἔχουσι . . .: this unnecessary
parenthetical sentence is simply an effective device of narrative art, tending to
increase the author's credibility: see Fehling, pp. 53–4.   Εὐρώπην: daughter of
Agenor (or Phoenix), sister of Cadmus, later mother of Minos and Sarpedon (I
173,2; IV 45,4–5; 147,4); for bibl., esp. on the iconography, see M. Robertson,
LIMC IV 1 1988, pp. 76–92. This is a rationalized version of the original Cretan
myth according to which Europa arrived at Crete riding the back of a bull-shaped
Zeus. For the etymology of Europa see L. Deroy, *RIO* XI (1959), 1–22;
Dombrowski. According to Herodotus' chronology (see II 145,4) the abduction
of Europa would be dated to about 2100 BC; this, however, does not agree with
VII 171,1, where Minos (assuming he should be identified with Europa's son:
I 173,2) belongs to the third generation before the Trojan war, as in Homer
(roughly 1340–130 BC, according to Herodotus' chronology; see II 145,4
and the note on 4,2–3).

2. καταπλώσαντες: Herodotus refers here to the Argonaut expedition to
Colchis (modern Georgia), set in the generation before the Trojan war (i.e.
*c.*1300 BC according to Herodotus' chronological system). The μακρὴ νηῦς (a
'warship': cf. 70,2; V 81,3; VII 48,2; VII 21,1) is the legendary Argo, a fifty-oared
ship (penteconter). 'Colchian Aia' is the legendary city of Aietes, king of the
Colchians. The Phasis (cf. 104,1, etc.), modern Rioni, was thought to connect the
Black Sea to the Ocean (see note on 202,4) and to separate Europe from Asia.
See O. Lordkipanidze, *LIMC* VII, 1 1994, pp. 368–9; P. Dräger *DNP* I (1997),
306–7 and 1066–9; Braund, ch. 1.   διαπρηξαμένους . . .: the accomplishment
of the challenges set by Aietes and the recovering of the golden
fleece.   Μηδείην: granddaughter of Helios and daughter of Aietes, a witch
or immortal demigoddess. The story of the abduction of Medea by Jason was
already known to Hesiod (*Theog.* 992–9), Pindar (*Pyth.* IV,9 ff.), and Pherecydes
(*FGrHist* 3 F 31–2; 105–13). Herodotus possibly knew the story also through
Euripides' famous play, staged in 431 BC. In the traditional version she is not
abducted but willingly leaves her country together with the Argonauts, motivated

by her love for Jason (as Io does in the Phoenician version: 5,2). In Herodotus, Medea is also the eponym of the Medes (VII 62,1). On Medea see M. Schmidt, *LIMC* VI 1 1992, pp. 386–98; on the Colchians in Herodotus cf. I 104,1; II 104–5, etc.   αἰτέειν τε δίκας ... ἔδοσάν σφι δίκας: cf. 3,1–2. These formulas are common in Herodotus. They express his own moral conception on retribution (see Introduction, pp. 38 ff.). Cf. D. Lateiner, *CQ* XXX (1980), 30 ff.

3,1. δευτέρῃ δὲ λέγουσι γενεῇ: the sons of the Argonauts participated in the Trojan war. From Homer onwards, Helen's abduction was traditionally seen as the achnowledged 'cause' of the Trojan war. However, in Book II Herodotus prefers the 'Egyptian' (or Stesichorean) version of the myth, according to which Helen never went to Troy but stayed in Egypt, until after the war Menelaus came to take her home (II 113–20). So, in a sense, Herodotus rehabilitated Helen, as did his contemporary Gorgias of Leontini in his *Encomium of Helen* (82 B 11 DK); see H. Pelliccia, *YCS* XXIX (1992), 63–84. Herodotus also knew that Helen had been abducted earlier by Theseus (IX 73,2), and that a temple at Therapne, near Sparta, was dedicated to her (VI 61,3). The messengers sent to Troy to reclaim Helen were Odysseus and Menelaus. The abduction of Helen was the subject of sophistic treatises in the late 5th and early 4th cents. See L. B. Ghali-Kahil, *Les Enlèvements et le retour d'Hélène dans les textes et les documents figurés*, Paris 1955; Long, pp. 39–50; L. Kahil, *LIMC* IV 1 (1988), 498–563.

4,1. Ἕλληνας ... γενέσθαι: Herodotus mentions the Trojan war also at II 145,4 and dates it to about 1280–1270 BC; cf. VII 20, 2 ff. and 43, where the Trojan war is explicitly compared to Xerxes' expedition. In Herodotus' time the moral problem of the Trojan war was a live issue in the Athens of the Delian league and the Peloponnesian wars, as the Trojan plays of Euripides reveal. Plutarch, *Mor.* 856 f. was shocked by reading in this chapter that 'the noblest and greatest exploits of Greece' were just 'an act of folly caused by a worthless woman'. See F. J. Groten, *Phoenix*, XVII (1963), 79–87; J. W. Neville, *G&R* XXIV (1977), 3–12.

2. τὸ μέν νυν ἁρπάζειν γυναῖκας...: the dispute between Asia and Europe is deeply rooted in the two peoples' different attitudes to social and moral issues such as the abduction of women. Here Herodotus gives his own interpretation of the rivalry as an ethnologist. See Benardete, pp. 7 ff.; on Herodotus' interest in sexual issues (not confined only to ethnographic passages), see, in Book I, 8 ff; 61,1; 93,3–4; 105,4; 135; 196; 198–9; 203,2; 216,1. See also P. Walcot, *Arethusa*, XI (1978), 137–47; and above, note on 1–5.

4. ἔθνεα: see note on 6,1.

5,1. Πέρσαι...: in Herodotus' view, the Persians consider themselves the legitimate rulers of Asia and therefore the legitimate heirs of all historical rights and claims connected with Asia. This Persian position was sometimes accepted also by the Greeks (e.g. by Aeschylus), even at the cost of recognizing Persian rule over Ionia.

2. **Φοίνικες**: the 'Phoenician' version is perhaps modelled on the episode of Eumaeus' maid in the *Odyssey* (XV 415 ff.) or on the traditional myth of Medea (see note on 2,2).

3. **ἐγὼ δὲ...**: the introductory digression ends with these programmatic statements. Rather than *chercher la femme* in the mythical world, about which nothing definite is known, Herodotus prefers to discuss recent characters and events, beginning with Croesus. If in the age of myth the responsibility for the conflict rests on the Greeks, in the historical period—the period that counts—it rests on the Asians. By adding this corrective Herodotus the 'philobarbarian' re-establishes a certain degree of impartiality. See Flory, p. 25 and p. 116, n. 5.   **πρῶτον**: for 'the first' in Book I cf. 6,2; 23; 26,3; 94,1; 102,1; 103,1; 163,1; 171,4.   **σμικρὰ...ἐπεξιών**: with this wise saying, Herodotus introduces the reader to the *logos* of Croesus, in which the problem of the instability of human fortune is crucial. We have here in a nutshell the earliest appearance of the 'cyclical (or rather, hemicyclical) theory' of history as Herodotus understands it. For similarities between this passage and Sophocles, *Electra* 916 f., see G. Donini, *Maia*, XXIII (1971), 65. For ἄστυ in the sense of 'town' (to be distinguished from the acropolis), both Greek and non-Greek, see e.g. 14,1 and 84,5, etc. For the difference between ἄστυ (city as an aggregation of buildings and people) and πόλις (city-state in the political sense) in Herodotus, see M. Casewitz, *Ktema*, VIII (1983), 75–83 (the two terms are not equivalent in Herodotean usage, as P. Musiolek *AAntHung* XXIX (1981), 133–8 believes). For the so-called 'aporia' between chs. 5–6 and 14 see Introduction to Book I, pp. 62 f.

6,1. Κροῖσος ἦν Λυδὸς μὲν γένος...: a famous passage which is often quoted, above all by the Greek rhetors; see also Strabo XII 1,3 and 3,9. According to Dionysius of Halicarnassus, who translates it into Attic *koiné* and gives two stylistic adaptations (*De Compositione Verborum* 26–7), Herodotus' ἱστορίη begins here. On Herodotus' usage of the terms γένος and ἔθνος see C. P. Jones, *CQ* XLVI (1996), 315–20. Croesus is called τύραννος, a term which not always carries a negative connotation in Herodotus: it is sometimes equivalent to βασιλεύς in the neutral sense of king, ruler, etc.: see e.g. I 15 and III 52,3–4. See A. Ferrill, *Historia*, XXVII (1978), 385–98; J. L. O'Neil, *Antichthon*, XX (1986), 34 ff.; E. Lévy, *Ktema*, XVIII (1993), 7–18. Cf. note on III 42,2. A group of epigraphic fragments from the Artemisium of Ephesus show that Croesus called himself βασιλεύς in Greek (*Syll.* 6); see Müller II, p. 474, Abb. 24, and cf. note on 92,1.   **Ἅλυος**: on the river Halys and its adjacent countries, see 72,1–2 and note on 72,2. **Σύριων**: see 72,1 and note. For the variants Σύροι—Σύριοι in Herodotus see L. Weber, *RFIC* XVII (1939), 171 f.

2. **πρῶτος τῶν ἡμεῖς ἴδμεν**: cf. 5,3. A typical Herodotean expression: cf. 14,2; 23; 94,1 (for the other books see Powell, *Lexicon*, s.v. οἶδα). See B. Shimron, *Eranos*, LXXI (1973), 45–51. For the treaty with Sparta see chs. 69–70.   **ἐς φόρου ἀπαγωγήν**: cf. 27,1. φόρος was the official term for 'tribute' in the Athenian empire in Herodotus' time.

3. πρὸ δὲ τῆς Kροίσου ἀρχῆς: see Introduction, p. 62 f.   ἐλεύθεροι: i.e. politically free from foreign control; for the same meaning, the most common in Herodotus, see 126,6 and 210,2; similarly ἐλευθερίη means independence at 95,2 and 170,2; for different meanings cf. 62,1,5 and 116,1, 3. On the senses of ἐλευθερίη in Herodotus see note on III 142,2. On the Cimmerians see ch. 15.

7,1. ἡ δὲ ἡγεμονίη...: in this interesting and important chapter the notions of Lydian genealogy and chronology that could have been obtained in Sardis and in Ionia in Herodotus' time are reflected. The names of the oldest Lydian kings are eponyms of local peoples or tribes. For Lydus cf. I 171,6 and VII 74,1. Lydus has a brother, Tyrsenus (I 94,5), or Torrhebus (Xanthus of Lydia, *FGrHist* 765 F 16); for variants see Dionysius of Halicarnassus, *Ant. Rom.* I 27,1–2. Asies is a son of Cotys, brother of Atys; both are sons of Manes: I 94,3; IV 45,3; other sons of Atys are Car and Mysus, I 171,6. All the names result from artificial reconstruction, popular or erudite. The tradition about the 'Heraclid' dynasty suggests that the hellenization of the Lydians was held by the Ionians to have occurred much earlier than Gyges. The first three Heraclids did not rule in Sardis; one of them, Alcaeus, is said to have been a son of Heracles and of 'a slave of Iardanus' (eponym of a river), i.e. of Omphale (a famous myth; for sources see Pedley, p. 12 ff.). Of the other two, Belos is the main god of Babylon (see note on 181,2) and Ninos is the eponym of Niniveh. The whole story is thus a Greek construct that, in order to link the oldest oriental dynasties to Heracles, artificially extends them by the insertion of spurious names. Apart from that, the direct succession from 'father to son' does not usually extend for more than eight or ten generations without moving to collateral branches of the family; nevertheless, an average of 23 years per reign (505/22: see 7,4) seems normal for historical dynasties of this kind, and the last two kings in the Heraclid line (Myrsus and Candaules) may be historical. However, a reliable average length of reigns, if used automatically, may misdate every single reign in the list. See M. Miller, *The Sicilian Colony Dates*, New York 1970; for African analogies and other examples of genealogical manipulations see the bibl. cited in the Introduction, p. 16, n. 43. The genealogy of the Mermnads was also, for various reasons, the result of an artificial calculation: 5 reigns in 170 years = 1 century (three Herodotean generations: II 142,2) + two-thirds of a century (66/7 years) + the 3 extra years assigned to Croesus' reign (I 91,3; see R. Ball, *CQ* XXIX (1979), 277 f.). In order to translate Herodotus' list of the Lydian kings into absolute dates we must start from 546 BC, usually taken to be the year of the Persian conquest of Sardis (see bibl. at the end of this note). On this basis a list of reigns may be obtained (see Fig. 2).

Adding the 505 years of the Heraclid dynasty, we can date the founder Agron to 1221 BC and Heracles to around 1350 (this corresponds precisely to the calculations made by Herodotus in II 145,4 where Heracles' age is put about 900 years before Herodotus' time (cf. Introduction, p. 31), and to the dates he gives for the Assyrian dynasty: I 95,2 with note). Though this chronology

Gyges	38 years (ch. 14,4)	716–678 BC
Ardys	49 years (ch. 16,1)	678–629
Sadyattes	12 years (ch. 16,1)	629–617
Alyattes	57 years (ch. 25,1)	617–560
Croesus	14 years (ch. 86,1)	560–546
TOTAL	170 years	716–546BC

FIG. 2. The Lydian kings

is of almost no historical value, tradition about the two Lydian dynasties cannot be entirely fictional. Nicolaus of Damascus (*FGrHist* 90 F 44–7) reports a tradition possibly based on Xanthus of Lydia differing in names and in details, but essentially similar. Bibl.: Mazzarino, ch. 4; H. Kaletsch, *Historia*, VII (1958), 1–47; R. van Compernolle, *Étude de chronologie et d'historiographie siciliotes*, Brussels–Rome 1960, pp. 63–138; Talamo, pp. 13 ff., 37 ff., table facing p. 160; C Masetti, *Helikon*, XI–XII (1971–2), 279–82; M. Lombardo, *Entretiens Hardt*, XXXV (1990), 181 ff.; A. I. Ivantchik, *Les Cimmériens au Proche-Orient*, Fribourg 1993, pp. 104–14. For Herodotus' chronology see Introduction, pp. 30 ff. and nn.   ἡγεμονίη: here it means the 'kingship' of the ruling dynasty (cf. VII 2,1); for other meanings see note on 46,1.   Μερμνάδας: 'Mermnadae' means the descendants of Mermnas. However, since such a name is unknown to all our sources, Mermnads was usually taken to mean 'dynasty of hawks' (μέρμνος, -ης, see e.g. Andron of Halicarnassus, *FGrHist* 768 F 3), assuming that the hawk was the cultic symbol of the family. See W. Fauth, *Hermes*, XCVI (1968), 257–64.

2. Κανδαύλης: Myrsilus, a name of Hittite origin, is supposed to be the first name, whereas Candaules is taken to be a cult title, perhaps connected to the Carian cult of the dog (see J. G. Pedley, *JHS* XCIV (1974), 96–9), which the Greeks identified with Hermes. Yet Candaules is also the name of the Lydian historian Xanthus (*FGrHist* 765 T 1a), a contemporary of Herodotus. Myrsus and Myrsilus are common Lydian names, although Herodotus thought they were Greek or hellenized. It is hard to understand why he preferred Candaules to these names; see J. A. S. Evans, *GRBS* XXVI (1985), 229–33. Nicolaus of Damascus (*FGrHist* 90 F 47) calls him Sadyattes or Adyattes, son of Myrsus.   Σαρδίων: αἱ Σάρδιες (Ionic; Σάρδεις Attic) Lydian *Sfard-*, Aramaic *Sfrd byrt*, 'the citadel of *Sfarda*' (probably to be identified with biblical *Sfrd*: Obadiah 20; today Sart); Sardis was the ancient capital of the Lydian kings in the Hermus valley. After 546 BC it became the administrative centre of the Persian satrapy *Sparda-* (see note on III 90,1). Though captured and burned during the Ionian revolt (V 102,1), it remained a thriving and cosmopolitan town. The use of at least five languages is attested (Lydian, Aramaic, Persian, Greek, Carian). The main goddess, Cybebe (Hdt. l.c.), or Cybele, of Phrygian origin, was identified or associated by the Greeks with Artemis. A younger contemporary of Herodotus, Xanthus of

Sardis (Lydia), wrote a history of the Lydian people in Greek (*FGrHist* 765). See J. G. Pedley, *Sardis in the Age of Croesus*, Norman, Okla. 1968; see also notes on ch. 84; Pedley; G. M. A. Hanfmann (ed.), *Sardis from Prehistoric to Roman Times*, Cambridge, Mass.–London 1983; C. H. Greenewalt, Jr., *PAPS* CXXXVI (1992), 247–71 and in P. Briant (ed.), *Dans les pas des Dix-Mille* (*Pallas*, 43), Toulouse 1995, pp. 135–45; T. Ganschow, 'Sardeis', *LIMC* VIII 1 (1997), 1076–7; E. Simon, 'Kybele', ibid., pp. 744–66; Müller II, pp. 681–722; on Lydia and the Lydians, ibid., pp. 565–9.

3. *Μηίων*: used by Homer and in poetry; in prose the ethnic adjective is *Λυδός*. However, the Maeonians and the Lydians are not always equated (Strabo XII 8,3). For bibl. see F. Baroni, *EAA* 1961, s.v. 'Maionia'.

4. *θεοπροπίου*: a common term in Herodotus for all sorts of oracular responses; cf. I 165,1; see Huber, p. 48 and nn. This first oracle legitimizes the dynasty of the Heraclids (as later that of the Mermnadae: 13,1–3); see Crahay, p. 189; Kirchberg, pp. 11–12.

8–12. The story of Gyges and Candaules' wife is the first short story told by Herodotus and one of the most famous. It is one of the versions current in antiquity of Gyges' rise to power (Pedley, pp. 15–17; it is impossible to unite all the versions into a coherent whole, K. F. Smith, *AJPh* XXIII (1902), 261–82; 361–87; XLI (1920), 1–37). Though rationalized, it preserves the oriental flavour of a court tale. The fantastic elements of the other versions are lacking: there is no reference to Gyges' ring, the 'serpent stone', or the double pupils of the queen's eyes (H. J. Rose, *CQ* XXXIV (1940), 78–81); it is lightened by a humorous touch, but also contains clear tragic elements. In form it is a mixture of dialogues (Aly, pp. 34 ff.; Heni, pp. 142 f.) and vivid scenes. This all suggests the use of poetic and dramatic rather than historical sources (the name of the queen is missing: in other sources she is called Nysia, Clytia, Habro, Toudo: see Nicolaus of Damascus, *FGrHist* 90 F 47 and Ptolemy Hephaistion in Photius, *Bibliotheca* 190, p. 150 Henry). The hypothesis that Herodotus' source is the Lydian Xanthus has rightly been rejected by H. Herter, *Bonner Beiträge* XV 1966, p. 53, n. 103, cf. K. H. Tomberg, 'Die Kaine Historia des Ptolemaios Chennos', Diss. Bonn 1967, pp. 169–70, n. 99. See on this story Long, pp. 9–38; Erbse, *Studien*, pp. 3–9; Arieti, pp. 16–23. Some have thought that Herodotus' story is an elaboration of a *hypothesis* of a five-act tragedy with three actors and a chorus. A papyrus fragment of the 2nd or 3rd cent. AD containing sixteen iambic trimeters (*TGF* II, fr. 664) shows that the story was actually dramatized in antiquity. Its publication by E. Lobel in 1950 kindled a heated debate on the dating of the play to pre-Herodotean or Hellenistic times: for the various hypotheses see Q. Cataudella, in *Studi Calderini-Paribeni*, II, Milan 1957, pp. 103–16; for the pre-Herodotean dating see B. Snell, *ZPE* XII (1973), 197–202 and A. Garzya, in *Studi in onore di Bruno Gentili* (a cura di R. Pretagostini), Rome 1993, II, pp. 547–9. For Gyges' rise to power see J. Th. Kakridis, in *Mélanges Delebecque*, Aix-en-Provence 1983, pp. 213 f. For the fortunes of the Herodotean story from antiquity to the present see R. Pichler, 'Die Gygesgeschichte in der griechischen Literatur und ihre neuzeitliche Rezeption', Diss. Munich 1986.

8,1. ἠράσθη...: apparently an unusual occurrence in Herodotus' view. On Gyges see note on 12,2.   **ἦν γάρ...μάλιστα:** parenthetic clause introduced by γάρ, quite common in Herodotus: cf., in this chapter, para. 2, χρῆν...κακῶς and ὦτα...ὀφθαλμῶν. See J. Kerschensteiner, *MSS* XVII 1964, pp. 29–50.
2. χρῆν...γενέσθαι κακῶς: cf. ἔδεε, δεῖν, μέλλειν with the same meaning of fatality of a 'bad end' (γενέσθαι κακῶς, etc.); I 12,1; 34,1; II 133,2; 161,3; IV 79,1; 135,3; IX 109,2. Famous 'bad ends' in Herodotus include Polycrates (III 125,2), Cleomenes (VI 84,1), Miltiades (VI 135,3), and Pheretime (IV 205). Cf. Drexler, p. 107; P. Hohti, *Arctos*, IX (1975), 31–7; Shapiro, op. cit., pp. 360–2; cf. Introduction, p. 37.   **ὦτα...ὀφθαλμῶν:** three sayings or proverbs follow one another in this dialogue. 'Ears are less trustworthy than eyes' is, for Herodotus, a methodological rule of research, as for Polybius (XII 27), who attributes the maxim, in a different form, to Heraclitus of Ephesus (22 B 101a DK; see also Luc., *Hist. Conscrib.* 20; *De Domo* 20; Marincola, pp. 63–86 ('Eyes, ears and contemporary history')). The principle is sometimes questioned by the orators. The second proverb, 'a woman who undresses, etc.', is also quoted as a maxim by Theano, Pythagoras' wife or pupil (Diog. Laert. VIII 43); cf. Ovid's paraphrase in *Am.* III 14 and 27 f. Plutarch discusses and approves the proverb (*Mor.* 37d and 139c). αἰδώς is variously translated in this proverb as 'modesty', 'decency', 'respect', 'dignity': see D. Cairns, *CQ* XLVI (1996), 78–83. The third saying, 'may everyone look after his own things', was also attributed to Pittacus of Mytilene (*Anth. Pal.* VII 89). Even gods are supposed to look after their own things (see e.g. VIII 36,1; Xen. *Hell.* VI 4,30; Diod. XXII 9,5; Tac. *Ann.* I 73), a Homeric notion (*Il.* V 430, etc.). See R. Harder in *Studies Robinson* II, Saint Louis 1951, pp. 446–9; E. Raubitschek, *RhM* C (1957), 139–41; H. Barth, *Philologus*, CXII (1968), 288–91. On dress and αἰδώς in ancient iconography see G. Ferrari, *Métis*, V (1990), 185–204. Another chapter in Book I with a number of sayings is 32, cf. also 96,2 and 207,1–2. See Lang, pp. 58 ff.
3. δέσποτα: for this form of address to an oriental king cf. 90,2; 115,2, etc.; see Dickey, pp. 95–8, 235–8, 271–4.

9,1. ἀρρωδέων: cf. 111,1; 156,1, etc.; for the Attic form ὀρροδέω, represented for our passage by few mss (A²CD²), cf. *Etym. Magn.*, s.v. ὀρρωδῶ καὶ ἀρρωδῶ; B. Hemmerdinger, *BollClass* XIV (1993), 57 and A. Colonna, *Paideia*, L (1995), 97–98. For καταρρωδέω see I 34,3.   **2. θύρης:** one of the two wings of the door.   **θρόνος:** a chair; elsewhere in Herodotus, a 'throne,' esp. of kings (I 14,3; III 30,2, etc.), priests, judges, etc.; see Powell, *Lexicon*, s.v.; 'seat' of statues of gods: I 183,1; II 149,2.

10,1. ὥρη τῆς κοίτης: cf. V 20,2; dinner time: I 119,4; VII 119,4; 'hour' of day or night: IV 158,2; VIII 14,2; IX 52. More commonly, ὥρη is a 'season' of the year in Herodotus (see Powell, *Lexicon*, s.v.). See also 31,2 and note.

2. ἐν νόῳ ἔχουσα: cf. 27,3; 77,1; III 64,2; 143,1; etc.   τείσασθαι: cf. 123,1; 124,1; 190,1, etc.; for the notion of 'revenge' or 'retribution' in Herodotus see the Introduction, p. 41.

3. παρὰ...φέρει: a typical ethnographic comment. Herodotus knew that the Lydians, though ashamed of nakedness, prostituted their own daughters (I 94,1). Nakedness of both men and women was taboo also in Greece in a very early period, until, for men, nudity in athletic contests was introduced (by the Cretans and the Spartans). The barbarians, and in particular the Asians, continued to use a loincloth in athletic competitions (Thuc. I 6,5–6; Plato, *Resp.* V 452c; Dio of Prusa, *Or.* XIII 24; Moretti, n. 16). For Herodotus' interest in sexual questions see note on 4,2.

11,1. ὡς δὲ ἡμέρη...: for the divisions of day and night in Herodotus see note on III 104,2.

2. ἐμέ τε καὶ τὴν βασιληίην: the storyteller apparently assumed that in Lydia (as in medieval countries ruled by the Salic law) women were excluded from succession to the throne, and that therefore the new husband of a widow-queen automatically became king and the founder of a new dynasty (and not just a prince-consort) Nevertheless, the regicide provoked a riot, and even Delphi legalized the change with a warning (13,1–2). In nearby Caria, Artemisia obtained the sovereign power (τὴν τυραννίδα) after the death of her husband (VII 99,1); cf. the status of Tomyris, the queen of the Massagetae (I 205,1). It is, however, hazardous to reconstruct social institutions on the basis of such stories. See Talamo, pp. 113 ff.; A. Moreau in *Femmes et patrimoine dans les sociétés rurales de l'Europe méditerranéenne*, Paris 1987, pp. 227–37.

4. ἀναγκαίη...ἀναγκαίην: the fatal course of events is stressed again.

5. ἐκ τοῦ αὐτοῦ μὲν χωρίου: a good example of symbolism of the same place; cf. 12,1 (τὴν αὐτὴν θύρην).

12,1. ἔδεε: see note on 8,2.   ἐγχειρίδιον: cf. 214,3, etc.: 'short sword, always non-Greek', and apparently unattested before Herodotus (Powell, *Lexicon*, s.v).

2. Γύγης: has been identified with *Guggu*, king of *Luddi* of Assyrian texts of Assurbanipal's time (669–626 BC): see, in English translation, Pedley, pp. 82–3. *Guggu* had asked for help against the Cimmerians c.662, then he stopped paying homage to the Assyrian king and sent troops to Egypt (657–656 BC); he eventually died during a Cimmerian attack at around 652 BC. He is also supposed by some scholars to be the prototype of Ezekiel's Gog (Ezek. 38–9); for the theory that he himself was a Cimmerian *condottiere* hired by the Lydian king see Wells, pp. 19–26. Guggu's successor, Herodotus' Ardys, renewed the homage to Assurbanipal c.648–4. This chronology is inconsistent with that of Herodotus (cf. note on 7,1), whereas it agrees (by chance?) with the one given by the Armenian version of Eusebius (687–652 BC), according to which the entire Mermnad dynasty lasted only 141 years (687–546 BC); see the analysis and tables in van Compernolle, *Étude de chronologie et d'historiographie siciliotes*, Brussels–Rome 1960, pp. 63 ff.; M. Cogan and H. Tadmor, *Orientalia*, XLVI (1977), 65–85; and S. J. Spalinger, *JAOS* XCVIII (1978), 400–9, with bibl.

Herodotus is not interested in Gyges' politics in the East, which were largely determined by the threat of Cimmerian attacks and the rivalry between Assyria and Egypt. In the second quarter of the 6th cent. Lydia controlled also Phrygia, the Ionian coast, and the Troad, with its outlets to the Aegean and the Black Sea. The Greeks remembered Gyges as a famous usurper and a great and fabulously wealthy τύραννος (see his contemporary Archilochus, fr. 79 West) who eventually obtained the support of Delphi (13,1–2). For Greek evidence and legends on Gyges, see Pedley, pp. 18–21, esp. Plato, *Resp.* II 359d–360b; Nicolaus of Damascus, *FGrHist* 90 F 47 (said to be derived from Xanthus' *Lydiaka*); and Plutarch, *Mor.* 302a. Gyges' funerary monument, already known to Hipponax, has been located at Bin Tepé (see note on 93,2) on 'Gyges' lake' (93,5; sources and bibliography in Pedley, pp. 77–8), but see C. Ratté, *JHS* CXIV (1994), 157–61. For the tomb of the woman loved by Gyges see Clearchus of Soli, fr. 29 Wehrli. For another Gyges, a Lydian contemporary of Polycrates, see III 122,1 and V 121; for a mythical Gyges, the son of Gē and Uranus, see Hesiod, *Theog.* 149. Gyges' father, Daskylos (8,1), is also a common name in Asia Minor, and looks like the eponym of Daskyleion, the capital of the Persian Hellespontine satrapy, and of lake Daskylitis near Cyzicus (see note on III 90,2 and 120,2). In mythology, one Daskylos is a son of Tantalus and another is his grandson, who joined the Argonauts as a guide (both are therefore related to the same northwestern area of Asia Minor). See R. Bloch, s.v., *DNP* III (1997).   [τοῦ . . . ἐπεμνήσθη]: Archilochus would have been the first lyric Greek poet quoted by Herodotus; cf. Introduction to Book I; but the phrase must be an interpolated one, a gloss by a reader, rather than a marginal note by the author: ἐν ἰάμβῳ τριμέτρῳ is in fact a technical expression of a period later than Herodotus (at 174,5 he uses τριμέτρῳ τόνῳ). Moreover, in Herodotus' time it would not have been necessary to quote Archilochus for a king so well known. The fragment is no. 19 West: 'Gyges and all his gold don't interest me. I've never been prey to envy, I don't marvel at heavenly things, or yearn for great dominion (τυραννίδος). That's all beyond the sights of such as me' (tr. M. L. West, *Greek Lyric Poetry*, Oxford 1994). For poetic quotations in Herodotus and other historians see H. W. Parke, *Hermathena*, LXVII (1946), 80–92.

13,1–2. ἐκ τοῦ . . . χρηστηρίου: the first appeal to the Delphic oracle in Herodotus (the response mentioned in 7,4 is not explicitly attributed to Delphi). The delegates of the two Lydian factions are sent to interrogate the oracle. Nicolaus of Damascus' version is more concise, but it includes in the delegation also a competitor to the throne, a certain Lixus, said to belong to the family of Tylonios (*FGrHist* 90 F 47 (5)), and presumably claiming Heraclid descent. The punishment, or revenge, is postponed to the fifth generation after commitment of the crime. Cf. the case of Sperthias and Bulis in VII 133–6. On the notion of hereditary punishment and its criticism see Plutarch's essay *De Sera Numinis Vindicta* (*Mor.* 548a–568a); cf. G. E. M. de Ste Croix, *G&R* XXIV (1977), 146–7, and Arieti, pp. 24–30. The response was composed *ex eventu*, after Croesus' fall, in order to reassert the truth of Apollo's earlier oracles which were favourable to the Mermnadae. See P–W II, no. 51; Crahay, pp. 189–91; Kirchberg, pp. 12–14; Fontenrose, Q 96; on the Delphic oracle and Lydia see P–W I, ch. 5. For another enquiry to Delphi on Gyges' part, which is composed on the model of the dialogue between Croesus and Solon on human happiness (chs. 30–1), see P–W II, no. 244 = Fontenrose, Q 97.

2. τίσις: on Herodotus' concept of retribution see Introduction, p. 38. λόγον οὐδένα ἐποιεῦντο: human neglect of prophecies is a recurrent motif in Herodotus; see e.g. VIII 20,1; 96,2.

14,1. τυραννεύσας: 'as soon as he became king' (cf. note on 6,1). ἀναθήματα: ἀνάθημα in Herodotus is any (votive) offering 'set up' in a temple (cf. 24,8; 53,2; 91,1; 4; 163,3; 183,3; etc.), esp. at Delphi (cf. 25,2; 51,3 and 5; 90,5; etc.), usually as a sign of thankfulness. The offering thus became the sacred property of the temple. An important group of ἀναθήματα in Herodotus are the Hellenic victory-offerings from the spoils of the Persian wars, dedicated at Delphi and elsewhere either as 'tithe' (δεκάτη) or 'first-fruits' (ἀυροθίνια; cf. 86,2; 90,4): see esp. VIII 121–2 and IX 81, 1–2. Cf. W. Gauer, *Weihgeschenke aus der Perserkriege*, Tübingen 1968. Monuments and offerings in Herodotus: Erbse, *Studien*, pp. 146–56. Herodotus' sources on the offerings made by Midas and the Lydian kings (this chapter and chs. 50–1) are his direct observation and information obtained from local guides, whose accounts he sometimes corrects. See Crahay, pp. 202–5; Talamo, pp. 130 ff.   μνήμην ἄξιον: cf. Drexler, pp. 30 ff. κρητῆρές: cf. 51,2 with note ad loc.

2. Κορινθίων θησαυρῷ: it is the most ancient treasury at Delphi (rooms or chests containing the offerings of kings and cities); cf. Strabo IX 3, 4. Archaeological traces of the Corinthian treasury have been found on the 'via sacra' opposite the portico of the Athenians. Kept there were also some of Croesus' offerings (50,3; 51,3) and a thurible dedicated by Euelthon, king of Cyprus (IV 162,3); cf. Paus. X 13.5. The treasury, built by Cypselus in the 7th cent. BC, was named after the tyrant until the Corinthian dynasty fell; then it was named after the *polis* (Plutarch, *De Pythiae Orac.* 13 = *Mor.* 400e; E. Bourguet, *BCH* XXVI (1912), 658 ff.). On Cypselus see V 92; J. B. Salmon, *Wealthy Corinth*, Oxford 1984, pp. 186–96, with bibl. Despite the exceptional privileges they were granted at Delphi (ch. 54), the Lydians had their own treasury not at Delphi but at Delos (the Etruscans of Caere were probably the only non-Greeks who had a treasury at Delphi: note on 167,2). Other treasuries at Delphi mentioned by Herodotus are the Clazomenian (51,2) and the Siphnian (III 57,2–3 and note ad loc.).   τριήκοντα τάλαντα: about 775 kg in weight (by Attic–Euboic standard). For τάλαντον as a weight cf. I 50,3; 183,1–2; 194,3; etc.); as a sum of money, see notes on III 89,2 and 95,1.   πρῶτος ... ἴδμεν: cf. note on 6,2. Midas and Gordies are names found in Phrygian dynasties. Three different Midases need to be distinguished in Herodotus: one is the fabulously rich mythological character, a son of Cybele: Tyrt. 12,6 West (see the legend of the embalmed gardens and Silenus: VIII 138,2–3; the music competition, Dionysus, the asses' ears, the magic gold, etc.); another Midas is a historical Phrygian king, presumably the one

mentioned here; the third is Adrastus' grandfather (35,3). Eusebius dates the historical king to 738–696 BC (*Ab Abramo* 1278 and 1320). He is probably to be identified with Mita, king of Muški, who, according to Assyrian sources, refused to pay tribute to Sargon II (721–705 BC) in 717 BC, only to be forced to recognize Assyrian hegemony ten years later: see Lie, ll. 72, 120, 125, 199, 446, 452 and Luckenbill II, para. 8. D. Hawkins, *CAH*² III 1, pp. 417 ff.; and *RLA* VIII (1994), pp. 271–3; M. Mellink, *CAH*² III 2, pp. 622 ff.; A. J. N. W. Prag, *AS* 1989, pp. 159–165; G. B. Lanfranchi, in A. Aloni and L. De Finis (eds.), *Dall' Indo a Thule: i Greci, i Romani, gli altri*, Trento 1996, pp. 94–101. It is not at all certain that the throne seen by Herodotus was in fact a gift of this king. It was 'worth seeing' as a work of art and a symbol of oriental magnificence; see A. Tamburello, *EAA* 1961, s.v. *Trono* (cult object? Crahay, pp. 207 f.). On the so-called 'tomb of Midas' at Gordium see C. A. Pinelli, *EAA* 1961, s.v. 'Mida, città di'; P. E. Pecorella, *EAA* 1966, s.v. 'Yazılıkaya', with bibl. M. Mellink, *CAH*² III 2, pp. 633–4 with bibl.; for a tentative reconstruction of Midas' original title (*midai lavagatei wanahtei* = 'to Midas the λαϝαγέτας and ἄναξ'), based on an archaic inscription on Midas' monument at Yazilikaya see M. Lejeune, *Athenaeum*, XLVII (1969), pp. 179–92. Midas is not an uncommon anthroponym in the Greek world (see the listings in *LGPN*).

3. ἀξιοθέητον: cf. 184, etc.; θέης ἄξιος: 25,2, etc.   θρόνος: see note on 9,1. Γυγάδας: information typically provided by Delphic guides (Herodotus even keeps the Doric form). On Gyges' coins see 94,1 and note.

4. καὶ οὗτος: so Croesus was not the first; see Introduction, pp. 62 f. Gyges' raids against Ionian cities testify to the Lydians' expansion towards the Aegean under the Mermnads; see Huxley, pp. 52–4. According to Herodotus, Gyges attacked Miletus and Smyrna (which had been Ionian from before 688 BC: see 150,1 and note) and occupied the lower city (τὸ ἄστυ: see note to 5,3) of Colophon (including the sanctuary of Clarus? see Talamo, *PP* XXVIII (1973), 345 ff.); Alyattes occupied Smyrna (16,2 and note). Nicolaus of Damascus adds Magnesia to the list (*FGrHist* 90 F 62). Smyrna, however, apparently succeeded in routing the Lydian cavalry in the Hermus plain (Mimnermus fr. 14 = *IEG II*² West; Paus. IV 21,5; IX 29,4). Miletus had to ask Gyges' permission to colonize Abydos in the Hellespont (Strabo XIII 1,22) which was then under Lydian control. On the Ionian cities see 142,3 and note.   μέγα...ἔργον: cf. the proem (in particular the note on 2–4).   βασιλεύσαντος: 'notwithstanding the fact that he ruled 38 years.' On Gyges' politics in the East, which Herodotus does not consider worth mentioning, see note on 12,2.

15. Ἄρδυος: Ardys corresponds to Alyattes I in Nicolaus of Damascus' list of Lydian kings (*FGrHist* 90 F 62); for sources see Pedley pp. 13–14. According to Herodotus, he ruled from 678 to 629, but in fact his reign did not begin before 652/1 (cf. notes on 7,1 and on 12,2). On Priene see 161 and note. The Cimmerians (Gimiraa in Assyrian texts, Gomer in the Old Testament) are traditionally said to have abandoned their settlements on the northern coast of the Black Sea as a result of Scythian pressure at the end of the 8th cent. (cf. I 103,3 and IV 11,1–2).

They crossed the Caucasus and the Hellespont and invaded the Middle East, and contributed to the decline of the Assyrian empire in the late 7th cent. In around 676 they invaded Phrygia, and King Midas was forced to commit suicide. The lower town of Sardis was apparently captured by the Cimmerians and then by the Treri. The Cimmerians invaded Ionia and seem to have settled permanently in some areas of Asia Minor, e.g. at Sinope (IV 12,2) and at Antandros (Kimmeris) in the Troad. The memory of the invasion was utilized for political purposes in a boundary dispute between Samos and Priene in 283/2 BC (*Inschriften v. Priene*, no. 500 = CB. Welles, *Royal Correspondence in the Hellenistic Period*, New Haven 1934, no. 7, ll. 14–18). Very little is known about them, for they did not leave any distinctive archaeological traces. They already had a mythical status in antiquity, from Homer onwards, and were said to live in a number of different areas (near Hades, Avernus in Campania, etc.). They were sometimes identified with the Cimbri (e.g. Posidonius, *FGrHist* 87 F 31). For the Greek sources on the Cimmerians see Pedley, pp. 21–2, with bibl. Today their country of origin is located somewhere between Armenia and Media, and they are thought to be culturally Iranian. The phases of their invasion and settlement in Anatolia are a matter of dispute. A. Kammenhuber, *RLA* V (1980), coll. 594–6; I. M. Diakonoff, *The Cimmerians*, *AI* XXI (1981), 103–40, and in *CHI*, p. 93 ff; T. Sulimirski and T. Taylor, *CAH²* III 2, pp. 555–60; G. B. Lanfranchi, *I Cimmeri*, Padova 1990; A. I. Ivantchik, *Les Cimmériens au Proche-Orient*, Fribourg 1993; V. Parker, *Klio*, LXXVII (1995), pp. 7–34. The fanciful identification of the Cimmerians with the lost 'Ten Tribes' of Israel is still alive: see A. K. G. Kristensen, *Who Were the Cimmerians and Where Did They Come From?*, Copenhagen 1988.   βασιλεύσαντος ... τυραννεύοντος: see note on 6,1.   ὑπὸ Σκυθέων τῶν νομάδων: cf. 73,3. The 'nomadic' Scythians are distinguished by Herodotus from the 'cultivators' (ἀροτῆρες, IV 17,2) and the 'husbandmen' (ἀγροικοί, IV 18,1).   ἐξ ἠθέων: 'from their accustomed place' (cf. II 142,4; V 14,1; 15,3; VII 75,2).

16,1. Σαδυάττης: 629–17 BC in Herodotus' chronology; also called Adyattes (a 'Hittite' name), cf. Nicolaus of Damascus, *FGrHist* 90 F 63, who probably follows the 5th-cent. BC historian Xanthus of Lydia. On the chronology and history of Sadyattes' reign see M. Lombardo, *ASNP* III 10: 2 (1980), 307–62. In the genealogy of Nicolaus of Damascus (*FGrHist* 90 F 44–7) four kings in the Heraclid dynasty are also called Sadyattes; for a homonymous Lydian merchant contemporary with Croesus, see Nicolaus of Damascus, ibid., F 65. Ἀλυάττης: 617–560 BC in Herodotus' chronology; for other sources see Pedley, pp. 22–5. Alyattes, the father of Croesus, was an important king, regarded by some scholars as the true founder of Lydian power. For his war against the Medes, see chs. 73–4. Apart from his campaigns against Ionian cities known to Herodotus (16–22), he arguably may have besieged Priene (Diog. Laert. I 83). Nicolaus of Damascus tells of a campaign in Caria, *FGrHist* 90 F 65. For his contacts with Delphi cf. ch. 25; for his funerary monument, cf. 93,2–5. On Alyattes and the Ionians, see Huxley, pp. 75–84.

2. *Σμύρνην...*: cf. Nicolaus of Damascus, *FGrHist* 90 F 64. Smyrna, which had already been attacked by Gyges (I 14,4), was subsequently occupied and destroyed by Alyattes *c*.600 BC; see R. M. Cook, *ABSA*, LXXX (1985), 25–8, and *JHS* CIX (1989), 165. It ceased to exist as a *polis* for about three centuries (see note on 150,1). On Alyattes and the cavalry of Colophon, see Polyaenus VII 2,2 (which may be based on Xanthus, see Talamo, *PP* XXVIII (1973), 348 ff.). *κτισθεῖσαν*: for *κτίζειν* in the sense of 'to found' or 'to colonize' in Herodotus, see B. Virgilio, *AAT* CVI (1971–2), 378 ff.; and M. Casevitz, *Le Vocabulaire de la colonisation en grec ancien*, Paris 1985, pp. 32 ff.   *Κυαξάρη...*: see note on 103,1; on Deioces, note on 96,1.   *Κλαζομενάς*: the failed attack on Clazomenae, which was then situated at Chytrion on the south-west coast of the gulf of Smyrna, must be connected with the conquest of Smyrna. See Müller II, pp. 527–33.   *ἀπεδέξατο*: see the proem.   *ἀξιαπηγητότατα*: cf. 177; see Drexler, pp. 13 f.

17,1. *Μιλησίοισι*: the campaigns of Sadyattes and Alyattes against Miletus (chs. 17–22) apparently lasted for eleven years (622–12, according to Herodotus' chronology: see 18,1). They coincided with Periander's rule (see 20,2), if we accept for him the dates 625–585 (see note on III 48–53 and 48,1). The story of these campaigns is anecdotal, rich in stratagems and wonders. Herodotus quotes Delphic and Milesian sources (ch. 20), which are perhaps not wholly fictional. On Miletus see Müller II, pp. 584–606.   *ὑπὸ συρίγγων...*: the *σύριγξ* is the shepherds' pipe, made of one or more reeds tied together (the so called 'Pan-pipes'); see G. Haas, *Die Syrinx in der griech. Bildkunst*, Vienna 1984. The *πηκτίς* is a sort of harp with several strings, similar to the Lydian *μάγαδις*; see M. L. West *CQ* XLVII (1997), 48–50. The *αὐλός* is a pipe, in its Phrygian and Lydian form usually made of two reeds (*tibiae*) of unequal length, the shorter emitting high-pitched 'female' sounds, the longer low-pitched, 'male' sounds; see J. Curtis, *JHS* XXXIV (1914), 89–105, and A. Pepin, *REA* LIII (1951), 107, *OCD*[3], p. 1005. Aulus Gellius I 11,7 grossly misunderstood Herodotus. Central to this passage is precisely the religious theme, the ritual of abuse or propitiation before battle. The Greeks too, however, when marching to attack, sang the paean to the sound of the flutes; a standing institution in the Spartan army, flute-music had nothing to do with religion (see Thuc. V 70 on the battle of Mantinea in 418 BC). Other peoples, from the Persians to the Lusitani, had similar customs. See W. Kendrick Pritchett, *The Greek State at War*, I, Berkeley 1971, pp. 105–8; R. Lonis, *Guerre et religion en Grèce à l'epoque classique*, Paris 1979, pp. 117–28.

2. *οἰκήματα*: sparing the farmsteads during an invasion appeared an unusual stratagem (explained at para. 3) to men who witnessed the Spartan incursions into Attica at the beginning of the Peloponnesian war; the realities of ancient farmsteads have become much better known to us as a result of recent excavations in areas surrounding various Greek cities, and especially Greek colonies, from Metapontum to Tauric Chersonesus. The archaeological remains scattered in the south and south-east coastal areas of Miletus, which sometimes lie as far as 15 or 20 km. away from the city, have not yet been studied systematically.

See J. Pečírka in M. I. Finley (ed.), *Problèmes de la terre en Grèce ancienne*, Paris 1973, pp. 103–33, with bibl.

3. τῆς γὰρ θαλάσσης ...: Herodotus, or his Ionian source, envisaged a period of Milesian 'thalassocracy' (θαλάσσης ... ἐπεκράτουν; for θαλασσοκρατέω see III 122,2, and for θαλασοκράτωρ, V 83,2) during the 7th cent.; cf. the 'List of Thalassocracies' in Diod. VII 11. To 5th-cent. Greeks it was obvious that a siege of a naval power's city with land forces has little practical effect. Alyattes, like Croesus, had no fleet (see 27,1).

18, 1. ἔτεα ἔνδεκα: see note on 17,1.   διφάσια: 'twice'; elsewhere the meaning of the term (apparently unattested before Herodotus) is either 'of two kinds' (II 36,4) or 'two (different, conflicting) causes or opinions' (I 70,2; III 122,1). For τριφάσιος see I 95,1 and note.   Λιμενηίῳ: the name suggests a small port in the hinterland, perhaps located in the Latmian gulf, or on the south-west coast. See Müller II, p. 564. Archaic Miletus, grouped around its acropolis on Mt Kalabak Tepe, did not yet have its famous four harbours (Strabo XIV 1,6). The Milesians were heavily defeated for the second time on the plain of the river Meander, north of Miletus' territory, which could suggest that they were counter-attacking on Lydian ground. The Meander (Büyük Menderes) marks the border between Lydia and Caria; see Müller II, pp. 569–75. The 'Meander' as an ornamental pattern of lines winding in and out is named after this winding river.

3. οὐδαμοὶ Ἰώνων: the passage does not lack a grain of anti-Ionian malice. Chios had Miletus as ally in its conflict with Erythrae, Samos, and Phocaea. The rivalry between Chios and Erythrae arose from the geographical position of the two cities, situated on two opposite sides of a strait largely controlled by Chios through the Oenussae islands (165,1); see Huxley, p. 49. For the περαία (mainland territory) of Chios see note on 160,4; for the dialect spoken at Chios and Erythrae see 142,4.

19,1. Ἀσσησίης: cf. Nicolaus of Damascus, *FGrHist* 90 F 52–3. Assesos is a cult centre of the χώρα surrounding Miletus. The divinity to which the sanctuary, located outside the city walls (today at Mengeres Tepe; see Müller II, pp. 430–4), was dedicated must have been of Anatolian origin. On this episode see Mazzarino, pp. 225–6 and Huxley, pp. 50 f. For other Ionian sanctuaries outside the city walls, see I 26,2; 70,3; 150,1; 157,3; etc.

2. ἐνόσησε: cf. 22,5 and 25,2. On medical issues in Herodotus see D. Brandenburg, *Medizinisches bei Herodot*, Berlin 1976; and note on III 1,1; for other enquiries of oracles concerning medical problems in Book I, see 167,1–2 and 174,4–5.   θεοπρόπους: 'sacred messengers' sent officially by a ruler or city-state to consult an oracle; cf. 48,2; 67,2–3; 78,2; 158,1–2; 174,4; etc. Aesch. *Prom.* 659. In Homer θεόπροπος means 'seer', 'prophet' (*Il.* XII 228; as an adjective, 'prophetic': *Il.* XIII 70).   εἴτε δὴ συμβουλεύσαντός τευ: cf. 191,1. On the 'wise counsellor' see note on 27,2. On Alyattes' appeal to Delphi see P–W I, pp. 128 f.; II, n. 50; Crahay, pp. 87 and 191–3; Kirchberg, pp. 14–16; Fontenrose, Q 98. The Delphic version (ch. 20) may be authentic. For the fulfilment of the order see 22,4. On Alyattes' offerings to Delphi see 25,2.

20. προστιθεῖσι: the Delphic version is confirmed in substance by the Milesian; see Fehling, p. 91.　Περίανδρον: on Periander, see also 23; 24,1, and in particular III 48–53 (with notes) and V 92; for the relationship between Periander and Thrasybulus, cf. V 92ζ. See J. B. Salmon, *Wealthy Corinth*, Oxford 1984, pp. 197–205 and 224–6, with bibl. Periander is the first of six archaic luminaries, all mentioned by Herodotus in Book I, all synchronized in the early 6th cent. BC, and all later included in lists of the 'Seven Sages.' The others are Bias of Priene, Pittacus of Mytilene (27,2; 170,1), Solon of Athens (29,1), Chilon of Sparta (59,2), and Thales of Miletus (74,2). The one missing name in Herodotus is Cleobulus of Lindus. The canon was probably already formed by Herodotus' time, but it is not attested explicitly before Plato (*Prot.* 343a). But see Hermippus of Smyrna, *FGrHist* (cont.) 1026 F 9–20 and commentary. Being a tyrant, Periander was struck out of some lists and eventually replaced by Myson of Chen (Plato l.c.) or the Scythian Anacharsis (Herod. IV 76–80: see Plutarch's 'Banquet of the Seven Sages', *Mor.* 146b). According to Ephorus, all the Wise Men except Thales met at Croesus' palace (*FGrHist* 70 F 181). The problems of chronology posed by such a meeting are insoluble, but the whole story is a legend and should be seen as such. See B. Snell, *Leben und Meinungen der Sieben Weisen*, Munich 1971[4]; P. v. der Mühl, *MH* XXII (1965), 178–80; A. Mosshammer, *CSCA* IX (1976), 165–80; D. Fehling, *Die Sieben Weisen und die frühgriechische Chronologie*, Bern 1985 (criticized by J. Bollansée, *FGrHist* (cont.) IV A,1, Leiden 1998, pp. 112–21, with full bibl.); T. S. Brown, *AHB* III (1989), 2–4. Thrasybulus is the first tyrant in the history of archaic Miletus known to us with certainty, if we disregard the obscure Amphitres and Epimenes (Nicolaus of Damascus, *FGrHist* 90 F 52–3). We do not know how he came to power: it is assumed that the aristocratic πρύτανις became τύραννος (cf. Arist. *Pol.* 1305a17), perhaps during a crisis in the war against Alyattes; see Mazzarino, pp. 225 ff.; Berve, p. 101 and note. Thrasybulus' power was apparently recognized by the Lydian king, if the herald's formula of a truce with 'Thrasybulus and the Milesians' (21,1) is, as it seems to be, authentic (cf. 22,4; cf. also the distinction made between Thrasybulus' provisions and those of private citizens: 21,2). The anecdote about Thrasybulus recommending, through a messenger of Periander's, the elimination of all prominent citizens, is famous (V 92ζ; cf. Arist. *Pol.* 1284a27 and 1311a20, where the anecdote is inverted). The peace with Alyattes secured for Miletus a period of economic and cultural prosperity (colonies, coinage, etc.).　ξεῖνον ἐς τὰ μάλιστα: cf. 22,4, etc., 'bound very closely by ξεινίη' (cf. 27,5), or 'ritual friendship', including mutual hospitality and help; see G. Herman, *Ritualized Friendship and the Greek City*, Cambridge 1987, and in *OCD*[3], 'Friendship, ritualized,' pp. 611–13; P. Spitzer, *REG* CVI (1993), 599–606.

21,1. ἀπόστολος: cf. V 38,2.　σαφέως προπεπυσμένος: cf. Polyaenus VI 47. A similar stratagem is attributed to Bias the Wise during a siege of Priene (note on 16,3); for another anecdote see Polyaenus VII 36. Frontinus attributes to Thrasybulus also another stratagem during the siege of the harbour of Sicyon (*Strateg.* III 9,7).

2. χρᾶσθαι: or χρῆσθαι. for the dialect forms of this verb in Herodotus' Book I see Rosén, p. 122.

22,2. διαλλαγή: the proposed 'truce' (21,1) turns into a permanent 'reconciliation', i.e. into an alliance between the two rulers, who also become ξένοι.

3. ἐλπίζων: cf. 27,3–4; 30,2; 50,1; 54,1; 56,1; 71,1; 75,2; 77,4; etc. The sense is 'to expect' on the ground of rational considerations. Herodotus' ἐλπίς (see 80,5 and note) has not much in common with our 'hope'. Rather, it meant reasonable expectation, almost always vain or erroneous, as in our passage. For ἔλπομαι see 65,3 and note. See J. L. Myres, *CR* LXIII (1949), 46; F. W. Hamdorf, 'Elpis', *LIMC* III 1 1986, pp. 722–5; A. Dihle, in *RAC* XV 1991, p. 1162 (and the bibl., pp. 1248–50); Nenci, note on V 30,25–6.

4. ξυμμάχους: for the term ξύμμαχος in the language of international relations see H. B. Rosén, *East and West* I, Munich 1982, p. 403. Herodotus is the only source for this treaty (*StV* II, n. 105; ὡς ἐγὼ πυνθάνομαι may express reservations about the reliability of his source); in his view, the only reason for the reconciliation was Thrasybulus' stratagem; we may think also of the Cimmerian danger and Periander's mediation. It is uncertain whether Miletus obtained full autonomy with this agreement. For Miletus' treaty with Cyrus see 141,4.

23–4. The mention of Periander (ch. 20) leads, by association, to the famous tale of Arion, included here for no other purpose than to celebrate a marvellous event illustrating the mutability of fortune (a main moral message of the story of Croesus, in which this digression is embedded); see Cobet, pp. 146–50; A. D. Skiadas, *EEAth* XXV (1974–7), 36–42; R. Vignolo Munson, *Ramus*, XV (1986), 93–104; J. T. Hooker, *G&R* XXXVI (1989), 141–6. An ordinary reader could not have detected the alleged parallels with the story of Alyattes by (for a different view see Cobet, pp. 145–7, with bibl.). For style and structure see A. Borgogno in *Studi classici in onore di Q. Cataudella* I, Catania 1972, pp. 379–82; and Long, pp. 51–60. The core of the story certainly pre-dates Herodotus. He could have invented the Corinthian and Lesbian sources (ch. 23) but not the statue at Cape Taenarum (24,8); for the theory that the story was told by the poet himself in a dithyramb or in some early form of tragedy, see Erbse, *Studien*, pp. 153–6; for a different view see Fehling, pp. 21–4. This monument, with or without an inscription, and whether it was an αἴτιον of the story or had been inspired by it, must have existed before Herodotus. Other legends of people saved or guided by dolphins circulated in seafaring cities such as Corinth (Melicertes), Methymna (Enalus and the virgin), and Tarentum (Taras, Phalanthus); there is no lack of representations on local coins (see note on 24,8). Various mythological and popular themes contributed to the creation of such legends: the dolphin was sacred to Apollo and to other divinities, a friend of sailors and fishermen, fascinated by music, etc. A possible, and very general, thematic connection with Eastern legends (the story of Jonah) cannot be proven. To claim the truth of this story from modern observations of the behaviour of dolphins in New Zealand is no more than an amusing fantasy (T. F. Higham, *G&R* VII (1960), 82–6). Though a boy can pirouette on a dolphin's back for half-an-hour, he cannot circumnavigate half the Peloponnese (for the calculation of distances see Plut. *Mor.* 162d).

23. Περίανδρος: see ch. 20 and note.   Ἀρίονα: Arion, considered a century ago as a mythical character like Orpheus, was active in Corinth in the age of Periander (his floruit is dated c.628–625 or 617 BC: see M. R. Cataudella, *Maia*, XVI (1964), 219–25). He was a famous citharode and, according to tradition, a πρῶτος εὑρετής in the field of music (Kleingünther, pp. 49 f.). The transformation of the dithyramb into a choral lyric song with a narrative content is attributed to him (he was not the first to use the term 'dithyramb', if that is what Herodotus meant to imply by ὀνομάσαντα in this chapter: the term was already known to Archilochus, fr. 120 West); others ascribed to him the first tragic drama, the 'cyclic choruses', etc. Arion's travels to Sicily and Magna Graecia have suggested the theory of his influence on Stesichorus. No fragments from Arion's work have survived, the text quoted by Aelian, *Nat. An.* XII 34 (= *PMG* 949) cannot be authentic; for a collection of testimonia on his life and work see *GL* III, pp. 16–25 Campbell. Arion's fame is largely due to the legend told by Herodotus, repeated and embellished by Plutarch (*Mor.* 160a–162b); for a free Latin adaptation see Aulus Gellius XVI 19. Bibliography: A. W. Pickard-Cambridge, *Dithyramb, Tragedy and Comedy*, Oxford 1962², pp. 97–100. C. M. Bowra, *MH* XX (1963), 121–34; G. F. Brussich, *QUCC* XXI (1976), 53–6; J. Schamp, *AC* XLV (1976), 95–120; H. A. Cahn, 'Arion', *LIMC* II 1 1984, pp. 602–3; Long, pp. 51–60; J. T. Hooker, *G&R* XXXVI (1989), 141–6; Arieti, pp. 35–9; E. Robbins and A.-M. Wittke, 'Arion', *DNP* I (1996), 1083–4; and also in general C. Sprimont, *Le Dauphin dans l'antiquité gréco-romaine*, Liège 1969. On Methymna see 160,2 and note.   Ταίναρον: cf. para. 8 and VII 168,2. It is the central peninsula of Southern Peloponnesus (today Mani), separating the Laconian gulf from the Messenian; see Müller I, pp. 858–62. A temple of Poseidon stood on the cape (now called Matapan), a recognized refuge for Helots. On the 'curse of Tainaron' see Thuc. I 128,1 ff.   πρῶτον ... ἴδμεν: cf. 6,2 and note.

24,1. ἐς Ἰταλίην: cf. 145; III 136,1; 138,2; etc. The southern coasts of Italy, called by the Greeks Μεγάλη Ἑλλάς (Magna Graecia). See L. Ronconi, in *Atti dell' Instituto Veneto*, CXLVII (1988–9), 185–97.   χρήματα μεγάλα: Herodotus is full of admiration for people who manage to get rich (see e.g. IV 152,3).

2. ἐκ Τάραντος: cf. III 136,1; 138,1–3. Taras was a colony of Sparta, but Arion preferred to sail in a Corinthian vessel. Herodotus muses, not without a touch of malicious irony, upon the groundlessness of Arion's confidence in Corinthians.

4. ἐδωλίοισι: quarterdecks, of which merchant ships had two, one at the bow and one at the stern. Arion stood on the stern deck: cf. Plut. *Mor.* 161c.

5. *νόμον*: a tune or melody sung to the accompaniment of the lyre or the flute, with a definite rhythm. *Nomoi* were traditionally introduced by Terpander of Lesbos (7th cent. BC) to perform epic poetry. The *νόμος ὄρθιος* was a traditional citharodic song in honour of Apollo, well known to Aeschylus and Aristophanes. According to Pollux, IV 65, *ὄρθιος* is a metrical term for an *arsis* of four *morae*, and a *thesis* of eight: ———⏑⏑. Polymnestus of Colophon, perhaps an older contemporary of Arion, was said to have composed *ὄρθιοι*. The introduction of sumptuous clothing for singers, attributed to Chrysothemis of Crete, a mythical propitiator of Apollo, may have pre-dated the invention of the *νόμος* itself. See H. Grieser, *Nomos. Ein Beitrag zur griech. Musikgeschichte*, Heidelberg 1937. M. L. West, *Ancient Greek Music*, Oxford 1992, pp. 215–17 and 352–3, n. 119. For the usual meanings of *νόμος* in Herodotus see note on 35,1.

6. *ἀποπλέειν . . . χωρέειν*: Arion, making his way on foot from Taenarum to Corinth (some 170 km. as the crow flies) in all his attire, allegedly arrived before the ship (see para. 7).

7. *ἱστορέεσθαι*: see Introduction, p. 8.   *ἐλεγχομένους*: 'confuted' (cf. 117,2; II 115,3).

8. *ἀνάθημα χάλκεον . . .*: Taras, the eponymous hero of Tarentum, is represented riding on a dolphin on coins of Tarentum of all periods (see Head, p. 53; for good reproductions see e.g. C. M. Kraay, *Greek Coins*, New York 1966, pls. 104 ff.). The same story was told of Phalanthos, the 'historical' founder of Tarentum. The statue of Taenarum may be related to the Laconian foundation of Tarentum, albeit interpreted by Herodotus (or by local informants) as an offering for Arion's safe arrival. For *ἀνάθημα* in Herodotus see note on 14,2.

25,1. *μετέπειτα*: according to Herodotus' chronology, Alyattes died in 560 BC, more than half-a-century after the peace settlement with Thrasybulus.

2. *τῆς οἰκίης ταύτης*: for *οἶκος* and *οἰκίη* in the sense of 'dynasty', cf. 120,4 and 207,1, etc.; see also Drexler, pp. 180 ff.   *κρητῆρα*: see note on 51,1.   *θέης ἄξιον*: cf. 14,2; indicates direct knowledge and admiration for the technique of iron-soldering: cf. 68,2; see Drexler, pp. 38 f. The support is described as a vessel stand by Hegesander of Delphi in the 2nd cent. BC (*FGrHist* IV p. 421). Pausanias, however, describes it as resembling a tower, with wide base and narrow top, made up of a series of iron circles soldered together (X 16,1–2). It still existed in the time of Athenaeus (*c.* AD 200), who describes it as a work 'truly worth seeing' on account of the reliefs of animals, insects, and plants which decorated it (V 210b–c).   *Γλαύκου τοῦ Χίου*: though known to other sources as well, nothing is known about this artist except for what Herodotus tells us. The saying *Γλαύκου τέχνη*, known to Plato (*Phdr.* 108d and schol.), is perhaps connected with him. The soldering of two pieces of red-hot metal together was known to the Egyptians, but the technique of soldering two pieces of metal by means of a third piece of a different (type of) metal does not seem to have been known (the issue is, however, debated). See *EAA* 1960, s.v. 'Glaukos di Chio', and C. Panseri, *EAA* 1961, s.v. 'Metallurgia', with bibl.; on ironworking technology see R. F. Tylecote, *A History of Metallurgy*, London 1992², pp. 47 ff.

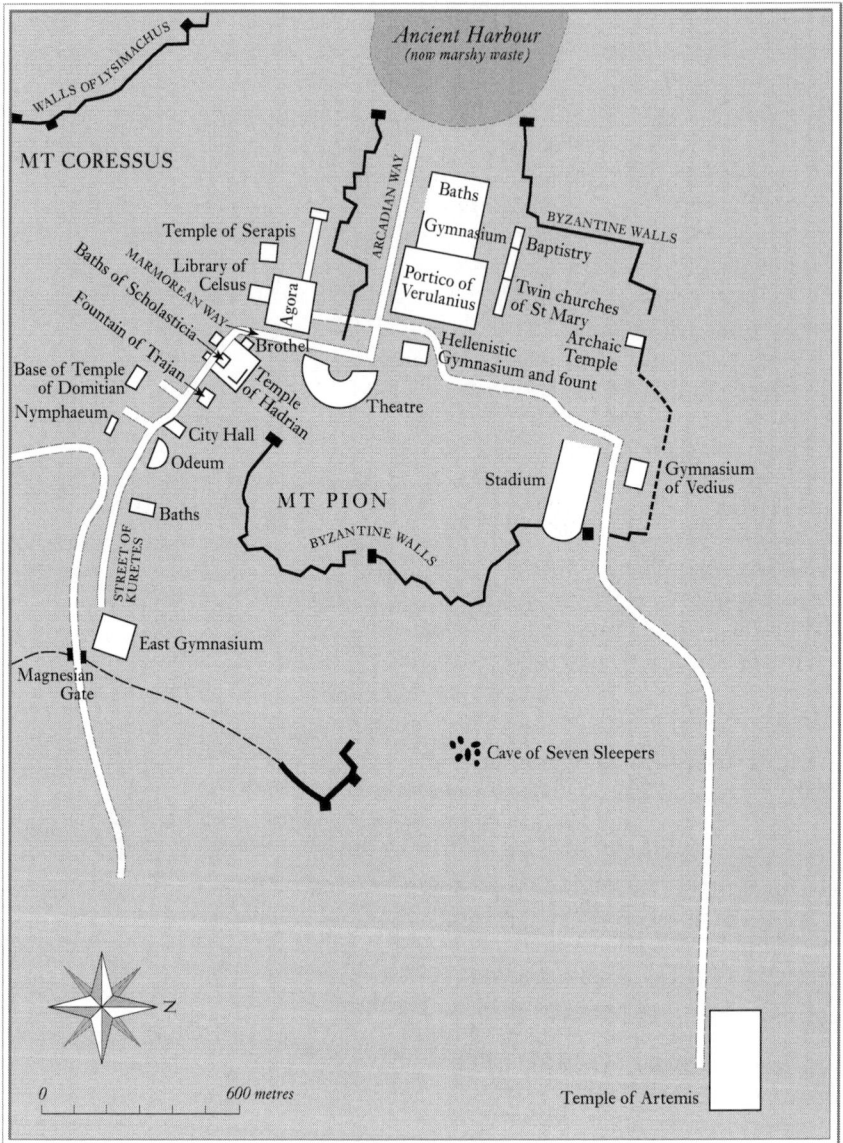

Map 14. Ephesus

26,1. Κροῖσος: strictly speaking, the Croesus *logos* begins here. Before rising to power, Croesus had apparently been governor of Adramyttium and of the plain of Thebes in the Troad; during Alyattes' Carian campaign (see note on 16,3), he is said to have made friends with some rich Ionians, among them the banker Pamphaes. On the dynastic crisis which brought Croesus to power, see 92,2–4 and note. For bibl. on the Croesus *logos* see Introduction, p. 59, n. 3. Ἐφεσίοισι: the siege of Ephesus should be dated to about 555 BC. Archaic Ephesus lay in the area between the mouth of the river Caÿster and the west side of Mt. Pion (Panayır Dağı), where the acropolis must have been. According to Herodotus the city was surrounded by walls. The rope mentioned in this passage supposedly connected the city walls on Mt. Pion and the temple of Artemis about 1200 m. north-east of the walls (near modern Selçuk). In Herodotus' time the suburbs east of Mt. Pion extended as far as the temple (hence the qualification παλαιῆς πόλιος at para. 2). Today there are practically no remains of the famous Artemisium which, in Hellenistic times, was considered one of the Seven Wonders of the World. The first Greek temple was probably constructed there already in the 8th cent.; it was twice rebuilt between the reigns of Gyges and Croesus, and a third time around the middle of the 6th cent., with the collaboration of famous architects. The last archaic building, referred to in the present chapter, was a gigantic Ionic peripteral temple (155 × 55 m. with 127 columns, 36 of which were *caelatae*); after peace had been made, Croesus contributed, with his offerings, to its beauty and wealth (see 92,1). It burned down two centuries later and was rebuilt in the second half of the 4th cent. BC. See P. Romanelli, *EAA* 1960, s.v. 'Efeso', with an updated and exhaustive bibl. by B. Palma in the 1973 Suppl.; D. Knibbe (and others) *RE* Suppl., XII 1970, coll. 248–364, 1588–604, 1654–73; A. Bammer, *Das Heiligtum der Artemis von Ephesos*, Graz 1984. L. Boffo, *I re ellenistici e i centri religiosi dell' Asia Minore*, Florence 1985, pp. 150–6; W. A. P. Childs, *JDAI* CVIII (1993), 399 ff. Müller II, pp. 454–75. For other Ionic temples outside the city walls see note on 19,1.

2. σχοινίον: in antiquity the rope linking temple to city walls symbolized the dedication of the entire city to the goddess; cf. Aelian, *Var. Hist.* III 26, and Polyaenus VI 50. In other words, the sanctity of the temple was communicated to the city through a conductor, in this case the rope; cf. the famous stratagem of the Cylonians at Athens; or the chaining of the island Rheneia in Polycrates' time to Delos. The Ephesian tyrant Pindar, son of a sister of Croesus, supposedly invented the stratagem (Berve, p. 99 and notes). Herodotus, interested only in the strategem itself, does not relate its outcome. According to Strabo (XVI 1,21), Croesus introduced a Lydian garrison into the city, whereas according to Aelian (loc. cit.), he set the city free after having expelled the tyrant.; cf. *StV,* no. 109.

3. καὶ Αἰολέων: e.g. Sidene on Mt. Granicus (Strabo XIII 1,42); see Berve, p. 90 and note; V. La Bua, *MGR* V (1977), 14.   αἰτίας... ἐπαιτιώμενος: charges or pretexts (Bornitz, p. 155; cf. Introduction, p. 40).

27,1. ἐς φόρου ἀπαγωγήν: cf. 6,2 and note.   νέας ποιησάμενος: Croesus is generally credited by modern scholars with a plan of making Lydia a naval power, either by building a fleet in order to conquer the Greek islands (Lesbos, Chios, and Samos) or through establishing bonds of ξενίη (para. 5) with the same islands, in order to obtain access to their fleets; but Lydia's entry in the 'List of Thalassocracies' preserved by Diodorus (VII 11) is referred to mythical times. Expansionist trends beyond hereditary or natural boundaries are seen by Herodotus as posing moral and historical philosophical problems: see Introduction, pp. 38 f., 40 ff., cf., in this book, 66,1; 73,1; 153,4; 177; 190,2; 206,2; sometimes expansionist policies are seen as the cause of wars, e.g. 96,2 and 205,1. See Drexler, pp. 129 ff.; Wood, pp. 25 ff. On islands in Herodotus, esp. in Book I, see P. Caccarelli, in *Impressions d'îles. Textes réunis par F. Létoublon*, Toulouse 1996, pp. 41–55.

2. **Βίαντα**: for Bias, cf. 170,1–3 and note on 170,1; on Priene see 161 and note. This anecdote, that adds favourable touches to Herodotus' characterization of Croesus, belongs to the literary genre of apophthegm and of didactic dialogues between wise men and tyrants: from Plato and Xenophon onwards, the genre became popular in Greek literature. It has no historical value, as can be inferred from Herodotus not even being certain of the name of the wise man who spoke with Croesus. The anecdote simply serves to report a witty answer and, at the same time, explain why Croesus did not conquer the islands. Both Bias and Pittacus were included in the list of the Seven Sages (see note on 20,1): their choice as Croesus' interlocutors is therefore appropriate. **Πιττακὸν**: Pittacus, the famous αἰσυμνήτης of Mytilene, a contemporary of the poet Alcaeus and the Olympic victor Phrynon (636 BC), belongs to the time of Alyattes, not that of Croesus; he died in 570 BC, i.e. about ten years before Croesus came to power. Attempts to downdate all the persons involved may be considered unsuccessful; on the chronological problem of the meeting between Croesus and Solon, see note on 29–33. On the character and function of the 'wise counsellor' in Herodotus, see Bischoff (an extract from his work can be found in Marg's collection, pp. 302–19); R. Lattimore, *CPh* XXXIV (1939), 24–35 (who usefully distinguishes between 'tragic', or rather 'didactic', and 'pragmatic' counsellors); Immerwahr, pp. 74 f., and J. Wikarjak, *Filomata* (1962–3), 158–65. See also Introduction, pp. 43 ff. These counsellors, whose practical advice is not always the right one, serve in Herodotus to predict and foreshadow the future, as do oracles, dreams, and portents. The dialogue has well-defined rules: it contains gnomic sentences, a general didactic warning, and sometimes also practical advice; the king or tyrant usually rejects the general warning, but often accepts the practical advice. In Book I, in addition to the advice of the 'wise men' mentioned above, cf. the advice given to Gyges (8,4), Sandanis (71,2–4), and Croesus himself (88–9; 155,2–4; 207).

3. **ὦ βασιλεῦ**: this is the usual form of address to an oriental king or to a Greek tyrant in Herodotus; Solon too uses it (30,3), but also the unexpected **Κροῖσε** (32,1 and 4); see Dickey, pp. 90–5, 236–7, 271.   **ἐλπίσαντα**: see note on 22,3.   **Λυδῶν παῖδας**: poetic (cf. III 21,3).   **σὺν ἵπποισι**: the Lydian cavalry (cf. 79,3), well known to Ionian lyric poets already in the 7th cent., represents here the typical army at the service of a continental state, as opposed to the fleets used by thalassocracies.

5. κάρτα τε ἡσθῆναι: excessive joy or laughter of kings and tyrants is often an ominous sign in Herodotus; cf. in Book I, 56,1; 69,3; 119,5. See D. Lateiner, *TAPhA* CVII (1977), 173–82.   τῷ ἐπιλόγῳ: this term, here in the sense of 'conclusion', or 'what comes after the reasoning', used by Herodotus only here, is apparently unattested in earlier sources.   ξεινίην: cf. 69,3, etc.; see note on ch. 20.

28. πλὴν γὰρ Κιλίκων...: this list of peoples subjected by Croesus in Asia Minor is neither complete nor faultless; but it should not, for this reason, be rejected as a reader's gloss. It includes thirteen peoples (three of which are Greek), whereas Ephorus lists sixteen peoples, and even his list is not complete (the Lydians and the 'mixed' peoples are missing: see *FGrHist* 70 F 162, with the criticism of Strabo XIV 5,23–5). For other lists of peoples in Asia Minor in Herodotus see III 90–4; V 49, and in particular VII 72–7 and 91–5. Actually they were conquered by Alyattes, not Croesus: Croesus was left with the task of unifying the administration, the army, and the tax system. The inclusion of the Lydians is not a mistake, since they too are subject to the king. On Phrygia and the Phrygians see 14,2 and 35,1–3; on Mysia see 36,1. The Mariandynians lived on the coast of Eastern Bithynia (the report on Croesus' campaign against Bithynia is doubtful: Strabo XII 4,3); see Müller II, pp. 177–8. The Chalybes, a half-mythical Homeric people, eventually associated with iron manufacture, are located usually to the East of the river Halys; ibid., pp. 111–12. Ephorus (loc. cit.) identified them with the Homeric Halizones, later located to the west of the Halys. On the Paphlagonians see 6,1 and 72,2. On Caria see 171 and 174–5. On the three Greek tribes see 141–51; on Lycia 173 and 176. In Pamphylia, there were Greek or mixed colonies and hellenized cities since the archaic period (Phaselis, Aspendus, Side). On Cilicia see 74.   πλὴν...Κροῖσος: a historical and geographical parenthesis (see note on 8,3–4).

29–33. The dialogue between Croesus and Solon on human happiness is one of the most famous passages of Book I, a focal point in the whole Croesus *logos* and Herodotus' work at large, and one of the most important sources for Herodotus' ethical, religious, historical, and philosophical views. Solon has seen the treasures of Croesus and ought to have concluded that its owner is the happiest man on earth. However, Croesus is twice disappointed by his guest, who assigns the first place in 'felicity' to a certain Tellus of Athens (30,3–5), and the second to two Argive brothers, Cleobis and Biton (31,1–5). Croesus' irritation prompts a didactic sermon by the wise Athenian. The terms for human well-being that recur in the dialogue are four: ὄλβος, εὐτυχίη, εὐδαιμονίη, μακαρίζω; but the fundamental distinction is between permanent 'happiness' (ὄλβος) and transient good luck (εὐτυχίη): see 32,7. In Herodotus, ὄλβος can also mean 'wealth' (30,1), and is not associated in any way with spiritual, subjective, or mystical happiness, etc., as opposed to the material and objective pleasures of this world. The two terms, ὄλβος and εὐτυχίη, are not mutually exclusive: the 'lucky' man can become 'happy', if he does not incur misfortune before his life ends in a glorious (Tellus) or a peaceful death (Cleobis and Biton). Both εὐτυχίη and ὄλβος signify the sum of the same series of material goods: good health, good children, good looks, physical strength, and a good income. The only significant distinction is that between a temporary state of well-being and a secure, permanent one, immortalized in the memory of future generations (see T. Krischer, *WS* LXVII (1964), 174–7); C. de Heer, *ΜΑΚΑΡ, ΕΥΔΑΙΜΩΝ, ΟΛΒΙΟΣ, ΕΥΤΥΧΗΣ: A Study of the Semantic Field Denoting Happiness in Ancient Greek to the End of the 5th Century B.C.*, Amsterdam 1969; N. Hinske, *Philosophisches Jahrbuch* LXXXV (1978), 317–30; P. W. Sage, 'Solon, Croesus and the Theme of the Ideal Life', Diss. J. Hopkins 1985; T. Krischer, *RhM* CXXXVI (1993), 213–22; G. Crane, *Arethusa*, XXIX (1996), 57–85. Any book on the 'fragility of goodness' in ancient thought, like the famous one by M. C. Nussbaum (Cambridge 1987), should start from this dialogue. Solon's view of happiness is extremely conventional and 'bourgeois', an *aurea mediocritas* which finds its trivial expression in public honours, in other people's envy, in funerals, monuments, etc. That this view of happiness, certainly shared by Herodotus, was in fact held by Solon is shown by the fragments of his poetry (see S. O. Shapiro, *ClassAnt* XV (1996), 348–64), on which Herodotus' characterization of Solon must ultimately be based; see above all frs. 23–4 West, with the translation and commentary by I. M. Linforth, *Solon the Athenian*, Berkeley 1919, pp. 130 ff.; cf. K. Nawratil, *WS* LX (1942), 1–8. Instability of prosperity, the end of life as a test of lasting happiness, partial luck as being within reach in human life, are typical Herodotean notions; see esp. the story of Polycrates' ring (III 40–3) and the remarks (e.g. at VII 190; 233,2; VIII 105,2), echoing the maxims of archaic wisdom, of which Solon is a prominent representative. Similar ideas about happiness are expressed in the last words of the chorus in Sophocles' *Oedipus Rex* (these may not be authentic: see B. Arkins, *CQ* XXXVIII (1988), 555–8). Aristotle's famous study of happiness (*Eth. Nic.* 1099b8, 1169b3, 1178b33) demonstrates that such views were not alien to Greek culture.

The meeting between Solon and Croesus also symbolizes the confrontation between wisdom and arrogance, moderation and excessiveness, etc. Although the examples of civic and filial virtue are taken from the Greek *polis*, the ethical opposition between Solon and Croesus is fundamentally human and universal. The ethno-cultural interpretation, that finds in the dialogue an expression of the conflict between Western 'freedom' and Eastern 'despotism' (Regenbogen, etc.), has insufficient support in these chapters. The dialogue is Herodotus' literary composition on a well-known theme, conforming to the conventions of a pre-existing and stylized literary genre (for the dialogue as an example of 'oral technique', see Lang, ch. 2; on dialogues with 'wise counsellors', see note on 27,2). The subject matter, the first oral and perhaps even written elaborations of the dialogue, must have been developed after Croesus' death in Athens, where Herodotus could have come to know them, together with other data of the tradition and myths about Solon (which he utilized only partially, in addition to our dialogue; see I 86, II 177, and V 113), and Solon's poems, which he must have studied attentively for composing the dialogue.

The historicity of the meeting is a controversial problem: it was doubted already in antiquity (Plutarch, *Sol.* 27,1). Herodotus dates it three years before Cyrus' revolt against Astyages (46,1), i.e. in 553 BC (see note on 130). Thus Croesus reached the peak of his 'happiness' after seven years of reign (560–554); then followed seven years of misfortunes, anxieties, and defeats before his final ruin (546). This structure is too symmetrical to be historical (Myres would call it 'pedimental'; see Introduction, p. 36); for Croesus' 'twice-seven-year' reign cf. 86,1–2 and note. Chronologically it could have been possible for Solon, already in his seventies, to have visited Amasis (30,1), Philocyprus of Salamis (Solon, fr. 19 West; Herod. V 113), and Croesus; though journeys of such a kind might not be easy at his age. The historicity thesis may be acceptable on three conditions: (1) the beginning of Solon's ἀποδημία, his residence abroad (29,1, 6), must be linked to the rise of Pisistratus (*c.*561/60 BC) and not to Solon's archonship (usually dated to 594/3); (2) the νομοθεσία must be downdated to the late seventies of the 6th cent.; (3) 559/8 must be rejected as the date of Solon's death (Phaenias of Eresus, fr. 21 Wehrli).

The story of Croesus and Solon was popular in antiquity; many sources tell it anew, from Aristotle to the end of the Byzantine period: see P. Oliva, *Altertum*, XXI (1975), 175–81. The dialogue is discussed in all modern monographs on Solon; see also Long, pp. 61–73; Fehling, pp. 211–12; for a review of modern discussions see G. Schneeiweiss, in *Apophoreta für Uvo Hölscher*, Bonn 1975, pp. 161–87. For a bibliography on Solon in Herodotus see A. Martina, *Solon. Testimonia veterum*, Roma 1968, pp. 430 ff. For the chronological problems see S. Markianos, *Historia*, XXIII (1974), 1–20; M. Miller, *Klio*, XLI (1963), 58–94; G. Maddoli, *Cronologia e storia*, Perugia 1975, pp. 20–5.

29,1. καὶ... Λυδοῖσι: these words are considered by some editors as interpolated (Stein, Legrand); cf. T. S. Brown, *AHB* III (1989), 2. The present form προσεπικτωμένου = 'acquiring additional' territory (Powell, *Lexicon*) may in fact seem unsound; see Immerwahr, pp. 29–30, n. 43. σοφισταί: 'wise men', not 'Sophists' in the more common (and sometimes negative) sense of the term. For Herodotus, Solon is certainly a 'sage', as Aelius Aristides rightly understood (46,311); Plutarch also knew perfectly well the use of the term, though he criticized Herodotus on this issue (*Mor.* 857 f). Other Herodotean σοφισταί are those who introduced into Greece the cult of Dionysus (II 49,1), and Pythagoras (IV 95,2). In the 4th cent. the seven canonical sages (see note on 20) are often called 'sophists'. See Stein's note ad loc. and T. S. Brown's criticism in *AHB* III (1989), 2–4. ἀνὴρ Ἀθηναῖος: this qualification seems unnecessary for an Athenian public (see Powell, *History*, pp. 36 ff.). νόμους: here written laws; cf., for the same meaning, 82,7–8; 132,3; 137,1; 144,3; for other meanings, I 24,5; 35,1; 61,1. On Solon's legislation see E. Ruschenbusch, ΣΟΛΩΝΟΣ ΝΟΜΟΙ. *Die Fragmente des solonisches Gesetzeswerkes mit einer Text- und Überlieferungsgeschichte*, *Historia* Einzelschriften, IX, Stuttgart 1966 (1983²) is fundamental. ἀπεδήμησε ἔτεα δέκα: see note on 29–33. In Aristotle, *Ath. Pol.* 7,2 and Plutarch, *Sol.* 25,1 the Athenians swore to obey Solon's laws for 100 years. See Rhodes,

Commentary

pp. 169–70. On Solon's travels see I. M. Linforth, *Solon the Athenian*, Berkeley 1919, pp. 297–302. κατὰ θεωρίης: cf., in Book I, 30,1 and 2. Aristotle adds to the 'desire for knowledge' also commercial aims (*Ath. Pol.* 11,1). Herodotus too travelled out of 'desire for knowledge': see Drexler, pp. 26 ff.; on Herodotus the 'tourist,' see J. Redfield, *CPh* LXXX (1985), 97–118; cf. Introduction, pp. 5 ff. πρόφασιν: cf. 156,1, etc. In Herodotus πρόφασις indicates the official or ostensible reason, which is not necessarily the true motive but also not always a false one. See L. Pearson, *TAPhA* LXXXIII (1952), 205–33, and esp. 208 ff., H. R. Rawlings III, *A Semantic Study of Prophasis to 400 BC*, Wiesbaden 1975.

30,1. Ἄμασιν: *Hnmw-ib-Re*, the last great pharaoh in the Saïte dynasty (*c.*569–525 BC), chiefly known through Herodotus (esp. II 154,3; 162; 169; 172–82; III 39–43). For Solon's visit to Egypt see the sources collected in Martina, *Solon*, nos. 33, 62–9, among them the famous Platonic passage: *Tim.* 20d–27b. On the law of Amasis that Solon introduced in Athens see II 177,2. ἡμέρῃ τρίτῃ ἢ τετάρτῃ: 'three days' is a 'typical' unit of time not only in Herodotus (cf. I 113; 185; 206,2) but in almost all ancient literatures; 'three or four' fosters credibility. See Br. Czajkowski, *Eos*, XXVIII (1925), 87–103; J. W. S. Blom, *De typische Getallen bij Homeros en Herodots. I. Triaden, hebdomaden en enneaden*, Nijmegen 1936; Fehling, pp. 216–39.

2. ξεῖνε Ἀθηναῖε: cf. 32,2; IX 120,2; for forms of address with ξεῖνε and an ethnic see Dickey, pp. 145–9; 283–4. φιλοσοφέων: the verb appears in Herodotus only here, and is apparently unattested in earlier Greek literature. νῦν ὦν ἵμερος: for an attempt to versify in iambic trimeters this and other utterances in the dialogue, see Myres, p. 77, n. 2. εἰ...πάντων: questions expressed in the superlative are typical of popular storytelling of all times; cf. W. M. Bloomer *ClAnt* XII (1993), 30–50. Herodotus made his own choice among the characters usually mentioned in this context (Gyges and the oracle: cf. note on 13,1–2; Aglaus of Psophis, a contemporary of Croesus, according to Paus. VIII 24,13; Tellus, etc.).

3. ἐλπίζων: see note on 22,3. Τέλλον: mentioned also in other sources depending on Herodotus. Perhaps a stele with an epitaph to Tellus could still be seen at Eleusis in Herodotus' time; but he must have used a narrative source. It is possible that the stories of Tellus, Cleobis, and Biton were mentioned in Solon's poems. Herodotus evidently guessed that Solon would tend to give the first place to a good patriot. There is no reason to doubt that Tellus actually existed and died in a battle between the Athenians and the Megarians at the end of the 7th cent., when the two neighbouring cities were fighting over the control of Salamis. See L. Weber, *Philologus*, LXXXII (1927), 154–66. For the hypothesis that the war was against independent Eleusis see K. W. Welwei, *Athen. Von neolitischen Siedlungsplatz zur archaischen Grosspolis*, Darmstadt 1992, pp. 66 and 144.

4. εὖ ἠκούσης: cf. εὖ ἥκοντι below. Cf. also I 102,2; V 62,3; VIII 111,2 (the meaning is analogous to εὖ ἔχειν, see Rosén, p. 218). Cf. III 82,5 and note. ὡς τὰ παρ' ἡμῖν: with this light and slightly ironic comment, Herodotus compares two

different life-styles (cf. Archilochus, fr. 19 West, on Gyges). Plutarch adds a touch of Hellenic nationalism (*Sol.* 27,8).

5. δημοσίη τε ἔθαψαν: it was an archaic Greek tradition to give soldiers a public burial on the battlefield. After the Persian wars the fallen Athenians began to be brought to Athens for public burial in the Ceramicus. Probably at the same time the funeral oration was instituted. The precise date of this change is debated: see Rhodes, pp. 650–1; C. E. Clairmont, *Patrios Nomos: Public Burial in Athens during the Fifth and Fourth Centuries BC*, Oxford 1983; N. Robertson, *EMC* XXVII (1983), 78–92; Pritchett, *GSW* IV (1985), 94–259.

31,1. δευτερεῖα: cf. VIII 123,2; the idea of a 'second prize' is non-aristocratic: the Homeric aspiration was 'always to be the first and to surpass the others' (*Il.* VI 208) in competitions and battles (only those 'unacquainted with prizes' count goods and profits (*Od.* VIII 159–64). However, there were exceptions, especially in horse and chariot races (see *Il.* XXIII 536–8). Cf. in Herod. VIII 123,2. Κλέοβίν τε καὶ Βίτωνα: this famous story too is repeated in later sources (e.g. Plut. *Sol.* 27,7). Cicero translates into Latin a different version (*Tusc.* I 47,113; see W. E. Blake, *AJPh* LXV (1944), 167–9). Plutarch knew the name of the mother, Cydippe, and that she was a priestess of Hera (*Mor.* 108 f; fr. 133 Sandbach). Pausanias mentions a bas-relief that portrays the scene, kept in his time in the temple of Apollo Lycius at Argos (II 20,3). The most interesting testimonies for this story are two archaic kouroi (today in the museum at Delphi) commonly identified with Cleobis and Biton, though the possibility that they represent two anonymous athletes or the Dioscuri cannot be ruled out; see C. Vatin, *BCH* CVI (1982), 509–25; P. Faure, *AC* LIV (1985), 56–65; D. Sansone, *Nikephoros*, IV (1991), 121–32. The inscriptions on the base of the statues (Jeffery, pp. 154 ff. and pl. 26,4), written in the dialect and alphabet of Argos, are dated to the first half of the 6th cent. BC. Their discovery fuelled a lively debate about Herodotus' truthfulness; see M. Guarducci, in *Studi in onore di U. E. Paoli*, Florence 1955, pp. 365–76, with bibl. In the inscription, [Πολυ]μεδες is a conjecture: see *EAA* 1965, s.v. 'Polymedes'. On the narrative structure of the story see A. Borgogno, in *Studi classici in onore di Q. Cataudella* I, Catania 1972, pp. 383–6. On the moral message see M. Lloyd, *Hermes*, CXV (1987), 22–8.

2. βίος τε ἀρκέων: the possession of two oxen (or mules, according to Plutarch, *Mor.* 108 f) suggests that they belong to the class known at Athens as the *zeugitai*, the (idealized) middle class. The ending in -βις is rare for Greek personal names, and has suggested to some that the family was of pre-Dorian origin. ἐούσης ὁρτῆς τῇ ῞Ηρῃ: see Eur. *El.* 171–4; cf. F. I. Zeitlin, *TAPhA* CI (1970), 645–69, and Aen. Tact. 17,2–4. The festival of Hera at Argos ('Heraia', also known as 'Hekatombaia') was the main annual celebration of the patron-goddess of the city. It included a procession to the temple, sacrifices, and athletic and musical contests, lasting probably for three days. See W. Pötscher, *AAntHung* XXXVII (1996–7), 25–36. οὐ παρεγίνοντο ἐν ὥρῃ: cf. Blake, article cited in note on 31,1. ἐν ὥρῃ: here, 'in time'; for other meanings of ὥρη in Herodotus, see note on 10,1. πέντε καὶ τεσσεράκοντα: taking 1 stadium = 180 m. (the usual unit,

which is *not* necessarily the one known to Herodotus: see note on 104,1), 45 stadia would be accurate: the distance between the famous Heraeum of Argos and the city itself is in fact roughly 8 km. (between the Heraeum and Mycenae about 5 km.). The most ancient archaeological remains of the temple are dated to the 7th cent. The temple was burned down in 423 BC and rebuilt further south. See L. Laurenzi, *EAA* 1958, s.v. 'Argo', with bibl.; and R. A. Tomlinson, *Argos and the Argolid*, London 1972, pp. 203–4, 230–47; T. Kelly, *A History of Argos to 500 B.C.*, Minneapolis 1976, pp. 51–72; F. De Polignac, *Cults, Territory, and the Origins of the Greek State*, Chicago and London 1995, pp. 41–54 (with bibl. pp. 169–70). A list of the priestesses of Hera, kept in the temple, was used by Hellanicus as a source. On sanctuaries in Herodotus see Bowden.

3. ὁ θεὸς: not a monotheistic sense: according to Powell's *Lexicon*, in 30 out of 146 times θεός is used 'monotheistically', and our passage would be the first time: incorrectly, however, since at para. 4 the mother invokes τὴν θεόν in front of the statue of Hera. ὁ θεός seems rather a collective or abstract term (cf. τὸ θεῖον, 32,1) more or less equivalent to our 'divinity' or 'deity'. In Herodotus this usage is mostly related to non-Greek religions, esp. the Persian (see note on 131,1); but see also e.g. in the speeches of Themistocles (VIII 60γ) and Lampon (IX 78,2). See Lachenaud, pp. 198–9; in general, G. François, *Le Polythéisme et l'emploi au singulier des mots theos et daimon dans la littérature grecque d' Homère à Platon*, Paris 1957, pp. 201–9.   περιχαρὴς: full of sudden joy (cf. 119,2, etc.); an 'ominous word' in Herodotus: see Ch. C. Chiasson, *Hermes*, CXI (1983), 115–18.   τὸ ἀνθρώπῳ...ἐστι: the notion that death is the greatest good (cf. VII 46,3–4) belongs to traditional Greek pessimism from Hesiod onwards. Neither Herodotus nor Solon believed in the immortality of the soul: they were fascinated by the possibility of a peaceful end to existence (during sleep, as in the golden age: Hesiod, *Op.* 116). See J. Elayi, *IA* XIV (1979), 147–8, with a review of different interpretations.

5. εὐωχήθησαν: cf. the similar myth of the brothers Agamedes and Trophonius in Pindar, fr. 2 Snell–Maehler, compared by Plutarch to our story (*Mor.* 109a). In both cases the happy death is preceded by a banquet.   εἰκόνας: see note on para. 1.   ὡς...γενομένων: perhaps an epigraphic formula?

32,1. εὐδαιμονίης: the commonest term for 'happiness', here equivalent to ὄλβος/ὄλβιος.   πᾶν...ταραχῶδες: see Introduction, pp. 38 f. This conception of the divine, implied by Homer and Pindar, becomes a fundamental principle in Herodotus' theology of history; cf. III 40,2 and note; VII 10ε. See Plutarch's assessment in *Mor.* 857f–858a. For a collection of passages on φθόνος θεῶν in Herodotus see Drexler, pp. 106 ff.; for modern interpretations see K. Nawratil, *PhW* LX (1940), coll. 125 f.; W. C. Greene, *Moira*, Cambridge, Mass. 1944, pp. 84–8; H. Lloyd-Jones, *The Justice of Zeus*, Berkeley–London 1983², pp. 55–78; M. W. Dickie, *A&R*, XXXII (1987), pp. 113–125. On φθόνος and its personifications see J.-R. Gisler, 'Phthonos', *LIMC* VIII 1 (1997), 992–6. For ὁ θεός as a collective noun equivalent to τὸ θεῖον see n. on 31, 3.

2. ἐν γὰρ... χρόνῳ: cf. V 9,3; see Soph. *Phil.* 305–6; for other echoes of this chapter in Sophocles, see P. Keseling, *PhW* LVII (1937), coll. 910–2. ἑβδομήκοντα: according to Solon, a lifetime should ideally last seventy years (fr. 27 West; cf. Diog. Laert. I 55, but he subsequently prolonged it to eighty (fr. 20 West, cf. Diog. Laert. loc. cit.), as a reaction to Mimnermus' hope to reach 60 without disease and worry (fr. 6 West); see A. Masaracchia, *Solone*, Florence 1958, pp. 322 ff., 334 ff. Seventy, being a multiple of 7 and 10, is a mystic number and certainly not the result of a demographic study: life-expectancy in archaic Greece was much lower. On the age of 70 see also Arist. *Pol.* 1335b32, 1336b38; [Hippocrates], Περὶ ἑβδομάδων 5 (VIII, p. 636 Littré); on the theory of the hebdomads and its application in historiography see R. van Compernolle, *Étude de chronologie et d'historiographie siciliotes*, Brussels–Rome 1960, pp. 252 f. and the bibl. quoted in the note on 30,1; A. Dreizehnter, *Die rhetorische Zahl: Quellenkritische Untersuchungen anhand der Zahlen 70 und 700*, Munich 1978; Fehling, pp. 225 ff. For peoples setting a limit to human life, see note on 216,5–6.

3. ἡμέρας: the calculation is simplified. Only six 'full' months in the Greek lunar calendars were thirty days long. Each pair of months was fifty-nine days long and the whole lunar year comprised 354 days, not 360, as Herodotus' calculation entails. The intercalation of a thirteenth month every two years is the most ancient system for harmonization with the solar year by ensuring that a pair of lunisolar years is either 737 or 738 days long: see Herodotus' discussion of this system, which he compares to the solar system adopted by the Egyptians (II 4,1). In Herodotus' time the Athenian astronomer Meton reformed the traditional system by introducing seven intercalary months within a cycle of nineteen years, as in the Babylonian system. There is no evidence, however, that the Metonic system was adopted in Athens or elsewhere in the 5th cent. or that Herodotus knew about it. On the calendar reforms attributed to Solon see A. Martina, *Solon. Testimonia veterum*, Rome 1968, 369a–371b (esp. Plut. *Sol.* 25). For bibl. see Bickerman, ch. 1.

4. πᾶν... συμφορή: an expression of popular wisdom; συμφορή, lit. 'bringing together', means 'coincidence', 'chance', usually in the negative sense of 'misfortune' or 'disaster'. It is the key word in the story of Atys and Adrastus, following immediately (chs. 34–45); cf. Immerwahr, p. 157; Arieti, p. 58.

5. τύχη: here 'luck', or 'chance'. It appears in Herodotus also in the plural, and sometimes with adjectives or demonstrative pronouns; it may have the neutral meaning of 'chance', 'circumstance', 'situation' (e.g. VII 236,2) as well as that of 'good luck' (e.g. I 118,2 and 124,1), 'happy occasion' (I 119,1) and also of 'bad luck' (VI 16,2). At VII 10,2 the word appears twice, once in the sense of good luck and once in the sense of misfortune. For the formula θείη τύχη, 'by divine providence', see e.g. I 126,6; Myres, pp. 48 f.; Drexler, pp. 103–6; cf. note on 111,1). Herodotus' τύχη influences the life of individuals or human destiny, not the historical process, as in Thucydides or Polybius). For the iconography of τύχη, see L. Villard, *LIMC* VIII 1 (1997), 115–25. πολλοὶ μὲν... εὐτυχέες: cf. the story of Ameinocles (VII 190), which perhaps recalls that of Croesus (καὶ τοῦτον). The distinction between the unhappy rich and the happy people of moderate

means is popular wisdom common to all cultures (see Arist. *Eth. Nic.* 1178b33, who quotes this passage), and should not be seen as a contradiction of the belief in the omnipotence of 'chance'. See J. Audiat, *REA* XLII (1940), 3–8.

6. ἄτην: the only 'technical' term in the cycle ὕβρις–κόρος–ἄτη in this dialogue; the word occurs several times in Solon's fragments, but only here in Herodotus (see however VI 61,1: ἄτη codd., ἄγη edd.), and is very rare in Greek prose; see Benardete, p. 17; R. E. Doyle, Ἄτη: *Its Use and Meaning*, New York 1984; M. Neuberg, in *Nomodeiktes*, pp. 491–504. For Atys as a personification of ἄτη, see note on 34–45. For κόρος ὕβριος υἱός in an oracle of Bakis, see VIII 77,1; for ὕβρις, cf. I 106,1, etc.

7. πρὶν δ᾽ἂν τελευτήσῃ: 'call no man happy until he is dead' is a λόγος ἀρχαῖος according to Sophocles (*Trach.* 1 ff.; see the scholium ad loc.). It is variously attested by Simonides (521 *PMG*) and Aeschylus (*Agam.* 928–9) before Herodotus.

9. ὁ θεὸς: see note on 31,3.

33. ἀμαθέα: this is what Croesus thinks of a man who is considered very wise by everyone else (cf. 30,2).

34–45. The logical and moral connection between Croesus' arrogance and the subsequent story of the tragic death of his son is clear. Croesus apparently had two sons and a daughter (Nanis: Hermesianax fr. 6 Diehl). It was well known in Lydia that one of his sons met a violent death, but everything else is fiction. The very names Atys and Adrastus were thought symbolic, standing for Misfortune (ἄτη) and Necessity (ἀδράστεια), respectively. However, Atys is a known Lydian name (I 7,3; VII 27,1). The story of Atys' death may also be connected to the myth of Attis, the son and companion of the Phrygian goddess Cybele, who according to the Hellenistic poet Hermesianax (in Paus. VII 17,10) was killed by a boar. See M. J. Vermaseren, *The Legend of Attis in Greek and Roman Art*, Leiden 1966; *Cybele and Attis: The Myth and the Cult*, London 1977; 'Attis', *LIMC* I 1986, pp. 22–44; Mora, pp. 139–142; G. Sfameni Gasparro, *Soteriology and Mystic Aspects in the Cult of Cybele and Attis*, Leiden 1985; P. Borgeaud, *La Mère des dieux. De Cybèle à la Vierge Marie*, Paris 1996, pp. 56–88, 131–68. Adrastus, a namesake of the leader of the Seven Argives against Thebes, is also the eponym of the Mysian city Adrastia, where there was a temple dedicated to Nemesis, the key goddess of the entire story (see note on 34,1). It seems likely that the story has its origin in a local aetiological saga. See E. Maass, *BNJ* V (1926–7), 179–83. Herodotus has organized his tale in a binary structure (two victims and two pairs of dialogues), rationalized it, and made it tragic (Croesus is the tragic hero). The story does not seem to have had much impact in antiquity. For bibl. see Immerwahr, pp. 70 f.; J. Meunier, *Didaskalion*, XXIII (1968), 1–12; R. Riecks, *Poetica*, VII (1975), 23–44 (esp. for the sources and the place of the story in the 'dramatic structure' of the *logos* of Croesus); and M. Szabo, *ACD* XIV (1978), 9–17; Long, pp. 74–105; Arieti, pp. 54–66.

34,1. νέμεσις: a *hapax* in Herodotus. As the goddess of 'Retribution' or 'Revenge', Nemesis had a well-known temple at Rhamnous, not far from Marathon. For the Homeric concept of *nemesis* and its iconography, see P. Karanastassi, 'Nemesis', *LIMC* VI (1992), 733–62, with bibl. ὄνειρος: in Herodotus, dreams (like oracles, portents, and wise counsellors) are literary constructions which serve as a means of warning and of foretelling the future. See Frisch; H. Schawbl, Ἀρετῆς μνήμη. *Stud. I. Vourveris*, Athens 1983, pp. 17–27; cf. Introduction, pp. 42 f. Herodotus may have occasionally used sources, suited to each case, of an oracular, narrative, or other type. What we have here is a king's dream on the future of his heir or dynasty: cf. the dreams of Astyages (I 107–8) and Cyrus (I 209,1). The dreamer usually believes the prophecy and also tries to avert it; see R. Bichler, *Chiron*, XV (1985), 125–47; Arieti, pp. 55–6, 128. As with oracles, the main problem is that of interpretation; see Crahay, pp. 186 f. τῶν μελλόντων γενέσθαι: see note on 8,2.

2. οὕτερος μὲν διέφθαρτο: on this son, see 85,1–4.

3. καταρρωδήσας: see note on 9,1. ἄγεται...: cf. Croesus' advice to Cyrus for making the Lydians effeminate (155,4). ἐωθότα δὲ στρατηγέειν...: as did other Anatolian princes (e.g. the Trojan Hector and the Hittite Mursili II); see P. Högemann, 'Atys'(2), *DNP* II, col. 264. Such analogies did not of course enter Herodotus' mind. ἀνδρεώνων: see Hartog, p. 111 = ET p. 93.

35,1. παρελθών...: presumably presenting himself as a 'suppliant' (ἱκέτης): cf. 73,3 and note. κατὰ νόμους: here, as most often in Herodotus, νόμος means ethnic 'custom'. Cf. in Book I, 94,1; 131,1; 172,1; 196,5; 197,1; 198,5; 200,1; 216,1. For other meanings see notes on 24,5; 29,1; 61,1; and Immerwahr, pp. 319–22. καθαρσίου: here in the sense of καθαρμός, purification; cf. the epithet of Zeus at 44,2. This problem invites Herodotus the ethnographer to add a digressive sentence on the customs of Greeks and Lydians (cf. 74,5). On the importance of pollution and the rites of purification from the Homeric age onwards, see R. Parker, *Miasma: Pollution and Purification in Early Greek Religion*, Oxford 1983. A murderer is polluted on account of bloodshed: he must be ritually purified before obtaining access to sacred and public areas. The most common Greek rite in cases of murder is expiatory sacrifice. It is noteworthy that in this instance the purification precedes the enquiry of the murderer's identity.

3. ὤνθρωπε: for this form of address, which may be neutral, as here, but may be used also in a derogatory sense, cf. I 85,4; III 63,1; VIII 125,2; see Dickey, pp. 150–4 and 285. Adrastus is addressed also by his name (44,1) or by ὦ ξεῖνε (45,2). Croesus first takes care of the stranger and then asks for his name—a Homeric form of courtesy: cf. Arieti, p. 57. ἐπίστιος: cf. Zeus' epithet at 44,2. Γορδίεω...: Adrastus comes from the Phrygian royal family, as can be deduced from the hereditary links of vassallage and guest-friendship between the Phrygian and the Lydian dynasty since the time of Alyattes. Adrastus' grandfather, Midas (not to be confused with King Midas, cf. 14,2–3), may perhaps be identified with the husband of Hermodice of Aeolic Cyme (Heraclides Lembus, *Excerpta politiarum* 37 Dilts; Pollux IX 83). In accordance with the customary treatment by oriental kings of prisoners or hostages of importance, Adrastus lives in Croesus' palace (35,4; cf. note on 130,3). For another Adrastus at Argos and Sicyon see V 67–8.   ἀέκων: cf. 45,2. The two murders committed by Adrastus are unintentional. For the distinction between premeditated and unintentional murder in Attic law (that does not of course apply to the whole of Greece, let alone to Lydia), see D. M. MacDowell, *Athenian Homicide Law in the Age of the Orators*, Manchester 1963; M. Gagarin, *Drakon and Early Athenian Homicide Law*, New Haven–London 1981; R. W. Wallace, *The Areopagus Council to 307 B.C.*, Baltimore–London 1985. According to Ptolemy Hephaestion, Adrastus' brother was called Agathon and seems to have been killed following a quarrel about a quail: see Photius, *Bibliotheca* 190, p. 146b Henry; cf. K. H. Tomberg, 'Die Kaine Historia des Ptolemaios Chennos', Diss. Bonn 1967, pp. 168–9, n. 97.

36,1. δίαταν εἶχε: 'lived'; cf. 136,2 etc.; for δίαιτα in the sense of 'way of life' see 202,2 and note.   ἐν τῷ Μυσίῳ Ὀλύμπῳ: Mysia is the north-west district of Asia Minor, stretching from Propontis and the Hellespont in the north to the river Hermus in the south, and bordering on Bithynia and Phrygia in the east. Alyattes, rather than Croesus, had annexed this region to the Lydian kingdom. Herodotus considers the Mysians 'colonists' of the Lydians (VII 74,2). On the eponym Mysus, cf. I 171,6. Mt. Olympus (today Ulu Dağ; 2,400 m.) marked the north-east border between Mysia and Bithynia. See Müller II, pp. 886–8. The local people were called Ὀλυμπιηνοί (VII 74,2). It is possible that under the Persians the area was a hunting reserve (Xen. *Cynegeticus* 11,1).   ὑός: the boar-hunt as adventure, sport, competitive activity, or test of manhood dates back to Homer. In mythology the chosen heroes of Greece hunted the Calydonian boar. Nets, javelins, and spears were employed in the hunt considered difficult and dangerous. In general, for the Greeks, the hunter is a hero and the hero is a hunter. For the techniques used in this hunt see Xen. *Cyneg.* 10. Hunting is connected with the cult of Artemis, the goddess that represents the opposite lifestyle to that of Aphrodite (Atys himself flees the bridal chamber to participate in the hunt). On hunting in Greece and the East see L. Vlad Borrelli, *EAA* 1959, s.v. 'Caccia'; W. Fauth, *Persica*, VIII (1979), 1–53; W. Heimpel–L. Trümpelmann, *RLA* V (1980), coll. 234–8, with bibl.; J. K. Anderson, *Hunting in the Ancient World*, London 1985.

2. λογάδας: cf. para. 3; 43,1; 82,4, etc. 'picked men', as for war.

3. τὸ κυνηγέσιον πᾶν: 'the whole hunting establishment'; cf. Xen. *Cyneg.* 10,4; also the 'hunt' itself: ibid. 6,11, etc. The term is apparently unattested before Herodotus.

37,2. πρότερον...νῦν δέ...: a consciousness of Lydian decline is implied; cf. 155–6.   ἀγορήν: this may in fact refer to the place of the artisans and the market on the banks of the Pactolus (V 101,2); but here it is rather an expression for public areas in general.

38,1. οὐδὲν ἄχαρι παριδών: cf. 108,5; συμφορῇ ἀχάρι: 41,1; παθήματα ἀχάριτα: 207,1; etc.

40. γνώμην ἀποφαίνων: cf. 37,3 (λόγῳ ἀνάπεισον). Herodotus is a deep believer in the force of 'reasoning', but is aware of the greater force of irrational powers.

41,2. κλῶπες κακοῦργοι: unlike boars, these can use iron arrowheads. The woods around Mt. Olympus in Mysia were full of bandits even in Strabo's time: XII 8,8. **3.** ἀπολαμπρύνεαι τοῖσι ἔργοισι: cf. VI 70,3. For the notion of 'glorious deeds' see proem and notes.

43,2: ὁ ξεῖνος...Ἄδρηστος: Herodotus presents his hero again to the reader (cf. 45,3), in reference to his main deeds (cf. note on III 69,6). ἁμαρτάνει: see Introduction, p. 39. **3.** ἐξέπλησε: cf. 199,5 (to fulfil the law); III 142, 3 (to fulfil his destiny); see also the use of ἀποπίμπλημι, 'to fulfil' a prophecy, VIII 96,2 (and cf. συμπεσεῖν τὸ πάθος, VI, 18). Biblical formulas, as τότε ἐπληρώθη, καὶ ἀναπληροῦται, ἵνα πληρωθῇ, etc. for 'fulfil' a prophecy are common (see e.g. Matt. 1: 22; 2: 17; 8: 17; 13: 14.

44,2. περιημεκτέων: cf. 114,4; 164,2; etc.   Δία καθάρσιον...ἐπίστιόν... ἑταιρήιον: the god Croesus invokes and the epithets he uses are Greek; Herodotus' explanation for the three epithets could not be better. For Zeus καθάρσιος, who is closely connected to Zeus ἐπίστιος (Ionian for ἐφέστιος) the protector of guests and suppliants (cf. Zeus ξείνιος), see R. Parker, *Miasma*, p. 139 and n. 143, with bibl. Zeus ἑταιρήιος is the patron of friendship. For other epithets of Zeus in Herodotus (sixteen in total) see Powell, *Lexicon*, s.v. 'Zeus'; on Zeus and his epithets see M. Tiverios *et al.*, 'Zeus', *LIMC* VIII 1 (1997), 310–99, with bibl.   τὸν αὐτὸν...θεόν: see note on 31,3.

45,1. παρεδίδου ἑωυτὸν: this act of self-delivery is simply a theatrical tragic gesture, not a part of penal procedures or ritual. **2.** τόν τε Ἄδρηστον κατοικτίρει: Croesus' tragic humanity seemed to other authors superhuman. According to Diodorus (IX 29,1–2), Croesus begins by threatening to burn the murderer alive.   ὅς μοι καὶ πάλαι...τὰ μέλλοντα ἔσεσθαι: these words seem like an allusion to Solon's speech on the instability of fortune. But Croesus here refers to 'some god', not to Solon: he will remember Solon's words only when he finds himself on the pyre (86,3). **3.** ἔθαψε ὡς οἰκὸς ἦν: 'Croesus buried his son with all the proper ceremony' (A. De Sélincourt). μνῆμα † τωτος in a corrupt fragment of Hipponax (7 Degani = 54 Knox, Loeb edn.) has been emended to Ἄτυος. For a tentative identification of Atys' tomb at Bin Tepe (cf. note on 93,2), see C. Ratté, *JHS* CXIV (1994), 161.

46–70. These twenty-five chapters consist of four digressive *logoi*, tenuously connected to the main narrative, of which the subject is Croesus' search for supporters and allies in Greece for the impending war against the Persians. The connection consists of an introductory sentence on Cyrus' rise to power and the Persian threat (46,1); some passages about the Lydian delegations to the oracles and the responses received (46,2–48; 53; 55); a sentence on the need for information about the available Greek powers (56,1); and the last two chapters

(69–70), devoted to the alliance and exchange of gifts between Croesus and Sparta. Apart from these passages, all the rest (and even some parts of the chapters mentioned) is accessory material, disproportionately detailed in comparison with the economy of the main narrative. Chronologically the period of Croesus' preparations for the war should be placed between Cyrus' revolt against Astyages (550 BC, see note on 130) and the end of Croesus' kingdom (546 BC). The gifts to Delphi must have been offered before the temple was burned in 548 BC (see 50,3; for the date see Paus. X 5,13). When Croesus makes his enquiries (see note on 59–64), Athens is already under Pisistratus' rule (59,1), and Anaxandridas II and Ariston, who were kings together since about 550, rule at Sparta (67,1). The alliance between Croesus and Sparta can thus be dated to approximately 548/7 BC. This period of preparation corresponds roughly to the 'three extra years' that Apollo conceded to Croesus (91,3): 549–547 BC. There is no lack of difficulties (still only partially resolved) within this chronological frame.

46,1. δύο ἔτεα: mourning lasted for two years, approximately from 552 to 551, and was interrupted by the events in Media: see M. Miller, *Klio*, XLI (1963), 72 ff. On the causes of war between Croesus and Cyrus see esp. 73,1; Herodotus emphasizes several times Croesus' responsibility (see, in this ch., para. 3; also 53,2; 71,1; 73,1; 75,2; 87,3).   **Ἀστυάγεος . . .**: see note on 107,1; on Cyrus' revolt against Astyages see 107–30 and notes.   **ἡγεμονίη**: 'empire', cf. III 65,6, etc.; the term used by Herodotus for 'empire' is more commonly ἀρχή (see 53,3 and note). Elsewhere ἡγεμονίη usually refers to the supreme military command of the Hellenic coalition against Xerxes. See J. Wickersham, *Hegemony and the Greek Historians*, Lanham–London 1994, ch. 1. Cf. Introduction, p. 43.

2. ἀπεπειρᾶτο τῶν μαντηίων: also Mardonius tested several oracles in 479: Abae in Phocis and the oracles in Boeotia; VIII 133–5. In both cases the enquirer is a barbarian, who has no obligation to believe blindly in the truthfulness of Greek oracles. In an atmosphere of widespread scepticism in Herodotus' time, the idea of testing the oracles must have been pleasing chiefly as a clever trick (see the self-criticism of Croesus in the work of a Greek conformist: Xenophon, *Cyr.* VII 2,17). Some modern critics have regarded the story as a Delphic advertising stunt, and indeed only the oracles of Delphi and Amphiaraus (see 49 and note) pass the test. The details of the story are certainly fictional. There are seven oracles involved, a symbolic number; the list does not reflect the historical reality of the 6th cent.: missing from it are famous oracles of Asia Minor, Claros, and Patara, that a Lydian king could have consulted before sending envoys to Greece. Although the Milesian oracle of Branchidae did not pass the test, Croesus rewarded it with gifts, just as he did that of Delphi (92,2). The oracle of Ismenian Apollo in Boeotia is not in the list, but received gifts from Croesus (92,1). Other famous oracles are missing, such as that of Apollo at Ptoion (see VIII 134; 135,1) and that of Zeus at Olympia. In addition to these inexplicable oddities, it is technically impossible to carry out just in two years all the series of tests, the main enquiries, and the offerings. For the practical difficulties involved see note on 47,1. For sources on Croesus and the oracles see Pedley, pp. 33–5. Oracles mentioned in Herodotus are:

Apollo at Abae (VIII 27,4–5; 33; 134,1); Branchidae at Miletus (I 157,3); Zeus at Dodona (II 52–7); Amphiaraus at Thebes (I 49; 52; 92,2; III 91,1; VIII 134,1–2); Trophonius at Lebadeia (VIII 134,1); and Zeus Ammonius in the oasis of Siwah (III 25,3; 76). On the testing of oracles see above all Crahay, pp. 193–7; Klees Kirchberg, pp. 16–18; and Huber, pp. 50 f. On Herodotus and Delphi see Bowden, pp. 84–6, 146–68; and Introduction, p. 4.

3. Ἄμμωνα: see II 18,1, etc.; III 26,1 and note. On the origin and diffusion of Zeus Ammon's cult see A. M. Bisi, in *Cyrenaica* pp. 305–17; for a possible connection between the test of this oracle and the alliance between Croesus and Amasis (77,2) see V. La Bua, *MGR* V (1977), 39 ff.   δεύτερα: see 53.

47,1. ἑκατοστῇ ἡμέρῃ: if this is the correct reading (v.l. ἕκαστος τῇ A), it must mean that the sacred envoys left Sardis at the same time in order to be all present at their seven different destinations after 100 days. The oracles were supposed to be tested on the same day (cf. 48,2). Similarly, the plan presupposes that reserving an audience and securing access to the oracles was always possible, and that they were all open on the same days. This assumption contradicts all we know about Delphi, where in the archaic period the oracle was open only one day per year (in a later period once a month); see H. W. Parke, *CQ* XXXVII (1943), 19–22; Amandry, pp. 81–5. Even Croesus would have found it impossible to ensure that on the 100th day from departure all oracles would be open.   συγγραψαμένους: cf. 48,1; either some of the Lydian envoys knew Greek, or there were bilingual προφῆται in the temples (see VIII 135,2–3). At Delphi the προφήτης often dictated the response to the enquirer or gave him a copy of the text in a sealed tablet (as here: 48,1).

2. τὰ λοιπὰ τῶν χρηστηρίων: Herodotus limited himself to the information collected at Delphi; see Drexler, pp. 69 f. Is this a 'trick of lying literature'? See Fehling, p. 126.   μέγαρον: here it must be equivalent to ἄδυτον, 'which cannot be entered' (cf. I 159,3; VII 140,1 and 3), the inaccessible recess room in a temple between the cella and the opisthodomus, sometimes synonymous with ἄβατον, 'which cannot be trodden'. See A. Chanioth, 'Abaton', *DNP* I, 8–9, with bibl. Access was granted after preliminary sacrifices. Here the Pythia spontaneously utters the response when she sees the envoys enter (cf. I 65,2; V 92,2; VII 140,1); this may be a characteristic trait of mythological responses: see Fontenrose, p. 116.   ἐν ἑξαμέτρῳ τόνῳ: cf. 62,4; V 60; 61,1; VII 220,3; ἐν τριμέτρῳ τόνῳ: I 174,5; ἐν ἰάμβῳ τριμέτρῳ: I 12,2 and note. Both ἑξάμετρος and τρίμετρος are technical terms apparently unattested before Herodotus. On verse oracles see Plutarch's essay 'On the oracles at Delphi no longer given in verse' (*Mor.* 394d–409d), and cf. Fontenrose, ch. 6.

3. "οἶδα...δ' ἐπίεσται": the first Delphic response quoted by Herodotus word for word is formulated in hexameters and in proverbially enigmatic terms. See P-W II, no. 52. On the 'number of sand grains' or the 'measures of the sea', see A. Y. Campbell and A. S. F. Gow, *CR* XLV (1931), 117 ff., 172 f.; *CR* XLVI (1932), 203; and Crahay, pp. 193 ff.; sand, sea, and stars represent immeasurable entities also in Eastern literatures. 'I understand even the mute' is a proverbial

saying, not an allusion to Croesus' deaf-and-dumb son (34,1 and note). For a comparison with the formulas in the Homeric Hymn to Hermes see M. Dobson, *AJPh* C (1979), 349–59. The response is composed of proverbs and a riddle, adapted to the story of Croesus; see Fontenrose, *Q* 99 and pp. 111 ff. Wormell's numismatic interpretation (*Hermathena*, XCVII (1963), 2–22) can be regarded as a joke.

48,1. μοῦνον εἶναι μαντήιον τὸ ἐν Δελφοῖσι: see note on 46,2.

2. θεοπρόπους: see note on 19,2.   **φυλάξας…:** see note on 47,1.

49. Ἀμφιάρεω: cf. note on 46,2. Probably the sanctuary near Thebes is meant (see I 52; VIII 134,1–2) rather than the one at Oropus (in the border area between Attica and Boeotia), which was not yet famous outside Greece in the 6th cent. BC. The place where the legendary seer Amphiaraus was swallowed by the earth (see note on 52) was located by some just south of the city (Strabo IX 2, 10; Paus. IX 8,3) and by others at a site called Harma (= chariot) to the east of Thebes (Paus. IX 19,4). The exact location of the Theban Amphiareion is uncertain, but since it was somehow linked to the temple of Apollo Ismenios (see 52 with note) it should perhaps be located nearby. Consultation of Amphiaraus was by oneiromancy, but Theban citizens had no access. See I. Krauskopf, 'Amphiaraos', *LIMC* I 1 1981, pp. 691–713; A. Schachter, *Cults of Boiotia* I, London 1981, pp. 19–26; S. Symeonoglou, *The Topography of Thebes, from the Bronze Age to Modern Times*, Princeton 1985, pp. 108, 177–8; T. K. Hubbard, *HSPh* XCIV (1992), 103–7; Parker, *AR*, pp. 146–9. On the Amphiareion at Oropus see Travlos, pp. 301–18.

50,1. θυσίῃσι μεγάλῃσι: a great propitiatory sacrifice consisting of a hecatomb and a pyre of objects symbolizing material wealth. On Croesus' gifts to Delphi see H. W. Parke, *GRBS* XXV (1984), 209–32. Cf. note on 14,1.   **κλίνας…:** for other lists of oriental objects symbolizing extravagant wealth see IX 80,1–2; 82,1–2; 83,1. On Lydian and Persian gold in Herodotus see M. Lombardo, *REA* XCI (1989), 197–212.   **εἵματα πορφύρεα:** purple is a Homeric symbol of royalty (e.g. *Il.* VIII 221), whereas in Herodotus it is a specimen of oriental luxury (cf. I 152,1; III 20,1; 22,1).   **ἐλπίζω:** see note on 22,3.

2. ἡμιπλίνθια: rectangular blocks of 6 'palms' in length (παλα(ι)στή or δῶρον, about 7.5 cm.), 3 in width, and 1 palm in height (about 45 × 22.5 × 7.5 cm.). Two such blocks constituted the unit 'brick'. Croesus offered four blocks of gold and 113 of 'white gold', i.e. electrum (an alloy of gold and silver). The sand of the Pactolus was rich in gold and electrum, and the first Lydian coins were made of electrum. Gold and silver bricks were widely used in the construction of temples and palaces of the East.   **τρία ἡμιτάλαντα:** the mss., lit. 'three half-talents'. The correction τρίτον ἡμιτάλαντον ('two-and-a-half talents', cf. 50,3 and Pollux IX 54–5) does not solve the difficulty: a brick of pure solid gold, of the dimensions given by Herodotus, is in any case much heavier (about 146 kg, i.e. between 3.7 and 5.6 talents, depending on the standard used). Perhaps the bricks were not made of solid gold, or were hollow, or perhaps the dimensions are wrong: see L. I. H. Pearson, *CR* XLV (1931), 118–19, and H. Buesing, *JDAI* XCVII

(1982), 1–45. The weight of the bricks of electrum depends on the unknown ratio between gold and silver in the alloy used for this particular offering. Herodotus probably copied the measurements and weights of the gifts, which could be obtained in the mid-5th cent. from lists and the remains still extant after the fire of 548 BC (cf. 50,3).

3. λέοντος: the lion rested on 117 bricks, probably arranged in four layers forming a rectangular base with steps (see Stein ad loc.). The lower layer would then measure 4.05 × 1.57 m. and the height of the entire base would be 4 palms (approximately 30 cm.). The lion is the heraldic animal par excellence in Eastern art and in Greek sculpture and ornamentation, from the Mycenean age. In Lydia the lion appears on weights and coins; and from there it spread also to Greek cities as Miletus, Samos, etc. It was connected with the Lydian cult of Sandon and Cybele and with the myths about the foundation of Sardis (84,3). In the 4th cent. it was generally held that Gyges (14,1–2) and Croesus had been the first to donate gold to Delphi, which had earlier been content with bronze. The Delphic oracle directed those who wanted to purchase gold to Croesus (Paus. III 10,8). After 480 BC the Deinomenids of Syracuse tried to emulate the Lydian kings (Theopompus, *FGrHist* 115 F 193). For another statue of a lion in Herodotus see VII 225,2. ἐπείτε κατεκαίετο: in 548 BC. Two centuries later, in 347/6, Phayllus, tyrant of Phocis, melted down the metals that had survived the fire in order to coin money; see Diod. XVI 56,6, who used a source that simplified and rounded off Herodotus' data, making a muddle of Croesus' offerings and those of others. ἐν τῷ Κορινθίων θησαυρῷ: see I 14,2. Herodotus' precise description points to autopsy.

51,1. κρητῆρας: craters are vases of various shapes, capacities, and materials (the bell-crater, the column-crater, the volute-crater, etc.), used to mix wine and water. Craters of all types and ages have been found, mostly made of clay or bronze. Croesus' two craters are probably comparable to the biggest ones found (cf. note on 51,2). For other craters of gold in Herodotus, see I 14,1; VII 54,3; 119,2; IX 80,1; of silver: I 25,2; VII 119,2; of bronze: I 70,1–3; IV 81,3–6; of other materials: I 207,6; III 11,2–3; IV 66. The typical crater in Croesus' day was the volute-crater, with handles rising higher than the rim. Croesus' craters must originally have been placed in the *pronaos* (see para. 2), at either side of the entrance to the cella. The silver crater remained in its place: cf. VIII 122.

2. ἐν τῷ Κλαζομενίων θησαυρῷ: Clazomenae belonged then to Lydia (I 16,2). Usually the Lydian gold was kept in the Corinthians' treasury (14,2; 50,3; 51,3; cf. Paus. X 13,5). εἴνατον... μνέας: 'eight talents and a half plus twelve minae.' The mina (μνέα or μνᾶ, first mentioned by Hipponax, fr. 36,3 West) is a silver weight unit equivalent to 1/60th of a talent. It is a loan-word from Semitic languages (*manu* Accadic, *mnh* Royal Aramaic, etc.). By the Attic–Euboic standard the mina is thought to weigh about 431 gr. and the talent about 26 kg. Croesus' golden crater therefore weighs about 500 minae = 220 kg. See also note on III 95,1. ἐπὶ τοῦ προνηΐου τῆς γωνίης: cf. VIII 122. This is a corner of the *pronaos* ('fore-temple'; cf. 92,1 and note), at the meeting-point of the wall of the cella and one of its *antae*. ἀμφορέας ἑξακοσίους: ἀμφορεύς is appar-

ently unattested in sources earlier than Herodotus. It is usually an earthenware
jar, with a narrow neck and two handles used for keeping wine, milk, etc.; cf. IV
163,1; 164,3; 195,3; VIII 28. As a capacity measure (cf. I 70,1; IV 81,4), one
ἀμφορεύς equals more than 40 litres. Croesus' silver crater therefore had the
capacity of over 20,000 litres, the same as the Scythian crater at Exampaeus (IV
81,2–6), while the crater donated by Croesus to Sparta was half the size (I 70,1).
The capacity of the silver crater was known because (γὰρ) it was still used at the
Theophania (or perhaps Theoxenia?—see E. Paribeni, *EAA* 1966, s.v. 'Teossenie'),
a spring festival in honour of all the gods (W. G. Forrest, *ABSA* LXXVII (1982),
83 f.). It may seem fantastically large, almost twenty times larger than the crater of
Vix (n. 70,1); see O. K. Armayor, *HSPh* LXXXII (1978), 51 ff., with Pritchett's
criticism, pp. 248 ff.; J. G. Griffith, *Festinat senex*, Oxford 1988, pp. 5–23. The
silver crater was melted down in 347/6 BC together with Croesus' other gifts, and
was replaced ten years later by a new one made by Athenian and other artists.

3. **Θεοδώρου τοῦ Σαμίου**: a famous architect, smelter of iron and bronze, and
engraver, who flourished *c*.560–20 BC. Herodotus' esteem for him is clear. The
invention of technical instruments (the square, lever, lathe, level) was attributed to
Theodorus, and he and Rhoecus were also credited with the discovery of a new
method of smelting and moulding bronze and iron. Herodotus attributes to
Theodorus the famous, but legendary, ring of Polycrates (III 41,1; cf. Paus. VIII
14,8); others claim that he was the creator of the golden vine which adorned the
chamber of the Persian kings (VII 27,2), of a statue of Apollo in Samos, etc. In the
field of architecture Theodorus contributed to the creation of the Ionic order, and
collaborated with Rhoecus (III 60,4) on the construction of the Heraeum at Samos
(60,3 and note). See A. Stewart, *Greek Sculpture: An Exploration*, New Haven–
London 1990, pp. 244–6.   **πίθους**: the πίθος (*dolium* in Latin) is a rounded pot
or vessel with handles, shaped like a barrel, usually made of clay (cf. III 96,2). Archaic
πίθοι with bas-reliefs have been found on the islands, in Boeotia and elsewhere. The
Delphic πίθος which was destroyed in 87/6 BC (Plut. *Sulla* 12,6) may have been that of
Croesus.   **περιρραντήρια**: basins for lustral water used for sprinkling or ablution.
They were placed at the entrance of temples and other sacred areas for public use, and
belong to the ritual inventory common to all temples. At Sardis a special minister
acted as 'sprinkler' (περιρραντής). For the archaeological evidence see J. Ducat, *BCH*
LXXXVIII (1964), 577–606. The silver sprinkler, melted down with everything else in
347/6 BC, was later replaced by a new one made by Athenian artists.

4. **ἐπέγραψε**: this is the most ancient Greek testimony of a false inscription.
Herodotus reports rumours current at Delphi in his time. He knows the name
of the falsifier, but does not reveal it: cf. II 123,3 and IV 43,7, and the passages
collected by Drexler, pp. 63 ff. Ptolemy Hephaestion does mention a name, for
what it is worth: a certain Aethus of Delphi (Photius, *Bibliotheca* 149b Henry),
unknown elsewhere. On Herodotus' criticism, see Verdin, pp. 55–7. Prontera, *RA*
(1981), 253–8 (with bibl.) claims that the false inscription is part of the Alcmaeonid 'schemes', when in exile at Delphi (from 514 BC), to win over the Spartans.
Herodotus quotes few inscriptions; cf. 93,3 and 187. See H. Volkmann, in

Convivium. Festschrift K. Ziegler, Stuttgart 1954, pp. 41–65; Fehling, pp. 133–40; S. West, *CQ* XXXV (1985), 278–305.

5. οὐκ ἐπίσημα: 'without inscriptions', and cf. the ἄλλα ἀναθήματα at 92,1. The remains of chryselephantine statues as well as of a bull were found under the Sacred Way at Delphi, and attributed for chronological reasons to the 'many other offerings' of Croesus; see P. Amandry, *BCH* LXIII (1939), 86–110; *Études delphiques*, Athens–Paris 1977, pp. 273–93.   χεύματα: casts of melted silver poured into round moulds.   εἴδωλον: cf. VI 58,3 (in the same sense as portrait statue).   τρίπηχυ: = about 1.35 m. (cf. I 178,3 and note).   τῆς ἀρτοκόπου: Croesus' baking-woman saved him from the poison that had been put into the bread by order of the Ionian wife of Alyattes (Plutarch, *Mor.* 401e). The anecdote should be connected with the conspiracy of Pantaleon (92,2–3). It has been suggested that the golden statue represented a votary of Cybele holding a tympanum, misinterpreted as a baking-woman by Herodotus or his informants at Delphi; see D. Harvey, in J. Wilkins *et al.* (eds.), *Food in Antiquity*, Exeter 1995, pp. 278–81. The statue was melted down, together with everything else, in 347/6 BC (Diodorus XVI 56,6). The name of Croesus' wife is unknown (cf. Xen. *Cyr.* VII 2,26–8). According to Bacchylides (31, lines 33 and 50), she climbed with her daughters onto Croesus' pyre; according to Ctesias, *FGrHist* 688 F 9(4), she killed herself when Sardis was captured.   τὰ ἀπὸ τῆς δειρῆς: i.e. necklaces; Herodotus' term for a soldier's necklace or torque is στρεπτός (III 20,1; 22,2; IX 80,2).   τὰς ζώνας: ζώνη and ζωστήρ are used interchangeably by Herodotus for 'girdle' or 'belt', mostly worn by Iranian kings and warriors (I 215,1; IV 9,4; 10,1; VII 61,1; VIII 120) but also by Athenian hoplites (IX 74,1). The sumptuous girdle of Persian queens was financed by revenues from certain cities and villages (see note on III 91,2).

52. τήν τε ἀρετὴν καὶ τὴν πάθην: a famous episode of the Theban cycle, known to Pindar, the tragedians, and Herodotus (VIII 134,2). Amphiaraus, a pious and wise seer, fought bravely on the side of the Seven against Thebes, but died swallowed up by a chasm in the earth, as he himself had predicted (Apollodorus, *Bibl.* III 6,2–8). For bibl. see note on 49.   ἀρετή: here, as elsewhere in Herodotus, is military valour: see Immerwahr, pp. 308 f. Croesus' admiration for Amphiaraus is an element of Herodotus' tragic characterization of the Lydian king.   τοῦ Ἰσμηνίου Ἀπόλλωνος: this famous temple has been located on the hill now called Ayios Loukas, south-east of the Electra gate of Thebes, on the river Ismenus. The archaic building (see Pindar, *Pyth.* XI 1–11) occupied the site of a previous temple, destroyed by fire c.700 BC. A later building was started in the 4th cent. BC but left unfinished; it was described by Pausanias (IX 10,2–3) in the 2nd cent. AD. The temple owned a collection of tripods, some of them inscribed (V 59–61), and statues attributed to Phidias and Scopas. See P. W. Wallace, *Strabo's Description of Boeotia: A Commentary*, Heidelberg 1979, p. 133; A. Schachter, op. cit., 132–3, 180–1, 236–9. Cf. note on 49. On the festival of Daphnephoria held at this temple see Pindar (loc. cit.), with P. Angelis Bernardini, in *Boiotika. Vorträge vom 5 Internationalen Böotien-Kolloquium*, Munich 1989, pp. 39–47.

53,1. τὰ χρηστήρια: of Delphi and of Amphiaraus. Nicolaus of Damascus adds an oracle of Zeus: *FGrHist* 90 F 68(8).

3. ἢν στρατεύηται ... καταλύσειν: cf. the apology at 91,4 and the indirect allusions at 69,2; 75,2; 86,1. This response is the most famous example of oracular ambiguity: see e.g. Lucian (*Iupp. Trag.* 43), who calls it ἀμφήκης 'double-edged', διπρόσωπος 'with two faces', like the double Hermae, and ἀμφιδέξιος 'ambiguous'. Aristotle (*Rhet.* 1407a38) and Diodorus (IX 31,1) quote it in hexameters; Cicero gives a Latin version (*Div.* II 115–16), and expresses doubts about its authenticity, comparing it with the oracle delivered to Pyrrhus in Ennius' *Annales*; see the criticism of Petrarch, *Rer. Mem.* IV 26; cf. J. A. S. Evans, *CJ* LXIV (1968), 11–12. The usage of the third person is rare even when responses are related through sacred envoys. See P–W II, no. 53; Crahay, pp. 197–9; Kirchberg, pp. 18–21; according to Fontenrose, Q 100 and pp. 113 f., it is 'not genuine'. It was clearly composed *post eventum*: the war might have ended without the fall of any empire. For ἀρχή in the sense of an oriental 'empire', cf. in Book I, 86,1; 91,4; 95,1; 104,2; 106,2; 185,1; 207,3; for bibl. cf. note on 46,1.

54,1. στατῆρσι: the Lydian stater (of electrum or silver) is equivalent to the oriental *šql* (60 staters equal a Mesopotamian mina). Here, however, the staters are made of gold. According to Plutarch, *Mor.* 556 f., every citizen of Delphi was entitled to 4 gold minae.   **ὑπερήσθη:** cf. 90,1; III 22,3; see above, note at 27,5.
2. προμαντηίην ...: the usual privilege granted by Greek cities to foreign individuals or cities in return for beneficial deeds, gifts, etc. Προμαντεία is the right of priority in consulting an oracle; ἀτέλεια at Delphi is the waiving of payment for consultation; προεδρία is the right to a front seat in public feasts, games, etc. Other privileges are προξενία (public hospitality conferred by the state on foreigners), ἀσυλία (immunity and inviolability of person and goods), and προδικία (priority of trial). Herodotus echoes the official formula used in decrees of this kind, but this does not mean that he copied an original archaic inscription from Delphi (for a tentative reconstruction of a possible original text, see *Syll.* III no. 7, and cf. 548 and n. 3).   **καὶ ἐξεῖναι ...:** Delphi apparently also granted to Croesus and the Lydians the right of citizenship for those who wanted to settle there permanently. This would be the most ancient example of potential or honorary citizenship (ἰσοπολιτεία) granted to members of an entire foreign community. See G. Gawantka, *Isopolitie*, Munich 1975, pp. 169 f. In 211 BC Sardis obtained a renewal of these privileges: *Syll.* III, no. 548.

55, 1. μουναρχίη: cf. III 80,3 and 6; 82,3 and 4; VII 154,1.
2. "ἀλλ' ὅταν ... εἶναι": see P–W II, no. 54. This response, clearly composed after Croesus retreated to Sardis (80,1–6), was included in Croesus' myth when the Greeks became aware of Cyrus' mixed Medo-Persian origin (91,5–6; 107 ff.). Abydenus, *FGrHist* 685 F 5b(3), assumes the same version concerning a prophecy by Nebuchadnezzar about the 'Persian Mule'. See Crahay, pp. 199–201; Kirchberg, pp. 21–3; Fontenrose, Q 101 and p. 114; R. Bichler, *GB* XV (1988), 47–59. It is, however, possible that an oracular riddle, perhaps composed for a different

purpose, existed before Croesus made his enquiry.   ἀλλ' ὅταν: cf. III 57,4; VI
77,2; VIII 77,1; this is a traditional opening formula of verse oracles (Fontenrose,
pp. 166 ff., 185).   ἡμίονος: the product of an ethno-socially mixed marriage;
see 91,5–6; for another prophecy concerning a mule see III 151,2 and
note.   Μήδοισι: cf. I 56,1; in the first four books Herodotus usually
distinguishes the Medes from the Persians as Simonides did earlier (fr. 13
IEG II² West; 'Simonides' *GL*); for other exceptions see I 163,3; 206,1; IV
197,1.   ποδαβρέ: a rare adjective evoking the typical ἀβροσύνη (luxury) of
Ionians and Lydians; cf. 71,4; on Lydian softness, see 34,3 and esp. 155–7;
yet the only ἀβρότατοι in Herodotus are the Scythian Agathyrsi, who are
very fond of wearing gold (IV 104).   Cf. πάναβρος Σαρδανάπαλλος: Apostolius,
XIII 89 = *Paroemiographi Graeci*, ed. Leutsch-Schneidewin.   Ἕρμον: the
modern river Gediz marked the northern border of Ionia; see Müller II,
pp. 494–8.   φεύγειν: see the interpretation of Dio of Prusa, *Or.* 13,6–7.

56–8. A connective passage introduces a true and proper digression dedicated to the
two main ethnic groups of Greece, the Dorians and the Ionians, with a parenthesis
on the language of the Pelasgians and the Tyrrhenians. Two further digressions are
then introduced: one on Athens (59–64) and one on Sparta (65–70). The section is
an important source for 5th-cent. ideas about the origins of the Greeks: the
autochthony of the Athenians, the migrations of the Dorians, the pre-Hellenic
population, the linguistic distinction between Hellenes and pre-Hellenes, etc.
In Book V the search for allies in Greece also gives rise to two long digressions on
Sparta and Athens (39–48 and 55–96 in 'reverse' order: it is the second city that
makes the alliance). In this respect Croesus foreshadows Aristagoras of Miletus.

56,1. πολλὸν τι μάλιστα πάντων ἥσθη: see note on 27,5.   ἐλπίζων: 'being
convinced'; see note on 22,3.   τῆς ἀρχῆς: the sense in this passage, as
ἡγεμονίη at 7,1, is the 'kingship' of the ruling dynasty.   ἐφρόντιζε: a typical
enquiry; cf. 153,1 and note. Croesus' trust in the god of Delphi does not rule out
the need of preparation for war.
2. ἱστορέων: see Introduction, p. 8.   προέχοντας: the hegemonic 'dualism' of Athens and Sparta dominates the political scene in the 5th cent., which
Herodotus tends to refer back to the 6th. However, what follows clearly shows
that at that time Sparta was the only hegemonic power (see 59,1 and
65,1).   Δωρικοῦ γένεος...: the Dorians and the Ionians are the two most
important ethnic and linguistic groups; other groups are the Aeolian/Thessalian,
Arcadian, and Achaean in the Peloponnese. These ethnic groups are clearly
differentiated not only by language, but also by tribal organization, cultic institutions, traditions, etc. In the 5th cent. a more profound consciousness of identity
started to be associated also with lifestyle and worldview, giving rise to stereotypes such as the 'Dorian landed aristocracy' and the 'Ionian naval democracy'.
During the Peloponnesian war these stereotypes were exploited by political
propaganda, especially in Sicily, where even earlier they had assumed violent
forms. For a good review of modern studies of this issue see E. Will, *Doriens et*

Ioniens, Strasburg 1956. On ethnic identity in Ancient Greece see J. Alty, *JHS* CII (1982), 1–14; J. M. Hall, *Ethnic Identity in Greek Antiquity*, Cambridge 1997; D. Asheri, *I Greci* II 1, pp. 14–19.   τὰ προκεκριμένα: see the textual analysis of R. A. McNeal, *AJPh* CII (1981), 359–61; id., *ICS* X (1985), 11–21; C. P. Jones, *CQ* 46 (1996), 317–18. The sense is clear: ταῦτα are the Athenians and the Spartans, τὸ μὲν the Athenians, τὸ δὲ the Spartans; thus also in the next sentence.   τὸ δὲ πολυπλάνητον κάρτα: while the Athenians, the Arcadians, and other people traditionally believed themselves to be autochthonous, the Spartans were always aware that they were not indigenous to Laconia, but came from outside and had conquered it by force. Autochthony (cf. 171,5 and note), conquest (or colonization), inheritance, and purchase supplied the ideological and legal basis for legitimizing the private, public, and 'historical' possession of the land. The official Spartan tradition, known already to Tyrtaeus and Pindar, was a rationalized form of the myth of the 'return of the Heraclids', and became amalgamated with the myth of the 'Dorian migration'. Many modern scholars have accepted the basic historicity of this myth and used it to explain the origin of the linguistic topography of the Peloponnese in historical times. Some have argued that the Dorians, who came from northern Greece (Epirus or western Macedon), were responsible for the destruction of the Mycenaean civilization in the 13th and 12th centuries BC. Others attribute to the Dorians certain technical innovations, such as the diffusion of iron, cremation, and protogeometric art, as well as certain demographic changes, such as the abandonment of some old settlements and the foundation of new ones. There is no lack of scholars who, like Beloch, absolutely deny the historicity of the Dorian migration. Today there are various tendencies that, on the basis of linguistic and archaeological data and the study of the ancient tradition, on the one hand emphasize that the same cultural phenomena can be detected in both Doric and non-Doric areas (e.g. in Attica), and on the other reject the theory of a sudden and complete break between the Mycenaean and Dorian civilizations, because of the existence of some intermediary archaeological phases between the late Mycenean and the protogeometric period. Modern scepticism about the historicity of Dorian migration has made possible an alternative theory of social and linguistic changes within the Mycenaean kingdoms themselves, replacing invasion by revolution. For this trend see A. M. Snodgrass, *The Dark Age of Greece*, Edinburgh 1971; see also the important linguistic analysis by A. Bartoněk in R. A. Crossland and A. Birchall (eds.), *Bronze Age Migrations in the Aegean*, London 1973, pp. 305–11; I. Malkin, *Myth and Territory in the Spartan Mediterranean*, Cambridge 1994. For a discussion of the entire issue see D. Musti (ed.), *Le origini dei Greci. Dori e mondo greco*, Rome–Bari 1985.

3. γῆν τὴν Φθιῶτιν: the stages of the migration are connected with places which preserved local Dorian traditions in historical times. Achaean Phthiotis is the place of origin of the eponymous Dorus. Histiaeotis is wrongly located in the north-east of Thessaly, in the area of Thessaliotis (57,1). Pindus, the mountain chain, is also the name of a city in Doris (see Müller I, pp. 544–6): one would expect to find the *ethnicon* Μακεδνοί in an area bordering on Macedonia, but the Pindus which the Dorians used as their base for the conquest of the Peloponnese

(VIII 43) must be a city: the problem is debated. Dryopis (between Mt. Oeta and Mt. Parnassus) was later called Doris (Müller I, pp. 483–4); the Dryopes were deported by Heracles to the Peloponnese, and then dispersed: I 146,1; VIII 46,4; 73,2). Herodotus does not mention the routes used by the Dorians to invade the Peloponnese, but he knew that Hyllus had chosen the road through the Isthmus: IX 26,3; 27,2. The route better known to other sources is the crossing between Rhium and Antirhium, south of Naupactus. According to Herodotus, the movements of the Dorians should be dated between the age of Deucalion (the son of Prometheus who survived the flood) and the conquest of the Peloponnese (a period of ten generations according to Hellanicus: *FGrHist* 4 F 125). Dorus is the son of Hellen and a grandson of Deucalion. Dorus and Heracles came to represent, in the Spartan national saga, the two allies who cooperated in the conquest of the Peloponnese and Sparta, i.e. the Dorians and the (Achaean) Heraclids; see Tyrtaeus, fr. 2 *IEG* II^2 West; Simonides, fr. 13 ibid.; Pind. *Pyth.* I 119 ff.; Thuc. I 12,3; Ephorus, *FGrHist* 70 F 15; cf. Herod. V 72,3 and VIII 114, 2. The Cadmeans were expelled from Thebes at the time of Laodamas, son of Eteocles (V 61,2), an event that can be dated to the time of the Trojan war (*c*.1280–1270 BC according to Herodotus, see note on 4,2–3). The invasion of the Peloponnese took place three generations after Hyllus (V 52,1), son of Heracles, came back from Troy, when Cadmus was king of Athens (V 76: according to Herodotus' chronology *c*.1180–1170). Hellenistic chronographers downdate these events by about a century: according to Eratosthenes's system (*FGrHist* 241 F 1), following Thucydides (I 12.3) the Heraclids returned to the Peloponnese in 1104/3, eighty years after the fall of Troy. Ephorus of Cyme began his universal history with the return of the Heraclids: *FGrHist* 70 F 15–18; 116–18.

57,1. γλῶσσαν: the most common term in Herodotus for 'language', both spoken and written, is γλῶσσα (see 58; 73,3; 110,1; 142,3–4; 172,1; etc.); φωνή is rarely used in this sense (see e.g. II 32,6). For διαλέγω = 'speak' a language see I 142,3–4 (διάλεκτος is not found in Herodotus) (on-line). For Herodotus' conception of foreign languages see T. Harrison, *Histos* II (1998).   οἱ Πελασγοί: Herodotus is the most remarkable representative of the so-called 'Pelasgian theory', according to which pre-Hellenic Greece was called Pelasgia and inhabited by an autochthonous population (cf. II 56,1; VIII 44,2). The Greek tribes that, in historical times, considered themselves autochthonous (such as Arcadians, Thessalians, Athenians, etc.) were seen as 'hellenized' Pelasgians. Only the Dorians, not autochthonous but Greek-speaking, could not claim descent from the Pelasgians, and therefore came to be considered 'Hellenic' in origin. According to this theory, the Pelasgians became 'hellenized' when the Greek language prevailed (thus the distinction is linguistic, not ethnic) thanks to one ethnic group (presumably the Dorians) that imposed its own language on the majority at large. We do not know how this theory developed. Homer furnished poetic epithets, such as 'Pelasgian Argos' (Thessaly), or 'Pelasgian Zeus' (at Dodona), etc. Other poets and genealogists invented the eponymous Pelasgus. The tradition of the autochthony of the Athenians and a wall on the acropolis named the Πελαργικόν

(V 64,2; cf. VI 137–9) are the origin of the Pelasgian theory at Athens. Finally the need to explain the origin of non-Hellenic linguistic islands in other areas of the Greek world in historic times contributed to generalizing the Pelasgian theory. Modern research no longer attempts to identify the Pelasgians with a specific pre-Hellenic ethnic group such as the Phoenicians, the Illyrians, or the Mycenaean Achaeans; see V. Pisani, *Paideia* VII (1952), 323–7. On the other hand, the study of the various linguistic strata of the Greek language and the attested remains of pre-Hellenic languages (Linear A, Cretan hieroglyphics, the Etruscan (?) inscription in Lemnos, the Eteo-Cypriot and the Cyprio-Minoan dialects) continues. What still remains of the so-called 'Pelasgian' language is a limited body of place-names ending in -*sa*, -*ssos*, etc., conventionally called 'Pelasgian,' and between 5,000 and 6,000 non-Greek words assimilated into the Greek vocabulary, mostly names of plants, animals, and tools. For post-Herodotean sources see Ephorus, *FGrHist* 70 F 133, 119, 142, and Strabo V 2,4; VII 7,10. For modern discussions of the Pelasgian theory see J. L. Myres, JHS XXVII (1907), 170–225; L. Pareti, *RFIC* XLVI (1918), 153 ff., 307 ff., Lloyd, *Commentary 1–98*, pp. 232 ff. with bibl.   ἀτρεκέως: see Introduction, p. 21 and note 60.   τεκμαιρόμενον: cf. para. 2; on Herodotus' terminology of evidence and proof, and on his so-called 'empiricism' see Introduction, p. 22 f.   Κρηστῶνα: this Creston, 'beyond the country of the Tyrrhenians' and bordering on the Thessaliotis (56,3), must be Creston in Thrace, known also to Hecataeus and Pindar. Herodotus certainly refers to the same area when he writes about the Κρηστωνική (γῆ) and the Κρηστωναῖοι (V 3,2 and 5; VII 124; 127,2; VIII 116,1), though here (para. 3) the form used is Κρηστωνιῆται. See also Thuc. II 99,6 and 100,4. Creston is the main centre of the tribe of the Crestonians, who lived north of the Chalcidice and to the west of it as far as the river Axius, which borders on Thessaliotis; see Müller I, pp. 178–9. Thucydides knew about Pelasgians in the Chalcidice, Tyrrhenians on Lemnos, as well as about Crestonians and 'bilingual barbarians' (IV 109,4). Other authors follow suit but, echoing Herod. IV 145,2; V, 26; VI 137, substitute Pelasgians with Tyrrhenians on Lemnos and Imbros. For 'Tyrrhenian' traces in Macedonia see N. G. L. Hammond, *A History of Macedonia*, I, Oxford 1972, pp. 119, 192, 302; for the location of the 'Tyrrhenians' at Tirsae in Mygdonia, see E. Wikén, *Hermes* LXXIII (1938), 129–32.
2. καὶ τῶν Πλακίην τε καὶ Σκυλάκην: east of Cyzicus, on the coast of the Propontis (IV 38,2); see Müller II, pp. 907–8 and 939–40 respectively. On the Dolones of Cyzicus, cf. Ephorus, *FGrHist* 70 F 61 and Strabo XII 8,11. These are probably either Thracian groups originally coming from the Crestonian area or a particular Phrygian group: see Strabo XIII 1,8.   οἳ σύνοικοι ἐγένοντο Ἀθηναίοισι: 'they had lived together with the Athenians' (perhaps a reference to the hellenized Pelasgians in Attica), before they were expelled; see VI 137–40 and cf. II 51,2–3; V 64,2 and VIII 44,2. See also A. G. Laird, *AJPh* LIV (1933), 97–119. Herodotus apparently wants to remind both the Spartans and the Athenians that they had once been 'neighbours' of the Pelasgians, or 'cohabitating' with them.   μετέβαλε: cf. para. 3, μεταβολῇ; for Herodotus' usage of these terms, see Immerwahr, p. 150, n. 3.
3. καὶ γὰρ...ἐν φυλακῇ: Dionysus of Halicarnassus quotes this passage (*Ant. Rom.* I 29,3) to show that the Pelasgians and the Tyrrhenians are different people.

While all our mss read Κρηστωνιῆται, Dionysius' copy read Κροτωνιῆται, i.e. the Pelasgians of Cortona in Umbria. Since the Krotoniates did *not* speak Etruscan (as one might have inferred from Herodotus), Dionysius argued that Hellanicus was wrong when he claimed that the Tyrrhenians or Etruscans were the Italian Pelasgians and that they had first colonized Cortona and then the rest of Etruria (Hellanicus, *FGrHist* 4 F 4, quoted by Dionysius, *Ant. Rom.* I 28,3). Some modern scholars (Pasquali, p. 313; see the editions by Costanzi and Legrand ad loc.) think that Dionysius' reading is the original one, whereas Κρηστωνιῆται and Κρηστῶνα are corrections. Yet, apart from the fact that all our manuscripts read Κρηστωνιῆται and Κρηστῶνα (see also the indirect testimony of Stephanus of Byzantium, s.v. Κρήστων), and that the area in question is said to be bordering on Thessaliotis, not on Etruria, it is easy to maintain that the correction is likely to be, as always, the *lectio facilior* (Croton, which in Greek is homonymous with the city in Umbria, was a well-known city of Magna Graecia, whereas Creston was obscure even to scholars). The Roman family of Herodotean manuscripts make a similar correction at III 136,2 (see note ad loc.). See D. Briquel, *Les Pélasgues en Italie*, Rome 1984, and especially chs. 5–6, with ample bibl. For the interpretation followed here, see E. Gabba, *RAL* XXX (1975), 44 and n. 22.

58. τὸ δὲ Ἑλληνικὸν: the Dorians and the hellenized barbarians of Pelasgian Greece.   ἀποσχισθὲν: cf. 60,3 (ἀπεκρίθη).   προσκεχωρηκότων: implies hellenization or a transformation above all linguistic.

59–64. This digression on the archaic history of Athens seems to be based on oral Attic traditions still current in Herodotus' day: the existence of a pre-Herodotean written 'History of Attica' is still a matter of debate. It should be read in conjunction with Thucydides' digression at VI 54–9 and with chs. 13–16 of Aristotle's Ἀθηναίων πολιτεία. What should have been essentially a chapter on the economic, social, and constitutional history of Athens *c.*560–46 BC is reduced in this digression to a series of anecdotes, portents, rumours, and stratagems bearing upon tyranny. Still the background against which the anecdotes are set—the warring factions, the passive role of the people, the links with foreign cities—are of great value for understanding the views of 5th-cent. Athenians on their *ancien régime*. Herodotus' own attitude towards Pisistratus is a mixture of admiration, criticism, and praise that reflects the ambiguous attitude of the Greeks towards archaic tyrannies. The chronology of the tyrannies and of the exiles of Pisistratus is one of the most debated problems of archaic Greek history. In short: Herodotus thinks that the tyranny of Pisistratus and his sons lasted for thirty-six years in all (V 65,3) and that Pisistratus' second exile lasted ten years (I 62,1), the latter round figure being of relative value. Aristotle, *Ath. Pol.* 19,2 and 6, gives an absolute date, accepted and repeated unanimously by ancient sources: according to him the tyranny ended in 511/10 BC. Taking this date as a base, the continuous tyranny of Pisistratus and his sons would begin in 547/6, and the second exile *c.*557/6. Previous chronology remains uncertain, but if we accept the date of the archon Comeas in 561/60, the first two tyrannies and the first exile must have taken place approximately within five years (561–557 BC). Among recent works see Bornitz, pp. 9–29; J. S. Ruebel, *GRBS* XIV (1973), 125–36; J. G. F. Hind, *CQ* XXIV (1974), 1–18; G. Maddoli, *Cronologia e storia*, Perugia 1975, pp. 25–31; Rhodes, pp. 191–9, and *Phoenix*, XXX (1976), 219–33; J. H. Schreiner, *SO* LVI (1981), 13–17; F. J. Frost, in *Essays in Honor of G. C. Starr*, Lanham 1985, pp. 57–78; V. Gray, *Histos*, I 1996/7 (on-line). On Herodotus and tyrants see Waters; on Herodotus and Athens see Immerwahr, pp. 206–25; Myres, pp. 177–84; J. A. S. Evans, *AC* XLVIII (1979), 112–18; W. G. Forrest, *Phoenix*, XXXVIII (1984), 1–11; G. Maddoli, *Storia della storiografia*, VII (1985), 101–12; on Pisistratus see A. Andrewes, *CAH*² III, pp. 392–416. On archaic tyranny see Berve I, pp. 3–167; K. H. Kinzl, *Die ältere Tyrannis bis zu den Persenkriege*, Darmstadt 1979; L. de Libero, *Die archaische Tyrannis*, Stuttgart 1996.

59,1. τοῦτον τὸν χρόνον: Croesus' envoys *c.*548/7 found Pisistratus ruling again after his return from ten years of exile. Hence either Herodotus did not establish a synchronism between the battle of Pallene (62,3–63,2) and the capture of Sardis, or he did not start his calculations from 511/10, or he dated the capture of Sardis a couple of years later. The problem cannot be solved. He clearly paid no attention to chronology when he decided to insert the digression on Athens within the story of Croesus. At any rate, Croesus' envoy to Athens was invented to parallel the embassy sent to Sparta, and to foreshadow the mission of Aristagoras of Miletus (V 55,1 ff.).   Ἱπποκράτεος: see Davies, p. 445. The Olympiad may be that of 608 or that of 604.   τέρας: 'portent', with dative of reference (cf. 78,1 as well as 74,2 and 175). See F. J. Frost, in *The Eye Expanded: Life and Art in Graeco-Roman Antiquity*, ed. F. B. Titchener and R. F. Moorton, Jr., Berkeley 1999, pp. 9–18. For the terminology see Huber, pp. 26 f. For dreams and portents on the birth of important persons see I 107,1–8 (Cyrus); V 92,2–3 (Cypselus); VI 131,2 (Pericles). For the function of portents, etc. in Herodotus' work see Introduction, pp. 42 f.

2. Χίλων: a famous ephor, active in the middle of the 6th cent. The meeting with Hippocrates at the end of the 7th cent. is chronologically impossible. Chilon here plays the role of the 'wise counsellor'; see note on 27,1. He was included in the list of the 'Seven Sages' (see note on ch. 20). His reform raised the ephorate to a level almost equivalent to that of the kings. His figure is connected with propaganda and Spartan resistance against tyranny, with the establishment of the Peloponnesean league, and with the 'great change' in lifestyle and regime which developed at Sparta during the 6th cent. Chilon had a hero-cult at Sparta. See, in Herod., also VII 235,2; another Chilon, also from Sparta, is mentioned at VI 65,2. See G. L. Huxley, *Early Sparta*, Shannon 1962, pp. 69–71; C. M. Stibbe, *Castrum peregrini*, CXLVIII–CXLIX (1981), 72–101; A. Griffin, *Sikyon*, Oxford 1982, pp. 45–7; L. Thummen, *Lakedaimonion Politeia*, Stuttgart 1996, pp. 76–8.   γυναῖκα ... τεκνοποιὸν: in Attic terms, lawful wife (γαμετή), mother of lawful children (γνήσιοι). This advice may perhaps be the origin of one of the ancient interpretations of the saying ἐγγύα, πάρα δ᾽ ἄτα, 'get engaged, the catastrophe is near', attributed to Chilon (Diod. IX 10,4, etc.). ἐκπέμπειν: 'repudiate the wife'. ἀπείπασθαι: indicates the withdrawal of the father's formal recognition pronounced at the birth of his son, an act similar to disinheriting a son, ἀποκήρυξις. See A. Wurm, *Apokeryxis, Abdicatio und Exheredatio*, Munich 1972, pp. 6–7.

3. στασιαζόντων: the three social and regional 'factions' (στάσεις) of 6th-cent. Attica are first attested by Herodotus in this chapter using the terminology current in his own time; cf. Arist., *Ath. Pol.* 13–15 and Plut., *Sol.* 13,1–2; 29,1. The men of the 'Plain' (Πεδιάς, Πεδιακοί) would be rich landowners, centred in the plain of western Attica, and politically oligarchic; the men of the 'Shore' (Παραλία, Παραλοί) would be traders and fishermen, centred along the coasts of southern and eastern Attica, and politically moderate; and the men of the 'Hill' (Ὑπεράκριοι, Διάκρια, Διάκριοι) mostly farmers and shepherds living in the mountainous area of eastern Attica, and politically radical. This traditional tripartite division is too schematic. There certainly were not clear-cut geographical or professional distinctions. The city of Athens itself was politically divided: at any rate, the leaders of all factions could find support in it, and the leadership of all factions was in the hands of locally based aristocratic clans. Cleisthenes' reforms were aimed at demolishing the old regional and class divisions. See F. Ghinatti, *I gruppi politici ateniesi fino alle guerre persiane*, Rome 1970; P. J. Bicknell, *Studies in Athenian Politics and Genealogy*, Wiesbaden 1972; F. Kluwe, *Klio*, LIV (1972), 101–24; H. K. Kinzl, *AHB* III (1989), 5–9. On faction-leaders, families, and properties see Davies, pp. 348 ff., 368 ff., 444 ff. Megacles is usually taken to be the husband of Agariste, daughter of Cleisthenes of Sicyon; but see F. W. Mitchell, *TAPhA* LXXXVIII (1957), 127–30. For the Alcmaeonidae in Herod. cf. V 62–5; 69–71; VI 121–31. Lycurgus belongs to the aristocratic γένος of the Eteobutadae. Pisistratus had some property in Brauron, south of Marathon (cf. 62,2), in the Hyperacria (VI 20) and he had connections with the powerful clan of the Philaidae. It is uncertain whether he was the founder of this third faction, as Herodotus implies. See Arist., *Ath. Pol.* 13,4. The famous hypothesis of P. N. Ure, *The Origin of Tyranny*, Cambridge 1922 (repr. 1962), pp. 33 ff., that Pisistratus was a mine-owner and the chief of a mass of contractors and miners, has found little following, not least because the mines at Laurion, unimportant in the 6th cent., are part of the Paralia. τρωματίσας...: cf. Arist., *Ath. Pol.* 14,1; Plut. *Sol.* 30,1. 'One who is aiming at a tyranny asks for a bodyguard' (Arist. *Rhet.* 1357b30); cf. Plato, *Resp.* 566b.

4. πρὸς Μεγαρέας: this war against Megara cannot be dated before 575–70, i.e. before Pisistratus reached the age of 30, the minimum age for military commands in the 5th cent. According to one tradition Pisistratus and Solon fought together against Megara: see Plutarch, *Sol.* 8,2; but see Arist., *Ath. Pol.* 17,2. The evidence is extremely confused. Νίσαιάν: Nisaea is the port of Megara on the Saronic gulf; see Müller I, pp. 576–9. Herodotus is the only source that attributes its occupation to Pisistratus; see however the stratagem described by Aeneas Tacticus IV 8–11; cf. R. P. Legon, *Megara*, Ithaca–London 1981, pp. 136 f.). From 461

onwards Nisaea was mostly under Athenian control and connected to Megara by two long walls.   ἀποδεξάμενος: see note on proem.

5. ὁ δὲ δῆμος: the author of this ψήφισμα was a certain Arist(i)on, see Arist., *Ath. Pol.* 14,1; Plut., *Sol.* 30,2. The aged Solon's opposition to this proposal is famous.   κορυνηφόροι: 'club-bearers'; according to Plutarch, *Sol.* 30,2, they were fifty in number, according to other sources 300 or 400 (scholium to Plato, *Resp.* 566b; Diog. Laert. I 66). The term, obsolete already in the 4th cent., recurs as a nickname of peasants also at Sicyon, see Pollux III 83 and Stephanus of Byzantium, s.v. Χῖος.

6. οὔτε τιμὰς...: this is inconsistent with Herodotus' negative portrayal of the third tyranny (para. 1); cf. Arist., *Ath. Pol.* 14,3.

60,1. τὠυτὸ φρονήσαντες: the strength or weakness of these coalitions depends on the position of the unstable 'centre'. The uncompromising anti-tyrannical faction is composed of Lycurgus' oligarchic πεδιακοί. The Alcmaeonidae were responsible for Pisistratus' rise to power and for his first restoration, in spite of later propaganda attempts to obscure this fact (V 62–3; VI 121; 123). See Plutarch's acute observation at *Mor.* 858c and 863b. Herodotus is the primary source on the three tyrannies of Pisistratus; cf. H. K. Kinzl, *AHB* III (1989), 9; on Pisistratus' rise to power in Herodotus see Ubsdell I, pp. 142–53 and nn.; B. M. Lavelle, *CQ* XLI (1991), 317–24; id., *The Sorrow and the Pity*, Stuttgart 1993, pp. 90–5. V. Gray, *Histos* I (1996–7) (on-line), with bibl.   ἐξελαύνουσί μιν: the first exile was short, perhaps a couple of months. Aristotle's five years (*Ath. Pol.* 14,3) must be wrong. He probably did not leave Attica, but withdrew to the Diacria, and was restored to power in the archonship of Hegesistratus (560/59).

3. πρῆγμα εὐηθέστατον: Herodotus apparently rationalized a previous, less sophisticated version of this famous anecdote (see H. J. Rose, *CQ* XXXIV (1940), 81–2), which presumably presented the procession of Phye and Pisistratus on a chariot as a miraculous epiphany of the goddess bringing back her chosen protégé to her acropolis and to power. Scenes of gods or heroes with mortals (mostly warriors or bridegrooms) on a chariot are depicted on Attic archaic vases; see also the scene on Polinices' shield in Aesch. *Sept.* 642–8. Pisistratus may well have exploited a familiar motif for propaganda; but it is worthy of note that heralds had to be sent to explain to the populace the meaning of the show. Re-creating epiphanies as a kind of religious performance with popular participation are known in ancient Greece, in medieval Europe, and even today. Herodotus believed that, in his day, a stratagem of this sort would have fooled no one, but he liked the idea nonetheless. Apparent is the arrogant irony of a 5th-cent. intellectual regarding the naivety of the previous century, and his scepticism regarding the stereotypical opposition between 'Greek intelligence' and 'barbarian naivety', and the supposed wisdom of the Athenians. Yet, one should not forget that in other reported cases of divine epiphany Herodotus is less sceptical (see e.g. II 91,3; VI 105; VIII 38–9; 84,2). On this anecdote, as well as on the hypothesis that Pisistratus was dressed up as Heracles, and on the

possibility of political manipulation of myth in archaic Athens in general, see
W. R. Connor, *JHS* CVII (1987), 40–50; J. Boardman, *JHS* CIX (1989), 158–9;
R. H. Sinos, in C. Dougherty and L. Kurke, *Cultural Poetics in Archaic Greece: Cult,
Performance, Politics*, Cambridge 1993, pp. 73–91; Parker, *AR*, Oxford
1996, pp. 83–4; H. Brandt, *Chiron*, XXVII (1997), 315–34; U. Huttner, *Die
politische Rolle der Heraklesgestalt in griechischen Herrschertum*, Stuttgart 1997,
pp. 25–42.   ἀπεκρίθη: refers to the separation of the Hellenes from the
Pelasgians (cf. ch. 58). On the various readings and interpretations of this passage
see P. Shorey, *CPh* XV (1920), 88–90; R. Lamacchia, *A&R* IV (1954), 87–9;
W. Burkert, *RhM* CVI (1963), 97–8; B. Laurot, *Ktéma*, VI (1981), 42–3 (with
the observation of E. Lévy at p. 48); A. Colonna, *Paideia*, L (1995), 98–101.
If we accept the reading in A (τὸ βάρβαρον ἔθνος τοῦ Ἑλληνικοῦ), the sense would
be: in ancient times the barbarians must have been cleverer than the Greeks if even
the Athenians, supposedly the wisest of the Greeks, were fooled like that. For other
interpretations of the stratagem see G. F. Else, *Hermes*, LXXXV (1957), 36–7;
Delcourt, pp. 177–80. Aristophanes may have parodied this passage in the *Birds*:
see C. Bonner, *AJPh* LXIV (1963), 208–10.

4. ἐν τῷ δήμῳ τῷ Παιανιέï: in pre-Cleisthenic Attica δῆμος is just a 'village', not
an administrative unit. Paiania is located on the eastern slopes of Mt. Hymettus
(near modern Liopesi), about 12 km. to the east of Athens. Demosthenes was
from Paiania; see Müller I, p. 684.   Φύη: the democratic Atthidographers
demystified the story of Phye by making her a Thracian flower-seller
(Arist. *Ath. Pol.* 14,5); according to Cleidemus (*FGrHist* 323 F 15) she later
married Hipparchus, son of Pisistratus. The exceptional height of the girl
(about 1.70 m.) was impressive: Phye, therefore, looks like a pun-name
(φυή = 'stature'). Polyaenus I 21,1 connects the story of Phye to the battle of
Pallene, perhaps following sources that confused or assimilated the two restorations of Pisistratus to power.   σκευάσαντες: for examples of women ritually
dressing as goddesses see Dittenberger, *Syll.* III 736, IV ll. 23–5; Polyaenus
VIII 59.   σχῆμα: 'garb', 'attire'; the term occurs only here in Herodotus
(σχημάτιον: VI 129,3). On the meanings of *schema* in Greek literature of classical
times see M. L. Catoni in *I Greci* II 2 (1997), 1013–60.

61,1. Μεγακλέα: see note on 59,3. The name of the daughter is unknown; cf.
Arist. *Ath. Pol.* 15,1.   παίδων: Hippias (*c.*570–490 BC), Hipparchus (killed in
514/13), and Hegestistratus (or Thessalus). Pisistratus may also have had a
daughter.   ἐναγέων: the clan of the Alcmaeonidae had been 'impure' collec-
tively and by heredity—the living, the dead, and their future descendants—ever
since the conspiracy of Cylon, outlaws and perpetually banned, without the
possibility of an amnesty. Even their bones were to be exhumed and thrown
outside the borders of the state. In practice, however, political and economic
considerations prevailed: Megacles, Cleisthenes, and other members of the clan
held the highest offices in Athens, despite the ἄγος which was formally still valid
and repeatedly used for political propaganda (e.g. in 508/7 (V 70,2 ff.) and, for
the last time, in 432/1 (Thuc. I 126–7)). Cf. B. Lavelle (*op. cit.* note 60,1).

οὐ κατὰ νόμον: here in the sense of 'rule', whether correct or conventional (cf. 90,2 and 195,2). See note on 35,1. On the anecdote, cf. Plut., *Mor.* 858c.

2. τῇ ἑαυτῆς μητρί: probably Agariste (see note on 59,3). κατηλλάσσετο... ἀπαλλάσσετο: see J. E. Powell, *CR* LI (1937), 105; Bornitz, p. 13, n. 20. τὸ παράπαν: the ten-year exile of the Pisistratids begins (557–47?), initially voluntarily (cf. Arist. *Ath. Pol.* 15,1), but later by condemnation involving confiscation of property, which only one citizen, Callias, had the courage to buy (VI 121,2). ἐς Ἐρέτριαν: the only residence of the exiles mentioned by Herodotus (who is summarizing: cf. para. 4). At that time Eretria was a flourishing city ruled by an oligarchy of knights; see Müller I, pp. 401–5. From this base the exiles could have gone to Thebes, Argos, and Naxos to collect money and mercenaries, then settling in Rhaikelos on the Thermaic gulf and in the gold-bearing area of Mt. Pangaeum: Arist. *Ath. Pol.* 15,2–4.

3. Ἱππίεω: from the very beginning Herodotus presents Hippias as the most 'tyrannical' of Pisistratus' sons: cf. V 62,1–2; 91,1; 93–4; VI 1–2; 107. Hippias and Marathon provide a link between the events of 547/6 and those of 490; see Bornitz, pp. 15 ff. Θηβαῖοι: Thebes was ever interested in weakening Athens.

4. Ἀργεῖοι μισθωτοί: they were 1,000 altogether, led by Hegestistratus son of Pisistratus (Arist., *Ath. Pol.* 17,4). Λύγδαμις: see note on 64,2.

62,1. Μαραθῶνα: Marathon is the natural landing-place for ships coming from Eretria (cf. VI 102, in 490 BC), and one of the townships in Diacria that supported Pisistratus. ἐλευθερίης: here in the sense of 'free system of government', as opposed to tyranny or monarchy; cf. III 142,4; VI 5,2. For other meanings, see note on 6,3.

3. ἐπὶ Παλληνίδος Ἀθηναίης ἱρὸν: Pallene, near modern Stavros, controls the pass between Mt. Pentelicon and Mt. Hymettus; see Müller I, pp. 685–6.

4. Ἀκαρνὰν: the correction Ἀχαρνεὺς is based on [Plato], *Theag.* 124d, who calls this seer ἡμεδαπός, 'of our land'. He may have been an Acarnanian by origin who was then given Athenian citizenship by Pisistratus; cf. M. M. Lavelle, *CQ* XLI (1991), 317–24; W. Lapini, *Il POxy 664 di Eraclide Pontico e la cronologia dei Cipselidi*, Florence 1996, pp. 180–4. Before Cleisthenes, the usage of the demotic is in any case anachronistic. For another travelling seer from Acarnania see VII 221. Some think that the prophecy is genuine, but the distich can be applied freely to any 'round-up' (by enemies, etc.). On the Pisistratids and oracles cf. I 64,2; V 90,2; VII 6,3. ἐν ἑξαμέτρῳ τόνῳ: see note on 47,2.

63,1. ἐνθεάζων: 'inspired by god'. The verb appears only here in Herodotus and is apparently unattested in earlier sources. δέκεσθαι: for δέκομαι in the precise sense of 'accepting' a prophecy, etc. cf. IV 15,3; VII 178,2; VIII 115,1; IX 91,2. ἐπῆγε τὴν στρατιήν: other sources for the battle of Pallene: Arist. *Ath. Pol.* 15,3; 17,4, Androtion, *FGrHist* 324 F 35; Polyaenus I 21,1. Herodotus is perhaps contrasting the Athenians' indifference and lack of organization in 547/6 to their effective resistance in 490, but his main message seems to be that sluggishness helps tyranny. πρὸς κύβους: warriors playing dice is a well-known motif of archaic vase-painting (e.g. Aias and Achilles on the Exekias amphora, Mus. Vat. 344). See J. Boardman, *AJA* LXXXII (1978), 11–24; R. Osborne, *Hephaistos*, V–VI (1983–4), 61–70 and pls. 1–2.

2. ἀναβιβάσας: for a possible aetiological connection between the way of Pisistratus' entering Athens and the horse-race known as *anthippasia* (Xen. *Hipparch.* 3,10–13) see N. Robertson, *Festivals and Legends: The Formation of Greek Cities in the Lights of Public Ritual*, Toronto 1992, pp. 140–3.   ἀπιέναι ἕκαστον ἐπὶ τὰ ἑωυτοῦ: the citizens are required to mind their own private business and not to meddle with politics.

64,1. ἐπικούροισί: with mercenaries (cf. 154, etc.).   συνόδοισι: a rare form for προσόδοισι. Pisistratus' income from Attica consisted in the 5 per cent and 10 per cent taxes, from Strymon the gold supplied by the mines of Mt. Pangaeum. For Pisistratus' politics and economics, see Arist., *Ath. Pol.* 16; see Müller I, pp. 104–7. ὁμήρους: the hypothesis that these hostages were 100 in number, had been freed by the Spartans *c.*524 BC, and had followed Dorieus to Sicily *c.*512–10 BC, is based on an uncertain reading in Paus. III 16,4: Ἀθηναίων ρω. See H. T. Wade-Gery, quoted by T. J. Dunbabin, *The Western Greeks*, Oxford 1948, p. 352, n. 4; Berve II, p. 547.

2. καὶ γὰρ...Λυγδάμι: a parenthetic explanation: see note on 8,1. The relationship between Pisistratus and Lygdamis and that between Lygdamis and Polycrates of Samos (Polyaenus, I 32,2) are taken as evidence for the existence of an 'international mafia' of tyrants. On Naxos see Müller I, pp. 984–6. On Lygdamis see Berve I, pp. 78 f.   Δῆλον: cf. Thuc. III 104,1. Delos, consecrated to Apollo and an amphictyonic centre in the Aegean since the 8th cent., became under Pisistratus an Athenian protectorate which, together with the alliance between Athens and Naxos, secured the Athenian hegemony in the Cyclades.   ἐκ τῶν λογίων: see Crahay, pp. 86 f. Cf. Thuc. III 104,2 for the year 426/5 BC. On archaic Delos see M. Gallet de Santerre, *Délos primitive et archaïque*, Paris 1958.

3. μετ' Ἀλκμεωνιδέων: those who accept the mss reading Ἀλκμεωνίδεω assume that Herodotus is referring to the new clan leader, Alcmeonides brother of Megacles, known from two dedicatory inscriptions (*IG* I³ 597; *CEG* I, 302). However, it is unlikely that Herodotus should mention him without any introduction. On the exile of the Alcmaeonidae cf. VI 123,1.

65–70. A brief connecting sentence introduces the digression on Sparta (chs. 65–8), which leads to two concluding chapters on the alliance with Croesus (69–70). Sparta is by convention the opposite of Athens. While Athens is oppressed and weakened by tyrants, Sparta has by now overcome, once and for all, its period of bad government and the difficulties caused by wars with foreign countries. It is already famous for its model government, and is becoming a great power. The comparison with Athens leads Herodotus to two main subjects: the regime of Lycurgus (65) and the wars against Tegea (66–8). For a bibl. on archaic Sparta see Cartledge, pp. 364–83; for a bibl. of publications organized by subject matter, 1965–82, see J. Ducat, *REG* XCVI (1983), 194–225; to the monographs there cited should be added M. Clauss, *Sparta*, Munich 1983, with a vast bibl.; O. Murray, *Early Greece*, London 1993², ch. 10; D. M. MacDowell, *Spartan Law*,

Edinburgh 1986. For Herodotus and Sparta see Myres, pp. 184–90; Immerwahr, pp. 200–6; and K. M. Cragg, 'Herodotus' Presentation of Sparta', Diss. Michigan 1976; Ubsdell I, pp. 98–110 and nn.; P. Vannicelli, *Erodoto e la storia dell' alto e medio arcaismo*, Rome 1993, pp. 21–98; cf. Introduction, pp. 47 ff.

65,1. Τεγεητέων: Tegea (see Müller I, pp. 866–9) controlled the route from Sparta to the Isthmus, hence her strategic importance. The *polis* was formed by synoecism of nine local villages. Tegea is regarded as a *polis* in a mid-6th-cent. BC treaty inscribed on a stele on the bank of the Alpheius, preserved by Aristotle (fr. 592 Rose; *StV* II no. 112) and by Herodotus himself; but the historical date of the synoecism is uncertain and much disputed; see M. Moggi, *I sinecismi interstatali greci* I, Pisa 1976, pp. 131–9. For the Spartan wars against Tegea see chs. 66–8. **ἐπὶ γὰρ Λέοντος . . .**: the common rule of these two kings is usually dated to *c.*575–560 BC. The 'other wars' are those fought against the tyrants of Corinth and Sicyon.

2. καὶ ξείνοισι ἀπρόσμικτοι: for Herodotus, this lack of interchange with foreigners is a symptom of κακονομίη, but the official Spartan doctrine attributed to Lycurgus the expulsion of foreigners (ξενηλασία) and the prohibition of Spartans from living abroad: thus, either Herodotus is criticizing these measures, or he has misunderstood his informants. Seventh-century Sparta was an open, lively, and hospitable city, importing and exporting goods and hosting foreign artists and poets. See P. Janni, *La cultura di Sparta arcaica*, I–II, Rome 1965–70. The so-called Spartan 'exclusiveness' developed gradually during the 6th cent., though its isolation was more a matter of myth than of reality. Poets and artists such as Stesichorus, Theodorus of Samos (note on 51,9–10), and Bathycles of Magnesia visited it in the 6th cent.; Simonides, Eupolis, Cratinus, Herodotus, and others in the 5th. For a balanced evaluation of Spartan 'austerity' see M. I. Finley, *The Use and Abuse of History*, London 1975, ch. 10.   **μετέβαλον**: cf. note on 57,2. εὐνομίη, a term already used by Tyrtaeus, is the 'good order' attributed officially to Lycurgus, the opposite of κακονομία (not in Herodotus, who has only the superlative adjective κακονομώτατοι: para. 1): see [Xen.], *Ath. Pol.* 1,8–9. Cf. Thuc. I 18,1 with the note of S. Hornblower, *A Commentary on Thucydides*, I, Oxford 1991, pp. 51–3. We are confronted here with 5th-cent. Spartan theory and political propaganda. The passage poses a well-known chronological problem. On the one hand Herodotus implies that the turn towards εὐνομίη happened shortly before the rule of Leon and Hegesicles (and thus should be dated *c.*600 BC). On the other, it is clear that he places Lycurgus centuries earlier (para. 4). The difficulty may be solved by assuming that, whereas according to the official Spartan tradition the whole existing κόσμος had been created all at once by Lycurgus, on the other hand the memory of certain phases and changes, some quite recent, was preserved. Modern scholarship usually distinguishes between the formation of the *polis* with its main political institutions (the great ῥήτρα), which took place before the age of Tyrtaeus, and the transformation of Sparta into a closed, militarized city. The beginning of this second phase can be dated archaeologically to *c.*600 BC. See W. G. Forrest, *A History of Sparta 950–192 BC*,

London 1968, pp. 40–68; Cartledge, chs. 8–9. On the chronological problem see Gomme I, pp. 128 ff. On εὐνομίη, see A. Andrewes, *CQ* XXXII (1938), 89–102; V. Ehrenberg, *Polis und Imperium*, Zurich 1965, pp. 139–58.   Λυκούργου: the first to mention him was Simonides of Ceos (fr. 123 PMG = Plutarch, *Lyc.* 1,4). Ancient scholars had neither genealogical nor other means of dating him. Herodotus says he was the uncle of King Leobotes (65,4), who in his own list of Agiads (VII 204) belongs to the 12th generation before Leonidas (died in 480 BC), thus placing him in the 10th or 9th cent. BC. Other ancient datings vary between the return of the Heraclidae and the 7th cent., a stretch of time of more than five centuries (hence Plutarch's scepticism at *Lyc.* 1). Lycurgus' entire biography is surely legendary. The author of the Delphic response quoted here expressed doubts whether Lycurgus was a man or a god; and in fact Lycurgus, like many other legislators and founders of cities, had a hero-cult in Sparta (66,1). But the hypercritical hypothesis that Lycurgus was originally a 'solar god' or a 'wolf-god' seems groundless: real human beings participated in the formation of the Spartan state in historical times, and there seems to be no reason why one of them should not have been called Lycurgus.   τὸ μέγαρον: see note on 47,2.

3. "ἥκεις...ὦ Λυκόοργε": the response is a spontaneous tribute to Lycurgus on the part of the Pythia (or perhaps a response to a question on whether Lycurgus was a god or a hero). It does not answer to any enquiry about the constitution. The response may have been composed in connection with the establishment of the hero-cult of Lycurgus at Sparta (66,1). Herodotus in any case knew that the origin of the Spartan constitution was attributed to Delphi (65,4). Shortly before 394 the Spartan king Pausanias wrote a treatise about Lycurgus' laws, including in it texts of relevant oracles. Later citations of the oracle include two lines on the Spartan constitution (Diod. VII 12,1): see P–W I, pp. 85 ff.; II, nn. 29 and 216; Crahay, pp. 149–53; Kirchberg, p. 60; Defradas, pp. 264–7; Fontenrose, Q 7 and pp. 115 f.   ἔλπομαι: in Herodotus means 'I think', 'I suppose', 'I suspect'; cf. II 11,4; 26,2; etc.; but in this pre-Herodotean response it would make sense to translate 'I believe'.

4. ἐκ Κρήτης: the Cretan theory is a 5th-cent. rationalization of the Spartan regime, based on what we would now call the method of comparative criticism. Plato, Ephorus, Aristotle, and others noted some similarities between the political systems of Sparta and Crete: see Polybius' criticism at VI 45–7. Herodotus certainly sympathized with the Cretan theory and attributed it to the Spartans (see Fehling, pp. 111 f.), who officially believed in the Delphic origin.

5. τὰ ἐς πόλεμον ἔχοντα...: Herodotus mentions here only a few examples of Spartan military units (he knew others: IX 53,2). The ἐνωμοτίαι, 'divisions of sworn' soldiers, were squadrons of between thirty-two and thirty-six men; and since τριακάδες, a term otherwise unknown, should mean 'unit of thirty men', it may be an explanatory gloss. The *syssitia* (called φιδίτια in Sparta), the famous common messes which were greatly admired in antiquity, in the classical period numbered fifteen men. Active participation in these messes, to which each member contributed produce from his own κλῆρος (inherited lot), was a requirement for holding full citizenship. See J. F. Lazenby, *The Spartan Army*, Warminster

1985; M. Lavrencic, *Spartanische Küche*, Vienna 1993, esp. pp. 129–33.   τοὺς
ἐφόρους καὶ γέροντας: Herodotus again selects only a few examples: he does not
mention the tribal divisions (φυλή, ὠβά) or the assembly (ἀπέλλα). The attribution of the ephorate to Lycurgus was debated by the Spartans themselves in the
Hellenistic period: see Plut. *Cleom.* 10. Aristotle, *Pol.* 1313a26, attributed it to
King Theopompus. Although the official list of ephors is said to start with the
year 754/3 BC, the first known historical ephor was Chilon (59,2 and note). See
N. Richer, *Les Éphores. Études sur l'histoire et sur l'image de Sparte* (*VIIIᵉ–IIIᵉ siècles
avant Jésus Christ*), Paris 1998. The γερουσία numbered thirty, the two kings and
twenty-eight citizens 60 years old or more, elected for life by the ἀπέλλα.

66,1. μεταβαλόντες: cf. note on 57,2. The cult of Lycurgus consisted in yearly
sacrifices, presumably of 'heroic' or chthonian type.   ἔν τε χώρῃ ἀγαθῇ...:
Herodotus couples a rational explanation, based on economic and demographic
considerations, with a religious, irrational one; see Huber, p. 104. In historical
times the 'Spartan chronic *malaise*' was the lack of men, *oligandria* or *oligan-
thropia*, which became a serious problem from the 4th cent. onwards. On the
moral issues raised by expansionism in Herodotus, see Introduction, p. 43, and
note on 27,1.   Ἀρκάδων: after Messenia, annexed and helotized before the
end of the 7th cent., came the turn of Arcadia, which Sparta preferred not to
annex, but eventually to keep under hegemonic control by a more varied system
of alliances, which was the basis of the Peloponnesian league.

2. "Ἀρκαδίην... διαμετρήσασθαι": the first oracle on Tegea and a much-quoted
one; see P–W II, n. 31; Fontenrose, Q 88 and pp. 123 f. It is a typical ambiguous
response, composed after a Tegean victory, and then quoted by the guides to the
temple of Athena Alea in order to explain to the visitors the origin of the fetters
hung up there (66,4). The first three words look like an independent saying,
which may have existed before the response was composed.   βαλανηφάγοι: on
the *topos* of the enemy's primitivism see 71,2 (with note). For the oracles on Tegea
see Crahay, pp. 150, 153–5, and Kirchberg, pp. 60–3; for criticism of Herodotus'
account and his chronology see L. Moretti, *RFIC* XXIV (1946), 87–103.
δώσω: the verse is quoted by Polyaenus I 8.

3. κιβδήλῳ: cf. 75,2, means 'false', 'tampered with', and is applied to money,
goods, etc. Here it means that the oracle is deceptive (cf. Philostr. *Vit. Soph.* II 5
(575); Huber, p. 46); the responses quoted by Herodotus at V 91,2 (cf. 63,1 and
90,1) are also false. Cf. χρηστήριον...ἄσημον: 'unintelligible response' (V
92β,3); ἀτέκμαρτον, 'inexplicable' (92γ,1); ἀμφιδέξιον, 'ambiguous' (92ε,1);
ποικιλώτερον, 'intricate' (VII 111,2). For the meaning of ἐξανδραποδίζω see
note on 155,1.

4. πέδας: rather than putting the enemy in chains and dancing with joy, the
Spartans were themselves forced to stamp the ground and measure it with the
rope. Here, as elsewhere, Herodotus enjoys the ambiguity of the oracle, the pun,
and the reversal of fortune. Later sources relate various anecdotes on a Spartan
defeat by the Arcadians, which may be the same as the one mentioned by
Herodotus. According to Theopompus (*FGrHist* 115 F 69), the Cretan seer

Epimenides (fl. *c.*600 BC) foretold the defeat, which eventually took place near Orchomenos; for the supposed historicity of this defeat see D. M. Leahy, *Phoenix*, XII (1958), 141–65. Pausanias (VIII 48,4–5) refers a defeat to the time of King Charillos (*c.*775–750 BC; see Herod. VIII 131,2), and tells an aetiological story about the women of Tegea who alone put the Spartans to flight; see M. V. García Quintela, *Gallaecia*, XI (1989), 267–305. For a story about King Theopompus (*c.*720–675 BC), imprisoned by the Tegeans and freed by his wife, see Polyaenus VIII 34. On fighting-style in 6th-cent. Peloponnese see K. Adshead, *Politics of the Archaic Peloponnese*, Aldershot 1986; H. W. Singor, *Lampas*, XX (1987), 182–203. For other offerings of fetters cf. I 90,2 and V 77,3–4; see also note on III 129,3.   τῆς Ἀλέης Ἀθηναίης: cf. IX 70,3. One of the most famous temples in the Peloponnese. The archaic sanctuary was destroyed by fire in 395/4 BC; the remains of the 4th-cent. temple built by the architect Scopas are still visible near modern Piali. From the archaic temple there survived in antiquity a statue of Athena and various relics, among which were the Spartan fetters (see Paus. VIII 45,4–47,4). The Ἀλώτια festival, traditionally in memory of the Tegean victory, was celebrated in the temple. Other temples of Athena Alea were at Alea and Mantinea (Paus. VIII 23,1; 9,6); outside Arcadia she was venerated at Amyclae in Laconia (Paus. III 19,7). See M. Joot, *Sanctuaires et cultes d'Arcadie*, Paris 1985, pp. 106–9.

67,2. θεοπρόπους: see note on 19,2.   ἡ δὲ Πυθίη...ἐπαγαγομένους: the second oracle on Tegea. Herodotus inserts in the digression on the wars with Tegea a response on the cult of Orestes at Sparta, which he received at Delphi. By the removal of the bones of a hero and protector, his protection shifts from the inhabitants of the old place to those of the new, the common belief being that the bones protected the land where they were buried. In Herodotus' view, in fact, the removal of Orestes' bones was the origin of Spartan superiority in the Peloponnese, and thus explains why Croesus sought an alliance with Sparta. Cf. the removal of Theseus' bones to Athens, which Pausanias III 3,7 compares with the bones of Orestes. There are various traditions on the death of Orestes. According to Pindar he died at Amyclae, in Laconia; Pausanias saw his tomb at Sparta, but knew that his bones had originally been buried at Tegea (III 11,10; VIII 54,4). Others noticed that no tomb of Orestes was visible at Argos or Mycenae (Lucian, *Tox.* 5–6). As a nephew of Menelaus, Orestes could easily be declared a Spartan; it seems, however, that also the bones of Agamemnon and of Tisamenus, son of Orestes, were transferred to Sparta at the same time. The propagandistic significance of these transfers is clear. Possibly, the oracle originally indicated that Sparta assimilate non-Dorian cults as a means of reconciliation with other cities; however, the new cults actually served to legitimize Sparta's expansionism in Arcadia and in other parts of the Peloponnese, and her panhellenism in general. In VII 159 Agamemnon is a Spartan symbol of panhellenism. Chilon (59,2) could have been a promoter of such propaganda. But Tarentum too had a cult of the Agamemnonids ([Arist.], *De Mirab. Auscult.* 840a6), and the city, according to tradition, was founded *c.*706 BC. It is therefore possible that the cult of Orestes at Sparta existed since the 8th cent. at least. On the oracle see P–W I pp. 95 f., and Fontenrose, Q 89, pp. 75 and 123 f. On the 'politics of bones' see H. T. Wade-Gery, *CAH* III (1925), 565 ff.; and G. L. Huxley, *Early Sparta*, Shannon 1962, pp. 67 ff. D. Boedeker, in C. Dougherty and L. Kurke (eds.), *Cultural Politics in Archaic Greece*, Cambridge 1993, pp. 164–177.

4. "ἔστι"…"ἔσσῃ": the third and last oracle on Tegea; see P–W I, pp. 95 f.; II, n. 33; Fontenrose, Q 90 and pp. 74 f., 81 and 123 f.; and Crahay, pp. 150, 155–9. The first three hexameters are a popular riddle, the last two are the response proper. The whole text assumes knowledge of the discovery of the bones, thus solving the riddle. Orestes, pursued by the Erinyes, had found refuge in a place in Arcadia called Orestia or Oresteion; others said that he had died at Oresteion or that he had been buried between Tegea and Thyrea. It is possible that these legends originated from a confusion between Orestes and Orestheus, son of Lycaon and eponym of Oresthasion, a well-known place in Arcadia, south-west of Tegea (see Pritchett, pp. 29–63); cf. the various readings Ὀρεσθείῳ—Ὀρεστείῳ in IX 11,2, and in particular Paus. VIII 3,1–2. It is clear from Herodotus' account that at Tegea nobody knew about Orestes' bones. See G. L. Huxley, *GRBS* XX (1979), 145–8.   λευρῷ ἐνὶ χώρῳ: cf. Homer, *Od.* VII 123.   τύπος ἀντίτυπος: see E. Orth, *PhW* LII (1932), coll. 429 f.   Ἀγαμεμνονίδην: cf. Homer, *Od.* I 30. κατέχει φυσίζοος αἶα: cf. *Il.* III 243; *Od.* XI 301.   ἐπιτάρροθος: epic for ἐπίρροθος, means 'protector' in Homer and is used chiefly of a god who helps combatants in battle.

5. τῶν ἀγαθοεργῶν: men who were at least 30 years old and had served for at least twenty years. When serving outside Sparta they were exposed to the dangers of contact with foreigners. The homonymous statesman Lichas, an Olympic champion in 420 BC, and πρόξενος of the Argives in Sparta, may be a great-grandson of the Lichas mentioned here. The ἱππεῖς to which this passage refers are the bodyguard of the kings; according to law, they numbered 100 (VI 56), but in 480 Leonidas was granted 300 (VII 205,2). For military units of 300 horsemen at Sparta see VIII 124,3; Thuc. V 72,4; perhaps they should be identified with the 300 horsemen of Xenophon, *Lac. Resp.* IV 3, headed by three ἱππαγρέται chosen by the ephors. In historical times these ἱππεῖς no longer fought on horseback.

68,1. ἐν θώματι: the technique of iron manufacture excites admiration: cf. 25,2. Note the repeated use of θωμ- composites in the next paragraph.

2. χαλκεύς: a 'smith' in general; for 'the deme of the κορυθεῖς' = smiths (?), at Tegea, see Paus. VIII 45,1.

3. ἑπταπήχεϊ: about 3 m. (but seven is a symbolic number), though the Greeks thought that a height of 1.70 m. would be sufficient even for a goddess (60,4). The belief that the heroes of myth were gigantic reappears in Herodotus in connection with Perseus (II 91,3) and Heracles (IV 82). Pliny and Gellius attributed to Homer the view that heroes were taller than common men, and mentioned Orestes as an example. For a collection of data on gigantic bones see Phlegon of Tralles (*FGrHist* 257 F 36 (XI–XIX)). The entire story is of course an aetiological legend, and should be seen as such. The amusing theory that the

bones found at Tegea were those of a prehistoric monster has been revived again: see Huxley, *GRBS* XX (1979), 145–8; *PRIA* LXXXIII (1983), 5 f.; cf. Pritchett, pp. 45 f.   τῆδε συμβαλλόμενος: a good example of oracle interpretation. For iron as a source of misfortune cf., with reference to this response, Diod. IX 36,3 and Paus. III 3,6.

5. ἐκ λόγου πλαστοῦ: since these were times of peaceful contacts between Sparta and Tegea (para. 1), it is plausible that the charges were brought by the ephors or personal enemies of Lichas who were suspicious of his relationship (of ξενία?) with the smith. Lichas was subsequently readmitted together with the bones of Orestes. On ξενία and treason, see G. Herman, *Ritualised Friendship and the Greek City*, Cambridge 1987, pp. 156 ff.   αἰτίην: see Bornitz, p. 150. Herodotus may have heard the version of the trial of Lichas known to his descendants, among them perhaps also the homonymous Olympic winner (see 67,5 and note).

6. κατυπέρτεροι: Tegea was forced to make an alliance with Sparta; on the treaty (*StV* II, no. 112), preserved by Aristotle, see note on 65, 1.

69,2. Ἕλληνα φίλον προσθέσθαι...κατὰ τὸ χρηστήριον...τὸ θεοπρόπιον: this advice is unattested in the extant oracular responses given to Croesus (P–W II, no 52–6; 249–50).   ἄνευ τε δόλου καὶ ἀπάτης: for this formula, presumably taken from Greek international treaties, cf. VIII 140a,4 and IX 7a,1 (all passages in which the formula occurs are in direct speech).

3. ἥσθησάν: see note on 27,5.   ὅρκια...καὶ συμμαχίης: the historicity of the treaty between Croesus and Sparta (cf. I 77,2–3; 83; III 47,1; Paus. IV 5,3) dated c.548/7 BC, is debated; see *StV* II, no. 113; V. La Bua, *MGR* V (1977), 36 ff., with bibl. The unusual voting procedure of the 'Lacedaimonians' only (i.e. of the Apella), without mention of previous deliberation by the kings, ephors, and gerousia, is somewhat surprising, unless Herodotus is just summarizing the substance of the process. On the other hand, there are traces of authentic formulae in Herodotus' text. See L. Moretti, *RFIC* XXVI (1948), 213–22.   εὐεργεσίαι: cf. III 47,1; 67,3; etc.; see P. Karavites, *RIDA* XXVII (1980), 69–79.

4. χρυσὸν: Sardis is the right place to buy gold.   ἐν Θόρνακι: a hill north of Sparta, on the left bank of the Eurotas, where there was a sanctuary of Apollo and a statue similar to that at Amyclae (see the account known to Pausanias III 10,8). See Müller I, p. 870.

70,1. κρητῆρα χάλκεον: this splendid crater that Herodotus evidently saw in the Heraion in Samos (para. 3; cf. III 47,1) is one of the last examples of refined Spartan art. For its capacity see 51,1 and note 2. An idea of its appearance may be gained from the famous crater of Vix, discovered in 1953 on Mt. Lassois, south-east of Paris (R. Joffroy, *Vix et ses trésors*, Paris 1979, pp. 49–73 and plates). On Spartan art and its decline in the 6th cent. see L. Vlad Borrelli, *EAA* 1959, s.v. 'Sparta'; C. Rolley, *Ktema* II (1977), 125–40; Cartledge, pp. 154 ff.; Bowden, pp. 44–5.

2. δι᾽ αἰτίας διφασίας: here αἰτίη means a 'cause' (in the sense of 'fault', Bornitz, pp. 156 f.) told in different or conflicting ways. Since the theft of the crater became a *casus belli* in 525 BC (III 47,1), it is probable that the two versions

date back to the time of Polycrates, when Samos and Sparta were hostile to one-another. The Spartan version implies that also in 547/6 there were no agreements of ἀσυλία between the two cities. See Plut. *Mor.* 859b–d. Herodotus, though apparently preferring the Samian version, understands that the Spartans may have believed theirs in good faith.

3. ὑστέρησαν: the delays of the Spartans are proverbial; cf. 83 and note.   τὸ *Ἡραιον*: one of the most famous and biggest Greek temples in antiquity; see III 60,4 and note.

71–94. Two-thirds of the last chapters of the *logos* of Croesus continue the main narrative and have the form of a typical *logos* of military history: the causes and the plans for the war against Cyrus (chs. 71 and 73), the march of the Lydians and the counter-march of the Persians, the preparations in Cappadocia, the battle in Pteria and its consequences (Croesus' retreat, the battle on the plain of Sardis, the siege: 75–81), the capture of the city; thereafter, the famous episode of Croesus on the pyre, and the dialogues between Croesus and Cyrus (84–91). For other sources on these events, see Pedley, pp. 36–42. The events take place in the years 548/7–547/6 BC. Three digressions intersect the narrative: on Cappadocia and the river Halys (72), on the relations between the Lydians and the Medes (73–4), on the wars between Sparta and Argos for the possession of the Thyraeatis (82). All the digressions are directly connected to the subjects of the main narrative. The *logos* ends with three other digressive chapters on various Lydian topics: final offerings of Croesus (92), marvels in Lydia (93), customs and emigration of the Lydians to Etruria (94).

71,1. ἁμαρτὼν τοῦ χρησμοῦ: see 53,3.   ἐλπίσας: see note on 22,3.   ἐς *Καππαδοκίην*: cf. 72,1–2; 73,1; 76,1; etc. See note on III 90,2.

2. Σάνδανις: another Herodotean 'wise counsellor' (cf. note on 27,2). Sandanis is a theophoric Lydian name (of the god Sandon). Some suggest that this parenthetic addition is interpolated or transposed from another line (possibly after τις Λυδῶν) or from the margin.   ἐπ᾽ ἄνδρας τοιούτους: the Persians are portrayed here as an uncouth but virile people in contrast with the Lydians, who are civilized but effeminate; cf. 34,3; 79,3; 155–7. Except for a vague hint concerning the Arcadians in the oracle quoted at 66,2; this is the first example of Herodotus' motif of the 'primitivism' of the enemy, that a wise counsellor advances for dissuading a reckless king from a dangerous war against such a people. 'Primitivism' is, of course, a comparative notion. Between the conquest of Lydia and that of Babylon, the Persians actually become transformed into a refined people (ch. 135) that nevertheless continues to acquire wealth in wars against more 'primitive' peoples: the Massagetae, the Ethiopians, the Scythians, and the Greeks themselves. For all aspects of this issue see Cobet, pp. 104–17, and the Introductions, pp. 43 ff., and 67 ff. Croesus himself will use Sandanis' very argument when a counsellor of Cyrus during the war against the Massagetae (207,6).   ἀναξυρίδας: a Persian word? See V. Pisani, *ZDMG* XCVI (1942), 82 f. For the Greeks, trousers were a typically oriental outfit, possibly recalling

to their mind the appearance of a bag (see Ar. *Vesp.* 1085 and schol.; Eur., *Cycl.* 182–3 with R. A. S. Seaford's note (Oxford 1988); cf. e.g. III 87; V 49,3; VII 61,1; Xen. *Anab.* I 5,8 (ποικίλαι ἀναξυρίδες). In Persian iconography common soldiers wear trousers; on the Median origin of Persian dress, see ch. 135; A. Bovon, *BCH* LXXXVII (1963), 579–602; W. Raeck, *Zum Barbarenbild in der Kunst Athen im 6 und 5 Jahrhundert v. Chr.*, Bonn 1981, pp. 101–63; S. Bittner, *Tracht und Bewaffnung des persischen Heeres zur Zeit der Achaimeniden*, Munich 1987², pp. 186–8; R. Hurschmann, 'Anaxyrides', *DNP* I (1996), 674–5 (with bibl.).   χώρην ἔχοντες τρηχέαν: Persia, a mountainous country, is set against flat land (Babylonia and Lydia) also in Herodotus' last chapter (IX 122). On Persian landscape and geography in Greek (esp. Athenian) literature see C. Tuplin, *Achaemenid Studies*, *Historia* Einzelschriften, XCIX, Stuttgart 1996, pp. 136–41. The contrast is of course not only topographical but also moral, the contrast of roughness and luxury.

3. οὐ σῦκα: since the Greeks thought of Lydia as a country which produced wine, oil, and figs, figs were considered a food common but necessary: therefore, οὐ should not be deleted (for a different view, see R. Merkelbach, *RhM* XCV (1952), 288); the testimonies of Strabo XV 3,8 and Plutarch, *Art.* 3,2 should not be referred to the age of Persian 'primitivism'. Apart from that, the entire sentence is built upon a series of negative particles.

72.1. οἱ δὲ Καππαδόκαι: in Herodotus Cappadocia includes also parts of Pontus and Galatia (the borders varied in the course of time); see also VII 72,1. The Greeks called the local people Syrians and Leucosyrians; cf. I 6,2; III 90,2 and note; V 49,6; VII 72,1. The strategic importance of Cappadocia is due to the routes of communication that cross it. For sources on ancient Cappadocia (in French trans.) see L. Franck, *RHA* XXIV (1966), 5–122; for bibl. see R. Schmitt, *RLA* V (1980), coll. 399–400; Müller II, pp. 123–9.

2. ὁ Ἅλυς: cf. 6,1. Its modern name is Kizil Irmak (915 km. long). In antiquity it marked the border between κάτω and ἄνω Ἀσίης, i.e. between western Asia Minor and the northern part of the Middle East; cf. 95,2; 103,2; 130,1; 177. See Müller II, pp. 117–21. The 'Royal Road' crossed it (V 52,2). For the sources of the Euphrates in Armenia see 180,1. For a general discussion of rivers marking political borders see v. Scheliha.   Ματιηνούς: they must have been a people bordering on the Phrygians in Cappadocia; (cf. VII 72,1–2); Müller II, pp. 179–80. They have nothing to do with the region of Matiene between Armenia and Cissia (I 189,1; 202,3; III 94,1; V 49,6–7; 52,5–6). See note on III 94,1. On Armenia see Müller II, pp. 100–8.

3. τῆς Ἀσίης τὰ κάτω: the 'low' seaward regions of Asia Minor (cf. 142,1 and 177), as opposed to the ἄνω Ἀσίης (95,2; 177), the 'high' or inland parts of it. Hence, κατάβασις is the 'descent' towards the western coasts, and ἀνάβασις the 'expedition up' into Asia.   αὐχήν: cf. II 34,2; for Herodotus' usage of this term in topographical contexts see G. Kahl, *Spudasmata*, LXIX (1998), 99–106. The data and the calculation are wrong. The narrowest 'neck' of Asia Minor, between Akçakoca and Side, is approximately 460 km.; the line between Sinope and the

Cilician coast is about 550 km. long, but by the 4th cent. BC it was used to divide
Asia Minor in two (Isocr. V 120). Given the mountainous character of the
country, there are no direct routes. In any case one would have to cover
112 km. per day, which may be the record of a professional runner (VI 106,2),
not that of just a 'good walker', who covers on average 36 km. in a day (IV 101,3;
cf. I 104,1). Herodotus' mistake was corrected in many late sources; see Janni,
p. 154 and notes. Besides, 'five days' is a standard expression (cf. note on 30,1).
On Herodotus' distances see note on 104,1.

73,1. τῶνδε εἵνεκα: the three causes of the war represent respectively rational and
political factors, religious and irrational factors, and a personal element. One may
add, without contradiction, the fear of Persian expansionism (46,1). As this
passage shows, it is clearly wrong to deny Herodotus intuitive or analytic perception of historical, impersonal causality (see Introduction, pp. 40 ff.). To the
causes singled out by Herodotus may be added the legacy of the hostilities
between Lydians and Medes, the precariousness of the treaty of 585 and of the
marriage alliances (74,3–4), and the excessive trust in the alleged coalition
between Lydians, Babylonians, and Egyptians against the Persians. On Cyrus'
conquest of Media cf. 127–30 and notes; on Astyages see note 107,1.

3. Κυαξάρης ὁ Φραόρτεω τοῦ Διόκεω: see resp. notes on 103,1; 102,1; and
96,1.	**ἱκέτας:** 'suppliants' to a man; cf. 159,1–4 and notes; V 51,1; IX
76,2–3. Most 'suppliants' turn to a god (i.e. seek refuge in a temple or by an
altar): I 159,4; V 71,1; VI 108,4; VII 141,1; VIII 53,3.

3–6. Σκυθέων ... ἱκέται ἐγένοντο: this digression on the Scythians in Media (see
for the context 103,3–106,1) refers presumably to events that happened at the
beginning of the 6th cent. It is well integrated into the main narrative of the war
between Croesus and Cyrus, seeking to explain its antecedents. The possibility of
wars between Lydians and Medians on account of the Scythians cannot be ruled
out a priori, but the macabre story of the banquet at para. 5 belongs to the same
motif of popular saga as the one at ch. 119. For the 'nomadic' Scythians see ch. 15
and note.

3. τὴν γλῶσσαν: cf. the famous *trivium* of Persian *paideia* (136,2 and note).

74,1. πόλεμος: this five-year war should be dated to 590–586 BC, since the 'battle
of the eclipse' took place in the sixth year (585 BC; see notes on 74,2 and 103,
3–106,2). In the same year Cyaxares apparently died (ch. 130 with note), perhaps
soon after the battle; other sources (among them *POxy 2506*, fr. 98) allude to a
war between Alyattes and Astyages, Cyaxares' successor. See G. L. Huxley, *GRBS*
VI (1965), 201–6; H. M. T. Cobbe, *Hermathena*, CV (1967), 21–33.	**ἐν
δὲ ... ἐποιήσαντο:** rather than an interpolated gloss, the sentence seems to be a
brief introduction to the eclipse episode: ἐν δὲ refers to the war between the
Lydians and the Medes in general; but see Legrand ad loc.

2. τὴν ἡμέρην ... γενέσθαι: cf. 103,2; a total eclipse of the sun. Within the chronological limits of the reigns of the two kings who fought the battle (617–585 BC),
the only total eclipse (97% of the total) visible in Cappadocia occurred a few
minutes before sunset on 28 May 585. The partial eclipse of 21 September 582 is

hardly preferable. Clement of Alexandria (*Strom.* I XIV 65,1), drawing on Eude-
mos of Rhodes (fr. 143 Wehrli), dates the event around the 50th Olympiad
(= 580–577 BC). It is not certain that in the time of Thales it was possible to
predict what eclipses would be visible in which geographical areas. It is also
doubtful whether Hellenistic chronographers had access to reports about this
eclipse unrelated to the calculations of Thales' *acme* (including his inclusion in
the list of the Seven Sages: see note on ch. 20), which was dated precisely to 585.
But the admiration of Thales began with Xenophanes and Heraclitus. The
problem is complex: see L. Blanche, *RPh* XCIII (1968), 153–99; O. Neugebauer,
The Exact Sciences in Antiquity, New York 1969; A. A. Mosshammer, *TAPhA* CXI
(1981), 145–55; D. W. Roller, *LCM* VIII (1983), 58–9. On Thales see A. Maddalena,
Ionici. Testimonianze e frammenti, Florence 1963. On Thales in Herodotus see
further chs. 75 and 170. For other eclipses in Herodotus see VII 37,2–3; IX 10,3.
For a list of eclipses attested in ancient sources see Boll, *RE* VI (1909), coll.
2352–64.   μεταβολή: here in the sense of extraordinary change in the order
of nature (cf. note on 57,2).

3. Συέννεσίς...: Syennesis seems to be the name adopted by the semi-independent
reguli of Cilicia; cf. V 118,2 and VII 98.   Λαβύνητος: the Greek form of
Nabû-na'id (Nabonidus), the last king of the neo-Babylonian dynasty (556–539
BC): cf. 77,2; 188,1. In 585 Nabonidus was still young, but he may have acted as the
plenipotentiary mediator of King Nebuchadnezzar (see J. Melkman, *Mnemosyne*, IX
(1941), 105–11). According to Herodotus, the father of the last Babylonian king was
also called Labynetus (188,1 and note); but this is probably incorrect. He may have
postulated two Labyneti because he did not think it possible that the Labynetus
active in 585 could be the same as the king who was deposed by Cyrus in 539; see
Beaulieu. Nabû-na'id was the son of Nabû-balaṭsu-iḳbi and Adad-guppi; see note
on 185–7; he became king in 556 after Nebuchadnezzar's son Labaši-Marduk was
killed. He lived in retirement at Teima in northern Arabia from 553 to about 543;
during his absence the regency was in the hands of Bal-šar-usur (Belshazzar/
Balthasares). His reign lasted until Cyrus' conquest of Babylon (see 188–91 and
notes); cf. P. Garelli, *Dictionnaire de la Bible*, Suppl. VI 1960, coll. 269–86. It is
actually possible that the Labynetus mentioned here is in fact Nebuchadnezzar
himself (605–562 BC), who in any case was the promoter of the mediation. For bibl.
see R. Schmitt, *RLA* VI 1983, coll. 411–12. Nabonidus' religious policy is much
debated; see A. Kuhrt, in M. Beard and J. North (eds.), *Pagan Priests: Religion and
Power in the Ancient World*, London 1990, pp. 117–56.

4. ὅρκιον...: on the treaty see *StV* II, no. 107, with bibl.

5. ὅρκια...ἀλλήλων: a very brief ethnographic digression (cf. 35,2). For analogous blood-rituals in alliances and affiliations cf. III 8,1 (Arabs); IV 70 (Scythians). See Hartog, pp. 130 ff = ET pp. 113 ff.; G. Herman, *Ritualised Friendship
and the Greek City*, Cambridge 1987, pp. 32 f.; for a general discussion,
H. Tegnaeus, *Blood Brothers*, Stockholm 1952.

75,1. μητροπάτορα: cf. 107,1–2.   αἰτίην: it was Astyages' guilt (Bornitz,
pp. 140 f.); see chs. 107 ff.

2. κιβδήλου: cf. 66,3 and note: a false oracle, but paid by Croesus with genuine gold.

3. διεβίβασε τὸν στρατόν: not all the bridges across the Halys known to Herodotus (V 52,2) existed already in 547/6 BC (cf. 75,4). Crossing the natural boundary between two empires or continents is, in Herodotus' view, an act of moral transgression (ὕβρις), as it implies a violation of the limits of the μοῖρα assigned by god to men. Croesus therefore foreshadows Cyrus (the crossing of the Araxes: 205,2 ff.), Darius (the Danube), Xerxes (the Hellespont) and Mardonius (the Asopus); see Introduction, pp. 43 f. For the moral issues raised by expansionism, cf. also note on 27,1.

4. τὸν Θαλῆν: the canalization of the Halys, attributed in Ionia to Thales (cf. Diog. Laert. I 38) recalls the Babylonian canalizations (185–6). It is itself also an act of ὕβρις, as it offends against nature. Cf. the digging at Cnidus (174,3–4), the Gyndes (189,2–4), and Mt. Athos (VII 22–4).

5. μηνοειδέα: cf. VIII 16,1, 'crescent shaped', like the waxing or waning moon.
ἀμφοτέρῃ: from both banks of the old stream, not both the old stream and the canal (cf. para. 6, where αὐτόν must refer to the canal).

76,1. ἡ δὲ Πτερίη ... κειμένη: a parenthetic sentence on a geographical matter (cf. note on 8,1). The traditional identification of Pteria with Boğgazköy, ancient Ḫatti or Ḫattusas, the capital of the Hittite kingdom and an important crossroads (see Müller II, pp. 208–13), was challenged by S. Przeworski (AO I (1929), 312–15), who proposed instead the fortified ruins discovered a few years earlier on Kerkenes Dağ, on the same meridian as Sinope (κατὰ Σινώπην is taken to mean 'on the line of Sinope') to the south-east of modern Josgad. For the suggestion that this site was a Median (cf. Steph. Byz. s.v. Πτέριον) military settlement founded by Astyages soon after the 'battle of the eclipse' (see note on 74,1) and destroyed by Croesus less than forty years later, see G. D. Summers, AS XLVI (1996), 201–34, and JNES LVI 2 (1997), 81–94.   κατὰ Σινώπην πόλιν: a renowned Milesian colony, on a promontory on the Euxine. See D. M. Robinson, Ancient Sinope, Baltimore 1906; for bibl. see K. Liampi, 'Sinope', LIMC VIII 1 1997, pp. 1135–7; Müller II, pp. 218–20.   τῶν Συρίων: see 72,1 and note.

2. οὐδὲν ἐόντας αἰτίους: a serious crime deserving punishment. The evacuated cities were to be used for quartering the troops or for a military colonization of the border area.   Κῦρος ...: according to the Chronicle of Nabonidus (col. II, lines 16 ff. ANET, p. 306), Cyrus arrived at the river Tigris in the month of Nisan (of 547 BC) and moved on to Lu-u[ddi?] in the following month. During his march he may have enlisted contingents of Medes, Syrians, Cappadocians, Cilicians, and others. Cf. Xen. Cyr. VI 2,4; VII 1,1 ff. Cf. J Cargill, AJAH II (1977), 97–116.

3. κήρυκας: the plural may indicate direct contacts with the individual Ionian cities (on Miletus see Diog. Laert. I 25), the singular (κήρυκα AB) direct contact with the league of the Panionium (141,3–4).

4. μάχης δὲ καρτερῆς: according to Herodotus this 'fierce battle' was inconclusive, but Cyrus still held the area across the Halys that Croesus had invaded, and

the Lydian king had to retreat to Sardis. According to late sources the battle of Pteria took place in the middle of winter and was a decisive defeat for Croesus: Castor, *FGrHist* 250 F 11. For a stratagem employed in the retreat cf. Polyaenus VII 8,2.

77,1. παρακαλέσας: the alliances with Amasis and Nabonidus (*StV* II, no. 114), if they are historical, should be dated between 550 and 547 BC; cf. 69,3 for the alliance with Sparta. See the fictitious account by Xenophon, *Cyr.* VI 2,10. For Egyptian mercenaries of Croesus see *Cyr.* VII 1,45; *Hist. Gr.* III 1,7. Perhaps, the treaties provided for military help only in the case of attacks by third parties, see V. La Bua, *MGR* V (1977), 47 f.

2. Λαβύνητος: see note on 74,3.

4. ἐς πέμπτον μῆνα: cf. 81; this must mean 'in the fifth month' from now. Assuming that Croesus returned to Sardis in autumn, the 'fifth month' would fall in early spring.

78,1. τὸ προάστιον: the 'space in front of the town' (cf. πρὸ τοῦ ἄστεος, 80,1), i.e. a 'suburb' outside a main gate; for the προάστιον τῶν Λυδῶν at Sardis cf. V 12,2; at other towns: III 14,1, etc. (Memphis); 84,3, etc. (Susa); 142,1 (Samos); IV 78,2 (Olbia); V 1,2 (Perinthus); VIII 129,2 (Potidaea).　　**ὀφίων:** Herodotus' snakes are sometimes related to portents or symbolic events; see IV 9,1 and VIII 41,2; for another invasion of snakes see IV 105,1. More often snakes appear in geo-ethnographic sections; I 140,3; II 74; 75,2, etc.; III 107,2, etc.; 109,3; IV 183,4; 189,1; 191,4; 192,2. See in general E. Küsten, *Die Schlange in der griechischen Kunst und Religion*, Giessen 1913; L. Bodson, *IEPA ZΩIA. Contribution à l'étude de la place de l'animal dans la religion grecque ancienne*, Bruxelles 1978, pp. 68–92; I. Malkin, 'Snakes,' *OCD*[3], pp. 1417–18; on the Greek snake vocabulary see M. Sancanano, *Athenaeum*, LXXXIV (1996), 49–70.

2. θεοπρόπους: see note on 19,2.　　**Τελμησσέων:** the Telmessian seers, who had already been consulted by the legendary king of Sardis, Meles (84,3), were famous. They must have come from Telmessus in Caria, which was under the rule of Croesus, and not from the homonymous city in Lycia, where there was a famous oracle of Apollo. The question is debated: see G. Daux, *RPh* XV (1941), 11–17; J. Elayi, *IA* XIII (1978), 98 and n. 1; C. Le Roy, *RHDFE* LXII (1984), 614, with bibl.; Müller II, pp. 382–6.

3. τάδε ἔγνωσαν...: this interpretation is manifestly *ex eventu*, in spite of Herodotus' οὐδέν κω εἰδότες.　　**τοὺς ἐπιχωρίους:** cf. 181,5; see note on 1,1.　　**ὄφιν εἶναι γῆς παῖδα:** in Greek mythology the serpent is a symbol of autochthony (for bibl. see note on para. 1).

79,2. ὡς δέ... ἄγγελος: for an attempt to turn this passage into iambic trimeters see Myres, p. 77, n. 2.

3. ἦν δέ... τοῦ Λυδίου: a digressive ethnographic sentence about the virility of the Lydians and their prowess in war, before they became effeminate (see 155,4 and note). On ethnic superlatives in Herodotus see W. M. Bloomer, *ClassAnt* XII (1993), 30–50. On the Lydian cavalry cf. 27,3. Cf. the melancholy saying about Miletus, πάλαι ποτ' ἦσαν ἄλκιμοι Μιλήσιοι (Anacreon, 426 *PMG*).

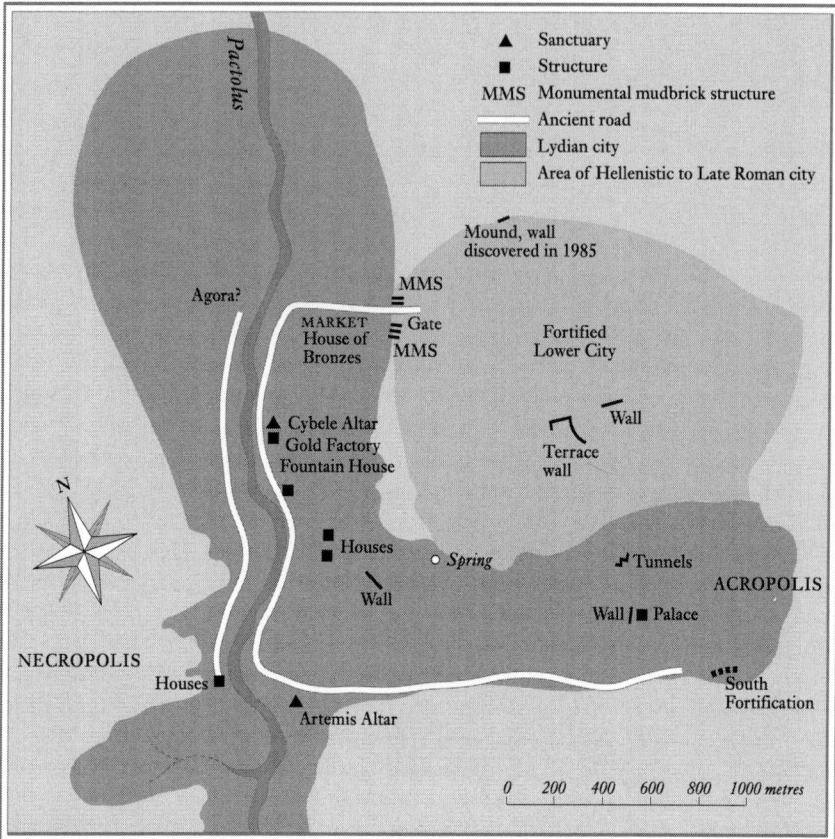

Pactolus

▲ Sanctuary
■ Structure
MMS Monumental mudbrick structure
—— Ancient road
Lydian city
Area of Hellenistic to Late Roman city

Mound, wall
discovered in 1985

Agora?

MMS

MARKET ≡ Gate
House of   MMS
Bronzes

Fortified
Lower City

▲ Cybele Altar
■ Gold Factory
Fountain House
■

Wall

Terrace
wall

■
■ Houses
○ *Spring*

Tunnels

Wall

ACROPOLIS

Wall / ■ Palace

NECROPOLIS
Houses ■

South
Fortification

▲
Artemis Altar

0   200   400   600   800   1000 metres

N

Map 15. Sardis

80,1. τὸ πεδίον: the plain of the Hermus, north of the city. On the topography of the area see the bibl. in note on 7,2. The sources of one branch of the river are on Mt Dindymon (1820 m.), on the border between Lydia and Phrygia. 'Mother Dindymene' is Kybele, venerated on this mountain; cf. Strab. XII 5,3 and Steph. Byz., s.v. Δίνδυμα. See Müller II, pp. 450–3. According to Xenophon (*Cyr.* VI 2,11; VII 1,45) the battle was fought at Thymbrara, a site known as a parade square at the time of the Achaemenids. It has been located in various ways: see J. Keil, *RE* VI A (1936), coll. 697 f.   κατὰ Φωκαίην πόλιν: on Phocea see note 163,1.

2. Ἁρπάγου: see 108,3 and note. Here he appears as a wise counsellor of the 'practical' sort; cf. note on 27,1.   κάμηλοι: the camel (from Semitic *gml*) was known to the Greeks as the typical animal for riding and transport used by the Medes and the Persians (cf. III 103 and note; VII 125). Agesilaus, king of Sparta, introduced camels to Greece in 395 BC (Xen. *Hist. Gr.* III 4,24). For horses and camels see Xen. *Cyr.* VII 1,27.

5. ἡ ἐλπίς: here a positive but deceitful 'hope', cf. 141,2, etc. See note on 22,3.
6. δειλοί: cf. 79,3 and note.
81. ἐς πέμπτον μῆνα: cf. 77,4 and note.

82–3. The digression on contention between Sparta and Argos over the Thyreatis is connected to the main narrative by Croesus' appeal to his allies, and seeks to justify the failure of the Spartans to help. It is linked to the previous digression on Sparta (chs. 65–8) and is continued in two further digressions on the reign of Cleomenes (V 39–48; VI 51–84). The Thyreatis (see note on 82,1) was an apple of discord between Sparta and Argos for centuries (see note on 82,4). Its fate was decided from time to time by fighting, arbitration, or semi-ritual athletic contests. Ritual elements here (82) are the number of fighters, the survivor who commits suicide, and the hairstyle (the same elements recur in the battle of Thermopylae: VII 208,3; 232). According to Chrysermus of Corinth, *FGrHist* 287 F 2(a), certain 'amphictyons' imposed a similar contest. These sorts of contest served as an aetiological explanation for a number of Laconian traditions, such as the hairstyle, the 'Thyreatic wreaths' at the Spartan festival of Gymnopaedia (see VI 67,2), and the Parparonia festivals (and the dedications at Delphi: see e.g. Paus. X 9,12; N. Robertson, *Festivals and Legends: The Formation of Greek Cities in the Light of Public Ritual*, Toronto 1992, pp. 179–207). Bibl.: L. Moretti, *RFIC* XXVI (1948), 204–13; A. Brelich, *Guerre, agoni e culti nella Grecia arcaica*, Bonn 1961, pp. 22–34; Piccirilli, nos. 8 and 29, with bibl.; T. Kelly, *A History of Argos to 500 BC*, Minneapolis 1976, pp. 137–9; Cartledge, pp. 140 and 233; Pritchett, *GSW* IV (1985), 160–1; P. Vannicelli, *Erodoto e la storia dell' alto e medio arcaismo*, Rome 1993, pp. 67–85.

82,1. ἔπεμπε: Croesus possibly also sent an envoy to enlist mercenaries in the Peloponnese: Ephorus, *FGrHist* 70 F 58 (a–d). This may seem anachronistic for the 6th cent.; see, however, H. W. Parke, *Greek Mercenary Soldiers: From the Earliest Times to the Battle of Ipsus*, Oxford 1933, pp. 3–10; M. Bettalli, *I mercenari nel mondo greco, I. Dalle origini alle fine del V sec. a. C.*, Pisa 1995. For Arcadian 'deserters' seeking employment in the Persian army (480 BC) see VIII 26,1. συνεπεπτώκεε: for συμπίπτω in the sense of 'coinciding' chronologically cf. VII 206,2; VIII 15,1; IX 100,2.   Θυρέης: see Pritchett, pp. 64–74; Müller I, pp. 871–6. The Thyreatis is a fertile plain in northern Cynuria, on the route from Sparta to Argos (see P. B. Phalakris, Ἀρχαία Κυνουρία, Athens 1990), controlled by the fleet of Argos together with the coastal area to the east of Parnon as far as Cape Malea and Cythera (82,2). It is not known whether and when the 'thalassocratic' dominion of Argos was a historical reality. It cannot be excluded that Herodotus had in mind the heroic era, known today as the Mycenaean period. Argos is not in the Diodoran 'list of thalassocracies' (VII 11).
2. Κυθηρίη νῆσος: see 105,3 and note.
4. μαχομένων δέ...: the history of this famous battle was later distorted for rhetorical purposes: see e.g. Isocrates 6,99; Strabo VIII 6,17; Chrysermus, *FGrHist* 287 F 2 (a–b); Theseus, ibid. 453 F 2. Plutarch thought that the Herodotean version of the suicide was hostile to Sparta: *Mor.* 858c–d, although λέγουσι at

para. 8 can easily refer to Spartan informants. According to the official Argive version, Othryadas was killed by Perilaos, the son of one of the two Argive survivors (Paus. II 20,7). The battle was fought at Parparon, where the tombs of the soldiers were located (Paus. II 38,5). For Hellenistic epitaphs for Othryades see *Anth. Pal.* VII 430; 431 = LXV *FGE* Page (attributed to Simonides), and 526.

7. κατακειράμενοι: this ending makes the whole episode resemble a pure and simple αἴτιον. In Aristophanes' day, long hair suggested laconism: *Av.* 1281 f.

8. νόμον: 'law', whether written or not (cf. note on 29,1). Cf. the suicides of the Spartan survivors from Thermopylae (VII 229–32 and IX 71,3–4); on Spartan suicides see L. Piccirilli, *ASNP* III, XXV 4 (1995), 1387–1400. For the suicide of a Massagetan warrior cf. 213.

83. ἄλλη ἀγγελίη: this is the second Spartan delay in Herodotus: cf. 70,3; the third and most famous delay was at Marathon (VI 105–6; 120).

84,2. Μάρδος: cf. 125,4. The *ethnicon* of Hyroiades seems reliable. The impregnability of the acropolis of Sardis is an assumption common to various anecdotes, such as the story of the betrayal of Croesus' daughter (Hermesianax, *FGrHist* 691 F 1) or the stratagem reported by Ctesias, *FGrHist* 688 F 9 (b–c), and repeated in other sources. Cf. the version of Xen. *Cyr.* VII 2,2–4. For other sources on the siege of Sardis see Pedley, pp. 37–40.

3. Μήλης: the name of two other kings of the dynasty of the Lydian Heraclidae (Nicolaus of Damascus, *FGrHist* 90 F 16 and 45); see K. von Fritz, *RE* Suppl. IX 1962, coll. 309–411.   τὸν λέοντα: cf. 50,3 and note. It is unclear why it was a concubine who had to give birth to this lion (a portent, not a dream as at VI 131,2). An oriental omen predicted that 'if a woman gives birth to a lion, the city will be captured and the king will be put in chains' (cf. Cicero, *Div.* I 53); however in Herodotus' account the lion guarantees impregnability. See G. Bunnens, in *Hommages à Marcel Renard*, II, Paris 1969, pp. 130–4. For anthropological analogies of vulnerable points in 'magic circles', see E. S. McCartney, *CJ* XXXIX (1943–4), 408–12; cf. Crahay, pp. 88 f. On the Telmessians cf. 78,2, and note. On the lion as a heraldic animal cf. above, note on 50,3.   πρὸς τοῦ Τμώλου: the side facing south, cf. 93,1; V 100–1; Müller II, pp. 744–7. The modern name is Boz Dağ. There are few remains of pre-Achaemenid Sardis, some of which reach back to the 9th cent. On Sardis see the bibl. on note 7,2. On the eponymous hero Tmolos see T. Ganschow, *LIMC* VIII 1 1997, pp. 44–5.

4. ἐφράσθη καὶ ἐς θυμὸν ἐβάλετο: a Homerism (see *Od.* XIX 485).

85,1. παῖς: cf. 34,2. For other stories about Croesus' sons and daughters during the capture of Sardis, see Xen. *Cyr.* VII 2,26, and Ctesias, *FGrHist* 688 F 9. εὐεστοῖ: 'prosperity', see the scholia ad loc. For Herodotus' vocabulary of happiness, see note on 29–33.   καὶ ἐς Δελφοὺς...: see on this response P–W II, no. 55; Fontenrose, Q 102 and p. 114; Crahay, pp. 186–8; and Kirchberg, pp. 24–6. The response, which according to some seems genuine, is closely connected to the miracle and must therefore have been composed after the capture of Sardis, when anecdotes and legends about the death of Croesus started to circulate. The impolite vocative 'foolish Croesus' (cf. Hesiod, *Op.* 633; cf. Fontenrose,

p. 139) indicates a change in the tone of the oracle with respect to its old benefactor.

4. πρῶτον ἐφθέγξατο: Cicero quotes Herodotus in connection with Croesus' son who, *cum esset infans, locutum* (*Div.* I 121); *infans (a non fando)* was understood by Pliny to mean 'baby': *NH* XI 270: *semestris locutus est Croesi filius*. See A. S. Pease, *CPh* XV (1920), 201–2.

86–7. The scene of Croesus on the pyre is one of the most famous in Herodotus. Through the story of the dialogues with Cyrus and the mission to Delphi (86–91) it is connected to the usurpation of Gyges (8–12) and ends the account of the dynasty of the Mermnadae with a disputable moral: an unaware descendant is punished for the sins of an ancestor (see W. H. Friedrich, *A&A* XVIII (1973), 126 ff.; the moral is a biblical one as well). The plot is tragic; yet the attractive theory that Herodotus was inspired by a tragic trilogy which focused on the sin of Gyges (for the papyrus fragment see note on chs. 8–12), on the story of Atys and Adrastus (34–45), and on the punishment of Croesus (the mutilated images on a Corinthian *hydria* dated to 470–50 BC are not sufficient evidence for the existence of a tragedy on this subject), seems unsupported by serious evidence; see B. Snell, *ZPE* XII (1973), 197–205, with bibl.; and R. Riecks, *Poetica*, VII (1975), 22–44. This scene, however, together with the dialogue of Croesus and Solon (29–33) on the one hand, and Croesus' advice to Cyrus on the other (207), forms the philosophical and historical axis of the whole first book; cf. Introduction, pp. 65 ff. The story of Croesus on the burning pyre is depicted on the so-called 'Myron vase' dated to the early 5th cent. (see L. Vlad Borrelli, *EAA* 1959, s.v. 'Creso' and pl. 1189), and is told by Bacchylides in his third ode (468 BC), where Croesus is saved by Apollo and taken to the land of the Hyperboreans (58 ff.). Hence the story has not been invented by Herodotus, though in the earlier versions it is Croesus who attempts to kill himself in order to avoid slavery (see C. Segal *WS* V (1971), 39–51). Herodotus' version had no following. According to Xenophon, Croesus became the advisor of Cyrus without the pyre or other unpleasant surprises (*Cyr.* VII 2,9 ff. and cf. Philostratus, *Imag.* II 9). Ctesias relates how Croesus took refuge in the temple of Apollo and Cyrus honourably relegated him to Barene, near Ecbatana (*FGrHist* 688 F 9). Others say that Croesus was exhibited in Cyrus' 'triumph' and deported to Persia (e.g. Castor, *FGrHist* 250 F 11). According to Nicolaus of Damascus (following Xanthus of Lydia?), he died on the pyre surrounded by weeping Lydians (*FGrHist* 90 F 68); cf. *Mythographi Vaticani* I 196; II 290, and see M. Toher, *ClassAnt* VIII (1989), 164–7. All these versions are either legends or conjectures that originated after 546 in Lydia, Delphi, and elsewhere about an event about which nothing certain was known. Herodotus chose the version that best served his didactic purposes, allowing a tragic figure and a benevolent monarch to converse on human happiness and destiny (see Fehling, pp. 206 f.). Eastern sources do not solve the historical problem of Croesus' fate. The Chronicle of Nabonidus (*ANET*, p. 306 = *Chroniques mésopotamiennes*, ed. J.-J. Glassner, Paris 1993, p. 203) only says that 'in *Lu-* - (= Lydia?), Cyrus *šurru-su iduk* the king of that country', which may mean either 'he killed its king' or 'he routed its king' (for the meanings of the Akkadian verb *dâku* see H. Tadmor, *JNES* XVII (1958), 129–41). We are therefore left with three possible options: (1) Croesus committed suicide on the pyre or by setting fire to the palace, like other known oriental kings and governors in a similar situation (cf. VII 167,1–2 on the suicide of Hamilcar at Himera, and Boges at Eion, VII 107,1–2; the most famous example is Sardanapalus at Nineveh); (2) he was executed on a pyre by order of Cyrus, a possibility that should not be ruled out a priori in spite of the Mazdaic prohibition on contaminating fire (131,2); (3) Croesus was a prisoner-guest at the court of Cyrus or became a vassal-king (of Lydia: Diod. IX 31,3) according to a practice common to many Eastern courts (including the Achaemenids; see III 15,1–4 and notes; on the treatment of Astyages and Nabonidus see notes on 130,3 and 188–91). This last option may seem the most plausible, but actually any preference would be arbitrary: the fate of Croesus remains for us a mystery. His tomb was probably shown at Sardis (Strabo XIV 5,28). For other sources see Pedley, pp. 40–2; on Herodotus' and earlier versions see Long, pp. 106–25; M. I. Flower, in M. A. Flower and M. Toher (eds.), *Georgika: Greek Studies in Honour of G. Cawkwell*, London 1991, pp. 73–7; M. Flusin, in *Orient–Occident, cultures et échanges*, Paris 1995, pp. 71–8; G. Crane, *Arethusa*, XXIX (1996), 63–84; on the historical problem see L. Moretti, *RFIC* XXVI (1948), 219 f.; F. Cornelius, *Gymnasium*, LXIV (1957), 346–7; V. la Bua, in *Studi di storia antica offerti dagli allievi a E. Manni*, Rome 1976, pp. 177–92; J. A. S. Evans, *CJ* LXXIV (1978), 34–40; M. Mallowan, *CHI*, pp. 412 ff.; on the various stages of the ancient tradition on the fate of Croesus see W. Burkert, *Catalepton (Festschrift B. Wyss)*, ed. Chr. Schäublin, Basel 1985, pp. 4–15. Greek idealization of Cyrus starts with Aeschylus (*Pers.* 768–72) and Herodotus' Book I; see esp. the studies of Xenophon's *Cyropaedia* by J. Tatum (Princeton 1989), B. Due (Aarhus 1989), D. Gera (Oxford 1994), and C. Mueller-Goldingen (Stuttgart 1995).

86,1. τεσσαρεσκαίδεκα...: all numbers in paras. 1–2 are symbolic: a reign of twice-seven years (cf. note on 29–33), a siege of twice-seven days, etc.
2. δὶς ἑπτά: cf. Bacchylides, *Dith.* III 2, about the 'twice seven' Athenian boys and girls sent to Minos.   εἴτε... εἴτε... εἴτε: Herodotus tries to find an acceptable explanation for Cyrus' seemingly inhuman deed. On Greek idealization of Cyrus see note on 130.   ἀκροθίνια: see note on 14,1.
3. ἑστεῶτι ἐπὶ τῆς πυρῆς: Croesus' metamorphosis begins on the pyre: from arrogant king he gradually becomes a wise counsellor; cf. note on 27,2.   τὸ μηδένα εἶναι τῶν ζωόντων ὄλβιον: a simplified summary of Solon's doctrine (32,5–9).
4. τοὺς ἑρμηνέας: cf. II 125, 6; 154,2; 164,1; III 38,4; 140,3; IV 24. Herodotus is aware of the problems of language communication; for bibl. see Introduction, p. 17, n. 45.   πᾶσι τυράννοισι: 'to all rulers' (see note on 6,1).
5. ἐς ἅπαν τὸ ἀνθρώπινον: 'to all mankind'; cf. VII 46,2. The term seems unattested in sources earlier than Herodotus.

6. μεταγνόντα: cf. the 'changing of mind' (μετάγνωσις, 87,1) of Darius and Xerxes before executions (III 132,2; IV 43,2–3; VII 194,1–2) and of the Egyptian kings at II 151,3. See also Herodotus' opinion of a Persian rule concerning the death-penalty (I 137,1 and note) and of Persian good behaviour towards valiant enemies (VII 238,2).   **τίσιν:** on Herodotus' concept of retribution see Introduction, p. 38.

87,3. Κροῖσε: the formal, obsequious ὦ is usually omitted by Herodotus whenever an inferior is addressed by a superior: cf. ὦ Κροῖσε at 32,1, as against the condescending Κροῖσε here (cf. 90,1, 3; 155,1). See G. H. Macurdy, *CPh* VII (1912), pp. 77–8.   **ἐγὼ ταῦτα ἔπρηξα…:** the first sentences of the new 'wise man' express three ideas: predestination, the responsibility of the gods, and a moral condemnation of war (for the latter cf. VIII 3,1; see Drexler, p. 132).

88,2. κότερον λέγειν: a question of two alternatives, see Lang, pp. 52 ff. We are presented with the problem of freedom of speech at the court of a despot; see P. Hohti, *Arctos*, VIII (1974), 19–29.

89,2. ὑβρισταὶ: for Herodotus' concept of ὕβρις (see in I 106,1 and 189,1) see Introduction, p. 38.

3. δεκατευθῆναι τῷ Διί: on δεκάτη see note on 14,1. Though Croesus' favourite Greek god is Apollo (cf. 90,2), he seems here to assign the tithe of Persian booty to Zeus. Herodotus possibly had in mind the major Persian deity Ahura Mazda, called Zeus by the Greeks (see 131,2 and note).

90–1. Croesus and Delphi: the rendering of accounts. Croesus' claim is very simple: he has been deceived by an ungrateful god. His reaction implies neither atheism nor theodicy. The oracle's apology is based on the three responses addressed to the Lydians (13,1–2; 53,3; 55,2), and on the 'dogma' of predestination in its extreme form. The passage is important for the understanding of Herodotean (and Delphic) pessimism; see P–W II, n. 56; Fontenrose, Q 103 and pp. 114 f.; Crahay, pp. 201 f.; Kirchberg, pp. 26 ff.

90, 2. τὰς πέδας: see note on 66,4.

3. γελάσας: see note on 27,5.

4. ἀκροθίνια: Croesus' fetters are presented ironically as the 'first-fruits' (see note on 14,1) of his campaign.

91,1. τὴν πεπρωμένην μοίραν: the 'predetermined fate'; for μοίρη in this sense cf. I 121,1; III 142,3; IV 164,4; see Myres, p. 48. πεπρωμένην (cf. para. 3 and III 64,5) also belongs to the vocabulary of predestination; see N. Marinatos, *Saeculum*, XXXIII (1982), 258 ff. On personified Moirai see S. De Angelis, *LIMC* VI 1 1992, pp. 636–48.   **ἁμαρτάδα:** cf. para. 6; as well as 119,1 and 167,2. See Lachenaud, pp. 608 ff. and Introduction, p. 38.

2. Λοξίεω: an obscure epithet of Apollo, mainly poetic (e.g. Bacchyl. XIII 148; Aesch. *Eum.* 19). It was explained by the ancients in various ways, either in connection to the 'flexuosity' of sunlight, or to the 'obliquity' of the ecliptic path of the sun in its imaginary movement from east to west, or to the 'tortuosity' of Delphic responses. Its recurrent use by Herodotus in this chapter may indicate a poetic (Delphic?) source.

3. ἐπαναβάλετο: 'caused to be deferred' (Powell, *Lexicon*); for ἀναβάλλω see III 85,2, etc.   τρία γὰρ ἔτεα: adding these three extra years to the five reigns of the Mermnadae, (one and two-thirds centuries) we arrive at a total of 170 years (716–546 BC). See note on 7,1.

92,1. κατὰ μὲν ... ἔσχε οὕτω: a good example of a closing sentence at the end of a *logos* in Book I; cf. 94,7; 130; 169; 191,6.   τὴν πρώτην καταστροφήν: Ionia was first subjected by Croesus (6,2) and then by the Persians (169,2). Cf. the Spartans' 'first campaign' in Asia c.525 (III 56,2) and their second in 479 BC (IX 96 ff.); the Persians' 'first' and 'second' conquest of Babylon (I 191,6; III 159,1); and the 'first' and 'second' Ionian revolts (IX 104). Enumeration of historical events for mnemonic rather than comparative purposes is typical of oral cultures.   τὰ εἰρημένα: cf. 50–2, and notes on 14,1 and 51,5.   Ἀπόλλωνι τῷ Ἰσμηνίῳ: cf. note on 52. On the Artemisium at Ephesus see 26,2 and note. Fragments of dedicatory inscriptions carved on the bases of three columns of the Artemisium (now in the British Museum), and written in the archaic Ionic alphabet, may be read as Βασιλεὺς Κρ[οῖσος] ἀνέθηκεν (*Syll.*³6 = *Tod I* 6).   ἐν δὲ Προνηίης: the archaic sanctuary of Athena Pronaia (or Pronoia), in the 'Marmara', east of the well-known *tholos*, was probably destroyed in 480 by an avalanche of rocks from Mt Parnassus (VIII 37,2–3); a few Doric capitals survive. It was rebuilt after the Persian wars. A new temple was built in the 4th cent. BC, next to the *tholos*, on the north-western end of the row (see [Dem.] XXV 34; Diod. XI 14,4; Paus. X 8,6–7). See Müller I, pp. 467 ff.; J.-F. Bommelaer (ed.), *Marmaria. Le sanctuaire d'Athéna à Delphes*, Bordeaux 1996. The epithet Προνηίη (cf. Aesch. *Eum.* 21, etc.) means 'who stands in front of the νηός' (i.e. in front of Apollo's temple within the great *temenos*; cf. προνηίος 51,2). The form Πρόνοια, 'the provident' (Aeschines III 108; 110–12; etc.), seems an alteration of the original epithet.   τὰ δ' ἐξαπόλωλε: lost, stolen, or destroyed during the century between c.550 BC and Herodotus' visit. Croesus' golden shield was said to have been stolen by Philomelus in 356 BC (Paus. X 8,7).

2. ἐν Βραγχίδῃσι: cf. 46,2 and note on 157,3. In 499 Hecataeus proposed to use the offerings to finance the Ionian revolt. They were lost in 494 (V 36,3–4 and VI 19,3, with references to this chapter).   ὡς ἐγὼ πυνθάνομαι: Herodotus could not have seen the gifts; see T. S. Brown, *AJPh* XCIX (1978), 70.   Ἀμφιάρεω: cf. 46,2; 49; 52.   ἀπαρχήν: cf. IV 71,4; 88,1; the 'first-fruits'. The priority of Delphi is stressed again. In Herodotus' time ἀπαρχή was the official term for one-sixtieth of the tribute (φόρος) paid yearly to Athens by members of the Delian league.   ἐξ ἀνδρὸς ... ἐχθροῦ: this 'enemy' may be identical with the merchant Sadyattes in Nicolaus of Damascus, *FGrHist* 90 F 65; cf. also Plut. *Mor.* 401 e–f, and Herod. I 51,5. See V. La Bua, *MGR* V (1977), 11 f.

4. ἐπὶ κνάφου: a 'combing-card', here an instrument of torture, cf. Plut. *Mor.* 858e–f.

93,1. θώματα: here natural wonders, as distinct from human ἔργα. Xanthus of Lydia actually discusses the 'burnt' volcanic land in the valley of the upper

Hermus (*FGrHist* 765 F 13). Scythia too does not have natural marvels (IV 82). ψήγματος: sand mixed with specks of gold, mentioned by Herodotus also elsewhere (e.g. III 102,3; 106,2; IV 195,2). On the gold of the Pactolus see also V 101,2; for other sources see Pedley, pp. 70–2.

2. Ἀλυάττεω... σῆμα: cf. Strabo XIII 4,7. The tomb of Alyattes (perhaps already mentioned by Hipponax, fr. 27 West), is today identified with a giant mound in the Lydian necropolis north of the river Hermus (BIn Tepe), but the measurements of this mound (1080 m. of circumference and 360 m. of diameter) are less than those of Herodotus (between 1140 and 1270 m. of circumference and 390–455 m. of diameter). Since Herodotus' stadium equals 6 plethra (II 149,3), the ratio between circumference (38 plethra) and diameter (13 plethra) of the tomb is not that of a perfect circle (see para. 5): the measurements seem to have been obtained empirically, not by calculation. See, however, P. Keyser, *CJ* LXXXI (1986), 230–42. The mound contains a complex network of tunnels and a funerary chamber of marble blocks. For bibl. see Pedley, p. 77; C. Ratté, *JHS* CXIV (1994), 157–61.

3. οὖροι: two pillars of phallic shape have been preserved, but without inscriptions. For inscriptions and epigraphy in Herodotus, cf. note on 51,4. According to Strabo (XIII 4,7), Alyattes' tomb was called by some a 'monument of prostitution' (πόρνης μνῆμα).

4. πορνεύονται πᾶσαι: an amusing view for a Greek public. This is not an example of sacred prostitution (as at Babylon, cf. 199). However, see Strabo XI 14,16. For a Herodotean reminiscence in Plautus, *Cistellaria* 562–3, see M. Renard, *Latomus*, II (1938), 77–83.

5. Γυγαίη: for other sources, from Homer onwards, see Pedley, pp. 69 f. This lake, also called Coloe (today Marmara Gölü), is situated just north of the Lydian necropolis. Cf. Strabo XIII 4,7.

94,1. νόμοισι: ethnic 'customs' (cf. note on 35, 1). Herodotus justifies the description (Mazzarino, p. 174) of a 'greco-lydian cultural *koinè*'. νόμισμα: Herodotus' theory of the Lydian origin of coinage is today the accepted view (see already Xenophanes, 21 B 4 DK); on the Lydians as 'first inventors' of coinage and other things, see Kleingünther, pp. 42 and 60; N. K. Rutter, in *Studi per Laura Breglia* I, Rome 1987, pp. 59–62. The connection between commerce and the origin of coins, which Herodotus implicitly assumes, is debated. See R. M. Cook, *Historia*, VII (1958), 259 ff.; J.-M. Servet, *Nomismata. État et origines de la monnaie*, Lyon 1984. The most ancient Lydian coins were of electrum (an alloy of gold and silver), oval, and of varying weight (either 168 gr. according to the Babylonian standard, or 220 gr. according to the Phoenician), with a lion head on the obverse as a symbol and incuse squares on the reverse. A re-examination of the hoard of Greek and Lydian coins found at the site of the Artemisium of Ephesus permits the dating of the earliest coins to 640–630 BC. To Croesus is attributed the striking of gold and silver coins (rather than electrum), and the introduction of new symbols. Autonomous Lydian coinage came to an end with the Persian conquest, but it influenced Persian and Greek coinage. See C. M. Kraay,

146 Commentary

Archaic and Classical Greek Coins, London 1976; on the Ephesus hoard see
S. Karwiese, *RE* Suppl. XII (1970), coll. 297–9, with bibl.   κάπηλοι: 'shop-
keepers', 'hucksters', 'retail traders'; cf. II 141,4; 164,1; V 9,3. King Darius was
remembered as a κάπηλος (III 89,3). On the term and concept of κάπηλος,
καπηλεύω, etc. see M. Lombardo, *I Greci* II 2 (1997), 699–705; on the equation
of retail trade with deceit see L. Kurke, *AJPh* CX (1989), 535–44.

2. τάς παιγνίας: Herodotus is the first to attribute to the Lydians the invention of
popular Greek games of his day: dice (six-sided cubes); *astragaloi* (knucklebones
of various shapes and values, and sometimes of artificial material); and the ball;
only πεσσοί (draughts: Athenaeus I 16e ff.) were not claimed by the Lydians as an
invention of their own. Dating the invention of these games to the time of Atys,
i.e. before Heracles (cf. note on 7,1), Herodotus knew very well that the Homeric
heroes played πεσσοί, ball, and knucklebones (but Athen. I 19a claims categorically that the heroic age preceded the time of Atys). According to Pliny, the ball
was invented by Gyges (*Nat. Hist.* VII 205). A different theory attributed the
invention of games to Palamedes; see R. Goossens, *RBPh* XXX (1952), 146–56.
For the Egyptian origin of games see Plato, *Phdr.* 274c. The connection between
games and hunger, variously interpreted (fertility rites, etc.) recurs also in the
sources on the myth of Palamedes. On games in antiquity see J. Dörig, *EAA* 1960,
s.v. 'giocattolo'.

3. Μάνεω: cf. Herodotus IV 45,3. See Talamo, pp. 16 ff.

5–7. δύο μοίρας ... Τυρσηνούς: Herodotus is the progenitor of the 'oriental'
theory of the origin of the Etruscans. It looks like a local Lydian tradition that
Herodotus reports without commenting; this version (unknown to Xanthus of
Lydia; but see H. H. Scullard, in *Studies Ehrenberg*, Oxford 1966, pp. 225–31) was
accepted, with or without variations, by the greater part of Greek poets and
historians (see *FGrHist* 706 [*Anhang*] and Pedley, pp. 10–12), and was also used
for political purposes (see Tacitus, *Ann.* IV 55). Dionysius of Halicarnassus is the
only representative of the theory of Etruscan autochthony (*Ant. Rom.* I 25–30).
Among modern scholars the oriental theory still prevails, supported today by new
linguistic considerations (the inscription of Lemnos, etc.); there exists also a
school of autochthonists who consider the Etruscans a pre-Indo-European
residual population transformed into a linguistic island by the (hypothetical)
invasion of the Italic peoples. A third modern school, with no ancient precursors,
believes in a northern origin from Rhaetia. Pallottino, already in his *Elementi di
lingua etrusca*, Florence 1936, set out the problem in terms of the cultural
formation of the Etruscan 'nation' rather than in terms of an ethno-geographical
origin—in other words, of a civilization formed in Italy, with an addition of
Anatolian elements. For a review of ancient and modern views see D. Briguel (op.
cit. in note on 7,1). On the Tyrrhenians in Herodotus see also chs. 166–7.

5. Τυρσηνόν: an artificial eponym; cf. Dion. Hal., *Ant. Rom.* I 27–8; Strabo V 2,2;
Paus. II 21,3, etc., with different genealogies and other variants.

6. Ὀμβρικούς: the 'Umbrians', cf. IV 49,2, vaguely located by Herodotus in
central Italy. See the bibl. quoted in note to paras. 5–7.

95–106. This is the most ancient 'history of the Medes' that we have, constructed around the paradigmatic personalities of the first three kings: the founder (Deïoces), the failure (Phraortes), and the great emperor (Cyaxares). The fourth, Astyages (107–30), was the king/tyrant who provoked revolt and the end of the kingdom. These kings foreshadow the great Persian monarchs from Cyrus to Xerxes. Herodotus attempted to write a true history, with personal evaluation of the political, judicial, social, and military activities of the kings, and with reflections on the origins and vicissitudes of despotism. It is possible to translate Herodotus' chronology of the Median reigns into absolute dates, starting from 550 BC (the fall of Astyages, cf. note on 130) and keeping the 'year of the eclipse', 585 BC (74,2 and note), as the last year of Cyaxares (see Fig. 3).

Deïoces	53 years (102,1)	700–647 BC
Phraortes	22 years (102,2)	647–625 BC
Cyaxares	40 years (106,3)	625–585 BC
Astyages	35 years (130,1)	585–550 BC
Total	150 years	700–550 BC

FIG. 3. Median reigns

Herodotus' total of 128 years, excluding (πάρεξ) twenty-eight years of Scythian hegemony (130,1 and note) which he seems to include (σὺν) in the forty-year reign of Cyaxares (106,1 and 3, and notes) is wrong. By inverting the lengths of the first two reigns, the total of the last three (Phraortes 53, Cyaxares 40, Astyages 35) is 128 (see Stein ad loc.). This alteration does not solve the main problem, although it may provide an explanation of the origin of Herodotus' mistaken total. It has, however, the advantage of causing Phraortes' reign (which would last from 678 to 625) to overlap with that of the Assyrian king Essarhaddon (681–669), a useful coincidence if we want to keep alive the widely accepted identification of Phraortes with the Kaštariti mentioned in an oracular enquiry by Essarhaddon (see note on 102,1). Yet Eastern sources provide us with two more names: Daiaukku, mentioned in the annals of Sargon II (722–705) and recalling Herodotus' Deioces, and the Scythian Par-ta-tua, who asked for an alliance with Essarhaddon (see note on 103,3). Besides, we have from Eastern sources the epochal date of the fall of Niniveh (612 BC), which Herodotus does not date but attributes to the last part of Cyaxares' reign (see 106 and note). To fit all these data into Herodotus' Median chronology, a recent attempt has been made to explain the σὺν at 106,3 in the sense of '*excluding*' (contrary to all expectation), thus adding the twenty-eight-year Scythian interregnum to the total of Cyaxares' reign (which would then last sixty-eight years, from 653 to 685, *including* the interregnum). As a result, Deioces' reign would last from 728 to 675, overlapping that of Sargon II. See J. A. Scurlock, *IA* XXV (1990), 149–63.

Herodotus may have used Eastern sources, both oral (among them the Median Harpagids of Xanthus in Lydia?: see Introd., p. 17 and note on 176,2) and

written, with the help of bilingual interpreters, as well as Greek treatises of
Περσικά, e.g. by Hecataeus; see J. V. Prášek, *Klio*, IV (1904), 193–208. A substratum of popular sagas underlies the story of Deïoces (96–101). Modern scholars are
perhaps excessively sceptical about the historical value of this Median *logos*: the
very notion of a 'Median empire' has been questioned. In fact, we owe it
exclusively to Herodotus and later Greek sources, since archaeologically, a
'Median' phase of material culture has not yet been identified. See B. Genito,
East & West, XXXVI (1986), 11–81; H. Sancisi-Weerdenburg, *AH* III (1988),
197–212. Nevertheless, Herodotus' is the only Greek account of the Medes which
is partly supported by our Eastern sources. For the sake of comparison see
Diodorus' summary based on an unrecognizable 'Herodotus' at II 32,2–3 (derived
from Ctesias?); or the fanciful chronology of Ctesias (*FGrHist* 688 F 1 and 5). Among
recent works, with bibl., see M. Miller, *The Thalassocracies*, Albany 1971, pp. 114–28;
P. R. Helm, *Iran*, XIX (1981), 85–90; and I. M. Diakonoff, *CHI*, pp. 36–148 (an
updated summary of his *History of Media*, published in Russian in 1956); S. Brown,
AH III (1988), 71–86; H. Sancisi-Weerdenburg, *AH* VIII (1994), 39–55; Briant,
Histoire, pp. 23–38, 908–9 = ET pp. 13–28; 879–80.

95,1. καὶ τριφασίας ... ὁδούς: the four 'types' of stories known to Herodotus,
must have been versions of Median or Persian origin, already elaborated and
rationalized by previous Greeks: the 'type' that Herodotus chooses, as well as
those chosen by Xenophon (popular sagas and songs about Cyrus: *Cyr.* I 2,1), by
Ctesias (*FGrHist* 688 F 66), and by the author summarized by Diodorus (see note
on 95–106) seem to suggest as much. The three types of story rejected by
Herodotus 'exalted' or 'departed from the truth in order to exalt' (cf. σεμνοῦν:
III 16,7) the king, either by emphasizing supernatural elements (see 122,3) or by
portraying Cyrus' parents as 'great kings' of Anšan (as the official Achaemenid
version). We know, however, other accounts that tended not to exalt Cyrus'
personality: e.g. Darius barely mentions him among his predecessors in the
Bisitun inscription (*DB* I §§10 ff. Kent); and Nicolaus of Damascus (following
Ctesias?) says that he was the son of a bandit. Herodotus chose a middle course:
even though he declares himself a lover of truth, he prefers a version that already
exists and does not reconstruct one of his own (see Drexler, pp. 57 ff.) This
version, though idealizing Cyrus, has at its centre the tragic figures of Astyages
and Harpagus; it certainly is not the official Achaemenid version, but neither is it
hostile to them (perhaps it goes back to a Median version told by the descendants
of Harpagus).

2. Ἀσσυρίων ...: since Herodotus apparently dated Deïoces to 700–647 BC (cf.
note on 95–106), he probably dated the beginning of the Assyrian hegemony to
1220 BC (= 700 + 520 years, or 13 generations of 40 years) in order to syn-
chronize it with the beginning of the Lydian Heraclid dynasty (cf. note on 7,1). It
thus seems too optimistic to look for historical parallels of the eponymous King
Ninus with Assyrian kings such as Tiglath-Pileser I (*c*.1130 BC) or Tukulti-
Nikurta I (1242–1206 BC); see e.g. E. A. Speiser, *Eretz Israel*, V (1958), 32–6;
I. M. Diakonoff, *CHI*, pp. 89 f. Herodotus may well have been acquainted with

the series of the three universal monarchies, probably formed in Ionia soon after the fall of Lydia; see the Introduction, p. 36. His Assyrian empire, however, includes the neo-Babylonian period as we call it today (from the fall of Niniveh to Cyrus' conquest of Babylon, 612–539 BC); see 178,1 and 184 with note. His sequence Assyria–Media is therefore a transitional 'succession' involving long periods of coexistence of rival empires. τῆς ἄνω Ἀσίης: see note on 72,3. ἐλευθερίης: here meaning political independence from foreign rule; cf. Introduction, pp. 43 f., and note on 6,3.

96,1. Δηιόκης: approximately half the Median *logos* is devoted to the story of Deïoces (chs. 96–101). The tyrant-founder was chosen as king by the grateful people (cf. Diod. VIII 16, and Polyaenus VII 1). He personifies the fair judge, the promoter of building works, and the unifier of the nation: all are ἔργα worthy of mention. See A. Piatkowska, in *Acta Conventus XI Eirene 1968*, Prague 1971, pp. 391 ff. Deïoces has generally been identified with Daiaukku mentioned in Assyrian sources dated to 724–725 BC, during the reign of Sargon II. A Daiku of Saparda paid tribute to the Assyrian king in 716 (see L. D. Levine, *Royal Ontario Museum*, XXIII (1972), 40 f.); in the following year the governor of Mannea, called Daiaukku, an ally of the king of Urartu (Lie, pp. 16 ff.; Luckenbill II, pp. 27 ff.) was deported by Sargon to Hamath in Syria. The Elamitic form of the name is *Da-a-hi-uk-ka* (with variants; see *PFT*, n. 681b; cf. O. K. Armayor, *AncW* I (1978), 152). *Dah-yu-ka* was proposed as the original Median and Persian version (see R. Schmitt, *AAWW* CX (1973), 137–47). The conjecture *[Bit-Da]iaukku* in the *Annals* of Sargon (713 BC) seems groundless. It is not easy to harmonize these data on the rebellious squire Daiaukku with Herodotus' account of Deïoces the 'unifier of the nation'. During the years 716–713 Media was in turmoil and there is no possibility of talking about Median unity for another forty years. To maintain the identification, one needs to assume that, after Sargon's death Daiaukku managed to return from Hamath to Media and become there the fair judge and governor, whose conduct merited the support of many Median villages. 2. ἐρασθεὶς τυραννίδος: cf. III 53,4 (τυραννίς ... πολλοὶ δὲ αὐτῆς ἐρασταί εἰσι). The story of Deïoces is a parable on the subject of the rise of tyranny, as seen by an intellectual Greek. κατὰ κώμας: Herodotus describes in Greek terms a rural society on its way to synoecism. Archaeologists have been able to identify very few Median settlements; see D. Stronach, *CHI*, pp. 832–7. δικαιοσύνην: Deïoces is a model judge. The exceptional concentration of terms of the δικ- family in these chapters (96–7; 100) arouses the suspicion that Deïoces might be, after all, a symbolic name. See C. Coulet, *REG* CV (1992), 371–84. τῷ δικαίῳ τὸ ἄδικον πολέμιόν ἐστι: a maxim of Ionian philosophy, not of Mazdaic 'dualism'; but see Arieti, p. 118.

97,1. κατίζειν ... προκατίζων: in the East judges arbitrate at the city gates, and the courts are built there; see e.g. 2 Sam. 14: 1 ff. and Ruth 4; cf. Herod. V 12,2. 3. φέρε στήσωμεν: cf. 1 Sam. 8: 5 ff.

98,3. ἐν πόλισμα: an act of synoecism. In Herodotus, at least, πόλισμα is not a 'small πόλις', as some scholars presume: Assyria is full of πολίσματα μεγάλα,

including Niniveh and Babylon (178,1–2).   Ἀγβάτανα: this is the form used
by Herodotus: cf. I 110,3; 153,3; III 64,4; 92,1. The usual Greek form is Ἐκβάτανα.
Old Persian has *Hagmatana* ('place of assembly'?); the Aramaic form is *Aḥmetha*.
It has been located near modern Hamadan, a crossroads 2,000 m. above sea-level,
on the Iranian plateau between the mountain chains of Elburz and Zagros.
Ctesias, *FGrHist* 688 F 1 (13,5–8) supposes that Ecbatana existed from the time
of Semiramis, while the Book of Judith attributes its foundation to a Median
king named Arphaxad (Harpagus). The Achaemenids used it as their summer
residence. For a homonymous small city in Syria see III 64,4. For bibl. see
A. Pagliaro, *EAA* 1960, s.v. 'Ecbatana'; P. Calmeyer, 'Hamadan', *RLA* IV 1972,
pp. 64–7.   ἕτερον ἑτέρῳ κύκλῳ...: Herodotus describes an imaginary citadel
of seven storeys, modelled on the Mesopotamian *ziqqurat* (see A. Bisi, *EAA* 1966,
s.v. 'Ziqqurat', updated by R. Ghirshmann in the 1973 Suppl.). The technique of
glazing bricks with various colours was widely known in Mesopotamia from the
3rd millennium BC. The dominant colours at Khorsabad are yellow and blue,
whereas at Nimrūd there is greater variety: white, black, red, yellow, blue, and
green. It is generally held that the Babylonians, and later the Medes and the
Persians, used seven colours to paint royal palaces and temples, seven being a
sacred number (cf. note on 181,5). These seven colours—as also metals, precious
stones, flavours, etc.—corresponded in Chaldaean astrology to the seven Mesopotamian divine planets: e.g. golden yellow was the colour of Šamaš, the sun;
scarlet was the colour of Nergal, Mars, etc.; the correspondence, however, is not
always certain. The outer circumference of the palace is surprisingly large: almost
9 km., like the walls of Athens in Herodotus' day; see Thuc. II 13,7, with the
commentary by Gomme ad loc. The other ancient descriptions of the citadel of
Ecbatana (Polyb. X 27,8–31; Judith 1: 2–3; Diod. XVII 110,7; Joseph., *Ant. Iud.* X
264–5) do not correspond with that of Herodotus. The restorations of the
Achaemenid and the Seleucid periods may have transformed the building. The
site has not been excavated.

4. προμαχεῶσι: here the word refers to the highest merlons or turrets projecting
from every wall: cf. I 164,1; III 151,1. See J. E. Powell, *CQ* XXIX (1935),
73 f.   κατὰ τὸν Ἀθηνέων κύκλον: Herodotus is of course addressing a Greek,
but not necessarily an Athenian, audience; for similar comparisons see 202,1, and
the Introduction, p. 5.

99,1. πρῶτος: Deïoces is also credited with having been the 'first inventor' of
court ceremonies and bureaucracy. In fact, the Medes imitated the Assyrians, and
in turn were imitated by the Persians (the Greek historians imagined the court of
Ecbatana as modelled on the Persian, known to them; see e.g. Nicolaus of
Damascus, *FGrHist* 90 F 66). In the palaces of Darius at Susa and Persepolis
audience was granted, according to routine procedure, in the *apadana*, a large
hypostyle throne hall, where the king, sitting in semi-darkness, could hardly have
been seen through the gaps between the columns. Under the Sassanids a scarcely
transparent curtain separated the Great King from the few privileged subjects and
guests who were granted audience. The inaccessibility of the king was an

important element in Persian etiquette that influenced court ceremonies of the Roman emperors from Diocletian onwards. Scenes of royal audience are respresented in Eastern sculpture from the Assyrian period; see G. Walser, *Audienz beim persischen Grosskönig*, Zürich 1965; H. Gabelmann, *Antike Audienz- und Tribunalszenen*, Darmstadt 1984, pp. 7–21; Briant, *Histoire*, pp. 230–5, 939–40 = ET pp. 217–23, 913–14; M. C. Miller, *Athens and Persia in the Fifth-Century B.C.: A Study of Cultural Receptivity*, Cambridge 1997, pp. 125 ff. For Persian bureaucracy see also 114,2 and 120,2; for the προσκύνησις, see 119,1 and 134,1 and note; for clothing, see 135. γελᾶν... αἰσχρόν: it would have been disgraceful for anyone to laugh or spit in the presence of the king. For an analogy with Sparta, see Plut. *Agis* 19,6; 21,2 (see U. Albini, *A&R* VI (1961), 95–6). Cf. Xen. *Cyr.* I 2,16; VIII 1,42.

2. ἑτεροῖός: Herodotus' explanation is rational and typically Greek, but he rightly assumes that Median kings, like the Persian ones, thought that their power was granted by divine will: king 'by favour of Ahura Mazda' is actually the common Achaemenid formula, hence their almost divine nature; cf. 204,2 and 207,2.

100,1. δίκας γράφοντες: no one doubts the Medes were literate, though epigraphic evidence is missing. The procedure here described resembles the *rescripta* of the Roman emperors. For the theory that written responses were given by Queen Atossa, see Hellanicus, *FGrHist* 4 F 178a.

2. κατ' ἀξίην: the punishment is neither stated by law nor inflicted arbitrarily, but in proportion to one's guilt. See note on 96,2. οἱ κατάσκοποί τε καὶ κατήκοοι: inspectors or spies (cf. Cassius Dio XLII 17,2), the precursors of the 'eyes and ears' of the Persian kings; see 112,1 and 114,2.

101. γένεα: the Median ἔθνος is said to consist of six γένεα; see for the terminology C. P. Jones, *CQ* XLVI (1996), 318. This list is not given much credit. Strabo places the Paretaceni in the area between Susiana and Media; they may be the same as the Paricani (III 92,1 and note; VII 68; 86,2). See H. Treidler, *RE* Suppl. X 1965, coll. 478–82; A. M. Piemontese, *RSO* XLIV (1969), 109–42. On the Magi see 140,2. The other ethnic tribes mentioned here are unknown. Stephanus of Byzantium has five Median ἔθνη: Αἰγηλοί, Βούδειοι, Βοῦσαι, Καρδούχοι, and Μάγοι (s.v. Μαγία). For the supposed Old Persian or Elamite original names of the Median tribes see O. K. Armayor, *AncW* I (1978), 152.

102,1. Φραόρτης: since Darius, in the Bisitun inscription (p. 531 below § 24), mentions a Median rebel-king called Fravontis (see O. K. Armayor, loc. cit.) who in 522 BC declared himself to be Kaštariti (Khšaθrita in Old Persian) and a descendant of Uvakhštreh, it has been suggested that Herodotus' Phraortes also had two names, or a private name and a royal title. On this ground our Phraortes is usually identified with the Kaštariti mentioned in Esarhaddon's oracular enquiries of the years 675–673 BC: see note on 95–106. At that time Kaštariti was the governor of Kar-Kašši (in the central Zagros area); he attacked and threatened various cities under Assyrian control and was also the leader of an anti-Assyrian coalition of Medes, Cimmerians, and Manneans (for the unified army see 101,2). See E. G. Klauber, *Politisch-religiöse Texte aus der Sargonidenzeit*, Leipzig 1913, nos. 1–15. However, the identification of Phraortes with Kaštariti presents a serious historical difficulty, since at the time of Esarhaddon and Assurbanipal Media was still in a fractured state and repeatedly invaded by the Assyrians. See R. Labat, *JA* CCXLIX (1961), 1–21, and the bibl. quoted in note on 95–106. στρατευσάμενος ἐπὶ τοὺς Πέρσας: Herodotus' Phraortes who waged war with the Persians penetrated the Zagros as far as Anšan and Parsumaš, which in the 7th cent. were under the sway of the first Achaemenids. These Achaemenids are supposed to have become vassals of the Median Phraortes, not of the Assyrian Esarhaddon; but some thirty years later (646 BC) Kuruš, king of Parsumaš, paid homage to Assurpanipal (see note on 107,2): hence Anšan and Parsumaš could be permanently annexed to the kingdom of the Medes only after this date.

2. οἳ Νίνον εἶχον: Phraortes attacked the Assyrians whose capital was Niniveh (as distinct from the Assyrians of Babylon): for Herodotus, pre-Achaemenid Babylonia is the remaining part of the Assyrian empire after the fall of Niniveh: cf. note on 95,1. He does not say that Phraortes attacked Niniveh itself.

103,1. Κυαξάρης: Ú-ak-sa-tar in Assyrian, Uvakhštrah in Old Persian. For the length of his reign see note on 95–106. Cyaxares is the king-conqueror and diplomat; he is the most important of the Median kings and the first who may be considered as a historical hegemonic emperor in the Middle East after the fall of the Assyrian empire. During his reign Niniveh (612 BC) and the rest of the northern Assyrian kingdom were conquered; the kingdom of Urartu in Armenia disappeared, and the whole of Cappadocia up to the river Halys was annexed (74,3–5); Babylon became an ally, Anšan and Parsumaš vassal-states; Lydia also became an ally and the Parthians were subjected. Only the Cadusii (between Mt. Elburz and the Caspian Sea) remained independent. The empire of the Medes reached its peak in the years 612–585. Cyaxares found his way into popular Median sagas: in 522 two usurpers, the Mede Fravartiš and the Sagartan Ciçatakhma, declared themselves descendants of Cyaxares. Greek sources later than Herodotus present some variants. In Ctesias' list, *FGrHist* 688 F 5(34), the second-to-last king of the Medes is called Astibaras and, according to Xenophon (*Cyr.* I 5,2), Cyaxares is the son and successor of Astyages. See the bibl. on 95–106, and also W. Hinz, *RLA* VI 1983, coll. 399–400.   πρῶτος ...: again, the motif of the 'first' inventor; see Introduction, p. 35.   κατὰ τέλεα: cf. VII 87, etc. Herodotus has in mind the ethnic contingents of the Persian multinational army.

2. ὅτε νύξ: see 74,2 and note.   ἐπὶ τὴν Νίνον: this first siege of Niniveh may be identified with the attack mentioned in the Gadd Chronicle (see note on 106,2), in the month of Ab in the twelfth year of the kingdom of Nabopolassar (July/Aug. 614 BC); for an earlier date see E. Cavaignac, *RAss* LI (1957), 28–9. It was preceded by a campaign in the area around Arrapha (between the river Tigris and the Zagros), and followed by attacks against Tarbiṣ and Assur. The Chronicle of Gadd also mentions a meeting between the king of Akkad (= Nabopolassar) and U-ma-kiš-tar (= Cyaxares) at Assur which ended with an agreement; cf. the alliance between Arbakes and Belesys in Ctesias, *FGrHist* 688 F 1 (24) and Nicolaus of Damascus, *FGrHist* 90 F 3; other Greek sources (probably following

Berossus) add that, on this occasion, Nebuchadnezzar took as his wife Amytis, daughter of Aždahak (= Astyages: chronologically impossible). On the Scythians in this siege nothing is known from other sources; for the presence of Bactrians see Ctesias, *FGrHist* 688 F 1 (26).

3. *Μαδύης Προτοθύεω παῖς*: Protothyes may be identified with *Par-ta-tu-a*, king of the Išguza (= Scythians), who had asked Esarhaddon for a wife and an alliance; see Klauber, op. cit., no. 16. Years later this alliance is supposed to have saved Niniveh from the first siege of Cyaxares. For Madyes see Strabo, I 3,21.

103,3–106,2. Digression on the Scythians in the Middle East. Herodotus is saying that the Scythians arrived in the Middle East during the first siege of Niniveh, when their twenty-eight-year-long 'hegemony' in Asia started (cf. 104,2; 106,1; IV 1,2–3); for 'Upper Asia', cf. IV 1,2; VII 20,2: see R. P. Vaggione, *JBL* XCII (1973), 523–30. The Scythian hegemony lasted until Cyaxares massacred their leaders (106,2; IV 1,3). For the chronology of the Scythian hegemony see notes on 95–106 and 106,3. Assyrian sources testify to the presence of Iškuza in the Middle East since the time of Esarhaddon (681–668 BC), when a Scythian kingdom had probably been established in modern Kurdistan, south of lake Urmia. The Old Testament vaguely alludes to the menace of Scythians at the end of the 7th cent. and in the early 6th cent.; see e.g. Jer. 1: 13–4; 4: 6–7; 47: 1–7; 51: 27; Zeph. 2: 4–7, 13–15. Various archaeological finds in Iran (the 'treasure of Ziwiyeh', the bronzes of Luristan) were attributed by some to Scythian civilization; but their style is mixed and points to acculturation (cf. Herodotus' anecdote at 73,3). Anyway the oriental sources on the Scythians do not confirm the notion of hegemony as a stable supremacy with regular tributes (106,1). The Scythians never replaced the existing kingdoms and did not prevent the Medes and the Babylonians from sharing the spoils of the Assyrian kingdom. Herodotus himself assumes that Cyaxares remained in power also during the Scythian 'hegemony', despite what he says at 104,2; cf. IV 1,2. It seems plausible to suppose that, for a certain time, Cyaxares relied on the cavalry of the Scythians, and that he was forced to donate land and money to their leaders in order to prevent sudden incursions (see 106,1; in Philistia see 105). See the bibl. in the note to 95–106; L. Piotrowicz, *Eos*, XXXII (1929), 473–508; A. Ivantchik, in Tsetskhladze, *Ancient Greeks* pp. 497–520.

103,3. *Κιμμερίους*: for the Cimmerians see note on ch. 15.

104,1. *ἀπὸ τῆς λίμνης*: lake Maiotis (cf. IV 3,2, etc.) is the Sea of Azov; on the river Phasis and Colchis see 2,2 and note. The distance is about 500 km. when travelling along the coast (cf. 72; and note). The implied average march per day, 17 km., is rather low for a 'good walker' when compared to other averages in Herodotus: see III 5,3 and note (*c.*24 km.); V 53 (27 km.); IV 101,3 (36 km.). Such calculations are of course extremely speculative, owing to uncertainty about the distances assumed by Herodotus in each case, and about his unit of *stadium* (148.85 m. according to O. Viedebantt, *Klio*, XVI (1920), 100–8; the average *stadium* is usually taken to be 600 feet = 180 m.). Cf. P. M. Fraser, *Cities of*

Alexander the Great, Oxford 1996, pp. 76–7 and n. 2.   Σάσπειρες: they inhabited a part of Armenia between Colchis and Media; cf. VI 37; 40,1; Müller II, 216–17. For the Saspeires in the Persian empire see III 94,1 and note; VII 79. East of the Saspeires, other peoples inhabited the coastal areas of the south-western Caspian Sea, among them the Caspians, well known to Herodotus (III 92,2 and note).

2. ἀλλὰ τὴν κατύπερθε ὁδόν: the Cimmerians turned west, along the Colchian coast towards Sinope and Phrygia (see ch. 15), while the Scythians took the way north of the Caucasus presumably passing through the 'Caucasian' or 'Albanian' gates (by way of Derbent, on the Caspian coast). On the Caucasus see I 203,1 and note.

105,1. ἐν τῇ Παλαιστίνῃ Συρίῃ: Herodotus calls 'Palestinian Syria' the coastal strip of land between Phoenicia and the Egyptian border: see III 5,1; IV 39,2; VII 89,1; as part of the Persian empire, III 91,1 and note; VII 89,1. Παλαιστίνη is a Greek transliteration of the Hebrew Plšth, 'the land of the Philistines'. Herodotus knew some of the five biblical cities of Philistia: Cadytis (possibly Gaza: II 159,2; III 5,1 and note), Ascalon, and Azotos (Ašdod: II 157). For the civilization of the Philistines see N. Avigad, *EAA* 1960, s.v. 'Filistea, ceramica'; and T. Dothan, *The Philistines and their Material Culture*, Jerusalem 1982. Herodotus is our only source for the Scythian incursion through Palestine, about which he may have gathered evidence in Egyptian temples, in the temple of Ascalon, or in Scythia. The incursion is dated to the time of Psammetichus I (*c*.663–609 BC), but it is impossible to be more precise (modern hypotheses vacillate between 626 and 609): evidently it must have been a brief raid into Philistia. It is absurd to extend over the whole of Palestine the twenty-eight years of Scythian hegemony, and to maintain that it left its trace in the name of the city Scythopolis (Beth-Šean, south of the Sea of Galilee; see A. Mazar and G. Foerster, in E. Stern (ed.), *The New Encyclopedia of Archaeological Excavations in the Holy Land*, I, Jerusalem 1993, pp. 214–35). Scythopolis is a Hellenistic settlement of the 3rd cent. on a site previously uninhabited for at least four centuries; see V. Tcherikover, *Hellenistic Civilization and the Jews*, New York 1977, p. 103.   ἀντιάσας: 'went to meet them'; cf. 166,2, etc.

2. Ἀσκάλωνι: Aškanu in Egyptian texts of the 2nd millennium BC, Ašklon in the Old Testament. It is situated about 16 km. north of Gaza, and was an important centre of communication between Egypt and Syria on the coastal road of Philistia. It was a Philistine city since the 12th cent. BC, tributary and rebelling under the Assyrians. Nabuchadnezzar conquered it in 604 BC. The historian Xanthus of Sardis thought it had been founded by the Lydians: *FGrHist* 765 F 5; cf. Nicolaus of Damascus, ibid. 90 F 18. See M. Avi-Yonah, *EAA* 1958, s.v. 'Ascalon', with bibl.; L. E. Stager, in Stern (ed.), op. cit. I, pp. 103–12.   τῆς οὐρανίης Ἀφροδίτης: cf. 131,3. A Greek interpretation of the local form or variant of the 'dea Syria': Atargatis or Aštart; see Strabo XVI 4,27, possibly following Posidonius, *FGrHist* 87 F 105b; cf. Philo of Byblos, ibid. 790 F 2; Herodian V 6,4; Derketo is another Greek form: see Ctesias, *FGrHist* 688 F 1d; Diod. II 4,2–3. For Derketo the mother

of Semiramis see Lucian, *De Dea Syria* 14. At Ascalon the goddess was Aštart, in the shape of a fish with the head of a woman; fish and doves were sacred to her. The Eastern epithet *malkat-hašamaljm* ('queen of heaven') may perhaps explain the Greek identification with Urania; cf. Paus. I 14,7. See B. M. Felletti Maj, *EAA* 1960, s.v. 'Dea Syria'; G. Garbini, *EAA*. 1961, s.v. 'Ishtar'; and M. Delcar, 'Astarte', *LIMC* III 1 1986, pp. 1077–85.

3. τὸ ἐν Κύπρῳ ἱρὸν: cf. Hesiod, *Theog.* 192 f. and West's note; Paus. I 14,7, and Diod. V 77,5. The temple and cult of Aphrodite Paphia (at Palaipaphos, near the modern village of Kouklia) were famous in antiquity; see Homer, *Od.* VIII 363 ff. and *Hymn. Hom. Aphr.* 58 ff. See Müller II, pp. 993–1000. On Cyprus in the Persian empire see III 91,1 and note; for sacred prostitution in Cyprus see I 199,5. On the temple at Cythera see Paus. III 23,1; it has been located tentatively to the west of Palaiokastro (the ancient acropolis of the city of Cythera); H. Waterhouse and R. H. Simpson, *ABSA* LVI (1967), 148–58; on Cythera see J. N. Coldstream and G. L. Huxley, *Cythera: Excavations and Studies*, London 1972; Müller I, pp. 790–4; on the Phoenicians at Cythera see J. Yakar, *Anatolica*, IV (1971–2), 133–7; and Cartledge, pp. 122 f.   ὡς αὐτοὶ Κύπριοι λέγουσι: on Herodotus' epichoric sources see note on 1,1.

4. θήλεαν νοῦσον: for the 'androgynous Enarees', a caste of Scythian seers devoted to Aphrodite, cf. IV 67,2; Hartog, pp. 125–6, 132. According to the Hippocratic Περὶ ἀέρων, the illness is a form of impotence, caused by excessive riding, a practice of noble and rich Scythians (ch. 22). See A. Ballabriga, *Mètis*, I (1986), 121–38. Cf. also Arist. *Eth. Nic.* 1150b15. 'Transexual shamans': D. Margreth, *Skythische Schamanen? Die Nachrichten über Enarees-Anarieis bei Herodot und Hippokrates*, Schaffhausen 1993. The modern hypothesis that Herodotus is alluding to pederasty makes no sense. For other theories see G. Dumézil, *Latomus*, V (1946), 249–55.

106,1. ὕβριος: on the concept and function of ὕβρις in Herodotus see Introduction, p. 38. For ὀλιγωρίη and ὀλίγωρος, both apparently unattested in sources earlier than Herodotus, cf. III 89,3 and VI 137,3.   φόρον ἔπρησσον: see 6,2 and note.

2. ξεινίσαντες: Herodotus divided a popular tale into two (see 73,3–6). The structure of his two stories is identical; the differences of detail are not an obstacle to reconstructing the original.   τὴν τε Νίνον εἷλον: the conquest of Niniveh by the Medes and Babylonians is one of the most decisive events in the history of the ancient Orient; Herodotus intended to treat it in his 'Assyrian *logoi*' (see 184,2 and the note ad loc.). It took place in 612 BC; it should be stressed, however, that apparently Herodotus dated it a couple of decades later; since his Scythian twenty-eight-year interregnum is included in the forty-year reign of Cyaxares (625–585 BC), his date of the fall of Niniveh, which followed the end of the interregnum, must be around 590 BC; cf. the anecdote at 73,3–74,1, which actually relates events datable around 590. Herodotus' Scythian interregnum would therefore extend approximately from 618 to 590 BC. See notes on 95–106 and 103,3–106,2. On Niniveh after 612 BC see S. Dalley, *AOF* XX (1993), 143–7.

Our main oriental source for the event is the Gadd Chronicle, ed. C. J. Gadd, *The Fall of Niniveh*, London 1923; cf. A. K. Grayson, *Assyrian and Babylonian Chronicles*, New York 1975, no. 3. According to this chronicle, Nabopolassar, together with the Umman-manda (possibly the Medes: see the collection of texts and the discussion by G. Komoróczy, *AAntHung* XXV (1977), 43–67) and U-ma-kiš-tar (= Cyaxares), attacked the city and plundered it; afterwards the two kings with their armies returned to their respective countries. In Greek sources the fall of Niniveh is almost a legendary event. Xenophon passed the ruins of the city in 401 without knowing it, confusing the Medes, Assyrians, and Persians in his pseudo-history of the conquest (*Anab.* III 4,7–12). The prophet Nahum expresses the widespread jubilation at the downfall of the corrupt and hated city, and delights in vague descriptions of the city flooded, plundered, and left in total desolation. In the destruction of 612 everything was obliterated: the famous temple of Ištar, the palace of Sennacherib, the library of Assurbanipal, the parks; the entire Assyrian civilization was erased. See H. W. F. Saggs, *The Might that Was Assyria*, London 1984. This great catastrophe, followed within the course of two generations by the fall of Ecbatana (550 BC) and Babylon (539), deeply shook the age-long sense of continuity of Middle Eastern civilizations, and according to some scholars originated the ancient theory of the 'Succession of Empires'. For bibl. see note on chs. 95–106.

107–30. The story of Astyages and Cyrus seems to provide a link between the *Mêdikos logos* and the rise of Cyrus to power, although the two sections are interrupted by ten chapters on Persian ethnography (131–40). The story is divided into two parts: the birth and youth of Cyrus (107–22); and the revolt against Astyages (123–30). The story presents a number of elements characteristic of popular saga and storytelling, but is organized biographically from the birth of Cyrus to his rise to power. It continues in chs. 75–81 and 84–90 (the conquest of Lydia); 188–91 (the conquest of Babylon) and 204–14 (the campaign against the Massagetae up to Cyrus' death). Some biographical elements of Greek and oriental heroes are prominent: dreams of kings wrongly interpreted, exposed baby princes, constant changes of scene between village and palace, court intrigues, recognition scenes, etc. A series of dialogues constitutes the essence of the story and contributes to its dramatic effect. See Long, pp. 126–75; P. Payen, *Les Îles nomades*, Paris 1997, pp. 49–62; on Greek idealization of Cyrus see the bibl. in note on 86–7.

107,1. Ἀστυάγης: *Arštiwaiga* in Old Persian, *Ištumegu* 'šar Umman-manda' in Babylonian sources. See O. K. Armayor, *AncW* I (1978), 151. Astyages is unknown to Greek sources earlier than Herodotus. According to Aeschylus (*Pers.* 765 ff.), Cyrus' grandfather is called Medos, a fictitious eponym of the Medes. Ctesias' last Median king is named Aspandas, 'whom the Greeks call Astyages' (*FGrHist* 688 F 5 (34,6)). In Herodotus' *logos* Astyages is depicted as a beaten and wounded tyrant who is ultimately the victim of the Magi's evil influence. He should be compared to the impotent tyrant in Nicolaus of Damascus, *FGrHist* 90 F 66, probably based on Ctesias; and to the Median king in Xenophon's *Cyropaedia*, presented as the paradigmatic opposite of Cyrus. On Astyages in cuneiform sources see D. O. Edzard, *RLA* V (1980), col. 212.   Μανδάνην: cf. Charon of Lampsacus, *FGrHist* 687 b F 2, and Xen. *Cyr.* I 2,1. Mandane may be a speaking name (*manda* = 'the Median woman'?; O. K. Armayor, *AncW* I (1978), 152). The oracle about the 'mule' relates to Cyrus' mixed origin (55,2 and 91,5–6). In other versions Cyrus and Astyages are not related at all: see Ctesias, *FGrHist* 688 F 9; and Nicolaus of Damascus, ibid. 90 F 66, where Cyrus' mother is called Argoste and is a shepherdess of the Mardian tribe.   ἐν τῷ ὕπνῳ: Astyages' dreams and their false interpretations provoke a series of actions and reactions on which depend a chain of events; at the same time they predict the end of the Median dynasty. The two dreams (107,1 and 108,1) are similar and convey the same message; see Bischoff, pp. 40 ff.; Frisch, pp. 6–11; Fehling, p. 143; C. Pelling, *CQ* XLVI (1996), 68–77; cf. note on 34,1. For the first dream, cf. Nicolaus of Damascus, *FGrHist* 90 F 66 (9), where it is the mother who dreams and the interpreter of the dream is a Chaldaean who becomes her mentor. The second dream was known also to Charon of Lampsacus (see above). See also Justin I 4,2; cf. the dream of Clytaemnestra in Sophocles' *Electra*, 419–23. Urine symbolizes the birth of a child also in Assyrian sources (see A. L. Oppenheim, *The Interpretation of Dreams in the Ancient Near East*, Philadelphia 1956, p. 265; J. Bottéro, *Ktema*, VII (1982), 5–18, esp. 12). The vine symbolizes success, salvation, etc. also in the East (e.g. Gen. 40: 9–13. For the golden vine of the Achaemenids, see note on 51,3). Though this dream symbolism is universal, one cannot rule out the possibility that Herodotus used Eastern sources.   τῶν μάγων τοῖσι ὀνειροπόλοισι: cf. 108,2 and 128,2; apparently not all Magi were entitled to interpret dreams. On the Magi see 140,2 and note.

2. **Καμβύσης**: *Kabūjia* in Persian, *Kam-bu-zi-j*a in Accadian, *Kanbuzi* in Aramaic. The hypothesis that this anthroponym may derive from the adjectival ethnic of the Indo-Iranian tribe of the *Kanboja* is debatable; see J. Chargentrier, *ZII* II (1923), 140–52; W. Eilers, *BzN* XV (1964), 180–236, and *AI* III (1974), 3–9; J. Harmatta, *AAntHung* XIX (1971), 5–8; O. K. Armayor, *AncW* I (1978), 149. Four 'Great Kings', 'Kings of Anshan', are named in the Cylinder of Cyrus (see note on 188–91; cf. note on 209,2): Teispes, Cyrus I, Cambyses I, and Cyrus the Great. This is what Herodotus calls the 'paternal genealogy' of Cyrus (III 75,1). Darius, in the Bisitun inscription, counted eight Achaemenid kings before himself, but named only his five direct predecessors: Achaemenes, Teispes, Ariaramnes, Arsames, and his father Hystaspes (who was not king) (see *DB* I § 2 (below, pp. 529 ff.)). The missing names are those of Cyrus' branch, two of which (Cyrus II and Cambyses II) are mentioned in the following historical section (ibid., § 10–11). See Balcer, *Prosopographical Study*, pp. 344–5. Herodotus tried to combine the two branches in a continuous Achaemenid line (VII 11,2), but the result is both confused and incomplete: Cyrus I and Cambyses I, both well known to him (111,5; III 66,2), are missing. The commonly accepted reconstruction of the genealogy is as shown in Fig. 4.

The historical plausibility of this reconstruction has been challenged, on the ground that Darius' attempt to relate the two branches (*DB* I § 4: *duvitāparanam*: 'in two lines'?) to each other as 'Achaemenids' is a piece of legitimist propaganda; see P. Miroschedji, *ZA* LXXV (1985), 280–3., and *IA*,

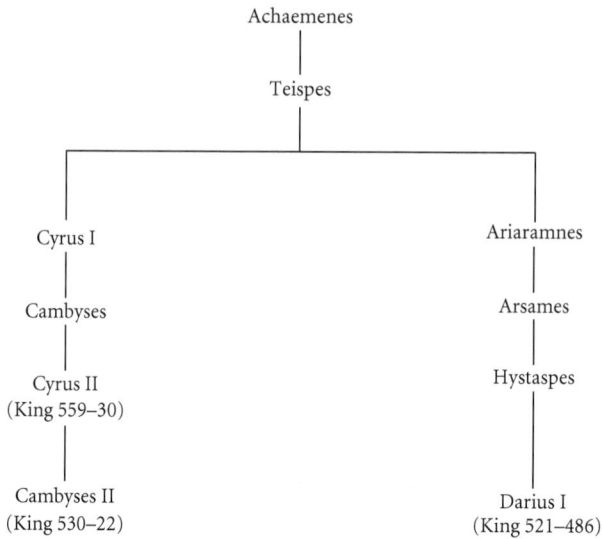

Fɪɢ. 4. Achaemenid genealogy

XXV (1990), 47–95; M. Brosius, *Women in Ancient Persia 559–331 B.C.* Oxford 1996, pp. 58–62; J. Wiesehöfer, *Encyclopedia Iranica*, IX (1999), 334. See also note to III 88,1. Aeschylus' genealogy at *Persae* 765 ff. has no historical value. The first Achaemenids clearly were vassal-kings, first of the Assyrian kings, and later of the Median kings. The theory that the two Achaemenid branches reigned contemporaneously, one at Anšan, and the other in Parsumaš, seems to have no basis, if it is true that the two place-names refer to the same region, Fars; (the city of Anšan has been located at Tall-i-Malyan, about 70 km. west of Persepolis: see J. Hanfman, *CHI*, pp. 25–35). Herodotus' Cyrus chronology is not very clear. When Cyrus reached 'manhood' (123,1 and note), i.e. between 16 and 17, he began his twenty-nine-year reign, which ended in 530 BC, a firm Herodotean dating confirmed by oriental sources (214,3 and note). He is therefore presumed to have been born in about (559 + 16–17) = 576/5 BC. We may be surprised to hear that, at the birth of his grandson, Astyages was already an 'old man' and unable to produce a male heir (109,3): a grandfather may well be in his forties and in his prime, especially one who about twenty years later was still able to lead an army to battle and to survive his own deposition (128,3; 130,3). However, in a folk-tale context the popular image of the grandfather as an old man prevailed over chronological considerations. A different tradition recorded that Cyrus lived to his seventieth year after a reign of thirty years (Dinon, *FGrHist* 690 F 10, etc.). Those who, following Ctesias (*FGrHist* 688 F 9(1)), deny the existence of kinship between Cyrus and Astyages, feel free to date his birth to 600 BC, as Dinon and others did, and to identify Cyrus I, his paternal grandfather, with Kuraš, king of Parsumaš, who in 646 BC was a subject of Assurbanipal; see E. F. Weidmer, *AO* VII (1931–2), 1–7; R. Campbell-Thompson and M. E. L. Mallowan, *LAA* XX (1933),

79–98; and W. Hinz *RLA* VI 1983, coll. 400–1. Yet Herodotus' lower dating may find support in the Sippar cylinder, where in reference to the revolt of 550 BC Cyrus is called 'the young vassal' (*arad-su ṣa-ah-ri*): see note on 130. In this case, however, it would be necessary to extend the genealogy of the first Achaemenids. It should be stressed that the contamination of the two versions is inadmissible. On the early Achaemenids see D. Heguy, *AAntHung* XXI (1973), 76–7; M. Dandamaev, *Persien unter den ersten Achämeniden*, Wiesbaden 1976 (trans. from the Russian); id., *AAntHung* XXV (1977), 39–42; id., *A Political History of the Achaemenid Empire* (Engl. tr. by W. J. Vogelsang), Leiden 1989, pp. 5–9; P. Briant, *IA* XIX (1984), 71–118; Frye, pp. 87–137; J. M. Cook, *CHI*, pp. 200–91, with an exhaustive bibl.; R. Schmitt, 'Achaemenid Dynasty', *Encycl. Iranica* I (1985), pp. 414 ff. See Balcer, pp. 35–42. P. Briant, *Histoire* I pp. 21–38; II, pp. 905–9 = ET, pp. 13–28, 877–80. On Herodotus' Ἀχαιμενίδαι see I 125,3 and note.

108,3. Ἄρπαγον: *Arbaka in Median, *Arppakuh* in Lycian; see O. K. Armayor, *AncW* I (1978), 151. The Greek form is associated with the verb ἁρπάζω and the word ἅρπαγος, 'hook'. Harpagus is a key character in the *logos* of Cyrus. Later he became a general and an adviser to Cyrus, satrap, and the conqueror of western Asia Minor. On the Lycian and Iranian offspring of Harpagus see note on 176,1.   5. παρεῖδες ... ἄχαρι: cf. 38,1.

109,3. πολλῶν δὲ εἴνεκα...: an idiomatic opening; cf. 138,1; 204,2, etc. See R. Renehan, *HSCPh* LXXX (1985), 29–35.   γέρων: see note on 107, 2.

110,1. Μιτραδάτης: one of the numerous Mithras-compound anthroponyms (see 131 and note); the original Old Persian form might be *Mithradate*; see O. K. Armayor, *AncW* I (1978), 152. It has been suggested that this Mithradates symbolizes Mithras' protection of Cyrus. Mithridates is the well-known dynastic name of the Hellenistic kings of Pontus; it was also the name of an Athenian archon of the 1st cent. AD (see *LGPN* II, s.v.). Another anthroponym of the same type is Mitrobates (III 120,1, etc.).   Σπακώ: the Iranian form of the word is unknown; see O. K. Armayor, loc. cit. The dog is a sacred animal for the Persians, especially in the cult of Mithras: see 140,3. On the original form of the legend see 122,3.
2. πρὸς βορέω...: the region described here could be Mannaea and northern Parsha. On the Saspeires see 104,1.

111,1. κως κατὰ δαίμονα: '... par l'effet d'une influence surnaturelle': G. François, *Le Polythéisme et l'emploi au singulier des mots θεός, δαίμων, dans la littérature grecque d' Homère à Platon*, Paris 1957, p. 208: supernatural elements are not totally absent from this story (cf. 118,2; 119,1; 121; 124,1; 126,6; 127,2, and note on 113,2). The popular belief in the 'tutelary genius' of an individual is common to all civilizations, Greek and Roman included. For the Avestan equivalent **huarnah-* or *hvarenah* see J. Duchesne-Guillemin, in G. Gnoli, *Iranica*, Naples 1979, pp. 375–86; *Altorientalische Forschungen* XXIII (1996), 171–80. See also the bibl. in the Introduction to Book III, App. I.
2. ὦ γύναι: 'Wife!' Cf. II 181,3; III 134,4 and 6; 'Woman!': III 119,3 and 5; V 72,3; IX 76,3. For this form of address see Dickey, pp. 84–9, 270–1.

5. *Καμβύσεω τοῦ Κύρου*: see note on 107,2.

112,1. *κατασκόπους*: see 100,2 and note.

3. *βασιληίης ταφῆς*: cf. 113,3.

113,1. *τὸν μὲν ἔφερε...*: for a different version see Isocrates V 66 and 132. The motif of an exposed child who miraculously survives (nursed by an animal or brought up among poor people or, on the contrary, kept in the palace of a king), and after many vicissitudes is finally recognized as the heir of a kingdom or of a fabulous fortune, or either becomes king himself or marries the daughter or the widow of his predecessor, etc., is a favourite theme of popular sagas and romances of all peoples, with endless variations. This type of story has its roots in the social and economic practice of infanticide (for the problem in ancient Greece see C. Patterson, *TAPhA* CXV (1985), 103–23). It is sometimes used to provide a pseudo-historical legitimation for controversial usurpation, change of dynasty, foundation of a kingdom, a cult, etc. Darius, a self-legitimized usurper, was also said to have been exposed by his mother and nursed by a mare (see Ptolemy Hephaistion, quoted by Photius, *Bibliotheca* 190, p. 148b Henry). In Eastern mythologies the best-known exposed children are Semiramis, Sargon, and Moses; in Greek and Roman mythology, Oedipus, Perseus, Paris, Neleus and Pelias, Romulus and Remus; see also the plots and scenes of recognition in comedies and novels of Hellenistic and Roman times. In medieval Persian literature there are some famous legends in the *Book of Kings* by Firdusi (*c.* AD 1000), such as Fredun, Zal, Khosrav (Cosrhoes), Darab, and Shapur. See G. Widengren, *AI* I 1 (1974), 88–9. The legend of Cyrus may be a mixture of oriental and Greek sagas. See L. Gierth, *Griechische Gründungsgeschichten*, Clausthal–Zellerfeld 1971, pp. 12 ff.; G. Binder, *Die Aussetzung des Königskindes, Kyros und Romulus*, Meisenheim am Glan 1964; R. Drews, *JNES* XXXIII (1974), 387–93; B. Lewis, *The Sargon Legend*, Cambridge, Mass. 1980; Delcourt, *passim*. Cf. the story of Cypselus, V 92, *β–ε*.

3. *οὔνομα ἄλλο*: Agradates, according to Strabo XV 3,6.

114,2. *διέταξε...*: cf. 120,2. Herodotus has succeeded in staging the 'game of being king' using as a model elements of the Medo-Persian court. The king nominates his ministers, who are thought of as 'servants' (cf. 120,2). The Persian title of the minister in charge of public buildings is unknown; in the Achaemenid inscriptions it is always the king himself who builds palaces or other buildings, with the favour of Ahura Mazda. According to a 4th-cent. version (Dinon, *FGrHist* 690 F 9; cf. Arist. *Pol.* 1312a) Cyrus himself was the commander of the guards in Astyages' court. The famous 'King's Eye', well known to the Greeks already since Aeschylus, is the chief inspector or spy; other 'eyes' and 'ears' are his subordinates and inspect individual provinces: cf. 100,2; 112,1; Xen. *Cyr.* VIII 2, 10–12. For modern conjectures on the original term (*gaušaka?*) see H. Lommel, *AI* II (1974), 91–100; and O. Bucci, *RIDA* XXV (1978), 33; for Greek sources see C. Autran, *Humanitas*, III (1950–1), 287–91; J. M. Balcer, *AJPh* XCVIII (1977), 252–63, and the collection by S. W. Hirsch, *The Friendship of the Barbarians: Xenophon and the Persian Empire*, Hanover–London 1985, pp. 131–9. The usher (probably called *hazarapatis* = chiliarch; cf. the ἀζαβαρίτης in Ctesias, *FGrHist* 688 F 15 (46)) announces and introduces embassies; see note on III 34,1; these ushers, who should not be confused with ordinary porters (θυρωροί or πυλουροί in Herodotus), were eunuchs: see III 77,2 and note. Herodotus might have also mentioned the chief cupbearer (III 34,1 and note) and the house-steward (III 61,1 and note). For modern reconstructions of Persian bureaucracy based on the Persepolis tablets see R. T. Hallock, *CHI*, pp. 588–609, with bibl.

3. Ἀρτεμβάρεος: a common Iranian name, possibly Arta-bara in Old Persian; see O. K. Armayor, *AncW* I (1978), 151. In the version of Nicolaus of Damascus, *FGrHist* 90 F 66 (5–7), Artembares is Astyages' chief cupbearer. For another Artembares, counsellor of Cyrus, see IX 122,1–2 (probably a different person); but see Macan's note *ad* IX 122, and Demand, p. 184, n. 11. Aeschylus' Artembares in *Pers.* 29 may be a fictitious character.

4. ἐς πόλιν: presumably Ecbatana. A noble family is supposed to live in the city, not in a poor village with cowsheds (114,1).

115,2. σὺ δὴ ἐών...: on the problem whether σύ is here syntactically a 'free' or 'bound' form, see Dickey, p. 24.   πρώτου παρ' ἐμοί: for the 'first Medes' at Astyages' court see 123,2; at the Persian court, see III 84,2 and note. ὦ δέσποτα: see note on 8,3.

116,1. ὑπόκρισις ἐλευθεριωτέρη: Cyrus' answer shows freedom of speech and is therefore worthy of a free man; cf. the usage of ἐλευθέρως, -ίως in V 93,2; VII 46,1; and VIII 73,3. A conventional assumptions of recognition scenes in Greek drama is that nobility of birth is preserved even after years of living among common and uneducated people. Cf. the didactic dialogues between Cyrus and Astyages in Xen. *Cyr.* I 3–4.

4. ἐς ἀνάγκας: a euphemism for 'torture'; cf. Antiphon VI 25, etc. At Athens torture was the usual procedure for eliciting testimony from slaves.

117,2. μόρῳ: always refers in Herodotus to violent death; see Lachenaud, pp. 91 f.

5. εὐνούχων: commonly explained from εὐνή and ἔχω, 'bedchamber attendant', a position held by castrated men in oriental courts. In Herodotus eunuchs are employed as porters, guards, or guardians of the harem at the palace of Susa (III 77,2, etc.; cf. Esther 1: 10, etc.), in Egypt (III 4,2) and, according to our passage, at Ecbatana. Many eunuchs followed Xerxes to Greece in 480 BC (VII 187,1–2); see the gruesome story of Hermotimus at VIII 105. The influence of eunuchs at court became a much-exploited motif in Graeco-Roman didactic rhetoric. See A. Hug, 'Eunuchen', *RE* Suppl. III 1918, pp. 449–55; G. Meyer, *RLA* II 1938, pp. 485–6; M. San Nicoló, ibid., pp. 402–3; P. Guyot, *Eunuchen als Sklaven und Freigelassenen in der griechisch-römischen Antike*, Klett–Cotta 1980; L. Stork, *LdÄ* III (1980), 354–5; Briant, *Histoire*, pp. 279–88, 944–5 (bibl.) = ET pp. 269–77, 919–20.

118,2. τῆς τύχης: see 111,1 and note.

119,1. προσκυνήσας: see note on 134,1.   ἐπὶ δεῖπνον: another blood-stained banquet; cf. I 73,5–6; and 106,2. The mythological model is the banquet of Atreus and Thyestes; see Burkert, *Homo Necans*, pp. 103–9.   ἐπὶ τύχῃσι χρηστῇσι: see note on 111,1.

2. περιχαρὴς: see 31,4 and note.

3. σφάξας: cf. 73, 5.   τῆς ὥρης γενομένης: see notes on 10,1 and 31,2.

4. ἐπὶ κανέῳ: a basket of reed or cane (LSJ), a semitic loan-word (*qn* Ugaritic, *qn'* Aramaic, *qnh* Hebrew); a *hapax* in Herodotus; cf. Hom. *Il.* IX 217; *Od.* XVII 343.

5. εἰ ἡσθείη … κάρτα ἡσθῆναι: see 27,5 and note.

7. ἀρεστὸν εἶναι: cf. Presaxpes' words at III 35,4.

120,2. καὶ γὰρ δορυφόρους …: see 114,2 and note.

4. οἴκῳ τε τῷ ἐμῷ: for οἶκος in the sense of the king's 'house', 'family', or 'dynasty', cf. I 207,1; V 31,4; VI 9,3; VII 52,2; 194,2; VIII 102,2; IX 107,1.

ἐόντα Πέρσην: Cyrus is Persian because he is the son of a Persian father. This is at variance with the rule prevalent in antiquity, according to which one's membership in an *ethnos* was inherited from the mother (see note on 173,5).

ἐόντες Μῆδοι: on the Magi as a Median γένος see 101; on the Magi see note on 140,2.

121. ἐχάρη: see 27,5 and 31,4 and notes.   τῇ σεωυτοῦ δὲ μοίρῃ: see note on 111,1.

122,1. ἀποπέμπει …: cf. the farewell to Cyrus in Nicolaus of Damascus, *FGrHist* 90 F 66 (21–3).

3. τραφῆναι …: cf. 110,1. The original myth recurs in the versions that 'exalted' Cyrus (95,1). Trogus preserved it: Cyrus is fed by a bitch and the foster-mother is afterwards given the name Spargos (Justin I 4,10–14). The rationalizing version may have existed before Herodotus. See Fehling, pp. 110 ff.

123,1. ἀνδρευμένῳ: at the age of 16 or 17: see Xen. *Cyr.* I 14,16 and 5,41; cf. note on 107,2. Cyrus succeeded his father Cambyses as 'Great King' and 'king of Anšan' in 559/8: see note on 130. Herodotus knows that Cyrus' reign lasted twenty-nine years, from 559 to 530 BC (217,3), but he does not distinguish between his accession as vassal-king of Anšan and his seizure of power in Ecbatana.

3. ὁδῶν φυλασσομένων: cf. Justin I 5,10 and Polyaenus VII 7. The 'Royal Road' was under surveillance in Achaemenid times (V 35,3 and VII 239,3 with similar episodes). For the sending of secret letters cf. Aeneas Tacticus XXXI. Secret messages in Herodotus are always written in a readable language: they are not cryptograms (on ancient cryptography see E. C. Reinke, *CJ* LVIII (1962–3), 113–21). For letters in Herodotus and the Greek formulae they feature, such as here, 'O son of Cambyses', see M. Van den Hout, *Mnemosyne*, II (1949), 25–33; for Persian letters in Greek sources, see ibid. 141–52; for the theory that letters were first invented by Queen Atossa see Hellanicus, *FGrHist* 4 F 178b.

124,1. τὰ δὲ γράμματα ἔλεγε: written texts sometimes, as it were, 'speak' (cf. IV 13,1; IV 91; VI 137,1); see C. W. Hendrick, Jr., in *Nomodeiktes*, p. 22; a common manner of expression in all languages even today.   ὦ παῖ Καμβύσεω: for this form of address cf. III 14,10 (ὦ παῖ Κύρου); 71,3 (ὦ παῖ Ὑστάσπεως), etc.; see

Dickey, pp. 52–6, 264. For Cambyses I see note on 107,2.　σὲ γὰρ θεοὶ ἐπορῶσι: see note on 111,1.

125,2. ἀλίην: ἀλία and ἀλίαια are archaic names for the assembly in various Dorian cities, in mother country and in the colonies. When he became the vassal-king of Anšan Cyrus may have led a parade of the Persian contingent of the multinational Median army. On this anecdote, cf. Justin I 6,4–6 and Polyaenus VII 6,7.　**δρέπανον:** elsewhere in Herodotus the sickle or scythe is a weapon, used by Carians and Lycians (V 112,2; VII 92–3). For chariots carrying scythes on their axles (ἄρματα δρεπανηφόρα) in Medo-Persian armies, see Nic. Dam. *FGrHist* 90 F 66 (31) (in Cyrus' army); Xen. *Anab.* I 7,10; Polyb. V 53,10; Diod. XVII 53,1. A combination of spear and scythe was the δορυδρέπανον used in sieges and sea-fights (Plato, *Laches* 183c–184a; Strabo IV 4,1; Polyb. XXI 27,4). It may have been a sacred object in the Persian rites of initiation, as it certainly was in late Mithraism; see R. Merkelbach, *Numen*, VI (1959), 154–6.

3. ἔστι δὲ...: a connective sentence attempts to ease the reader into this short digression on Persian clans, which interrupts the narrative abruptly and would more naturally belong in chs. 131–40 on Persian ethnography. See G. Klamp, *PhW* XLIX (1929), coll. 1597–9. Herodotus lists ten clans, Xenophon speaks of twelve φυλαί (*Cyr.* I 2,5). Strabo's list of φῦλα at XV 3,1 is altogether different. For the supposed Old Persian, Elamite, and Hittite forms of these names see O. K. Armayor, *AncW* I (1978), 151. On the Persian clans see A. Christensen, *Kulturgeschichte der alten Orient*, Munich 1933, pp. 236–9; H. von Gall, *AMI* V (1972), 261–83; R. Ghirshmann, *CRAI* (1973), 210–21.　**ἀρτέαται:** Stephanus of Byzantium understood the verb as the name of a clan, see s.v. **Πασαργάδαι:** *Parsa-gada* supposedly means 'Persian camp' (Anaximenes of Lampsacus, *FGrHist* 72 F 19). For a nobleman belonging to this clan see IV 167,1. The homonymous city αἱ Πασαργάδαι (never mentioned by Herodotus), traditionally founded by Cyrus on the site of his victory over Astyages, lies to the north-east of Persepolis; it remained the holy centre of the Achaemenids. See D. Stronach, *Pasargadai*, Oxford 1978, and *CHI* II 838–55 (with bibl. at p. 926). For Cyrus' tomb at Pasargadae see note on 214,5.　**Μαράφιοι, Μάσπιοι:** the Maraphii have not been located (cf. Μάραφις in Aesch. *Persae*, post v. 777, in the apparatus of Page, Oxford 1972; for Amasis the Maraphian see IV 167,1). The Maspii are unknown, see the strange gloss of Stephanus of Byzantium, s.v. **Ἀχαιμενίδαι:** *Haxāmanišiyā* in Old Persian (see *DB* I § 3). They are seen by Herodotus as a φρήτρη within the γένος of the Pasargadai (in Greek common use the γένος is a subdivision of the φρατρία, and not the other way round). Cf. the district Ἀχαιμενία (Stephanus of Byzantium, s.v.). Herodotus here alludes to the mythical offspring of Perses, son of Perseus (a hellenized Assyrian, see VI 54), which is pure Greek invention; cf. VII 61,3; 150,2; 220,4. It is impossible to guess how Herodotus connected the forefather Achaemenes (III 75,1; VII 11,2) with the Perseidae. Besides the members of the royal family (III 65,6), there were also various members of the 'phratry' of the 'Achaemenidae' who never became kings (e.g. Darius' father Hystaspes, see I 209,2 and note).

4. Πανθιαλαῖοι...: also the Panthialii and the Derusii are unknown. The Germanii are the inhabitants of Carmania (Kirman), along the Hormuz straits. Δάοι...: the Daoi (Daai or Dasai) are supposed to be a Scythian nomad tribe living in the eastern Caspian area. From the Aparni, a sub-group of this clan, originated the Parthian dynasty of the Arsacids. Daos (Lat. Davus) is a common name of slaves in Attica. The Mardi (cf. 84,2), or Amardi, remained famous as a nomad tribe of bandits (in Persia and in the Caspian area). The Dropici are perhaps identical with the Caspian Derbici (?). The Sagartii (*Asagarta* in Old Persian) were a Persian-speaking nomadic tribe (Kuhistan and Yazd); cf. III 93,2 and note and VII 85.

126,1. προεῖπε ἐξημερῶσαι ἐν ἡμέρῃ: Cyrus' orders to the army are meant to puzzle the reader, and the whole scene (called λόγος by Herodotus: para. 4) looks like an enigmatic fable; see R. Merkelbach, in *Hestia und Erigone. Vorträge und Aufsätze*, Stuttgart–Leipzig 1996, pp. 460–1.

3. ἐς λειμῶνα: cf. Herodotus' description of the 'Table of the Sun' at III 18.

5. ἄνδρες Πέρσαι: cf. VII 8a, 1; VIII 118,3; see Dickey, pp. 177–84, 293–5. βουλομένοισι...: for a biblical choice between well-being and misfortune offered by a leader to his people see Deut. 28.

6. θείη τύχη γεγονὼς: see note on 111,1.

127,2. ὥστε θεοβλαβὴς ἐὼν: cf. VIII 137,4, and see note on 111,1.

3. στρατευσάμενοι: the Chronicle of Nabonidus mentions the desertion in relation to the only (and decisive) battle (see note on 128,3). See the version of Nicolaus of Damascus, *FGrHist* 90 F 66 (29).

128,1. ἀλλ' οὐδ' ὡς Κῦρός γε χαιρήσει: possibly a memorable, or, proverbial, saying.

2. ἀνεσκολόπισε: 'impaled' (cf. III 132,2), synonymous with ἀνεσταύρωσε, 'crucified' (see III 125,3 and note). These Magi die as martyrs for Cyrus' cause.

3. ἐσσώθη...: cf. the Chronicle of Nabonidus, II 1–4 *BHT* and the Sippar cylinder, 28–33 *ANET*. According to Nicolaus of Damascus, the battle took place near Pasargadae; see *FGrHist* 90 F 66. For Cyrus and Astyages at Ecbatana and the removal of the treasure to Pasargadae, see ibid. 90 F 66 (45).

130. This chapter is an important historical summary. From the preceding chapters we gather that Cyrus' revolt was based on the cooperation between a faction of the Median nobility at the court of the king and the Persian contingent led by the 'king of Anšan', eager to free himself from his tributary vassalage. The eastern sources do not contradict these basic data and add some more factual details, such as the liberation of Ḥarran and the sack of Ecbatana (they are, however, contradicted by the Greek versions deriving from Ctesias: see, above all, the romanticized story in Nicolaus of Damascus, *FGrHist* 90 F 66). It would be impossible to reconstruct a plausible history of the revolt solely on the basis of the oriental sources without a good dose of imagination (e.g. the alleged alliance between Cyrus and Nabonidus against Astyages is pure fantasy). Herodotus condenses in his *logos* events that took place over almost ten years. According

to him, Cyrus' reign lasted twenty-nine years; if the date of his death is certain (the summer of 530: I 214,3 and note), he became king of Anšan in 559. But it is almost certain that the Chronicle of Nabonidus dated Cyrus' revolt to the sixth year of Nabonidus' reign (= 550/49 BC; see *BHT*, pp. 100–1). Into the subsequent nine years have to be fitted the Persian military reorganization, Harpagus' conspiracy, the revolt itself, and the battles. This solution does not disturb Herodotus' chronological grid for the last two Median kings (Cyaxares, 625–585, and Astyages, 585–550: see note on 95–106). Some modern scholars, however, prefer a somewhat earlier date for the revolt: 553 BC, basing their calculations on two other cuneiform sources: the Sippar cylinder (= Nab. 1) and the inscription Nab. 8. The revolt, may of course have lasted for a few years. For a complete discussion see C. J. Gadd, *AS* VIII (1958), 35–92; E. Vogt, *Biblica*, XL (1959), 88–102; P. Garelli, 'Nabunaid', in *Dictionnaire de la Bible*, Suppl. VI 1960, coll. 269 ff.; P. Sacchi, *PP* XX (1965), 223–33; H. Tadmor, in *Studies in Honour of B. Landsberger*, Chicago 1965, pp. 351–64; and R. Drews, *Historia*, XVIII (1969), 1–11. For bibl. on Cyrus the Great see G. Gnoli, 'Ciro il Grande', in *I protagonisti della storia universale* II, Milan 1968, pp. 1–28; see also the first three volumes of *AI* (1974), with the proceedings of the 1971 conference at Shiraz and other studies; W. Hinz, *RLA* VI 1983, coll. 401–3; M. Mallowan, *CHI*, pp. 392–419; Beaulieu, pp 104–15; Briant, *Histoire*, pp. 41–61, 909–914 (with bibl.) = ET, pp. 31–50, 881–6. On Greek idealization of Cyrus see note on 86–7.

130,1. πάρεξ ἤ . . . : see note on 95–106.

2. ἀπέστησαν ἀπὸ Δαρείου: this is the only reference in Greek sources to a Median revolt against Darius. In the Bisitun inscription Darius relates in detail the story of the Median usurper Fravartiš, defeated in two battles and finally impaled at Ecbatana (*DB* II §§ 24–5 and 31–5). Trogus mentions a series of wars against the Medes during the reign of Cyrus (cf. Justin I 7,2–3). See also note on III 127,1.

3. εἶχε παρ' ἑωυτῷ: in other words, Astyages lived at the court of his grandson, in accordance with the traditional treatment of royal prisoners in the Eastern kingdoms; cf. the controversial case of Croesus (note on 86–7) and that of Nabonidus (note on 191,7); cf. also Ctesias (*FGrHist* 688 F 13 (10)), on the last Egyptian king (the Herodotean Psammenitus), deported to Susa; see also III 15,2–3 with 5th-cent. examples. For biblical parallels see e.g. 2 Kings 25: 27–30. On the fate of Astyages cf. the vague report in Ctesias, *FGrHist* 688 F 9. According to Xenophon Cyrus kept 'Cyaxares' in Babylon (*Cyr.* VIII 5,17); according to Trogus he became the governor of Hyrcania (cf. Justin I 6,16).   ὡς εἴρηταί μοι πρότερον: in 76 ff.   πάσης τῆς Ἀσίης ἦρξε: this must mean that, by conquering Lydia, Cyrus united under the same empire the two main regions of northern Asia—Asia Minor and Media (cf. 72,3 and 103,3).

131–40. This very interesting digression on Persian ethnography is a mixture of objective data, curiosities, and idealized information, which Herodotus sometimes personally approves. The only connection with the main narrative is the treatment of subjects conventionally found in *Persika* (see for a different view Cobet, pp. 117 ff.). Herodotus honestly distinguishes between facts that he knows for certain and others which are spoken of in secret (140,1); but our usual doubts about his receptive ability with respect to foreign cultures (see Introduction, pp. 17 ff.) certainly apply to this section. It has been argued, for example, that Herodotus could not have been admitted to the sacrifices and esoteric rites of the Magi; however, artistic representations of Persian sacrifices, such as the famous bas-relief at Dascylium, were available, as well as the existing written accounts in Greek *Persika* or *Magika*. A great amount of information could have come from bilingual guides and Greek interpreters. See Immerwahr, pp. 185 ff.; and Drexler, pp. 171 ff.; cf. Strabo's Persian ethnography, XV 3,13–22, partially based on Herodotus. The passages devoted to religion (131–2; 140) are particularly interesting. Two main problems have been at the centre of modern criticism since the 19th cent.: whether the religion described by Herodotus is Zoroastrianism, and whether Zoroastrianism was the religion of the Achaemenids; see É. Benveniste, *The Persian Religion According to the Chief Greek Texts*, Paris 1929. Yet Herodotus' description is an amalgam of elements which can be attributed to earlier Iranian religion, of others which may be related to Mazdaic doctrines, and of foreign influences (see the distinction of Herodotus himself at 131,3). This mixture of elements should not surprise us: after all, Mazdaic predominance never became exclusive, not even among the Magi: it was rather the old paganism which absorbed Zoroastrianism. It remains, however, the fact that in a Greek treatment of Persian religion it seemed right to omit the name of Zoroaster (already known to Xanthus of Lydia). Bibl.: M. Boyce, *A History of Zoroastrianism* I–II, Leiden–Cologne 1975–92; *CHJ* I (1984), 279–307; G. Gnoli, *Zoroaster's Time and Homeland*, Naples 1980, with a vast bibl. Mora, pp. 27–40; A. De Jong, 'Traditions of the Magi: Zoroastrianism in Greek and Latin Literature', Diss. Utrecht 1996 (with a commentary on Herod. I 131–2: pp. 51–83). For Greek and Roman sources on Persian religion see C. Clemen, *Fontes Historiae Religionis Persicae*, Bonn 1920. For Greek views on the civilization and religion of the Persians, see A. Momigliano, *Alien Wisdom*, Cambridge 1975, ch. 6.

131,1. νόμοισι: ethnic 'customs'; cf. 35,1.   ἀγάλματα: cf. Dinon, *FGrHist* 690 F 28; Berossus, ibid. 680 F 11; Cicero, *Leg.* II 26; and Strabo XV 3,13. The Persians did not have temples with statues of the Greek type, but they did have sanctuaries (*brazmadana?*) of different types: square towers with a raised chamber where the sacred fire burned, and open-air altars (131,2). Perhaps there were no proper images of Persian deities in Herodotus' time; even if the bust emerging from the winged circle on the Bisitun rock and elsewhere represents Ahura Mazda (but see A. Shapur Shahbazi, *Gymnasium*, LXXXV (1978), 496 f.), it is still halfway between iconography and symbol. Perhaps in this passage a covert criticism of Greek anthropomorphism is present; but Herodotus is usually more interested in rites than in dogmas.

2. Διί...Δία: Herodotus surprisingly does not mention the Persian name of the supreme god, though he does mention that of the main goddess (para. 3). 'Zeus' equals 'Ahura Mazda', a 'great god, who created this earth, who created yonder sky, who created man, and who created happiness for man' (*DNa* 1 ff. Kent; cf.

DSs, etc.); he is the 'greatest god' (*DPd* 1–2 Kent), but not the only one, though he is the only god mentioned by name in Darius' inscriptions as the guardian god of the royal dynasty. To speak of 'Mazdaic monotheism' is therefore incorrect. There is no reference in Herodotus to Ahriman (Ἀρειμάνιος), the Principle of Evil; nor to the famous Mazdaic dualism (which perhaps was not yet sufficiently widespread in his time).   ἡλίῳ: cf. 138,1; VII 54,2–3. For sacrifices to the sun and the earth see Xen. *Cyr.* VIII 3,24; see B. Jacobs, in J. Kellens (ed.), *La Religion iranienne à l'époque achéménide, IA* Suppl., V, Gand 1991, pp. 49–80; for sacrifices to the winds see VII 191,2; for the cult of fire see III 16,3. For fire altars at Pasargadae and elsewhere see C. A. Pinelli, *EAA* 1963, s.v. 'Naqsh-i Rustam'; and R. Naumann, ibid. 1973 Supplement, s.v. 'Takht-i Suleiman', with bibl. In Mazdaic theology fire became also the symbol of the universal judgement. On the prohibition against contaminating the 'four elements', cf. 139–40.

3. τῇ Οὐρανίῃ...Μίτραν: for Urania, cf. 105,2–3; for Mylitta, cf. 199,3 (*Mullittu* or *Mu allidtu* may be an epithet of Ištar; alternatively, perhaps from Semitic *ba'alath* = 'lady'?). See G. Wilhelm, in T. Abusch *et al., Lingering Over Words: Studies in Ancient Near Eastern Literature in Honor of W. L. Moran*, Atlanta 1990, p. 505, n. 1. The correct Persian name for the goddess is held to be *Anah^ata* (Anahita, Ἀναΐτις), whose cult is supposed to have been introduced by Cyrus (for its introduction in Lydia see Tacitus, *Ann.* III 62), and to have spread throughout the empire under Artaxerxes II (405–359 BC). The Greeks, however, usually identified Anahita with Artemis (*Diana Persica*), not with Aphrodite. See T. Corsten, *IA* XXVI (1991), 163–80.   Ἀλιλάτ: probably corresponds to the Arabic *al-Alahat* (also *al-Ilahat*; Allat in the Koran) which means 'the goddess'; see note on III 8,3. Perhaps she was sometimes identified with Athena. On the Arabs (Ἀράβιοι in Herodotus, Ἄραβες in later sources) cf. 198 and esp. III 8,1–3; 107–13, and the notes. Μίτραν is an inexcusable error: either Herodotus confused Anahita with Mithras, or he or a copyist wrote Μίτραν instead of Μητέραν (= the Mother goddess): in any case, Mithras is a male deity; see the correction of Strabo XV 3,13. The attempts to rehabilitate Herodotus are not convincing; see M. Bussagli, *RHR* CXL (1951), 129–54; A. Tourraix, *DHA* II (1976), 380–1; M. J. Edwards, *AJPh* CXI (1990), 1–4. According to a widespread modern theory, Cyrus' favourite god was Mithras. The bibl. on the cult of Mithras is enormous (especially for the Roman imperial period); see the two volumes *Mithraic Studies* (ed. J. R. Hinnels), Manchester 1975; M. Boyce, *AI* IV (1975), 69–76; *Études mithriaques, AI* XVII (1978); R. Merkelbach, *Mithras*, Hain 1984; D. Ulanssey, *The Origins of the Mithraic Mysteries*, Oxford 1990; R. Vollkommer, 'Mithras', *LIMC* VI 1 1992, pp. 583–626 (with bibl.).

132,1. θυσίη: the ritual described here cannot be Mazdaic, if it is true that Mazdaism forbade slaughtering animals for sacrifice. The Magi themselves presided over the sacrifices. Herodotus compares them with Greek sacrifices: the sacred fire does not burn the meat, there are no libations of wine into the fire (though sometimes libations are made of pure water or of the inebriating liquor *haoma* (?): see e.g. VII 54,2; cf. I 202,2).   οὐλῇσι: cf. I 160,5. Grains of spelt

were sprinkled over the head of the victim during Greek sacrifices.   τὸν
τιάραν: cf. III 12,4; VII 61,1; VIII 120 (τιήρη); also in the feminine in later
sources. The tiara, already known to Aeschylus (*Pers.* 661: βασιλείου τιήρας; see
commentary of E. Hall ad loc.), is the typical Persian felt turban, conical in shape.
Only the Great King wore an 'upright' tiara (ὀρθός): other people, including
satraps and generals, wore it floppy (ἀπαγής: see VII 61,1); cf. Cleitarchus,
FGrHist 137 F 5. Iconographic representations of tiaras include Persian reliefs,
Greek vase-paintings and coins. See P. B. Sirch and W. Hinz, *RE* Suppl. Bd. XIV
1974, pp. 786–96; S. Bittner, *Tracht und Bewaffnung des Persischen Heeres zur Zeit
der Achaimeniden*[2], Munich 1987, pp. 193–9. The tiara decorated with myrtle
seemed to Herodotus entirely different from the Greek στέμμα worn by priests or
put on sacrificial victims (see VII 197,2).
2. τῷ θύοντι: should not be expunged (see J. E. Powell, *CQ* XXXII (1938), 211); it
is necessary for understanding what follows (καὶ αὐτὸς γίνεται is the person who
sacrifices, not the Persian king; for a different interpretation, see O. Bucci, *RIDA*
XXV (1978), 20).
3. θεογονίην: seems to be an ἐπαοιδή, or liturgical hymn (cf. ὑμνεῖν: Xen. *Cyr.* VIII
1,23), or *yašt*, of the type preserved in the Gathas, but Herodotus certainly
understood θεογονίη as an account of the 'origin of the gods' (cf. II 53,2 on the
'theogony' of Homer and Hesiod; see Hesiod, *Theogony*, ed. M. L. West, Oxford
1966, pp. 1–16). The concept of 'theogony' seems foreign to the type of Zoroastrianism that conceived of the divine as eternal, not foreign perhaps to the dualist
doctrine (known to 4th-cent. Greeks) of Good (Ormuzd) and Evil (Ahriman), as
the twin sons of Time or Destiny (Zuruan); see R. C. Zaehner, *Zuruan*, Oxford
1955. The hymn mentioned here may be a poetic evocation of this myth (perhaps
portrayed on a Luristan lamina; see B. Brentjes, *Wissensch. Zeitschrift d. M. Luther
Univ. Halle-Wittemberg, Gesell. u. Sprachwiss. Reihe*, XIV (1965), 513–14;
M. Papatheophanes, *IA* XXV (1985), 130–1, 136–42).

133,1. ἡμέρην... τῇ ἕκαστος ἐγένετο: see W. Schmidt, *Geburtstag im Altertum*,
Giessen 1908. This is the birthday banquet called τύκτα in Persian (perhaps
meaning 'perfect': IX 110,2): see Athenaeus IV 143 ff. θakata in Old Persian is
used for 'time passed' (see e.g. *DB* I, ll. 37–8 Kent), but in Greek τυκτός (from
τεύχω) means also 'completed' or 'perfect'. The hypothesis that this passage is
parodied by Aristophanes (*Ach.* 85 ff.) is worthless.   βοῦν καὶ ἵππον: on realities and Greek stereotypes of Persian food and dinners see H. Sancisi-Weerdenburg, in J. Wilkins *et al.* (eds.), *Food in Antiquity*, Exeter 1995, pp. 286–302 (with
bibl.); on the King's dinner see D. M. Lewis, *AH* II (1987), 1–6; eating and
drinking in Iranian art: A. Gunter, *Asian Art*, I (1988), 7–54.
2. ἐπιφορήμασι: various dishes served after dinner; see Athenaeus, XIV 640f ff.
3. οἴνῳ: when the Persians were still an unrefined people they drank water: 71,3.
The drunken Persian king is a stock character both in Herodotus and in the Book
of Esther. Cf. the law known to Duris of Samos, *FGrHist* 76 F 5. See P. Orsi,
Anc. Soc. XIX (1988), pp. 155–8.   μεθυσκόμενοι...: this famous custom is

presented with sympathy as an amusing curiosity; on the *Germani*, cf. Tacitus, *Germ.* 22,2–4.

134,1. προσπίπτων προσκυνέει: the προσκύνησις, a well-known act of supplication, hierarchical self-humiliation, and adoration towards the gods, kings, and one's own superiors, common throughout the East (for its Egyptian form, see II 80,2) became an essential element of court ceremonial. It consisted, literally, in blowing a kiss (προσ-κυνεῖν) with a small bow; sometimes, however, it was accompanied by genuflection and prostration on the ground. Both forms are attested in bas-reliefs, but the exact significance of the gestures is debated. Cf. I 119,1; III 86,2; VII 13,3; 136,1; VIII 118,4. In Homer and the tragedians supplication involves embracing the knees and kissing the hands of the person that is being entreated. The official Greek position in Achaemenid times was that προσκύνησις should be an act reserved for the gods; see the story of the Spartan ambassadors in VII 135–6 and Xen. *Anab.* I 6,10; III 2,13. Superficially interpreted as an act of veneration (but see G. Widergren, *The Sacral Kingship of Iran*, Leiden 1959), προσκύνησις became in the 4th cent. BC an ideological issue; in practice, however, ambassadors had to comply or devise stratagems. Alexander's attempt at introducing προσκύνησις at his court renewed the polemics and influenced later accounts of some episodes. Eventually it was accepted in various forms at the Roman and Byzantine courts, and became common in medieval and modern monarchies until the present. See J. Horst, *Proskynein*, Gütersloh 1932; F. Altheim, *Paideia*, V (1950), 307–9; E. J. Bickerman, *PP* XVIII (1963), 241–55; R. N. Frye, *IA* IX (1972), 102–7; E. Vissen, in *Festschrift z. 150 jährigen Bestehen des Berliner Ägyptischen Museums*, Berlin 1974, pp. 453–7; A. Sh. Shahbazi, *AI* XXV (1985), 503; A. B. Bosworth, *Alexander and the East*, Oxford 1996, pp. 109–14.

2. τιμῶσι...: it is evident that Herodotus is interested in notions of social class; cf. 91,6 and 107,2; see Drexler, pp. 51 ff. His speculation is based exclusively on the accepted fact of cultural affinity of Medes and Persians. The Ionians as well as the Indians must be included among the marginal peoples of the periphery (cf. III 38,3–4 and notes). In Achaemenid inscriptions the farthest countries are India and Sparda (= Sardis), the Scythians beyond Sogdiana and Ethiopia (see e.g. *DPh* l. 3 ff. Kent). In Herodotus' view all peoples think of themselves as better and superior to all others (see Introduction, p. 44).

3. Μήδων ἀρχόντων: the Median hierarchical system here described is imaginary. It may be based on the distinction between Median 'protectorates' with vassal-kings, and direct Persian rule through satraps. See Immerwahr, p. 185.
τὸ ἔθνος: 'every people', not just the Medes and the Persians. On Herodotus' use of this term see note on 6,1.

135. ἐσθῆτα: cf. VII 62,1; leather breeches, see I 71,2. The magnificence of Median clothing became proverbial in Greek sources and a symbol of luxury. According to Ctesias, *FGrHist* 688 F 1 (6,6), it was Assyrian in origin; cf. Justin I 2,3. The conventional distinction between Median and Persian clothes, on the bas-reliefs at Persepolis and elsewhere, is still discussed; see G. Thompson, *Iran,*

III (1965), 121–6; A. Sh. Shahbazi, *Gymnasium*, LXXXV (1978), 487–500; J. M. Cook, *CHI*, pp. 278 ff.; P. Calmeyer, *RLA* VII (1990), 615–17; B. Jacobs, *IA* XXIX (1994), 125–56. Fashions certainly changed over time, but Greek descriptions of oriental dress should be taken with caution. See e.g. A. Demandt, *IA* IX (1972), 94–101, and O. K. Armayor, *TAPhA* CVIII (1978), 1–9; Bittner, op. cit. ἀπ' Ἑλλήνων μαθόντες: cf. Athenaeus XIII 603a. This is an example of Herodotus' 'malice', contradicted according to Plutarch (*Mor.* 857b–c) by the fact that the Persians practised castration before they came into contact with the Greeks. In Herodotus the Persians are the opposite of the Egyptians and the Scythians (people hostile to foreign customs: II 91,1; IV 76,1).   κουριδίας γυναῖκας: lawful wives, as opposed to παλλακαί or concubines; cf. V 18,2. For marriage between kinsmen see III 31,1–6 and notes. On the harem of Persian kings see III 68–9; 88,2–3; among later sources see e.g. Heraclides of Cyme, *FGrHist* 689 F 1; and Esther 2:8–14. Polygamy and the harem were common institutions in the ancient Orient (also in Egypt, *pace* II 92,1), including Homeric society (*Il.* XXIV 496 ff.).

136,1. δῶρα: on gift-exchange in the Persian empire see H. Sancisi-Weerdenburg, *Historia*, XXXVII (1988), 372–4; id., in P. Briant-C. Herrenschmidt (eds.), *Le Tribut dans l'empire perse*, Paris–Louvain 1989, pp. 129–46; Briant, *Histoire*, pp. 314–55, 948–9 = ET pp. 302–43, 900–00.   τὸ πολλὸν: what counts in Persia is quantity—among Greeks quality: see e.g. the dialogue of Xerxes and Demaratus, VII 102–4.

2. παιδεύουσι…: This famous *trivium* of the ideal Persian *paideia* is in all likelihood a Greek interpretation of some oriental formulae of royal self-glorification from Assurbanipal to Xerxes to Arbinas of Xanthus, whereby the kings present themselves as good horsemen, good archers, etc. Persian education apparently did not include reading and writing; it was nevertheless idealized by Greek conservatives no less than the Spartan; see e.g. Xen. *Anab.* I 9,2–6; *Cyr.* I 2,3–12; Plato, *Alc.* I 121e–122a; Onesicritus, *FGrHist* 134 F 35; Nic. Dam. ibid. 90 F 67. See P. Orsi, *Anc.Soc.* XIX (1988), 150–5; Briant, *Histoire*, pp. 339–42, 949–50 (with bibl.) = ET pp. 327–30, 924–5. On Lydian education see I 155,4 and note. Truth and Lie (see 138,1) are often coupled in the Achaemenid inscriptions; Dandamaev, pp. 120 f.; see also Herodotus' sophistic interpretation at III 72,4–5; and cf. Xen. *Cyr.* I 6,28–46.

137,1. τὸ μὴ μιῆς αἰτίης: another idealizing interpretation. Cf. note on 86,6; on the search for precedents see O. Bucci, *RIDA* XXV (1978), 22; on the punishments inflicted on guilty judges see V 25,1; Heraclides of Cyme, *FGrHist* 689 F 4.

2. ἀποκτεῖναι: cf. Isocrates' boastful claim about Athens (XII 121–3).

138,1. λέπρην ἢ λεύκην: it is almost impossible to diagnose these diseases. In Greek sources λέπρα is a curable form of scabies, vitiligo, or psoriasis; whereas in the LXX λέπρα is the Greek for the Hebrew *sare'ath*, which refers to serious wounds, festering blisters, or putrescent spots, even on clothes. The two diseases mentioned here do not correspond to leprosy in the modern sense (*lepra Arabum* or *elephantiasis*). In the ancient Orient the *lepra* was always considered an impurity, and the sick were quarantined or expelled. See e.g. Lev. 13–14 and the parables in Matt. 8: 2–3, and Luke 16: 20 ff. See R. D. Briggs, *RLA* VI 1983, col. 605, with bibl. On Persian medicine in Herodotus see P. Huyse, *Anc. Soc.* XXI (1990), 141–8; see also note on 19,2.

2. αὐτὴν αἰτίην: see Bornitz, pp. 151 f. White doves are perhaps ritually linked to these diseases. They are supposed to have appeared in Greece for the first time in 479 BC: see Charon of Lampsacus, *FGrHist* 262 F 3.   σέβονται ποταμοὺς μάλιστα: cf. Strabo XV 3,14 and 16; and *Anth. Pal.* VII 162. On the sacrifice of white horses at the river Strymon see VII 113,2. It is not at all certain that the cult was restricted to fresh waters (Xerxes punished the salty waters of the Hellespont, but Cyrus punished the Gyndes, a freshwater river: I 189,3). Cf. Introduction, p. 38.

139. τὰ οὐνόματά...: this double linguistic rule, perhaps formulated by Herodotus himself, is not entirely wrong. The meaning (often uncertain) of many Persian personal names falls within Herodotus' definition (e.g. Aršāma, Aspacanah, Darayavahus, etc. designate personal or physical qualities, nobility, etc.). The rule does not apply to theophoric names (Mithra-data, Baga-data, etc.). See R. Schmitt, *ZDMG* CXVII (1967), 119–45 (updated in *AAntHung* XXIV (1976), 25–35). For the meaning of Persian royal names, cf. VI 98,3. For Persian names in Herodotus and their supposed meaning, see the list, with sources and bibl., in O. K. Armayor, *AncW* I 1978 (reprint 1986), pp. 147–51. The rule about the *sigma* holds only for the hellenized form of masculine names (which shows that Herodotus was unfamiliar with the original pronunciation). The name of the letter σίγμα is apparently unattested in sources earlier than Herodotus; σάν occurs in Pindar, *Dith.* II 3 Maehler = Dion. Hal., *De Comp. Verb.* 14 = Athen. X 455c. *Sigma* derives from the proto-Canaanite, Phoenician, and Hebrew *šin*, which is closer to the Dorian 'san' (used in the 5th cent. also in Ionian areas). For another short linguistic note on endings see 148,2.

140,1. πρὶν ἂν ὑπ᾽ ὄρνιθος...: cf. Strabo XV 3,20. It may be a Mazdaic custom which has left traces up to modern times (the 'towers of silence'). In Zoroastrianism cremation and burial are both forbidden, because they contaminate fire and earth. Heraclitus of Ephesus, who was devoted to fire and was in contact with Darius, was said to have arranged to have his body thrown to the dogs (22 A 1a DK).

2. κατακηρώσαντες: embalming was probably reserved for kings and noblemen. On the usage of wax also for Scythian kings see IV 71,1. The Spartans used wax because of a shortage of honey; for the usage of honey in Babylon, cf. 198; for embalming in Egypt, cf. II 86 ff.   μάγοι: *maguš* in Old Persian. The etymology is uncertain; in the Avesta *maga* indicates a particular state of ecstasy. In Darius' Bisitun inscription *maguš* is the title of the usurper Gaumata (*DB* I § 11, etc.). Several names of Magi are mentioned in the Elamite Persepolis Fortification Tablets (see *PFT*). In Greek sources μάγος first appears in a fragment of Heraclitus (fl. 500 BC), if it is a full verbal quotation (22 B 14 DK). Heraclitus has been taken to provide a link between the doctrines of the Magi and Ionian philosophy (see

M. L. West, *Early Greek Philosophy and the Orient*, Oxford 1971; M. Papatheophanes, *IA* XX (1985), 101–61). In Herodotus the Magi are a Median caste or a
tribal brotherhood (ch. 101), who act as priests and seers, and therefore comparable to the Chaldaeans and the Levites. They preside over sacrifices and libations
(e.g. VII 43,2; 113,2–114,1; 191,2); some Magi of the court interpreted dreams
(107–8; 120; 128,2 at the Median court; VII 19,1–2) and other portents (VII
37,2–3). According to later sources, they guarded the sacred fire and the tombs of
the kings. The esoteric nature of the caste and the hostile propaganda (under
Darius, see III 79 and note) were the origin of malicious rumours; in Greek μάγος
means also a quack (e.g. Soph. *Oed. Tyr.* 387). Some scholars distinguish between
the Median Magi, persecuted by Darius and Xerxes, and the Persian Magi,
employed by the Achaemenids in their stead. The Greeks had no clear views
about the Magi, although they started writing Μαγικά already in the 5th cent.
(see e.g. the Μαγικά of Xanthus of Lydia, who included also a chronological list of
Magi). Zoroaster was considered the first Magus, and Zoroastrian tenets and
practices were attributed to the Magi. See the bibl. quoted in the note on 131–40;
E. Benveniste, *Les Mages dans l'ancient Iran*, Paris 1938; J. Bidez and F. Cumont,
Les Mages hellénisés I–II, Paris 1938; and R. C. Zaehner, *The Teachings of the Magi*,
London 1956; for a critical reassessment of the position of the Magi under the
Achaemenids, see E. J. Bickerman, in E. Gabba and M. Smith (eds.), *Religions and
Politics in the Hellenistic and Roman Periods*, Como 1985, pp. 629 ff.
3. μύρμηκας…: perhaps ants represent the embodiment of Evil (as creatures of
Ahriman). The dog had an important role in the story of Cyrus (110,1; 122,3),
and was sacred to Mithras. The whole rite here described is thought to be
Mithraic.   ἄνειμι δὲ ἐπὶ τὸν πρότερον λόγον: a good example of transition
between separate sections in Book I (see the Introduction, p. 11): with these
words Herodotus closes the Medo-Persian *logos* (95–140), refers the reader to the
end of the Lydian *logos* (6–94), and introduces the Ionian *logos*.

141–76. The Ionian *logos* deals with the Persian conquest of western Asia Minor
(*c.*546 and 542 BC), and contains three important digressions, only in part
ethnographic: Ionia, Aeolis, and Doris (142–51); the Phocaeans in the West
(163–7); Carians, Caunians, and Lycians (171–6). For other Greek sources on
the Persian conquest of Asia Minor see Pedley, pp. 46–7. For bibl. see L. Boffo,
MAL XXVI (1983), 6–70; Briant, *Histoire*, pp. 45–8, 910–11 = ET, pp. 35–8,
882–3.

141,1. ἔπεμπον ἀγγέλους: to retain their power, the Ionian and Dorian elites are
ready to switch their support from the Lydians (λυδίζοντες) to the Persians
(μηδίζοντες); during the revolt of 500–494 they were even prepared to become
patriotic.   ἔλεξέ σφι λόγον: a famous parable included in Aesop's collection of
fables; see B. E. Perry, *Babrius and Phaedrus*, LCL, London 1965, Introduction
and no. 9; P. Payen, *Les Îles nomades*, Paris 1997, pp. 62–74; probable allusions in
Matt. 11: 17 and Luke 7: 32; a different story in Diod. IX 35,1–3. For a socio-
economic and structural interpretation see E. S. Hirsch, *CJ* LXXXI (1986), 222–9.

4. τείχεά τε περιεβάλοντο ἕκαστοι: see the case of Phocaea (163,3–4). The common assumption is that previously Ionian cities had no walls. Herodotus, however, knew that some cities had walls (Smyrna, 150,1; Ephesus, 26,2; Miletus, 17–22). Perhaps he thought that the more ancient city walls had been dismantled by order of Croesus. Some scholars think that previously only citadels were fortified.   συνελέγοντο: this is the first testimony on the Ionian league in Herodotus (cf. V 109,3) and on decisions taken in common (κοινῷ λόγῳ). For subsequent activities of the Ionian league, see chs. 152 and 170; on the Panionium, see ch. 148. Probably an amphictyonic league of the twelve cities, with common festivals at the Panionium, had been in existence since 700 BC, assuming a political character only in situations of extreme emergency, such as Cyrus' conquest and the Ionian revolt. It never developed into a permanent federal organization. See C. Roebuck, *CPh* I (1955), 26–40; O. Murray, *CAH²* IV (1988), pp. 481–2.   πλὴν Μιλησίων: Cyrus may have renewed the conditions of alliance and ξενία that Alyattes had established with Miletus at around 611 BC (22,4); cf. *StV* II, nn. 105 and 115.

142,1. οἱ δὲ Ἴωνες: Ἰάονες (Hom. *Il.* XIII 685), [Ἰ]αονίας (Sol., fr. 4a West), *Yaunā*, Old Persian (DPe l. 12 f. Kent, etc.), *Ywn*, Old Testament (Gen. 10: 2, etc.); on the problem of Ionian origins, cults, cities, and dialects see F. Cassola, *La Ionia nel mondo miceneo*, Naples 1957; M. Sakellariou, *La Migration greque en Ionie*, Athens 1958; J. M. Cook, *The Greeks in Ionia and the East*, London 1962 and *CAH²* IV 2, 782–90, 796–804; Huxley; O. Murray, *CAH²* IV, pp. 461–6. On the Panionion see 148,1 and note.

3. γλῶσσαν...: this interesting classification of the Ionian dialects cannot be verified from the epigraphic evidence, except in the case of Chios and Erythrae, which in fact belong to the same group. It is plausible to assume that epichoric languages, especially Carian and Lydian, influenced the Ionian dialects. The four groups are all said to be παραγωγαί 'alterations', apparently a pejorative term, perhaps as compared to a 'pure' literary Ionian (Homer?); see Erbse, pp. 173–9. Herodotus wants to emphasize the Ionians' lack of unity in all areas: language, ethnicity, politics, etc.; cf. esp. ch. 146. On Herodotus and the Ionians see note on 146,1. Smyrna (150) and the Aeolian Magnesia (161) are not included in the canonical list of the twelve cities.

143,1. Φοίνικες: Phoenicia fell into Persian hands after the conquest of Babylon (539 BC).

2–3. ἀπεσχίσθησαν...Σμυρναῖοι: for ἀπεσχίσθησαν, cf. ch. 58. The following οὗτοι refers to the Ionians in Asia Minor, who were separated from the other Ionians in the motherland: Herodotus is here alluding to the Ionian migration (cf. 145,1 and 146,1–3), which allegedly took place in a period of 'weakness' of the Greeks in general and of the Ionians in particular. The settlers in Asia Minor are supposed to have redeemed the name 'Ionians', which had fallen into disrepute in the motherland. See G. Maddoli, *PP* XXXIV (1979), 256–66, with criticism of other interpretations. Herodotus therefore wishes to explain the common usage of his time, when the name 'Ionians' was reserved for the settlers living in Asia

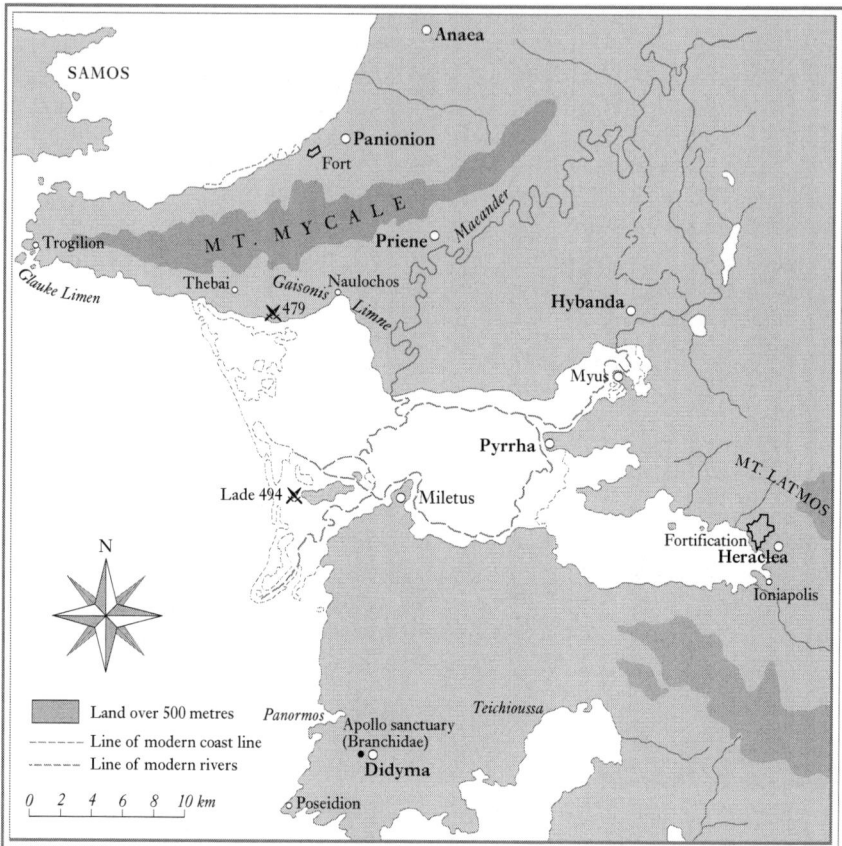

Map 16. Environs of Miletus

Minor, and on the other hand to allude to the current contempt for the same Ionians of Asia Minor as models of softness and servility (cf. 143,3; V 69,1). The brief allusion to their arrogance and cultural exclusiveness prepares the reader for the harsh criticism in ch. 146. Cf. Plutarch, *Mor.* 858 f., where this contempt is advanced as as an example of Herodotean 'malice'. The assumption that the name 'Ionians' was imported from the motherland is confirmed by common institutions (the four tribes, the festival of the Apaturia at 147,2, 6–7, the eponym Ion, etc.), and by linguistic affinities. See the bibl. quoted in note on 142,1.

144,1. Δωριέες: this sub-digression on Asiatic Doris is inspired by the criticism of the ethnic exclusiveness of the Ionians (its proper place would most naturally be after ch. 148 or 151). Herodotus was well aware that ethnic exclusiveness was a general rule in the Greek world (see e.g. V 72), but the case of Halicarnassus touched him personally. The Dorian pentapolis, a cultic league (cf. 144,3), was formed following the Dorian colonization from the Peloponnese. The minor

Dorian islands, such as Nisyros, Calydna, etc., and some Doricized sites on the mainland would be the πρόσοικοι that were never admitted to the league. Cf. Dion. Hal., *Ant. Rom.* IV 25. **Τριοπικὸν ἱρόν**: the Pandorian sanctuary of Apollo was located on the Triopium or Cape Crio (Deveboynu Burnu), i.e. on the western tip of the Cnidian headland; see Müller II, pp. 390–5, and cf. note on 174,2. There are no archaeological traces of the temple, though the festivals and the athletic contests continued to be celebrated into the Roman period. Some coins from Cos, with a discobolus and a tripod, have been thought to have been minted in relation to these festivals. See K. Hanell, *RE* VII A, 1939, coll. 174 f.; J. M. Cook, *CAH*[3] II 2, pp. 790–6; for the eponym see C. Saletti, *EAA* 1973 Suppl., s.v. 'Triopas'; N. Vogeikoff, s.v. 'Triopas', *LIMC* VIII, 1 1997, pp. 55–6.

3. **Λίνδος καὶ Ἰήλυσός τε καὶ Κάμιρος**: the three Dorian states on the island of Rhodes remained independent *poleis* until they synoecized in 408/7 to form a federal state, with the new city of Rhodes as capital. On Lindos see III 47,2 and note; on Cos, the homeland of Hippocrates and a famous centre of medical studies, cf. IX 76,2, etc.; cf. Müller I, pp. 948–9, 956, and 973–5; on Cnidus see I 174,1–6 and note. See S. Hornblower, *Mausolus*, Oxford 1982, pp. 115–37. **Ἁλικαρνησσόν**: Halicarnassus, Herodotus' mother country, was traditionally a Dorian city, a colony of Troezen (VII 99,3); but in the 5th cent. it had a mixed Greek and Carian population, and the Ionian dialect and calendar were dominant. It is generally assumed that the city was excluded from the league for this reason, but actually the date of its expulsion is unknown. For bibl. on Halicarnassus, see L. Rocchetti, *EAA* 1958, s.v. 'Alicarnasso'; Hornblower, op. cit.; Müller II, pp. 254–62.

145. Ἀχαιῶν: in Herodotus Ἀχαιοί has three different meanings: the Homeric Ἀχαιοί (for 'Greeks' in general), II 120,3; the pre-Dorian population of the Peloponnese (IX 26,3); the historical district of Achaea on the northern coast between Sicyonia and Elis (as in our passage and I 146,1; VII 94; VIII 36,2; 47). In some other passages the meaning is uncertain (V 61,2; 72,3). Herodotus apparently believed that the pre-Dorian Achaean population in the Peloponnese migrated to the historical district, possibly as a result of the Dorian invasion, while the Arcadians never left their country. This theory does not explain the presence of Achaeans outside the Peloponnese, e.g. in Phthiotis, in colonial Magna Graecia, and on the north-eastern coast of the Euxine. See W. Goegebeur, *AC* LIV (1985), 116–51; M. Giangiulio, *Ricerche su Crotone arcaica*, Pisa 1989, pp. 163 ff.; Y. Laford, *DNP* I (1996), 62–69 (with bibl.); C. Morgan and J. Hall, in M. H. Hansen (ed.), *Introduction to an Inventory of Poleis*, Copenhagen 1996, pp. 164–232. In Roman times Achaea was the name of the senatorial province of Greece. On the Achaean Dodecapolis here described, cf. Polyb. II 41; Strabo VIII 7,1–5; and Paus. II 18,6–8; VII 1, 1–9. According to a widely accepted ancient theory, the Ionians-Achaeans originally left the Peloponnese and, after a stay at Athens, settled in Asia Minor. The belief that the Ionians were originally Achaeans is based on a pair of concrete data: the number of twelve districts and the epithet *Helikonios* for Poseidon. However, 12 is a typical number for tribe divisions in the ancient world, and the etymology of *Helikonios* is controversial (note on 148,1). In any case, the federal god of the

Achaean league in historical times was Zeus Homarius. On the Hellenistic Achaean league see J. A. O. Larsen, *Greek Federal States*, Oxford 1968, pp. 80–9, with bibl.; Walbank, III, pp. 406–14.   *Πελλήνη*...: all these localities are mentioned by Herodotus only here; see Walbank II, p. 41; Müller I, pp. 733–879, *passim*. On Sicyon see V 67,1 etc.; A. Griffin, *Sikyon*, Oxford 1982; G. Kavradis, *LIMC* VIII 1 1997, pp. 1107–8.   *Κρᾶθις*: the river Crathis (modern Akrata) in Achaea flows from Mt. Chelmus (Aroania), with the waterfalls of Styx (Mavronero); see Müller I, pp. 788–9. For the river Crathis in Italy, cf. V 45,1.

146,1. *οὗτοι "Ιωνές εἰσι*: the doctrine of the ethnic purity of the Ionians, which Herodotus harshly criticizes here, was developed in Asia Minor as an element of national identity and an ideological means of increasing the political and cultural cohesion of the Dodecapolis. It was used to justify the cultic exclusiveness of the Panionium and, in the 5th cent., to legitimize the inclusion of Ionia into the Delian league. Herodotus' hostility towards the Ionians manifests itself also elsewhere (e.g. at II 16,1–2), particularly in regard to their role during the Graeco-Persian conflict. On Herodotus and the Ionians see the ample bibl. in D. Gillis, *Collaboration with the Persians*, Wiesbaden 1979, Pt. I; Masaracchia, pp. 7–44; and Hart, pp. 181–2; M. Van der Valk, in *Stemmata. Mélanges J. Labarbe*, Liège–Louvain–Neuve 1987, pp. 242–8; L. Moscati Castelnuovo, in Daniele Foraboschi (ed.), *Storiografia ed erudizione: scritti in onore di Ida Calabi Limentani*, Bologna 1999. Modern scholars generally accept the Herodotean view of the mixed character of the Ionian migration and of the ethnic fusion achieved only on Asian soil. But while the ancients thought of the Ionian migration as an event restricted to a limited period of time (one generation or even a single year: the generation of Neleus, the founder of Miletus, following that of his father Codrus, the Athenian king contemporary with the Dorian invasion: V 76; IX 97; 1044/3 bc, according to Eratosthenes, *FGrHist* 241 F 1a), modern scholars imagine a long process lasting over centuries, between the later part of the 2nd millennium and the beginning of the 1st. For all these issues see the bibl. quoted in note on 142,1. On the 'national' identity of the Ionians in Asia Minor see D. Asheri, in *I Greci* II 2 (1997), 14–16; M. Corsaro, ibid. 27–59.   *Ἄβαντες*...: the Abantes are an Euboean people, probably pre-Hellenic, known already to Homer (*Il.* II 536 ff., etc.); Abantis is a poetic epithet for Euboea (Strabo X 1,3; Paus. V 22,3). On Orchomenos see Müller I, pp. 529–31. On the Orchomenian Minyans see IV 145,3 ff.; for the Cadmeians see I 56,2 and note; for the Dryopes see VIII 43, etc.; for the Phocians see I 46,2; the Molossians (VI 127,4) are the main Epirote tribe, ruled by the hellenized dynasty of the Aeacidae (see N. G. L. Hammond, *Epirus*, Oxford 1967).   *Ἀρκάδες*...*'Επιδαύριοι*: as autochthonous the Arcadians are Pelasgians; cf. note on 57,1. According to Pausanias, VII 4,2, the Epidaurians were Ionian.

2. *ἀπὸ τοῦ πρυτανηίου*: the prytaneum is the residence of the *πρύτανις*, the chief magistrate in the *polis* (see F. Gschnitzer, *RE* Suppl. XIII 1973, coll. 801–9). The most ancient prytaneum must have been built in Athens after the synoecism of Theseus (Thuc. II 15,2 and the scholium ad loc.); it was situated on the acropolis. Up to the time of Solon it was the residence of the eponymous archon; the *βασιλεύς* lived nearby, in the *βουκολεῖον*, but sat in judgement at the prytaneum in some cases of homicide. After the Persian fire of 480 the prytaneum was rebuilt, perhaps not far

from the original site. The laws of Solon were kept there. The prytaneum should not be confused with the θόλος in the agora, the residence of the πρυτάνεις of Cleisthenes' βουλή. Greek prytanea were generally sacred to the public Hestia, on whose altar burned the sacred fire of the city (see W. Fuchs, *EAA* 1961, s.v. 'Hestia', and O. Hansen, *AC* LIV (1985), 276, n. 4). Certain meritorious citizens and guests of honour were entertained to meals in a refectory attached to the prytaneum. See the description of the prytaneum at Olympia in Paus. V 13, 8–12. In general see S. G. Miller, *The Prytaneion: Its Function and Architectural Form*, Berkeley 1978. It is held that Herodotus is here alluding to the tradition whereby Athenian oecists lit a torch at the altar of Hestia to bring the fire of the mother city to the colony; this would be a Herodotean concession to the theory of the συγγένεια of Ionians and Athenians, which was used as a formal pretext for the creation of the Delian league in 478 BC (Thuc. I 95,1–2, etc.). The tradition is, however, attested only in late sources of disputed value; see Malkin, ch. 3. The notion of connection between Athens and the Ionians is as old as Homer (*Il.* XIII 685–90). Athens represented the Ionians at the Amphictyony of Delphi, her four pre-Cleisthenic tribes and the old dress of Athenian men and women were known as 'Ionian', the Apatouria (see 147,2 and 2) were celebrated at Athens, and Solon described Attica as 'the oldest Ionian land' (fr. 4a West). But the doctrine of the formal 'foundation' of the Ionian dodecapolis by Athens as its metropolis seems to have emerged later, in connection with the establishment of the Delian league, and thereafter used to the full as imperial propaganda. The first literary evidence may be Pindar, *Paean* II,28 ff. Cf. Hdt. V 97, 2; VII 22,1; IX 97 and 106,3; see J. Barron, *JHS* LXXXII (1962), 1–6; LXXXIV (1964), 35–48; Meiggs, pp. 293–8.   οὐ γυναῖκας ἠγάγοντο: in fact the settlers were often young single men (IV 153); but there is no lack of examples where entire families migrated abroad (e.g. the Phocaeans at 164,3). On the role of women in colonization see A. J. Graham in *Atti del Centro di ricerche e di documentazione sull'antichità classica*, XI (1980–1), Milan 1984, pp. 293–314, with bibl. Cases of the expulsion or massacre of male natives and the abduction of women were not rare, but there is no lack of examples in Ionia of peaceful cohabitation (Samos, Erythrae, Phocaea), and mixed examples of expulsion and cohabitation (Ephesus, Colophon, Chios) also occur. According to our earliest sources, from Homer to Ephorus, the native population of Miletus was Carian and Lelegian.

3. μή κοτε ὁμοσιτῆσαι: Herodotus gives a rational aetiology for the widespread custom of sex-segregation at meals; cf. the Cretan and Spartan syssitia, the Greek symposia in general, and the banquets of the Macedonians (V 18,3) and the Persians; the Caunians are an exception (172,1). For anthropological parallels see M. M. Westington, *CJ* XL (1944–5), 495–6. The Milesian women's custom of abstaining from calling their husbands ὀνομαστί is probably a Carian tradition which outlived the hellenization of the city. It is seen by Herodotus as a strange or exceptional custom; cf. Dickey, p. 225, n. 49.

147,1. βασιλέας: 'kings' of individual cities are meant here (on the federal 'king of the Ionians' see note on 148,1); there is evidence for the existence of some of them (P. Carlier, *La Royauté en Grèce avant Alexandre*, Strasbourg 1984, pp. 432–50). In historical times the βασιλεῖς were magistrates who presided over cults, or

descendants of ancient aristocratic dynasties who continued to enjoy some privileges. Glaucus was a leader of the Lycians at Troy (*Il.* II 876) who fell fighting over the corpse of Achilles. According to a well-known but fanciful theory, the 'descendants of Glaucus' would be the ruling house at Xanthus in Lycia, at whose court Homer would have sung the heroic deeds of their ancestor. The Caucones lived in Triphylia on the western Peloponnese; but Herodotus is here referring to the Neleids of Pylos, who were considered ancestors by oecists and dynasties of several Ionian cities, among them Miletus (see IX 97 on Neleus founder of Miletus); see the sources in *FGrHist*, Commentary 323a F 11, n. 5; Carlier, op. cit., pp. 432–40; E. Simon, 'Neleus', *LIMC* VI 1 1992, pp. 727–31.   συναμφοτέρους: indicates that in some cities the Glaucids and the Neleids ruled simultaneously or alternately.
2. Ἀπατούρια: ancient Ionian festivals; in Athens they were the festivals of the phratries. The most likely etymology comes from ὁμοπατόρια: 'festivals of the sons of the same father', i.e. the *phrateres*. According to an aetiological myth the name derived from ἀπάτη, Melanthus' 'cheat' during his combat with Xanthus of Boeotia. Herodotus' proof remains questionable, because the Apaturia was celebrated in some cities that never considered themselves Athenian colonies (e.g. Delos), and not in others (e.g. Ephesus). See the bibl. in note 142,1. On the Athenian Apatouria see H. W. Parke, *Festivals of the Athenians*, London 1977, pp. 88–92; Parker, *Polytheism*, pp. 458–61.

148,1. Πανιώνιόν: cf. 141,4; 142,1; 143,3; 170,1; VI 7; the amphictyonic, federal sanctuary of the Ionian Dodecapolis was located at Otomatik Tepe (or Profitis Ilias), at the foot of the spurs of Mt Mycale (on Mycale see IX 90,1 ff.). The 1957 excavations have uncovered a 6th-cent. BC altar and, perhaps, the remains of a 4th-cent. *bouleuterion.* No traces of the temple of Poseidon have yet been found. It may have been located on the land taken from the city of Melia in the 8th cent. For bibl. see U. von Wilamowitz-Moellendorf, *Kleine Schriften*, Berlin V 1937, pp. 38–57; G. Kleiner *et al., Panionion und Melie* (*JDAI* Ergänzungsheft 23), Berlin 1967; G. E. Bean, *Aegean Turkey*, London 1979, pp. 178–80; Shipley, p. 267; Müller II, pp. 606–62. For Panionios as an anthroponym see VIII 105–6.   Ποσειδέωνι Ἑλικωνίῳ: Helikonios is a Homeric epithet of Poseidon, probably in connection with Achaean Helike (*Il.* VIII 203–4; XX 404), as Herodotus too seems to imply (for Helike see ch. 145); yet many modern scholars think that the epithet Heliconius is connected with Mt. Helicon in Boeotia (see *Hymn. Hom.* XXII 3). A 'king of the Ionians' presided over the federal festivals at the Panionium: these continued into the Roman period, when the 'king of the Ionians' was normally a citizen of Priene. During the Peloponnesian war and the first decades of the 4th cent. the festivals were celebrated at Ephesus, for reasons which are unclear; see A. Momigliano, *V Contributo*, Rome 1975, 205–10; S. Hornblower, *Historia*, XXXI (1982), 241–5; L. Boffo, *I re ellenistici e i centri religiosi dell'Asia Minore*, Florence 1985, p. 123.
2. ἐς τὠυτὸ γράμμα: e.g., τὰ Ὀλύμπια (ἱερά), etc.; for the endings of Persian names, cf. ch. 139.

149,1–2. Αἰολίδες: broadly speaking, the Aeolis is the area colonized by Lesbos on the mainland, between the river Hermus and the Propontis. Herodotus, however, makes a clear distinction between the Troas and the territory of the Dodecapolis which extends from the area south-east of Cyme, through the Hermus valley, to the coast north of the Caïcus mouth. Linguistically, the Aeolians belong to the Thessalo-Boeotian group. The list of cities seems an artificial choice of Aeolian villages (except Cyme, which is an important centre: see 141,1 and note) created on the model of the Ionian Dodecapolis. Nothing is known about an Aeolic league with political functions, except for what Herodotus tells us (cf. 141,1; 150,2; 151,2; 152,1). It is possible that an amphictyonic centre developed around the oracle of Gryneion. It is not even certain that there was an Aeolian league in the Hellenistic period. See J. Bérard, *RA* (1959), 1–28; Huxley, pp. 36–9; J. M. Cook, *CAH*³ II 2, pp. 776–82; Müller II, pp. 416–29, 485–9, 541–7, 555–8.

150,1. Σμύρνην: cf. 14,4; 16,2; 94,6; 143,2; 144,1; II 106,2; archaic Smyrna was on the site of the modern suburb of Bayralki (near modern Izmir), about 8 km. north-west of the Hellenistic city of Smyrna and the modern city of Izmir. The excavations on the rise of Tepekule have brought to light an elegant city, that in the 7th cent. had circular city walls, an urban plan with parallel streets and blocks of spacious houses, and a sacred area. For bibl. see A. M. Mansel, *EAA* 1966, s.v. 'Smirne'; see also R. Martin, *L'Urbanisme dans la Grèce antique*, Paris 1974², pp. 289 f.; L. Moscati Castelnuovo, *Siris*, Brussels 1989, pp. 75–9; E. Akurgal, *Alt-Smyrna I. Wohnschichten und Athenatempel*, Ankara 1983; Müller II, pp. 723–9. The archaic city was destroyed by Alyattes (16,2), and ceased to exist as a *polis* at about 600 BC, though some of the inhabited areas, the temples, and the necropolis survived. Various stories about the foundation of Smyrna were current in antiquity. Traditionally Smyrna was also the name of an eponymous Amazon (see R. Vollkommer, *LIMC* VIII 1 1997, pp. 1145–7). It was one of the supposed birthplaces of Homer. According to the later Ionian version, it was a colony of Ephesus; see Strabo XIV 1,4.　**Κολοφωνίους**: Herodotus' version may seem unfavourable to the Colophonians, but he probably chose it because the cunning stratagem appealed to him. Mimnermus thought that the conquest of Smyrna was a sign of divine providence (fr. 9 West). The causes of the στάσις in Colophon are unknown. There are a number of parallels for the stratagem: e.g. the episode of the Samians at Zancle (VI 23–4). Cities with sanctuaries outside the walls had to take precautions so that a part of the population remained in the city; see Aen. Tact. XVII. According to Paus. V 8,7 Smyrna had already become Ionian in 688 BC. See *EAA* 1959, s.v. 'Colofone'; *StV* II, no. 101; and G. Fogazza, *QUCC* XVIII (1974), 23–38; and the bibl. quoted at n. on 142,1.

151,1. ἐν τῇ ῎Ιδῃ: Mt. Ida (the peak Kaz Dağ, 1,700 m.) faces the gulf of Adramyttium and extends further north. The mountain was sacred to Zeus Idaeus and to the Phrygian Great Mother (see Müller II, pp. 844–6), and was sometimes confused with the homonymous mountain in Crete. ῎Ιδη means 'timber' for the construction of ships: see IV 109,2. On the Troad in general see Strabo XIII 1,1–70 and J. M. Cook, *The Troad*, Oxford 1973.

2. πέντε μὲν πόλιες: Mytilene (I 160,1 and note), Methymna, Eresus, Antissa, and Pyrrha. There may have been a pan-Lesbian sanctuary in the centre of the island in the time of Alcaeus. Arisba (Müller I, pp. 929–30) should not be confused with the homonymous city of the Troad mentioned by Homer (*Il.* II 836, etc.). On Eresus see ibid., pp. 946–7. See G. Labarre, *Les Cités de Lesbos aux époques*

hellénistique et impériale, Paris 1996. The Dorian hexapolis too became a pentapolis; see 144,3.   Μηθυμναῖοι: Methymna, a powerful city-state and a rival of
Mytilene, was the birthplace of Arion (see 23,1). See H.-G. Buchholz, *Methymna*,
Mainz 1975; Müller I, pp. 977–8, 980–1.   ἐν Τενέδῳ: modern Bozcaada,
about 7 km. away off the coast of the Troad; see Müller II, pp. 949–52. It was
famous as the base to which the Achaeans retired in order to deceive the Trojans
before their final attack.   Ἑκατὸν νήσοισι: a group of small islands (much less
than a hundred) between Lesbos and the continent; see Strabo XIII 2,5, where
Ἑκατόν is taken to be an epithet of Apollo. The 'only one *polis*' referred to by
Herodotus must be Pordoselene (Strabo loc. cit.).

152,1. ἐς τὴν Σπάρτην: this chapter refers back to 141,4 and resumes the main
narrative (152–62). The failed Ionian embassy to Sparta foreshadows the more
famous one of Aristagoras (V 49–51). For Croesus' embassy to Sparta, cf. chs.
69–70. There is a moral message in these and other diplomatic meetings, whether
real or fictitious (e.g. those at III 46 and 148): they portray the contrast between two
cultural models, pomp and verbosity on the one hand, laconian austerity on the
other. The image of Sparta that emerges from this chapter is of a city extremely
narrow-minded, patriotic, arrogant, panhellenic in words but totally ineffective in
practice; for a different interpretation see Arieti, pp. 151–2. As in the case of Croesus'
representation, no kings or ephors are mentioned (see note on 69,3). The envoys
contrived an audience with a device that amused Herodotus, but was of course
inadmissible according to Spartan procedures. The name Pythermus may be a trace
of an authentic Spartan tradition (a contemporary of his may be the homonymous
poet and musician of Teos: Athen. XIV 635C). On purple see note on 50,1.

3. γῆς τῆς Ἑλλάδος: that the Greeks of Asia Minor belong to Greece is a notion of
5th-cent. Greek ideology and anti-Persian propaganda; cf. Diod. IX 36,1 (from
Ephorus?) on the συγγένεια of the Spartans and the Greeks of Asia Minor. Lacrines
personifies the 5th-cent. stereotype of the arrogant Spartan herald. Only the report
about the meeting at Sardis may contain an element of authentic tradition.

153,1. τίνες ... προαγορεύουσι: a typical question of kings and satraps in Herodotus, cf. e.g. I 56,1; V 73,2; 105,1. In his answer Cyrus refers to Greek civilization in
general and to the Ionians in particular. Herodotus must have perceived the
non sequitur (at para. 2), but he did not correct it, leaving us with a doubt whether
the answer may belong to a different dialogue: only the last sentence is appropriate
to a dialogue with mainland Greeks who try to get involved in Asiatic affairs.
ἄνδρας τοιούτους: Herodotus contrasts two stereotypes: the primitive Persians (cf.
71,2) and the sophisticated mercantile Greek society of his times. The reduction of
the agora from a civic institution to a centre of deception seems to be lifted from
anti-democratic Greek propaganda from Theognis (53–60) to Xenophon (*Cyr.* I
2,3). Cf. also Diog. Laert. I 104–5 on the Scythian Anacharsis' view of the agora. See
L. Kurke, *AJPh* CX (1989), 535–44. However, Herodotus may well be using 'agora'
in the sense of 'marketplace' (cf. II 39,2; III 42,2; VII 23,4), which (after all)
non-Greek cities may also possess (cf. I 37,2; 197; II 138,4; V 101,2; VII 26,3).

3. *Ταβάλῳ*: for the supposed original form and meaning of this name see O. K. Armayor, *AncW* I (1978), 150. Tabalus is the first satrap of Sardis; Cyrus nominated also his successor, Oroetes (III 120,1). Pactyes was in charge of κομίζειν, of 'transporting' the gold' (T. S. Brown, *AJPh* XCIX (1978), 65, n. 6), not of keeping it safe or managing it; cf. the sack of Ecbatana (note on 128,3).

4. *Βαβυλών...*: the list is not arranged in chronological order. Ctesias mentions Cyrus' campaigns against the Bactrians and the Sacae, *FGrHist* 688 F 9 (2–3), but his testimony is doubtful. The probable chronological order of Cyrus' campaigns is: Media, Asia Minor, Babylon, eastern Iran, Massagetae. Cf. 177–8,1; 190,2. See the bibl. quoted at 130.   ἄλλον ... στρατηγόν: Mazares (156,2).

154. *τοὺς Λυδοὺς ἀπέστησε*: on Pactyes' rebellion (154–61) see Briant, *Histoire* pp. 47–8, 911 = ET pp. 37–8, 882–3 (with bibl.).

155,1. *Κροῖσον*: Croesus continues his career as 'wise counsellor' (cf. note on 27,2). On this dialogue see Heni, pp. 117 ff.   ἐξανδραποδίσασθαί: cf. 66,3 and 161, etc.; ἐξανδραπόδισις: III 140,5 in the sense of 'deport into captivity', the practice that the Achaemenids inherited from the Neobabylonians, who in turn took it from the Assyrians, cf. VI 94,2 etc. For ἀνδραποδίζω see III 59,3; 137,3; 147,1; etc. The expressions ἀναστάτους ποιέω (para. 2) and ἐξαναίστημι (para. 3) have a similar meaning: they all refer to the annihilation of a city through mass-deportation of its inhabitants; cf. notes on III 25,3 and 93,2.   ὡς εἴ τις πατέρα: an epic reminiscence (Cypria fr. XXV Allen).

4. *ὅπλα*: cf. Nymphodorus of Amphipolis, *ap. Schol. Soph. Oed. Col.* 337; Just. I 7,2–3; Polyaenus VII 6,4. For the motif see also [Xen.], *Cyrop.* VIII 8; Dion. Hal. *Ant. Rom.* VII 9,3–5, and Plut. *Mor.* 173c. The new Lydian *paideia* is the exact opposite of the Persian (I 136,2); cf. L. Kurke, *AJPh* CX (1989), 539. On the effeminacy of the Lydians cf. 34,3; 55,2; 71,2. Lydian luxuriousness and effeminacy is a well-known Ionian *topos* already current in the pre-Persian period; see e.g. Xenophanes of Colophon, 21 B 3 DK.

156,1. *ἀξιόχρεον πρόφασιν*: an excellent example of Herodotus' use of the term. The 'adequate reason', a basic concept of the Greek art of persuasion, is not necessarily the true one, but rather that most effective for persuading one's opponent. On this passage see R. Sealey, *CQ* VII (1957), 6; cf. the bibl. quoted at 29,1.   *Μαζάρεα*: cf. 157,2–3; 160,2; 161; for the supposed original form and meaning of this name see O. K. Armayor, *AncW* I (1978), 152.

157,1. *ἐς Κύμην*: cf. I 149,1. 'Aeolic Cyme' (VII 191,1; Hes. *Op.* 636; etc.), to distinguish it from Euboean and Campanian Cyme. According to Charon of Lampsacus, *FGrHist* 262 F 9, Pactyes escaped from Sardis to Mytilene and then to Chios. Cyme is the most important town in the Aeolis, see *EAA* 1973 Suppl., s.v. 'Kyme'; and C. Talamo, *PP* XXVIII (1973), 361 ff.; Müller II, pp. 541–7 and cf. the bibl. at note on 149,1–2.

2. *τὴν πᾶσαν δίαιταν τῆς ζόης*: cf. 79,3; 155,4 and notes.

3. *Μαζάρης*: Herodotus relates the story of Pactyes' extradition, which extends to 161,1, with literary skill and attention to the moral and religious dilemma arising from the conflict between the sacred immunity of the suppliant (ἱκέτης) and the

request for extradition (ἔκδωσις). Seen as a conflict between religion and politics, this theme inspired a number of Attic tragedies, from Aeschylus' *Supplices* to Euripides' *Heraclidae*. Cf. I 73,6–74,1 and VI 108,4. The story of Pactyes presents two possible choices: the religious one of Cyme (157,1–160,1) and the political one of Mytilene (160,1–2) and Chios (160,3–5). Herodotus must have collected his information in the cities involved in the events: at Miletus he could have heard the local account of the behaviour of the Branchidae. One cannot rule out the use of Hecataeus as a written source who knew everything about Didyma during the Ionian revolt (see V 36, 2–3). τὸν ἐν Βραγχίδῃσι: cf. 46,2 and 92,2. This famous temple and oracle of Apollo at Didyma (VI 19,2) was situated about 16 km. south of Miletus. The surviving archaeological remains include the sacred precinct and porch of the 7th cent., the temple and peristyle of the 6th cent., statues, etc. A *via sacra* connected the sanctuary to Miletus. Temple and oracle were administered by the Branchidai (οἱ Βραγχίδαι: 158,1), a priestly clan so-called probably after an artificial ancestor Branchos (see Strabo IX 3,9). The sanctuary was sacked by the Persians after the Ionian revolt (VI 9,2–3); the Branchidai were later deported to Sogdiana, probably by Xerxes to save them from their own fellow-Ionians (Strabo XI 11,4; XIV 1,5; XVII 1,43). A very hostile tradition about the Branchidai did indeed prevail in antiquity and eventually served to justify the massacre of their supposed descendants perpetrated by the soldiers of Alexander in 329 BC. An imposing and perfectly preserved temple was rebuilt at Didyma towards the end of the 4th cent. BC. For bibl. see G. Colonna, *EAA* 1963, s.v. 'Mileto'; H. W. Parke, *The Oracles of Apollo in Asia Minor*, Oxford 1985; id., *JHS* CV (1985), 59–68; J. Fontenrose, *Didyma: Apollo's Oracle, Cult and Companions*, Berkeley–London 1988; K. Tuchelt, 'Didyma', *DNP* III (1997), 544–9; Müller II, pp. 438–50; N. G. L. Hammond, *CQ* XLVIII (1998), 339–44.

158, 1. θεοπρόπους: see note on 19,1.

158,2. Ἀριστόδικος ὁ Ἡρακλείδεω: possibly an ancestor of the tyrant of Cyme of Darius' time (IV 138,2; V 37,1). The anthroponym is common in all areas, especially in the Aegean. On Aristodicus' puzzling story see R. Merkelbach, in *Hestia und Erigone. Vorträge und Aufsätze*, Stuttgart–Leipzig 1996, p. 468.   ἀπιστέων: the initial charge was of 'false embassy' (cf. the legal term is παραπρεσβεία), not of a false oracular response. Cf. the reaction of the Athenian θεοπρόποι to the Delphic response at VII 141,1–2. A new embassy is the outcome of party quarrels in the *polis*. Later, however, Aristodicus tested the same oracle in an irreverent manner (159,3).

159,1. ὦναξ: used by Herodotus only as an address to Apollo (cf. IV 150,3; 155,4; VII 141,2) or as an oracular epithet of Apollo (IV 155,3). Homer and the tragedians use it also for mortals in the original (Mycenaean *wa-na-ka*) sense of 'lord', 'master' (e.g. ἄναξ ἀνδρῶν Ἀγαμέμνων, *Il.* I 442, etc.; οἴκοιο ἄναξ, *Od.* I 397), or 'king' (ἄναξ Ξέρξης: Aesch. *Pers.* 5; ἄναξ Δαρεῖε, ibid. 787). See P. Carlier, *Le Royauté en Grèce avant Alexandre*, Paris 1984, pp. 44–107, 142, 215–21. The same rules apply to the feminine ἄνασσα (e.g. *Od.* VI 149, to a mortal lady; III 380, to a goddess). The plural ἄνακες is an epithet of the Dioscuri, and ἀνάκειον is their temple. For ἀνάκτωρ = ἄναξ, of a god, see Aesch. *Choeph.* 357. For ὦναξ as an address in prose writers see Dickey, pp. 101–3, 27–3.

3. ἐκ τοῦ ἀδύτου: see note on 47,2.

4. ναὶ κελεύω...: Apollo has lost his patience and self-assurance. Herodotus could not expect his public, who already knew the story of Croesus and the oracles (chs. 46–8), to realize immediately that the Cymaean enquiry was irreverent and sacrilegious (cf. VI 86γ,2). Herodotus was perfectly aware that the oracle had suggested a pro-Persian political move, but found itself compelled to contradict itself or to interpret its own response in order to justify itself before Aristodicus. As far as Aristodicus is concerned, he managed to camouflage astutely his own irreverence (and his anti-Persian political stand) as religious 'fundamentalism'. Eventually, he stands out as more likeable, more intelligent, and perhaps even more moral than the god of the Branchidae, whom Herodotus too probably disliked. For a different view see T. S. Brown, *AJPh* XCIX (1978), 64–78. On Herodotus' attitude towards oracles see Introduction, pp. 41 f.

160,1. ἐς Μυτιλήνην: Mytilene (also Mitylene) was the main city of archaic and classical Lesbos; see the bibl. in A. Archontidou, 'Mytilene', *LIMC* VIII 1 1997, pp. 863–4, and cf. note on 151,2.

2–3. οἱ δὲ Μυτιληναῖοι...ἐξεδόθη: cf. Plutarch, *Mor.* 859a–b.

3. Ἀταρνέος: on the Aeolian coast east of Pergamon. It became the περαία (sc. γῆ or χώρα), of Chios, i.e. the opposite shore on the mainland controlled by an insular city-state across the straits; for περαίη, cf. VIII 44,1. Herodotus often refers to this fertile plain (VI 28,2; 29,1; VII 42,1; VIII 106,1). Cf. πέρην = 'across', or 'on the other side of', the sea (e.g. VI 28,2; 44,2; 97,1). On Atarneus see Müller II, pp. 434–7; E. Schwertheim, *DNP* II (1997), 147, with bibl.

5. οὐλὰς κριθέων: cf. 132,1. The aetiological story aims to explain the origin of the Atarnean ritual described here.   ἐπέσσετο: cf. II 37,4 and VIII 137,2.

161. Πριηνέας: cf. Paus. VII 2,10. The entire population was not deported if in 494 BC the city was able to contribute twelve ships for the battle of Lade (Herod. VI 8,1); but it later became unimportant and virtually disappeared. It was re-established by the reign of Alexander as a 'Hippodamic' planned city on a spur of Mt. Mycale; see for sources *Inschriften von Priene*, Berlin 1906; Müller II, pp. 674–80; on the Hellenistic city see R. Martin, *L'Urbanisme dans la Grèce antique*², Paris 1974, pp. 113–14, 234–5; E. J. Owens, *The City in the Greek and Roman World*, London–New York 1991, pp. 65–6, with bibl. ἐπέδραμε: the verb refers to incursions, not deportations.   αὐτίκα νούσῳ τελευτᾷ: αὐτίκα suggests a divine punishment, presumably for the depopulation of Priene; cf. the case of Otanes, III 149 and note.

162,1. Ἅρπαγος: a repeat of of what has been said and a reference back to ch. 119. 2. χώμασι: for the technique described here see L. Boffo *MAL* XXVI (1983), 32 and notes.

163–7. The digression on the Phocaeans in the West opens with two chapters on Phocaea, the city walls, and Arganthonius (163–4), and passes to the vicissitudes of the emigrants in Corsica and Velia with a sub-digression on Agylla (165–7).

The *logos* is important for the archaic history of the West. It is only superficially a chain of local histories of Phocaea, Corsica, and Lucania, which cannot be understood without the Etruscan, Punic, and Greek background. Herodotus once again displays his narrative art and his humanity in this scenario of 'total' history: feats of arms, adventures, customs, oracles, feelings, and mentalities. Bibliography: three volumes of *Parola del Passato* are devoted to the Phocaeans in the West and to Velia: XXI 1966, XXV 1970, and XXXVII 1982; the first includes a critical edition and a commentary on these chapters by M. Gigante (pp. 295–317). For a review of studies published between 1966 and 1975 see J.-P. Morel, *BCH* XCIX (1975), 853–96; an updated bibl. can be found in *CAH*[2] III 3, 1982, pp. 480 ff.; M. Bats, *AION* (ASA) 1 (1994), 133–48; M. Gras, in *I Greci* II 2, pp. 61–77. For a commented collection of texts see V. Krings, *Carthage et les Grecs c. 580–480 av. J.-C., Textes et histoire*, Leiden–Boston–Cologne 1998.

163,1. *Φωκαίη*: though Phocaea had been introduced as the city leading the resistance against Cyrus (151,1 and 3), paradoxically it represents in this *logos* the most defeatist reaction to the Persian conquest. Emigration *en masse*, an act which expresses desire for freedom, was presented as the best solution for all the Ionian cities (170,1–2), and was also chosen by Teos (ch. 168; Teos is the city proposed by Thales as the capital of a unified Ionian state: 170,3). Changes from illusion to disillusionment, such as here, are certainly not unintentional in Herodotus. For bibl. on Phocaea (at modern Eski Foça) see B. Pace, *EAA* 1969, s.v. 'Focea'; on Herodotus and mass-emigration in the Persian wars see N. Demand, *AJPh* CIX (1988), 416–23; Demand, pp. 34–44.   *πρῶτοι*...: from Thucydides onwards Phocaea was regularly included among the ancient thalassocracies: in Diodorus' list (VII 11) it was supposed to have dominated the sea for forty-four years (576–533 BC?); see Miller, pp. 106 f.

2. *οὐ στρογγύλῃσι νηυσὶ ἀλλὰ πεντηκοντέροισι*: not a mercantile, but a war fleet. The penteconter was a ship about 32 m. long, with twenty-five oars on each side and a ram at the prow; the crew could consist of up to eighty men (so VII 184,3), fifty of whom were rowers. This type of ship dominated the sea until the early 5th cent., when it was gradually replaced by the trireme. For Polycrates' fleet (*c.*532–522 BC), a mixture of penteconters and triremes, see III 39,3; 44,2 and notes.   *Ταρτησσὸν*: the area between Huelva, Sevilla, and Cadiz, near the mouth of the river Guadalquivir, inhabited in antiquity by the Turdetani. In Stesichorus' view (184 *PMG*) Tartessus was a river and its springs were 'silver-rooted', hinting perhaps at the mines. The location of a (mythical?) 'city' named Tartessus and its identification with the biblical Taršiš are a matter of debate. Traditions about Rhodian seafaring to Iberia 'earlier than the First Olympiad' (Strabo XIV 2,10) are better explained as an invention of Hellenistic Rhodian historians. According to Hdt. IV 152,1–3 the Samians first discovered this area in the second half of the 7th cent. BC. Greek objects of the 7th cent. and later have been found in the area, but they may attest only to commercial relations. Whether Mainake (Malaca?) is a Greek or Phoenician settlement is a problem much disputed. See A. Schulten, in *Fontes Hispaniae Antiquae* II, Barcelona 1925, pp. 26–9; id., *Tartessos*[2], Hamburg

1950; U. Täckholm, *ORom* V (1965), 143–200; ibid. X 3 (1976), 41–57; J. M. Blázquez, *Tartessos y sus problemas*, Barcelona 1969; id., *Tartessos y los orígenes de la colonización fenicia en occidente²*, Salamanca 1975; Y. B. Tsirkin, *Oikoumene*, V (1986), 163–71; J. M. Alonso Nuñez, *AC* LVI (1987), 243–9; M. E. Aubet (ed.), *Tartessos. Arqueología protohistórica del Bajo Guadalquivir*, Barcelona 1989; F. Javier Gómez Espelosín *et al.*, *La imagen de España en la antigüedad clásica*, Madrid 1995.   Ἀργανθώνιος: the character belongs to the cluster of legends that developed in the 6th cent. around the mirage of Tartessus; he is one of the μακρόβιοι. Cf. Anacreon, fr. 361 *PMG*, Cicero, *De Senect.* 69 (with M. Manfredini, *RFIC* XCVIII (1970), 278–91), and Lucian, *Macr.* 20. Earlier speculations about Etruscan (*arcnti*) or Celtic (*argant* = silver) connections are now generally discarded, but some still believe that a historical figure may hide behind the myth. Arganthonius' friendly relations with the Greeks have been explained historically against the background of hostility between Iberians and Phoenicians in southern Spain (though προσφιλέες at para. 2 has no political connotation; cf. 123,1). See the bibl. quoted above.

3–4. τεῖχος ... συναρμοσμένων: Herodotus could have seen the ruins of the walls of Phocaea. His description of the 'large blocks of stone skilfully fitted together' (συναρμοσμένων) was understood to indicate a polygonal construction of the 'Lesbian type', such as those at Aeolic Larisae (149,1) and at Velia; see F. Prontera, *RA* (1981), 259–60. Herodotus' terminology, however, is not unambiguous: cf. II 124,5 and 148,7, which refer to non-polygonal constructions. In fact, the remains of the archaic walls of Phocaea, discovered in 1992, are made of long, rectangular, non-polygonal blocks; see Ö. Ozyğit, *REA* XCVI (1994), 77–109; H. Tréziny, ibid. 115–35.

164,1. προμαχεῶνα: cf. 98,4 and note; οἴκημα (cf. 179,3) is the curtain wall between towers. Harpagus is content with a symbolic act of surrender.

2. δουλοσύνῃ: on the meaning of περιημεκτέοντες and the motif of freedom in this passage see Gigante, *PP* XXI (1966), 302 f.   ἡμέρην μίαν: a mass evacuation of a city cannot be completed in one day nor under the eyes of the enemy.

3. ἀναθήματα: see note on 14,1.   ἐρημωθεῖσαν ἀνδρῶν: only the men of substance emigrated according to Antiochus of Syracuse, who used other sources (*FGrHist* 555 F 8).

165,1: τὰς Οἰνούσσας: at the northern entrance of the channel between Chios and Erythrae; see Müller I, p. 990. The term ἐμπόριον, a 'commercial centre', is apparently not attested before Herodotus. See M. Casevitz, in *L'Emporion*, textes réunis par A. Bresson and P. Rouillard, Paris 1993, pp. 15–17.   ἐκ θεοπροπίου: cf. 7,4 and note; a typical colonization oracle: See P-W I, p. 142; II no. 49; Fontenrose, p. 68 and Q 93; and Crahay, pp. 138–40. ἀνεστήσαντο: 'had founded' a city; the correction ἐνεκτήσαντο, proposed by Herwerden and accepted by Legrand in his edition, has been understood to mean 'they had taken possession' of an inhabited area. 'Twenty years earlier' is *c.*560 BC. The excavations at Alalia, modern Aleria, attest traces of habitation already in the early iron age, but this does not justify the textual correction. For bibl. see P. Pergola, *EAA* 1973–94 Suppl. and *EAA* I (1994²), s.v. 'Aleria'; J. and L. Jehasse, *Aléria antique*, Paris 1987.

3. μύδρον σιδήρεον: a famous archaic ritual for taking solemn oaths, probably known to Alcaeus (see fr. 77 Voigt, and scholia *ad loc.*), repeated in a similar form in the sources on the foundation of the Delian league. The anecdote underlines the perpetual validity and irrevocability of the oath; cf. VIII 143,2. For a similar anecdote about the Epidamnians see Diodorus IX 10,3. Echoes of this passage are found in Callimachus (fr. 388 Pfeiffer and scholia *ad loc.*) and in Horace, *Epod.* 16, 17–22; see M. Gigante, *Maia*, XVIII (1966), 223–31; S. J. Harrison, *CQ* XXXIX (1989), 273–4. Μύδρος here simply means 'block of (red-hot?) iron'.   ἀπέπλεον ὀπίσω: for an electrum coin, perhaps minted at Phocaea after the return of the 'perjurers', see F. Chiesa, *Numismatica e antichità classiche*, V (1976), 27–31. To the battle of Lade (494 BC) Phocaea sent only three ships (VI 8,2).

166,1. κοινῇ: according to the terminology of Greek colonization, the newcomers become the σύνοικοι of the first settlers (what rights were associated with this status is not stated). A transformation of a new settlement into a thriving naval city is not a matter of five years (a 'typical' figure of narrative art, not to be taken literally; cf. the similar case of the Samians at Cydonia: III 59,2). According to various sources, on this occasion a part of the Phocaeans also founded Massalia (mentioned by Herodotus at V 9,3 in a totally different context); but the issue is debated. See the bibl. in note on 163–7.   τοὺς περιοίκους ἅπαντας: the Etruscans and the Carthaginians, who must have been damaged by raids at sea and on the Etruscan coast. For this view see M. Gras, *Latomus*, XXXI (1972), 698–716; Y. B. Tsirkin, *Oikumene*, IV (1983), 209–21.   κοινῷ λόγῳ: from the 6th cent. onwards the Etruscans and the Carthaginians had commercial treaties; see S. Cataldi, *ASNP* IV 4 (1974), 1235–48. Also Etruscan Rome (unmentioned by Herodotus) established a link with Carthage with the famous 'first treaty', which Polybius dates to 508 BC (III 22–3).   ἑξήκοντα: sixty ships on each side; therefore the Phocaeans had to face a fleet twice as large as their own: these are typical numbers, expressing the idea of the equivalence of the allies and the inferiority of Phocaea, thus having no historical value; cf. VI 8,2; VII 95,1; 168,2; 185,3 on Greek fleets; and VII 36,1 and 89,1 on Phoenician fleets. However, sixty ships seems to be the standard size of Phoenician fleets also in other sources: see R. Rebuffat, *Semitica*, XXVI (1976), 74. If Thucydides is referring to the battle of Alalia at I 13,6, he does not mention the Etruscans; Diodorus' account at V 13,4, brief and inaccurate, does not mention the Carthaginians.

2. ἀντίαζον: see 105,1 and note. The 'Sardinian Sea' separates the coast of Tuscany and Latium from Sardinia and Corsica; cf. Strabo V 2,1.   Καδμείη τις νίκη: the famous battle of Alalia, once dramatically considered a decisive disaster for the Greeks in the West, is now revalued and seen as a local episode relevant only to Corsica; see the bibl. in note on 163–7. The Phocaeans continued their trade in the Tyrrhenian sea well into the early 5th cent. Corsica was probably not seized by the Etruscans (but see Diod. V 13,3–5; XI 88,5) and the balance of power in the West was not substantially changed. A 'Cadmean victory', like a Pyrrhic victory, is a victory obtained at a high cost, so called after the legendary Theban wars; cf. Plato, *Leg.* I 641C; Diod. IV 65,9; XI 12,1; XXII 6; Plut. *Mor.* 10a; 488a; *Suidas*, s.v.; in the sense of 'great victory': Arrian, *FGrHist* 156 F 21a–b.

τοὺς ἐμβόλους: the iron or bronze poles projecting from the prow could bend when colliding with enemy rams. Battles between penteconters proceeded by a series of rammings; the stricken ships sank, but most of the crew survived (hence the great number of prisoners).

3. ἔπλεον: here the imperfect seems to indicate several journeys (but see above, 165,3). Twenty penteconters could apparently carry about 1,600 persons. The question of whether the Greek evacuation of Corsica was total or partial is disputed by archaeologists.

167,1. οἵ τε Καρχηδόνιοι... κατέλευσαν: with some effort, it is possible to understand the meaning of the transmitted text without emendation: the Τυρσηνοί are the Tyrrhenians of Agylla; αὐτῶν refers to τοὺς ἄνδρας (the Phocaean prisoners); πολλῷ πλείους are the Phocaean dead. See J. Jehasse, *REA* LXIV (1962), 249 f.; A. Colonna, *Paideia*, XLIV (1989), 62–3. ἐξαγαγόντες κατέλευσαν: the stoning took place in the territory of Agylla, or Caere (*Cisra* in Etruscan), modern Cerveteri (48 km. north of Rome). Together with Veii, Tarquinia, Vulci, Clusium, and other cities, Caere belonged to the league of the Etruscan Dodecapolis. The city is famous for its large necropolis. See M. Cristofani, 'Cerveteri', *BTCGI* V (1987), 251–66, with full bibl.; S. Bianchetti, *DNP* II (1997), 906–7. A huge temple, dating to the late 6th cent. BC, is supposed to have been built where the massacre occurred as an act of expiation; see M. Torelli, in *Le Délit religieux dans la cité antique*, Rome 1981, pp. 1–7. Stoning (λευσμός: Aesch. *Eum.* 189), either as a ritual of expiation, a mass-lynching, or a legal form of execution, is common in many ancient, medieval, and even in some modern cultures, especially for crimes against the community or for causing pollution. Greek tragedy abounds in examples; see V 38,1 and IX 5,2. M. Gras, *Du châtiment dans la cité. Supplices corporels et peine de mort dans le monde antique*, Rome 1984, pp. 75–88; V. J. Rosivach, *ClAnt* VI (1987), 232–49. Sacrifice of prisoners is also well-attested in ancient Greece (see e.g. Phaenias of Eresus, fr. 25 Wehrli) and Rome; for the Etruscans cf. Livy VII 15,10. See P. Ducrey, *La Traitement des prisonniers de guerre dans la Grèce antique*, Paris 1968, pp. 201–15; D. D. Hughes, *Human Sacrifice in Ancient Greece*, London–New York 1991; M. Halm-Tisserant, *Réalités et imaginaire des supplices en Grèce ancienne*, Paris 1998, pp. 139–48.

2. ἐγίνητο διάστροφα: see M. Delcourt, *Stérilités mystérieuses et naissances malifiques dans l'antiquité classique*, Liège 1938 (repr. Paris 1986), pp. 29–66. ἐς Δελφούς: the connections of Agylla and Delphi are attested by the treasury of the Agylleans (Strabo V 2,3). Herodotus could have obtained information at Delphi or in Magna Graecia; τὰ καὶ νῦν... ἔτι at para. 2 may even indicate direct knowledge. Since the response is expiatory, not prophetic, it may actually be authentic; see P–W I, p. 142 f.; II no. 64; Crahay, p. 80 f.; Fontenrose, Q 133 and *CSCA* I (1968), 97 f.; but it is told as an αἴτιον for the games. The cathartic nature of the oracle is typical of Delphi, but the institution of games as expiation is Italic and Etruscan; see J.-P. Thuillier, *Caesarodunum* (Suppl. 52) (1985), 23–32. On the relations between Caere and Delphi see D. Briquel, *Les Pélasgues en Italie. Recherches sur l'histoire et le légende*, Rome 1984, pp. 214–21.

3–4. ἐκτήσαντο... ἔκτισαν: they 'procured for themselves a city', i.e. they bought from the Oenotrians a plot of land on which they founded the city. The area seems to have been previously unoccupied; cf. Strabo VI 1,1. See C. Bencivenga Trillmich, in J.-P. Descoeudres (ed.), *Greek Colonists and Native Populations*, Canberra–Oxford 1990, pp. 365–71; J.-P. Morel, in F. Krinzinger and G. Tocco (eds.), *Neue Forschungen in Velia*, Vienna 1999, pp. 19–22.   Ὑέλη: the hellenized form of a local place-name. The excavations of Velia (modern Castellamare della Bruca) have revealed an archaic village with polygonal walls and a system of non-orthogonal streets south of the acropolis. According to Pseudo-Scymnus, 250 ff., Massalian settlers participated in the foundation of Velia: this would explain the obscure toponym Ἰταλία Μασσαλιωτική (see J. Brunel, *REA* LXXVI (1974), 29–35). Xenophanes of Colophon settled in Velia and Parmenides was born there. On the basis of Herodotus, the foundation of the city should be dated roughly between 535 and 530 BC (we do not know the precise date of the Persian conquest of Phocaea, nor how long the migration of the Phocaeans and their stay in Alalia and Rhegium lasted). Herodotus calls the area around Velia 'Oenotria', one of the names used by the western Greeks for southern Italian areas known to them; it corresponds to modern Bruzio-Lucania. See Hecataeus of Miletus, *FGrHist* 1 F 64–71; Antiochus of Syracuse, ibid. 555 F 2–6, 9 and 12; for Oenotrian legends see D. Asheri, in *L'incidenza dell'antico. Studi in memoria di Ettore Lepore*, II, Naples 1996, pp. 151–63. For the 'Oenotrian islands' opposite Velia, cf. Strabo VI 1,1 and Pliny, *NH* III 85.

4. ὡς τὸν Κύρνον ... οὐ τὴν νῆσον: P–W II no. 49; Fontenrose, Q 93 and p. 68; Crahay, pp. 138–40. The oracle was originally intended for the founders of Alalia (165,1). Herodotus, however, assumes that it involves also the Phocaeans who had fled to Rhegium. Until then both the founders and the new settlers had understood the order κτίσαι (τὴν) Κύρνον to have the obvious meaning 'colonize Corsica'. The learned interpreter from Poseidonia (Paestum) assumed a misunderstanding of the true meaning; his interpretation freed the Phocaeans from the obligation of colonizing Corsica, but required them to establish a cult to Cyrnus; see E. Greco, *PP* XXX (1975), 209–11. This the Phocaeans had not done yet, since their interpretation of the oracle was different. Cyrnus, son of Heracles, is the eponym of Corsica, but he could be worshipped elsewhere too. The Phocaeans did not make further enquiries at Delphi, but proceeded to found Velia, where they presumably instituted the cult of Cyrnus. But why Velia? Herodotus does not explain: he only implies that the new interpretation of the oracle allowed the Phocians to choose freely the site for their *polis*, provided that they instituted the cult of Cyrnus. The fact that no traces of this cult have yet been found at Velia is an argument of little weight. Apart from the bibl. already quoted, see M. Lombardo, *ASNP* III 2 (1972), 82–5; Malkin, pp. 72–3.

168. Τήιοι: the same spelling as at III 121,1 and VI 81,1; Τέως: I 142,3; 170,2; II 178,2. On Teos (at modern Sigacik) see Müller II, pp. 732–9.   χώματι: cf. 162,2. Ἄβδηρα: cf. VI 46,2 and VIII 120. Abdera is on the Thracian coast (Cape Balustra), north-east of Thasos; see Müller I, pp. 37–41. The toponym seems Phoenician (*'abd* means 'slave'), and there was a Phoenician colony of the same name on the coast of Spain. It had its own eponym: Abderus (known to Pindar, *Paean* II 2), a Locrian in origin, who was killed in Thrace. According to a local tradition Abderus' lover Heracles founded Abdera near his grave and instituted

athletic games in his honour; see [Apollodorus] II 5,8; Philostr. *Imag.* II 25; J. Boardman, s.v. *LIMC* I 1 1981. The cult of Timesius, the first historical settler, was added to that of Abderus and was later observed also by the colonists from Teos. The Clazomenian settlement is dated by Eusebius to 655 BC (= *ab Abramo* 1362; cf. M. Miller, *The Sicilian Colony Dates*, New York 1970, pp. 25–6); on Clazomenae see I 16,2; 51,3; 142,3; etc., and the bibl. quoted in note on 142,1; the Tean settlement should be dated *c.*540 BC. The Teian poet Anacreon took part in the colonization. Either the emigration from Teos was not total, or many came back: other Teians are said to have founded Phanagoria, on the Taman peninsula, at about the same time (Arrian, *Byth.* 55 Roos); and less than half-a-century later Teos was able to contribute seventeen ships to the battle of Lade (VI 8,1). On Abdera during the Persian war see VII 120 and VIII 120. On the history of Abdera see J. M. F. May, *The Coinage of Abdera, 540–345 BC*, London 1966; Isaac, pp. 73–108; C. M. Danov, in J.-P. Descoeudres (op. cit. at n. on 167, 3–4), pp. 151–5; on town-planning see W. Hoepfner and E.-L. Schwandner, *Haus und Stadt in klassischen Griechenland*, Munich 1994, pp. 180–7. ὑπὸ Τηίων τῶν ἐν Ἀβδήροισι: this should not be taken to mean that the settlers remained 'Teians', i.e. citizens of Teos in Abdera (cf. Protagoras 'the Teian' in Eupolis, fr. 157 K–A), although in this case the relations between the colony and mother city continued to be exceptionally close for centuries. On the relations between Teos and Abdera in Hellenistic and Roman times see Seibert, pp. 175–8; L. and J. Robert, *Journal des Savants* (1976), 153–235; P. Herrmann, *Chiron*, XI (1981), 1–30; Demand, pp. 39–43; A. J. Graham, *JHS* CXII (1992), 44–73; C. Marek, *Tyche*, XII (1997), 169–77.

169–70. In these two chapters Herodotus summarizes the main features in the Persian conquest of Ionia and reflects on the ethical and political problem of the options open to the Ionians. They had three alternatives: emigration *en masse*, armed resistance, or voluntary submission. Herodotus fully understands the first option, the expression of horror in the face of slavery (169,1; 170,2; cf. 164,2); he also appreciates the more noble choice of resistance (169,1; cf. 170,4); but he does not comment on voluntary submission, the choice of Miletus and the islands (169,1–2). The peoples of Caria and Lycia were also facing three alternatives (see note on 171–6).

169,2. ὡς καὶ πρότερόν μοι εἴρηται: see 141,4.   τὸ δεύτερον: see notes on 92,1 and 196,6.   οἱ τὰς νήσους ἔχοντες Ἴωνες: Chios and Samos. The statement contradicts 143,1; cf. 174,3. No other source confirms this report that the islands gave submission to Cyrus. Persian hegemony over the islands developed through the collaboration of vassal-tyrants during the reigns of Cambyses and Darius.

170,1. Βίαντα: cf. 27,2 and note. Bias is one of the 'Seven Sages' (see note on 20), hence dated as their contemporary. However, some sources date him to the time of Alyattes, Periander, and Thrasybulus, the second Messenian war, and the war between Samos and Priene (Piccirilli, no. 4). Others, as Herodotus, consider him to be a contemporary of Croesus and Cyrus. Bias, as Thales also, represents the figure of the 'wise counsellor'.

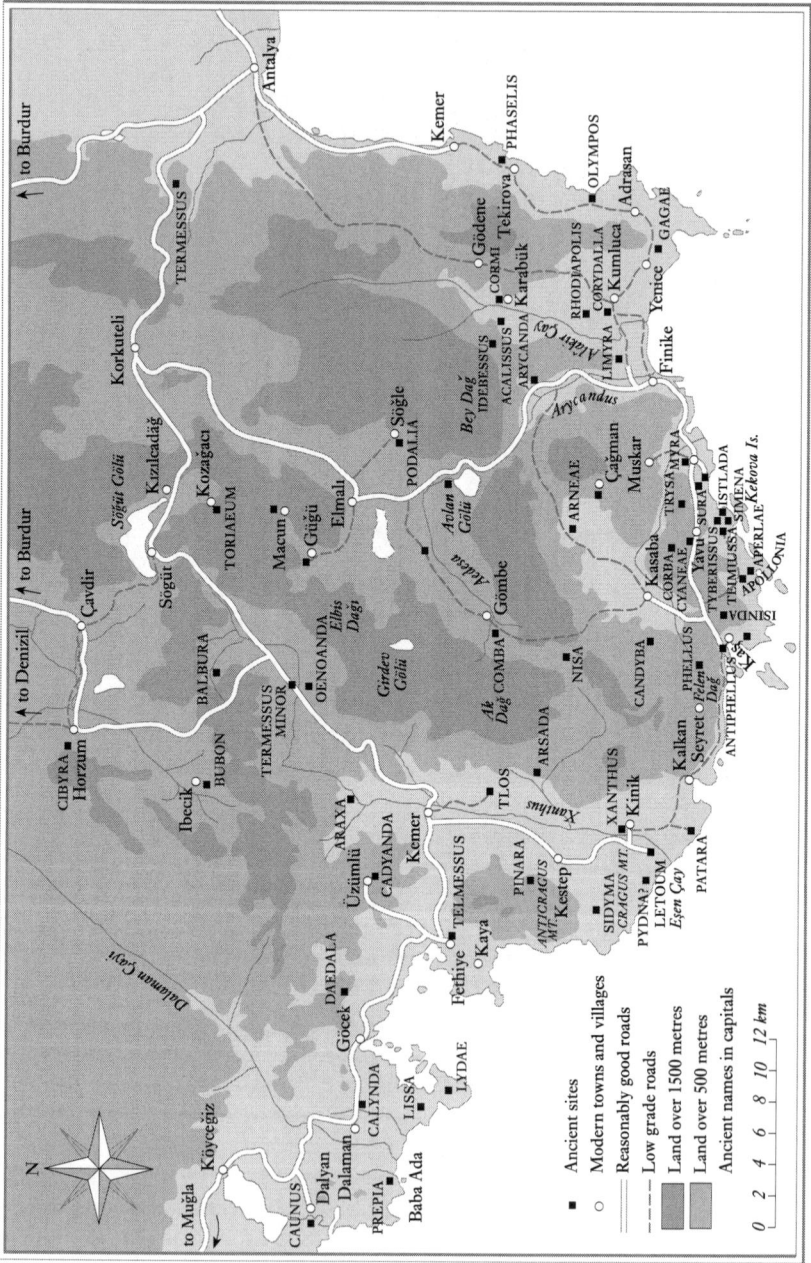

Map 17. Lycia

2. κοινῷ στόλῳ: Herodotus attributes to Bias, as well as to Thales, an initiative in support of Ionian unity. The option of mass emigration, already chosen by Phocaea and Teos (chs. 163–8), presented itself again after the Ionian revolt and even after the battle of Mycale. The project of a Panionian colony in Sardinia or Sicily seemed particularly appealing (V 124,1; VI 22 ff.); cf. Histiaeus' plans at V 106,6 and VI 2,1, and the debate at IX 106. Many in antiquity believed that Sardinia was the largest island in the Mediterranean (including [Scylax] 114 and Timaeus, *FGrHist* 566 F 65; however, Strabo rightly claimed that Sicily is the largest; see R. J. Rowlands, *CW* LXVIII (1975), 438–9; M. L. Chaumont, *QS* XLIX (1999), 142–3. These projects of mass emigration involved the mirage of the Island of the Blest. In fact, in the 6th cent. Sardinia was under Carthaginian hegemony, and therefore closed to Greeks immigration. For an echo of Herodotus in Horace (*Epod.* 16,41 ff.), see M. Gigante, *Maia* XVIII (1966), 226 ff. On the Greeks in Sardinia see J. M. Davidson, in M. S. Balmuth and R. J. Rowland (eds.), *Studies in Sardinian Archaeology*, I, Ann Arbor 1984, pp. 67–82.

3. χρηστὴ ...'Ιωνίην: Thales' proposal is not just 'useful', but also morally 'good' and noble, see J. Elayi, *IA* XIV (1979), 197. It may be inferred from the text that, according to Herodotus, the proposal was made at the Panionium before the final subjection of Ionia to the Persians. However, we are not told when exactly the proposal was made, nor whether it was intended as a permanent constitutional reform or as a temporary measure to ensure united resistance (see E. Marinoni, *Acme*, XXIX (1976), 179–231). It is also unclear how a Milesian 'delegate' (πρόβουλος: cf. VI 7) could have proposed a plan of united resistance to the Ionian league, to which Miletus itself, as an ally of Cyrus, must have been opposed (cf. 141,4; 143,1). But perhaps Herodotus simply wanted to contrast Bias' unitarian proposal with a different unitarian alternative.   ἐόντος Φοίνικος: the best Panionian 'national' plan is not proposed by one of the most noble Ionians descended from those who left the prytaneum of Athens (146,2), but by a barbarian (a good example of Herodotean 'malice': Plut. *Mor.* 857 f). Democritus (55 B 115 Diels), Leander of Miletus (*FGrHist* 492 F 17), and Duris of Samos (*FGrHist* 76 F 74) all knew of Thales' Phoenician origin; cf. Diog. Laert. I 22. What these sources mean is that he was a descendant of the Phoenicians who came to Greece with Cadmus. The tradition may be based on a misinterpretation of Φοινίκη, a poetic epithet of Caria, to which Miletus belongs. For Phoenicia as a federal model (?), see B. Soyez, *AC* XLIII (1974), 74–82. On Thales, cf. 74,2 and note.   ἐν βουλευτήριον: a single assembly replacing the assemblies of individual cities, which would be abolished. In Herodotus' view the proposal amounts to a transformation of the Ionian league into a unified Ionian state, with a capital in its geographical centre, Teos. The other cities would lose their political autonomy. That the idea is modelled on the Attic synoecism is clear even from the terminology (cf. I 60,5; 62,1; V 69,2; Thuc. II 15,2). The project has all the appearance of a political utopia, conceived in the intellectual circles of Miletus between the Persian conquest and the Ionian revolt. For other interpretations see Moggi, n. 16, with ample bibl. The term βουλευτήριον is first applied by Aeschylus to the Athenian Areopagus (*Eum.* 570, etc.).

171–6. The subject of the Persian conquest of Caria and Lycia is treated in two separate sections: three chapters (171–3) are devoted to the history and ethnography of the Carians, Caunians, and Lycians; and three (174–6) relate the conquest itself. Each section has three parts, but there is no absolute correspondence between them. In the narrative section the three parts represent three different human and political reactions to invasion (as was done in respect of the Ionians, but here too there is no absolute correspondence): voluntary submission (Carians and Cnidians), sensible resistance (Pedasians), and collective suicide (the Lycians of Xanthus, and the Caunians).

171, 2. *Κᾶρες:* cf. I 28, etc. *Karka* in Persian and Aramaic, *Kar* or *Qar* in the Old Testament, *Kar-sa* in Accadian. The Carians were in close and stable contact with the Greeks of Asia Minor, especially on the coast between Miletus and Halicarnassus (for ethnic mixing at Miletus see 146,3–4; at Halicarnassus see note on 144,3). They also served as mercenaries outside Asia Minor and were in contact with Greeks in the settlements in Egypt. Under Croesus and Cyrus they suffered a similar fate to that of the Ionians, were included within the same satrapy (*Yaunā* or *Sparda*), and participated in the Ionian revolt with similar plans for submission or mass emigration. See III 91,1; V 103,2; 117–21; VI 25,2. Bibl. in S. Hornblower, *Mausolus*, Oxford 1982, and in *CAH*² VII, ch. 8a; Müller II, pp. 276–82. *ἐκ τῶν νήσων:* the Cretan version perhaps derives from the city of Praesus, where Herodotus thought he had found information about the age of Minos (VII 171,1). It is a flattering version that elevates the Carians to the status of allies of Minos. Contrast the version of Thuc. I 4; 8,1. *Λέλεγες:* Homer distinguishes between Carians and Leleges (*Il.* X 428–9), and includes the first in his Catalogue of Ships (*Il.* II 867), but not the second (the issue was debated in antiquity, cf. Strabo XIII 3,1). Other authors too distinguished between the two peoples: see Aristotle (frs. 473–4 Rose), Philip of Theangela (a Hellenistic historian of Lelegan origin (?): *FGrHist* 741 F 2), and Strabo himself (esp. VII 7,2 and XIII 1,58–9; at XIV 2,27 he summarizes Herodotus). See W. Aly, *Philologus*, XXIII (1909), 428–44, and the sources collected in A. Laumonier, *Les Cultes indigènes en Carie*, Paris 1958, pp. 16 ff., and Müller II, pp. 322–3. In stories about origins, the transformation of the *ethnicon* through a mythical eponym is a conventional element (Fehling, pp. 33–49). *φόρον:* cf. 6,2 and note; Herodotus refers to the period of Minos' thalassocracy. The model of allies as privileged subjects exempt from tribute seems to be derived from the conventions of the Delian league. Herodotus' research about the tributes is aimed at contradicting those who maintained the contrary; see M. Giuffrida, in *Studi di storia antica offerti dagli allievi a Eugenio Manni*, Rome 1976, pp. 133–52. Unlike later sources, Herodotus does not know of a Carian thalassocracy independent from that of Minos. See W. G. Forrest, *CQ* XIX (1969), 98 ff.; and R. Ball, *CQ* XXVII (1977), 317–22. For possible connections between this passage and other chapters dealing with Crete (I 173; VII 169,2; and 171,2), see Cobet, pp. 50 ff.

4. *τριξὰ ἐξευρήματα:* a typically Herodotean triad (see note on 30,1). This passage forms part of the *elogium* of the Carians in the Cretan version. They were traditionally considered the 'first inventors' of certain weapons: see Alcaeus'

Carian crest (fr. 388 Page), and the shield-handle 'of Carian make' mentioned in Anacreon (401 Campbell), both quoted by Strabo XIV 2,27. For 'Carian' weapons found at Delos in 426 BC, see Thuc. I 1,8. Other inventions were attributed to the Carians (some sorts of clothes, a type of ship, drugs, musical tunes, etc.); but on the whole the Carians are to the Greeks as the Samnites are to the Romans: their superiority in the manufacture of weapons was fully recognized by the respective cultures, who adopted them. Herodotus dated these inventions to the time of Minos, i.e. before the Trojan war (Homer knew the crested helmets, the round shields, and the ornaments that identified the warrior); today, however, it is believed that these and similar inventions belong to the 'hoplite revolution' in the early 7th cent., and were Greek, not Carian, though Carian mercenaries may have eventually spread them in the East (see e.g. the ὄχανα in Sennacherib's army, II 141,5). In reality the passage may refer to new types of crests (in some cases simple ribs holding together the two halves of the helmet), to straps in the inside middle of the shield, and handles on the sides; and to standard emblems, mostly birds, other animals or initial letters. Archaeological finds do not so far support the Carian origin of these innovations. See A. M. Snodgrass, *JHS* LXXXIV (1964), 107–18.   τὰ σημήια: cf. the ἐπίσημον on Sophanes' shield (IX 74,2). On decorations and capital initials on Greek shields see G. H. Chase, *HSPh* 13 (1902), 61–127; A. M. Snodgrass, *Arms and Armour of the Greeks*, Ithaca, NY, 1967, pp. 54–5, 67, 95–6 (with sources and bibl. in the notes).   ἄνευ ὀχάνων: the most ancient shields were fastened by shoulder-straps (τελαμῶνες). Famous in the *Iliad* are Ajax's large 'tower' shield (σάκος: *Il.* VII 219 ff.) and Patroclus' ἀσπὶς τερμιόεσσα that touches the ground (*Il.* XVI 802–3; see C. Picard, *RA* XLVI (1955), 68–71).

5. αὐτόχθονας: cf. 172,1, etc.; for αὐτόχθονος = αὐτῇ τῇ χθονί, 'grounds and all', see Aesch. *Agam.* 536. Pherecydes of Athens wrote a treatise called Ἀυτόχθονες (*FGrHist* 3 T 2). The literal sense of αὐτόχθων, in Herodotus and later writers, seems to be '(sprung from) the very soil', as the Spartoi at Thebes and some legendary kings of Attica (see Erechtheus γηγενής, VIII 55); but the usual meaning is 'indigenous', or just 'a people which never left its own land', like the Athenians, the Arcadians, and many other Greek tribes; cf. note on 56,2. The opposite is ἔπηλυς, 'immigrant', 'newcomer': see 78,3; 176,2; and esp. the distinction at IV 197,2 and VIII 73,2. On the 'autochthony' of the Athenians see Parker, *AR* pp. 138–9, with bibl.; A. H. Shapiro, in D. Boedeker and K. Raaflaub (eds.), *Democracy, Empire, and the Arts of Fifth-Century Athens*, Cambridge, Mass., 1998, pp. 127–51.

6. Διὸς Καρίου: the Carian league started celebrating the amphictyonic cult of Carian Zeus in the early 6th cent. at least (there are possible archaeological remains of this cult at Peçin Kalesi, on the site of the acropolis of Mylasa). For the cult Διὶ Καρίῳ (codd.; Ἰκαρίῳ?) in the family of Isagoras at Athens, see V 66,1. At Labraunda, which had close links with Mylasa, there was an important and exclusively Carian cult of Zeus Stratios (V 119,2). Mylasa is the most important Carian town; see N. Bonacasa, *EAA* 1963, sv. 'Mylasa'; see G. E. Bean, *Turkey Beyond the Maeander*, London–New York, 1980, pp. 31 ff.; Hornblower, op. cit.; Müller II, pp. 339–46.   τὸν γὰρ Λυδὸν ... ἀδελφεούς: for

Lydus see 7,1 and note; for Mysus, the Mysians, and Mysia see 36,1. According to Aelian (*Nat. An.* XII 30), Kar is the son of Zeus and Crete. Triads of patriarchs are common, and not only in the ancient world (see M. L. West, *The Hesiodic Catalogue of Women*, Oxford 1985, pp. 11–30); this particular triad is perhaps modelled on that of the sons of Hellen. For the Scythian triad see IV 10,1.

172,1. Καύνιοι: cf. 171,1; 176,3; V 103,2; Strabo XIV 2,3. On the ruins of Caunos at Dalyan see G. E. Bean, *JHS* LXXIII (1953), 10–35; Müller II, pp. 286–92. The cultural characteristics of the city are the dialect, the cults, and the legends of its origins (with links to Miletus and Crete; see F. Cassola, *PP* XII (1957), 192–209). On the eponymous Caunus, son of Miletus and Cyanee, see H. Walter, s.v., *LIMC* VIII 1 1997, pp. 670–1. The love-affair between Caunus and his sister Byblis is well known.   **γλῶσσαν:** it is impossible to assess the linguistic problem posed here, and left open. Carian, documented by over 100 inscriptions and graffiti, remains incomprehensible, and there is even a lack of agreement on whether it belongs to the Indo-European group. See the review of previous studies and the bibl. in O. Masson, *BSL* LXVIII (1973), 187–213; R. Schmitt, *RLA* V 1980, coll. 423–5; I.-J. Adiego, *Studia Carica*, Barcelona 1993. The Caunus inscriptions published by G. E. Bean (*JHS* LXXIV (1954), 85–110) have not solved the problem.   **ἐς πόσιν:** cf. note on 146,3.
2. (ἔδοξε ... θεοῖσι): the parenthesis aims at explaining the apotropaic rite described here. The procession towards Calynda may indicate cultural hostility towards the Lycians. For the cults of Caunus, see *Fouilles de Xanthos*, VI, Paris 1979 (on the trilingual inscription), esp. pp. 32 ff. Calynda is about 15 km. east of Caunos, across the river Indus, which marks the border between Caria and Lycia. It is homonymous with a Dorian island north of Cos and subject to Halicarnassus, better known as Calymna (VII 99,2; VIII 87,2 and 88,3). See Walbank III, pp. 469 f.; G. E. Bean, *Lycian Turkey*, London 1978, pp. 33 ff.; Müller II, pp. 272–6.

173,1. Λύκιοι: the Cretan version of the origin of the Lycians must be a fruit of Homeric exegesis: the Lycian hero Sarpedon, son of Zeus and Laodamia (the daughter of Bellerophon), was confused with the homonymous son of Zeus and Europa (the brother of Minos). In order to resolve the chronological difficulty, the Homeric hero became the grandson of the Cretan one, or else he was said to have had an exceptionally long life; see D. von Bothmer, *LIMC* VII 1 1994, pp. 696–700; Arieti, p. 169. The predominance of Cretan traditions in Caria and Lycia should not be disregarded. On Lycia and the Lycians see Bean, op. cit.; *Actes du Colloque sur la Lycie antique*, Paris 1980; T. R. Bryce, *The Lycians*, Copenhagen 1986; A. G. Keen, 'A Political History of Lycia and its Relations with Foreign Powers 545–300 B.C.', Diss. Manchester 1992; B. Jacobs, in J. Borchhardt and G. Dobesch (eds.), *Akten des II. Intern. Lykien-Symposions*, ÖAW-Denkschr. CCXXXI, Vienna 1993, pp. 61–9.
2. Μιλυάς ...: Herodotus believed that Milyas was the ancient name of Lycia, and that it was inhabited by the Solymi who later changed their name to the Milyae. Cf. Strabo XII 8,5. The historical Milyas was north and north-east of Lycia. For the Milyae in the Persian empire see III 90,1; VII 77. See Müller II, pp. 336–9, 380–1.

3. *Τερμίλαι*: it seems that this national *ethnicon* of the Lycians (*trmm̃is* and *trmm̃yl* in Lycian inscriptions) is originally Anatolian; see E. Laroche, *RA* (1976), 15–19. The form *Τρεμίλαι*, known to Hecataeus, Panyassis, and, perhaps, Menecrates of Xanthus, seems to be closer to the original Lycian form; see Dombrowski, pp. 34 ff. Panyassis told the story of the eponymous Tremiles, father of the eponymous founders of the main Lycian cities.   *Λύκος*: cf. VII 92. The name of a people typically changes with a new eponymous hero (cf. 171,2). Lycus features in the myth of Theseus, who is of political significance also in Lycia, especially when the region was part of the Delian league (*c.*460–440 BC). Without much chronological concern, Lycus (who belonged to the generation before Theseus) was made to emigrate to Lycia in old age, during the last years of the reign of Sarpedon, who belonged to the generation of Theseus and Minos. Different etymologies for the name of the Lycians are given by Hecataeus (the nymph Lycia: *FGrHist* 1 F 256), Menecrates (the good wolves who helped Leto: *FGrHist* 769 F 2; cf. T. R. Bryce, *Historia*, XXXII (1983), 1 ff.), and Philip of Theangela (the Lelegan bandits Lycus and Termerus: *FGrHist* 741 F 3); cf. the etymological connections given to Lycus himself (Kearns, p. 182). Several modern scholars identify the Lycians with the *ruki* and the *lukka* of Egyptian and Hittite texts of the 2nd millennium.

4–5. *καλέουσι...τὰς μητέρας*: Lycian inscriptions do not confirm the usage of matronymics; see S. Pembroke *JESHO* VIII (1965), 217–47; id., *JWI* XXX (1967), 1–29. It is possible that Herodotus is reporting a malicious rumour current among the neighbouring peoples (similar to other rumours, e.g. that they were bandits, were ruled by women, and had no laws; see e.g. Aristotle, fr. 611,43 Rose). Ever since Bachofen and Engels, Lycia is conventionally quoted among the examples of matriarchy (*Mutterrecht*), conceived as a stage in the history of civilization.

5. *ἢυμέν γε γυνὴ ... γίνεται*: the legal rule reported here is almost the same as that related by Pollux III 21, regarding the Athenians; the only difference, but a substantial one, is that, according to Attic law, only the son of an Attic woman legally married to an Athenian citizen is *γνήσιος* (*γενναῖος* in our passage). It thus seems that in Lycia, since the concept of *iustae nuptiae* was lacking, the son born of the union of a free woman and a slave is also legitimate (see, however, the restrictions in the Gortyn law code: *IC*, no. 72, col. VI, line 56–VII, line 4); this seems to be another element in the negative stereotype of the Lycians as having no laws, etc. It should be observed that, in spite of the use of precise Attic legal terms (*ἀστή*, *ἄτιμα*), our passage is not referring to rights of citizenship, but to personal legitimacy, upon which, however, depends whether an individual belongs to the *ethnos* (the Lycians, in other words, followed the *mater certa* principle, which after all determined the individual's ethnic status among almost all ancient peoples). Even at Athens, with the famous law of 451 BC the legal status of the mother became decisive. It cannot be ruled out that Herodotus alludes here to the similarities between the Lycians and the Athenians, and is even insinuating that whereas the Lycian law applied equally to all, the Athenians made exceptions for their 'first' citizen (Pericles, who succeeded in having naturalized the son of his

concubine). At any rate, bias towards Pericles cannot be detected either here or elsewhere in Herodotus (Fornara, pp. 53 f.; and W. G. Forrest, *Phoenix*, XXXVIII (1984), 4 and 10 f.; Mora, pp. 242–5; P. Vannicelli, *Erodoto e la storia dell'alto e medio arcaismo*, Rome 1993, pp. 93–4).

174,2 *Κνίδιοι*: cf. 144,3; II 178,2; III 138,2–3 (and the notes); the Cnidians are mentioned because of their exceptional story. The location of archaic Cnidus is debated: it may have been at Cape Crio (Tekir), where the Hellenistic city was located, or at Bengaz (near modern Datça) on the south coast of the strip of land connecting the Triopion (see note on 144,1) and the Bubassia. See G. E. Bean and J. M. Cook, *ABSA* XLVII (1952), 171–212; Hornblower, op. cit. p. 101 and n. 180, who summarizes the controversy; Demand in *ClassAnt* VIII (1989), 224–37, and *Urban Relocation*, pp. 146–150; D. Berger, *MDAI(A)* XLIV (1994), 5–16; Müller II, pp. 246–51 and 298–317; A. Bresson, *REA* CI (1999), 83–114. Syme is an island between Cnidus and Rhodes; see the bibl. quoted by A. Andrewes, in Gomme V, p. 88 and Müller I, p. 1044. On Rhodes see the bibl. in *OCD*[3] (1996), s.v.

3. *πέντε στάδια*: about 900 m., but the exact width is 1.5 km. The story is based on the assumption that the Persians had officially declared the islands to lie outside their hegemony (see 143,1 and 169,2).

4. *θειότερον*: digging the canal is considered an act of *hybris* against nature (cf. 75, 3–6, and the Introduction, p. 38). For parallels, cf. E. S. McCartney, *CPh* XXXV (1940), 416–20.   *θεοπρόπους*: see note on 19,2.

5. *"Ἰσθμὸν... ἐβούλετο"*:   the response is a command, and could be authentic. Herodotus, however, relates the Cnidian story without involvement. He does not corroborate it from Delphic sources and draws attention to the unusual metrics (for oracles in iambic trimeters see P–W I, p. 44, n. 73). Another difficulty is raised by the appeal to Delphi, instead of the Branchidae of Didyma (157,3). All in all, this response looks very much like a *post eventum* composition by the Cnidians themselves, in order to justify the failed excavation and the submission to Harpagus. See P–W II, no. 63; Crahay, p. 327 f.; Kirchberg, p. 38; Fontenrose, Q 112; J. Elayi, *IA* XIV (1979), 96 f.; R. B. Kebris, *The Paintings in the Cnidian Lesche at Delphi and their Historical Context*, Leiden 1983, pp. 39–40.

175.   *Πηδασέες*: cf. VIII 104 and Strabo XIII 1,59. Pedasa is a common place-name in Asia Minor. Here it refers to a Lelegan city near Gökçeler (north of Halicarnassus); see Müller II, pp. 363–7. Another Pedasa (or Pidasa) was in the area of Mt. Grion (at modern Danisment), belonging to Miletus before 494 BC (cf. VI 20). See L. Robert, *BCH* CII (1978), 500; Müller II, pp. 368–72.   *μεσόγαιαν*: the 'inland country' (cf. II 7,1, etc.), probably a term already used by Hecataeus (see *FGrHist* 1 F 64–71).   *τρίς... ἐγένετο*: the portent happened three times (only twice at VIII 104) in the history of Pedasa. If it took place in the time of Harpagus, we have here a direct connection to the main narrative.

176,1. *ἐς τὸ Ξάνθιον πεδίον*: the main valley of Lycia, crossed by the river Xanthus, where the main Lycian cities are located, including Xanthus (*Arnna* in Lycian and *Wrna* in Aramaic), a city famous for the Letoön (a large sanctuary of

Leto, mother of Apollo and Artemis, about 4 km. south-east of the city), and for many works of art and buildings in the archaic Greek and in the Graeco-Persian style of the classical period (for the archaeological excavations see the periodical series *Fouilles de Xanthos*, ed. P. Demargne, H. Metzger *et al.*, vol. I ff., Paris 1958 ff.; cf. Müller II, pp. 396–406. After the Persian conquest Xanthus became the administrative capital (*byrta*) of the area, with a mixed Lycian and Iranian ruling class only superficially hellenized. Since Harpagus (*Arppakuh* in Lycian: see note on 108,3) is a recurrent name in the ruling dynasties of the 5th cent., one is tempted to infer that the conqueror himself or one of his relatives later settled in Xanthus and began a line of Harpagids. According to a well-known hypothesis, these supposed Harpagids were a source of information to Herodotus on Median history and the Persian conquest of Asia Minor (see Introduction, p. 68). τάς τε γυναῖκας...: Xanthus and Caunus (para. 3) represent the choice of self-destruction for the love of freedom. It is not a typical Lycian characteristic, since Alexander's arrival met with no resistance. Yet they committed suicide again when Brutus besieged them in 42 BC (Appian, *Bell. Civ.* VI 80).

3. ὀγδώκοντα ἱστιέων: these 'families' were probably a pro-Persian faction in exile, repatriated and restored to power by Harpagus (Mazzarino, p. 405), rather than just 'happening' (ἔτυχον) to be abroad for the summer season. For ἱστίη = 'family', cf. VI 86δ; in the sense of 'hearth' (as symbol of the home), cf. IV 68,1–2; V 40,2; for Ἱστίη the goddess of the home: II 50,2; IV 59,1–2; 127,4; on the cult of Hestia among the Scythians see Hartog, pp. 119–25 = ET, pp. 102–9.

177–200. The Babylonian *logos* is divided into three parts: the description of the city of Babylon (178–87), the account of the siege and the Persian conquest (188–91), the geography and ethnography of Babylonia (192–200). The three chapters of the main narrative are inserted between two digressions, closely linked to the subject of the Persian conquest (Cobet, pp. 103–4, 124–7). It is possible that these chapters were part of a larger collection of Assyrian and Babylonian material (note on 184,2). There is no reason to doubt that Herodotus visited the city and the satrapy of Babylon about a century after the Persian conquest of 539 BC. What he saw, or could have seen, was the Babylon of the time of Artaxerxes I Longimanus (465–424 BC). What he gathered from his local informants was data that partly referred to the past, mainly of the reign of Nebuchadnezzar II (605–562 BC) and the early Persian period, and partly to the present. He may have read Greek accounts, e.g. in Hecataeus, which reflected the times of Darius and Xerxes (Herodotus sometimes uses the present tense to describe things that no longer existed in his time). Not all of his informants were competent persons; nevertheless, many of his reports are confirmed by archaeological excavations, cuneiform lists, and topographical descriptions, as well as by other Greek sources. The Babylonian *logos* is therefore a mixture of imaginary data and measurements, misunderstandings, and extraordinarily accurate descriptions. It is, in any case, one of our most important sources for ancient Babylon. The main source of evidence is, of course, the archaeological excavations (1899–1917). See R. Koldewey, *The Excavations at Babylon*, London 1914. On Herodotus and Babylon, see esp.

Ravn; F. Wetzel, *ZAss* XIV (1944), 45–68; W. Baumgartner, *AO* XVIII (1950), 69–106; D. J. Wiseman, *Nebuchadnezzar and Babylon*, Oxford 1985; J. MacGinnis, *BICS* XXXIII (1986), 67–86; R. H. Sack, *Images of Nebuchadnezzar: The Emergence of a Legend*, New York 1991, pp. 72–92. For topographical cuneiform texts, cf. the edition by E. Unger, in F. Wetzel, *Die Stadtmauern von Babylon*, Leipzig 1930; id., *Babylon. Die heilige Stadt*, Berlin–Leipzig 1931; A. George, *Sumer*, XLIV (1986), 7–24; for a new cuneiform text see O. R. Gurney, *Iraq*, XXXVI (1974), 39–52. For the description in Ctesias see J. M. Bigwood, *AJAH* III (1978), 32–52; in Curtius Rufus, L. Prandi, *Fortuna e realtà nell'opera di Clitarco*, Stuttgart 1996, pp. 133–6. For a critical survey of modern research on most problems of the Babylonian *logos* see R. Rolliger, *Herodots Babylonisches Logos*, Innsbruck 1993.

177. κάτω τῆς Ἀσίης ... τὰ δὲ ἄνω αὐτῆς: see note on 72,3.   ἀξιαπηγ-ητότατα: see 16,2 and note. For Herodotus' view of the neo-Babylonian reign as part and continuation of the Assyrian empire cf. note on 95,2.

178, 1. Βαβυλών: *Babilu, Bab-ili,* or *Bab-ilani* ('gate of god' or 'of the gods') in Accadic; *Ká.dingir.(RA)ki* in Sumerian, *Babel* in Hebrew. The ruins are spread over an area of about 850 hectares, 85 km. south of Baghdad, on the river Euphrates. Most of them date to the time of Nebuchadnezzar: what Herodotus saw are apparently the ruins that have survived to the present. On Babylon as part of Assyria cf. notes on 95,1 and 184.

2. μέγαθος ...: these measurements (a circumference of 88–96 km.) are pure fantasy, as are those given by Ctesias and other Greek sources (360–5 *stadia*, a mystic-cosmological figure). Measurements of this sort served to create among the Greeks the notion of a mirage of a gigantic and supernatural oriental city, for which the concept of the *polis* seemed totally inapplicable (see Arist. *Pol.* 1276a28). The partial excavations of the city walls permit the calculation of 7.5 km. for the length of the external walls facing south and east (built by Nabopolassar and Nebuchadnezzar); if we add the wall built by Nabonidus along the east bank of the Euphrates, the perimeter of the triangle would be about 12 km. Inside the external walls was a second wall, almost rectangular, on both sides of the Euphrates, surrounding the residential area, the temples, and the palaces. The circumference of the internal wall is about 8.3 km., and with the addition of the walled stretches on the two river banks, about 11–12 km. altogether. Attempts at reconciling Herodotus' measurements with those of the excavations are unconvincing: it has been argued, for example, that Herodotus quadrupled the length of the circumference because he thought that it was the length of one side only; or that he confused the circumference of the city with that of the entire district. It is, however, possible that Herodotus made a mistake with his units of measurement; cf. Diodorus' account at II 7,4.

3. τάφρος: two long ditches, filled with water from the Euphrates, turned Babylon into a double island. One ditch circled the external walls, the other surrounded the internal ones. The ditches were wide, in places up to 70–100 m., with embankments of baked bricks and quays near the city gates.   μετὰ δὲ τεῖχος ...: Herodotus applies his measurements to the only set of walls he has mentioned: the 'square' one. Their width, 50 royal cubits, about 27 m., does allow for the passage of two quadrigas, even where the curtain walls rise to a turret (see 179,3; cf. Diod. II 7,4). This measurement corresponds to the archaeological findings of double external walls, on top of which ran a road. On the other hand, the height of 200 cubits (110 m.) is pure fantasy. The height given by Strabo XVI 1,5, Curtius Rufus V 1,26, and the writers mentioned by Diodorus at II 7, 4 (50 cubits) is more realistic: 1.5 plethra high (about 45 m.) according to Philostratus, *Vita Apoll.* I 25.

179,1. ὄντινα τρόπον ἔργαστο: the Babylonian technique for baking bricks was well known in the East (see e.g. Gen. 11: 3) and in Greece (e.g. Aristophanes, *Av.* 552). Herodotus' description is accurate. The backing of reeds was meant to prevent disintegration in case of floods; it seems that as a rule one mat of reeds was tucked into every 8–10 rows of bricks. The hypothesis that lines 1124 ff. of Aristophanes' *Birds* presuppose knowledge of this passage by the poet or his Athenian public rests upon a very fragile basis; see the Introduction, p. 51.

3. ἐπάνω δὲ τοῦ τείχεος: Herodotus' description of these parapets (cf. 164,1), called προμαχεῶνες at III 151,1, situated on the front of the city walls, cannot be confirmed archaeologically because nothing remains from the upper section of the walls. It seems that Herodotus knew that the walls were double. In fact, towers protruded only from the external wall.   **πύλαι ... ἑκατόν**: 'hundred gates' is a Homeric reminiscence (*Il.* X 383). The excavations have not revealed any gates in the external walls; but according to cuneiform tablets there were at least eight gates made of cedar with bronze frames, of palm wood covered with asphalt according to Xenophon, *Cyr.* VII 5,22. Some gates have been identified in the so-called 'wall of Nabonidus' (cf. 180,4). The five gates mentioned by Herodotus elsewhere (III 155,5–6) must have belonged to the internal rectangular walls.

4. Ἴς: *Id, Idu* in Sumerian, *Hit* in Arabic, and *ittû* in Akkadian, meaning raw bitumen. The site is on the Euphrates, about 180 km. due north-west of Babylon; the road along the tortuous course of the river is much longer, but eight days' journey seems excessive. For the extraction of asphalt, cf. VI 119,2–3.

180,1. Εὐφρήτης: cf. 179,4; one of the major rivers of the Middle East. 'Mesopotamia' is the land 'between the rivers' Euphrates and Tigris; see Müller II, pp. 112–17, 225–33. The two rivers were connected by a system of canals (see 185,2–6 and notes).   **ἐξ Ἀρμενίων**: cf. on the sources of the Halys at 72,2.   **Ἐρυθρὴν θάλασσαν**: the Persian Gulf is part of the 'Red Sea' of the Greeks (see note on 1,1).

2. τὸ ὦν δὴ τεῖχος ἑκάτερον: Herodotus probably intends to say that the north and south walls of the 'square' city reached the banks of the Euphrates, and there formed a right angle with the two dry-stone walls (αἱμασιή; cf. 185,5). This almost rectangular wall is better known: it consisted of two series of walls, an external one (*Nemetti-Enlil*), 3.70 m. wide and an internal one (*Igmur-Enlil*), 6.50 m. wide, both of air-dried bricks and separated by a road. Towers and bastions protruded from both walls. The Babylonian names of some of the gates are known, and it is

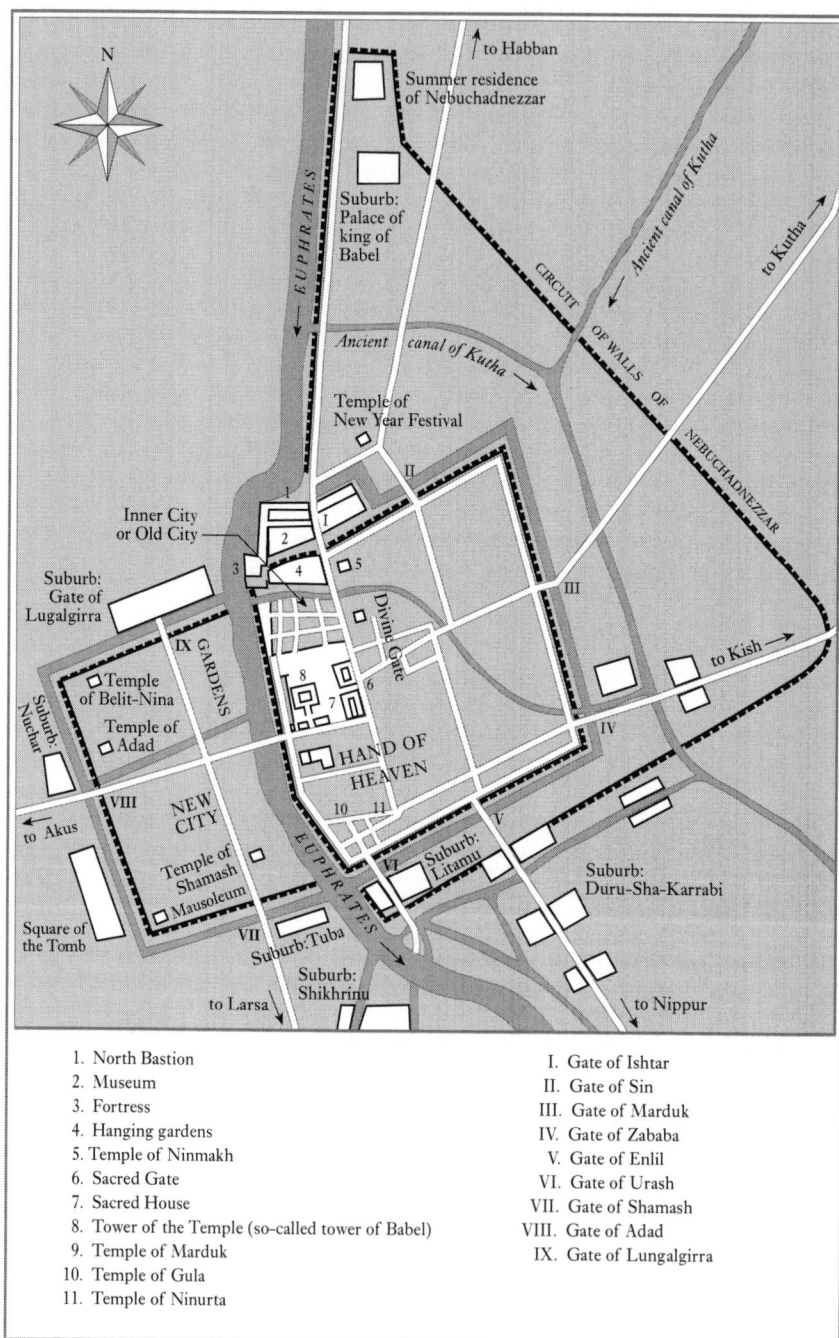

1. North Bastion
2. Museum
3. Fortress
4. Hanging gardens
5. Temple of Ninmakh
6. Sacred Gate
7. Sacred House
8. Tower of the Temple (so-called tower of Babel)
9. Temple of Marduk
10. Temple of Gula
11. Temple of Ninurta

I. Gate of Ishtar
II. Gate of Sin
III. Gate of Marduk
IV. Gate of Zababa
V. Gate of Enlil
VI. Gate of Urash
VII. Gate of Shamash
VIII. Gate of Adad
IX. Gate of Lungalgirra

Map 18. Babylon

possible to match them with those found in Herodotus (III 155,5–6): the most famous and most monumental gate is the 'gate of Ištar' (of Semiramis?), facing north. The 'wall of Nabonidus' on the east bank is 7.60 m. wide; on the west bank a dry-stone wall about 1,700 m. long connected the ends of the two internal walls. Cf. 186,2.

3. οἰκιέων τριορόφων καὶ τετρορόφων: houses with three or four roofs, not 'storeys', built on superimposed terraces; see Ravn, pp. 79 f.   **τὰς ὁδοὺς ἰθείας:** Herodotus schematically 'Hippodamizes' the urban plan of his square Babylon. A plan almost at right angles did in fact exist in the quarter called Merkes ('the centre'), east and north-east of *Etemenanki* (cf. note on 181,5).

181,1. τοῦτο μὲν δὴ τὸ τεῖχος: not an apt description of the wall last mentioned, which can hardly be called the armour of Babylon; nor is this definition suitable for the external wall of the rectangular fortification which, contrary to what our passage says, is narrower than the internal wall.

2. ἐν δὲ φάρσεϊ ἑκατέρῳ: this plainly contradicts the topography of the city in the neo-Babylonian period, as well as the archaeological excavations: all the monumental buildings were on the east bank of the river. In order to save Herodotus' credibility, a hypothesis was formed that the course of the Euphrates was altered in the early Achaemenid age, and made to flow west of the temple and east of the palace; see Ravn, pp. 61–6.   **τὰ βασιλήια:** the system of palaces and fortresses in the so-called Qasr, the north-west corner of the city, was extended beyond the city walls by Nebuchadnezzar.   **Διὸς Βήλου ἱρὸν:** Belu in Accadian and *Bel* (*Ba'al*) in the Old Testament, is the 'Lord' of Babylon, i.e. Marduk. The area sacred to Marduk, containing the 'high temple' on the tower described here, and the 'low temple' (cf. 183,1), was a square area with sides of 400 m. (tallying perfectly with Herodotus' 2 stadia). Herodotus describes here the *ziqqurat* (note on 98,3) of Babylon, called *Etemenanki* ('the foundation of heaven and earth'), of which the base still remains in the area called *Sachn*: it is an enormous square of 91 m. (about half a stadium) per side, i.e. half the length given by Herodotus. The 'Smith tablet' found in the 'low temple' contains the measurements of the *Etemenanki*: it had seven storeys (not eight) of various heights, totalling about 90 m., with the temple on the seventh storey. The problem of the stairs is debated and has inspired numerous modern attempts at reconstruction. The inscriptions of Nabopolassar and Nebuchadnezzar claim that the *Etemenanki* 'reaches the sky'. Cf. the 'tower of Babel' in Gen. 11: 4. In the Babylonian Talmud the tower of Babel is identified with the *ziqqurat* of Borsippa (*Sanhedrin* 109a), not of Babylon. The *Etemenanki* existed in Herodotus' day: he describes it with admiration and with his usual blend of precise detail and wrong measurements. For another description see Strabo XVI 1,5. Apart from the bibl. quoted *ad* 177–200, see F. Wetzel and F. H. Weissbach, *Das Hauptheiligtum des Marduk in Babylon, Esagila und Etemenanki*, Leipzig 1893 (repr. Osnabrück 1967); A. Parrot, *Ziggurats et Tour de Babel*, Paris 1949; E. Klengel-Brandt, *Der Turm von Babylon. Legende und Geschichte eines Bauwerkes*, Berlin–Leipzig 1992. For an English translation of the 'Smith tablet' see R. Koldewey, *The Excavations at Babylon*, London 1914, pp. 192 f.

5. *νηὸς ἔπεστι μέγας*: according to the Smith tablet, it seems that this 'large' high temple on top of the *Etemenanki* was 21–2 m. wide, 24 m. long, and 15 m. high (but the interpretation of the text is debated). In it there were three chambers sacred to Marduk, one of them with a large bed and a throne; there is no mention of statues. Herodotus' description corresponds on the whole to that of the tablet.   *Χαλδαῖοι*: in Herodotus they are a tribe or an order of priests. Herodotus knew of a 'Chaldaean gate' at Babylon (III 155,5), and of Chaldaeans in Xerxes' army (VII 63). Originally they were the Aramaic inhabitants of Kaldu, in southern Babylonia, usually identified with the Biblical *Ksdym*. From the ethnic 'Chaldaean', often synonymous with 'Babylonian', the name came to designate a priestly order that in addition to the cult of Marduk cultivated various sciences, e.g. astrology (II 109,3), magic, genethliacology (and even historiography: Berossus was a Chaldaean and a priest of Belos). But 'Chaldaean' too, just like 'Magus', became synonymous with visionary and charlatan. See D. O. Edzard, *RLA* V (1980), coll. 291–7; A. Kuhrt, op. cit. in note on 74,3.

182,1. *τὸν θεὸν αὐτὸν*: Herodotus may have misunderstood an allusion to the myth of the 'sacred wedding' between Marduk and Ṣarpanitu, which was ritually enacted at the New Year festival; cf. 183,2. But see P. Panitschek, in H. D. Galter (ed.), *Kulturkontakte und ihre Bedeutung in Geschichte und Gegenwart des Orients*, Graz 1986, pp. 43–50.   *ἐν Θήβῃσι τῇσι Αἰγυπτίῃσι*: the high priestess of Ammon (Zeus), who was considered also the wife of the god, ruled at Thebes (Karnak) for almost two centuries. For the sacred women at the temple of Thebes, cf. II 54,1; 56,1. Various similarities between Egyptian Thebes and Babylon were found in antiquity: enormous buildings, 'one hundred gates' (cf. 179,3), fabulous treasures, astronomers; both were plundered by the Persians, etc.

2. *ἐν Πατάροισι*: Pttara in Lycian, south of Xanthus (today at Kelemis) (see Müller II, pp. 356–62), with the famous oracle of Apollo, active in the winter months (when the oracle of Delos was closed).

183,1. *ἔστι δὲ τοῦ ἐν Βαβυλῶνι ἱροῦ ...*: this 'low' temple is supposed to be the Esagila on the Tell Amran, south of the *Etemenanki*, in the quarter *Eridu* (cf. O. R. Gurney, *Iraq*, XXXVI (1974), 39–52). The main palace was almost square (78 × 86 m.), with a rectangular area to the east. Babylonian inscriptions praise the marvels of this temple; Herodotus' description does not correspond in detail, but conveys the same impression.

2. *λιβανωτοῦ*: see note on III 107,1.   *ἔτεος ἑκάστου*: this may be an allusion to the New Year festivities (*akitu*, *zagmukku*) which took place in Mesopotamian cities between the 1st and the 11th of the month of Nisan (March/April), with sacrifices, processions, and liturgical recitations. At Babylon the divine power of the king, whose presence was required during the festivities, was also ritually renewed every year. See *Testi sumerici e accadici*, ed. G. R. Castellano, Turin 1977, pp. 735–43; and Frankfort, *Kingship*, pp. 313–33.   *ἔτι τὸν χρόνον ἐκεῖνον*: in the time of Cyrus. It is probably the statue of Bel-Marduk, a symbol of the Babylonian kingdom and of its independence (the statue is briefly described in the preceding paragraph: Herodotus must have confused two different statues).

The cult of Marduk was not disturbed by the Persian conquest. For propaganda purposes Cyrus even presented himself as 'chosen by Marduk' and as the 'restorer of the *Esagila* and the *Ezida*'. In the first months of 538 BC Cyrus restored to Marduk the privileged position he had enjoyed before Nabonidus' religious reforms. For Darius in Babylon see III 151–9; on his father Hystaspes see note on 209,2. Less pious than Cyrus the 'Father', Darius the 'Shopkeeper' desecrated Nitocris' tomb (187,1). Finally, Xerxes the *hybristes* stole a statue, or so at least a hostile local tradition said. Sometime during Xerxes' reign the title 'king of Babylon' held by the Achaemenids was abolished. Herodotus does not mention a Babylonian revolt under Xerxes (perhaps he dated it after 478 BC?). Ctesias mentions one (*FGrHist* 688 F 13 (25)), and dates it earlier than 480. On the politics of Cyrus in Babylon (and the coronation of Cambyses as 'king of Babylon' at the Esagila New Year festival) see A. L. Oppenheim, *CHI*, p. 545 ff., 554 ff.; on Xerxes in Babylonia see A. T. L. Kuhrt, *PCPhS* XXXIV (1988), 60–76; M. A. Dandamaev, *Bull. of the Asia Institute*, VII (1993), 41–7; for bibl. on the revolt against Xerxes see R. Drews, *AJPh* XCI (1970), 182, n. 5.

184. πολλοί...: 'There were many kings of this city of Babylon, of whom I shall make mention in my Assyrian account, who further adorned the fortifications and the temples; and among the sovereigns there were two women' (David Grene's translation, Chicago–London 1987, p. 116). Otherwise, taking τῶν as partitive genitive, the sense might be that Herodotus is going to mention here— i.e. in these 'Assyrian' chapters—only those kings who adorned, etc. (as he did in the case of Egypt). The interpretation of this sentence is directly related to the problem of the 'Assyrian *logoi*', which has been discussed for over a century, initially in order to resolve more general issues, such as the various stages in the composition of Herodotus' work and its ultimate incompleteness: see Introduction, pp. 20 f. Three facts seem to be beyond doubt: (1) Herodotus collected Assyrian material that does not appear in our *Histories*, such as the list of kings promised here and the account of the conquest of Niniveh promised at 106,2; (2) he was informed enough about Assyria to write a monograph that could contain, for example, data on topography, cities, climate, local products, customs; he had information about a number of kings, about the fall of Niniveh, and the transfer of the capital to Babylon; he also had his own opinions about chronology (95,2); (3) for Herodotus, Babylon was geographically and historically part of Assyria: he did not distinguish, as we do today, between the Assyrian period and the neo-Babylonian one (cf. I 106,2; 178,1; 188,1; 192,1–2; 193,1–2; 199,3; III 92,1; 155,2; IV 39,1; see also note on I 95). From these data, it is legitimate to conclude that Herodotus collected material for 'Assyrian *logoi*'; that a part was used for drafting chs. 177–200 in our book, another part sporadically for other passages of the work that we possess; and that the rest of the material does not survive, for reasons that perhaps it is useless to search after. It is possible that some writings about Assyria circulated in antiquity under the name of Herodotus, but their presumed traces are rather questionable. Bibl.: Focke, pp. 14 ff.; Powell, *History*, pp. 18–23; Maddalena, pp. 17–35; G. Huxley, *GRBS* V (1965), 207–12; R. Drews,

AJPh XCI (1970), 181–91; J. G. Macqueen, *CQ* XXXVIII (1978), 284–91; Erbse, pp. 162–9; S. Zawadzki, *Eos*, VII (1984), 253–67 (who considers the 'promises' made at 106,2 and in this passage to be marginal notes of the author); S. Douglas Olson, *Historia*, XXXVI (1987), 495–6.   Σεμίραμις: Herodotus' Semiramis lived 'five generations' before Nitocris, the mother of Labynetus (188,1). Five is a typical number, not a historical one; in any case, Herodotus placed her *c.*800 BC, in the time of Sammu-ramat, the wife of Šamši-Adad V (824–810 BC), who was Assyrian and possibly a regent during the childhood of her son Adad-Neraris III (810–782). She was an important figure, known from a number of inscriptions. It cannot be excluded that some military campaigns and hydraulic works were attributed to Sammu-ramat. Herodotus is rather cautious in regard to Semiramis (he admires Nitocris more). The origin of the Greek legend about Semiramis, later transmitted to European culture and art, is to be found in Ctesias. See W. Eilers, *SAWW*, CCLXXIV 2, (1971); W. Nagel, *Ninus und Semiramis in Sage und Geschichte*, Berlin 1982. On the problem of Sammu-ramat's regency see W. Schramm, *Historia*, XXI (1972), 513–21; for Assyrian-Babylonian queens see H.-J. Seux, *RLA* VI 1983, coll. 161–2. On monuments in Herodotus see note on 14,1.   ἀξιοθέητα: cf. 14,3.

185–7. These three chapters on Nitocris connect the Babylonian digression to the main narrative on the Persian conquest, perhaps because the conquest took place during the reign of Nitocris' son (188,1), or because certain actions attributed to Nitocris were seen by Herodotus as defensive preparations in face of the Medo-Persian danger (see Cobet, pp. 125 ff). No queen or wife of an Assyro-Babylonian king with this or a similar name appears in oriental texts. The mother of Nabonidus, the last Neobabylonian king (see 74,3 and note), is very well known from her inscriptions and those of her son, but her name is Adadguppi: she died in 546 BC, when she was more than 100 years old; see Nabonidus Chronicle, *ANET*, p. 306 = *Chroniques mésopotamiennes*, ed. J.-J. Glassner, Paris 1993, p. 203. She was a woman of great influence at court, nor can it be excluded that some buildings in the age of Nebuchadnezzar and Nabonidus became associated with her name in Babylonian popular memory. The hypothesis that Adad-guppi was the historical person on whom the figure of Nitocris is based (put forward by W. Röllig, in *Festschrift F. Altheim*, Berlin 1969, I, pp. 127–35) is plausible, but it does not explain the origin of the name Nitocris (possibly it arose from a confusion with the Egyptian queen Nitocris at II 100,2, rather than with the name of Nebuchadnezzar or of Naqî-a-Zakutun, the wife of Sennacherib). See E. Dhorme, *RA* XLI (1947), 1–21; Beaulieu, pp. 67–79, 197–8.

185,1. τὴν Μήδων ὁρῶσα…: Herodotus may have attributed to Nitocris hydraulic and defensive works of Nebuchadnezzar; including anecdotes, measurements, and explanations collected on the spot and interpreted in his own way. From Nebuchadnezzar's inscriptions an image emerges of an enormous water reservoir (its circumference, about 200 km., must be an exaggeration) situated in a square area of which the angles were Babylon, Kiš, Opis, and Sippar, made of baked bricks with dams and walls, intended to water the fields in peace time and to flood the area in the case of an enemy invasion from the north or north-east. See Ravn, pp. 38–42, with bibl.

2. Ἀρδέρικκα: an unknown place (not to be confused with the Ardericca in Cissia mentioned at VI 119,2). The typical number three recurs three times in this passage, illustrating the symbolic value of Herodotean triads; but see the graphic reconstruction of How–Wells ad loc.

4. ἔλυτρον λίμνῃ: cf. 186,1. The circumference given by Herodotus of c.45 km. is much smaller than that mentioned in the Nebuchadnezzar inscription (cf. note on para. 1), which corresponds to Ctesias' measurement (1,200 stadii: *FGrHist* 688 F 1,9 [1]), and to that given by Abydenus (40 parasangs: ibid. 685 F 6). Abydenus attributes the lake to Nebuchadnezzar and places it near Sippar; see ibid. 685 F 6 (7). To such works are to be related also the so-called 'Median wall' (Xen., *Anab.* I 7,15; II 4,12; for archaeological evidence see H. Gasche *et al.*, in *Northern Akkad Project Report* I (1987), and II (1989), 23–70; and in P. Briant (ed.), *Dans le pas des Dix Milles* (*Pallas* 43), Toulouse 1995, pp. 201–16), the *nahar-malka* (see note on 193,2), and the 'wall of Semiramis' between the Tigris and Euphrates near Opis (Eratosthenes, quoted by Strabo II 1,26); all these works are ascribed today to Nebuchadnezzar. For ἔλυτρον, cf. I 186,1 and IV 173.   παρατείνουσα: 'extending it'; L. Weber reads παρακλίνουσα, 'diverting it' and linking the lake to the river through a canal: *PhW* LXI (1941), coll. 236 f.

5. κρηπῖδα: probably a high embankment or a pier for containing the waters; cf. II 170,2.

6. τὸ ὄρυγμα πᾶν ἕλος: this must mean that, in the event of an enemy invasion, the lake could flood the entire region (Herodotus seems not to have understood the function of the lake).

186,1. παρενθήκην: here an 'additional' or 'accessory construction'; for the meaning of 'excursus' *et sim.*, see VI 19,1; VII 5,3; 171,1. For the topography of Babylon see note on 178,2 and bibl. in note on 177–200.

2. γέφυραν: the archaeological finds confirm that the bridge rested on eight pylons, with bases of baked bricks. There are no traces of metal bindings. The bridge was large, at least 5–6 m. wide and 115 m. long; it continued the road between the *Esagila* and the *Etemenanki*. Herodotus does not describe the technique of disassembly, though it must have been done regularly to allow the passage of ships, as well as for reasons of security. For a description of the same bridge, accurate in part, see Diod. II 8,2–4.

187,1. ἀπάτην τοιήνδε: a typically Greek anecdote of 'deceit' hostile to Darius, a notoriously greedy king (see III 89,3 and note). Nitocris' deceit consists first in tempting the visitor to desecrate her tomb and then reproaching his greed. The story is fictitious; cf. the similar anecdote of Xerxes at the 'tomb of Belos' (Aelian, *Var. Hist.* XIII 3). Herodotus, however, was mainly interested in the queen's shrewdness. Mesopotamian tombs are underground, though the idea of a 'tomb in the air' would not be alien to Achaemenid funerary customs. There are no tombs near the gates of Babylon, nor was the historical mother of Nabonidus buried in Babylon (see note on 185–7). See J. Dillery, *CPh* LXXXVII (1992), 30–8; A. Tourraix, *DHA* XXII 2 (1996), 109–25. On Herodotus' women see note on 1–5. λεωφόρων: Röllig's criticism of certain incredible translations of this adjective (op. cit. I, p. 132, n. 17) is obvious, but nevertheless needed. The 'most frequented' gate of Babylon is the Ištar gate (see note on 180,2).

2. τῶν τις ἐμεῦ: such formulae were actually used at the beginning of Babylonian funerary inscriptions. For Herodotus and inscriptions see note on 51,4.   οὐ γὰρ ἄμεινον: cf. Ael. *Var. Hist.* XIII 3. The same expression is put by Herodotus twice in Darius' mouth (III 71,1–2, and note; 82,5). It recalls Hesiod's μηδ᾽ ἐπ᾽ ἀκινήτοισι καθίζειν, οὐ γὰρ ἄμεινον (*Op.* 750), probably referring to 'undisturbed tombs' (cf. para. 3, τάφος ... ἀκίνητος); see also Homer, *Il.* XXIV 52. λώϊον καὶ ἄμεινον, 'better and finer', is also an oracular formula (see e.g. Parke, *Oracles of Zeus*, p. 261, n. 5, etc).

4. ὅτι ὑπὲρ κεφαλῆς ...: this is Herodotus' explanation. The scruple of avoiding walking under a corpse is matched by the unscrupulous opening of the tomb, a manifest inconsistency from any point of view, including Zoroastrian doctrine (see note on 140,1).

188–91. These chapters are devoted to the Persian conquest of Babylon (autumn 539), which ended the neo-Babylonian dynasty founded in 625 BC by Nabopolassar, one of the most significant eras in the history of the ancient Near East. In Herodotus, however, the history of this memorable event is reduced to a string of anecdotal descriptions and selected episodes: Persian logistics (188), the incident of the white horses and the canalization of the river Gyndes (189), the battle outside the city (190), the draining of the Euphrates, and the surprise entrance into Babylon (191). The Nabonidus chronicle and other cuneiform texts allow the arranging of the main events in precise chronological order. Cyrus first attacked Opis on the river Tigris, then, on the 14th of the month of Tašritu (Sept./Oct.), Sippar opened its gates and Nabonidus escaped to Babylon. Two days later, Ugbaru (or Gubaru, Gobryas), general of Cyrus and governor of Ḳutu (Gutium, across the Tigris, north of Opis), captured Babylon without striking a blow; the cult at the *Esagila* continued undisturbed and Nabonidus was taken prisoner. On the 3rd of the month of Araḫsammu (Oct./Nov.), Cyrus triumphantly entered Babylon and Ugbaru, who had become satrap of the new province, nominated the subordinate governors; on the 11th of the same month, Belšazzar (Bel-sar-u ṣur) the son, co-ruler of Nabonidus, and regent of Babylon, was executed. The statues of gods that Nabonidus had transported to Babylon were returned to their original cities (see P.-A. Beaulieu, *JNES* LII (1993), 241–61), and commercial documents soon began to be dated to the first year of Cyrus' reign. Among post-Herodotean Greek sources see Xen., *Cyr.* VII 5,1–36 and Berossus, *FGrHist* 680 F 9a (151–3). Greek and Babylonian sources agree on two important events: the battle outside the city and the almost peaceful capture of Babylon. But Herodotus, or his informants, may have confused or identified Belšazzar with

Nabonidus, as others also did (see Josephus, *AI* X 231 on 'Baltasares, called Nabuandelos by the Babylonians'; Georgios Syncellus identifies Belšazzar with Neriglissar: pp. 275–6 Moss-Lammer). Xenophon has a story (taken seriously by some scholars) about Gobryas' defection to Cyrus (*Cyr.* IV 6,1 ff.). For bibl. see M. A. Dandamaev, *CHJ* I (1984), 326–34; M. Mallowan, *CHI*, pp. 408 ff.; A. L. Oppenheim, pp. 529 ff.; A. Kuhrt, in D. Cannadine and S. Price (eds.), *Rituals of Royalty: Power and Ceremonial in Traditional Societies*, Cambridge 1987, pp. 20–55; K. Głombiowski, *Das Altertum*, XXXVI (1990), 49–55. For a collection of cuneiform texts see *ANET*, esp. pp. 306–7 = *Chroniques mésopotamiennes* (ed. J.-J. Glassner), Paris 1993, pp. 203–4; for the Cyrus cylinder see W. Eilers, *AI* II (1974), 25–34 (with a French translation); and P. R. Berger, *ZAss* LXIV (1975), 192–234 (with a German translation); for Cyrus' decree concerning the temple of Jerusalem (Ezra 1: 2–4) see E. J. Bickermann, *JBL* LXV (1946), 249–75; for the 'Dynastic Prophecy' see G. F. Hasel, *Journal for the Study of the Old Testament*, XII (1979), 17–30. On the reign of Nabonidus see note on 74,3 with bibl.

188,1. Λαβυνήτου: cf. note on 74,3.   στρατεύεται... ποταμοῦ: a brief parenthetic digression of Persian ethnography. The Great King, who was also invested with priestly rank, apparently had to observe some particular taboos or dietary rules. Xerxes allegedly established the rule that the Persian king should not eat or drink foreign food; Dinon, *FGrHist* 690 F 12. Agathocles of Cyzicus (ibid. 473 F3) speaks of 'golden water' that only the king and the king's firstborn son could drink. Water, as well as fire, is a sacred element also in the Avesta; see Y. Béquignon, *REA* XLII (1940), 20–4; and esp. P. Briant, in L. Milano (ed.), *Drinking in Ancient Societies: History and Culture of Drinks in the Ancient Near East*, Padua 1994, pp. 45–65. On the cult of water and rivers in Persian religion see 131,2 and 138,2. For the river Choaspes, cf. V 49,7; 52,6; and Strabo XV 3,4; the epichoric name Ulai (Dan. 8: 2) left a trace in the Greek form Εὔλαιος (modern Karkheh and Kârûn). For pack-animals and provisions, cf. VII 187. On Susa see note on III 91,4. The motif of water pervades the history of the conquest of Babylon (and that of Veii); see D. Briquel, *BAGB* (1981), 293–306.

189,1. ἐπὶ Γύνδη ποταμῷ: cf. V 52,6. Herodotus assumes that, starting from Susa, Cyrus reaches the river Gyndes (modern Diyala), which flows into the Tigris about 20 km. south of Opis. On the Matieni see note on 72,2; the Dardani are unknown. Opis was a very ancient commercial settlement on the west bank of the Tigris, where the river is linked to the Euphrates by several canals (among which the *nahar malka*: see note on 193,2); see Eratosthenes, quoted by Strabo II 1,26, etc.). Opis was the scene of a famous mutiny against Alexander in 324 BC (Arr., *Anab.* VII 7,8 ff., etc.).   ἱρῶν ἵππων τῶν λευκῶν: the horse was sacred to Ahura Mazda and Mithras. For a tribute of white horses in Herodotus see III 90,3; cf. Strabo XI 13,7. For sacred horses in Herod. see VII 40,2–3; cf. III 106,2 and IX 20. At VII 40,4 the chariot of Persian 'Zeus' was drawn by white horses; cf. VII 55,3; VIII 115,4; and Xen. *Cyr.* VIII 3,12. For a sacrifice of white horses to the river Strymon see VII 113,2. On the famous 'Nisaean horses' see III 106,2 and note.

3. ὀγδώκοντα καὶ ἑκατόν: 360 (see 190,1), as the total number of days in the twelve months of the Egyptian solar year (not including the five supplementary days) became a symbolic or cosmic number; cf. Fehling, p. 232. This should not in itself cast doubts on the report that Cyrus caused the flooded area between the Tigris and the Euphrates to be drained; see G. G. Cameron, *IA* I (1974), 46–8. At para. 4, and again at 190,2, Herodotus seems to dislike the canalization, apparently seen as an act of *hybris* against nature and against the river's sacred water. Cf. note on 75,4.

190,1. τὸ δεύτερον ἔαρ ὑπέλαμπε: no precise chronological value should be attached to this joyful expression: Babylon was captured in autumn.   ἑσσωθέντες τῇ μάχῃ: see note on 188–91.

2. παντὶ ἔθνεϊ ὁμοίως ἐπιχειρέοντα: a harsh criticism of Persian aggressive expansionism is implied in these words.   ἐτέων κάρτα πολλῶν: since Media was the first victim, the 'very many years' cover roughly the decade 550–540 BC. First Belšazzar, and then Nabonidus (upon his return from Teima, *c*.543), would be in charge of the preparations. See notes on 74,3 and 188–91.

191,1. ἄλλος: a 'wise counsellor'?; cf. note on 27,2.

3. ἐπὶ τὴν λίμνην: the narration of this anecdote is topographically accurate, but its main purpose is didactic, to illustrate the futility of human projects. The lake excavated with such skill by Nitocris for the defence of Babylon (185,4–7) eventually helped the enemy to conquer the city.

6. ὑπὸ δὲ μεγάθεος τῆς πόλιος: cf. Arist. *Pol.* 1276a28; for a somewhat similar account of the conquest of Megalopolis by Cleomenes in 223/2 see Plut. *Cleom.* 23,4.   ὁρτήν: cf. Xen. *Cyr.* VII 5,15 and the story of Balthassar's famous feast (Dan. 8). According to some scholars, the capture of Babylon coincided with the *Harran akitu* festival (see note on 183,2), celebrated in the capital by the supporters of Nabonidus (Beaulieu, p. 226).   πρῶτον: the first conquest prepares the reader for the account of the second one (under Darius: III 159,1); cf. note on 92. Herodotus does not tell us anything about the fate of Nabonidus. According to Berossus (*FGrHist* 680 F9a), he was exiled to Carmania; Xenophon, *Cyr.* VII 5,29–30, relates how the last Babylonian king was killed in the palace by Gobryas.

192–200. The ethnography of Babylonia, consisting of a collection of *mirabilia* and various curious, and sometimes spicy, stories. Perhaps part of the material had been collected for the Assyrian *logoi* (see note on 184,2). Sometimes Herodotus compares the past to the present (e.g. at 196,5); hence the frequent use of the imperfect tense (which need not necessarily point to the use of written sources). The vast ethnographic information allows Herodotus to make some comparisons (193,1–2; 196,1; 198; 199,5; cf. above 182,1–2). He takes a moral stance only over sacred prostitution (199,1). On Babylonian customs cf. Strabo XVI 1,20. See on this group of chapters S. Muñiz Rodríguez, *Gallaecia*, XIII (1992), 351–67.

192,1. πάρεξ τοῦ φόρου: the ninth satrapy ('Babylon and the rest of Assyria') paid an annual tribute of 1,000 Babylonian silver talents (about 30 tons), and of 500 castrated boys (III 92,1 and note), as well as the other services mentioned here. In Herodotus' time the value of Babylon was no longer that of 'one-third of Asia': perhaps there is a confusion with an earlier time, when the provinces of Babylon and ʿAbar-nahara (Syria, Phoenicia, and Palestine) were ruled by a single satrap whose residence was in Babylon. See note on III 91,1.

2. σατραπηίην: cf. III 89,1; the usual Herodotean term for a satrapy is νομός (for satrap, ὕπαρχος, or ἄρχων, as in para. 4) in Old Persian term is khšaθrapavan, in Aramaic ḥaštarpna. The Greek form σατράπης is not attested before Xenophon. Τριτανταίχμη: probably Ciçataxma in Old Persian (see O. K. Armayor, *AncW* I (1978), 151); but the rebel Ciçataxma of 522/1 BC was a Sagartian (*DB* II, l. 79 Kent). Tritantaichmes was probably the satrap of Babylon in Herodotus' day. His father Artabazus is perhaps the general who participated in the campaigns in Greece of 489–479 BC. For another Tritantaichmes, possibly of the same family see VII 82; 121,3; VIII 26,2. On Babylon under the Persians see A. L. Oppenheim, *CHI*, pp. 529–87; Briant, *Histoire*, Index.

3. (ἡ δὲ ἀρτάβη ... Ἀττικῆσι): 1 medimnus is equivalent to about 50 litres, a choenix to about 1 litre.

4. τέσσερες τῶν ἐν τῷ πεδίῳ κῶμαι: for this kind of regional tribute or service in the Persian empire see note on III 91,2.

193,1. κηλωνηίοισι: probably big wheels, or wheel rims with buckets to channel water from the river to the canals used for field irrigation.

2. ἡ μεγίστη: the *nahar-malka* ('the king's river') canal had been repaired by Nebuchadnezzar: it connected the Tigris and the Euphrates between Opis and Sippar, where the distance is minimal (about 30 km. apart). The water flowed southeastwards from the Euphrates into the Tigris (πρὸς ἥλιον ... τὸν χειμερινόν). Cf. note on 189,1.   ἀρίστη...: a list of marvels begins, recalling popular descriptions of Earthly Paradise and the Land of Plenty; cf. note on III 26,1. Herodotus here seems afraid of compromising his own credibility (para. 4), see Drexler, pp. 62 ff. But the extreme fertility of the irrigated area is an ascertained fact. The 'fruit of Demeter' is of course corn. IV 198,2 refers back to this passage. It is, however, incorrect to say that the Babylonians had no knowledge of fig trees, vines, or olive trees. On Babylonian agriculture see K. Butz, *RLA* VI 1983, coll. 470–86; for food and cooking see J. Bottéro, ibid., coll. 277–98.

5. συκέων τρόπον: Herodotus describes accurately the technique of caprification, well-known to the Greeks: it involved tying the inflorescence (syconia) of the male fig (ὄλονθος), where gall-flies nest, to branches of female fig-trees, in order to facilitate pollination (cf. Arist. *Hist. An.* 557b25). Having learned in the East that date palms too are 'male' and 'female', Herodotus automatically assumed that the same technique was also applicable to palms. However, the pollination of palms does not depend on gall-flies or other insects: the pollen of the 'male' tree is carried by the wind or human agency to the flower, not the fruit, of the 'female' one. See L. Georgi, *CPh* LXXVII (1982), 224–8, with bibl.

194,1. θῶμα: Herodotus admires the ingenuity of the technique described here. Round boats with two pairs of rowers feature on Assyrian bas-reliefs; one type of round boat, the *gúfah*, is still in use today on the Euphrates. They could not possibly have carried a load of 5,000 talents (about 150 tons).

2. βίκους: cf. Xen. *Anab.* I 9,25 (βίκους οἴνου). It may be a Semitic loan-word (*bq* = 'potsherd' in Royal Aramaic; cf. *bqbwq* in Hebrew, translated as βίκον by LXX).

195,1. ἐσθῆτι: the wool industry is very old in Mesopotamia. No mantles, however, are depicted in art. Cuneiform texts confirm the existence of the ointment industry, and the use of staffs and emblems (used to seal letters and documents). See W. Reimpell, *Geschichte der babylonische und assyrische Kleidung*, Berlin 1921; E. Strommenger, *RLA* VI (1983), coll. 18–38; H. Waetzold and R. M. Boehmer, ibid., coll. 197–210; A. R. Millard, ibid., coll. 135–40.   ἐμβάσι: open slippers. In Greece they were usually worn by old or poor people.   μίτρῃσι: cf. VII 90; common turbans, to be distinguished from the Persian tiara (see 132,1 and note).

196,1. ὁ μὲν σοφώτατος: Herodotus judges foreign customs according to a moral scale. We start with the 'most wise'; for the 'next one in wisdom' see 197,1; and for the 'most shameful' see 199,1. The custom here described is 'most wise' because of the principle of social justice it expresses; cf. the utopian redistribution of dowries proposed by Phaleas of Chalcedon (Arist. *Pol.* 1266b3). No Babylonian evidence exists for such a custom, and the entire description gives the impression of a utopian, half-comic Greek fantasy. See Mora, pp. 240–2; R. A. McNeal, *Historia*, XXVII (1988), 54–71.   πυνθάνομαι...: an implied reservation towards the trustworthiness of the report. Herodotus thought that the Eneti (or Veneti) were of Illyrian origin (perhaps to distinguish them from the Homeric Eneti from Paphlagonia). In any case, he located them vaguely on the Adriatic coast (cf. V 9,2). But whether he is alluding here to an Illyrian tribe is a matter of dispute; see H. Krahe, *RhM* LXXXVIII (1939), 97–101. For ancient theories on the origins of the Veneti, see L. Braccesi, *La leggenda di Antenore*, Venice 1997[2].

3. ἀμορφεστάτην: instead of ἀμορφοτάτην (influenced by the preceding εὐειδεστάτας: see E. Schwyzer, *PhW* XLII (1922), coll. 527 ff.).

5. ἵνα...ἄγωνται: some scholars think that the sentence contains a lacuna, others delete it altogether, or place it elsewhere. The sense is that prostitution (whether alleged or practised for securing a dowry; cf. the Lydian custom at 93,4) protects the girls from the violation of guarantees. The biblical stories about girls taken to the king's harem are well known (1 Kings 1: 2–3; Esther 2: 2–8). On the economic situation of Babylon under the Persians see M. A. Dandamaev, in *Ancient Mesopotamia*, Moscow 1969, pp. 296–311. A. L. Oppenheim, *CHI*, pp. 529–87 (with bibl. at pp. 905–14).

197. οὐ γὰρ δὴ χρέωνται ἰητροῖσι: not only therapeutic magic (*asiputu*), but also medicine (*asutu*) flourished in Babylon. The custom described by Herodotus may have arisen in impoverished rural communities under the Persian rule. A comparison with the Persians' attitude towards the sick is implicit (138,1–2). See A. L. Oppenheim, *BHM* XXXVI (1962), 97–108; J. Oates, *Babylon*, London 1979, pp. 180–3; R. D. Biggs, *RLA* VII 1987–90, pp. 623–9.

198. μέλιτι: for a similar custom at Sparta see e.g. Xen. *Hell.* V 3,19; Plut. *Ages.* 40,3; on palm-honey in Babylonia see 193,4; for another implicit comparison with the Persians, cf. note on 140,2. For Egyptian funerary laments, cf. II 79. ὁσάκις δ᾽ἂν μειχθῇ...: for similar customs among the Caffa in Abyssinia and other East African tribes see R. Pettazzoni, *SMSR* IX (1933), pp. 238–41. Ἀράβιοι: see note on 131,3.

199,1. αἴσχιστος τῶν νόμων: cf. LXX Epist. Jerem. 42–3; and Strabo XVI 1,20. On Herodotus' judgement of Babylonian customs, cf. note on 196,1. Herodotus' moralistic attitude did not prevent the deleting of this chapter in some ancient editions, as the mss RSV testify. Sacred prostitution, or 'sacred slavery' (ἱεροδουλία) for prostitution purposes, was widespread in the East, especially in Asia Minor and Armenia, besides Babylon and Cyprus (para. 5) as attested in our chapter; but also in some Greek temples of Aphrodite (Corinth, Locri Epizephyri in southern Italy, probably also at Eryx in Sicily; for Cythera see 105,4 and note). At Athens, Solon was said to have founded a temple of Aphrodite Pandemos from the profits of prostitutes (Nicander of Colophon, fr. 10 Schneider, quoted by Athen. XIII 509d). Usually sexual intercourse in a sanctuary was judged by the Greeks as an act of sacrilege; see Archilochus frs. 36–7 West, and M. L. West, *ZPE* CII (1994), 3–4; cf. Herod. IX 116,3; the same in Egypt, II 64,1, but at Egyptian Thebes the tombs of the 'concubines of Zeus' were shown to visitors (Hecataeus of Abdera, *FGrHist* 264 F25 (47,1)); cf. Strabo XVII 1,46. It is worth noting that even at Babylon intercourse was permitted only outside the sacred area (para. 3: ἔξω τοῦ ἱεροῦ; cf. Strabo l.c.: 'far away (ἄπωθεν) from the sacred precinct'); hence what shocked Herodotus was not sacrilege, but the institutionalization of prostitution. See R. Parker, *Miasma: Pollution and Purification in Early Greek Religion*, Oxford 1983, pp. 74–103; L. Santi Amantini, *MGR* IX (1984), 39–62; H. D. Saffrey, *RBi* XCII (1985), 359–74; B. MacLachlan, *Studies in Religion/Sciences religieuses*, XXI (1992), 145–62; S. G. Pembroke, 'Prostitution, sacred', *OCD*[3], pp. 1263–4. Cuneiform evidence for official prostitution in Babylonian temples is a matter of dispute; see D. Arnaud, *RHR* CLXXXIII (1973), 111–15; G. Wilhelm, in T. Abusch *et al.*, *Lingering Over Words*, Atlanta 1990, pp. 505–24. Sacred prostitution should not be confused with secular, commercial prostitution (see 93,4; 196,5).

3. Μύλιττα: see 131,3 and note.

5. Κύπρου: cf. Just. XVIII 5,4. See 105,3 and note.

200. πατριαί...: cf. Strabo XVI 1,20, and Diod. III 22. For other ichthyophagi on the African coast of the Red Sea and on the coast of the Persian Gulf see III 19,1 ff.; 98,3 and notes; cf. Paus. I 33,4. The hypothesis that the ichthyophagi of our chapter were Sacae living in the Caspian area (cf. 202,3 and 216,3; Strabo XI 8,7) presents some difficulties (Strabo thought that they were Babylonian, XVI 1,20). See J. G. Macqueen, *CQ* XXXVIII (1978), 284–91. διὰ σινδόνος: '*fine cloth*, usually *linen*', LSJ, and anything made of it; see e.g. Aesch., fr. 153 Radt; in Herodotus, II 86,6 (a shroud, used for wrapping a mummy); 95,3 (a sheet); VII

181,2 (used for dressing a wound). σινδών may be a semitic loan-word: *saddinu* Accad., *sdyn'* Aram.; *sdyn* Hebrew (translated as σινδών by LXX, Judg. 14: 12).

201–16. The Massagetan *logos* is a digression on the geography and ethnography of this people in two parts (201–3; 215–16), into which the account of Cyrus' last campaign (204–14) is inserted. The narrative and didactic passages are important: through Croesus' speech, the dream of Cyrus, and the suicide of Spargapises Herodotus conveys his ethical, historical, and philosophical reflections on the entire episode (cf. Introduction, pp. 61 f.). Croesus reappears in the role of 'wise counsellor' (see note on 27,2): once again he meditates on the mutability of human fortune and insinuates a warning against the consequences of *hybris* and the risks of a war against a rustic people—reflections that Croesus himself had heard some years earlier from Solon (29–33) and Sandanis (71), to no avail. Croesus eventually gives Cyrus the wrong practical advice: to cross the river Araxes. Cyrus' fate is thus linked to that of Croesus. Tomyris, the queen of the Massagetae, adds the motif of the violation of natural boundaries between peoples and raises once again the moral issue of territorial expansionism. Herodotus' initial liking for Cyrus, particularly evident in the dialogues with Croesus (86–90) and in the childhood legend (107–30), gives way to a rather stern and critical portrayal of the king, not necessarily attributable to the use of different sources (possibly stemming from Darius' branch of the Achaemenid family; see 209–10), but rather to Herodotus' moral stance in the face of a new situation. There were various contradictory versions of the last campaign of Cyrus and his death in antiquity. The enemy were the Derbices and the Indians, according to Ctesias *FGrHist* 688 F 9 (7); the Dahae according to Berossus, ibid. 680 F 10; the Scythians according to others. The version chosen by Herodotus has no more historical value than the others. No Eastern source relates the circumstances of Cyrus' death. That he invaded Sogdiana (modern Turkestan) may perhaps be indirectly attested by the place-name Cyroupolis or Cyreschata on the river Jaxartes (E. Benveniste, *JA* CCXXXIV (1943–5), 163–6); but we know nothing of the chronology of such a campaign. The general historical value of the *logos* is very slight. Cf. also the note on 214,3.

201. Μασσαγέτας: a nomad people like the Scythians. They lived in Sogdiana, between the rivers Oxus (*Amu Darya*) and Jaxartes (*Sir Darya*). The area remained little known to the Greeks even after it became part of the Persian empire (the Persian name was *Suguda* or *Sugda*; cf. Sogdi, Chorasmi, etc., in the 16th satrapy: III 93,3 and note), and even after Alexander the Great conquered it. The archaeological finds convey the nature of the material culture of the peoples of Sogdiana: see D. Mazzeo, *EAA* 1966, s.v. 'Sogdiana, Arte della'; and K. Jettmar, *EAA* 1963, s.v. 'Oxus, Tesoro dell'. Some later sources identified a part of the Massagetae with the Alani (see e.g. Arrian, *FGrHist* 156 T 5). On the Massagetae see A. Herrmann, *RE* XIV (1930), coll. 2123–9; on the Massagetae in Herodotus see I. V. Pyankov, *VDI* CXXXII (1975), 46–70 (in Russian, with an English summary).   μέγα... καὶ ἄλκιμον: Herodotus prepares the reader for the de-

scription of bloody fights with this people and for its ethnographic characterization: the profound connection between the ethnographical digression and
the historical narrative is in this *logos* very clear. Herodotus does not give an
idealized presentation of the Massagetae as 'noble savages', contrary to some parts
of the Scythian *logos* (IV 1–82) and to other ancient writings about Σκυθικά.
Ἰσσηδόνων ἀνδρῶν: an epic formula, taken perhaps from the *Arimaspea*
of Aristeas of Proconnesus (IV 13,1–2; 16,1; 26–7). The Issedones are a half-
mythical people like the Hyperboreans, located by the ancients in modern
Kazakh, east of Sir Darya.

202,1. Ἀράξης: see Müller II, p. 99; the course of the river described here may
correspond, with some difficulties, to that of the river Aras, which flows from
Armenia to the Caspian Sea (cf. 202,4; IV 40,1). Herodotus may have confused it
with the Oxus which today flows into the Aral Sea, or even with the Rha (Volga).
He may have made the same mistake at IV 11,1; cf. Strabo XI 8,6. Herodotus was
followed by Callisthenes, *FGrHist* 124 F 38; cf. Strabo XI 14,13.   Ἴστρου: the
Danube. Cf. esp. II 33,3–4.   Λέσβῳ: the comparison may perhaps have been
taken from Hellanicus of Lesbos' Σκυθικά (if published while Herodotus was still
alive): φασι εἶναι may allude to a written source. For similar comparisons see I
98,5, and the Introduction, p. 5.

2. δένδρεα...: probably a type of Indian hemp, from which hashish is extracted;
cf. IV 74–5,1. See C. J. Vooys, *Hermeneus*, XXVII (1956), 152–3. It has been linked
to the Iranian inebriating liquor known as *haoma*, also used for cultic purposes
(see note on III 34,2).   δίαιτα: as 'way of life' cf. 215,1 and III 102,1. The term
was most famously used to describe the Spartan discipline.

3. ὅθεν περ ὁ Γύνδης: ch. 189. The moral message of this pointed (but incorrect)
geographical association between the Araxes and the Gyndes is obvious. Forty is a
standard number for lengths, periods, fleets, etc. (cf. 166,2). On the Matieni see
note on 72,2.

4. Κασπίη θάλασσά: cf. 203,1; 204,1; IV 40,1; also called Hyrcanian. From
Hecataeus to the Hellenistic and Roman geographers, the prevalent opinion
was that the Caspian Sea was a gulf of the northern Ocean. For example, it was
believed that the Argonauts travelled from the Black Sea to the Ocean by sailing
along the river Phasis (2,2 and note) and returned to the Mediterranean along the
Nile (Hecataeus, *FGrHist* 1 F 18a–b, 302c). Herodotus' views constitute an
impressive exception: he rejects with scorn the whole idea of an Ocean surrounding the continents and of the Nile connecting it to the Mediterranean (II 21 and
23; IV 8,2; 36,2). Herodotus' view was finally rehabilitated by Ptolemy, in the 2nd
cent. AD. The measures for the Caspian Sea given by Herodotus (203,1) entail that
the width and the length are in the proportion 8 : 15, whereas the correct
proportion is approximately 8 : 22 (450 km. in width and 1,250 km. in length).
It is thus impossible to calculate the average distance covered by a rowing-ship
per day according to Herodotus (for a similar difficulty see II 11,1). Clitarchus'
estimate that the Caspian Sea is as large as the Black Sea (*FGrHist* 137 F 12) is
satisfactorily correct. On the Caspian Sea in antiquity see M. Cary and E. H.

Warmington, *The Ancient Explorers*, Harmondsworth 1963, pp. 163–7, 185–6, 198–9; A. B. Bosworth, *From Arrian to Alexander*, Oxford 1988, pp. 129–32. On Herodotus' geography see Introduction, pp. 23 ff.

203, 1. ὁ Καύκασος: cf. 104,3; IV 12,3. The name refers to the entire mountain chain. The highest peak, Elbruz, is over 5,600 m. high. Mt. Demavend, in the Elbruz chain south of the Caspian Sea, is even higher. See Braund; A. Nercessian, 'Kaukasos', *LIMC* V 1 (1990), 973 (bibl.). **ἔθνεα:** the Colchians, the Albanians, and the Iberians. See S. Ferri, *EAA* 1959, s.v. 'Caucaso, Culture del', with bibl. For Herodotus' use of the term ἔθνος see n. on 6,1.

204, 2. ἡ γένεσις: the death of Cyrus is linked to his birth and miraculous childhood (Immerwahr, pp. 165 f.). Herodotus only sees the personal reasons for the campaign, considers Cyrus' overconfidence as a sign of *hybris*, and prepares the reader for the reversal of fortune. Presumably Cyrus, like Darius after him, believed himself chosen and protected by Ahura Mazda.

205,1. Τόμυρίς: it is impossible to determine the historicity of this queen. 216,1 does not suggest that Massagetan women did enjoy a privileged position: perhaps Herodotus wanted to sharpen the contrast between Cyrus' illusory good-fortune and his miserable death by the hand of a woman. He thought that by marrying Tomyris he would have inherited the kingdom of the Massagetae; cf. the case of Gyges and Candaules' wife (11,2 and note). See K. M. T. Atkinson, *JAOS* LXXVI (1956), 175.

2. γεφύρας τε ζευγνύων ...: for ζευγνύω meaning to 'subjugate' a river or a strait with a bridge see III 134,4 and note; IV 83,1; 87,2; 89,1–2; VII 8 β,1, etc; note on 75,3.

206,1. ἔλεγε τάδε: for a discussion of Tomyris' and Croesus' speeches (206–7) and the moral issue of expansionism see P. Payen, *Métis*, VI (1991), 253–81.   **ὦ βασιλεῦ Μήδων:** only hostile foreign messengers address the king of Persia as 'king of the Medians' (cf. VII 136,2; VIII 114,2), a title, which, though not incorrect, does not express full recognition of the Great King's status as βασιλεὺς Περσῶν (which never occurs) would do; see Dickey, p. 95.

207,1. Κροῖσος ὁ Λυδός: this famous speech is not out of place here. See G. Klamp, *PhW* L (1930), coll. 890–3; Bischoff, p. 44, n. 1.   **οἴκῳ τῷ σῷ:** the house of the Achaemenids; cf. 25,2 and note.   **τὰ δέ μοι παθήματα...:** this resembles a popular saying.

2. ὡς κύκλος ...: a succinct cyclical presentation of history in terms of the rise, success, and decline of great individuals; cf. Introduction, pp. 36 ff.

5. διαβάντας προελθεῖν ...: cf. Cambyses' reproach to Croesus at III 36,3.

6. ἀγαθῶν ... ἄπειροι: cf. 71,2. For the stratagem, cf. Justin I 8,4 ff. (with some variants); for Tomyris' stratagem against Cyrus, cf. Frontinus, *Strat.* II 5,5, and Polyaenus VIII 28. We would not expect a 'wise counsellor' to give such advice.

208.   Καμβύσῃ...: cf. Ctesias, *FGrHist* 688 F 9 (8), and Xen. *Cyr.* VIII 7,11. On Cambyses son of Cyrus see note on III 1,1; for the Achaemenids and Cambyses see also the bibl. quoted at 107,2 and 183,2.

209,1. ὄψιν: as in the cases of Croesus and Astyages, Cyrus' dream also concerns the future of the dynasty, as well as being a 'death dream'. The winged man is a well-known element in the royal iconography of the Achaemenids (cf. e.g. the winged genius on a pillar in Cyrus' palace at Pasargadae: see G. Ambrosetti, *EAA* 1963, s.v. 'Pasargadae', table 1197; M. C. Root, *AI* XIX (1979), 46 ff. and table 1): it is the charismatic symbol of the king, the chosen one of Ahura Mazda (for the Assyrian model see M. Mallowan, *CHI*, pp. 392 ff.). For the eagle as a symbol of the Achaemenids see G. Binder, *Die Aussetzung des Königskindes. Kyros und Romulus*, Meisenheim am Glan 1964, pp. 45 f. The image of the winged Darius predicts the shift of rule to Hystaspes' branch; the two wings cover the two continents over which Hystaspes' descendants in fact will rule. See H. Aigner, *RhM* CXVII (1974), 215–18; R. Bichler, *Chiron*, XV (1985), 128 f.

2. Ὑστάσπεϊ: *Vištaspa* in Old Persian; see O. K. Armayor, *AncW* I (1978), 151. He must have been about 50 years old in 530 BC. He was the governor of Parthia and suppressed a rebellion there in 522–521 (*DB* II § 35); according to Herodotus, he was governor of Persia (III 70,3). Darius' father has been identified by some scholars with the homonymous protector and follower of Zoroaster, after whom a part of the Avesta is called (*Vištasp Yašt*). The names of Hystaspes' father Arsames (*Aršāma*) and grandfather Ariaramnes (*Ariyāramna*) are written in Old Persian on two gold tablets from Hamadan (Ecbatana): see *AmH* and *AsH* Kent. They are called 'Great King, King of Kings, King of Persia'; the authenticity of the tablets is, however, extremely doubtful; see P. Lecoq, *AI* III (1974), 48–52; C. Herrenschmidt, in *Pad Nam I Yazdan*, Paris 1979, pp. 5–21; M. Cook, *CHI*, pp. 209–10; Briant, *Histoire*, pp. 26–7, 905–6 = ET pp. 16–17, 877. Arsames was still alive at a very old age when Darius ascended the throne (*Dsf* l. 12 ff.; *Xlf* Kent). ἀνδρὶ Ἀχαιμενίδῃ: cf. III 2,2; IV 43,1; VII 62,1; for the Old Persian *Haxāmanišiya* = 'Achaemenian' see R. Schmitt, *Beiträge zur Namenforschung*, XXII (1987), 243–7. For the genealogy of the first Achaemenids see note on 107,2.

210,1. περιχωρέοι ἐς Δαρεῖον: Cyrus' successor, however, was his son Cambyses, but Xerxes, a grandchild of Cyrus on his mother's side, reunited the two branches of the dynasty. However, the simplest interpretation of the dream suggests a prediction of Darius' rule over the two continents.

2. μὴ εἴη ἀνὴρ Πέρσης: Herodotus' assumption is that no Persian would ever revolt against the Great King. But in 522/1 BC the Persian Vahyazdata was the leader of a rebellion in Persia against Darius (*DB* II §21; III §40–3).

211,3. οἱ δὲ Πέρσαι ἐπελθόντες: cf. Strabo XI 8,5 on Cyrus' attack against the Sacae. Σπαργαπίσης: this is also the name of a mythical horse-breeder who was the first to feed the baby Darius when he was exposed (Ptolemy Hephaistion, in Photius, *Bibliotheca* 190, p. 148b Henry). Cf. the Scythian anthroponym Spargapeithes at IV 76,6; 78,2. It may be the hellenized form of an authentic Iranian name, possibly reinterpreted to mean the 'one who is persuaded by, or trusts on, the σπάργανα' (the objects left with an exposed child for recognition).

212,3. ἥλιον: cf. 216,4 and note.

213. διεργάζεται ἑωυτόν: cf. note on 82,8.

214,1. ταύτην τὴν μάχην: a great action on the part of two barbarian peoples. The description of the two stages of the battle agrees with what we know about the tactics of the cavalry of semi-nomad Iranian peoples (even in late antiquity). The enemy was first worn down by a shower of arrows and then attacked frontally by the infantry or the cavalry with battering and cutting weapons. For the Persian losses, cf. Ctesias, *FGrHist* 688 F 9 (6), and Justin I 8,11–12.

3. βασιλεύσας τὰ πάντα: 'in total', i.e. including the period of rule as vassal-king of Astyages in Anšan (559–550 BC; cf. note on 130), would be a correct historical interpretation, much better than 'over all the lands', since Cyrus took the title of 'King of Lands' only in 539 BC. But we cannot be sure that Herodotus was aware of this, and that this is what he meant in this passage. The twenty-nine years span the period between 559 and 530 BC. The year 559/8 is calculated by adding the reigns of Darius (36 years), Cambyses (8), and Cyrus (29) to the year 486/5, marking the end of Darius' reign. Babylonian commercial documents allow us to date the end of Cyrus' reign to August 530: see W. H. Dubberstein, *AJSL* LV (1938), 417–19; R. A. Parker and W. H. Dubberstein, *Babylonian Chronology 626 BC–AD 75*, Providence, RI, 1956 (repr. 1971), p. 14.

5. πολλῶν λόγων λεγομένων: e.g., according to Ctesias, Cyrus was wounded by an Indian and taken to the camp by his relatives, where he died three days later. Cambyses then took care of bringing his body to Persia, and of burying it (*FGrHist* 688 F 9 (6–8)). According to Diodorus, Cyrus was captured and crucified by the queen of the Scythians (II 44,2); while according to Onesicritus (*FGrHist* 134 F 36), Cyrus died of a broken heart on hearing of his son Cambyses' misdeeds. Xenophon reports that he died in his own bed in Persia, surrounded by his children, friends, and officers (*Cyr.* VIII 7). See H. Sancisi-Weerdenburg, *AI* XXV (1985), pp. 459–71, and S. W. Hirsch, in *The Greek Historians: Literature and History. Papers Presented to A. E. Raubitschek*, Stanford 1985, pp. 81 ff. Herodotus' version leaves unexplained the fact that Cyrus' corpse was recovered by the Persians and that it somehow found its way to Pasargadae, where it was embalmed and buried in a park. The funerary monument described by the historians of Alexander the Great (for the sources see H. Treidler, *RE* Suppl. IX 1962, coll. 784 ff.) is usually identified with the so-called 'tomb of Solomon's mother' at Pasargadae; see D. Stronach, *Pasargadae*, Oxford 1978, pp. 24–43; *CHI*, pp. 838–41.

215,1. ὁμοίην τῇ Σκυθικῇ: cf. IV 23,2: ἐσθῆτι δὲ χρεώμενοι Σκυθικῇ. In Herodotus' Scythian *logos* dress is surmised as an element of culture (see also IV 78,4 and 106), but never described. The military attire of the Sacae = Scythians is described at VII 64,2.   σαγάρις: simple or double axe, used by the Scythians as well (IV 70; VII 64,2) and by other nomad people. Gold was used in the Urals and Sogdiana from very ancient times; the mountainous area of Samarkand and Ferghana are rich in copper. On the arms of the Massagetae, cf. Strabo XI 8,6, derived mainly from our chs. 215–16. On the function of the girdle (ζωστήρ) see P. Jamzadeh, *IA* XXII (1987), 267–73.

2. χαλινούς ...: cf. IV 64,2; 72,4. The harnesses were probably made of gilded bronze. Cf. χρυσοχάλινος ἵππος, IX 20.

216,1.   γυναῖκα μὲν ...: Herodotus knows four types of marriage: *de facto* monogamy with institutionalized concubinage (the most widespread system among the Greeks); completely legal polygamy and concubinage (the Persian system: ch. 135); monogamy or polygamy with regulated sexual promiscuity (monogamy among the Massagetae and polygamy among the Nasamones: IV 172,2); the system of the Agathyrsi cannot be classified: IV 104; cf. the custom of the Gindan women at IV 176. In the last two types of marriage, adultery would be equivalent to disregarding certain semi-ritual habits (such as hanging the quiver or other objects in the house of the woman). For ancient examples of limited promiscuity (e.g. restricted to the husband's brothers) see the Spartan polyandry described by Polybius at XII 6b,8; and the Arab habit described by Strabo at XVI 4,25. Legalized prostitution of unmarried girls, whether for economic or sacred purposes (I 93,4; 196,5; 199), is not a system of matrimony; the habit of public intercourse (cf. 203,2; IV 180,5) can, in theory, coexist with any form of marriage. Herodotus is fascinated by the diversity and relativism of human habits. For shared women in Herodotus see V. Andò, in Φιλίας χάριν. *Miscellanea E. Manni*, I, Rome 1980, pp. 85–102; in later sources see e.g. Ephorus, *FGrHist* 70 F 42 (on the Scythians); Theopompus, ibid. 115 F204 (on the Etruscans); and the famous regulations in Plato's *Republic* (V 457c–d, etc.).   φασὶ "Ελληνες: perhaps a reference to Greek Σκυθικά (Hellanicus?). The Scythian community of women, sons, and goods was sometimes idealized (e.g. by Ephorus, *FGrHist* 70 F 42).

2. οὗρος δὲ ἡλικίης: in contrast to other peoples who set a limit of a certain age (e.g. 70 years); see Strabo XI 11,3 and Aelian, *Var. Hist.* IV 1, on the Derbices and the Caspians. At Ceos the limit was once 60 (see Strabo X 5,6, etc.). At Rome *sexagenarii de ponte* was no more taken literally during the Republic, but rather meant that men over 60 did not have access to the *pontes* which led to the *ovilia* for the voting. For 70 as the ideal limit of human life, cf. 32,2 and note.   ἐπεὰν δὲ γέρων γένηται...: cf. Strabo XI 8,6. The Massagetae kill and eat their old people (as some Indian tribes also did; see III 99,1–2 and 38,4; cf. the Derbices in Strabo XI 11,8). The Issedones do not kill them but eat them after death (IV 26,1); finally other peoples kill the old but do not eat them (the Bactrians, the Sardinians, and the Caspians, etc.). Herodotus rationalizes this form of cannibalism, which must in fact have had both 'Malthusian' and magical origins. Killing the old is attested also in some medieval and modern societies. For anthropophagy in Lydia see Xanthus of Lydia, *FGrHist* 765 F 18.

4. γαλακτοπόται: cf. IV 186,1, and the Scythian γλακτοφάγοι in Homer (*Il.* XIII 6) and Hesiod (fr. 151 Merkelbach–West). Cf. Hartog, p. 182 = ET, p. 168. μοῦνον ἥλιον: cf. 212,3. For the cult of the sun among the Persians see 131,1 and 3; at Heliopolis in Egypt see e.g. II 59,3; 73,3–4; 111,4; among the Libyans, IV 188; among the Ethiopians, III 18 and note. Among the Greeks, apart from its identification with Apollo, the sun as such was worshipped at Apollonia on the Ionian sea (IX 93,1), and especially at Rhodes, where the sun was the principal

god, in Crete and other cities, mostly Dorian (Troezen, Corinth, Taenarum (I 23 and note), Thermos in Aetolia), but also at Athens. For solar symbolism in Macedonia see VIII 137,4. But as far as the Massagetae are concerned it was allegedly their only cult, a form of heliotheism which in Greek eyes might have appeared as monotheism. The Scythians (IV 61,2; 62,2; etc.), the Persians (see note on 189,1), the Parthians, the Romans, and other peoples also sacrificed horses, though not exclusively to the sun; see Walbank II, p. 328 for sources and bibl. Herodotus' interpretation of the horse sacrifice to the sun is rationalizing and typically Greek (the 'chariot of the sun'). For bibl. see H. Sichtermann, *EAA* 1960, s.v. 'Helios'; N. Yalouris and T. Visser-Choitz, 'Helios', *LIMC* V 1 1990, pp. 1005–34; C. O. Pavese, *ZPE* CXII (1996), 57.

BOOK II

Alan Lloyd

I

The second book of Herodotus' *Histories* reflects over two centuries of Greek involvement with pharaonic Egypt. This fact was of great importance both in providing a substantial corpus of widely available information on the country and in generating a long history of direct Greek participation in Egyptian political and military affairs which became an integral part of his subject matter. It is, therefore, essential that any commentary on Book II should provide a summary of Greek activities in Egypt during the archaic and classical periods up to the mid-fifth century.[1]

Herodotus himself identifies three categories of Greek visitors at III 139,1: 'When Cambyses, son of Cyrus, was marching against Egypt, other Greeks also went there, some, as one would expect, for purposes of trade, others as soldiers, and yet others to see the country itself.' These groups, however, were certainly not confined to this sixth-century context. Greek merchants and soldiers are detectable in the country from a much earlier period, whilst evidence of tourists or scholars, though less clear and reliable, is, nevertheless, indisputable. These groups, however, may not exhaust the possibilities; for in the seventh–sixth centuries there is a distinct possibility that Greeks were also active as naval experts.

After the long hiatus of the Dark Ages it was as merchants that Greeks first reappeared in Egypt early in the reign of Psammetichus I (664–610 BC), and by the end of the seventh century the Milesians had established a major commercial centre there at Naucratis near Sais, the capital of the XXVIth Dynasty which ruled Egypt from 664 to the Persian conquest in 525. Ideally suited as a base for export and import trade, it rapidly developed and attracted first Aeginetans and Samians in some strength and subsequently contingents from Chios, Teos, Phocaea, Clazomenae, Rhodes, Cnidus, Halicarnassus, Phaselis, and Mytilene. In, or about, 570 BC this position was consolidated as a result of the anti-Greek movement which brought Amasis to the throne of Egypt; the city was then made the centre through which all Greek trade within the country had to be channelled (178–9). The main focus of this Greek commercial interest was corn, but objects of faience were also acquired and, possibly, linen, papyrus, and ivory. In exchange the Greeks imported into Egypt pre-eminently silver and wine.[2]

Mercenaries are also clearly identifiable in the early years of the reign of Psammetichus I, when Carian and Ionian troops played a crucial role in winning

---

[1] In general see Austin; Lloyd, *Introduction*, pp. 1 ff.; Boardman, *Greeks Overseas*, pp. 111 ff.; T. F. R. G. Braun, in *CAH*² III 3, pp. 32 ff.

[2] Austin, pp. 22 ff.; Lloyd, *Introduction*, pp. 24 ff.; Boardman, *Greeks Overseas*, pp. 118 ff.; Braun, pp. 37 ff.

MEDITERRANEAN SEA

Phatnitic / Bucolic Mouth
Mendesian Mouth
Tanitic / Saïtic Mouth
Pelusiac Mouth

MOUNT CASIUS
Lake Serbonis (Bardawil)

Gaza

Sebennytic Mouth

Bolbitinic Mouth

Canopic Mouth
Tower of Perseus
Canopus
Salt Pans
Alexandria
Anthylla
Marcia
Lake Archandropolis
Mareotis
Plinthinete
Gulf

Apis

Naucratis
Sais
Siouph?
Bouto
Chemmis
Sebennytos
Bousiris
Onouphis
Mendes
Anysis?
Tanis
Pelusium
Salt Pans Magdolos
Daphnai
Pharbaithos
Ismailia

Thmouis
Myekphoris
Leontopolis
Bubastis
Canal of Darius
Tell el-Mashkuta
Canal

Atarbechis?
Athribis
Saft el-Hina

Momemphis
Heliopolis
Erythrabolos?
Cairo GEBEL AHMAR
Giza Tura
Abu Gurab Abusir
Saqqâra Memphis
Dashur
El-Lisht

Aphroditopolis (Atfih)

ARABIAN

Kerkasoros
Wenkhem?

Maidum
Crocodilopolis
(Medinet el-Faiyum)
Sedment'
Herakleopolis (Ihnasiya)
Hawara
el-Lahun
Teuzoi (el-Hibeh)

Nile

Sheikh Fadl

Siwa
Oasis

Lake Moeris
(Birket Qarun)

Oxyrhynchus (el-Bahnasa)

el-Minya
Antinoopolis (Sheikh Ibada)

Hermopolis (Ashmunein)

LIBYAN

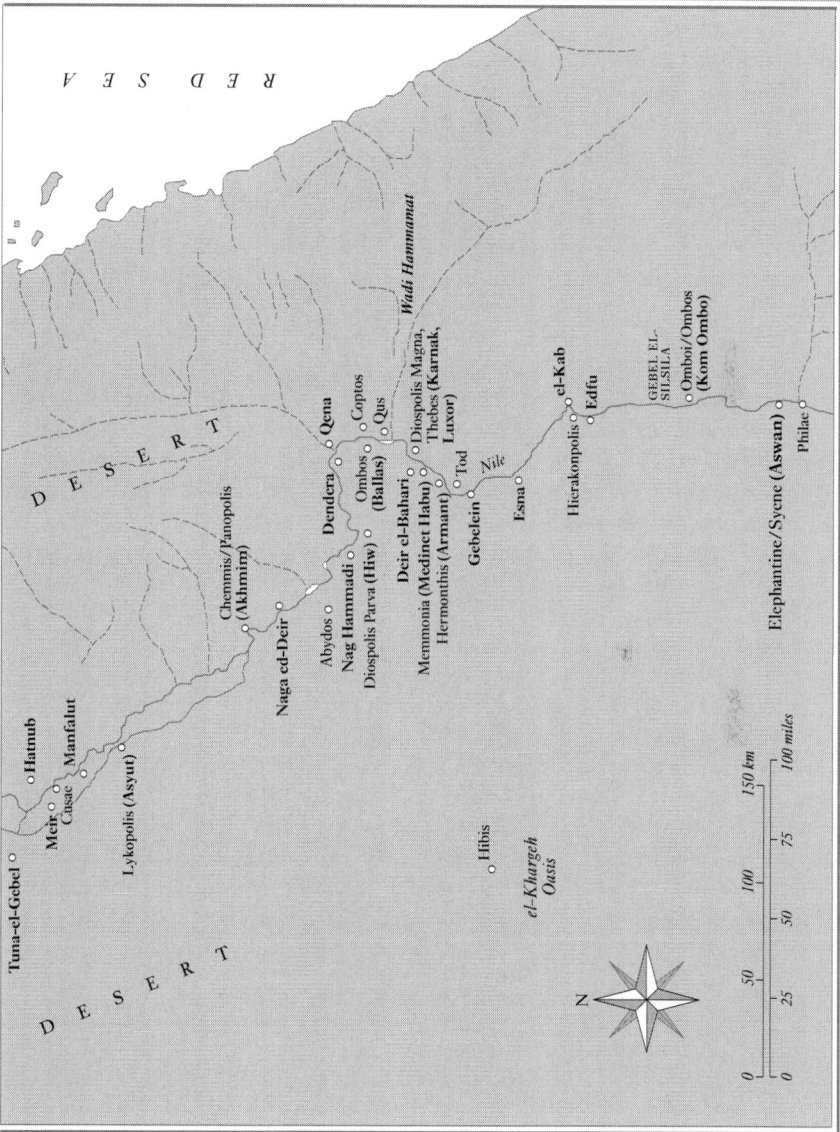

Map 19. Egypt

Egyptian independence from Assyrian domination and also in Psammetichus' re-establishment of a centralized and unified government in the country by 656.[3] He subsequently settled them in permanent camps on the north-eastern frontier, of which remains have been unearthed at Daphnae, Migdol, and probably Tell Kedwa. Here they were clearly intended to provide a barrier against invasion by dangerous Asiatic imperial powers such as the Assyrians, Chaldaeans, and, later, the Persians. These troops were, however, also employed in Egypt's own aggressive foreign policy, the best-known example being the invasion of Nubia in 593/2 during the reign of Psammetichus II which took them at least as far as the Third Cataract and, in the by-going, gave one contingent of Greek soldiers an opportunity on their return to record their passing in inscriptions on one of the colossi of Ramesses II at Abu Simbel. In this, and probably all other contexts, they functioned under the operational command of Egyptian officers.[4]

Mercenaries were not, however, the only Greek military personnel to be found in Egypt during the archaic and classical periods. The Athenians and other members of the Confederacy of Delos were also present there in considerable numbers as allies between *c.*460 and 455 BC, when they went to the support of the revolt of Inarus against the Persian rulers of Egypt. Their catastrophic defeat in this adventure evidently dissuaded the Athenians from any further major Egyptian commitments of this kind.[5]

According to Herodotus, sheer curiosity also brought many Greeks to Egypt. Of these some would have been tourists, but others could doubtless be described as students. Up to his time many famous figures in the history of Greek culture were alleged to have visited Egypt and acquired wisdom or knowledge there, for example Homer, Lycurgus, Solon, and Pythagoras. In general, the historicity of such traditions is highly questionable, but in the case of the artists Telecles and Theodorus at least, a strong case can be made.[6]

More problematic are the implications of Herodotus' claim that the pharaoh Necho (610–595 BC) employed triremes in his fleet (159,1). Some scholars regard this assertion as an anachronism, but there can be no doubt that these ships were either biremes or triremes, and that situation raises the distinct possibility that they were designed and built by Greek experts and that initial training in their use was also obtained from the same source, but, without

    [3] Recent discoveries at Tell Kedwa include Greek pottery and suggest that it was a Saite fort: see L. Giddy, *Egyptian Archaeology*, XIV (1999), 28, with map on p. 29.

    [4] Austin, pp. 15 ff.; Lloyd, *Introduction*, pp. 14 ff.; Boardman, *Greeks Overseas*, pp. 114 ff., 133 ff.; Braun, op. cit., pp. 35 ff., 43 ff., 49 ff.

    [5] For the details see R. Meiggs, *HSCPh* LXVII (1963), 1 ff.; Salmon, pp. 90 ff.; E. Robinson, *Class-Ant.*, XVIII (1999), 132 ff.

    [6] T. Hopfner, *Orient und griechische Philosophie*, Beihefte zum Alten Orient, IV, Leipzig 1925; Lloyd, *Introduction.*, pp. 49 ff. On Telecles and Theodorus and the more general question of early Egyptian influence on Greek art see Lippold, *RE* VA 2, 1919; G. Richter, *Kouroi*, London 1960; Morenz, *Die Begegnung*, pp. 72 ff.; Boardman, *Greeks Overseas*, p. 144.

further evidence, the precise historical background to Herodotus' claim must remain obscure.[7]

Relations between these Greek visitors and the Egyptians were certainly strained at times and could break out into open and violent hostility. The Saite military policy of preferring Greek mercenaries to native troops naturally offended the native Egyptian warrior class or *Machimoi*, and we hear that in the reign of Psammetichus I a large contingent emigrated to Ethiopia (i.e. Nubia) where, no doubt, they felt they would be treated with greater respect (30). This resentment reached disastrous proportions in the reign of the pharaoh Apries (589–570 BC) and led to a great revolt of native troops which cost the king at first his crown and ultimately his life (161,3–4–163; 169). As a result, the mercenaries were stripped of their privileges, at least temporarily, being withdrawn from their camps on the north-eastern frontier and stationed in the city of Memphis itself (154,3). The reason for this move was doubtless to replace them with contingents from the *Machimoi*, who were evidently offended at the slight to their honour of stationing Greek troops at the most dangerous frontier of the country.

Religious taboos could also create problems. Herodotus writes as follows:

And the Egyptians, one and all, venerate cows much more highly than any other animal. This is the reason why no native of Egypt, whether man or woman, will give a Greek a kiss or use the knife of a Greek, or his spit, or his cauldron, or taste the flesh of an ox, known to be pure, if it has been cut with a Greek knife. (41,2–3)

[Again:] . . . then they slay the animal, and, cutting off its head, proceed to flay the body. Next they take the head, and, heaping imprecations on it, if there is a market-place and a body of Greek traders in the city, they carry it there and sell it instantly; if, however, there are no Greeks among them, they throw the head into the river. (39,1–2)

Generally, however, the two peoples seem to have been able to work out a satisfactory *modus vivendi*. We hear in Aristagoras of Miletus of half-castes called *Karomemphitai* and *Hellenomemphitai* (*FGrHist* 608 F 9), presumably the product of mixed Carian/Greek and Egyptian marriages. It is also possible that we have evidence of this phenomenon from a tomb in the oasis of Siwa where we find a representation of the owner, who may have been a Greek, clad in Egyptian clothes, depicted according to the conventions of Egyptian mortuary art, and accompanied by a son who is represented entirely in the Greek fashion. Dating problems are acute in the case of this tomb, but there is at least a possibility that it should be assigned to the period with which we are concerned. Be that as it may, it is evident that liaisons between Greeks and Egyptian women were common, and that there was no legal impediment of any sort against marriage between foreigners and Egyptians as far as the Egyptians themselves were concerned.[8]

---

[7] L. Basch, *JHS* XCVII (1977), 1 ff.; Lloyd, *JHS* C (1980), 195 ff. See also my study 'The Saite Navy', in J. Oliver *et al.*, *The Sea in Antiquity* (BAR International Series 899), Oxford 2000, pp. 81 ff.

[8] Austin, pp. 19, 28; Lloyd, *Introduction*, pp. 18 ff.

Whatever problems might arise in other contexts, there was one area, at least, where the attractions of Egypt proved almost irresistible to the Greeks. The appeal of Egyptian religion to the inhabitants of the Greek world, once established, endured for centuries. We have already commented upon the evidence of the assimilation of Egyptian mortuary practices by a Greek who was buried at Sîwa, but Herodotus himself refers to a similar phenomenon in his description of Carian involvement in the cult of Osiris at Busiris which reached spectacular proportions:

The ceremonies at the feast of Isis in the city of Busiris have been already spoken of. It is there that the whole multitude, both of men and women, many thousands in number, beat themselves at the close of the sacrifice, in honour of a god whose name a religious scruple forbids me to mention. The Carian dwellers in Egypt proceed on this occasion to still greater lengths, even cutting their faces with their knives, whereby they let it be seen that they are not Egyptians but foreigners (61).

II

The precise date of Herodotus' visit to Egypt cannot be determined. All we can say is that he was certainly there after *c*.459 because he mentions the battle of Papremis, which took place about this time, and that the probabilities favour a date between 449 and 430 BC. Identifying the season of the year in which his journey fell is even more problematic. Sourdille believed that it must have been the inundation season, but the truth of the matter is that we do not have the evidence to establish the point.[9]

The question of where precisely Herodotus went in the country must be approached with care. We cannot simply assume that he visited every place which he mentions. Fortunately, he indicates at many points in Book II that he has seen a particular area, and, if we accept that such statements are true, they provide a list of localities certainly visited by Herodotus covering all the major areas of the country.[10] In the Delta, or Lower Egypt, he visited Pelusium, where he speaks of seeing the skulls of Egyptians and Persians killed in the battle of Pelusium in 525 (III 12,1). He also visited Bubastis, which he describes as being built on a large *tell*, or mound, in the centre of which stood the great temple of Bastet (137,5 ff.). Only meagre ruins of this temple have survived into modern times, but his detailed description excites no qualms in the Egyptologist. He also journeyed to Western Buto (Tell el-Farâ'în) and provides a description

---

[9] For a detailed analysis see Lloyd, *Introduction*, pp. 61 ff. The discussions of Sourdille (*La Durée*) and v. Fritz (I, pp. 136, 154 ff.) should be treated with extreme care.

[10] Among the more modern sceptics we may mention Oertel; Fehling (see also his 'The Art of Herodotus and the Margins of the World', in Z. von Martels (ed.), *Travel Fact and Travel Fiction: Studies on Fiction, Literary Tradition, Scholarly Discovery and Observation in Travel Writing*, Brill's Studies in Intellectual History, LV, Leiden 1994, p. 1 ff.); O. K. Armayor, *JARCE* XV (1980), 59 ff.; S. West, Review of Lloyd, *Introduction, Commentary 1–98, CR* NS XXVIII (1978), 231 ff. For searching discussions of this important issue and its implications see C. Dewald and J. Marincola, *Arethusa*, XX (1987), 26 ff.; W. K. Pritchett, *The Liar School of Herodotus*, Amsterdam 1993; J. L. Moles, in C. Gill and T. P. Wiseman (eds.), *Lies and Fiction in the Ancient World*, Austin and Exeter 1993, pp. 88 ff.; R. Thomas, *JHS* CXVI (1996), 175 ff.; G. S. Shrimpton, *History and Memory in Ancient Greece*, Montreal 1997.

of the temple of Wadjet, which was the site of the most veracious of Egyptian oracles and contained an extraordinary monolithic shrine (155–6). He also speaks of a place in the area called Chemmis which was alleged to be a floating island. His scepticism is clearly expressed, but he did succeed in obtaining good information on the mythology connected with it. In the vicinity of Eastern Buto (Tell el-Far'ûn) he visited a site where the skeletons of flying serpents were to be seen (75). Not surprisingly, the city of Sais was also subjected to his personal attention. Here he extracted information from a scribe of the sacred treasury of Neith on the sources of the Nile, saw statues of the servants of Mycerinus' daughter, and corrected the legend that, in real life, they had had their hands cut off. He also saw the shrine of the goddess Neith (28,1; 131,3; 170,2). On the battlefield of Papremis he examined the skulls of Persians killed by Inarus (III 12,4). At Heliopolis he discussed the tradition of the antiquity of Egypt with the priests of the city (3,1), and at Memphis he not only debated this same question with the local priests but also gained a thorough knowledge of the monuments of the city, though his attention was typically concentrated on those which were connected with major figures in Egyptian history (2,5; 3,1; 99 ff.).

In Upper Egypt the list of sites stated to have been personally visited is shorter. He went to the Fayûm, where he observed the general configuration of the land and collected a quantity of suspect legends (5,1; 10,1; 150,2). He also had an opportunity to view the Labyrinth, whose origins and structure receive due attention (148). He visited Akhmîm, or Chemmis, and saw the temple of Min-Hor as well as gaining information on the athletic games conducted there and the connection of Perseus with the area (91). Herodotus also visited Thebes, and the priests of the city discussed with him the question of the antiquity of the Egyptian nation, the origins of the oracles of Zeus at Sîwa and Dodona, and the genealogy of Hecataeus (3,1; 55; 143). In connection with the latter he was admitted to a *megaron*, presumably one of the hypostyle halls. Finally, he visited Elephantine on the First Cataract (29,1).

In addition to statements about specific sites located on the alluvium, there are general references to observations of geographical and geological conditions made both in Upper and Lower Egypt as well as in the western desert, where Herodotus also has much to say on the Gîza pyramid field (8,3; 10,1; 12,1; 15,2; 125,6; 127,1).

This information summarizes all that we know for certain about the movements of Herodotus in the country, but we must not fall into the trap of assuming that this is all that there was. Since the list of sites covers the whole of Egypt, many other areas which he mentions may have been subjected to his personal attention, even though he does not explicitly say so; it is also intrinsically probable that he visited many sites to which he does not even refer.

III

The account of Egypt which emerged, at least in part, from Herodotus' experience of Egypt shows a remarkable breadth of interest. It falls into two main sections: chs. 1–98, which are largely devoted to the description of the country and its culture, and chs. 99–182, which deal pre-eminently with history. In the first section there is hardly any aspect of Egypt or Egyptian life which does not receive attention. The first thirty-five chapters are dominated by geographical and geological issues, in particular, the physical structure and dimensions of Egypt (4; 14–18) and the behaviour of the Nile (19–34), but Herodotus also touches briefly on the problem of the antiquity of the Egyptian people (2), the calendar (4), the religions of Egypt and Ethiopia (3; 4; 29), zoology (32,7), ethnic distribution (32,2), and physical anthropology (32,6–7). Chs. 35–98, on the other hand, are mainly concerned with Egyptian ethnography. Here Herodotus discusses the factors giving rise to cultural differences between Egypt and others (35), and enumerates areas where Egyptian practices are diametrically opposite to those of other people in the distribution of labour between sexes, methods of carrying burdens, weaving techniques, organization of the priesthood, mourning customs, food, clothing, sailing technology, and methods of writing (35–6). In chs. 37–98 religious practices are given much attention, including taboos, animal cults (a subject of intense interest), methods of sacrifice, the cults of Isis, Osiris, Neith/Athene, Ares, Perseus, the Egyptian role in the development of Greek religion, the pig in cult, oracles and omens, festivals, and mortuary practices; but this material is supplemented by more secular observations on the hunting of crocodiles, food, attitudes to the elderly, dress, medical practices, marriage customs, oil-production, techniques for coping with mosquitoes, and shipbuilding and sailing. This material is periodically interspersed with non-ethnographical comment: Herodotus' zoological interests surface in his discussions of the crocodile (68), the hippopotamus (71), the horned viper (74), the ibis (76), fish (93), and two creatures, the phoenix (73) and the winged serpents (75), which are fabulous to us but were clearly treated by him as genuinely existing. A concern for things botanical is also in evidence in the descriptions of the rose lotus at 92,2–5 and the castor-oil plant at 94,1–2.

The historical section proper occupies chs. 99–182, though similar material does occur sporadically in the earlier part of the book (1; 4; 30). It falls into two halves: chs. 99–142 (the reigns of Min to Sethos) and 147–82 (the reigns from the Dodecarchs to Amasis). The kings are discussed in what Herodotus believed to be their chronological sequence (see below, pp. 236 ff.), though he made serious errors in this respect, and the narrative is interrupted by numerous excursuses on a wide range of topics (see below, p. 234). In this account Herodotus recognizes the major distinction made by the Egyptians between the dynasties of the gods and human kings (4,2; 144–5), and in the discussion of the kings from Min to Psammenitus rulers of most of the major periods of Egyptian history are mentioned (see below, p. 238).

IV

The character and quality of the information summarized in the previous section was inevitably to a large extent determined by the nature of the sources to which

Herodotus had access.[11] He makes several explicit statements about his policy in this respect:

Up to this point my statements are based on what I myself saw (ὄψις), my own opinion (γνώμη), and personal enquiry (ἱστορίη), but from this point I shall proceed by retailing Egyptian traditions as I heard them; these will be supplemented also in some measure by what I myself saw. (99,1)

This, then, is what the Egyptians themselves say, but from now on I shall record all those things which both other men and the Egyptians say happened in this land. This will be supplemented in some measure also by what I myself saw. (147,1)

Once these [*sc.* Carian and Ionian mercenaries] had been settled in Egypt, we Greeks, through intercourse with them, have accurate knowledge of all Egyptian history from the time of king Psammetichus onwards. (154,4)

At 123,1 he also indicates his attitude to what he was told: 'Now, as for the statements of the Egyptians, let him use them whoever finds such things credible; for my part, it is my principle throughout my narrative to record what is said by each informant as I heard it (ἀκοῇ).' This policy is expressed in similar terms at VII, 152,3: 'As for me, I am bound to retail what is said, but I am not bound to believe everything, and let this principle hold good for me in the whole of my narrative.'

Ὄψις is emphasized as the major source in 99,1, for the preceding chapters of Book II.[12] It is described as a supplementary source at 147,1, for the account of Egyptian history which is provided after that point. In the first half of the book (1–98) it features explicitly in discussions of geology and geography (5,1; 8,3; 10,1; 12,1; 29,1), the temples of Heracles at Tyre and Thasos (44,2, 4), the picture of the phoenix (73,1), the skeletons of the flying snakes at Eastern Buto (75,1), and probably in the account of Chemmis/Akhmîm at ch. 91 (see wording at 91,5). Subsequently, it figures explicitly only in Herodotus' treatment of monuments (the stelae of Sesostris in Syria/Palestine, 106,1; the description of the pyramids at Gîza, 125,6; 127,1; the statues of the servants of Mycerinus' daughter, 131,3; Bubastis, 137,5; Thebes, 143,3; the Labyrinth, 148; lake Moiris, 150,2; Sais, 170,2). In six of these cases the ὄψις was used as part of an argument to support or reject a tradition in which Herodotus was interested.

Γνώμη, 'opinion', was a major source up to 99,1. The use of this technique is often betrayed by the use of some such word as δοκέω.[13] As we should expect from Herodotus' own statement at 99,1, there are many examples in 1–98 where it appears particularly when he is dealing with historical, legendary, or mythological traditions (2,5; 43,3; 44,5; 45,2; 49,1; 50,1–56,1). It does, however, surface in the treatment of other topics: the Egyptian calendar (4,1), the geology of Egypt and the definition of what Egypt is (5,1; 6,1; 10–18), the Nile (19–28; 33–4), the

---

[11] v. Fritz I, pp. 158, 407 ff.; Oertel, pp. 5 ff; Lloyd, *Introduction*, pp. 77 ff.; Dewald–Marincola, op. cit. pp. 26 ff; J. Marincola, *Arethusa*, XX (1987), 121 ff.

[12] v. Fritz I, pp. 158, 409 ff.; Oertel, pp. 58 ff.; Lloyd, *Introduction*, pp. 78 ff.; id., 'Herodotus' Account', pp. 23 ff. In general see Schepens.

[13] v. Fritz, p. 158; Lloyd, *Introduction*, pp. 77 ff., 82, 89 ff.; id., *Historia*, XXXVII (1988), 23 ff.

etymology of the word Ἀμμώνιοι (42,5), the question of the Egyptian invention
of festivals (58), the role of environmental determinism in Egyptian culture
(77,3), and zoology (93,6). Subsequently, although Herodotus ignores the fact
in his catalogues of sources, he still employed γνώμη when he was in a position to
do so. In nearly all cases where this arises he was concerned with establishing the
veracity of received traditions and had at his disposal data which he felt confident
of assessing (103,1; 104,1; 116; 120; 131,3; 134–5): one of these issues is largely
ethnographical (104,1), two are archaeological (103,1; 131,3), and in four cases he
is dealing with Greek traditions (116; 120; 134–6). At 109,3 he also offers the
opinion that Sesostris' activities were responsible for the invention of geometry.

Ἱστορίη, 'enquiry', is mentioned specifically as a major source at 99,1.[14] It is
best treated together with ἀκοή, 'hearsay', from which it differs in that it insists on
the attempt of the aural recipient to acquire information by questioning. From
99,1 Herodotus regarded hearsay as his major source, and its pre-eminence is
reiterated at 147,1 and 154,4. The wording of 99,1 implies that from this point his
stance towards hearsay traditions was more passive than previously, and that
squares with the disinclination to adjudicate on traditions expressed both at
123,1, and VII 152,3. In Book II Herodotus explicitly recognizes that his oral
informants changed according to subject matter: for 1–98 he is unspecific on
their nature; for 99–147,1 they were Egyptians; from 147,1 they were Egyptians
and 'other men', and it emerges from 154,4 that the latter were pre-eminently
Greeks.

In chs. 1–98 ἱστορίη or cognates occurs four times. In three cases Herodotus is
dealing with problems associated with the Nile (19,3; 29,1; 34,1) and in one case
with the problem of the nature of Heracles (44,5). Ἱστορίη also features at 113,1
and 119,3, in his discussion of the tradition of Helen's sojourn in Egypt. Here he
is evidently insisting that he had made a conscious attempt to acquire information on these topics by interrogating possible sources. This list of cases is
surprisingly restricted, but we can be confident that he engaged in 'enquiry' on
Egyptian matters far more often than he claims, not least because he describes his
entire work in the introduction as an 'enquiry'.

Ἀκοή and related words occur frequently. A survey of specific examples shows
that Herodotus' distinction between Egyptian and non-Egyptian informants is
amply borne out. Egyptian priests are the most frequent and important sources,
generally those of Thebes, Memphis, and Heliopolis. They feature at many points
(2,5; 3,1; 10,1; 13,1; 19,1; 28; 54–5; 73,1; 99–143), and provide information on
religion, secular culture, history, and geography and also assist in evaluating
Greek tradition. The general opinion of older scholars that they were low-grade

[14] B. Snell, *Die Ausdrücke für den Begriff des Wissens in der vorplatonischen Philosophie, Philologische Untersuchungen*, XXIX, Berlin 1924; F. Müller, *Mnemosyne*, LIV (1926), 234 ff.; J. C. Keuck, *Historia. Geschichte des Wortes und seiner Bedeutungen in der Antike und den romanischen Sprachen*, Münster 1934; H. Barth, in *Neue Beiträge zur Geschichte der Alten Welt. Zweite Internationale Tagung der Fachgruppe Alte Geschichte der Deutschen Historiker-Gesellschaft vom 4. bis 8. September 1962 in Stralsund*, Berlin 1964, I, pp. 173 ff.

members of the hierarchy has little to be said for it. It is far from improbable that Herodotus had access to high-ranking priests, and the distorted and confused information which he obtained from them, particularly on history, is by no means inconsistent with that view. Egyptian priests were certainly not as well informed as we are inclined to think.[15]

Other identifiable Egyptian oral sources are the citizens of Chemmis on the hero Perseus (91,3), an interpreter who provided dubious information on inscriptions (125,6), doorkeepers at the Labyrinth (148), and local inhabitants at 150,1 and III 12,1. There are also numerous references to 'Egyptians' or 'Egyptian tradition' where the precise status of the informants is open to question (15,2; 19,3; 28,1; 43,2; 104,2; 127,1; 142,1; 147,1). As for Herodotus' non-Egyptian oral informants, these are explicitly indicated at several points and comprise Libyans (28,1), Colchians (104,1), and Greeks, either generally or specifically (28,1; 32,1; 45,1; 53,3; 55,3).

Whatever the precise origin of a particular oral source, it is essential to grasp that the reliability of the information is likely to be impaired. As with any other source, the oral information may be based on a partial view or knowledge of the data, and the memory itself may be uncertain. Furthermore, if the tradition has passed through several intermediaries over a period of time of any extent, the historically specific tends to be eroded: the historical protagonists can be assimilated to stereotypes; folk-motifs may accrete to the narrative; and the teller's sense of dramatic propriety easily leads to modifications which give his version greater impact on the listener. It must also be remembered that oral informants use and purvey only what is relevant to their purpose, and that the longer a tradition exists, the more likely it is to lose elements under the influence of this tendency.

When Herodotus refers to what Greeks say, it is extremely probable that he does not only mean what was passed by word of mouth but also what they had written. We can assume with considerable confidence that the Ionians of 15,1 include Ionian writers who had committed themselves to paper on Egypt. Of these the most important by far was Hecataeus of Miletus, though the influence, direct or indirect, of the epic tradition, Euthymenes of Massilia, Anaximander, and Scylax of Caryanda must also be borne in mind.[16] Since Hecataeus' work survives only in fragments, it is impossible to establish for certain the precise limits of Herodotus' use of him as a source. He is mentioned only once in Book II (143,1), and the fact that he is named only to be criticized is probably symptomatic; for the relationship was far from that of source and recipient, but rather a situation where the later author is engaged in a continuous critical dialogue with his predecessor when matters of common interest arise. It is, however, certain that Hecataeus exercised a considerable influence on the formulation of Herodotus' general thinking on geography and chronology, and we can postulate a measure of dependence at a number of specific points: the numerous references to Greek

[15] For an example of the older view see Spiegelberg, *Glaubwürdigkeit*, pp. 17 ff. (trans. A. M. Blackman: *The Credibility of Herodotus' Account of Egypt in the Light of the Egyptian Monuments*, Oxford 1927). The arguments against this attitude are given in detail by Lloyd, *Introduction*, pp. 94 ff.

[16] See v. Fritz I, pp. 48 ff., 407 ff.; Lloyd, *Introduction*, pp. 127 ff.; Mora, esp. pp. 249 ff.

historical, legendary, and mythological traditions (2,5; 43; 44,4–5; 45; 49,5; 91; 98; 104; 112–20; 143,3–4; 146; 156,1–2; 171,3); the discussions of geography and geology (5,1; 8; 10–12; 15–17; 23; 32,1–5; 33–4); some of the zoology (71; 73); Egyptian food (77,4); botany (92; 94; 96); shipping (96); and possibly the discussion of the *Machimoi* (165–6).

V

The character and accuracy of Herodotus' Aἰγύπτιος λόγος is not, however, determined simply, or even perhaps mainly, by the nature of his sources. The cast of the mind which processed the data must also have had a major impact. This, in turn, was the product largely, if not entirely, of the cultural environment within which the writer was raised and lived. The effects of this programming manifest themselves both in his attitude to human life and history and in his scholarly interests.

We should begin the analysis with Herodotus' own conception of the nature of his work which emerges unequivocally in the proem: 'This is the publication of the enquiry of Herodotus of Halicarnassus in order to ensure that neither should the remembrance of actions of men be lost through the passage of time nor should the great and wondrous deeds, some performed by Greeks, others by non-Greeks, lack their due meed of glory, both other things and, in particular, the reason why they fought each other.'

There are several points of emphasis here: first, and most obviously, the enquiry is intended to commemorate remarkable deeds, and secondly it is to be concerned with laying bare their causes—and it very quickly emerges on further reading that, when Herodotus speaks of causes, he means the sum total of moral factors giving rise to the great conflict between Persia and the Greeks. In short, the intention of the work is both commemorative and didactic. It is further to be noted that Herodotus is here recalling the same two points of emphasis as appear in the introductions to the *Iliad* and the *Odyssey*,[17] and thereby implicitly places himself within the epic tradition, an affinity which is also expressed by the explicit intention of making war his main theme.[18] It should also be observed that he insists that the focus will be on μεγάλα τε καὶ θωμαστά, that there is to be equal recognition of Greek and non-Greek achievements, and that the work as a whole is claimed to be an ἱστορίη or 'enquiry'. The ramifications of all this are easily detectable in Book II.

The moral and didactic dimension on which the proem insists is in evidence throughout Herodotus' work, and is a function of a conceptual framework which was in essence typical of the archaic and early classical periods, receiving its most

---

[17] The emphasis in the introductory lines of the *Iliad* is on the μῆνις of Achilles and its consequences, i.e. a moral issue, whereas the proem of the *Odyssey* insists that the work is concerned with a man and his achievements.

[18] On Homeric influence on Herodotus see below and also e.g. Gomme, *Greek Attitude*; L. Huber, in *Synusia: Festgabe für W. Schadewaldt*, Pfullingen 1965, pp. 29 ff.; H. Strasburger, in *Sitz. Heidelberger Ak. Wiss. Jahrg. 1972*, I, Heidelberg 1972.

potent expression in the epic tradition. Herodotus envisaged the context within which human beings functioned as having two interpenetrating dimensions, the human and the divine.[19] It was dominated by the concept of a cosmic law ($\delta i \kappa \eta$) according to which every element had its time and place, its fixed boundaries or limitations which must be observed. Human beings were obliged to recognize this framework and integrate themselves with it. If they did, they were $\delta i \kappa a \iota o \iota$ and won the favour of the gods; if they did not, they were $\ddot{a} \delta \iota \kappa o \iota$. This state of $\dot{a} \delta \iota \kappa i \eta$ was reached pre-eminently by the transgression of boundaries in relation to gods or human beings, and exposed the $\ddot{a} \delta \iota \kappa o \varsigma$ to divine retribution; it could arise either through actions or simply through nurturing a presumptuous attitude of mind. Within this body of concepts an important role was played by the principle of fate, which was normally in Herodotus far from being an amoral deterministic force but rather 'a symbol of the fixed and implacably self-maintaining order of the universe'.[20]

Of the nature of the gods themselves, Herodotus says very little when speaking in his own person. Of their existence he is convinced, and he is usually confident of the justice of their dealings, but their names and cults were to him largely a matter of convention. Links between them and men, which are frequently mentioned, were provided by such agencies as oracles, dreams, portents, seers, and warner figures. Given the subject matter of Book II, there is less scope for Herodotus to give expression to this corpus of ideas than in most other parts of his work, but aspects of it are clearly evident at many points in the historical section of the book (111,2; 112–20; 133; 139; 141,6; 147,4; 151–2; 158,5; 161,2–3 with 169,2: cf. III 10; 36; 39–47).

To Herodotus none of these theological factors impaired man's responsibility as a moral agent, and he shows a willingness to impute to his characters a wide range of motives, of which the most important relate to the complex of social values encapsulated by the principle of $\tau \iota \mu \eta$, 'prestige'. These include vengeance (100,2; 108,1; 152,3), commemoration (110; 121; 135,3; 136,3; 148), the desire to get the better of opponents (121ϵ,3; 133,5), the desire to surpass one's ancestors (136,3), and the determination to demonstrate the superiority of one's own cultural practices (100,1). Other motives explicitly stated or clearly implied are imperial aggrandizement (102 ff.), curiosity (2), desire to improve living conditions (108,4), arrogance ($\dot{a} \tau a \sigma \theta a \lambda i \eta$, 111,2), malice (113,3), the bonds of $\xi \epsilon \iota v i \eta$ (115,4 and 6; 182,2), artistic considerations (116,1), hatred (119,3; 128), self-preservation or preservation of others (120; 121a,2; 147,4; 154,3), preservation of property (121a), trust (121ζ,2), wickedness (126,1), grief (129,3), sexual desire (131,1; 181,1), indignation (133,2; 161,4), economic difficulties (136,2), religious scruples or belief (139,3; 141,4; 175,5; 182,2), anger (162,5), a ruler's reaction to pressure from one's subjects (169,3), and favouritism (178,1).

---

[19] Legrand, *Introduction*, pp. 131 ff.; Immerwahr, pp. 306 ff.; Lloyd, *Commentary 99–182*, pp. 1 ff.; K. A. Raaflaub, *Arethusa*, XX (1987), 221 ff.

[20] Lloyd, *Historia*, XXXVII (1988), 29.

Despite his conviction that divinely sanctioned moral laws worked in the world of men, Herodotus had a keen awareness of the savage ironies of human life. This also emerges in Book II: it is the very fair-mindedness of the Dodecarchs at 151,3 which leads to their deposition at 152,5; at 162–3 and 169 it is the very person sent by Apries to put down the rebellion of the *Machimoi* who brings the uprising to a successful conclusion with the deposition of Apries himself; and at 133 we have a particularly intriguing case where Mycerinus, *despite his just behaviour,* is condemned to a short life because the time appointed by fate for Egypt to suffer oppression had not yet elapsed. Here we see exemplified a willingness to concede the bleak fact that the laws of the universe may sometimes operate in ways which run directly counter to any human perception of justice, and can assume the appearance of a blind fate whose workings are both amoral and immutable.

The thinking just described is itself, in very large measure, a legacy of epic, but epic influence is also detectable in many other areas throughout the *Histories,* and Book II is no exception: the mixture of speeches and narrative is less marked than elsewhere, Herodotus preferring to use *oratio obliqua,* but examples of speeches do occur at chs. 114–15 and 173, where they deal, typically, with moral issues raised by their context; the *colour* of the language is frequently reminiscent of epic (e.g. 13,1; 14,2; 32,3; 42,3; 148,4); there is a recurrent interest in war (102–6; 110; 137; 141; 152; 154; 157; 159; 161–3; 169); material derived from epic tradition features in the narrative (112–20); the list of *Machimoi* nomes at 164–6 irresistibly recalls Homeric catalogues;[21] and the relative looseness of structure also has its origin in the same tradition. This characteristic manifests itself with particular clarity in the ease with which Herodotus indulges in excursuses which are a recurrent feature of his work.[22] He himself comments at IV 30,1, προσθήκας ... μοι ὁ λόγος ἐξ ἀρχῆς ἐδίζητο (cf. VII 171,1), and of this phenomenon Book II itself must be regarded as an example. The narrative of the rise of Persia has brought him to the assault on Egypt by Cambyses at II 1, and this triggers a book-long excursus on Egypt fuelled above all by Egypt's position as a land of marvels (see below). This great excursus, in turn, contains further excursuses: an exercise in Homeric criticism (116–17), the discussion of the doctrine of metempsychosis (123), the description of the temple of Bubastis at ch. 138; the account of the Labyrinth at 148; the treatment of Buto and its shrines at 155–6; the discussion of the royal cemetery of Sais at 169,4–5; and the survey of the Egyptian class structure at 164–8. All of these are closely integrated with their context. Two other examples, however, are blatant digressions: the account of lake Moiris at chs. 149–50 and the discussion of the cult of Osiris at 170–1.

The concern with μεγάλα τε καὶ θωμαστά is strikingly in evidence in Book II. Their importance in attracting Herodotus to write such a long and detailed account emerges clearly at 35,1: ἔρχομαι δὲ περὶ Αἰγύπτου μηκυνέων τὸν λόγον,

---

[21] For this and other catalogues see T. W. Allen, *The Homeric Catalogue of Ships,* Oxford 1921, pp. 22 ff.; O. K. Armayor, *TAPhA* CVIII (1978), 12 ff. The list of Persian forces at Herod. VII 60 ff. lies firmly within this tradition.

[22] For a detailed discussion see Cobet.

ὅτι πλεῖστα θωμάσια ἔχει καὶ ἔργα λόγου μέζω παρέχεται πρὸς πᾶσαν χώρην, 'I shall speak at some length of Egypt because beyond all lands it possesses very many marvels and offers works which surpass all power to describe'. The word θῶμα and cognates are not themselves particularly common in the book, though they do appear in several passages: actions are mentioned under this heading at 121β,1, ζ,2, and monuments at 148,6; 149,1; 155,3; 156,1; 175,1, 3; amazement is also explicitly in evidence at 156,2, where Herodotus uses the word τέθηπα when referring to the floating island of Chemmis. However, his perception of Egypt as a land of colossal and marvellous things cannot be confined to cases where such words are explicitly used. It clearly played a pervasive role in orientating him in choice and treatment of subject matter: it motivates the discussion of customs at 35 (cf. 91,1), sacred animals (65–76), geography (6; 10; 13–14; 19,3; 31; 77,3; 97), personalities and deeds (e.g. Sesostris, 102–10; Rhampsinitus, 121–2), zoology (68; 71; 74; 75–6; 93), and, in particular, buildings (the temple of Ptah at Memphis, 101; 108; 110; 121; 136; 153: cf. 112; 176; the pyramids, 124–35; Necho's Red Sea canal, 158; the monuments of Sais, 169–70; and Amasis' building operations, 182).

Paradoxically, Herodotus' awareness of marvels in Egypt also creates an acute sensitivity to similarities with Greek practices. Examples of this phenomenon occur in religion (48,2; 91,2 ff.; 170–1), social behaviour (80,1), and social organization (164–8). This trait can, however, lead to pernicious consequences, since Herodotus has a marked tendency to assume that such similarities are the result of cultural influence, that is, that the older culture has bequeathed the feature to the younger (the *post hoc ergo propter hoc* fallacy). As a cultural historian, therefore, Herodotus presents himself as a committed hyperdiffusionist. Clear instances of this characteristic arise in the discussion of circumcision at ch. 104, geometry at 109, the doctrine of transmigration of souls at 123, the νόμος ἀργίας at 177, and his attitude to the relationship between Egyptian and Greek religion (see above, p. 228).

Another conspicuous feature which emerges in the proem is Herodotus' even-handed willingness to concede barbarian achievements on the same terms as those of Greeks. This was doubtless encouraged by his firm conviction that social values were culture-specific and that the notion that one's own civilization was superior to those of others was untenable. This idea is clearly expressed at III 38,1:

πανταχῇ ὦν μοι δῆλά ἐστι ὅτι ἐμάνη μεγάλως ὁ Καμβύσης· οὐ γὰρ ἂν ἱροῖσί τε καὶ νομαίοισι ἐπεχείρησε καταγελᾶν. εἰ γάρ τις προθείη πᾶσι ἀνθρώποισι ἐκλέξασθαι κελεύων νόμους τοὺς καλλίστους ἐκ τῶν πάντων νόμων, διασκεψάμενοι ἂν ἑλοίατο ἕκαστοι τοὺς ἑωυτῶν· οὕτω νομίζουσι πολλόν τι καλλίστους τοὺς ἑωυτῶν νόμους ἕκαστοι εἶναι,

In every way, therefore, is it clear to me that Cambyses was afflicted with a great madness; for ⟨otherwise⟩ he would not have tried to make mock of religious customs. For if one were to enjoin all men to choose the finest customs, each, after reviewing them all, would choose his own; to such a degree does each society think that its own customs are much the finest.

This led not only to a marked disinclination to make negative judgements on foreign customs, but to an unusual willingness to express admiration for foreign achievements and practices, even to the point of disparaging those of his fellow-countrymen. This tendency, which led pseudo-Plutarch to describe him by the distinctly uncomplimentary epithet φιλοβάρβαρος,[23] appears at several points in Book II (2,5; 10,1; 45,1; 118,1; 119; 143; 148,2).

It would, however, be quite mistaken to think of Herodotus simply as a latter-day Homer composing a prose epic. He did not simply look back to, and draw upon, the thinking and traditions of the archaic period; he was also profoundly influenced by contemporary scientific, philosophical, and rhetorical developments. This point is signalled in the proem itself, where he describes his entire work as an ἱστορίη, a word which could not fail to indicate to a mid-fifth-century reader that the author perceived his work, amongst other things, as scientific enquiry.[24] The effects of this situation in the treatment of Egypt's geography, geology, zoology, botany, and ethnography have already been discussed (see above, p. 230), but it emerges also in several other areas: an interest in the problems of epistemology surfaces at 3,2,[25] and contemporary medical thought is clearly in evidence at 35,2 and 77,2–3; and an awareness of methods of argument typical both of rhetoric, philosophy, and science shows itself at many points: the use of argument by induction, normally based on observation (5; 10–14; 22; 24–7; 104); εἰκός, or probability (22; 25,2; 27; 43,2–3; 45; 49,2–3; 56; 93); empiricism (12; 14; 28; 45; 57; 156); analogy (10; 20; 33; 150); *reductio ad absurdum* (15); and exposing a fallacy (21; 23). His willingness to argue a case also manifests itself in the use of archaeological τεκμήρια (44; 103; 106; 131,3; 135), arguments from tradition (43; 112), and by chronology (134).

Chronology was another major contemporary scholarly concern. One of Hecataeus' two major works, the *Genealogiai*, was devoted to this topic, and in it he attempted to bring traditions on the relationships of gods and heroes into some sort of coherent order. This work indisputably had an influence on Herodotus (see above, p. 231), and his interests in this area are apparent in a number of ways in Book II: he attempts to grapple with the chronological problems presented by Greek mythological traditions (43–4; 142–6); there is an interest in the contradictions between Greek and Egyptian chronology (143); and there is an uncompromising determination to provide a clear chronological framework for Egyptian history. It is likely, though undemonstrable, that the latter is Herodotus' own creation,[26] but it clearly reflects Egyptian tradition, on which he claims to rely, though inaccuracies are not infrequent. It shows the traditional distinction between the dynasties of gods and humans (4,2; 144–5), and then deals with the human kings in what Herodotus believed to be their chronological order. These rulers are divided into two groups: kings from Min to

---

[23] *De Herodoti Malignitate* 12 (*Mor.* 857a).

[24] This meaning emerges clearly in the Hippocratic *On Ancient Medicine* 20, which probably dates *c.*430 BC.

[25] Cf. e.g. the speculations of Xenophanes, Heraclitus, Parmenides, and Empedocles (KR², pp. 179 ff., 186 ff. (esp. p. 188), 244 ff., 284 ff., 309 ff.).

[26] Lloyd, *Introduction*, pp. 175 ff.

Sethos (Shabataka), a total of 342 kings (99–142), and the Dodecarchy and the kings of the Saite (XXVIth) Dynasty down to Amasis (147–82), though this continues into Book III with the account of the reign of Psammenitus. When Herodotus or his contemporaries needed to fix events or personalities in time they normally either simply used generations or they converted a generation count into calendar years on the basis of a fixed generation length. Herodotus indicates that his system was to assume three generations to 100 years, though it is evident that this scheme was not applied with any great arithmetical rigour (142).

We need finally to mention two further features of Herodotus' mind which operate at a much less conscious level than those hitherto discussed. In the first place, he shows a typically Greek curiosity about the way things work or are made. The detailed description of Egyptian methods of boat-building at ch. 96 is an excellent instance of this, and the lengthy account of the technology of building pyramids is, if anything, an even more striking example. Secondly, he shows a marked predilection for arranging his data into neat but oversimplified patterns. This process of over-schematization led in several cases to severe distortion: the catalogue of Egyptian customs at chs. 35–6 can frequently be convicted of this deficiency; the neat tripartite division in the account of mummification is untenable (86–9); such evidence as we have on the Labyrinth does not support Herodotus' elegant parallelism between the subterranean chambers and those above ground (148); and the chronological simplicity injected into the building of the *temene* at Naucratis is clearly at variance with archaeology (178).

VI

When we come to evaluate this account, what is our verdict? On Egyptian culture Herodotus knew a great deal. The catalogue of customs at chs. 35–6 shows much keen observation (e.g. on weaving techniques, priests, and filial obligation), but the picture is severely distorted by over-schematization. At ch. 37 the punctilious attention to ritual obligation by priests and laity is well remarked, and most of the other comments can be substantiated. Much space is also devoted elsewhere to things religious: on the cult of the gods his statements are, in the main, consistent with Egyptian evidence (38–48; 58–76; 83), and, even when confirmation is lacking, the Egyptologist does not normally find the comments startling (e.g. 40). However, Herodotus' determination to identify Greek and Egyptian gods produces an entirely unhistorical view of the relationship between Greek and Egyptian religions (49–57; 91), and at times he also falls victim to his besetting sin of oversimplification (41, 65). The account of the cult of the dead again shows considerable knowledge of Egyptian practices (85–90), but is equally guilty of over-schematization. On Egyptian medicine many of his comments are not without justification, but, again, the account presents a much less complex picture than Egyptian evidence suggests (84), and the same can be said of the discussion of Egyptian agriculture at ch. 14. Herodotus' descriptions of Egyptian boat-building and sailing techniques are commendably accurate (29; 36; 96), but his firm determination to ascribe cultural priority to Egypt in the invention of the calendar, altars, statues, and temples (4) is misplaced, and his reference to Egyptian use of goat's milk as a drink is certainly incorrect (2). On the few occasions when he comments on Egyptian words or linguistic habits his statements are unexceptionable (42,5; 69,3; 143,4; 158,5), and throughout the work Egyptian place- and personal names are usually rendered with accuracy. He rarely comments on the character of the Egyptian people. When he does, his statements are sound, but they are isolated observations (37,1; 45,2; 158,5), and there is no coherent perception of the fundamental ethos or ideology of Egyptian culture. The organization of the kingdom occupies him little. We hear of kings and nomes, and he is aware of the status of Thebes, Memphis, Heliopolis, and Sais as major cities, either politically or in religious terms, and he also has some knowledge of the taxation system (98). All in all, however, Egyptian culture is perceived against a background of Greek culture; it is pre-eminently points of similarity or difference with the Greek world which attract his attention.

Herodotus' account of Egyptian history is very much of a piece with that of Egyptian civilization. Half of the names of rulers are well rendered; of the rest five are certainly corrupt (Moiris, Sesostris, Rhampsinitus, Psammis, Psammenitus), two probably so (Asychis, Sethos); two are certainly false names (Pheros and Proteus), and one probably so (Anysis). When genuine names are employed, they are the names which we should expect Egyptians themselves to use. The chronology is often inadequate: the pyramid-builders are badly displaced (124,1), and their reign-lengths are incorrect (127,1, 3; 133,1, 5), as is that of Sabacos (137,2; 139,3); the order of succession is sometimes wrong (127,1; 129,1); and attempts to locate rulers in terms of years erroneous (13,1; 140,2; 142, 2–3). However, infelicities of this kind are concentrated in the first half of the historical section, and the chronology of the account of the Saite rulers from Psammetichus onwards is much more accurate (see, however, 161,2).

The narrative of events has a hard core of genuinely historical material, and rulers of most of the major periods are mentioned: the Archaic Period (Min), the Old Kingdom (Nitocris, Cheops, Chephren, Mycerinus), the Middle Kingdom (Sesostris, Moiris), the New Kingdom (Rhampsinitus), the Libyan Period (Asychis), the Ethiopian (Nubian) Period (Sabacos, Sethos), the Saite Period (Psammetichus to Amasis, continuing with Psammenitus in Book III), and the Persian Period (Cambyses, Darius). In terms of accuracy and detail the section on Saite history is undoubtedly superior to the first; indeed, it provides the earliest and most important consecutive account of the period in any language. Throughout, however, this historical core is overlaid and distorted by non-historical or pseudo-historical elements of many different kinds: folklore and other narrative-fiction influences are pervasive (100; 107–9; 111; 121–2; 126; 131; 133; 140–1; 151; 160; 162; 172; 175; 181); Egyptian propaganda, both political and cultural, is in evidence (103; 110; 152; 169; 172–4) and possibly also Greek propaganda (163); Egyptian and Greek ethical and ideological preoccupations are a recurrent feature (99; 102–10; 111; 120; 136; 137; 139; 140; 141; 151–2; 161; 169); probable cases of the intrusion of faded myths can be identified (137; 140; 141); different rulers can be combined or confused (110; 120–1; 137–40; 152); time-scales can be foreshortened (124–9; 154; 161–3 and 169); Greek traditions or practices can contaminate the record (99 [possibly]; 108; 109; 114; 125; 134; 136; 151); there is a clear and sometimes pernicious concern with real or imaginary Egyptian analogies to items in Greek culture (2; 28; 113; 123; 144–5; 164–8; 170); there is undue concentration on issues of interest to Greeks or impinging upon them (103; 104; 105; 106; 112–20; 134–5; 157; 159; 160; 161; 178–82); and finally Herodotus in his Egyptian history, as elsewhere, feels at liberty to mobilize all his literary skills to make the account as dramatic and compelling as possible (114–15; 121; 151; 172–4).

In addition to Egyptian culture, Herodotus also refers *en passant* to elements in the culture and geography of Phrygia, Nubia, and Libya. His claim that the word βέκος was the Phrygian word for bread is probably correct (2,4); on the political life and culture of Nubia he is sound (29–30); but his observations on the geography and tribal distribution of Libya are considerably oversimplified (33–4; 42).

If we turn to Herodotus' account of the non-human aspects of Egypt, we are confronted with a similarly variegated picture. In his discussion of geography and geology (in particular 5–34) the overall impression left on the reader is the scientific spirit which he shows throughout and his independence of mind (e.g. 15–34), though at times the organization of his material is not as logical as it might have been (21). On the configuration of the country he is, on the whole, good, though his measurements are not reliable (e.g. 15); his comments on the inundation of the Nile and rates of sedimentation are sometimes infelicitous (13); his location of sites can be inaccurate (15) and descriptions of them imprecise (28); he is misleading on the nature of the Bolbitinic branch (17) and confused and inaccurate on the area south of the First Cataract (29–31, 33); his discussions of buildings contain much of merit but must be treated with caution.[27] However, these errors in the main are venial since he was usually very much at the mercy of his informants and would not have found their information easy, or indeed possible, to check.

On fauna and flora the picture is far from monochrome. In zoology, paradoxography is a recurrent feature: the ornithology is generally good (22; 75–6). He does make the error of treating the phoenix as a creature which really existed (73), but he was clearly led to this belief by Egyptians, and we must always remember that what is clearly fabulous to us was not necessarily as clearly so to the ancients. In his account of quadrupeds eccentricities certainly arise (66,3; 68), the description of the hippopotamus being conspicuously inaccurate (71). The discussion of the behaviour of *Tilapia* at ch. 93 shows some acute observation but is nevertheless marred by confusion, whilst the description of the flying serpents at ch. 75 is one of the most perplexing *cruces* in Herodotus. Botanical comment is less problematic; errors there are, but good information was clearly available (92; 96).

---

[27] Id., in A. Powell (ed.), *The Greek World*, London–New York 1995, pp. 273 ff.

Summary of Book II

problem of the Third Pyramid of Gîza and the career of Rhodopis. 136 The reign of Asychis. 137 Anysis and Sabacos. 138 The great temple at Bubastis. 139–40 Anysis and Sabacos. 141 Sethos and Sennacherib. 142 Egyptian chronology. 143 Hecataeus and the Theban priests. 144–6 The Egyptian dynasty of the gods and the problem of the Egyptian origin of Heracles, Dionysus, and Pan. 147 Sources, the Dodecarchs. 148 The Labyrinth. 149 Lake Moiris. 151–7 The reign of Psammetichus, including an *excursus* on Buto and floating island of Chemmis (155–6). 158–9 The reign of Necho. 160 The reign of Psammis (Psammetichus II). 161–9 The reign of Apries, including an *excursus* on the Egyptian class structure (164–8). 169–82 The reign of Amasis, embracing not only political and military history but also descriptions of the royal tombs at Sais (169,4–5), the alleged mysteries of Sais (170–1), and the Greek settlement at Naucratis (178).

1,1. τελευτήσαντος ... παῖς: cf. the Bisitun inscription of Darius I (*DB* I § 10 Kent p. 530 below). Cambyses (Old Persian *Kambūjia*, cf. Kent, pp. 178b ff.) became Great King in 530 and died in 522 (Parker–Dubberstein, p. 14). **Κασσανδάνης τῆς Φαρνάσπεω**: Pharnaspes was an Achaemenid (III 2,2). The alternative tradition that Cambyses was the son of Nitetis, daughter of the Pharaoh Apries, was clearly Egyptian propaganda (Alan B. Lloyd, in A. Kuhrt and H. Sancisi-Weerdenburg (eds.), *Achaemenid History III, Method and Theory*, Leiden 1987, pp. 55). **προαποθανούσης ... ποιέεσθαι**: Herodotus has an inordinate taste for alliteration with π (cf. III 58; 60,2). The function is emphatic.

2. ὡς ... ἐνόμιζε: the verb is here treated as a verb of perceiving and constructed with the participle. It normally takes the infinitive (Goodwin, *Moods and Tenses*, p. 361). **ἐπὶ δὲ Αἴγυπτον ... στρατηλασίην**: the invasion took place in May/June 525 BC (Posener, p. 173 ff.). It had been impending since the time of Cyrus and had been provoked by the anti-Persian foreign policy of the pharaoh Amasis (570–526 BC) (Kienitz, pp. 31 ff.). **Αἴγυπτον**: probably the Egyptian Ḥwt-k3-Ptḥ, 'House of the Spirit of Ptah', a name of the city of Memphis (Gardiner, *AEO* II, p. 124*). **ἄλλους τε ... ἐπεκράτεε**: the heterogeneous character of the invading force is confirmed by the Egyptian inscription of Udjahorresnet (Posener, pp. 6, B.11–12, 14, 18–9) and by the 5th-cent. Elephantine Aramaic papyri (N. Aimé-Giron, *Textes araméens d'Egypte*, Cairo 1931, p. 58). It was typical of the Persian army (Cook, pp. 101 ff.).

2–4. The antiquity of Egypt.

2,1. Ψαμμήτιχον: Egyptian (Gauthier, *Le Livre* p. 66 ff.), Psammetichus I (664–610 BC), the founder of the XXVIth Dynasty. **ἑωυτούς**: we should expect the nominative and infinitive since the subject of the infinitive is identical with that of ἐνόμιζον. The accusative is emphatic, insisting on the contrast with Φρύγας (cf. Schwyzer, *Gr. Grammatik* II, p. 376).

1–5. ἐπειδὴ δὲ Ψαμμήτιχος ... γυναιξί: for this famous pseudo-historical episode see also, *int. al.*, Aristophanes, *Nu.* 398, with schol., and Pollux V 88; Herod. II 28, 4 offers an intriguing parallel. The tale appeared in some form in Hecataeus (de Meulenaere, p. 47; Lloyd, *Commentary 1–98*, pp. 8 ff.) and is patently an Ionian invention (J. A. K. Thomson, *The Art of the Logos*, London 1935, pp. 56 ff.; Aly, pp. 62 ff.). For a discussion of the implications for Herodotean linguistics see T. Harrison, *Histos*, II (1988), 13 ff.

1. Φρύγας: the Phrygians, who invaded Asia Minor from Europe after 1200 BC, made a powerful impression on Greek historical consciousness (cf. I 14; 35; 45). The ill-founded notion of their extreme antiquity may reflect a confusion between Phrygians proper and the much older cultures which had prevailed in their area of settlement for centuries before (cf. R. D. Barnett, *CAH*³ II, pp. 417 ff.).

2. παιδία... αἶγας: note that the experiment is very carefully controlled. Experimental enquiry, while not common, was far from unknown in Greek science (B. Farrington, *Science in Antiquity*, Oxford 1969², Index, s.v. 'experiment, scientific'). ἐς τὰ ποίμνια: the ἐς is *praegnans*: 'take to his flocks and raise them there.' τὴν ὥρην... γάλακτος: the Egyptians did not drink goats' milk, though that of cows was a favourite beverage (G. Lefebvre, *Revue d'Égyptologie*, XXI (1960), 59 ff.). Greeks, on the other hand, did (L. A. Moritz, *KP* III, pp.1293 ff.). τὴν ὥρην: 'at the right time' instead of ἐν ὥρῃ. The accusative normally denotes extent rather than a specific point in time and perhaps even here suggests a point of some duration.

3–4. βεκός... τὸν ἄρτον: probably correct; for the word occurs in Phrygian inscriptions (J. Friedrich, *Kleinasiatische Sprachdenkmäler*, Berlin 1932, nos. 33 and 86) and probably in the linguistically related Samothracian (P. M. Fraser, *Samothrace: The Inscriptions on Stone*, II 1, London 1960, p. 64). Such linguistic arguments are typical of 5th-cent. Greek anthropology.

5. τῶν ἱρέων: for Herodotus' priestly sources see above, pp. 230 ff.   τοῦ Ἡφαίστου: the Egyptian *Ptḥ*, 'Ptah', the chief god of Memphis (Kolta, *Die Gleichsetzung*, pp. 123 ff.).   ἐν Μέμφι: see note on 99,4.   Ἕλληνες δὲ λέγουσι: variant versions feature frequently in Herodotus and probably reflect his determination to report what he had heard even when he did not accept it (F. J. Groten, *Phoenix*, XVII (1963), 79 ff.). This variant is likely to be Hecataean (Lloyd, *Commentary 1–98*, pp. 8 ff.) and is probably rejected because it violated Herodotus' belief in the basic humanity of the Egyptians (note on ch. 45).

3,1. κατὰ μὲν... ἐτραπόμην: i.e. Herodotus entered into discussions with priests in the three pre-eminent religious centres of the country. The concern to cross-check his traditions is typical (see above, pp. 228 ff.).   Θήβας: etymology dubious. It appears to derive, by assimilation to Greek Θῆβαι, either from *Ṭ3mt*, the name for the western district of Thebes, or from *t3'Ipt*, 'Luxor' (Gardiner, *AEO* II, pp. 25* ff.). Thebes, the mighty capital of the Egyptian empire during the New Kingdom, was greatly in decline in Herodotus' time, but was still a major ecclesiastical centre as the focal point of the cult of Amon-re, to whose priesthood Herodotus' informants belonged.   Ἡλίου πόλιν: Egyptian *'Iwnw*, *'Iwnw R'*, sited at Tell Hisn, *c*.12 km. north-east of Cairo. It was the centre of the worship of the sun god Re (Gardiner, *AEO* II, pp. 144* ff.).   λογιώτατοι: λόγιοι in pre-Socratic philosophy can designate men of outstanding intellect who have promoted the development of civilization (cf. Democritus, 68 B30 DK); this meaning could well be at issue here.

2. τὰ μέν νυν θεῖα... ἐξηγέεσθαι: one of many instances where Herodotus expresses an unwillingness to discuss theological issues, but, in this case, his motive is stated (see further Linforth, *UCPCPh* VII 9 (1924), 259 ff.; id., *UCPCPh* IX 7 (1928), 201 ff.). τὰ μὲν... θεῖα: i.e. what belongs to the trans-physical world, such as myths, divine attributes, and the forms of the gods. These things cannot be objects of

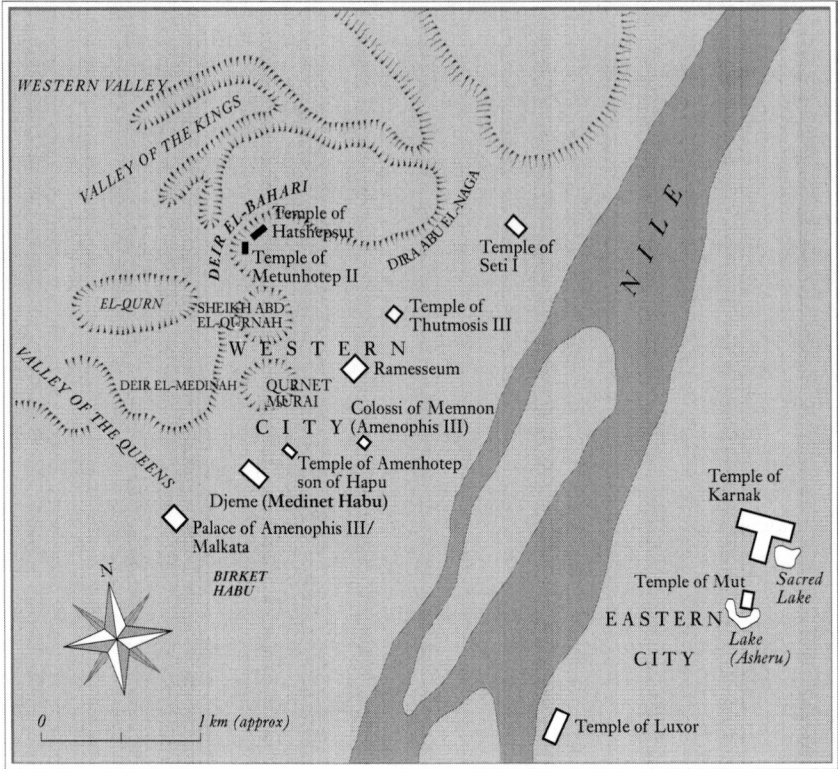

Map 20. Thebes

sense-perception and are not susceptible to ἱστορίη. They are distinct from
ἀνθρωπήϊα (4,1), which belong in man's sphere of activity and can be subjected
to ἱστορίη.   τὰ οὐνόματα αὐτῶν: οὔνομα probably means no more than 'name' in
our sense (note on 43,2). αὐτῶν here and in περὶ αὐτῶν below is probably masculine
plural, referring to the θεοί implicit in θεῖα.   νομίζων ... ἐπίστασθαι: 'considering
that all men have equal knowledge concerning them (sc. θεοί)', i.e. all men have
equal lack of knowledge of them.   ὑπὸ τοῦ λόγου ἐξαναγκαζόμενος: Herodotus
recognizes that his narrative will at times absolutely compel him to break this rule-
of-thumb, e.g. in the discussion of the genealogy of Heracles at chs. 43–4, and the
excursus at 142–6. The ἐξ- prefix is used intensively to emphasize the absolute
nature of the compulsion (cf. H. Thesleff, *Studies in Intensification in Early and
Classical Greek*, Helsingfors 1954, p. 157).

4,1. ὅσα ... πρήγματα: see note on 3,2.

1–2. πρώτους ... ἐγγλύψαι: for Ancient Egyptians an entirely credible assertion,
given their inordinate self-esteem (cf. Plato, *Tim.* 21a–22b; Gardiner, *Egypt of the
Pharaohs*, p. 37).

1. πρώτους...τὸν ἐνιαυτόν: cf. Diod. I 50,1–2; Strabo XVII 1,29 (C806), 1,46 (C816). Herodotus is not simply claiming that the Egyptians discovered the year; he implies that they then passed it on to others (see above, p. 235). The Egyptian civil calendar was introduced in 2770 and post-dates by several centuries its Sumerian counterpart (S. H. Langdon, *Babylonian Menologies and the Semitic Calendar*, London 1935, p. 10).   δυώδεκα μέρεα...ἔλεγον: clearly the civil year, which consisted of 12 months of 30 days each. These were grouped into three 4-month seasons and supplemented by the 5 epagomenal days. The priests' ἐξευρεῖν ἐκ τῶν ἄστρων is only correct insofar as this system was a reaction against the anomalies of the old luni-solar calendar (in general see Parker).   ἄγουσι...τῶν ὡρέων εἵνεκεν: the Greek civil calendars used a solar year of 12 months of 29 or 30 days. An intercalary month (ἐμβόλιμος) was added every other year (διὰ τρίτου ἔτεος) to keep in step with the astronomical year (Bickerman, pp. 27 ff.).   ἐμοὶ δοκέειν: this absolute use of the infinitive first appears in the 5th cent. and is extremely common in Herodotus with or without ὡς preceding. It is often used in parenthesis, as here, to indicate the writer's attitude (Schwyzer, *Gr. Grammatik* II, pp. 378 ff.).   Αἰγύπτιοι...παραγίνεται: 5 epagomenal days were indeed added at the end of the Egyptian civil year, but, since this only raised the number of days to 365, and the astronomical year is c.365.25 days, the practice failed to keep the year in step with the seasons (Parker, pp. 51 ff.).

2. δυώδεκά τε θεῶν ἐπωνυμίας: probably ἐπωνυμίας here is synonymous with οὐνόματα at 50,1. The Egyptians did not group gods in twelves; probably they were talking of one of their equivalents to the Greek canonical Twelve, e.g. the Heliopolitan Ennead, many of whose members had been identified with members of the Twelve (Lloyd, *Commentary 1–98*, pp. 28 ff.).   βωμούς...ἐγγλύψαι: in all cases demonstrably untrue: older altars in A. Moortgat, *Die Entstehung der sumerischen Hochkultur, Der alte Orient*, XLIII, Leipzig 1945, p. 42); older divine statues in J. Mellaart, *CAH*³ I, pp. 312 ff.); older temples in H. Schmökel, *Das Land Sumer*, Stuttgart 1966³, pp. 102 ff.; and older stone relief sculpture in H. Frankfort, *The Art and Architecture of the Ancient Orient*, Pelican History of Art, VII, Harmondsworth 1954, pp. 9 ff.   τούτων...ἔλεγον: for the common λόγος–ἔργον antithesis see G. Kennedy, *The Art of Persuasion in Greece*, London 1963, Index, s.v. 'antithesis'. For Min see ch. 99.

3. ἐπὶ τούτου...ἀνὰ τὸν ποταμόν: geomorphology was a major preoccupation of Ionian geography (notes on chs. 5–14). Egyptian assent to this notion was probably gained because they were thinking in terms of some such mythological event as the emergence of the primeval hill from the waters of chaos (for which see Bonnet, *RÄRG*, pp. 847 ff.).   τοῦ Θηβαϊκοῦ νομοῦ: cf. 91,1. Clearly not the Theban Nome, i.e. the 4th Nome of Upper Egypt, but the whole of Upper Egypt from Elephantine to the entrance of the Fayûm (cf. Ball, *Egypt*, pp. 112 ff.). λίμνης τῆς Μοίριος: for the lake of Moeris see notes on chs. 149–50. ἀνάπλοος...ποταμόν: this presupposes an average of c.35 miles (56 km.) a day, which is entirely plausible (cf. R. Caminos, *JEA* L (1964), 84, n. line 11).

5–34. An essay on the physical geography of Egypt.

5,1. καὶ εὖ μοι ἐδόκεον ... περὶ τῆς χώρης: Herodotus begins a series of τεκμήρια designed to support the priests' claim (cf. notes on chs. 7, 10, 12–13).　　δῆλα γάρ ... ἔχει: the major source is ὄψις (see above, p. 229), but ἀκοή was also available, not surprisingly since sedimentation was of considerable interest to Ionian geographers (e.g. Xanthus, *FGrHist* 765 F 13), and Hecataeus had discussed its role in precisely this context (ibid. I F 301). His account was certainly in Herodotus' mind here (Jacoby, *Kommentar*, ad loc.).　　ὅτι Αἴγυπτος ... τοῦ ποταμοῦ: this can hardly be anything but the Hecataean doctrine. Αἴγυπτος ... ναυτίλλονται: the following clause makes it clear that the limit was lake Moiris (J. Gwyn Griffiths, *JNES* XXV (1966), 58).　　καὶ τὰ κατύπερθε ... τοιοῦτον: Herodotus' modification of Hecataeus based on ὄψις.　　μέχρι τριῶν ἡμερέων: this would be a maximum of 168.95 km. south of Beni Suef (cf. note on 4,3). The only feature which might have led Herodotus to treat the area on the same terms as the Delta was the Bahr Yusuf, which could have been regarded as the remnant of an old water-course left behind by gradual depositions of alluvium (cf. note on ch. 10).

2. πρῶτα ... πρόχυσιν τῆς γῆς ἐοῦσαν: τεκμήριον 1. The effects of sedimentation have been observed well in excess of 48.27 km. from the coast (Ball, *Egypt*, p. 13), but the details here perplex. In Herodotus, a day's journey by sea is 700 stades, i.e. 130.33 km. (IV 86), whereas the 11-fathom line is not even encountered 19 miles from the coast. The easiest solution is to treat ἡμέρης δρόμον not as reflecting a measurement taken at right angles to the coast without regard to sailing conditions, but simply as an indication of the time it took Herodotus or his source to get from the 11-fathom line to the coast on one particular occasion. ἀνοίσεις ... ἔσεαι: both tense and person are designed to create a sense of immediacy by involving the reader imaginatively in the action.

6,1. αὐτῆς δὲ τῆς Αἰγύπτου ... σχοῖνοι: spectacularly wrong: on Herodotus' count (6,3), 60 schoinoi amount to 3600 stades; at 179 m. per stade, the shortest known pre-Hellenistic measurement (*Artemis Lexikon*, 3424), this totals 644.40 km., whereas the correct measurement is *c*.476.26 km. (Ball, *Egypt*, p. 13). If the long stade of 213 m. is used, all other figures become correspondingly higher. The error might have arisen in two ways: the schoinos could vary in length in Egypt (see below), and it may be that Herodotus' authority meant 60 schoinoi of 30 or 40 stades. Using the low stade, we should then get distances of 322.20 km. or 429.60 km. respectively; alternatively, the figure might be based on information on the time taken to pass by sea between the two points, i.e. it might reflect a journey of 5 days in adverse conditions converted at the rate of 700 stades per day (see note on 5,2).　　κατὰ ἡμεῖς ... τείνει: Herodotus insists on his autonomy; the Ionians measured from the Pelusiac to the Canopic Branch (note on ch. 15).　　κατά: for κατ' ἅ, as often in Herodotus (Powell, *Lexicon*, p. 185).　　εἶναι: cf. VII 47,1 for Herodotus' use of the infinitive with διαιρέω. This infinitive seems to hover between the final and consecutive uses.　　τοῦ Πλινθινήτεω κόλπου: the Arabian Gulf (Ball, *Egypt* p. 13).　　Σερβωνίδος λίμνης: the Sabkhet el-Bardawil (ibid.).　　τὸ

Κάσιον ὄρος: Katîb el-Qals, west of lake Bardawil (ibid.).   *ἄπο*: this anastrophe of *ἀπό* is unique in Herodotus (Powell, *Lexicon*, p. 38). The effect is to throw *ταύτης* into sharp relief.

3. *δύναται... στάδια*: this information, together with 149,3 and V 53, yields the following Herodotean table: 1 schoinos = 2 parasangs = 60 stades; 1 parasang = 30 stades; 1 stade = 6 plethra = 100 orguiai; 1 orguia = 4 cubits or 6 feet; 1 cubit = 6 palms; 1 foot = 4 palms. Unfortunately, Herodotus never provides enough information to convert this table accurately into modern metrological systems.   *ὁ δὲ σχοῖνος... Αἰγύπτιον*: the schoinos was an Egyptian measurement widely used in the Mediterranean and Near East in Herodotus' time. Its length could vary in Egypt from 30 stades in the Delta to 120 in Middle Egypt and 60 in the Thebaid (Strabo XVII 1,24 (C804)), but it was the 30-stade measure which prevailed abroad (Schlott, pp. 144 ff., 156).

7,1. *ἐνθεῦτεν... ἰλύς*: *τεκμήριον* 2 (note on ch. 5), the physiography of the Delta. *ὑπτίη*: 'flat, horizontal'. Today the average slope of the plain is 1–10,600 (J. Ball, *Contributions*, p. 47).   *ἔνυδρος καὶ ἰλύς*: an accurate description (notes on chs. 10, 17,4–6, 19 ff., 92–3).   *ὁδῷ... φερούσῃ*: this well-known landmark was constructed in 522/1 BC by Peisistratus, grandson of the tyrant, in the agora opposite the Stoa of Zeus. As the starting-point of major roads out of the city, it was frequently used in calculations of distance (e.g. *IG* II² 2640) (H. A. Thompson, *The Athenian Agora*, Athens 1962², pp. 22, 35, 66 ff.).   *Πῖσαν*: though used by Herodotus as a synonym for Olympia, it was strictly the name of a district, probably the group of Eight Cities of Pisatis mentioned by Apollodorus (Strabo VIII 3,31 (C356)) (Meyer, *RE* XX 2, 1732 ff.).   *τὸν νηὸν*: the Doric temple of the Olympian Zeus erected by Lison between 471 and 456 BC (Wiesner, *RE* XVIII, 84 ff.).

2. *τὸ μή... εἶναι*: cf. Sophocles, *OT* 1232, 1388; *Phil.* 1241. The article serves simply to reinforce the infinitive (cf. Burguière, p. 102 ff.).   *ἡ μὲν γάρ... χιλίων*: 1500 stades = 268.5 km. and 15 stades = 2.69 km. at 179 m. per stade (note on 6,1). The true distance via Corinth, Sicyon, Orchomenus, Sirai, Thelpusa, and Stratos exceeds 241.35 km. On these figures, therefore, Herodotus is not far wrong.   *ἡ δὲ ἐς Ἡλίου πόλιν... τοῦτον*: the distance from the sea to Heliopolis along the modern Rosetta Branch is *c*.265 km. Herodotus' estimate is, therefore, very accurate, if he was using the 179 m. stade.   [*ἐς*] *τὸν ἀριθμὸν τοῦτον*: the preposition *ἐς* is unusual with *πληρόω* but is read by virtually all mss and is also the *lectio difficilior*.   *ἀπὸ δὲ Ἡλίου πόλιος... Αἴγυπτος*: Egypt proper extended to Aswan, a distance from Heliopolis of *c*.1006.44 km.; the valley width varies from *c*.28.98 km. to no more than that of the river at some points (e.g. Gebel es-Silileh, cf. Baedeker, *Egypt*, map between pp. 244–5).

8,1. *τῆς Ἀραβίης ὄρος*: the genitive is dependent on *ὄρος*. Herodotus habitually divides Upper Egypt between Arabia and Libya (see note on ch. 16).   *ἀπ' ἄρκτου... καὶ νότον*: Herodotus' system of orientation combined astronomical principles with the use of winds connected with the four cardinal points. Both appear here (Berger, pp. 127 ff.).   *τὴν Ἐρυθρὴν καλεομένην θάλασσαν*: strictly, synonymous with 'the Southern Ocean' (IV 37,1), but the phrase not infrequently refers to the Red Sea (cf. II 158,2; IV 39,1; 42,3). The name probably originates from the reddish-brown algae which cover large tracts of water during summer (*Admiralty Geographical Handbook Series. B.R.527. Western Arabia and the Red Sea, Naval Intelligence Division*, June 1946, p. 66). ἐν τῷ αἱ λιθοτομίαι ἔνεισι...τὸ ὄρος: the Mokattam Hills east of Cairo, which produce extremely fine limestone. The casing blocks of the pyramids of Cheops and Chephren and those of the upper part of that of Mycerinus emanated from there (S. Clarke and R. Engelbach, *Ancient Egyptian Masonry*, Oxford 1930, Index s.v. 'Tura quarries'). δύο μηνῶν...πρὸς ἑσπέρην: badly wrong; modern times by camel are 4–11 days (Baedeker, Egypt, p. 372 ff.). The mistake probably arose through combining the erroneous conviction that frankincense occurred at the eastern boundary of the Arabian mountain and information on the lengthy Egyptian expeditions to Eritrea–Somaliland to obtain that commodity (Lloyd, *Commentary 1–98*, pp. 51 ff.). εἶναι: attracted into the infinitive by proximity to ἐπυνθανόμην (cf. III 14,11; IV 5,1; V 10).

2. τὸ δὲ πρὸς Λιβύης...φέροντα: the north-east sector of the Libyan desert (Kees, *Ancient Egypt*, pp. 127 ff.). αἱ πυραμίδες: usually the Gîza pyramids (chs. 12, 97, 124–8, 134–5), but others were known to Herodotus (chs. 101, 136,3–4, 148–9). κατειλυμένον: cf. Homer, *Od.* XIV 136.

3. ὡς εἶναι Αἰγύπτου: limitative, lit. 'The territory beyond Heliopolis is no longer much land so as to belong to Egypt'. ὅσον τε ἡμερέων...Αἴγυπτός ἐστι: Herodotus is thinking of the πέλεκυς theory whereby the shape of Egypt was thought to resemble a double axe:

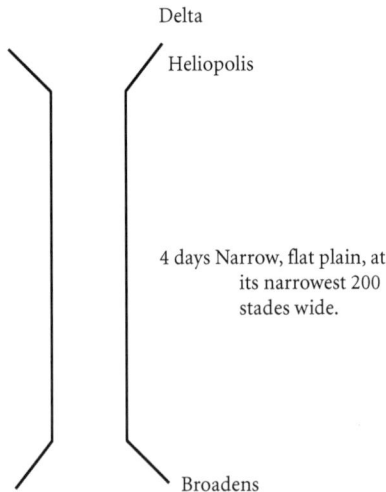

Delta

Heliopolis

4 days Narrow, flat plain, at its narrowest 200 stades wide.

Broadens

(so Hecataeus and pseudo-Scylax, *FGrHist* I F301, *Kommentar*, ad loc.). Between Helwan and El-Wasta (roughly 98.22 km.) the valley is indeed very narrow and then broadens out to 20.13–24.15 km. as far as Farshut (V. Ehrenberg, *Klio*, XVI (1920), 321 ff.); 98.22 km. would take about 3 days in a modern sailing dahabiyeh (cf. Baedeker, *Egypt*, p. 204). The addition of <καὶ δέκα> after τεσσέρων proposed by Dietsch is quite unnecessary and is contradicted by Aristides XXXVI 46.   στάδιοι...οὐ πλέους: 200 stades = 35.8 km., much too high; even at El-Wasta the width is only *c.*13.69 km., but Herodotus would not have found it easy to get an accurate figure (cf. Sourdille, *La Durée*, pp. 140 ff.).

9,1. ἐννέα ἡμερέων: at least 13 days would be needed by sailing boat (Ehrenberg, op.cit. p. 320 n. 2). Presumably a slip of memory or an error in recording is to blame for the mistake.   στάδιοι ἐόντων: 4860 stades/81 schoinoi = 869.94 km. at 179 m. per stade. The correct distance is 722.5 km. The discrepancy here, and below, is probably due to imprecise methods of calculation.
2. τὸ μὲν παρὰ θάλασσαν...τρισχιλίων: see note on ch. 6.   ὅσον δέ... ἑξακισχίλιοι: 6120 stades = 1095.48 km. at 179 m. per stade. The correct distance is *c.*890 km.   τὸ δὲ ἀπὸ Θηβέων...εἰσι: 1800 stades = 322.2 km. at 179 m. per stade. The true distance is *c.*220 km.

10,1. Ταύτης ὧν τῆς χώρης...Αἰγυπτίοισι: cf. 4,3; 5.   τῶν γὰρ ὀρέων... κόλπος θαλάσσης: only to a point 3 days' travel south of lake Moeris (note on 5,1). The claim is strikingly apposite: the sea invaded the entire valley during Pliocene times (began *c.*10 million years ago) but retreated as far as the Fayûm before the Pleistocene (began *c.*700,000 years ago). Subsequently, the river has been depositing sediments of sand, gravel, and mud to create the Delta and the rich margins of agricultural land along its banks. The Delta reached approximately its present extent *c.*10,000 BC (Ball, *Contributions*, pp. 17 ff.).   ὥσπερ...πεποίηκε: τεκμήριον 3 (see note on 5,2), one of many Herodotean arguments κατ' ἀναλογίαν (see above, p. 236). Hecataean influence is certain in this section (cf. FGrHist I F102c, 109, 221–4, 239–41, with Commentary).   τά τε περὶ "Ιλιον: the Hissarlik plain received sediment from the Old Scamander and the Simois (W. Leaf, *Strabo on the Troad*, Cambridge 1923, pp. 158 ff.).   Τευθρανίην: the port of Teuthranie, main city of the district of the same name, stood on an alluvial plain created by the river Caicus (Bürchner, *RE* X, 1501 ff.).   "Εφεσόν: the depositions of the river Cayster have long since completely isolated this ancient port from the sea (G. Bean, *Aegean Turkey*, London 1966, pp. 160 ff.).   Μαιάνδρου πεδίον: the river's alluvium was slowly filling up the Latmian Gulf in Herodotus' time, with disastrous effects for the cities of Old Priene, Myous, and particularly Miletus.

1–2. ὡς γε εἶναι...ἐστι: the Florentine mss and the Parisinus read ὥστε, but the analogy of IV 99,5 suggests that ὡς, the reading of the Roman group, is preferable. The use of ὡς/ὥστε with the infinitive in a limiting conditional sense is paralleled outside Herodotus (Moorhouse, p. 311). Here εἶναι is equivalent to ἐξεῖναι. The emphasis on the inordinate size of things Egyptian and the willingness to denigrate Greek ideas are conspicuous Herodotean habits of mind (see above, pp. 235 ff.).
2. πενταστόμου: see note on 17,3–6.
3. καὶ οὐκ ἥκιστα...πεποίηκε: cf. pseudo-Scylax, *GGM*, p. 37; pseudo-Scymnus, *GGM*, p. 215; Thuc. II 102. Alluviation on the plain of Achelous was so voluminous that it forced the abandonment of the old city of Oeniadae and the

construction of a replacement nearer the sea (Strabo X 2,2 (C450)) (A. Philipp-son, *Die griechischen Landschaften*, II 2, Frankfurt a. M. 1958, pp. 400 ff.).

11,1–4. ἔστι δέ... ἐργατικοῦ: strictly not a τεκμήριον (note on 5,2) but a hypo-thetical analogy illustrating the thesis of chs. 5 and 10.

1. τῆς᾿ Ἀραβίης χώρης: see note on ch. 15.   κόλπος θαλάσσης: i.e. the Southern Ocean (note on 8,1).   τῆς Ἐρυθρῆς καλεομένης: i.e. the Southern Ocean (ibid.).   ὡς ἔρχομαι φράσων: in such periphrastic forms the weight of meaning is always borne by the participle (Goodwin, *Moods and Tenses*, p. 354).

2. μῆκος... χρεωμένῳ: the figure is too high: 40 days at 700 stades per day (note on 5,2) = 5012 km. at 179 m. to the stade, whereas the distance from Suez to Abd al-Kuri is *c*.3059.58 km. and that to the Bab el-Mandeb 2093.40 km. Either Herodotus' informant used a slower rate of sailing (e.g. the standard 500 stades a day, which would reduce the distance to 3580 km.) or the figure reflects the length of a specific voyage including all the stops and delays.   εὖρος δέ... πλόου: the Red Sea at its widest is *c*.354.27 km. (Baedeker, *Egypt*, p. 424), which at 700 stades per day would take about 3 days. Confusion between the Gulf of Suez and the Red Sea is the most likely explanation.   ῥηχίη... γίνεται: a great θῶμα (see above, pp. 234 ff.). The tides vary from *c*.2.13 m. at Suez to the virtually imperceptible at some points (*Admiralty Geographical Handbook Series*. B.R. 527, op. cit., p. 61).

3. ἐκ τῆς βορηίης... τῆς νοτίης: see note on 158,4.

4. χωσθῆναι: the Roman group of mss has the simplex, but ἐκχωσθῆναι has better ms authority and also seems to give an added punch to the argument.

12,1. τοῖσι λέγουσι... ἰδών τε: the informants in question were Egyptian priests (4,3) and Greeks such as Hecataeus, but Herodotus typically emphasizes con-firmation by autopsy (see above, pp. 229 ff.).

1–3. τὴν Αἴγυπτον... ἐοῦσαν: despite the specious nature of several τεκμήρια (see below), the scientific spirit of this passage is impressive (cf. J. O. Thomson, p. 103).

1. τὴν Αἴγυπτον... γῆς: τεκμήριον 4 (see note on 5,1), a sound argument since the Nile Delta is a classic delta formation which has pushed itself out into the sea with depositions of sediment as far as the offshore currents permit (Ball, *Contributions*, pp. 13 ff.).   κογχύλιά: τεκμήριον 5, which has several parallels within the tradition of Ionian science (21 A33, 5 DK; *FGrHist* 765 F12: cf. KR, p. 140). The deserts contain an abundance of marine fossils (W. Hume, *Geology of Egypt* I, Cairo, 1925, pp. 3, 65 ff.; Ball, *Contributions*, p. 22), but relatively few reflect the Pliocene invasion of the valley by the sea (ibid. p. 26 ff.). Herodotus' argument may well have been based on quite the wrong type.   ἅλμην... δηλέεσθαι: τεκμήριον 6, unsound. Surface incrustations of salt are plentiful (Hume, op. cit., pp. 161, 172), but they are not in any way evidence of Herodotus' prehistoric sea.   δηλέεσθαι: salt incrustations created by capillary action within the masonry of buildings are a serious cause of damage in Ancient Egyptian monuments (T. G. H. James, *An Introduction to Ancient Egypt*, London 1979, p. 192). ψάμμον... ἔχον: τεκμήριον 7, unsound. The Libyan plateau is liberally covered with sand (Ball, *Contributions*, pp. 9 ff.), but it does not have a marine origin.

2–3. πρὸς δὲ... ἐοῦσαν: τεκμήριον 8, a sound argument.

2. οὐ μὲν οὐδὲ: this connective combination is not uncommon in Herodotus (Denniston, *Greek Particles*, p. 363). μελάγγαιόν: the soil is a blackish-brown mud (hence the Egyptian name *Kmt*, 'the Black Land', for Egypt) and can become deeply fissured (καταρρηγνυμένην) (Hurst, pp. 45 ff.). ὥστε: for ἅτε as often in Herodotus (Powell, *Lexicon*, p. 392, I, 1). ἐξ Αἰθιοπίης: in fact, from the Abyssinian Highlands (Hume, op. cit., pp. 175 ff.).

3. ἐρυθροτέρην: the area was often called *Dšrt*, 'the Red Land', by the Ancient Egyptians (*Wb.* V, pp. 494, 5–13). Συρίην: clearly here the area on the south-east coast of the Mediterranean between lake Serbonis and Ienisus (cf. τῆς γὰρ Ἀραβίης... νέμονται above and III 5,2). Herodotus' grouping of that district with the desert east of the Nile valley is geologically quite sound (Sourdille, *La Durée*, p. 118). ὑπόπετρον: the eastern desert is considerably more rocky than the western (T. Barron and W. Hume, *Topography and Geology of the Eastern Desert of Egypt: Central Portion*, Cairo 1902).

13,1. ἔλεγον... τεκμήριον: τεκμήριον 9, based on ἀκοή (see above, pp. 230 ff.). We are neatly returned to 4,3, a good example of ring composition (see in general Beck). The argument is specious, being based on misinterpreted evidence (see below). ἐπὶ Μοίριος βασιλέος: Amenemhet III, *c.*1842–1797 BC (Lloyd, *Historia*, XXXVII (1988), 31 ff.). ὅκως ἔλθοι... ἐς τὴν χώρην: the level of the inundation was not uniform throughout the country. Heights of 8 cubits (*c.*4.75 m.) and 15 or 16 cubits (8 or 8.53 m.) fit well modern figures for maxima at Sais in the Delta and Roda at Cairo (Bonneau, *La Crue*, p. 23). Clearly, therefore, Herodotus' figures refer to two quite different parts of Egypt and are useless for proving his thesis. ἀρδέσκε: the Ionic iterative imperfect (Goodwin, *Moods and Tenses*, p. 56). ἔτεα εἰνακόσια: the date is 500 years too low (see above). εἰ... ἀναβῇ: εἰ with subjunctive without ἄν is Homeric (Chantraine, *Grammaire* II, p. 279). It can be used, as here, when stating an undesirable hypothesis.

2. Αἰγυπτίων... οἰκέοντες: cf. 4,3. Herodotus seems to ignore 5,1. ἦν οὕτω... πείσεσθαι: quite untrue. The riverbed has risen at the same rate as the level of the alluvium on either side (8.89 cm. per century in antiquity: Ball, *Contributions*, pp. 175 ff.).

3. πυνθανόμενοι... μοῦνον: a typical Egyptian view (S. Sauneron, *BIFAO* LI (1952), 41 ff.). εἰ μὴ... αἱρεθήσονται: the future in protasis makes the conditional more emphatic: if the condition is fulfilled, the apodosis is certain to follow. The construction is frequent in threats or warnings (Goodwin, *Moods and Tenses*, pp. 165 ff.).

14,1. εἰ σφι... πεινήσουσι: see notes on 13,1–2. The apodosis has a future indicative where an optative with ἄν might be expected. This construction indicates the absolute certainty of the conclusion if the condition is fulfilled. ἡ χώρη ἡ ἔνερθε Μέμφιος: inconsistent, cf. 5,1 and 13,2. εἰ μήτε γε ὕσεταί: cf. note on 13,3 for the tense. Herodotus prefers to use middle for passive with this verb. Egypt's average rainfall is *c.*1 cm. per annum, though the Mediterranean coast receives *c*.20 cm. (Ball, *Contributions*, pp. 2 ff.). This is quite inadequate for agricultural purposes.

2. ἡ γὰρ δὴ νῦν...κομίζεται: cf. Diod. I 36, who recognizes that conditions are essentially the same throughout the country. Herodotus, unlike Strabo (XVII 1,3 (C788)), ignores the extremely laborious irrigation system which made Egyptian agriculture possible (F. Hartmann, pp. 87 ff.). The Egyptian peasant's life was by no means enviable (cf. Baedeker, *Egypt*, p. liv).   οὔτε ἀρότρῳ...πόνους: frequently true, since seed could often be broadcast immediately onto the damp alluvium. Greeks, on the other hand, might need to plough as many as three times before sowing (Homer, *Il.* XVIII 541 ff.).   ἄρσῃ...ἄρσας: for this *figura etymologica* cf. Homer, *Il.* I 595 ff.   ὗς: exemplified for the New Kingdom (Wreszinski I, pl. 97b) and the Hellenistic period (M. Schnebel, *Die Landwirtschaft im hellenistischen Ägypten*, I, Munich 1925, p. 174). ἀποδινήσας: pigs are never shown in this role, though cattle frequently are (F. Hartmann, pp. 134 ff.). Nevertheless, there is no reason to doubt Herodotus' assertion.

15–18. The problem of the definition of Egypt: 15–16, critique of the Ionian view; 17–18, Herodotus' opinion.

15,1. Εἰ ὦν βουλόμεθα...Ἀραβίης εἶναι: cf. Aeschylus, *Prom.* 813, the Ionian view championed by Hecataeus (Jacoby, *RE* VII, 2678 ff.).   βουλόμεθα: the indicative in protasis is picked up by the optative with ἄν in the apodosis. Stein's βουλοίμεθα is quite unnecessary (cf. Goodwin, *Moods and Tenses*, 190 ff.). The conversational looseness of the whole sentence is quite remarkable.   Περσέος καλεομένης σκοπιῆς: cf. Euripides, *Hel.* 769; Strabo VII 1,18 (C801). It lay east of the Bolbitinic mouth of the Nile beyond Agnou keras (Strabo, loc. cit.). Herodotus appears to have located it erroneously further west near the Canopic mouth (Ball, *Egypt*, pp. 18, 65 n.*).   Ταριχηίων τῶν Πηλουσιακῶν: cf. 113,1, and Stephanus of Byzantium, s.v. Mendes and Taricheai. Pickling fish was a highly prosperous Ancient Egyptian industry (Kees, *Ägypten*, pp. 61, 119). Pelusium is the modern El-Faram, 40 km. south-east of Port Said (Gardiner, *AEO* II, p. 156*).   τεσσεράκοντά...σχοῖνοι: 2400 stades = 429.6 km. at 179 m. to the stade (note on 6,1). Since the true distance is *c*.300 km., Herodotus is badly wrong (cf. note on 6,1, for possible explanations).   Κερκασώρου πόλιος: cf. II, 17, 97. Probably El-Warrâq, north-west of Cairo (Ball, *Egypt*, pp. 14, 17, 25, 63, 71).   Κάνωβον: this city lay west of Abukir and 22 km. from Alexandria (PM IV, p. 2). It was certainly discussed by Hecataeus (*FGrHist* I F308–9 with *Kommentar*, p. 369).   τὰ δὲ ἄλλα...εἶναι: see note on ch. 16.

1–3. ἀποδεικνύοιμεν...ὑποκαταβαίνοντας: objection I to the Ionian view: if the Delta alone were Egypt, the country would be a recent creation (cf. ch. 13), and the Egyptians would not claim to be the most ancient people. Since they do (ch. 2), the country itself must be of great antiquity. It was originally the Thebaid alone.

2. ὡς λόγῳ εἰπεῖν: see note on 4,1.

3. αἱ Θῆβαι: here the area south of a point 3-days' journey from the lake of Moiris (note on 5,1), i.e. essentially the Thebaid.   τῆς τὸ περίμετρον... ἑξακισχίλιοι: 6120 stades = 1095.48 km. at 179 m. per stade. If we regard αἱ Θῆβαι as running from approximately Deirout to Aswan, the distance is c.611.92 km; τὸ περίμετρον should be twice that plus twice the width of the valley, i.e. Herodotus' figure is well over 130 km. too low.

16,1–2. εἰ ὦν ἡμεῖς... γίνοιτ' ἄν: objection 2. The Ionians are inconsistent: their doctrine of continents commits them to regarding the Delta as a fourth continent. The argument is irrelevant: 'Herodotus' objection is valid whether or not the Delta be equated with Egypt' (J. E. Powell, *CQ* XXIX (1935), 75), i.e. he stands convicted of muddled thinking.

1. τρία μόρια: continents were a major interest of Ionian geographers (Berger, pp. 82 ff., 87 ff.). Initially, they claimed that there were two; the tripartite division probably originated with Hecataeus (*FGrHist* I, *Kommentar*, pp. 366 ff.). Λιβύην: i.e. Africa.

2. ὁ Νεῖλός... τῇ Λιβύῃ: water boundaries were a standard means of demarcating continents, and the Nile was the acknowledged frontier between Libye and Asie (Scheliha, pp. 34 ff.). Clearly the Ionians had not realized the implications of the doctrine for the Delta: it must either be a fourth continent or an island.   τῇ Λιβύῃ: for this very unusual dative cf. IV 180,1. A parallel using χωρίζομαι occurs at IV 28,2.

17,1. ἡμεῖς... λέγομεν: Herodotus proceeds to his own definition, also attributed to the 'Greeks', that Egypt is simply the country inhabited by Egyptians.   κη: so Reiske, but all mss read καί. If this is correct, we should translate 'also'.   Αἴγυπτον... ὑπὸ Ἀσσυρίων: proof 1, argument κατ' ἀναλογίαν (see above, p. 236).

3–6. ὁ γὰρ δὴ Νεῖλος... ἀλλ' ὀρυκτά: in general see Ball, *Egypt*, pp. 22 ff. The claim that the Nile was πεντάστομος is unique; the standard view made it ἑπτάστομος (e.g. pseudo-Scylax, *GGM* I, p. 80; Diod. I 33,7; Strabo XVII 1,18 (C801). Herodotus differs in regarding the Bolbitinic and Bucolic branches as artificial. Hecataeus probably supported the ἑπτάστομος doctrine and is the likely target at this point (Jacoby, *RE* VII, 2680).

3. Κερκασώρου: see note on 15,1. τριφασίας ὁδούς: consistent with pseudo-Scylax (loc. cit.) and the Ramesside Onomasticon of Amenemope (Gardiner, *AEO* II, pp. 153* ff.).

4. τὸ δὲ ἀπὸ τούτου σχίζων... στόμα: called 'the Great River' in Amenemope (see above), it provides Herodotus' solution to the demarcation problem of chs. 15–16: the Sebennytic branch splits the Delta into 'Libye' to the west and 'Asie' to the east.

5. Σαϊτικὸν: here Tanitic (J. v. Beckerath, *Tanis und Theben, Äg. Forschungen*, XVI, Glückstadt 1951, p. 33).

6. τὸ δὲ Βολβίτινον... ἀλλ' ὀρυκτά: certainly untrue for the Bolbitinic (K. W. Butzer, *Studien zum vor- und frühgeschichtlichen Landschaftswandel der Sahara. III. Die Naturlandschaft Ägyptens während der Vorgeschichte und der dynastischen Zeit*, Wiesbaden 1959, pp. 32 ff.).

18,1. μαρτυρέει δέ μοι τῇ γνώμῃ... ἐπυθόμην: proof 2, the oracular response of Zeus Ammon.   τὸ Ἄμμωνος χρηστήριον: see note on ch. 42.

2. Μαρέης τε πόλιος: cf. Thuc. I 104,2; Diodorus I 68,5; and modern Arabic Mariût for the neighbouring lake (Montet, *Géographie* I, pp. 63 ff.). It lay adjacent to the south shore of lake Mareotis, but the ruins have never been certainly identified (Kees, *RE* XIV, 1676 ff.).   Ἄπιος: probably the Egyptian *Nỉwt nt Ḥpy*, 'Town of Apis' (Montet, *Géographie* I, p. 64), plausibly identified with Taposiris (modern Abusir) (Ball, *Egypt*, p. 17).   αὐτοί τε δοκέοντες εἶναι Λίβυες: in antiquity the western Delta had a strongly Libyan character (Gardiner, *AEO* I, pp. 114* ff.); even in the 4th cent. AD a Greek papyrus clearly distinguishes between Μαρεωταί and Αἰγύπτιοι (Wilcken, I 2, pp. 379, 322, n.4).   καὶ ἀχθόμενοι... ἔργεσθαι: cows were sacred to Isis (n. II, 41), and the worship of her husband Osiris was firmly established in the area (Gauthier, *DG* III, p. 54).   ἐς Ἄμμωνα: one of the earliest known consultations of the oracle. On the oracular method see Parke, *Oracles of Zeus*, pp. 214 ff.

3. φὰς Αἴγυπτον... πίνουσι: correct. Textual evidence demonstrates that, to the Egyptians, their country consisted of the alluvium watered directly by the Nile between Elephantine and the sea (Schlott, *passim*).

19–34. The two major Nile problems: the cause of the inundation (19–27, with a subsidiary problem at 19,3) and the river's sources (28–34).

19, 1–2. ἐπέρχεται... θερινέων: stage 1, statement of the problem.

1. τοῦ Λιβυκοῦ... τοῦ Ἀραβίου: both are partitive genitives dependent on ἐνιαχῇ.   ἐπὶ δύο ἡμερέων: in the valley proper the distance from the Nile to the western cliffs is *c.*20 km. at Beni Suef, but usually the cliffs are much closer on both sides. However, the flood could travel from the Delta along the Wadi Tumilat in Arabia for *c.*60 km., a journey of 1–2 days, and on the Libyan side in the Fayûm the waters might be regarded as getting as far as the extreme west of the basin, i.e. a distance of *c.*80 km. or 2 days' sail.   τοῦ ποταμοῦ δὲ... ἱρέων: priestly views on the subject were mythological (Bonneau, *La Crue*, pp. 229 ff., 243 ff., 263 ff., 299 ff.), and would not have counted as scientific explanations of the kind that Herodotus required.

2. τροπέων τῶν θερινέων: June 22–3. The Nile rose at Aswan about the beginning of June and *c.*20 days later in the Cairo area. Herodotus was, therefore, using information gathered in the north (cf. Sourdille, *La Durée*, pp. 15 ff.).   ἐπὶ ἑκατὸν ἡμέρας: the ancients claimed 90–100 days (C. Palanque, *Le Nil à l'époque pharaonique*, Paris 1903, p. 21), and this fits well with modern experience (Bonneau, *La Crue*, pp. 20 ff.).

3. [παρὰ] τῶν Αἰγυπτίων: the παρά is present in all mss but is deleted by Krueger. He was probably correct since it reads very awkwardly in the context and would be the most natural of glosses after παραλαμβάνω. τῶν Αἰγυπτίων would then become a partitive genitive dependent on οὐδενός. If the preposition is retained, we must postulate a slight anacoluthon: 'Concerning these matters, then, I was able to obtain no information from anyone, (I mean) from the

Egyptians.' τὰ ἔμπαλιν πεφυκέναι: the Nile's paradoxical behaviour (cf. 24,1) explains Herodotus' and the recurrent Greek fascination with the river. It was a θῶμα (see above, pp. 234 ff.). αὔρας ἀποπνεούσας ... οὐ παρέχεται: a subsidiary problem: several Greek writers speak of the capacity of rivers to exhale cool breezes from their surface (Hippocrates, *Aer.* 19: Theophrastus, *Vent.* III 25; Diod. I 38,7; Aristides, *Or.* 36, 14); the Nile does not do so. For Herodotus' explanation see ch. 27. αὔρας: particularly of cool breezes which blow from water (LSJ, p. 248a, s.v. αὔρα 1).

20,1. Ἀλλὰ Ἑλλήνων ... ὁδούς: stage 2, the demolition of unacceptable explanations.

2. ἡ ἑτέρη μὲν λέγει ... τὸν Νεῖλον: the theory of Thales (11 A16 DK), later adapted, amongst others, by Euthymenes of Massilia (*FGrHist* 647 F 1(5)) and frequently mentioned in classical writers (Bonneau, *La Crue*, pp. 151 ff.). τοὺς ἐτησίας ἀνέμους: since they occur after the summer solstice and the Heliacal rise of Sirius (Arist. *Mete.* II 5(361b)), i.e. roughly at the beginning the Nile's inundation, a correlation between the phenomena was a natural assumption.

2–3. πολλάκις δὲ ... ὁ Νεῖλος: the theory is skilfully destroyed by observing the inconsistency of the correlation and by an argument κατ' ἀναλογίαν (see above, p. 236). Herodotus was not the only critic (Bonneau, *La Crue*, pp. 154 ff.).

2. ἔπνευσαν: the 'typical' use of the aorist often employed to describe something which is a regular occurrence (Chantraine, *Grammaire* II, pp. 185 ff.).

3. χρῆν: the omission of ἄν in apodosis is normal with all words expressing necessity or obligation (Goodwin, *Moods and Tenses*, pp. 151 ff.).

21. ἡ δ' ἑτέρη ... ῥέειν: the counter-argument is illogically postponed until ch. 23 (cf. note on ch. 50). The theory was that of Hecataeus (*FGrHist* I F 302; *RE* Suppl. II, 427), who may have owed something to Euthymenes of Massilia (*FGrHist* 647 F 1(5)); it enjoyed a long career (Bonneau, *La Crue*, pp. 145 ff.). In Herodotus' version it does not explicitly indicate how the inundation took place, but Euthymenes claimed that it resulted from the pressure of the Etesian winds at the Nile's starting point on Ocean. τὸν δὲ Ὠκεανὸν: cf. Homer, *Il.* XVIII 607 ff., XXI 194 ff.; Hesiod, *Theog.* 338; Herod. IV, 8.

22,1. ἡ δὲ τρίτη ... ἐς Αἴγυπτον: the view of Anaxagoras of Clazomenae (59 A45, 5 A91 DK), widely current in the 5th cent. and for that reason the object of Herodotus' particular attention. He appears to have destroyed its credibility (Bonneau, *La Crue*, pp. 161 ff.). Melting snow has, in fact, nothing to do with the inundation (ibid., p. 15).

2–4. κῶς ὦν ... ἐλέγχει: argument κατὰ τὸ εἰκός (see above, p. 236) using four μαρτύρια. Herodotus is correct in dismissing the theory, but his reasoning is specious since it is based on the erroneous, though standard, conviction that the Greek Αἰθιοπίη lay at the edge of the world in its hottest zone, i.e. the possibility of a cooler zone to the south was excluded (Bonneau, *La Crue*, pp. 161 ff.).

2. ἀπὸ τῶν θερμοτάτων ... ἐστι: All mss are corrupt here. The Florentine group reads ῥέων ἐς τὰ ψυχρότερα τῶν τὰ πολλά ἐστι; Hude transposes the τῶν after ἐς and deletes τά. An easier remedy, proposed by Stein, would be to delete τῶν

and translate: '...flowing into places of which the majority are colder.'
οἱ ἄνεμοι... θερμοί: the Khamsîn, which blows from March to the beginning of
June (Hurst, pp. 171 ff.).

3. ὕσαι ἐν πέντε ἡμέρῃσι: untrue (cf. Gellius, *Epit.* VIII 4). The claim is probably
popular weather lore (cf. Rawlinson, *Herodotus* II, p. 33, n. 7).   μέλανες: for
Herodotean anthropology see note on 104,2.

4. ἰκτῖνοι: kites are certainly resident in Egypt and the Sudan (Meinertzhagen, II,
pp. 410, 412).   χελιδόνες: the Egyptian swallow is a common resident species
(ibid. I, pp. 305 ff.).   γέρανοι: cranes are common migrants to Egypt and the
Sudan (ibid. II, pp. 627 ff.).

23. ὁ δὲ... λέξας: cf. note to ch. 21. The doctrine is rejected as a *petitio principii.*
Herodotus consistently refuses to accept the existence of Ὠκεανός (cf. IV 8,2;
36,2); in this, as in much else, he exemplifies the rising swell of criticism of Ionian
geography (cf. Berger, pp. 5, 87).   Ὅμηρον δὲ... ἐσενείκασθαι: cf. Solon, fr. 29
IEG; Pindar, *Olymp.* I 28 ff. Herodotus shows similar scepticism at ch. 53.

24,1. εἰ δὲ δεῖ... ἀποδέξασθαι: stage 3, Herodotus' own explanation. Note, however, his awareness of the epistemological difficulties (cf. P. Foucart, *BIE* XXV
(1943), 95 ff.).

1–2. τὴν χειμερινὴν ὥρην... τῶν ποταμῶν: Herodotus invokes two factors: the
apparent seasonal movement of the sun (it is, in fact, the earth which moves) and
evaporation. He is correct in both cases: the inundation arises from moisture
generated by evaporation as the sun crosses and recrosses the equator during
March–September. This moisture is then brought to Ethiopia by the south-east trades
and monsoons and deposited over the Ethiopian highlands to yield an annual rainfall
of 75–150 cm., which subsequently drains off into the Nile (Bonneau, *La Crue*,
pp. 14 ff.).   ἀπελαυνόμενος: early thinkers considered the cosmos to be a hemisphere of relatively small compass within which the sun and other heavenly bodies
moved so close to earth that they could be affected by winds (cf. Anaximander, KR,
p. 138; Anaximenes, KR, pp. 154 ff.; and probably Diogenes of Apollonia, KR, p. 439).
2. ὡς... δηλῶσαι: See notes on 4,1; 10,1.

25,1. ὡς... δηλῶσαι: see previous note.   ἄτε... ψυχρῶν: perceptive. 'Evaporation is affected by the dampness of the atmosphere, and by the wind and temperature' (Hurst, p. 253). In Egypt and the Sudan as far as Khartoum it is heavy.
2. ἕλκει: firmly in the tradition of early Greek thought on meteorological phenomena where evaporation and condensation are prominent (cf. Hesiod, *Op.*
550 ff.: Anaximander, KR 131; Anaximenes, KR 161; Xenophanes, KR 186;
Diogenes of Apollonia (64 A18 DK); Hippocrates, *Aer.* 8: see in general
O. Gilbert, *Die meteorologischen Theorien des griechischen Altertums*, Hildesheim
1967 (1907), pp. 439 ff.).   ἕλκει... ἑλκύσας: see note on 14,2.
3. ὑπολείπεσθαι: presumably as nourishment (cf. W. K. Guthrie, *History of Greek
Philosophy*, I, Cambridge 1962, p. 67).
5. ὑποδεέστερος: cf. Oenopides of Chios (41 A11 DK). The notion that the
inundation reflected the Nile's proper size fits Herodotus' conviction that things
in Egypt were larger than elsewhere (see above, pp. 234 ff.).

26,1. ξηρὸν: atmospheric moisture in the northern Sudan sometimes falls to virtually zero; to the south, however, it rises sharply during the rainy season (Hurst, pp. 173 ff.).   αὐτῷ: most mss read αὐτῷ which Waddell tries implausibly to rescue as a dative of disadvantage referring to τὸν ἠέρα (p. 146). Stein and many other editors read ἑωυτοῦ which seems otiose. The dative reflexive ἑωυτῷ is an easy correction and yields exactly the required sense.

2. εἰ δὲ ἡ στάσις... τὸν Νεῖλον: a vivid hypothetical analogy comparable to that in ch. 11.   τὸν Ἴστρον: the Danube is consistently treated as Europe's counterpart of the Nile (see note on ch. 33).

27. τῆς αὔρης ... ἀποπνέει: this comment harks back to 19,3. Editors have generally preferred the reading of the Florentine group of mss and omitted the ἀπὸ τοῦ Νείλου inserted by the Roman group after ἀποπνέει, but the relationship to the foregoing discussion strongly favours retention.   ὡς κάρτα ... ἀποπνέειν: lit.: 'that it is not probable that anything should blow from very hot places.' In the light of the previous note, the χώρων of the Roman group gives a much better sense than the χωρέων of the Florentines. The latter probably arose from confusion in scribal minds created by the earlier comments on winds which blow from particular lands (22,2; 25,2). With the abandonment of χωρέων the θερμέων of Stein and Hude would lose its *raison d'être*, and the θερμῶν read by all mss could be reinstated. For a detailed discussion of this passage see J. W. Baxendale, *Mnemosyne*, XLVII (1994), 433 ff.   κάρτα: the separation from θερμέων gives greater emphasis (cf. I 88).   οἰκός: for argument κατὰ τὸ εἰκός see above, p. 236.

28,1. τὰς πηγὰς: the second major Nile problem. It occupies Herodotus until ch. 34.   οὔτε Αἰγυπτίων... Ἀθηναίης: Herodotus proceeds with ἱστορίη (see above, p. 230). This, in conjunction with *petitio principii*, leads him to his own conclusion at ch. 33.   Σάϊ: Egyptian *S3w*, modern Sa el-Hagar, one of the great cities of the Late Period and home of the kings of the XXVIth Dynasty who occupy Herodotus from ch. 147 on. Only about 16 km. from Naucratis, it was easily accessible to Greeks.   ὁ γραμματιστὴς: probably a *sš pr ḥḏ n Nt*, 'Scribe of the Treasury of Neith'. Whether he was a priest is an open question, but he must have possessed a modicum of learning.   τῆς Ἀθηναίης: the Egyptian goddess Neith, the major deity of Sais (Sabri Kolta, *Die Gleichsetzung*, pp. 96 ff.).

2–3. ἔλεγε δὲ ... ῥέειν: cf. Plato, *Ti.* 22d; Seneca, *QN* IV 2,3 ff.; Aristides, *Or.* 36, 47 ff.; Strabo XVII 1,52 (C819). It was standard Egyptian doctrine in Herodotus' time that the sources (the *Tpḥt*, 'cavern', or *Qrty*, 'two holes') lay in this area, but some located them at Elephantine and others at Biggeh (P. Barguet, *La Stèle de la famine à Séhel*, Cairo 1953, p. 18).

2. δύο ὄρεα... Ἐλεφαντίνης: there is nothing of the kind between the island of Elephantine and Syene on the east bank, but the Famine stele (ll. 13 ff.) refers to two rocky features which are clearly identical with Krophi and Mophi (Barguet, op. cit., p. 22, n. 14). These evidently lay amongst the great granite boulders protruding from the water immediately south of Elephantine (cf. G. A. Wainwright, *JHS* LXXIII (1953), 106 ff.). Herodotus' mistaken location presumably reflects a confusion, possibly a mistranslation, but his failure to

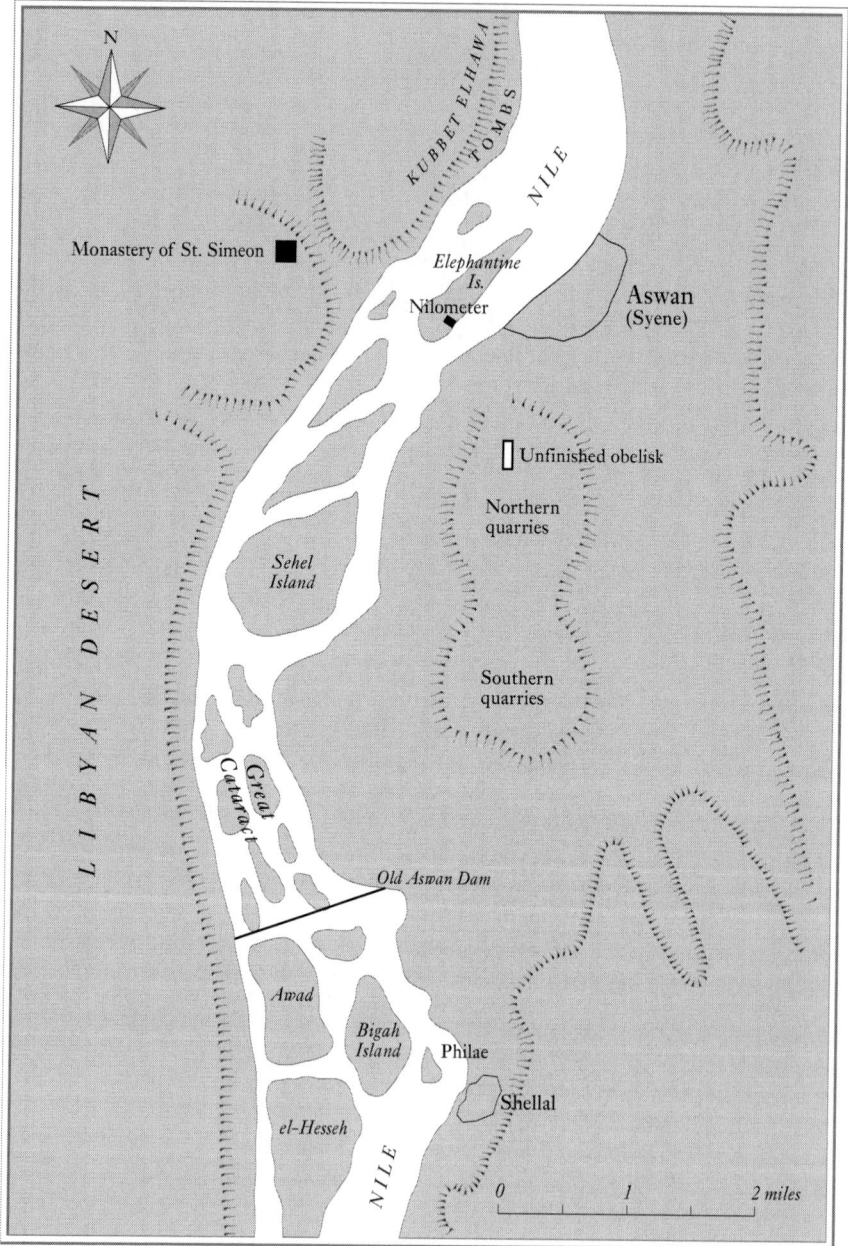

Map 21. Elephantine and the First Cataract

correct it cannot be used as evidence that he never visited Elephantine (see note on 29,1).   ἀπηγμένα: here and at VII 64 all the best mss read ἀπιγμένα. This is not impossible in the light of the capacity of ἀπικνέομαι for use in metaphorical contexts, but Bekker's widely accepted emendation is probably preferable insofar as it permits an easy reconciliation of the ms variants at this point. τὰς κορυφὰς is an accusative of respect.   Συήνης: Egyptian *Swnw*, modern Aswan (Gardiner, *AEO* II, p. 5*).   Ἐλεφαντίνης: Egyptian *3bw*, 'Elephantine' or 'Ivory Town' (ibid., p. 2*).   τῷ μὲν Κρῶφι, τῷ δὲ Μῶφι: the name Κρῶφι, which appears in the Famine Stele, ll. 13 ff., as *grf 3bw*, 'geref of Elephantine', may be related to the Coptic *krof*, 'evil' (W. Westendorf, *Koptisches Handwörterbuch*, Heidelberg 1965–77, p. 69); Μῶφι may originate from the Egyptian *nfr*, 'good' (*Wb.* II, pp. 253 ff.).

3. τὸ μὲν ἥμισυ...νότου: before the construction of the Low Dam a violent countercurrent ran for 100 km. south of Aswan (Wainwright, op. cit., pp. 105 ff.).

4–5. ὡς δὲ ἄβυσσοί...ἰέναι: the second apocryphal experiment attributed by Greeks to Psammetichus I (see note on ch. 2). Observe, however, that the XXVIth Dynasty to which he belonged was extremely active in this area (PM V, pp. 245 ff.).

5. ὡς ἐμὲ κατανοέειν: cf. note on 4,1.   δίνας τινὰς: whirlpools were a major hazard in the region, e.g. the Sheimat el-Wah, 'The Whirlpool of the Oasis' (Wainwright, op. cit., p. 106).

29,1. Ἐλεφαντίνης: see note on 28,2.   αὐτόπτης ἐλθών: disbelieved by some (e.g. Aristides, *Or.* 36, 48 ff.; A. H. Sayce, *Journal of Philology* XIV (1885), 257 ff.), but the case is not strong (see above, pp. 226 ff.).

2–3. ἀπὸ Ἐλεφαντίνης...διεκπλῶσαι: the First Cataract. Longinus (*De Subl.* 26) rightly emphasizes the vividness of the writing in this passage. The Cataract did not extend for 12 schoinoi as far as Tachompso but ended at the island of Hesse, *c*.11 km. south of Elephantine, i.e. about 4 hours' journey by land (cf. Sourdille, *La Durée*, p. 230). From that point the river was navigable, though not always with ease, as far as the Second Cataract. Clearly Herodotus has confused the First Cataract region with the Dodekaschoinos which ran as far as Hierasykaminos (K. Sethe, *Dodekaschoinos, das Zwölfmeilenland an der Grenze von Ägypten und Nubien, Untersuchungen*, II, Leipzig 1901, pp. 59 ff.).

2. διαδήσαντας: a common practice in Ancient Egypt (note on 96,3).

3. Μαίανδρός: see note on 10,1.   Ταχομψὼ: Egyptian *Tkmsi*, here the island of Djerar, though the name was also borne by a settlement on the adjacent bank (Kees, *RE* IVA, 1987).

4. Αἰθίοπες...Αἰγύπτιοι: this ethnic mix (cf. Strabo XVII 1,49 (C818)) and the fact that Herodotus located the island at the end of what he thought to be the First Cataract indicate that he had confused Tachompso with Philae. Αἰθίοπες: 'Burnt-faces'. Herodotus used the term Αἰθιοπίη to cover everything south of Aswân (Herminghausen, pp. 2 ff.).   ἔχεται...ἐκδιδοῖ: the stretch from Hierasykaminos to the Second Cataract, where navigation once more varies from the difficult to the impossible (Hurst, pp. 73 ff.).   λίμνη

μεγάλη: exaggerated. It could only be a broadening of the river (Ball, *Egypt*, p. 15 n.). *νομάδες Αἰθίοπες*: i.e. Beduin such as the modern Bedja. They are explicitly distinguished from their sedentary neighbours in the valley (*οἱ ἄλλοι Αἰθίοπες* below, cf. Strabo XVII 1, 53 (C819)).

5. *ἡμερέων τεσσεράκοντα*: according to V 53, 1 day's journey by land was 150 stades, i.e. 26.85 km. at 179 m. to the stade (*c*.24 km. would be a good daily average in Africa: O. G. S. Crawford, *The Fung Kingdom of Sennar*, Gloucester 1951, App. 10). Forty days' journey would, therefore, be 1074 km. This figure is not badly wrong, since the first practicable point to re-embark would be Abu Hamed, *c*.966.18 km. along the valley from the Second Cataract.

6. *δυώδεκα ἡμέρας*: according to 29,3, a distance of 12 schoinoi could be covered in 4 days. At 179 m. to the stade this yields 32.22 km. per stade. Therefore, in 12 days it would be possible to travel *c*.386.64 km. The actual distance from Abu Hamed is *c*.418.68 km. *Μερόη*: the oldest occurrence of the name anywhere. It certainly refers to Meroe below the Sixth Cataract and not Napata as often claimed (Lloyd, *Commentary 1–98*, pp. 123 f.).

7. *Δία θεῶν καὶ Διόνυσον μούνους*: Amun (Zeus) was the major god in Nubia from the New Kingdom (Shinnie, p. 141); Osiris is less in evidence but clearly identifiable (F. Hintze, *Studien zur meroitischen Chronologie und zu den Opfertafeln aus den Pyramiden von Meroe*, Berlin 1959, pp. 11 ff.). Other gods are, however, known (Shinnie, pp. 81 ff.). *μαντήιον Διός*: cf. Diodorus III 9: Strabo XVII 2,3 (C822); Pliny, *NH* VI 186; Heliodorus, *Aeth. passim*. The influence of the oracle of Amun was pervasive, and it is known to have pronounced on military campaigns (Kees, *Ägypten*, pp. 351 ff.).

30,1. *ἐν ἴσῳ χρόνῳ ἄλλῳ*: i.e. 56 days. At *c*.32.22 km per day (note on 29,3) this amounts to *c*.1804.32 km. *ἐς τοὺς αὐτομόλους*: cf. Arist. *Rh.* III, 16; Diod. I, 67; Strabo XVI 4,8 (C770); XVII 1,2 (C787); Pliny, *NH* VI 191 ff.; Ptolemy, *Geog.* IV 20 ff. All available evidence points to a location in the Gezirah immediately south of Khartoum and the Blue Nile in the vicinity of Soba. If so, the time of 56 days is far too high (Lloyd, *Commentary 1–98*, pp. 126 ff.); 7 days would be quite sufficient. *Ἀσμάχ...βασιλέϊ*: also called *Makhloiones* (Hesychius s.v.) and *Sembritae* (Strabo XVI 4,8 (C770–1); XVII 1,2 (C786)). The term *Ἀσμάχ* probably derived from Egyptian *smḥy*, 'left' (cf. de Meulenaere, p. 42). *ἐξ ἀριστερῆς χειρός*: apparently the left side was regarded as less honourable than the right (J. Gwyn Griffiths, *ASAE LIII* (1956), 146 ff.).

2–3. *ἀπέστησαν...Αἰγύπτια*: although the story has been embellished, it has a clear historical parallel from the same period in the inscription of Neshor (de Meulenaere, pp. 41 ff.).

2. *αὗται*: for *οὗτοι* by attraction to *μυριάδες*. *τέσσερες καὶ εἴκοσι μυριάδες*: cf. Diod. I 67. The number cannot be taken seriously, though its precise source is debatable (cf. Fehling, p. 232). *τῶν μαχίμων*: see note on 164,2. *ἐπὶ Ψαμμητίχου...ἄλλη*: Elephantine was Egypt's southern frontier in the Saite period and exposed to attack from the powerful Meroitic kingdom to the south (de Meulenaere, pp. 38 ff.). In Psammetichus' time Daphnae protected Egypt against attacks from the Assyrians (probably *οἱ Σύριοι*), the Chaldaeans,

and desert nomads (οἱ Ἀράβιοι) (ibid., pp. 33 ff.). To the west the Libyans were a recurrent problem (Gardiner, *AEO* I, pp. 114* ff.).

3. ἐπ᾽ ἐμεῦ: Marea was not garrisoned in Herodotus' time because Cyrenaica to the west was under Persian control (Kienitz, pp. 55 ff.).   ἀπέλυε: more probably they were disgruntled at undue preference shown to Greek mercenaries (de Meulenaere, pp. 41 ff.).

4. τὸ αἰδοῖον: obscenity is a common motif in folklore (Thompson, *Motif-Index* VI, s.v. 'Obscene').

5. τῷ Αἰθιόπων βασιλέϊ: possibly they maintained some allegiance to the XXVth (Nubian) Dynasty recently expelled from Egypt by Psammetichus I (de Meulenaere, p. 43).   διάφοροί: disorders within the Nubian kingdom are exemplified (M. F. L. Macadam, *Temples of Kawa*, I, Oxford 1949, pp. 46 ff., 50 ff.). μαθόντες: Nubian culture was permeated with Egyptian influence, but it goes back much earlier than Herodotus thought, since Egyptians were present in the country from the Old Kingdom onwards (Adams, pp. 66 ff.).

31. τεσσέρων μηνῶν: strictly 112 days (note on 30,1); Herodotus has rounded up the figure.   ἀπὸ ἑσπέρης τε καὶ [ἡλίου] δυσμέων: i.e. the entire course of the Nile ran west to east above Elephantine (Bunbury I, pp. 266, 303). It, therefore, flowed parallel to its European counterpart the Danube (cf. 33,2).   καύματος: it was canonical doctrine from Hecataeus onwards that the entire world was surrounded by a belt of desert (Berger, pp. 77 ff.).

32,1. ἀνδρῶν Κυρηναίων: see above, p. 231.   τὸ Ἄμμωνος χρηστήριον: see note on 42,4. Zeus Ammon was the chief Cyrenaean deity in Herodotus' time. Ἐτεάρχῳ: the Greek name is quite plausible, given the close links between Sîwa and Cyrene (Morenz, *Die Begegnung*, p. 78).   βασιλέϊ: whether a Persian vassal or an independent ruler is unclear (Parke, *Oracles of Zeus*, pp. 205 ff.). Νασαμῶνας: cf. IV 172–3; Diod. III 49; Strabo II 5,33 (C131); XVII 3,20 (C836). They lived south-east of Syrtis Major, south-west of Euesperides, west of the Auschisae, and north of the Psylloi (Windberg, *RE* XVI, 1776 ff.).

3. δυναστέων: 'chieftains', presumably the leaders of a loose agglomeration of tribes (Gsell, *Hérodote*, p. 200).   ἴδοιεν... ἰδομένων: for the shift from active to middle with this verb cf. Homer, *Il.* I 262. In Herodotus the aorist active seems to refer to the fact of seeing purely and simply whereas the middle implies seeing with some result.

4. τῆς γὰρ Λιβύης... ἔρημος πάντων: cf. IV 168–99. Herodotus' highly schematized Libyan geography, which derived largely from Hecataeus (*FGrHist* I F 329–57, with *Commentary*, pp. 371 ff.), divided the north sector from north to south into four zones: ἡ οἰκουμένη, ἡ θηριώδης Λιβύη, ἡ ὀφρύη ψάμμης, and ἡ ἔρημος.   παρὰ πᾶσαν: sc. θάλασσαν.   [τὰ κατύπερθε]: this phrase is quite meaningless here and must be deleted. It presumably arose by dittography from τὰ δὲ κατύπερθε below.   ψάμμος: dunes are extensive south of the Sîwa Depression (J. Leclant, *BIFAO* XLIX (1950), pp. 196 ff.).

5–7. ἐπεὶ ὦν... κροκοδείλους: the journey probably followed the line Augila–Fezzan–Tibesti to end in the Bodele Depression (Carpenter, pp. 231 ff.)

6. ἄνδρας σμικρούς: pygmies were found much further north in antiquity than today (R. Watermann, *Bilder aus dem Lande des Ptah und Imhotep*, Cologne 1958, pp. 55 ff.).   ἐκείνων τοὺς Νασαμῶνας ... τῶν Νασαμώνων: note the chiasmus.
7. κροκοδείλους: for the spelling see note on 68,1. Crocodiles were certainly present in the Bodele Depression in antiquity (G. Nachtigal, *Sahārā und Sūdān*, II, Berlin 1881, pp. 77 ff.).

33,1. γόητας: in modern times the Makari of the Logone region south-east of lake Chad in the Bodele area enjoyed a similar reputation (Nachtigal, op. cit., pp. 533 ff.).
2. ὁ λόγος: γνώμη operating κατ᾽ ἀναλογίαν, as often in early Greek geography (M. Ninck, *Die Entdeckung von Europa durch die Griechen*, Basle 1945, pp. 45 ff., 49, 54, 80). Here the analogy consists of the groundless contemporary conviction that the Nile was the mirror-image of the Danube (see above, p. 257). This allowed Herodotus to locate the course of the Nile on the same line of longitude (ἐκ τῶν ἴσων μέτρων) as that of the Danube.   τοῖσι ἐμπανέσι: cf. Solon's maxim τὰ ἀφανῆ τοῖς φανεροῖς τεκμαίρου (in Stobaeus, *Flor.* I 79,β (Meineke)).
3. Ἴστρος ... Εὐρώπην: this erroneous conviction may well derive from a verbal misunderstanding, e.g. Herodotus or his source may have been told: 'The Danube route leads to the Pyrenees', and then assumed that the river rose there (R. Dion, *RPh* XLII (1968), 7 ff.).   τε: this is not answered by a καί but picked up by περὶ δὲ τῶν τοῦ Νείλου πηγέων in 34,1.   Κελτῶν: probably the Cempsi, who were settled on the Spanish coast west of the Straits of Gibraltar (S. Lambrino, *Bull. des Études Portugaises*, XIX (1956), 5 ff.).   Πυρήνης: cf. Mela II 81 ff.; Pliny, *NH* III 8; Avienus, *Or. Mar.* 558 ff. Almost certainly *Portus Pyrenaei*, the modern Port Vendres at the east end of the Pyrenees (Dion, op. cit., p. 9).   Κυνησίοισι: cf. IV 49,3. They occupied at the very least the territory from the Guadiana area to Cape St Vincent and north as far as the river Mira (Lambrino, op. cit., pp. 8 ff., 15).
4. Ἰστρίην: in fact it lies *c*.40 km. south of the Danube's mouth. It was founded by Milesians in the late 7th or early 6th cent. BC (Boardman, *Greeks Overseas*, pp. 242, 247 ff.).

34,1–2. ἡ δὲ Αἴγυπτος ... κεῖται: another erroneous line of longitude (cf. note on 33,2; Berger, p. 92). The later Olbia–Rhodes–Alexandria meridian was better but still inaccurate (Ninck, op. cit., 65).

35,1. θωμάσια: see above, pp. 234 ff.
2–4. Αἰγύπτιοι ... βουλομένῃσι: this section and the following chapter are riddled with overschematization (see above, p. 237). Note throughout the skilful stylistic variation to avoid the monotony which could easily arise in such a catalogue.
2. ἅμα ... νόμους: cf. Soph. *OC* 337 ff. Herodotus was a convinced exponent of environmental determinism (cf. Hippocrates, *Aer.* 12–24; Sigerist II, pp. 247, 280 ff.).   ἀγοράζουσι: there was no fixed rule in Egypt (cf. Lepsius, *Denkmäler* II, pls. 96, 103; Klebs, *NR*, pp. 230 ff.). In Athens men did go to market (Lacey, p. 168).   καπηλεύουσι: contradicted for Egypt by Herodotus (141,4; 164,1) and pharaonic evidence (Klebs, *NR* I, pp. 231 ff.) and for Greece by literary

references (e.g. Aristophanes, *Lys.* 457 ff.).   ὑφαίνουσι: true for the New King-dom and later (C. Johl, *Altägyptische Webestühle, Untersuchung,* VIII, Leipzig 1924, fig. 39). In Greece it was woman's work (cf. H. Long Roth, *Ancient Egyptian and Greek Looms,* Halifax Barkfield Museum Notes, II 2, Halifax 1913).   οἱ μὲν ἄλλοι ἄνω... κάτω: the Egyptian double-beamed loom allowed the weft threads to be beaten in 'downwards', whereas the weft threads on the warp-weighted loom used in Greece and widely elsewhere could only be beaten in 'upwards' (Singer *et al.* I, pp. 425 ff.; II, pp. 211 ff.).

3. τὰ ἄχθεα: untrue (e.g. Wreszinski I, pls. 63, 232).   οὐρέουσι: true for Egyptian males (L. Borchardt, *Zeitschrift für Bauwesen,* LXVI Jahrg. (1916), 542) but also exemplified in Greece (Hesiod, *Op.* 731 ff.).   εὐμαρείη: toilets and *chaises percées* are known from Ancient Egypt (P. Ghalioungui, *Magic and Medical Science in Ancient Egypt,* London 1963, pp. 154 ff.), but modern Egyptian practice suggests that Herodotus greatly exaggerates. The use of chamber-pots in 5th-cent. Greece indicates no great distinction (Aristophanes, *Th.* 485; *Vesp.* 805 ff.).   ἐσθίουσι: Egyptians certainly did eat in the open (e.g. Klebs, *AR,* p. 106, fig. 87), but this was far from invariable (cf. N. de Garis Davies, *MMS* I (1929), 33 ff.).

4. ἱρᾶται: no Egyptian woman performed the divine cult or occupied a position which made her a priestess in the Greek sense; they were simply assistants of the priests (cf. Blackman, *HERE* X, p. 295; Woodhouse, ibid., p. 302 ff.). τρέφειν: sons were certainly not bound by law, though they were under moral pressure, but women were legally required to support their fathers (E. Seidl, *Atti Ximo congr. intern. di papirologia, 2–8 sett. 1965,* Milan 1966, pp. 149 ff.). In Athens the legal compulsion on the son was absolute (Lacey, pp. 116 ff.).

36,1. ξυρῶνται: cf. 37,2. A clean-shaven head was common for priests from the New Kingdom and compulsory by the Graeco-Roman Period (Bonnet, *RÄRG,* p. 389).   τοὺς μάλιστα ἱκνέεται: the subject is probably κῆδος with τούς as direct object (cf. IX 26,6 (accepting the ms reading)).   αὔξεσθαι: unkempt hair, beards, and moustaches were indeed a sign of mourning in Egypt, whereas shorn hair was customary in Greece (C. Desroches-Noblecourt, *BIFAO* XLV (1947), 185 ff.).   ἐξυρημένοι: facial hair was a rarity after the Old Kingdom and short hair the norm (Kees, *Ägypten,* p. 90, n.8).

2. πυρῶν καὶ κριθέων: πυρός, 'naked wheat' (*Triticum vulgare*) and κρῖθος, 'bar-ley' (*Hordeum vulgare*) were the standard cereals in Greece and Palestine (N. Jasny, *The Wheats of Classical Antiquity,* Baltimore 1944, pp. 14 ff., 148 ff.).   ὄνειδος: to the Egyptians food was a canonical means of distinguish-ing between foreigners and themselves (S. Sauneron, *Kush,* VII (1959), 63 ff.).   ἀπὸ ὀλυρέων... καλέουσι: in the strict sense ὄλυρα is probably soft emmer wheat and ζειά hard emmer (Jasny, op. cit., p. 129). Emmer was the normal Egyptian bread cereal in the Late Period (Kees, *Ancient Egypt,* p. 74).

3. τοῖσι ποσί: it could also be done by hand (e.g. N. de Garis Davies and A. H. Gardiner, *The Tomb of Antefoker,* London 1920, pl. 8, bottom register), and that

was the norm in Greece.   τῇσι χερσί: πηλός, 'mud, clay', could be kneaded by hand or foot (G. A. Reisner, *Mycerinus*, Cambridge, Mass. 1931, pp. 72 ff.). καὶ ... ἀναιρέονται: This comment rudely breaks the pattern of balanced antithesis prevailing in this section. Deletion would be rash in view of the good ms authority; it seems preferable, with Legrand, to postulate a lacuna pointing up a contrast between Greek and Egyptian practice. The Greeks certainly employed dung as manure, the Egyptians presumably as fuel (cf. A. Wiedemann, *Das alte Ägypten*, Heidelberg 1920, p. 188).   ἔμαθον: cf. 104,2–4. It is exemplified almost worldwide as a ritual act (Foucart, *HERE* III, pp. 659 ff.).   περιτάμνονται: cf. 37,2; 104,2 ff. Circumcision was never universal in Ancient Egypt and only compulsory for priests and royalty (Ghalioungui, op. cit., p. 96).   δύο: a linen tunic and woollen mantle (81,1). It was not uncommon for men to be more elaborately dressed than women (Erman–Ranke, *Ägypten*, pp. 231 ff.).   ἐν ἑκάστῃ: presumably the simple linen dress often depicted on servants (e.g. Lepsius, *Denkmäler* III, pls. 42, 91h), but it must have been supplemented by other garments during the winter season.

4. τῶν ἱστίων ... ἔσωθεν: in Greece κρίκοι, 'rings', were fixed to the sail's leading edge and κάλοι, 'reefing/brailing ropes', fitted through them for the purpose of reefing or furling the sail (J. S. Morrison and R. T. Williams, *Greek Oared Ships*, Cambridge 1968, pp. 299 ff.). The Egyptians fitted theirs on the windward side (Chassinat, *Edfou* XIII, pls. CCCC, LXX, CCCCLXXI, DVIII, DXXX). γράμματα ... ἀριστερά: hieratic and demotic are invariably written from right to left; hieroglyphs normally are, but the reverse direction is possible (Gardiner, *Egyptian Grammar*, p. 25).   ψήφοισι: here ψῆφος means 'number' (LSJ, p. 2023, s.v. ψῆφος, II,1). Translate 'they perform their calculations' (J. Gwyn Griffiths, *ASAE* LIII (1956), 142).   ποιεῦντες ταῦτα ... ἐπαρίστερα: probably a pun, ἐπὶ δεξιά meaning 'rightly' and ἐπ' ἀριστερά 'wrongly' (W. Spiegelberg, *Hermes*, LVI (1921), 436).   τὰ μὲν αὐτῶν ... καλέεται: the first is hieroglyphic (cf. 106,4) and the second demotic. Hieratic is omitted (cf. Spiegelberg, op. cit., pp. 434 ff.).

37,1. θεοσεβέες: amply confirmed: cf. Diod. I 83; Cic. *Tusc.* V 27; Tac. *Hist.* I 11; Aelian, *VH* II 31; Bonnet, *RÄRG*, p. 438.   χαλκέων ποτηρίων: bronze cups were widely used in Egypt (Hellanicus, *FGrHist* 4 F 53; W. C. Hayes, *The Scepter of Egypt*, II, New York 1959, p. 406). Since bronze was thought to have sanctifying powers (Bonnet, *RÄRG*, p. 636) priests may well have preferred them.

2. νεόπλυτα: personal cleanliness was essential to ritual purity (Blackman, *HERE* X, p. 477).   περιτάμνονται: cf. 36,3. Ritual purity probably was the motive (cf. Lichtheim, *Late Period*, p. 80).   ξυρῶνται: cf. 36,1. Depilation was also practised (e.g. R. O. Faulkner, *JEA* XXII (1936), 122). Purity was certainly the motive (Bonnet, *RÄRG*, p. 389).

3. λινέην: cf. Pliny, *NH* XIX 14; Plutarch, *DIO* 3–4 (*Mor.* 352). Woollen garments were absolutely forbidden to priests in the Graeco-Roman period (*BGU* I, no. 16; V, 71, 75).   βύβλινα: cf. Philostratus, *VA* VIII, 7 (333); Apuleius, *Met.* II 28. Papyrus sandals are known (Lucas–Harris, *AEMI*, p. 137), but there is no pharaonic evidence that priests had to wear them.   λοῦνται δὲ δίς: Chaeremon, who was a priest, says three times (in Porphyry, *Abst.* IV 7). Purification with water was believed both to remove dirt and to recharge with new life and power (Blackman, *HERE* X, pp. 476 ff.).   μυρίας: cf. Chaeremon, loc. cit.; R. Merkelbach, in P. Derchain (ed.), *Religions en Egypte hellénistique et romain,* Paris 1969, pp. 69 ff.   ὡς εἰπεῖν λόγῳ: see note on 4,1.

4. οὐκ ὀλίγα: priests received a regular stipend in kind from the temple estates and offerings made in the temple apart from incidental perquisities and private earnings (Kees, *Ägypten,* pp. 246 ff.).   σιτία . . . πεσσόμενα: the verb is not simply periphrastic for the unitary present passive (as Waddell, p. 161); the participle should be given full force. Transl. '. . . they also have sacred loaves which are baked for them'. They used special white bread according to one text (A. H. Gardiner, *The Admonitions of an Egyptian Sage,* Leipzig 1909, p. 76). ἰχθύων: cf. Chaeremon, loc. cit.; Plutarch, *DIO* 7 (*Mor.* 353). For fish in Egyptian religion see ch. 72.

5. κυάμους: beans certainly were used as food in Ancient Egypt (Hartmann, p. 54).   οὐδὲ ὁρέοντες ἀνέχονται: the taboo is confirmed by Aristagoras, *FGrHist* 608 F 7; Plutarch, *DIO* 5 (*Mor.* 352); Diodorus I 89,4; Pharaonic evidence is limited but tends to confirm classical statements (Lloyd, *Commentary* 1–98, pp. 168 ff.).   πολλοί: the Greek practice of appointing one priest at a time (Diod. I 73,5) was not followed in Egypt, where temples could have a very large number of them divided into various categories and under the overall supervision of a high priest (Bonnet, *RÄRG,* pp. 596 ff.).   ἀρχιέρεως: on the form and accentuation see Rosén, *Sprachform,* p. 91.   ἀντικατίσταται: cf. 143,3; Diod. I 88,2. The hereditary principle was certainly strong at most periods, but technically it was pharaoh's right to appoint anyone he liked as a priest, and this right was frequently exercised. Only in the Graeco-Roman period was priestly birth essential (H. Kees, *Das Priestertum im ägyptischen Staat,* Leiden–Cologne 1953, pp. 1 ff.).

38,1. τοῦ Ἐπάφου: cf. II 153; III 28. Epaphus was identified with the Egyptian *Ḥpw,* 'Apis' (Linforth, *UCPCPh* II(1910), 81 ff.). The cult of the Apis, the sacred bull of Memphis, was of great antiquity and achieved major importance in the Late Period (E. Otto, *Beiträge zur Geschichte der Stierkulte in Ägypten,* Leipzig 1938, pp. 11 ff.).

1–3.   τρίχα . . . καθαρός: cf. III 28; Pliny, *NH* VIII 184; Eusebius, *PE* III 13. The examination was intended to ensure that the animal was free of the markings of an Apis so that a prospective Apis was not sacrificed in error (Hopfner, *Tierkult,* p. 72).   ἴδηται: cf. note on 32,3.

2. τῶν τις ἱρέων: initially a *web*-priest, but in Greek times it was the duty of the μοσχοσφραγισταί (W. Otto, *Priester und Tempel im hellenistischen Ägypten,* I, Leipzig–Berlin 1908, p. 84).

3. τὸν δακτύλιον: it depicted a man on his knees, hands bound behind his back and sword at his throat (cf. G. Daressy, *Fouilles de la vallée des rois* (CGC), Cairo 1902, p. 37, no. 24089). In Roman times a tax was levied on each sealing (Wilcken, p. 115).   θάνατος: cf. 65,5; *BGU* V, pp. 79, 72. The death-penalty

is not confirmed in other sources, but from year 7 of Hadrian a certificate had to be presented to the central administration indicating that the law had been fulfilled (Wilcken, p. 116).

39,1. ἀγαγόντες: cf. H. E. Naville, *The Temple of Deir el Bahari*, IV, London 1901, pl. CXI.   βωμὸν: for examples of Egyptian altars see Wreszinski I, pl. 143; W. Wolf, *Das schöne Fest von Opet*, Leipzig 1931, pp. 19 ff., 25.   πῦρ: ritually fire was employed to cook offerings when they were conceived of as food and to destroy them when they were regarded as the enemies of the recipient deity (Bonnet, *RÄRG*, pp. 124 ff., 547, 549 ff.).   οἶνον: wine offerings are amply documented and served a variety of cultic purposes (ibid., pp. 863 ff.). Here it probably served to purify and dedicate the offering.   ἐπικαλέσαντες: the ritual is described in Egyptian as *ỉnt nṯr r šb(w).f*, 'inviting the god to his offering' (Naville, op. cit. II, pl. XXVIII).   σφάζουσι: cutting the throat was standard Egyptian practice (e.g. Klebs, *AR*, pp. 112 ff.; id., *MR*, pp. 17 ff.). ἀποτάμνουσι: decapitation was normal but not invariable (cf. Lepsius, *Denkmäler* IV, pl. 25).

2. δείρουσι: for representations of this rite see ibid. II, pls. 66–7. καταρησάμενοι φέρουσι: cf. Plutarch, *DIO* 31 (*Mor.* 363); Aelian, *HA* X 21. Heads of cattle and antelope frequently feature as offerings (e.g. Nelson, *Medinet Habu* III, pl. 172). Egyptian sources do not describe the subsequent removal of the head.   ἔμποροι: see above, p. 221.   ἀπ'ὧν ἔδοντο: for the gnomic aorist of habitual action see note on 20,2.

3. καταρῶνται: for a Hebrew parallel see Lev. 16: 6, 21. A curse directed against heads is known from one sacrificial context (*Urk.* VI 48 ff.), but the content is quite different.

4. κεφαλῆς: this general taboo is not substantiated from any Egyptian source.

40,1. ἄλλη . . . κατέστηκε: differences certainly existed between cults (e.g. Alliot, *Le Culte* II, p. 521), but detailed confirmation is not possible.   μεγίστην τε δαίμονα: Isis at this period (J. Bergman, *Ich bin Isis*, Uppsala 1968, pp. 132 ff.). ἔρχομαι ἐρέων: cf. note on 11,3.

2. κοιλίην μὲν κείνην: the removal of intestines is described at Edfu (Alliot, loc. cit.). κείνην is equivalent to τὴν κείνου, though Kenrick (*Egypt*, p. 63) preferred κεινήν, 'empty'.   ἐξ ὧν εἶλον: for the gnomic aorist of habitual action see note on 20,2.   σπλάγχνα: the Greeks removed them (cf. Homer, *Il.* I 464; *Syll.* 1002, 5). The statement on Egypt is inaccurate since the heart, which formed part of the σπλάγχνα, was frequently extracted (e.g. *Urk.* VI 82).   τὴν πιμελήν: 'soft fat, lard' often features in Egyptian sacrifices (e.g. Chassinat, *Edfou* VII, pp. 102, 213).   σκέλεα: there are many representations of this practice (e.g. Lepsius, *Denkmäler* II, pls. 66–8, 128–9; H. E. Naville, *The Temple of Deir el Bahari*, I, London 1895, pls. IV, VI–VII).   τὴν ὀσφὺν . . . τὸν τράχηλον: these presumably figured amongst the *stpwt*, 'choice joints', so often presented to the gods (*Wb.* IV, pp. 336,14–337,1).

3. τὸ ἄλλο σῶμα . . . θυωμάτων: in general true (cf. Alliot, *Le Culte* II, p. 521), but the details cannot all be confirmed.   ἄρτων καθαρῶν: loaves are common

offerings (e.g. Chassinat, *Dendera* IV, pl. CCLXXIII), but there is no evidence of their use in this way. μέλιτος: frequently offered to the gods (e.g. Nelson, *Medinet Habu* III, pl. 146), but this employment is unverified. ἀσταφίδος: as yet raisins are unknown from Ancient Egypt. σύκων: 'figs' are frequently offered to the gods (e.g. Lepsius, *Denkmäler* III, pl. 125b). λιβανωτοῦ καὶ σμύρνης: 'frankincense' and 'myrrh' were used in the offering service throughout Egyptian history (Bonnet, *RÄRG*, pp. 624 ff.). ἔλαιον: oils of various kinds were frequently employed in the cult (ibid., pp. 647 ff.).

4. προνηστεύσαντες: fasting is exemplified in Ancient Egypt (S. Schott, *Abhand. Akademie der Wissenschaften und der Literatur in Mainz*, X (1950), 10), but there is no evidence of it, as yet, in this context. τύπτονται: expressions of grief for the defeat of Seth occurred in Osirian ritual (*Urk.* VI 15), but there is no evidence, as yet, that it was a general practice. δαῖτα: offerings formed part of the stipend of temple and mortuary priests (see note on 37,4).

41,1 τὰς δὲ θηλέας...Ἴσιος: cf. 18,2; Plutarch, *DIO* 39 (*Mor.* 366); Apuleius, *Met.* XI 11; Athanasius, *Hist. Arian.* 56; Porphyry, *Abst.* II 11. Examples of cow sacrifice are rare and always early (Bonnet, *RÄRG*, p. 405). Ἴσιος: Egyptian *3st* (*Wb.* IV, pp. 8, 11–13).

2. βούκερων: this is normal (G. Daressy, *Statues de divinités* (CGC), Cairo 1905–6, pp. 217 ff.), but the horns can be replaced by the throne sign which spells her name in hieroglyphic (Roscher, *Lexicon* II, pp. 367 ff.). κατά περ...γράφουσι: from about the middle of the 5th cent. BC Io is often depicted as a horned maiden (Eitrem, *RE* IX, 1732 ff.). μάλιστα μακρῷ: the wide popularity of the Isis cult guaranteed the general currency of cow worship (Bonnet, *RÄRG*, p. 402).

3. φιλήσειε: this claim cannot be substantiated, but it is consistent with Egyptian attitudes to foreigners in general (cf. W. Helck, *Saeculum*, XV (1964), 103 ff.).

4. ἐς τὸν ποταμὸν: this practice is not confirmed by Egyptian sources, but since drowning in the Nile was thought to deify (note on ch. 90) and since the Nile could be identified with Osiris (Bonnet, *RÄRG*, pp. 527 ff.), the action can be given a plausible religious interpretation. τοὺς δὲ ἔρσενας...νήσου: the state of surviving mummified bodies can be used to substantiate this claim (cf. Gaillard–Daressy, *La Faune momifiée*, p. 17; Lortet–Gaillard, *La Faune momifiée* I, pp. 41 ff.). τὸ κέρας...εἵνεκεν: this phrase must be construed as being in apposition to τοὺς ἔρσενας (cf. 133,5; 166,2; IV 71,1). The protruding horns would facilitate finding the corpses. The description is paralleled by Buchis-bull burials at Armant, in which the horns were fixed more or less vertically (Sir Robert Mond and O. M. Myers, *The Bucheum*, I, London 1934, p. 58). Προσωπίτιδος...νήσου: cf. ch. 165; Thuc. I 109; Strabo XVII 1,20 (C802); Ptolemy, *Geog.* IV 5,9. The island was probably formed by the Canopic and Sebennytic branches of the Nile and a waterway joining them to the north.

5. σχοῖνοι ἐννέα: i.e. *c.*96.66 km. at 179 m. to the stade (note on ch. 6). Ἀτάρβηχις: probably K(ôm Abu Billu. This city was not situated within the

νῆσος but may well have lain within the Prosopite Nome (Lloyd, *Commentary 1–98*, pp. 187 ff.). A large cattle cemetery has been found nearby (Bonnet, *RÄRG*, p. 791).

6. **ἐς ἕνα χῶρον**: this cannot be literally true, since bull cemeteries are known from many parts of Egypt (PM III, pp. 205 ff.; V, p. 158; Bonnet, *RÄRG*, p. 520), but the practice of collecting the bodies of sacred animals for burial is exemplified (F. Preisigke and W. Spiegelberg, *Die Prinz Joachim Ostraka*, Strasbourg 1914, pp. 2, 14, n. 5). Herodotus has probably exaggerated the range of activity of Atarbechis' agents.

42,1. **Διὸς Θηβαιέος**: cf. I 46; II 18; 32; 55. The identification of the Egyptian Amon-re, 'King of the Gods', with Zeus/Jupiter was standard classical practice (cf. Diod. I 12, 97; Strabo XVII 1,27 (C805), 46 (C816)). He was worshipped throughout Egypt.   **νομοῦ τοῦ Θηβαίου**: here the 4th Nome of Upper Egypt.   **ὄϊων ἀπεχόμενοι**: wherever rams were worshipped, there would normally have been a general prohibition on sacrificing all members of the species (note on ch. 65).

2. **τοῦ Μένδητος**: the Egyptian *B3-nb-ḏd*, 'Soul Lord of Djedet'. The ram was his canonical incarnation (L. Keimer, *ASAE* XXXVIII (1938), 695).   **αἰγῶν ἀπεχόμενοι**: strictly Mendes' sacred animal was a ram of the species *Ovis longipes palaeoaegyptiacus*, but the disappearance of this animal from Egypt led to its replacement by the goat (*Hircus mambrinus*) (Keimer, loc. cit.).

3–6. **Θηβαῖοι ... αὐτόν**: cf. Hyginus, *Fab.* CXCVI. The tale is an aetiological myth designed to explain the ritual of sacrificing the ram and clothing the statue with its fleece. The purpose of the rite was presumably to endue the god's statue with the life and power of the sacred animal.

3. **Ἡρακλέα**: probably Chonsu, Amon-re's son (J. Gwyn Griffiths, *JHS* LXXV (1955), 23).   **ἰδέσθαι**: see note on 32,3.   **τὸν**: the Homeric demonstrative pronoun (Chantraine, *Grammaire* II, pp. 158 ff.).   **<τοιάδε>**: Herold and Hude read τάδε and Fritsch τοιόνδε. τοιάδε is preferable since it is Herodotus' normal word after μηχανάομαι.

4. **κριοπρόσωπον**: this is canonical (cf. Daressy, op. cit., pl. XXIX). **Ἀμμώνιοι**: the inhabitants of the Sîwa Oasis, site of the oracle of Zeus Ammon (Parke, *Oracles of Zeus*, pp. 202 ff.).   **ἄποικοι**: Sîwa is inhabited today by a mixture of Berbers, Beduin, and Sudanese (A. Fakhri, *The Oasis of Siwa*, Cairo 1950, p. 1). Egyptians were undoubtedly there in antiquity (ibid., pp. 41, 121 ff.), and a Nubian element is extremely probable (J. Leclant and J. Yoyotte, *BIFAO*, LI (1952), 28, n.6). Libyans were also present (Gardiner, *AEO* I, pp. 116 ff., 120). **φωνήν**: the ethnic mix would inevitably create a heterogeneous linguistic environment.

5. **δοκέειν**: cf. note on 4,1.   **Ἀμοῦν**: Egyptian *'Imn*, 'The Hidden One' (*Wb.* I, pp. 83 ff.).

6. **τύπτονται**: cf. 40,4; 61; Lucian, *Sacr.* 15.   **ἐν ἱρῇ θήκῃ**: ram cemeteries are found throughout the country (D. Kessler, *LdÄ* VI, pp. 579–80), but no known mummy shows the mutilation described by Herodotus.

43,1. Ἡρακλέος: the Egyptian prototype here is Shu (Gwyn Griffiths, op. cit., p. 23). He was often identified with Chonsu, who clearly lies behind the Heracles of II 42.   τῶν δυώδεκα θεῶν: strictly, the Ennead, which was the Egyptian counterpart of the Greek Twelve Gods (ibid., p. 22).   τοῦ ἑτέρου: i.e. the hero; for the Greeks regarded Heracles both as a god and a hero (L. Farnell, *Greek Hero Cults*, Oxford 1921, pp. 97 ff.).

2. τὸ οὔνομα: 'name', not simply 'personality, concept', as often claimed (e.g. Linforth, *UCPCPh* VII (1924), 285), i.e. Herodotus believed that 'Heracles' was an Egyptian name imported into Greece (Lloyd, *Commentary* 1–98, pp. 203 ff.). It is, of course, Greek, probably Ἥρα + κλέος (Farnell, op. cit., pp. 99 ff.). τεκμήρια: Herodotus skilfully applies γνώμη to the problem, using three arguments in this chapter, two based on tradition (43,2 and 4) and the other on probability (43,2–3). The argument continues into ch. 44.   τὸ ἀνέκαθεν: proof 1. Both were descended from Perseus, who had close Egyptian affinities (ch. 91). οὔτε Ποσειδέωνος οὔτε Διοσκόρων: proof 2. They were sea gods, and their names would have been known in Egypt if they had travelled to Greece and acquired the name there.

4. ἐς Ἄμασιν: proof 3. Amasis ascended the throne in 570 BC (note on ch. 162). Therefore the Egyptian Heracles was much older than the Greek hero.   ἐκ τῶν ὀκτὼ θεῶν: the Ogdoad of Hermopolis (Gwyn Griffiths, op. cit., pp. 21 ff.).

44,1–4. καὶ θέλων … γενέσθαι: two further proofs, this time based on ἱστορίη (see above, p. 230).

1. ἱρὸν: argument 4. It probably stood on the site of the modern Cathédrale des croisés (M. H. Chéhab, in *Mélanges Mouterde*, II, Beirut 1962, p. 17).   Ἡρακλέος: i.e. Melqart, who was predominantly a sea god in Herodotus' time (E. Dhorme and R. Dussaud, *Les Anciennes Religions orientales*, II, Paris 1945, p. 366).

2. εἶδον … μέγαθος: the building probably consisted of a court with the cult objects in the centre enclosed in a roofed building (cf. G. Contenau, *La Civilisation phénicienne*, Paris 1928, pp. 162 ff.).   στῆλαι δύο: cf. Theophrastus, *Lap.* IV 25; Pliny, *HN* XXXVII 75. They were round-topped and stood on a rectangular base. The dual number probably reflected the fact that Melqart was a fusion of the two gods Ba'al Hadad and Yam (Comte du Mesnil du Buisson, *RHR* CLXIV (1963), 133 ff.).   μέγαθος: if correct, this noun must be employed adverbially, but such a usage would be highly untypical Herodotean Greek. No emendation inspires confidence: Reiske's μέγα φῶς seems forced; Wesseling's μεγάλως, accepted by Legrand, is easy but does not seem to be paralleled with λάμπω and is not, in any case, particularly apposite since it does not adequately convey the notion of 'brightness' which the context evidently requires. The temptation to delete is strong, but the possibility remains that the μέγαθος conceals a corruption of some kind.

3. τριηκόσια καὶ δισχίλια: i.e. c.2750 BC. Since the cult of Melqart does not occur before the 10th cent., Herodotus is presumably referring to his predecessor Ba'al Hadad. Tyre certainly existed in the 14th cent. BC. There is, as yet, no evidence of it in the 3rd millennium, but such a date is not impossible (cf. D. Harden, *The Phoenicians*, Harmondsworth 1971, pp. 44, 217, n. 35). εἶδον ... εἶναι: this shrine will reflect the activities of Thasian traders in the Levant (J. Pouilloux, *Recherches sur l'histoire et les cultes de Thasos*, I, Paris 1954, pp. 21, 54, 356 ff.). Θασίου: cf. *IG* XII, Supp., 414; Paus. VI 11,2. εἶναι: this prolative infinitive is frequent after ὀνομάζειν and similar words and expressions.

4. ἐς Θάσον: argument 5. This Thasian cult was renowned throughout the Greek world (M. Launey, *Le Sanctuaire et le culte d'Héraklès à Thasos*, Paris 1944).

5. διξὰ Ἡράκλεια: ambiguous: either 'two temples of Heracles' or 'a double temple of Heracles'. The latter is probably correct here, since the Herakleion at Thasos seems to have included a double shrine for the god and hero (ibid., p. 167). θύουσι ... ἐναγίζουσι: the correct technical terms for the different types of offering cults. For details of variations see Nilsson, *GgrR* I, pp. 378 ff., 715 ff.

45,1. λέγουσι ... λέγουσι: cf. Hecataeus, *FGrHist* I F1. ὡς αὐτὸν ... καταφονεῦσαι: the action is usually ascribed to the legendary Egyptian king Busiris (v. Gärtringen, *RE* III, 1074 ff.). Since the tale was used by Panyassis, Herodotus' uncle (*EGF* I, p. 253), he is conceivably the target here.

2–3. ἐμοὶ μέν ... φονεῦσαι: the tradition is neatly demolished as being incompatible with Egyptian character and physically impossible to boot (see above, pp. 236 ff.). There is no unequivocal evidence of human sacrifice in Egypt after the Ist Dynasty (for discussions see Bonnet, *RÄRG*, pp. 453 ff.; J. Gwyn Griffiths, *LdÄ* IV, 64–5). The story probably arose from Egyptian xenophobia and traditions on human sacrifice amongst the Ethiopians (*FGrHist* 609 F 2, 3a–c, pp. 48 ff.; I. Hofmann, *Die Kulturen des Niltals von Assuan bis Sennar*, Hamburg 1967, Index, s.v. 'Menschenopfer'). This amalgam may then have been further contaminated by accounts of human sacrifice in the Tauric Chersonese (cf. IV 103).

3. κῶς φύσιν ἔχει: impersonal: 'How is it natural?'

46,1. Τὰς δὲ δὴ αἶγας καὶ τοὺς τράγους: see notes on 42,1–2; 65. τὸν Πᾶνα: the Egyptian Mendes (46,4). τῶν ὀκτὼ θεῶν ... τῶν δυώδεκα θεῶν: the Ogdoad and Ennead respectively (43,1 and 4). No Egyptian text speaks of Mendes as a member of the Ogdoad, but he is sometimes treated as one of the primeval gods, the category to which the Ogdoad belongs (Bonnet, *RÄRG*, pp. 869 ff.).

2. γράφουσί ... γλύφουσι: 'Paint' and 'carve' respectively. αἰγοπρόσωπον: Mendes is almost always represented as a ram, though the animal used as his incarnation in Herodotus' time was the goat (note on 42,2). Pan can be depicted entirely as a goat (e.g. R. Dawkins, *The Sanctuary of Artemis Orthia at Sparta*, London 1929, pp. 262, 269, pls. 184, 19; 189, 23–5), but anthropomorphic elements are evident from an early period and can predominate (H. Sichtermann, *EAA* V, pp. 920 ff.).

3. σέβονται: see notes on chs. 42, 65. πένθος μέγα: this would be normal for all beings perceived as divine (cf. note on 66,4).

4. ἐμίσγετο: confirmed by Pindar (fr. 190 (Bowra)), Aristides (*Or.* 36, 112), and Clement (*Protr.* II 32,4). Furthermore, a mould from the city of Mendes depicts

the act (G. Michaelidis, *BIFAO* LXIII (1965), 139 ff.). Women also frequently exposed themselves before the sacred animal to gain fertility (Hopfner, *Fontes*, p. 742).

47,1. ὗν ... εἶναι: pigs were raised in Egypt from prehistoric times (L. Keimer, *BIE* XIX (1937), 147 ff.), but they were certainly regarded as unclean in most contexts (ibid. 148 ff.). **τοῦτο μέν ... τοῦτο δέ:** here, as often, to introduce specific examples of a general proposition. **ἀπ'ὧν ἔβαψε:** the gnomic aorist of habitual action (cf. note on 20,2). **οἱ συβῶται:** for representations see J. J. Tylor and F. Ll. Griffith, *The Tomb of Paheri*, London 1894, pl. III. The prohibition on their entering temples is not substantiated but is entirely credible for the Late Period (Kees, *Ancient Egypt*, p. 91). **ἐκδίδοσθαι:** Herodotus exaggerates. It was normal practice for people to marry within their own socio-economic group (P. Pestman, *Marriage and Matrimonial Property in Ancient Egypt*, London 1961, p. 14).

2. τοῖσι μέν νυν ἄλλοισι θεοῖσι ... τῶν κρεῶν: pigs were commonly sacrificed in Greece (P. Stengel, *Griechische Kultusaltertümer*, Munich 1920³, pp. 121 ff.). This was a rare event in Egypt but can be identified in the cults of the Osirian group of gods (e.g. Nelson, *Medinet Habu* III, pl. 158; Alliot, *Le Culte* I, p. 231). **Σελήνη:** she is Isis and Dionysus Osiris (Bonnet, *RÄRG*, p. 691). Sacrifice at the full moon is confirmed by classical and Egyptian sources (Manetho, *FGrHist* 609 F 23; Plutarch, *DIO* 8 (*Mor.* 354); Alliot, loc. cit.). **δι' ὅ τι ... θύουσι:** the ultimate reason was health, but from an early stage the taboo was reinforced by associating the pig with Seth, Osiris' arch-enemy and the Egyptian equivalent of the devil (Bonnet, *RÄRG*, pp. 690 ff.). The λόγος is probably that of Seth's attack on the moon (i.e. Osiris) (cf. Griffiths, *The Conflict*, pp. 108 ff., 124 ff.).

3. θυσίη: cf. II, 39 ff. The details are impossible to confirm. **κατ' ὦν ἐκάλυψε:** cf. ἀπ' ὧν ἔβαψε above. **οὐκ ἄν ἔτι γευσαίατο:** the potential optative here approximates to a pure future: 'they will not taste (under any circumstances)' (Goodwin, *Moods and Tenses*, 80). Pigs were eaten during the New Kingdom (Keimer, op. cit., p. 149), but a general prohibition in the Late Period is not impossible. **σταιτίνας:** the use of ritual models of dough and bread is exemplified in the cult of Osirian deities (Alliot, *Le Culte*, p. 789; Chassinat, *Le Mystère*, pp. 151, 164 ff.).

48,1. Τῷ Διονύσῳ ... τῶν συβωτέων: see note on 47,2. **ἀποφέρεσθαι:** final infinitive (cf. Goodwin, *Moods and Tenses*, p. 308 ff.).

2. χορῶν: 'choral dances' (LSJ, p. 1999,b,1). **φαλλῶν:** they were of major importance in the cult of Dionysus (Nilsson, *GgrR* I, pp. 118, 590 ff.). Here and in the worship of Osiris the phallic element reflects the god's fertility aspect. **ἄλλα ... σώματος:** the ithyphallic Osiris features frequently in Egyptian sources (Bonnet, *RÄRG*, p. 59). **νευρόσπαστα:** no cult images of this kind have survived, but toys with parts moved by strings are well known (e.g. Garstang, pp. 152 ff.). The festival is probably the Pamylia described by Plutarch (*DIO* 12, 36 (*Mor.* 355, 365)). **νεῦον τὸ αἰδοῖον:** probably correct and standing in loose apposition to ἀγάλματα (cf. note on ch. 41), but the temptation to emend to νεύον<τα> τὸ αἰδοῖον is strong.   αὐλός: cf. note on 60,1. ἀείδουσαι: festival hymns occur frequently in Egyptian sources (e.g. W. Wolf, *Das schöne Fest von Opet*, Leipzig 1931, pp. 56 ff.).

3. λόγος: the reticence is typical (cf. Linforth, *UCPCPh* VII (1924), 259 ff.). The λόγος probably related to the myth that, when Isis was trying to reconstitute the body of Osiris after its dismemberment by Seth, she was unable to find the phallus and used a model (Plutarch, *DIO* 18 ff., 36 (*Mor.* 358, 365)).

49,1. Μελάμπους: cf. Homer, *Od.* XI 285 ff.; XV 225 ff.; Apollodorus I 9, 11 ff. He features in Greek legend as a great ἰατρόμαντις, and in this capacity developed a close connection with the Dionysiac cult (Nilsson, *GgrR* I, Index, s.v. 'Melampus').   τοῦ Διονύσου... οὔνομα: not Dionysus, son of Semele (145,4), but the much older Egyptian god whom Herodotus calls Dionysus (cf. the case of Heracles, 43,1).   τό τε οὔνομα: see note on 43,2.

2–3. Ἕλλησι... νόμαιον: Herodotus supports his thesis by two arguments (see above, pp. 235 ff.).

2. ὁμότροπα: argument I: 'For they (sc. Dionysiac practices) would be identical in character to Greek practices...', i.e. if Greek Dionysiac worship agreed by accident (συμπεσεῖν) with its Egyptian counterpart, it would have been a native growth and would have shown standard Greek features. In fact, the cult is identifiable in Greece as early as the late bronze age (L. Palmer, *Mycenaean Greek Texts*, Oxford 1963, p. 255), but later foreign influences are certainly detectable (Nilsson, *GgrR* I pp. 564 ff., 578 ff.).

3. οὐ μὲν οὐδὲ... νόμαιον: argument 2. Essentially the *post hoc ergo proper hoc* fallacy (see above, p. 235).   Κάδμου: cf. II 145; IV 147; V 57–9. He was in origin a god, the Πάϊς of the Theban Kabeirion, but subsequently acquired the status of a ἥρως. His intimate connection with Dionysus arose through the latter's great popularity in Boeotia. The Phoenician affinities probably reflect nothing more than the close Greek contact with the Near East during the orientalizing and archaic periods (Lloyd, *Commentary 1–98*, pp. 226 ff.).

50,1. σχεδὸν δὲ... Ἑλλάδα: logically this chapter belongs after ch. 52.   τὰ οὐνόματα: see note on 43,2.

2. ὅτι γὰρ... εἴρηται: cf. 43,2.   καὶ Διοσκόρων: they were indisputably Greek. The Pelasgian origin theory presumably arose from their rather primitive nature (Nilsson, *GgrR* I, pp. 407 ff.).   Ἥρης: her Greek credentials are as good as those of any deity. It may have been her connection with Arcadia, a major 'Pelasgian' area, which led to Herodotus' notion on her origins (cf. ibid., pp. 427 ff.).   Ἱστίης: her Greek antecedents are certain (ibid., p. 337). The idea that she was Pelasgian may have originated from her rather amorphous personality (cf. 52,1).   Θέμιος: the name is Greek, but her connection with Thessaly, a 'Pelasgian' area (Homer, *Il.* II 681), and her role as a primeval deity provide adequate explanations for Herodotus' mistake.   Χαρίτων: 'the Gift-' or 'Grace-givers' (J. A. Harrison, *Themis*, Cambridge 1912, p. 185). They are certainly Greek, but their cult could be very primitive and might well have suggested a pre-Greek origin (cf. Escher, *RE* III, 2150).　　*Νηρηΐδων*: again a Greek origin is beyond question (Herzog-Hauser, *RE* XVII, 1 ff.). Perhaps it was their function as sea deities which suggested a non-Greek provenance (cf. 43,2).　　*Πελασγῶν*: cf. I 57–8; 146,1; II 56,1; 171,2–3; VII 94–5; VIII 44. The Pelasgians figure prominently in Greek tradition as the pre-Dorian, non-Greek inhabitants of Greece, but they are largely fictitious, an ingenious but misguided product of early Greek historical speculation (Lloyd, *Commentary 1–98*, pp. 232 ff.).

2–3. *τοῦτον... αἰεί*: Poseidon's Indo-European antecedents are certain (F. Scha-chermeyr, *Poseidon und die Entstehung des griechischen Glaubens*, Bern 1950). His cult in North Africa cannot pre-date the 8th cent.; the notion of its great antiquity probably arose because the Greek god had been identified with an older Libyan deity (Lloyd, *Commentary 1–98*, pp. 237 ff.).

3. *νομίζουσι... ἥρωσι οὐδέν*: *νομίζουσι* is constructed with the dative like *χράομαι* (cf. Powell, *Lexicon*, p. 233, II, 3). 'Heroes' in Greece were an intermediate group between men and gods. There was no pharaonic counterpart, since great men translated to a higher status after death were regarded in Egypt as gods (Bonnet, *RÄRG*, p. 856).

51,1. *τοῦ δὲ Ἑρμέω... ὦλλοι*: the classical ithyphallic herm does appear to be of Athenian origin (J. F. Crome, *MDAI(A)* LX 1 (1935–6), 300 ff.).

1–2. *πρῶτοι... νομισθῆναι*: on the Pelasgians see note on 50,2. Herodotus had two traditions on their history in Attica: (a) The Athenians had originally been Pelas-gians but had subsequently been transmuted into Greeks (*Ἀθηναίοισι... τελέουσι*) (cf. VIII 44); (b) Pelasgians had once lived in Attica alongside the Athenians (cf. VI 137 ff.). Here the two traditions are combined.

2. *ὅθεν περ*: 'since when they (sc. the Pelasgians) also began to be considered Greeks', i.e. the Pelasgian colony was assimilated. Like most things Pelasgian, this colony was a pseudo-historical fabrication (Meyer, *Forschungen* I, pp. 8 ff.).　　*τὰ Καβείρων ὄργια*: the Kabeiroi were usually a pair of male gods, one older than the other, the older usually bearing the name Kabeiros. Strictly, they were never worshipped on Samothrace; Herodotus has identified them with the similar *Μεγάλοι θεοί* or *Σαμόθρᾳκες θεοί* who were worshipped there. It was with the older male that the ithyphallic Hermes was usually identified. The rites were greatly influenced by the Eleusinian mysteries during the classical period (B. Hemberg, *Die Kabiren*, Uppsala 1950, pp. 49 ff., 92 ff., 104 ff., 261 ff.). *παρὰ Πελασγῶν*: the Samothracian cult seems to have been an indigenous phenomenon with some Asiatic influence (Lloyd, *Commentary 1–98*, pp. 242 ff.). The claim that it was Pelasgian probably reflects its primitive char-acter, the presence on Samothrace of a non-Greek linguistic element, and the connection of the Kabeiroi with Lemnos, a well-known Pelasgian area (cf. VI 136,2; 138 ff.).

3. *πρότερον*: i.e. before Herodotus' own time.

4. *λόγον*: this was presumably connected with the ritual of the *ἱερὸς γάμος*. For the cult's phallic aspect see K. H. De Jong, *Das antike Mysterienwesen*, Leiden

1919², p. 78).   τά: in loose apposition to λόγον, indicating that the latter is made up of many details.

52,1. ἔθνον . . . αὐτῶν: Herodotus claims that Greek religion evolved through three phases: undifferentiated and unnamed gods; the introduction of names and personalities from Egypt by the Pelasgians; and the systematization of this material by the Greeks, particularly Homer and Hesiod. This perspective has its origins partly in the Hesiodic theogonic tradition (note on ch. 53) and partly in pre-Socratic speculation on the nature of religious traditions and on evolutionary theories of social and biological development (cf. Jaeger, pp. 172 ff.). ἐπωνυμίην: 'epithet'. Epithets were assigned by Homer and Hesiod, whereas names like Zeus and Dionysus came from Egypt (note on 53,2).   θεούς: cf. Plato, *Cra.* 397d. The etymology of θεός is still debated (H. Frisk, *Griechisches etymologisches Wörterbuch*, Heidelberg 1960–72, pp. 662 ff.; W. Burkert, in Alan B. Lloyd (ed.), *What is a God? Studies in the Nature of Greek Divinity*, London 1997, pp. 15 ff.). Such etymologizing was regarded in early Greek theology as a means of penetrating to the very essence of divine beings (Jaeger, pp. 68 ff.).   θέντες . . . εἶχον: not simply a periphrastic tense (*pace* W. J. Aerts, *Periphrastica*, Amsterdam 1965, p. 150). The two elements appear to retain much of their independence, as often: 'having established all in due order and all allotments, they kept them (there)' (cf. Goodwin, *Moods and Tenses*, pp. 14 ff.).

2. ἔπειτε: the Ionic form of ἔπειτα (cf. Powell, *Lexicon*, p. 129). As the *lectio difficilior* it is preferable to the variant ἔπειτα.   ἐν Δωδώνῃ: see notes on chs. 54–7. It was normal Greek practice to obtain divine approval for cult changes (Parke, *Oracles of Zeus*, pp. 39, 110, 113, 189).   μοῦνον: cf. Plato, *Phdr.* 275b. Both Homer and Hesiod connect the shrine with Zeus Pelasgikos (*Il.* XVI 233; Hesiod, fr. 240 (Merkelbach–West), and its Pelasgian affinities are frequently mentioned later (e.g. Aeschylus, *Supp.* 249 ff.; Strabo VII 7,10 (C327; IX 2,4 (C402)). The shrine's great antiquity admits of no doubt (Parke, op. cit., pp. 7 ff., 97 ff.).

3. ἀνέλωνται . . . ἀνεῖλε: for the pun cf. J. E. Powell, *CR* LI (1937), 104. ἀναιρέω is the standard word for delivering an oracular response; it presumably reflects the method of obtaining oracles by picking up beans or lots which was commonly used both at Dodona and Delphi (P–W, pp. 18 ff.).

53,1. ὅθεν . . . λόγῳ: Herodotus mistakenly assumes that the beginning of his evidence reflects the introduction of the phenomenon. In reality, epic theology had a long history behind it (Guthrie, p. 27).   ὡς εἰπεῖν λόγῳ: see note on 4,1.

2. τετρακοσίοισι ἔτεσι: cf., for Homer, Aristarchus in *Plutarchi Vita* II 16–20 (Allen); Pliny, *HN* VII 16; Tzetzes, *H* XIII 639 ff.; *FGrHist* 239 F 28; Jacoby, *Apollodors Chronik*, pp. 118 ff.; for Hesiod, Archemachus, *FGrHist* 424 F 3; Tzetzes, *H* XIII 643 ff. An 8th-cent. date for both is not likely to be seriously wrong (G. S. Kirk, *CAH*³ II 2, pp. 848 ff.; M. L. West, *Hesiod. Theogony*, Oxford 1966, pp. 40 ff.).   οὗτοι . . . σημήναντες: cf. Arist. *Met.* I, 3(983b). The central role of these two authors in defining the gods' epithets (ἐπωνυμίας), attributes (τιμάς τε καὶ τέχνας), and forms (εἴδεα) is beyond dispute and exercised a potent influence down to the end of classical paganism both in literature and art (W. K. Guthrie, *CAH³* II 2, pp. 887 ff.). However, not all Greeks regarded their influence as wholesome (e.g. Xenophanes, 21 frs. 10–11 DK; Plato, *Rep.* 606e).

3. ὕστερον: it was sometimes claimed that Homer was descended from Orpheus (Pherecydes, *FGrHist* 3 F 167; Hellanicus, ibid. 4 F 5; Damastes, ibid. 5 F 11) or Musaeus (Gorgias, 82 B25 DK). ἔμοιγε δοκέειν: see note on 4,1. τούτων...λέγω: as often in controversial matters, Herodotus is meticulous in stating his sources (see above, pp. 228 ff.).

54,1. χρηστηρίων δὲ πέρι: the beginning of the discussion of the origin of the oracle at Dodona, which extends to ch. 57. We are given the traditions of the priests of the Theban Zeus (54) and of the Dodoneans (55), and these are then subjected by Herodotus to a searching criticism (56–7). There were several other legends on the foundation of the oracle which Herodotus ignores (Parke, *Oracles of Zeus*, pp. 38 ff.). ἱερείας: contradicted by 35,4. Females would be a necessary part of the tradition, since the Dodonean oracle was administered by women in Herodotus' time (note on 55,1). ὑπὸ Φοινίκων: cf. I 1 for another example of the Phoenicians' piratical bent. ἐς Λιβύην: i.e. to the oracular shrine of Zeus Ammon at Sîwa, on which see note on 18,2. The doctrine that the cults of Sîwa and Dodona had a common origin was apparently established in Greece before Herodotus discussed the issue (Parke, op. cit., pp. 57 ff.).

55,1. αἱ προμάντιες: the oracle was originally served by male priests, the Ἑλλοί or Σελλοί, but they were subsequently relegated to a subordinate position by priestesses (Strabo VII 7,12 (C329); Parke, *Oracles of Zeus*, pp. 69 ff.). Herodotus' claim that there were three is confirmed by Euripides (schol. ad Soph. *Trach.* 172), Strabo (VII F 1), and Eustathius (*ad Od.* XIV 327). πελειάδας: πελειάς is used generically for birds of the pigeon family (Thompson, *Greek Birds*, pp. 225 ff.); the species honoured at Dodona was probably the ring dove or wood pigeon (*Columba palumbus palumbus*). The bird's connection with Zeus is not unique to Dodona (Parke, *Oracles of Zeus*, pp. 43 ff.).

2. φηγὸν: 'the Valonia oak' (*Quercus macrolepis*). A tree of this species was held sacred to Zeus at Dodona and served as the focus of the cult there (Parke, op. cit., pp. 20 ff.). Its location has probably been identified south of the Acropolis and east of the *hiera oikia* (S. Dakaris, Ἀρχαιολογικὸ Δελτίον, XVI (1960), 37 ff.). μαντήιον: the oracular Zeus worshipped at Dodona was Zeus Naios. The cult was of great antiquity, having been brought into Greece by Indo-European invaders in the late 3rd millennium BC; it had no Egyptian affinities (Parke, op. cit., pp. 68, 98). σφεα: so Krueger. All mss read σφεας, but the word is intolerable after αὐτούς...αὐτοῖσι. Krueger's σφεα would refer to the content of the oracle. Herodotus can certainly use this neuter anaphorically (cf. Powell, *Lexicon*, p. 347), but in the present case a disconcerting element of tautology would arise with ἐκ τούτου. It therefore seems preferable to delete σφεας as a gloss.

3. οἱ ἄλλοι Δωδωναῖοι: these were possibly the Ἑλλοί priests (cf. Homer, *Il.* XVI 234 ff.).

56,1. ἐγὼ δ'ἔχω...γνώμην τήνδε: in this and the following chapter Herodotus attempts to extract the truth by argument from the traditions retailed to him (see above, pp. 229–31).

1–3. εἰ ἀληθέως...ἐπρήθη: argument I, based on εἰκός (see above, p. 236).

1. Πελασγίης: cf. note on 50,2; 51,1–2.   Θεσπρωτούς: in the early period Dodona was undoubtedly under the Thesprotians (*Od.* XIV 314 ff.; XIX 287), but in Herodotus' time it was controlled by the Molossians (Parke, *Oracles of Zeus*, p. 11). Nevertheless, it remained the focus of Thesprotian religious life until the end of the 5th cent. (cf. Euripides, *Phoen.* 982).

2. ἱρὸν: 'shrine, holy place'. Since there was no temple until *c*.400 BC (Parke, op. cit., pp. 98 ff.), Herodotus must be thinking of the establishment of a *temenos* only.

3. τὴν Ἑλλάδα γλῶσσαν: strictly it would have been Pelasgian (52,3).

57,1–3. πελειάδες...ἀπιγμένη: argument 2, the sheer impossibility of the Dodonian tradition (cf. 45,3). Herodotus' attitude is uncompromisingly rationalistic (see above, pp. 228 ff., 236).

3. ἡ δὲ μαντηίη: originally the oracular response seems to have been derived from the rustling or creaking of the sacred oak, but in the 5th cent. questions were written on small strips of lead and the answers probably obtained by a priestess drawing lots (Parke, *Oracles of Zeus*, pp. 27 ff., 75 ff., 84, 100 ff.). This technique has close similarities to the standard Egyptian method (note on ch. 83). ἔστι...ἀπιγμένη: the use of the periphrastic perfect probably emphasizes the permanence of the state which had come into existence as a result of the verbal action (cf. P. Chantraine, *Histoire du parfait grec*, Paris 1927, p. 249). Divination based on the behaviour of burning offerings was practised at Olympia and at Thebes (Parke, *Oracles of Zeus*, pp. 164, 184). The fact that this chapter is concerned with Zeus suggests that Herodotus had Olympia specifically in mind. The Egyptians are not known to have employed this method, but their interest in omens suggests that it may have occurred from time to time (cf. Bonnet, *RÄRG*, pp. 542 ff.).

58. πανηγύριας...μεμαθήκασι: for the alliteration cf. note on 1,1; 60,2. πανηγύριας: 'general assemblies, national festivals'. The term is normally applied to a festival attended by many people from many different areas, e.g. the Olympic Games or the Panionia (cf. Nilsson, *GgrR* I, pp. 826 ff.). Egyptian parallels were numerous (note on 59–63).   ἄρα: Herodotus shares with Homer a taste for this particle to introduce an explanatory detail (Denniston, *Greek Particles*, pp. 33 ff.).   πομπὰς: 'solemn processions' accompanying a statue or offerings, e.g. the Panathenaic Festival at Athens (L. Deubner, *Attische Feste*, Berlin 1932, pp. 22 ff.), but the fact that Herodotus distinguished between πομπαί and προσαγωγαί (see below) indicates that he used the former pre-eminently of processions concerned with divine statues. πομπαί have many similarities with the Egyptian *prwt nṯr*, 'emergence of the god' festivals, e.g. the Festival of Opet (cf. W. Wolf, *Das schöne Fest von Opet*, Leipzig 1931).   προσαγωγὰς: 'solemn approaches' bringing offerings to the deity

(Lloyd, *Commentary 1–98*, p. 266). The term could have been applied to many Egyptian festivals.   τεκμήριον: one of many examples in Herodotus of the *post hoc ergo propter hoc* fallacy (see above, p. 235).   νεωστί: not as recently as Herodotus thought; for festivals are clearly identifiable in the Aegean world during the Bronze Age (Nilsson, *GgrR* I, pp. 303 ff.).

59,1. πανηγυρίζουσι . . . συχνάς: the festival calendar at Medinet Habu mentions festivals for every third or fourth day (Bonnet, *RÄRG*, p. 185), but only a small number would have been πανηγύριες. Note that Herodotus' list is confined to the Delta; he makes no mention of important Upper Egyptian examples such as the Festival of Opet and the Festival of the Valley (Wolf, op. cit.; S. Schott, *Das schöne Fest vom Wüstentale*, Wiesbaden 1953). This situation clearly reflects the Lower Egyptian bias of his information.   Βούβαστιν . . . τῇ Ἀρτέμιδι: cf. chs. 67, 137–8, 166. The city's name derives from the Egyptian *Pr-B3stt*, 'House of Bastet'. The site lies at Tell Basta in the eastern Delta (L. Habachi, *LdÄ* I, 873–4).   τῇ Ἀρτέμιδι: the cat/lion-headed Egyptian goddess *B3stt*, 'She of *B3st*' (Kolta, pp. 24 ff.). She is called Boubastis at chs. 137 and 156. For the splendid temple at Bubastis see note on 137,5.   Βούσιριν . . . τῇ Ἴσι: this city (Egyptian *Pr-Wsir*, 'House of Osiris') lay in the centre of the Delta at Abu Sîr, 5.5 km. south of Samannûd (J. von Beckerath, *LdÄ* I, 883–4).   τῇ Ἴσι: see notes on ch. 41.
2. Ἴσις . . . Δημήτηρ: cf. 156,5. On the identification see Kolta, op. cit., pp. 52 ff.
3. Σάϊν . . . τῇ Ἀθηναίῃ: see notes on 28,1, and 62.   Ἡλίου πόλιν τῷ Ἡλίῳ: see notes on 3,1 and 63,1.   Βουτοῦν . . . τῇ Λητοῖ: cf. 63,1. The name of the city occurs frequently (63,1; 75; 83; 111,2; 133,1; 152,3; 155–6; III 64) and, with the exception of II 75, always refers to the ancient city whose ruins lie at Tell el-Farâin in the north-west Delta.   τῇ Λητοῖ: the cobra goddess *W3dt* (Kolta, op. cit., pp. 145 ff.).   Πάπρημιν . . . τῷ Ἄρεϊ: cf. 1; 71; 165; III 12,4. The exact site is unknown, but it probably lay in the north-west Delta, somewhere within the canonical 7th Nome of Lower Egypt (Lloyd, *Commentary 1–98*, pp. 270 ff.).   τῷ Ἄρεϊ: probably Horus or Onuris (cf. ch. 63).

60,1. ἐπεὰν κομίζωνται: several major festivals were celebrated at Bubastis in honour of Bastet. Herodotus is probably referring to that on the 18th of the 2nd month of the *šmw* season which was even attended by the cult image of the goddess Hathor of Dendera (Alliot, *Le Culte* I, p. 232).   πλέουσί: both individual parties and ceremonial barks bearing the divine images of the gods would have wound their way by water to Bubastis (cf. Bonnet, *RÄRG*, pp. 613 ff.).   βάρι: cf. 96,5. The word derives from the Egyptian *br* (*Wb*. I, p. 465, 8–9) which is frequently used of freighters.   κρόταλα: 'clappers' were widely employed in Egyptian music (Wreszinski I, pl. 419; H. Hickmann, *Instruments de musique* (CGC), Cairo 1949, pp. 32 ff.).   αὐλέουσι: the Greek *aulos* was a reeded instrument comparable with the modern clarinet or oboe (K. Schlesinger, *The Greek Aulos*, London 1939). The Egyptian instruments used here would probably have been flutes, double clarinets, or oboes (cf. Hickmann, op. cit., pp. 115 ff.). Herodotus rightly assigns them to the men (cf. E. Brunner-Traut, *Der Tanz im alten Ägypten*, *Äg. Forschungen*, VI,

Gluckstadt–Hamburg–New York 1938).   ἀείδουσι: cf. 48,2. Music was particularly apposite to Bastet, who was closely associated with joy and merriment
(Bonnet, *RÄRG*, p. 81), but it featured prominently in the cult of all Egyptian
gods (ibid., p. 490 ff.).   κροτέουσι: handclapping featured prominently in
Egyptian music at all periods (cf. Klebs, *AR*, p. 111; Lepsius, *Denkmäler* II, pl. 53a).
2. ἐγχρίμψαντες: both simplex and compounds are poetic (LSJ, s.v.). τωθάζουσι:
the mockery was probably intended to avert the evil eye (cf. the Roman *Fescen-
nina iocatio* in marriage ceremonial, C. J. Fordyce, *Catullus*, Oxford 1965,
pp. 247 ff.).   ὀρχέονται: dancing as a cult act is frequently exemplified in
Egyptian sources and was usually performed by women (Brunner-Traut, op.
cit.).   ἀνασύρονται: displaying the pudenda is a well-known Egyptian ritual
act (e.g. S. Sauneron, *Les Fêtes religieuses d'Esna aux derniers siècles du paganisme*
(*Esna* V), Cairo 1962, pp. 41 ff.). In this case the aim was probably to impart
fertility to the people and the land on the banks.   ταῦτα . . . ποιεῦσι: for the
alliteration cf. notes on. 1,1; 58.
3. οἶνος: drunkenness and other forms of excess are easily paralleled in our
sources, e.g. the Festival of Drunkenness celebrated in honour of Hathor, who
had close affinities with Bastet (Alliot, *Le Culte* I, p. 239).   ἐς ἑβδομήκοντα
μυριάδας: the figure is startlingly high and must be taken as symbolic (see note
on 163,1), but in modern times festivals in Egypt have been known to attract up
to half a million participants.   ὡς . . . λέγουσι: see above, p. 229.

61,1. ἐν δὲ Βουσίρι πόλι . . . πρότερόν μοι: cf. notes on 40; 59,1. Strictly, the festival
was concerned with the death and resurrection of Osiris, but since the role of Isis
was pre-eminent in both cult-myth and ritual, Herodotus regards the festival as
being held in her honour. Both Diodorus I 20 and Plutarch, *DIO* 27 (*Mor.* 361)
claim that she founded the rites.   τύπτονται . . . ἀνθρώπων: Herodotus distinguishes between a θυσίη and a period of lamentation. The festival is clearly the
Festival of Khoiak, which ran from the 18th to the 30th of the 4th month of the
season of Akhet (the month of Khoiak, i.e. the 4th of the year). In Herodotus'
time this festival had both funerary and fertility dimensions and centred upon the
re-enactment of the death, resurrection, and triumph of Osiris. Pharaonic evidence indicates that the period of lamentation proper occupied days 23–5,
though in Plutarch's time four days were needed (*DIO* 39 (*Mor.* 366)). Herodotus
says nothing of the period of rejoicing which followed the lamentations (in
general see Chassinat, *Le Mystère, passim*; G. Gaballa and K. A. Kitchen, *Orientalia*, XXXVIII (1969), 1 ff.).   μυριάδες κάρτα πολλαὶ ἀνθρώπων: for the number see note on 60,3.   τὸν δὲ τύπτονται . . . λέγειν: the god was Osiris.
Herodotus shows his usual reticence in giving such information (see note on 3,2).
2. Καρῶν: for Carians in Egypt see above, p. 221.   μαχαίρῃσι: the Carians
identified Osiris with their own deity Attis, whose character as a dying god of
vegetation made him an obvious counterpart. During the rituals of lamentation
of the *dies sanguinis* celebrated for Attis at the vernal equinox the Archigallus and
the Galli mutilated themselves with knives and potsherds and sprinkled the altar
and sacred tree with their blood (Cumont, *RE* II, 2247 ff.; Strathmann, *RAC* I,

889 ff.). These practices the Carians had clearly imported into their worship of Osiris.　καὶ τούτῳ … Αἰγύπτιοι: cf. note on 45,2.

62,1. ἐς Σάϊν δὲ πόλιν: see note on 59,3.　τῆσι θυσίῃσι: this phrase has caused difficulty. Legrand reads τῆς θυσίης ἐν τῇ νυκτί, invoking the variant of the Roman group for the second phrase. The reading of the Florentines is, however, perfectly acceptable, the case being explained as a locative dative or a dative of purpose (cf. Kühner–Gerth, *Gr. Grammatik* II 1, pp. 441 ff.).　ἔν τινι νυκτί: this festival took place on the 13th day of the 3rd month of the season of Shomu (the month of Epiphi, i.e. the 11th of the year) (S. Sauneron, *Le Temple d'Esna* (*Esna* III), Cairo 1968, no. 207, 22–23; id., *Les Fêtes religieuses d'Esna aux derniers siècles du paganisme* (*Esna* V), Cairo 1962, pp. 245 ff., 302). λύχνα … κύκλῳ: festivals of torches were a common feature of Egyptian cult (Erman–Ranke, *Ägypten*, p. 166). Several were held in honour of Neith/Athene, who is frequently depicted carrying a torch (P. Perdrizet, *Les Terres cuites grecques d'Egypte de la Collection Fouquet*, I, Nancy–Paris–Strasbourg 1921, pp. 68, 169, with LVIII–LIX). The festival of the 13th of Epiphi re-enacted the triumphal arrival of Neith at Sais at the creation of the world after the destruction of the forces of disorder and darkness. One late text describes it as follows: 'Burning of torches in abundance within this temple. Let men and women make festival! Let this whole city raise cries of joy, and let none sleep until sunrise!' (Sauneron, *Les Fêtes*, loc. cit.).　τὰ δὲ λύχνα … τὸ ἐλλύχνιον: floating-wick lamps of this type were widely used in Ancient Egypt (Forbes VI, p. 144; F. W. Robins, *JEA* XXV (1939), 184 ff.).　ἁλός: this ingredient ensured the absence of smoke and also gave the flame a bright yellow colour (Forbes VI, p. 147).　ἐλαίου: see note on ch. 94.　τῇ ὁρτῇ … λυχνοκαΐῃ: i.e. amongst the Greeks. Herodotus ignores the fact that the Egyptians will have had their own name.
2. ἀνὰ πᾶσαν Αἴγυπτον: the Saite Calendar Papyrus describes a fire-festival in the month of Epiphi as follows: καὶ ἐν Σάι πανήγυ[υρις] Ἀθηνᾶς καὶ λύχνους κάουσι κατὰ τὴν χώραν (P. Hib. I 27). The day is lost, but the text could well refer to the ritual described by Herodotus.　ἱρὸς … λόγος: the myth was a cosmogony describing the birth of Neith and the ensuing establishment of the cosmic order (Sauneron, *Le Temple*, no. 206, 13–15; *Les Fêtes*, pp. 269 ff.).

63,1. ἐς δὲ Ἡλίου τε πόλιν: cf. 59,3. Several major festivals associated with celestial phenomena were probably or certainly celebrated at Heliopolis: the Festival of the Pillar, the New Year's Festival, and the *išd* Festival (Kees, *Götterglaube*, pp. 224 ff.). The second was the festival of the birth of Re/Helios and might well be the ritual described by Herodotus, but proof positive is lacking.　καὶ Βουτοῦν: cf. 59,3. Probably the Festival of Horus, celebrated on the 12th–17th of the 2nd month of Shomu (the month of Payni, the 10th of the year) (E. Drioton, *BIE* XXV (1943), 16 ff.). Herodotus' claim at 59,3 that it was held in honour of Wadjet/Leto is inaccurate but reflects her great importance in this ritual.　θυσίας μούνας: incorrect for Buto at least, since we know that the Festival of Horus included a ritual battle (Drioton, op. cit., p. 6). Παπρῆμι: cf. 59,3.　τὤγαλμα: i.e. the cult statue (see note on 4,2).

1–3. οἱ δὲ πολλοί...οὐδένα: ritual battles are exemplified in the cults of Horus at Letopolis, Osiris at Abydos, and Min at Buto as well as in the ritual of the Raising of the *Djed* Pillar (Lloyd, *Commentary 1–98*, p. 285). Representations of stick-fights also occur, but their precise nature is unclear (J. A. Wilson, *JEA* XVII (1931), 211 ff.).

2. ἐν νηῷ...κατακεχρυσωμένῳ: portable shrines were a standard feature of Ancient Egyptian temples. They were frequently placed on model boats bearing figureheads which represented the divine owner (G. Roeder, *Naos* (CGC), Leipzig 1914), and they were often constructed of gilded wood (e.g. ibid., no. 70024).   μικρῷ: σμικρῷ is preferable. The 's' form occurs in no ms at this point, but occurrences of μικρός in the received text of Herodotus suggest that this was the form which he used after a word ending in sigma (cf. Powell, *Lexicon*, p. 334; H. W. Smyth, *The Sounds and Inflections of the Greek Dialects: Ionic*, Oxford 1894, p. 313). Since there is no preceding sigma, the 's' form should be restored.   τετράκυκλον ἅμαξαν: portable shrines were normally transported by means of carrying poles or sleds, but wheeled vehicles are occasionally exemplified from the New Kingdom onwards (e.g. H. Schäfer (trans. J. R. Baines), *Principles of Egyptian Art*, Oxford 1974, pl. 40; G. Lefebvre, *Le Tombeau de Petosiris*, I, Cairo 1924, pp. 129 ff.; III, Cairo 1923, pl. XXX).

4. οἱ ἐπιχώριοι: see above, pp. 230 ff.   τοῦ Ἄρεος: the Egyptian god was probably Horus or Onuris (cf. H. Altenmüller, *JEOL* XVIII (1964), 276 ff.).   τὸν Ἄρεα...τὴν μητέρα: mother–son incest is a well-authenticated Egyptian mythological concept, and extant cases include Horus, who is a likely Egyptian prototype of Ares here (in general see Griffiths, *The Conflict*, pp. 92 ff.).   ἐξανδρωμένον: for the intensive ἐξ- see note on 3,2.   συμμεῖξαι: 'have intercourse with' (Griffiths, *The Conflict*, p. 86). Hude reads συμμεῖξαι, but the -ι- form appears in all mss and is entirely acceptable (cf. Rosén, *Sprachform*, pp. 130, 135–6, 138).

64,1. καὶ τὸ μὴ μίσγεσθαι...θρησκεύσαντες: the Egyptians, like many peoples, ancient and modern, associated sexual activity with impurity (Porphyry, *De Abst.*, IV 20; Gardiner, *Egyptian Grammar*, Sign List, D53). It was essential to prevent such miasma contaminating the gods (cf. notes on ch. 37).   τὸ μὴ μίσγεσθαι γυναιξὶ ἐν ἱροῖσι: cf. Clement, *Strom.* I 16,2. Egyptian sources confirm the prohibition (e.g. *Book of the Dead*, CXXV, Intro B12: 'I have not copulated (in the pure places of my city god)': cf. Alliot, *Le Culte* I, pp. 185 ff.). There is, however, some late evidence of temple prostitution at Thebes, though this possibly arose under Persian influence (Strabo XVII l,46 (C816); L. Delekat, *Katoche, Hierodulie und Adoptionsfreilassung*, Munich 1964, pp. 65, 68, 70 ff.).   μηδὲ ἀλούτους...ἐσιέναι: there is clear evidence that the Egyptians laid great store by washing after sexual intercourse (W. K. Simpson, *The Literature of Ancient Egypt*, New Haven–London 1973, pp. 17 ff.; E. Miller, *RA* 3rd ser. II (1883), 181 ff.; Porphyry, *De Abst.* IV 6–8).   πρῶτοι θρησκεύσαντες: the interest in the πρῶτος εὑρετής elements in human culture is an aspect of the *post hoc ergo propter hoc* fallacy (see above, p. 235) and was a deeply rooted Greek obsession which Herodotus fully shared. Inevitably, the Egyptians featured prominently in such

discussions (see, in general, Kleingünther).   οἱ μὲν γὰρ ἄλλοι... ἐς ἱρόν: Herodotus is thinking pre-eminently of temple prostitution, which was widespread in the
non-Greek eastern Mediterranean world, e.g. Canaan, Babylonia, and Phoenicia
(G. A. Barton, *HERE* VI, pp. 672 ff.).   Ἑλλήνων: the Greeks were most strin-
gent in the matter. Plutarch recommended several days' abstinence before visiting the
temple (*Quaest. Symp.* III 6,4 (*Mor.* 655)) and chastity was required of many
officiants in Greek temples (E. Fehrle, *Die kultische Keuschheit im Altertum*, Giessen
1910, pp. 98 ff., 155 ff.).   [ἀνιστάμενοι]: this word is deleted by Naber, but its
removal would be a great loss, and it has good ms support.
1–2. νομίζοντες... ποιέειν: a patent piece of Greek rationalization which may owe
something to current criticism of the illogicality of cult practices (e.g. Heraclitus,
KR 244–6; Hippocrates, *Morb. Sacr.* 1: cf. Herod. I 157–60). The reasons for such
permissiveness probably lay in some cases in the conviction that sexual
intercourse could be dangerous for either or each participant; in other cases,
the hierodules might be identified with the deity and hence become sources of
virility and fertility (Fehrle, op. cit., pp. 40 ff.).
2. εἶναι: the verbs of subordinate clauses are often attracted into the infinitive in
oratio obliqua, but cases with εἰ are infrequent and almost confined to Herodotus
(Kühner–Gerth, *Gr. Grammatik* II 2, pp. 550 ff.; Goodwin, *Moods and Tenses*,
pp. 303 ff.).   οὗτοι... οὐκ ἀρεστά: Herodotus remains fully convinced of the
correctness of Greek practice.

65–76. A discussion of animal worship and the zoology of Egypt.

65,2. Ἐοῦσα: concessive: 'Although Egypt borders on Libya...' (cf. notes on
chs. 8, 16).   τὰ δὲ ἐόντα: sc. θηρία, assumed from θηριώδης.   καὶ τὰ μὲν
σύντροφα... τὰ δὲ οὔ: Herodotus does not exaggerate by much. Ancient writers
mention about thirty-four species of sacred animal, but Egyptian evidence
demonstrates that this figure is too low (cf. Hopfner, *Tierkult*, pp. 10 ff.). Some
animals were held sacred throughout the country (e.g. the cow of Hathor, the ibis
of Thoth, and the hawk of Horus), but the cults of many species were much more
localized (Bonnet, *RÄRG*, pp. 812 ff.).   τῶν δὲ εἵνεκεν... λέγοιμι: the reticence is typical (note on 3,2). Other ancient writers do venture on explanations,
some not unperceptive (e.g. Diod. I 21, 86–7, 89, 90; Plutarch, *DIO* 72 (*Mor.*
379–80); Lucian, *De Astr.*, 7; Alexander of Lycopolis, *In Man. Op. Disp.*, 14). In
all probability, the explanation usually lay in a mixture of wonder, admiration,
and fear for the mysterious powers which animals were felt to possess. Such
reactions would naturally lead to a cult based on *captatio benevolentiae* (Lloyd,
Commentary 1–98, pp. 291 ff.).   [τὰ] ἱρά: the article occurs in all mss, but
most editors follow Valckenaer and delete it, treating ἱρά as predicative and
making the θηρία assumed from θηριώδης the subject: 'If I were to give the reason
why they are consecrated <so as to be> sacred...' This is certainly correct, since
the presence of the article could only mean that there were other animals in Egypt
which were not regarded as sacred, and that possibility Herodotus has explicitly

excluded in the previous sentence. For ἀνίημι in the sense 'to consecrate, dedicate' see LSJ, p. 143,b.II,6, and for the use of the perfect in such contexts cf. notes on chs. 72, 81, 91.

3–5. νόμος δέ ... ἀποδέδεκται: cf. Diod. I 83,2–3. Sacred animals also enjoyed the fruits of special allotments of land (cf. P.Teb. I, 62, 19, and 23) as well as donations from the crown (e.g. Urk. II, 42 ff.).

3. μελεδωνοί: cf. Strabo XVII 1,38 (C812). Greek documents often yield titles reflecting the species for which they cared (e.g. κροκοδιλοβοσκός, BGU III, 734, 2, 7, 33). In pharaonic times the priesthood of a sacred animal could be as elaborate and hierarchized as that of any other deity (cf. W. Spiegelberg, ZÄS XLIII (1906), 129 ff.).

5. τὸ δ' ἄν τις ... ἀνάγκη: cf. Diod. I 83,6–9; Aelian, NA XI 27. Egyptian sources neither confirm nor refute these claims. It would be wise to suspect an element of exaggeration; it is more than likely that cases of wilful killing of a treasured sacred animal led to summary lynchings and that such incidents were transmuted by classical tradition into a regular legal process.

66,1. πολλῶν δὲ ... θηρίων: the genitive absolute is used despite the fact that its subject is identical with that of the main verb. This usage is rather infrequent and is probably intended to give greater prominence to the subject matter of the absolute (see note on 111,1). Observe the alliteration of π throughout the sentence (cf. note on 1,1).   αἰελούρους: originally used of the wild cat, αἰέλουρος (later αἴλουρος) refers here to the Libyan cat (Felis maniculata), the ancestor of the modern domestic cat, though some cross-breeding with the marsh lynx (Felis chaus) seems to have occurred (Anderson, Zoology: Mammalia, pp. 171 ff.; J. Malek, The Cat in Ancient Egypt, Philadelphia 1993, pp. 13 ff.). These animals qualified as a θῶμα for Herodotus since they have not been identified in Europe until the 1st cent. AD (O. Keller, Die antike Tierwelt, I, Leipzig 1909, pp. 73 ff.).

1–2. ἐπεὰν τέκωσι ... τὸ θηρίον: for feline lust cf. Aelian, NA VI, 27: Arist. HA V 2. Male cats certainly kill kittens for this and other reasons.

3. πυρκαϊῆς ... πῦρ: this claim is entirely without foundation and must be firmly consigned to the realm of paradoxography (see above, pp. 232, 234 ff., 239). διαδυνόντες: many editors, following Cobet, have preferred this form. The Hippocratic Corpus shows διαδύνω and at I 9,2 Herodotus uses ἐκδύνω. Elsewhere, however, the mss show the -δύω form. In view of the ποικιλία of Herodotus' style it seems preferable to accept διαδύοντες. ὑπερθρῴσκοντες: construed with simple accusative as in Homer (cf. H. Ebeling, Lexikon Homericum, London–Paris 1885, s.v.).

4. ταῦτα δὲ γινόμενα: an odd construction, best explained as accusative absolute (Kühner–Gerth, Gr. Grammatik II 2, p. 89). Goodwin comments: 'The accusative absolute used personally without ὡς or ὥσπερ is very rare. It occurs chiefly with neuter participles which are regularly impersonal' (Moods and Tenses, pp. 339 ff.).   πένθεα ... τὴν κεφαλήν: the cat cult is identifiable in Egypt

from at least the New Kingdom and enjoyed an enormous popularity in the Late
Period. In cult the animal was associated with Bastet of Bubastis (note on 59,1),
and in that context embodied her fertility and erotic dimensions. Mythologically
its snake-killing capacities led, in particular, to its association with the sun-god Re
whom it was claimed to protect against the malevolent serpent Apophis (N. and
B. Langton, *The Cat in Ancient Egypt*, Cambridge 1940; Bonnet, *RÄRG*, pp. 371 ff.;
Malek, op. cit., pp. 73 ff.).   ἐν ὁτέοισι... κεφαλήν: cf. Diod. I 84,2–3. These
practices are not identifiable in any Egyptian source and contrast curiously
with that described for human bereavements at 36,1. There is, however, no
intrinsic reason to doubt that such customs existed at least in some part of
Egypt.   κύων: see note on 67,1.

67,1. ἀπάγονται... ταριχευθέντες: cat mummies are extremely numerous and
usually carefully finished with well-moulded heads and elaborate bandaging
(Lortet–Gaillard, *La Faune momifiée* I, pp. 19 ff; Malek, op. cit.,
pp. 123 ff.).   ἐς ἱρὰς στέγας: at Bubastis great pits were used, whose walls
and bases were faced with brick or clay. The largest had a capacity of no less than
20.38 m.³ (E. Naville, *Bubastis (1887–1889)*, London 1891, p. 53).   ἐν
Βουβάστι πόλι: Bubastis was undoubtedly the major centre of cat worship and
burial from the XXIInd Dynasty onwards (ibid., pp. 52 ff.), but it was certainly
not the only one; for cat cemeteries are known throughout the country, e.g.
Saqqâra (Bonnet, *RÄRG*, p. 81), Speos Artemidos (ibid., p. 578), and Thebes
(Hopfner, *Tierkult*, p. 39).   τὰς δὲ κύνας: cf. Strabo XVII 1,40 (C812); Aelian,
NA X 45; Plutarch, *Quaest. Conv.* VII 3 (*Mor.* 703). The Greeks used the term
κύων in this Egyptian context to refer generally to wild dogs, foxes, and jackals, a
practice which admirably reflects the Egyptian tendency to treat all such species
alike both linguistically and for cult purposes (Kees, *Götterglaube*, pp. 28 ff.;
L. Keimer, *Bibliotheca Orientalis*, V (1948), 22 ff.).   ἐν τῇ ἑωυτῶν... θήκῃσι:
the most important centre was Cynopolis or Hardai (modern Esh-Shêkh Fadl),
the capital of the 17th Nome of Upper Egypt (cf. Strabo, loc. cit.; Aelian, loc. cit),
near which a substantial canid cemetery has been identified (Gardiner, *AEO* II,
pp. 98 ff.). However, canid cults and cemeteries occur widely elsewhere in the
country, e.g. Saqqâra, Siut, and Thebes (Hopfner, *Tierkult*, pp. 50 ff., 54; Bonnet,
RÄRG, p. 450).   ὡς δὲ αὔτως... θάπτονται: the ἰχνευτής (later ἰχνεύμων) or
Nile mongoose (*Herpestes ichneumon*) was associated particularly with Horus of
Letopolis, Re-Atum of Heliopolis, and Wadjet of Buto. There is also evidence of a
cult at Tanis, Sais, Athribis, Bubastis, Herakleopolis, and Akhmîm. Much the
largest group of mummies was unearthed at Tanis (in general see E. Brunner-
Traut, *Nachrichten Ak. Wiss. Göttingen*, VII (1965), 124 ff.).   ὡς δὲ αὔτως: for
ὡσαύτως. The tmesis occurs elsewhere in Herodotus (Powell, *Lexicon*,
p. 391).   τὰς δὲ μυγαλᾶς: the μυγαλῆ, 'shrew-mouse, field-mouse', was
associated with Horus of Letopolis and certainly enjoyed a cult at Buto
(Brunner-Traut, op. cit., pp. 133 ff., 161).   τοὺς ἴρηκας: the term ἴρηξ can be
used generically of all the smaller hawks and falcons (Thompson, *Greek Birds*,
p. 114). The original species of the Egyptian sacred hawk remains to be

determined, *Falco babylonica*, *Falco feldeggi*, or *Hierofalco saker* all being possibilities. The species of mummies, however, vary greatly and indicate a considerable degree of either confusion or indifference in the matter (cf. L. Lortet and C. Gaillard, *ASAE* III (1902), 18 ff.). Cemeteries were certainly not confined to Buto and have been identified throughout the country (D. Kessler, *LdÄ* VI, 579 ff.). τὰς δὲ ἴβις ... πόλιν: for zoology see notes on chs. 75–6. The bird was sacred to Thoth/Hermes and examples were certainly interred in large numbers in the cemetery of Tuna el-Gebel which was the necropolis of his great centre of Hermopolis Magna (modern Ashmunein: Kessler, *LdÄ* VI, 798 ff.). *Pace* Herodotus, however, they do occur elsewhere, e.g. Hermopolis Parva, Saqqâra, and Abydos (Bonnet, *RÄRG*, pp. 295, 320 ff.).

2. τὰς δὲ ἄρκτους ἐούσας σπανίας: certainly correct. The only evidence of bears in Ancient Egypt consists of seven representations of the now extinct *Ursus syriacus* (L. Keimer, *Archiv für Orientforschung*, XVII (1956), 337 ff.). Herodotus is probably correct in claiming that no special arrangements were made for burial.   τοὺς λύκους ... μέζονας: these creatures were clearly not wolves in the strict sense (*Canis lupus*). The description would fit the jackal (*Canis lupaster*), the Egyptian fox (*Canis vulpes aegyptiacus*), or the desert fox (*Canis zerda*). The bodies of jackals would not normally have been treated in the cavalier fashion described by Herodotus (see above), but those of either of the other two might have been.

68,1. Τῶν δὲ κροκοδείλων: for other classical accounts of the crocodile see Arist. *HA* II 10; Diod. I 35; Pliny, *NH* VIII 89; Aelian, *NA* III 11; VIII 25; XVII 6; and, in general, D. Arnould, *RPh* LXX (1996), 13 ff. Herodotus' source is uncertain; it is only the description of hunting the animal at ch. 70 which certainly derived from Hecataeus (*FGrHist* I T 22 F 324). For etymology and spelling see note on ch. 69, 3. τοὺς χειμεριωτάτους: cf. Aelian, *NA* X 21. Crocodiles do not hibernate (A. Bellairs, *Reptiles*, London 1970³, p. 104).   χερσαῖον καὶ λιμναῖόν ἐστι: cf. Aelian, *NA* XI 37.   τίκτει ... ἐκλέπει: the number varies between 25 and 95, and they are indeed approximately the same size as those of geese (Bellairs, op. cit., p. 102). The crocodile remains near them and also helps to release the young from the nest, but it does not, in the strict sense, 'hatch them'.   τὸ πολλὸν ... τῆς δρόσου: correct.

2. πάντων δὲ ... ἔτι: cf. Aelian, *NA* XVII 6. Newly born crocodiles measure 15–20 cm.; a fully grown adult may attain *c*.6 m., considerably less than Herodotus' 17 cubits (9 m.) (Bellairs and R. Carrington, *The World of Reptiles*, London 1966, p. 131).

3. [κατὰ λόγον τοῦ σώματος]: this phrase is deleted by Gomperz, but it occurs in all mss and certainly adds something to the sense.   γλῶσσαν ... ἔφυσε: incorrect, but it is short and difficult to detect (Anderson, *Zoology: Reptilia*, p. 19).   οὐκ ἔφυσε: for this gnomic or typical aorist see note on 20,2. οὐδὲ κινέει ... τῇ κάτω: cf. Arist. *HA* I 11. This is the result of its normal stance, not the consequence of any anatomical deficiency.

4. τυφλὸν ... ὀξυδερκέστατον: cf. Arist. *HA* II 10. Of its keen sight on land there is no doubt (Bellairs, op. cit., p. 101).   βδελλέων: there are no leeches in Egypt. The creatures in question are parasitic worms (Anderson, op. cit., p. 20).

5. τὸν τροχίλον: cf. Aelian, *NA* III 11; VIII 25. This bird is generally identified with *Pluvianus aegyptius*, but no one species seems to have a unique right. τροχίλος is best regarded as a generic which could also includes such species as *Hoplopterus spinosus* and *Aegialites cunonica* (cf. Meinertzhagen, p. 528; Thompson, *Greek Birds*, p. 288).

69,1. τοῖσι μὲν ... περιέπουσι: such lack of uniformity is typical of Egyptian animal cults. Attitudes to the crocodile depended on the god with whom it was associated in a given area. When connected with Sobk (the major crocodile god), Horus, or Neith, the animal was accorded religious veneration, e.g. in the Fayûm. When associated with Seth, it was normally treated with detestation, e.g. at Edfû (Kees, *Götterglaube*, pp. 14 ff.).   οἱ δὲ περί τε Θήβας ... ἱρούς: accurate. In the Theban area the main crocodile cult was that of Hermonthis. Cults do, however, occur elsewhere in Upper Egypt, e.g. at Crocodilopolis, south of Thebes, Antaeopolis, and Coptos. In the vicinity of lake Moiris the major cult was at Crocodilopolis (modern Medinet el-Fayûm), the centre of the worship of the crocodile-headed god Sobk (F. Gomaà, *LdÄ* III, 1254 f.).

2. ἕνα: it was the practice in many animal cults to choose one animal to function as the incarnation of the deity, the most famous example being the Apis bull (see note on ch. 38). The other members of the species were regarded as sharing in this divinity and were revered accordingly, but they did not have the same status and did not receive the same distinctive honours (Bonnet, *RÄRG*, pp. 812 ff.).   ἀρτήματά ... πόδας: several crocodile mummies found at Thebes had holes bored into their skulls in the vicinity of the ear (Hopfner, *Tierkult*, p. 128). Other details of Herodotus' description cannot be substantiated but are not intrinsically improbable.   καὶ σιτία ... ζῶντας: cf. note on 65,4. Strabo provides a detailed account of feeding the sacred crocodiles at Crocodilopolis at XVII 1,38 (C812); cf. J. de Morgan *et al.*, *Kom Ombos*, II (*Catalogue des monuments et inscriptions de l'Egypte ancienne*), Vienna 1894–1909, pp. 312, 422).   ἀποθανόντας ... θήκῃσι: mummies have been found in great numbers and are often distinguished by elaborate and careful bandaging (Lortet–Gaillard, *La Faune momifiée* I, pp. 181 ff.). Cemeteries are widespread, e.g. the Fayûm (note on ch. 148), Kom Ombo, and Tehne (D. Kessler, *LdÄ* VI, 579 ff.).

3. οἱ δὲ περὶ Ἐλεφαντίνην ... εἶναι: crocodiles were eaten both at Apollinopolis Magna (modern Edfû) and Apollinopolis Parva (modern Qus near Dendera) (Plutarch, *DIO* 50 (*Mor.* 371); Aelian, *NA* X 21), but there is, as yet, no evidence of this practice at Elephantine. Indeed, at Syene, which lay opposite Elephantine island on the east bank of the Nile, the crocodile is known to have been worshipped (J. de Morgan, *Catalogue de monuments et inscriptions de l'Egypte antique*, I. *De la frontière de Nubie à Kom Ombos*, Vienna 1894, p. 50). καλέονται ... αἱμασιῇσι: cf. Hipponax, fr. 155 (West) and D. Arnould, *RPh* LXX (1996), 13. The older spelling of κροκόδιλος apparently did not show an -ε- (LSJ, pp. 997 ff., s.v. κροκόδιλος). The word basically means 'lizard' and is derived by H. Frisk (*Griechisches etymologisches Wörterbuch*, II, Heidelberg 1970, p. 23) from κρόκη, 'pebble', and δρῖλος, 'worm'. Herodotus' χάμψαι derives from the Egyptian

msḥ, 'crocodile', preceded by the plural indefinite article (cf. Coptic *han-msah*, 'some crocodiles': J. Černý, *ASAE* XLII (1943), 346 ff.) and is gratifyingly accurate.

70,1. ἄγραι ... παντοῖαι: Diodorus confirms (I 35,5).

1–2. ἥ δ' ὦν ... πόνῳ: Hecataeus certainly contributed to this section (*FGrHist* I F 324). Egyptian representations of crocodile hunting are extremely rare (cf. J. Capart, *Primitive Art in Egypt*, London 1905, p. 204, fig. 161; Klebs, *MR*, pp. 95 ff.). We also encounter late representations of gods harpooning crocodiles (e.g. Chassinat, *Edfou* III, pls. LXXVII, LXXXII; XIII, pls. DXXVIII–DXXIX), but these must be treated as theological statements, not reflections of contemporary practice. Nowhere is there any Egyptian corroboration for the activity described by Herodotus, but the method has been observed in modern times both in Africa and America (Hopfner, *Tierkult*, p. 134).

1. ἐπεὰν νῶτον ... ποταμόν: this ellipse of a self-evident subject is not uncommon (cf. Kühner–Gerth, *Gr. Grammatik* II 1, pp. 32 ff.).

2. κατ' ὦν ἔπλασε: cf. note on 39,2.

71. Οἱ δὲ ἵπποι οἱ ποτάμιοι ... οὐκ ἱροί: not so, but the Egyptian attitude was certainly ambivalent. Where the animal was identified with Seth/Typhon as a negative cosmic force of destructive and terrifying power, it was an object of hatred. Its slaying is frequently depicted and mentioned in the great cult centre of Seth's arch-enemy Horus at Edfû (e.g. Chassinat, *Edfou* XIII, pls. DVIII, DX, DXII–DXIII; Alliot, *Le Culte* II, pp. 524, 699, 779, 784 ff.), and this attitude was undoubtedly the most common. Nevertheless, the animal could be connected with protective goddesses associated with maternity such as Ipet and Taurt, and cult centres of such deities are easily identifiable in e.g. Thebes, the Fayûm, and Gebel es-Silsileh (D. Meeks, *LdÄ* III, 172 ff.; R. Gundlach, *LdÄ* VI, 494 ff.). Hippopotamus cults were, therefore, more widely current than Herodotus realized, but they were, for all that, far from common.   **ἵπποι οἱ ποτάμιοι:** the term 'river-horse' presumably reflects the rather horse-like appearance of the creature's head. The term may also be another example of the Greek predilection for using rather jesting names for foreign phenomena (cf. note on 9,3). *Hippopotamus amphibius* was a native Egyptian species until relatively modern times (Anderson, *Zoology: Mammalia*, pp. 356 ff.).   **νομῷ μὲν τῷ Παπρημίτῃ:** on the identification of this area see notes on 59,3; 165. The dative is locative, a usage which is almost entirely poetic (cf. Kühner–Gerth, *Gr. Grammatik*, II 1, pp. 441 ff.).   **φύσιν δὲ ... ἐξ αὐτοῦ:** cf. Diod. I 35 (with some improvements). Herodotus' description, which clearly derived much from Hecataeus (*FGrHist* I F 324), is riddled with inaccuracies: the feet of the hippopotamus are not cloven (δίχηλον) and quite unlike those of an ox; it could be called 'snub-nosed' (σιμόν), but it does not have a mane (λοφιήν); tusks it certainly has, but its exiguous tail does not resemble that of a horse nor is its bellowing in the least equine; it is also considerable larger than even the largest ox (fully grown, *c.* 4 m. long and 2–3 metric tons in weight, Anderson, op. cit.). For possible explanations of these oddities see Lloyd, *Commentary 1–98*, pp. 313 ff.   **τετράπουν ... μέγιστος:** for

the vivid staccato descriptive style cf. 73,2; 76,2.   τὸ δέρμα... ἐξ αὐτοῦ: shields
and helmets were made of it according to Pliny (*NH* VIII 95), but there is no
confirmation in any ancient author of Herodotus' statement. Nevertheless, it is a
quite credible material for throwing spears, inasmuch as sticks are still made of
hippopotamus hide in modern Africa (O. Keller, *Die antike Tierwelt*, I, Leipzig
1909, p. 406).   [ἀκόντια]: Schaefer and others delete as tautologous with
ξυστά, but the case for retention is much stronger: not only does it appear in all
mss, but the collocation is supported by Hesychius' phrase ξυστὸν ἀκόντιον (s.v.)
and Arrian's ξυστὰ δόρατα (*Tactica* 40,4).

72. ἐνύδριες: the otter (*Lutra vulgaris*) has been claimed to be an ancient Egyptian
species (L. Keimer, *BIE* XXXVI (1955), 458 ff.), but doubt has recently been
expressed on the identification of the relevant representations (P. F. Houlihan,
The Animal World of the Pharaohs, London 1996, pp. 126 ff.). There is no evidence
of a cult apart from Herodotus' claim. However, since Ammianus Marcellinus
can speak of it as a kind of ichneumon, it is possible that it was included in the
cult of that animal (cf. note on 67,1).   ἤγηνται: as often, the perfect should be
translated as a present: 'they consider' (cf. P. Chantraine, *Histoire du parfait grec*,
Paris 1927, pp. 146 ff.).   λεπιδωτὸν: *Barbus bynni*, an extremely common
edible Nile species (Boulenger, p. 203). It was honoured throughout Egypt in
Hellenistic and Roman times (Strabo XVII 1,40 (C812)), but the major cult
centre was Lepidotonpolis (modern Mesheikh) in Upper Egypt where it was
connected with Mehit and Onuris. Mummies are known and figurines
common.   τὴν ἔγχελυν: the eel (*Anguilla vulgaris*) is not common in Egypt
(Boulenger, pp. 402 ff.), but there is evidence of a cult connection with the
creator-god Atum (G. Daressy, *Recueil de travaux*, XXVI (1904), 133 ff.). Figurines have been found at Sais and mummy cases at Naucratis (W. M. F. Petrie,
Naukratis I (1884–5), London 1886, pp. 41 ff.).   ἱροὺς δὲ τούτους τοῦ
Νείλου: fish cults were more numerous than Herodotus implies; he says nothing
of the highly popular oxyrhynchus, latus, and phagrus cults (Hopfner, *Tierkult*
pp. 150 ff.). He is probably correct to emphasize the role of the Nile in their
divinization; for these fish were normally connected with female deities and that
irresistibly suggests that a conceptual link had been established with the fertility
of the river.   τοὺς χηναλώπεκας: Herodotus is almost certainly referring to
the Egyptian *smn*-goose (*Chenalopex aegyptiaca*). Extant Egyptian sources do not
connect it with the Nile but usually with Geb or Amon-re in their aspect as
creator gods (C. Kuentz, *L'Oie du Nil*, Arch. mus. hist. nat. Lyon XIV, 1926). It
would be perfectly natural theologically to extend this creator-god association to
the Nile god Hapi, but there is, as yet, no evidence that this was done.

73,1. ῎Εστι... φοῖνιξ: despite the bird's extraordinary behaviour, Herodotus'
wording makes it clear that he regarded it as having an objective existence
comparable to that of the *Chenalopex* of the preceding chapter. The name
φοῖνιξ derives from the Egyptian *bnw*, '*bnw*-bird', with assimilation to the name
Φοῖνιξ (Lloyd, *Commentary 1–98*, p. 317). In Egyptian contexts it was originally
a small bird resembling the water wagtail, but representations from the Middle

Kingdom onwards show it either as a purple heron (*Ardea purpurea*) or a grey
heron (*Ardea cinerea*).   ἐγὼ μέν...γραφῇ: note Herodotus' care in defining
the basis of his description. It is clear from explicit statements in this chapter that
ὄψις and ἀκοή played a major role (see above, pp. 229 ff.). In addition, he
undoubtedly drew on Hecataeus (*FGrHist* I F 324).   καὶ γὰρ δὴ καὶ σπάνιος
ἐπιφοιτᾷ: the classical phoenix legend, which evolved with the addition of ever-
more fantastic elements in antiquity, must be seen as a Greek reworking of
Egyptian mythology. In Egyptian myth the *bnw* was associated with the primeval
hill, the source of all created things, and, as such, was frequently regarded as the
manifestation of Re-Atum, the great creator-god of Heliopolis. It was also associated at Heliopolis with the *išd*-tree, on whose leaves were allegedly recorded great
events such as royal accessions, an association which led to a connection with the
passing of time (see, in general, R. T. Rundle Clark, *University of Birmingham
Historical Journal* II 1(1949), 1 ff.; II 2(1950), 105 ff.; Sabri Kolta, pp. 111 ff.). The
Greeks speak of the phoenix as early as the Hesiodic corpus (fr. 304 Merkelbach–
West), and by the 5th cent. had introduced into the legend the concept of a cyclic
return, the bird's brilliant colouring, the connection with Arabia, the ball of incense,
and the relationship with its father, much of which may have its seeds in Egyptian
sources but does not appear there explicitly. Subsequent additions include, in
particular, the idea that it underwent periodic rebirth by being consumed in fire
and reborn from it, and the concept that it was eternal, a notion enthusiastically
taken up by the Christian Church (R. van den Broek, *The Myth of the Phoenix
According to Classical and Early Christian Traditions*, Leiden 1972).   σπάνιος
...πεντακοσίων: the classical phoenix cycle is normally given as 500 years, but
other totals do occur, e.g. Tacitus gives 1,461 years (*Ann.* VI 28), i.e. virtually a Sothic
cycle. In Egyptian mythology the *bnw* has several general connections with time,
but no such cycle is ever mentioned. Clearly we are confronted with an example
of Greek reworking. (Lloyd, *Commentary 1–98*, pp. 320 ff.).   Ἡλιοπολῖται: cf.
3,1. Heliopolis is the city most often mentioned in relation to the *bnw* (see above).
2. τὰ μὲν αὐτοῦ...τὸ μέγαθος: for the style see note on ch. 71. The Egyptian *bnw*
never looks like this. Reddish plumage is sometimes seen on herons, but the
gold colouring, which clearly reflects the bird's solar affinities, suggests that
we are here in the realm of myth rather than ornithology. Traditions on its
splendid plumage become ever more baroque until the phoenix comes to resemble a peacock. It could also be identified with the eagle (Türk, in Roscher, *Lexicon*
III, 3470).
3. ἐξ Ἀραβίης: frequently so, but other areas to the east are also mentioned
(cf. Ovid, *Met.* XV 392–407). The connection clearly reflects the phoenix's solar
affinities.   ἐν σμύρνῃ: the phoenix is frequently related to myrrh, a substance
associated both by Egyptians and Greeks with the east.
4. ᾠόν: the egg often features as a symbol of birth/rebirth in Egyptian mythology.
There is even a representation of a *bnw* emerging from one (A. Wiedemann, *ZÄS*
XVI (1878), 104).   ὅσον [τε]: the Roman group of mss and the Parisinus
read τε after ὅσον whilst other mss have nothing at all. ὅσον in the sense

'approximately' is common in Herodotus (Powell, *Lexicon*, p. 272), but the present use with a verb looks unique, though it does appear in epic with a connotation of habitual action (cf. Denniston, *Greek Particles*, pp. 524 ff.). Schweighaeuser emends to τι, which is neat and fits perfectly.

74. Εἰσὶ δὲ ... ἱρούς: sacred serpents were a conspicuous feature of Egyptian religion. The basis was normally a *captatio benevolentiae* inspired by their dangerous nature. It is always the cobra (*Naja haje* L.) which features in extant Egyptian material, being connected, in particular, with the tutelary goddesses Wadjet, Renenutet, and Meritseger (Kees, *Götterglaube*, pp. 52 ff.). *Pace* Herodotus, there is no conclusive evidence of a cult of the viper (see below).   περὶ Θήβας: for the place-name see note on 3,1. The snake goddess Meritseger was popular in the Theban area (B. Bruyère, *Mert Seger à Deir el Médineh*, *MIFAO* LVIII (1930)), but a cult relationship with vipers remains to be demonstrated.   ἱροὶ ὄφιες ... τῆς κεφαλῆς: cf. IV 192,2; Philumenus, *Ven.* XVIII 1. The horned viper (*Cerastes cornutus*), a common N. African desert species, is widely current in Egypt (Anderson, *Zoology: Reptilia* pp. 326 ff.). It is possible, but no more, that some representations of Meritseger depict the viper. It is also alleged that viper mummies have come to light (Wilkinson–Birch, IV, p. 248; V, pp. 124, 247; H. Vyse and J. S. Perring, *Operations Carried on at the Pyramids of Gizeh in 1837*, III, London, 1842, App., p. 88), but the identification cannot be confirmed and is best left an open question. That the animal did enjoy a cult in the Theban area during the Late Period is far from improbable, but there is, as yet, no proof.   ἀνθρώπων οὐδαμῶς δηλήμονες: this use of the adjective with objective genitive is pre-eminently poetic (Kühner–Gerth, *Gr. Grammatik* II 1, p. 371). The claim is untrue. The bite would not normally be fatal but could be expected to give rise to very unpleasant and painful symptoms (Anderson, op. cit., pp. 333 ff.). It would, however, be easy to imagine circumstances which could give rise to such a misundertanding (Lloyd, *Commentary 1–98*, p. 324). μεγάθεϊ ἐόντες σμικροί: the average length is *c.*45 cm.; it rarely exceeds 70 cm., though measurements as high as 73. 5 cm. are recorded (L. Keimer, *Études d'égyptologie*, VII, Cairo 1945, p. 15, n.1).   μεγάθεϊ: cf. VI 44. The dative of respect is considerably less common than its accusative counterpart (Kühner– Gerth, *Gr. Grammatik* II 1, p. 440). The pleonasm of μεγάθεϊ σμικροί is typically Greek (ibid. II 2, p. 583).   δύο κέρεα: they consist of two spines protruding above each eye. Cases are mentioned in ancient and modern literature with more than two, but anything above that will be native embellishment (Keimer, op. cit., p. 11).   τοὺς θάπτουσι ... εἶναι ἱρούς: there is nothing intrinsically improbable here. Sacred animals could be buried in the temples of gods with whom they were associated (cf. note on 148,5), and Amun does have connections with snakes (K. Sethe, *Amun und die acht Urgötter von Hermopolis*, Berlin 1929, pp. 38, 106, 110; Bruyère, op. cit., figs. 80, 85). As yet, however, no mummies of horned vipers have been found in the temple area of Amon-re nor is there evidence of any connection of the animal with him.   ἐν τῷ ἱρῷ τοῦ Διός: without qualification we should expect this phrase to refer to the great temple complex of Karnak at Thebes, though Herodotus could conceivably be treating the closely linked complexes of Karnak and Luxor as one large ἱρόν (for this entire area see Kees, *Ancient Egypt*, pp. 252 ff.). His reticence on the architectural marvels of these installations has often excited comment, much of it misguided (see above).

75,1. Βουτοῦν: this name was borne by several Egyptian cities. Here it is ᾿Imt (modern Tell Fara᾿ûn), about 13 km. south-east of Tanis in the north-eastern Delta (Gardiner, *AEO* II, pp. 170* ff., 191* ff.).   πυνθανόμενος: ἱστορίη in action (see above, p. 230). It is possible that Herodotus is here pursuing a topic already broached by Hecataeus (Lloyd, *Commentary 1–98*, p. 326).   τῶν πτερωτῶν ὀφίων: cf. III 107; Mela III 82; Aelian, *NA* II 38; Pliny, *NH* X 75; Isaiah 30: 6. The identification of these creatures has given rise to much debate. The easiest solution is to assume an amalgam in which several ingredients have interacted: the starting-point might have been Egyptian iconography which often attributed wings to the cobra goddess Wadjet of Buto (Sethe, *RE* III, 1088), or the horned viper's habit of flinging itself through the air to attack its victim (Anderson, *Zoology: Reptilia*, p. 333), or a combination of both; this material could then have been contaminated by information on the flying lizards of South-East Asia which fit the description of 76,3 very well (O. Keller, *Die antike Tierwelt*, II, Leipzig 1913, p. 301; K. Morta, *Eos*, LXXXII (1994), 311 ff.).   ἀπικόμενος δὲ...οὗτοι: on Herodotus and ὄψις see above, p. 229. He may well here be guilty of some exaggeration. If a substantial proportion of the bones were indeed snake skeletons, and if reptile-eating ibises (note on 76,1) were responsible for them, we should have to assume that there was an unusual profusion of snakes and ibises in this area. Neither situation is inconceivable, but some have preferred to regard the difficulties of this passage as evidence that Herodotus' claims to autopsy are not always to be trusted (e.g. Fehling, pp. 24 ff.).

2. ἐσβολὴ...μέγα: probably the pass on the El-Kantareh road between lake Menzalah and the Abbasiyah canal south of Tell el-Defennah (Baedeker, *Egypt*, inset map between pp. 184–5).

3. ταύτης τῆς χώρης: a rather odd possessive genitive. Trans. 'into this land' (sc. Egypt).

4. τὴν ἲβιν...ταύτας: strictly the sacred ibis was *Ibis aethiopica*, not the crested ibis which is at issue here (notes on 76,1–2). Herodotus may well have been given the explanation for its divinization outlined here, and Egyptians may well have agreed, but the true reason was almost certainly its apparently infallible instinct in searching and finding which led to its being associated with wisdom and hence with Thoth, the god of learning (Kees, *Götterglaube*, p. 48).   Ἀράβιοι: sc. the people inhabiting the Isthmus of Suez (note on 12,2).

76,1. εἶδος...ἰδέη: almost certainly the crested or hermit ibis (*Geronticus eremita*), which frequents rocky mountain ranges (cf. 75,2) and does indeed eat reptiles (Meinertzhagen I, p. 67), but the claims of the glossy ibis (*Plegadis falcinellus*) are also strongly supported (P. F. Houlihan, *The Birds of Ancient Egypt*, Warminster 1988, p. 27).   μέλαινα...κρέξ: on style see note on ch. 71. Both colour and shape are well described (Meinertzhagen II, p. 438), but the size is very inaccurate. The hermit ibis can attain a length of 68 cm., which is over twice the size of the κρέξ, whether the latter is identified with the corncrake (*Rallus crex*) or the black-winged stilt (*Himantopus rufipes*) (Thompson, *Greek Birds*, p. 177).   μέγαθος: ms D reads δέ after this word and has been followed by Hude and Waddell. However, D is not a good authority; the parallel in ch. 71, though not exact, gives considerable support for omission, and the absence of a connective would be compatible with the staccato nature of the style at this point. It seems preferable, therefore, to follow Stein, Legrand, and Godley in dispensing with δέ.

1–2. τῶν δ' ἐν ποσὶ ... τῇ ἑτέρῃ: the sacred ibis (*Threskiornis aethiopicus*), which is described with great precision (Meinerzhagen II, p. 437). Mummified examples are legion (D. Kessler, *LdÄ* VI, 579 ff.).

1. διξαί: ancient Egyptian sources show three, but there are five main African species (L. Keimer, 'Quelques hiéroglyphes représentant des oiseaux', *ASAE* XXX (1930), 20 ff.). None now breeds in Egypt, though migratory specimens are still to be seen.

2. τῶν ὕδρων: the term ὕδρος can be used of two European species: the grass snake and *Tropidonotus bilineatus* Jan. (Gossen-Steier, *RE* II, 2nd ser., 554 ff.).

3. μάλιστά κη: this adverbial phrase does not simply reinforce the superlative but also emphasizes τοῖσι τῆς νυκτερίδος πτεροῖσι. Trans.: 'The wings it has are not covered with feathers but, to take the best comparison, are very similar to the wings of a bat' (cf. Kühner–Gerth, *Gr. Grammatik* II 1, pp. 27 ff.).

77,1. μέν: the answering δέ does not appear until 92,1.   τὴν σπειρομένην Αἴγυπτον: i.e. the part of Egypt south of the marshes of the northern Delta (cf. 92,1). The latter area was largely unsuitable for arable farming (Kees, *Ancient Egypt*, pp. 29 ff.).   μνήμην ... ἀπικόμην: an impressive corpus of king-lists, annals, and historical narratives has survived which covers the entire range of Egyptian history (D. B. Redford, *Pharaonic King-lists, Annals and Daybooks: A Contribution to the Study of the Egyptian Sense of History*, SSEA Publication, IV, Mississauga 1986; *BAR* I–V). This material would probably not have exceeded in bulk the historical records of such ancient peoples as the Babylonians and Assyrians, but was considerably more voluminous and covered a considerably greater time-span than anything with which Herodotus was familiar.   λογιώτατοί: see note on 3,1.

2. συρμαΐζουσι ... κλύσμασι: purges and enemata were indeed a major feature of Egyptian medicine (H. Grapow, *Grundriss der medizinischen Texte*, III, Berlin 1956, pp. 28 ff.; G. Morgan, *Mnemosyne*, XLIV (1991), 415 ff.).   τρεῖς ἡμέρας ... ἑκάστου: the commonest figure in extant Egyptian medical prescriptions is four days (F. Jonckheere, *Le Papyrus médical Chester Beatty, La Médecine égyptienne*, II, Brussels 1947, VI–VIII, 14). It is possible that Herodotus' marked predilection for the number 3 has contaminated the tradition here (cf. Alan B. Lloyd, *Historia* XXXVII (1988), 41, n. 53).   νομίζοντες ... γίνεσθαι: cf. Diod. I 82. Egyptian medical texts confirm this claim (P. Ghalioungui, *BIFAO*

LXVI (1968), 37 ff.; A. Volten *Das demotische Weisheitsbuch*, Analecta Aegyptiaca II, Copenhagen 1942, p. 169). The doctrine was, however, widely current in contemporary Greek medicine (Sigerist II, pp. 103, 110, 242).

3. εἰσὶ ... ἀνθρώπων: this is a startling comment to anyone familiar with health conditions in modern Egypt. Possible practical explanations of the disparity have been offered by Sigerist (ibid., I, pp. 222 ff., 246 ff.), but it is possible that Herodotus' claim is simply assumption: current Greek medical doctrine taught that climatic change is a major cause of disease (ibid., pp. 280 ff., 320 ff.); such changes in Egypt are slight or non-existent; therefore, the incidence of disease there must be less.   τῶν ὡρέων ... μάλιστα: for Greek thought on the matter see previous note. Egyptian doctors also recognized that climate could affect health (Grapow, op. cit. III, p. 42).   ἐμοὶ δοκέειν: so Hude and Legrand, following the Roman group of mss. The reading δοκέειν ἐμοὶ has the authority of the superior Florentine group and is also entirely consistent with Herodotean usage (cf. Powell, *Lexicon*, p. 93, so also Godley).   ὅτι οὐ μεταλλάσσουσι: the claim is exaggerated but intelligible. The Egyptian winter and summer show clear climatic differences (Baedeker, *Egypt*, pp. lxxvi ff.), but by European standards they are far from spectacular. μεταλλάσσω, like so many Greek verbs referring to movement or change, can be used either transitively or intransitively (Kühner–Gerth, *Gr. Grammatik* II 1, pp. 91 ff.).

4. ἀρτοφαγέουσι ... ὀνομάζουσι: cf. Hecataeus, *FGrHist* I F 322–3, who undoubtedly contributed something to this discussion.   ἐκ τῶν ὀλυρέων: emmer wheat was certainly the main Egyptian bread cereal in Herodotus' time (note on 36,2).   κυλλήστις: a good rendering of the Egyptian name *kršt* (*Wb.* V, p. 136, 2–3). This type of unleavened bread was very popular (Kees, *Ägypten*, p. 32).   οἴνῳ ... διαχρέωνται: beer was the favourite Ancient Egyptian drink and was frequently made of barley, though other materials could be used (H. L. Lutz, *Viticulture and Brewing in the Ancient Orient*, Leipzig 1922, pp. 72 ff.).   οὐ γάρ ... ἄμπελοι: cf. 37,4. Vineyards were to be found in the oases, which could not possibly be included in ἡ σπειρομένη Αἴγυπτος, but they also occurred in the Delta (Hartmann, pp. 156 ff.). If Herodotus knew of these Delta vineyards, he presumably excluded them because he regarded the areas where they lay as being ἐν τοῖσι ἕλεσι rather than ἐν τῇ σπειρομένῃ Αἰγύπτῳ.   ἰχθύων: fish, both dried and pickled in salt, were a major item in the Ancient Egyptian diet (Kees, *Ägypten*, pp. 58 ff.).

5. ὀρνίθων ... προταριχεύσαντες: quails were not a popular food but were certainly eaten (Wreszinski I, pls. 33, 108). Ducks, however, were a great favourite (Erman–Ranke, pp. 268, 529).   ἄλλα ὅσα ... ὁκόσοι: note the change of gender: ὁκόσοι picks up the masculine plurals ὀρνίθων ἢ ἰχθύων rather than the preceding neuter.   ὀπτοὺς ... σιτέονται: the first technique was standard, though not invariable (Montet, *Everyday Life*, pp. 84 ff.).

78. ἐν δὲ τῇσι συνουσίῃσι: see also Plutarch, *DIO* 17 (*Mor.* 357); id., *Sept. Sap. Conv.* 2 (*Mor.* 148a–b); Lucian, *Luct.* 21; and cf. Petronius, *Sat.* 34. No Egyptian source refers to this practice, but it is compatible with Egyptian attitudes and archaeological

evidence and is entirely credible (see below). τοῖσι εὐδαίμοσι: the dative hovers somewhere between a dative of advantage and a possessive dative. Trans.: 'of their wealthy class.' νεκρὸν... δίπηχυν: objects are known which are reminiscent of this description and which may well have been used for the same purpose (Budge, p. 98; Montet, *Everyday Life*, p. 98; B. J. Peterson, *Opuscula Atheniensia*, VII (1967), 21 ff.). The exact appearance created by the painting (γραφῇ) and carving (ἔργῳ) is unclear. The bodies may have represented emaciated corpses like the figures discussed by Peterson or they may have resembled the mummiform figures of Budge and Montet. πάντῃ: this word occurs in all mss but is deleted both by Stein and Godley. How–Wells and Waddell (ad loc.) retain it and render 'altogether, in all'. Context and linguistic considerations strongly favour removal. Where πάντῃ occurs elsewhere in Herodotus it means 'in every direction, on every side' (cf. I 181,2; II 168,1), and this is its normal significance in other authors. To describe the corpse and its coffin as 'approximately a cubit or two cubits in every direction' is patent nonsense. Certainly, πάντῃ can also be employed as an intensive in the sense 'in every respect, altogether' (LSJ, p. 1300,a, s.v. πάντῃ (n. II)), but this usage is most unlikely here before an adjective describing dimensions. ἐς τοῦτον... τοιοῦτος: this sentiment is easily paralleled in Ancient Egyptian texts, e.g. the Harper Song from the tomb of King Inyotef (Lichtheim, *Old and Middle Kingdoms*, pp. 194 ff.).

79,1. πατρίοισι... ἐπικτῶνται: cf. also 91,1. τοῖσι... νόμιμα: on Herodotus' inordinate respect and admiration for Ancient Egyptian culture see above, pp. 235 ff. ἐπάξιά: so the Roman group of mss and the Parisinus; the reading of the Florentines is corrupt (cf. VII 96,2, where ἐπάξιος is usually read by conjecture). The word is generally regarded as equivalent to ἀξιόλογος and ἀξιαπήγητος and translated 'noteworthy' *vel sim.* (LSJ, p. 610,a, s.v. ἐπάξιος 3; Powell, *Lexicon*, p. 127). Such a meaning would fit the context and Herodotean usage very well. However, this view is open to the serious objection that, where ἐπάξιος is used absolutely elsewhere, the respect in which someone or something is worthy is either stated by an adverbial adjunct (e.g. infinitive or genitive noun) or can easily be supplied from the context. Since there is no suggestion in our passage of speech, neither condition is fulfilled. Given this linguistic difficulty and the mss problem, the reading ἐπάξιος must be regarded as suspect, but, if it is correct, two possible explanations suggest themselves: either ἐπάξιος reflects a specialized use, possibly Ionic, unexemplified elsewhere, and is equivalent to ἀξιόλογος; or it does not mean ἀξιόλογος *vel sim.* at all. The first alternative could only be acceptable as a last resort; if, on the other hand, we pursue the second, a ready solution presents itself. The simplex ἄξιος often means 'of worth, estimable' (LSJ, p. 171,a, ἄξιος, II,1). By analogy we might postulate a semantic evolution of ἐπάξιος from 'worthy' through 'of worth' to 'estimable'. This hypothesis is much less bold than the traditional rendering of ἐπάξιος and yields an entirely acceptable sense.

1–2. καὶ δὴ καί... Μανερῶς: Herodotus shows a marked predilection for identifying similar phenomena, a tendency which greatly encourages his taste for hyperdiffusionism (see above, p. 235). Herodotus' attention is drawn to this particular νόμιμον above all by the question of origins.

1. ἓν ἐστι: so modern editors, accepting Wesseling's emendation of the ἔνεστι read by all mss. This emendation, like the misguided interpretation of καὶ... γενέσθαι below on which it is presumably based, must surely be rejected as patent nonsense. The mss reading is perfectly viable: 'they have both other estimable customs, and, in particular, there is amongst them [sc. the customs] a song...'   Λίνος: the name derives from the cry αἴλινος (LSJ, p. 38,a, s.v. αἰλίνος), which may originate, in turn, in a Semitic expression such as 'oi lanu, 'woe to us'. Linus first appears as a dying god of vegetation similar to Adonis (cf. Homer, *Il.* XVIII 561 ff.), but in Greek mythology he features pre-eminently as a famous singer who met a tragic and untimely end (W. Kroll, *RE* XIII, 715 ff.).   ὅς περ... ἔχει: Herodotus has in mind such parallels as the Near Eastern Tammuz/Adonis, the Phrygian Lityerses, and the Bithynian Bormus/ Borimus.

2. συμφέρεται... εἶναι: the verb is constructed with an epexegetic infinitive rather than the more usual dative noun or pronoun (cf. 80,1; Powell, *Lexicon*, p. 343). Lit. 'he corresponds so as to be the same as...'.   ἀποθωμάζειν: τὸ θωμάσιον is one of Herodotus' standard criteria in choice of subject-matter (see above, pp. 234 ff.).   [τὸ οὔνομα]: clearly a gloss, since it is almost immediately contradicted by ἔστι δὲ... Μανερῶς below.   Μανερῶς: also discussed by Plutarch, *DIO* 17 (*Mor.* 357), Paus. IX 29,7, Pollux IV 54, and Hesychius, s.v.: cf. Suidas, s.v. Several ingenious attempts have made to identify an Egyptian proto- type for the name (e.g. J. Černý, *Miscellanea Gregoriana*, Vatican 1941, p. 60), but they amount to nothing more than guesses and inspire no confidence.

3. ἔφασαν... τιμηθῆναι: the king in question was Menes (note on 99,2). Plutarch's account substitutes the king of Byblos (loc. cit.) and incorporates a number of other variations.   θρήνοισι τούτοισι: we should expect a song resembling the Linus to be a dirge connected with agriculture. In Egypt this would almost certainly relate to Osiris, who had close affinities with corn (Bonnet, *RÄRG*, pp. 391 ff.). Confidence in this correlation is strengthened by the fact that Osiris, like Linus, met an untimely death and also by classical references to farmers singing a dirge in an Osirian context (Diod. I 14; Firmicus Maternus, *De Errore Prof. Rel.*, 2 (6–7): cf. G. Roeder, *ZÄS* LV (1918), 55, l. 5).   ἀοιδήν... γενέσθαι: what exactly does Herodotus mean here? It has usually been understood: 'and this was the first and only song they had', i.e. 'ever had', but this would be an incredible statement for an Egyptian to make and a very difficult one for anyone to credit. In this chapter Herodotus is affirming the indigenous nature of Egyptian customs in general and in this context is concerned, in particular, to establish the absolute priority of the Egyptian version of the Linos song. Surely, καὶ μούνην is intended simply to reinforce πρώτην, i.e. he is arguing that the Maneros song was introduced so early that the Egyptians had not got around to inventing any other songs. Translate: 'this was the first and only song they had <at that time>' (so also A. de Sélincourt, *Herodotus: The Histories*, Harmondsworth 1972, p. 159).

80,1. συμφέρονται... ὑπανιστέαται: cf. note on 35,4. An awareness of the wisdom brought by age emerges frequently in Egyptian texts, and respect for one's elders is a recurrent theme (e.g. Z. Žabà, *Les Maximes de Ptahhotep*, Prague 1956, pp. 17, 10–13). τόδε ἄλλο: accusative of respect. Lit: 'in respect of this other matter...' (cf. τόδε μέντοι ἄλλο below and ταῦτα at 81,2). μούνοισι Λακεδαιμονίοισι: the claim on the similarity of Spartan practice is confirmed by Xenophon, *Lac.* X 1–3; *Mem.* III 5, Plutarch, *Inst. Lac.* 10 (*Mor.* 237)), Cicero, *Sen.* 18,63, and Gellius II 15. This level of respect was apparently a thing of the past in classical Athens (Aristophanes, *Nu.* 993). ὁδοῦ: genitive of separation dependent on εἴκουσι (Kühner–Gerth, *Gr. Grammatik* II 1, p. 395).

2. τόδε μέντοι... τὴν χεῖρα: cf. I 134,1. References to this practice are numerous in Ancient Egyptian texts (e.g. *Wb.* III, pp. 231, 2–12; 367, 1–4; Žabà, op.cit., 5, 71; 13, 9). In Greece προσκύνησις before a human was repugnant (e.g. Isocrates, *Pan.* 151), but it featured prominently in the cult of the gods (W. Fauth, *KP*, IV, 1189).

81,1. ἐνδεδύκασι... θυσανωτούς: linen was the normal material for textiles in Ancient Egypt (Lucas–Harris, *AEMI*, p. 142). The majority of representations and surviving garments do not correspond to Herodotus' description, but examples of tunics with fringed hems have survived from the New Kingdom (E. Schiaparelli, *La tomba intatta dell' architetto Cha nella necropoli di Tebe*, II, Turin 1927, pp. 93 ff., figs. 68–9), and they are also represented on the Busiris Hydria (on which see note on ch. 45). Presumably garments of this kind were much in vogue during the Late Period and came to be regarded as the typical Egyptian dress, but we may suspect that Herodotus exaggerates in claiming that all tunics were of this kind. ἐνδεδύκασι: 'they wear', an excellent example of the perfect used to express a present situation created by past action (cf. Kühner–Gehrt, *Gr. Grammatik* II 1, p. 148). καλασίρις: no surviving Egyptian text uses this word of Egyptian tunics. It seems probable that it is connected with the name of the Καλασίριες warrior class (note on ch. 164) and refers to a type of dress which was originally particularly associated with them. The word was eventually fully assimilated into Greek, where it denotes chitons of an exotic kind which have nothing to do with Egypt (LSJ, p. 1993, s.v. χιτών). εἰρίνεα εἴματα: εἷμα frequently denotes an ἱμάτιον in Herodotus (LSJ, p. 487,b, s.v. εἷμα). Garments which could be described as ἱμάτια are often represented (H. Bonnet, *Die ägyptische Tracht bis zum Ende des Neuen Reiches, Untersuchungen*, VII, Leipzig 1917, pp. 62 ff.), but the evidence suggests that they were of linen. Surviving woollen garments are uncommon (Lucas–Harris, *AEMI*, pp. 146 ff.), but, in view of the taboo on burying them with the dead (see below), this need not surprise us. Since sheep were certainly reared on some scale (L. Störk, *LdÄ* V, 522 ff.), we must give Herodotus the benefit of the doubt (cf. Diod. I 87,2). οὐ μέντοι... εἰρίνεα: woollen garments were absolutely fobidden to priests in the Hellenistic and Roman periods on grounds of impurity (Plutarch, *DIO* 3 ff. (*Mor.* 352); Graf W. Uxkull-Gullenband, *Der Gnomon des Idios Logos, Griech. Urkunden Berlin*, V 2, Berlin 1934, p. 77).

There is no specific confirmation from earlier times, but Herodotus' claim is entirely credible in the light of the strict provisions for priestly purity described in ch. 37.   οὐδὲ συγκαταθάπτεταί σφι: examples do occur in graves, but they are exceedingly uncommon (Lucas–Harris, *AEMI*, pp. 146 ff.). The association of wool with ritual impurity will explain this taboo (see above).

2. ὁμολογέουσι . . . θαφθῆναι: 'Ορφικά refers to the ritual practices and religious beliefs ascribed to the legendary seer Orpheus, though it questionable whether they formed a clearly defined corpus in Herodotus' time. In this passage they are evidently regarded as having affinities with Βακχικά, i.e. the Dionysiac cult, a view which is indisputably correct. Herodotus is the first extant author to compare the Orphics and Pythagoreans, but it subsequently became common practice (KR², pp. 21, 30, 220 ff.). For Herodotus' claim that these systems were of Egyptian origin see notes on chs. 49, 123.   ταῦτα: see note on 80,1.   Βακχικοῖσι . . . καὶ: this section is omitted in all the Florentine mss, but the arguments for postulating an omission in this group are considerably stronger than those for interpolation in DRSV (Dodds, p. 169, n. 80). On the general issue of Egyptian influence on Orphism see R. Merkelbach, *ZPE* CXXVIII (1999), 1 ff.   οὐδὲ γὰρ . . . θαφθῆναι: rules of abstinence were typical of Pythagoreanism and the religious systems with which it had affinities (KR², pp. 220 ff., 230 ff.).   ἔστι . . . λεγόμενος: such reticence is common in Herodotus (note on ch. 3), but it is possible that the notorious Pythagorean secrecy on matters of doctrine may have exercised an additional influence in this case (cf. KR², pp. 227 ff.).

82,1. μείς . . . ὅτευ ἐστί: the association of months with specific gods is well documented from the New Kingdom onwards, such deities functioning as the tutelary god of the relevant month (L. Borchardt, *Die altägyptische Zeitmessung*, Berlin–Leipzig 1920, pp. 6 ff.; PM VI, p. 264).   ἡμέρη . . . ὅτευ ἐστί: in several Ptolemaic temple texts each day and even each hour are placed under the protection of a specific deity (PM loc. cit.). Herodotus' statement provides welcome evidence that this concept already existed in the pharaonic period. Though he does not mention the fact, individual gods were also thought to preside over the hours of the day (Bonnet, *RÄRG*, pp. 753 ff.).   τῇ ἕκαστος . . . ἔσται: the incidence of hemerology in Ancient Egypt is amply confirmed; indeed, Egyptian prowess in this area was acknowledged even in Ancient Rome (Hopfner, *Fontes*, pp. 522 ff., 647). It clearly had its origin in the association of particular days with particular mythological events which indelibly stamped them with a specific character, though astrology exercised a powerful influence during the Roman period (G. Roeder, *Zauberei und Jenseitsglauben im alten Ägypten*, Zurich–Stuttgart 1961, pp. 126 ff.).   οἱ ἐν ποιήσι γενόμενοι: 'those engaged in poetry . . .' For this use of ἐν see Kühner–Gerth, *Gr. Grammatik* II 1, pp. 462 ff. The reference is pre-eminently to Hesiod (*Op.* 765–828). The latter's scheme is based on the lunar month, unlike the fully developed pharaonic system which uses the year. This difference alone invalidates Herodotus' claim of Greek dependence in the matter. Hemerology is a worldwide phenomenon and has developed quite independently in many different cultures. As so often, Herodotus has fallen victim to the *post hoc ergo propter hoc* fallacy (see above, p. 235).

2. τέρατά ... ἀνθρώποισι: portents feature infrequently in Egyptian texts but do occur occasionally (Bonnet, *RÄRG*, pp. 542 ff.). The most important category is *biȝyt*, 'marvels', which are extraordinary phenomena sent by the gods to indicate to a specific pharaoh that his actions have divine approval (Alan B. Lloyd, *JEA* LXI (1975), 57 ff.). **γενομένου ... ἀποβήσεσθαι:** the fragments of Manetho contain several entries which might well have emanated from such collections (*FGrHist* 609, pp. 18, 20, 46), but, as yet, no examples of these books have come to light. The preservation of texts designed to help in the interpretation of dreams also justifies confidence in the existence of such documents even though the format which they employ differs from that ascribed by Herodotus to books of portents (cf. Volten).

83. ἀνθρώπων ... μετεξετέροισι: Herodotus means that there was nothing in Egypt comparable to Greek human prophetic media such as μάντεις; all prophecies proceeded directly from the gods. Divine oracles were certainly very important in Egypt from the New Kingdom onwards, and could be invoked to solve any difficulty, domestic or public, but were particularly prominent in political and legal contexts (L. Kákosy, *LdÄ* IV, 600 ff.). **καὶ γὰρ ... ἐστί:** the gods in this list can be identified as follows: Heracles = Onuris, Apollo = Horus, Athene = Neith, Artemis = Bastet, Ares = Montju, Zeus = Amun, and Leto = Wadjet. There was nothing to prevent any Egyptian god from giving oracles, but only Onuris and Amun can be demonstrated to have done so (Bonnet, *RÄRG*, p. 564). There is, however, indirect evidence that nearly all the others functioned in this way also (Lloyd, *Commentary 1–98*, p. 347). Important oracular deities not mentioned by Herodotus are Isis, Bes, Ptah, and sacred animals (Kákosy, op. cit., 603). **διάφοροί:** the standard method was to put questions orally or in writing to the cult image while it was being carried in procession by the priests. It would then be made to approach or recoil to signify the god's approval or disapproval. Other methods probably or certainly used were incubation, the interpretation of the movements of sacred animals, oral communication by the god, and the behaviour of sacred objects during solemn processions, e.g. the divine bark could become too heavy to move, or the god's statue carried could shake (Lloyd, op. cit., pp. 348 ff.).

84. ἡ δὲ ἰητρική: Egyptian medicine enjoyed a very high international reputation in antiquity (Homer, *Od.* IV 228; Herod. III 1; 129; the inscription of Udjahorresnet speaks of an Egyptian in the entourage of Darius I: Posener, p. 22). There is clear evidence that medicine was considered as a series of areas of special expertise, and there are indications of a degree of specialization, but Herodotus exaggerates in claiming rigid departmentalization. Individuals such as the well-known Iri could lay claim to competence in many of these areas, and this was probably common throughout Egyptian history (Jonckheere, p. 24; H. Grapow, *Grundriss der Medizin der alten Ägypter*, III, Berlin 1956, pp. 97 ff.). **σφι:** best interpreted as dative of the agent, though Waddell (note ad loc.) prefers to regard it as dative of advantage from which datives of the agent are often virtually or actually indistinguishable. The latter are not uncommon with perfect or pluperfect passives but are otherwise rare (Kühner–Gerth, *Gr. Grammatik* II 1, pp. 422 ff.). ὀφθαλμῶν ἰητροί: cf. the Egyptian title *swnw irty pr ʿ3*, 'the Eye Physician of the Palace' (F. Jonckheere, *CdE* XXVI (1951), 242 ff.). Eye-complaints were endemic in Ancient Egypt and feature prominently in medical literature (Grapow, op. cit. V, pp. 71 ff.). οἱ δὲ κεφαλῆς: remedies for the head certainly appear in medical texts (ibid., IV 1, pp. 34 ff.), but there are no extant titles confirming the existence of specialists in this area. οἱ δὲ ὀδόντων: cf. the Egyptian *ibḥy*, 'He of the Tooth', and *irw ibḥ*, 'He who deals with Teeth' (Jonckheere, pp. 125 ff.). There is substantial evidence on Egyptian dentistry which indicates that its effectiveness was low (in general see F. Filce Leek, *JEA* LIII (1967), 51 ff.). οἱ δὲ τῶν κατὰ νηδύν: cf. the Egyptian *swnw ḥt pr ʿ3*, 'The Body Physician of the Palace' (Jonckheere, *CdE* XXVI (1951), 258 ff.). Maladies in this area must have been rife, and remedies are well documented in the medical papyri (Grapow, op. cit. V, pp. 145 ff.). οἱ δὲ τῶν ἀφανέων νούσων: the Greek may reflect such Egyptian titles as *ʿḥmwt št3t*, 'He who knows(?) of the Mysterious Things' and *ʿmw m-ḥnw ntntt*, 'He who knows(?) the Hidden Water within the Ntntt* (Jonckheere, *CdE* XXVI(1951), 243 ff.).

85–90. An excursus on the Egyptian cult of the dead, containing a discussion of θρῆνοι (85), a detailed description of mummification (86–9), and an account of the treatment of those who had drowned or were killed by crocodiles (90).

85,1. θρῆνοι: the preliminary stage in the mortuary cult immediately following death is only represented twice in extant documentation: in the Old Kingdom of Isesi at Saqqâra and in an XVIIIth Dynasty representation at El-Amarna (G. Foucart, *Le Tombeau d'Amonmos, MIFAO* (LVII 3–4 1935), pp. 7 ff.). Both are much earlier than Herodotus and provide inadequate evidence for refuting or confirming his description of this particular phase of the obsequies. We must, however, allow for the possibility that Herodotus has elevated a general tendency into a hard-and-fast rule. ᾖ: the omission of ἄν in indefinite relative clauses with subjunctive is a poetic usage but is paralleled elsewhere in Herodotus (Goodwin, *Moods and Tenses*, p. 208).
1–2. τὸ θῆλυ γένος πᾶν ... ἄνδρες: the El-Amarna evidence (see above) shows no such demarcation, but it is perfectly plausible that the practice, or at least a general tendency, existed in the 5th cent. BC. In modern Egypt a distinction is certainly made in the role of the sexes (E. Lüddeckens, *MDAI(K)* XI (1943), 9).
1. κατ' ὦν ἐπλάσατο ... πηλῷ: this custom is confirmed both by representations and texts, but some of the evidence indicates that both sexes could practise it (Goyon, pp. 11 ff.). In modern Egypt, however, it is confined to women (Lüddeckens, op. cit., p. 15). κατ' ὦν ἐπλάσατο: see note on 39,2. λιποῦσαι: Herodotus switches to a feminine plural after τὸ θῆλυ γένος by a

constructio ad sensum. τύπτονται: this practice is well documented, e.g. in the representations in the tomb of Isesi and at El-Amarna (see above). ὑπεζωμέναι: 'girt up' (Powell, *Lexicon*, p. 368, some mss reading ὑπεζωσμέναι). Both here and below the mss tradition offers ἐπεζωμένοι, 'girt on', as an alternative. Since ὑποζώννυμι is an attested Herodotean word (Powell, loc. cit.) whilst ἐπιζώννυμι does not seem exemplified before the Hellenistic period (LSJ, p. 633,b, s.v), the former must be preferred. Unequivocal examples of this custom are difficult to isolate but do occur (e.g. I. E. S. Edwards, *Revue d'Égyptologie*, XXVII (1975), 117 ff., with the suggestion that ἐπεζωσμέναι (οἱ) was used of women and ὑπεζωσμέναι (οἱ) of men). φαίνουσαι τοὺς μαζούς: for examples of this common practice in mourning contexts see M. Werbrouck, *Les Pleureuses dans l'Egypte ancienne*, Brussels 1938. σὺν δέ σφι: σύν with the dative in the sense of 'together with' is rare in classical Greek prose. Here it may well have a poetic colouring (cf. Kühner–Gerth, *Gr. Grammatik* II 1, p. 467 n.).

2. ταρίχευσιν: Herodotus here introduces a lengthy discussion of mummification to which his attention was drawn pre-eminently by its character as a θῶμα (see above, pp. 234 ff.). The process in its most developed and elaborate form involved two main stages: removal of the perishable organs from the body, i.e. brain, stomach, liver, entrails, and kidneys (86, 1–5; 87,1–2; 88); and drying out the body with natron, i.e. the ταρίχευσις, 'pickling', proper (86,5; 87,2; 88). This could be followed by the insertion of packing to give the body a more lifelike appearance, and the procedure was concluded by bandaging (86,6). All of these activities would have been accompanied by appropriate rituals and incantations which ensured that the operation took considerably longer than purely technological considerations required (see, in general, Lucas–Harris, *AEMI*, pp. 270 ff.).

86,1. εἰσὶ δέ ... ταύτην: the Egyptians usually refer to the embalming house either as the *wᶜbt*, 'pure place', or as the *sḥ nṯr*, 'divine booth'. Some were clearly temporary structures erected near the tomb, but there is evidence of more permanent installations (W. R. Dawson, *JEA* XIII (1927), 40 ff.; A. Altenmüller, *JVEG* XXII (1972), 307 ff.). In the Late Period embalmers were very numerous and constituted a hereditary calling (Diod. I 91,3). The head of each group was designated the *ḥry sšt3*, 'chief of mysteries', and the rank-and-file were described by the general term *ḥryw ḥbt*, 'lector priests' (W. Spiegelberg, *ZÄS* LVI (1920), 3 ff.). Their relationship to the deceased was modelled on the mythological role of Anubis, who was believed to have invented embalming, first employing it on the corpse of Osiris with whom all the dead were identified, but this ritual function did not save the embalmers from considerable loss of respect in the Late Period. See in general C. Andrews, *Egyptian Mummies*, London, 1998², pp. 16 ff.

2. δεικνύουσι ... μεμιμημένα: these models probably depicted no more than the external appearance, particularly the bandaging, of the different styles of embalming. τῇ γραφῇ: 'in painting' (cf. ch. 78). τοῦ οὐκ ὅσιον ... ὀνομάζειν: cf. note on ch. 3. Herodotus is referring to Osiris. τὴν μὲν σπουδαιοτάτην ... εὐτελεστέρην: cf. Diod. I 91; Porphyry, *Abst.* IV 10; Plutarch, *Sept. Sap. Conv.* 16 (*Mor.* 159). Herodotus' description is the most

informative account of mummification in any ancient language and formed the basis of that of Diodorus. According to the latter, the first method cost a talent, the second 20 minae, and the third much less. Though there were certainly differences in technique (Lucas–Harris, *AEMI*, pp. 299 ff.), Egyptian sources give no indication of this neat tripartite structure. Since Herodotus shows a predilection for grouping phenomena in threes (see above, note on 77,2), it would be wise not to press the division too far.

3. μισθῷ: dative of price (cf. Kühner–Gerth, *Gr. Grammatik* II 1, p. 438). πρῶτα...ἐξάγοντες: this is normal, though not invariable, from the XVIIIth Dynasty onwards. The brain could also be removed through the back of the head at the base of the skull or by way of a trepanning orbit; alternatively, it could be left in the body (W. R. Dawson, *Proc. of the Royal Soc. of Medicine*, XX (1927), 832 ff.).   τὰ δὲ ἐγχέοντες φάρμακα: it is likely enough that the Egyptians cleared out the brain cavity in this way at some stage, but there is no evidence, as yet, of removing the brain itself by such a technique.

4. λίθῳ Αἰθιοπικῷ ὀξέϊ: i.e. obsidian (Lucas–Harris, *AEMI*, p. 416). This substance was certainly employed to make false eyes for mummies, but no obsidian knives of the historic period are known from Egypt. It is not improbable that they were of flint (cf. ibid. p. 411).   παρασχίσαντες...πᾶσαν: evisceration was by no means invariably carried out. The incision was almost always made on the left side. The stomach, entrails, lungs, and liver were normally removed, but the heart and kidneys were generally left in the corpse. The parts removed were usually deposited in four Canopic jars each of which was associated with one of the four sons of Horus (Dawson, *JEA* XIII (1927), 48).   ἐξ ὧν εἷλον: see note on 39,2.   ἐκκαθήραντες...τετριμμένοισι: palm wine was certainly used in Ancient Egypt, but no trace of its employment in mummification has ever been identified (Lucas–Harris, *AEMI*, p. 301).   θυμιήμασι: here the word refers to fragrant spices which were presumably intended to serve as a deodorant.

5. ἔπειτα τὴν νηδὺν...ὀπίσω: these substances were inserted as a temporary packing and might have functioned as a dehydrating agent, a deodorant, or a support for the body wall (Lucas–Harris, *AEMI*, p. 301).   σμύρνης: 'myrrh', derived from various species of Balsamodendron and Commiphora, was undoubtedly employed in mummification (ibid., p. 323).   κασίης: cassia, derived from *Cinnamon cassia*, has never been conclusively identified in mummies (ibid., pp. 308 ff.).   λιβανωτοῦ: frankincense was derived from trees of the genus *Boswellia* and also from *Commiphora pedunculata*. For material evidence of its use in mummification see ibid., p. 92.   συρράπτουσι ὀπίσω: such an act is most improbable at this stage since there would be no point in sewing up the wound after a preliminary packing. Presumably, Herodotus has inadvertently transposed the final sealing to this point (see below).   ταῦτα δὲ...λίτρῳ: the body was dried out by being covered in dry natron (natural soda) which occurred in great quantities along the Wadi Natrûn in the western desert (ibid., pp. 278 ff.). The old notion that a natron solution was used has been demonstrated to be unsound.   ἡμέρας ἑβδομήκοντα: Herodotus exaggerates. This is the classic figure for the entire series of rituals

from death to burial (W. R. Dawson and P. Gray, *Catalogue of Egyptian Antiquities in the British Museum*. I. *Mummies and Human Remains*, London 1968, p. x).   πλεῦναs ... ταριχεύειν: there is no doubt that the procedure was governed by a strict body of rules (cf. S. Sauneron, *Le Ritual d'embaumement*, Cairo 1952).

6. λούσαντες: this process is clearly identifiable (Lucas–Harris, *AEMI*, pp. 301 ff.). For the ritual significance of lustration by water see note on ch. 37. κατειλίσσουσι ... κατατετμημένοισι: before beginning this stage the embalming wound would be closed. It might be sewn up, as Herodotus claims (see above), but this method was rare. Normally the incision was simply covered with a plate of metal or beeswax fixed in position by molten resin (Smith–Dawson, pp. 100, 152 ff.). Bandaging was an elaborate process and tended to become more complex and decorative the later the mummy.   τῷ κόμμι: Egyptian ḳmyt (*Wb*. V, p. 39, 3–14). Liquid resin was normally poured over a mummy after wrapping (Lucas–Harris, *AEMI*, pp. 312 ff.).

7. ξύλινον τύπον ἀνθρωποειδέα: wooden anthropoid coffins are amongst the commonest surviving Egyptian artefacts (A. Niwinski, *LdÄ* V, 430 ff.). ἐσεργνῦσι: this compound is a Herodotean *hapax legomenon*.   ἐν οἰκήματι θηκαίῳ: 'in a sepulchral chamber'. Diodorus describes these installations as οἰκήματα πολυτελῆ (I 91,7).

87,1. τοὺς δὲ ... βουλομένους: this technique is reminiscent of that employed for the Apis bulls (cf. W. Spiegelberg, *ZÄS* LVI (1920), 1 ff.).

2–3. ἐπεὰν ... ἐξάγει: κέδρος in classical texts refers to a type of juniper, not cedar as we know it (A. Lucas, *JEA* XVII (1931), 13 ff.). It is quite impossible that an oil of this tree could have had the massively corrosive effect described here (Lucas–Harris, *AEMI*, pp. 15 ff.). If Herodotus has correctly identified the oil, it probably served to arrest decomposition until the body could be desiccated. When released, it could well have brought portions of viscera with it, but this would have been an incidental result of natural decomposition, not an intentional consequence (cf. Dawson, *JEA* XIII (1927), 48). Embalmers using such a technique would, therefore, be concerned essentially with no more than desiccation, saving time and effort by omitting the evisceration process. At least one mummy appears to exemplify such a process (R. Engelbach and D. E. Derry, *ASAE* XLI (1942), 248).

2. ἐν ὦν ἔπλησαν: see note on 39,2.   οὔτε ἀναταμόντες ... τὴν νηδύν: some mummies do indeed show these features (Engelbach and Derry, op. cit., pp. 246 ff.).   τὰς προκειμένας ἡμέρας: see note on 86,5.

3. ἀπ᾽ ὦν ἔδωκαν: see above.   οὐδὲν ἔτι πρηγματευθέντες: they could hardly have dispensed with bandaging.

88. ἡ δὲ τρίτη: see note on 86,2.   συρμαίη ... τὴν κοιλίην: the use of the term συρμαίη, 'purge', suggests that this process was intended simply to evacuate waste from the stomach and no more (Lucas–Harris, *AEMI*, p. 302). Again, therefore, the evisceration process is omitted. Such a technique would be nothing but a variation of that described in the previous chapter.   τὰς ἑβδομήκοντα

ἡμέρας: see note on 86,5.   καὶ ἔπειτα...ἀποφέρεσθαι: as in 87,3, we should
assume that the embalmers at the very least bandaged the corpse.   ἀπ' ὧν
ἔδωκαν: see note on 39,2.   ἀποφέρεσθαι: this use of the infinitive to express
purpose is common after verbs of giving (Schwyzer, *Gr. Grammatik* II, pp. 362 ff.).
Lit.: 'so as to carry <it> away.'

89,1. τὰς δὲ γυναῖκας: delays in mummification were clearly frequent (e.g.
Engelbach and Derry, *ASAE* XLI (1942), 255, 261), but there is no evidence
that they were commoner in the case of women. Probably they are to be explained
in most cases as the result of pressure of work. The connection with sexual abuses
of the kind described by Herodotus may be nothing more than Greek gossip-
mongering.   τριταῖαι ἢ τεταρταῖαι: since the number 3 is much used by
Herodotus as a typical or symbolic number, it is advisable never to regard it as
accurate unless there is good reason to do so. Here, as often, it is probably being
employed simply to generate an impression of precision (see above, note on 77,2).

90,1. ὃς δ' ἂν...ἁρπασθείς: it seems improbable that this was universal since
veneration for the crocodile did not occur everywhere in Egypt (note on ch. 69),
and texts, both earlier and later than Herodotus, paint a very different picture
(Lichtheim, *Old and Middle Kingdoms*, p. 222); *Urk.*, I, 23; Manetho, *FGrHist* 609,
p. 28). Aelian mentions Ombos (modern Kôm Ombo), a major centre of crocodile worship, as a place where death by crocodile was regarded as a joyful event
(*NA* X 21: cf. Maximus of Tyre II 5; Josephus, *Ap.* II 7 (86)); and the very fact
that he singles this city out tends to confirm the suspicion that the notion
of apotheosis by crocodile, if it existed, was a localized phenomenon (H. Kees,
in S. R. K. Glanville (ed.), *Studies Presented to F. Ll. Griffith*, London 1932,
p. 404).   ἢ ὑπ' αὐτοῦ τοῦ ποταμοῦ...τεθνεώς: the Egyptians certainly believed
in apotheosis by drowning (ibid., pp. 402 ff.).

1–2. τούτους...θάπτουσι: this is no more than we should expect of a divine
being. The account of the obsequies of Neneferkaptah, who suffered this fate in
the demotic tale of Setem Khaemwese, probably gives a good idea of what could
be expected (Lichtheim, *Late Period*, p. 132).

1. τούτους: Herodotus switches to the plural by a *constructio ad sensum* (cf.
Kühner–Gerth, *Gr. Grammatik* II 1, p. 54).   ἐν ἰρῇσι θήκῃσι: in some areas,
these may have been communal vaults similar to those used for sacred animals
like the Apis (PM III 2, pp. 780 ff.), but, in the one case of a drowned person
known to me, the Graeco-Roman burial of Isadora at Tuna el-Gebel, an individual tomb of the standard type for the period is employed (PM IV, p. 174).

2. ἄλλον οὐδένα: Herodotus normally employs a dative after ἔξεστι, but the
accusative and infinitive is paralleled elsewhere in his work (Powell, *Lexicon*,
p. 125).

91,1–6. Ἑλληνικοῖσι...ἐπιτελέειν: cf. 79,1. To Herodotus the Greek character of
the festival of Perseus was so striking in the light of Egyptian distaste for foreign
customs that it became a θῶμα (see above, pp. 234 ff.).

1. τὸ δὲ σύμπαν εἰπεῖν: for this limitative infinitive see note on 4,1.
μηδ'...μηδαμῶν: infinitives dependent on verbs embodying a negative idea are

frequently preceded by an expletive μή (Goodwin, *Moods and Tenses*, p. 326). Herodotus chooses not to place one before χρᾶσθαι, but both negatives here are treated as though he had. The best mss precede μηδαμῶν with μηδαμά, but it does not fit well and is best deleted as a product of dittography.   *Χέμμις*: the name derived from the Egyptian *ḥnty Mnw*, and the modern name Akhmîm is a lineal descendant. It was the capital of the 9th Nome of Upper Egypt and is not to be confused with the Lower Egyptian Chemmis discussed at ch. 156 (Gardiner, *AEO* II, p. 40*).   νομοῦ τοῦ Θηβαϊκοῦ: cf. Diod. I 18,2. Here νομός does not mean 'nome', as so often in Herodotus' account of Egypt, but more generally 'administrative area' (cf. Powell, *Lexicon*, p. 233).   *Νέης πόλιος*: this enigmatic town has never been firmly identified, but a case can be made for its being a Greek settlement of some kind on the site of Ptolemais Hermiou (modern El-Manshah) (Alan B. Lloyd, *JHS* LXXXIX (1969), 80).

2. *Περσέος τοῦ Δανάης*: the legend of Perseus brought him into close contact with Egypt, Libya, and Ethiopia. At Chemmis he had evidently been identified with a local deity who must be either Horus or Min-Hor (Lloyd, *Commentary 1–98*, pp. 368 ff.).   ἰρὸν ... τοῦ Περσέος: Chemmis certainly boasted several major temples in ancient times, but remains are now few (S. Sauneron, *BIFAO* LI (1952), 123). Herodotus' description mentions several of the features to be expected, but it is impossible to determine the temple to which it relates.   πέριξ δὲ αὐτοῦ: cf. I 179,3. The accusative is more common after this preposition, both in Herodotus and other authors (Kühner–Gerth, *Gr. Grammatik* II 1, p. 453).

3. σφι: all mss read σφι, but, since a reflexive is required, Herwerden's addition of <σι> should be accepted.   σανδάλιόν ... δίπηχυ: flying-shoes given by Hermes feature prominently in the Perseus legend and, not surprisingly, they appear on Graeco-Roman coins from Akhmîm and also in the late writer Nonnus who came from that city. Reflexions of them in Egyptian myth would have been easy to find in this area: Antaeopolis, called *Ṯbw*, 'Sandal Town', in Egyptian, and sited not far from Akhmîm, was alleged to be the place where Horus made himself a pair of sandals from the hide of Seth, and the idea was also current in this area that the feet of a god brought prosperity wherever they trod (Lloyd, op. cit., pp. 368 ff.).   εὐθενέειν: Hude and several other editors have preferred this form, but all mss read εὐθηνέειν, and that is perfectly acceptable in Herodotus (cf. LSJ, p. 714,b, s.v.).

4. ποιεῦσι: the description of the games depicts them as entirely Greek in character. If it is trustworthy, it invalidates all suggestions that Herodotus is referring to the Climbing Ceremony celebrated at Akhmîm on behalf of Min or Min-Hor (so e.g. Sabri Kolta, pp. 151 ff.). We can only assume that, when Perseus was identified with the local god, Greeks resident in the area introduced games of a Hellenic type which were celebrated in association with the cult of the Egyptian god (Lloyd, op. cit., pp. 85 ff.).   ἔχοντα: 'extending' (cf. I 199,2; II 108,3; in general Powell, *Lexicon*, p. 156).

6. ἐκμεμαθηκότα: as usual, the perfect emphasizes a state of being: '<having learned and now> knowing' (cf. Chantraine, *Histoire du parfait grec*,

p. 155).   παρὰ τῆς μητρός: the preposition παρά is often used after πυνθάνομαι instead of the pure genitive (Kühner–Gerth, *Gr. Grammatik* II 1, p. 360).   αὐτοῦ κελεύσαντος: Herodotus is assuming, or had been told, that Perseus/Min-Hor had made an oracular pronouncement (see notes on ch. 83). Oracles are frequently involved in determining matters of cultic practice in Greek contexts (cf. I 167; P–W I, pp. 320 ff.).

92,1. οἱ κατύπερθε τῶν ἑλέων ... κατοικημένοι: the marsh area in question lay in the northern sector of the Delta (cf. Strabo XVII 1,15 (C800), 18 (C801), 20–1 (C802–3); Ball, *Contributions*, p. 4).   τοῖσι μὲν ... Αἰγύπτιοι: clearly Herodotus is not referring to the marsh-dwellers proper, who followed a unique lifestyle which could not possibly be described in this way (Heliodorus, *Aethiopica* I 5 ff.; Montet, *Everyday Life*, pp. 126 ff.). He must have in mind the inhabitants of villages or towns within, or closely associated with, the marshlands.   γυναικί μιῇ ... συνοικέει: Diodorus claims that, apart from priests, the Egyptians could have as many wives as they wished (I 80,1), and there are possible cases of polygamy in late texts (M. el-Amir, *BIFAO* LXII (1964), 103 ff.). Perhaps Herodotus' comment reflects standard practice rather than the full range of legal options.   ἀτὰρ ... ἐξεύρηται: cf. 77,4 for the situation elsewhere.   σφι: dative of the agent (note on ch. 84).

2. λωτόν: the flower was not called λωτός by the Egyptians but *sšn* (*Wb*. III, pp. 485, 486, 1–14). However, the slip has its parallels elsewhere (e.g. Diod. I 34,10). Here Herodotus is referring either to the white lotus (*Nymphaea lotus* L.), or the blue lotus (*Nymphaea caerulea* Savigny). They both now only occur in the Delta, though the latter is extremely uncommon (L. Keimer, *Egypt Travel Magazine*, XXV (Aug. 1956), 26).   ταῦτ' ἐπεὰν ... πυρί: loaves made from lotus seeds, which have a very high nutritional value, are well documented for pharaonic and post-pharaonic times, and Herodotus' description of their preparation squares well with more modern practice (W. Spanton, *Ancient Egypt* (1917), I, p. 4 ff.).

3. ἔστι δὲ ... μῆλον: we can accept this claim with confidence, in spite of the lack of Ancient Egyptian evidence, since rhizomes of Nymphaeaceae have certainly been eaten in post-pharaonic times (Keimer, op. cit., p. 26).   ἐὸν ... στρογγύλον: in general statements predicative adjectives often appear as neuters singular functioning like neuter nouns (cf. Kühner–Gerth, *Gr. Grammatik* II 2, pp. 59 ff.). ἐόν should strictly be feminine singular but is attracted into the neuter by proximity to στρογγύλον.

4. ἄλλα κρίνεα ... ἐμφερέα: Herodotus is discussing the Indian or rose lotus (*Nelumbo nucifera* Gaertn.). This is the earliest evidence of it in Egypt, but it is subsequently mentioned frequently under the name of κύαμος Αἰγύπτιος (e.g. Strabo XVII 1,15 (C799 ff.) (Keimer, op. cit., pp. 21, 28).   ὁ καρπὸς: the 'fruit', i.e. the seed and seed vessel together (cf. Theophrastus, *HP* I 2,1).   ἐν ἄλλῃ κάλυκι: κάλυξ here means 'flower, calyx' (Lloyd, *Commentary 1–98*, p. 373). Herodotus' wording indicates that he thought there was one κάλυξ with a fruit and another without. This is quite incorrect. All κάλυκες contain a fruit, though it would certainly have been more obvious in some cases than

others.   κηρίῳ ... ὁμοιότατον: the description is very apt (Keimer, op. cit., p. 27).   ἐν τούτῳ τρωκτὰ ... συχνά: the seeds are about the size of a small acorn and are imbedded in cavities on the upper surface of the fruit. 5. τὴν δὲ βύβλον ... τρώγουσι: Herodotus' comments on the papyrus (*Cyperus papyrus*) are impeccable. It was last recorded wild in Egypt in the early 19th cent. but is now extinct there as a natural growth since the marshy conditions which it requires have largely disappeared, though it is 'farmed' for the modern tourist papyrus industry. It was abundant in antiquity and harvested regularly both for food and industrial purposes such as boat-building, rope-making, paper-manufacture, and carpets (Täckholm–Drar II, pp. 104 ff.).   οἳ δὲ ἂν ... τρώγουσι: it could also be eaten raw (Sir Armand Ruffer, *Mémoires de l'institut d'Egypte*, I (1919), 67).   οἱ δέ τινες ... σιτέονται: cf. note on 77,4. Herodotus must be exaggerating, since an exclusive diet of fish is not feasible. Again, he has taken a tendency and made too much of it.

93,1. οἱ ἀγελαῖοι: Herodotus here anticipates 4th-cent. zoological theory where a clear distinction is made between τὰ ἀγελαῖα and τὰ μοναδικά (Arist. *HA* I, 1 ff.; *Pol.* I 8 (1256a); Plato, *Pol.* 264d). The following description makes it clear that he is using the term here pre-eminently, if not exclusively, of the genus *Tilapia*.   ἐν μὲν τοῖσι ποταμοῖσι: i.e. the Delta arms of the Nile (for which see 17,3–6).   οὐ μάλα γίνονται: 'are not born at all'. For οὐ μάλα in this sense see Powell, *Lexicon*, p. 213,a, μάλα, I.   ἐν τῇσι λίμνῃσι: i.e. the lakes of the northern Delta, precursors of, if not identical with, modern lakes such as Burullus and Menzala (cf. Strabo XVII 1,7 (C793), 14 (C799), 21 (C803); Ptolemy, *Geog.* IV 5,44; Ball, *Egypt*, p. 22).   ἐπεάν σφεας ... ἐς θάλασσαν: fish of the genus *Tilapia*, which are clearly at issue here, are fresh- or brackish-water species and do not migrate to the sea, though some Nile species, e.g. the mullet, are known to do so (Boulenger, pp. 92, 402, 447, 459).

1–3. ἡγέονται ... γίνονται: this account, redolent of paradoxography (see above, pp. 232, 234 ff., 239), is based on the breeding habits of *Tilapia nilotica* L. and picks up the fact that, when the female has laid her eggs, she takes them into her mouth followed by the semen of the male. The fertilized eggs are then retained in the mouth until they hatch. The process has, however, been badly misunderstood; in particular, Herodotus believes that it is the male which takes the eggs into his mouth, and that they are being eaten rather than incubated (in general see M. Dambach and I. Wallert, *CdE* XLI (1966), 273 ff.).

3–4. οἳ δ' ἂν αὐτῶν ... ῥόον: pure paradoxography (cf. Aelian, *NA* IX 42). The *Tilapia* has a spot, which might be misinterpreted as a bruise, on both sides of its head (Boulenger, p. 525).

3. τὰ ἐπ' ἀριστερὰ: accusative of respect.

4. ἁμάρτοιεν: the optative after a primary tense in final clauses is highly irregular but does occur several times in Homer (Goodwin, *Moods and Tenses*, p. 115). Kühner–Gehrt (*Gr. Grammatik* II 1, pp. 59 ff.) suggest that, unlike the subjunctive, the optative presents the verbal action as merely conceived of rather than expected.

5–6. ἐπεὰν δὲ...οἱ ἰχθύες: ingenious but untrue. The pools acquired their fish by way of canals as the waters of the inundation rose.

5. διηθέοντος τοῦ ὕδατος: for the phenomenon of filtration see Bonneau, *La Crue*, p. 63 ff.   καὶ αὐτίκα...πίμπλαται πάντα: the parataxis is typical of Herodotus (cf. Kühner–Gehrt, op.cit. II 2, p. 231).

94,1. οἱ περὶ τὰ ἕλεα οἰκέοντες: cf. 92,1. The use of castor oil by the inhabitants of this area is understandable since they were amongst the poorer elements of Egypt, and this type of oil was cheap (Strabo XVII 2,5 (C824); Schnebel, pp. 197 ff.). σιλλικυπρίων: the castor-oil plant (*Ricinus communis* L.) (Lucas–Harris, *AEMI*, p. 332).   κίκι: an accurate rendering of the Egyptian name *k3k3* (*Wb.* V, p. 109, 2–7).   παρὰ τὰ χείλεα...ταῦτα: information from pharaonic times is limited, but the castor-oil plant was widely cultivated in Hellenistic times and is still common, particularly in Upper Egypt (Lucas–Harris, *AEMI*, p. 332). It is entirely credible, though undemonstrable, that Herodotus' marsh-dwellers grew it in the manner described.

2. τοῦτον...ἀπιποῦσι: cf. Pliny, *NH* XV 25, and Dioscorides IV 161.   οἱ δὲ...συγκομίζονται: Herodotus may be in error here, since Pliny excludes this method for Egypt (loc. cit.). However, Pliny wrote long after Herodotus, and the method is known elsewhere in the ancient world (loc. cit.). It seems, advisable, therefore, to keep an open mind on the matter.   ἔστι δὲ πῖον... παρέχεται: castor oil was certainly used for lamps in Ancient Egypt, though it burns with a loud crackling noise (L. Keimer, *Die Gartenpflanzen im alten Ägypten*, I, Hamburg 1924, p. 119).   τοῦ ἐλαίου: olive oil was standard for such purposes in the Greek world (A. S. Pease, *RE* XVII, 2466), but the Egyptian variety burned with an unpleasant smell and was never popular (Lucas–Harris, *AEMI*, p. 333).

95,1. τοὺς κώνωπας: 'gnats, mosquitoes' (LSJ, p. 1019,a, κώνωψ). Such insects are extremely numerous in Egypt, where the heat and large expanses of water create ideal conditions for them (Sigerist I, p. 253).   τὰ ἄνω τῶν ἑλέων: cf. note on 92,1.   οἱ πύργοι: it is still common in Egypt to sleep on house roofs (Lane, p. 158), but the precise significance of πύργος is puzzling. It may refer to elevations which are occasionally represented on the rooftops of houses (N. de Garis Davies, *Metropolitan Museum Studies*, I 2 (1929), 245 ff.). Alternatively, it could denote the narrow towers shown next to temples and other buildings in the Palestrina Mosaic (G. Gullini, *I mosaici di Palestrina*, Suppl. di *Archeologia Classica*, I, Rome 1956, pl. I).

2. τοῖσι δὲ...μεμηχάνηται: marsh-dwellers used much simpler dwellings than most other Egyptians, often contenting themselves with low cabins of reeds which could not offer the advantage of height (cf. O. Bates, *Harvard African Studies*, I (1917), 267).   πᾶς...ἔκτηται: the northern Delta area has been of paramount importance in Egypt's freshwater fishing industry in modern times (ibid., pp. 199 ff.), and there is no reason to doubt that the same held true in antiquity. Fishing-nets would, therefore, have been a widespread, if not universal, possession.   ἰχθῦς: the nets could also be used for fowling (ibid., p. 267).

τῆς μὲν... τὴν δὲ νύκτα: the genitive indicates time during which, the accusative total extent. Trans.: 'during the day... through the night' (cf. Kühner–Gerth, *Gr. Grammatik* II 1, p. 446, n. 7). τὴν δὲ νύκτα... κατεύδει: a bed-canopy, possibly intended as a mosquito net, is known (G. Reisner and W. S. Smith, *Giza*, II, Cambridge, Mass. 1955, pp. 23 ff.). Fishing-nets would not have been very efficient, but seine nets as long as 100 m. with meshes as small as 1/8 inch are known (Bates, p. 267). If these were folded over on themselves several times, they might well have been capable of reducing the nuisance to tolerable proportions.

3. διὰ δὲ τοῦ δικτύου... ἀρχήν: this comment smacks strongly of paradoxography (see above, pp. 232, 234 ff., 239). ἀρχήν: for this common adverbial use of the accusative of ἀρχήν in the sense of 'to begin with, at all' see Powell, *Lexicon*, p. 48.

96,1. τὰ δὲ δὴ... φορτηγέουσι: Herodotus is describing freighters only; other types of vessel are clearly excluded. ἐστὶ... ποιεύμενα: for such periphrastic forms see notes on 37,4; 52,1. τῆς ἀκάνθης: 'acacia' (Egyptian *šnḏt*, *Wb.* IV, pp. 520, 9–13, 521, 1–15). In Greek shipbuilding it was used only for interior work, but ships were frequently made of it in Egypt (B. Landström, *Ships of the Pharaohs, Architectura Navalis*, I, London 1970, Index, s.v. 'acacia'). τῷ Κυρηναίῳ λωτῷ: generally identified with the common N. African species *Zizyphus lotus* (L.) Willd. (Steier, *RE* XIII, 1515), but the two types of tree are only alike in both possessing thorns. κόμμι: acacia gum (Egyptian *ḳmyt nt šnḏt*) is frequently mentioned in Egyptian texts (cf. W. Wreszinski, *Die Medizin der alten Ägypter*, III. *Der Papyrus Ebers*, Leipzig 1913, pp. 54, 16, 17, 19). ὅσον τε διπήχεα: the knotty character of the acacia means that it is impossible to extract long planks from it (G. Jéquier, *BIFAO* XIX (1922), 31 ff.). πλινθηδόν: 'after the fashion of brickwork'. Since short planks had to be used to construct the hull, they were fitted in such a way that the vertical joins 'broke bond' and created a pattern of horizontal and vertical lines resembling the joins in a brick wall (cf. P. E. Newberry, *Beni Hasan*, I, London 1893, pl. XXIX).

2. περὶ γόμφους: the γόμφοι, lit. 'pegs, pins, dowels' (Lloyd, *Commentary 1–98*, pp. 385 ff.) were tenons, sometimes as much as 6–10 inches long, which were fitted into mortices cut in the edge of planks in order to bind them together vertically. The technique is frequently exemplified in representations and surviving examples of Egyptian boatbuilding (Landström, op. cit., pp. 28 ff., 38, 90) and continued into modern times (J. Hornell, *Water Transport*, Cambridge 1946, p. 215). A boat built in this way during the Persian period was excavated at Mataria, Cairo, in 1987 (C. W. Haldane, 'Ancient Egyptian Hull Construction', Diss. Texas A & M University, Ann Arbor 1994, pp. 240 ff.). ζυγὰ: lit. 'thwarts, benches' (LSJ, p. 757,a, s.v. ζυγόν III). Structurally they tied the vessel together in a lateral sense, but they could be used as benches or as supports for deck planking. In vessels designed to carry particularly heavy burdens there were frequently several superimposed rows of them (Landström, op. cit., pp. 28 ff., 41, 54, 71, 84, 90 ff., 99 (317), 101 (319), etc.). νομεῦσι: 'frames, ribs'. These were certainly used in Egypt to help a vessel retain its shape once built, but they were far from being an invariable feature. Even those vessels in which they occurred

will normally have been built without them, only acquiring them at a late stage in their life when strengthening the hull became necessary (Alan B. Lloyd, *CQ* ns XXIX (1979), 45 ff.). Herodotus' comment is, therefore, an accurate reflection of standard practice.   ἐν ὧν ἐπάκτωσαν: for the gnomic aorist with tmesis see note on 39,2. Traditionally the verb has been rendered 'caulk', but recent research strongly supports the translation 'bind, fasten', i.e. Herodotus is referring to the practice of binding hull planks together with rope, as in the Khufu boat preserved at Gîza (C. W. Haldane and C. W. Shelmerdine, *CQ* XL (1990), 535 ff.; S. Vinson, *ZPE* CXIII (1996), 197 ff.).   τῇ βύβλῳ: if caulking were at issue, nothing would be more likely than the use of this readily available material. In modern times even strips of the sailors' clothing could be used (Hornell, op. cit., p. 218). If, on the other hand, the reference is to tying hulk-planks together—and that is the more probable view—it is papyrus ropes which are at issue.

3. πηδάλιον δὲ ἕν: no doubt this was normal, but more could be carried (Landström, op. cit., *passim*). In Greece the standard number was two (Casson, pp. 224 ff.).   καὶ τοῦτο...διαβύνεται: steering-oars could certainly be fitted in the centre line at the stern in a notch specially designed to hold it (e.g. Landström, op. cit., pp. 71 ff., 74 ff.). In the strictest sense, however, Egyptian ships did not have a keel (τρόπις).   ἱστῷ δὲ ἀκανθίνῳ: if the mast was indeed made of acacia, it would normally have been constructed from several pieces of timber fished together (A. Köster, *Das antike Seewesen*, Berlin 1923, p. 17).   ἱστίοισι δὲ βυβλίνοισι: there is no proof from pharaonic sources of the use of papyrus for sails, but it is inconceivable that so cheap and obvious a material should not have been employed. This suspicion is confirmed by observation of modern Egyptian sailing-boats which show an extraordinary range of nondescript materials used for sake of cheapness. In modern times papyrus sails are used most effectively on lake Titicaca (Hornell, op. cit., p. 227).   ταῦτα τὰ πλοῖα...ὧδε: this distinction in techniques is amply documented (Landström, op. cit., pp. 46, 55, 117 (361)). The strong current of the Nile would certainly need to be counteracted by a stiff northerly breeze (λαμπρὸς ἄνεμος), but this is a common phenomenon and frequently provides ideal sailing conditions for vessels travelling south.

4–5.   ἔστι...τὸν πλόον: there is no absolutely unimpeachable Egyptian evidence of this practice, but possible examples or hints of it have been identified (Lloyd, *Commentary 1–98*, pp. 389 ff.).

4. ἐπιφέρεσθαι: this final infinitive is common after verbs of sending (cf. Goodwin, *Moods and Tenses*, pp. 308 ff.).

5. πλήθεϊ πολλά: For the alliteration and construction see notes on 1,1; 74.

97,1. αἱ δὲ πόλιες μοῦναι...ὑπερέχουσι: cf. Diod. I 36; Hurst, pp. 40, 313. It was the practice throughout the country to build settlements on the highest available land which would have kept them safe from all but the most exceptional floods (K. Butzer, CAH³ I p. 66).   πορθμεύονται...τοῦ πεδίου: this is confirmed by many sources, ancient and modern (e.g. Aristides, *Or.* 36,83; Hurst, p. 195).

2. ἐς μέν γε...ὁ πλόος: at the height of the inundation it would have been perfectly feasible for boats to skirt the edge of the desert plateau on which the

Gîza pyramids stand, since Egyptian ships were of very shallow draught and the average depth of the flood was between 1 and 2 m. ἔστι δὲ οὐκ οὗτος: the verb has an unusually strong existential nuance, hence the emphatic position: 'But this is not (the real) water-route but rather via the apex of the Delta and city of Kerkasôros.' Κερκάσωρον πόλιν: see note on 17,3. Ναύκρατιν: see note on ch. 178. Κανώβου: see note on 15,1. ἥξεις: for this vivid use of tense and person see note on 5,2. Ἄνθυλλάν: for this city see also Stephanus of Byzantium, s.v. Ἄνθυλλάν; Athenaeus I 33; *P ZenCol* IV, p. 11. Available evidence is quite inadequate for locating the site, though Gynaecopolis has been claimed as a possibility (cf. A. Calderini, *Dizionario dei nomi geographici*, I, Cairo 1935, p. 44). τὴν Ἀρχάνδρυ καλευμένην: also mentioned by Stephanus of Byzantium (s.v. Ἀρχανδρούπολις) and Geogr. Ravenna (s.v. *Archa*). As with the previous town, attempts have been made to pinpoint the location, but the data are quite inadequate for this purpose (cf. Calderini, op. cit., p. 224).

98,1. ἐς ὑποδήματα: cf. Diod. I 52; Plato, *Alc.* I 123b–c. In the Persian empire taxes could be paid in the form of a regular monetary tribute or in kind. Imposts of the latter type are known from other contexts to have been paid to the household of the Great King (A. Andreades (rev. C. N. Brown), *A History of Greek Public Finance*, Cambridge, Mass. 1933, pp. 89 ff.). According to Athenaeus (I 33) Anthylla was responsible for girdles, not slippers. ἐξ ὅσου... Αἴγυπτος: i.e. since 525 BC. As often, this present use of εἶναι denotes a situation which came into existence in the past and continues into the present (Goodwin, *Moods and Tenses*, p. 9).

2. ἡ δὲ ἑτέρη...πόλις: for this section the readings of *P Rylands* I 55 are available in addition to those of the mss (Paap, pp. 41 ff.). They are significantly different at several points and raise the question of the authority of papyrological evidence as against the mss. It is universally agreed that the papyri and mss reflect the same recension. The papyri are earlier, but that in itself does not mean that they are more accurate. Patent errors in *P. Rylands'* recording of this and other chapters indicate that its testimony here should be treated with caution. The best policy is to take each problem individually, and, on this principle, *P Rylands* only seems preferable in its much more forceful positioning of γε after Αἰγύπτιον. Archander and his brother Architeles were Achaean heroes whose legend was closely related to that of Danaus and his daughters. It was presumably the latter affinity which led to the heroes' connection with Egypt. Herodotus' genealogy is by no means the only one extant (cf., in general, v. Geisau, *KP* I, 501). εἴη δ'ἄν...τὸ οὔνομα: on Herodotus' methods of argument see above, p. 236. For this use of the potential optative to indicate something which might prove to be true see Goodwin, *Moods and Tenses*, p. 79.

99–182. These chapters are mainly devoted to Egyptian history. They fall into two sections: chs. 99–142 (kings Min to Sethos) and 147–82 (kings Psammetichus I to Amasis). For a discussion of the salient features see above, pp. 238 ff.

99–142. The rulers of Egypt from Min to Sethos are discussed: Min (ch. 99), Nitocris (100), Moiris (101), Sesostris (102–10), Pheros (111), Proteus (112–20), Rhampsinitus (121–4), Cheops, Chephren, Mycerinus (124–34), Asychis (136), Anysis (137, 140), Sabacos (137, 139), and Sethos (141).

99,1. μέχρι μὲν ... ὄψιος: one of Herodotus' periodic statements about sources. For its implications see above, pp. 228 ff.   λέγουσά ἐστι: cf. notes on 37,4; 52,1. **2.** Μῖνα: cf. 4,3. Min, called Menes by Manetho (*FGrHist* 609, pp. 16 ff.), was claimed by the Egyptians from at least the New Kingdom to be their first historical king and, as such, would have ascended the throne *c*.3200 BC. Some scholars regard him as entirely unhistorical, but there is a good case for identifying him with Narmer, the first king of the Ist Dynasty (Lloyd, *Commentary 99–182*, pp. 6 ff; A. J. Spencer, *Early Egypt: The Rise of Civilisation in the Nile Valley*, London, 1993, pp. 63 ff.).   οἱ ἱρέες: the priests were a major source for Herodotus' Egyptian history (see above, pp. 230 ff.).   τοῦτο μὲν ἀπογεφυρῶσαι ... ῥέειν: cf. I 75 for a suspiciously comparable enterprise. The project ascribed to Menes would have been quite impossible. The tradition is probably pure legend based on several factors: the belief that Menes founded Memphis; the fact that Menes developed into an embodiment of the ideal of kingship and, as such, must be concerned with irrigation projects (note on 108,2); and the fact that flood protection was a perennial problem in this area down to modern times (I. E. S. Edwards, *CAH*[3] I 2, p. 15).   τοῦτο μὲν: strictly, not answered by the expected τοῦτο δέ, but it is restated in para. 4 and this second τοῦτο μέν is subsequently answered in the usual way.   παρὰ τὸ ὄρος ... πρὸς Λιβύης: cf. note on 8,2. **3.** ὑπὸ Περσέων: Egypt became a province of the Persian empire in 525 BC as a result of the conquest by Cambyses (note on ch. 1).   ὡς ἀπεργμένος ῥέῃ: so Hude, but the text is problematic. All mss read ῥέει and all but one ὡς. If we accept these readings, the clause becomes causal: 'since it flows...' However, *Laur.* LXX 6 reads ὅς for ὡς, yielding a relative clause which runs considerably more smoothly. As for the participle, the mss vacillate between the perfect ἀπεργμένος and the present ἀπεργόμενος. The former, 'in a state of being dyked off', is far preferable to the present, 'in the process of being dyked off'. **4.** πόλιν ... καλέεται: this city certainly dated from the very beginning of Egyptian history. It was originally called 'Inb ḥḏ, 'the White Wall', and was established to guarantee control of the northern part of the country after its conquest by Narmer/Menes (Edwards, op. cit., p. 16). It did not acquire the name Memphis (Egyptian Mn-nfr) until the beginning of the VIth Dynasty (*c*.2345–2181 BC) (Gardiner, *AEO* II, p. 122* ff.). Herodotus' conviction that Menes' activities were still reflected in the hydraulic régime of the area in his time is almost certainly unsound, since there is increasing evidence that the site of Memphis at the beginning of Egyptian history lay significantly to the north of the later location (L. Giddy, *JEA* LXXVII (1991), 6).   ἔξωθεν ... ἀπέργει: the claim that Memphis was largely surrounded by water is confirmed by Egyptian and classical sources (Lichtheim, *Late Period*, pp. 75 ff.; Strabo XVII 1,32 (C808)).   τοῦτο δὲ ... ἀξιαπηγητότατον: the assertion that the temple of Hephaestus (the

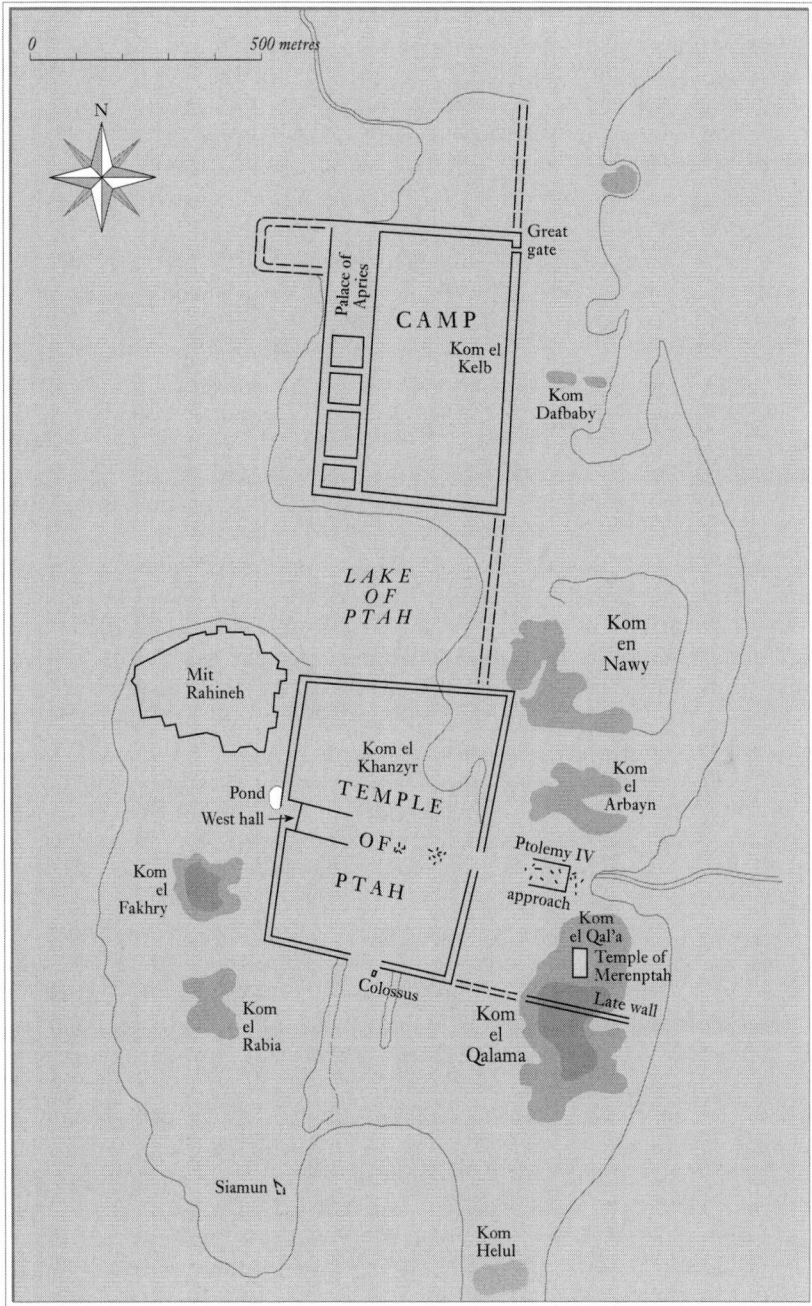

Map 22. Memphis (sketch map by Flinders Petrie)

Egyptian Ptah, see 3,1) was built by Menes certainly conforms to Egyptian tradition (cf. A. Badawi, *Memphis als zweite Landeshauptstadt im Neuen Reich*, Cairo 1958, p. 13). It became one of the most important of all Egyptian shrines and amply merited Herodotus' glowing eulogy (Kees, *Ancient Egypt*, pp. 147 ff.). He subsequently mentions royal building-works on the site on many occasions (chs. 101, 108, 110, 121, 136, 153: cf. 112, 176).

100,1. οἱ ἱρέες: see above, pp. 230 ff.   ἐκ βύβλου: this papyrus presumably contained a king-list comparable to the Turin Canon which, when complete, catalogued the kings of Egypt from the Dynasty of the Gods down to the XIXth Dynasty (cf. Gardiner, *Egypt*, pp. 47 ff.).   τριηκοσίων τε καὶ τριήκοντα: this figure is meant to embrace all the kings of Egypt between Min and Sethos (i.e. Shabataka, note on ch. 141), and is strikingly close to the total of 323 for the same period which appears in Manetho (Alan B. Lloyd, *Historia*, XXXVII (1988), 33 ff.).   ὀκτωκαίδεκα μὲν Αἰθίοπες: for this Ethiopian or Nubian XXVth Dynasty see notes on chs. 137, 139.   οἱ δὲ ἄλλοι ἄνδρες Αἰγύπτιοι: this claim predictably ignores the Asiatic Hyksos rulers of the Second Intermediate Period and also glosses over the Libyan antecedents of the XXIInd–XXIIIrd Dynasties (cf. Gardiner, *Egypt*, p. 324 ff., 441).

2–4. τῇ δὲ γυναικὶ...γένηται: for other classical versions of the Nitocris legend see Manetho, *FGrHist* 609, pp. 26 ff., Eratosthenes, ibid., 610 F 1<κβ>, Dio Cassius LXII 6; LXXIX 23, and Julian, *Or.* III 129b. Like most Herodotean traditions on Egyptian history, this narrative contains a grain of historical reminiscence but is heavily overlaid with folklore. It also shows evidence of confusion with the famous courtesan Rhodopis (note on ch. 135: in general see Lloyd, *Commentary 99–182*, pp. 13 ff.).

2. ἥτις: simply 'who' without any indefinite nuance. ὅστις can be used in this way in Homer (Kühner–Gerth, *Gr. Grammatik* II 2, p. 400).   τῇ Βαβυλωνίῃ: cf. I 185 ff. She was probably a legendary reflex of Adad-Guppi, the mother of the Babylonian king Nabonidus (W. Röllig, in *Beiträge zur Alten Geschichte und deren Nachleben*, Festschrift für Franz Altheim, I, Berlin 1969, pp. 127 ff.). Νίτωκρις: the name in Egyptian was *Nt-ἰḳr.tἰ*, 'Neith is excellent', which was particularly common in the Late Period (Ranke, pp. 181, 27). The historical prototype of Herodotus' Nitocris must be the queen Nitocris/*Nt-ἰḳr.tἰ* located at the end of the VIth Dynasty by Manetho and the Turin Canon (Gardiner, *Egypt*, pp. 102, 436).   τὴν ἔλεγον τιμωρέουσαν...τούτῳ τιμωρέουσαν: for this anaphoric use of a demonstrative with repetition of the verb cf. II 152,1; III 14,1; IV 145,2; VI 42,2. This rather loose stylistic feature probably reflects the affinity of Herodotus' style with that of oral narrative (Kühner–Gerth, *Gr. Grammatik* II 1, p. 661). Vengeance frequently figures in the corpus of motives ascribed by Herodotus to his characters (see above, p. 233).

3. ποιησαμένην...μεγάλου: the common folk-motif of the *fête fatale* (Lloyd, *Historia*, XXXVII (1988), 39).   καινοῦν: the present infinitive expresses intention (cf. Goodwin, *Moods and Tenses*, p. 9).   καλέσασαν [δὲ] μιν: Abicht's

widely approved deletion of δέ is unjustified. Here it stands for γάρ as often in Homer, though the usage is rare in prose (Denniston, *Greek Particles*, pp. 169 ff.).

101,1. τῶν δὲ ἄλλων βασιλέων: the genitive is possessive dependent upon οὐδεμίαν ἔργων ἀπόδεξιν, and its position is highly emphatic. Trans. 'As for the other kings,...'   γὰρ: an example of the anticipatory γάρ of explanation (cf. Denniston, *Greek Particles*, pp. 70 ff.). It indicates the reason for omitting all the kings except Moeris. Lit. '...inasmuch as they denied that any of their works were of any degree of renown, except for one, the last of them, Moeris...'   Μοίριος: i.e. Amenemhet III. The Greek name is best regarded as a corruption of his prenomen *Nĭ-m3ʿ-rʿ* one pronunciation of which would have sounded like *Amuaria*. A part may also have been played by the name of lake Moeris, which was closely associated with him. In Herodotus' chronological scheme he is placed *c.*1350 BC, whereas his correct dates are *c.*1842–1797 BC (Lloyd, *Historia*, XXXVII (1988), 32).

2. τοῦτον δὲ ... προπύλαια: cf. Diod. I 51. For this motif see note on 99,4. In this case the tradition is confirmed by the discovery of remains of a gateway of Amenemhet III in the northern part of the temenos wall. Other evidence of building or artistic work in the XIIth Dynasty, to which this king belonged, is also known (PM III 2, pp. 832, 835–7, 847, 849).   λίμνην τε ... ἐπιμνήσομαι: see notes on 149–50.

102–10: An account of the reign of Sesostris in which are discussed his conquests (102–6, 110), an attempt on his life (107), and his benefactions to Egypt (108–9). The core of Herodotus' narrative is provided by an Egyptian tradition which presented Sesostris as a model of the ideal of kingship. This certainly contained an historical element, but it has been supplemented and contaminated by folklore, nationalist propaganda, and Greek attitudes (Lloyd, *Commentary 99–182*, pp. 16 ff.; A. I. Ivantchik, *Historia*, XLVIII (1999), 395 ff.).

102,1. Σέσωστρις: the name originates from the Egyptian royal name *S-n-wsrt*, 'Man of <the Goddess> Wosret', borne by three kings of the XIIth Dynasty (M. Malaise, *CdE* XLI (1966), 244 ff.). The historical prototype of the legendary Sesostris was either Senwosret I or III or a combination of the two. Diodorus, unlike Herodotus, places Sesostris seven generations after Moeris (I 53,1).

2. οἱ ἱρέες: see above, pp. 230 ff.   πρῶτον μὲν ... βραχέων: cf. Diod. I 53,5; 55,2; Strabo XVI 1,6 (C687); XVI 4,4 (C769); 4,7 (C770). Herodotus presumably had in mind the coast of Saudi Arabia, but no Egyptian pharaoh ever subdued this area. The tradition may be a distortion of historical Egyptian activities in Sinai and the Red Sea, but more probably has its origin in anti-Persian propaganda in that Sesostris' conquest of Arabia would present him as surpassing Achaemenid achievements (Braun, p. 16).   ἐκ τοῦ Ἀραβίου κόλπου: i.e. the Gulf of Suez (Alan B. Lloyd, *JEA* LXIII (1977), 268).   τὴν Ἐρυθρὴν θάλασσαν: here the Red Sea, but the term can have a much wider application (note on 8,1).   ἐς ὃ πλέοντά ... βραχέων: no such obstacles exist or could have existed. This ingredient in the tradition cannot be of Egyptian origin, and is best explained as a piece of Greek rationalism intended to explain why Sesostris turned back.   ἀπικέσθαι: for this infinitive see note on 64,2.

3–5. ἐνθεῦτεν... ἀνάλκιδες: cf. Diod. I 55; Manetho, *FGrHist* 609, pp. 30 ff.). Sesostris' conquests grow ever more extensive as time goes on and come to embrace the whole of Asia as well as parts of Europe. This tradition was inspired partly by Egypt's historical activities in Asia during the Middle Kingdom and later and partly by nationalist propaganda (Malaise, op. cit., pp. 264 ff.).

4. ὁτέοισι...: see also ch. 106; Manetho, loc. cit.; Diod. I 55,7 ff. This tradition is not consistent with the attitudes of Ancient Egyptians, who would have been most disinclined to admit the valour of any of their defeated enemies, and must have been injected into the Sesostris legend by Greeks (Lloyd, *Commentary 99–182*, pp. 20 ff.). Syntactically, note that we have two μέν clauses (ὁτέοισι μέν, τούτοισι μέν) followed by two δέ clauses (ὁτεων δέ, τούτοισι δέ). This arrangement has many parallels and is always highly emphatic (Kühner–Gerth, *Gr. Grammatik* II 2, pp. 269 ff.).   ἀλκίμοισι: this word has a distinctly poetical colouring (LSJ, p. 67,b, s.v.).   [περί]: the employment of the preposition is a unique usage and almost certainly an interpolation, since γλίχομαι elsewhere in Herodotus takes a straight genitive and in other authors a genitive or accusative (LSJ, pp. 351,b–352,a).

5. αἰδοῖα γυναικὸς: there is a hieroglyphic sign which reflects the genitals of a woman (Gardiner, *Egyptian Grammar*, Sign List, N41), but it would have been quite unrecognizable as such to a non-Egyptian observer. We can be confident that it played no part in the evolution of this tradition.   ἀνάλκιδες: Herodotus is the only prose author to use this word, and that only in the present passage (LSJ, p. 111,b, s.v.).

103,1. τὴν Εὐρώπην... τοὺς Θρήικας: for other classical accounts in the same vein cf. Manetho, *FGrHist* 609, pp. 30 ff.; Diod. I 55,4 ff.; Strabo XV 1,6 (C686–7). The claim is totally unhistorical and has its origin in nationalist propaganda aimed at making Sesostris' conquests equal or even surpass those of the Persians (Malaise, *CdE* XLI (1966), 264 ff., 270 ff.).   ἐν μὲν γὰρ... οὐκέτι: note the use of γνώμη to justify Herodotus' claim (see above, p. 229). It is possible that the stelae were local monuments erroneously attributed to Sesostris, but it seems equally likely that they never existed at all and were simply the product of some such thought-process as: 'Sesostris recorded his conquest with stelae. He conquered Scythia and Thrace. Therefore, there must be stelae in these countries.' For a detailed discussion see S. West, *Historia*, XLI (1992), 117 ff.

2. ἐπὶ Φάσι ποταμῷ: cf. Diod. I 55,4. The Phasis (modern Rion), which flows into the eastern end of the Black Sea, was generally, though not universally, regarded in early Greek geographers as the boundary between Europe and Asia (Lloyd, *Commentary 1–98*, pp. 83 ff.).

104,1. φαίνονται... Αἰγύπτιοι: this notion became firmly rooted in classical tradition (e.g. Diod. I 28; 55, 4 ff.; Ammianus Marcellinus XXII 8,24), but Colchis was only one of a series of colonies which the Egyptians were alleged to have founded (cf. Istrus' 'Colonies of the Egyptians', *FGrHist* 334 F 43–6). Herodotus

proceeds in this and the following chapter to argue for the Egyptian origin of the Colchians, using an impressive series of proofs based on physical similarities, customs, mode of life, and language.   *Κόλχοι*: i.e. the inhabitants of the area through which the Phasis ran.   *νοήσας... Κόλχων*: i.e. in the elucidation of this problem Herodotus mobilized γνώμη, ἀκοή, and ἱστορίη. Note that he insists on the independence of his own conclusions in the matter (see above, pp. 228 ff.).
2. *μελάγχροές εἰσι καὶ οὐλότριχες*: '... they are swarthy and curly-haired'. This description need not apply to negroes, as sometimes claimed (e.g. by O. K. Armayor, *HSCPh* LXXXII (1978), 58). Odysseus is called μελαγχροιής at *Od.* XXVI 175, and Plutarch can describe a Syrian as οὐλοκόμην καὶ μελάγχρουν (*Aratus* 20). Herodotus' adjectives characterize well a common Egyptian physical type, though many other physiognomies were, and are, in evidence. Colchis probably showed many physical types, since there is good evidence of a considerable ethnic diversity there in antiquity (Strabo XI 2,16 (C497–8). The inhabitants of the Phasian marshes were sallow-skinned (Hippoc. *De Aere* 15), but the presence elsewhere of a substantial number of people comparable to Herodotus' Egyptians or Plutarch's Syrian is far from improbable.   *ὅτι μοῦνοι... τὰ αἰδοῖα*: cf. 36,3. Some slight archaeological support for Colchian circumcision has been offered (Gardiner, *AEO* I, p. 199*), but our ethnographical knowledge of ancient Colchis is too limited to provide independent confirmation of the currency of the practice there. It would, however, be surprising, in view of the long Greek acquaintance with the area, if Herodotus were mistaken.
3. *Φοίνικες... μεμαθηκέναι*: circumcision amongst Semitic peoples was certainly not of Egyptian origin (Barton, *HERE* III, p. 679). The basis of this mistaken notion lies in Herodotus' predilection for the *post hoc ergo propter hoc* fallacy (see above, p. 235).   *Σύριοι δὲ... Παρθένιον*: here Cappadocians (cf. I 6, 72, 76; V 49; Ruge, *RE* XII, 2291 ff.). Since these would have been Indo-Europeans, it is surprising to find them practising circumcision. Perhaps they inherited the practice from their predecessors in the area (Lloyd, *Commentary 99–182*, pp. 23 ff.).   *Θερμώδοντα*: the modern Terme Tshai.   *Παρθένιον*: the modern Bartinsu.   *Μάκρωνες*: they lived around or above Trapezus (Herrmann, *RE* XIV, 815, s.v. *Makrokephaloi, Makrones*) and were also mentioned by Hecataeus (*FGrHist* I F 206). There is no direct confirmation from any source of their practising circumcision, but we have no good reason to doubt the claim.
4. [*κατὰ τὰ αἰδοῖα*]: the combination of this phrase and τὰ αἰδοῖα in the next clause makes for a very clumsy sentence. It seems preferable to follow Gomperz and delete as a gloss.
105. *λίνον... κατὰ ταὐτά*: on the famed Colchian linen industry see Strabo XI 2,17 (C498), and on Egyptian linen cf. note on 37,2. Herodotus' comment presumably means that he believed that they both used the double-beamed vertical loom (on which see note on 35,2).   *ἡ ζόη πᾶσα*: the Phasian marsh-dwellers led a life that was comparable to that of their counterparts in the Delta marshes of Egypt (see notes on chs. 92, 104,2). Colchians in general also shared with the Egyptians a predilection for linen (see above), and it may be that there

were other points of similarity which we are unable to detect, but it is always possible that Herodotus' claim is based on no more than these two points.   ἡ γλῶσσα: ancient Colchis was afflicted with considerable linguistic diversity (Strabo XI 2,16 (C498)). We have no means of knowing what the language was which Herodotus regarded as specifically Colchian, but any similarity between that and Egyptian will have been superficial and entirely coincidental.   Σαρδονικὸν: also called *Phasianikon/Phasianon* (Pollux V 26). The origin of the adjective is unclear, but it is not impossible that there is a connection with the ancestors of the historical Sardinians, who may well have had links with the Colchis area (Lloyd, *Commentary 99–182*, p. 26).

106,1. τὰς δὲ στήλας . . . περιεοῦσαι: see note on 102,4; 103,2. Strictly the phrase τὰς στήλας should be in the nominative, and αἱ στῆλαι is indeed read by the Florentines and the Parisinus. However, the attraction into the accusative under the influence of the following word is easily paralleled (*attractio inversa*, cf. Kühner–Gerth, *Gr. Grammatik* II 2, pp. 413 ff.) and is preferable as the *lectio difficilior*.   ἐν δὲ τῇ Παλαιστίνη Συρίῃ: i.e. somewhere between Gaza and the southern frontier of Phoenicia (Lloyd, *Commentary 99–182*, p. 23). As yet no such monuments have been identified in this area. Those at the mouth of the Nahr el-Kelb, whose claims have often been canvassed, are too far north.   καὶ τὰ γράμματα . . . αἰδοῖα: see 102,4–5.

2. περὶ Ἰωνίην: lit. 'at several spots in Ionia' (J. Friedrich, *Annuaire de l'Inst. de Philologie et d'Histoire Orientales de l'Université Libre de Bruxelles*, V (1937), 387).   τῇ τε ἐκ τῆς Ἐφεσίης . . . ἐς Σμύρνην: Herodotus is not referring to the point of intersection of these two highways but to two separate places, one on the road from Ephesus to Phocaea, the other on the road from Sardis to Smyrna. The monuments at the former point are usually identified with the Hittite reliefs at Karabel (ibid., pp. 386 ff.).   ἔρχονται: sc. 'people'. For the ellipse of such indefinite subjects see Kühner–Gerth, *Gr. Grammatik* II 1, pp. 33 ff.

3–4. ἑκατέρωθι . . . ἐγκεκολαμμένα: cf. Diod. I 55,9. This description does not fit the sculptures at Karabel. Possibly Herodotus is describing the other figure, as yet unidentified, on the Sardis–Smyrna road.

3. πέμπτης σπιθαμῆς: c.1.30 m. as against Diodorus' figure, which amounts to c.2.40 m. The main Karabel relief is 2.30 m., the second 2.08 m.   τῇ μὲν δεξιῇ χειρί: inconsistent with both Karabel reliefs, in which the lance is held in the left hand.   τῇ δὲ ἀριστερῇ: at Karabel, where detectable, the bow is on the right shoulder.

4. ἐκ δὲ τοῦ ὤμου . . . διήκει: an inscription in this position would not be incompatible with Hittite practice but does not occur there on the main relief at Karabel. There is, however, a text in Hittite hieroglyphs running between the head and lance (Friedrich, op. cit., pp. 387 ff.).   ἐγὼ . . . ἐκτησάμην: the translation is pure fabrication, though we cannot establish who was responsible. It was indubitably based on the wording of Achaemenid royal inscriptions (for Herodotus as epigraphist see S. West, *CQ* XXXV (1985), 278 ff.).   ὅστις δὲ . . . δεδήλωκε: see 102,4.

5. *Μέμνονος*: Memnon was probably in origin the epitome of the heroic warrior, but at an early period he became the king of the Ethiopians. Once he had evolved to this point, nothing was easier than finding evidence of his activity in the oriental world (cf. M. E. Clark and W. D. Coulsen, *MH* XXXV (1978), 65 ff.).

107,1–2. *Τοῦτον δὴ ... πατρί*: Diod. I 55,10; 57,6 ff. and Manetho, *FGrHist* 609 F 9, 98 ff. also have versions of this tale. It is possible that it vaguely reflects the conspiracy which confronted one of Sesostris' historical prototypes, Senwosret I, at the beginning of his reign, but such events were so common in the ancient Orient that a correlation must remain no more than an intriguing possibility.

1. *πολλοὺς ἀνθρώπους ... κατεστρέψατο*: it was common Pharaonic practice to bring back prisoners-of-war to Egypt where they were often settled in camps and used as a labour force as required (Kees, *Ancient Egypt*, pp. 82, 89, 125, 290).   *ἐν Δάφνῃσι τῇσι Πηλουσίῃσι*: the modern Tell Defenneh in the north-eastern Delta (see note on 30,2).   *τὸν ἀδελφεὸν*: the treacherous brother is a common folk-motif (Thompson, *Motif-Index*, K2211).   *ἐπὶ ξείνια*: the *fête fatale* motif, for which see note on 100, 3.   *τοὺς παῖδας*: the role of the children in this tale possibly arises from their presence on the monument described at 110,1, i.e. the tale may contain an element of *Monument-novelle* (Spiegelberg, *Glaubwürdigkeit*, p. 26 ff.).   *ὑποπρῆσαι*: for fire in folk-tales cf. Thompson, *Motif-Index*, H1199.10, F848.4; S12.22).

2. *μαθεῖν*: see note on 64, 2.   *τὴν δέ ... τρόπῳ τοιούτῳ*: the Life of Pythagoras (A. Westermann, *Vitarum scriptores graeci minores*, Brunswick 1845, pp. 437–8) has a close parallel which may well derive from Herodotus (R. Hallo, *Klio*, XIX (1925), p 472 ff.). Folk-tales where the son saves his father are far from uncommon (Thompson, *Motif-Index*, R154.2 and 3; H1162.2).

108,1. *τεισάμενος*: vengeance figures as a common motive throughout Herodotus' *Histories* (cf. note on 100,2).   *τῷ μὲν ὁμίλῳ*: cf. Diod. I 56,2 ff. On Egyptian use of prisoners-of-war see note on 107,1.

2. *οἱ*: dative of advantage.   *ἐς τοῦ Ἡφαίστου τὸ ἱρόν*: cf. note on 99,4; 110. Diodorus ascribes to Sesostris a wide-ranging programme of temple-building (I 56,2). This was a classic activity of the Egyptian king and is one of several features in the Sesostris legend reflecting his role as an embodiment of the pharaonic ideal.   *μεγάθεϊ περιμήκεας*: 'huge in bulk'.   *τὰς διώρυχας ... ὤρυξαν*: cf. 137,4; Diod. I 57,2 ff. The Egyptian canal-system was much older than the XIIth Dynasty (W. Schenkel, *LdÄ* III, 311), the period to which the historical prototypes of Sesostris belong. The claim, however, does not originate in historical reminiscence but in the fact that by Herodotus' time Sesostris had become an embodiment of the ideal of Egyptian kingship and, as such, would naturally be connected with irrigation (Lloyd, *Commentary 99–182*, pp. 30 ff.). The notion that he invented the system probably also reflects a tendency to regard him as a culture hero (on which see Thompson, *Motif-Index* I, A510 ff.). *ἱππασίμην ... πᾶσαν*: the claim is anachronistic, since horses and wheeled transport did not appear in Egypt until the Second Intermediate Period (*c*.1786–1570 BC), considerably later than the historical context of Sesostris' historical

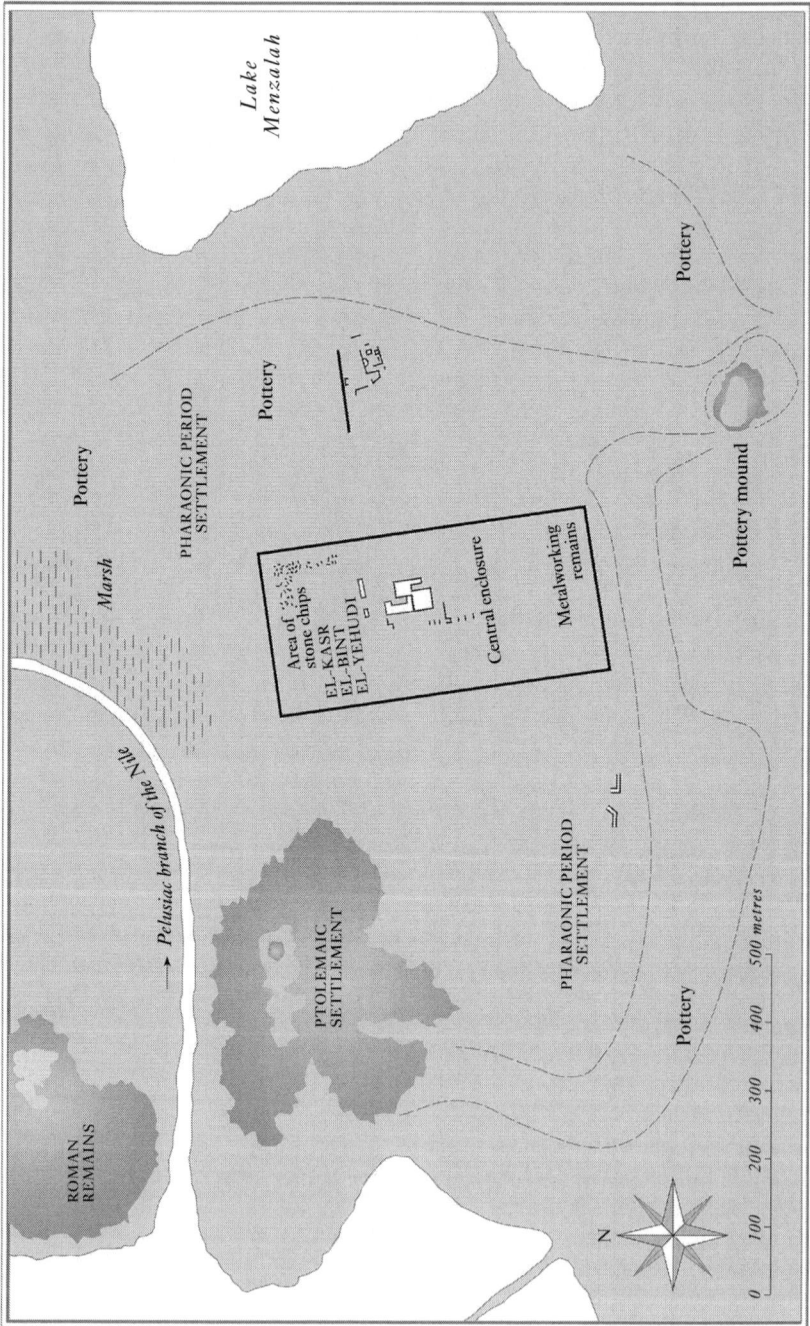

Map 23. Site of Daphnae (Tell Defenneh)

protoypes (cf. note on 102,1). However, throughout pharaonic history travel by road was severely impeded by canals and was much less important than water transport (S. Clarke and R. Engelbach, *Ancient Egyptian Masonry*, Oxford 1930, p. 88).

4. ὅσοι... χρεώμενοι: cf. Diod. I 57,2. The canal-system was devised for irrigation purposes. Herodotus foists onto Sesostris a motivation which reflects contemporary Greek concern with the effects of different types of water on health (cf. III 23,2–3; Sigerist II, pp. 247, 280 ff.). Well-water is claimed in the Hippocratic corpus to be unsuitable for drinking (*De Aere*, 7).   [τε]: most perplexing. Since it cannot be interpreted as a connective, it has been suggested that it is a survival of the epic frequentative or generalizing τε (e.g. Denniston, *Greek Particles*, p. 524), but this occurs nowhere else in Herodotus with ὅκως, and in other respects the style of the passage does not show and does not require an epic heightening. Stein and Legrand (nn. ad loc.) propose a lacuna after ποταμός, but rather than accept this desperate remedy, it seems preferable, with Krueger, to delete. The τε might conceivably be a dittograph originating in the -τε- of πλατυτέροισι.

109,1. κατανεῖμαι... διδόντα: so also Diod. I 54,2 ff. This claim of a radical economic reorganization may be a recollection of Senwosret III's administrative reforms (on which see W. C. Hayes, *CAH*³ I 2, pp. 505 ff.), but, more probably, it is partly a reflection of Sesostris' culture-hero aspect (note on 108,2) and partly a product of the idea that the Egyptian pharaoh was theoretically the owner of all the land of Egypt. Note also that Herodotus' account shows Greek contamination of the tradition in its very un-Egyptian insistence on equal treatment for all (ἴσον ἑκάστῳ).   καὶ ἀπὸ τούτου... κατ᾽ ἐνιαυτόν: the Ancient Egyptians did not have a money economy and taxes were paid annually in kind (Kees, *Ägypten*, pp. 22 ff.).

2. εἰ δέ... τελέοι: cf. Strabo XVII 1,3 (C787). Such surveys were conducted annually by 'scribes of fields' for taxation purposes (Helck, *Zur Verwaltung*, pp. 139 ff.). The humane attitude described by Herodotus is confirmed by Egyptian sources (e.g. A. H. Gardiner, *JEA* XXVII (1941), 19 ff.).   ἄν... ἐσήμαινε: '...he would indicate...'. For this use of the imperfect with ἄν to indicate customary action see Goodwin, *Moods and Tenses*, p. 56.

3. γεωμετρίη: this conviction that Greek geometry originated in Egypt was widespread (e.g. Diod. I 69,5; 81,3; 94,3; Strabo XVII 1,3 (C788)) and quite unfounded. What is called Egyptian geometry is no more than a system of surveying techniques; geometry proper, i.e. the systematic study of the mathematical properties of forms, is entirely Greek in origin (Sir Thomas Heath, *A History of Greek Mathematics*, I, Oxford 1965, pp. 118 ff.).   πόλον: 'a concave sundial' (LSJ, p. 1436,a,IV).   γνώμονα: 'pointer' (LSJ, p. 354,b,II,2), i.e. a vertical fixture used to cast the sun's shadow for measuring time. It could be inserted into the πόλος and used as part of a sundial, but it could also be employed entirely on its own (cf. S. West, *CQ* NS XXIII (1973), 61 ff.).   τὰ δυώδεκα μέρεα τῆς ἡμέρης: this is the earliest reference in any Greek text to

hours (cf. H. Diels, *Antike Technik*, Leipzig–Berlin 1924, pp. 158 ff.).   παρὰ
Βαβυλωνίων: all of the items in question are known to have been used in
Babylonia. There is some evidence to suggest that the πόλος and γνώμων may
have been imported from there by Anaximander (Lloyd, *Commentary 99–182*,
pp. 34 ff.), and the division of the day into twelve hours may also have derived
from the same area, but the possibility remains that the Greek claims are based on
nothing more than the *post hoc ergo propter hoc* fallacy (see above, p. 235).

110,1. Βασιλεὺς ... ἦρξε: Αἰθιοπίη, i.e. 'Nubia', was conquered and integrated
into the Egyptian state preeminently by Senwosret I and III, the two most
important historical prototypes of Sesostris (B. Kemp, in Trigger, pp. 130 ff.). It
is, therefore, possible that historical reminiscence lurks here, but it is equally
likely that this element reflects no more than the Egyptian ideal of kingship for
which control of this and other areas was a canonical theme (Lloyd, *Commentary
99–182*, pp. 16 ff.).   μνημόσυνα ... ἕκαστον: cf. Diod. I 57,5. For the motif see
note on 99,4. The two larger statues may well be the granite and limestone colossi
of Ramesses II still extant at Memphis (Lange, p. 23), but there is no trace of
statues of children.

2–3. τῶν δὴ ... ἔργοισι: this tale provides clear evidence of the role of Egyptian
nationalist propaganda in developing the Sesostris legend, particularly the claims
on the extent of his conquest: the alleged success of Sesostris in Scythia (103,1) is
contrasted with the historical failure of Darius in the same area between 516 and
511 BC (cf. Cook, pp. 62 ff.). Subsequently, the Sesostris legend is also used to
provide an Egyptian counterpart to Alexander the Great (Lange, pp. 24 ff.).

2. Δαρεῖον: king of Persia 521–485 BC. Unlike Cambyses, Darius was generally
popular in Egypt. This situation is reflected in the acquiescent response attributed
to him in this passage (cf. Alan B. Lloyd, *JEA* LXVIII (1982), 173 ff.).

3. μὴ οὐκ ὑπερβαλόμενον: for the use of μὴ οὐ with participles to express
negative conditions see Goodwin, *Moods and Tenses*, p. 56.   συγγνώμην
ποιήσασθαι: trans. 'agreed', not 'pardoned' (Powell, *Lexicon*, p. 340).

111,1. Φερῶν: cf. Diod. I 59,1; Malalas, *FGrHist* 609 F 5, p. 83, line 28; *Anagra-
phae*, ibid. 610 F 1). The name derives from the Egyptian royal title pr-ʿ3, 'the
Great House, Pharaoh' (H. de Meulenaere, *CdE* XXVIII (1953), 250). This
situation indicates that Pheros originally exemplified the anonymity so common
to folk heroes, but an attempt was subsequently made to identify him with a
specific historical figure; for in some sources he is given the name Nencoreus *vel
sim.* (e.g. Pliny, *NH* XXXVI 74), a variant which clearly originates in Nbw-k3w-rʿ,
one of the names of the XIIth Dynasty king Amenemhet II.

1–4. συνενειχθῆναι ... ὀκτὼ πήχεων: cf. Diod. I 59; Isidore, *Etym.* XVIII 31. That
this tale is essentially Egyptian admits of no doubt (de Meulenaere, op. cit.,
pp. 248 ff.), but Greek contamination is equally indisputable (see below).

1–2. συνενειχθῆναι ... τυφλωθῆναι: cf. Diod. I 59; III 29–30, offers an interesting
parallel. Eye-complaints, including blindness, were common in Ancient
Egypt (Sigerist I, pp. 224, 274, 334, 343), and blindness certainly featured
there as a divine punishment (de Meulenaere, op. cit., pp. 255 ff.).   τοῦ

ποταμοῦ...πήχεας: the genitive absolute is employed, despite the fact that its subject is identical with that of the main verb (see note on 66,1). ἐπ' ὀκτωκαίδεκα πήχεας: cf. 13,1. To judge from other ancient evidence, 18 cubits would be two cubits above the ideal (n. ad loc.). Floods were certainly a recurrent hazard (e.g. *BAR* IV, 742 ff.).

2. ἀτασθαλίῃ χρησάμενον: a clear case of *interpretatio Graeca* (see above, pp. 238 ff.). αἰχμὴν: the spear appears frequently in folklore in a wide variety of contexts (Aly, p. 66; Thompson, *Motif-Index*, Index, pp. 735 ff.). δέκα...ἄπειρος: oracles which look easy but prove difficult to fulfil are part of the stock-in-trade of folklore (Crahay, p. 225). The number 10 is prominent in the same context as a formulistic number (Thompson, op. cit., Index, s.v. 'Ten', etc.). ἐκ Βουτοῦς πόλιος: see note on ch. 83. οὔρῳ: urine was commonly used as a therapeutic agent in Egyptian medicine (de Meulenaere, op. cit., pp. 257 ff.); it has also played an important role in folklore worldwide (Thompson, op. cit., Index, p. 832). ἥτις...ἄπειρος: sexual purity is a recurrent theme in folklore, and the notion that deliverance can only be achieved through a chaste woman is easily paralleled (Aly, loc. cit.).

3. καὶ τὸν πρώτης...πειρᾶσθαι: folklore has much to say on the immorality of woman (Meulenaere, op. cit., pp. 250 ff.), and the theme is far from unknown in Egyptian literature (e.g. Lichtheim, *Late Period*, pp. 133 ff.). Ἐρυθρὴ βῶλος: 'Red Glebe' (cf. Diod. I 59). Several attempts have been made to identify this site, but none has been successful (Lloyd, *Commentary 99–182*, pp. 40 ff.). ὑποπρῆσαι: incineration was rarely used as a mode of execution in Ancient Egypt, and always for criminals whose crime was regarded as so heinous that only their total destruction was considered an adequate punishment. Adultery certainly fell into that category, though other punishments were also invoked (cf., in general, C. Sander-Hansen, *Der Begriff des Todes bei den alten Aegyptern*, Copenhagen 1940, p. 10). σὺν αὐτῇ τῇ πόλι: the dative of accompaniment with αὐτός would have been quite adequate. The addition of σύν is rare in prose (Kühner–Gerth, *Gr. Grammatik* II 1, pp. 433 ff.).

4. τῆς δὲ νιψάμενος...ἀνέβλεψε: Diodorus claims that she was a gardener (I 59,3). ταύτην δὲ: Herodotus frequently uses an apodotic δέ after a relative protasis, but in this case the δέ should be treated as a reduplication of that of the relative clause and serves to re-emphasize the antithesis with the treatment of the other women (Denniston, *Greek Particles*, pp. 178, 184). ἔσχε: all mss read the imperfect, but Krueger's emendation ἔσχε has been generally accepted. The aorist is certainly not without its attractions, but the imperfect, which insists on the continuity of the verbal action, seems perfectly viable (so also Kallenberg). καὶ...γε: this pairing, which is very common in Attic, has the effect here of throwing particular weight on the relative clause τοῦ...ἔχειν (cf. Denniston, *Greek Particles*, p. 157 n). ἐς τοῦ Ἡλίου τὸ ἱρὸν: i.e. the temple of Re at Heliopolis (cf. note on ch. 3). ὀβελοὺς: lit. 'spits'. For the Greek tendency to jest at things Egyptian see note on 69,3. Obelisks were frequently set up in pairs on either side of temple doorways; in this context they were regarded as embodying

the protective power of the creator-god guarding the shrine. At Heliopolis they were clearly very numerous, but only one is now standing there (cf. PM IV, p. 60). ἐξ ἑνὸς ἐόντας... πήχεων: obelisks were normally monolithic, but Herodotus' figure for the height (*c*.45.6 m.) is greater than that of any known example (the unfinished obelisk at Aswan, the largest extant, is *c*.41.8 m. long). A width of *c*.3.6 m., on the other hand, though considerable, is not implausible since it falls below that of the Aswan obelisk (*c*.4.1 m.).

112–20. A discussion of the reign of Proteus, which falls into four sections: Introduction (112), Helen's sojourn in Egypt (113–15), Homeric traditon on her wanderings (116–17), and Egyptian priestly tradition on the matter (118–20).

112,1. *Τούτου δὲ ἐκδέξασθαι... εἶναι*: cf. Diod. I 62. On Proteus' chronological location see Lloyd, *Introduction*, pp. 187 ff.   *Πρωτέα*: the name derives from that of the sea-god of *Od.* IV 351 ff., and has nothing to do with any Egyptian antecedent, despite the many attempts to find one (e.g. Herter, *RE*, XXIII 1, 952). He presumably acquired this human status through assimilation to the Thon of *Od.* IV 228, but the reasons behind this evolution must remain a matter of speculation (Alan B. Lloyd, *JHS* C (1980), 196).   *εἶναι*: for the infinitive see note on 64,2.   *τοῦ νῦν τέμενός... κείμενον*: the precise location has never been established, but this shrine probably lay south-east of the great temple of Ptah in the Kom el-Qala area (for the site see D. G. Jeffreys, *The Survey of Memphis*, I, London 1985).

2. *Τυρίων στρατόπεδον*: apart from a possible mention in a Ptolemaic text (Montet, *Géographie*, I, p. 33), Egyptian sources are silent on this installation. Nevertheless, camps for foreigners are known from the New Kingdom onwards, and there is ample evidence of Phoenicians in Egypt during the Late Period and Hellenistic times (e.g. J. Leclant, in W. A. Ward (ed.), *The Role of the Phoenicians in the Interaction of Mediterranean Civilizations*, Beirut 1968, pp. 16 ff.; *P Hib* II, 261, [4], 262). Herodotus' camp was probably a base for military and/or naval personnel.   *ἔστι δὲ... ξείνης Ἀφροδίτης*: cf. Strabo XVII 1,31 (C807). The temple appears in papyri as the *Aphrodision*. The goddess was called in Egyptian ᶜstr(t) ḫ3rw, 'Astarte of Syria'. Her prominence in Memphis may well be due to her widely current identification with the Egyptian goddess Sekhmet, consort of Ptah, the major Memphite god (S. Mercer, *Egyptian Religion*, III (1935), 192 ff.).   *καὶ τὸν λόγον... ἐπικαλέεται*: on Herodotus' care in justifying a thesis where possible see above, pp. 228 ff.

113,1. *ἔλεγον... ὧδε*: for priests as a source in Herodotus see above pp. 230 ff., and on the role of ἱστορίη in his work see above p. 230.

1–3. *Ἀλέξανδρον... Θῶνις*: the tradition that Helen never got to Troy but was left in Egypt occupies Herodotus until ch.120. It occurred, in some form, as early as Hesiod (fr. 358 (Merkelbach–West)) and appears highly developed in Euripides' *Helen* (in general see N. Austin, *Helen of Troy and her Shameless Phantom*,

New York, 1995). The origin of Herodotus' variant may well have been Hecataeus (Lloyd, *Commentary 99–182*, pp. 46 ff.).

1. ἐξῶσται ἄνεμοι: i.e. the Etesian Winds (cf. note on 20,2).   Κανωβικὸν καλεύμενον στόμα: on the Canopic branch of the Nile see note on 15,1.

Ταριχείας: lit. 'Pickling-factories'. This place must have been so named because at some stage in its history it was a centre for producing salted fish (on which see note on 15,1).

2. Ἡρακλέος: the Egyptian prototype is open to debate. Chonsu (note on ch. 42) and Shu (note on ch. 43) are demonstrable Herodotean equivalents, but other possibilities, e.g. Onuris, are also available. Strabo locates the temple east of Canopus (XVII 1,18 (C801)).   ὅτευ ὦν ἀνθρώπων: the construction is elliptical, ὅτευ standing for ὅστις ἐστιν with attraction of the relative into the genitive of the antecedent (cf. Kühner–Gerth, *Gr. Grammatik* II 2, p. 411). ὦν with the indefinite relative emphasizes the universal application of the phrase (Denniston, *Greek Particles*, p. 422).   στίγματα ἱρά: plausible in the case of οἰκέται at any rate, since there is clear evidence for branding temple-slaves in Ancient Egypt (e.g. *BAR* IV, 405).   οὐκ ἔξεστι τούτου ἄψασθαι: cf. Eustathius on *Od.* IV 228. The right of asylum is well known in Egypt during the Ptolemaic Period, but this passage is the earliest example of its existence before that time (E. Lüddeckens, *LdÄ* I, 514 ff.).

3. πάντα λόγον: the omission of the article in this phrase is rare (Kühner–Gerth, *Gr. Grammatik* II 1, pp. 633 ff.).   φύλακον: this officer's precise rank is unclear. He may simply have been a local garrison commander, but we do hear of a much more elevated official, the *imy-r ꜥꜢw ḫꜢswt Wꜣḏ-wr*, 'Overseer of the Frontier with the Foreign Lands of the Great Green', who was active in this area and clearly exercised a wide supervisory control over the northern coast of Egypt (cf. P.-M. Chevereau, *Prosopographie des cadres militaires égyptiens de la Basse Epoque*, Paris, 1985, p. 94).   Θῶνις: this name has its origin in that of the Thon mentioned in *Od.* IV 219 ff. The Greek name Thonis, in turn, probably gave rise to the Delta place-name Thonis (cf. Kees, *RE* VIa, 330).

114,1. ἀκούσας δὲ τούτων: Herodotus frequently uses this genitive of the thing heard where other writers would tend to use an accusative (cf., however, 115,1; in general see Kühner–Gerth, *Gr. Grammatik* II 1, p. 358).   τὴν ταχίστην: Herodotus' insistence on the pressing nature of the problem injects a psychological dimension into the narrative which considerably enhances the sense of drama (see above, p. 239).

2–3. Ἥκει…λέξει: On the function of speeches in Herodotus' historical narrative see above, p. 234.   ἀνόσιον: i.e. it was worse than an ἄδικον; for he had committed an offence against Zeus Xenios (see below). ξείνου…χρήματα: cf. 115,4–6; 118,3. Thonis, like Homer (*Il.* VII 360 ff.; XIII 623 ff.), pinpoints two wrongs done to Menelaus: Alexander's offence against ξενία and the theft of property (cf. M. Finley, *The World of Odysseus*, Harmondsworth 1956, pp. 115 ff., 143). Note that the language and the social values are unequivocally Greek.   κότερα δῆτα: the conversational liveliness of the particle δῆτα is particularly apposite to Thonis' earnest and urgent enquiry (cf. Denniston, *Greek Particles*, pp. 269, 271).

3. ἀνόσια ἐξεργασμένος: Krueger, followed by Hude, inserts <ὁ> before ἀνόσια, but the reading of the mss seems quite acceptable, the slight looseness of construction being explained by the rather chatty context.   εἰδέω: so Hude, but all mss read εἰδῶ which could well be an Herodotean form (cf. Rosén, *Sprachform*, p. 155).   τί: so Hude, but the Florentine group of mss reads ὅ τι, and there seems no good reason to prefer Hude's reading. For relatives in such contexts see Kühner–Gerth, *Gr. Grammatik* II 2, p. 438).   καί: this particle serves to stress the interrogative dimension in τί/ὅ τι (cf. Denniston, *Greek Particles*, p. 313).

115,1. ἀκούσας ... ἱκέτας: note the accumulation of detail, a standard Herodotean device for creating verisimilitude (see Lloyd, *Historia*, XXXVII (1988), 50).   ἀκούσας δὲ ταῦτα: see note on 114,1.

2–3. ἀνακομισθέντων ... τοῦ ἀδικήματος: for a parallel to the general situation cf. I 24, 7–8. Note that the narrative at this point uses indirect speech to record the exchange between Alexander and Proteus. Proteus' succeeding denunciation, on the other hand, is delivered in *oratio recta*. This device has the effect of throwing the dénouement into sharper and more dramatic relief.

2. καὶ δὴ καί: this emphatic grouping of particles is used more frequently by Herodotus than any other author (Denniston, *Greek Particles*, p. 255).

3. λάβοι: instead of ἔλαβες in *oratio recta*. The use of the optative in indirect questions to replace an indicative in historic sequence is rare (cf. Kühner–Gerth, *Gr. Grammatik* II 2, p. 538).

4–5. τέλος ... ἥκεις: on the content of the denunciation see note on 114. Proteus' respect for the obligations of ξενία is made to contrast forcefully with Alexander's disregard for them.

4. ὅτι: the use of this conjunction before *oratio recta* is uncommon, and this case is the earliest extant example (Goodwin, *Moods and Tenses*, §711).

6. γυναῖκα μὲν ταύτην: the omission of the article arises because ταύτην does not have full demonstrative force but is equivalent to a locative adverb such as 'there, here' (Kühner–Gerth, *Gr. Grammatik* II 1, p. 629).   τριῶν ἡμερέων: one of many examples in Herodotus of the number 3 used as a formulaic number (see note on 77,2).   ἅτε πολεμίους: this use of ἅτε in the sense 'as if' is frequent in Herodotus (Powell, *Lexicon*, pp. 50 ff.) but is otherwise a poetic usage (cf. Denniston, *Greek Particles*, p. 526).

116,1–6. δοκέει ... οἰκέουσι: on Herodotus' methods of argument see above, p. 236.

1. ἀλλ' οὐ γάρ: the ἀλλά belongs with the main clause and γάρ with the subordinate. Herodotus is the only prose writer who commonly uses these particles in this way (Denniston, *Greek Particles*, p. 99).   [ἐς ὅ]: these words occur in every ms but are evidently unacceptable. Stein's emendation to ἑκών is palaeographically not unattractive, but the sense fails to convince. It seems preferable to delete with Bekker. Perhaps an intrusive 'o' arose at some stage as a dittograph from the

preceding -το, and a misguided scribe then added ἐς and accents to make what he considered to be a viable construction.

2–5. δῆλον δέ...ἑκατόμβας: the references are *Il.* VI 289–92 and *Od.* IV 227–30 and 351–2. Since the tradition of Helen's sojourn in Egypt is probably post-Homeric (see above, note on ch. 113), even the first passage is suspect evidence for Herodotus' purpose. The second, however, is almost certainly irrelevant, since it probably refers to the *nostos* of Menelaus whilst the third passage undoubtedly does. Schaefer favoured deleting the two *Odyssey* passages as a gloss. The conclusion of the chapter and the beginning of the next clearly proceed as though they were not there, but it is not inconceivable that they appeared in Herodotus' ms as afterthoughts which were never properly worked into the text (cf. J. E. Powell, *CQ* XXIX (1935), 76).

2. κατά παρεποίησε: all mss read κατὰ γάρ, which is impossible. Bekker emended to παρεποίησε and was followed by Hude, but παραποιέω is not securely attested in the required sense and is, in any case, not a certain 5th-cent. word at all (LSJ, pp. 1321 ff.). Reiz's κατά περ ἐποίησε is much the best alternative.   τε δή: Herodotus shows a marked predilection for this combination of particles, with over sixty examples. The δή probably simply serves to stress the τε (Denniston, *Greek Particles*, pp. 259 ff.).

117. κατὰ ταῦτα...αὐτήν: on Herodotus' methods of argument see above, p. 236.   οὐκ ἥκιστα ἀλλὰ μάλιστα: for this use of litotes reinforced by its opposite cf. IV 170.   οὐκ Ὁμήρου: cf. Arist. *Pol.* 23(1459a). Homeric authorship was accepted by Pindar (fr. 265 (Snell–Maehler)) and Aelian (*VH* IX 15), but the work was also ascribed to Stasinus and Hegesias (e.g. Athenaeus 682d).   τὰ Κύπρια: this poem was concerned with the events leading up to the Trojan war.   εἴρηται...λείη: the *testimonia* on the poem contradict this statement, asserting that Paris visited Cyprus and Phoenicia before returning home (Apollodorus, *Epit.* III 1 ff.). Perhaps the best explanation is that Herodotus has confused two different poems on the subject of Paris' return to Troy.

118,1. τοὺς ἱρέας: see note on 113,1.

3. ἀπαιτέειν...Ἀλέξανδρος: see note on 114,2.

3–4. τοὺς δὲ Τευκροὺς...Πρωτέα: see note on ch. 113.

3. τότε...ἀνωμοτί: on Herodotus' exploitation of detail in historical narrative to create a sense of actuality see note on 115,1.   μὴ μέν: the negative of the grouping ἦ μέν frequently employed to introduce an oath (Denniston, *Greek Particles*, pp. 389 ff.).

119,1–2. καὶ ξεινίων...ὅσιον: yet again is the generosity of Egyptian treatment of Greeks contrasted with the injustice of Greek behaviour (cf. note on 115,6).

2. ἄπλοιαι: the Etesian winds would often have created impossible sailing conditions for travellers intent on voyaging northwards (cf. note on 20,2).

2–3. ἐπειδή...ἐποίησε: the inspiration for this episode lies ultimately in *Od.* IV 351 ff., but Homer makes no mention of human sacrifice. That element has probably been taken over from the tradition of Agamemnon's sacrifice of Iphigenia at Aulis (cf. Fehling, p. 62.).

3. ἐπάϊστος ἐγένετο: Herodotus uses the personal construction in preference to the impersonal to keep attention firmly fixed on the action's protagonist (for this example and parallels with δῆλος and φανερός see Goodwin, *Moods and Tenses*, p. 360).   ἰθὺ Λιβύης: Menelaus' visit to Libye was already known to Homer (*Od.* IV 81 ff.) and played a major role in Cyrenean legend (Chamoux, pp. 69 ff.).

120,1–5. ἐγὼ... εἴρηται: Herodotus concludes his discussion by submitting the priestly tradition to evaluation by γνώμη. The argument is based on εἰκός (see above, p. 236).

2. οὐ γὰρ δὴ οὕτω γε: 'Usually, though not invariably... used for clearing the ground by ruling out at least one possibility' (Denniston, *Greek Particles*, p. 243). Trans.: 'For Priam was certainly not so insane...'

3. τούτων δὲ τοιούτων: the δέ is resumptive and harks back to the temporal protasis ἐπεὶ... ἀπέθνησκον (on this usage see ibid., p. 183).   γε δή: highly emphatic. Translate 'especially' *vel sim.* (cf. ibid., p. 245).

4. οὐ μὲν οὐδέ: this combination is much favoured by Herodotus (Powell, *Lexicon*, p. 275,b). Here it is simply employed to introduce a further argument.

5. ἀλλ' οὐ γάρ: as often, this grouping of particles indicates that a stated condition has not been fulfilled (Denniston, *Greek Particles*, p. 104).   ὡς μὲν ἐγώ: an example of the μέν *solitarium* where the contrasted element (viz. other commentators) is only implied.   τοῦ δαιμονίου... θεῶν: on the theology see above, pp. 232 ff.

121–3.   The reign of Rhampsinitus. For chronology see above, pp. 236 ff.

121,1. Ῥαμψίνιτον: cf. Diod. I 62,5. The name is a combination of the Egyptian Rᶜ-ms(w)-sw, 'Ramesses', a common royal name during the XIXth and XXth Dynasties, and s3-Nt, 'son of Neith', an epithet frequently applied to kings in the Late Period (Lloyd, *Historia*, XXXVII (1988), 32). Whatever his historical antecedents, he had become almost entirely a figure of of legend by the 5th cent. For a stylistic analysis of the *logos* see R. V. Munson, *AJPh* CXIV (1993), 27 ff.   ὃς μνημόσυνα...Ἡφαιστείου: cf. note on 99,4, for this recurrent theme. Evidence of building at Memphis by Pharaohs bearing the name Ramesses is plentiful (PM I 2, pp. 830 ff.).   ἀντίους...πήχεων: traces of a statue of Ramesses III have indeed come to light in the area (W. M. F. Petrie and J. H. Walker, *Memphis*, I, London 1909, p. 2); 25 cubits (*c.*11.5 m.) is a plausible height for such a statue. τὸν μὲν πρὸς βορέω...ἔρδουσι: the two seasons will be the hot season (May to September) and the cool season (October to April). Probably the first was connected with the north because it is then that the northerly Etesian winds blow (note on 20,2). The connection of the southern statue with winter would be a natural corollary. The difference in cultic response probably originated in a perception of summer as a bringer of blessings, particularly the inundation, and winter as a source of difficulties, e.g. the falling of the Nile to a low level and the incidence of the unpleasant southerly Khamsîn wind (Bonneau, *La*

Crue, p. 37).   πρὸς βορέω: in the next clause πρός is used with the accusative. The difference in case arises because Herodotus presupposes that the viewer is looking north, so that one statue is 'on the northern side' whilst the other is 'towards the south' (cf. Kühner–Gerth, *Gr. Grammatik* II 1, p. 515).   τοῦτον μέν: the repetition of the μέν with an anaphoric demonstrative is emphatic (cf. ibid. II 2, p. 269; cf. Denniston, *Greek. Particles*, p. 385).   προσκυνέουσί: see note on 80,2.

α,1. πλοῦτον δὲ τούτῳ τῷ βασιλέϊ: the well-known story of the treasury of Rhampsinitus, which is a veritable string of folk-motifs, in particular that of the wily thief, and has parallels and descendants throughout the world (Aly, pp. 67 ff.; C. W. Müller, in id. (ed.), *Zum Umgang mit fremden Sprachen in der griechisch-römischen Antike: Kolloquium der Fachrichtungen Klassische Philologie der Universitäten Leipzig und Saarbrücken am 21. und 22. November 1989 in Saarbrücken* (Palingenesia, XXXVI), Stuttgart 1992, pp. 37 ff.). Herodotus' tale is firmly rooted in an Egyptian context, but the extent, origin, and character of the Egyptian source material continues to excite debate (e.g. ibid.).   τὸν οὐδένα...ἐλθεῖν: for the attraction of verbs of subordinate clauses into the infinitive in *oratio obliqua* see note on 64,2.   βουλόμενον...ὑπὸ ἑνός: note that here and throughout this episode Herodotus devotes great attention to detail in order to make the story as concrete and credible as possible (see note on 115,1). A stone chamber would have been an unlikely component of an Egyptian palace and is probably inspired by the stone crypts sealed by movable blocks which feature in Egyptian temples (Bonnet, *RÄRG*, p. 401).

β,1. τῶν τε σημάντρων: it was standard Egyptian practice to seal doors with mud sealings bearing the owner's name (O. Koenigsberger, *Die Konstruktion der ägyptischen Tür, Äg. Forschungen*, II, Glückstadt 1936, pp. 40 ff.).   τρὶς ἀνοίξαντι: on 3 as a formulaic number see note on 77,2.   πάγας: for examples of Egyptian animal traps see N. de Garis Davies, *Five Theban Tombs*, London 1913, pls. 23–4.

β,2. ὃς εἴη: in such constructions ὅς seems to retain its relative force (sc. [the person] who he was) and should not be treated as a simple equivalent to τίς *vel sim.* (Kühner–Gerth, *Gk. Grammatik* II 2, p. 438).

δ,1. ὄνους: throughout Egyptian history the donkey appears in texts and representations as the ubiquitous beast of burden, and even today continues to play an important role in this capacity (cf. Kees, *Ägypten*, pp. 20, 122, 139 ff.).

δ,4. πεισθῆναί τε δή: for this sequence of particles see note on 116,2. Here it serves to stress the infinitive.

δ,6. τῶν φυλάκων...παρηίδας: cf. 2 Sam. 10: 4–5. The claim that the guards were bearded means that they were not envisaged as being Egyptian (cf. note on 36,1). The creators of the tale evidently conceived of them as foreign mercenaries, who were used in great numbers in Late Period Egypt (cf. Roeder, *RE* IA, 145).

ε,2. τὴν θυγατέρα...ἐπ᾽ οἰκήματος: for the motif where a father prostitutes his daughter see note on 126,1. On the episode in general cf. H. Neitzel, *Würzburger Jahrb. für die Altertumswissenschaft*, XIX (1993), 215 ff.

ζ,1–2. ὡς δὲ καὶ ταῦτα... ἀνθρώπων: such reversals of fortune are part of the stock-in-trade of folklore (cf. notes on ch. 134).

ζ,2. Αἰγυπτίους... Αἰγυπτίων: on Egyptian self-esteem see note on 158,5.

122,1–3. μετὰ δὲ ταῦτα... χωρίον: this tale has many parallels in world folklore (Aly, pp. 67 ff.). It was probably in origin a myth connected with the royal accession (see below), but had degenerated by Herodotus' time into little more than legend.

1. τοῦτον τὸν βασιλέα: wealth and the Underworld are often linked in myth and folktale, a fact which may well explain why the story was told of Rhampsinitus rather than of some other Egyptian king (Aly, loc. cit.).   Ἀίδην: many editors prefer to print this epic form instead of the mss's Ἅιδην (*vel sim.*), on the assumption that this is what Herodotus would have written, but in the light of the ποικιλία of his style this must remain a questionable assumption (so also Godley). By the Egyptians it was normally called ᾿Imnt/Imntt or Dw3t (Wb. I, pp. 84,13, and 86,1 ff.; V, pp. 415,3 ff.).   συγκυβεύειν... χρύσεον: the game will have been *snt*, which was played with pieces on a board resembling a draught-board, but the moves were determined by throwing dice or knucklebones. Since it features prominently in mortuary beliefs in a variety of contexts, its appearance here is not surprising (cf. E. B. Pusch, *Das Senet Brettspiel im Alten Ägypten*, MÄS XXXVIII, Munich–Berlin 1979). Folklore abounds in cases where privileges are won in a game, and Egyptian examples are not lacking (Plutarch, *DIO* 12 (*Mor.* 355); Lichtheim, *Late Period*, pp. 132 ff.).   τῇ Δήμητρι: i.e. Isis (see note on 59,2).   χειρόμακτρον χρύσεον: this is almost certainly the *nms*-headdress, i.e. the yellow headcloth with blue stripes worn by Egyptian kings (cf. H. E. Winlock, *Bull. of the Metropolitan Museum of Art*, XI (1916), 238 ff.). Here its acquisition probably symbolizes the acquisition of the kingly office.

2. ἀπὸ δὲ τῆς Ῥαμψινίτου καταβάσιος: this festival is best interpreted as a ritual re-enactment of the journey to the Underworld of the dead king (= the blind-folded priest) and the accession of the new king (= the returning priest, who had probably had his blindfold removed and came back carrying the gold kerchief to symbolize the kingship acquired from his mother Demeter/Isis) (for detailed discussion see Lloyd, *Commentary 99–182*, p. 58).

3. φᾶρος... ἐξυφήναντες: this activity has parallels in the Festival of Khoiak (Chassinat, *Le Mystère*, pp. 477, 585 ff.).   κατ' ὦν ἔδησαν: see note on 39,2.   αὐτῶν: so all mss, but, since the context requires a reflexive, Stein's ἑωυτῶν seems preferable.   ὑπὸ δύο λύκων: i.e. two priests who impersonated the jackal-headed divine herald Wp(w)-w3wt, 'the Opener of the Ways'. He often appears in duplicate, one for Upper Egypt and the other for Lower (Bonnet, RÄRG, pp. 842 ff.). On the Greek confusion over canid sacred animals see note on ch. 67.   τῆς πόλιος: possibly Letopolis, *c.*13 km. north-west of Cairo (Lloyd, op. cit., p. 59).

123,1–3. τοῖσι μέν νυν... ἀκοῇ γράφω: see above, pp. 230 ff.

1. ἀρχηγετεύειν... Διόνυσον: the Egyptian equivalents are Isis and Osiris respectively (notes on 42,2; 59,2). Osiris appears as king of the dead from the Old Kingdom onwards (Griffiths, *The Origins*, pp. 173 ff.), but Isis is never their queen

in extant evidence. Herodotus' claim may have arisen from a combination of *interpretatio Graeca* (Isis = Demeter, who occupied an important position in the Greek Underworld) and the fact that she was the wife of Osiris. It is also possible that Isis had acquired the status of queen in the Late Period without its leaving any trace in our extant sources.

2. πρῶτοι... ἔτεσι: the doctrine of transmigration of souls was certainly not Egyptian (H. Brunner, *LdÄ* 813). Herodotus' conviction that it was probably arose partly from misinterpretation of Egyptian beliefs or representations, partly from an obsessive interest in the πρῶτος εὑρετής of cultural material, and partly through the misguided application of the *post hoc ergo propter hoc* fallacy (see above, p. 235; Mora, pp. 167 ff.).   ἐν τρισχιλίοισι ἔτεσι: a 3,000-year cycle is nowhere mentioned, but the number 3 is a common significant number (note on 77,2) and does feature in parallel contexts, e.g. Empedocles claims that the cycle of reincarnation occupied 30,000 seasons (KR², pp. 40l, 471). Herodotus' statement may, therefore, be accurate.

3. τούτῳ τῷ λόγῳ... οὐ γράφω: Herodotus will have particularly in mind Pythagoras, Empedocles, and the Orphics (KR², pp. 260–1, 401–10; W. K. Guthrie, *Orpheus and Greek Religion*, London 1952², pp. 167 ff.). There is no reason to doubt that it was a native Greek product (Nilsson, *GgrR* I, pp. 691 ff.).

124–35. The reigns of the Pyramid Builders of the IVth Dynasty (*c.*2613–2494 BC) and an account of their monuments in the Gîza necropolis near Cairo. The chronology is badly wrong but is easily explained (see Lloyd, *Introduction*, pp. 188 ff.; B. Shimron, *Athenaeum*, LXVIII (1990), 191 ff.).

124,1. εὐθενέειν: the form εὐθηνέειν seems preferable to the εὐθενέειν read by Cobet and Hude since the -ε- form occurs in no ms at this point, whereas the -η- form appears in the Homeric hymns and is also probable in Hippocrates (LSJ, p. 714,b).   Χέοπα: the Greek is a good rendering of the Egyptian *ḥw.f-wi*, an abbreviated form of the name *Ḥnm-ḥw.f-wi*, 'May Khnum protect me' (Alan B. Lloyd, *Historia*, XXXVII (1988), 31). He was the second king of the IVth Dynasty and ruled from *c.*2596 to 2573 BC.   ἐς πᾶσαν κακότητα: there is no trace of an anti-Cheops tradition in Old Kingdom texts, but elements of one do appear in the Middle Kingdom Westcar Papyrus (Lichtheim, *Old and Middle Kingdoms*, pp. 218 ff.), and there are signs of negative attitudes to the Old Kingdom in general elsewhere in Egyptian literature. It is furthermore possible that the tradition on Cheops was affected by assimilation of the name *ḥw.f-wi* (via the late pronunciation *Shufu**) to such Egyptian words as *šft*, 'sin', and it is equally possible that it was contaminated by the folk motif of the tyrannical ruler (Lloyd, *Commentary 99–182*, pp. 62 ff.).   ἐργάζεσθαι... Αἰγυπτίους: since compulsory service (*corvée*) was an essential element of the Egyptian economic system throughout pharaonic times (Kees, *Ägypten*, Index s.v. 'Frondienst'), there was nothing unusual in Cheops' command.

2. ἐκ τῶν λιθοτομιέων: i.e. the Tura quarries in the Mokattam Hills east of Cairo (note on 8,1). Only the casing blocks came from this area; the rest of the stone

was quarried locally (Edwards, p. 99).   ἐκ τουτέων: such anaphoric use of demonstratives serves for emphasis. Here it draws attention to the extraordinary nature of the feat (cf. Kühner–Gerth, *Gr. Grammatik* II 1, p. 660).   ἕλκειν: this was standard practice. The blocks were placed on a sledge which was dragged along a slipway of dampened Nile mud (J.-P. Lauer, *BIFAO* LXXIII (1973), 131 ff.).   πλοίοισι: the freighters used in such contexts are frequently mentioned in inscriptions of the period (e.g. *BAR* I, 308, 321 ff.: cf. n. 96).

3. κατὰ δέκα μυριάδας: the number is not implausible as a total for the workforce when a maximum effort was being exerted (Butzer, p. 87, n. 4), but Herodotus, or his source, has misrepresented the system. During the inundation season a large force would be mobilized to stockpile materials, but for most of the year a much smaller staff was used for the construction work (cf. Edwards, pp. 270 ff.).   τριβομένῳ τῷ λεῷ: for this dative in temporal expressions see Kühner–Gerth, *Gr. Grammatik* II 1, p. 425).

3–4. τῆς ὁδοῦ . . . γενέσθαι: Herodotus has clearly confused the causeway of the pyramid with a building-ramp. The causeway was a limestone corridor running from Nazlet es-Semman up the desert to the mortuary temple on the east side of the pyramid (width *c.*18.35 m. as against Herodotus' *c.*18.5 m.; length *c.*658.6 m. as against Herodotus' *c.*924 m.). Building-ramps were quite separate from such features; they were constructed to enable the Egyptians to raise blocks to the working area and were normally removed once the building work was completed (Edwards, pp. 257 ff., 267 ff.).

4. ὡς ἐμοὶ δοκέειν: for the infinitive see note on 4,1.   ὑψηλοτάτη . . . ἑωυτῆς: this use of the superlative with a reflexive pronoun is common in Herodotus. It insists that the quality in question (in this case, height) is characteristic of the entity described, but that this instance was its most conspicuous manifestation (Kühner–Gerth, *Gr. Grammatik* II 2, p. 314).   τῶν ἐπὶ τοῦ λόφου . . . ἐσαγαγών: there is only one chamber ὑπὸ γῆν, the rest being constructed within the body of the pyramid. There is no island and no canal, but the notion does reflect the highly apposite Egyptian mortuary concept of the Osiris-grave, which consisted of an island surrounded by water on which the god himself was buried (Helck, *RE* XXIII 2, 2202). The accusative with ὑπό implies 'extending under'.

5. εἴκοσι ἔτεα: this figure is acceptable (Lloyd, *Commentary 99–182*, p. 66). ὀκτὼ πλέθρα: there are slight variations between sides: modern measurements give *c.*230 m. as against Herodotus' 237.6 m. (converting at 1 plethron = 29.7 m., m., the lowest figure possible: *Artemis Lexikon*, 3424).   ὕψος ἴσον: the vertical height was *c.*146.7 m. and the height up the side *c.*186 m. Herodotus' figure is, therefore, rather too high.   λίθου δὲ ξεστοῦ . . . τὰ μάλιστα: the casing blocks only survive at the base of the Great Pyramid, where the masonry is of extreme accuracy (Edwards, p. 262).   τριήκοντα ποδῶν: much too high a figure. As often with 3 and multiples, we should treat the number as symbolic, i.e. it simply means 'big' (cf. Lloyd, *Historia*, XXXVII (1988), 41, n. 53).

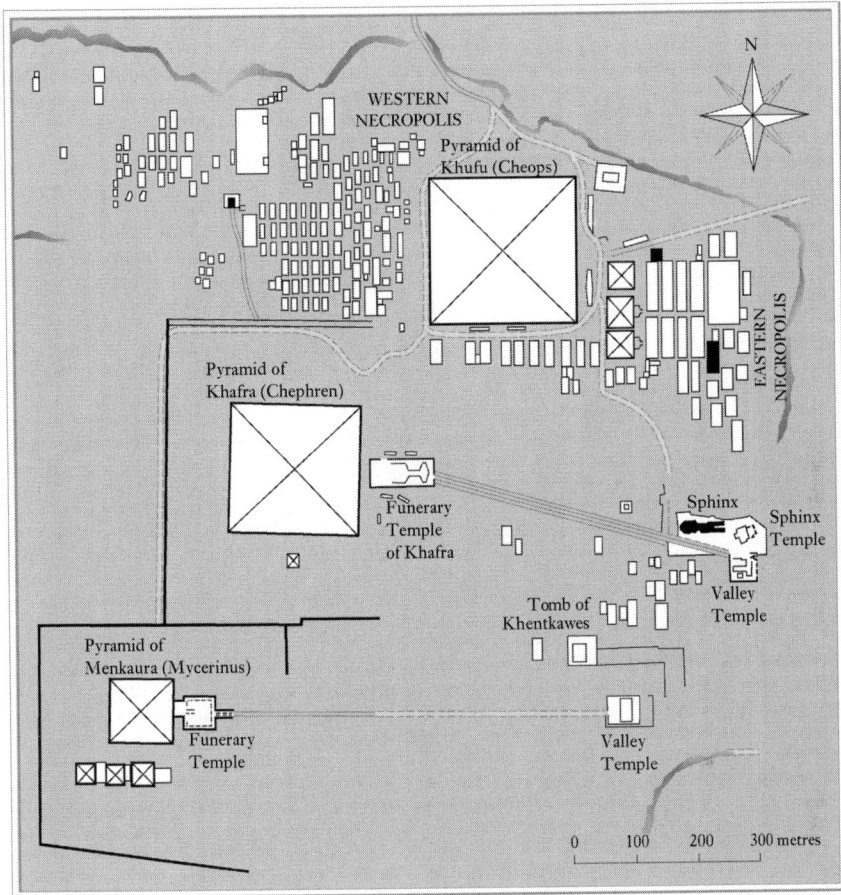

Map 24. The Pyramids of Gîza

125,1. ἐποιήθη ... ὀνομάζουσι: i.e. it was constructed initially as a step pyramid and finished off by filling in the steps. The problematic κρόσσαι were probably battlements of a Near Eastern type whose outline resembled that of a step pyramid (Lloyd, *Commentary 99–182*, pp. 67 ff.).

2. μηχανῇσι ... πεποιημένῃσι: a clear anachronism. μηχαναί are cranes (J. J. Coulton, *JHS* XCIV (1974), 7 ff.), but the only known Egyptian device for lifting weights was the building-ramp (note on 124, 2–3). Herodotus, or his source, has simply assumed that the Egyptians built according to contemporary Greek practice. They are probably claimed to be made of short pieces of wood because Herodotus and other Greeks were aware that Egyptian trees only yielded short lengths (see note on 96,1).

4.[γὰρ]: this word only appears in mss C and P. Hude brackets it, but the authority of these mss is good, and the Greek reads better if it is retained.

5. ἐξεποιήθη . . . ἐξεποίησαν: this must refer to the finishing process applied to the casing blocks which could only be carried out from the top down (Edwards, pp. 257 ff.).

6. σεσήμανται . . . πυραμίδι: the surface of the pyramid certainly bore inscriptions, but they were, in the main, visitors' graffiti whose content was quite different from that described by Herodotus (G. Goyon, *Les Inscriptions et graffiti des voyageurs sur la Grande Pyramide*, Cairo 1944, pp. xxvi ff.: cf. Helck, *RE* XXIII 2, 2202).   ὅσα . . . τοῖσι ἐργαζομένοισι: radishes, onions, and garlic were certainly important elements in Egyptian diet (Kees, *Ancient Egypt*, p. 77; L. Keimer, *Die Gartenpflanzen im alten Ägypten*, II, Mainz am Rhein 1984, pp. 60 ff.), but the list omits many items which we should expect, e.g. bread, beer, and fish. There can be no doubt that the interpreter invented the translation (see also below).   ἑξακόσια . . . τετελέσθαι: again, clearly a fabrication. The Egyptians of pharaonic times did not operate a money economy; the workmen will have been paid in kind (cf., in general, Helck, *Wirtschaftsgeschichte*).

7. σίδηρον: another anachronism. The tools used were of stone or copper (Edwards, pp. 248 ff.). The claim that iron was employed is based simply on the assumption that the Egyptian tools had been made of the same metal as those of 5th-cent. Greeks.

126,1–2. ἐς τοῦτο . . . πλέθρου: cf. 121,ε,2–3. This episode is intended, in part, to account for one of the subsidiary pyramids attached to the Great Pyramid, i.e. it is a *Monument-novelle* (see note on 107,1), but, through the prostitution episode, which has many parallels in world folklore (Thompson, *Motif-Index*, T455), it also serves to cast Cheops in a particularly unfavourable light.

1. ἀργύριον ὁκόσον δή τι: this element clearly arose from Greek contamination of the Egyptian tradition (cf. notes on 125,6–7; S. von Reden, *JHS* CXVII (1997), 172).   οὐ γὰρ . . . ἔλεγον: note the care in recording sources, or lack of them (see above, pp. 228 ff.).   [ἐν τοῖσι ἔργοισι]: this phrase reads awkwardly as part of the girl's request, though it would go well with the preceding infinitive. Valckenaer deletes, but it would be a very odd gloss. Werfer, on the other hand, reads ἐπί for ἐν, giving the sense 'for the purpose of' which suits the context perfectly.

2. τὴν ἐν μέσῳ . . . πυραμίδος: there is a line of three small pyramids running north–south on the south-east side of the pyramid and intended for queens of Cheops (Vandier, *Manuel* II 1, pp. 75 ff.). The owner of the middle structure is unknown, and it is far from clear why it became the focus of this tale.   ὅλου καὶ ἡμίσεος πλέθρου: i.e. 44.5 m., if we use the shortest known length for the plethron (note on 124,5). The true length is 49 m. (Vandier, op. cit., p. 75, n.3).

127,1. πεντήκοντα ἔτεα: the figure is far too high, since regnal year 25/6 is the latest known in contemporary texts. For the probable source of this error see Lloyd, *Historia*, XXXVII (1988), 35.   τὸν ἀδελφεὸν αὐτοῦ Χεφρῆνα: cf. Diod. I 64,1. Herodotus' Greek name is a good rendering of the Egyptian ḥꜥ.f-rꜥ;

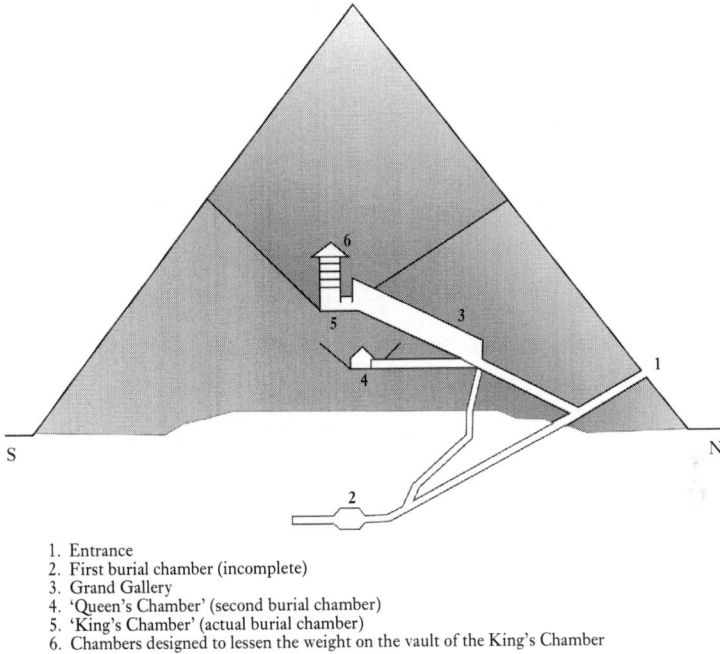

1. Entrance
2. First burial chamber (incomplete)
3. Grand Gallery
4. 'Queen's Chamber' (second burial chamber)
5. 'King's Chamber' (actual burial chamber)
6. Chambers designed to lessen the weight on the vault of the King's Chamber

Map 25. The Pyramid of Khufu (Cheops)

He was the son, not brother, of Cheops, and was not his immediate successor, being preceded by his brother Djedefre. Since the latter can be omitted even in Egyptian sources, the error in Herodotus' tradition could well have an Egyptian origin (Lloyd, op. cit., p.36).   καὶ τοῦτον δὲ: this combination of particles is rare in Herodotus (Denniston, *Greek Particles*, p. 201).   ἐς μὲν τὰ ἐκείνου ... ἐμετρήσαμεν: cf. Aristophanes, *Av.* 1130. The length of side is *c*.215.7 m., i.e. *c*.14.6 m. shorter than that of the Great Pyramid, whereas the height is *c*.143.5 m., i.e. *c*.3 m. lower than its predecessor (cf. Edwards, p. 131). Herodotus' claim to have measured the structure is one of his many assertions of autopsy (see above, p. 227). It presumably refers to the length of side, which could be determined relatively easily by pacing the distance.   ταῦτα γὰρ ὦν: when used with γάρ, the particle ὦν always imparts a particularly powerful emphasis to a statement (Denniston, *Greek Particles*, p. 446).

2. οὔτε γὰρ ὕπεστι ... Χέοπα: cf. 124,4. The section has only a very tenuous logical connection with what precedes and looks like an interpolation. This need not mean, however, that it is not from Herodotus' hand. He may simply have inserted the passage as a note, intending to return and integrate it with the text, and never did so (cf. J. E. Powell, *CQ* XXIX (1935), 77 ff.). *Pace* Herodotus, there are two subterranean chambers in Chephren's pyramid (Edwards,

pp. 131 ff.).   ὑπὸ γῆν: sc. 'extending under', the standard meaning of the preposition with the accusative.

3. ὑποδείμας ... ποικίλου: it is the first two courses of the casing only which are constructed of granite, the rest being of limestone (V. Maragioglio and C. Rinaldi, *L'architettura delle piramidi Menfite*, V, Rapallo 1966, p. 48).   λίθου Αἰθιοπικοῦ: material genitive (cf. I 194,2; V 62,3); Kühner–Gerth, *Gr. Grammatik* II 1, p. 376).   τεσσεράκοντα ... οἰκοδόμησε: if this extremely gauche Greek were correct, we should have to treat τεσσεράκοντα πόδας as an accusative of extent, τῆς ἑτέρης as a genitive of separation dependent on ὑποβάς, and τὠυτὸ μέγαθος as adverbial accusative: lit. 'having descended forty feet lower than the other in respect of the same size ...'. It is just possible that Herodotus wrote this phrase as a note for later development, but there is a great temptation to follow Wiedemann and Legrand in emending τὠυτό to τό, which yields a great improvement for minimal loss (cf., however, Powell, *CQ* XXXII (1938), 213). The second pyramid of Gîza was only *c.*3 m. shorter, not *c.*12 m. as Herodotus claims. For a possible explanation of the error see Lloyd, *Commentary 99–182*, p. 75.   ἓξ καὶ πεντήκοντα ἔτεα: as with Cheops, the figure is much too high. The reign length is known to have been about twenty-six years. For the likely explanation see above.

128. εἶναι ... ἀνοιχθῆναι: for the infinitives see note on 64,2.   Φιλίτιος: cf. chs. 134–5. This story looks very much like a folk-tale; the widely current view that Philitis reflects a dim memory of the Hyksos invaders of the 2nd Intermediate Period (Manetho's 'Shepherd Kings', *FGrHist* 609 F 8,82) is entirely without foundation. The name is problematic, but it could well derive from the Egyptian *p3-nr-i3wt*, 'herdsman' (which may have been pronounced approximately *Pi-l-i*) with the addition of the suffix -τις (Lloyd, *Commentary 99–182*, p. 76).

129,1. Μυκερῖνον: the Greek name is a good rendering of the Egyptian *Mn-k3w-r*ᶜ (Lloyd, *Historia*, XXXVII (1988), 31). He was the son of Chephren, not of Cheops, and there is good reason to believe that he was not Chephren's immediate successor but was preceded by Baufre (W. Stevenson Smith, *CAH*³ I 2, p. 71).   τῷ τὰ μὲν τοῦ πατρὸς ἔργα: there are traces of a positive tradition on Mycerinus in Egyptian sources (Wildung, pp. 214, 223). These might be connected with the fact that his pyramid is smaller than those of his predecessors.   ἀπαδεῖν: for the infinitive see note on 64,2.   τά τε ἱρὰ ἀνοῖξαι ... θυσίας: see note on 124,1.

1–2. δίκας δέ ... τὸν θυμόν: Mycerinus is one of several Egyptian kings who feature prominently in classical literature in connection with legal administration (cf. Diod. I 64,9; 65,2–3; 79; 94–5). It is also possible that the folk-motif of the just ruler has played a part in the development of the tradition (cf. Thompson, *Folktale*, p. 266).

3. πρῶτον κακῶν: cf. 133,1.   τὴν μοῦνόν ... τέκνον: certainly untrue (Stevenson Smith, *CAH*³ I 2, pp. 176 ff.). For the infinitive see note on 64,2. ποιήσασθαι ... θυγατέρα: cf. chs., 130–2. The basis of this description was clearly a cult image consisting of a hollow, gold-covered wooden figure of the goddess Isis in the form of a cow, which contained the headless mummy of her husband Osiris. Such images were used in the rituals of the Osirian Festival of Khoiak

(Chassinat, *Le Mystère*, p. 599). Why such a figure should have been connected specifically with Mycerinus is unclear. [ταύτην]: impossibly harsh. It must be deleted either as a gloss or as a dittograph arising from the second ταύτην (so Krueger).

130,1. ἐν Σάϊ: on the city of Sais see note on 28,1. It was a major centre of Osiris worship, in which the wooden image of a cow played an important role (see notes on 129,3; 170). ἐν τοῖσι βασιληίοισι: at first sight this is a surprising location for such a cult statue, but palaces and temples could form part of the same complex in Ancient Egypt (cf. Vandier, *Manuel* II 2, pp. 760 ff.), and it should also be remembered that Osiris played a central role in the mythology of kingship. θυμιήματα: on the use of incense in the Egyptian cult see note on 40,3. νύκτα...παρακαίεται: on rituals of illumination see note on 62.

2. ἔλεγον...ἱρέες: on priests as sources see above, pp. 230 ff. ξύλινοι... ἐργασμέναι: wooden statues of women survive in considerable numbers, but the impression of nakedness is usually an illusion created by the Egyptians' characteristically cursory rendering of close-fitting dresses (cf. Vandier, *Manuel* III, pp. 91, 111, 237 ff., 437). If these statues really existed, they were presumably effigies of attendants of Isis and/or Osiris. οὐκ ἔχω...λεγόμενα: here Herodotus follows his normal practice of recording traditions as they were reported to him, whatever their deficiencies (see above, pp. 228 ff.).

131,1–2. οἱ δέ τινες...ἔπαθον: this unseemly tale presumably began as a *Monument-novelle* intended to explain the absence of hands on the statues (see note on 107,1), but has also drawn upon the incest motif which is widely current in folklore (cf. Thompson, *Motif-Index* V, pp. 383 ff.). The τινες were probably not priests, but there is no means of identifying the source precisely.

3. ταῦτα δέ λέγουσι...ἐς ἐμέ: argument by ὄψις (see above, p. 229). ταῦτα γάρ ὦν: see n. II, 127,1.

132,1–2. ἡ δέ βοῦς...ζωή: entirely plausible. Many of these features are known to have been characteristic of the iconography of the Saite cow-goddess Methyer who had close affinities with Isis, the goddess undoubtedly embodied in Herodotus' wooden cow (cf. S. Sauneron, *Les Fêtes religieuses d'Esna* (*Esna* V), Cairo 1962, pp. 268 ff.).

1. μεταξύ δέ τῶν κερέων...χρύσεος: this attribute was a prominent element in the iconography of Isis and related goddesses during the Late Period (Bonnet, *RÄRG*, pp. 277, 404, 459).

2. μέγαθος...ζωή: the cow image at Dendera was only 1 cubit long (note on 129,3), but, since size was not normally critical in such matters, we can accept Herodotus' claim without qualms. ἐκφέρεται...πρηγματι: i.e. at the Festival of Khoiak. The god in question was Osiris (cf. note on 129,3). The reticence is typical (note on 3,2). τύπτωνται: constructed with the accusative by analogy with such verbs as ὀδύρομαι (cf. Kühner–Gerth, *Gr. Grammatik* II 1, p. 299).

3. φασὶ γὰρ δή... κατιδεῖν: this comment is an aetiological legend which betrays a total misunderstanding of the rationale of the festival. It does, however, add an element of pathos to the tale which considerably enhances its emotional impact (see above, p. 239).

133,1. ἐλθεῖν οἱ μαντήιον: another element derived from folklore, where death prophecies are a recurrent theme (Thompson, *Motif-Index*, M341).   ἐκ Βουτοῦς πόλιος: given the reputation of this oracle, the pronouncement had a particularly compelling force (cf. note on ch. 83).   ἐξ ἔτεα... τελευτήσειν: the chronology is badly wrong, since Mycerinus probably ruled for twenty-eight years. The figure is best explained as another element emanating from folklore where 7 and its multiples are common formulaic numbers (Lloyd, *Historia*, XXXVII (1988), 35). The character of the response suggests that it has an Egyptian origin (Klees, pp. 31, 60).

2. τὸν δὲ δεινὸν ποιησάμενον: this reaction and its aftermath are not without parallel in Egyptian texts (Klees, p. 36), but they could not have featured in official sources. We are probably again dealing with material derived from folk contexts.   ὁ μὲν αὐτοῦ πατήρ: a rare example of the positioning of the genitive of the non-reflexive pronoun between the article and the noun. Here it probably occurs because αὐτοῦ is logically, though not formally, reflexive. ἐβίωσαν: the aorist can be employed to refer even to a long period of time if the verbal action is conceived of simply as a self-contained event without any accessory idea such as evolution or continuity (cf. Kühner–Gerth, *Gr. Grammatik* II 1, p. 155).   χρόνον ἐπὶ πολλόν: this word-order is common in poetry but unusual in prose. With this preposition, however, it is frequent in Herodotus where its flavour is both poetic and emphatic (cf. ibid., p. 555).   εὐσεβέων: so Hude, but this verb does not occur elsewhere in Herodotus (Powell, *Lexicon*, p. 153). Godley and Legrand wisely read εὐσεβὴς ἐών with the best mss.

3. δεῖν γὰρ Αἴγυπτον... ἑκατόν: forecasts of disaster for Egypt are not difficult to parallel in pharaonic literature, e.g. the Prophecy of Neferty (W. K. Simpson (ed.), *The Literature of Ancient Egypt*, New Haven and London 1973, pp. 234 ff.).   δεῖν: '... it was fated...', an extremely common meaning of the word in Herodotus (Powell, *Lexicon*, p. 82).

4–5. ταῦτα ἀκούσαντα... ποιεύμεναι: unsuccessful attempts to forestall a prophecy are part of the stock-in-trade of folklore and legend (Thompson, *Motif-Index*, M370 ff.).   πίνειν: Egyptian kings can acquire a ritual association with drunkenness in Egyptian texts (Brunner, *ZÄS* LXXIX (1954), 81 ff.), but in our context this ingredient is best treated as no more than a natural consequence of Mycerinus' decision to defy the oracle.   τὰ ἕλεα: cf. Strabo XVII 1,15 (C799 ff.). Nothing could be more natural; hunting, fowling, and fishing in the marshlands were at all periods favourite pastimes of the wealthy (Decker, pp. 38 ff.).   τὰ ἄλσεα: groves of trees such as palm and acacia were obvious places of refreshment and enjoyment in the hot climate of Egypt (Kees, *Ancient Egypt*, pp. 78 ff.).

5. ἀποδέξαι: so Hude, but ἀποδεῖξαι has good ms authority and is accepted by Rosén as a genuine Herodotean form (*Sprachform*, p. 29).

134,1. πυραμίδα . . . κατελίπετο: the third and smallest of the kings' pyramids at Gîza.　πολλὸν ἐλάσσω: the area covered by this pyramid is less than a quarter of that of the Great Pyramid (Edwards, p. 139).　τοῦ πατρός: to Herodotus this was Cheops (note on 129,1).　εἴκοσι ποδῶν . . . τριῶν πλέθρων: at the shortest known length for the pous and plethron (note on 124,5) this amounts to 83.16 m., whereas the true length is *c*.108.5 m. (Edwards, loc. cit.).　κῶλον ἕκαστον: accusative of respect dependent on καταδέουσαν.　ἐούσης τετραγώνου: strictly, Herodotus should have used accusatives dependent on πυραμίδα. On such irregular genitives absolute see note on 66,1.　λίθου . . . Αἰθιοπικοῦ: genitive of material (cf. note on 127,2). This was true of the casing blocks only. Aswan granite was a much-coveted stone but very difficult to work. It was only used for the lower third of the pyramid, the upper casing consisting of the Tura limestone normally employed for such purposes (V. Maragioglio and C. Rinaldi, *L'architettura delle piramidi Menfite*, VI, Rapallo 1967, pp. 34 ff.).　τὴν δὴ μετεξέτεροί . . . εἶναι: although there are differences of detail, this story gained wide currency (e.g. Diod. I 64,14; Strabo XVII 1,33 (C808); Pliny, *HN* XXXVI 82). It originated with the visit of the historical Rhodopis to Egypt, but was subsequently contaminated by a number of influences such as the Nitocris tradition (note on ch. 100) and folk elements like the reversal-of-fortune motif (Lloyd, *Commentary 99–182*, pp. 84 ff.).　οὐκ ὀρθῶς λέγοντες: one of several cases in Book II where Herodotus repudiates a received tradition (cf. chs. 2, 16, 45, 131).

2. οὐδὲ ὦν . . . ἀναισίμωνται: the first argument against Rhodopis' ownership of the pyramid: her historical circumstances made it impossible. The point is developed in greater detail in the next chapter.　οὐδὲ ὦν οὐδὲ: for the duplication of οὐδὲ see Denniston, *Greek Particles*, p. 197.

2–3. πρὸς δὲ . . . ἐγένετο: the second argument is based on chronological impossibility. This is supported by her connections with Aesop (134,3–4) and Sappho (135).

2. κατὰ Ἄμασιν: Amasis ruled from 570 to 526 BC.

3. Ἰάδμονος: also Admon and Idmon (e.g. Suidas, s.v. Ῥοδώπιδος ἀνάθημα; Plutarch, *De Sera Num. Vind.* 12 (*Mor.* 556).　καὶ γὰρ οὗτος . . . ἐγένετο: Herodotus even feels obliged to prove the connection between Aesop and Iadmon, Rhodopis' master. He refers to the tradition, which exists in several versions, that the Delphians had unjustly executed Aesop and been visited with divine punishment. To extricate themselves and on the instructions of the oracle they sent embassies throughout the Greek world to invite someone to accept compensation for his death (for details see B. E. Perry, *Aesopica*, I, Urbana, I11. 1952, pp. 220 ff.).　διέδεξε: intransitive: 'it appeared' (Powell, *Lexicon*, p. 87).

135,1–6. Ῥοδῶπις . . . πέπαυμαι: see note on 134,2.

1. Ξάνθεω τοῦ Σαμίου: Samians had major commercial interests in Egypt from at least the late 7th cent. (note on 178,3).　χρημάτων μεγάλων: genitive of price. Μυτιληναίου: for Mytilene and Egypt see note on 178,2.　Σαπφοῦς τῆς μουσοποιοῦ: Sappho lived *c*.612–*c*.550 BC (D. Page, *Sappho and Alcaeus*, Oxford

1955, pp. 223 ff.). Amongst the remains of her work Frs. 5 and 15b both mention her brother's liaison with a certain Doricha, who is probably identical with Rhodopis (ibid., pp. 48 ff.).

2. ὡς [ἂν] ... ἐξικέσθαι: though the ἄν is read in all mss, it is preferable to delete with Krueger (cf., however, Kühner–Gerth, *Gr. Grammatik* II 1, p. 509). The straight limitative infinitive with ὡς is common in Herodotus (note on ch. 4). Certainly, the potential nuance of ἄν is not unattractive, but the sequence ὡς + ἄν + infinitive has no parallel in Herodotus in such contexts. Perhaps the ἄν is a dittograph arising from the following syllable.

3–4. τῆς γὰρ τὴν δεκάτην ... τοῦ νηοῦ: one of several cases where Herodotus supports a tradition with an archaeological proof (see above, p. 236). The existence of the dedication is confirmed by Athenaeus (XIII 596c) and epigraphic evidence (Jeffery, p. 102).

3. τὸ μὴ τυγχάνει: the μή probably arises through the generic flavour of the relative clause (cf. Moorhouse, pp. 323 ff.).

4. ὀβελοὺς ... σιδηρέους: such dedications are paralleled elsewhere, both archaeologically and epigraphically. Apart from their practical uses, iron spits were used in early times as a medium of exchange. However, in such cases as this they were probably simply a symbol of devotion to the god (Jeffery, p. 124; S. von Reden, *JHS* CXVII (1997), 173).   ὄπισθε ... τοῦ νηοῦ: cf. Athenaeus XIII 596d. The Chian altar was dedicated *c.*475 BC; the area in which it was set up was very prominent and, as such, much favoured at all periods for dedications (E. Kirsten and W. Kraiker, *Griechenlandkunde*, I, Heidelberg 1967⁵, pp. 259 ff.).

5. φιλέουσι ... ἑταῖραι: cf. Athenaeus XIII 596d.   οὕτω ... ἐξέμαθον: the use of ὡς for ὥστε in consecutive clauses is rare (see Goodwin, *Moods and Tenses*, pp. 232 ff.).   Ἀρχιδίκη: also Archedike (cf. Aelian, *Var. Hist.* XII 63).

136,1–4. μετὰ δὲ Μυκερῖνον ... ἀποδέξασθαι: the reign of Asychis. On the chronological error see Lloyd, *Introduction*, pp.186 ff.

1. Ἄσυχιν: the name is derived from the Egyptian royal name *Ššnk* borne by four rulers of the XXIInd (Libyan) Dynasty (*c.*945–730 BC). Here Herodotus is referring to the greatest of them, i.e. Sheshonk I (*c.*942–924 BC) (Lloyd, *Commentary 99–182*, pp. 87 ff.; cf. K. A. Kitchen, in John Baines *et al.* (eds.), *Pyramid Studies and Other Essays presented to I. E. S. Edwards*, EES Occasional Publications, VII, London, 1988, pp. 148 ff.).   τὸν τὰ πρὸς ἥλιον ... προπύλαια: for this recurrent theme see note on 99,4. There is archaeological evidence of building activity of Sheshonk I both at Memphis and elsewhere (PM III 2, p. 841; M. L. Bierbrier, *LdÄ* V, 585). If Herodotus' location is accurate, this gateway presumably lay somewhere to the west of that of Ptolemy IV (cf. W. M. F. Petrie and J. H. Walker, *Memphis* I, London, 1909, pl. 1).   τύπους ... μακρῷ μάλιστα: these reliefs will have been concerned with the king's martial prowess. Herodotus' enthusiasm is entirely credible since sculptures of Sheshonk's reign from other parts of Egypt are of very high quality (e.g. Lepsius, *Denkmäler* III, pls. 252–5).

2. ἐπὶ τούτου ... θάψαι: there is no Egyptian tradition extant on Sheshonk as a lawgiver, but the idea does occur elsewhere in classical literature (Diod. I 94,3).

The notion probably arose from the interaction of several factors: the strong impression made by his reign; the Egyptian ideal of kingship in which lawmaking was an essential ingredient (note on ch. 109); and the folk-motif of the wise ruler (cf. Thompson, *Motif-Index*, D1711.1.1, 1711.7, 1711,7.1). ἀμειξίης ἐούσης πολλῆς χρημάτων: again Herodotus anachronistically ascribes a money economy to pharaonic Egypt (note on 125,6; 126,1). We know of no such economic difficulties in Sheshonk's reign, but both before and later in the dynasty problems certainly did arise (Kitchen, pp. 3 ff., 255 ff., 287, 313 ff.). γενέσθαι νόμον ... θάψαι: this claim is the earliest evidence of such a law in any source. It certainly applied in Ptolemaic and Roman times (R. Taubenschlag, *The Law of Graeco-Roman Egypt*, Warsaw 1955², pp. 30, 276).

3–4. ὑπερβαλέσθαι ... ἐξεποίησαν: Sheshonk's tomb, which has yet to be discovered, must have lain in the temple of Amun at Tanis and was certainly not a pyramid (cf. M. Römer, *LdÄ* VI, 203 ff.). Herodotus' fictitious tradition is probably an amalgam of three main elements: pyramids were typical royal monuments; they could be made of mud-brick; and the paradox motif derived from folklore (Thompson, *Motif-Index*, L140 ff.).

137–40. The reign of Anysis, which also includes an account of that of the Ethiopian king Sabacos (137, 139).

137,1. ἐξ Ἀνύσιος πόλιος: cf. notes on ch. 111. This city lay somewhere in the north-eastern Delta (cf. 166,1); there is a strong temptation to identify it with Herakleopolis Parva whose Egyptian name *Nnì-nsw* (Hebrew *Hanes*, cf. Gardiner, *AEO* II, p. 176*) could well have been the origin of Herodotus' place-name. Ἄνυσιν: the name probably arose by transference from that of the town mentioned previously. It is unlikely that he represents any specific king but rather stands for the entire XXIIIrd (Tanite) Dynasty (Lloyd, *Commentary 99–182*, pp. 91 ff.). ἐπὶ τούτου βασιλεύοντος ... Σαβακῶν τὸν Αἰθιόπων βασιλέα: Shabaka's conquest of Egypt took place c.715–714 BC (Kitchen, pp. 362 ff.). Αἰθίοπάς: sc. 'Nubians' (cf. note on 29,4). Σαβακῶν: a good rendering of the Egyptian *Š3-b3-k3* (Assyrian *Sha-ba-ku-u*) (Roeder, *RE*, IA, 1523 ff.).

2. ἐς τὰ ἕλεα: cf. note on 92,1. Throughout Egyptian history the Delta marshes were constantly used as a place of refuge for rebels or fugitives from the law (cf. Thucy. I 110,2; M. Rostovtzeff, *The Social and Economic History of the Hellenistic World*, II, Oxford 1953, p. 898). ἐπ' ἔτεα πεντήκοντα: far too high, since Shabaka was king of Egypt for about fourteen years only. The figure is best explained as reflecting the fifty-year period which elapsed between the completion of Shabaka's conquest of Egypt in c.714 and the accession in 664 of Psammetichus I who brought the Ethiopian/Nubian domination of the country to an end. ἀποδέξασθαι: for the infinitive see note on 64,2.

3. ὅκως τῶν τις Αἰγυπτίων ... τῶν ἀδικεόντων: cf. Diod. I 65,2. On pharaohs as the fount of law cf. note on 136,2. This pro-Ethiopian tradition is paralleled elsewhere (cf. Diod. I 60; in general see Hofmann–Vorbichler,

pp. 76 ff.), but some classical sources take quite the opposite view of the invader (cf. Manetho, *FGrHist* 609 F 2, 3a–b, pp. 48 ff.).   καὶ οὕτω... ἐγένοντο: cf. note on 138,2.

5. ἡ ἐν Βουβάστι πόλις: cf. note on 59,1.   Βουβάστιος: i.e. the Egyptian goddess Bastet (cf. note on 59,1).   μέζω μὲν γὰρ ἄλλα... μᾶλλον: excavation on the site has revealed that this is by no means an exaggerated claim (H. E. Naville, *Bubastis (1887–1889)*, London 1891, pp. 10 ff., 46 ff.).

138,1–4. πλὴν τῆς ἐσόδου... ἔχει: an archaeological proof is used to substantiate the historical tradition of the preceding chapter (see above, p. 236).

1. πλὴν τῆς ἐσόδου... δένδρεσι κατάσκιος: traces of these canals have been identified in modern times (Naville, op. cit., p. 3). They served an important cultic purpose in that they created an *išrw*, i.e. a crescent-shaped lake enveloping the temple on three sides. Such features were a common element in the shrines of goddesses such as Bastet (cf. S. Sauneron, *BIFAO* LXII (1964), 50 ff.).   δένδρεσι κατάσκιος: trees were clearly a standard accompaniment of the *išrw* (ibid., p. 51, fig. 1).

2. τὰ δὲ προπύλαια... ἀξίοισι λόγου: this gate lay on the east side of the temple. The sculptures were probably the work either of Ramesses II or Osorkon I (cf. Naville, op. cit., p. 3).   ἐὸν δ' ἐν μέσῃ τῇ πόλι... ἔσοπτόν ἐστι: correct. The ruins lie in a depression measuring *c.*274.3 × 304.8 m. (Naville, loc. cit.).

3. περιθέει... τύποισι: this feature was apparently made of black basalt (Naville, loc. cit.).   ἄλσος... πεφυτευμένον: the trees symbolized the protective presence of the goddess in the temple (cf. Bonnet, *RÄRG*, p. 85).   νηὸν μέγαν... τὦγαλμα ἔνι: the νηός was the main temple building. Its exact dimensions cannot be established, but it is improbable that it was much more than 121.9 m. in length (cf. Naville, op. cit., pp. 3 ff.).   εὖρος δὲ καὶ μῆκος... ἐστί: these measurements presumably refer to the entire sacred enclosure, which was probably *c.*228.6 m. long and *c.*176.7 m. broad (Kitchen, p. 318, fig. 3).

4. ὁδὸς λίθου... ὡς τεσσέρων πλέθρων: such processional ways were common in Egyptian temples (cf. PM II, plans I and XXIV). Traces extant in modern times suggest that Herodotus' measurement is much too short (3 stades = at least 537 m.; true length *c.* 685.8 m.). The width has never been determined, but it cannot have been anywhere near 3 plethra (not less than *c.*89 m.). The best explanation is that, as often in Herodotus, the figure 3 is being used impressionistically and that neither he nor his audience would have insisted on its literal accuracy, i.e. he simply means 'a substantial number of stades' and 'a substantial number of plethra' (cf. note on 124,5).   λίθου: genitive of material (see note on 127, 3).   ἐς Ἑρμέω ἱρόν: i.e. a temple of Thoth. In the relevant area there are remains of a temple built by Osorkon I, but it is unclear whose cult it served (L. Habachi, *Tell Basta*, Suppl. to *Annales du Service des Antiquités*, XXII, Cairo 1957, pp. 119 ff.).

139,1. τέλος δὲ τῆς ἀπαλλαγῆς: cf. Homer, *Il.* III 309.   ὄψιν... διαταμεῖν: cf. 141,3–6 and S. West, *CQ* XXXVII (1987), 262 ff. The Egyptians believed that dreams were one of the means by which gods could communicate with men, and

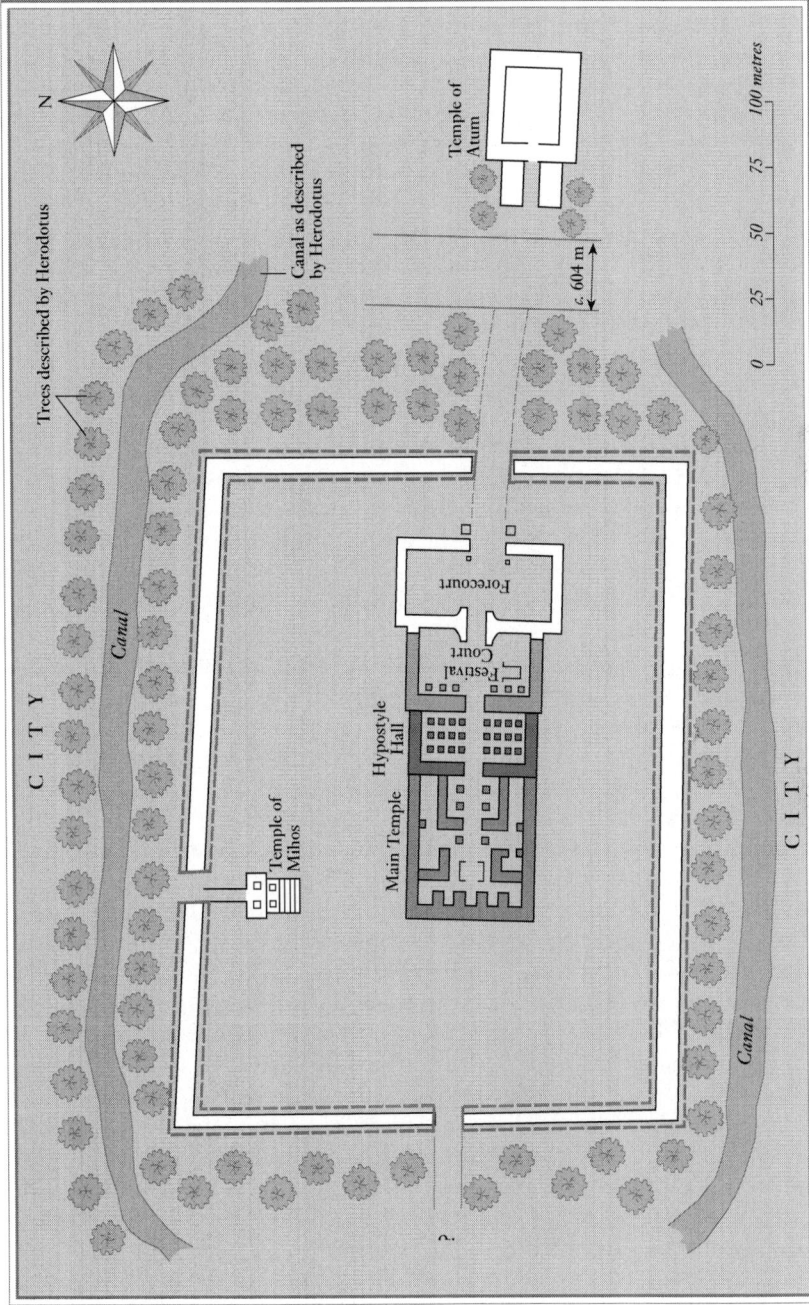

Map 26. The temple of Bubastis (conjectural reconstruction).
Main Temple: Dyns. 12–21; Hypostyle Hall: Osorkon I–II; Festival Court: Osorkon II; Forecourt: Osorkon I.

even developed handbooks to assist in their interpretation (Sauneron *et al.*, pp. 19 ff.). This notion was certainly shared by the Nubians/Ethiopians, and Herodotus is quite correct in claiming that they could treat dreams as the basis for major political and military decisions (e.g. the Dream Stele of Tanutamun (664–*c*.655 BC), *BAR* IV, 922). However, since dreams figure prominently in folklore, we should also make allowance for the possibility of influence from that source (cf. Thompson, *Motif-Index*, Index, p. 228).   μέσους διαταμεῖν: cf. VII 39; Gen. 15: 10–17; Livy XL 6,1–2; T. W. Africa, *JNES* XXII (1963), 255, n. 15.
2. ἰδόντα δὲ τὴν ὄψιν...ταῦτα: cf. I 158–9,4. For this pro-Ethiopian tradition see note on 137,3.   οὐκ ὦν: for the adversative use of this sequence in the sense of Latin *nec vero* or *non tamen* see Kühner–Gerth, *Gr. Grammatik* II 2, p. 161.   ἀλλὰ γάρ: trans.: 'For, on the contrary,...' (cf. Denniston, *Greek. Particles*, p. 107).   τὸν χρόνον...ἐκχωρήσειν: oracles were of major importance in determining state policy in Nubia (note on ch. 29). Note, however, that folklore may also have exercised some influence, here since it contains many prophecies of downfall or death (Crahay, p. 227).   κεχρῆσθαι: for the infinitive see note on 64,2.
3. ἔτεα πεντήκοντα: see note on 137,2.   ὡς ὦν...ὁ Σαβακῶς: cf. 152,1. This narrative is quite unhistorical. The Nubian XXVth Dynasty came to an end in 656 during the reign of Tanutamun, over three decades after the death of Sabacos, and was certainly not as peaceful as Herodotus believed (Kitchen, pp. 391 ff.).

140,1. ἄρα: the particle expresses keen interest in the event under discussion (Denniston, *Greek Particles*, p. 34).   οἴχεσθαι: for the infinitive see note on 64,2.   αὖτις τὸν τυφλὸν...ἀπικόμενον: this element may well owe something to folklore, where the return-of-the-king motif is of common occurrence (Thompson, *Motif-Index*, F451.6.12; J1189.3; R191).   πεντήκοντα ἔτεα: cf. note on 137,2.   νῆσον...οἴκεε: this ingredient in the tradition looks very much like a faded myth dealing with the death and resurrection of the king. The island frequently features in mythological contexts as the place of creation and, as such, plays an important role in rituals of kingship. Furthermore, in some texts this island can appear as the *iw nsrsr*, 'the Isle of Flame', a concept which may well be reflected in the connection of Herodotus' island with σποδός, 'ash' (Lloyd, *Commentary 99–182*, pp. 98 ff.).   φοιτᾶν...προστετάχθαι: for the infinitives see note on 64,2.
2. Ἀμυρταίου: for this anti-Persian rebel see III 15,3; Thuc. I 112,3.   ἔτεα ... Ἀμυρταίου: on the chronological problems presented by this figure see Lloyd, *Introduction*, p. 188.   ἔτεα ἐπὶ πλέω: cf. note on 133,2.   Ἐλβώ: cf. Stephanus of Byzantium, s.v. The site has never been identified.

141,1. Μετὰ δὲ τοῦτον...Σεθῶν: the chronology is correct, since Sethos is certainly to be identified with Shabaka's successor Shabataka (702–690 BC), and the campaign of Sennacherib did indeed take place in his reign (see below).   τὸν ἱρέα τοῦ Ἡφαίστου: Sethos' Nubian nationality has either been ignored or forgotten. However, the fact that he is transmuted into a priest of a major

Egyptian temple is a striking testimony to the power of the pro-Nubian strand in Egyptian tradition (cf. note on 139,2) and may also reflect the undoubted interest shown by the Nubians in the shrine of Ptah/Hephaestus at Memphis (cf. H. v. Zeissl, *Äthioper und Assyrer in Ägypten*, *Äg. Forschungen*, XIV, Glückstadt 1944, p. 81). Σεθῶν: the name is probably a corruption of the Egyptian Š3-b3-t3-k3 (Alan B. Lloyd, *Historia*, XXXVII (1988), 32). τῶν μαχίμων ... δυῶδεκα ἀρούρας: for the *Machimoi* and their privileges see notes on 164,2. ἐς αὐτοὺς: the accusative of the person suffering the action is more normal in such contexts (Kühner–Gerth, *Gr. Grammatik* II 1, 324).

2. μετὰ δὲ ἐπ' Αἴγυπτον ... Ἀσσυρίων: Herodotus' picture is distorted since, although Sennacherib was at war with Shabataka, his forces were not marching against Egypt when the events in question took place (Kitchen, pp. 154 ff., 383 ff.). Σαναχάριβον: a good rendering of the Assyrian *Sin-ahhê-eriba* (cf. G. Roux, *Ancient Iraq*, Harmondsworth 1964, p. 288). Ἀραβίων: it was standard Assyrian practice to draw troops from subject nations as required, and Arabians were certainly no exception (ibid., p. 279).

3. ἐπελθεῖν ... στρατόν: cf. note on 139,1. Incubation was certainly an Egyptian practice (Bonnet, *RÄRG*, p. 837).

4. τούτοισι δή μιν πίσυνον: this phrase is followed by τοῖσι ἐνυπνίοισι in the Florentine mss and by Αἰγυπτίοισι in the Roman group. This uncertainty strongly suggests that both are glosses on τούτοισι and that Gomperz was correct in deleting. τούτοισι refers loosely to the content of the dream just described. καπήλους ... ἀνθρώπους: for κάπηλοι see 35,2; 164,1. The prominence of these groups, none of which would have enjoyed high prestige in Egyptian society, probably reflects the influence of the reversal-of-fortune motif so common in folklore (Thompson, *Motif-Index*, L300 ff.).

5. ἐνθαῦτα ... πολλούς: for alternative versions see Isa. 37; 2 Kings 19; 2 Chro. 32; Josephus, *Ant. Iud.* X 1,3,5; Berossus, *FGrHist* 680 F 7(a). The disaster befell an Assyrian force besieging Jerusalem and probably took the form of an epidemic of typhoid or cholera (Lloyd, *Commentary 99–182*, pp. 102 ff.). μῦς ἀρουρ-αίους ... μῦν: it seems probable that this tale originated as an attempt to explain a statue in Memphis dedicated by Shabataka to Horus of Letopolis, a god who had close cultic affinities with the shrewmouse (cf. note on 67,1; Spiegelberg, *Glaub-würdigkeit*, pp. 26 ff.). This statue may well have been set up as a thank-offering for the god's assistance against the Assyrians. κατὰ μὲν ... κατὰ δὲ: tmesis of a compound verb with μέν and δέ where the δέ is not followed by the simplex of the verb is a Homeric construction which occurs not infrequently in Herodotus (Kühner–Gerth, *Gr. Grammatik* II 1, p. 537). [ἀνόπλων]: the Roman group and the Parisinus read ὅπλων which would be dependent on γυμνῶν; other mss have ἀνόπλων. Both should be deleted. The first is an unnecessary expansion of γυμνῶν, and ἀνόπλων is a gloss on the phrase γυμνῶν ὅπλων, both errors perpetrated by scribes unfamiliar with the Homeric use of γυμνός in the sense 'unarmed'.

6. οὗτος ὁ βασιλεὺς ... μῦν: such a statue would be well within Egyptian artistic convention (e.g. Vandier, *Manuel* III, pl. CXXXII 2). λέγων διὰ

γραμμάτων... ἔστω: no Egyptian inscription could possibly have been couched in these terms; the 'translation' is indisputably a Greek invention and clearly demonstrates that the Egyptian tale of Sethos' triumph has been reworked for Greek consumption.

142–6. This section consists of a chronological excursus inspired by the previously described panorama of Egyptian history and the contradictions with Greek traditions which it presented (see above, pp. 229 ff.). There is a distinct possibility that it was no part of Herodotus' original draft but was added as an afterthought (J. E. Powell, *CQ* XXIX (1935), 78 ff.).

142,1. Ἐς μὲν τοσόνδε τοῦ λόγου... ἔλεγον: from 147,1, non-Egyptians become a major source of information (see above, pp. 229 ff.).		**ἀπὸ τοῦ πρώτου βασιλέος... γενομένους**: cf. note on 143,4. The number of generations is indeed 341, but the correct number of kings is 342. Herodotus has ignored the fact that Anysis and Sabacos were contemporaries (chs. 137, 140).
2. καίτοι τριηκόσιαι... ἐστι: the equation 3 generations = 100 years is a good rule-of-thumb and was intended simply as that. It should not be taken to mean that Herodotus considered 1 generation to be $33\frac{1}{3}$ years (see above, pp. 236 ff.).		**μιῆς δὲ... ἔτεα**: by strict arithmetic 41 generations would total 1,366 years, but such niceties are of no interest to Herodotus, who has simply given the nearest round number—a clear indication of the level of precision he observed and expected in such matters.
3. θεὸν... τοιοῦτον: Herodotus points up the blatant contradiction between Egyptian tradition and Greek mythical and legendary chronology. This was evidently a matter of major interest to himself and his contemporaries (cf. v. Fritz I, pp. 182 ff.).		**οὐ μὲν οὐδὲ**: Hude and Legrand read μέν with the Romans and the Parisinus, but the best mss read μέντοι and the adversative dimension is certainly apposite (so also Stein and Godley).
4. ἐν τοίνυν τούτῳ τῷ χρόνῳ... καταδῦναι: cf. Mela I 9,8; Solinus 32. Herodotus has in mind the recurrent cosmic cycles which featured in the systems of several Greek thinkers (e.g. Empedocles, KR², pp. 287 ff.). This concept was foreign to Egyptian thought, but we do find mythological references to disruption of the movements of heavenly bodies (cf. C. Sander-Hansen, *Die Texte der Metternichstele*, Analecta Aegyptiaca, VII, Copenhagen 1956, pp. 64, 203 ff.). Probably Herodotus or his Egyptian informants mistakenly identified these two very different notions.		**τοίνυν**: the particle is rather colloquial and is relatively infrequent in narrative contexts in Herodotus (Denniston, *Greek Particles*, p. 569).		**ἐξ ἠθέων**: the use of ἐκ in the sense of ἔξω/ἐκτός has an epic flavour (Kühner–Gerth, *Gr. Grammatik* II 1, p. 459).		**καὶ οὐδεν ... θανάτους**: given Herodotus' views on environmental determinism (cf. 35,2; 77,3), he would expect such cosmic changes to have radical effects on the mode of life of those subjected to them.		**οὔτε τὰ ἀπὸ τῆς γῆς... γινόμενα**: these phrases reflect such common Egyptian expressions as *ddt pt ḳm3t t3 ỉnnt Ḥp*, 'that which heaven gives, earth creates, and the Nile brings forth' (*Wb.* V, p. 35, 7–8). This situation

confirms the involvement of Egyptian sources in creating this tradition. ἀπό...ἀπό: so Hude, but the best mss prefer ἐκ in both cases.

143,1–4. πρότερον δέ...κἀγαθός: Herodotus' first argument against traditional Greek legendary chronology.

1. Ἑκαταίῳ τῷ λογοποιῷ: Herodotus' most important predecessor (see above, p. 231 and S. West, *JHS* CXI (1991), 144 ff.). ἐς ἑκκαιδέκατον θεόν: i.e. at the traditional date of the Ionian Migration (1086/5 or 1076/5 BC, *FGrHist* 239 F 27). οἱ ἱρέες τοῦ Διός: they were probably the priests of Amon-re at Karnak.

2–4. ἐσαγαγόντες...αὐτούς: the demolition of Hecataeus' genealogical pretentions and, *ipso facto*, his concept of early Greek chronology. At first sight the details are difficult to credit, but the narrative becomes comprehensible if we regard it as a conflation of a report in Hecataeus' *Genealogies*, Herodotus' experiences during his confrontation with the priests, and interpretations and afterthoughts on both (for detailed discussion see Lloyd, *Commentary 99–182,* pp. 107 ff.).

2. τὸ μέγαρον: probably the Great Hypostyle Hall at Karnak, which measured *c.*51.7 m. east–west and *c.*102.9 m. north–south. The nave was *c.*24 m. high (Baedeker, *Egypt,* pp. 268 ff.). ἐξηρίθμεον...εἶπον: the expression is very loose. According to 142,1 the number was 341; at 143,4 it is 345. Herodotus has simply taken for granted the four generations and statues which would have been added between the time of Sethos and Hecataeus' visit. ἐξηρίθμεον: for the intensive use of the prefix ἐξ- see note on 3,2.

2–3. κολοσσοὺς ξυλίνους...ἁπάσας αὐτάς: the presence of a large number of statues in such a context was quite normal. A large cache of them discovered at Karnak included some of high priests, and many carried genealogical inscriptions. Some were of wood, but the majority followed standard practice and were of stone (G. Legrain, *Statues et statuettes de rois et de particuliers* (CGC), I–III, Cairo 1906–25).

3. παῖδα πατρὸς...διὰ πασέων: the hereditary principle was well established in Herodotus' time (cf. 37,5), but it was certainly not applied so consistently over the enormous, not to say impossible, time-span indicated by Herodotus. The Egyptians were, however, capable of deliberately misleading statements on such matters (cf. Posener, pp. 98 ff.).

4. κολοσσοὺς: this word is followed in mss either by πίρωμιν ἐκ πιρώμιος γενόμενον or πίρωμιν ἐπονομαζόμενον, both of which make the run of the sentence very awkward. It seems preferable with Stein to delete. The first was probably an interpolation based on the preceding πίρωμιν ἐκ πιρώμιος γεγονέναι and the second perhaps a gloss on the interpolation. πίρωμις: the word is derived from the Egyptian *p3 rmṯ,* 'the man', which can be used in the sense of 'a man of importance' (*Wb.* II, p. 422,10).

144,1–2. ἤδη...γλῶσσαν: the Egyptian tradition on the Dynasty of the Gods. This discussion begins a further argument against Greek chronological ideas which continues until ch. 146, i.e. they are contradicted by Egyptian theology. For ἤδη ὦν in the sense 'well now' to introduce such additional arguments see Powell, *Lexicon,* p. 160.

2. τὸ δὲ πρότερον...τὸν κρατέοντα εἶναι: impeccable. The Dynasty of the Gods was a constant element in the Ancient Egyptian concept of history, though opinions differed on its composition (cf. Wb. II, p. 457, 9–12; Manetho, FGrHist 609, pp. 11 ff.); Egyptian texts are perfectly capable of treating them on the same terms as historical kings (e.g. Re in the Myth of the Destruction of Mankind, Lichtheim, New Kingdom, pp. 197 ff.).   ὕστατον...ὀνομάζουσι: this was canonical doctrine (cf. Bonnet, RÄRG, pp. 228 ff.). On the identification of Horus and Apollo see notes on chs. 155–6.   Τυφῶνα: cf. 156,4–5. The Egyptian god in question was Seth, brother of Osiris and uncle of Horus (Kolta, pp. 161 ff.).   Ὄσιρις...γλῶσσαν: cf. notes on 42,4; 47,2; 48,2–3.

145,1. Ἐν Ἕλλησι...Πάν: for purposes of the argument of chs. 145–6 Herodotus treats these three gods as one coherent group: anything which he can prove for one must hold true for all.   Πὰν μὲν...θεῶν: sc. the Egyptian god Mendes. There is, as yet, no evidence that he belonged to the Ogdoad, but it is perfectly possible that he was included in it at some religious centres during the Late Period (note on ch. 46; Alan B. Lloyd, Historia, XXXVII (1988), 33).   Ἡρακλέης: sc. the Egyptian Shu. Since Herodotus' group of twelve gods is to be identified in this context with the Egyptian Heliopolitan Ennead, his theology here is impeccable (note on 43,1).   Διόνυσος: sc. Osiris (note on 144,2). The 'third group' will have been one of the lesser Enneads of Heliopolis (on which see Bonnet, RÄRG, pp. 523 ff.).

2. δεδήλωταί μοι πρόσθε: cf. 43,4.

2–4. Διονύσῳ...ἐς ἐμέ: this calculation places Dionysus in the later 15th cent. BC (see above, pp. 236 ff.). After χίλια all mss read ἑξακόσια ἔτεα καί. The numeral must be deleted if the arithmetic is to work (Lloyd, Introduction, p. 179); the καί is pointless, and we should expect μάλιστα to be closely adjacent to the phrase which it qualifies (cf. ὀκτακόσια μάλιστα below).

4. Ἡρακλέϊ...εἰνακόσια: i.e. c.1350 BC. For his parentage see note on 43,2.   Πανὶ δὲ τῷ [ἐκ] Πηνελόπης: cf. Apollodorus, Ep. VII 38; Cicero, De Nat. D. III 56. This genealogy is probably the oldest, but there were differences of opinion on Pan's lineage (e.g. Hymn. Hom. Pan 27 ff.).   ἐλάσσω ἔτεά...ἐμέ: sc. c.1250 BC. Herodotus' date for the Trojan war fell within the period c.1330–1250 BC (see Lloyd, Introduction, p. 178).

146,1. τούτων ὦν ἀμφοτέρων: partitive genitive dependent upon τοῖσί...μᾶλλον. The phrase refers to the two opinions on the date of the three gods mentioned in ch. 145.   ἐμοὶ δ' ὦν...ἀποδέδεκται: cf. chs. 43–9.

1–2. εἰ μὲν γὰρ φανεροί...τὴν γένεσιν: since this passage sits awkwardly in the context and is far from clear in expression, it may well be an Herodotean afterthought (cf. J. E. Powell, CQ XXIX (1935), 78 ff.). Herodotus argues that the Greek chronology for the birth of Heracles, Dionysus, and Pan is incorrect by demolishing what he regards as the only alternative: it might be claimed that these three had been born in Greece as men and had subsequently acquired their names from previously existing gods. This cannot be true, since there would have been detailed information on their early careers in Greece, and that was not the case.

The truth is that these three deities arrived in Greece from Egypt at a late date and that the Greeks assigned their birth to the time when they got to know them.

1. καὶ οὗτοι: i.e. the three ancient deities of 145,1–3. The καί recalls the fact that at 50,2 Herodotus has argued that there was a small group of gods which had originated exclusively in Greece.   κατά περ...ὁ ἐκ Πηνελόπης γενό-μενος: *pace* Stein *et al.*, there is no break in sense before καὶ δὴ καί. To Herodotus all three stand on the same footing.   ἔφη...θεῶν: as with Heracles, ancient texts sometimes claim that there were two Pans (e.g. Aeschylus, fr. 25b (Radt); Eustathius, *ad Odyssey* II 84).   καὶ τούτους ἄλλους: lit. 'these others also'. The expression and possibly thinking are confused. Herodotus means: 'Dionysus, son of Semele, and Pan, son of Penelope, <like Heracles, son of Amphitryon in II, 43>'. The sense would have been much clearer if he had simply written τούτους.

2. νῦν δὲ Διόνυσόν...Ζεύς: for details see Apollodorus IV 2 ff.   ἐς Νύσαν: cf. III 97,2. Dionysus is alleged to have been reared in Nysa and to have planted there the first vine. Herodotus' siting of the place is one of many in ancient sources which locate it in widely differing parts of Europe, Africa, and Asia (cf. Herrmann, *RE* XVII, 1654 ff.).   καὶ...γε: see note on 111,4.

147–82. A discussion of the history of the Saite Period (XXVIth Dynasty) covering approximately the years 664–529 BC. Since it is the earliest and fullest consecutive account in any language, it is, for all its deficiencies, of great historical importance (see above, p. 238).

147,1. Ταῦτα μέν...ὄψιος: again Herodotus is explicit on his sources (see note on 142,1).

2–4. ἐλευθερωθέντες Αἰγύπτιοι...συνελέγοντο: cf. Diod. I 66. Herodotus' account of the Dodecarchs, which continues at chs. 148, 151–2, is the first part of his narrative of the reign of Psammetichus I (664–610 BC). His history of this ruler is based on a core of sound information, but this is overlaid with Egyptian propaganda (152) and folklore (note on ch. 147) and distorted by Greek tradition and attitudes (notes on chs. 151–2).

2. τὸν ἱρέα: Sethos (see ch. 141).   ἄνευ βασιλέος: a sound assessment. To the Egyptians kingship was not simply the only feasible type of government; it was the most important single element in the conceptual infrastructure of their world (Frankfort, *Religion*, pp. 30 ff.).   δυώδεκα βασιλέας: this multiplicity of kings is a reflection of the collapse of central authority and fragmentation of power during the Nubian and Assyrian Periods (cf. Kitchen, pp. 398, 456, 459). Why Herodotus should speak specifically of twelve is uncertain, but the number may reflect that of the courts in the Labyrinth which was associated with the Dodecarchs (cf. 148,4; Griffith, *Catalogue* III, p. 71).   δυώδεκα μοίρας: many mss read ἐς before this phrase, but it is omitted in the Roman group and is against Herodotean usage (Powell, *Lexicon*, p. 72).

3. ἐπιγαμίας: in Egypt, as elsewhere, political marriages were commonplace (e.g. *BAR* I, p. 282 ff.).

4. ἐκέχρηστό σφι... Αἰγύπτου: cf. ch. 151. This element in the tradition might well emanate from folklore, where accession prophecies are of frequent occurrence (Thompson, *Motif-Index*, M310). The format is not Egyptian, but the fact that prophecies concerned with royal appointments do occur in pharaonic sources justifies the strong suspicion that the story has an Egyptian origin (cf. de Meulenaere, pp. 25 ff.).   ἐκέχρηστό: χράω in the the sense of 'give an oracular response' normally takes a present or aorist infinitive rather than the future (Goodwin, *Moods and Tenses*, p. 30).   ἐν τῷ ἱρῷ τοῦ Ἡφαίστου: see note on ch. 151.   συνελέγοντο: this statement could well be early evidence of the existence of priestly synods which are not, as yet, securely attested before the Ptolemaic Period (cf. Bonnet, *RÄRG*, pp. 603 ff.).

148,1–7. καὶ δή σφι... πεποίηται: an excursus on the Egyptian Labyrinth, one of the Egyptian monuments most admired in antiquity (cf. Diod. I 61; 66,3–6; Strabo XVII 1,37 (C811); 1,42 (C813); Pliny, *NH*, XXXVI 13 (19); Mela I 9,56).
1. καὶ δή σφι... κοινῇ: untrue. The Labyrinth was built much earlier by Amenemhet III (for whom see note on 13,1). It combined the functions of a mortuary temple for the king buried in the adjacent pyramid and probably that of a cult centre for the local gods of the Fayûm area (Alan B. Lloyd, *JEA* LVI (1970), 91 ff.).   δόξαν: accusative absolute, which is normally used instead of the genitive construction with impersonal verbs (Goodwin, *Moods and Tenses*, pp. 338 ff.). The *figura etymologica* with the preceding ἔδοξε is typical of Herodotus, who commonly employs it as a method of linking clauses (cf. note on 14,2).   λαβύρινθον: the word is pre-Greek and probably means 'House of the Double Axe' (H. Frisk, *Griechisches etymologisches Wörterbuch*, II, Heidelberg 1970, p. 67). Attempts to relate it to homophonous Egyptian words have been ingenious but unconvincing (Lloyd, op. cit., pp. 92 ff.).   τῆς λίμνης τῆς Μοίριος: see notes on 4,3; 149–50.   Κροκοδείλων καλεομένην πόλιν: the Ancient Egyptian city of Šdyt (modern Medinet el-Fayûm), which was a major cult centre of the crocodile god Sobk. The importance of this god in the area explains the Herodotean name for the place. In Hellenistic and Roman times it was known as Arsinoiton polis/Arsinoe (see, in general, Gardiner, *AEO* II, pp. 116* ff.).   εἶδον: ὄψις in action (see above, p. 229).
1–3.   λόγου μέζω... ὑπερβάλλει: the Labyrinth was a clear case of a θῶμα (cf. above, pp. 234 ff.). The disparaging attitude towards things Greek is not without parallel in Herodotus (see above, pp. 235 ff.).
2. τὰ ἐξ Ἑλλήνων τείχεά: the genitive would have been quite sufficient, but the addition of the prepositions ἐκ or ἀπό in such contexts is not without parallel. Here the preposition serves to throw Ἑλλήνων into sharper relief and emphasizes the contrast with Egyptian achievements (Kühner–Gerth, *Gr. Grammatik* II 1, p. 336).   ὁ ἐν Ἐφέσῳ... νηός: i.e. the Croesus or archaic temple of Artemis which measured c.54.8 m. × 109.6 m. along the stylobate as against c.243.6 m. × 304.5 m. for the Labyrinth (cf. D. S. Robertson, *Greek and Roman Architecture*, Cambridge 1943², pp. 90 ff.).   ὁ ἐν Σάμῳ: i.e. the temple of Hera, which seems to have been begun by Polycrates, tyrant of Samos c.533–522 BC. At

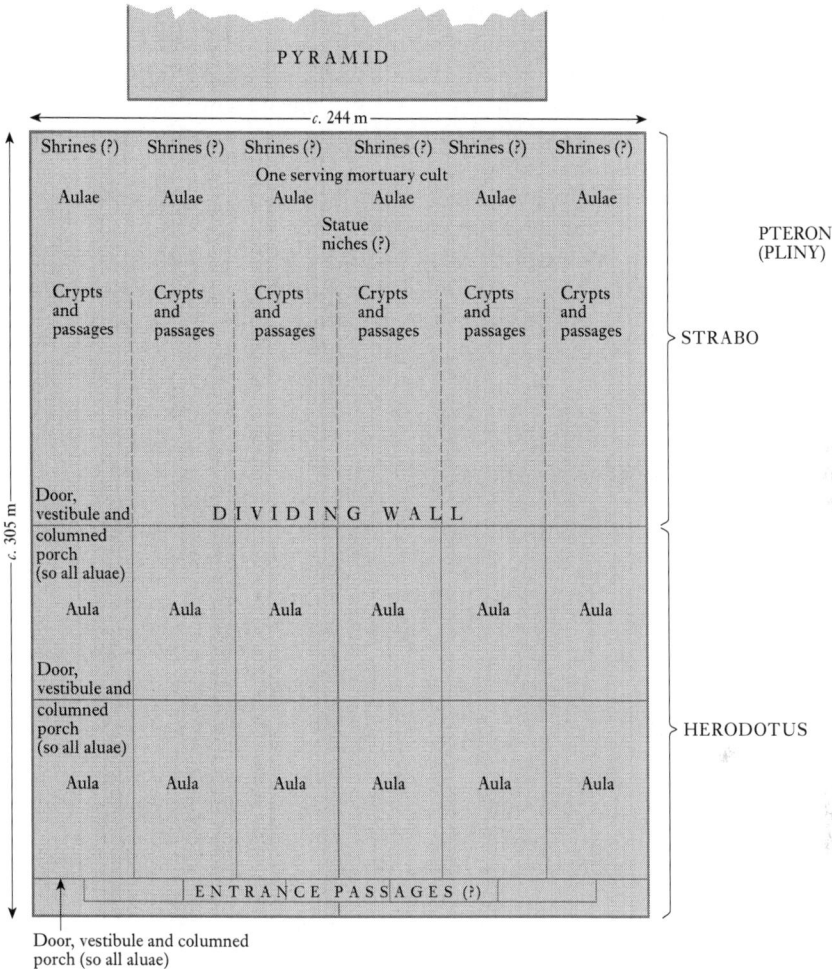

PYRAMID

c. 244 m

Shrines (?)	Shrines (?)	Shrines (?)	Shrines (?)	Shrines (?)	Shrines (?)
		One serving mortuary cult			
Aulae	Aulae	Aulae	Aulae	Aulae	Aulae
		Statue niches (?)			
Crypts and passages	Crypts and passages	Crypts and passages	Crypts and passages	Crypts and passages	Crypts and passages

PTERON (PLINY)

STRABO

c. 305 m

Door, vestibule and columned porch (so all aluae)

DIVIDING WALL

| Aula | Aula | Aula | Aula | Aula | Aula |

Door, vestibule and columned porch (so all aluae)

| Aula | Aula | Aula | Aula | Aula | Aula |

HERODOTUS

ENTRANCE PASSAGES (?)

Door, vestibule and columned porch (so all aluae)

Sketch plan

Map 27. The Egyptian Labyrinth (conjectural reconstruction)

*c.*54.5 m. × 111.4 m. along the stylobate it also fell far below the Labyrinth in size (cf. ibid., pp. 95 ff.).

4. τοῦ γὰρ δυώδεκα: τοῦ is being used as a simple demonstrative (cf. 124,4, where it is also preceded by γάρ).   αὐλαὶ κατάστεγοι: 'roofed courts', but Egyptian architectural practice suggests that the roofing would only have been partial and would have left a square opening in the centre (Lloyd, op. cit., p. 82). At 148,7 the courts are said to be surrounded by columns, a feature which has many extant parallels.

4–5. οἰκήματα δ' ἔνεστι ... κροκοδείλων: the claim that there was a subterranean series of chambers exactly parallel to that above ground should be treated with extreme reserve (see above, p. 237), but underground rooms certainly occur in temples of Sobk, and it is not improbable that some of them were used for either or both of the purposes mentioned by Herodotus (Lloyd, op. cit., p. 94; D. Arnold, *MDAI(K)* XXXV (1979), 7 ff.).

6. διὰ τῶν στεγέων: here στέγη may mean 'vestibule' (Lloyd, op. cit., p. 83, n. 1).   παστάδας: 'columned porches' (ibid., pp. 81 ff.).

7. λίθου λευκοῦ: i.e. limestone, of which abundant fragments can still be seen on the site (ibid., p. 83, n. 4).   τῆς δὲ γωνίης ... τεσσερακοντόργυιος: Herodotus' memory or informant played him false, for the pyramid stands on the centre line of the Labyrinth. It is now badly ruined, but in its original state it measured *c.*57.9 m. high and *c.*106.6 m. square. Herodotus does not indicate the dimension to which his 40 orguiai (*c.*73 m.) refer, but it does not fit either well. ὁδὸς ... πεποίηται: a passage led from the south side of the pyamid by a very devious route to the burial chamber in the centre (Edwards, p. 218).

149–50.   An excursus on lake Moeris. Unlike most such digressions in Herodotus it is completely irrelevant (Lloyd, *Historia*, XXXVII (1988), 49).

149,1. θῶμα: see above, pp. 234 ff.   ἡ Μοίριος καλεομένη λίμνη: cf. note on 4,3. This lake survives as the much smaller Birket Karûn in the Fayûm. It was a subject of recurrent fascination and misunderstanding amongst classical writers (cf. Diod. I 51–2; Strabo XVII 1,4 (C789); 35 (C809); 37 (C810 ff.); Pliny, *NH*, V 50; Mela I 9,5).   Μοίριος: Amenemhet III (note on ch. 13). Classical sources frequently speak of his activities in this area. There is no direct confirmation by Egyptian evidence, but the tradition is supported in general by the fact that the XIIth Dynasty, to which Moeris/Amenemhet III belonged, has left a substantially larger corpus of monuments in the area than any preceding age (PM IV, pp. 96 ff.).   ὁ λαβύρινθος: see note on 148,1.   τὸ περίμετρον ... τὸ παρὰ θάλασσαν: i.e. *c.*666.1 km. It could never at any time have reached this size, and in the mid-5th cent. stood at a mere *c.*270 km. (Lloyd, *Commentary 99–182*, p. 125).   κεῖται ... νότον: since the lake would have lain on the 20 m. contour line in Herodotus' time, the orientation is correct (ibid.). πεντηκοντόργυιος: i.e. *c.*93 m. It would probably not have been deeper than *c.*73 m. (Ball, *Contributions*, p. 207).

2. χειροποίητός: untrue. The basin which the lake partly occupied is a geological formation (Ball, pp. 178 ff.).   ἐν γὰρ μέσῃ τῇ λίμνῃ ... θρόνῳ: cf. Diod. I 52. Herodotus must be referring to the two Biahmu colossi, which were *c.*12 m. high and stood on pedestals *c.*6.4 m. high. It is the latter which Herodotus describes as πυραμίδες, but the claim that they rose 50 orguiai (*c.*93 m.) above water and went down 50 feet below is grossly exaggerated (for a possible explanation see Ball, loc. cit.).

4. τὸ δὲ ὕδωρ ... αὖτις: water normally flowed into the lake via the Bahr Yusuf, and for long periods in Egyptian history no efflux would have been possible. However, in Herodotus' time the level of the lake was such that for part of the year

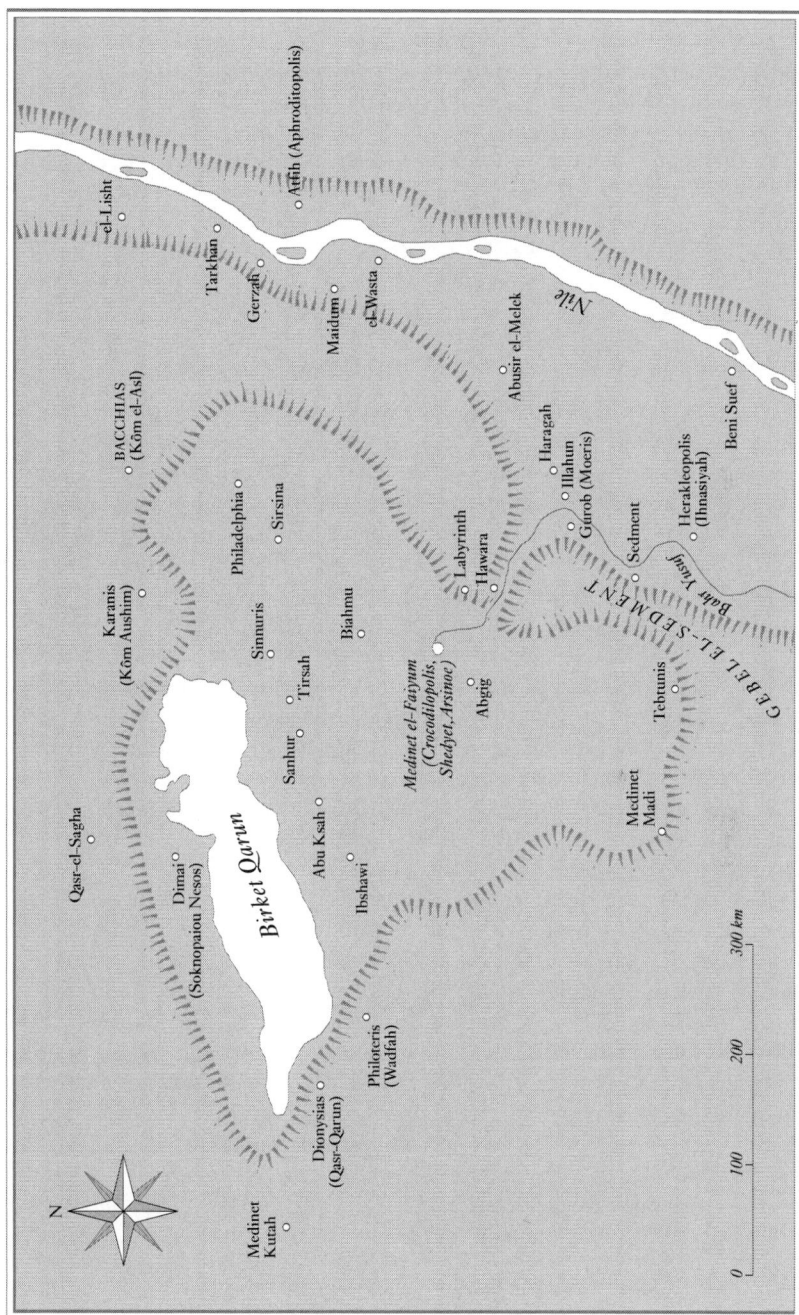

Map 28. The Fayûm

water would indeed have flowed out (Butzer, p. 37).   ταύτῃ: Reiske, followed by many editors, added < ἡ > before the demonstrative to provide ἄνυδρος with a subject (sc. 'the <land> here'), but the resultant phrase, which requires an ellipse of γῆ or χώρη, is odd and does not inspire confidence. The parallel at I 84,3 suggests that some such expression as ἡ γῆ may have dropped out at the end of the sentence.   κατὰ διώρυχα: i.e. the Bahr Yusuf.

5. καὶ ἐπεὰν...μνέας: cf. II 98,1; III 91. The Fayûm fisheries have always been lucrative, and the yield claimed by Herodotus is quite plausible (Ball, *Contribution*, pp. 290 ff., 300).   ἡ δὲ τότε: apodotic δέ with temporal protasis is very common in Homer (see Denniston, *Greek Particles*, p. 179).   ἐς τὸ βασιλήιον καταβάλλει: taxes in fish were certainly levied in pharaonic times (Helck, *Zur Verwaltung*, pp. 263 ff.).

150,1. οἱ ἐπιχώριοι: 'local inhabitants' are mentioned several times by Herodotus as sources (see above, pp. 230 ff.).   ἐς τὴν Σύρτιν...ὑπὸ γῆν: for other cases of underground channels in Book II cf. 100,3 and 124,4. There is no such effluent; the level of lake Moiris is largely maintained by evaporation, though a small amount of water is lost by percolation into the surrounding land (Ball, *Contributions*, pp. 201, 282 ff.). However, equally mistaken and closely similar notions have been current in the Nile valley even in modern times (cf. G. Maspero, *Recueil des travaux*, XXXVIII (1917), 20).   ὑπὸ γῆν: on ὑπό with the accusative see 124,4.

2. ἐπείτε δὲ τοῦ ὀρύγματος: Herodotus shows meticulous care in checking his sources (see above, pp. 228 ff.).   τοῦ ὀρύγματος τούτου: the phrase has caused difficulty but is best interpreted as a blanket reference applied to the cavity for the lake, the canal which fed it, and the subterranean channel which was supposed to take off water into Syrtis (Lloyd, *Commentary 99–182*, p. 128).   ᾔδεα γὰρ...τοιοῦτον: cf. notes on 121a,1 ff.   Νίνῳ: Niniveh, the administrative capital of the Assyrian empire, the ruins of which lie north-east of Mosul on the east bank of the Tigris (Weidner, *RE* XVII, 635 ff.).

3. Σαρδαναπάλλου: cf. Hellanicus, *FGrHist* 4 F 63; Ctesias, ibid. 688 F 1 (23). The name might be derived from that of Ashur-danin-aplu, a son of Shalmaneser III, or that of king Assurbanipal, but the Sardanapallus *logos*, despite some historical influences, belongs mainly to the realm of folklore (cf. Weißbach, *RE* IA, 2436 ff.).   Νίνου: cf. I 7. According to Ctesias (loc. cit.), Sardanapallus was the thirtieth ruler after Ninus.   μεγάλα χρήματα: enormous wealth is a consistent ingredient of the Sardanapallus tradition.   σταθμεόμενοι: such vivid detail is frequently employed by Herodotus to add a sense of actuality to his narrative (see note on 115,1).   ἐς τὸν Τίγρην...Νίνον: at first sight a startling comment, since the river now flows some distance to the west. In antiquity, however, it ran much further east (H. R. Hall, *The Ancient History of the Near East*, London 1963[11], map facing p. 172).

151,1–3. Τῶν δὲ δυώδεκα...Αἰγύπτου: see note on 147,2–4.
1. Τῶν δὲ δυώδεκα...χρεωμένων: strictly the dative should have been used in agreement with σφι below. For such irregular genitives absolute see note on 111,1.   ἐν τῷ ἱρῷ τοῦ Ἡφαίστου: i.e. the temple of Ptah at Memphis (notes

on 2,5; 99,4). From an early period this city formed part of the territory of the Saite Dynasty, to which Psammetichus belonged (Kitchen, pp. l45 ff., 172 ff.).

2. περιελόμενος...ἔσπενδε: metal helmets were used in Egypt from the New Kingdom onwards (R. Krauß, *LdÄ* II, 1113 ff.). It is possible that the tale is an aetiological legend, since Psammetichus' name may have been understood to mean 'the man' or 'vendor of wine' (Griffith, *Catalogue* III, pp. 44, n. 5; 201, n. 3). κυνέας... ἔχοντες: this practice would certainly not have been out of place in the grave political uncertainties of the 8th–7th cent. BC, of which the Dodecarchs are a legendary reminiscence.

3. Ψαμμήτιχος...τῇ ἄλλῃ Αἰγύπτῳ: an example of the widely current prophecy-fulfilled motif (see note on 133,4–5). προνοίης: the issue of intention was of critical importance in Athenian homicide law, though not, apparently, in other contexts (MacDowell, pp. 114 ff.). On the other hand, there is no indication that it was a factor recognized in the Egyptian legal system. Evidently Herodotus, or his source, was viewing the situation in the light of Greek judicial practice. ἐς δὲ τὰ ἕλεα: see note on 137,2. Observe the irony of this situation: it is the very forebearance of Psammetichus' colleagues which brings about their deposition (see above, p. 234).

152,1. τὸν δὲ Ψαμμήτιχον...εἰσι: on the περιπέτειαι of Psammetichus' career see Lloyd, *Historia*, XXXVII (1988), 50. Σαβακῶν: see ch. 137. ὅς...ἀπέκτεινε: incorrect. Necho I was killed fighting the Nubian king Tanutamun, probably at Memphis in 664 (Kitchen, p. 393). τοῦτον φεύγοντα: for this use of the demonstrative see note on 100,2. ἐς Συρίην: Psammetichus was, at this stage, an ally of the Assyrians. Since Syria and Assyria were often confused, it may well be the latter which is meant here (Kitchen, p. 393, n. 883). κατήγαγον...εἰσι: incorrect. Psammetichus was restored by his overlords the Assyrians, whose role in these events is consistently ignored in the Herodotean tradition (cf. Kitchen, pp. 145 ff., 172 ff.).

2. πρὸς τῶν ἕνδεκα βασιλέων: for πρός with the genitive expressing the agent see note on 75,4.

3–5. ἐπιστάμενος...τοὺς βασιλέας: the last of Psammetichus' περιπέτειαι (see above note on 152,1).

3. περιυβρισμένος: again the thinking is Greek (cf. 151, 3). ὕβρις, best described in such contexts as the arrogant and insulting diminution of someone's τιμή, was a recurrent and disruptive factor in Greek social behaviour (N. R. E. Fisher (ed.), *Social Values in Classical Athens*, London 1976, Index, s.v. 'Hybris'). The maintenance of the victim's social standing required him to exact retribution (see above, p. 233). ἐς Βουτοῦν πόλιν: see note on ch. 83. This important city fell firmly within the territory controlled by Psammetichus' family (Kitchen, maps at pp. 346, 367, 401). ἔνθα δή: here the δή serves to emphasize the importance of the city to which the relative adverb ἔνθα refers (cf. Denniston, *Greek Particles*, pp. 218 ff.). τίσις: see above, p. 233.

4. τῷ μὲν δή: the δή emphasizing the μέν throws into dramatic relief the contrast between Psammetichus' expectations and what actually took place (cf. Denniston, *Greek Particles*, pp. 257 ff.).

4–5. χρόνου δὲ οὐ πολλοῦ... τοὺς βασιλέας: cf. Diod. I 66,12; Polyaenus, *Strat.* VII 3. The chronology is typically vague. The historical kernel of this episode probably lies in the troops dispatched by Gyges of Lydia to Psammetichus *c.* 660 BC to assist him in his war of liberation against the Assyrians, but the narrative has clearly been contaminated by the *Odyssey* (XIV 245 ff., XVII 424 ff.) and also by Egyptian propaganda which has led, in particular, to the complete eradication of the Assyrians (Lloyd, *Introduction,* pp. 14 ff.).

4. Ἰωνάς τε καὶ Κᾶρας: on Ionians in Egypt see notes on 178,2–3. The Carians from south-western Asia Minor were renowned soldiers whose presence in Egypt is amply confirmed by archaeological and epigraphic evidence (Alan B. Lloyd, *JEA* LXIV (1978), 108 ff.; J. D. Ray, *JEA* LXVIII (1982), 181 ff.).   κατὰ ληίην: lit.: 'for the purpose of plunder'. For κατά in this sense see Kühner–Gerth, *Gr. Grammatik* II 1, p. 478.   ὁπλισθέντας χαλκῷ: the reference is to Greek plate armour of a type presumably unfamiliar to Egyptians of the 7th cent. BC. The only known pharaonic armour of bronze was made of metal scales fixed to leather base (cf. W. Wolf, *Die Bewaffnung des altägyptischen Heeres*, Leipzig 1926, pp. 96 ff.).

5. ἅμα τοῖσι [μετ᾿ ἑωυτοῦ] βουλομένοισι: the mss follow the definite article with the words μετ᾿ ἑωυτοῦ, which are meaningless and rightly deleted by Krueger. They probably arose by dittography from the μετ᾿ ἑωυτοῦ of the preceding sentence. Psammetichus' support in the early part of his reign embraced most, if not all, of the western half of the Delta (Kitchen, p. 400).   τοὺς βασιλέας: initially these troops would have been used against the Assyrians, but they would certainly have been employed subsequently to remove any opposition which Psammetichus could not neutralize by carefully calculated diplomatic measures (Lloyd, *Introduction,* p. 16).

153. κρατήσας δὲ Αἰγύπτου πάσης: Psammetichus achieved total control of the country in 656 (Kitchen, p. 403).   ἐποίησε τῷ Ἡφαίστου: see notes on 99,4: 101; 151,1. There is, as yet, no archaeological support for this claim.   αὐλήν... πλέην: cf. Diod. I 84; Strabo XVII 1,31 (C807). This cult-centre was called in Egyptian *Ḥwt šḥn nt ḥp ʿnḥ(w)*, 'the dwelling-house of the living Apis', or *t3 st Ḥp*, 'the place of Apis', and appears in Greek texts as the *Apieion* (M. el Amir, *JEA* XXXIV (1948), 51 ff.). It must have lain in the general vicinity of the Saite embalming-house of the Apis bulls (cf. PM III 2, pp. 830 ff.).   τῷ Ἄπι: see note on ch. 38.   περίστυλον: courts surrounded by columns are extremely common in Egyptian religious architecture.   τύπων πλέην: 'covered with reliefs'. Such decoration is a recurrent element in Egyptian temples.   ἀντὶ δὲ κιόνων... τῇ αὐλῇ: Herodotus describes the supports as caryatids, but they were probably pseudo-caryatids in the form of pillars fronted by statues of Osiris (cf. Jéquier, *Manuel,* p. 162).   δυωδεκαπήχεες: i.e. at least 5.35 m.   ὁ δὲ Ἄπις... Ἔπαφος: see note on 38, 1.

154,1. Τοῖσι δὲ Ἴωσι... Στρατόπεδα: Psammetichus retained these troops both to neutralize the threat to royal authority posed by the native Egyptian warrior class (on which see notes on chs. 164–9) and for defence against attack by Egypt's powerful Asiatic neighbours (Lloyd, *Introduction*, pp. 16 ff.). The Saite pharaohs also employed mercenaries of Near Eastern origin such as Jews and Phoenicians (cf. *BAR* IV, 994; B. Porten, *Archives from Elephantine*, Berkeley–Los Angeles 1968). ἐνοικῆσαι: for this final infinitive see note on 96,4. τε δή: see note on ch. 116,2.

2. παῖδας ... γεγόνασι: such a measure may well have been necessary initially, but, if the Ancient Egyptians' linguistic facility was anything like that of their modern descendants, a working knowledge of Greek would quickly have become current. It must, therefore, be questionable whether the 'interpreters' were, in the main, descendants of these lads.

3. χρόνον ἐπὶ πολλόν: see note on 133,2. εἰσὶ δὲ οὗτοι οἱ χῶροι ... τοῦ Νείλου: there is a good case for identifying these sites with the mercenary camps at Daphnae (Tell Defenneh to the west of the Pelusiac branch, H. de Meulenaere, *LdÄ* I, 990) and the recently discovered 'Migdol' to the east (cf. Boardman, *Greeks Overseas*, pp. 134 ff.; Lloyd, *Commentary 99–182*, p. 137). τούτους ... πρὸς Αἰγυπτίων: this move probably dated to 570 or immediately afterwards and is best regarded, *pace* Herodotus, as a restrictive anti-Greek measure motivated by the tide of xenophobic fervour which brought Amasis to the throne (notes on 161,4–163; 169,1; in general Lloyd, *Introduction*, pp. 137 ff.). There is ample evidence, literary, documentary, and archaeological, of the Greek and Carian presence at Memphis (e.g. Aristagoras, *FGrHist* 608 F 9; Boardman, op. cit., pp. 152 ff.; J. D. Ray, *JEA* LXVIII (1982), 181 ff.).

4. τούτων ... κατοικίσθησαν: on Herodotus' source-awareness see above, pp. 228 ff. πρῶτοι ... κατοικίσθησαν: Herodotus is probably thinking specifically of the 7th cent. and later, but earlier parallels certainly existed (e.g. Kitchen, pp. 244 ff.).

5. οἵ τε ὁλκοὶ τῶν νεῶν: '... the slipways of their ships ...', probably of stone or mud brick. Since slipways were only used for warships (Casson, pp. 363 ff.), the camps must have been naval as well as military bases. ἐρείπια τῶν οἰκημάτων: i.e. mainly their mud-brick walls.

155–6. An excursus on Buto and its monuments (see above, p. 234). It is badly integrated into its context and may have been a later addition.

155,1. Τοῦ δὲ χρηστηρίου ... ἤδη: cf. 83; 152,3. ὡς ἀξίου ἐόντος: typically, it is the site's θώματα which attract Herodotus' attention (see above, pp. 234 ff.). [τὸ ἐν Αἰγύπτῳ]: these words are extremely clumsy after the preceding τοῦ ἐν Αἰγύπτῳ and are best deleted (so Cobet). Λητοῦς: i.e. Wadjet (note on 59,3). ἐν πόλι δὲ μεγάλῃ: the ruins lie at Tell el-Farâ'in in the Delta and still cover at least 175 acres. It was a major settlement throughout Egyptian history (H. Altenmüller, *LdÄ* I, 887 ff.). κατὰ τὸ Σεβεννυτικὸν καλεόμενον στόμα ... ἄνω: cf. Strabo XVII 1,18 (C802). The expression is very lax since the city lies on the Sebennytic branch whether one travels upstream or not. Presumably Herodotus means that, if one travels upstream to Buto from the Mediterranean, one travels via the Sebennytic branch; if, however, the traveller starts from some other quarter the route would be different. Powell prefers to solve the problem by emendation (*CQ* XXIX (1935), 80). The precise course of the Sebennytic branch remains problematic, but it certainly lay to the east of the city (M. Bietak, *Tell el-Dab'a*, II, Vienna 1975, pp. 148 ff.).

2. *Βουτώ*: see note on 59,3.   *Ἀπόλλωνος καὶ Ἀρτέμιδος*: i.e. Horus and Bastet (notes on clrs. 83, 137, 156,5). The existence of Butic cults of both deities is corroborated by Egyptian sources (Gardiner, *AEO*, II, p. 189*; V. Seton-Williams and D. Redford, *JEA* LV (1969), 7 ff., 21).   *καὶ ὅ γε νηὸς τῆς Λητοῦς...ὀργυιέων*: the remains indicate a very substantial structure in which a massive brick temenos wall, partly Ramesside and partly Saite, enclosed a shrine of limestone and quartzite dating to the reign of Amasis (570–526 BC) (Seton-Williams and Redford, op. cit., pp. 5 ff.). It would have amply justified Herodotus' eulogy.   *καὶ...γε*: see note on ch. 111,4.   *δέκα ὀργυιέων*: i.e. at least 17.82 m.

3. *θῶμα*: see above, pp. 234 ff. Hude, like many editors, follows the Roman group of mss and prints *ἦν* before *θῶμα*, but the best mss omit, and the Greek construes without it.   *νηὸς ἐξ ἑνὸς λίθου...ἐς μῆκος*: 'a shrine which is monolithic as far as height and length are concerned'. This comment excludes the roof, which is also claimed to be monolithic (see below).   *τούτοισι ἴσος*: *τούτοισι* is either a dative of respect ('equal in respect of these (sc. height and length)') or an instrumental dative ('equal to the following (sc. 40 cubits)'). Either way, the shrine emerges as a perfectly cubic structure which has, as yet, no parallel in extant temple architecture. Powell again prefers to emend (art. cit., p. 81).   *τεσσεράκοντα πήχεων*: i.e. at least 17.82 m. A monolithic shrine of such proportions is a practical impossibility. Probably it was built of numerous blocks so carefully fitted together that the joins were not readily visible (cf. note on 124,5).   *τὸ δὲ καταστέγασμα*: in apposition to the subject *λίθος*. As often, the apposition indicates the result or purpose of the verbal action (Kühner–Gerth, *Gr. Grammatik* II 1, p. 284).   *ἄλλος...λίθος*: if true, this statement would mean that the roof was a monolithic block *c.* 400 m.² in extent, but this is not possible. Again, Herodotus may have been misled by the skill of Egyptian stonemasons.   *τὴν παρωροφίδα*: the word is *hapax legomenon*. It clearly refers to the cornice which curved outwards at roof level from the top of the walls (so already Kenrick, *Egypt*, p. 200).

156,1. *θωμαστότατον*: see above, pp. 234 ff.

1–6. *τῶν δὲ δευτέρων...λέγουσι*: this topic had been discussed by Hecataeus (*FGrHist* I F 305), whose narrative was certainly in Herodotus' mind's eye (see above, pp. 231 ff.).

1. *Χέμμις*: the name derives from the Egyptian *3ḫ bìty*, whose later form *ḫb* became *Χέμβις*, then *Χέμμις* in Greek (H. Altenmüller, *LdÄ* I, 921 ff.). It is not to be confused with the Chemmis of ch. 91.

2–6. *ἔστι...λέγουσι*: cf. Mela I 9; Heliodorus, *Aethiopica* II 18. Chemmis is mentioned as early as the Pyramid Texts (2190a; see Faulkner, p. 306) and appears frequently in late literature (e.g. W. Spiegelberg, *Der Sagenkreis des Königs*

Petubastis, Demotische Studien, III, Leipzig 1910, pp. 14 ff.). Edgar believed that the lake was situated to the east of Tell el-Farâ'in (*ASAE* XI (1911), 89).

2. βαθέη: probably mere literary embellishment, since deep lakes are unknown in the Delta.   λέγεται ... πλωτή: on Egyptians as sources see above, pp. 230 ff. Islands of papyrus can indeed float, but no Egyptian text claims that Chemmis did. Probably the notion was injected into Butic tradition by Greeks who had identified Chemmis with their own floating island of Ortygia/Delos on which Leto was believed to have given birth to Artemis and Apollo (cf. Griffiths, *The Conflict*, p. 93).   αὐτὸς μὲν ἔγωγε ... πλωτή: on Herodotean autopsy see above, pp. 229 ff.

3. ἐν δὴ ὦν ταύτῃ ... ἄφορα πολλά: entirely consistent with Egyptian descriptions (Kees, *Götterglaube*, p. 50; Chassinat, *Edfou* VI, p. 51, XVIII).   βωμοὶ τριφάσιοι: probably in honour of Isis, Wadjet, and Horus, given the myth narrated immediately below.

4–6. λόγον δὲ τόνδε ... λέγουσι: the only consecutive account of this myth in any language, but elements of it occur in a variety of Egyptian texts.

4. Λητὼ ἐοῦσα ... γενομένων: cf. 43,4. Leto/Wadjet is never described by the Egyptians as belonging to the Ogdoad, but she is a cobra goddess and may well well have been identified in some areas with one of the four cobra goddesses included in that group.   ἵνα δή: see note on 152,3.   ὁ Τυφῶν: Seth (note on 144,2).

5. Ἀπόλλωνα δὲ καὶ Ἄρτεμιν ... παῖδας: standard theology as far as Apollo/Horus is concerned, but no Egyptian text corroborates the claim for Artemis/Bastet (Gwyn Griffiths, loc. cit.).   Λητοῦν δὲ τροφὸν αὐτοῖσι ... γενέσθαι: the theology here is impeccable (cf. Gwyn Griffiths, loc. cit.).   Αἰγυπτιστὶ δὲ ... Βούβαστις: see notes on chs. 59, 144.

6. ἐκ τούτου ... Δήμητρος: Hecataeus could well have been Aeschylus' immediate source (Powell, *CQ* XXIX (1935), 82).   μοῦνος δή: the use of the emphatic δή with adjectives is much more restricted in prose than verse but is frequent with μόνος (Denniston, *Greek Particles*, pp. 204 ff.).   διὰ τοῦτο: the demonstrative clearly refers to the narrative ending at Ὀσίριος τὸν παῖδα, despite the intervention of the explanatory matter in the section Ἀπόλλωνα ... Δήμητρος.

157. ἐβασίλευσε: for the aorist see note on 133,2.   τέσσερα καὶ πεντήκοντα ἔτεα: correct (Lloyd, *Introduction*, pp. 189 ff.).   τὰ ἑνὸς δέοντα τριήκοντα: the length of this siege is incredible. Several explanations have been offered, e.g. that the city was besieged twice with an interval of *c.*30 years and the notion then arose that there had been an unbroken siege between these two points (Kienitz, p. 17), but it is more than possible that 30 is no more than a symbolic number meaning 'an extremely long time' (see note on 124,5). The truth of the matter remains obscure.   Ἄζωτον: i.e. the northern Philistine settlement of Ashdod, a city of great strategic importance which Psammetichus had to control to open up a route northwards through Syria–Palestine. The traces of destruction in stratum 3a of the mound probably reflect this assault which may tentatively be dated somewhere between 655 and 630 BC (Lloyd, *Commentary 99–182*, pp. 146 ff.).   αὕτη ... ἴδμεν: note that it is the extraordinary nature of this

event, not its strategic or general historical importance, which Herodotus emphasizes (see above, pp. 234 ff., 238 ff.).

158–9.   The reign of Necho II (610–595 BC).

158,1. Νεκῶς: a good rendering of the Egyptian *Ny-k3w* (cf. Manetho's Νεχαώ, *FGrHist* 609, pp. 48 ff., F 2–3c; p. 111, F 28).   ὃς τῇ διώρυχι...φερούσῃ: cf. Diod. I 33,8 ff.; Strabo XVII 1,25 (C804). There is no confirmation of this enterprise from Egyptian sources, but it is consistent with Necho's interest in the Red Sea (II 159,1; IV 42) and need not be doubted. Such a canal could have served both military and commercial purposes.   πρῶτος: probably correct. There is, at present, no good evidence of a navigation canal in this area before Necho's time (Lloyd, *Commentary 99–182*, p. 151).   ἐς τὴν Ἐρυθρὴν θάλασσαν: translate either 'Red Sea' or 'Southern Ocean' here (cf. note on 8,1).   τὴν Δαρεῖος...διώρυξε: so also IV 39,1, but cf. Arist. *Meteor.* I,14 (352b), Diod. I 33,8 ff., Strabo XVII 1,25 (C804), and Pliny, *NH* VI 165 ff. Herodotus' tradition is confirmed by epigraphic evidence (Posener, pp. 48 ff.). The canal was begun *c*.510 BC and completed in 497 as part of an elaborate communications network designed to tie the Persian empire together.   τῆς μῆκος...ἡμέραι τέσσερες: for the construction cf. 29,3. Herodotus' figure presupposes a speed of *c*.30 km. per day, which is comparable to the speed of a tourist sailing dahabiyeh in modern times but slow for commercial or official traffic (cf. Lloyd, *Commentary 1–98*, pp. 121 ff.).   εὖρος δὲ ὠρύχθη...ἐλαστρευμένας: cf. VII 24. For this to be possible a width of at least 30.48 m. would be necessary, a figure which is entirely acceptable since at least one later canal was 45.72 m. wide (Strabo XVII 1,26 (C805); Baedeker, *Egypt*, p. 180). The Persian canal was certainly used by war-galleys (Posener, p. 57, l. 19).

2. ἦκται...ἐς τὴν Ἐρυθρὴν θάλασσαν: there are remains of ancient canal construction along much of this line (J. Clédat, *BIFAO* XXIII *Bulletin de* (1924), 62 ff.).   ἦκται δὲ...ἦκται δὲ: for continuative δέ with repetition of the main verb see Denniston, *Greek Particles*, p. 164.   κατύπερθε ὀλίγον Βουβάστιος πόλιος: for Bubastis see note on 59,1. The starting-point probably lay south of the city in the general area of Mina el-Kamh.   παρὰ Πάτουμον: '...past Patoumos...'. The city was called in Egyptian *Pr-itm*, 'House of Atum', which appears in the Old Testament as Pithom (D. B. Redford, *LdÄ* IV, 1054 ff.). It is probably to be located in the Wadi Tumilat at Tell el-Maskhutah, south-east of which traces of an ancient canal have been identified (C. Redmount, in K. Bard (ed.), *Encyclopedia of the Archaeology of Ancient Egypt*, London 1999, 786 ff.).

2–3. ὀρώρυκται δὲ πρῶτον...πρὸς τὴν ἠῶ: this description refers to the first major section of the canal running eastwards across the alluvium from approximately Mina el-Kamh to the eastern desert and then north-eastwards to the entrance of the Wadi Tumilat.

2. λιθοτομίαι: cf. 8,1; 124,2.

3. καὶ ἔπειτα...ἐς διασφάγας: i.e. the second major section of the canal running through the Wadi Tumilat.   φέρουσα...Ἀράβιον: the third main stretch which ran south from Nefisheh to Suez.

4. ἐκ τῆς βορηίης θαλάσσης...ἐς τὴν νοτίην: the Northern Ocean occupied the northern and north-western segment of the earth and included the Mediterranean Sea; the Southern Ocean was its counterpart to the south and comprised all seas and oceans in the area, e.g. the Red Sea, Persian Gulf, and Indian Ocean.   τοῦ Κασίου ὄρεος: see note on 6,1.   στάδιοι <ἀπαρτὶ> χίλιοι: cf. IV 41; Strabo XVII 1,21 (C803). Hude *et al.* read <ἀπαρτὶ>, 'exactly', after στάδιοι, but the word features neither in the mss nor in *P Oxy* 1092, and, since 1,000 stades would be at least 179 km., whereas the actual distance is *c.*115 km., its introduction into the text is a positive embarrassment.

5. σκολιωτέρη: this description would certainly fit the modern irrigation canal in the area as well as the traces of its ancient counterpart or counterparts (Baedeker, *Egypt*, map between pp. 184–5).   δυώδεκα μυριάδες: this prodigious total is best not taken literally, but we need not doubt that the casualty figure was large, since during the construction of the Mahmudieh Canal in 1819 no fewer than 20,000 men died in a period of six months (Erman–Ranke, p. 567). Νεκῶς...προεργάζεσθαι: Strabo claims that death intervened (XVII 1,25 (C804)). The oracle sounds suspiciously like an *ex-eventu* cautionary prophecy which is almost certainly Greek and entirely unhistorical (cf. Crahay, p. 329, and see above, pp. 238 ff.).   μεταξὺ: on this positioning and use of adverbs with temporal participles see Goodwin, *Moods and Tenses*, 858. βαρβάρους...ὁμογλώσσους: the Ancient Egyptians indubitably held a firm conviction of cultural superiority (36,2; W. Helck, *Saeculum*, XV (1964), 103 ff.).

159,1. παυσάμενος...στρατηίας: this chronology would mean that the canal only occupied Necho's attention for one year, because his Asiatic campaigns were certainly in train during 609. Strabo, however, describes the canal construction as lasting throughout his reign (XVII 1,25 (C804)), and this seems intrinsically more probable. The military operations were designed to neutralize the threat to Egypt posed by the rise of the Chaldaean empire and, despite serious reverses, were successful in maintaining Egyptian independence (Kienitz, pp. 20 ff.).   τριήρεες: this term may have been used anachronistically, but there is a distinct possibility that it is an accurate description of the vessels used. They could have been Greek or Phoenician in origin (Lloyd, *Commentary 99–182*, pp. 159 ff.).   ἐπὶ τῇ βορηίῃ θαλάσσῃ: see note on 158,4. Here the ships would be used in conjunction with Egyptian land forces operating in the Levant.   ἐν τῷ Ἀραβίῳ κόλπῳ ἐπὶ τῇ Ἐρυθρῇ θαλάσσῃ: see note on 8,1. Here the ships were presumably intended to protect Egyptian trading vessels operating in the Red Sea (Alan B. Lloyd, *JEA* LXIII (1977), 145 ff.).   ὁλκοί: see note on 154,5.

2. Σύριοισι: a term of wide application (note on ch. 104,3), which refers in this context to the Chaldaeans. The reference is to Necho's victory over the forces of Nebuchadnezzar II on the eastern frontier of Egypt in 601–600 BC (Lloyd, op. cit., pp. 159 ff.).   Μαγδώλῳ: undoubtedly Migdol near Pelusium (Kees, *RE* XIV, 299 ff.).   Κάδυτιν: i.e. Gaza (Gardiner, *AEO* I, p. 191*).

3. ἐν τῇ δὲ ἐσθῆτι...τὰς Μιλησίων: cf. his dedications at Ialysus (J. Leclant, *Orientalia*, XLVIII (1979), 406) and the parallels in the reign of Amasis

(ch. 182), all designed to win good-will in the Greek world. Necho could hardly have chosen a better place for such a demonstration than the famous oracular shrine of Branchidae 18 km. south of Miletus (on the site see K. Tuchelt, in *PECR*, pp. 272 ff., s.v. 'Didyma'), but he may also have wanted to acknowledge the assistance of Ionian mercenaries in these campaigns.   ἐν τῇ δὲ ἐσθῆτι: this position of δέ in such phrases is rare; it would be more normal to place it after the noun (Denniston, *Greek Particles*, p. 186).   ἐκκαίδεκα ἔτεα τὰ πάντα: strictly the total was nearer fifteen (Lloyd, *Introduction*, pp. 192 ff.). Presumably, Herodotus or his source simply rounded up the figure.   Ψάμμι: Psmṯk in Egyptian, i.e. the same name as Herodotus' Ψαμμήτιχος (cf. Diod. I 68). The short version may have been based on a genuine Egyptian abbreviation which he took over as a convenient means of distinguishing this king from his predecessor.

160–1,1. An account of two episodes in the reign of Psammis (Psammetichus II) (595–589 BC).

160,1–4. Ἐπὶ τοῦτον... ὑπεθήκαντο: cf. Diod. I 95; Plutarch, *Plat. Quaest.* 2 (*Mor.* 1000a). Diodorus places the episode in the reign of Amasis. It is quite unhistorical, being an amalgam of Greek cult politics, traditional narrative motifs (the wisdom of the Egyptians, the wise ruler, and the test or riddle), and current Greek attitudes towards the organization of the Olympic Games (Lloyd, *Commentary 99–182*, pp. 165 ff.).   Ἠλείων ἄγγελοι: the Eleans only obtained control of the games c.570 BC, almost twenty years after the death of Psammis (A. Hönle, *Olympia in der Politik der griechischen Staatenwelt von 776 bis zum Ende des 5. Jahrhunderts*, Tübingen 1968, pp. 29 ff.). It is probable that this tale, despite the addition of some criticism, originally formed part of a programme of propaganda designed to justify Elean administration of the games.   τοὺς σοφωτάτους ἀνθρώπων Αἰγυπτίους: the wisdom of the Egyptians is a recurrent theme in ancient literature (Froidefond, pp. 137 ff.).

2. ὁ βασιλεὺς οὗτος: for the motif of the wise ruler see Thompson, *Folktale*, p. 268; Alan B. Lloyd, *JEA* LXIII (1977), 153 ff.

2–4. συνελθόντες... ὑπεθήκαντο: riddles and problem-solving are part of the stock-in-trade of folklore throughout the world (Thompson, *Folktale*, p. 494). The debate demonstrates that criticisms of the organization and content of the games were already being made as early as Herodotus' time (Aly, p. 292).

2. σφέας: the accusative is unusual after κατήκει, the standard case being the dative (Powell, *Lexicon*, pp. 191 ff.).

4. οὐδεμίαν... τὸν ξεῖνον: the construction is most unusual. Expressions such as οὐδεμίαν εἶναι μηχανήν are normally followed by the infinitive, which is sometimes preceded by ὥστε. Herodotus uses here a ὅκως clause as though it were preceded by ποιεῖν vel sim. in the sense of 'take care' (Kühner–Gerth, *Gr. Grammatik* II 2, pp. 9 ff.).

161,1. ἓξ ἔτεα μοῦνον: Egyptian records indicate five full years and an undetermined part of regnal year 6 (Lloyd, *Introduction*, pp. 192 ff.). Again Herodotus or

his source has rounded up the figure (cf. note on 159,3).   στρατευσαμένου ἐς
Αἰθιοπίην: Ethiopia here means Nubia (note on 29,4), to which the Saite kings
were consistently hostile. The expedition, which is mentioned in several Egyptian
texts, took place in 593/2 and penetrated at least as far as the Fourth Cataract
(S. Sauneron and J. Yoyotte, *BIFAO* L (1952), 173 ff.; Alan B. Lloyd, in Trigger,
p. 281; R. Gozzoli, *Discussions in Egyptology*, XXXVIII (1997), 5 ff.). Herodotus'
interest in Ethiopia and also in this expedition may to some extent reflect the
area's powerful Greek mythical and legendary associations (cf. F. M. Snowden,
Blacks in Antiquity, Cambridge, Mass. 1970, pp. 144 ff.).   μεταυτίκα: since
Psammis died in 589 the adverb is hardly appropriate, but at least one Egyptian
source makes the same error (Griffith, *Catalogue* III, p. 92).   Ἀπρίης: a good
rendering of the Egyptian *W3ḥ-ib-r*. He ruled from 589 to 570 BC (Lloyd,
Introduction, pp. 191 ff.).

2. ὃς μετὰ Ψαμμήτιχον ... βασιλέων: since the country was certainly invaded
by the Babylonians in 582 (H. de Meulenaere, *LdÄ* I, 358 ff.), Apries' εὐδαιμονία
was not unremitting. Herodotus, or his source, has cast his career in the form
of an example of the εὐδαιμονία–ὕβρις–τίσις syndrome and may well have
exaggerated Apries' success in order to throw his fall into sharper relief (Alan B.
Lloyd, *Historia*, XXXVII (1988), 41 ff.).   ἐπ' ἔτεα πέντε καὶ εἴκοσι ἄρξας: cf.
Diod. I 68,1. The figure is odd. Apries ruled from 589 to 570 BC, when he was
deposed, but he lived on until 567 (note on 163,1). Therefore, the maximum total
would be twenty-three years. The discrepancy may have arisen from a general
confusion about the precise date of Apries' death created by the propagandist
tradition of II 169, 2 ff.   ἐπί τε Σιδῶνα ... τῷ Τυρίῳ: cf. Diod. I 68,1, who
includes Cyprus in these operations. They are best dated to the period *c.*574–570
BC and were clearly intended to counter the threat to Egypt of Chaldaean
expansion down the east coast of the Mediterranean (Lloyd, *Commentary
99–182*, pp. 170 ff.).

3. ἔδεε: cf. 169,2. For this verb in the sense of 'to be fated' see note on
133,3.   ἐγένετο ... ἀπηγήσομαι: see IV 159; Hellanicus, *FGrHist* 4 F 55;
Diod. I 68,2 ff.; Athenaeus XIII 560e. It is conceivable that Herodotus obtained
some, at least, of his information on this event from Cyrene.

4. ἀποπέμψας ... προσέπταισε: this campaign, which must be dated *c.*571–570
BC, was the result of an appeal to Egypt by the local Libyan population on whose
territory the Cyrenaeans were encroaching (IV 159). The troops used were
Machimoi, i.e. members of the native warrior class who were themselves Libyan
in origin (notes on chs. 164–8) and, therefore, well suited to this enterprise.
From Apries' point of view the expansion of Cyrene will have made it both a
threat and a rich prize.   μεγάλως προσέπταισε: this disaster took place on
the Spring of Thyeste in the district of Irasa (IV 159,5). Hude reads μεγάλως
instead of μεγαλωστί, but the latter is preferable since it is the reading of the
Florentines and is a securely attested Herodotean form (Powell, *Lexicon*,
p. 216).   Αἰγύπτιοι ... ἐκ τῆς ἰθέης: the defeat was probably no more than
the last straw since the *Machimoi* must have been seething with indignation
for some time at the privileged position of their Greek mercenary colleagues

(A. Spalinger, *Orientalia*, XLVII (1978), 25 ff.). For a mercenary revolt during this reign see *BAR* IV, 989 ff.   ἵνα ... ἄρχοι: this change of mood in the final clause is easily paralleled. Arnold's principle that the subjunctive expresses the immediate consequence and the optative the more remote would fit this example very well (Goodwin, *Moods and Tenses*, p. 321; Kühner–Gerth, *Gr. Grammatik* II 2, p. 387). The use of δή after ἵνα is very common in Herodotus (see note on 93,4). Here it may express, as often, an element of indignation (cf. Denniston, *Greek Particles*, p. 232).

162–82. The reign of Amasis (570–526 BC).

162.1–6. πυθόμενος ... Ἀμάσι: the first phase of the conflict of Apries and Amasis which continues until 169,3 (cf. Hellanicus, *FGrHist* 4 F 55; Diod. I 68,2–6).
1. Ἄμασιν: a good rendering of the Egyptian 'I'ḥ-msw (cf. Manetho's Ἄμωσις, *FGrHist* 609 F 2–3c, pp. 50 ff.).   κατελάμβανε ... μὴ ποιέειν: the imperfect is conative ('tried to restrain') and takes μή before the dependent infinitive like standard verbs of preventing (Goodwin, *Moods and Tenses*, pp. 322 ff.). λέγοντος αὐτοῦ: strictly the dative should have been used in agreement with οἱ (see note on 151,1).   κυνέην: cf. 151,2 and contrast Hellanicus, *FGrHist*, loc. cit. This episode may obliquely reflect the importance of the ritual of coronation in converting the crown-prince into pharaoh (cf. Bonnet, *RÄRG*, pp. 395 ff.).
2. καὶ τῷ: καὶ τόν and καὶ τήν in the sense *et eum/et eam* in accusative and infinitive are common in prose, but Herodotus also admits other oblique cases as here (Kühner–Gerth, *Gr. Grammatik* II 1, p. 585).
3. Πατάρβημις: Hellanicus calls him Patarmis (loc. cit.). The name occurs neither in Egyptian nor papyrological sources and may be a corruption of the common Patarbekis.   ὁ Ἄμασις ... ἀπάγειν: cf. Stobaeus, *Florilegium* 115,24. The episode looks very much like an import from folklore, where obscenity is commonplace (cf. Thompson, *Motif-Index* VI, s.v. 'Obscene'). ἐπάρας: '... having lifted up his leg, having risen up ...' (LSJ, p. 604a), '... having risen in the saddle ...' (Powell, *Lexicon*, p. 127a).
5. τὸν δὲ ... τὴν ῥῖνα: Herodotus abruptly switches to *oratio obliqua*, presumably because he is particularly conscious at this point of purveying a tradition which he has been told (cf. I 86,3). *POxy* 1092 records an alternative version for part of para. 5 of the chapter: [ἀπικομένου δὲ] τούτου καὶ οὐκ ἄ[γοντος τὸν Ἄμασι]ν Ἀπρίης οὐδέ[να λόγον αὐτῶι δοὺς] ἀλλὰ περιθύ[μως ἔχων λέγεται τά]ξαι περιταμεῖν [αὐτοῦ τήν τε ῥῖνα] καὶ τὰ ὦτα. This variant is best explained as a scribal correction designed to remove this slightly disconcerting transition (Paap, p. 53).
5–6. οὐδένα λόγον ... διακείμενον: cf. note on 161,2. Apries hybristically ignores Atarbemis' moral and legal rights and thereby exposes himself inevitably to divine vengeance. His presumption is explicitly made responsible for his fall at 169,2 (see above, pp. 232 ff.).

5. περιταμεῖν . . . τὴν ῥῖνα: this punishment was commonly exacted in Egypt for a wide range of offences (Kees, *Ägypten*, pp. 23, 244–5).

6. οὐδένα δὴ χρόνον: the use of δή to strengthen negatives is rare (Denniston, *Greek Particles*, p. 222).

163,1–2. ὁ Ἀπρίης . . . ξείνους: Herodotus leaves us in no doubt of the ethnic dimensions of the conflict (cf. 163,2; 169,1). His narrative of the struggle appears to be garbled and combines different stages. The actual course of events seems to have been that Apries was defeated at Momemphis in 570 but survived for three years, possibly in Babylonia, returned to Egypt with a Babylonian force in 567, and was then killed in the ensuing struggle (E. Edel, *GM* XXIX (1978), 13 ff.; Lloyd, *Commentary 99–182*, pp. 178 ff.). This chapter describes the build-up to the first clash.   Κᾶράς τε καὶ Ἴωνας ἄνδρας: in other contexts Apries certainly employed mercenaries of other nationalities as well (*BAR* IV, 994), but the Amasis stele supports Herodotus' claim that at this stage he relied on Carians and Ionians (cf. Edel, op. cit., p. 19).   τρισμυρίους: cf. Diod. I 68,4 (probably not independent). Herodotus' frequent use of 3 and multiples as symbolic numbers suggests caution in taking this figure literally (Alan B. Lloyd, *Historia*, XXXVII (1988), 41).   τὰ βασιλήια: Sais was a royal residence even in Ptolemaic times (*Urk.* II, 79). Its ruins are still significant, but no trace of this palace has been identified. Nevertheless, the remains of Apries' palace at Memphis demonstrate that Herodotus' admiration would have been amply justifed (B. J. Kemp, *MDAI(K)* XXIX (1977), 101 ff.; id., *GM* XXIX (1978), 61).

2. τε: though followed by καί, this cannot be translated 'both'. It functions as a simple connective (Denniston, *Greek Particles*, p. 261).   Μωμέμφι: cf. Stephanus of Byzantium, s.v. Μώμεμφις, and Diod. I 68,5. It should probably be identified with Kom el-Hisn (later Terenuthis) in the western Delta (Ball, *Egypt*, p. 18; Lloyd, *Commentary 99–182*, pp. 181 ff.).

164–8.   An excursus on Egyptian social structure, a favourite theme of Greek writers on Egypt (e.g. Plato, *Tim.* 23–4; Isocrates, *Busiris* 15 ff.). Only the priests and the *Machimoi* feature consistently in their lists of classes, and it is clear that they all oversimplify, distort, and create a quite misleading impression of rigidity (cf. Froidefond, pp. 145 ff., 169 ff., 242).

164,1. ἑπτὰ γένεα: it is, at first sight, surprising that Herodotus does not include the χειρώνακτες and ἀγοραῖοι ἄνθρωποι of 141,4, and also groups such as farmers. Perhaps γένος here retains something of its old sense of clan and implies a group of free men with a clearly defined legal or social identity. If so, the social groups which we miss may well have been omitted because they did not square with this definition.   οἱ μὲν ἱρέες: see notes on 36,1; 37,3 ff.; 143.   οἱ δὲ μάχιμοι: see notes on 30,2; 141,1 ff.; 164. They were the descendants of Libyan prisoners and immigrants who had become a major element in the Egyptian population from the New Kingdom onwards and even gave Egypt the kings of the XXIInd Dynasty. *Machimoi* also occur during the Ptolemaic period (Kienitz, pp. 35 ff.;

M. Rostovtzeff, *The Social and Economic History of the Hellenistic World*, III, Oxford 1953, Index, s.v. μάχιμοι), but there is some doubt as to whether they were descendants of those described by Herodotus (K. Goudriaan, *Ethnicity in Ptolemaic Egypt*, Dutch Monographs on Ancient History and Archaeology, V, Amsterdam 1988, pp. 121 ff.). κεκλέαται: trans. 'bears the names' (see note on 72). οἱ δὲ βουκόλοι: cattle-raising was an important branch of Egyptian agriculture, and herdsmen were numerous, particularly in the Delta (see Vandier, *Manuel* V, pp. 13 ff., 195 ff., 250 ff.). οἱ δὲ συβῶται: see notes on 47,1; 48,1. οἱ δὲ κάπηλοι: see notes on 35,2; 141,4. οἱ δὲ ἑρμηνέες: see notes on 125,6; 154,2. οἱ δὲ κυβερνῆται: navigation on the Nile presents many problems, and the existence of an elite corps of 'steersmen, pilots' in antiquity is entirely credible. They certainly exist in modern Egypt (cf. Lane, p. 337).

2. οἱ δὲ μάχιμοι...Ἑρμοτύβιες: this division may have been the product of purely administrative convenience or the result of more deeply rooted historical factors, but the evidence is not available to establish the truth of the matter (cf. Gyles, p. 85; Kees, *Ägypten*, p. 238, n. 6). Καλασίριες: cf. VII 89; IX 32. The term derives from the Egyptian *kri/gl-šry*, 'young lad, young recruit, soldier' (J. K. Winnicki, *Historia*, XXVI (1977), 267). It is also used of a style of tunic (note on 81,1). The Kalasiries are first mentioned in Egyptian texts during the XXth Dynasty and are in evidence subsequently down to the Greek period (ibid., pp. 257 ff.). Ἑρμοτύβιες: cf. IX 32,1, with VII 89,2–3; Aristagoras of Miletus, *FGrHist* 608 F 1. The first element of the name may well be the Egyptian word *rmṯ*, 'men', but the etymology of the remainder is uncertain (Grapow, *RE* VIII, 905). They have never been securely identified in Egyptian texts. νομούς: the nomes, roughly equivalent to English counties or French provinces, are a recurrent feature of Egyptian administration in antiquity. Herodotus mentions eighteen, Strabo thirty-six, and Ptolemy forty-seven (Ball, *Egypt*, pp. 49, 60, 120 ff.). The canonical number in Egyptian texts in Graeco-Roman times was forty-two (in general W. Helck, *Die altägyptischen Gaue*, Wiesbaden 1974). διαραίρηται: trans. 'is divided' (see note on 72,1).

165. Ἑρμοτυβίων...νομοί: it emerges from the following list that all Hermotybian nomes lay in the west and central Delta. Βουσιρίτης: i.e. wholly or mainly the 9th Nome of Lower Egypt (cf. note on 59,1). Σαΐτης: i.e. wholly or mainly the 5th Nome of Lower Egypt (cf. note on 28,1). Χεμμίτης: this nome only appears in Herodotus. On the basis of ch. 156 we may identify it with the canonical 6th Nome of Lower Egypt. Παπρημίτης: again a nome only mentioned in Herodotus. It must be either wholly or in part the 7th Nome of Lower Egypt (cf. 59,3). νῆσος ἡ Προσωπῖτις καλεομένη: mainly or entirely the 4th Nome of Lower Egypt (note on 41,5). Ναθῶ τὸ ἥμισυ: the name possibly derives from the Egyptian *N3y-t3-ḥwt* (Gardiner, *AEO* II, pp. 146* ff.). Its location is problematic, but there is a good case for placing it in the 11th Nome of Lower Egypt (Lloyd, *Commentary 99–182*, p. 189). γενοίατο: so Hude, but the indefinite optative gives a very odd sense. The aorist indicative ἐγένοντο of the Florentine mss is clearly preferable. ἑκκαίδεκα μυριάδες: cf. 30,2; Diod.

I 67,3. With the figure in 166,2 we have a *Machimoi* population of 410,000, exclusive of their families, out of an overall population which probably did not exceed 3 millions (cf. Diod. I 31,7–8; Butzer, p. 83). The *Machimoi* figure does not seem unreasonable (Alan B. Lloyd, in Trigger, pp. 299 ff.).   καὶ τούτων βαναυσίης ... ἐς τὸ μάχιμον: a dubious claim. Herodotus and later writers show a marked predilection for assimilating the *Machimoi* to the Spartan ὅμοιοι (notes on chs. 167–8), and this comment looks suspiciously like an example of that phenomenon. Egyptian sources are silent on *Machimoi* methods of working their land allotments, but the most plausible guess would be that they spent a large part of their life as farmers and only functioned in military contexts when called to the colours or on occasional training exercises (cf. Rostovtzeff, op. cit. I, pp. 284 ff.).

166,1. *Καλασιρίων ... εἰσι*: apart from the Theban nome (see below), all Kalasirian territory lay in the southern and eastern Delta.   Θηβαῖος: i.e. the 4th Nome of Upper Egypt (cf. note on 42,1), where *Machimoi* are identifiable as late as the Ptolemaic period (Winnicki, *Historia*, XXVI (1977), 261), but see note on 164,1.   *Βουβαστίτης*: essentially, if not completely, the 18th Nome of Lower Egypt (see note on 59,1).   *Ἀφθίτης*: the location is debatable, but a good case can be made for the 14th Nome of Lower Egypt (Lloyd, *Commentary 99–182*, pp. 191 ff.).   *Τανίτης*: i.e. largely, if not completely, the 19th Nome of Lower Egypt (cf. Helck, op. cit., pp. 195 ff.).   *Μενδήσιος*: mainly, if not entirely, the 16th Nome of Lower Egypt (cf. note on 42,2).   *Σεβεννύτης*: Sebennytus was the capital of the 12th Nome of Lower Egypt (ibid., pp. 179 ff.). *Ἀθριβίτης*: essentially, if not entirely, the 10th Nome of Lower Egypt (cf. ibid., pp. 175 ff.).   *Φαρβαιθίτης*: more or less identical with the 11th Nome of Lower Egypt (cf. ibid., p. 197).   *Θμουΐτης*: Thmouis was the later capital of the Mendesian Nome mentioned above. There is no doubt that Herodotus, or his source, is in error in treating the Thmouite Nome as different from the Mendesian (cf. ibid., pp. 191 ff.).   'Ονουφίτης: cf. Pliny, *NH* V 49; Ptolemy, IV 5,22. This nome still needs to be firmly located, but there are indications that it lay in the western Delta north of Tanta around Mehallat Menûf (Lloyd, op. cit., pp. 193 ff.).   *Ἀνύτιος*: cf. 137,1; Stephanus of Byzantium, s.v. This nome lay in the vicinity of the south-east corner of lake Menzalah in the eastern Delta (ibid., pp. 194 ff.).   *Μυεκφορίτης*: this nome is mentioned nowhere else. There are arguments for locating it in the 20th Nome of Lower Egypt, but uncertainty remains on the matter (ibid., p. 195).

2. γενόμενοι ... μοῦνα: see notes on ch. 165.   γενοίατο: ἐγένοντο is preferable (see note on ch. 165).   παῖς παρὰ πατρὸς ἐκδεκόμενος: the hereditary principle was deeply rooted in Egyptian society (cf. note on 37,5), and it certainly operated amongst the *Machimoi* (Winnicki, loc. cit.).

167,1–2. εἰ μέν νυν καὶ τοῦτο ... τοὺς χειροτέχνας: *pace* How–Wells (p. 250), Herodotus is still thinking here along diffusionist lines (on which see above, p. 235). His difficulty was to determine whether the source was Egypt or somewhere else.

1. εἰ μέν νυν καὶ τοῦτο ... οἱ Ἕλληνες: Greek social values were, of course, a native product and originated in the attitudes of the free Greek peasant farmer and the aristocratic ideal. These led almost inevitably to a general negative valuation of industrial activity, which was aggravated by the major role played in industry by slaves (cf. M. M. Austin and P. Vidal-Naquet, *Economic and Social History of Ancient Greece: An Introduction*, London 1977, pp. 11 ff., 44 ff., 107 ff.). μεμαθήκασι: see note on 72,1.   Θρήικας: cf. V 6,2. Thracian military prowess was a recurrent matter of comment in ancient sources (e.g. Tacitus, *Ann.* IV 46–51: cf. S. Casson, *Macedonia, Thrace and Illyria*, Groningen 1968, pp. 202 ff.).   Σκύθας: the Scythians had a formidable reputation as fighting men (IV 1–82, particularly 64–6; cf. Talbot Rice).   Πέρσας: the martial predilections of the Persians made a deep impression on Herodotus and other Greek writers (I 136; VII 181; IX 107; Xen. *Cyr.*; Arrian, *Anab.*, I 13 ff.; III 7 ff.; cf. Cook, p. 1 ff.).   Λυδοὺς: Herodotus has in mind the fighting qualities of the Lydian aristocracy, which must have been largely responsible for the imperial expansion described at I 6 ff. (in general see Keil, *RE* XIII, 2169 ff.).

2. Λακεδαιμόνιοι: the mode of life of the elite corps of Spartan ὅμοιοι was erroneously explained in later literature as an imitation of the Egyptian *Machimoi* (e.g. Isocrates, *Bus.* 6–8; Plutarch, *Lyc.* 4,5; cf. Froidefond, pp. 145 ff., 172, 242 ff.); it appears from this passage that the notion had already taken firm root in Herodotus' time.   ἥκιστα ... τοὺς χειροτέχνας: this claim cannot be substantiated in other sources but is hardly likely to be incorrect. Certain it is that Corinth was a place unusually conducive to industrial innovation and progress (E. Will, *Korinthiaka*, Paris 1955, pp. 326 ff.).

168,1. γέρεα ... πάρεξ τῶν ἱρέων: cf. 141,1. Priests certainly received many γέρεα (37,3–4), but payment for state service by means of land-grants was normal Egyptian practice. Such allotments would only be at the disposal of the beneficiary as long as he served the crown; they did not become his absolute property (Helck, *Wirtschaftsgeschichte*, pp. 56 ff., 249 ff.).   ἄρουραι ... ἑκάστῳ: i.e. *c*.3.2 hectares (see below). If this figure is correct, Herodotus' *Machimoi* were treated very generously; for Ptolemaic *Machimoi* normally received 5, 7, or 8 *arourae* (D. Crawford, *Kerkeosiris*, Cambridge 1971, pp. 69 ff.), and 12 would have been over twice the quantity required to feed a family. It is also strange that Herodotus indicates no distinctions of rank (cf. ibid). Probably he is guilty of considerable oversimplification.   ἀτελέες: this phenomenon is easily paralleled in Egyptian texts (Kees, *Ägypten*, pp. 43, 106, 235).   ἡ δὲ ἄρουρα ... τῷ Σαμίῳ: if, as is probable, the Egyptian cubit in question is the royal cubit of 0.523 m., the *aroura* was 2735.29 m.^{2}, a measurement paralleled as early as the IIIrd Dynasty (Crawford, op. cit., p. 12, n. 2).

2. ἐν περιτροπῇ: Herodotus probably exaggerates. Egyptian administrative practice suggests that fiefs would have changed hands when a *Machimos* ceased to function as such, normally on death, but otherwise he would have enjoyed undisturbed tenure.   Καλασιρίων χίλιοι ... τὸν βασιλέα: an unnervingly close parallel to the annually selected 300 Spartan ἱππέες (I 67,5; A. H. Jones, *Sparta*,

Oxford 1967, p. 63). Has Herodotus' account been contaminated here by Spartan practice? τούτοισι ὦν ... ἐδίδοτο: such ration-payments were a standard feature of ancient Egyptian economic life (Helck, *Wirtschaftsgeschichte*, pp. 231 ff.), but, if the figures are accurate, the bodyguard was treated with considerable generosity. If we convert using the Attic mina of 436.6 g., these guards received 2.18 kg. of bread and 873.2 gr. of meat per day, and if we take the *aryster* as a fraction less than 0.28 litres, they received *c*.1.12 l. of wine per day. It should also be noted that wine and meat counted as luxury foods in Egypt (in general Lloyd, *Commentary 99–182*, p. 201).   ἐπ᾽ ἡμερῃ ἑκάστῃ: this temporal use of ἐπί with dative is mainly a poetic and late prose usage. It is rare in Attic (Kühner–Gerth, *Gr. Grammatik* II 1, p. 500).

169,1 Ἐπείτε ... συνέβαλον: see notes on ch. 163.   πλήθεϊ δὲ πολλῷ ἐλάσσονες: this may have been the explanation for the defeat, but the claim could have been motivated by little more than Greek national pride (Alan B. Lloyd, *Historia*, XXXVII (1988), 41).

2. Ἀπρίεω ... ἐδόκεε: see notes on 161,2–3; 162,5–6.

2–3. καὶ δὴ τότε ... ἀπέπνιξαν: this account is flatly contradicted by the Amasis stele, our one explicit Egyptian source, which states that Apries was killed in the final battle (see notes on 163,1). Herodotus' version, which exonerates the usurper Amasis of all blame, is probably pro-Amasis propaganda (Lloyd, op. cit., p. 40).

2. βασιλήια: see note on 163,1.

3. ἐν τῇσι πατρωίῃσι ταφῇσι: the Amasis stele speaks of Amasis himself as carrying out the obsequies. This was a duty traditionally incumbent on a king's successor, and its execution would have strengthened Amasis' claim to legitimacy (cf. R. Stadelmann, *MDAI(K)* XXVII (1971), 112).

4–5. αἱ δέ εἰσι ... ἡ θήκη ἐστί: there are no identifiable traces at Sais, but Herodotus' description rings true inasmuch as such temple-court tombs were typical of the Late Period (ibid., pp. 111 ff.).

4. ἐν τῷ ἱρῷ τῆς Ἀθηναίης: sc. 'in the temple of Neith', the major deity of Sais (cf. note on 28,1).   τοῦ μεγάρου: sc. 'the hall' (cf. 141,3), the section of the main temple-building which would be encountered on passing from the court.   ἔθαψαν δὲ Σαῖται ... ἐν τῷ ἱρῷ: cf. III 10; Strabo XVII 1,18 (C802). ἐκ νομοῦ τούτου: the omission of the article with demonstratives is common in poetry and occurs frequently in Herodotus when the demonstrative follows the noun (Kühner–Gerth, *Gr. Grammatik* II 1, p. 630).

5. καὶ γὰρ τὸ τοῦ Ἀμάσιος ... τοῦ ἱροῦ: the location of Amasis' tomb in the royal necropolis of the XXVIth Dynasty provides another example of his efforts to gloss over his usurpation (cf., however, note on ch. 172).   παστὰς: lit. 'a columned portico', but in this instance the word is being used by a σχῆμα καθ᾽ ὅλον καὶ μέρος of a mortuary temple fronted by this feature (Alan B. Lloyd, *JEA* LVI (1970), 83, n. 3).   στύλοισί τε ... μεμιμημένοισι: palm-leaf capitals were widely used in Egyptian architecture from the Old Kingdom onwards. For the symbolic implications see note on 138,3.   καὶ τῇ ἄλλῃ δαπάνῃ: i.e. painted relief sculpture

presumably representing the mortuary cult and, inside the structure, the post-mortem fate of the king.   διξὰ θυρώματα: probably 'two doors', one behind the other, as in the parallel structures at Medinet Habu (Stadelman, op. cit., pp. 114 ff.).   ἡ θήκη: almost certainly the area beyond the doors was the mortuary chapel for the cult of the dead king; the θήκη proper would have been a vault beneath the floor (Stadelmann, loc. cit.).

170–1.   A brief excursus on the cult of Osiris at Sais suggested by the mention of the temple of Neith in the previous chapter and aspects of the cult which appeared to have parallels in Greek religion.

170,1. εἰσὶ δὲ ... τοίχου: on Herodotus' reticence in such matters see note on 3,2. His reserve will have been strengthened in this instance by his belief that the rituals were μυστήρια (note on 171,1).   αἱ ταφαὶ ... τοίχου: the god was Osiris, who was second only to Neith in importance at Sais. His shrine in the sacred enclosure was the Ḥwt-bìty, 'The Mansion of the King of Lower Egypt', which contained a ritual tomb of the god in an installation called the Ḥwt-Ḥm3g, 'The Mansion of Hemag (sc. Osiris)' (R. el-Sayed, *Documents relatifs à Sais et ses divinités*, BdE LXXXVI, Cairo 1982, pp. 199 ff., 208, 211).

2. ὀβελοὶ ... λίθινοι: for the ritual significance of obelisks see note on 111,4. Examples are known to have been made for Neith in the Saite period (el-Sayed, BIFAO LXXIV (1974), 41 ff.).   λίμνη: sacred lakes were a standard element of ancient Egyptian temples (cf. note on 138,1). The site of the specimen at Sais has never been securely identified, but it is explicitly mentioned in a late inscription (J. Leclant and H. de Meulenaere, *Kêmi*, XIV (1957), 36).   λιθίνη κρηπῖδι: i.e. a stone border around the edge like that surrounding the sacred lake at Dendera (Chassinat, *Dendera* I, pls. XI, XV–XVI, XXV–XXVI).   ἐργασμένη εὖ κύκλῳ: trans. '... well worked on all sides'. It should be borne firmly in mind (*pace* Rawlinson II, p. 255, *et al.*) that the adverb κύκλῳ implies nothing about the shape of the lake. We can be quite confident that it was rectangular (Lloyd, *Commentary 99–182*, pp. 208 ff.).   καὶ μέγαθος ... τροχοειδὴς καλεομένη: on the Delian lake, which was oval-shaped, see Theognis I 5 ff.; Aeschylus, *Eum.* 9; Euripides, *Iph. Taur.* 1104. It lay near Scardana, north-east of the temple of Leto. Since it measured *c.*100 m. north–south and *c.*70 m. east–west, it was larger than any known Egyptian sacred lake.   ὡς ἐμοὶ ἐδόκεε: on Herodotean autopsy see above, p. 229.

171,1. ἐν δὲ τῇ λίμνῃ ταύτῃ ... Αἰγύπτιοι: this ritual was 'the Navigation of Osiris' which formed part of the Festival of Khoiak and normally took place on the 24–25th of the month of Khoiak (the fourth of the Egyptian civil year). It certainly could not be described as *mysteria* in the Greek sense (notes on ch. 61; Alliot, *Le Culte*, pp. 244 ff., 696).   περὶ μέν νυν τούτων ... εὔστομα κείσθω: see notes on 61; 170, 1.

2. καὶ τῆς Δήμητρος τελετῆς πέρι ... καλέουσι: the Thesmophoria was restricted to women and celebrated in honour of Demeter Thesmophoros. At Athens it took place on the 11th–13th of the month of Pyanepsion (H. W. Parke, *Festivals of the Athenians*, London 1977, pp. 82 ff.). The erroneous association with the cult of Osiris arose through the identification of Demeter with Osiris' sister-wife Isis (notes on 59; 122–3; 156,5).

3. αἱ Δαναοῦ θυγατέρες…τὰς Πελασγιώτιδας γυναῖκας: on Herodotus' view, largely mistaken, of the origins of Greek religions see notes on chs. 43–58. αἱ Δαναοῦ θυγατέρες: their sex and Egyptian origin made them ideal intermediaries. For their legend see Rose, *Handbook Greek Mythology*, Index, s.v. τὰς Πελασγιώτιδας γυναῖκας: for Herodotus' mistaken notions on the Pelasgians see note on ch. 50. μετὰ δὲ…Δωριέων: the concept of *exanastasis*, 'population displacement', clearly played a major part in 5th-cent. thinking about early Greek history (Thuc. I 2,12). The Dorian invasion probably took place in the 11th cent. BC, but Greek memories of it were confused and should be treated with extreme caution (cf. V. Desborough, *The Greek Dark Ages*, London 1972, pp. 324 ff.). καὶ οὐκ…μοῦνοι: an unsurprising claim; for the Arcadians were themselves considered to be Pelasgians (note on ch. 50) and were greatly devoted to the cult of Demeter (cf. Nilsson, *GgrR* I, pp. 448 ff.).

172,1. Ἀπρίεω…ἐβασίλευσε Ἄμασις: this statement completely ignores the overlap between the accession of Amasis and the death of Apries (on which see note on ch. 163). νομοῦ μὲν Σάϊτεω: cf. Plato, *Tim.* 21e. There is no explicit Egyptian confirmation, but the Saite kings of the XXVIth Dynasty would certainly have had a marked tendency to prefer people from Sais as their henchmen. Σιούφ: this place-name does not certainly occur in any other context, and modern attempts to locate it are pure guesswork (cf. J. Yoyotte, *MDAI(K)* XVI (1958), 414 ff.).

2–5. τὰ μὲν δὴ πρῶτα…δουλεύειν: cf. Diod. I 95; Plutarch, *De Virt. Mul.* 25 (*Mor.* 261c ff.); Polyaenus, *Strat.* VII 4. This pseudo-historical tale is probably Greek in origin and is built around several motifs: reversal-of-fortune, the wise ruler, the trick, and obscenity (Lloyd, *Commentary 99–182*, p. 212).

2. ἅτε δὴ δημότην…οὐκ ἐπιφανέος: cf. Hellanicus, *FGrHist* 4 F 55; Diod. I 95. Egyptian sources give no indication of the status of Amasis' family, but the evidence of Egyptian efforts to defame him suggests extreme caution in accepting the historicity of the Herodotean tradition (cf. H. de Meulenaere, *JEA* LIV (1968), 183 ff.).

3. κατ' ὦν κόψας: on the tmesis see note on 39,2.

5. εἰ γὰρ πρότερον εἶναι δημότης: for the attraction of the finite verb into the infinitive in subordinate clauses see note on 64,2.

173,1–4. ἐχρᾶτο…ἀμείψατο: note that, whereas in the previous tale the denouement is given in indirect speech, in this chapter Herodotus uses *oratio recta* (see above, pp. 234, 239).

1. τὸ δὲ ἀπὸ τούτου…παιγνιήμων: cf. 174,1; Plutarch, *Sept. Sap. Conv.* 6 (*Mor.* 151b ff.); Aelian, *VH* II 41. It is safe to postulate an Egyptian origin for the tale, since Amasis' drunkenness also features in the the Egyptian tale of Amasis and the Boatman (Spiegelberg, *Demotische Chronik*, pp. 30 ff.: cf. in general C. W. Müller, in *Ak. der Wissenschaften und der Literatur Mainz 1949–1989*, Stuttgart 1989,

pp. 209 ff.: J. Quaegebeur, *Anc.Soc.* XXI (1990), 240 ff.), but Greek contamination is clear in the Herodotean version (see below). The tradition should not be regarded as historically accurate, but it does show an irreverent attitude to kings and kingship which is easily paralleled in Egyptian literature (Alan B. Lloyd, in Trigger, p. 296).

2–4. ἀχθεσθέντες ... ἀμείψατο: Aly emphasizes the tragic colouring of the language of this section (*Volksmärchen*, p. 61).

2. οὐκ ὀρθῶς ... οὐδαμῶς: such a critique is not inconceivable in Late Period Egypt (Alan B. Lloyd, *Historia*, XXXI (1982), 42 ff.). σὺ ἄμεινον ἤκουες: the alternative reading ἄμεινον σὺ ἂν ἤκουες has stronger ms support, and the word-order is also more forceful.

3–4. ὁ δ᾽ ἀμείβετο ... ἀμείψατο: cf. Ovid, *Her.* IV 89 ff. For the use of *apophtheg-mata* as the basis for a speech see Heni, p. 132. Since the bow-metaphor is un-Egyptian and is used here in a very un-Egyptian way, we must accept that severe Greek contamination of the Egyptian original has taken place. The *figura etymo-logica* ἀμείβετο ... ἀμείψατο is a typical Herodotean feature (cf. 14,2).

4. ὅ γε: demonstrative ὁ followed by γε is very rare and here has a strong epic flavour (Kühner–Gerth, *Gr. Grammatik* II 1, pp. 586, 656 ff.).

174,1. λέγεται: this account, unlike those in the two preceding chapters, is presented entirely in narrative form (cf. note on 173,1). Here too we are probably confronted with the Herodotean version of an ultimately Egyptian tale. The use of ὁ Ἄμασις as the subject of λέγεται is a variant of a common form of prolepsis whereby the subject of a subordinate clause is transferred into the main clause as a direct object, e.g. οὗτος ὁ Ὀτάνης πρῶτος ὑπώπτευσε τὸν μάγον ὡς οὐκ εἴη ὁ Κύρου Σμέρδις (III 68). The construction throws particular emphasis on to the transferred element (cf. Kühner–Gerth, *Gr. Grammatik* II 2, pp. 577 ff.). φιλοπότης ... ἀνήρ: cf. note on 173,1. κλέπτεσκε ἄν: for the verbal form see note on 13,1. For the imperfect with ἄν in such contexts see note on 109,2. Note that, unlike the peccadilloes mentioned earlier, theft was a crime, and Amasis is being presented here as a criminal. This tradition may well derive from anti-Amasis sources which existed at least as early as the Persian Period (see note on 172,2). οἱ δ᾽ ἄν ... μαντήιον: the use of oracles to solve legal problems was widespread in Late Period Egypt (note on ch. 83). ἄγεσκον: on the form see note on 13,1.

2. ὅσοι ... ἐπεμέλετο: doubts about the reliability of some oracular shrines and also divination were certainly current in 5th-cent. Greece (cf. I 47–9; IV 68–9; Parke, *Greek Oracles*, pp. 107 ff.), and these may well have played a part in turning Greek attention to this tale. ὅσοι μὲν ... τούτων μὲν: for this duplication of μέν see Denniston, *Greek Particles*, p. 386. ἀπέλυσαν ... κατέδησαν: both verbs are used in a pregnant sense as verbs of saying with dependent infinitive (Kühner–Gerth, *Gr. Grammatik* II 2, p. 5).

175,1–5. καὶ τοῦτο μὲν ... ἐσελκυσθῆναι: in this and the following chapter Hero-dotus discusses Amasis' building achievements, to which his attention was drawn pre-eminently by their status as θωμάσια (see above, pp. 234 ff.).

1. ἐν Σάϊ: for this city see note on 28,1. It is badly ruined (note on 169,4), but there is clear evidence of Amasis' architectural activity on the site (e.g. PM IV, p. 48; VII, p. 414; H. Ranke, *MDAI(K)* XII (1943), 107 ff.).   προπύλαια: cf. notes on 101,2; 121,1; 136,1.   κολοσσοὺς μεγάλους: remains of such statuary of the relevant date have been found on the site, but nothing which can be attributed specifically to Amasis (F. M. Wasif, *Oriens Antiquus*, XIII (1974), 328).   ἀνδρόσφιγγας: i.e. sphinxes with the body of a lion and the head of a king, in this case Amasis (cf. C. de Wit, *Le Rôle et le sens du lion dans l'Egypte ancien*, Leiden 1951, pp. 39 ff.). Sphinxes of the reign of Amasis are known from various sites (e.g. PM IV, p. 73; VII, pp. 299, 414).

2. ἐκ τῶν κατὰ Μέμφιν ἐουσέων λιθοτομιέων: see note on 124,2. As yet no inscriptions of Amasis have been identified here, but other kings of the dynasty to which he belonged have left several.   ἐξ Ἐλεφαντίνης πόλιος: see note on 134,1. Inscriptions of Amasis have been preserved in this area (PM V, pp. 226, 243, 252, 256).   πλόον ... ἀπὸ Σάϊος: this distance is *c.*1100 km. and could well have been covered in 20 days (cf. notes on 8,3–9).

3. οἴκημα μουνόλιθον: clearly a *naos*. The dimensions (*c.*9.26m. high, 6.17 *m.* in depth) are plausible, though unusually large. One of Amasis' surviving *naoi* measures *c.*6.00 m. in height and *c.*3.6 m. in width (H. E. Naville, *Ahnas el Medineh (Heracleopolis Magna)*, London 1894, p. 17), and many smaller specimens are known.   ἐπ' ἔτεα τρία: see note on 77,2.   δισχίλιοι: since in one XIth Dynasty expedition a team of 3,000 sailors was used in a similar context (*BAR* I, 390), Herodotus' figure must be treated with respect. κυβερνῆται: see note on 164,1.

4. ἀτάρ: for the use of ἀτάρ after μέν with adversative force see Denniston, *Greek Particles*, p. 54.   <τὸ δὲ εὖρος δυώδεκα πήχεων>: so S, but this ms has little authority. Since a measurement of width seems necessary, we should probably postulate a lacuna.

5. ἔσω γάρ μιν ... ἐσελκυσθῆναι: on the use of alternative versions in Herodotus see note on 2,5. Observe that the attitude to Amasis is favourable in both. οἷά: equivalent to ἅτε, as often in Herodotus (Powell, *Lexicon*, p. 262). ἐνθυμητὸν: so Hude, but the reading ἐνθυμιστὸν has strong ms support, and the word is also epigraphically attested at Thasos in the required sense (J. Pouilloux, *Recherches sur l'histoire et les cultes de Thasos*, I, Paris 1954, pp. 372 ff.). ἤδη: here used to introduce a variant account, as elsewhere in Herodotus (Kühner–Gerth, *Gr. Grammatik* II 2, p. 123). Trans. 'Further, as well'.

176,1. ἀνέθηκε ... ἀξιοθέητα: there is abundant archaeological evidence of Amasis' temple-building in many parts of Egypt and outlying areas (addition to old shrines, e.g. PM II, pp. 192 ff.; IV, pp. 35 ff., 45 ff.; complete temples, e.g. at Philae, Elephantine, and Abydos, S. Farag, G. Wahba, and A. Farid, *Oriens Antiquus*, XVI (1977), 315 ff; PM V, p. 43).   ἐν δὲ ... μῆκος: cf. 99,4; 110,1; 151,1. At 29.4 cm. to the *pous* this statue, either fallen or never erected, would have been at least 22 m. high, i.e. even taller than the colossi of Memnon (*c.*21 m.).

Large it probably was, but such a size is difficult to accept, especially in view of the recurrent inaccuracy of Herodotus' measurements (notes on chs. 8, 124, 148). ἐπὶ δὲ τῷ αὐτῷ βάθρῳ... τοῦ μεγάλου: i.e. the group formed a triad (cf. Vandier, *Manuel* III, pp. 21 ff.). The addition of smaller figures to a colossal statue is a well-known feature of Egyptian sculpture (e.g. Baedeker, *Egypt*, p. 404). These figures (*c*.5.8 m. high) will have represented queens, princes, or princesses.
2. ἔστι δὲ λίθινος... ἐν Μέμφι: no colossus has survived in whole or in part from Sais which can certainly be ascribed to Amasis, but remains of a red-granite specimen, probably of his dynasty have been discovered (F. M. Wasif, *Oriens Antiquus*, XIII (1974), 328). τῇ Ἴσι... ἀξιοθεητότατον: this is the earliest substantial Isis temple known from Memphis (J. Bergman, *Ich bin Isis*, Uppsala 1968, pp. 241 ff.). Amasis' temple-building on the site is confirmed archaeologically (PM III, pp. 840, 851), and he certainly built in honour of Isis at Philae (PM VI, p. 235; G. Haeny, *BIFAO* LXXXV (1985), 197 ff.), but as yet no trace of the Memphite Isis temple has come to light. τε: on the use of τε to connect sentences see Denniston, *Greek Particles*, p. 499. It normally appears in second position but commonly recedes when preceded by article and noun (ibid., p. 516). ἐξοικοδομήσας: the ἐξ- is intensive (cf. note on 3,2, and parallels at II 180,1; V 62,2); the verb, therefore, means 'build from beginning to end', and Herodotus is insisting on Amasis' sole responsibility for the structure.
177,1. Ἐπ' Ἀμάσιος... τὰς οἰκεομένας: cf. Diod. I 60,1; 95,1. The quantity and quality of building and artistic work and the plethora of administrative documents confirm this claim (notes on chs. 175–6; Griffith, *Catalogue* III, pp. 20 ff.). μάλιστα δή: as often, the δή strengthens the superlative, a usage particularly common in Thucydides (Denniston, *Greek Particles*, p. 207). καὶ τὰ ἀπὸ τοῦ ποταμοῦ... τοῖσι ἀνθρώποισι: see note on 142,4. καὶ πόλις... τὰς οἰκεομένας: taken literally, this figure is unacceptably high. Perhaps πόλις is being used loosely to cover settlements ranging from large hamlets to cities; alternatively, Herodotus, or his source, may simply have exaggerated (Lloyd, *Commentary 99–182*, pp. 219 ff.).
2. νόμον τε Αἰγυπτίοισι... ὁ καταστήσας: cf. Diod. I 95,1. The tradition of Amasis the lawgiver is probably no more than a reflection of a programme of reorganization undertaken after his defeat of Apries (on which see note on 163,1). ἀποδεικνύναι... βιοῦται: cf. Diod. I 77,5. Amasis certainly did not initiate this (D. Cohen, *Mnemosyne*, LIII (1925), 82 ff.). μὴ δὲ: in such contexts δέ is often postponed to a position after the participle. The present location serves to emphasize the opposition of negative and positive ideas (Denniston, *Greek Particles*, p. 187). Σόλων δὲ ὁ Ἀθηναῖος... νόμῳ: cf. I 30,1. The tradition on Solon's visit and, in particular, his relations with Amasis is suspect and should be treated with extreme caution (Lloyd, *Introduction*, pp. 55 ff.; S. S. Markianos, *Historia*, XXIII (1974), 7 ff.). τοῦτον τὸν νόμον... ἀμώμῳ νόμῳ: Herodotus is probably referring to the Athenian νόμος ἀργίας which made ἀργία a criminal offence and is variously ascribed to Draco,

Solon, or Peisistratus (E. Ruschenbusch, *ΣΟΛΩΝΟΣ ΝΟΜΟΙ*, *Historia* Einzelschriften, IX, Wiesbaden 1966, fr. 148). It is certain that it was not in any way a product of Egyptian influence.

178,1. φιλέλλην δὲ γενόμενος: trans. 'having become a lover of the Greeks', i.e. after initial hostility (see notes on 161,1–2; 163). Amasis' measures concerning Naucratis were probably restrictive and intended as a limitation of Greek trade after the nationalist revolt of 570 (cf. v. Fritz I, pp. 201 ff.), but evidence of conciliation of the Greeks in the latter part of his reign is easily found (180,2; 182; III 47).   τοῖσι ἀπικνευμένοισι: Greeks went to Egypt in considerable numbers and for a variety of motives (see above, pp. 221 ff.).   Ναύκρατιν: the name is pure Greek, though it does occur in the Egyptian form *Nἰwt-krt*; the city also bore the Egyptian name *Pr-mryt*, 'Harbour-house'. It lay in the north-west Delta on the east side of the Canopic Branch of the Nile where the mound of Tell Neqrash still preserves its name. It was certainly founded in the reign of Psammetichus I by Milesians, the first settlers appearing perhaps as early as the 650s, though the oldest archaeological material dates to 620–610 BC (Austin, pp. 22 ff.; Lloyd, *Commentary 99–182*, pp. 222 ff.; J. W. Drijvers, *Mnemosyne*, LII (1999), 16 ff.).   ἐνοικῆσαι ... ἐνιδρύσασθαι: the infinitives are final (see note on 96,4).

2. χρησιμώτατον: 'most made use of, most frequented' (LSJ, p. 2006a, s.v. χρήσιμος, I,3).   Ἑλλήνιον: this temenos lay in the north-east sector of the site. Archaeological evidence points to a foundation firmly within the sixth century (Boardman, *Greeks Overseas*, p. 120; for doubts about the correctness of this identification see H. Bowden, in M. H. Hansen and K. A. Raaflaub (eds.), *More Studies in the Ancient Greek Polis*, *Historia* Einzelschriften, CVIII, Stuttgart 1996, pp. 22 ff.).   Χίος ... μούνη: with the exception of Halicarnassus and Phaselis, the presence of members of all these states can be confirmed at Naucratis (Boardman, op. cit., pp. 122 ff.; Lloyd, op. cit., pp. 224 f.).

3. τούτων ... τὸ τέμενος: the national affinities of the finds from this part of the site confirm Herodotus' claim.   προστάτας τοῦ ἐμπορίου: cf. Athenaeus IV 149. Translate '*prostatai* of the trading post', the term ἐμπόριον referring to the entire city, as often (C. Roebuck, *CPh* XLVI (1951), 215). It is possible that they were the supreme magistrates of the city, but the evidence is insufficient to establish their precise status (cf. Bowden, op. cit., p. 33).   Αἰγινῆται: Aegina, the only mainland Greek state listed here, certainly had close connections with Egypt (Boardman, *Greeks Overseas*, pp. 112, 122–3, 125, 128–31, 142).   ἱδρύσαντο: the correlation between τὸ μέν νυν and χωρὶς δέ shows that Herodotus thought all the *temenē* were built at the same time as a result of the policy of Amasis. It is clear, however, that those mentioned below were constructed before the Hellenium.   τέμενος Διός: this structure has never been identified, but substantial parts of the site remain to be explored.   Σάμιοι: there is ample corroboration of their presence (Boardman, op. cit., pp. 113–15, 120, 122, 124, 127, 129–30, 132: cf. pp. 142, 147).   Ἥρης: the temenos was discovered in the northern part of the site

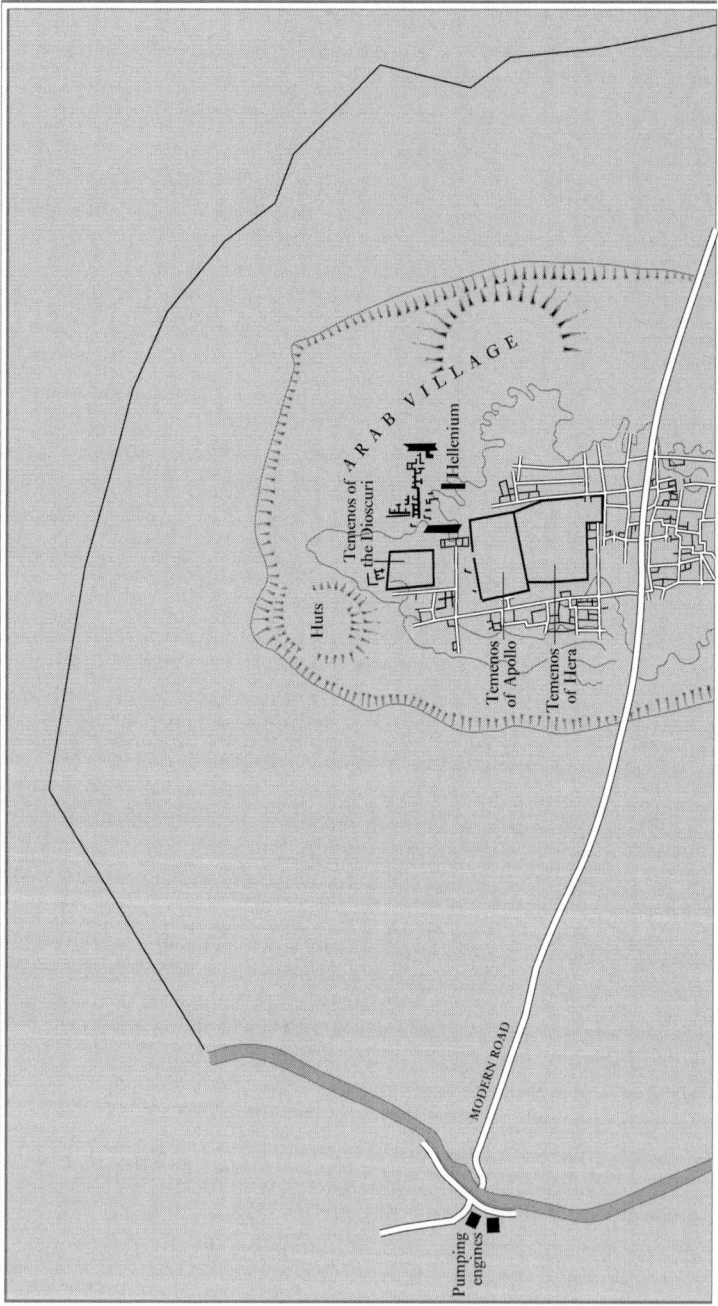

ARAB VILLAGE

Temenos of
the Dioscuri

Hellenium

Huts

Temenos
of Apollo

Temenos
of Hera

MODERN ROAD

Pumping
engines

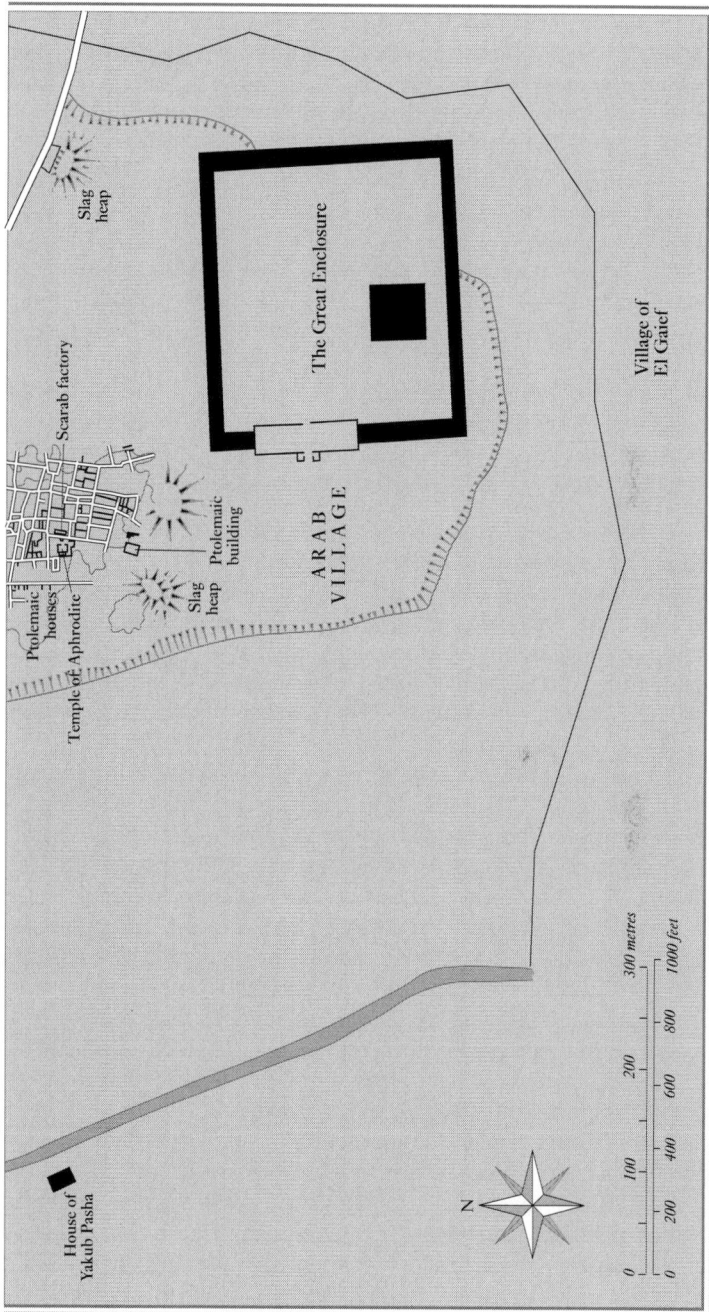

Map 29. Site of Naucratis

House of
Yakub Pasha

Ptolemaic
houses

Temple of Aphrodite

Scarab factory

Slag
heap

Slag
heap

Ptolemaic
building

ARAB
VILLAGE

The Great Enclosure

Village of
El Gaief

N

0   100   200
0   200   400   600   800   1000 feet

300 metres

and was one of the earliest to be built.   *Μιλήσιοι*: traditionally it was Milesians who founded the city, and there is no difficulty in confirming their presence there (Boardman, op. cit., pp. 113, 120, 124, 130: cf. p. 146).   *Ἀπόλλωνος*: the temenos stood in the northern part of the site and was founded no later than *c*.600 BC (Lloyd, *Commentary 99–182*, p. 229).

179. *τὸ παλαιὸν*: i.e. before Herodotus' time. The restriction in question was almost certainly introduced by Amasis at the beginning of his reign (cf. note on 178,1).   *μούνη Ναύκρατις ἐμπόριον*: i.e. it was the only trading post, but other types of settlement for Greeks were not excluded.   *εἰ δέ τις... Κανωβικόν*: such controls were well within Egyptian tradition. Amongst other things they facilitated the levying of customs dues, which were probably set at 10% (Kees, *RE* II, 1959 ff.).   *μὴ μὲν*: see note on 118,3.   *πρὸς ἀνέμους ἀντίους*: i.e. the northerly Etesian winds (note on ch. 20).   *τὰ φορτία... τὸ Δέλτα*: water levels in the Delta were a recurrent hazard to navigation and necessitated the use of specially designed shallow-draught vessels (cf. Strabo XVII 1,18 (C801)).   *ἐτετίμητο*: probably a misunderstanding (note on 178,1).

180,1–2. *Ἀμφικτυόνων... μνέας*: one of several cases where Amasis attempted to ingratiate himself with Greek states (cf. notes on 178,1; 181–2).

1. *Ἀμφικτυόνων... κατεκάη*: cf. I 50,3; V 62. This conflagration took place in 548/7 BC. The Delphian or Pylaean Amphictyony, which was responsible for the administration of the temple and the Pythian Games, consisted of representatives of major *ethnē* of central and northern Greece (P–W, pp. 100 ff.; E. Kirsten and W. Kraiker, *Griechenlandkunde*, I, Heidelberg 1967, pp. 248 ff.).   *μισθωσάντων... ταλάντων*: 'put out to tender'. This was the standard method of organizing the construction of public buildings in ancient Greece. The individual contracts were usually very small, but a total cost of 300 talents is entirely plausible (cf. A. Burford, *The Greek Temple Builders at Epidauros*, Liverpool Monographs in Archaeology and Oriental Studies, Liverpool 1969, pp. 81 ff.).   *ἐξεργάσασθαι*: for the meaning see note on 176,2. The infinitive is final (see note on 96,4).   *αὐτόματος*: there was clearly much debate on this issue; it was even claimed by some that the Peisistratids were behind the disaster (schol. on Pindar, *Pyth*. VII 1).

1–2. *τοὺς Δελφοὺς δὴ ἐπέβαλε... ἠνείκαντο*: the 75 talents required of the Delphians could only be paid by obtaining contributions from other sympathetic states. It is, however, evident that appeals of this kind usually met with a favourable response (Burford, op. cit., pp. 35 ff., 81).

2. *χίλια στυπτηρίης τάλαντα*: the substance was probably alum, which was mined in the Dakhla and Kharga Oases. One thousand talents in weight would be equivalent to *c*.26 metric tons if Herodotus was using the Attic talent. Such a contribution was extremely generous since it would have amounted to more than half the Egyptian alum production in medieval times (Lucas–Harris, *AEMI*, pp. 257 ff.).   *εἴκοσι μνέας*: i.e. 8.73 kg., if Herodotus is using the Attic mina. This figure is extremely low and may reflect an error or misunderstanding on Herodotus' part, e.g. it may be based on a damaged inscription.

181,1. *Κυρηναίοισι... συνεθήκατο*: cf. note on 161,4. Amasis' calculated philhellenism again shows itself in his diplomatic efforts to regulate relations with his Cyrenaean neighbours (cf. E. Edel, *GM* XXIX (1978), 14 ff.; in general notes on 178,1; 180).   *φιλότητος Κυρηναίων εἵνεκα*: we can be confident that the marriage was a shrewd diplomatic move to cement good relations.

2. *γαμέει... Λαδίκη*: on alternative versions in Herodotus see note on 2,5. If the marriage was part of Amasis' grand strategy, it is infinitely more probable that Ladike was the daughter of King Battus.   *Βάττου τοῦ Ἀρκεσίλεω*: Battus II, who ruled *c.*590–*c.*560 BC and was the son of Arcesilaus I (*c.*606–*c.*590).

2–5. *τῇ ἐπείτε... ἄστεος*: this pseudo-historical tale appears to be a combination of Amasis' historical relations with Cyrene, *Monument-novelle* (i.e. a desire to explain a statue at Cyrene, see note on 107,1), folklore (the sex motif, Thompson, *Motif-Index*, T), and, possibly, anti-Amasis propaganda (cf. note on 172,2).

3. *κατά με ἐφάρμαξας*: tmesis of a compound verb by an enclitic pronoun is the least common Herodotean form of tmesis (Kühner–Gerth, *Gr. Grammatik* II 1, p. 537). Here it highlights the *με* and imparts a greater element of vehemence to Amasis' claim.

4. *ἡ δὲ Λαδίκη... ἐς Κυρήνην*: Aphrodite was popular both in Cyrene and Cyrenaica at large; numerous statues of her were found in the city at a small temple south of the Odeion (A. Rowe, *New Light on Aegypto-Cyrenaean Relations*, Cah. *ASAE* XII, Cairo 1948, p. 21).

5. *ταύτην τὴν Λαδίκην... ἐς Κυρήνην*: initially the Cyrenaeans were allied with the Egyptians against Cambyses (Diod. X fr. 15), but they swiftly made their peace with him after the Persian conquest (Herod. III 13,3–4). Probably Cambyses' return of Ladike was intended to consolidate good relations with the Cyrenean royal house (Lloyd, *Commentary 99–182*, pp. 234 ff.).

182,1–2. *Ἀνέθηκε... Ἄμασις*: cf. notes on 159,3; 178,1; 180; 181,1.   *ἐς Κυρήνην... Ἀθηναίης*: cf. note on 181,1. On Athena at Cyrene see Pindar, *Pyth.* IX 97; Chamoux, p. 270). The identification of Athene with the Egyptian Neith, a favourite deity of Amasis' dynasty, makes this dedication easily intelligible (cf. note on 28,1).   *εἰκόνα ἑωυτοῦ γραφῇ εἰκασμένην*: trans. probably 'a painted portrait of himself'. For surviving paintings of Amasis see T. G. H. James, *JEA* LXVIII (1982), 156 ff.).   *τῇ ἐν Λίνδῳ Ἀθηναίῃ*: the Lindian Chronicle also mentions ten bowls (C. Blinkenberg, *Die lindische Tempelchronik*, Kleine Texte für Vorlesungen und Übungen, CXXXI, Bonn 1951, p. 25). Lindus was the most powerful of the Rhodian cities in Amasis' reign. The famed temple of Athene Lindia, to which the dedications were made, was rebuilt between 550 and 525 by the tyrant Cleobulus (R. E. Wycherley, in *PECS*, pp. 755 ff.).   *ἀγάλματα λίθινα*: probably in the Egyptian style and representing Neith. They are mentioned in the Lindian Chronicle (Blinkenberg, loc. cit.).   *θώρηκα λίνεον ἀξιοθέητον*: cf. II 159,3; III 47,1–3; Blinkenberg, *Lindos. Fouilles de l'Acropole 1902–1914. II. Inscriptions*, I, Berlin–Copenhagen 1941, p.173; Pliny, *NH* XIX 2,12. The manufacturing technology is discussed by Ch. Picard, in 'Hommages à Waldemar Deonna', *Collection Latomus*, XXVIII (1957), 363 ff. Linen breastplates are known to have been used by the Egyptians, but none has survived (W. Wolf, *Die Bewaffnung des altägyptischen Heeres*, Leipzig 1926, p. 98). ἐς Σάμον τῇ Ἥρῃ: cf. II 148,2; III 60. It was the temple being rebuilt by the tyrant Polycrates (see below) which received these dedications. εἰκόνας ἑωυτοῦ... ξυλίνας: statues of kings made of this material are unusual in modern collections but were clearly numerous and normally of very high quality (Vandier, *Manuel* III, pp. 552 ff.).

2. ἐς μέν νυν Σάμον... Πολυκράτεος τοῦ Αἰάκεος: cf. III 39–45, 54, 56, 120–5, 142. Polycrates was tyrant from 533/2 to *c*. 522 BC. The alliance between Egypt and Samos was a mutual defence pact against the Persians; according to Herodotus it was eventually abandoned by Amasis (see, in general, B. Mitchell, *JHS* XCV (1975), 75 ff.; Andrewes, pp. 117 ff.). ἐς δὲ Λίνδον... παῖδας: Herodotus is probably wrong. Amasis was surely interested in Lindus for the same economic and strategic motives as operated in the case of Samos (Lloyd, *Commentary 99–182*, p. 239). ὅτι δὲ... παῖδας: see note on 171,3. εἷλε δὲ Κύπρον... ἀπαγωγήν: cf. Diod. I 68,1. Cultural contact was certainly close in Saite times (Boardman, *Greeks Overseas*, pp. 74, 112, 120, 124, 127, 139, 141, 234), and Apries seems to have had close links of some kind (E. Edel, *GM* XXIX (1978), 19). Amasis attacked the island at the beginning of his reign (ibid.), but the date of its conquest remains uncertain. πρῶτος ἀνθρώπων: certainly incorrect. The Hittites, Phoenicians, and Assyrians all exercised control of substantial parts, if not all, of it.

BOOK III

David Asheri

INTRODUCTION TO BOOK III

The third book of Herodotus—its traditional muse is Thalia—is connected thematically and chronologically to the great *excursus* on Egyptian history that constitutes the second part of the second book (II 99–182), as well as to the main narrative of Persian history begun in Book I with Cyrus' birth and his rise to power (I 107–30), and broken off with his death on the battlefield (I 214; cf. the hint of connection at II 1,1). Herodotus immediately introduces the two representatives of this double Persian and Egyptian plot: Cambyses and Amasis. The first chapters report certain previous anecdotal episodes from the last years of Cyrus and the first years of Cambyses. However, the actual and proper narrative of the third book starts with the Egyptian campaign of 525 BC. The preparations for the campaign (4,3; 7 and 9) can be dated to the previous two or three years (see note on 1–38); whereas at the opposite time limit the Persian subjection of Samos (144–9) and the siege of Babylon (150–60) constitute the latest events of the book. Herodotus connects the two events chronologically (150,1), so that they both can be assigned to the initial period of Darius' reign: *c*.520/19, although it can be inferred from the oriental sources that the last Babylonian revolt against Darius was suppressed in December of 521 (see note on 150–60). Therefore it is ten years at the most that the main narrative of Book III relates.[1] It is mainly Persian history: the reign of Cambyses (529–22), the usurpation of the throne by the Magus, the conspiracy of the seven, the accession of Darius (522/1), the restoration and reorganization of the empire, certain armed conflicts which took place in the very first years of Darius' reign. The chapters on Egyptian history (1–37) and the three important sections on the history of Samos (39–60; 120–8; 139–49) are thematically and chronologically interwoven with the main narrative of Persian history. In a few digressive chapters Herodotus mentions events of the previous century: Samos' help to Sparta during the second Messenian war (end of seventh century: see note on 47,1); the tyranny of Periander (perhaps 625–585; cf. note on 48–53); certain episodes shortly preceding the Persian conquest of Sardis, or contemporary with it (about 548–546; cf. 47,1–2); Polycrates' rise to power (perhaps in 533/2; cf. note on 39,1). There is no lack of other sporadic allusions to later events, not only subsequent to those at the end of Book III, but also to those that conclude the *Histories* of Herodotus: the battle of Papremis in 462/1 (12,4), the insurrections of Inarus and of Amyrtaeus *c*.450 (15,3); the desertion of Zopyrus the Younger to Athens (probably shortly after 440; cf. 160,2). Nevertheless, apart from these rare temporal leaps, the essential chronological frame of the book is rigorously circumscribed.

Also from a structural point of view, Book III presents a solid main narrative, formed from a series of Persian *logoi*, sometimes moral or symbolic in content,

---

[1] Cf. the roughly thirty years covered by Book I; see above, p. 59.

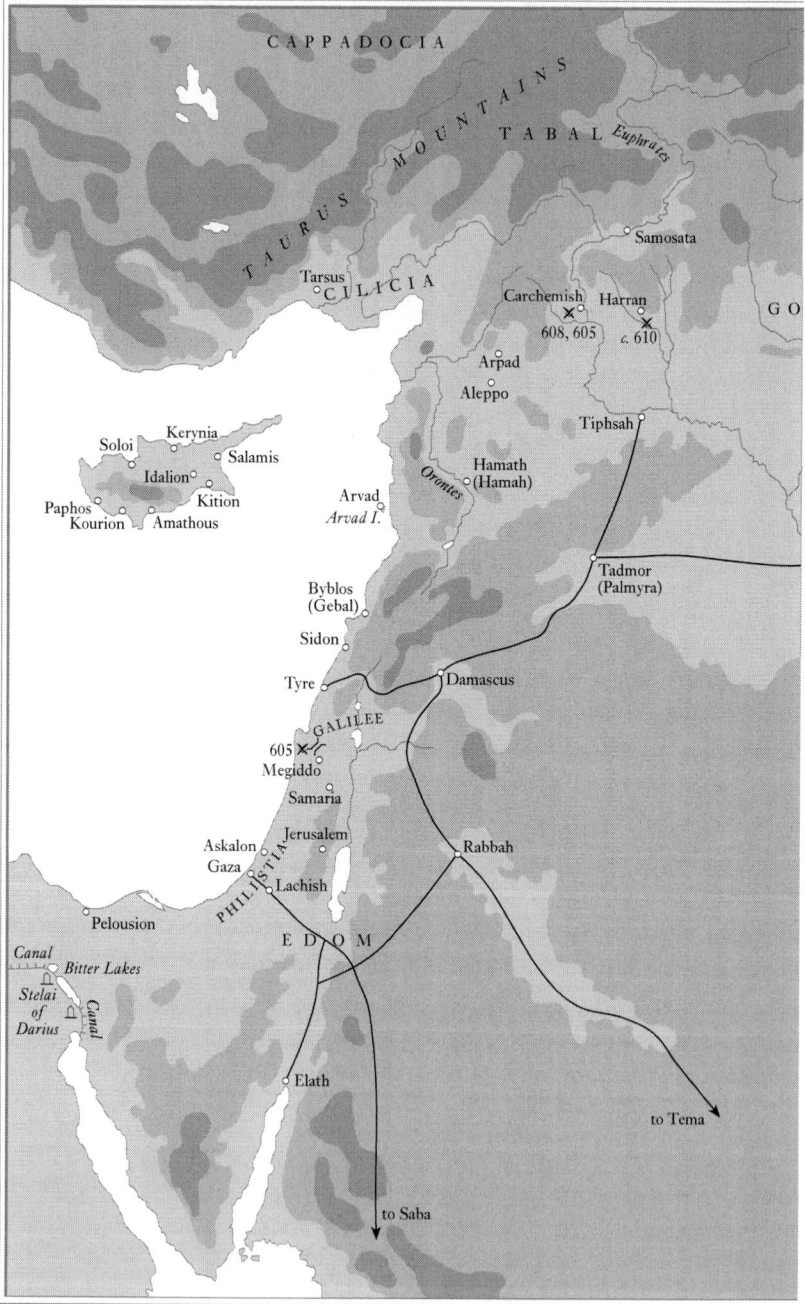

Map 30. The Fertile Crescent

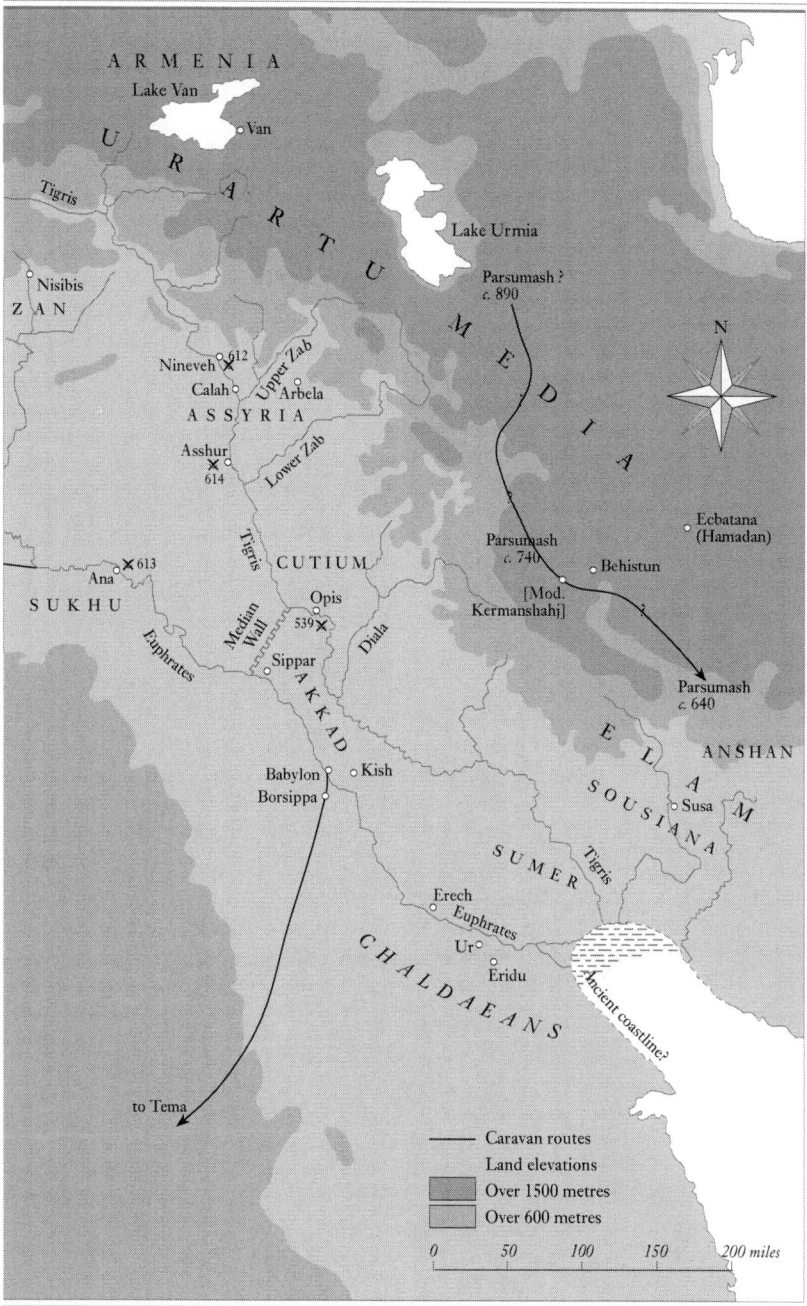

ARMENIA
Lake Van
Van
URARTU
Tigris
Lake Urmia
Parsumash ?
c. 890
Nisibis
ZAN
MEDIA
Nineveh ✗ 612
Upper Zab
Calah
Arbela
ASSYRIA
Asshur
✗
614
Lower Zab
Ecbatana
(Hamadan)
Tigris
CUTIUM
Parsumash
c. 740
Behistun
✗ 613
Ana
SUKHU
Median Wall
Opis
539 ✗
Diala
[Mod.
Kermanshahj]
Euphrates
Sippar
AKKAD
Parsumash
c. 640
ELAM
ANSHAN
Babylon
Borsippa
Kish
SOUSIANA
Susa
SUMER
Tigris
Erech
Euphrates
CHALDAEANS
Ur
Eridu
Ancient coastline?
to Tema

Caravan routes
Land elevations
Over 1500 metres
Over 600 metres
0   50   100   150   200 miles

purposely chained together by means of chronological links.[2] The first Persian *logos* (1–38) is dedicated to the reign of Cambyses. It centres on the Persian conquest of Egypt: its 'cause' (1–3), preceding events and preparations (7–9), the battle of Pelusium (10–12), the siege of Memphis and its fall, the voluntary submission of the Libyans, the Cyreneans, and the Barceans (13). After three chapters on the sufferings and humiliations inflicted upon the living and the dead members of the Egyptian royal family and nobility (14–16), Herodotus turns to the three expeditions planned by Cambyses, all of which had Egypt as their point of departure and ultimately failed (17): against Carthage (19), against the oasis of Ammon (26), and against Ethiopia (17–25). Only the last campaign, ending in catastrophe, is described in detail, in chapters rich in ethnological material. When Cambyses returns from Ethiopia Herodotus focuses on the character, the behaviour, and the actions of the king, ultimately representing him as a victim of a mental illness (33). Cambyses orders the death of his brother Smerdis, suspecting him of conspiracy; he personally kills his sister, who was also his wife and pregnant; he kills the son of his faithful courtier Prexaspes; he orders the living burial of twelve Persian nobles. At the height of his madness, according to Herodotus, Cambyses commits a series of sacrilegious acts against the Egyptian gods, temples, and priests, causing in particular the death of the new Apis (27–9). The aged Croesus returns to the scene one last time in his role of 'wise counsellor', but does not succeed in stopping the king's excesses (30–7). This part of Cambyses' 'biography' ends with a famous anecdote of an ethnographic and moralizing nature (38); finally, the last events and the king's death are narrated as an epilogue (64–6). Among the numerous episodes of this first *logos*, four function as thematic and moral links to later events narrated in the second great Persian *logos* of Book III (61–88): the killings of Apis, of his brother, of his sister-wife, and of Prexaspes' son are connected, respectively, to the death of Cambyses (64–6), the reign of the false Smerdis (61–3; 67–79), the extinction of the offspring of Cyrus (66,2), and the tragic fate of Prexaspes (74–5). Thus, the function of these four episodes within the book extends beyond the thematic limits of the first *logos*. The main narrative is here interrupted by various geo-ethnographic or anecdotal digressions, which in general are well integrated in Cambyses' 'biography': the geography of the Palestinian coast (5), the wine-jars in Egypt (6), the customs of the Arabs (8), the Table of the Sun in Ethiopia (18), the customs of the Ethiopians (20–4). A novelistic collection of dreams (30,2; 65,2), portents (32,1), and oracles (64,4) is ably used to demonstrate the linkage of events.[3]

---

[2] Bernadete, pp. 93–4, n. 45, divides Book III into thirteen sections; S. Cagnazzi, *Hermes*, CIII (1975), 393–4, divides it into three great *logoi* (1–38; 39–60; 61–160). On Herodotus' *Persergeschichten* and their sources see K. Reinhardt, in: Marg. pp. 32–69, with A. Köhnken's criticism, *RhM* CXXXIII (1990), 115–37.

[3] For other dreams, oracles, prophecies, and portents in Book III, see 57.3 ff.; 76,3; 86,2; 125,4; 149; 151,2 and 153,1. Cf. above, pp. 41 ff.

The story of the false Smerdis, of the conspiracy of the seven, and of Darius' ascent to the throne is the pivot of the main narrative of Book III. On the one hand, it directly continues the *logos* of Cambyses; on the other, it serves as a prelude to the description of the satrapies and the tributes of the empire (89–96), restored and reorganized by the new, great Achaemenid king. The events of the short reign of the Magus provide a prelude to the dramatic account of the conspiracy (67–79), which is immediately followed by the debate of the victorious conspirators about political systems (80–2), and by the tale of the election of Darius as king (83–7). The *logos* ends with a chapter on Darius, his family, and his monument (88). The main narrative of this second Persian *logos*, into which clusters of perfectly integrated dialogues and speeches are woven, contains no real and proper digressions, apart from a very few parenthetic phrases of explanatory nature (e.g. 69,6; 79,3). On reading the *logos*, all the elements of Herodotus' creativity emerge: his great art of story-writing, his love for the exotic, the paradoxical, the incredible, the intellectual amusement; his tragic vision of life, well illustrated by the examples of Cambyses and Prexaspes; the foreboding of a profound conflict between falsehood and truth in the drama of human history. As always, Herodotus seeks a moral and divine significance behind the individual events. The entire narrative centres on the thoughts and actions of a few great persons. Herodotus is not primarily interested in the social, economic, and spiritual problems that agitated the Persian empire at that time. He passes beyond the limits of the particular, transforming it into a moral *exemplum*.

The grand 'catalogue' of the satrapies and of tributes follows (89–96); then five minor Persian *logoi*, all chronologically connected to the initial period of Darius' reign: the death of Intaphernes (118–19), of Polycrates and Oroetes (120–8), the vicissitudes of the court doctor, Democedes (129–38), the restoration of Syloson in Samos (139–49), and the siege of Babylon (150–60). Within the Persian *logoi* of Book III, or inserted between them, are several digressive sections of narrative and ethnological character. A long Samian *logos* (39–60), which probably existed before the final editing of the book, is inserted between the story of Cambyses and that of the usurpation of the Magus; that in turn contains two sub-digressions; one on the tyranny of Periander (48–53), and one on the adventures of the Samian exiles in the Aegean (57–9). The 'catalogue' of the Persian empire has as an appendix two sections on the rim (or peripheral areas) of the inhabited world, to the east (India, 98–106), and to the south (Arabia, 107–13); these are followed by a few chapters on diverse *mirabilia* found at other extremities of the world (114–17). Usually, these historical and geo-ethnographical digressions are well regulated, and nearly always convincingly integrated into the general frame of the narrative.[4] Even the famous debate on political constitutions, which many scholars deemed a foreign body of Greek political theory inserted by Herodotus at the centre of Persian history, constitutes actually an example of

---

[4] Information on Persian ethnography which could have found a place in Book III, is instead in Book I (chs. 131–40); this can be integrated with other information present in the entire work of Herodotus (cf. Immerwahr, pp. 185 ff.); e.g. III 31,2–4; 79,3.

intentional integration of an *excursus* into the main narrative, aiming to better characterize the personalities (see note on 80–2). The debate is at the centre of the book, not only because it occupies chapters 80–2, and not even in the sense attributed to it by those who consider the speech of Otanes (82) a eulogy of democracy of the Athenian variety, the sole glimmer of light in a book dominated by the darkness of tyrannical regimes.[5] It is the explanation of the centre of the book in the sense that it constitutes a key to interpreting the political transform-ation of the Persian empire during the course of the great crisis.

In this Persian book, the Greek world is rather marginal; for the East, it does not represent an alternative of political nature or of cultural order. Its most eminent representatives—Polycrates, Periander, and Syloson—are tragic figures of tyrants, psychologically or morally not fundamentally different from the Persian kings. Nevertheless, the Greek sections have a clear role within the book: they create an alternation between West and East; anticipate that technique of Greek–Persian 'parallel history', military and political, characteristic of the last three books of the *Histories*; and prepare the reader for the scene and the developments of the great conflict.

The reading of the book immediately reveals the threefold intertwining of narrative, research (ἱστορίη), and didactic reflection. As he had done at the beginning of Book I, Herodotus also poses at the beginning of Book III a primary historical problem: the 'cause' (αἰτίη) of Cambyses' expedition to Egypt (1,1). However, since for Herodotus 'causality' is generally equivalent to the search for a 'fault', a transgression or a personal responsibility,[6] the analysis of the historical problem consists of a few harem episodes, with two women as protagonists (1–3).[7] Nevertheless, perhaps to avoid dispelling the illusion of 'research', Herodotus does not forget to cite different versions of these stories; to criticize one eruditely, to refute categorically the credibility of another (2–3). In Book III there are two other examples of queens or concubines of the Great King with well-defined 'causal' roles: one is Phaedima, Otanes' daughter, who uncovers the fraud of the false Smerdis (68–9); the other is Atossa, Darius' wife, who goads him to undertake the expansionist campaigns in the west (134). In these scenes, Herodotus is revealed as a creator of a new genre of story-writing. The underlying assumption is that the destiny of these people—Egyptian, Persian, and Greek—is ultimately determined in the Great King's bed, influenced by his women. The same assumption guides the author of the Book of Esther.[8] Inevitably a picture emerges of an effeminate and decadent court, destined to become standard in *Persika* from Ctesias onwards. Herodotus was no doubt familiar with the role of the Queen Mother in Aeschylus' *Persians*, performed

---

[5] See G. M. Hirst, in *Collected Classical Papers*, Oxford 1938, pp. 97–110; cf. Bernadete, pp. 93–4.

[6] Cf. Asheri, above p. 1; on 'Speech as a cause' in Book III see Bernadete, p. 70.

[7] On female characters in Book III and in Herodotus in general, see note on 1,40.

[8] On the Book of Esther as a 'Persian chronicle' see R. Gordis, *JBL* C (1981), 359–88; M. Hutter, in H. D. Galter (ed.), *Kulturkontakte und ihre Bedeutung in Geschichte und Gegenwart des Orients*, Graz 1986, pp. 51–66.

in Athens in 472; moreover, thanks to his journeys and researches, he also had ideas of his own on the functioning of the Achaemenid government. He does not, however, seem to have had any difficulty in ascribing the first conventional symptoms of 'decadence' to the times of Cyrus, the founding-father of the empire, and the symbol of virility and wisdom of government (IX 122,3–4). A similar story-line is also present in the chapters on military history. The narration of the battle of Pelusium and of the conquest of Memphis (11–14), the two most important military events of the Egyptian campaign, contains two pairs of horrifying and astonishing anecdotes. However, the spirit of rationalistic ἱστορίη survives, thanks to the quoting of oral informants, the author's direct testimony,[9] and an interesting pseudo-scientific argumentation (12). As for the Ethiopian campaign (25), the dramatic narration of the events is appropriately interrupted by historical, explanatory, and didactic reasoning on the madness of the Persian king (25,5); whereas in the description of the disappearance of Cambyses' army in the dunes of the Libyan desert (26) there prevails a sceptical reservation about the credibility of his source. The chapters dedicated to the crimes and sacrilegious acts of Cambyses in Egypt (27–37) also offer a mixture of repulsive descriptions, generally credible ethnological information on Egyptian cults and customs, and philosophical reflections on the theme of ὕβρις, senseless tyranny, and divine retribution.

These thoughts directly prepare the reader for his encounter with Polycrates, the great tyrant of Samos. In fact, the first Samian *logos* contains a jewel of ancient novelistic art: the story of Polycrates' ring (41–2), which, although evidently delightful, also fulfills the explicit aim of presenting a theological interpretation of this great tyrant figure, compared with Cambyses, the mad Persian king, in his ambitions and tragic end. Here Herodotus confirms yet again his dramatic vision of human life and of history. The great tyrant of Samos almost reaches the height of the greatest Persian monarchs: tragic figures who, at the peak of success, lose their reason. They transgress the limits imposed upon human desires by nature, the gods, morals, customs, or treaties, therefore exposing themselves to danger by foolish and catastrophic acts. Again the problem of human happiness and divine jealousy emerges,[10] a problem already fully dealt with in Book I, thanks to the famous dialogue between Croesus and Solon (29–32). However, even in the narration of the parable of Polycrates, it is possible to distinguish unmistakable signs of a rationalizing 'enquiry': the verbal quotation of a fictitious letter (40), the mention of a contemporary artisan (41,1), a conclusive 'serious' reference to the sole significant historical event related to this parable (the breaking off of the alliance between Samos and Egypt on the eve of Cambyses' campaign: 43; 44,1). Also in the stories of the Samian exiles there are sometimes presented double versions (45,1; 47,1); details which excite a certain degree of credibility (e.g. 47,2–3; 54,1–2; 57,2; 59); critical or sceptical argumentations (e.g. 45,3; 55,1; 56,2); a very rare reference to an oral informer whose name is disclosed

---

[9] The presence of Herodotus' 'I' in Book III is minimal: see the statistics of Beltrametti, pp. 37 ff.
[10] Cf. Asheri, above p. 38.

(55,2); and a conclusive historical hint of the 'first' Spartan campaign in Asia (56,2), probably intended to prepare the reader for the story of the 'second' (at Mycale in 479: IX 96 ff.). Even the sub-digression on Periander (48–53), which could, at first sight, appear as a mixture of a romantic story and dramatic dialogue, has a precise aetiological aim (48,1), contains an interesting speculative argument (49,1) and is rich in moral reflections on the problem of tyranny.

The story of the false Smerdis and the conspiracy of the seven is a masterpiece of the ancient art of storytelling (61–88). It can be read simply as a romance comparable to that of the Book of *Esther*, perfectly adapted to the exotic and legendary world of oriental courts and harems, with its ushers and eunuchs, courtiers and concubines, adventures and conspiracies of cloak and dagger. However, it can also be read as a parable on the theme of falsehood and truth. There is no lack of philosophical reflection; although the external elements of 'research' are reduced to a minimum, almost so as not to weigh down the reading, they are enough to remind the reader that, after all, Herodotus is also an acute researcher of oral traditions. The description of the revolt actually ends with a short aetiological remark on the 'massacre of the Magi' (79,3); the episode of Darius' election to the throne thanks to his horse (85–7)—it is possible to claim—ends with a 'self-parody' of the 'double-version' technique (87).

Suddenly, and without forewarning, the catalogue of the satrapies begins— whoever prefers more amusing reading can skip over it without any harm. With it is immediately re-established the equilibrium between the two greatest skills of Herodotus, an equilibrium that is maintained even more solidly in the last *logoi* of the book. Here also the substratum is composed of anecdotes, with frequent interweaving of dialogues: it is enough to recall the romanticized story of Poly-crates' death (123–5), the adventures of Democedes (129–38), the tale of Darius and Syloson (139–40), the stratagem of Bagaeus in Sardis (128), the self-mutila-tion of Zopyrus during the siege of Babylon (153–8). Nevertheless, it is a substratum laced with 'research'. There are double versions (120–1), sceptical and ironic reservations (122,2), details that add credit to the story (e.g. 123,1; 127,1; 137,5; 138; 142,2; 149; 160,1–2), among which those concerning the medical art are particularly interesting.[11] There is no lack of evaluations of aetiological and historical order: on the greatness and fall of Polycrates (125,2–4); the role of Atossa in the expansionistic policy of Darius (134); the first Persian explorations in Greece and in the Greek West (138,4); the reasons that drove Otanes to repopulate Samos (149). Finally there are also some per-ceptive and significant comments on political theory and practice in the world of the *polis* (142–3).

In the ethnographic parts of Book III the typical mixture of apparently accurate description, legendary or utopian fiction, and moral-theological reflection continues to appear. From this point of view, the Ethiopian *logos* (17–25) and the *excursus* on the extremities of the world (98–117) are paradigmatic. The former reflects a combination of information on Persian Nubia, idealized

---

[11] See e.g. 129,2; 130,3; 133,1. On the material relevant to medicine in Herodotus see note on 1,1.

descriptions partly drawn from epic, and second thoughts of a moralizing nature on Persian expansionism and on the civilization of 'primitive' people. In turn, in the *excursus* on the extremities of the world, in digressing on cults and customs, on harvesting of spices in Arabia, on mining of gold in India and the country of the Arimaspians, Herodotus willingly abandons ethnological 'research' for expressing ideas and stereotypes of epic origin—from Homer to Aristeas of Proconnesus—on the flora, the fauna, and the fabulous treasures at the ends of the world, and for reflecting philosophically on phenomena of ecological imbalance and the workings of divine providence (see esp. 108–9). In these sections too there is no lack of the usual expressions of scepticism (e.g. 18; 24,1; 111,1; 115; 116,1–2). Moreover, Herodotus seizes the opportunity to express yet again his ideas and notions on the relativity of human customs: whereas they exert within each culture an absolute and undisputed power, they also lead the sharp and sophisticated observer to a particular form of relativism: on the one hand the observer is capable of accepting the values of his own culture with conviction and sincere attachment, and on the other, he is also capable of respecting the values of other cultures (38).

As already underlined, tyranny is a central theme of Book III. It is set forth in theoretical form in the speech of Otanes (80), and in paradigmatic form in the 'biographies' of Cambyses and Polycrates.[12] Their portraits, though tragic and dark, are not deprived of humanity. These are persons whom success and power have deprived of reason and driven to calamity: 'If Cambyses, seeing what was happening, had changed his mind and led his army back despite his initial error, he would have shown himself to be sensible; but instead he paid no attention to what was happening, and continued his advance' (25,5). 'Your great good fortune does not please me,' says Amasis to his ally Polycrates, 'since I know that the gods are envious . . . I have never yet heard of a man fortunate in all his undertakings, who did not end in utter ruin' (40,2–3). Cambyses, who has been epileptic since birth, reveals his insanity on his return from Ethiopia (30,1; 33; etc.); Polycrates, blinded by Persian gold, does not suspect the trap that Oroetes is laying for him, and ends up being impaled in Magnesia (123,1; 125,2–4). Tyranny for Herodotus is, first of all, a human problem, not exclusively Greek or Persian, nor specifically Western or Eastern, though he is well aware of certain differences: in Persia it is the legitimate king who degenerates into a tyrant, whereas in Greece it is an ambitious and unscrupulous citizen who seizes power violently. Although the contexts are obviously very different, the moral of the parables of Cambyses and Polycrates is essentially the same. In Herodotus also the problem of freedom is a human problem, not exclusively Greek. In Susa,

---

[12] The other tyrants of Book III are all Greek: Maeandrius, Lycaretus, and Syloson in Samos (139–49), Cypselus and Periander in Corinth (48–53), Lycophron in Corcyra (50–3), Procles in Epidaurus (50–2), Aristophilides in Tarentum (136,2 with note). On the study of tyrants in Herodotus see Waters, 42 ff., with the criticism of J. G. Gammie, *JNES* XLV (1986), 171–95. On the figure of the tyrant in Greek literature and the Persian 'model' see S. Borzsák, *Gymnasium*, XCIV (1987), 289–97.

Otanes proposes *isonomia* instead of tyranny to the Persians (80,6); Herodotus insists, despite his incredulous and arrogant fellow-countrymen, that such a proposal was actually made (80,1; cf. VI 43,3). In Samos, the ruler Meandrius wants to be remembered by posterity as the 'most just of men', renouncing tyranny and establishing freedom (142,1). All men love *isonomia*—which is, as Otanes says (80,6), the most beautiful word of all—but everywhere they succumb to one-man rule. This continuous alternation of Persian and Greek history aims at emphasizing not only the differences, but also the similarities of several political and moral phenomena, which, on the two sides of the ethnic-cultural barrier, manifest similar symptoms.

Closely related to tyranny is the problem that ancient monarchies have with unlimited and insatiable territorial expansionism, a moral criticism attributed to the king of the Ethiopians: 'Had [the Persian king] been a just man, he would not have coveted a country not his own, nor brought slavery on men who never wronged him' (21,2). The reader, remembering what the herald of Tomyris, queen of the Massagetae, said to Cyrus (I 206), and reading subsequently the words of the Scythian king Idanthyrsus to Darius (IV 127), cannot fail to see the connection of this 'anti-imperialistic' message, ascribed to the leaders of the conquered 'primitive' peoples, to the warnings of the 'wise counsellors' of the court.[13] Greek tyrants irresistibly coveted hegemony, too. Polycrates, a new Minos, was the first tyrant of the historical period to aim at 'ruling the sea' (θαλασσοκρατέειν, 122,2); these expansionist desires, directed not only at the Aegean islands but also at the continent of Asia Minor, ultimately determined, according to Herodotus, the fall of tyranny in Samos. A prominent element of this problem is the repatriation of exiles: a tool, a pretext, or an occasional cause of expansionist politics. Book III offers a series of paradigmatic examples on this subject: the story of the Egyptian oculist, who succeeded in opposing Cambyses to Amasis, and thus led to the enslaving of his own country by the enemy (1); the adventures of another doctor, Democedes of Croton, who, in order to return home, guided a group of Persians, spies, and explorers through Greek waters (129–37); the story of Gillus of Tarentum, exiled in Iapygia, who vainly tried to return to his fatherland with the help of the Persians (138); the story of Syloson, who actually returned to Samos thanks to Persian arms (139–49). These examples not only indicate the complexity of the problem of imperialism and 'collaborationism' in the archaic Greek world, but also anticipate the problem of the repatriation of political exiles, destined to have a decisive role in the development of the most important events of the great Graeco-Persian conflict in the following books of Herodotus. It is enough to consider, for example, the relation between the attempted repatriation of the Naxian exiles and the origins of the Ionian revolt (V 30 ff.); or the attempted repatriation of the Pisistratids by the Persian army at Marathon (VI 102; 107; 109,3; 121) and in Athens (VII 6,2–5; VIII 52–5).

---

[13] Cf. Asheri, 43 ff.

The leitmotif of Book III is, essentially, the metaphysical and moral conflict between falsehood and truth.[14] This is the theme that unifies the various Persian *logoi* from beginning to end, characterizes personalities and situations, words and events, and reappears with notable frequency in a great part of the episodes, dialogues, and speeches. The book opens with the story of an intrigue and a false wife (1–3). According to a version considered untrustworthy by Herodotus, even after his death Amasis tried to deceive the Persian conqueror Cambyses with a false mummy at Sais (16,5–7). In Memphis, Cambyses (who personifies truth, or falsehood, or false truth) orders the execution as liars of the priests who had told him the truth (27,3). The same king wounds the Apis bull to demonstrate that he is a false god (29,2); and he kills the son of his most faithful servant to show that the Persian nobles lie when accusing him of madness, though by this very act he demonstrates the truth of their diagnosis (35,1–4). Meanwhile a false Smerdis, similar in appearance and name to the real one, seizes power; Cambyses begins to suspect that the false one is actually the real one and that Prexaspes has deceived him; however, it is the herald of the false Smerdis who, not lying at all, makes the king and his minister understand the truth of the deceit (62–3). On his deathbed Cambyses reveals the truth, whereas Prexaspes is forced to lie; the Persians believe Prexaspes (and thus what is false) and are convinced that the false Smerdis is the true brother of Cambyses, never actually killed by Prexaspes (66). A woman of the harem will discover the truth, that the false Smerdis is an impostor (68–9): finally the reversal is complete. Cambyses had told the truth, Prexaspes had lied to save his own life; then the loyal minister promises to the false Smerdis to deny in public that he had killed the real one; however, at the last moment he reveals the truth and kills himself (74–5), a victim of the inevitable cosmic and moral conflict between falsehood and truth, a conflict which men are called to re-create throughout history. Meanwhile Darius presents his fellow-conspirators with his theory of human behaviour: 'When it is necessary to lie, let a lie by spoken. For whether men lie or speak the truth, it is with one and the same object' (72,4); then, thanks to a stratagem, he contrives his election as king (85–7). The *motif* also reappears in the last *logoi* of the book. Oroetes the satrap deceives Maeandrius with false gold (123–4); Darius causes the death of Oroetes by a sophisticated strategem (128); Zopyrus, the false deserter, betrays the Babylonians who completely trusted him (153–9). Herodotus' work is indeed full of frauds and stratagems: they please the writer, a great admirer of technical ingenuity, and entertain the public. Nevertheless, Book III is distinct from the other books in its continuous examination of the dilemma or conflict between falsehood and truth, as if it were the philosophical pivot of the whole story.[15] It is legitimate to ask whether it was only a coincidence that Herodotus chose exactly this dilemma or conflict as a basis for a collection of *logoi* dedicated to the Persians and to Darius:

---

[14] Cf. Benardete, pp. 69–98.

[15] The exceptional frequency in Book III of expressions that indicate truth ($\dot{a}\lambda\eta\theta\dot{\eta}s$, $\dot{a}\lambda\eta\theta\epsilon\dot{\iota}\eta$), trust ($\pi\dot{\iota}\sigma\tau\iota s$, $\pi\iota\sigma\tau\dot{o}s$, $\pi\iota\theta\alpha\nu\dot{o}s$) and falsehood ($\psi\epsilon\hat{\upsilon}\delta os$, $\psi\epsilon\dot{\upsilon}\delta o\mu\alpha\iota$) has also been noted. Cf. Bernadete, p. 79, n. 9.

the Persians who, according to Herodotus, educated their children 'in three things alone—to ride, to draw the bow, and to speak the truth' (I 136,2; cf. 138); Darius who, on the rock of Bisitun, declared that after the death of Cambyses 'The Lie grew greatly in the land, in Persia, Media, and the other countries' (Appendix I, §10); who revealed the true name of the Magus (Gaumata) who had 'lied to the people' under the false name of Bardiya (Smerdis); who disclosed the names of the other usurpers and rebels who equally 'lied to the people' by assuming false names and titles; Darius who saw in 'the Lie' the root of every rebellion (ibid., §54); who bade his future heir to punish severely the followers of 'the lie' (§55; cf. §64) and the reader of the inscription to believe everything written in it (§57: 'I will take Ahura Mazda's anger upon myself that I did this truly (hašiyam), and not falsely'); who declared that he was indeed firmly convinced of having received divine help 'because I was not disloyal, I was not a follower of the Lie. I was no evilddoer' (§63).[16]

Was Herodotus familiar with this message of political and theological propaganda, communicated by Darius in all languages and in all provinces of the empire? Did he know anything about the mazdaic dualism of Ormuz and Ahriman, of the principles of Good and Evil, True and False, in eternal conflict in the souls of humans? Could he, perhaps, on finding this dualism, this antinomy in the Ionian philosophical tradition or in the sophistic movement of his own time, not suspect its possible oriental origins? In fact, the relativism of truth and falsehood is a premise of Greek thought since Homer. From Odysseus, the personification of 'noble deception', to Plato's *Republic* and onwards, views that not even gods refrain from 'just deception' (Aeschylus, fr. 301 Radt); that falsehood is permissible, even a duty, in order to avoid disasters (Sophocles, fr. 352 *Radt*); that truth has to be said 'when useful' or 'because it is very useful' (Democritus, 55 B 225 DK); that rulers have the licence to lie for the good of the state (Plato, *Resp.* III 389b), were repeatedly expressed, debated, accepted, and criticized. These were ideas theorized straightaway in special dissertations titled *On Truth* ($\Pi\epsilon\rho\grave{\iota}\ \dot{\alpha}\lambda\eta\theta\epsilon\acute{\iota}\alpha\varsigma$), starting with Antiphon and Protagoras in the second half of the fifth century.

Some might find it more convenient to avoid such problems—and the choice they impose 'between East and West'—supposing that, ultimately, this *leitmotif* is the result of internal logical necessity, without obvious or hidden external influences, mazdaic or sophistic; hence that it is a product of the very narrative, composed entirely of deceptions, conspiracies, and stratagems. This last solution is, in my opinion, only a way of avoiding the difficulty instead of facing, let alone solving, it. The 'choice', in this case, forces the making up of one's mind on the preliminary problem of Herodotus' sources in drafting the Persian *logoi*: a complicated problem, which today sometimes tends to be emblematically summed up in the simplified phrase 'Herodotus and Bisitun', but is actually far broader.[17] Even a superficial reading of Book III reveals an evident substratum of

[16] Cf. Darius' words in the inscription of Naqš-i Rustam (*DNb* Kent); see Balcer, pp. 46 ff.
[17] See the bibl. quoted in the note on chs. 61–88 and in the introductory note on Appendix I.

oriental material; to deny it would be absurd: it is visible in names of characters, in the tendentiousness of Cambyses' vicissitudes in Egypt, in the oriental colouring of the stories of the palace and harem; and in a particularly notable way in the extraordinary correspondence, in both content and tendentiousness, between Herodotus' account and the evidence deducible from Persian and Babylonian epigraphic sources. Especially relevant is the correspondence in the names of the conspirators (see note on 70,1), the essential core of the usurpation story and the Magus' death, with the whole chronological frame of the reigns of Cambyses, of the Magus, and of Darius. There are indeed divergences, but the material is Persian. However—notwithstanding the Iranian *paideia* known to Herodotus and a certain modern orientalizing romanticism—'Persian' does not *a priori* equal 'true'. The inscription of Bisitun is a text of political propaganda, with an explicit intention of publicly legitimizing a controversial act of usurpation. Therefore it cannot be cited either to confirm or to refute the veracity of Herodotus; but it is useful for confirming the Persian origin of various materials that Herodotus had collected and used in the drafting of the Persian *logoi*. Part of these and other oriental materials had already entered the Greek world in the early fifth century, as seen from certain verses of Aeschylus' *Persians* (774–9), fragments of historians more or less contemporary with Herodotus (especially the first writers of *Persika*: see Dionysius of Miletus, *FGrHist* 687 F 2), and the notice of a poem of Simonides on the reigns of Cambyses and Darius (Suidas, s.v. Σιμωνίδης). Many accounts of Persian origin were discovered or rediscovered, repeated or reworked, also after Herodotus' death.[18] The intermediate stages of this transition are unknown and can barely be hypothesized: only the ends of the chain are accessible. It is certainly a chain of historical traditions: but the truth is bound to elude us. On the one hand, Herodotus relates the information he succeeded in gathering from his Greek and bilingual informants; on the other, the inscription of Bisitun theateningly imposes the 'truth' of Darius and terrorizes the incredulous, falsifying history in the service of propaganda. Herodotus and Bisitun are thus two prisms—connected but in no way identical—through which passes the same ray of 'truth' or historical reality, refracted and altered: the drama of the miraculous year 522/1 BC. Naturally, in both appear names of persons and places, dates and events, the veracity of which there is no sufficient reason to doubt. But Herodotus' reshaping of the material is the result of his narrative creativity; whereas the Bisitun inscription is a product of ideology and of uncompromising political propaganda.

Finally, the 'catalogue' of the satrapies and tributes stems from a written Persian document: for this kind of material seems to exclude oral information. However, it is here also necessary to postulate between Herodotus and the original document (which cannot be absolutely identified with any of the surviving Persian epigraphic lists)[19] a series of intermediate stages during

---

[18] See e.g. Ctesias, *FGrHist* 688 F 13 (11–18); Plato, *Leg.* III 695a–e; Strabo XV 3,24; Justin I 9,7–10,14.

[19] See the bibl. quoted in note on chs. 89–96 and in the introductory note on Appendix II.

which the list was translated, changed, contaminated with others, rationalised, hellenized, and so on. Herodotus represents one of these stages, perhaps the last one in a chain of transmission of which we know neither its specific starting point nor its length, width, or degree of conductivity: the field is open for hypotheses (cf. note on 89–96).

With the Samian *logoi* the situation is profoundly different. For these *logoi*, we can confidently claim the use of sources essentially oral and local, but also direct autopsy of the city, its topography, monuments, and inscriptions, thanks to Herodotus' sojourn in the Ionian island (cf. note on 39–60). For the stories of Democedes and Gillus we can also add the use of Western Greek sources, gathered during Herodotus' stay in Thurii (cf. note on 129–38). He also alludes to a Spartan source concerning Samian events in ch. 55,2. Finally, it should be noted that Herodotus' use of Greek written sources is often assumed for the composition of chs. 80–2 (see note ad loc.), and various sections of ethnographic character.

Book III is therefore not only a masterpiece of ancient narrative art, but also an indispensable source for every historical reconstruction of the Persian empire and of the Eastern Aegean in the decade between 530 and 520 BC. In all of ancient historiography there does not exist a work of superior or equal value. Herodotus also provides a chronological and historical background to the extraordinarily rich and important materials from Eastern sources (epigraphic and iconographic). Book III constitutes undoubtedly the only complete attempt by an ancient historian to examine, understand, and interpret the great crisis that shook the East in the years of the fateful passage from the tyranny of Cambyses to the restored monarchy of Darius.

Summary of Book III

Phoenicians to take part in the expeditions against Carthage; the voluntary submission of Cyprus to Cambyses (19). Cambyses sends to Ethiopia, with gifts to the king, several bilingual Icthyophagi as envoys and spies; customs of the Ethiopians (20); dialogue between the envoys of Cambyses and king of the Ethiopians (21–2); visit of the envoys to Ethiopia, with description of various customs and *mirabilia* (23–4); the Persian invasion of Ethiopia and the catastrophic retreat of the army (25).

26   The failure of the Persian expedition in the Libyan desert against the Ammonians.

27–37   The sacrilegious and criminal acts of Cambyses after the return from Ethiopia: the killing of Apis (27–9), with information on the identification and cult of the sacred bull (28,2–3); the killing in Persia of Smerdis by the hand of Prexaspes (30); the killing in Egypt of the sister-wife of Cambyses (31–2), with short digressions on the marriage customs of the Persian kings and on the royal judges (31,2–6); the madness of Cambyses and its diagnosis (33); Cambyses and his advisers (34–6); the killing of the son of Prexaspes and of twelve Persians (35); the clash with Croesus (36); sacrilegious acts of Cambyses in the temples of Memphis (37).

38   Concluding digression on the relativity of human customs, with the episode of the confrontation between Greeks and Indians at the court of Darius.

39–60   *First Samian logos*

39,1   Synchronic link between the Egyptian campaign of Cambyses and the Spartan expedition against Samos.

39–45   Historical digression on the tyranny of Polycrates and on the beginning of the Samian thalassocracy (39); story of Polycrates' ring (40–2); breach of the alliance between Polycrates and Amasis (43); the Samian fleet, sent by Polycrates to Egypt, changes route and arrives in the Peloponnese (44–5).

46–7   The Samian exiles in Sparta ask for and obtain military help against Polycrates (46); the reasons for the Spartan intervention.

48–53   Historical digression on the tyranny of Periander in Corinth, aimed at explaining the reasons for the Corinthian participation in the expedition against Samos.

54–6   Anecdotes on the Spartan siege of Samos and its failure.

57–9   More vicissitudes of the Samian exiles in the Aegean (in Siphnos: 57–8; in Hydrea and in Cydonia) up to their final taming by the hand of Aegina (59).

60   Concluding digression on the marvellous buildings of Samos.

61–88   *The revolt of the Magi and Darius' accession to the throne*

61   The revolt of the false Smerdis during Cambyses' absence.

62–6   The death of Cambyses in Syria on the way to Susa.

67   The consolidation of the false Smerdis' authority after the death of Cambyses.

68–9   The discovery of the deceit thanks to the daughter of Otanes, bride of the false Smerdis.

70–9   The conspiracy of the seven; Darius (70–3); the suicide of Prexaspes (74–5) and the killing of the Magi (76–9).

80–2   Debate of the conspirators on political constitutions.

COMMENTARY

1–38. The first *logos* of Persian history is directly linked with the historical part of the Egyptian *logos* (through Amasis, the last king that Herodotus mentions in Book II: 172–82) and with the main thread of Persian history, interrupted at the end of Book I with the death of Cyrus (214,3); cf. Introduction p. 381. At the centre of this 'biography' of Cambyses are three main themes: the Persian conquest of Egypt (chs. 1–14), the campaign against Ethiopia (17–25), and the criminal and sacrilegious acts of Cambyses in Egypt on his return from Ethiopia (27–37). From the beginning of the campaign against Egypt until the fall of Memphis (1–13) the figure of Cambyses is that of a king who acts on legitimate and rational grounds. After the conquest the picture changes rapidly. His personality begins to be tinged with dark hues, transforming finally into that of a cruel and insane despot. Herodotus openly criticizes his behaviour, especially the sacrilegious acts, but he does not neglect his more humane traits and his rare moments of sanity. He attributes to the Ethiopian king a strong condemnation of the aggressive expansionism of the Persians. Thanks to these and to other explicit warnings, as well as to a series of implicit links, parallelisms, and contrasts, the reader can guess the impending catastrophic outcome of all the events. The dark picture of Cambyses' personality elaborated by Herodotus was substantially accepted in the ancient literary tradition, as if the king had fallen victim to an irreparable *damnatio memoriae*: he reappears, for example, in Ctesias, Plato, Diodorus, Strabo, and in Latin writers as a paradigm of ferocious tyranny. Only modern criticism, with the aid of Eastern documents, has attempted to redeem the figure of Cambyses at least partially. For that purpose the problem of Herodotus' sources has been raised (see Jacoby, coll. 427–8). They were thought to come essentially from the so-called 'tendentious Graeco-Egyptian novel' (Prášek), or from stories of Irano-Babylonian origin reworked at the court of Darius with a hostile bias towards Cambyses, before reaching Egypt (Hofmann–Vorbichler, pp. 86–105). Today the prevailing tendency is to attribute the core of the demoniac representation of Cambyses to oriental propaganda sources, reinterpreted by Herodotus in the light of his personal convictions tinged with Ionian philosophy, Greek religion, and Attic tragedy. The Egyptian inscriptions also contribute towards a more exact historical evaluation of the king, either by correcting, even radically, several of Herodotus' informations (e.g. the killing of the Apis bull), or by allowing interpretations in a political or economic vein of certain repressive measures, which had been interpreted by hostile propaganda as symptoms of madness or religious intolerance.

1,1. Καμβύσης: Cambyses (*Kambūjiya* Pers., *Kanbuzi* Aram., *Knbwd* Egypt.) was also the name of his paternal grandfather (I 107,2). The hypothesis that the name derives from the ethnic adjective of the Indo-Iranian tribe of the *Kanboja* (J. Charpentier, *ZII* II (1923), 140–52) is very controversial (J. Harmatta,

AAntHung XIX (1971), 6 ff.). Cambyses, eldest son of Cyrus and Cassandane
(2,2)—also the parents of Smerdis and at least one of his sisters (30,1; 31,1)—
participated in 539 BC with his father in the conquest of Babylon, of which he was
king for a certain time; his coronation at the Esagila, where he presided over the
celebration of the New Year on the 1st Nisan (27 March) 538, provoked a scandal.
The precise chronology of his new titulature is a matter of dispute. As 'Son of the
King' he was associated with his father's reign; see H. Petschow, *RAss* LXXXII
(1982), 78–82; J. Peat, *J. Cuneiform Studies*, XLI (1989), 199–216. After the death
of Cyrus in August 530 Cambyses ascended the throne, and on the 1st Nisan 529
he inaugurated his official 'first year' by assuming the title of 'King of Lands',
which he kept until 522. The rules of succession to the Achaemenid throne began
then to be formulated. He had his father's body transported to Persia: see Ctesias,
FGrHist 688 F 13 (9). The disorders which erupted in several regions after the
death of Cyrus (Xen. *Cyr.* VIII 8,2) detained the new king in Persia for about five
years (530–526 BC); in this period his brother Smerdis, who had allegedly been
appointed governor of some provinces (Ctesias, *FGrHist* 688 F 9 (8); Xen. *Cyr.*
VIII 7,11), was executed (see 30,1 and note). Cyrus was survived also by two
daughters, Atossa and Artystone (see 88,2 and note). It was only in the year 526/5
that Cambyses could dedicate himself to the Egyptian campaign. The oriental
sources (epigraphical, archaeological, papyrological) permit verifications, corrections, and additions, but not an independent reconstruction of his reign. Fundamental are the collection of the Egyptian texts edited by Posener and the
inscription of Bisitun (see App. I). Amongst the papyri, of particular importance
are the demotic text on the reverse of Pap. Louvre 215, an Aramaic papyrus of
Elephantine of the year 408, an Egyptian ritual text of the 4th cent. (see note on
37,1), and the Coptic story of the conquest of Egypt (see note on 11,2). On the
figure of Cambyses in Herodotus see Waters, pp. 53–6; Hofmann–Vorbichler,
pp. 86–105; K. Głombiowski, *Meander*, XXXV (1980), 463–6; T. S. Brown,
Historia, XXXI (1982), 387–403; Balcer, pp. 70–100; A. B. Lloyd, *AH* III (1987),
55–66. For links and parallels in the *logos* of Cambyses, H. Fahr, 'Kambyses. Ein
Beitrag zur Herodotsinterpretation', Diss. Hamburg 1959, pp. 59–72; Erbse,
pp. 45–55. On Herodotean 'biography', H. Homeyer, *Philologus*, CVI (1962),
78–9. On Cambyses and the conquest of Egypt see Prášek, *passim*; Olmstead,
pp. 86–93; Meulenaere, pp. 124–34; A. Klasens, *JVEG* III (1944–6), 339–49;
Kienitz, ch. 5; W. Hinz, *RLA* V (1980), coll. 328–30; I. Hofmann, *Studien zur
Altägyptischen Kultur*, IX (1981), 179–99; Frye, pp. 96 ff.; T. C. Young, *CAH*[2] IV,
pp. 36–41. On Cambyses in Babylon, A. Kuhrt, ibid., pp. 120 ff. On the Persian
satrapy of Egypt see 91,2–3 and note to 91,2; P. Högemann, *Das alte Vorderasien
und die Achämeniden. Ein Beitrag zur Herodot-Analyse*, Wiesbaden 1992,
pp. 194–202.   ἄλλους ... Αἰολέας: cf. II 1,2. The ethnic contingents of the
peoples subdued by Cyrus; among them were the Greeks of Asia Minor, who
served in the fleet (13,1 and note).   δι' αἰτίην τοιήνδε: with this formula
Herodotus opens and ends (at 1,5) a short digression on previous events, an
oral narrative technique already used by Homer; T. E. V. Pierce, *Eranos*, LXXXIX
(1981), 87–90; for the Herodotean formulae of 'ring-composition', cf. Beck,

passim. On the concept of αἰτίη and on Herodotean 'causality', cf. above p. 40 ff. with bibl. Here (and at 1,5) the αἰτίη is the deceit attempted by Amasis: a moral 'fault' that becomes, for the Persians, a 'pretext' (cf. IV 167,3) or *casus belli.* However, according to Herodotus himself the conquest of Egypt was already intended by Cyrus (I 153,4). Cf. Bornitz, pp. 157 f. Only indirectly is the 'cause' a woman (but see M. L. Lang, *Proc. of the American Phil. Soc.,* CXVI (1972), 410–4), whereas in turn the 'fault' of Amasis is the last link of the chain, with two fortuitous 'accidents' (the eye-illness of Cyrus and the mention of the true patronymic of Cambyses' wife) and three moral 'faults' (the exile of the oculist, his advice to Cambyses, and the deceit of Amasis); cf. the medical 'case' of Atossa and its historical consequences (ch. 133 ff.). The two versions of the marriage of Cambyses or of Cyrus with the daughter of Apries were probably widespread in Persia and Egypt under Cambyses or Darius; their aim was to legitimate the conquest by linking again the Achaemenid house to the 26th Saite dynasty overthrown by Amasis around the year 570 BC (see note on 16,1). See K. M. T. Atkinson, *JAOS* LXXVI (1956), 167–77.   θυγατέρα: on female characters in Herodotus see note on I,1–5; C. Dewald, in H. P. Foley (ed.), *Reflections of Women in Antiquity,* New York–London–Paris 1981, pp. 91–125. ἐκ συμβουλίης: cf. para. 2: τῇ συμβουλῇ. L. Weber (*PhW* LXI (1941), coll. 285–6) reads βουλῆς, in the sense of 'deceit'. The Egyptian oculist is the first 'adviser' in Book III: Croesus and Prexaspes will follow (14,11; 30,3; 34,4–5; 36); on the figure of the 'wise adviser' in Herodotus see Bischoff; Lattimore, *CPh* XXXVI (1939), 24–35; Fehling, pp. 145–9; K. D. Bratt, 'Herodotus' Oriental Monarchs and their Counsellors', Diss. Princeton 1985. Ctesias, *FGrHist* 688 F 13 (9), mentions various characters influential at Cambyses' court. ἰητρὸν ὀφθαλμῶν: on Egyptian oculists (*swnw i rty* = 'oculist' in Egyptian) see II 84 and note; Lloyd, *Commentary 1–98,* p. 349; for lesions or maladies of the eyes in Herodotus see also I 174,4; VII 229,1. The frequency of eye maladies (trachoma, etc.) in the ancient East explains the high level reached by Egyptian ophthalmology and the privileged status enjoyed by the oculists. Fundamental for Egyptian medicine is the collection of H. Grapow, *Grundriss der Medizin der alten Ägypten,* I–IX, Berlin 1954–73 (for ophthalmology see in the Index, s.v. 'Auge'). Cf. also M. Helbing, *Der altägyptische Augenkranke, sein Artz und seine Götter,* Zürich 1980, and P. Ghalioungui, *The Physicians of Pharaonic Egypt,* Cairo 1983. For Egyptian physicians in Herodotus cf. II 77,2–3; 84; III 129,2–130,3. For a general guide, S. Curto, *Medicina e medici nell' antico Egitto,* Turin 1970, with bibl.; M. H. Marganne, *L'Ophtalmologie dans l'Egypte gréco-romain,* Leiden 1994; for medicine in Herodotus see D. Brandenburg, *Medizinisches bei Herodot,* Berlin 1976; P. Huyse, *Anc. Soc.* XXI (1990), 141–8. Some scholars identify the oculist of this chapter with the physician Udjahorresne (on whom see note on 16,1). Another famous physician in this book is the exile Democedes (129–37).

2. τῇ δυνάμι ...: see the treaties of Amasis with Croesus and Nabonidus against Cyrus (I 77,1 with note; Xen. *Cyr.* I 5,3; cf. *StV* II no. 114, with bibl.) and with Polycrates against Cambyses (39,2 and note on 40,1).   ὡς παλλακήν: concubine, because she is a foreigner or because she does not belong to the

high Persian aristocracy (cf. 84,2). The names of two daughters of Amasis are known from Egyptian inscriptions: Tacherenêse and Nitocris (namesake of the Nitocris mentioned in II 100,2–4 as daughter of Psammetichus); cf. H. de Meulenaere, *JEA* LIV (1968), 183–7.

3. θυγάτηρ... εὐειδής: Herodotus usually links height to beauty in women (I 60,4; V 12,1).   Νίτητις: cf. the similar version of Ctesias (*FGrHist* 688 F 13a) as an example of a war started because of a woman. The motif of the fraudulent exchange of wives is well known from the popular novelistic tradition of the ancient East (e.g. Gen. 29: 21 ff.); from the very beginning Herodotus presents the Persian king as engaged in a continuous battle against falsehood (see Introduction, p. 391 ff.). On Apries cf. II 161–3; 169; IV 159,4–6.

5. τὸ ἔπος: see Benardete, p. 20: 'Speech as a cause... underlies most of the stories in the Third Book'; cf., in causal contexts, 21,3; 32,3; 36,1; 42,2; 50,3; 51,1; 120,1; 130,4; 134,6; 151,1.   οὕτω μέν... Πέρσαι: the first example in this book of a 'double version'; cf. the General Introduction, p. 20 ff., with bibl.

2,1. οἰκηιεῦνται Καμβύσεα: 'lay claim to Cambyses', as if he were an Egyptian Pharaoh, and the legitimate heir of Apries (cf. 1,1 and note). For the verb cf. I 4,4; 94,3; IV 148,1. The Egyptian version, rejected by Herodotus, was substantially accepted by Dinon (a 4th cent. BC historian) in his *Persika* (*FGrHist* 690 F 11), and by Lykeas of Naucratis in his *Aigyptiaka* (*FGrHist* 613 F 1); cf. Polyaenus VIII 29. It is a plausible hypothesis that Cyrus had offered an alliance to Amasis, sealed by a marriage bond, in order to inherit his kingdom; cf. Cyrus' proposal to the queen of the Massagetae in I 205,1. Xenophon ascribed the conquest of Egypt to Cyrus (*Cyr.* I 1,4; VIII 6,2–21); see G. Radet, *REA* XI (1909), 201–10, and K. M. T. Atkinson, *JAOS* LXXXVI (1956), 171 ff.

2. νόμιμα: closer to νόμοι than to νόμαια (cf. note on 38,1), thus more in a legal sense than in that of custom and ritual, etc. Herodotus is here thinking about the Persian laws of succession; elsewhere (I 65,5) the same word refers to Spartan public institutions. However, see II 79,1 and VII 136,2. Herodotus rejects the Egyptian version, since it presupposes the impossible breach of a 'national' law (cf. 38); see J. A. S. Evans, *Athenaeum*, XLIII (1965), 148.   νόθον: Herodotus interprets the Persian law in Greek terms. The son of a male citizen and a foreign female was considered, according to Pericles' law of 451 BC, a νόθος (cf. V 94,1), not γνήσιος ('legitimate'); he was considered as the child of a concubine or a slave. Cf. the Lycian law known to Herodotus (I 173,5). For Persian concubinage see I 135; on the νόθοι children of Xerxes see VIII 103 (and note). γνησίου παρεόντος: i.e. Smerdis.   Κασσανδάνης...: Cassandane died before her husband Cyrus, who mourned her deeply (II 1,1). According to M. Boyce, *AI* XXIII (1984), 67–71, she must have been buried in Zendan-i Suleiman at Pasargadae. Pharnaspes, Cyrus' father-in-law, cannot be identified with the homonymous father of Otanes (68,1 and note). According to Ctesias, *FGrHist* 688 F 9 (2) and 13 (11), the mother of Cambyses was called Amytis and was the daughter of the last Median king, Astyages; we are

facing an obvious confusion with the Mandane of Herodotus, mother of Cyrus (I 107).

3,1. τῶν Περσίδων...ἐσελθοῦσά τις...: this harem tale presupposes a third version which, if it shared with the Egyptian version the marriage between Cyrus and Nitetis, nevertheless denied that Nitetis could be the mother of Cambyses (and therefore was unable to confer on Cambyses the status of a legitimate heir of Apries). The story looks like a learned compromise by a Greek who, perhaps for chronological reasons, accepted the view that it was Cyrus, not Cambyses, who had married Nitetis, while knowing that Cambyses' mother was a Persian noblewoman. Herodotus does not believe the story of the conversation between the Persian woman and Cassandane, but perhaps had no reason to reject the version about Nitetis as wife of Cyrus. On the function of this short 'aetiological' dialogue cf. Heni, pp. 112–3. For other harem scenes in Book III see 68,3–5; 69,6; 88,2–3; 130,4–5. Cf. also Introduction, p. 386.

4,1. Φάνης: see Hofstetter, no. 252; G. F. Seibt, *Griechische Söldner in Achämenidenreich*, Bonn 1977, pp. 25–7. Herodotus may have been able to obtain information about Phanes at Halicarnassus from descendants of his family (Jacoby, col. 428); however, the sons of Phanes were executed immediately before the battle of Pelusium (11). A famous stater, probably of Ephesus, with the legend Φάνεος ἐμὶ σῆμα (Head, pp. 571–2), was once attributed to our captain, but actually belongs to an earlier date. On this and other similar coins see P. R. Franke and R. Schmitt, *Chiron*, IV (1974), 1–4; M. Vickers, *NC* CXLV (1985), 17–22; R. M. Cook, *JHS* CIX (1989), 165–6. In the version of Ctesias, *FGrHist* 688 F 13 (10), the betrayer of Amyrtaeus (rather than of Amasis) is the Egyptian eunuch Combaphis, cousin of one of Cambyses' eunuchs, who revealed secrets to the enemy in the hope of becoming governor of Egypt under the king of Persia. Cf. note on 16,1.

2. ἐλθεῖν ἐς λόγους: cf. e.g. 21,1; 68,5; 145,1.   τῶν εὐνούχων τὸν πιστότατον: cf. I 117,5; for the faithfulness of eunuchs among barbarian peoples cf. VIII 105,2.   τριήρεϊ: on the problem of triremes in the 6th cent. see note on 44,2; on Phoenician triremes in the time of Herodotus cf. 37,2 and note.   σοφίη: in the sense of ability, cunning, fraud, stratagem; cf. 85,1; 127,2; V 21,2. For σόφισμα cf. III 85,2 and 152. For σοφίζομαι cf. I 80,4; II 66,2; III, 111,3; VIII 27,3.

3. ὁρμημένῳ...: the usual Persian base against Egypt was at Ake (St John of Acre, today Acco, north of Haifa), see Diod. XV 41,3; Strabo XVI 2,25. τὸν 'Αραβίων βασιλέα: a 'king of Qedar', called Qainu bar Geshem, is known from an Aramaic votive inscription on a silver vase of the late 5th cent. found at Tell el-Maskhuta, about 18 km. west of Ismailia (see J. S. Holladay, *Cities of the Delta*, III. *Tell el-Maskhuta*, Malibu 1982); cf. I. Rabinowitz, *JNES* XV (1956), 1–9. On the 'kingdom of Qedar' and on the hypothetical identification of Geshem with 'Geshem the Arab', who around the year 445 BC opposed the rebuilding of the walls of Jerusalem (*Neh.* 2: 19; 6: 1–2), see the bibl. in the note on 8,1.

5,1. ἀπὸ γὰρ Φοινίκης...καλεομένων: the reference is to the Palestinian coast between Mt. Carmel, the southern border of Phoenicia, and Gaza. In the time of

Herodotus the most important cities of this stretch of coast were the ports of Dor, Jaffa, Asdod (Azotos: II 157), Ascalon (I 105,2 and 4), 'Eqron, and Gaza; the first of these cities was considered Phoenician, the last four Philistine. Some wrongly identify Dor with Doros, which Craterus (*FGrHist* 342 F 1) mentions as one of the Carian cities which were part of the Delian league: see Meiggs, pp. 420–1. The inhabitants of the region, 'the Syrians called Palestinians', at the time of Herodotus were a mixture of Phoenicians, Philistines, Arabs, Egyptians, and perhaps also other peoples. Some Phoenicians and 'Syrians called Palestinians' were, according to Herodotus, circumcised due to the influence of Egyptian culture (II 104,1–3), but according to the prophet Ezekiel, the Phoenicians of Sidon (Ezek. 32: 30) were not circumcised, while the Philistines of the Old Testament are *'arelim* ('the uncircumcised') par excellence (see e.g. Judg. 15: 18). Perhaps the circumcised 'Syrians called Palestinians' are the Arabs and the Egyptians of the Sinai coast; at the time of Herodotus there were few Jews in the coastal area (cf. Stern I, pp. 3–4, with bibl.); see, however, Lloyd, above note on II 104,2. The culturally mixed character of the southern coast between Gaza and Raphia is well illustrated, for the late bronze age, by the Phoenicio-Egyptian anthropoid sarcophagi of Dir el-Balakh, now in the Israel Museum of Jerusalem. On the peoples of Palestine in the Persian period see A. Lemaire, *Transeuphratene*, III (1990), 31–74. On the Arabs see note on 8,1. It is probable that Herodotus had travelled along the coast of Sinai and Palestine coming from Egypt (for evidence of a first-hand knowledge see II 106,1). For 'Syria-Palestine' in Herodotus see also I 105; II 106,1; III 91,1; IV 39,2; VII 89,1–2. For the submission of the Phoenicians to the Persians see 91,1.

2. **Καδύτιος**: cf. II 159,2. Kadytis is generally identified with Gaza (Γάζα) since I. Toussaint, *De Urbe Cadyti Herodotea*, Franequerae 1737, and F. Hitzig, 'De Cadyti urbe Herodotea dissertatio', Diss. Göttingen 1829; see E. Schürer, *The History of the Jewish People in the Age of Jesus*, Engl. edn. by G. Vermes and F. Millar, II, Edinburgh 1979, p. 99 and n.; Stern I, pp. 4–5 and Lloyd, *Commentary 99–182*, pp. 162–3. The old identification with el-Quds ('the Holy', i.e. Jerusalem) is pure fantasy. Gaza was an important port and a strategic point on the *via maris* between Syria and Egypt since the 2nd millennium; from the 12th cent. BC it was one of the five biblical cities of the Philistines, where some of the most famous episodes of Samson's story are located (Judges 16). At first it belonged to Egypt, later for a short time to the kingdom of David, then to Assyria under Tiglath-Pileser III and Sargon, finally again to Egypt (it was conquered by Pharaoh Necho at the end of the 7th cent.: II 159,2), with which it always had economic relations. In 526/5 it came under Persian rule. For Gaza in the Persian period see U. Rappaport, *Israel Exploration Journal* XX (1970), 75–80; A. Negev, in *PECS*, pp. 345–6; H. J. Katzenstein, *Transeuphratene*, I (1989), 67–86; A. Ovadiah, in E. Stern (ed.), *The New Encyclopedia of Archaeological Excavations in the Holy Land*, II, Jerusalem 1993, pp. 464–7. At the time of Herodotus it was a flourishing city, with commercial and cultural relations also with the Greek world (for the coins see Head, p. 805; for myths of its foundation see Stephanus of Byzantium, s.v. Γάζα). In 332 BC it withstood the siege of Alexander for five

months, flourished anew in the Roman period, and became a centre of learning in Byzantine times. See also Strabo XVI 2,30.   Σαρδίων: the comparison with Sardis indicates direct knowledge; but it does not show that Herodotus, in writing this paragraph, was necessarily thinking of an Ionian audience.   ἀπὸ ταύτης ... λίμνης: we move on to the Mediterranean coast of Sinai between Gaza and Pelusium. It is a sandy stretch of about 190 km., crossed over the centuries by caravans and armies headed for Egypt or Syria. On the ancient topography of this area see S. Mittmann, *ZDPV* XCIX (1983), 130–40 (with bibl.).   Ἰηνύσου πόλιος: the identification of this city with Khan Yunis ('Hospice of Jonah', a place-name of the Islamic period that, despite appearances, has no relation to Ienysus), was criticized by M. Abel, *RB* XLVIII (1939), 533–41 (who looked for Ienysus near el-'Arish = Rhinokolura), but is now in vogue (see Mittmann, op. cit.; the theory of Abel is taken up again by A. P. Figueras, *Scripta Classica Israelica*, VIII–IX (1985–8), 53–65). The distance between Khan Yunis and the eastern end of the Bu'az-a Zaranikh (a smaller lagoon that borders to the east on lake Serbonis) is about 72 km., corresponding exactly to 3 days' march (see 5.3), if calculated on the basis of the average distance established by Herodotus for the Royal Road (150 stadia = c.27 km. a day: V 53); however, it is only 2 days if calculated on the basis of the average distance of a 'fast man' (200 stadia = c.36 km. a day: IV 101,3); a much lower average distance is perhaps supposed in I 104,1 and note on I 72,3 ('three days', however, is a typical figure in Herodotus, that should not be understood literally). The name Ienysus does not appear in any other ancient source, apart from Stephanus of Byzantium, s.v. Ἰνυσσός, who quotes Herodotus; moreover Herodotus does not mention Raphiah (about 7 km. west of Khan Yunis). It seems as if the whole stretch of coast between Gaza and Ienysus, about 23 km., was monopolized by the Arabs (note on 8,1): the caravan routes of the spice trade (chs. 107–13), up to the emporia on the Mediterranean, seem to have been controlled by a local tribe, led by its sheikh (cf. note on 4,3). Probably this is the 'district of the Arabs' that was exempted from the Persian tribute (88,1 and 91,1).   Σερβωνίδος λίμνης: cf. II 6,1 and Pliny, *NH* V 68. Today Sabkhat al-Bardawil ('Baldwin's pond', named after the crusader king who died there in 1118) is a lagoon separated from the sea by a strip of land about 100 km. long and between 400 and 600 m. wide at the most, with openings to the east. The measurements of Strabo (200 × 60 stadia: XVI 2,32; cf. Diod. I 30,4) do not correspond to the actual measurements. Lake Serbonis was of particular interest to ancient scientists for demonstrating that the whole of Lower Egypt was once submerged under water, and also for its dangerous *barathra*, or 'chasms' (marshy areas covered with sand): see e.g. Strato of Lampsacus and Eratosthenes, in Strabo I 3,4; cf. XVI 1,12 and 2,26; for the confusion with the Dead Sea, XVI 2,34 and 42–4; cf. Diod. I 30,4–9 and XX 73,3 ff. In 342 BC part of the Persian army drowned in lake Serbonis (Diod. XVI 46,5). This episode, which recalls the disappearance of the Persian army in the Libyan desert (see 26,2–3), and other similar incidents in antiquity, have given rise to the modern hypothesis that lake Serbonis is the place of the miraculous passage across the Red Sea. On lake Serbonis see H. Kees, *RE* III 1, 1927, coll. 286–7; A. H. Gardiner, *JEA* VI

(1920), 99–116 (with a good map); Walbank I, p. 610.   *Κάσιον ὄρος*: cf. II 6,1. Mt Casius is identified with Mehemdiye, a dune with ruins on the western end of lake Serbonis. The relation between the name of Kasion, Qasiya (mentioned in the *Midraš*) and the Arabic Kathib el-Qasl is hypothetical. It was the site of a known Phoenician cult of Ba'al Safon, perhaps imported from the homonymous Mt Casius on the Orontes (Gebel Aqra', on the modern border between Syria and Turkey); the Greeks identified the god with Zeus Kasios, through several legendary etymologies (see P. Chuvin and J. Yoyotte, *RA* (1986), 41–63). Greek sources often mention the 'mountain' on lake Serbonis (e.g. Polybius V 80,2; Diod. XX 74,1–5; Strabo XVI 2,33; Stephanus of Byzantium, s.v. *βάραθρον*, *Κάσιον*), mainly as a regular stop of the troops that came from Raphia or from Pelusium; it retained its fame after Pompey was killed and buried there in 48 BC. See in general K. Steuernagel and H. Kees, *RE* X 2, 1919, coll. 2263–4; O. Eissfeldt, *Baal Zaphon, Zeus Kasios und der Durchweg der Israeliten durchs Meer*, Halle 1932. The anthroponymic *Κασ(σ)ιόδωρος* can be connected to the cult of Zeus Kasios.

3. *τὸν Τυφῶ*: Typho was a mythological monster with a hundred heads, son of Tartarus and Gea, father of monsters and winds (Hesiod, *Theog.* 820 ff.), enemy of the gods, who, in order to escape him, fled to Egypt where they transformed themselves into animals; finally Zeus mutilated him and sank him under Mt Casius; according to other legends, under various mountains or in volcanic or seismic areas: e.g. *εἰν Ἀρίμοις* (*Il.* II 782 ff.: in Cilicia-Syria?), in the cave of Coricus in Cilicia (Aeschylus, *Prom.* 351 ff.), in the 'burned land' of Mysia (Xanthus of Lydia, *FGrHist* 765 F 13a–b), or in Lydia, in Phrygia, in Boeotia, or in the Greek West (in Ischia, in the Phlegrean fields, or, especially, under Etna). According to the Herodotean Egyptian mythology, Typho reigned over Egypt until he was deposed by the last divine king, Horos (Apollo): II 144,2; 156,4. For the identification of Typho with Seth, see esp. Plutarch, *Mor.* 367d, 371b, and 376a. The connection of Typho with Mt Casius—either Mt Casius in Egypt, the marshes of which were called 'the gusts of Typho', or Mt Casius by the Orontes, where there was also a river called Typho—indicates an etymological link with Safon (see above), that in Phoenician and Hebrew means both 'hidden' and 'north'. Some affinities between the Greek myth and the Hittite epic of Kumarbi are explained in various ways by these very ancient cultural contacts in the area of Mt. Khazzi (Casius), between Ugarit (Ras Shamra) and Alalakh, south of the gulf of Alexandretta. See G. Seippel, 'Der Typhons Mythos', Diss. Greifswald 1939; O. Touchefeu-Meynier, *LIMC* VIII 1 1997, pp. 147–51; on ancient sources and 19th-cent. theories about Typho see J. Schmidt, in Roscher, *Lexikon* V, coll. 1426–54; on Typho and the gods, J. G. Griffiths, *Hermes* LXXXVIII (1960), 374–6; J.-P. Vernant, in *Mélanges Puech*, Paris 1974, pp. 101–6; on the Arimoi and Aramaeans in Syria-Cilicia, J. Fontenrose, in *Studies in Honor of H. Caplan*, Ithaca, NY 1966, pp. 64–82; for Hittite affinities A. Heubeck, *Gymnasium*, LXII (1955), 509 ff.; F. Vian, in *Éléments orientaux dans la religion grecque*, Strasbourg 1960, pp. 17–37; D. Thompson, *PP* XXII (1967), 241–51; Sabri Kolta, pp. 161–8; C. Bonnet, in *Studia Phoenicia*, V, Leuven 1987, pp. 101–43; Lloyd, *Commentary*

99–182, p. III.   ἀπὸ ταύτης ἤδη Αἴγυπτος: Herodotus thinks of the border between the satrapy of 'Abar Nahara (Syria–Phoenicia–Palestine: 91,1) and Egypt, a border that in his day ran between mounts Casius and Pelusium.

6,1. ἐς Αἴγυπτον ναυτιλλομένων: cf. II 5,1.   κέραμος... ἰδέσθαι: an obvious exaggeration. Numerous archaic Greek vases, especially of the 6th cent., were found in Egypt (in Naucratis, Daphnae, Memphis, Thebes, etc.); see Boardman, *Greeks Overseas*, pp. 111–59, with bibl. at pp. 290 ff. Perhaps Herodotus refers to the villages of the *chora*; cf. δήμαρχον (para. 2).

2. κοῦ δῆτα... φράσω: a colloquial expression rarely found in Herodotus. On rhetorical questions see Lang, pp. 39 ff. On the Herodotean use of δῆτα see C. C. Chiasson, *Phoenix*, XXXVI (1982), 157, n. 8.   δήμαρχον: in Attica indicates the head of a deme, here the head of a village of the Egyptian *chora*, subordinated to the νομάρχης (II 177,2). On the *nomarchoi* and wine in Scythia cf. IV 66.

7,1. κατὰ... ὕδατι: 'providing it with water in the way I have said' (sc. τὰ ἄνυδρα τῆς Συρίης; sc. κέραμον Wells, τὴν ἐσβολὴν Powell).

8,1. Ἀράβοι...: the first digression on the Arabs in Book III (the second is in chs. 107–13). The Arabia known to Herodotus is actually limited to the southern Palestinian coast (ch. 5), the northern part of Egypt east of the Nile, and the opening of the Suez gulf ('the Arabian gulf', ὁ Ἀράβιος κόλπος): cf. II 8; 124,2. It does not seem that Herodotus had a clear idea of the Negev or Sinai peninsula, let alone of the Arabian peninsula (see 107,1) and thus of the tribes of the Idumaeans, of *Arabia Petraea* and of *Arabia Deserta* south of the Euphrates; nor obviously of the oasis cities of Teima, el-'Ola, or Dedan (the 'Midianites') in northern Hejaz, not to mention the civilization of central and southern Arabia (Saba', Qataban, Hadramaut). The tribe of Qedar (see note on 4,3) was situated east of the Nile, in a cultural and economic symbiosis with the other populations of the area; they spoke Aramaic. The hypothesis of a great Arab 'empire' with the Qedarites at its head, extending from the Mediterranean to the Hejaz, where in the 6th and 5th cents. the Lihjanic dialect was predominant, does not have a sound base. See W. J. Dumbrell, *BASOR* CCIII (1971), 33–44. On the Arabs and Arabia in antiquity see A. Grohmann, *Arabien*, Munich 1963; F. Altheim and R. Stiehl, *Die Araber in der alten Welt*, I, Berlin 1964; Briant, *État et pasteurs*, ch. 3; I. Eph'al, *The Ancient Arabs*, Jerusalem–Leiden 1982 and in *CAH*² IV, pp. 161–4; T. Fahd (ed.), *L'Arabie pré-islamique*, Leiden 1989. In the following centuries the Mineans and ultimately the Nabateans prevailed; on the latter see R. Wenning, *Die Nabatäer. Denkmäler und Geschichte*, Freiburg 1987. According to Xenophon (*Cyr.* VI 2,9–10; VII 5,14), an Arabian king is said to have supported Croesus against Cyrus; later on, however, the Arabs are said to have taken part in the Persian siege of Babylon as subjects of Cyrus. On the Persian satrapy *Arabāya* see 91,1 and note; on the Arab troops in Xerxes' army see VII 69; 86,2.   πίστις: cf. in this sense e.g. 71,1 and 74,2. On similar blood rituals in contractual and brotherhood alliances see I 74,6 and IV 70; cf. A. M. Khazanov, *SA* (1972), 68–75; Hartog, pp. 130 ff. = ET pp. 113 ff.; G. Herman, *Ritualized Friendship in the Greek City*,

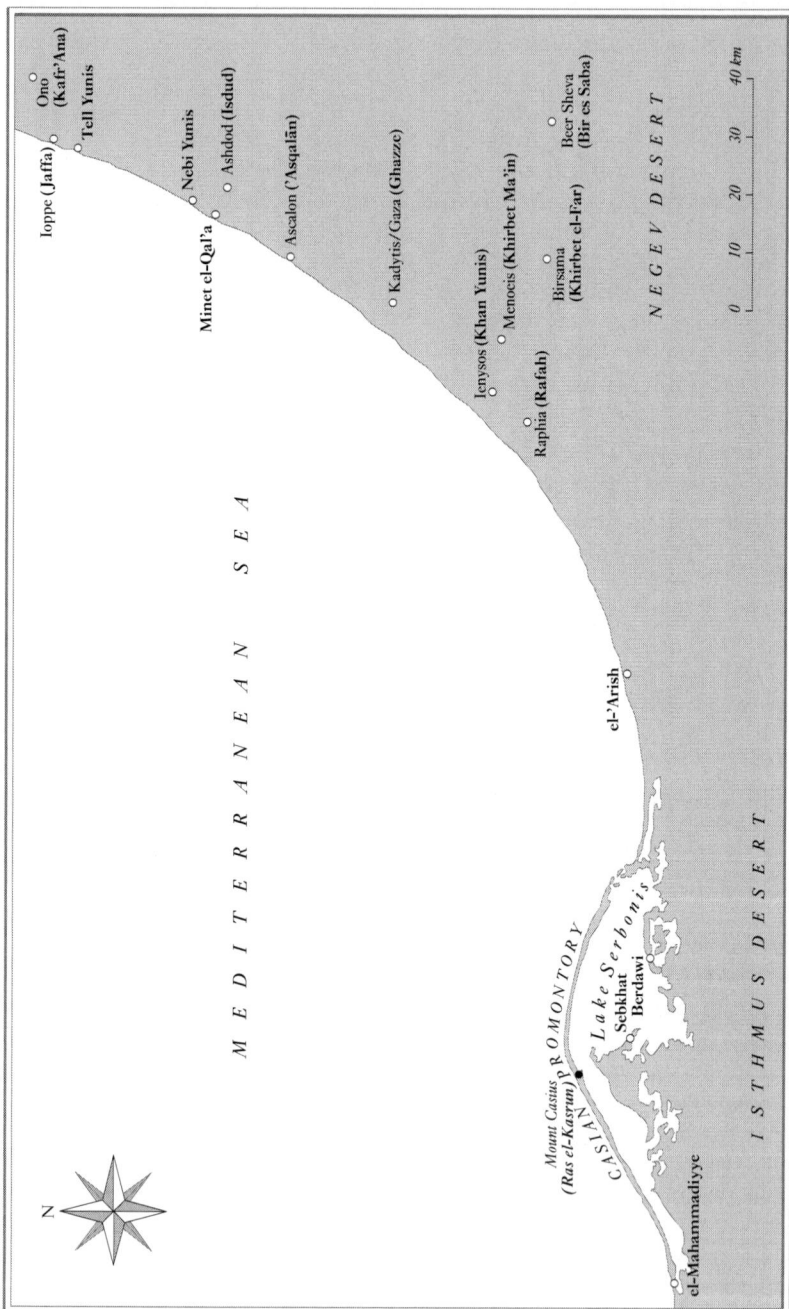

Map 31. The southern Palestinian coast

Cambridge 1987. Animal sacrifices are also common in these ceremonies: M. Weinfeld, *Ugarit-Forschungen*, VIII (1976), 401 ff. On stones as witnesses: e.g. Gen. 31: 44–54; Jos. 24: 26–7; in our passage the witnesses are the gods. In the ancient East the number 7 had a sacred and symbolic value.

2. ξεῖνον: opposed to ἀστόν; taken from the terminology of the Greek *polis*.

3. Διόνυσον... Ἀλιλάτ: cf. Celsus, and Origen, *Contra Cels.* V 34; 37–8; whereas Aristobulos (*FGrHist* 139 F 55–6) in the second half of the 4th cent. BC believed that the two most important Arab deities were Zeus, or Uranos, and Dionysus. These are worthless Greek simplifications. Pre-Islamic Arabs venerated several deities, mostly astral ones, although they might have had a propensity towards centring the cult on a more important divine couple (the Sun and the Moon); cf. the Ugaritic couple El and Asherah and the Israelitic one of Yahweh and Asherah. In Greece there were temples dedicated to both Dionysus and Urania: e.g. in Argos and in Megalopolis (Paus. II 23,8; VIII 32,2–3). See H. Petersmann, in T. Fahd, op. cit., pp. 401–12.   καὶ τῶν τριχῶν... κροτάφους: see the supposed representations of Arabs at the *Apadana* of Persepolis (Walser, *Völkerschaften*, pp. 97–9); cf. Jer. 9: 25 ('those who cut their hair, dwellers of the desert'). This is the type of haircut forbidden to the Hebrews (Lev.19: 27). Choerilos of Samos in the late 5th cent. BC is probably thinking about the Arabs, perhaps influenced by Herodotus, or about an Ethiopian tribe, when he describes those who speak 'Phoenician', with shabby heads 'shaved in a circle' (τροχοκουφάδες: *FGrHist* 696 F 34 and 557 Stern), in spite of Josephus, *Ap.* I 173–4. The Greeks cut their hair in a round shape but did not shave their temples; Dionysus, in Greek archaic and classical art, usually wears his curly hair tied up on the nape of the neck or on the temples; see C. Gasparri, *LIMC* III 1 1986, pp. 414–556; cf. T. H. Carpenter, *Dionysian Imagery in Archaic Greek Art*, Oxford 1986. The way hair is worn is of ethnological interest for Herodotus: cf. e.g. I 195,1; IV 168,1; 175,1; 180,1; 191,1.   Ὀροτάλτ: the search for the original Arab name of Orotalt has interested philologists and orientalists since the time of E. Pococke ('*Allah ta'ala*, 'may Allah be exalted', is a common Islamic formula). The text has been variously corrected: e.g. to Νουράλλα = *nūr Allah* ('light of Allah'), and to Ὀβοτάλτ, *Atthar* (the male equivalent of *Ishtar* = Aphrodite); for all these interpretations see J. H. Mordtmann, *Klio*, XXV (1932), 430–3 with bibl. Much credit is now given to R. Dussaud's theory, according to which Orotalt should be identified with the god A'arrā, the equivalent of *Dwsr* (Δουσάρης), the most important Nabatean deity, himself identified with Dionysus; see M. Höfner, in *Wörterbuch der Myth.* I, pp. 433–5, 459–60; H. J. W. Drijvers, *LIMC* III 1 1986, pp. 670–2.   Ἀλιλάτ: the problem of Ἀλιλάτ, in which already Scaliger and Selden were engaged, seems now to be solved: it seems to correspond to *al-Alahāt* or *al-Ilahāt* (*han-Ilahāt* at Tell al-Maskhuta: see note on 4,3; I. Rabinowitz, *JNES* XVIII (1959), 154 f. and P. Grelot, *Documents araméens d' Égypte*, Paris 1972, pp. 336 ff., nn. 78–9) the *Allat* of the Koran: 'the Goddess'; see Höfner, *Wörterbuch der Myth.* I, pp. 422–4. The Greek identification with Aphrodite Urania, whatever its value, draws the Arab goddess nearer to that of Ascalon and to the Babylonian Mylitta (I 105,2; 131,3; 199,3); however, the offerings to the goddess at Tell el-Maskhuta include

thousands of Attic tetradrachms with the effigy of Athena; see E. S. G. Robinson, *NC* VII (1947), 115–21.

9,1. ἐμηχανᾶτο: an example of technical ingenuity (cf. note on 4,2). On the problem of water in the desert and the relations between Arabs and Persians, see I. Epha'al, in *CAH*² IV, pp. 161 f.

2. οὗτος μὲν...ῥηθῆναι: typical example of *relata referre* by Herodotus; see General Introduction, p. 20 ff.   δεῖ...: Herodotus considers it right also to relate the less trustworthy versions, which he rejects; see ibid.   Κόρυς: no 'great river' exists in Arabia, neither at 12 days, nor at any other distance from the desert region. The Euphrates, well known to Herodotus, flows out into the 'Red Sea', a name that in antiquity also included the Persian Gulf (cf. note on I 1,1); however, the river does not pass through Arabia. Aqueducts, canalizations (also underground), and cisterns existed in various arid areas of the ancient East.

10,1. Πηλουσίῳ καλεομένῳ στόματι: cf. II 17,4; 154,3. It is this mouth of the Delta that marks the eastern border of Egypt. Here were the ἐσβολαί, the ways of access to Egypt (II 141,4) for the armies coming from Syria. The Pelusian mouth was in the area of the Salt Pans (II 15,1), by the city of Bubastis (now Tell Basta), where Psammetichus settled Ionians and Carians (II 154,3). Further south, on the same branch of the Nile, was Daphnae (now Tell Defenneh), the base for the garrison on the border between Egypt and the Syro-Arabic area (II 30,2; 107,1); then Patoumos (*Pitûmû*, the biblical Pithom, about 15 km. west of Ismailia) which Herodotus considers an Arab city (II 158,2). The ancient canal, which must have connected the Mediterranean with the Gulf of Suez, started from the Pelusian mouth. Ancient Pelusium is located at Tell Farama (in Coptic *Peremum* = 'Temple of Amon') about 20 km. east of the Suez Canal; Pelusium has left a toponomastic trace in the name of neighbouring Balusa. The toponym was understood by the Greeks as 'city of the marshes', or aetiologized as 'city of Peleus' (Strabo XVII 1,21; Eustathius, *Comm. Dion. Perieg.* 260). The site had already been fortified in the Pharaonic era (*śnw* = 'fortress'), and was an important border-station for commerce and customs also in the Hellenistic period, and scene of many battles up to Roman times. See H. Kees, *RE* XIX 1, 1937, coll. 407–15.   Ψαμμήνιτος: Psamtik II, son of Amasis and Tentkheta; see chs. 14–15. Manetho, *FGrHist* 609 F 2, p. 50, calls him Ψαμμεχερίτης, whereas Ctesias, ibid. 688 F 13 (10), confuses him with Amyrtaeus (cf. note on 15,3).

2. τέσσερα καὶ τεσσεράκοντα ἔτεα: Amasis reigned between 569 and 525 BC, according to a chronology substantially accepted by modern scholars. According to Diod. I 68,6 he reigned for fifty-five years. His death probably occurred in the autumn of 526. For bibl. see note on III 1,1.

3. φάσμα: cf. IV 79,1; VII 37,2; VIII 37,2 and 38. A typical Herodotean prodigy, which foretells an imminent disaster; cf. VI 27,1; see General Introduction, p. 41 ff. As elsewhere, it is an unusual phenomenon that has been dramatized by Herodotus or by his source (cf. VI 98,1–2; VII 129; Fehling, p. 91).   Θῆβαι αἱ Αἰγύπτιαι: cf. III 25,7 and 7; 26,1. On this famous city see Lloyd, *Commentary 1–98*, pp. 12 ff., with bibl.

11–12. On the battle of Pelusium, cf. Ctesias, *FGrHist* 688 F 13 (10); Diod. X 14,2; Polyaenus VII 9. On the siege of Memphis cf. ch. 13. For bibl. see note on 1,1. The episode of the killing of Phanes' sons may create the impression that Greek and Carian mercenaries were drawn up in the front line of battle in both camps; for Greeks in Cambyses' army, cf. II 1,2 and III 1,1; for the Carians in Egypt: II 152; Polyaenus VII 3; see O. Masson, *Bull. de la Soc. Française d' Égyptologie*, LVI (1969), 25–36, and *Carian Inscriptions from North Saqqara and Buhen*, London 1978. However, the anecdote narrated by Polyaenus VII 9, on the stratagem of Cambyses who ordered the sacred animals to be exposed (cf. Amasis' stratagem in Polyaenus VII 4), is based on the assumption that the Egyptian troops were drawn up against the enemy's front line.

11,1. μηχανῶνται: an example of brutal and vindictive 'ingenuity'; cf. note on 4,2.
2. τοὺς ἀγαγόντες: this macabre act probably stems from a blood rite. On the one hand, it imposes on the participants in the crime a reciprocal obligation, as if they were conspirators. On the other, the action of the Greek and Carian mercenaries seems to reveal the resurrection of a repressed, but never suppressed, practice of human sacrifice: a practice common to all the peoples in antiquity, including the Egyptians; on this matter see Lloyd, above, note to II 45 and *Commentary 1–98*, pp. 213 f. Occasions of propitiatory human sacrifices, especially of prisoners, before a war or a battle are not rare among the Greeks (see the example of Themistocles at the battle of Salamis: Phanias of Eresus, fr. 25 Wehrli), nor among civilized barbarians (see the example of the Persians at the battle of Artemisium: VII 180). According to the Coptic story of the Persian conquest of Egypt (Pap. Berol. 9009; L. S. B. MacCoull, *GRBS* XXIII (1982), 185–8; see H. L. Jansen, *The Coptic Story of Cambyses' Invasion of Egypt*, Oslo 1952), an Egyptian garrison threatened to kill Cambyses' sons, who—we must suppose—were thought to have fallen into Egyptian hands; cf. the medieval Ethiopian version of the Chronicle of John of Nikiu, on which see J. Schwartz, *BIFAO* XLVIII (1949), 67–8.
3. καὶ πεσόντων...πολλῶν: 50,000 Egyptians and 7,000 Persians, according to Ctesias, *FGrHist* 688 F 13 (10).

12,1. θῶμα: cf. 47,3; 112; 113,1; see General Introduction, p. 14 f. The passage is autobiographical, it attests autopsy and highlights well the presence of the historian himself in his book; see Beltrametti, pp. 38 f.; J. Marincola, *Arethusa*, XX (1987), 121–37.
2. αἴτιον: cf. note on 1,1. Herodotus relates the result of a typical experiment of the local guides. He really let himself be 'easily' convinced (εὐπετέως). The fallen soldiers, left unburied on the battlefield, would probably have been mostly Carian and Greek mercenaries of both armies; Persians and Egyptians were probably buried or embalmed, according to their customs. It is also probable that the two heaps of bones had been prepared by the guides for the spectacle. Besides, Herodotus had his own convictions: he knew that baldness was common amongst the northern populations similar to the Persians, e.g. beyond the Scythians (IV 23–5), whereas it was rare in Egypt; perhaps he even knew

the Hippocratic theory of humidity and fragility of the human body in Scythia (*De aeribus locis aquis* 20–22): cf. Fehling, pp. 28–30. This does not exclude the possibility that the 'locals', the Greeks of Naucratis or the Egyptian physicians, also knew similar theories. The autopsy and the oral testimony in this chapter should not, therefore, be considered fictitious. In fact the skulls of the ancient Egyptians are of normal hardness; in the case of the Persians it is possible only to say that the fragility of the skull and of the bones in general is a typical symptom of rickets, a disease more common in northern countries than in tropical ones, due to malnutrition and vitamin D deficiency. See D. Brandenburg, *Medizinisches bei Herodot*, Berlin 1976, p. 50; W. R. Dawson, *BICS* XXXIII (1986), 93 (with n. 32 of F. D. Harvey). Bones of fallen Persians with anomalies were found also in the battlefield of Plataea: IX 83.

3. *τοῦ μὴ φαλακροῦσθαι*: the shaving of the head was probably the privilege of priests (II 36,1; 37,2): on Egyptian monuments soldiers do not have shaved heads.
4. *σκιητροφέουσι*: cf. VI 12,4.   *πίλους τιάρας*: see note on I 132,1. *ἐν Παπρήμι*: cf. II 59,3; 63,1; 71; 165; see Lloyd, *Commentary 1–98*, pp. 270–2; *pprm* in Aramaic. A city and a district of disputed etymology and location; see Salmon, pp. 144–6, with an exhaustive review of modern hypotheses. It is generally thought to be located in the western area of the Delta; e.g. at Letopolis or Androupolis (H. Altenmüller, *JVEG* XVIII (1964), 271–9; E. Bresciani, *SCO* XXI (1972), 299–303); for a different location, between Heliopolis and Bubastis see A. Nibbi, *Ancient Byblos Reconsidered*, Oxford 1985, pp. 79 ff., 90 ff. The battle of Papremis is one of the few events posterior to 479 BC related by Herodotus; it is dated around 462/1. Other historians do not mention the site: Thuc. I 104; 109–10; Ctesias, *FGrHist* 688 F 14 (32) (see J. M. Bigwood, *Phoenix*, XXX (1976), 1–25); Diod. XI 71,3–6; 74,1–4; Aristodemos, *FGrHist* 104 F 11,3.   *ὑπὸ Ἰνάρω*: the battle of Papremis and the subsequent, partial conquest of Memphis are the most important military events of the autonomistic insurrection headed by Inarus (*Ienheru*), a Libyan prince who had probably presented himself to the people as 'son of Psammetichus' (see G. Dunst, *MDAI(A)* LXXXVII (1972), 153–5; O. Masson *Epigraphica Anatolica*, XI (1988), 173), i.e. as legitimate heir of the Saite dynasty. Inarus exploited the rising discontent in Egypt after the killing of Xerxes in 465 BC; see Diod. XI 71,3. At Papremis he defeated the Persian army, led by Achaemenes, brother of Xerxes and satrap of Egypt since 484; cf. VII 7 (who also participated in Xerxes' invasion of Greece in 480: VII 97; 236); Achaemenes fell in battle with 100,000 soldiers; see Ctesias, *FGrHist* 688 F 14 (32). Two hundred Athenian ships also took part in the revolt; however, the precise chronology of this intervention, which inaugurated the catastrophic Athenian expedition in Egypt, is uncertain. In the biased and rhetorical version of Diodorus (XI 71,3–6; 74,1–4), the Athenians participated in the battle victoriously. The revolt was finally suppressed by Megabyzus (160,2 with note); however, it perhaps survived in the marshy area west of the Delta, where the rule of Amyrtaeus remained autonomous for a certain time (see note on 15,3). Inarus was deported to Persia and impaled around the year 450 BC together with fifty Greek prisoners. About the son Thannyras see note on 15,3.

13,1. νέα Μυτιληναίην: Lesbos is supposed to have been under Persian hegemony during this period; on Coes, philo-Persian tyrant of Mytilene, see IV 97,2; V 11,1–2. Lesbos in the age of Pittacus (early 6th cent.) was included by the ancients in the list of 'thalassocracies'; in fact its fleet was important also in the late-6th and 5th centuries. Mytilene's relations with Egypt are well attested by its participation in the panhellenic sanctuary at Naucratis (II 178,2). See also II 135. For the Aeolians in Cambyses' army see II 1,2; III 1,1.

2. **ἐσελθοῦσαν**: the form ἐσελθοῦσαν indicates that the Nile passed through Memphis, or rather that the extramural districts stretched along the two banks of the river (see map on p. 311). Monuments and districts of Memphis in Herodotus include the temple of Hephaestus (37,2 and note), the temple of Aphrodite and the Phoenician quarter (II 112,1–2), the temple of Isis (II 176,2), market (III 139,2); statues (II 176,1), hills and pyramids in the west (II 150,1; 158,2, etc.), dam and artificial lake (II 99,2–3), Ionian and Carian quarters (II 154,3). See S. Donadoni, *EAA* IV 1961, pp. 996–7.   **ἐκ τοῦ τείχεος**: the famous White Castle of Memphis (cf. 91,3 with note), seat of the royal family and of a large garrison; see note to II 99,4.   **κρεοργηδὸν**: a *hapax* in Herodotus; there might be a reminiscence of it in Eunapius, *Vit. Soph.* VI 3,13 Giangrande. In the Coptic story of the conquest (cf. note on 11,2) a garrison wants to massacre the messengers of Cambyses, but renounces its intent; in the Chronicle of John Nikiu (cf. note on 11,2), the citizens of Memphis killed Cambyses' sons. Are the reminiscences of Herodotus confused in both cases?

3. **παρέστησαν**: with the fall of Memphis and the subsequent coronation of Cambyses as pharaoh (the first of the XXVIIth Dynasty of Manetho), the first Persian occupation of Egypt (525–402 BC) officially begins. The Egyptian documents date the reign of Cambyses from June/July 525, according to the Egyptian system which does not distinguish between the year of accession to the throne and the official 'first year' (a distinction observed by the Persian and Babylonian calendars), and therefore passes over the short reign of Psammenitus, and includes in the 'first year' of Cambyses the entire period after the death of Amasis. The Egyptian 'first year' corresponds in the Persian system to Cambyses' fifth year (Manetho, *FGrHist* 609 F 28, p. 112), calculated retroactively from 1 Nisan 529 (see note on ch. 1,1) also for Egypt. For Diodorus (I 68,6) it was the third year of the 63rd Olympiad, which ended in July/August 525. The *Tabula Capitolina* (*IG* XIV 1297 = *FGrHist* 252 B 7) postpones it one year (524/3); cf. J. M. Balcer, *HSCPh* LXXVI (1972), 99–132. The *terminus post quem* for the division of the Egyptian booty would be, according to Babylonian documents, the autumn of 525 (B. Meissmer, *ZÄS* XXIX (1891), 123 ff.). On the problems of correspondence between the Egyptian and the Persian calendars see R. A. Parker, *AJSL* LVIII (1941), 285–301; K. M. T. Atkinson, *JAOS* LXXVI (1956), 168, n. 13. It is thought—but only on the basis of Strabo XVII 1,27—that the city of Heliopolis resisted longer. On the Persian satrapy of Egypt see 91,2–3 and note. **οἱ δὲ προσεχέες Λίβυες**: cf. Diod. X 15. Libya in Herodotus starts just west of the Delta and the Nile. Herodotus here refers to the western Libyan tribes (the *Tehenou* of the Egyptian texts), especially the neighbouring and culturally

Egyptian ones (e.g. the Adyrmachidai, on whom see IV 168,1), who lived in the marshy area of Mareia and the oasis between Wadi Natrun and the Fayûm. On these tribes see IV 168 ff. On the Libyan tribute see III 91,2; on the Ammonians see 17; 25,3 and esp. 26.   Κυρηναῖοι καὶ Βαρκαῖοι: at the time Cyrene was ruled by the Battiad king Arcesilaus III, who, shortly before the Persian conquest of Egypt, had again seized power after several years of exile in Samos. The king of Barce was his father-in-law Alazeir (see IV 164,4). Arcesilaus apparently renewed with the new king of Egypt the alliance that Cyrene had made years before with Amasis, who had married a noblewoman from Cyrene (II 181; gift of Amasis to Cyrene: II 182,1). On the relations between Cyrene and Egypt see Chamoux, esp. pp. 149 ff.; on Cyrene within the Persian satrapy of Egypt see 91,2 with note.

14,1. ἡμέρῃ δὲ δεκάτῃ: a 'typical' number (Fehling, pp. 225–9). Here begins the famous scene of the psychological experiment (cf. διεπειρᾶτο . . . τῆς ψυχῆς) conducted by Cambyses in order to test the scale of human feelings. Psammenitus answers with a Greek motto (known to Bacchylides, fr. 2 Snell–Maehler, and to Pindar, *Pyth*. 4, 237 f.), whereas Croesus, necessarily present at the scene (at least in Herodotus), cries. Cf. S. Flory, *AJPh* XCIX (1978), 145–53. In this eminently didactic chapter, and in the following one, the figure of Cambyses has humane traits and is not fundamentally different from that of Cyrus in his dialogue with the prisoner Croesus (I 86–90): as for the rest, the parallels between the two scenes are evident and doubtless intentional. Note the rich terminology related to weeping, cries of pain, etc.; on 'non-verbal' forms of communication in Herodotus, D. Lateiner, *Arethusa* XX (1987), 83–119. The existence of a 'scale of feelings' is assumed by Homer (*Il*. IX 555 ff.; see F. Dornseiff, *Philologus*, XCIII (1938), 407), but the wicked idea of the experiment assumes also a despotic regime, that imposes collective punishments on entire families and offers the 'choice of mercy' to one of the victims (cf. 119,6 with note). The origin is perhaps oriental (Aly, pp. 81–2). Historically, the parade of prisoners roped around their necks through the streets of Memphis recalls other scenes of mass deportations in Herodotus (see note on 93,2) and in oriental iconography; according to Ctesias, *FGrHist* 688 F 13(10), the Egyptian king was deported to Susa with 6,000 men chosen by Cambyses.   προάστιον: port suburbs between the Nile and the White Castle.

2. ἐπ' ὕδωρ . . .: in Greek poetry, from Homer to the tragedians, fetching water is a typical task of slaves; cf. also V 12,2–4.

5. ὑπὲρ ἀνδρὸς ἑκάστου . . .: according to Herodotus himself the average number of crew in the classical trireme is 200 (VII 184,1; VIII 17). However, the Ionian ships of the early 5th cent. were pentaconters (39,3 and note on 44, 2), with an average crew of eighty men (VII 184,3).

10. ὦ παῖ Κύρου: a common form of address in Herodotus; see Dickey, pp. 52–6 and 264.

11. ὡς δὲ λέγεται ὑπ' Αἰγυπτίων: the source is fictitious: the Egyptians in fact did not know anything about Croesus (see Fehling, pp. 105, 208). On the figure of 'the wise counsellor' see note on 1,1.

15,2. ἐπεί ... τοὺς παῖδας: a wise practice of imperial administration, common to all ancient empires. For the period of Cyrus it is well documented by various Greek sources on the fate of Astyages, Croesus, and Nabonidus; see notes on I 86–7; 130,3; 191,6. The cases of Thannyras and of Pausiris belong to the second half of the reign of Artaxerxes I (465–424 BC).

3. 'Ἰνάρῳ παιδὶ Θαννύρᾳ: on Inarus see note on 12,4. Thannyras was probably recognized by Artaxerxes as the vassal-king of the bordering Libyans after the supression of Inarus' revolt around 455 BC. He might have still reigned when Herodotus visited Egypt. καὶ τῷ Ἀμυρταίου Παυσίρι: Amyrtaeus ('Amnerdâïs = 'gift of Ammon'; cf. Μυρταῖος· Ἀμμωνόδοτος in Eratosthenes, *FGrHist* 610 F 1 <κγ>, p. 114) probably barricaded himself on the artificial isle of Elbo (II 140,2), in the marshy area of the western Delta (cf. II 92–5). This area always had a history and a culture different from the rest of Lower Egypt, with an autonomistic tradition since the time of Anysis (II 137,2) and the twelve kings (II 151,3; 152,2–4). During the time of Cimon, in 450 BC, before the so-called Peace of Callias of 449/8 (see *StV* II 152), Amyrtaeus was supported by Athens: see Thuc. I 110,2; 112,3–4; Plutarch, *Cim.* 18–19. His fate is unknown. In 445/4 a new Psammetichus 'king of Egypt' made the Athenians a gift of wheat (Philochorus, *FGrHist* 328 F 119; Plutarch, *Per.* 37,3–4); a new Amyrtaeus, perhaps the nephew of the first one, if not a false pretender, stayed in power between 408 and 403 BC (see Manetho, *FGrHist* 609 F 2, p. 50). Pausiris is not mentioned in other sources; the name *Pasiri* is present in an Aramaic dedication at Tell el-Maskhuta and has been understood as 'the man (p³) coming from Phoenicia (*sir*)'.

4. ἀπιστάς: Psammenitus' attempt to revolt could have taken place during Cambyses' campaign in Ethiopia. αἷμα ταύρου: according to Ctesias, *FGrHist* 688 F 13 (12), it was Cambyses' brother who committed suicide with bull's blood. There was a belief in antiquity (also shared by the physician Ctesias) that bull's blood was poisonous, as it would block respiration by coagulating in the stomach. Among the suicides by means of bull's blood, note the mythological ones of Jason (or of his father Aeson) and of Midas; among the examples from the historical period, that of Themistocles is famous, imitated, according to some, by Flamininus. See the sources and the data collected by W. Roscher, *NJPh* XXIX (1883), 158–62; F. J. Frost, *Plutarch's Themistocles*, Princeton 1980, p. 227. In fact bull's blood is innocuous and part of the diet of many peoples. For the various modern attempts to explain the origin of the ancient belief and of the information given by Herodotus, see A. Touwaide, *AC* XLVIII (1979), 5–14; I. Gershevitch, *AAntHung* XXVII (1979), 340; Giraudeau, pp. 29–30. Ctesias' version, that the Egyptian king was deported to Susa (see note on 14,1), is preferred by some modern 'rehabilitators' of Cambyses.

16,1. Καμβύσης: Cambyses presented himself at Sais as Apries' legitimate heir (cf. note on 2,1) and was crowned, according with Egyptian tradition, with the titles *Horus Sm̉*, *T̉*, *.wj*, 'king of Upper and Lower Egypt', *Mś. tjw (?)-R̉*, 'son of Ra, Cambyses' (Posener, nos. 3–4; S. Hodjache and O. Berlev, *CdE* LII (1977), 37–9).

The visit to Sais is confirmed by the famous Vatican *naophoros* of Udjahorresne (see Posener, no. 1; A. Tulli, *Miscellanea Gregoriana*, Mon. Vat. VI, Vatican City 1941, pp. 211–80). It dates to the third or fourth year of Darius (519/8–518/7 BC). From the inscription, which covers the statue, it appears that Udjahorresnet (who was already admiral, prophet, and chief scribe under Amasis) became, under Cambyses, court physician, priest of Neith, director of the palace, and formulator of the royal titulature. He received Cambyses and accompanied him to the temples of Sais and the district; obtained from the new pharaoh the removal of some 'foreigners', probably soldiers or mercenaries, who had installed themselves in the temple of Neith; he also obtained the purification of this temple, the restoration of the clergy and of the sacred revenues, of the feasts, etc. Cambyses worshipped the goddess and made offerings and libations to her. This section of the text reflects an atmosphere of collaboration between the high clergy of Sais and the new monarch; this has been used by modern research to declare entirely false the tradition hostile to Cambyses (cf. note on 37,1). Udjahorresne has been identified by some with the ophthalmologist of Cyrus (see 1,1 with note): see A. Godron, in *Hommages à François Dumas*, Montpellier 1986, I, pp. 285–97; others identify him with Kombaphis in Ctesias, *FGrHist* 688 F 13(10). See the bibl. at note to ch. 1, to which should be added A. B. Lloyd, *JEA* LXVIII (1982), 166–80; P. Ghalioungui, *The Physicians of Pharaonic Egypt*, Cairo 1983, pp. 81–4; A. Spalinger, *LdÄ* VI 1986, coll. 822–4; T. Holm-Rasmussen, in *Studies in Ancient History and Numismatics presented to Rudi Thomsen*, Aarhus 1988, pp. 29–38; J. Blenkinsopp, *JBL* CVI (1987), 409–21; W. Huss, *Tyche*, XII (1997), 131–43. ἐς Σάϊν πόλιν: Sais was the capital of the Egyptian kingdom during the Saite dynasty. Its ruins are near Sâ el-Hagar, on the Saitic mouth of the Nile (II 17,5). Herodotus mentions its tombs, statues, palaces, and the famous temple of Athena (Neith) (II 28,1; 130; 163,1; 169,3–5; 170; 175; 176,2). See G. Matthiae Scandone, *Oriens Antiquus*, VI (1967), 145–68; R. el-Sayed, *Documents relatifs à Saïs et ses divinités*, Cairo 1975 (with S. Pernigotti, *SCO* XXVIII (1978), 223–35), and *La déesse Neith de Saïs*, I–II, Cairo 1982; Lloyd, *Commentary 99–182*, pp. 204 ff. On the festivals of Athena in Sais see II 59,3; 62. In some Greek historicized legends Sais became a colony or metropolis of Athens (see Plato, *Tim.* 21e and 23d–e; Anaximenes, *FGrHist* 72 F 20; etc.). ἐς τὰ τοῦ Ἀμάσιος οἰκία: in other words, in the royal palace, τὰ βασιλήϊα οἰκία; cf. II 150,3. The tomb of Amasis was situated, according to Herodotus (II 169,5), in a courtyard decorated with colonnades and annexed to the temple of Athena; but perhaps the temple and the palace were adjacent. τὸν Ἀμάσιος νέκυν: cf. Diod. X 14,2. This is the first sacrilegious act committed by Cambyses in Egypt. To outrage the corpse of a defeated enemy was not considered a sacrilegious act in Homeric epic; see Achilles' outrage of the body of Hector in *Il.* XXII 395–404; XXIV 14 ff.; cf. J.-P. Vernant, in G. Gnoli and J.-P. Vernant (eds.), *La Mort, les morts dans les sociétés anciennes*, Cambridge–Paris 1982, esp. pp. 64 ff. By Herodotus' time, however, the attitude had changed; see VII 238; IX 78–9; cf. Xen. *Anab.* III 1,17; Ctesias, *FGrHist* 688 F 21 (13). Some scholars consider Cambyses' act as an outburst of personal hatred towards the deceiving king (1,3; see e.g. T. S. Brown, *Historia*, XXXI (1982), 393), incarnation of the Lie (cf. Introduction, pp. 391 f.). Others explain the cremation of the mummy as a means to prevent the resurrection of the 'usurper' Amasis (e.g. K. M. T. Atkinson, *JAOS* LXXVI (1956), 171 ff.; Hofmann–Vorbichler, p. 92; E. Bresciani, *CHI*, p. 503). See bibl. in the note on 1,1. Perhaps related to this act is also a gesture of *damnatio memoriae* against Amasis: the chiselling-out of his name from the monuments that he constructed (see E. Bresciani, *SCO* XVI (1967), 277, 279); the high clergy of Sais also probably collaborated in the erasure of his name.

2. ὁ γὰρ...διεχέετο: on the Egyptian techniques of embalming see II 86–9.   οὐκ ὅσια: impiety from the religious and moral point of view; cf. e.g. II 119,2 and III 120,1.

2–3. Πέρσαι...ἀνθρώπου: on the cult of fire in Persian religion cf. I 131,2, with note.   νόμῳ: in the sense of 'usage', 'custom'; cf. the similar use in para. 4; and also 20,2; 38; 99,1 (v.l.).

3–4. Αἰγυπτίοισι...καταβρωθῇ: cf. Aristotle, *Parva Nat.* V 469b21, according to whom fire is extinguished when its nourishment is used up. The Egyptians allowed fires to blaze unchecked (II 66,3); yet during sacrifices they burned parts of the victims in the fire (e.g. II 39,1; 40,1 and 4; 47,3); Sesostris orders his children to be burnt alive (II 107,2). Herodotus is not interested in theology but in the techniques of embalming (II 86–9); cf. Lloyd, above, notes on II 85 ff. and *Commentary 1–98*, pp. 353 f., with bibl. on pp. 365 f.

5. ὡς μέντοι...: Herodotus criticizes again (cf. 2,2) an Egyptian version, as he considers it biased and perhaps even contrary to the character of Amasis, a man resigned to his fate (43,1). Nevertheless stratagems connected with tombs amuse him; cf. I 187.   τὴν...ἡλικίην: the word here means stature; cf. e.g. Demosthenes XL 56; Lucian, *Ver. Hist.* I 40.

6. ἐκ μαντηίου: Herodotus does not deny the veracity of this response, which Cambyses would then fulfil; cf. Kirchberg, pp. 50 f. A list of Egyptian oracles is supplied by Herodotus, II 83; the oracle of Leto at Buto is the most important; see also III 64,4 with note. On Amasis and oracles cf. II 174.

17–25. This famous 'Ethiopian' *logos* is a historical and ethnographical digression perfectly integrated in the main narrative. It starts from the historical events of the three main campaigns lost by Cambyses (ch. 17), and connects with the story of the sacrilegious acts performed by the mad Persian king. The *logos*, therefore, has a crucial role in the Herodotean 'biography' of Cambyses. The account of the Ethiopian campaign occupies only the last chapter, ch. 25; the other chapters contain an ethnographic account, mostly fictitious or idealized for didactic purposes; see the summary of Herminghausen, pp. 67 ff. The *logos* mixes a Greek traditional utopia with information of varying value gathered in Egypt from Greek-speaking informers tendentiously hostile to Cambyses. For the Greeks the Ethiopians generally represent the black peoples (αἰθίοψ, 'face burned' by the sun) well known from mythology which, from Homer onwards, conventionally divided them into two groups living in proximity to the rising and the setting of the sun (*Od.* I 22–3). The Ionian geographers and their successors sought more precise locations: e.g. in India and in Africa, from Nubia to the Atlantic coast; cf. VII 69–70. The Ethiopians thus became the *antichthones* of the northern peoples, as well as ἔσχατοι ἀνδρῶν, the 'noble savages' of antiquity. Herodotus thought that the Ethiopians were the tallest and most beautiful people in the world; that they lived for 120 years; that they were pious and righteous; that they elected their kings. Moreover, since he was interested in the problem of the Nile's sources, he studied the geography of Nubia, forming a (not necessarily wrong) view of the distances and nature of the area between the First Cataract (Aswan, or Syene, by Elephantine) and the Fifth or Sixth (Meroe). It is an area 750 km. long that corresponds to the modern Egyptian Nubia and to northern Sudan, as far as Khartoum. This is the Ethiopia of the ancients, which some modern scholars, in order to avoid mistakes, call *Kush* from the name of the Persian satrapy; see 97,2 with note. Most of the area was known to the Egyptians, who dominated it for 1,500 years, colonized it, and introduced their culture there. The so-called 'Ethiopian dynasty', the twenty-fifth in Manetho's list, ruled Egypt between the early 8th cent. and the middle of the 7th (see II 137–9). The Greeks and the Carians who in 593 BC had accompanied Psammetichus II to Ethiopia (II 161,1) also knew the area up to Kerkis (perhaps Abu Hammed, about 300 km. north of Meroe) and left their traces in the famous graffiti of Abu-Simbel (ML, no. 7). After Herodotus, in the 4th cent. BC Ephorus became interested in Ethiopia, *FGrHist* 70 F 30, 128–9; however, it was essentially the Hellenistic and Roman period that opened Nubia to trade and to Graeco-Roman culture. In ancient Nubia, from the 8th cent. BC, flourished an indigenous kingdom profoundly Egyptian in culture, with a religious centre in Napata, beyond the Fourth Cataract; from the 6th cent. the political capital gradually moved to Meroe, near modern Bagrawiya, about 160 km. south of the Fifth Cataract. Herodotus defines Meroe as the 'metropolis' of the 'other Ethiopians', i.e. the independent Ethiopians who lived beyond the borders of the Persian satrapy. At its peak the kingdom of Meroe dominated the whole area between Egypt and Kordofan; it flourished up to the time of the Roman expeditions under Augustus and Nero; and then declined. The end of the kingdom of Meroe is dated around the middle of the 4th cent. AD. It was a typically Nilotic culture, stretching along the two banks of the river as far as the desert sand-dunes. Today it is sufficiently well known thanks to exploration and extraordinary archaeological discoveries. For Herodotus' evidence on the Ethiopians, apart from this *logos*, see Herminghausen, pp. 80–92; among other classical sources should be mentioned Diod. II 14,4–15,5 and III 2–11; Strabo XVII 1,53–4; Mela III 85; Pliny, *NH* VI 178–97 and the fragments of *Aithiopiaka* (*FGrHist* 666–72 and *Anhang* 673). Of great interest are also the *Aethiopica* of Heliodorus, a novel of the 3rd cent. AD, on which see J. R. Morgan, *ClassAnt* I (1982), 221–65. On Herodotus' *logos* and his sources see Hofmann–Vorbichler, with exhaustive bibl. on all aspects of the problem. On the mythological and 'utopian' sources see M. Hadas, *CPh* XXX (1935), 113–21; T. Säve-Söderbergh, *Eranos*, XLIV (1946), 68–80; A. Lesky, *Hermes*, LXXXVII (1959), 27–38. On the black peoples in classical antiquity see F. M. Snowden, jr., *Blacks in Antiquity*, Cambridge, Mass. 1970; *Before Color Prejudice*, Cambridge,

Mass. 1983, with bibl.; and *Greeks and Barbarians*, ed. J. E. Coleman and
C. A. Walz, Bethesda 1997, pp. 103–21; R. Lonis, *Ktema*, VI (1981), 69–87. On
the civilization of Napata and Meroe see the bibl. compiled by F. F. Gadallah,
Kush, XI (1963), 207–16; I. Baldassarre, *EAA* Suppl. 1970, Rome 1973, pp. 552–9;
P. L. Shinnie, *CHA* II, pp. 742–5 and 697–9; Trigger, pp. 412–27. On the texts and
documents, E. A. W. Budge, *The Egyptian Sudan*, I–II, London 1907, is fundamental. On the notions of the Greeks about Nubia and Nilotic Africa see
Desanges, *Recherches*, pp. 217–305. Among works of comprehensive character
see F. Hintze, *Studien zur meroitischen Chronologie*, Berlin 1959; S. Curto, *Nubia.
Storia di una civiltà favolosa*, Novara 1965; P. L. Shinnie, *Meroe: A Civilization of
the Sudan*, London 1967; and *Ancient Nubia*, London 1996; D. O'Connor, *Ancient
Nubia*, Philadelphia 1993; D. Welsby, *The Kingdom of Kush*, London 1996. See the
survey of recent Nubian studies by L. Török, *SO* LXXIII (1998), 201–7. Of
particular importance is the series *Meroitica*, first published in 1973: see esp.
vols. I, IV, and VII with contributions to chronology, etc.

17,1 μετὰ δὲ ταῦτα...: the chapter introduces the story of the three failed
campaigns of Cambyses. Herodotus is particularly interested in the moral
problem of these campaigns, not in their strategic or logistical aspects. They
were actually aimed against the traditional enemies of the Egyptian pharaohs, in
the west and in the south. Two campaigns cannot be considered to have failed,
from a historical point of view, as both northern Nubia and the oasis of Ammon
became tributaries of the Persian empire (97,2 with note).   τριφασίας: a
typically Herodotean Ionian form: cf. I 95,1; II 17,3; 20,1; VI 119,3. For
διφάσιαι see III 122,1.   τοὺς μακροβίους Αἰθίοπας: the traditional Greek epithet for the Ethiopians, wrapped in an aura of legend. Longevity is a utopian
element, also attributed to other people inhabiting the outer ends of the world:
e.g. the Hyperboreans. On the Herodotean rationalizations see 22,4–23,3. The
hypothesis that μακρόβιοι also originally meant 'of the long bows' is unacceptable; see the criticisms of W. R. Halliday, *CQ* XVIII (1924), 53–4, and of
Herminghausen, pp. 31 ff.   τῇ νοτίῃ θαλάσσῃ: cf. II 11,3; the equivalent of
the Red Sea in Herodotus (II 158,4; IV 37), or also of the continuation of the Red
Sea to the south, beyond the Gulf of Aden (IV 42,3).
2. ὀψομένους... ἀληθέως: Herodotus ascribes to the Persian kings also ethnological interests (cf. 136,1; VII 43,1; 128); see M. Rener, 'Historie und Theorie als
Elemente der Personendarstellung bei Herodot', Diss. Göttingen 1973, esp.
pp. 21–8.
18. ἡ δὲ τράπεζα τοῦ ἡλίου: cf. 23,4. A digressive chapter—or an explanatory
note of the author—on an ethnological subject. The text is summarized by
Pomponius Mela (III 85); Pausanias (I 33,4; cf. VI 26,2) locates the Table of
the Sun at Meroe; however, we cannot exclude that Herodotus was thinking
of Nisa (97,2 with note). At the origins of this famous legend are the hecatombs
and banquets of the Ethiopians in Homer, in which the gods participate
(*Il.* I 423–4; XXIII 206–7; *Od.* I 22–5); and also the image of Ethiopia, for evident

reasons, as the land of the Sun. The rest was elaborated by Greek utopian writers, fascinated by the Hesiodic Golden Age and by the paradoxographical descriptions of the Lands of Plenty. Herodotus knew how to rationalize the legend without obscuring, even in terminology, its Greek characteristics, and attributes the less credible version to imaginary indigenous people; cf. Fehling, pp. 99, 111. λειμών ἐστι...: some modern scholars identify the 'meadow', where the table (or altar: τράπεζα τοῦ θεοῦ or τῷ θεῷ: see e.g. *Syll.* 996, l. 9; 1022; 1038, l. 11–2; 1042, l. 20; 1106, ll. 99 f.), was placed with the so-called Temple of the Sun discovered by J. Garstang at the beginning of the 20th cent. in an exceptionally fertile area about half a kilometre east of Meroe; cf. Pliny, *NH* VI 185; see bibl. in note on chs. 17–25. The identification rightly provoked much scepticism: see S. M. Burstein, *J. Soc. for the Study of Egyptian Antiquities*, XI (1981), 2–3. κρεῶν ἐφθῶν: for the notion of 'naturally boiled and cooked' meat, presumably by the Sun-god (an almost ambrosial food that confers long life, if not immortality, upon the banqueters, if not immortal), see J.-P. Vernant, in M. Detienne and J.-P. Vernant (eds.), *La cuisine du sacrifice en pays grec*, Paris 1979, pp. 239–49; *Bull. du Centre Th. More*, XXIII (1978), 3–14.

19,1. κατασκόπους: Cambyses ordered the spies to come from Elephantine to Saïs, aiming to send them later to Ethiopia; see J. E. Powell, *CQ* XXIX (1935), 150.   Ἐλεφαντίνης: *3bw* in Egyptian ('city of elephants' or 'of ivory'), *Yeb* in Aramaic. It was the station of one of the three Persian garrisons stationed in Egypt (II 30,2–3). A Jewish contingent stationed at Elephantine in Herodotus' time has left a rich documentation in papyri, in which Cambyses' stay in Egypt is mentioned; see B. Porten, *Archives from Elephantine*, Berkeley–Los Angeles 1968. Herodotus confirms that he personally visited Elephantine (II 29,1), but the issue is controversial (see Lloyd, above, and *Commentary 1–98*, pp. 115 ff.).   Ἰχθυοφάγων ἀνδρῶν: according to Pausanias (I 33,4) these fish-eaters are ἔσχατοι Ethiopians, who came from beyond Syene and inhabited the coasts of the Red Sea and the so-called 'gulf of the Ichthyophagi'. A city of the Ichthyophagi was Deire on the strait of Bab el-Mandeb; see Eratosthenes, in Strabo XVI 4,4; on the customs of the Ichthyophagi see Strabo XVI 4,13. Fish was the favourite food along the Nile and the Delta, although it was forbidden to the priests (II 37,4). In Greek, however, the epithet Ichthyophagi indicates, also in many writers after Herodotus, certain primitive coastal populations, semi-legendary or utopian, who lived on the outermost borders of the civilized world, especially on the Persian Gulf and on the Red Sea, in the area of the Caspian and on the coast of western India. Cf. I 200; 202,3; II 92,5; III 98,3. The pile-dwellers of Lake Prasias in Thrace also eat fish (V 16,4). For the sources see J. Tkač, *RE* IX 2 (1916), coll. 2524–31.   τοὺς ἐπισταμένους...: Herodotus perhaps attributes these bilingual Ichthyophagi to the class of 'interpreters' (ἑρμηνέες) formed in Egypt at the time of Psammetichus (II 154,2; the Scythians also had classes of interpreters: IV 24). On the Ichthyophagi as a culturally intermediate people, in Herodotus and in later ethnography, see O. Longo, *Materiali e discussioni per l'analisi dei testi classici*, XVIII (1987), pp. 9–55.

In eastern Nubia and along the Red Sea Kushitic languages are now spoken, among which is Beja, thought to be a language different both from Nubian (medieval and modern) and from ancient Meroitic. The ancient Meroitic alphabet, hieroglyphic and 'cursive', has been deciphered, but its vocabulary, and the linguistic family to which it belongs, are unknown; Meroitic is epigraphically attested only in the Hellenistic and Roman periods; see the bibl. collected by S. Wenig, *LdÄ* IV 1980, coll. 104–7. The multilingualism of ancient 'interpreters' was often associated, as in our case, with notions of espionage, treason, diplomatic deceits; see e.g. IV 78–80; VIII 135,2–3; cf. V. Rotolo, in *Studi classici in onore di Q. Cataudella*, I, Catania 1972, pp. 395–414.

2. ἐπὶ τὴν Καρχηδόνα πλέειν: Cambyses could as well have attempted a campaign by land, starting from Cyrene or from Barce (cf. 13,3). Ophellas was to do so in 309/8 BC, marching for more than two months and suffering great losses; see Diod. XX 40–2. In the time of Cambyses, Mago governed Carthage as the successor of Malchus; he was followed by his sons Hasdrubal and Hamilcar; the first fell in battle in Sardinia, the second fell or immolated himself at the battle of Himera, in 480 BC. This was the period of the formation of the Punic thalassocracy in the western Mediterranean; see the bibl. in *CAH*[2] IV, pp. 882 ff.; on Carthage in Herodotus, cf. I 166–7; IV 195–6; V 42–8; VII 165–7. Φοίνικες...: Herodotus interprets the Phoenician refusal in terms of Greek relations between mother city and colony, possibly with an implicit reference to relations previously not respected, such as e.g. between Corinth and Corcyra (see 49,1 with note). This does not exclude, however, that the Phoenician world also could have had similar conceptions: on Hellenistic coins Tyre is *'em Sidonim*, 'mother of the Sidonians'. It seems that the colonies of Tyre paid a tribute or a tithe to the metropolis and that the suspension of this payment was considered an act of rebellion; see e.g. Menander of Ephesus, *FGrHist* 783 F 1 (119). Carthage paid its tribute in the archaic age, then stopped (Diod. XX 14,1–2); but the relations with the metropolis continued to be maintained, despite the Babylonian and Persian conquests (573 and 538 BC, respectively), also in the Hellenistic and Roman periods. Apart from the information in Herodotus, the relations between Persia and Carthage after the reign of Cambyses are not well known. On the alleged 'treaty' between Xerxes and Carthage in 481 see *StV* II no. 129, with bibl. On Phoenicia in the Persian empire see 91,1 with note. οἱ λοιποὶ οὐκ ἀξιόμαχοι ἐγίνοντο: the fleet of the Ionians and Aeolians; much more is said of their fleet in Cambyses' Egyptian campaign (II 1,2; III 1,1; 13,1; 25,2 and 7; 44,2) than in the Phoenician one.

3. Καμβύσης...: Cambyses gives up for two reasons, a moral and a practical one; a positive trait of the king's personality emerges here. ἐδεδώκεσαν Πέρσῃσι: the Phoenicians probably submitted to Cyrus after the Persian conquest of Babylon (539 BC). Κύπριοι: at the time of Amasis Cyprus was a tributary of Egypt (II 182,2). On Cyprus in the Persian empire see 91,1 with note.

20,1. δῶρα...κάδον: the purple robe is a clear symbol of monarchy (cf. 139,2 with note). The necklace and the bracelets, presented as harmless ornaments, are interpreted by the king of the Ethiopians as signs of slavery (22,2); myrrh (cf. 112) and palm-tree wine (22,3 with note) symbolize refinement. Cf. the enigma and the symbolism of the presents that the Scythians give to Darius (IV 131–2). For other typical Persian gifts see Xen. *Anab.* I 2,27.   κάδον: 'pitcher', '*urceus, non poculum*' according to L. Weber, 'Anacreontea', Diss. Göttingen 1892, p. 80; a *hapax* in Herodotus; however, the term was already known to Archilochus (fr. 4,7 West) and to Anacreon (fr. 373 *PMG*). It is probably of Semitic origin (*kd* Hebr., Ugaritic, Royal Aramaic), but the Greeks thought it an Ionic form for κεράμιον (cf. 6,1; thus also Clitarchus Gnomologus, in Athenaeus XI 473b), or a characteristic word of the dialect of Soli in Cilicia (*Anecdota Graeca* I, p. 268, 18 Bekker).   μέγιστοι...: cf. ch. 114.

2. νόμοισι...: the historical Ethiopians, contrary to the mythical ones, were thoroughly Egyptianized (cf. note on chs. 17–25).   κρίνωσι... βασιλεύειν: since the Ethiopians were the tallest and most handsome of all men, their kings had to be the tallest (and most handsome) among the Ethiopians; see pseudo-Scylax 112; Arist. *Pol.* 1290b6; Bion of Soli, *FGrHist* 688 F 2; Nicolaus of Damascus, ibid. 90 F 103; on the Cathaei of India cf. Onesicritus, ibid. 134 F 21. The Hellenistic-Roman sources also ennumerate other criteria for electing the Ethiopian king: care in the rearing of livestock, virtue, wealth; see Diod. III 5,1; Strabo XVII 2,3; cf. O. Murray, *JEA* LVI (1970), 153–5. Diodorus (III 5,1), following Agatharchides of Cnidos, describes, in a Greek way, a mixed procedure, with a 'pre-election' made by the priests and a confirmation by the gods. The procedure that emerges from the epigraphic descriptions of the election of certain Nubian kings, from Aspelta (*c.*593–568 BC) to Nastasen (*c.*335–310 BC) is that of a very limited election generally held among the brothers of the dead king on the initiative of the military chiefs, followed by an oracular ratification by the temple of Ammon in Napata. The influence of the queen mother was probably considerable in the procedure of election. The king (*kwr*) of Kush was also considered Amon-re's adoptive son, therefore a semi-divine being, if not a direct incarnation of the god, as the Egyptian pharaoh. See the bibl. in the note on chs. 17–25; also B. G. Haycock, *Comp. Studies in Society and History*, VII (1964/5), 461–80; I. Hofman, *Studien zum meroitischen Königtum*, Brussels 1971. On Greek views of the Meroitic monarchy in the Hellenistic-Roman age, see J. Desanges, *BIFAO* LXVI (1968), 89–104.

21,1. τῷ βασιλέϊ: the king of Meroe in the time of Cambyses was Amani-Nataki-Lebte, according to the chronology of F. Hintze, *Studien zur meroitischen Chronologie*, Berlin 1959, pp. 22 ff. (see note on chs. 17–25).

2. ἀληθέα... δίκαιος: appropriate terms for one who represents an utopically just people. Cambyses, always struggling against the Lie, is here accused of fraud (cf. 22,1 and 3).   ἐπεθύμησε: a verb loaded with moralistic warnings, cf. 120,1 and 4; 127,1; 134,5. For the criticism of Persian expansionism see Introduction, pp. 390 ff.

3. τόξον: the only Persian who will be able to bend this bow will be Smerdis (30,1). Through the symbolism of the bow Herodotus creates a moral connection

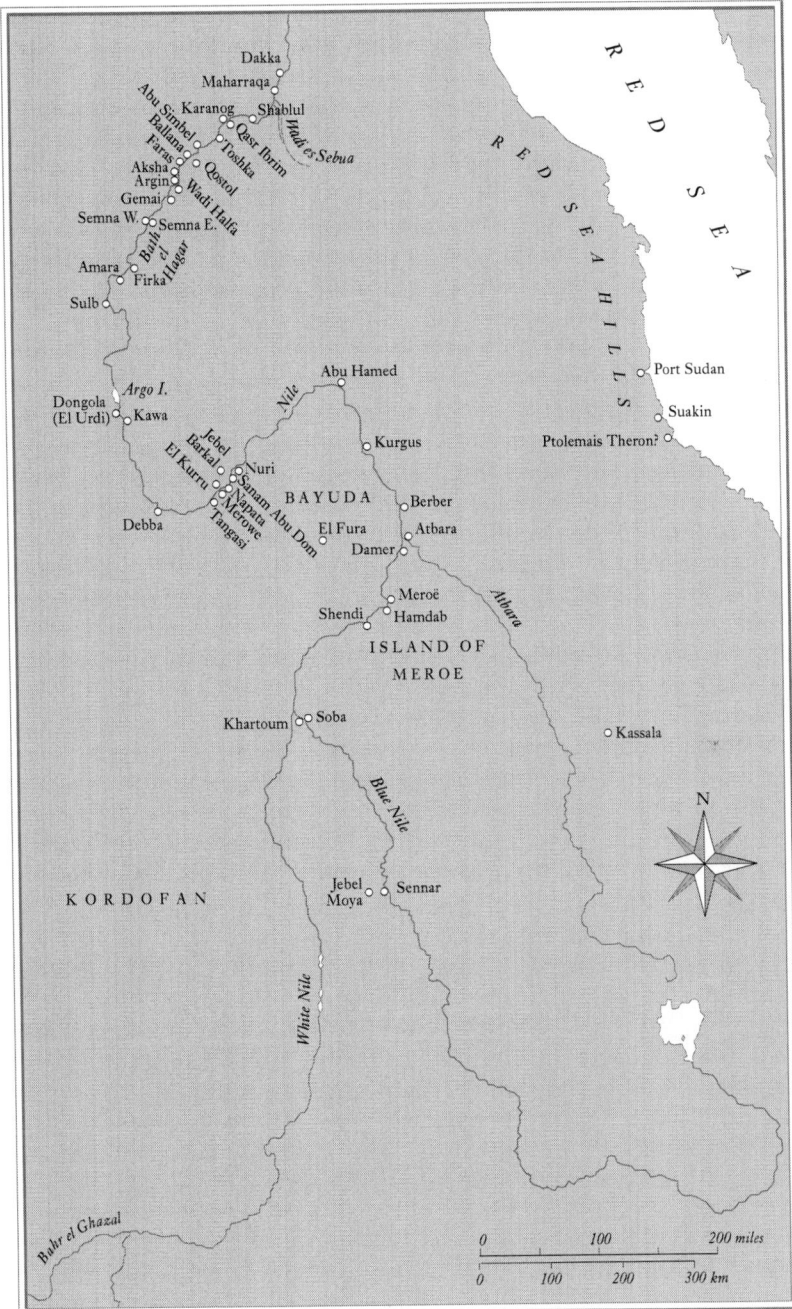

Map 32. Nubia

between the Ethiopian campaign, Cambyses' madness, and the problem of the succession to the throne. The motif of the bow in the Cambyses *logos* also recurs in the stories of Prexaspes (35,3), in that of Croesus (36,4), and in the killing of the false Smerdis (78,2–3). Cf. the story of Scythes and the bow of Heracles (IV 9,5 ff.); also the episode of the bow of the king of the Scythians and of Darius in the version of Ctesias, *FGrHist* 688 F 13 (17). The motif is Homeric: for the challenge of Odysseus' bow see *Od.* XIX 577–8, 586; XXI 75–6. It is also found in the popular novel; Aly, p. 85. The bow is, however, the symbol of Ethiopia both in Herodotus (VII 69,1), and in the Egyptian hieroglyphics and bas-reliefs of Meroe, where the bow is held in the hands of gods and of kings. For another ancient description of the Ethiopian bow see Strabo XVII 2,3.   οἳ οὐκ ἐπὶ νόον...: the historical Ethiopians of Nubia dominated Egypt during the XXVth Dynasty (cf. note on chs. 17–25).

22,1. δολεροὺς ... εἵματα: Greeks of the archaic age considered dresses and ointments as proverbially 'deceitful'; cf. Plutarch, *Mor.* 646b, and, with a variant, 270f; Clement of Alexandria, *Strom.* I 48,5, and *Paed.* II 65,1. Plutarch, *Mor.* 863e, qualifies with this motto the deceitfulness of the entire work of Herodotus. The real message intended by the sending of the purple robe seems to have been at most the assertion of Cambyses' monarchic power over the Ethiopians (the sending is probably related to a ceremonial request of 'earth and water' by the Great King).

2. πέδας: fetters are a symbol of slavery (20,1). For the golden chains see 23,4; 130,4.

3. μύρον: cf. 112.   τὴν ποίησιν: palm wine (cf. II 86,4) is a sugary juice extracted from the inflorescence of some palms (especially the *Arenga saccharifera*) of India, Malaya, and northern Africa; the juice, once fermented, is similar to wine. For date wine in Babylon see I 193,4.

4. ὀγδώκοντα δὲ ἔτεα: 'typical' figure for indicating a long period of time, more than the ideal length of a man's life, which is seventy years (I 32,2 with note).

23,1. ἐς εἴκοσί τε καὶ ἑκατόν: cf. the age of Arganthonius, in the Far West, who lived for 120 years and reigned for eighty (I 163,2). One hundred and twenty years—three generations of forty; cf. Nestor's age in *Il.* I 250–2—represent the maximum limit of a human life also in the Old Testament (e.g. Gen. 6: 3). Cf. the observation of Valerius Maximus VIII 13 *ext.* 5. κρέα ἑφθὰ καὶ πόμα γάλα: cf. Strabo XVII 2,2. On the meats of the Ethiopians cf. note on 18. For the ancients, the 'natural' diet was composed, for obvious reasons, of blood and milk (cf. I 216,3–4). On millet and barley in Ethiopia: Strabo XVII 2,2; Pliny, *NH* XVIII 100. On diet and longevity cf. Lucian, *Macrobii.*

2. κρήνην: cf., following Herodotus, Pomponius Mela III 88. According to Ctesias, *FGrHist* 688 F 1,11 (α'–γ'), the cinnabar-red water of this spring caused madness; cf. Philon (Hellenistic writer of *Aethiopica*), *FGrHist* 670 F 1; also, with more detail, Diod. II 14,4. Some modern scholars have hypothesized the existence of an oil-well; however, we have here a purely legendary element rationalized by Herodotus; it is perhaps of Homeric origin: see in *Od.* III 1–2 the περικαλλέα λίμνην that the sun leaves before rising in the sky.

3. οἷόν τ' εἶναι: see R. Neuberger-Donath, *Hermes*, CX (1982), 364. εἴ σφί...λέγεται: a typical Herodotean formula for expressing distance and scepticism.

4. ἐν πέδῃσι χρυσέῃσι: gold—which in developed societies is a symbol of wealth, greed, and arrogance—is less valuable than copper, or worth the same as terra-cotta (Tacitus, *Germ.* 5,4), or iron (Heliodorus, *Aethiopica* 9,1), in the utopian world where humanity lives in a state of nature. The Ethiopians, when subjects of the Persian empire, offered the Great King gifts of gold. Egypt, besides Aswan and Nubia, was famous in the ancient world for its gold-mines, as (generally for the same reason) were the outermost parts of the world; cf. on the gold of India, III 98 ff.; on that of the Arimaspians, 116,1. The gold-mines of the areas of Coptos, Wawat, and especially the Nilotic area between Wadi Halfa and Dongola are actually rather modest, and it seems that in the late 6th cent. the extraction and washing of gold there were in decline; see J. Vercoutter, *Kush*, VII (1959), 120–53. Herodotus does not allude at all to gold as an aim of Cambyses' campaign; cf., however, 97,3.   ὁ χαλκὸς: there are no copper-mines in Nubia; the working of iron only developed at Meroe from the 4th cent. BC; cf. VII 69,1; see D. Williams, in L. A. Thompson and J. Ferguson (eds.), *Africa in Classical Antiquity*, Ibadan 1969, pp. 62–80.

24,1. θήκας: Diodorus (II 15,1), evidently paraphrasing Ctesias, attributes to Herodotus the information that the Ethiopians poured glass around the mummy, and that the glazed mummy was then placed on a pillar. Herodotus, however, offers no such details. Ctesias asserts that the mummy was placed inside an effigy of the dead person, made of gold, silver, or terracotta according to social class, and then glazed; see Ctesias, *FGrHist* 688 F 1 b (15); cf. Diod. III 9,3; Strabo XVII 2,3.   ἐξ ὑάλου: ὕαλος can here indicate a sort of naturally transparent crystal, meltable and plastic; or natron (λίτρον), well known to Herodotus in relation to the Egyptian technique of mummification (II 86,5, and note), and with which glass objects were produced in Egypt from the 2nd millennium. Archaeology has not yet confirmed Herodotus' description, which does not seem totally imaginary, but rather slightly fanciful. In Meroe, as in Egypt, mummies were deposited in stone or wooden sarcophagi. Knowledge of Egyptian cultural influence on the funeral customs of Nubia emerges from this chapter (despite what is said at 20,2, with note).

25,1. αὐτίκα ὁ Καμβύσης...: in this dramatic chapter—paraphrased and extended by Seneca, *De Ira* III 20,2–4; see M. Giacchero, *Sandalion*, III (1980), 188—Herodotus traces the horrifying events of Cambyses' mad campaign in Ethiopia and his catastrophic retreat. The historical core of the story must be a Persian attempt to march south through the desert of Nubia, probably against Napata and Meroe (see note on 25,4). However, no confirmation of a similar attempt, datable to 524/3 BC, exists either in Egyptian or in Nubian sources. The inscription of Nastasen, found in Napata, which records a victorious campaign against a certain *Kmbswdn* or *Hmbswtn* north of Napata, was once thought to relate to Cambyses' failed campaign, but is currently dated much later, in the late 4th cent.; for an English translation, T. Eide, T. Hägg, R. Holton Pierce, and L. Török (eds.), *Fontes Historiae Nubiorum* II, Bergen 1996, Text 84. A demotic papyrus of Elephantine (Pap. Berol. 13615), dated April 529 BC, contains a list of persons or troops dispatched to Ethiopia; see W. Erichsen, *Klio*, XXXIV (1942), 56–61; Kienitz, pp. 129 f.; its date, however, does not correspond to the period during which Cambyses was in Egypt. Some modern scholars nevertheless believe in the historicity of a failed Persian attack against Napata and Meroe, especially on the basis of evidence derived from Greek sources, though late and of little value, on Cambyses the 'founder' of Meroe: Agatharchides of Cnidus, *FGrHist* 86 F 19 (33,1); Lucius Ampelius 13,2 Assmann; cf. Strabo XVII 1,5; Josephus, *Ant. Iud.* II 249; and on the basis of place-names such as Καμβύσου ταμιεῖα (Ptolemy, IV 7), *forum Cambusis* (Pliny, *NH* VI 181), and others (there is a site named *Kabushija*, 4 km. north of Meroe). The hypothesis that the transfer of the 'capital' of Nubia from Napata to Meroe (see note on chs. 17–25) must have been result of Cambyses' campaign, has been abandoned in favour of a new hypothesis that postulates a long process of transfer, begun in the early 6th cent. Cf. S. M. Burstein, *J. Soc. for the Study of Egyptian Antiquities*, XI (1981), 1–5. Cambyses joined the respectable list of the invaders of Ethiopia who had failed in their attempt, together with Dionysus, Heracles, and Semiramis; see Diod. III 3,1.   ὀργὴν: the fateful and arrogant anger of oriental monarchs or Greek tyrants (cf. I 73,4; 141,4; 156,2; III 52,3–4), or of other despotic persons (I 61,2; III 131,1). For Cambyses, cf. 35,1. On Cambyses' sardonic laughter see 29,1 with note.   οὔτε παρασκευὴν σίτου: the information contradicts not only the detailed account of the exploration and espionage (chs. 20–4), but also that of the preparations of Cambyses for the crossing of the desert (9).   ἐς τὰ ἔσχατα γῆς: ch. 98–116 of Book III are dedicated to the outermost borders of the world (Arabia, Ethiopia, India, Western and Central Europe). Darius also failed in his campaign to the outermost borders of the world: see IV 134–43; VII 10a, 2 ff. Egyptian 'nationalistic' propaganda of the 5th cent. juxtaposed the failures of the Persian kings to the success of Sesostris, the ideal pharaoh, who had also conquered Ethiopia and Scythia; see II 103,1; 110.

2. ἐμμανής τε ἐὼν καὶ οὐ φρενήρης: cf. 30,1; 35,4. The first explicit mention of Cambyses' madness (ch. 33); see R. Vignolo Munson, *Arethusa*, XXIV (1991), 43–65. The word φρενήρης also recurs in relation to two Spartans: King Cleomenes, contemporary of Cambyses (V 42,1) and Amompharetus, the fanatic commander who refuses the order of retreat in the battle of Plataea (IX 53–5).   Ἑλλήνων: Herodotus stresses the fact that the Greeks did not participate in the Ethiopian campaign.

3. ἐξανδραποδισαμένους: can be understood in the general sense of 'to subdue' (cf. I 66,3; VI 18) or in that of 'to deport in mass' (cf. I 155,1; 156,2; 161; VI 9,4; 94,2; VIII 126,2). The ἀνδράποδα are the prisoners-of-war (129,3 with note; cf. 125,3). For ἀνδραποδίζω see 59,3. On the Persian deportations see notes on 14,1; 93,2; and 149,1.

4. τὸ πέμπτον μέρος: an expression that indicates a small part of the whole. Supposing that the aim of the campaign was Meroe, the distance along the Nile from Elephantine is about 1,600 km., equivalent to about 56 days' march (3 schoeni = 180 stadia = 32 km. per day: see II 29, with Lloyd, *Commentary 1–98*, pp. 115 ff.). The fifth part, if taken literally, would be about 300 km.; the army, in other words, had not yet proceeded beyond Wadi Halfa, on the Second Cataract. It is presumed that Cambyses abandoned the Nile route at this point or at Korosko, in order to pursue a direct route towards Napata or Abu Hamed and Meroe, across the desert between the areas of the gold-mines. Strabo (XVII 1,54), however, locates the disaster in the 'dunes' north of Premnis (Wadi Halfa?). See R. C. C. Law, *CHA* II, pp. 98 f.

5. ἐγνωσιμάχεε: cf. VII 130,2; VIII 29,1, and see the clear definition of the word in the Λέξεις and in the scholia to Herodotus: γνωσιμαχεῖν τὸ γνῶναι τὴν ἑαυτοῦ ἀσθένειαν τήν τε τῶν ἐναντίων ἰσχύν). For this and other examples of judgement after the event see N. Demand, *AJPh* CVIII (1987), 7 (cf. also III 55,1).

6. ἐς τὴν ψάμμον: the sandstorm in Strabo (XVII 1,54) is perhaps borrowed from the story of the expedition against the Ammonians (26,3). Herodotus does not mention at all the problem of water for the crossing of this desert; it is otherwise in ch. 9.

7. ἀλληλοφαγίην: the hunger of the Persian soldiers is perhaps contrasted with the fabulous abundance of the 'Table of the Sun'; cf. Balcer, p. 85. For the motif of cannibalism in Persian campaigns, cf. Diod. XVII 81.

26,1. ἐπ' Ἀμμωνίους: the aim of this expedition against the Ammonians seems to be the placing of garrisons or military colonies in the oases scattered along the caravan route; it is easier to reach Sîwa from the Mediterranean coast or from Fayûm than from Thebes. The Ammonians were the inhabitants of the oasis of Sîwa, near the modern border between Egypt and Libya; they were named after the famous temple and oracle of Ammon. According to Herodotus (II 42,4) they were a mixed population of Egyptians and 'Ethiopians'; in fact they were Negroes, or rather Libyans of the desert. A very independent 'king' ruled over them (II 32,1). The archaeological remains (the palace and the temple of the oracle on the majestic fortress of Aghurmi; another temple of Ammon at Umm U-baydah; their tombs) and ancient descriptions (Hdt. IV 181,2–4; Diod. XVII 50; Curtius Rufus IV 7,16–24) suggest an Egyptian culture, or a Libyan influenced by Egyptian. See A. Fakhry, *The Oases of Egypt*, I. *Siwa Oasis*, Cairo 1973; J. Osing, *LdÄ* V 1984, coll. 865–8. The god Ammon (Amon, Haman?; against the modern identification of Ba'al Ḥammon and Zeus Ammon, see E. Lipinski in *Studia Phoenicia*, IV, Namur 1986, pp. 307–22) was already worshipped at Sîwa in the time of Amasis. Herodotus relates an ancient consultation of the oracle by 'autonomist' Egyptians (II 18,2–3); apparently he was consulted by Croesus (I 46,3), at that time an ally of Amasis. After the Persian conquest the god of Sîwa was introduced into the Greek world; first to the inhabitants of Cyrene, who identified him with Zeus; then also to the Greeks of the motherland, especially in the Peloponnese. Pindar (*Pyth.* 4,25 ff.) is said to have composed a hymn for the

Ammonians, still legible on a stele in the 2nd cent. AD; see Paus. IX 16,1. The oracle was consulted by the delegates of Cimon in 451 BC and by the Athenians in 415, before the Sicilian expedition. Perhaps Lysander tried to bribe it; see C. J. Classen, *Historia*, VIII (1959), 349–55. But it was the famous visit of Alexander the Great, in 331 BC, which assured to the oracle of Ammon a place of honour in literature and cultural history. The Libyan desert, with its oases between el-Kharga and Sîwa, and caravan routes between Egypt and Cyrene (J. Lectant, *BIFAO* XLIX (1950), 193–253; Desanges, *Recherches*, pp. 185–8), was under Persian control at least from 505 BC (IV 200–4). The sources of Herodotus on this event are probably Samian (acquired at Samos or Naucratis rather than at el-Kharga) or from Cyrene; for the local Ammonian tradition see note on 26,3. In general, Chamoux, pp. 64–6, 331–9; Parke, *Oracles of Zeus*, pp. 194 ff.; Lloyd, *Commentary 1–98*, pp. 195–200, with bibl.; Bosworth, pp. 269 ff.; V. Brouquier-Reddé, *Temples et cultes de Tripolitaine*, Paris 1992, pp. 255–65. Ὄασιν: name of Egyptian origin (*wḥ3t* or *uhat*, 'cauldron'); see A. G. McGready, *Glotta*, XLVI (1968), 249. According to Strabo (II 5,33; XVII 1,5; cf. also Stephanus of Byzantium, s.v. Αὔασις), the Egyptian word was used as a common name for oasis in general; the use was in practice limited to the oases of the Libyan desert to the west of the Nile. These oases were important caravan stations, with inhabited centres, temples, military bases, and frontier zones. In the Ptolemaic age there were seven, three of which belonged to Egypt; see Strabo XVII 1,42. Ptolemy (IV, 5,15) distinguishes between a 'Great Oasis' and a 'Small Oasis'. The Oasis mentioned in this chapter is generally identified with el-Kharga (Egyptian *Knmt*), about 200 km. west of Thebes; the distance equals the 7 days' march mentioned by Herodotus (26,1) if the average is 30 km. a day; but 7 is a symbolic number. The 'first oasis' of Strabo (XVII 1,42) is 7 days away from Abydos, about 90 km. north-west of Thebes. This oasis, rich in water and vineyards, was an inhabited centre since very ancient times; in the main site, Hibis, was a temple of Ammon, built under Darius. It flourished in Achaemenid times thanks to the caravan trade. In Roman imperial times it was used as a place of exile (*in Oasin relegare*: see J. Schwartz, *Mélanges A. Piganiol*, III, Paris 1966, pp. 1481–8). From el-Kharga to Sîwa the distance is about 650 km; therefore not 3 days' march, as perhaps implied by Herodotus in IV 181,2. See H. Kees, *RE* XVII 2 (1937), coll. 1681–6. For a different identification (el-Bahriya) see Chamoux, pp. 64 f. Cf. G. Wagner, *Les Oasis d'Égypte à l'époque grecque, romaine et byzantine, d'après les documents grecs*, Cairo 1987. Σάμιοι: probably an authentic detail, perhaps derived from Samos or Naucratis. It refers most probably to a garrison-colony of Samian veterans, installed in Oasis perhaps by Psammetichus or Amasis.   τῆς Αἰσχριωνίης φυλῆς: nothing of significance can be said of the Aeschrionian tribe, apart from the fact that Aeschrion is a personal name also common in Samos. See Shipley, p. 106 and n. 19 with bibl. The word φυλή can mean a tribe, a military unit based on the tribe (cf. VI, 1), or a clan or *genos* (cf. IV 149,111).   Μακάρων νῆσοι: the plural indicates poetic traditionalism: it is possible, though, that the metaphor adopted by the Samians could refer also to other 'islands of the desert';

Chares of Mytilene, in the 4th cent. BC, calls the oasis of Sîwa 'the island of Ammon' (Ἄμμωνος νῆσος, *FGrHist* 125 F 8). The origin of the famous eschatological utopia of the 'Islands of the Blessed' was Homer's 'Elysian Field', where Rhadamanthys and Menelaus lived eternal life (*Od.* IV 563–4). The Elysian Field is not necessarily an 'island', either in the sea or the desert; however, it was soon confused or identified with the 'Islands of the Blessed', mentioned for the first time by Hesiod (*Op.* 171) and traditionally located in the Atlantic; they were also called the Hesperides, and eventually identified with the Canary Isles, known to the Phoenicians. They were eternally inhabited by privileged heroes (e.g. Achilles and Diomedes) abducted by the gods. See A. Schulten, *RE* XXVII 1, 1928, coll. 628–32; V. Manfredi, *Le isole fortunate. Topografia di un mito*, Rome 1993. The Egyptians also had their Elysian Field, in the shape of green 'islands', fresh, fertile, and with enormous plants, where the souls of the 'justified' lived. Places like Abydos and el-Kharga, which were also centres of the cult of Osiris, could have been the origin of this belief. Cf. the 'Blessed Villages' in Hyrcania in Diod. XVII 75,4–7 and Curtius Rufus VI 4,21–2.

3. λέγεται...: cf. Justin I 9,3; Seneca, *Nat. Quaest.* II 30,2 on which M. Giacchero, *Sandalion*, III (1980), 178–9; Plutarch, *Alex.* 26,12. Strabo XVII 1,54, inserts this same episode in the story of the Ethiopian campaign. It is an official miracle version spread by Ammon's priests and also known in Egypt and in Cyrene in Herodotus' time; cf. the miraculous story of Delphi in VIII 36–9. Today there are many who credit this version with belief, citing even recent examples of caravans swallowed up by sands; see the information quoted by Balcer, p. 84, n. 44.   **καὶ τάδε:** καί is not superfluous: the Ammonians are mentioned as a direct and as an intermediate source in the previous para. also; for similar formulae cf. 87 and 108,1.

27–9. Killing an Apis bull was for the Egyptians the greatest possible sacrilege. The same sacrilege was ascribed to Artaxerxes Ochos, the second Persian conqueror of Egypt in 342 BC. Darius' respectful behaviour was contrasted with that of Cambyses (Polyaenus VII 11,7) as was Alexander's to that of Artaxerxes (Bosworth, p. 262). The stele and the sarcophagi found by A. Mariette west of Memphis in the hypogeum of Saqqara, where the mummies of the sacred oxen were deposited (plan of the hypogeum in J. Vercoutter, *Bibl. de l' École Pratique des Hautes Études*, CCCXVI, Paris 1962, p. 28), show that an Apis born, as it seems, in the twenty-seventh year of Amasis (543 BC), was deposited with the usual rites in November 524. The new pharaoh Cambyses (Posener, no. 4) dedicated his sumptuous granite sarcophagus, following a practice begun under Amasis; on the stele (Posener, no. 3) the king (?) is pictured on his knees, as if worshipping. It is unthinkable that this Apis was killed by Cambyses or that it was buried in secret; but cf. 29,3. The successor, born in May 525, at the time of the Persian conquest, died naturally in the fourth year of Darius (518/7 BC), when it was more than 8 years old (Posener, no. 5). Therefore Cambyses did not kill this one either. Since the coexistence of two Apises is theologically unacceptable (as there cannot exist simultaneously two incarnations of Ptah), it is supposed that the Apis buried in November 524 had died before the birth of its successor, i.e. in the spring of 525. Cambyses perhaps arrived in Memphis during the feasts of the birth or enthronement of the new Apis: if so, not on his return from Ethiopia as Herodotus affirms, but shortly after the conquest of Memphis itself; in Memphis he saw to the burial of the dead Apis, which strangely took place more than a year after its death; the irregularity can be explained by the general disorder that the Persian conquest created in Egypt. Today it is agreed by most scholars that the whole episode of the killing of Apis narrated by Herodotus is the fruit of propaganda hostile to Cambyses, and lacks historical basis. Cf. Justin I 9,2; Plutarch, *Mor.* 368f.; Clement of Alexandria, *Protr.* IV 52,6. To the bibl. quoted in note on 1,1 add L. Depuydt, *JNES* LIV (1995), 119–26.

27,1. ἐφάνη . . . καλέουσι: Apis (Ḥpw), the sacred bull of Memphis, incarnation of Ptah, became especially important under the XXVIth Dynasty. The bull, which was identified by certain signs (28,3), was enthroned in a court reserved to him (called Apieion by the Greeks; see Lloyd, note on II 153 and *Commentary 99–182*, pp. 135–6), where he lived an average of about seventeen to nineteen years until his death. After a period of mourning of seventy days he was mummified and buried in the hypogeum of Saqqara ('Serapeum'). See Lloyd, *Commentary 1–98*, pp. 171 f. with bibl.; J. Vercoutter, *LdÄ* I 1975, coll. 338–50; for photographs E. Winter, *Der Apiskult im alten Aegypten*, Mainz 1978. The Greeks identified Apis with Epaphus, the black son of Zeus and Io, herself in the myth first transformed into a cow, and finally restored to her human shape and settled in Canopus in Egypt: cf. II 41,2. Aeschylus, *Prom.* 850–1, suggests an etymology from ἀφή, divine 'touch'; cf. Plutarch, *Mor.* 718b, and note on 28,3. See Sabri Kolta, pp. 16–23; cf. Aesch. *Suppl.* 313–15 (Epaphus so called ἐκ τοῦ ἐφάπτεσθαι by Zeus ἐφάπτωρ); see R. D. Murray, Jr., *The Motif of Io in Aeschylus' Suppliants*, Princeton 1958, pp. 32–7.
2. τοὺς ἐπιτρόπους: the execution of these 'prefects' is the first act of sacrilegious violence attributed to Cambyses.

28,2. οἵη τε γίνεται: cf. note on 23,3.   σέλας ἐκ τοῦ οὐρανοῦ: cf. Aelian, *Nat. An.* XI 10. It was a 'touch' of the moon according to Plutarch, *Mor.* 718b. The mother of Apis lived in a court in front of the Apieion; after her death she was identified with Isis. See H. S. Smith, *Revue d'Égyptologie*, XXIV (1972), 176–87; *Bull. de la Soc. Française d'Égyptologie*, LXX–LXXI (1974), 11–27; and in A. B. Lloyd (ed.), *Studies in Pharaonic Religion and Society in Honour of J. G. Griffiths*, London 1992, pp. 201–25.
3. μόσχος . . . κάνθαρον: cf. II 38; see the variants of Strabo XVII 1,31; Pliny, *NH* VIII 184; Eusebius, *Prap. Evang.* III 13. According to Aelian, *Nat. An.* XI 10, the signs were twenty-nine and among other things symbolized the stars.

29,1. ὑπομαργότερος: cf. 145,1; VI 75,1.   ἐγχειρίδιον: a dagger or a short sword, that the Greeks in Herodotus never use; it is the weapon of Mithras Tauroctonos in Mithraic iconography of the Hellenistic-Roman age.   μηρόν: the wound on the thigh is common in Herodotus; for Cambyses see 64,3; 66,2; for others see 78,2; VI 5,2; 75,3; 134,2; 136,2–3; cf. Ctesias, *FGrHist*

688 F 14 (37) and (40); Plutarch, *Alex.* 20,8–9 etc. In mythology, e.g. Anceus was wounded on the thigh by the Caledonian boar (Pherecydes, *FGrHist* 3 F 36). Maybe, in the case of Apis, the wound has also a symbolic meaning, in addition to the one, evident in this chapter, of moral link between sin (Apis' wound on the thigh) and punishment (Cambyses' death by a wound on the thigh). In Mithraic iconography the bull's throat is slit.　　γελάσας: in Herodotus laughter and rage (cf. 25,1) are prerogatives of kings and great personalities, especially those who have lost their sanity or sense of their proper limits; laughter is a sign of *hybris*, a sardonic laughter that foreshadows catastrophe. See D. Lateiner, *TAPhA* CVII (1977), 173–82. The laughter of the king of the Ethiopians (22,2) is different. κακαὶ κεφαλαί: cf. Dickey, pp. 165–74; 289.

2. ἔναιμοί τε καὶ σαρκώδεες: it seems like a criticism of the zoomorphism and anthropomorphism of popular idolatry; the words, however, evoke the struggle of Mazdaism against the Lie, the invectives of the biblical prophets, and the satires of Greek 'atheists' (e.g. of Xenophanes, frs. 18–19 Gentili Prato = 14–15 DK).

3. λάθρῃ: see the versions of Plutarch, *Mor.* 355c and 368f, on Cambyses and Artaxerxes.

30,1. ἐμάνη...φρενήρης: cf. 25,2. The connection (here ascribed to the Egyptians) between the death of Apis and Cambyses' madness actually has a precise moral and literary function in the Herodotean 'biography' of the king. However, see the rationalistic interpretation at ch. 33.　　ἐξεργάσατο: according to the Bisitun inscription (see App. I, §10), Bardiya, the brother of Cambyses, was killed unbeknown to the people before the Egyptian campaign (cf. 63,2 with note). The murder could thus be explained by the disorders that erupted after the death of Cyrus over his succession.　　Σμέρδιν: *Bardiya* Old Persian, *Bar-zi-ia* Akkadian, *Bir-ti-ya* Elamite; in Greek Μάρδος (Aesch. *Pers.* 774) which also is the name of a Persian tribe (I 125,4), Μερδία (scholion to Aesch. *Pers.* 776 Dähnhardt) or Σμέρδις, a well-known Greek name. For the initial sigma cf. e.g. the case of (σ)μικρός; see Balcer, p. 36, n. 56 and p. 57. In Justin I 9,5 the name is *Mergis*. According to Xenophon, *Cyr.* VIII 7,11, and Ctesias, *FGrHist* 688 F 9 (8), the name of Cambyses' brother was respectively Tanaoxares or Tanyoxardes. ἐόντα πατρὸς...τῆς αὐτῆς: cf. the formula of the Babylonian text of Bisitun (§10 Voigtlander; see App. I, p. 530) and of Xenophon, *Anab.* III 1,17. The Old Persian text inverts the order: *hamātā hamapitā*: see App. I, §10; cf. the Elamite text (German translation of W. Hinz, *AMI* VII (1974), 124). On the death of Cambyses' brother see the very different versions of Ctesias, *FGrHist* 688 F 13 (11–12), and of Justin I 9,4–10, which partly contaminate various material from Herodotus on the 'true' and 'false' Smerdis.　　τόξον: cf. 21,3 with note.

2. ὄψιν: cf. 64,1; 65,2; see also Justin I 9,4. A prophetic dream, typical in Herodotus, of the fate of a dynasty, like the dreams of Astyages (I 107–8) and of Cyrus (I 209,1). It announces to the reader the following events. On the function of dreams and of portents in Herodotus see General Introduction, pp. 42 ff.; on the dream of Cambyses cf. also Huber, pp. 10 ff. For other dreams in Book III cf. 124; 149.　　ἄγγελον...ψαύσειε: the dream will be fulfilled in

62,1. The head touching the sky is a symbolic image in oriental monarchies, Egyptian (the king supports the sky: Shu, Seti I, Tarhaqa, and others) and Persian (see M. Mallowan, *CHI*, pp. 392 ff.; M. C. Root, *The King and Kingship in Achaemenid Art*, *AI* XIX 1979, esp. pp. 131–61 and 300–8); however, it also occurs in Greek mythology: Atlas supports the sky, Typho (cf. 5,3 and note) touches the stars; for the expression 'to touch the sky' in archaic Greek literature see Sappho, fr. 52 Voigt ψαύην δ' οὐ δοκίμωμ' ὀράνω), and it is common in popular folk-tales of all times and countries (bibl. in Thompson, *Motif-Index*, F 531 and 531.1.4.1).

3. *Πρηξάσπεα*: a compound noun of *aspa-*, in Median 'horse'; see O. K. Armayor, *AncW* I (1978), 150. On this remarkable character see chs. 34–5, 62–3, 74–5; cf. the Introduction, p. 391. With Prexaspes, Herodotus delineates a figure of a noble and tragic friend, faithful to the end. On Prexaspes' story and its probable oriental origin, cf. A. Szabo, *AAntHung* I (1951–2), 76–80. For another Prexaspes, perhaps the nephew of Cambyses' friend, cf. VII 97.   *ἀναβὰς ἐς Σοῦσα*: for the Greeks of the Asia Minor coast the journey to Susa was an 'ascent' (ἀνάβασις) and the journey in the opposite sense was a 'descent' (κατάβασις, cf. 136,1). In the Bible one 'goes up' from Egypt to Syria and 'goes down' in the opposite direction: this usage perhaps corresponds well to the case of Prexaspes and maybe also to that of Syloson (140,1).   *ἐπ' ἄγρην*: cf. the story of Atys son of Croesus in I 43; for a hunting accident in Book III see 129,1.   *ἐς τὴν Ἐρυθρὴν θάλασσαν*: evidently Herodotus does not intend to say that Smerdis was relegated to the islands of the Persian Gulf (93,2), as some modern scholars interpret it (e.g. Marquart II, p. 145; E. Herzfeld, *AMI* V (1933), 131).

31,1. *τὴν ἀδελφεὴν*: see the versions of Ctesias, *FGrHist* 688 F 13 (14), and of Strabo XVII 1,5. For the other daughters of Cyrus see 68,4–5 and 88,2. According to Strabo (loc. cit.) a sister and wife of Cambyses was named Meroe; cf. Josephus, *Ant. Iud.* II 249.

2. *ἔγημε...*: Cambyses apparently was the first Achaemenid king to marry his sister. Herodotus certainly knew that in his time such marriages were common, although he did not know how old this custom actually was in the royal houses of the ancient East. Other examples of the Achaemenid period are those of Darius II and Parysatis; Artaxerxes II and one (or two: Plutarch, *Artax.* 23,3–4) of his daughters; the satrap Terituchmes and his sister (Ctesias, *FGrHist* 688 F 13 (53)); the satrap Sisimithres and his mother (Curtius Rufus VIII 2,19). Xanthus of Lydia, *FGrHist* 765 F 31, knew that the Magi consorted with their mothers; cf. Strabo XV 3,20. In the *Avesta*, marriage between blood-relatives (*hvaētvadāθa*) is much praised; in Sassanid Persia it was institutionalized definitively in the royal family and in the aristocracy. Here Herodotus does not mean that marriage between blood-relatives became 'legal' in Persia from Cambyses onwards; on the contrary, from the related anecdote it may be deduced that what is exceptionally allowed to the king is nevertheless forbidden for all others. Besides, the anecdote of the royal judges is not unlike a Greek sophistic argument. See O. Bucci, *Ricerche intorno ad alcune forme di matrimonio nella esperienza giuridica delle*

genti iraniche, Rome 1980, pp. 53–81; C. Heerenschmidt, *AH* II (1987), 56–7. The Greeks ascribed only to the gods the 'sacred marriage' (ἱερὸς γάμος) between brother and sister (e.g. Zeus and Hera). Attic law forbade marriage between uterine siblings; the Persian custom was therefore cited by Greeks to illustrate the relativism of human customs (cf. *Dissoi logoi* II 15 Robinson). τοὺς βασιληίους ... δικαστάς: cf. 14,5; V 25,1–2 (with Diod. XV 10,1); VII 194,1. Herodotus considered these 'judges' as also jurisconsults and interpreters of the law. See O. Bucci, *RIDA* XXII (1975), 11–25; *L' impero persiano come ordinamento giuridico sovrannazionale*, I, Rome 1984, pp. 43–8. νόμος: would correspond here to the Persian *dātā*, 'law' in general, and in particular the traditional 'law of the Medes and Persians', 'immutable' according to Dan. 6: 8 and 15.

4. ὑπεκρίνοντο: in the sense of 'giving a response', 'pronouncing a judgement', cf. 46,1–2; 53,5; 119,4; 121,2; see G. K. H. Ley, *Philologus*, CXXVII (1983), 14–20. 6. ἄλλην ἀδελφεήν: i.e. Atossa.

32,1. διξὸς ... λόγος: in the sense of 'double version', cf. IX 74,1. Elsewhere in Herodotus διξοί indicates 'double' things, 'two types' of things, or even simply 'two'. For the citation of 'double' versions or of several versions in Herodotus, cf. note on 1,5. Here in paras. 1–2 a Greek version is cited and in paras. 3–4 an Egyptian one, but strangely no Persian version.

2. ἥδεσθαι θεώμενον ...: the king looks and enjoys himself, his sister listens thoughtfully; see D. Konstan, *Arethusa*, XX (1987), 69 and n. 21. Whereas the laughter of the Herodotean kings and tyrants is almost always an inauspicious sign (cf. note on 29,1), their 'enjoyment', or pleasure, can also be a sign of humanity and sometimes foreshadows acts of clemency; see 34,5; 42,2; 119,7; 130,4.   οὐκ εἴη ὁ τιμωρήσων: cf. 65,5; also the words of Cyrus to his sons in Xenophon, *Cyr.* VIII 7,14 ff.

3. τὸ ἔπος: cf. note on 1,5.   θρίδακα: the Egyptian origin of this version could perhaps be attested by the fact that lettuce is important in the Egyptian diet; see in this sense L. Keimer, *BIE* XXXVI (1953–4), 464–5. In Greek mythology lettuce is connected with the myth of the death of Adonis; see M. Detienne, *Les Jardins d'Adonis*, Paris 1972, pp. 130–8 and 229–41.

4. τὸν δὲ θυμωθέντα: cf. note on 25,2. The scene is repeated, not very differently, by Tacitus (*Ann.* XVI 6) concerning the death of Poppaea; cf. Suetonius, *Nero* 35,3; see E. Slijper, *Mnemosyne*, LVII (1929), 110. It seems that Cambyses actually died without offspring; cf. 66,2. Some modern historians, in an attempt to rehabilitate Cambyses, consider this episode a tendentious falsification of an accident: the woman perhaps died in childbirth; see the bibl. in the note on 1,1.

33. εἴτε καὶ ἄλλως ...: Herodotus cannot decide between the theological and the scientific interpretation of Cambyses' madness. Some modern scholars ascribe his madness, not only to the epilepsy ('the sacred disease') that afflicted him since birth, but also to the alcoholism of the king and his father; others suggest a cerebral syphilis. See the review of A. Giusti, *Bilychnis*, XXXIII (1929), 181–96.

34,1. ἐξεμάνη ...: the sources of these episodes on the sick madness of Cambyses, up to ch. 36, look like a complex of hellenized Persian traditions, all hostile to Cambyses and reworked by Herodotus in a moralizing and didactic way. A topical problem of tyranny emerges from them: the problem of relations between the despot and his counsellors or his courtiers (Prexaspes, Croesus, the Persian nobles), which Herodotus had already highlighted in relation to Astyages and Harpagus (I 107–29). In the dialogues the contrast between madness and sanity, adulation and falsehood, 'freedom of speech' and truth, betrayal and faithfulness is emphasized. In the background is the morbid obsession of a king with no heirs, constantly suspicious of conspiracies to depose him. On these dialogues and on the characterization of Cambyses see Heni, pp. 129–32, with the *Exkursus*, pp. 151–4. The scene is used as an *exemplum* by Seneca, *De Ira* III 14,1–4, with amplifications in a moral vein; cf. M. Giacchero, *Sandalion*, III (1980), 183–5.   **τὰς ἀγγελίας:** cf. 77,2; I 114,2 and 120,2. He was a high court official of the greatest trustworthiness (30,3), not to be confused with the subordinate ἀγγελιηφόροι (cf. 118,2), least of all with simple porters (cf. 72,5). It is thought that Herodotus is here referring to the Persian *hazarapatis*; see Hesychius, s.v. ἀζαραπατεῖς· οἱ εἰσαγγελεῖς; ἀζαβαρίτης: Ctesias, *FGrHist* 688 F 15 (46). The Greeks also called him 'chiliarchos': he was the chief usher who announced and introduced the embassies received by the Great King, performing the duties of a vizier; he carried a bow, a sword, or the royal axe. See Marquart I, pp. 56–65; P. J. Junge, *Klio*, XXXIII (1940), 13 ff.; J. M. Cook, *CHI*, pp. 232–3. For the bureaucracy of the Persian court, which today can be better reconstructed from the Persepolis tablets, see R. T. Hallock, *CHI*, pp. 588–609 with bibl.   **οἰνοχόος:** another important official, of the greatest trustworthiness; cf. Xenophon, *Cyr* I 3,8–10, and Nicolaus of Damascus, *FGrHist* 90 F 66 (5; 23), on the ἐπιστάτης of the cupbearers at the court of the king of the Medians (Nicolaus probably uses Ctesias). On Nehemiah, cupbearer of Artaxerxes, see Neh. 2: 1 ff.; on the wine-pourers of the Scythian kings, Herod. IV 71,4; on the wine-pourers in Greek banquets, Athenaeus X 424e ff. It is possible that Prexaspes had another son, cf. note on 70,1.   **ὦ δέσποτα:** cf. Dickey, pp. 96–7.

2. φιλοινίη: not alcoholism, but love or devotion to wine. On this vice, typical of the Persians, cf. e.g. I 133,3–4. According to a recently revived hypothesis, it is *haoma* and not wine, ecstasy and not drunkenness; see, e.g. Hofmann–Vorbichler, pp. 96 ff. But Herodotus did not mean this. For the relation between undiluted wine and madness, cf. the case of Cleomenes in VI 84.

4. Κροίσου: see 14,11. Croesus returns to the scene in his old role as counsellor of the Great King. On Croesus as counsellor of Cyrus see I 88–9; 155–6; 207–8.   **κοῖός τις ... Κῦρον:** Herodotus constantly compares Cyrus and his Achaemenid successors: see esp. 160,1; cf. 75,1–2; 89,3; 134,1 (where the comparison is implicit); 152; 159,1; VII 2,3; 8α,1–2; 51,1. In this sense see also IX 122. The comparison is common in the Greek literature idealizing Cyrus: see e.g. Aesch. *Pers.* 759 ff., and Xen. *Cyr.* VIII 8.   **τελέσαι:** 'ut ad patris exemplar perveniat sive eum equiperet' according to Wesseling (cf. LJS, s.v. τελέω II 4); but

see the criticism of L. Weber, *RFIC* XV (1937), 380–1, who reads ταλάσαι, from
*τλάω, 'to resist', 'to be strong(er)' than the father.

5. κρίσιν: 'sentence', or authoritative 'answer'; elsewhere in Herodotus it means
'dispute' or 'judgement': V 5; VI 131,1; VII 26,2. For ἀνάκρισις see 53,2. The
unexpected, witty, and subtly ironic answer of Croesus delights Herodotus no less
than his Cambyses.

35,1. τούτων ... ἐπιμνησθέντα ...: the chapter can be read as a doublet of I 119
(the killing of Harpagus' son by Astyages), with which it was in fact sometimes
confused in antiquity. In the story of Cambyses' growing madness it has a similar
role. Nevertheless the differences should be stressed (Harpagus deserts, whereas
Prexaspes remains faithful), as well as the problem of truth in the story of
Cambyses (cf. Introduction, p. 391), which is absent from the story of Harpagus.
On the novelistic motif see Aly, pp. 86–8.

2. προθύροισι: here the vestibule or the antechamber, from which one entered the
audience hall; cf. ch. 140,1. The word is Homeric; for the entrance to the αὐλή or
to the μέγαρον see e.g. *Od.* I 103; XVIII 101; XX 355. In Homer the word can also
indicate the porch at the entrance to the palace: *Od.* IV 20; X 220.

3. γελάσαντα: cf. note to 29,1.   **περιχαρέα:** the same Herodotean term of ill
omen (Ch. C. Chiasson, *Hermes*, CXI (1983), 115–18) recurs also in relation to
Harpagus; cf. I 119,2; III 157,3.

4. τὸν θεόν: a nameless god, whom a Greek could call 'Apollo the Archer' and a
Persian 'Mithras'.

5. ἐπὶ κεφαλὴν: cf. 75,3 ('head-down', 'headlong'). The torture, which is depicted
by Herodotus' hostile source as an act of arbitrary cruelty, could also be interpreted as a form of propitiatory ritual sacrifice to chthonic divinities. This is
suggested by the number 12, which has a symbolic or mystical value. Cf. the seven
couples (VII 114,2; and I 86,2; these were also twelve according to Plutarch, *Mor.*
171d); nine couples (VII 114,1). The torture could also be a punishment or
revenge: Ctesias, *FGrHist* 688 F 15 (45) and (56).

36,1. μὴ πάντα ... ἐπίτρεπε: cf. VII 18,2.   **πρόνοον:** cf. Aeschylus, *Supp.*
969.   **προμηθίη:** the virtue of Prometheus, the 'Foreseeing'.

3. χρηστῶς: cf. IV 117. Here it is said with irony.   **Ἀράξην:** cf. I 207,3–7.

4. τὰ τόξα: the scene is reminiscent of that of Saul and David in 1 Sam. 18: 10–11.

6. Κροίσῳ: cf. I 118,9; VIII 118,4.

37,1. ὁ μὲν ... ἐξεμαίνετο ...: the list of the wrongdoings of Cambyses in Egypt
ends with two last impieties: the violation of the tombs and the mockery of the
images of Egyptian divinities. The short account of the facts is amplified by the
author's explanatory notes. Herodotus relates a very precisely defined local
tradition of Memphis. However, during his time the propaganda hostile to
Cambyses in Egypt extended his sacrileges to all the temples of the country and
even referred to absolute destructions and plunder. Udjahorrense of Sais (note on
16,1) had already mentioned a 'storm' that hit his people under Cambyses. An
Aramaic papyrus of Elephantine of 408 BC records that, when Cambyses arrived,
'the temples of the gods of Egypt were all destroyed, but no one damaged this

temple' (Cowley, nos. 30–1, pp. 108 ff.; P. Grelot, *Documents araméens d'Égypte*, Paris 1972, pp. 408 ff., n. 102); for the Jewish tradition hostile to Cambyses cf. Josephus, *Ant. Iud.* XI 21–6. See also the text used for rituals or conjurations for defence of Egypt in the temple of Osiris in Abydos (the text was copied in 361 BC; see the edn. of Schott (1929) and cf. E. Drioton, *Pages d' égyptologie*, Cairo 1957, pp. 307–27), in which Seth, god of confusion and profanator of temples, perhaps represents Cambyses. Late Greek sources describe fire and pillaging of temples also at Thebes and Heliopolis: Hecataeus of Abdera, *FGrHist* 264 F 25 (49,5); Diod. I 46,4–5; 95,4; Strabo XVII 1,27. On the other hand, the so called Demotic Chronicle (Bibl. Nat. no. 215, ed. by Spiegelberg, 1914; see Kienitz, pp. 136 ff.; J. H. Johnson, *Enchoria*, IV (1974), 1–14, and in H. J. Thissen and K. T. Zaurich (eds.), *Grammata demotika. Festschrift für E. Lüddeckens*, Würzburg 1984, pp. 107–24; P. Kaplony, *LdÄ* I 1975, coll. 1056–60), composed in the 3rd cent. BC, which contains on its obverse a series of historical oracles of a prophetic-nationalistic orientation on events posterior to 404 BC, reports, on the reverse of the papyrus, an edict of Cambyses drastically reducing the revenues of the sanctuaries and the provisions of animals (with three exceptions, among them the temple of Memphis); see bibl. in the note on 1,1. In any case, the reduction or even the abolition of revenues is not the same as destruction or pillage; it might be an economic or fiscal measure not related to impiety nor, on the contrary, to 'religious tolerance' opposed to the traditional Egyptian theocracy. Cambyses' edict could be a part of a plan of administrative reforms undertaken by the Persian king for the organization of the new satrapy. The most plausible modern theory suggests that such steps provoked the hatred of the Egyptian clergy and that this hatred originated the hostile propaganda, a source from which Herodotus drew information eighty years later. It cannot be excluded that the Egyptian propaganda obtained the approval of Darius' government during its years of great restoration and legislative work (cf. note on 91,2). Besides, fiscal measures which affected possessions of Egyptian temples were also ascribed to the pharaohs Cheops, Chephren, and Amasis (II 124–8; 174); later to Tachos ([Aristotle], *Oec.* II 1350b33), and to Artaxerxes Ochus (Diod. XVI 51,2). The sacrilegious behaviour attributed to Cambyses in Egypt is part of the wider problem of Achaemenid religious 'tolerance', the destruction of Greek temples, etc.; see on these problems P. Tozzi, *RSI* LXXXIX (1977), 18 ff.; O. Bucci, *Utrumque ius*, XII (1985), 231 f.; G. Firpo, *ASNP* XVI (1986), 331 ff.

2. ἐς τοῦ Ἡφαίστου...: the famous temple of Ptah, south of the royal palace of Memphis, founded, according to Herodotus (II 99,4), by Min, the first Egyptian king, and later enlarged and enriched by various pharaohs, from Moeris to Psammetichus (II 108,2; 110,1; 136,1; 141,1 and 6; 153). Setho, a priest of this sanctuary, became pharaoh (II 141,1). For an anecdote of Darius in this temple see II 110,2–3 with note.   κατεγέλασε: cf. note on 29,1. τὤγαλμα: usually the statue of Ptah was anthropomorphic and stylized, with the body wrapped in a tight dress, like a mummy; a bald head covered by a cap, straight beard like that of the pharaohs, ornaments on the chest, and free hands with the sceptre. Later there are also representations of Ptah in the

form of a dwarf. The identification of Ptah with Hephaestus derives from the homophony of the names and the similar function of the two divinities: both are craftsmen, blacksmiths, etc. See the iconographic collection of M. Stolk, *Ptah*, Berlin 1911; fundamental is M. Sandman-Holmberg, *The God Ptah*, Lund 1946; for other bibl. cf. S. Morenz, in *Festschrift F. Zucker*, Berlin 1954, pp. 275–90; Sabri Kolta, pp. 118–25 and 140–4; S. Donadoni, *EAA* VI 1965, p. 535; H. te Velde, *LdÄ* IV 1980, coll. 1177–80.   τοῖσι Φοινικηίοισι Παταίκοισι: they could be 'small Ptahs'; the etymology is uncertain. Busts or full statues of deformed and grotesque dwarfs, certainly of apotropaic power, were placed on the prows of Phoenician ships. They are recognizable on Phoenician amulets and coins of the 6th–5th cent. BC. Herodotus possibly had in mind the Tyrian variety; see J. and A. G. Elayi, *American Numismatic Soc.—Museum Notes*, XXXI (1986), 1–5. It is still debated whether the Pataeci are of Egyptian or Phoenician origin. In Greek sources the Pataeci are also described as protectors of the table. See H. Herter, *RE* XVIII 2, 1949, coll. 2550–5; *KP* IV, coll. 543–4; P. Montet, *RA* XL (1952), 1–11; G. Becatti, *EAA* V 1963, p. 986; J. G. Griffiths, *LdÄ* IV, coll. 914 f.;V. Dasen, *Dwarfs in Ancient Egypt and Greece*, Oxford 1993, pp. 55–98 (with bibl.); A. Hermany, *LIMC* VII 1, 1994, pp. 201–2.   πυγμαίου: the pygmies are a legendary people, already known to Homer (*Il.* III 6) as fighting migratory cranes. They were located especially in Africa (cf. II 32,6–7), but also elsewhere. See E. Wüst, *RE* XXIII 2, 1959, coll. 2064–74.   μίμησις: the most ancient testimony of this famous term, here used in the simple sense of artistic representation.

3. ἐς τῶν Καβείρων: cf. Strabo X 3,21. The Cabeiri often formed a 'holy family' of father, mother, and son; they originated in Asia Minor and spread to several Greek cities. Ptah also, together with Sakhmet and their son Neferten, are a Memphite variant of the 'holy family'. See II 51,2 (Lloyd, *Commentary 1–98*, pp. 227–31 and 241–3, with bibl.); also S. G. Cole, *Theoi megaloi*, Leiden 1984; D. Vollkommer-Glökler, *LIMC* VIII 1, 1997, pp. 820–8.   οὐ θεμιτόν: cf. V 72,3.

38,1. πανταχῆ ὦν μοι...: this famous chapter concludes the *logos* of Cambyses. Herodotus takes the opportunity to express his severe judgement of the Persian king, stressing again the extenuating circumstances of his madness and reflecting, in ethnological and philosophical terms, on the theme of the supremacy of 'customs' (νόμοι) in different human cultures. Herodotus compares the madness of Cambyses with the sanity of Darius, with his famous ethnological experiment; he draws the conclusion that all human beliefs and customs belong to the history of civilization; that there is no objective measure for rating the merits and demerits of each culture; that therefore diversity deserves respect; and finally, that although 'customs' are very different on a universal level, their authority is absolute and undisputed within each culture. The choice of the individual is determined by a personal or collective attachment to tradition, or by a rational conviction. The relativistic spirit of Ionian science permeates this chapter, reinforced—as it seems—by a more recent experience of sophistic antilogy: if on the one hand it removes the basis for any absolute ethical judgement, on

436   *Commentary*

the other it remains fundamentally sceptical towards ethical-political utopias (see εἰ γάρ τις προσθείη …). The names of Protagoras, Hippias, and Prodicus have been suggested as possible inspirers of Herodotus' views in this chapter; but Herodotus could himself have inspired these and other famous contemporary Sophists. It should be stressed that Herodotus' position is not at all equivalent to a radical sophistic relativism, nor to the theory according to which the 'law' has to be obeyed only for the fear of punishment; see rightly S. C. Humphreys, *Arethusa*, XX (1987), 211 ff. On the contrary, Herodotus emphasizes the fear that 'law' itself instills in men; cf. VII 104,4.   νομαίοισι: Herodotus' νόμαια include divinities, rituals, and customs in a broad sense. νόμαια can be Greek, foreign, ancestral, of one's own and of others; see e.g. 80,5; 99,1. However, in this chapter we immediately move on to νόμος, a legal rather than ethnological term, maybe in a philological 'nod' to the Pindaric quote in para. 4.

3. Δαρεῖος … : the anecdote puts on the stage, from an Iranocentric point of view, the two peoples living beyond the eastern and western borders of the Persian empire, the Indians and the Greeks, both 'barbarians' for the Persian king, and both highly civilized, though different in culture; see H. Humbach, in *Musa iocosa. Festschrift A. Thierfelder*, Hildesheim–New York 1974, pp. 26–8.

4. καλέσας … καλεομένους: a pun according to J. E. Powell, *CR* LI (1937), 105.   Καλλατίας: the Kallatiai were already known to Hecataeus, *FGrHist* 1 F 298, with Jacoby's *Kommentar*. They could be identified as a distant, dark-skinned Indian tribe, south of the Persian empire, never conquered by Darius (101,2), perhaps vaguely known to the Persians after the explorations of Scylax; cf. IV 44. An etymological link between Kalatiai and the Sanskrit *kala*, 'black' has been suggested.   τοὺς γονέας κατεσθίουσι: the Kallatiai did not kill or sacrifice the elderly, as did the Padaei (99,1–2), the Massagetae (I 216,2 with note), and other people; they simply ate their flesh after death; cf. the customs of the Issedonians, IV 26. As is well known, the killing of the elderly, with or without cannibalism, was widespread in antiquity and even in medieval and modern times; for distinctions and examples see W. E. Arens, *The Man-Eating Myth*, Oxford 1975. It is worth noticing how in this passage cannibalism is a 'custom' or a 'law', thus an element of culture or civilization (cf. 99,1; IV 26,1); elsewhere it is a sign of lack of civilization or of primitiveness; see IV 106 and, more moderately, 26,2; for a possible Homeric reminiscence see *Od.* IX 215; cf. Hesiod, *Op.* 276 ff. See F. Heinimann, *Nomos und Physis*, Basel 1945, pp. 61 f.; H. D. Rankin, *Hermes*, XCVII (1969), 381–4.   δι' ἑρμηνέος: cf. 140,3 and 19,1 with note. Herodotus, who does not understand foreign languages, appreciates enormously the knowledge of interpreters, although he cannot always blindly trust their translations; see II 125,6–7.   κατακαίειν πυρί: cremation is represented as a Greek usage par excellence.   Πίνδαρος … : Herodotus alludes to a verse of Pindar (fr. 169 Maehler), partially quoted by Plato through Callicles (*Gorg.* 484b) and variously by other ancient sources; see A. Turyn, *Pindari carmina cum fragmentis*, Cracow 1948, pp. 350 ff.; D. E. Gerber, *Emendations in Pindar 1513–1972*, Amsterdam 1976, pp. 185 f.; *A Bibliography of Pindar 1513–1966*, Princeton 1969,

pp. 105 f. Pindar probably meant that mortals and the gods themselves are ruled by an irrational and arbitrary 'law' (νόμος ὁ πάντων βασιλεὺς θνατῶν καὶ ἀθανάτων), which there is no use opposing, even when it justifies acts of violence repugnant to universal moral sense: e.g. the violence of Heracles against Geryon and Diomedes. Anyway, Herodotus is not interested here in the original meaning of Pindar's text: he isolates the verse from its context and quotes it as a motto for his purposes of ethnological and moral comparison. Plato also used the same verse to explain the sophistic doctrine of the 'law of nature', which justifies the right of the strongest (*Gorg.* 488b; *Leg.* III 690b; IV 714e; X 890a). The modern interpretations of the Pindaric fragment are diverse: see the review and the analysis in Gigante, pp. 72–122, and of E. Des Places, *Pindare et Platon*, Paris 1949, pp. 171 ff. Among the editions and commentaries of the fragment see M. Ostwald, *HSCPh* LXIX (1965), 109–38; L. Castagna, *SIFC* XLIII (1971), 173–98; H. Lloyd-Jones *HSCPh* LXXVI (1972), 45–56; B. Gentili, in *Il mito greco*, Rome 1977, pp. 299–305; G. Kirkwood, *Selections from Pindar*, Chico 1982, pp. 347 ff. For the formula νόμος βασιλεύς cf. νόμος ἰσχυρός and δεσπότης νόμος in VII 102,1 and 104,4; νόμος τύραννος in Plato, *Prot.* 337d; see J. A. S. Evans, *Athenaeum*, XLIII (1965), 142–53; Waters, pp. 97 ff.; Giraudeau, pp. 128–33. For the mental affinities between Pindar and Herodotus, Ch. G. Starr, *Hermes*, XCV (1967), 393–403; on Herodotus and the Greek poets, H. Verdin, in *Historiographia antiqua. Festschrift W. Peremans*, Leuven 1977, pp. 54–65.

39–60. With a synchronic link (39,1 with note), Herodotus turns to the account of contemporary events, namely the siege of Samos by the Spartans and Corinthians (525 BC), the main subject of the first of the three Samian *logoi* of Book III; the other two are formed by chs. 120–5 and 139–49. However, neither the synchronism nor the relative importance of the narrated events can adequately explain the reasons for the insertion of this long *excursus* into the account of Persian history; Herodotus himself apologizes for its length (60,1 and 4). We can explain this simply by supposing that the *logos* already existed before the final draft of the book. Two digressions on two great tyrants of archaic Greece are interwoven with the main narrative: on Polycrates of Samos (39–43) and on Periander of Corinth (48–53); the *logos* ends with a chapter dedicated to the building-works of Samos (60). The sources are mainly oral, although in the 5th cent. archival documents and the first writings of local Samian history already existed: e.g. the Ὧροι of Euagon, *FGrHist* 535; cf. V. La Bua, *MGR* IV (1975), 1–40. Scholars have rightly underlined Herodotus' sympathy for the city that offered him hospitality, and the tendentiousness of his sources, mixed with nostalgic feelings for the city's past greatness and criticism of the tyrannical regime of Polycrates and his pro-Persian policy. Herodotus also had the opportunity in Sparta to collect some evidence on the siege of Samos (47,1; 55,2); he could have found information on the vicissitudes of the exiles in the Peloponnese, at Delphi, and in the Aegean (57–9). On the didactic value of the Samian *logos* see the Introduction, p. 387. On Herodotus and Samos see the useful collection of Tölle-Kastenbein. On the Samian *logos* cf. Cobet, pp. 159–63, and H. R. Immerwahr, *CJ* LII (1957), 312–22. On the sources see Jacoby, coll. 428–9; on the monuments E. E. Cole, *The Samos of Herodotus*, New Haven 1912; for the tendentiousness B. M. Mitchell, *JHS* XCV (1975), 75–91; V. La Bua, *MGR* VI (1978), 1–88. On the figure of Polycrates in Herodotus see H. J. Diesner, *AAntHung* VII (1959), 211–19; Waters, pp. 6 and 25–30; W. H. Friedrich, *A&A* XVIII (1973), 120–5. See also the bibl. in the note on 39,1. For bibliographies on the history of Samos cf. E. Meyer, *KP* IV, coll. 1534–7; Shipley, pp. 315–39; and the guide to Samos by R. Tölle, *Die antike Stadt Samos*, Mainz 1969.

39,1. Καμβύσεω…: the synchronism of Thuc. I 13,6 is more vague. A synchronic connection between Cambyses and Polycrates is also assumed by the late tradition of Pythagoras' exile from Samos by Polycrates, and his deportation from Egypt to Babylon after the Persian conquest; see Iamblichus, *De Vita Pythag.* 11–12; cf. Strabo XIV 1,16.   **Πολυκράτεα…:** Herodotus is the most important source on this famous tyrant (cf. Erbse, pp. 93–9); for other sources and bibl. see Gottlieb; Berve II, pp. 581–7; Hofstetter, no. 270; V. La Bua, *MGR* IV (1975), 1–40; Shipley, ch. 2; L. De Libero, *Die archaische Tyrannis*, Stuttgart 1996, pp. 249–310. For Aeaces father of Polycrates cf. II 182,2; III 139,1; VI 13,2. For the homonymous nephew see VI 13. An Aeaces, son of Brychon, appears in an inscription of the Heraion of Samos, datable around 500 BC; see ML, no. 16 with bibl.; G. Dunst, *MDAI(A)* LXXXVII (1972), 116–21; photograph in Tölle-Kastenbein, pl. 1b. This could be a son of a brother of Polycrates; see J. P. Barron, *CQ* XIV (1964), 210–29. For the theory that Polycrates' father was a great tyrant see M. White, *JHS* LXXIV (1954), 36–43. According to *Suidas*, s.v. Ἴβυκος, Polycrates' father was himself called Polycrates, and had ruled Samos during the time of Croesus (*c.*560–546 BC), when the poet Ibycus of Rhegium (fl. in the 54th Olympiad, 564–561 BC) arrived at his court. This is the basis for the modern hypothesis of two Polycrateses, father (*c.*572–539 BC) and son (the Polycrates of Herodotus, *c.*533–522 BC); see F. Sisti, *QUCC* II (1966), 91–102; G. Schmidt, *Annales du Midi*, LXXXVII (1972), 181–5; for a different solution of the chronological gap see J. Labarbe, *AC* XXXI (1962), 153–88. The hypothesis of a powerful tyranny before Polycrates has today a rather solid foundation; but the exact genealogical reconstruction is still uncertain. Herodotus' version is shown in Fig. 5.   **ἐπαναστάς:** the verb occurs frequently in Book III (16 of a total of 22 times), which is full of insurrections and *coups d'état*; see e.g. 61,2; 63,4; 65,3–4; 80,1; 120,3; 140,1; 150,1. For ἐπανάστασις see 44,2; 118,1; 119,21, with I. A. F. Bruce, *CQ* XI (1961), 168 and n. 5. On Polycrates' *coup d'état*, cf. III 120,3 (allegedly Polycrates carried it out with fifteen hoplites) and Polyaenus I 23,2; see also Polyaenus VI 45; E. Homann-Wedeking, *AE*, B (1958), pp. 185–91; cf. J. Labarbe, *Anc. Soc.* V (1974), 21–41; V. La Bua, in *Xenia. Scritti in onore di P. Treves*, Rome 1985, pp. 95–101. On *coups d' état* and extramural sanctuaries cf. I 150,1 with note. Herodotus clearly supposes that before Polycrates the regime

Aeaces I

(born *c.*600 BC)

Polycrates   Syloson   Pantagnotos
(born *c.*570)   (born *c.*570)

daughter   Aeaces II
(III 124, 1)   (born *c.*535)

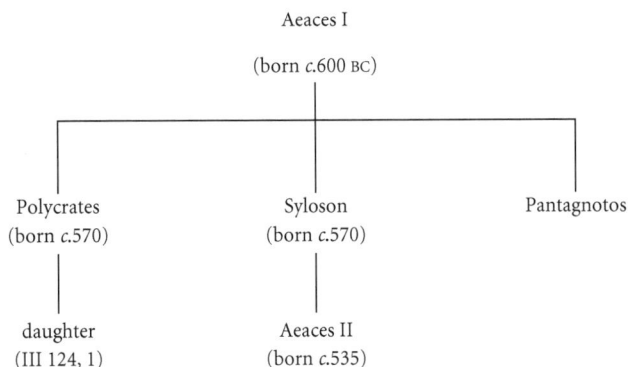

Fɪɢ. 5. Polycrates' genealogy

was not a tyranny; Plutarch mentions an archaic Samian oligarchy (maybe of restored γεωμόροι) in *Mor.* 303f ff. It is impossible to infer any precise chronology from ἐν χρόνῳ δὲ ὀλίγῳ; in Eusebius' *Chronicon* (Armenian and Latin) the date is *ab Abramo* 1484 = 533/2 BC, generally accepted by modern scholars, in the absence of better evidence; see A. A. Mosshammer, *The Chronicle of Eusebius and Greek Chronographic Tradition*, Lewisburg–London 1979, pp. 290–304; however, it is derived from an erroneous synchronism with Cambyses or with Pythagoras' *acme* (see Iamblichus, *De Vita Pyth.* 35). Some date the *coup d'état* of the three brothers to 538, and the beginning of Polycrates' own tyranny to 533/2, whereas others think that Polycrates ruled from the forties of the 6th cent. and that he had fought the Persians after the fall of Sardis (cf. note on 39,4).

2. τριχῇ δασάμενος: the tripartite division of the territory is contrasted with Polycrates' unified power over 'all Samos' (πᾶσαν Σάμον).   Συλοσῶντι: cf. 139,1 and note on chs. 139–49.

3. εὐτυχέως: cf., in reference to Polycrates, the adjective εὐτυχής, the substantive εὐτυχίη and the verb εὐτυχέειν at 40,1,2,4; 43,1; 44,1; 125,4; 12 times out of a total of 28 the forms of εὐτυχ- refer to Polycrates; cf. D. Lateiner, *RhM* CXXV (1982), 97–101. For this and other Herodotean terms indicating 'success', 'fortune', 'happiness', etc., see the dialogue between Croesus and Solon (I 29–33 with note). On Polycrates' proverbial 'good fortune', cf. Anacreon fr. 177 Gentili; Cicero, *Fin.* V 92; Val. Max. VI 9, *ext.* 5.   ἔκτητο...: the pentecónter, a boat about 32 m. long, with twenty-five rowers on each side and a total crew of eighty men (cf. VII 184,3), was the typical warship of archaic Greek fleets (cf. I 163,2; III 14,5). One hundred is obviously a 'typical' number, see Fehling, pp. 230–1. It is uncertain whether Polycrates also had triremes (44,2 with note); on the 'Samaina' see note on 59,3. Some of the archers (and foreign mercenaries) served in the fleet; see Berve II, p. 583, with bibl.

4. ἔφερε δὲ καὶ ἦγε…: Samian piracy did not originate with Polycrates; see I 70,2–3; III 47,1; cf. also the name Συλοσῶν, a compound of σύλη-, '(right of) seizure'; the anonymous fragment of *FGrHist* 544 F 3; Plut. *Mor.* 303d. On piracy in the time of Polycrates, Diod. I 95,3; X 16,1; Polyaenus I 23,1; Maximus of Tyre 29,8. The inscription of Aeaces (see note on 39,1) mentions the booty (τὴν σύλην) as a regular levy or tax, with official dedications to the goddess (however, the interpretation is still disputed). Apparently Polycrates compelled the delivery of the booty, or part of it, to the city. See P. N. Ure, *The Origin of Tyranny*, Cambridge 1922, pp. 68 ff.; H. Ormerod, *Piracy in the Ancient World*, Liverpool 1950, pp. 103 ff.   συχνάς: with respect to the cities of the mainland, this statement must be unacceptable after *c*.540, the date of the Persian conquest of Asia Minor, unless we understand ἀραιρήκεε in the sense of a temporary 'occupation' aimed at robbery, with a 'hope' (cf. 122,2) of a permanent domination. Some have ascribed these conquests on the mainland to Polycrates' father, others have moved the date of the beginning of Polycrates' tyranny to the forties of the 6th cent. (cf. note on 39,1). For the late version of Cyrus' falling in war against Polycrates see Malalas, *Chronica* VI 158; Cedrenus 138c. For the islands see Thuc. I 13,6 and III 104,2 (Rheneia); Κυ]κλάδων νῆσ<σ>ων in Pap. Heid. 1740, ed. with photographs by P. Tozzi, *Athenaeum*, LVIII (1980), 153–8; on Delos, *Suidas*, s.v. Πύθια καὶ Δήλια (for two different interpretations of the original meaning of this motto, see W. Burkert, in *Arktouros. Hellenic Studies presented to Bernard M. W. Knox*, Berlin–New York 1979, pp. 53–62, and F. Mora, in M. Sordi (ed.), *Santuari e politica nel mondo antico*, Milan 1983, pp. 105–16); H. W. Parke, *CQ* XL (1946), 105–8; the hypothesis of Polycrates' rule over Rhodes, with a homonymous son as governor, seems very artificial: Himerius 29,20 f. Colonna; C. M. Bowra, *CJ* XXIX (1934), 375–80; id., *Greek Lyric Poetry*, Oxford 1961, pp. 249–53; cf. D. L. Page, *Aegyptus*, XXXI (1951), 158–72. According to Herodotus, Polycrates was the first great ruler of the sea (122,2); cf. Thuc. I 13,6; Strabo XIV 1,16. On the Samian thalassocracy, lasting sixteen–seventeen years (539–522?), see W. G. Forrest, *CQ* XIX (1969), 105; Miller, pp. 22–37; L. Boffo, *MAL* XXVI (1983), 46 and n. 232; see also the bibl. in the note on 39,1. καὶ Λεσβίους…: aetiological information, probably obtained from local guides. εἷλε: according to G. Vollgraff, *Mnemosyne*, L (1922), 65 f., a number is missing after this verb. For the scene of chained prisoners cf. the story of Plutarch (*Mor.* 303f ff.) on the Megarian prisoners in Samos. A proverb ('the Milesians were once brave in war') is quoted in an oracular response given to Polycrates (schol. to Aristophanes, *Pl.* 1002).   τὴν τάφρον: the remains of a ditch around the archaic walls of Samos have been discovered on the western side of the city; cf. note on 54,1.

40,1. τὸν Ἄμασιν…ὁ Πολυκράτης: the relations between Polycrates, Amasis, and Cambyses (cf. 44,1) offer Herodotus an excellent opportunity for linking more closely the Samian *logos* to that of the Persian conquest of Egypt. Herodotus' true interest is not, however, on the diplomatic or military relations, but on the moral and theological problem of the fickle 'fortune' of powerful men and powerful states. This time it is Amasis, the old Egyptian usurper, who, becoming wise, warns the forcible Greek tyrant. The two do not meet in person: instead of a dialogue, we have here an exceptional case of epistolary communication; cf. Heni, pp. 61 ff., 76 ff. Amasis' letter assumes that Polycrates' fate is already sealed: it is therefore pure literary fiction. The only historical core of the story is the *volte-face* of Polycrates, who, for essentially practical reasons, decided around 526 BC to break his friendly relations with Amasis and cross over to Cambyses' side (cf. 43,2 with note; 44,2). See P. L. Tozzi, in Φιλίας χάριν. *Miscellanea di studi classici in onore di Eugenio Manni*, Rome 1980, VI, pp. 2087–99. Ἄμασις Πολυκράτεϊ: for Greek epistolary formulas see M. van den Hout, *Mnemosyne*, II (1949), 25–33.

2. φίλον καὶ ξεῖνον: Herodotus assumes personal relations between the two statesmen (cf. 43,2), not an 'alliance' in a political or military sense (as modern scholars generally understand it). See I. Koenig, *PP* XLIV (1989), 321–40. τὸ θεῖον ὡς ἔστι φθονερόν: a direct reference to Solon's words to Croesus (I 32,1), with an explicit parallelism of situations and morals. On the 'jealousy of the gods' in Herodotus cf. General Introduction, pp. 37 ff. and note to I 32,1 to its bibl. add M. W. Dickie's just criticism, *Athens & Rome*, XXXII (1987), 113–25 of an old interpretation resumed by H. Lloyd-Jones, *The Justice of Zeus*, Berkeley–London 1971, pp. 55–78.

3. πρόρριζος: another reference to Solon's words (I 32,9). To die 'uprooted' (i.e. with no progeny) is a grave calamity (cf. 66,2 with note; VI 86); to die 'with good progeny' (εὔπαις), on the other hand, is a sign of the greatest happiness (I 32,6). Cf. D. Lateiner, in *The Greek Historians. Literature and History. Papers Presented to A. E. Raubitschek*, Stanford 1985, pp. 98 ff.

41,1. ὁ Πολυκράτης...ἐδίζητο...: the superb tale of Polycrates' ring, famous in antiquity, is present also in modern literature (Schiller's ballad 'Der Ring des Polikrates'; Leopardi, *Zibaldone* 4478 of 31 March 1829); it directly follows the letter of Amasis; its purpose is to introduce the following story on the fortune and misfortune of Polycrates. It is a variation of the motif of a precious or miraculous object, lost and then unexpectedly found (a subject of countless popular oriental and European tales of every period; see Aly, pp. 90–2). It is certainly not by chance that a similar story was told about Minos (Bacchylides XVII = *Dith.* III 1–32 Snell–Maehler; Hyginus, *De Astr.* II 5 Bunte; Paus. I 17,3 with the note by Musti-Beschi), the great thalassocrat of Greek mythology (cf. III 122,2), who was overcome by Theseus, himself a symbol of 5th-cent. Athenian thalassocracy. Herodotus rationalizes the tale and transforms it into a parable, adding, in order to make it more credible, some precise details. Not everyone considers the tale of Polycrates' ring as having characteristic features originating in the genre of popular fable. Various interpretations have been attempted of the 'symbolic' act of throwing a ring into the sea: according to the most famous interpretation, it is a ritual act of 'marriage with the sea' inherited by the Venetian doges from Polycrates. Others interpret it as a form of hydromantic ordeal or a sacrifice by consultation. For a review of these and other interpretations see J. Van Oeteghem, *EC* IX (1940), 311–4; also Berve II, pp. 584–5. In Herodotus' version the ring symbolizes the false or ritual sacrifices that men are prepared to perform in order to deceive the gods. See Cicero, *Fin.* V 92; Strabo, XIV 1,16; Val. Max. VI 9, *ext.* 5; Pliny, *NH* XXXVII 3–4; for the Pap. Heid. 1740 see P. Tozzi, *Athenaeum*, LVIII 1980, pp. 155 ff.   τῶν κειμηλίων: 'relics' or 'curios' in the sense of precious objects or metals deposited (κεῖμαι) in the treasury, and therefore 'treasures'. They were mainly preserved for the exchange of gifts; see e.g. Homer, *Od.* I 312–13; *Il.* VI 47 f.; XXIII 618; Herod. VI 62,2. The term is rarely found in prose. See F. Fischer, *Germania*, LI (1973), 442–8. Polycrates' wealth, magnificence, and luxuries became proverbial; cf. 125,2; Plato, *Men.* 90a; Athenaeus XII 540d–e, who quotes Clytos of Miletus, *FGrHist* 490 F 2, and Alexis of Samos, ibid. 539 F 2. σφρηγὶς: description of a seal (cf. I 195,2; III 128,2 with note; VII 69,1) or of a gem engraved and set in gold; cf. Strabo XIV 1,16 and Paus. VIII 14,8. According to Clement of Alexandria, *Paed.* III 59,2, the engraving depicted a lyre; the lyre was the symbol of several archaic coins of the island of Calymnos; see C. Seltman, in H. Ingholt (ed.), *Centennial Publ. of the Amer. Num. Society*, New York 1958, pp. 595–601. According to Pliny, *NH* XXXVII 4, the gem must have been a sardonyx and not an emerald; in his times (*si credimus*) it was placed on a golden horn in the temple of Concordia in Rome.   χρυσόδετος: cf. Alcaeus, fr. 350,2 Voigt.   Θεοδώρου: on Theodorus, not only an engraver but also an architect, already dead at the time of Polycrates, cf. I 51,3 with note; on his career see also M. Vickers, *NC* CXLV (1985), 13 ff.

42,1. ἐπὶ τὰς θύρας: for other similar scenes, set in oriental palaces in Book III, cf. 117,5; 119,3; 120,2.   ἔφη...: on this lively dialogue see Heni, pp. 66 ff.

2. βασιλεῦ: here a title which indicates respect; the words βασιλεύς and τύραννος are usually neither synonymous nor neutral in Herodotus, contrary to what was once believed; see A. Ferrill, *Historia*, XXVII (1978), 385–98; J. L. O'Neil, *Antichthon*, XX (1986), 34 ff. E. Lévy, *Ktema*, XVIII (1993), 7–18; V. Parker, *Hermes*, CXXVI (1998), 161–5. Nevertheless there are still some ambiguous cases (52,3 with note; cf. note on I 6,1).   ἀγορήν: in the sense of 'market', cf. I 153,2; VI 58,3; VII 23,4.

43,1. ἔμαθε...: Amasis, an antiheroic figure, does not want to suffer. Cf. the reinterpretation, in an anti-tyrannical vein, of Diod. I 95,3. See note on 40,1.

2. διαλύεσθαι...ξεινίην: cf. Diod. I 95,3. Herodotus believes it was Amasis who severed the personal relations of ξεινίη with Polycrates (cf. note on 40,1). Today many hold that it was Polycrates who broke an 'alliance' with Amasis, precisely at the moment when Egypt was under threat from Persia. See, however, in the opposite sense, Berve I, p. 112; F. Mora, in M. Sordi (ed.), *Santuari e politica nel mondo antico*, Milan 1983, pp.110 ff. Bibl. in Lloyd, *Commentary 99–182*, pp. 238–9.

44,1. ἐπὶ τοῦτον...Λακεδαιμόνιοι...: we return to the main narrative of the Samian *logos*, reconnecting with the vicissitudes of Cambyses (44,2). The occasion, or the pretext, for the intervention of Sparta against Samos must have been the embassy of the exiles asking for armed support for their return. The Spartans, however, had earlier reasons of their own for deposing the tyrant (see notes to 47,1). In this aetiological complex which could, with a little effort, be read in terms of immediate cause and remote or final cause, Herodotus does not overstep the limits of personal and emotional motivations, based on feelings of aversion, gratitude, and revenge; cf. note on 1,1. Nevertheless, from these anecdotes emerges the notable existence of an inter-state conflict of the archaic age, provoked by struggle of factions, armed support for the return of exiles, and the Samian, Spartan, and Corinthian thalassocracies of the last quarter of the 6th cent. On faction struggles, and the return of exiles in the archaic and classical age see J. Seibert, *Die politische Flüchtlinge und Verbannten in der griechischen Geschichte*, I, Darmstadt 1979 esp. pp. 22–3 and notes; H.-J. Gehrke, *Stasis*, Munich 1985. Herodotus was well aware that without the military aid of others the repatriation of exiles usually remained a vain hope; however, here he appears more interested in the unusual vicissitudes of the Samian exiles in the Aegean than in the phenomenology of civil wars. πέμψας: refers to the period of Cambyses' preparations for the Egyptian campaign, around 526 BC. The reading λάθρη Σαμίων is a textual variant, accepted by many modern editors: it could indicate an example of secret diplomacy, normal for a tyrant. On the treaty with Cambyses see *StV* II no. 118. ἐδεήθη ... δέοιτο: for the second verb we would expect a pluperfect. It is a 'repetition for the pleasure of repetition', according to J. E. Powell, *CR* LI (1937), 105.

2. τοὺς ὑπώπτευε: perhaps oligarchic elements—e.g. γεωμόροι—traditionally hostile to the tyrant and linked to Sparta. This does not, however, exclude that among the 'suspects' were also members of the *demos*. A verse of Anacreon (fr. 21 Gentili) has been interpreted as referring to rebellious Samian fishermen; moreover, during Polycrates' rule Arcesilaus found followers in Samos who were attracted by the promise of land-distribution in Cyrenaica (IV 163,1). τεσσεράκοντα τριήρεσι: Herodotus perhaps thought that the shift in Greece from the penteconter to the trireme (see Thuc. I 13–14) had already begun in the time of Polycrates. However, since in 39,3 only penteconters are discussed, it is also possible that the triremes of this passage are to be understood in the more general sense of warships (cf. 136,1; V 85–6); see J. A. Davison, *CQ* XLI (1947), 18–24; J. S. Morrison and J. F. Coates, *The Athenian Trireme*, Cambridge 1986, with bibl.

45,1. οἱ μὲν ...: the first of these two versions, corresponding to two logical possibilities (Fehling, p. 109), preserves a detail that seems genuine. ἐν Καρπάθῳ: 'in the waters of Carpathos'; cf. ἐν Χίῳ at V 33,1. Carpathos in the Dodecanese is the most important island between Crete and Rhodes. A Doric island, known to Homer (Κράπαθος: *Il.* II 676), mostly in the orbit of Rhodian influence. See E. M. Craik, *The Dorian Aegean*, London 1980; Müller I, pp. 957–60.

2. οἱ κατιόντες: for the use of this verb in the sense of 'to return from exile', cf. e.g. I 62,3; IV 1,3; 163,3; 164,1; V 30,3; 62,2; VI 107,2; IX 26,2–4.

3. οὐκ ὀρθῶς ...: the argument is very interesting. If the rejected version is not Herodotus' pure invention, it could be ascribed to the boastfulness of the Samian oligarchs.

4. νεωσοίκους: docks or sheds for ships; cf. νεὼς οἶκοι in Paus. I 29,16, and the Homeric ἐπίστιον (*Od.* VI 265). The harbour of Samos must have had at least 100 for the penteconters; for the Roman period cf. Strabo XIV 1,14.

46,1. ἐπὶ τοὺς ἄρχοντας: the kings and the ephors; cf. I 83; 152,1–2 and notes, where there is allusion to an assembly. Plutarch (*Mor.* 223d) attributes the anecdote and the maxim to Cleomenes, who, however, had probably not yet ascended the throne; see Virgilio, pp. 146–51. Herodotus is perhaps the indirect source of various Spartan apophthegms, commonly aiming to depict, not without irony, the Laconic aversion to Ionian verbosity. On this chapter see J. Labarbe, in *Le Monde grec. Hommages à C. Préaux*, Brussels 1975, pp. 365–75.　　ὑπεκρίναντο: cf. note on 31,4. The verb also occurs in para. 2.　　θύλακον: the Samians show an empty bag and say 'it needs corn'; the Spartans reply that the bag was unnecessary. The dialogue was thus understood by Sextus Empiricus, *Adv. Math.* II 23, who attributes it to a negotiation on the export of corn. Cf. H. Bannert, in *Festschrift A. Betz*, Vienna 1985, pp. 41–6. For other interpretations e.g. Stein, ad loc.; Labarbe, op. cit., p. 375.

47,1. εὐεργεσίας ἐκτίνοντες: the version most favourable to Sparta is strangely attributed to the Samians and probably refers to an unknown event of the Messenian wars (probably the second one, the 'war of Tyrtaeus', at the end of the 7th cent.): these elements suggest a genuine tradition of Samian and olig-archic origin. Sparta would have wanted to repay the 'benefit' to the political heirs of the oligarchic regime, now in exile. On the concept of εὐεργεσία in Greek inter-state relations, cf. I 69,3; III 140,1; IV 165,2; see P. Karavites, *RIDA* XXVII (1980), 69–79. In a different sense 67,3 with note.　　ὡς τείσασθαι...: Plutarch (*Mor.* 859b–d), with remarkable acuteness and historical intelligence, remarks on the 'malignity' of attributing to the Spartans themselves this unworthy argument in favour of the intervention, which is considered by him as an exemplary case of the Spartan struggle against tyranny; on the 'myth' of an anti-tyrannical Sparta see R. Bernhardt, *Historia*, XXXVI (1987), 257–89. For the description and history of the Spartan crater see I 70 with notes. The idea of taking revenge on Polycrates for a theft perpetrated in 546, probably the year of the Persian conquest of Sardis, makes sense only if we suppose that, according to Herodotus or his source, Polycrates by then already ruled, alone or with his brothers: see note on 39,1. Herodotus does not place the Spartan thalassocracy in its historical context, nor does he link Spartan policy in the eastern Aegean with Spartan policy in the West (on Dorieus' expedition see V 42–8), nor consider as 'cause' of the conflict the commercial relations between Sparta and Samos, which are today also archaeologically documented (see G. Dunst, *MDAI(A)* LXXXVII (1972), 140–4). On these different historical aspects see L. Pareti, in *Studi minori di storia antica*, II, Rome 1961, pp. 1 ff; W. G. Forrest, *CQ* XIX (1969), 105; B. R. Sealey, *Klio* LVIII (1976), 339 ff.; Cartledge, pp. 145 ff.; *CQ* XXXII (1982), 243–65; L. Boffo, *MAL* XXVI (1983), 21 ff.

2. τῷ προτέρῳ ἔτεϊ: around 548/7 BC. Amasis was probably searching for allies in Greece after Cyrus' ascent to the throne. Herodotus must have seen the corslet of

Lindos (cf. para. 3 and II 182,1 with Lloyd, note ad loc. and *Commentary 99–182*, pp. 236 ff.), examined centuries later by Licinius Mucianus, *consul suffectus* in the seventies of the 1st cent. AD; see Pliny, *NH* XIX 12. The Persian soldiers wore Egyptian linen corslets (I 135); see E. D. Francis and M. Vickers, *BICS* XXXI (1984), 119–30. The corslets of the 'Assyrian' soldiers and of the Phoenician and Syro-Palestinian sailors in Xerxes' army was also made of linen (VII 63; 89,1). εἰρίοισι ἀπὸ ξύλου: this 'tree wool' (*Baumwolle* in German) is cotton, almost unknown to the Greeks before Alexander. Cf. 106,3; Pliny, *NH* XIX 14; Pollux VII 75. See M. Johnson, *CW* XXIV (1930), 63; A. Pedrikou-Gorecki, *DNP*, 1997, coll. 505–6.

3. θωυμάσαι ἄξιον: cf. ἀξιοθέητον in II 182,1.   τριηκοσίας καὶ ἑξήκοντα: 365 according to Pliny, *NH* XIV 12. The number is mystical; cf. 90,3 with note.

ἐν Λίνδῳ: cf. II 182. Lindos was the most important of the three cities of the island of Rhodes (the other two were Ialysos and Camiros) before the Rhodian synoecism and the foundation of the city of Rhodes in 407 BC. It was part of the Doric pentapolis (I 144,3). The ruins of its famous temple of Athena are still visible on the Acropolis. For sources and bibl. see Müller I, pp. 973–5.

48–53. In these chapters Herodotus explains, in two joint digressions dedicated to two different events of inter-state Greek history of the archaic age, the causes for the participation of Corinth in the Spartan campaign against Samos in 525 BC. The first digression (48–9) concerns the 'offence' of Samos against Corinth, dated by Herodotus to the preceeding generation (48,1 with note). The second (50–3) describes the reasons for the ill-will between Corinth and Corcyra at the time of Periander in order to explain the origin of the hatred of Corinth towards Samos. We have here a return to the past in two stages, connected by a causal association, also used by Herodotus elsewhere (see note on 1,1). The anecdotal and novelistic elements in these chapters prevail over historical analysis; see, however, 49,2. Herodotus does not cite different versions; on the other hand, he inserts a series of dialogues (50–3) whose language often seems to be influenced by poetry and tragedy. The figure of Periander, the last great tyrant of the Cypselid dynasty (perhaps 625–585 BC: the chronology is disputed; see the survey of A. A. Mosshammer, *The Chronicle of Eusebius and Greek Chronographic Tradition*, Lewisburg–London 1979, pp. 234–45 and nn. at pp. 342–4, with bibl.; cf. below note on 48,1), is at the centre of this double digression. Herodotus had already presented Periander favourably in Book I (20; 23–4); but in Book III, where monarchic figures tower over the narrative, Periander is reshaped into the tragic figure of a father and tyrant who tries in vain to find a solution to his own dynastic crisis, and reaches heights of excessive and vindictive cruelty. Only in Book V (92) will Herodotus depict Periander in darker colours, as an example of ferocious tyranny. On Periander in Herodotus see Waters, pp. 18–20; M. Stahl, *Hermes*, CXI (1983), 207–10; L. De Libero, *Die archaische Tyrannis*, Stuttgart 1996, pp. 137–78. Various criticisms could be levelled at Herodotus from a historical point of view. Plutarch (*Mor.* 859f ff.) could not understand how the free Corinth of 525 could have been thought the heir of the political grudges that arose during the tyranny. To this acute observation it is possible to raise the objection that alliances and hostility between cities generally outlast internal constitutional changes within the same cities. Besides the campaign of 525 was not directed against the 'Samians' in general, as Plutarch also rightly observed, but against Polycrates, in whose fall both rival sea-powers were interested. See the bibl. in J. B. Salmon, *Wealthy Corinth*, Oxford 1984; see also E. Will, *Korinthiaka*, Paris 1955, pp. 442 ff.; on the Corinthian reasons for the intervention, pp. 634 ff.

48,1. εἶχε ... γενόμενον: the text is 'untranslatable' according to J. E. Powell, *CQ* XXXI (1938), 214; nevertheless, the sense is clear: 'for there was in fact also an offence against the Corinthians by the Samians.' For ἐς τούτους εἶχε cf. V 81,2. **γενεῇ ...:** a well-known chronological *aporia*, which surprisingly synchronizes Alyattes (para. 2) with the end of the reign of Croesus (546 BC). Various attempts have been made to emend the text, either to <γ'> γενεῇ (based on Plutarch, *Mor.* 859 f) and to < οὐ > κατὰ δὲ τὸν αὐτὸν χρόνον, or by deleting κατὰ ... γεγονός as a gloss. Herodotus probably divided the period 625–525 BC into three generations (cf. II 142,2), represented respectively by Alyattes–Periander, Croesus–Cyrus, and Polycrates–Cambyses. He therefore should have said that the Samians insulted the Corinthians in the generation previous to that of the theft of the crater (Croesus), and not in the generation of the campaign against Polycrates. To hypothesize an 'early' chronology for the Cypselids in Herodotus does not solve the problem; the *aporia* arises from the erroneous synchronization of an episode dated to the period of Alyattes with an episode dated to the last year of Croesus. See P. Giannini, *QUCC* XLV (1984), esp. pp. 14–25 with critical apparatus; cf. J. Ducat, *BCH* LXXXV (1961), 418–25; Q. Cataudella, *Maia*, XVI (1964), 204–25; J. Servais, *AC* XXXVIII (1969), 28–81; Virgilio, pp. 152 ff.; H.-J. Gehrke, in W. Ax (ed.), *Memoria rerum veterum. Festschrift für C. J. Classen*, Stuttgart 1990, pp. 33–49; M. R. Cataudella, *Sileno*, XXII (1996), 38–41; W. Lapini, *Il POxy 664 di Eraclide Pontico e la cronologia dei Cipselidi*, Florence 1996, pp. 101–27; C. Neri, *Εἰκασμός*, VIII (1997), 91–5.

2. Κερκυραίων ... παῖδας ...: cf. Nicolaus of Damascus, *FGrHist* 90 F 59; Diog. Laert. I 94.   **τριηκοσίους:** a 'typical' number. Cf. I 82,3; VI 23,6; 44,3; VII 235,1; IX 21,3; see Fehling, pp. 222–3. On Corcyra see Müller I, pp. 901–2.   **ἱροῦ ... Ἀρτέμιδος:** the sanctuary of Artemis is today identified with the remains of the archaic age that have been excavated near modern Pythagorion; see K. Tsakos, *Ἀρχαιολογικὰ Ἀνάλεκτα ἐξ Ἀθηνῶν*, XIII (1980), 305–18; Shipley, p. 262 with bibl.

3. τοὺς ἱκέτας: for other cases of 'suppliants' in Herodotus cf. V 71,1; VI 91; 108,4; VIII 53,2. For the religious and moral problem created by the extradition of the suppliants see I 157–61 with note to 157,2.   **ὁρτήν ...:** clearly an aetiological story that Herodotus had heard from local guides.   **παρθένων τε καὶ ἠιθέων:** a Homerism; see *Il.* XVIII 593.   **τρωκτά:** cf. II 92,4.   **νόμον:** here in the sense of cultural 'law' or 'custom'; see note on 38,1.   **ἁρπάζοντες:** cf. the

ritual theft of cheeses at the sanctuary of Artemis Orthia at Sparta (on which e.g. Xenophon, *Lac. Rep.* II 9, etc.); see H. J. Rose, *HThR* XXXIV (1941), 1–5.
4. Σάμιοι: the Cnidians, according to Dionysius of Chalcis, *FHG* IV, fr. 13, and Antenor of Crete, *FGrHist* 463 F 2, quoted by Plutarch (*Mor.* 860b–c), who also knew (perhaps from these same sources) about decrees and privileges of Corcyra honouring the Cnidians. See also the miraculous story told by Pliny, *NH* IX 80. Another Corcyra, called the 'Black' (today Curzola), near the Dalmatian coast, was a colony of Cnidos; on the connections between Cnidos and the two Adriatic islands, see L. Braccesi, *Civiltà Adriatica*, Bologna 1977², pp. 104 ff. The existence of several versions in this case may be a sign of the popular aetiological origin of the entire story; cf. Aly, pp. 92 ff. For the value of this tale in the history of archaic Greek religion see J. K. Davies, *CAH²* IV, pp. 368 ff.

49,1. εἰ μέν νυν ...: an example of 'counterfactual conditional causal argument' in Herodotus, according to N. Demand, *AJPh* CVIII (1987), 746 ff.   αἰτίης: here perhaps the word has the neutral sense of 'motive'; see note on 1,1.   ἔκτισαν: they 'colonized', not 'founded'; cf. in this sense the analogies examined by Casevitz, pp. 33 ff.; also B. Virgilio, *AAT* CVI (1971–2), 378 ff. The ancients dated the Corinthian foundation of Corcyra (Corfu; cf. Müller I, pp. 902–4) to the same year as that of Syracuse (in 734 BC according to Thuc. VI 3,2). The colony soon became an important maritime city, with a fleet which, in the 5th cent., was believed to be inferior only to that of Athens. This was the cause of the commercial rivalry between the colony and the mother city, especially for the control of the Ionian and Adriatic seas. See Graham, pp. 118–53. Herodotus (VII 168), judges negatively on Corcyra concerning the events of the year 481/0 BC. εἰσὶ ... ἑωυτοῖσι for the various hypothetical attempts to bridge the apparent lacuna, see Rosén's long note, pp. 285–6.
2. ἀπεμνησικάκεον: cf. οὐ μνησικακέομεν in VIII 29,2. The first occurrence of this famous formula of reconciliation.

50,1. ἐπείτε γὰρ ...: in this second digression, extending to ch. 53 (see note on 48–53), unfolds the family tragedy of Periander, following the fatal dialogue between his children and their maternal grandfather; again, it is a speech that begins a series of events: see note on 1,5. The tragedy is narrated through dialogues or speeches made by one person only, with indirect references to the reactions or the replies of others (in this case Lycophron). The abundance of moral maxims, especially in the speech of Periander's daughter, re-creates well the atmosphere of archaic wisdom. The tragic hero is obviously Periander; see C. Sourvinou-Inwood, *OA* XVII (1988), 167–82. Three verifiable historical elements might be extracted: the temporary annexation of Epidaurus to Cypselid rule (52,7); the government of Lycophron in Corcyra (52,6; 53,7); the fact that Periander's successor was not his son, but Psammetichus, the son of his brother Gorgo (or Gordios). The family tree in Fig. 6 (simplified) shows the genealogy of the Cypselids according to Herodotus (see also V 92 and Diog. Laert. I 94).

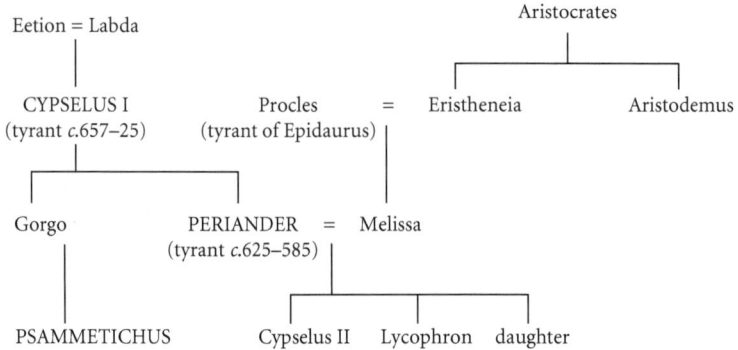

Fig. 6. Cypselid genealogy

According to Nicolaus of Damascus, *FGrHist* 90 F 59, Periander had four sons: Evagoras, Lycophron, Gorgo, and Nicolaus. For an 'Oedipal' reading of these chapters see J.-P. Vernant, *Le Temps de la réflexion*, II (1981), 235–55; *Arethusa*, XV (1982), 19–38.   Μέλισσαν: cf. V 92,η1–4, and Pythainetos, *FGrHist* 299 F 3. According to a version known to Diogenes Laertius (I 94), Periander had kicked his pregnant wife (as did Cambyses in 32,4). On the tombs of Melissa and Procles near Epidaurus see Paus. II 28,8.

2. Προκλέης: cf. Heraclides Ponticus, fr. 144 Wehrli; on the cruelty and the end of this tyrant see Plutarch, *Mor.* 403c–e. For a fictitious letter from Periander to Procles see Diog. Laert. I 100. Cf. Berve I, pp. 34–5 with notes.

3. ὁ μὲν πρεσβύτερος: the eldest son was νωθέστερος, 'dull-witted' (see 53,1 with note), and was called Cypselus (Heraclides Ponticus, fr. 144 Wehrli). Compare the sons of Croesus: one excellent, but who died young; the other deaf and dumb (I 34 ff.; 85).   ἱστορέοντι: cf. 51,1 and 77,2.

52,1. ζημίην: some scholars understand this word in the sense of 'fine', 'reparation' consecrated to the god. The columns of the temple of Apollo, north of the Corinthian *agora*, are well known.

2. στοιῇσι: the famous arcades of the Corinthian *agora*, rebuilt in the Roman age, are still visible.   ἐκαλινδέετο: cf. Thuc. II 52,2; see J.-P. Vernant, *Arethusa*, XV (1982), 37, n. 37.

3. τετάρτῃ δὲ ἡμέρῃ: a typical number in ancient storytelling; cf. I 30,1 with note.   τὴν τυραννίδα…: Herodotus does not think it strange to attribute to Periander (or his daughter: 53,3–4) the titles τυραννίς and βασιλεύς (para. 4) in reference to his own regime. In this unusual case the two terms are obviously equivalent (see note on 42,2). On ἀγαθά and tyranny, M. Stahl, *Hermes*, CXI (1983), 209 ff. For Herodotus the procurement and preservation of ἀγαθά are the arrogant aims of wars of conquest and of the usurpation of political power; cf. VII 8,γ1; see Drexler, pp. 133 ff.

4. *Κορίνθου τῆς εὐδαίμονος*: Corinth was described conventionally by fixed epithets of prosperity and wealth from Homeric times: e.g. ἀφνειός (*Il.* II 570; cf. Pindar, fr. 122,2 Maehler; Thuc. I 13,5); ὀλβία (Pindar, *Ol.* 13, 4). The epithet ὀφρυόεις, 'lofty', 'on the summit of the rock', in the oracle cited at V 92,β3, refers to the citadel of Acrocorinth.   *ὑποψίην ... ἔχεις*: cf. IX 99,2. Periander understands that his son suspects him of having killed his wife.   *μέτοχος*: the tyrant, who is also one of the Seven Sages, shows regret and refrains from explicitly referring to the 'disgrace' of which he speaks.

6. *ἐς Κέρκυραν*: the practice of Greek tyrants of appointing their sons or relatives to govern subject provinces is attributed also to Polycrates (cf. note on 39,4). On the colonial empire of the Cypselids see sources and bibl. in Berve II, pp. 526 f.

7. *αἰτιώτατον*: cf. IV 202,1; VI 50,1. Periander believes Procles to be mainly responsible for what had happened, and not himself to have provoked the death of Melissa.   *τὴν 'Επίδαυρον*: this important city of the Argolid, today famous for its great 4th-cent. BC theatre, had probably been subject to Periander since his marriage with Melissa; perhaps it was definitively annexed following an act of disloyalty by Procles. On archaic Epidaurus see also V 82–4; for the bibl. B. Conticello, *EAA* III 1960, pp. 358–67; Müller I, pp. 761–3.

53,1. *παρηβήκεε*: on Periander's old age, cf. Nicolaus of Damascus, *FGrHist* 90 F 59; Diog. Laert. I 94.   *νωθέστερος*: cf. Aeschylus, *Prom.* 62; νωθὴς τὸν νόον in Hippocrates, *Epist.* 17; for 'dull-witted' referring to animals see *Il.* XI 559; Plato, *Apol.* 30e.

2. *ἀδελφεήν ...*: she must have been older than her brother since in para. 3 she calls him ὦ παῖ.

4. *φιλοτιμίη ...*: the whole of para. 4 is composed of five maxims or sayings of archaic popular morality, more apt to the father than to the daughter. To Periander were attributed numerous moral maxims and a collection of these comprising 2,000 verses (Diog. Laert. I 97–8).   *μὴ τῷ κακῷ τὸ κακὸν ἰῶ*: cf. e.g. Aeschylus, fr. 349 Radt; Sophocles, *Aj.* 362 ff.; Euripides, *Bacch.* 839; Thuc. V 65,2.   *πολλοὶ ... προτιθεῖσι*: the moral superiority of equity as opposed to a purely formal justice is a common Greek notion, well known from Gorgias' *Epitaphios* and from the *Nicomachean Ethics* of Aristotle. Here the assumption would be that the homicide perpetrated by Periander, being involuntary (52,4), should be judged with more equanimity.   *τὰ μητρώια ... τὰ πατρώια*: the saying refers to the risks of inheritance suits. The heir who tries with excessive zeal to obtain his mother's inheritance (in Attic law, the bequest passed from the maternal grandfather through an ἐπίκληρος, or inheriting daughter) can risk either being disinherited by his father or contesting the parental inheritance with a claimant with a stronger right.

5. *ὑποκρινόμενος*: cf. note on 31,4.

54,1. *πρὸς τὸ τεῖχος ... τῆς πόλιος*: resumes the story of the siege of Samos. The archaic city walls fortified the citadel on the east, and on the north and west a great part of the hill of Ampelos, for a total length of nearly 6.5 km. The remains of the walls are sometimes several metres tall, with marble blocks each up to

1.5 m. long. The walled area is roughly 1.5 km. in diameter. It is possible that the work of fortification had already begun at the time of the Persian conquest of Asia Minor; see H. J. Kienast, *Die Stadtmauer von Samos*, Bonn 1978. For the moat encircling the walls see 39,4. The exact point of the Spartan attack from the sea must have been at the outermost south-west part of the walls, which, according to Herodotus, ended on the coast with a tower. West of this side of the walls extended a suburb (142,2), perhaps up to the mouth of the Imbrasos (today Rema Mylon); cf. Strabo XIV 1,14. For the topography of Samos see notes to 60,1. 2. τὸν ἐπάνω πύργον...: the remains of an archaic tower on the acropolis are perfectly preserved; see Shipley, pl. 12.   ἐπίκουροι: the mercenaries are clearly distinguished from the 'Samians themselves' (αὐτῶν Σαμίων); cf. 45,3; 145,3; 146,3–4.

55,1. εἰ μὲν νυν...: cf. note on 49,1.   ὅμοιοι: an ironic pun, at least if one thinks of the famous ὅμοιοι of Sparta; so B. Shimron, *RhM* CXXII (1979), 131–3; for ὅμοιοι at Samos see 142,3.

2. ἄλλῳ Ἀρχίῃ τῷ Σαμίου: Herodotus rarely discloses the names of his inform-ants; cf. II 55,32; IV 76,6; IX 16,1; when he does, their testimonies are personal and precise, accepted as true even by the most sceptical; they illustrate well those examples of biographical information on the author himself that are present in his work; see Beltrametti, ch. 1; J. Marincola, *Arethusa*, XX (1987), 121–37. Herodotus probably visited Sparta before 440 BC (thus already A. Kirchhoff, *Über die Entstehungszeit des herodotischen Geschichtswerkes*, Berlin 1878², pp. 49–56).   Πιτάνη: a village and residential quarter of Sparta, on the banks of the Eurotas, west and south-west of the acropolis (Müller I, p. 849); it had ancient and aristocratic traditions, numerous sanctuaries, and the tombs of the Agiad kings. It constituted one of the five ὠβαί (territorial tribes) and a military unit: see IX 53,2–3 and Thucydides' criticism, I 20,3; cf. D. H. Kelly, *GRBS* XXII (1981), 31–8; J. F. Lazenby, *The Spartan Army*, Warminster 1985, pp. 48–52. For a homonymous village in Aeolis (Asia Minor) see I 149,1. Σαμίου: he was born after his father's death, or received a second name after it. The younger Archias was probably born in the early 5th cent. and, when Herodotus met him, must have been *proxenos* of the Samians; cf. Plutarch, *Mor.* 860c. ταφῆναί...δημοσίῃ: cf. Plutarch, *Mor.* 860c.   ὑπὸ Σαμίων: the monument dedicated to Archias was certainly erected by the Samians once they were free, after the fall of tyranny.

56,2. ματαιότερος λόγος: Herodotus does not deny the exceptional minting of coins of gilded lead, but only the veracity of the version which, by stressing Polycrates' inventiveness and simultaneously ridiculing the Spartans (unaccus-tomed to money matters, according to the stereotype), established a connection between the great tyrant and the local Samian minting (ἐπιχώριον νόμισμα); in particular between a series of coins and the siege of 525 BC. Some Samian lead coins originally covered with electrum have been found; see J. P. Barron, *The Silver Coins of Samos*, London 1966, p. 17, with bibl.; however, the problem of the immediate purpose of such a coinage still remains open. The payment of mercenaries or another local need may perhaps appear a more reliable *logos* to us than to Herodotus. A premeditated devaluation has also been suggested: E. Condurachi, *Athenaeum*, XXXVI (1958), 238–47. πρώτην στρατιήν...: this is the first 'Asiatic' campaign (Samos is here considered as part of Asia) of the Lacedaemonians of Doric descent (the Lacedaemonians who fought at Troy were not Dorians). The second took place in 479 at Mycale (IX 96 ff.). Cf. the 'first' and the 'second' submission of the Ionians (I 92,1; 169,2), the 'first' and the 'second' Persian conquest of Babylon (I 191,6; III 159,1), the 'first' and 'second' Ionian secession from the Persian empire (IX 104).

57,1. οἱ... στρατευσάμενοι Σαμίων: this interesting digression continues, up to ch. 59, the story of the mutinous exiles started in chs. 45–6. From a chronological point of view, if we calculate the five years spent in Cydonia (59,2) and the previous adventures, we arrive at *c.*518 BC for the definitive defeat of this brave group of aristocratic exiles, transformed by necessity into pirates and colonizers. It is a very unlikely hypothesis that ancient chronographers also included these years in the period of the 'Samian thalassocracy' (Miller, pp. 31–7). A second period of Samian peregrination with a second five years of prosperity, this time at Zancle, started after the battle of Lade in 494 BC (VI 22–3). A systematic research would have led Herodotus to collect information on all the sites and stages of the Samian peregrinations, besides Samos and Sparta. It must be held, however, that Herodotus was satisified with the version known at Samos, eventually adding evidence gathered especially at Delphi.   καὶ αὐτοί: they moved away with the Spartan ships. It has been suggested that the Spartans took advantage of this occasion to overturn Lygdamis, tyrant of Naxos; see Berve I, pp. 78 f.   Σίφνον: Ionian island of the western Cyclades; it had fertile plains, schist rocks, marble, iron, and lead deposits, and, in antiquity, gold- and silver-mines. The homonymous city was situated on the promontory of the modern Kastro, on the eastern coast, with its acropolis on the hill. Siphnos did not submit to the Persians. In the Delian league it paid a high tribute (at first 3 and later 9 talents) and minted its own coins: both signs of wealth. On the institutions and laws of Siphnos in the early 4th cent. see Isocrates XIX. For bibl., L. Guerrini, *EAA* VII 1966, pp. 328–9; Müller I, pp. 1032–43.

2. τὰ δὲ τῶν Σιφνίων πρήγματα...: after the story of the false gold coins of Samos we pass on to the story of the true gold of Siphnos. Herodotus dates the 'acme' of the mineral wealth of the island, otherwise poor in resources, to around 525; see H. Montgomery, *OA* XV (1984), 122–33. When the mines were exhausted or flooded by the sea the island became impoverished, and declined; the ancients, however, interpreted the change in religious-moral terms; see Paus. X 11,2; Suidas, s.v. Σίφνιοι (Σ 511 Adler) = Aelian, fr. 345 Hercher. For traces of ancient mines sunken in the sea at Hayos Sostis see L. Bürchner, *RE* III A 1 1927, coll. 264 f.; G. A. Wagner and G. Weisgerber, *Archeophysika*, X (1979), 209–22.   ἤκμαζε: the verb occurs in Herodotus five times, of which four refer to prosperous cities that were subsequently conquered or destroyed: besides the present passage see I 29,1; V 28; VI 127,1. Cf. D. Lateiner, *RhM* CXXV

(1982), 97 f. The 'cycle' of prosperity and decadence of cities is already announced at I 5,3–4. **ἀπὸ τῆς δεκάτης:** according to Pausanias (X 11,2), the Siphnians were obliged by order of Apollo to pay a tithe regularly. The treasury of the Siphnians was identified in 1894 with the ruins of a pleasant little Ionic temple of the archaic age with caryatids and friezes, found next to the treasury of Sicyon on the Sacred Way of Delphi. The sculptures of this little temple, which are among the masterpieces of archaic Greek art, are preserved in the Delphi Museum. The dating of the ruins depends solely on the information given by Herodotus in this chapter (para. 3) and at 58,1. For an attempt to lower the date of the treasury to the 5th cent. see E. D. Francis and M. Vickers, *JHS* CIII (1983), 49–97, with R. M. Cook's criticism, *JHS* CIX (1989), 167. On the friezes see F. Vian, *La Guerre des géants*, Paris 1952, pp. 106–12. On a possible allusion of Pindar to a frieze of the Siphnian treasury see K. B. Shapiro, *MH* XLV (1988), 1–5. **διενέμοντο:** according to the normal practice, e.g. in Athens (VII 144,1; Aristotle, *Ath. Pol.* 22,7; Plutarch, *Themist.* 4,1 with Marr's commentary ad loc.).

3. **ἐχρέωντο . . . :** the Siphnians, thanks to their rich gifts to Delphi, had gained, in the 6th cent., the privilege of *προμαντεία*, the right of priority in the consultation of the oracle: see *Syll.* 17b; Croesus and the Lydians had obtained the same right and for the same reason: I 54,2.

4. **Ἀλλ' ὅταν . . . ἐρυθρόν:** this response is in fact a moral admonition which, under an enigmatic cover, establishes a 'causal' connection between excessive prosperity and divine nemesis. In other words, that tragic vision of history, already fully illustrated in Book III by the vicissitudes of Cambyses and Polycrates, reappears. On this response (cf. *Anth. Pal.* XIV 82) see P-W I, pp. 150–2; II, no. 65; Crahay, pp. 258–60; Kirchberg, pp. 23 f.; Huber, pp. 38 ff.; Fontenrose, Q 114 ('c. 520, not genuine') and p. 65. **Ἀλλ' ὅταν:** opening formula typical of archaic or archaizing oracular responses; cf. I 55,2 with note. **πρυτανήια:** cf. I 146,2 with note. **φράδμονος . . . φράσσασθαι:** a characteristic epic alliteration; cf. *Il.* XXIV 354. **ξύλινόν τε λόχον:** cf. the 'wooden wall' of the famous oracle at VII 141,3. **τοῖσι . . . ἠσκημένα:** since the agora and the prytaneum of Siphnos were already faced with marble when the oracle was asked, Herodotus obviously meant the *ἀλλ' ὅταν* of the response not as a prophetic reference to the future, but in a vaguely conditional sense ('in case': cf. I 55,2). Consequently, the part of the response that the Siphnians were unable to interpret was only the second (*τότε δὴ . . . ἐρυθρόν*). Cf. Legrand, *REA* XL (1938), 225 f., who criticizes the proposal to transfer the entire phrase *τοῖσι . . . ἠσκημένα* to 58,1. **Παρίῳ λίθῳ:** cf. V 62,3. The oldest reference in a literary text to the use of this famous marble.

58,1. **πρέσβεας:** only here in the sense of 'messengers' (perhaps an Atticism; see C. Saerens, *AC* XLIV (1975), 618–29). The usual words for 'messenger' in Herodotus are *κῆρυξ* and *ἄγγελος* —both occur in this chapter (in paras. 2 and 3 respectively).

2. **τὸ δὲ παλαιὸν:** for Herodotus' use of *παλαιός* see R. Weil, *SS* VII (1985), 28–37. **μιλτηλιφέες:** cf. the Homeric forms *νῆες μιλτοπάρῃοι* (*Il.* II 637,

with the scholia and the commentary of Eustathius; *Od.* IX 125) and φοινικοπάρῃοι (*Od.* XI 124; XXIII 271), said of 'red-cheeked' ships. Herodotus also knows that μίλτος (red ochre) was used by some African peoples to paint their body (IV 191,1; 194; VII 69,1). καὶ ἦν τοῦτο...: Herodotus interprets the response and rationalistically explains the decline of Siphnos as a consequence of the Samian attack and of the extortion of the 100 talents (para. 4). The religious-moral interpretation reported by Pausanias (X 11,2) reflects more closely the Delphic tradition.

59,1. παρὰ δὲ ῾Ερμιονέων...: the Samians force the Hermionians to give them, instead of money (ἀντὶ χρημάτων), the island of Hydrea: another violent extortion, not a legitimate purchase. The exiles now have enough resources (the 100 talents extorted from the Siphnians and the money borrowed from Troezen) to finance their last enterprise. The entire episode illustrates well the practice of archaic Greek piracy. Hermione (VIII 73,2), a very old city known to Homer (*Il.* II 560), considered by Herodotus a foundation of Dryopian immigrants (VIII 43). This was the birthplace of the poet Lasus, who is also known to Herodotus (VII 6,3). In the 5th cent. it was an ally of Sparta. Remains of walls, temples, and necropoleis are visible east of Mt Pron (Müller I, pp. 771–3). ῾Υδρέαν: the picturesque island of Hydrea, parallel to the southern coast of the Argolid, was known to Hecataeus, *FGrHist* 1 F 124; see Müller I, pp. 773–7. Τροιζηνίοισι: Troezen (Τροζάν, Τροιζήν), about 3 km. from the eastern coast of the Argolid, near the modern village of Damala, bordered in the west the territory of Hermione; it had two ports, one at Pogon (VIII 42,1) and the other at Psipha. Well known to Homer, it was held to be the birthplace of Theseus, and, though Doric or Doricized, it maintained links of close friendship with Athens. It was considered the metropolis of Halicarnassus (VII 99,3) and of Sybaris, called the 'Troezen of Italy'. In 480 it hosted a great number of the families that fled Athens during the Persian invasion (VIII 41–2): a Hellenistic copy or a reworking of the so-called 'decree of Themistocles' with the orders of evacuation was found at Troezen in 1959 (ML 23). See Müller I, pp. 880–2. αὐτοὶ δὲ Κυδωνίην...: the original plan of the Samians was to set sail for Zacynthus (Zante in the Ionian sea: IV 195,2; cf. Müller I, pp. 915–8) and to settle in the island in place of the inhabitants; however, for reasons that Herodotus does not specify, the Samians changed direction (probably when they reached the waters off Cape Malea) and sailed towards Crete, almost as the ships of Menelaus must have done when returning from Troy (*Od.* III 286–92). Cydonia was an important city of western Crete, near modern Chania, in the area of the Homeric Cydonians (*Od.* III 292; XIX 176). The Cydonians were considered an 'autochthonous' people, to whom should probably be ascribed the cult of Cydonian Athena, the Κυδώνια μᾶλα ('quinces') known already to Stesichorus, and also, for example, the mysterious toponym Cydonia in Sicily. The form Κυδών for 'Cretan' is of epic origin. Legend ascribed the foundation of Cydonia to Minos or to an eponymous Kydon; on Cydonia in the Mycenean age see L. Godart in D. Musti (ed.), *Le origini dei Greci. Dori e mondo egeo*, Rome–Bari 1986², pp. 174 ff.; however, we know nothing about a *polis* at Cydonia before the events narrated by Herodotus in this passage. For sources and bibl. see M. Guarducci, *IC* II, pp. 104–16; Müller I, pp. 966 f. On the sculptor Aristocles of Cydonia see Paus. V 25,11.   ἔκτισαν: they 'founded' (cf. 44,1) in the sense of 'colonized', see note on 49,1.   ἐκ τῆς νήσου: from Zacynthus, not from Crete: see Legrand, *REA* XL (1938), 226 ff.

2. εὐδαιμόνησαν: 'lived happily', 'prospered'; cf. in the sense of 'prosper' with reference to cities: I 170,1–2; II 177,1; V 28; 81,2; cf. III 52,4; V 31,3; VIII 2.   τὰ ἱρά: nothing of these temples remains. The cults of Cydonia are known mainly from coins. For the local feasts, Ephorus, *FGrHist* 70 F 29.

ἐόντα νῦν: the expression could indicate autopsy. Δικτύνης νηόν: an extramural sanctuary on the eastern coast of the Tityros peninsula, about 35 km. from Cydonia by the coast road. Remains of the temple of the Roman period have been excavated. Dikty(n)na, originally a Cretan 'mother-goddess', was assimilated by the Greeks to Artemis, the goddess of hunters and also of fishermen; in the popular etymology, Dikty(n)na is the goddess of the 'net' (δίκτυον). She was also variously confused, associated, or identified with the eastern Cretan nymph Britomartis and, outside Crete, with Aphaia of Aegina (Paus. II 30,3). She had a cult in Laconia, in Athens, and elsewhere. Sources and bibl. are collected by D. Williams, *LIMC* I 1 1981, pp. 876–7; C. Boulotis, ibid., III 1 1986, pp. 391–4; H van Effenterre, ibid., pp. 169–70; Müller I, pp. 943–5.

3. ἕκτῳ δὲ ἔτεϊ: around 518 BC.   Αἰγινῆται: this important maritime city had direct interests in ensuring the security of navigation in the western Aegean. On the fleet, thalassocracy, and prosperity of Aegina in the 6th cent., cf. V 81,2; 83,1–2.   ἠνδραποδίσαντο: cf. note on 25,3.   μετὰ Κρητῶν: these must be the Cretans expelled by the Samians five years earlier.   τῶν νηῶν καπρίους: here κάπριος (κάπρος in Homer) is an adjective. The 'Samaina', a Samian bireme attributed to Polycrates, had a 'prow shaped like a wild boar' (ὑόπρωπος); it figured on the Samian coins of Zancle and was described in various literary sources; see G. Dunst, *MDAI(A)* LXXXVII (1972), 159–61.   τὸ ἱρὸν τῆς Ἀθηναίης...: the famous archaic temple of Aphaia, situated about 4.5 km. east of Palaiochora, the site of ancient Aegina. The great group of sculptures that adorned the two pediments (today in the Glyptothek at Munich) clearly referred to the goddess Athena. The name Aphaia appears on an archaic inscription found near the sanctuary (τἀφαίαι hοῖϜος, 'temple of Aphaia': *IG* IV 15880). Aphaia was a well-known divinity of Aegina (see above all Paus. II 30,3), also identified with the Cretan Dikty(n)na (see note on 59,2). Her name probably became the Aeginetan epithet of Athena. Ἀθηναίης is not therefore a mistake that should be corrected to Ἀφαίης, as was thought immediately after the discovery of the inscription. The temple known to Herodotus, the impressive remains of which are still visible, was enlarged and transformed in the early 5th cent. BC. after a fire had destroyed the previous one. See A. Furtwängler, *Aegina. Das Heiligtum der Aphaia* I–II, Munich 1906; B. Conticello *EAA* III 1960, pp. 238–47 with bibl.; A. Invernizzi, *I frontoni del tempio di Aphaia ad Egina*, Turin 1965; R. A. Tomlinson, *Greek Sanctuaries*, London 1976, pp. 104–8; U. Sinn, *MDAI(A)* CII (1987), 131–67; D. Williams, *AA* (1987),

629 ff.; Müller I, pp. 736–43. The dedication of the Samian prows to the goddess of Aegina, venerated under another name also at Cydonia, must have had a cultic meaning. Herodotus, who had probably seen the prows, when recalling the vicissitudes of the Samian thalassocracy will have discovered in the dedication also a moral symbolic message. For an Aeginetan colony at Cydonia, perhaps after 518 BC, see Strabo VIII 6,16; for Aeginetan colonists in Crete in the 4th cent. see Plato, *Leg.* IV 707e.

4. ἔγκοτον: in Herodotus, rancour is a 'cause' of vindictive acts that then become 'causes' of wars (cf. αἰτίη at end of para. and IX 110,1); with διά or a causal genitive: VI 73,1; 133,1; VIII 29,1.   ἐπ' Ἀμφικράτεος...: typical eponymic formula that recalls a βασιλεύς as eponymous magistrate of archaic Samos. Others think of an actual and proper 'king', who in the 7th cent. would have commanded the Samian fleet against Aegina (perhaps during the Lelantine war?), or even a tyrant. See G. Schmidt, *MDAI(A)* LXXXVII (1972), 184 f.; R. Drews, *Basileus: The Evidence for Kingship in Geometric Greece*, New Haven 1983, pp. 27 f.; P. Carlier, *La Royauté en Grèce avant Alexandre*, Strasbourg 1984, pp. 445 f.; Shipley, pp. 37 ff. For βασιλεύς and τύραννος in Herodotus see note on 52,3.

60,1. ἐμήκυνα: the chapter starts and ends with this verbal form; cf. II 35,1. The 'length' of the Samian *logos* is better explained differently (see note on chs. 39–60). Some have thought ἐμήκυνα an epistolary aorist, with which the author asks the reader for a little more patience (see J. E. Powell, *CQ* XXIX (1935), p. 152; but see Erbse's reaction, pp. 146–7).   μέγιστα...ἐξεργασμένα: see the bibl. in the note on chs. 39–60. Herodotus does not explicitly attribute to Polycrates the great building-works of Samos; but Aristotle wrote of great ἔργα Πολυκράτεια, 'Polycratean works' (*Pol.* 1313b24), perhaps expressing the common opinion of his time. The chronology, based on archaeological excavations, dates the beginning of the works to the forties of the 6th cent. (cf. note on 39,1); their grandiosity is entirely worthy of the building policy of the Greek tyrants; see G. Bodei Giglioni, *Lavori pubblici e occupazione nell' antichità classica*, Bologna 1974, pp. 15 ff.   ὄρεος: the Ampelos hill, close to the city, was partly included within the city walls; it is 240 m. high; the 150 ὀργυιαί of Herodotus equal about 270 m.   ὄρυγμα: the aim of this very famous tunnel was to conduct into the city the water of a spring situated to the north, in the plain of Ayades. It was a tunnel with an underground aqueduct. It was discovered in 1882 and made known to the public two years later by E. Fabricius. The measurements correspond, very approximately, to those reported in this chapter: the length of the tunnel is 1050 m. (7 stades = 1,250 m.); the height and the width are *c.*175 cm. (8 feet = 240 cm.); the depth of the aqueduct is 20 cubits (880 cm.); this measurement, even if it refers to the entrance of the aqueduct, is excessive; the aqueduct's width is 3 feet, equal to 90 cm. The tunnel was excavated simultaneously from both ends and the excavators met halfway, with a horizontal deviation of about 2 m. and a vertical one of 3 m. It was a remarkable success for the levelling techniques of the time; there are various attempts to explain it: either by attributing to the architect notions evolved from geometric theory (Eupalinus

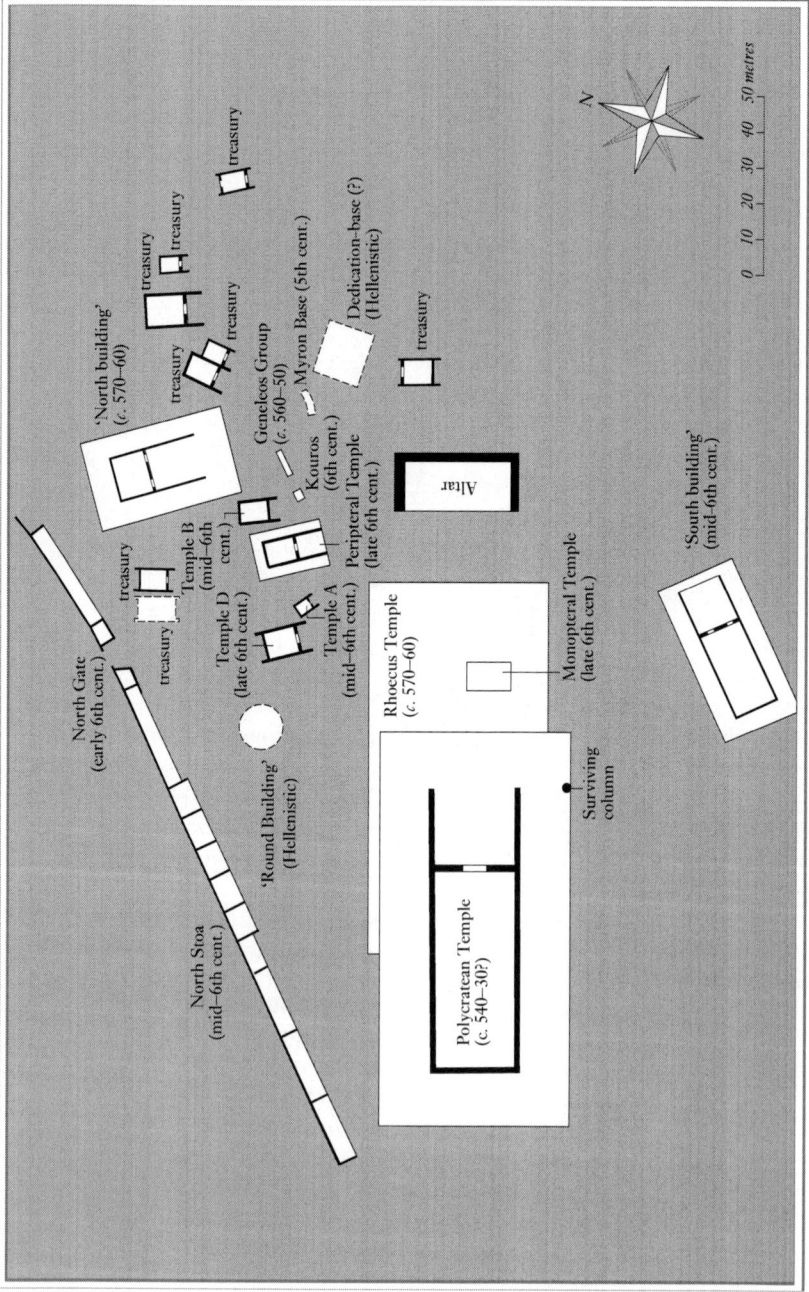

Map 33. The Samian Heraion c.500 BC

The labels on the map:

North Stoa (mid–6th cent.)

North Gate (early 6th cent.)

'Round Building' (Hellenistic)

treasury

Temple D (late 6th cent.)

Temple B (mid–6th cent.)

treasury

'North building' (c. 570–60)

treasury

treasury

treasury

treasury

Temple A (mid–6th cent.)

Geneleos Group (c. 560–50)

Kouros (6th cent.)

Myron Base (5th cent.)

Peripteral Temple (late 6th cent.)

Dedication-base (?) (Hellenistic)

treasury

Altar

Rhoccus Temple (c. 570–60)

Polycratean Temple (c. 540–30?)

Surviving column

Monopteral Temple (late 6th cent.)

'South building' (mid–6th cent.)

0 10 20 30 40 50 metres

N

and Pythagoras of Samos were almost contemporaries), or by examining the problem from an empirical point of view. In the East the technique is well attested in the late 7th cent. BC by Hezekiah's acqueduct in Jerusalem. See B. L. van der Waerden, *Science Awakening*, Groningen 1954, pp. 102–5 (with the criticism of J. Goodfield and S. Toulmin, *Isis* LVI (1965), 46–55); for the excavations see the reports of U. Jantzen (and others), *AA* (1973), 72–89, 401–4; (1975), 19–35; H. J. Kienast, *Architectura*, VII (1977), 97–117; T. E. Rihll and J. V. Tucker, in A. Powell (ed.) *The Greek World*, London 1995, pp. 403–31. The excavation of the tunnel is today dated to *c.*540–530 BC at the latest.

2. **ἄλλο ὄρυγμα**: the aqueduct.   **σωλήνων**: remains of pipes are preserved in the stretch that leads from the spring to the northern opening of the tunnel (about 850 m.), where the water flowed into the aqueduct; another pipe conducted the water into tanks situated inside the city walls.

3. **Εὐπαλῖνος**: to him is attributed also the restoration of a monumental fountain in Megara, built according to Pausanias (I 40,1) by the tyrant Theagenes (see Berve II, p. 536). A Megarean sculptor of the same name was active in the 3rd cent. BC **χῶμα**: cf. VIII 97,1. This double-branched mole, a continuation of the city walls, created a 'closed harbour', typical of Greek city ports of the Classical and Hellenistic periods. It was built with great marble blocks, still visible and partly reused in building the modern mole of Pythagorion (Shipley, pp. 76 f.). The length reported by Herodotus (more than 2 stades = 360 m.) seems right, whereas the depth (20 ὀργυιαί = 360 m.) would be double what can be observed today in the modern port.

4. **νηός ...**: the great and famous temple of Hera rising about 6 km. west of the city walls, near an anchorage (cf. IX 96,1) at the mouth of the river Imbrasos, in a place (today Kolonna) dedicated to the cult since Mycenaean times. The excavations revealed the various prehistoric and archaic phases of the construction. The so-called 'temple of Rhoikos', erected around the middle of the 6th cent., is believed to constitute the third phase. It was a giant dipteros (52 × 105 m.) with a total of about 136 columns and a great altar to the east. It was destroyed shortly after its construction by a fire, perhaps started by the Persians around 540 (see Paus. VII 5,4), or during the Spartan siege of 525, or again by the Persians during the conquest of Samos around 520 (chs. 144–9). This was probably the sanctuary mentioned by the poet Asios (see A. Veneri, *QUCC* XVII (1984), 81–93); the temple visited by Herodotus is the successive one, similar to the former in dimensions and style, built after the fire about 40 m. further west. Although it remained unfinished, it aroused admiration. The size of the temple, in fact, is not inferior to the great temples of Agrigento and Selinunte; along with the Artemisium of Ephesus (I 26,2) it was one of the major temples of Ionic art. For other references to it in Herodotus see I 70,3; III 123,1; IV 88,1; 152,4. To the bibl. quoted in the note on chs. 39–60 add R. A. Tomlinson, *Greek Sanctuaries*, London 1976, pp. 124–7; H. Walter, *Das Heraion von Samos*, Munich 1976; H. Kyrieleis, *Führer durch das Heraion von Samos*, Athens 1981, and in N. Marinatos and R. Hägg (eds.), *Greek Sanctuaries*, London 1993, pp. 125–53; Shipley, pp. 78 f., 262, with further bibl.   **τῶν ἡμεῖς ἴδμεν**: for this typically Herodotean idiom cf., in Book III, 94,2; 98,2; 122,2; see Powell's *Lexicon*, s.v. οἶδα.

ἀρχιτέκτων πρῶτος ἐγένετο ...: the attribution of the second temple to Rhoikos as 'chief architect' chronologically is perhaps not far from the truth, if its sense is that the temple was devised according to the model of the first dipteros. In any case the Samian tradition known to Herodotus did not connect the Heraion with the name of Polycrates. See A. E. Furtwaengler, *MDAI(A)* XCIX (1984), 97–103.   'Ροῖκος Φίλεω: Φιλαίου, according to Pausanias VIII 14,8; see J. E. Powell, *CQ* XXXII (1938), 214. This famous architect from Samos is sometimes associated with his fellow-countryman Theodorus (cf. 41,1; I 51,3; for Theodorus 'son' of Rhoikos see Diog. Laert. II 103) for his invention or perfection of fusion and working of bronze (Paus. VIII 14,8; IX 41,1; X 38,6). Various works were attributed to him, among them a female statue representing Night in the Artemisium at Ephesus (Paus. X 38,6). The rare anthroponym (ῥοικός = 'hunchback', 'bowed'), probably Ionian, occurs in an archaic inscription in Samian alphabet, found at Naucratis (Jeffery, p. 328). See P. Moreno, *EAA* VI 1965, pp. 672–3; A. Stewart, *Greek Sculpture*, New Haven 1990, pp. 244–6.

61–88. On the story of false Smerdis and Darius' ascent to the throne, which is the core of the main narrative of Book III, and on the general problem of sources, see Introduction, pp. 385 f., 387 f. Whether the events narrated in these chapters are historically true is a matter of dispute. Once it was believed that the Bisitun inscription gave truthful information (see App. I), the credibility of Herodotus increased also. Things changed when, at the beginning of the 20th cent., the inscription began to be considered as a propaganda text. Thereupon the theory that the Magus Gaumata (the false Smerdis) had never existed became popular: the story was simply an invention of Darius, modelled on other 'false kings', rebels and usurpers, aimed at justifying the *coup d'état* and thus legitimating his own power. Darius' very insistence on his struggle against 'the Lie' was rightly appraised as propaganda. From this perspective the real usurper would be Darius himself, who would have killed the *real* Smerdis (Bardiya), who himself had seized power in a moment of general disaffection shortly before the death of Cambyses. The invention of the false Smerdis would have then necessarily required the invention of the whole story of the assassination of the true Smerdis by order of Cambyses. We are faced with a theory that only seems to solve the problems, but which actually creates many others. It does, in fact, seem incredible that a brother of the Great King could be secretly eliminated, with no one at the court noticing his death for years; yet it is equally incredible that Darius could invent a false Smerdis after having killed the true one. The fact remains that Darius was fully convinced that his contemporaries would have accepted his version: in some regimes 'truth' is the official version that the government imposes on its subjects (see what Darius himself says at §56 ff. in the Bisitun inscription). Shortly after the death of Gaumata, a second false Smerdis appeared before the people (§40 ff.); in other provinces, false Nabuchadnezzars, false descendants of Cyaxares, and so on suddenly sprouted, all usurping names and titles of kings that had traditionally become symbols of the independence and greatness of their countries. These are symbolic names for impressing the masses in times of discontent and effective in inciting the people to revolt. In these situations the problem of historical 'truth' does not arise. The phenomenon of false kings has too many analogies in the ancient world (e.g. the false Neros) and in the medieval and modern periods (the false Fredericks) to be lightly considered a pure invention for propaganda purposes. Thus the case of Bardiya is not fundamentally different from other cases of rebel kings. In modern historical reconstructions, the origin of the Persian crisis of 522/1 BC is usually ascribed to opposition to the centralizing despotism of Cambyses; the crisis probably broke out openly after the catastrophe in Ethiopia. Emphasized here is the social and political conflict between the Persian high nobility (represented by the seven conspirators) and the inferior classes, the multitudes of peasants and peoples subjected to Persia, among whom Gaumata perhaps sought support in his seizure of power. Gaumata is sometimes presented in modern studies as a revolutionary, or even as a precursor of the famous 'Manichean-communist' Mazdak of the 5th cent. AD, whereas Darius is regularly seen as the restorer of the old regime. Others attach more importance to the rivalry between the two Achaemenid dynastic branches—that of Cyrus and Cambyses, and that of Hystaspes and Darius—and to their respective followers; or to the conflict between centralism (of the 'Median' variety, according to some) represented by Cambyses (and by Gaumata) and the satrapic 'federalism' instituted by Darius as a system; or to the religious tensions, sometimes violent, between uncompromising Zoroastrianism (according to some, championed by the Magi; according to others, by Darius, the chosen of Ahura Mazda) and the more ancient Iranic cultic traditions which privileged the nobles (these tensions would be finally resolved by the pragmatic syncretism imposed by Darius). The old interpretations along ethnic lines—conflict between Medes (the Magi) and Persians—although based on the version of Herodotus himself (see 65,6 with note), are nowadays less fashionable. In all these reconstructions many elements remain hypothetical and even fanciful: the same texts and the same words are often interpreted in completely different ways. There is agreement, however, on the fact that, in the sources at our disposal, the 'great history'—social, political, ethnic, and religious—of this period is reduced to a minimum: to what is required (on the one hand) by the needs of the legitimizing propaganda of Darius, and (on the other) by the requirements of Herodotus' narrative and didactic art. The bibl. is vast. (On the inscription of Bisitun see what is quoted in the introductory note on App. I.) On Herodotus and the inscription of Bisitun see Dandamaev; A. Martorelli, *RIL* CXI (1977), 115–25; F. Gschnitzer, *Sitzungsberichte der Heidelberger Ak. der Wiss.* (1977); Wiesehöfer; A. Köhnken, *Würzburger Jahrb. für die Altertumswissenschaft* (1980), 39–59; J. M. Cook, *CHI*, pp. 215–7; Balcer; T. C. Young, *CAH*[2] IV, pp. 53–66; for an unusual and unconvincing interpretation see E. J. Bickerman, *Athenaeum*, LVI (1978), 239–61; for a 'detective story' reading of the Herodotean *logos* see I. Gershevitch, *AAntHung* XXVII (1979), 337–51.

61,1. *Καμβύσῃ...ἀδελφεοί*: the synchronic connection refers not to the history of Samos, but to the events of Persian history. According to the inscription of

Bisitun (see App. I, §§11–13), the revolt of Gaumata started on 11 March 522; the Magus was acknowledged as king on 1 July and killed on 29 September of the same year.   μάγοι δύο ἀδελφεοί: there are two in chs. 61–6, 74, and 76–9 (also in Justin I 9,7–9 and in some Byzantine sources, e.g. *Chronicon Paschale*, p. 357 Migne (*PG* 92); Cedrenus I, p. 144 Bekker; Constantine Manasses, *Compendium Chronicum* 873 Bekker), whereas there is only one in chs. 67–73, in the inscription of Bisitun, and in Ctesias, *FGrHist* 688 F 13 (11 ff.). Other doubles in this *logos* are the two Smerdeis, the two Ecbatanas, the two identical wounds of Apis and Cambyses. On the Magi in Herodotus see I 140,2 with note. This *logos* probably has the earliest Greek use of the word μάγος in the common sense of impostor or in the more specific one of a conspirator in religious dress: e.g. Sophocles, *Oed. Tyr.* 585 ff. (cf. K. J. Rigsby, *GRBS* XVII (1976), 109–14); Plato, *Resp.* IX 572; and *Ep.* VII 337a (where the Magus is called 'a eunuch': see I. Lévy, *REG* XLII (1940), 234–41). For an ancient criticism of such hostile interpretations see Dio Chrys. *Or.* 36. In the inscription of Bisitun Gaumata is repeatedly called *maguš*.   τῶν οἰκίων μελεδωνόν: 'butler' (for ἐπίτροπος τῶν οἰκίων see 63,2; 65,5), or also 'custodian', 'administrator' (cf. II 65,3–4; VII 31; 38,3). On the office of μελεδωνοί at Samos, *Syll.* 976, l. 16; on the verb μελεδαίνω ('to tend' to a sick person) cf. VIII 115,3. It has been supposed that the original Persian title of this official was **pati-khšayathia* (from this *padishah, pasha*), 'viceroy', and that Herodotus (or his source) transformed the title into a proper name (Patizeithes), thus dividing the Magus into two persons; see Marquart II, p. 145; Altheim–Stiehl, *Die aramäische Sprache*, pp. 75–86. In the inscription of Bisitun, the usurping *Maguš* is not a court official; nor does he begin the revolt from inside the palace of Susa (cf. 64,2), but from a place called Paishiyauvada (§11), which some identify with Pasargadae.   ὡς ὀλίγοι...: first of all Prexaspes; Cambyses' sister-wife also knew or suspected it (32,2), but now she was already dead. According to Ctesias, the killing was known to four eunuch accomplices; and Amytis, Smerdis' mother, also discovered it and killed herself: *FGrHist* 688 F 13 (11–13).

2. τοῖσι βασιληίοισι: cf. in this sense 65,5.   οἰκὼς...τὸ εἶδος: cf. Ctesias, *FGrHist* 688 F 13 (12); Justin I 9,10. The motif of physical resemblance is a narrative element of storytelling missing from the Bisitun inscription. Herodotus' false Smerdis had no ears (69,3 ff.): for this reason, despite the physical similarity, he refrained from appearing in public (68,2).   καὶ οὔνομα τὠυτὸ εἶχε...: Herodotus (or his source) misunderstood or interpreted the original statement of the pretender: 'I am Bardiya, the son of Cyrus, the brother of Cambyses!' (Bis. inscr. §11). His real name was Gaumata, which becomes Cometes in Justin I 9,7. In Ctesias the name of the Magus is Sphendadates; in Justin I 9,9–10 it is Oropastas; in Aeschylus, *Pers.* 774 ff., the successor of 'the son of Cyrus' is Mardos, who was a disgrace as a king, but was neither a Magus nor a usurper. On the form Smerdis cf. note on 30,1.

3. Πατιζείθης: Πανξούθης in Dionysius of Miletus, *FGrHist* 687 F 2 (cited in the scholia to Herodotus), probably from his *Persika*. Cf. also the name Παζάτας in Xanthus of Lydia, *FGrHist* 765 F 32. In the Bisitun inscription and in

Ctesias there is no one whose role corresponds to that of Patizeithes. For the Persian original of the name see note on 61,1.

62,1. εὕρισκε... ἐν Ἀγβατάνοισι: a parenthetic phrase or a gloss of the author, that does not explain the motive for Cambyses' arrival in Syria; Cambyses for the first time became aware of the revolt when he arrived in Syria. For a hypothetical reconstruction of Cambyses' route from Egypt to Syria see P. Högemann, in G. Maddoli (ed.), *Strabone. Contributi allo studio della personalità e dell'opera*, Perugia 1986, pp. 159–69.   ἐς μέσον: 'at the centre', 'in the presence of'; cf. in this sense, in Book III, 129,3; 130,1; 140,3. In a different sense 80,2 with note. 2. ἐλπίσας: cf. in this sense 143,2; 151,2; 157,1.   ἀληθέα: on truth and falsehood in Book III see Introduction, pp. 391 ff.   εἶπε...: here begins a series of three dialogues (62,2–4; 63,1–2; 63,3–4), and a speech (65,1–7), which form the backbone of the account of Cambyses' tragic death; see Heni, p. 135. Πρήξασπες... διέπρηξας... πρῆγμα: on these alliterations see J. E. Powell, *CR* LI (1937), 104.
3. νεῖκος: a Homerism; in a similar sense cf. 120,2; VI 42,1; 66,1; 68,2; VII 158,2; VIII 87,3; IX 55,1.
4. ἀνεστέασι: the verb is used only here in Herodotus for the resurrection of the dead. But the belief is swiftly eliminated, since the resurrected would be the false Smerdis, identical to the true one in appearance and in name (61,2), ἐνεστεῶτα on the throne (67,1; cf. ἐνιστάμενος at 68,1). ἀνεστέασι seems to create with ἐπαναστήσεσθαι an intentional alliteration.   Ἀστυάγεα...: the last Median king and, according to Herodotus, Cambyses' maternal great-grandfather; he was deposed by Cyrus in 550 BC (see I 107–30 with note). The mention of Astyages is a first hint of the connection between the Medes and the revolt of the Magus (see 65,6 with note).   ἐπαναστήσεσθαι: cf. 39,1 with note.

63,1. Ὤνθρωπε: see Dickey, pp. 150–4 and 285.   ἄπιθι χαίρων: cf. I 121; IV 136,4.
2. ἐξ ὅτευ... οὔκω ὄπωπα: according to the Bisitun inscription, Bardiya was killed before Cambyses' Egyptian campaign (§10; cf. note on 30,1). Perhaps Herodotus has been led here to contradict his own moralizing theory, which seeks to establish a direct connection between Cambyses' madness and the assassination of his brother.
3. αἰτίην: fault or accusation of disobedience, in this specific instance; cf. note on 1,1.   ἐπιβατεύων... οὐνόματος: cf. 67,2; IX 95. Herodotus means the fraudulent usurpation in using the name of another.
4. ὦ βασιλεῦ: see Dickey, pp. 96–7.

64,1. ἔτυψε ἡ ἀληθείη: the drama of Cambyses, like that of Oedipus, unfolds tragically when he discovers the truth, or correctly reinterprets the events of his life.
2. ἀπέκλαιε... ἀποκλαύσας: on the terminology of lamentations see note on 14,1.   περιημεκτήσας: on the meaning of this typical Herodotean verb see M. Gigante, *PP* XXI (1966), 302 f.   ἐς Σοῦσα: cf. note on 61,1; on the city of Susa see 91,4 with note.

3. οἱ ἀναθρῴσκοντι...: when mounting on horseback, the mushroom-shaped tip (μύκης) of the scabbard (κολεόν) broke off, and the dagger penetrated his thigh; by ξίφος is probably meant the so-called ἀκινάκης (cf. 118,2; 128,5; VII 54,2), that the Persians carried on their left side. See G. Walser, in *Festschrift H. Bengtson*, Wiesbaden 1983, pp. 8–18; cf. Hinz, fig. 33; P. Calmeyer, *AH* II (1987), 13. The same terminology is found in a verbal quotation of Hecataeus (*FGrHist* 1 F 22) which Herodotus certainly knew. For the definition of μύκης see scholion to Nicander, *Alexipharmaca* 103. According to Herodotus, Cambyses accidentally wounded himself; cf. Justin I 9,8; according to Ctesias, *FGrHist* 688 F 13 (14) Cambyses wounded his thigh with his own dagger at Babylon while amusing himself by cutting a piece of wood; for the suicide of Cambyses, see Constantine Manasses, *Compendium Chronicum* 871 Bekker. In the Bisitun inscription Cambyses *uvāmaršiyuš amariyatā* (§11), 'died his own death', an expression that has often been understood as suicide; today it is generally held that the Persian text does not specify the manner of his death: its sense would then be the vague one of *suo fato obiit*, which perhaps excludes only the possibility that he was assassinated (possibly by Darius himself, according to a daring modern theory). See W. Schulze, *Sitzungsberichte der Preussischen Ak. der Wiss.*, XXXVII (1912), 685–703; H. H. Schaeder, *Nach. der Ak. der Wiss. Göttingen*, (1946–7), 26–36; J. P. Asmussen, *Acta Orientalia*, XXXI (1968), 9–14; J. Puhvel, in *Studia classica et orientalia A. Pagliaro oblata*, III, Rome 1969, 169–75; G. Lazard, *BSL* LXXI (1976), 175–92; Wiesehöfer, pp. 57–60; Balcer, pp. 93 ff. Cambyses' death is also the subject of a passage filled with lacunae, and restored in various ways, of the Demotic Chronicle (note on 37,1): see G. Farina, *Bilychnis*, XXXIII (1929), 455.   κατὰ τοῦτο...: it is unnecessary to look for an Egyptian source for this unmistakable Herodotean symbolism; cf. I 11,5. For the wound of Apis see 29,1–3 and notes.

4. ἐκ Βουτοῦς πόλιος: on this famous oracle see II 83; 152,3, 155, with Lloyd's notes, and *Commentary 1–98*, pp. 270 ff. and *Commentary 99–182*, pp. 140 ff., with bibl.. The sacrilegious king had consulted an Egyptian oracle. Μηδικοῖσι Ἀγβατάνοισι: on Ecbatana, summer capital of the Achaemenids, see I 98,3 and III 92,1 with notes.   ἐν Συρίῃ Ἀγβατάνοισι: cf. 62,1. According to Stephanus of Byzantium, s.v. Ἀγβάτανα, where Herodotus and Demetrius of Magnesia are quoted, the place was later called Βατάνεια. For *Acbatana* on Mt Carmel, Pliny, *NH* V 75, for the fortress Ἐκβάτανα in Batanea (Bashan, in Syria), Josephus, *Vita* 54 ff. Some located this Ecbatana at Hamath on the Orontes (Epiphaneia, modern Hama), a toponym that recalls the Aramaic *Ahmetha*, i.e. *Hamadan* = Median Ecbatana; however, the existence of an Ecbatana in Syria is generally denied. The interpretation of the ambiguous oracle is typically Herodotean: it seeks to show the infallibility of oracular responses, but also the deficiency of the human faculty of interpretation and the inevitability of fate; cf. I 53,3 and 91,4. Cf. Marquart II, pp. 151–6; Kirchberg, pp. 30–2. For similar examples of oracles on death with homonymy of place-names see Thuc. III 96,1; Plutarch, *Flam.* 20,3–4; Appian, *Syriaca* 11; Paus. VIII 11,10–1; Amm. Marc. XXV

3,9; Zonaras XIII 13; etc. Cf. Aly, pp. 97 ff. According to Ctesias, Cambyses died at Babylon (note on 64,3); according to Josephus, *Ant. Iud.* XI 30, at Damascus.

5. ἐκπεπληγμένος: the trauma causes the king to recover from his madness; differently Powell, *CQ* XXIX (1935), 152 f.   ἐστὶ πεπρωμένον...: a typical phrase of determinism; cf. N. Marinatos, *Saeculum*, XXXIII (1982), 258 ff.

65,4. ὁ δαίμων: for the divine origin of dreams, cf. VII 16 and 18,3.

5. ἔργον ἐξέργασται: cf. IX 75; Aeschylus, *Pers.* 759.

6. θεοὺς τοὺς βασιληίους: cf. V 106,6; Justin XI 15,10; Plutarch, *Mor.* 338 f. (Ζεῦ πατρῷε Περσῶν καὶ βασίλειοι θεοί); Dio of Prusa, *Or.* 74,14. The formula probably is of Persian origin: *Auramazdām hadā vithaibiš bagaibiš*, 'Ahura Mazda together with the kings' (?): *DPd* l. 13 ff. Kent.   Ἀχαιμενιδέων: see I 107 with notes.   ἐς Μήδους: from the initial assumption that the Magi were a Median caste (I 101), Herodotus concludes that their usurpation was a revolt of the Medes against the Persians. Cf. 73,1; 126,1 and the references to Astyages (62,4) and to Ectabana (64,4). Cf. Plato, *Leg.* III 695b. However, in the Persian texts the identification of the Magi with the Medes is not attested. Only in the Babylonian version of Bisitun is Gaumata the Magus called 'Median' (l. 15 Voigtlander); the fact that Gaumata was killed in Media (note on 78,5) is irrelevant. Cf. note on chs. 61–88. Herodotus knew of a Median revolt against Darius: I 130,2 and cf. the notes to III 126,1; 127,1.   εἴτε δόλῳ ... σθένεϊ: the end justifies the means: cf. 72,4–5. According to Aeschylus, *Pers.* 775, Mardos was killed σὺν δόλῳ.

7. γῆ τε καρπὸν...: an imprecation formula, found with many variants in several ancient civilizations; for the Persians see the Bisitun inscription, §§66–7; for the Greeks, e.g. Soph. *Oed. Tyr.* 269 ff.; Aeschines 3, 111; Tod, *GHI* II, no. 204, l. 39 ff.; *Syll.* 526, l. 44 ff.; 527, l. 85 ff. For the sterility of the earth, of women, and of flocks cf. VI 139,1; Soph. *Oed. Tyr.* 25 ff.; Myrsilus, *FGrHist* 477 F 8. Cf. Prexaspes' imprecation at III 75,3; on imprecations in Herodotus, Giraudeau, p. 31 ff.   ἐλευθέροισι: the political independence of the Persians from the yoke of the Medes; cf. I 126,6; 127,1; 210,2; III 82,5; VII 2,3. For ἐλευθερίη in the sense of 'freedom' from tyranny see 125,3 with note.

66,1. πάντες...διεχρέωντο: cf. VIII 99,2; Aesch. *Pers.* 537; Xen. *Cyr.* III 1,13; for other sources, see L. Belloni (ed.), *Eschilo, I Persiani*, Milan 1988, p. 101. The ripping of clothes is a very common expression of grief in ancient oriental cultures. See *Luciano, Il lutto*, ed. V. Andò, Palermo 1984, p. 131.

2. ἐσφακέλισε...ἐσάπη: cf. VI 136,3.   βασιλεύσαντα...: the Babylonian commercial documents and the Bisitun inscription confirm and more precisely define the chronology of Herodotus. The first Babylonian tablet is dated, by its mention of Cambyses, to 31 August 530; the last one to 18 April 522. Another is dated only a few days earlier, by its mention of Bardiya, who probably calculated his official 'first' Babylonian year from 1 Nisan 522: cf. note on 67,2. Cambyses therefore reigned for seven official years in total (1 Nisan 529–end of Adar 522), and for about seven additional months from his ascent to the throne to the

beginning of the 'first year' (August 530–March/April 529). Josephus (*Ant. Iud.* XI 30) counts six years for Cambyses and one year for the reign of the Magi, thus converting the tradition known to Herodotus into round figures. Apparently Herodotus did not include in his calculation the period when Cambyses was co-regent with his father Cyrus only in Babylon (538–530 BC); with the addition of this period, the total should be sixteen 'official' years. Cf. the eighteen years of Cambyses in Ctesias, *FGrHist* 688 F 13 (14), which (according to some) reflects the Babylonian calculation. Consequently, τὰ πάντα should be understood in this passage in the sense of 'in the whole (empire)' = 'King of lands', and not—as elsewhere—in the sense of 'in total' (e.g. I 214,3; II 159,3; VII 4). On the chronology of Cambyses see also Manetho, *FGrHist* 609 F 2; 3a–b; 11. See the bibl. in the note on III 1,1, and esp. A. Poebel, *AJSL* LV (1938), 130–41 (a fundamental work on the Persian calendar); *AJSL* LVI (1939), 121 ff.: G. G. Cameron, *AJSL*. LVIII (1941), 314 ff.; Parker–Dubberstein, pp. 10 f, 14; Balcer, pp. 106 ff. According to Ctesias, *FGrHist* 688 F 13 (15), the eunuch Izabates returned Cambyses' body to Persia. On the presumed 'tomb of Cambyses', left unfinished at Dašt-i Gohar, not far from the future Persepolis, see E. Porada, *CHI*, pp. 801 f.   ἄπαιδα...: cf. the case of Astyages (I 109,3) and for the phrase cf. VII 61,3; 205,1. The ἀπαιδίη (VI 139,1), an obsession and punishment of Cambyses, marks the end of the dynasty of Cyrus (cf. 32,4). See also note on 40,3.

3. ἀπιστίη...: cf. II 152,4. The Persian nobles were convinced, like some modern historians, that the story of the killing of the true Smerdis and the figure of the 'false' Smerdis were propaganda inventions. Cf. note on chs. 61–88.

67,2. μῆνας ἑπτά...πληρώσιος: cf. Ctesias, *FGrHist* 688 F 13 (16). In this passage the departing-point of Herodotus is the imprecise assumption that the reigns of Cambyses and the Magus followed each other, whereas in fact they were partially simultaneous. According to the Bisitun inscription (cf. note on 61,1), seven months separated the beginning of the revolt of the Magus from his death, but his acknowledged reign probably lasted only three months. From the Babylonian tablets it appears that Bardiya was the acknowledged king at least between 14 April and 20 September 522, i.e. for more than six months. See the bibl. to note on 66,2. Herodotus does not include the false Smerdis in his Achaemenid genealogy (e.g. 89,3; VII 8a,1; 11,2), as Photius in his Herodotean epitome saw (see C. E. Finch, *Classical Weekly*, XLIII (1949), 40 f.).

3. εὐεργεσίας: cf. VII 39,2; IX 18,3; in a different sense see 47,1 with note.   πόθον...: implicit here is a favourable judgement on the Magus' government; cf. Bisitun inscription §13, and the bibl. in the note on chs. 61–88.   πάρεξ αὐτῶν Περσέων: Herodotus, faithful to the thesis of a Median revolt (see note on 65,6), cannot include the Persians among those who enter-tained a 'nostalgic' longing for the reign of the Magus; the Bisitun inscription (§§40–3) records a second revolt in Persia headed by a second 'false Bardiya'. See Dandamaev, pp. 126 ff., 133 ff.; Wiesehöfer, pp. 77 ff.   πᾶν ἔθνος: cf. similar

phrases in Esther 1: 22; 3: 12; 8: 9.   ἀτελείην: according to Herodotus himself
(VI 59), the Persian kings normally remitted old debts at the beginning of their
reign. Here, however, an anticipated remission of the taxes due in the following
three years is described. Cf. Justin I 9,12; for Dionysius the Younger in
Syracuse see Justin XXI 1,5. See the distinction made by P. Briant, *AH* III
(1987), 141.

68–9. In these chapters Herodotus narrates though dialogues an amusing harem
story, certainly of Persian popular origin, and perfectly suited to the ambience
of the exotic and fantastic palace of Susa, like the macabre story of Xerxes and
the wife of Masistes (IX 108–13) and the dramatic but amusing story of Esther,
which offers quite a few analogies, both in the general plot and in some verbal
expressions.

68,1. ὀγδόῳ δὲ μηνὶ: in the Bisitun inscription too, the conspiracy and the *coup
d'état* rapidly unfold in the space of a month: September 522.   ᾽Οτάνης...:
Utāna, son of *Thukhra*, according to the Bisitun inscription (§68); *Hu-ud-da-na*
Elam., *U-mi-it-ta-na* Babyl.; *Hostanes* in Justin I 9,14 (on which A. von Gutschmid,
Kleine Schriften, ed. F. Rühl, V, Leipzig 1984, pp. 60 f.). The name of the father
Pharnaspes is a compound of *aspa*, 'horse'. Otanes is a common name among the
Persian nobility of Herodotus (V 25,1; VII 40,4; 61,2; 62,2; 82). The Otanes men-
tioned here, if he was the son of the Pharnaspes mentioned in 2,2, must then have
been a brother-in-law of Cyrus and so an uncle of Cambyses; in 522 he must have
been at least 50 years old. The family's genealogy according to Herodotus is shown in
Fig. 7.
In Herodotus the true hero of the conspiracy is Otanes, whereas Darius appears at
its end. Otanes is the wise initiator, moderate and of noble virtues, favourable

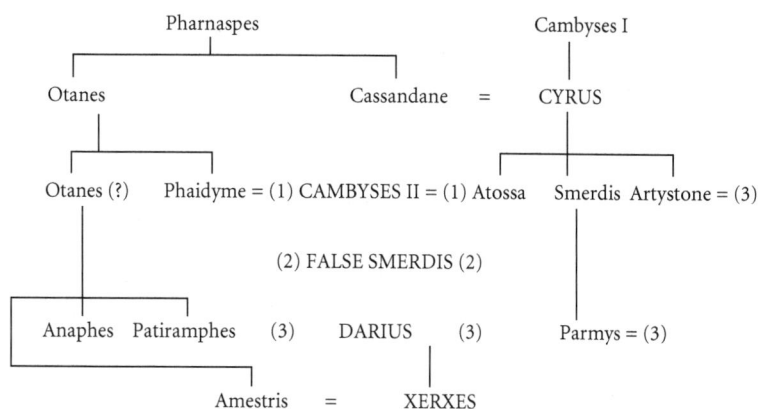

FIG. 7. Persian genealogy

towards democracy, who withdraws from the competition for the throne and receives the greatest honours. He comes back on the scene later, in relation to the Persian conquest of Samos (141–9). In this respect Herodotus departs from the official version of Darius in the Bisitun inscription (§68), as well as from the Aeschylean tradition, according to which Artaphernes is the only hero of the conspiracy (*Pers.* 775 ff.). Cf. C. Herrenschmidt, *AH* II (1987), 63 ff.

2. τῇδε συμβαλλόμενος: for this type of argument, cf. P. Hohti, *Arctos*, XI (1977), 5–14.   ἐκ τῆς ἀκροπόλιος: cf. 79,1 and τὸ βασιλήιον τεῖχος at 74,3. The ancient Elamite acropolis of Susa, destroyed in great part by Assurbanipal around 645–640 BC, was rebuilt by Darius after 521.   οὐκ ἐκάλεε...: see note on 84,2. The king's inaccessibility and even his invisibility are part of Eastern court ceremonial, whether true or imaginary, since the age of the Medes (I 99,1 with note); as for the Magus, his inaccessibility appeared excessive and caused suspicion. See the different interpretation of Justin I 9,11; 14.

3. Φαιδύμη: excellent Greek name, perhaps Hellenized, for a heroine (φαίδιμος, 'famous', 'glorious'); has nothing to do with Fatima. The harem of Cambyses, inherited by the false Smerdis, will in turn pass to Darius with all the regal patrimony (see 88,2–3).   πέμπων: the allusion is to secret contacts, or to contacts through intermediaries, between father and daughter; cf. the dialogue between Mordecai and Esther through a eunuch in Esther 4: 5–17.

5. τῶν συγκατημένων γυναικῶν: the women who 'live together' in the women's quarters; differently Powell, *CQ* XXXII (1938), 214. Cf. Justin I 9,16.

69,2. δεῖ σε...: cf. Esther 4: 13 ff.   δοῦναι δίκην: see D. Lateiner, *CQ* XXX (1980), 30 ff.

3. τὰ ὦτα: cf. Justin I 9,17. In the bas-relief of Bisitun the left ear of Gaumata was still visible at the beginning of the 20th cent.; see e.g. Hinz, fig. 36; Balcer, pp. 111 ff. According to Herodotus the Magus could not appear in public for fear of being recognized due to his missing ears. In other words, Herodotus supposes that the ears of the Persian king were usually visible when he wore ceremonial dress in public audiences, a detail confirmed by the iconography: see e.g. the head of Darius on the bas-relief of Bisitun. By contrast, in classical Greek iconography the ears of Persian kings were hidden under the tiara or a hood. See differently A. Demandt, *IA* IX (1972), 94–101, with photographs; S. R. West, in *Georgica: Greek Studies in Honour of G. Cawkwell*, London 1991, pp. 176–81.

5. ἀπέταμε: cf. Justin I 9,17. Mutilation of ears, nose, tongue, hands, feet, etc. is a well-known Persian punishment (generally practised in the Ancient East), inflicted on common offenders, rebels, and prisoners. Cf. III 118,2; IX 112; for the self-mutilation of Zopyrus see III 154,2. See the punishments inflicted by Darius on two rebels according to the Bisitun inscription (§§32–3). Perhaps the punishment was of Median origin; see C. Nylander, *AJA* LXXXIV (1980), 329–33.

6. ἐν περιτροπῇ ... Πέρσῃσι: parenthetic phrase of ethnological content; cf. Diod. XVII 7,7 and the 'turn' of Esther in Esther 2: 15. Phaidyme, like Esther, is

presented again to the reader, with her patronymic, at the decisive moment of her career. Cf. the cases of Adrastus (I 45,3) and Pausanias (IX 64,1). οὐ χαλεπῶς, ἀλλ᾽ εὐπετέως: the double assertion, negative and positive, interpreted by some as criticism of a different version, seems more simply an element of narrative art. Herodotus describes a comic scene of 'recognition', effected by acquired 'body signs' (Arist. *Poet.* 1454b19 ff.).

70,1. ὁ δὲ Ὀτάνης παραλαβών...: we have three full lists of the seven conspirators (see Fig.8).

Herodotus	The Bisitun inscription (§68)	Ctesias (*FGrHist* 688 F 13 (16))
1. Otanes	(Darius)	Onophas
2. Aspathines	Vidafarnā son of Vāyaspāra	Hydernes
3. Gobryas	Utāna son of Thukhra	Norondabates
4. Intaphernes	Gaubaru son of Marduniya	Mardonius
5. Megabyzus	Vidarna son of Bagābigna	Barisses
6. Hydarnes	Bagabukhša son of Dātuvahya	Ataphernes
7. Darius	Ardumaniš son of Vahauka	Darius

FIG. 8. The seven conspirators

Cf. Balcer, *Prosopographical Study*, pp. 59–60; 74–7; 99–103; 123–4; 126–7; 129. Seven is a typical number (cf. seven Persian ambassadors at V 17,1, with the note by Nenci); yet 'there must from time to time be the possibility that a correct number is also a typical one. For example, the Seven Years' War really lasted seven years' (Fehling, p. 220). In our case, six names out of seven in Herodotus correspond to names found among the seven names of the Bisitun inscription; three of these recur, with variants, also in Ctesias' list, where Onophas substitutes Otanes, and Mardonius occupies the place of Gobryas. On Otanes see note on 68,1; on Darius see note on 88,1. Ἀσπαθίνην: cf. 78,2; this is the only name in Herodotus without a correspondence in the Bisitun list, where instead there is Ar[duma]n[iš, a name restored on the basis of the Babylonian text, see R. Schmitt, *BzN* VI (1971), 1–8. An *Aspacanā*, carrier of Darius' bow and axe, is found in the inscription *DNd* Kent at Naqš-i Rustam (tomb of Darius, north of Persepolis); he could be a son of Prexaspes (VII 97); for seals of *Ašbazana* see M. Garrison, *AH* XI (1998), 151–31. In Constantine Manasses, *Compendium Chronicum* 873 Bekker, Aspathines is the name of the second Magus. Γωβρύην: Gobryas was Darius' father-in-law (VII 2,2), his brother-in-law (VII 5,1), and his faithful follower (III 73; 78,4–5). At Naqš-i Rustam he is Darius' spear-carrier; cf. the (anonymous) person on the left of the bas-relief at Bisitun; he is called *Pātišuvariš* (*DNc* Kent; the meaning of the title is disputed; some relate it to the clan of the Pateischoreis, known to Strabo XV 3,1). Gobryas suppressed the last rebellion in Elam (see the Bisitun inscription, §71) and participated in Darius' Scythian campaign (IV 132,2; 134,2–3). Some have identified this Gobryas with Gaubaru/Gobryas, the general of Cyrus during the conquest of Babylon (I 188–91 with note).

2. Ἰνταφρένεα: cf. 78,2. Intaphernes appears first in the Bisitun list (Vindafarnā, a compound of *farnah* = personal 'fortune' or 'glory', on which see P. Lecoq, *CRAI* (1987), 671–81); in Aeschylus, *Pers.* 776, he is the killer of Mardos. His name is Daphernes in Hellanicus, *FGrHist* 678a F 9. He suppressed the last Babylonian revolt around the end of 521 BC (Bis. inscr. §50). On his end and that of his family see chs. 118–19. Μεγάβυξον: Megabyzus will be the spokesman for oligarchy in the constitutional debate (ch. 81); for his son Zopyrus cf. 153,1. Ὑδάρνεα: if this is the same Hydarnes who took part in the campaigns against the rebels in Media in the winter of 522/1 (Bis. inscr. §25), he had several sons (VII 66,1; 135,1; 211,1 ff.; VIII 113,2; 118,1), and Orontes, one of his descendants, was governor in Armenia in Hellenistic times (Strabo IX 14,15). For the bibl. on the conspirators see note on chs. 61–88; on the 'seven' nobles of the Persian empire see 84,2 with note.

3. Δαρεῖος...: cf. note on 88,1. Darius had been in Egypt with Cambyses (139,2); but here he is said to have come from Persia. The contradiction can be resolved either by postulating the use of different sources, or better by supposing that Herodotus knew that Darius returned to Persia after Cambyses' death. On the father Hystaspes see I 209,2 with note; in 522/1, according to the Bisitun inscription (§35), he was in Parthia. For another Hystaspes, son of Darius and Atossa, see VII 64,2. ὕπαρχος: cf. notes to 89,1 and 120,1.

71–3. This first meeting of the conspirators (a second one in ch. 80–2) puts on stage the two main antagonists, Darius and Otanes (Gobryas is the faithful supporter of Darius), who represent the two stereotypical characters of every political debate: the determined authoritarian conspirator, who has clear plans and is ready to use every means, and the noble elder, experienced and moderate, who counsels caution and seeks the support of the majority. On the dialogue see Heni, p. 123 ff.

71,2. αὐτὸς μοῦνος...: cf. the Bisitun inscription §13. Herodotus does not explain the motives or the arguments that provoked Darius' suspicion. οὐ γὰρ ἄμεινον: with the same phrase Darius also concludes his speech on monarchy (82,5). Cf. I 187,2.

3. ὦ παῖ Ὑστάσπεος: Otanes addresses Darius as an adolescent (cf. note on 53,2), although he was almost 30 (I 209,2) and the father of three sons (VII 2,2). For the form of address see Dickey, pp. 52–6 and 264. πλεῦνας: first hint of Otanes' sympathies for democracy.

4. κέρδεα: cf. 72,4–5. Darius himself is no exception to the rule: 89,3.

72,2. λόγῳ μὲν... ἔργῳ δέ: Darius' sophistic argument begins.

3. ἡμέων... τοιῶνδε: cf. 77,1. The Magus was inaccessible even to the most noble (68,2 with note), contrary to the rule that will be established by the conspirators at 84,2; cf. 118,1.

4–5. ἔνθα γάρ... ἀληθής: cf. Introduction, pp. 391 ff.

5. **πυλουρῶν**: cf. 77,2; 118,2; 140,2–3; for those at the gates of Babylon cf. 156,2. These ushers or porters (also called θυρωροί at I 120,2) must be distinguished from the palace guards; they are sometimes called eunuchs (77,2; cf. Esther 2: 21; 6: 2), but have different functions from the subordinate ἀγγελιηφόροι (77,2).

73,1. ὦτα οὐκ ἔχοντος: the assertion is based on the assumption that a maimed man, especially if his maiming resulted from punishment, is barred from ascending the throne.

3. **τίθεμαι ψῆφον**: cf. VIII 123,2; the Attic terminology for the secret vote; it is used only here for a consultation in a non-Greek context.

74,1. κατὰ συντυχίην: cf. IX 21,1. 'Chance' or 'coincidence' does not exclude divine providence in Herodotus (IX 91,1).   **μοῦνος ἠπίστατο**: incorrect; cf. note on 61,1.

2. **πίστι...**: the plot of the 'three' against the 'seven'.   **μυρία**: a well-known Homerism; cf. II 136,1; 148,6; VI 67,3; VIII 119.

3. **ὡς ὑπὸ τοῦ Κύρου...**: the Magi suspect that the thesis of a 'false' Smerdis has already spread.

4. **δῆθεν**: cf. 136,2; 156,1.

75,1. ἐγενεηλόγησε: cf. II 91,5; 143,1 and 4; 146,2; VI 54; ἀντεγενεηλογέω at II 143,4. The verb belongs to the technical terminology of the early Greek genealogists. Prexaspes starts with genealogy, then tells the factual story, and finally ends with a 'sanction' (the imprecations at 75). This tripartite structure of the speech (exordium, narration, peroration) seems purely Greek, but it could be applied as well to Darius' Bisitun 'speech'.

3. **ἐπὶ κεφαλὴν**: 'upside down', 'headlong'; cf. 35,5.   **Πρηξάσπης... ἐτελεύτησε**: Herodotus concludes the episode with praise for the tragic hero who lived and died with dignity, and who has spoken the truth not in order to gain profit; cf. 71,4; 72,4–5. On Prexaspes as 'double' (or 'Janus') agent see M. Lang, *JNES* LI (1992), 201–7; on his heroic suicide cf. S. Flory, *AJPh* XCIX (1978), 411 ff. In Ctesias, *FGrHist* 688 F 13 (15), it is the faithful eunuch Hyzabates who reveals the true story to the troops, takes refuge in a temple, and is finally captured and beheaded. For a comparison of the death of Prexaspes and the martyrdom of St James (Hegesippus, in Eusebius, *Hist. Eccl.* II 23,4–18) see K. Geiser, in *Navicula Tubingensis für A. Tovar*, Tübingen 1984, pp. 133–43, who also mentions a drama *Prexaspes* in five acts by Peter Hacks (1978).

76,1. εὐξάμενοι τοῖσι θεοῖσι: in the Bisitun inscription Darius only prays to Ahura Mazda (§13).

2. **τῇ ὁδῷ μέσῃ**: the acquisition of information en route is a recurrent motif in Herodotus; see L. Boffo, *MAL* XXVI (1983), 25, n. 100.   **οἰδεόντων τῶν πρηγμάτων**: cf. 127,1.

3. **ἑπτὰ ζεύγεα**: see Powell, *CQ* XXIX (1935), 153. 'Seven pairs', like 'two times seven' (I 86,2; VII 114,2), is a symbolic or sacred unit (cf. Fehling, p. 226), probably of oriental origin; simplifying the numbers, they symbolize the clash between the seven conspirators and the two Magi. The ἴρηξ (Attic ἱέραξ) is in

Homer a symbol of speed; see *Il.* XIII 62; XV 237. αἰγυπιός is also a Homeric and poetic form. Cf. the 'Persian' portent with the eagle and the hawk in Aesch. *Pers.* 205 ff. (with Broadhead's note). Here as elsewhere in Herodotus, divine intervention prevails over human plans.

77,1. θείη πομπῇ χρεωμένους: cf. I 62,4; IV 152,2; VIII 94,2. According to Ctesias, *FGrHist* 688 F 13 (16), the conspirators were let in by two eunuchs, their accomplices. In Justin (I 9,19–20), the conspirators entered using force.
2. τοῖσι τὰς ἀγγελίας...: cf. 34,1; though here the reference is to eunuchs with specific functions, like the porters; cf. note on 72,5.   ἱστόρεον...: cf. note on 50,3.
3. ἐς τὸν ἀνδρεῶνα: cf. 78,3. The men's room, or *andron*, is in Herodotus the reception and banqueting room of royal and princely palaces; cf. I 34,3; III 121,1; 123,1; IV 95,3; see Hartog, p. 111 = ET pp. 93–4. In the houses of the wealthy in Greece, the men's room also functioned as dining-room, for the symposium, etc.; it can be considered as a derivation of the Homeric μέγαρον. See G. Matthiae, *EAA* I 1958, p. 364.

78,1. ἔσω: according to Ctesias, *FGrHist* 688 F 13 (16), the Magus was caught in the nuptial bed with a Babylonian concubine.
2. ὁ μὲν...ἐτράπετο: the Magus who seizes the bow is the one later killed by Darius, i.e. the false Smerdis. At audiences the bow and the spear of the king were carried by two high dignitaries (cf. note on 70,1). On the motif of the bow, cf. note on 21,3. In Ctesias' version, *FGrHist* 688 F 13 (16), the weapons had been removed by a eunuch.   Ἀσπαθίνην: cf. note on 70,1. According to Justin I 9,21, in this clash two of the seven were killed.   μηρόν: cf. note on 29,1.
3. τὰς θύρας: a door with two leaves; cf. I 9,3; II 121ε, 5; V 72,3.
4. ἐν σκότεϊ: cf. Justin I 9,22; the anecdote of Polyaenus VII 11,2, about the identification signal agreed by the conspirators, also presupposes darkness.
5. ὁρῶν δέ μιν...: the great number of different versions on the killing of the Magus is worth noting. According to Darius himself (Bis. inscr. §§13 and 68), the Magus Gaumata was killed in Media by Darius in the presence of his six collaborators. In Aeschylus (*Pers.* 775 ff.) it is Artaphernes who, together with his companions, kills Mardos in the palace 'with deceit' (σὺν δόλῳ). According to Ctesias, *FGrHist* 688 F 13 (15), it is Cambyses' faithful minister Hyzabates (in the role of Herodotus' Prexaspes) who reveals the plot to the troops: the Magus hides in a temple, and is dragged out and beheaded. Finally in Justin (I 9,22–3), it is Gobryas who in the struggle seizes the Magus, who is then killed by others in the obscurity of the palace (cf. Polyaenus VII 11,2). There is no compelling reason to prefer one version to another: for instance, Aeschylus' version is no better than that of the Bisitun inscription and vice versa (differently Balcer, pp. 153–66). In Herodotus, Darius is much more resolute in words than in deeds. According to the Bisitun inscription (§13) the place where the killing of the Magus took place is not the palace of Susa, but a fortress in the district of Nisaya, in Media, called Sikayuvatiš. It is today identified with the archaeological remains of Median age about 100 m. north of the inscribed rock of Bisitun, which thus perhaps com-

memorates the exact location of the decisive historical event in the life of Darius; see H. Luschey, *AMI* I (1968), 67; W. Kleiss, *AMI* III (1970), 156 f., with map opposite p. 133; H. von Gall, *AMI* V (1972), 281. Whether this castle, not far from Ecbatana, was a usual summer residence of the Persian kings, or a place of refuge to which the Magus and his followers had fled, is a matter of dispute. See the bibl. in the note on chs. 61–8.

79,3. ταύτην ... μαγοφόνια: cf. Ctesias, *FGrHist* 688 F 13 (18); Agathias II 26 (*HGM* II, p. 225). The story of the massacre of the Magi resembles an *aition*, intended to explain the origin of a festival; cf. the story of the massacres at Susa and other cities and the origin of the Jewish festival of Purim in Esther 8: 11–14; 9: 1–32. The suspicion is also strengthened by the official date of the killing of the Magus in the Bisitun inscription (§13): 10 *Bagayadiš* (29 September 522) falls in the month of the 'feast of Baga' (god), which seems to have been celebrated precisely on that day or the two following days; in later times the festival was called *Mithrakana*, 'festival of Mithras' (see G. Widengren, *Die Religionen Irans*, Stuttgart 1965, pp. 140 and 228 ff.). Moreover, the hypothesis that the conspirators had intentionally chosen a feast day for their plot derives from the combination of two sources: the Bisitun date of the killing of the Magus and the place of the plot (Susa) according to Herodotus. Alternatively, it has been suggested that the historical dates of the reign of the Magus were readapted to the mythological cycle of the Iranian calendar for propaganda purposes. On the 'massacre of the Magi' see Marquart II, pp. 132 ff.; Altheim–Stiehl, *Die aramäische Sprache*, pp. 99–105; Wiesehöfer, p. 175 ff.: Hofmann–Vorbichler, p. 103; Balcer, p. 113. The term *mwyzt* (from *mayu-zati*, 'magaphonia') occurs in a Sogdian Manichean text (TM 393) found near modern Turfan (Tulufan) in Sin-Kiang (north-west China) and published by W. B. Henning in 1944 (see text, English trans., and commentary, *IA* XV (1977), 139–50): it refers to the massacre of the Magi allegedly perpetrated by Alexander. From the fact that, despite the massacre and the subsequent persecutions, the Magi rapidly regained influence at the Achaemenid court, it can be seen that the contrast between the king and the Magi during the age of Darius was neither theologically profound nor politically insuperable; see J. Duchesne-Guillemin, in Walser, pp. 72 f. The hypothesis of two groups of Magi—one Median, Mithraic, and persecuted; the other 'reformed', Mazdaic, and left in power—does not find much support in the sources; see M. Papatheophanes, *IA* XX (1985), 148 ff.

80–2. This famous debate on political regimes, the second one of the conspirators, is also divided into three parts (for the first debate see chs. 71–3). It proposes a tripartite classification of political regimes (rule of one, of few, and of many), which had already been mentioned by Pindar about half-a-century earlier (*Pyth.* 2,158 ff.), and which did not yet have a proper terminology. After Herodotus the classification was resumed, extended, and variously modified by philosophers, orators, and historians (e.g. Plato, Aristotle, Isocrates, Polybius; see J. de Romilly, *REG* LXXII (1959), 88–99), remaining at the base of Western

political theories, ancient, medieval, and modern. The three speeches, forming an
ἀγών of thesis and antithesis, with three possibilities, contain various
rhetorical devices: rhetorical questions, tripartite rhythmical phrases, alliterations, colloquialisms, and *climax*. There is no lack of Atticisms, or even of
Ionicisms or poetical forms. The dominant theory was once that the three
speeches belonged to an Attic sophistic treatise, inserted by Herodotus in his
text with minimal adaptations. The theory's proponents even pretended to know
the name of the author of the treatise: Protagoras, Hippias, Antiphon, Prodicus.
In response have been pointed out stylistic traces of Ionian scientific prose, a lack
of real antinomies and of typically sophistic symmetrical arguments, the presence
of archaic religious ideas and of political doctrines not specifically Attic. Moreover, Otanes' optative-potential style contrasted with Darius' indicative-assertive
style, is a characteristic trait of the two main speakers already familiar from the
previous debate. These considerations, and Herodotus' insistence on the historicity of the debate, have led to a different evaluation of the text, which claims for
Herodotus a greater creative autonomy in the composition of his Persian *logos*
and Book III generally (cf. the Introduction, pp. 390 f.). In reaction, there has
been no lack of attempts to trace the Persian origin of the ideas expressed in the
debate, and therefore to vindicate their historicity, at least in part. Darius'
polemical references to the social and religious policy of the Magus (cf. Bis.
inscr. §14), his strong stand against all forms of injustice (by the powerful against
the weak and by the weak against the powerful), his ideal of a wise king (see esp.
DNb §8 Kent), seem genuine ideas that, through the Greek interpretation of
Herodotus' oral sources (perhaps the descendants of Otanes or Megabyzus), were
perhaps transformed in the speech that has come to us. Some have also suggested
the Iranian origin of contests of eloquence held in the king's court, with prizes for
the best speech or for the correct solution of a riddle; cf. 1 Ezra (LXX.) 1: 3–4;
Josephus, *Ant. Iud.* XI 33–63.

   The problem of the debate's historicity should be stated differently. In the form
that has reached us it is a Greek debate on Greek ideas, composed by Herodotus,
well integrated into the main narrative, and made emphatic at a time when the
Greek public was interested in problems of this type. Yet a more obvious context
for such a debate would be an assembly at Athens *c.*511 BC, with Cleisthenes,
Isagoras, and a Pisistratid as speakers on the three political regimes. The choice of
a Persian context presents the possibility that the crisis of the Persian empire in
522/1, the usurpation, and the legitimizing propaganda might have provoked
dissent and internal debates among the members of the restored high nobility.
The essential choice must have been between the continuation of the centralist-
'tyrannic' government of Cambyses (and Gaumata), and a return to the limited,
paternalistic, and idealized monarchy of Cyrus. Besides, different forms of kingship existed in the countries conquered under Cyrus and Cambyses—in Media,
Lydia, Babylonia, and Egypt (cf. P. Högemann, *Das alte Vorderasien und die
Achämeniden. Ein Beitrag zur Herodot-Analyse*, Wiesbaden 1992, pp. 351–5),
and were known to the Persians. We should exclude the possibility that a serious
alternative to a monarchic regime could have been proposed. Herodotus knew

very well that the empire had undergone a radical change after a severe crisis; he therefore tried to understand the phenomenon within the limits of his own frame of reference: the constitutional changes of the Greek *poleis*. Herodotus does not take sides in the debate, and attempts to discover his political ideas in these chapters have failed (see the balanced judgement of Wüst, pp. 47–62). For Herodotus what took place in 522/1 constituted a great θῶμα, worthy of being recorded. His insistence on the debate's historicity has a 'methodological' purpose of criticizing yet again false opinions of the Greeks about the barbarians; the 'didactic' aim of reminding his compatriots that 'democracy' is not a specifically Greek invention totally foreign to the world of the barbarians. In any case, he implies that democracy had been proposed in Susa more than ten years before its institution in Athens, and that the Ionian cities did not receive it from Athens but from the son of one of the seven Persian conspirators. Bibl.: see H. Apffel, 'Die Verfassungsdebatte bei Herodot (3,80–2)', Diss. Erlangen 1957, *passim*; P.T. Brannan, *Traditio*, XIX (1963), 427 ff.; W. R. Connor, *The New Politicians of Fifth-century Athens*, Princeton 1971, pp. 199–206; F. Gschnitzer, *Sitzungsberichte der Heidelberger Ak. der Wiss.* (1977), 31–2, n. 36; D. Lanza, *Il tiranno e il suo pubblico*, Turin 1977, pp. 225 ff. For the sophistic sources, W. Aly, *Formprobleme der frühen griechischen Prosa*, *Philologus* Suppl. XXI 3, Leipzig 1929, pp. 102–4; Ubsdell I pp. 396–9; for the monarchic theories of the Sophists, K. F. Stroheker, *Historia*, II (1953–4), 381–412; for Protagoras, F. Lasserre, *MH* XXXIII (1976), 65–84; for Hippias, A. J. Podlecki, *TAPhA* XCVII (1966), 359–71; for criticism of the sophistic theory, H. Erbse, *Glotta*, XXXIX (1960–1), 224–30; on the Persian sources, V.V. Struve, *VDI* III (1948), 12–35; Dandamaev, p. 163 ff.; G. Dumézil, *AI* XXIII (1984), 143–9; for hellenized oriental sources, F. Cassola, in *Xenia. Scritti in onore di P. Treves*, Rome 1985, pp. 27 f.; on the oriental competitions of eloquence, Sancisi-Weerdenburg, pp. 217–43.

80,1. ἐκτὸς πέντε ἡμερέων: a typical number in Herodotus; cf. I 72,3; II 22,3; 34,2; cf. Fehling, pp. 224–5. The passage is perhaps the basis of the tradition (late and not of much weight) of the Persian *interregna* with five days of *anomia*, in which massacres and plundering were allowed; see F. Lasserre, *MH* XXXIII (1976), 69–71. ἐλέχθησαν ... ἐλέχθησαν δ᾽ ὦν: the allusion here is to those who do not believe in the debate's historicity; cf. VI 43,3 for those who do not believe in Otanes' proposal. An example of direct relations between the author and his audience; cf. I 193,4; IV 99,5; VII 139,1; see Beltrametti, p. 44.

2. ἐς μέσον ...: what is common is placed 'in the middle'; in a political sense, cf. 83,1; 142,3; IV 161,3; VII 164; see also note on 80,6 and Theognis 678. See M. Detienne, *Les Maitres de vérité dans la Grèce archaïque*, Paris 1967, pp. 83 ff. In the sense of 'open to public discussion' see I 206,3; VII 8δ,2. In another sense see note on 62,1. ἐμοὶ δοκέει: this subjectivist phrase, common in Herodotus, seems appropriate to the 'democratic' spirit of Otanes. ἕνα ... μούναρχον: the criticism of monarchy, or rather, of tyranny begins here. From this criticism it is impossible to deduce anything about Herodotus' political ideas. On Herodotus and tyranny/monarchy see G. M. Hirst, *Collected Classical Papers*,

Oxford 1938, pp. 97–110; H. J. Diesner, *Forschungen und Fortschritte*, XXXIV (1960), 270–2; Waters, *passim*; *G&R* XIX (1972), 136–50; J. N. Davie, *G&R* XXVI (1979), 160–8; B. Gentili, *QUCC* XXX (1979), 152–6; J. G. Gammie, *JNES* XLV (1986), 171–85; Flory, esp. pp. 128–36; Lateiner, pp. 163–86. On the theme of tyranny in Book III cf. the Introduction, pp. 389 f.

3. κῶς ... τὰ βούλεται: a rhetorical question; cf. 81,2; 82,5. ἀνευθύνῳ: the term is not attested before Herodotus. It became a technical term, like ἀνυπεύθυνος, with an implicit note of blame to designate unconstitutional tyrants or special magistrates exempted from εὔθυνα, the rendering of accounts on the completion of their office. In a wider sense it also means 'irresponsible'; see e.g. Thuc. III 43,4. The opposite is ὑπεύθυνος; cf. on para. 6. στάντα ... στήσειε: a pun (J. E. Powell, *CR* LI (1937), 103). For tyranny as perverted βασιλεία cf. e.g. Arist. *Pol.* 1279b4; 1289a28. ὕβρις ... φθόνος ...: commonplaces of archaic religious thought applied to anti-tyrannical rhetoric; for a third commonplace, κόρος, see κεκορημένος in para. 4; cf. Soph. *Oed. Tyr.* 873 ὕβρις φυτεύει τύραννον.

6. οὔνομα ... ἔχει: cf. V 78; Plato, *Resp.* VIII 557c ff. ἰσονομίην: cf. 83,1; 142,3; V 37,1. The adjective ἰσόνομος occurs in the famous Attic *skolion* of the tyrannicides of the end of the 6th cent. and indicates freedom as opposed to tyranny. In Herodotus δημοκρατίη and δημοκρατέεσθαι (IV 137,2; VI 43,3), ἰσοκρατίη (V 92a,1; cf. IV 26,2), and ἐλευθερίη (III 142,2, with note) are also antithetical to tyranny. Alcmaeon, living *c.*500 BC and perhaps a Pythagorean, defined the healthy state as the 'isonomy of opposites', by contrast to the 'monarchy' of one of those opposites, the definition of the pathological state; see L. MacKinney, in J. Mau and E. G. Schmidt (eds.), *Isonomia. Studien zur Gleichheitsvorstellung im griechischen Denken*, Berlin 1964, pp. 79 ff.; C. Triebel-Schubert, *Klio*, LXVI (1984), 40–50. It is probable that ἰσονομία etymologically derives from ἴσος and νέμειν; the original sense being 'equal distribution' (of booty, of rights, of offices); it seems that only later was the term understood as 'equality before the law', as if derived from ἴσος and νόμος. The problem has given rise to excessive polemics: see e.g. V. Ehrenberg, *Polis und Imperium*, Zurich–Stuttgart 1965, pp. 279–86; G. Vlastos, *AJPh* LXXIV (1953), 337–66, and in *Isonomia* (op. cit.), pp. 1–35; M. Ostwald, *Nomos and the Beginnings of the Athenian Democracy*, Oxford 1969, pp. 96–136. Independently from its etymology, the term was used in the classical period for any 'free' regime, i.e. non-monarchic; an oligarchy can also be ἰσόνομος: Thuc. III 62,3. In this passage, however, it corresponds to πλῆθος ἄρχον (81,1; 82,4), in other words, to democracy (cf. VI 43,3). Isonomia is not, however, a synonym of democracy or of any other political regime: it is rather the *slogan* of free regimes, especially democracies; moderate aristocracies preferred εὐνομία. See also B. Borecky, *Eirene*, IX (1971), 5–24; K. H. Hinzl, *Gymnasium*, LXXXV (1978), 117–27; P. Frei, *MH* XXXVIII (1981), 205–19; Y. Nakategawa, *Historia*, XXXVII (1988), 260–5. The ἴσος δασμός, regretted by the aristocratic poet of the *Corpus Theognideum* (l. 678), has been defined an 'elegiac substitute' for isonomia (G. Cerri, *QUCC* XIII (1969), 97–104); cf. J. A. S. Evans, *QUCC* XXXVI (1981), 79–84, and the just

observations of S. Humphreys, *Arethusa*, XX (1987), 214 ff.). On Herodotus' political terminology see Apffel, pp. 59–70.

6. πάλῳ: cf. IV 94,2; 153. Election by lot was the system typical of democracies, in Athens and elsewhere.   ὑπεύθυνον: cf. note on 80,3; the term is already attested in Aeschylus, *Pers.* 213; *Choeph.* 715; *Prom.* 324.   τὸ κοινὸν: alludes to the *ekklesia*, the sovereign body of Greek democracies.   ἐν γὰρ τῷ πολλῷ ἔνι τὰ πάντα: 'in the many is everything', in other words, everything depends on the will of the majority. It is a lapidary statement, also translated in different ways (e.g. 'in the majority is the whole', etc.).

81,1. ἀξυνετώτερον: cf. VII 156,3 (ἀχαριτώτατον). This is a commonplace of oligarchic criticism of democracy.

2. χειμάρρῳ: a Homeric metaphor for the irresistible vehemence of heroes, used by Theognis 347–8, in a political sense it indicates the overflowing, impulsive mass of the people; cf. Sophocles, *Ant.* 712 f.; Isocrates 15,172 (on which F. A. Spencer, *TAPhA* LV (1924), pp. xxxi f.). For the uses of this metaphor in Greek literature, F. Rodriguez Adrados, *Emerita*, XXXIII (1965), 4–14.

3. οἳ Πέρσῃσι κακὸν νοέουσι: a flattering irony for an Athenian audience. καὶ αὐτοὶ ἐνεσόμεθα: an argument from self-interest; cf. 84,2.

82,2. ἀνδρὸς ... φανείη: a commonplace in Greek monarchic theories. ἀμωμήτως: cf. ἀμώμῳ νόμῳ at II 177,2.   δυσμενέας ἄνδρας: cf. VII 237,2; the opposite of εὐμενεῖς, 'friends'.

3. ἀρετὴν ἐπασκέουσι: ἀρετή in Herodotus usually indicates military or physical virtue; cf. e.g. VII 102,1; VIII 26,3; also of a horse at III 88,3. Only here and at VII 237,2 does it have the sense of civic or moral virtue.   ἐς τὸ κοινὸν ... ἐγγίνεσθαι: the two propositions are symmetrically opposed. The idea that personal rivalries between nobles or factions ultimately destroy the state is a commonplace of 4th-cent. Greek rhetoric and political theory. κορυφαῖος: cf. 159,1; VI 23,6; 98,2. The term, not documented before Herodotus, designated at Athens the leader of the tragic chorus; in the sense of 'faction leader' see Polybius XXVIII 4,5.   ἔχθεα μεγάλα ... στάσιες ... φόνος ...: a first series of ascending concepts, with a climax at para. 4. The notion of the inevitable transition from oligarchy to monarchy, a form of μεταβολὴ πολιτειῶν, is implicit. Monarchy is also born from ἀνομία: see already Solon, fr. 41,12 ff. Gentili–Prato, and Theognis 51 f.; for Herodotus cf. I 96,2 ff.

4. κακότητος ... μούναρχος ἐών: a second series of ascending concepts. The transition from demagogy to tyranny is a famous commonplace general to Greek political theory and especially to anti-democratic criticism. προστάς τις τοῦ δήμου: the head of the ruling faction in Greek democracies. There have been attempts to relate the προστάς of Herodotus to Thucydides' Pericles who προὔστη τῆς πόλεως (II 65,5); in such a view, the Athenian regime of the time would have been democratic only in theory, whereas it was in fact the rule of the first citizen (Thuc. II 65,9). Thucydides, however, did not see in Pericles' *prostasia* a warning sign of tyranny.

5. κόθεν...: rhetorical questions. The last arguments seem a pure invention of Herodotus, based on his notions of Persian history.　ἐλευθερίη: 'freedom' understood as political independence from foreign yoke; cf. 65,7 with note.　πατρίους νόμους: cf. 83,3. Darius believes that the monarchy should be preserved because it is the πάτριος πολιτεία of the Persians; whereas Otanes believes that the monarchy-tyranny subverts the νόμαια πάτρια (80,5). The controversy recalls the late 5th-cent. Athenian debates on πάτριος πολιτεία.　ἔχοντας εὖ: the sense is that the laws should be preserved as long as they 'are solid', 'work well'. For a possible connection between εὖ ἔχειν and the Greek interpretation of Darius' name ἐρξίης at VI 98,3, 'he who works for (or maintains) the good'—see R. Schmitt, *Historia*, XXVI (1977), 243 f. οὐ γὰρ ἄμεινον: cf. 71,2 with note.

83,1. οἱ δὲ τέσσερες: it is pointless for the other four to speak, since there are only three options.　ἐς μέσον: cf. note on 62,1 and 80,2.

2. κλήρῳ...μηχανῆ: ballot, election, or other non-isonomic 'means'. Cf. 84,3. οὔτε γὰρ ἄρχειν οὔτε ἄρχεσθαι: the maxim is worthy of a philosopher. Cf. the version of the scholia to Aesch. *Pers.* 776 Dähnhardt. Otanes embodies the Athenian democratic ideal of 'living as one pleases' (Thuc. II 37,2, etc.).

3. ἐκ μέσου κατῆστο: cf. IV 118,2; VIII 22,2; 73,3. According to Herodotus, he who 'gets out of the way' and declares himself neutral helps the strongest; see VIII 73,3; G. Nenci, *Il Veltro*, XXII (1978), 495–506.　καὶ νῦν...θέλει: Otanes, an Achaemenid and father of one of Darius' wives, became, at least in theory, a more independent satrap than others. Cf. Diod. XXXI 19,2, on the descendants of 'Anaphas' and their privileges. It cannot be excluded that either a bill of privileges, perhaps with an unusual title (different from the usual δοῦλος, used for all the subjects of the Great King, including satraps), or an oral tradition were preserved up to Herodotus' times, and that one of the two was the basis of the versions favourable to Otanes and to his love of liberty and *isonomia*.

84,1. ἐβουλεύοντο: the verb recurs five times in this 'deliberative' chapter. ἢν ἐς ἄλλον τινὰ...: Otanes has renounced the throne, so only six conspirators (οἱ ἕξ of 86,1)—including the wounded Aspathines and Intaphernes (78,2; 79,1)—participate in the competition; however, Otanes remains forever one of the 'seven'; see Erbse, pp. 169–73. For a different interpretation see J. E. Powell, *CQ* XXIX (1935), 153 f.　ἐξαίρετα: 'special privileges', the gifts 'chosen' in honour of someone; cf. 142,4; VI 57,2; IX 81,2. For lands selected for individual assignments see II 141,1; 168,1; V 45,2. In colonial assignments the χώρα ἐξαίρετος was the land not assigned by lot and reserved e.g. for cults and honours.　ἐσθῆτά τε Μηδικήν: cf. I 135 with note. For other honorific gifts see III 160,2 with note; cf. also e.g. Xen. *Anab.* I 2,27; Esther 6: 8–11; 8: 15.

2. παριέναι...συνεπαναστάντων: this 'bill' reflects a form of 'oligarchy' headed by a king who is a 'first amongst equals', or almost so. The tradition of the seven great Persian houses appeared in Achaemenid times and survived into the Sassanid age. It is probable that it pre-dates Darius' restoration of the Persian houses. Cf. Esther 1: 14: 'the seven princes of Persia and Media who saw the King's face and who sat

the first in the kingdom'; see also Ezra 7: 14 ('the seven counsellors'); Josephus, *Ant. Iud.* XI 31 ('the so called seven houses of the Persians'). Plato held that Darius had divided his empire in seven parts and that he governed it with his collaborators (*Leg.* III 695b–e; cf. *Ep.* 7,332a–b); the fact is that some oriental dynasties of the 4th cent. or of Hellenistic times (e.g. in Cappadocia, in Armenia, in Pontus, in Lydia, and in Ionia) related themselves to the seven conspirators. On the *epigamia* among the seven cf. e.g. 88,3; VII 2,2. For the iconographic representation of the Persian great nobles at Persepolis see e.g. G. Walser, *Audienz beim persischen Grosskönig*, Zurich 1965. For the free access to the throne-room see 72,3; 77; 118,1; cf. the grave fault of Aman in Esther 7: 8.

3. περὶ δὲ... ἔχειν τὴν βασιληίην: since election and lot are excluded, another μηχανή is chosen (cf. 83,2). With his masterly irony, Herodotus introduces us behind the scenes, which he enjoys revealing, whether out of his personal interest in ingenuities of all sorts (85,1); or to entertain his audience with oracular institutions (cf. e.g. II 151), or to return once again, at the end of the drama, to the central problem of falsehood and truth (cf. Introduction, pp. 391 ff.). Some scholars believe in the historicity of the anecdote narrated in chs. 85–7. In the Bisitun inscription Darius bases his right to the throne on his Achaemenid origin (§1–5) and the will of Ahura Mazda (§9, etc.); there is no mention of chance or portents. An allusion to 'chance' is found in Aeschylus, *Pers.* 779. The story of the neighing of the horse was accepted e.g. also by Ctesias *FGrHist* F13 (17); Justin I 10,3–10; Ptolomaeus Hephaestion (in Photius 190, p. 148b Henry); Plutarch, *Mor.* 340b; Polyaenus VII 10; Lucius Ampelius 13,2 Assmann. To the bibl. quoted in the note on chs. 61–88, add, on this anecdote, C. F. Lehmann-Haupt, *Klio*, XVIII (1923), 59–64. ὁ ἵππος ἡλίου ἐπανατείλαντος: the anecdote is aetiological; it interprets the inscription on Darius' equestrian bas-relief, on which see 88,3. However, it also uses Iranian cultic elements well known to Herodotus; the white horses sacred to the Sun, the cult of the Sun, the sacrifices of horses; cf. I 131,2; 189,1 with notes; III 90,3; 106,2. According to Justin (I 10,5), the Sun was the only god of the Persians and the horse was sacred to him; cf. what is said by Herodotus (I 216,4) regarding the Massagetae. Hippomantia with white horses was known to the Germans (see Tacitus, *Germ.* 10,3–5); Achilles' horse also had prophetic powers (*Il.* XIX 404 ff.). (For later Sassanian divination through horses see Agathias p. 261 B; Averil Cameron, *Dumbarton Oaks Papers* 23–4 (1969–70) p. 122) For the Vedic formulas on the neighing of the electing-horse G. Dumézil, *AI* XXIII (1984), 143–9.

85,1. σοφός: cf. note on 4,2. Οἰβάρης: *Ha-ba-ra* Elamitic, *Ubariia* in Nuzi; Οἰβάρας corresponds to ἀγαθάγγελος in Nicolaus of Damascus, *FGrHist* 90 F 66 (13). Here he plays the role of the cunning slave of ancient comedy, who finds a solution to every problem; see K. Glaser, *Humanistisches Gymnasium*, XLIII (1932), 202 f.; A. Köhnken, *RhM* CXXXIII (1990), 115–37. On μῆτις and the conquest of power in Herodotus see M. Dorati, *Acme*, LI (1998), 203–11. ἔλεξε...: dialogue between slave and master; cf. 42,2; see Heni, p. 140.

86,1. ἐχρεμέτισε: cf. Justin (I 10,17), where Zopyrus rebukes Darius for having become a king *non virtute sed auspicio, non iudicio hominum sed hinnitu equi.*

2. ἀστραπή ... καὶ βροντή: the portent here consists in the simultaneousness of the phenomena. On portents in Herodotus cf. General Introduction, pp. 42 ff.   προσεκύνεον: cf. I 134,1 with note.

87,1. οἱ μὲν ... οἱ δὲ: two possibilities because two different versions of the same event. For other variants, see scholia to Aeschylus, *Pers.* 776 Dähnhardt. ἀναξυρίσι: cf. I 71, 2 with note.

88,1. Δαρεῖος ...: the story of the reign of Darius starts; it will remain at the centre of the main narrative until the end of Book III, and then in Books IV–VI, until VII 4 (death of Darius). The figure of the great Achaemenid king is transformed from that of a revolutionary conspirator, authoritarian and unscrupulous, to that of a restorer, who re-establishes peace and reorganizes administration, not without humanity and paternalistic wisdom. However, missing in Herodotus is an idealization of Darius like that in Aeschylus' *Persians*; see B. Alexanderson, *Eranos*, LXV (1967), 1–11; A. Tourraix, *REA* LXXXVI (1984), 123 f.; Evans, *Explorer*, pp. 56–60; Erbse, *Studien*, pp. 56–73.

   Darius (*Dārayavauš* Persian and Elamite; *Da-ri-ya-muš* Babylonian; *T/Drwš* Egyptian; *Drywš* Hebrew; *Dryhwš* Aramaic), born *c*.550 BC, was king from 522 to 486; he brought to the throne the cadet branch of the Achaemenids (see I 107,2 with note). Herodotus knew little of the important events of his 'first year', which Darius describes in detail in the Bisitun inscription; see the commentary on the story of the siege of Babylon (chs. 150–60). For the bibl. see note on chs. 61–88; for iconography of Darius, H. Luschey, *AMI* I (1968), 71–4 and pl. 28 and 33; for Darius' physical beauty see the inscription quoted in IV 91,2; Polycleitus of Larissa, *FGrHist* 128 F 3a (with partial confusion between Darius and Artaxerxes 'Longimanus'); Justin I 10,13. As for the chronology, Gaumata was killed on 29 September 522 (see note on 67,2). A little later Darius' 'accession year' began, until 1 Nisan (March–April) 521, when according to the Babylonian calendar his official 'first year' started (his thirty-sixth year does actually fall in 486: VII 4). Some scholars held the official 'first year' was calculated retroactively from 1 Nisan 522, the initial date of Gaumata; see e.g. E. J. Bickerman, *RB* LXXXVIII (1981), 23–8. Darius declared that he had defeated all the rebels in nineteen battles 'in one and the same year' (*hamahyāhā tharda*, §52). The calculation and the exact chronological order of these battles are still discussed; it is, however, certain that if we calculate the time between the killing of Gaumata (perhaps the first 'battle') and the last victory over the Babylonians (27 November 521), the period is almost fourteen months long. But since the year 522/1 had an intercalary month, Darius' 'year' had thirteen months and an addition of two periods of time at the beginning and at the end of the year. These periods, since each was less than a complete month, could have been eliminated from the calculation without provoking criticism. It is certainly easier to confine the events within the chronological boundaries stated by Darius by excluding from the calculation the killing of Gaumata, in spite of it being the first great event of the year (and Darius could not have excluded it). In any case, since 'in a single year' is a well-known phrase of Assyrian, Hittite, Urartian and other royal inscriptions, Darius' statement does not have to be taken literally. See Balcer, pp. 131 ff. with bibl.; for the Babylonian chronology of the year 522/1 see Parker–Dubberstein, p. 30. Ἀράβιοι: cf. chs. 8–9; 107–13, with the relevant notes.

2. τοὺς πρώτους . . . Πέρσῃσι: cf. 84,2. Before 522/1 Darius had married one of Gobryas' daughters, by whom he had three sons (VII 2,2). On the juridical, political, and propaganda aims of Darius' marriages see Justin I 10,14. Xerxes, since he was the son of Darius and Atossa, unified in his person the two branches of the Achaemenid family.   Ἄτοσσαν: the Old Persian form of the name is unknown (*Hutaosa* in the Avesta; *Atahsu* Hittite). Atossa, daughter of Cyrus (and perhaps of Cassandane), wife first of her brother Cambyses, then of the false Smerdis, and finally of Darius, was extremely influential at court (cf. chs. 133–4); she had four sons, among them Xerxes, who was said to have ascended the throne thanks to his mother (VII 2–3; cf. 64,2; 82). In Aeschylus' *Persians* the queen-mother is anonymous. In Hellanicus, *FGrHist* 4 F 178a–b, Atossa is a semi-legendary figure, confused or identified with Semiramis; cf. Conon, *FGrHist* 26 F 1 (IX). See H. Sancisi-Weerdenburg, in *Images of Women in Antiquity*, London–Canberra 1983, pp. 20–33; on Darius' wives cf. Balcer, *Prosopographical Study*, pp. 86–9; 99.   Ἀρτυστώνην: *Ir-taš-du-na* Elamite; see A. Tourraix, *REA* LXXXVI (1984), 125, n. 10, with bibl.; M. A. Dandamaev, *SS* VII (1985), 98. She was Darius' favourite wife and mother of two commanders active in 480 BC; cf. VII 69,2; 72,2.

3. Πάρμυς: cf. VII 78.   Ὀτάνεω θυγατέρα: cf. 68,3 ff. Darius also married Phratagune, daughter of his brother Artanes; see VII 224,2.   τύπον: figure sculpted in bas-relief; cf. II 106,2 for a rock-cut bas-relief; II 136,1; 138,2–3; 148,7; 153; ἔστησε later in the paragraph seems, however, more appropriate to a proper statue. No equestrian representation of an Achaemenid king is preserved; there are some of Assyrian kings or described in Assyrian sources. Herodotus cannot be referring to the bas-relief of Bisitun, on which Darius is not represented on horseback.   ἐπέγραψε . . .: at best Herodotus reports here what bilingual guides told him. The statue and the inscription are at any rate the basis of the aetiological anecdote on the neighing of the horse (84,3–87). The motif of the horse and the groom, who take part in the conquest of the kingdom, is found in the *Annals* of Sargon II in relation to 714 BC; see H. Volkmann, in *Convivium. Festschrift K. Ziegler*, Stuttgart 1954, pp. 49 f., with bibl. For Herodotus and the inscriptions cf. General Introduction, pp. 17 f.

89–96. These eight chapters, which formally constitute a digression within the *logos* of Darius, contain a list of twenty ἀρχαί or satrapies that the new king is held to have organized immediately after his accession to the throne; but see *Chron. Paschale* I, p. 272 Dindorf (the reform should probably be dated *c.*520 BC: see T. Petit, *AC* LIII (1984), 35–46; *LEC* LV (1987), 175–9). It is the first of the two great Herodotean 'catalogues' of the Achaemenid empire (the second one, on the armed contingents, is at VII 61–98). The twenty 'satrapies' listed by Herodotus are multi-ethnic and fiscal conglomerates or νομοί (the usual term for the Egyptian districts), not always established according to a rigid criterion of

territorial continuity (89,1). For each νομός Herodotus usually records the names
of one or more tributary 'peoples' (ἔθνεα)—seventy units in total: 57 ethnic and
13 territorial districts (cf. the 72 'satrapies' under Seleucus I, Appian, *Syr.* 328)—
and the total tax paid by them (in silver Babylonian talents for the first nineteen
districts, in Euboic golden talents for the twentieth: cf. 89,2 and 95). The first six
districts in the west (from Ionia to Cyrenaica) follow each other in a well-defined
geographical order from the point of view of a Greek of Asia Minor; for the centre
and the East the list becomes chaotic and less comprehensible. The catalogue ends
with an allusion to additions, to later modifications, and to the method of storing
the tribute (96). The problem of the sources and of the credibility of this list
is much discussed. Some have suggested a source written in Greek, compiled on
the basis of a Persian or Aramaic document, official and authentic, composed
under Darius and ultimately handed to Hecataeus of Miletus by the satrap of
Sardis before the Ionian revolt (cf. V 36,2 and the famous 'map' at V 49,5–7, that
many attribute to Anaximander or to Hecataeus); this would involve a source
with revisions and changes made by the first Greek authors of *Persika*, and then
used by Herodotus. Others have supposed the existence of an oral or written
source, which Herodotus received directly from a good bilingual Persian informant (perhaps Zopyrus the younger: see 160,2 with note); in this case the list would
reflect the situation around the middle of the 5th cent. The other extreme is the
hypothesis that Herodotus composed almost freely a list on the Homeric model
of the 'catalogue of ships' in the second book of the *Iliad*. That Herodotus' list
cannot be a translation, word for word, of a Persian document, is shown by the
hellenocentric order of the satrapies (with the Ionians at the head), their number,
and their ethnics, which only approximately correspond to the data of Persian
sources (see the comparative table in App. II). On the other hand, that the list is
not the fruit of sheer fantasy is shown by the certain undeniable correspondences
with the same Persian sources. Since these Persian sources were not fiscal or
administrative documents of official character, but lists of 'peoples' (*dahyāva*) or
'lands inhabited by peoples' (the exact meaning is debated), lists that were
engraved or pictured on bas-reliefs for propaganda purposes, they should not
be held to be what they are not. Only about half of Herodotus' νομοί, and scarcely
a third of the Persian *dahyāva* correspond to the historical 'satrapies' known to us
from later sources: therefore any comparison with the Persian lists of the period
of Darius and Xerxes cannot decisively tip the scales either for or against
Herodotus' credibility. A better check is provided by Babylonian and Egyptian
documents and the evidence from the Greek sources on the history of the Persian
empire in the 5th and 4th cent. BC. Herodotus' catalogue, however, is the only
fiscal list in our possession (there remain two fragments from a work by Ctesias:
FGrHist 688 F 53–4; see also a fragment of Polycleitos of Larissa, ibid., 128 F 3a);
it is a document which, together with the military catalogue of Book VII, is
indispensable for any reconstruction of the administrative geography of the
Achaemenid empire. It must, however, be remembered: (1) that the later Greek
lists and sources (of the 4th cent. and the Hellenistic-Roman period, e.g. Diod.
XVIII 5–6 and 39,5–7) should be used only with extreme caution for the period of

Darius and Xerxes; (2) that the twenty satrapies constituted a great administrative network; that many of them were divided into sub-satrapies or districts with subordinate governors; that others were semi-autonomous with local dynasties of vassal-kings, tyrants, and sheiks (for a total of 127 *mdinh* see Esther 1: 1 and 8,9; and the fictitious letter of Artaxerxes, 1, p. 175 Hercher; 1 Ezra [LXX] 3: 2; Josephus, *Ant. Iud.* XI 3,2; 6,1; 120 'satraps': Dan. 6: 2); (3) that Darius' original organization, despite additions and modifications, remained substantially stable until Alexander; and (4) that within the satrapies, Achaemenid domination was concretely demonstrated by means of road networks (on the 'Royal Road' see V 52), fortresses, government palaces, garrisons, strongholds, military colonies, 'feudal' agrarian infrastructures, plantations, 'paradises', and cultic institutions, with their repercussions in the socio-economic, ethnico-linguistic, and cultural fields. Herodotus' list is examined in all the histories of the Persian empire (e.g. in those of Olmstead, Frye, J. M. Cook, and Briant) and in the studies dedicated to the Persian lists of ethnics and iconographic representations. On the Herodotean and Homeric catalogues, see O. K. Armayor, *TAPhA* CVIII (1987), 1–9. On the satrapies see also C. H. Lehmann-Haupt, *RE* II A 1,1921, coll. 32–138; Leuze, *passim*; Toynbee, pp. 580–689 (and pl. V–VII); Burn, pp. 109–11, 122–6; Herzfeld, pp. 288–349; Dandamaev, in Walser, pp. 15–58; J. M. Cook, *CHI*, pp. 204–5, 244–67; T. C Young, *CAH*[2] IV, pp. 70–99. On the Achaemenid imperial ideology, C. Herrenschmidt, *Studia Iranica*, V (1976), 35–65, and in the *Le Concept d' empire*, Paris 1980, pp. 69–102; T. Petit, *REA* LXXXVII (1985), 43–52; Dandamaev–Lukonin, pp. 96–116, 177–95. See also the bibl. cited in the note on chs. 61–88.

89,1. ἐν Πέρσῃσι: 'in the empire of the Persians'; cf. VII 106,2. ἀρχὰς... σατραπηίας: cf. I 192,2 with note.   ἄρχοντας: cf. I 192,4 and note on III 120,1. The form σατράπης does not occur in Greek sources before Xenophon. Darius probably extended a government system that already existed at a regional level; for the period of Cyrus and Cambyses see I 153,3; III 70,3; 120,1; IV 166,1; cf. the governors mentioned in the Bisitun inscription, §§38, 45 ff.; see also Xen. *Cyr.* VIII 6,7–8.   ἐτάξατο... ἔθνεα: the Persian tribute-system was arranged 'according to peoples', i.e. the single fiscal units normally corresponded to ethnic groups: e.g. to a group of Lydian villages. The regular φόρος was a *tributum soli*, perhaps about 12 per cent (cf. R. Descat, *REA* LXXXVII (1985), 97 ff.) of the estimated produce of every unit (cf. Theopompus, *FGrHist* 115 F 113). When a systematic centuriation of the empire was established (in Ionia, after 494 BC), the estimate of the land-tax was calculated according to a register of perimeters measured in parasangs (VI 42,2 with note; cf. I 192,1). The most common fiscal unit was the village, with a 'village-chief' (κώμαρχος) who was responsible to the regional government. Many units paid in metal; some also paid contributions in kind (90,3 with note). In addition to the royal 'tribute' each satrapy was also taxed for the payment of the 'salary' of the satrap, the subordinate governors, the commanders, and officials of every rank (cf. I 192). On the 'gifts' see 89,3 and 97,2–5; on the tribute system, in addition to the bibl. quoted in the note on chs. 89–96, see P. Briant, *JESHO* XVIII (1975), 163–86; P. Briant and

C. Herrenschmidt, *Le Tribut dans l'Empire Perse*, Paris 1989; on the 'salary' system, Lewis, pp. 4 ff.   πρὸς τοῖσι ἔθνεσι...: Herodotus means that minority populations were ascribed to, or associated with, the main peoples of each satrapy.

ὑπερβαίνων...: sometimes more distant peoples were assigned to the same tribute grouping, 'going beyond', 'jumping over' the closer ones.

2. χρυσίον: cf. 95,1.   τὸ δὲ βαβυλώνιον...: the Babylonian talent corresponded to 70 minae, not to 60 like the Euboic and Attic talent; cf. Pollux IX 89.   ἑβδομήκοντα: the addition of Reiz ⟨ὀκτὼ καὶ⟩ to read 78, although accepted by Hude and most modern editors, is wrong: see B. Hemmerdinger, *Boll Class* IX (1988), 51–6.

3. ἦν κατεστηκὸς: cf. 97,2–5. The distinction between 'tribute' and 'gift' (the two concepts do not necessarily exclude each other) is partly ideological: paying a tribute signified subjection, offering gifts meant alliance. In the 'gift' there is an element of reciprocity and ceremony that tribute lacks; see e.g. the gifts from the ethnic delegations to the king, and the reciprocal gifts from the king to the delegates, on occasions like festivals or banquets, and also the procession depicted in the *Apadana* of Persepolis (see the bibl. cited in the introduction to App. II): cf. Sancisi-Weerdenburg, pp. 145–83.   διὰ δὲ ταύτην τὴν ἐπίταξιν: the regular tribute, the diffusion of coins (cf. IV 166,2), and the systematic hoarding of precious metals (III 96,2) could have earned Darius the nickname of 'shopkeeper', which may be authentic. However, elsewhere in Herodotus Darius is not characterized as greedy; e.g. he is not mentioned in relation to the taxation of water at 117,6; cf. in later sources the anecdote about Darius halving the tributes imposed by the satraps (Plutarch, *Mor.* 172 f; Polyaenus VII 11,3); and cf. the anecdote of Herodotus about Cambyses at 13,4. For the idealization of Cyrus see note on 34,4. See N. Smith, *REA* XCI (1989), 208–12; R. Descat, *AH* VIII (1994), 161–6; B. Baldriga, *Studi micenei ed egeo-orientali*, XXXVII (1996), 131–9; M. Lombardo, in *I Greci* II 2 1997, pp. 699–706.

90,1. ἀπὸ μὲν δὴ Ἰώνων...: cf. νομὸς Ἰωνικός at 127,1. *Yauna* (Ionia) or *Yaunā tyaiy uškahya* ('Ionians of the continent') are found in the Persian lists. *Yauna* stretched along the western Asia Minor coast south of the gulf of Adramyttium, and extended into the Carian–Lycian–Pamphylian hinterland up to the border with Cilicia. It is noteworthy that the Dorians of Asia are missing from the list of peoples (see VII 93). On the Anatolian satrapies see M. Corsaro, *ASNP* III 10 (1980), 1166–73; M. Mellink, *CAH*[2] IV, pp. 211–33.   Ἰώνων...καὶ Αἰολέων: cf. note on 1,1. For the satrapal centre of Magnesia (modern Tekke) see 122,1; 125,2; Müller II, pp. 575–80.   Καρῶν: the *Karkā* are linked to the *Yaunā* only in *DSf* ll. 33 f. Kent: together they transport cedar of Lebanon from Babylon to Susa. In the past the identification of the *Karka* with the Carians was very controversial; see e.g. W. Eilers, *Orientalistische Literaturzeitung*, XXXVIII (1935), coll. 201–13. A separate satrapy of Caria and Lycia was created in 395 BC, with the dynasty of the Hecatomnids.   Λυκίων: cf. I 176,1 with note. On Lycia in the Persian empire see B. Jacobs, in *Akten des II Internationales Lykiens-Symposium, 1990*, Vienna 1993, pp. 163–9; P. Briant, *CRAI* (1998), 305–47.

Μιλυέων: cf. I 173,2 with note; Müller II, pp. 336–9.   *Παμφύλων*: cf. I 28 with note; Müller II, pp. 351–5.   ἀπὸ δὲ *Μυσῶν* ...: cf. νομὸς Λύδιος at 127,1; corresponding to the famous *Sparda* of the Persian lists, considered by Darius as the western extremity of his empire ('from India to Sparda': *DPh* Kent). It included the hinterland of Mysia and Lydia up to Cybira in Cabalia. The seat of the satrap was at Sardis; cf. 127,1. The satraps of Sardis, like e.g. Oroetes (120,1) and Artaphernes (V 25,1), had a major political role in the Aegean–Anatolian area both in the reign of Darius and later. On Achaemenid Lydia, cf. J. M. Balcer, *Sparda by the Bitter Sea*, Chico 1984; N. V. Sekunda, *REA* LXXXVII (1985), 7–29; M. Mellink, *CAH*² IV, pp. 217 ff. On the Lydians and the Mysians in the army of Xerxes see VII 74; for the Mysians in the Lydian satrapy, cf. M. J. Osborne, *GB* III (1975), 291–309; on Mysia, cf. Müller II, pp. 882–3.   *Λασονίων*: at VII 77 a different name for the *Καβηλέες*; here, however, the two peoples are distinct; they are not mentioned anywhere else.   *Καβαλίων*: also called *Μηίονες*, the ancient name of the Lydians (VII 741,77; cf. I 7,3 with note); some linked them to the Solymi (Strabo XIII 4,16) of the Lycian–Pisidian area; cf. O. Masson, *MH* XLI (1984), 139–45. Hecataeus, *FGrHist* 1 F 269 knew of a 'city' *Καβαλίς* (cf. Strabo XIII 4,17). Cf. Müller II, pp. 269–71.   *Ὑτεννέων* (Stein): some accept the reading *Ὑγεννέων* of some mss and unconvincingly link this people to the Sigynni of Herodotus, V 9,1; see Toynbee, p. 676; however, it is the *Ἐτεννεῖς* who in the Hellenistic age are known in this area: cf. Walbank I, pp. 599–600. They are probably a mountain tribe, with a town called Etenna in Pisidia; cf. Müller II, pp. 262–6.   *πεντακόσια τάλαντα*: perhaps partly paid in gold: see *DSf* ll 35 f. Kent.

2. ἀπὸ δὲ *Ἑλλησποντίων* ...: cf. νομὸς Φρύγιος at 127,1. This large satrapy, which the Greeks also called Dascylitis, from the name of the capital Dascylium (see note on 120,2), included the rest of Asia Minor up to Armenia, excluding Cilicia. In other words, it included areas that until 546 BC had been politically separated by the river Halys, namely the kingdom of Lydia and the Medo-Persian kingdom (see I 72,2 with note). Nevertheless, Cappadocia (*Katpatuka* in the Persian lists) probably had a separate and semi-autonomous government; the Halys also retained some of its role as a military and administrative border; cf. V 102,1. Among the peoples of this area there is no mention of the Chalybes (I 28 with note), the Ligyes, and the western Matieni (VII 72). On Phrygia see Müller II, pp. 190–8; on the Persian settlements in Phrygia, N. Sekunda, *AH* III (1987), pp. 175–96.   *Θρηίκων ... Ἀσίη*: the Thyni and the Bithyni of Bithynia (I 28), who, according to Herodotus, emigrated from Thrace (VII 75,2), as did the Phrygians themselves (VII 73); see P. Carrington, *AS* XXVII (1977), 117–26. For the phrase 'Thracians of Asia' cf. Pherecydes, *FGrHist* 3 F 27; Xen. *Anab.* VI 4,1–2. On Paphlagonia cf. Müller II, pp. 184–8.   *Μαριανδυνῶν*: cf. I 28 with note; Müller II, pp. 177–8.   *Συρίων*: the Cappadocians; cf. I 72,1; V 49,6; VII 72,1.   *ἑξήκοντα καὶ τριηκόσια τάλαντα*: see note on 90,3. According to Strabo XI 13,8, the tribute of Cappadocia also included 1,500 horses, 2,000 mules, and 20,000 sheep.

3. ἀπὸ δὲ *Κιλίκων*: *Khilakku* in the Assyrian texts, *khlk*, *khylky* in Aramaic coins and papyri, corresponds to the mountainous area of *Cilicia aspera* or τραχεία,

while Cilicia *campestris* (or Πεδιάς) is called *Que*; there is no equivalent in the Persian lists. In Herodotus Cilicia comprises both regions; its borders reach beyond the Halys (I 72,2) in the north, as far as Pamphylia in the west and the Euphrates in the east (V 52,3), including Commagene; for the border with Syria see 91,1. Aeschylus, *Pers.* 326 ff., mentions a Syennesis governor of the Cilicians. The frequent appearance of the name Syennesis (I 74,3; V 118,2; VII 98; Xen. *Anab.* I 2,12–27; Diod. XIV 20,2–3) gave rise to the view that it was a title, not a proper name. In the 5th cent. Cilicia was governed by a hereditary dynasty, vassal and tributary: it had its seat at Tarsus and possessed the right to mint coins. Herodotus considers Cilicia an ethnically homogeneous νομός, despite the presence of 'Achaean' colonies well known to him (91,1; VII 91). On Achaemenid Cilicia see A. Erzen, 'Kilikien bis zum Ende der Perserherrschaft', Diss. Leipzig 1940; M. Mellink, *CAH*² IV, pp. 226 f.; P. Desideri and M. Jasink, *Cilicia*, Turin 1990; A. Lemaine and H. Lozmachens, *Transeuphratene*, III (1990), 143–55; cf. also Müller II, pp. 148–55.   ἵπποι τε λευκοί: sacred to the Sun (cf. note on 84,3); for other tributes in kind see I 192,4; II 98,1; III 91,2–3 and 92,1; cf. Xen. *Anab.* I 4,9; IV 5,24, 34.   ἐξήκοντα καὶ τριηκόσιοι: the same number also occurs for the total royal tribute of Cilicia in silver talents; cf. 90,2; 92,2; 94,2. The number naturally has a symbolic value, connected with the Egyptian solar year and the cult of the Sun (cf. I 32,3; II 4,1), but not with the lunar year of the contemporary Persian calendar, nor probably with the Mazdaic solar year of 365 days, known to Curtius Rufus III 3,10. See Marquart II, pp. 202 ff.; Dandamaev–Lukonin, pp. 191–2.   πεντακόσια: cf. V 49,6. The 140 expended on the cavalry stationed in Cilicia must not be included in the total (95; cf. the distinctions concerning Egypt: 91,2–3). The sum is noteworthy, an indication of the wealth of Cilicia, amassed from the silver-mines of the Taurus, sea trade, and the Greek cities of the coast.

91,1. ἀπὸ δέ…μέχρι Αἰγύπτου: Herodotus here indicates the territorial limits, without giving a list of peoples. He refers to the whole coastal stretch of the eastern Mediterranean, between the Mt Casius of the north and the homonymous one of the south (see note on 5,2), about 600 km. of coast, whose fertile hinterland reached as far as the desert, east of the Orontes and of the Jordan. This νομός corresponds in the Persian lists to *Athurā* (cf. Ἀτουρία or Ἀτυρία, for the area of Niniveh, Strabo XVI 1,1–3; Arrian, *Anab.* III 7,7 [v.l.]; Dio Cassius LXVIII, fr. 26,4; Stephanus of Byzantium, s.v. Νῖνος), a territory that must have embraced, at least in part, the area of the old Assyrian kingdom (e.g. *Izalā*: cf. Bis. inscr. §29) and all the area 'beyond the Euphrates' (*Ebir Nari* Accadian, *'abr nhra* Aramaic, literally meaning 'beyond the river'; cf. πέραν Εὐ[φ]ράτου in the letter of Darius to Gadatas: ML 12, ll. 10 f.). In a trilingual inscription of Darius, *Athurā* is actually translated as *Ebir Nari* (*DSf* l. 32 Kent). The entire area, of great strategic and economic importance, had fallen to the Persians after the conquest of Babylon of 539 BC. Herodotus assumes that his fifth νομός was distinct from the ninth ('Babylon and the rest of Assyria': 92,1) from the time of Darius. In fact, *Athurā* and *Bābiruš* are distinct in all the unofficial Persian lists (see note on chs.

89–96); nevertheless, it is now clear from the Babylonian documents that during the entire reign of Darius both provinces were governed by a single satrap based in Babylonia. Thus, the governors of the fifth νομός in the period of Darius must have been subordinate to the satrap of 'Babylon and *Eber Nari*'; e.g. the famous Tattenai, *pḥa* of *Eber Nari* (Ezra 5: 6; 6: 6) was subordinate to the satrap Uštani. Subordinate satraps governed through regional *pḥoth* (e.g. Zerubbabel and Nehemiah in Judaea, Sanballat in Samaria, the Tobiads in the Ammonitis), sheiks (e.g. Geshem: see note on 8,1), kings, or despots in the Phoenician cities (cf. VII 98). The satrapal seat in Syria was, in 401 BC, north-west of Thapsacus, on the Euphrates; on the palace and its paradise see Xen. *Anab.* I 4,10–11. On the Achaemenid military base in northern Syria (Deve Hüyük) see P. R. S. Moorey, *Levant*, VII (1975), 208–17; on the royal paradise at Sidon see Diod. XVI 41,5. For the bibl. see Leuze, *passim*; M. W. Stolper, *JNES* XLVIII (1989), 283–305; Bengtson, pp. 402–8; A. F. Rainey, *Australian J. Biblical Arch.*, I (1969), 51–78; E. Stern, *CHJud*, pp. 78–87; E. Kuhrt, *CAH*² IV, pp. 130 f.; I. Eph'al, ibid., pp. 139–64; P. Calmeyer, *Transeuphratene*, III (1990), 109–29.   Ποσιδηίου πόλιος: cf. Stephanus of Byzantium, s.v.; called a πολίχνη in Strabo XVI 2,8 and 12; The name indicates a promontory; today Ras el-Basit, south of the mouth of the Orontes. Cf Müller II, pp. 205–7; P. Courbin, in J.-P. Descoeudres (ed.), *Greek Colonists and Native Populations*, Canberra–Oxford 1990, pp. 563–9. Coins (of Achaemenid times?): G. Le Rider, *BCH* CX (1986), 393–408; J. Elayi, *REG* CV (1992), 327.   Ἀμφίλοχος...: Herodotus alludes to the legend of Amphilochus, a famous seer like his father Amphiaraus, who, upon returning from Troy with Chalcas, founded an oracle at Mallus in Cilicia and several cities in Pamphylia, Cilicia, and northern Syria (cf. VII 91). In the West Amphilochus founded Amphilochian Argos on the gulf of Ambracia (Thuc. II 68,3). The legend, of which there are several versions, probably stems from the *Nostoi* and was already known to Hesiod and Callinus (both quoted by Strabo XVI 5,17; 4,3). See I. Krauskopf, *LIMC* I 1981, pp. 713–7. The archaeological excavations of Al-Mina, at the mouth of the Orontes, and at Tell Sukas, south of Posideion, have shown that the area had been visited by Greeks since 800 BC; see Boardman, *Greeks Overseas*, pp. 35–54 with bibl.   Ἀραβίων: cf. 5,1–2; 97,5. The nomads of the desert south of the Fertile Crescent between the Delta and the Euphrates were under Persian rule (*Arabāya* in the Persian lists). For the Arab contingents in Xerxes' army see VII 69; 86,2; 87; 184,4.   πεντήκοντα...φόρος ἦν: cf. 'the tribute of '*br nhra* (Ezra 6: 8), 'the tribute of the king' (Neh. 5: 4), did not include taxes and local tolls for the maintenance of the governor ('the bread of the *peḥa*'). On the 'villages of Parysatis', in northern Syria, for the girdle of the queen-mother, see Xen. *Anab.* I 4,9; cf. Plato, *Alcib.* I 123b–c; and see G. Cardascia, in *Marchands, diplomates et empereurs. Études offerts à Paul Garelli*, Paris 1991, pp. 363–9.   Φοινίκη: cf. note on 5,1. On Phoenicia in the Achaemenid period see J. Elayi, *Pénétration grecque en Phénicie sous l'empire perse*, Nancy 1988, with bibl.; *AH* IV (1990), 227–37.   Συρίη ἡ Παλαιστίνη καλεομένη: cf. 5,1 with note; see E. M. Laperoussaz and E. Lemaire (eds.), *La Palestine à l'époque perse*, Paris 1994.   Κύπρος: see II 182,2; III 19,3. There is no confirmation from

eastern sources that Cyprus was part of this satrapy. For the Cypriot fleet in
Xerxes' army see VII 90; 98. On Cyprus in the Persian empire, cf. P. Bocci, *EAA* II
1959, pp. 628–43; V. Karageorghis, *Cyprus*, Geneva 1968; A. Destrooper-Geor-
giades, *Studia Phoenicia*, V, Louvain 1987, pp. 339–55; C. Tuplin, *Achaemenid
Studies*, Stuttgart 1996, pp. 9–79.

2. *ἀπ' Αἰγύπτου*: *Mudrāya* in all the Persian lists; *Msrjm* in the Old Testament.
Darius left his indelible stamp on Egypt through his legislative and fiscal work,
the reconstruction of temples, building projects, and the excavation of the canal
(II 158; IV 39,1); information about these appears not only in Herodotus but also
in numerous inscriptions and papyri (see e.g. P. Grelot, *Documents araméens
d'Egypte*, Paris 1972, pp. 280 ff., 308 ff., 319 ff.). On the Persian satrapy of Egypt
see esp. E. Bresciani, in Bengtson, pp. 333–53; *CHJud*, pp. 358–72; *CHI*,
pp. 507–29; see also Kienitz, pp. 55–66; P. Briant, *AH* III (1987), 137–73;
J. D. Ray, *CAH*² IV, pp. 254–86. On Darius' work of codification in Egypt see
also R. Neith, *Mizraim*, I (1933), 178–85; Seidl, pp. 1 f., 84 f. See also the bibl.
mentioned in the note on 1,1.   *Λιβύων...Βάρκης*: cf. 13,3 with note; VII
71; 86,2.   *Μοίριος λίμνης*: lake Moeris was in the Fayûm; cf. II 148–9 with the
commentary of Lloyd's notes, and *Commentary 99–182*, pp. 120 ff. According to
Herodotus (II 149,5), the income from taxes on fishing in the lake was 240 talents
a year. It was probably a toll imposed in pharaonic times (cf. Diod. I 52,5); cf. II
98,1 on the city of Anthylla (perhaps close to Alexandria), which paid for the
shoes of the queen (and/or the girdle according to Athenaeus I 33 f.). On the
water of the Nile and ammoniac salt for the Great King see Dinon, *FGrHist* 690 F
23a–b. Cf. note on para. 4.

3. *Λευκῷ τείχεϊ*: cf. note on 13,2. The castle became the seat of the satrap, the
administration, and the treasury; it was also a garrison base. In Egypt
the pre-existing district subdivision into *νομοί* with local governors (*frtrk* in the
Aramaic documents) was maintained. For the other garrisons in Egypt see II
30,2–3; 99,3; III 19,1. On the Egyptian fleet in 480 BC cf. VII 89,2; VIII 17.

4. *Σατταγύδαι*: *Thataguš* in the Persian lists; the etymology of the name is
disputed. Herodotus jumps from Egypt to the extreme east of the empire.
Today the Sattagydians (missing at VII 66,1) are placed, with many uncertainties,
in the south of Gandara, between Drangiana (93,2), the Indus, and Arachosia
(*Harauvatiš* in the Persian lists; there is no equivalent in Herodotus; see
W. Vogelsang, *IA* XX (1985), 55–99). In other words, they possibly occupied
the territory between central-west Pakistan and southern Afghanistan. Another
hypothesis proposed locating them in Punjab and the area south of the Hindu
Kush. It was a rebel area in 522/1; see D. Fleming, *JRAS* (1982),
102–12.   *Γανδάριοι*: cf. VII 66,1. *Gadāra* in the Persian lists. They occupied
the basin of Kabul, between Bactria and Peshawar and beyond; see A. Foucher,
CRAI (1938), 339 ff.; I. Puskás, *AUB* V–VI (1977–8), 85 f. The name Gandara is
perhaps preserved in Kandahar. The population was Indian according to Hecataeus, *FGrHist* 1 F 294a–b (cf. Arrian, *Anab.* III 8,3), who considered also the city
of Kaspatyrus to be 'Gandarian' (see note on 102,1). In the Hellenistic period a
famous Graeco-Indian kingdom flourished in this area.   *Δαδίκαι*: cf. VII 66.

A 'Persian people' according to Stephanus of Byzantium, s.v. There is no equivalent in the Persian lists. According to modern conjectures they correspond to the Dardistan or Tadgiki.   *Ἀπαρύται*: cf. the *Παρυηταί* of Ptolemy VI 20; the ethnic has no equivalent in the Persian lists. According to modern conjectures it was a mountain tribe (cf. Arrian, *Anab.* III 8,4) corresponding to the modern Afridi north of Peshawar.   *ἑβδομήκοντα ...*: the lowest taxation of the entire catalogue.   *ἀπὸ Σούσων*: *Çūšā* in the inscriptions of Darius (*DSf* l. 22 Kent; *DSo*), *Šu-ša-an* Elamitic and Babylonian, *Šu-šn* Hebrew. The toponym means 'lily'. The city was situated on the site of the modern *Šuš*, on the river *Šahur*, a tributary of the Choaspes. In Herodotus, who does not mention Persepolis, Susa is the capital of the empire par excellence: he describes its palace, acropolis gates, and its towers; it was the destination of the kings returning from their campaigns, of ambassadors, and of suppliants asking for an audience. Herodotus knew the Greek legend of the foundation of Susa or its palace by Memnon (V 53; 54,2; VII 151); he knew that the river Choaspes flowed by the city (see I 188, with note); he records in passing the streets and the population of Susa (VIII 9,9). Much more concrete and picturesque are the descriptions of Susa in the Book of Esther. Susa was the ancient capital of the kingdom of Elam; even after the foundation of Persepolis it became the winter capital under the Achaemenids. Darius restored the walls and built a great palace, whose remains inspire admiration; the ruins of the eastern door were excavated in 1973; Darius himself described the construction of the palace in *DSf* Kent. See Ghirshmann, pp.126 ff.; A. L. Oppenheim, *JNES* XXIV (1965), 328–32; Hinz, pp. 177–82 with fig. 38 and bibl. on p. 251. Note that Susa, despite being the capital, paid tribute and was the seat of a regional satrap. For its treasuries see note on 96,2.   *Κισσίων χώρης*: cf. V 49,7; 52,6; for the 'Cissian gates' of Babylon cf. III 155,6; for the Cissians in Xerxes' army cf. VII 62,2; 86,1; 210,1. It corresponds to *Ūvja* or *Ūja* in the Persian lists, where it always occupies one of the first three places, with *Pārsa* and *Māda*; *hal-tam-ti* is the local Elamite name. In Greek the name can also have the form *Σουσίς* (Aesch. *Pers.* 119) or *Σουσιανή*. It was the area of the ancient kingdom of Elam, which separated Persis from Babylonia and Media. It rebelled in 522/1, and again later; cf. Bis. inscr. §§22–3 and 71. For the petroliferous areas belonging to the king see VI 119. In Cissia lived also other tribes, some of them quite autonomous mountain peoples, like the Ouxii and the Cossaei (Arrian, *Anab.* III 17,1; VII 15,1–2).

92,1. *ἀπὸ Βαβυλῶνος ...*: see I 177–200 with note; for the siege of Darius cf. III 150–60 and note. On Babylon as a Persian satrapy, cf. M. Meuleau, in Bengtson, pp. 354–85; A. L. Oppenheim, *CHI*, pp. 529–87; M. Dandamaev, *CHJud*, pp. 326–42; A. Kuhrt, *CAH*² IV, pp. 112–38 and *PCPhS* CCXIII (1988), 60–76.   *τῆς λοιπῆς Ἀσσυρίης*: lower Mesopotamia of the neo-Babylonian kingdom, conquered by Cyrus in 539 BC. Cf. I 183 f. with notes. On the satrapy of Babylonia—*Eber Nari* see note on 91,1. On the Babylonian tribute see also I 192,1 with note; Xen. *Anab.* II 4,27.   *ἀπὸ δὲ Ἀγβατάνων ...*: *Māda* in the Persian lists. For Herodotus Media is the area extending between the upper

Tigris, Armenia, and the 'Caspian gates' (between Media and Parthia, east of
Teheran), and to the south as far as Cissia and Persis. Media, subjected by Cyrus
from 550 BC, was a privileged but still tributary area. Cf. I 95–106 with notes; on
Ecbatana see I 98,3 with note; III 64,4. On the tribute see also 106,1; cf. Strabo XI
13,8. For the Medians in Xerxes' army cf. VII 62,1.   Παρικανίων: probably
identical with the Παρητακηνοί, a Median tribe (see I 101 with note); in this case
they would be different from the Παρικάνιοι of the seventeenth νομός (94,1); cf.
Stephanus of Byzantium, s.v. Παραίτακα; also Hecataeus, *FGrHist* 1 F 282. They
are thought to have lived in the region of modern Isfahan and up to the Caspian
Sea. On the etymologies of the name and modern hypotheses H. Treidler, *RE*
Suppl. X 1965, coll. 478–82; A. M. Piemontese, *RSO* XLIV (1969),
102–42.   Ὀρθοκορυβαντίων: among modern theories, the best-known claims
that this ethnic corresponds to the *sakā tigrakhaudā*, 'the Sakā with the pointed
hood', of the Persian lists (see note on 93,3).

2. **Κάσπιοι**: apart from the Caspians, the peoples here mentioned by Herodotus
are not found in any other source, and lack equivalents in the Persian lists.
Perhaps they were coastal populations of the south-western Caspian Sea (Qazwin,
west of Teheran); others think of the inhabitants of Hyrcania (on the south-
eastern coast of the Caspian Sea; see W. Vogelsang, *AH* III (1987), 121–35), which
do not appear in Herodotus' list (cf. 117,1 with note). For other Caspian peoples,
cf. 93,3.   Πανσίκαι: cf. the *Paesicae, Pestici* in the Caspian area (Mela III 39
and 42; Pliny, *NH* VI 50).   ἀπὸ δὲ Βακτριανῶν...: Bactria (*Bakhtriš* in the
Persian lists) corresponds approximately to northern Afghanistan and to the
southern areas of Tajikistan and Uzbekistan, in the basin of the high Amu
Daria north of Paropamisus. It was a vast and important satrapy, the seat of the
famous Graeco-Bactrian kingdom in the Hellenistic age, and a place of contacts
with India and China. Excavations at Ai-Khanum in eastern Bactria brought to
light the remains of a prosperous Hellenistic city. On Bactrian art see
O. M. Dalton, *The Treasure of Oxus*, London 1964; cf. K. V. Trever, *EAA* II
1959, pp. 23–30. Bactria, the traditional homeland of Zoroaster, was incorporated
by Darius into the Persian empire after the revolts of 522/1. Its main centre was
Bactra; see VI 9,4; IX 113,1; another Greek name of the city was Zariaspa. To the
Greeks Bactria (already known e.g. to Aeschylus, *Pers.* 306) was the extreme end
of their world; cf. Herod. VI 9,4. For the Barcaei in Bactria see IV 204. On the
Indians bordering with Bactria cf. III 102,1; on the Bactrians in the army of Xerxes
and Mardonius see VII 64; 86,1; VIII 113,2; IX 31,3; on the satraps of
Bactria, Dadaršiš and Masistes, see Bis. inscr. §38, and IX 113,1. On the gold
of Bactria see *DSf* ll. 35 f. Kent. Cf. in general Sancisi-Weerdenburg, pp. 122–44;
H. P. Frankfort, *CAH*² IV, pp. 165–93; for the Greeks in Bactria see W. W. Tarn,
The Greeks in Bactria and India, Chicago 1953³ (re-edited with additions and bibl.
by F. L. Holt, Chicago 1985); A. H. Narain, *The Indo-Greeks*, Oxford 1957;
S. Sherwin-White and A. Kuhrt, *From Samarkand to Sardis*, London 1993;
P. Bernard, in *History of Civilization of Central Asia*, II, London 1994,
pp. 99–129.   Αἰγλῶν: cf. the Αὔγαλοί of Ptolemy VI 12, and the Αὐγάσιοι

of Stephanus of Byzantium, s.v. For modern hypotheses, cf. A. G. Laird, *CPh* XVI (1921), 308 f.

93,1. *Πακτυϊκῆς*: this should be altogether distinguished from the homonymous region of India (102,1), unless it is a mistake (perhaps for *Katpatuka*, Cappadocia).   *Ἀρμενίων*: *Armina* in the Persian lists; *Ú-ra-aš-tu* (Urartu) in Babylonian. Herodotus uses this name to mean the territory bordered by Cilicia and Matiene, Assyria, and the Caucasus (see esp. V 49,6; 52,3 and 5; cf. I 194,2). Around 400 BC it was divided into two satrapies: eastern Armenia, east of the Tigris, and western Armenia as far as the Euphrates (Xen. *Anab.* III 5,17; IV 3,4; 4,4 and 7). The two provinces formed, in Hellenistic times, the kingdom of the Artaxiads (Strabo XI 14,5). In Roman times they were again divided into Armenia *Maior* (on the east) and Armenia *Minor*. Herodotus considered Armenia a great mountain area from which four great rivers flowed: the Euphrates, the Tigris, the Halys, and the Gyndes (I 72,2; 180,1; V 52,4–5); he viewed the Armenians as Phrygian 'colonists' (VII 73). Modern research shows that western Armenia was inhabited since 600 BC by the Haiks, a people speaking an Indo-European language. On the Armenian satrapy see G. A. Tiratsian, *AAntHung* XXIX (1981), 151–68, and R. H. Hewsen, *Rev. des Études Arméniennes*, XVII (1983), 123–43; M. Mellink, *CAH²* IV, pp. 231–3.   *καὶ τῶν προσεχέων*: Herodotus probably alludes to the area between the Kara Su and the coast of Pontus, from the Phasis to Trapezus, inhabited in Xenophon's time by autonomous or almost autonomous populations. The populations of the nineteenth *νομός* are not included among the peoples bordering on the Armenians (94,2).   *τετρακόσια τάλαντα*: according to Xenophon (*Anab.* V 5,24 and 34) they also paid tribute in kind. Strabo (XI 14,9) adds that every year the satrap of Armenia sent 20,000 colts to the Great King for the festival of Mitra (*Μιθρακήνοις* codd.; see note on 79,3).

2. *Σαγαρτίων*...: Iranian populations of the south-eastern area of Persis, between the gulf and Parthia. Sagartia, Drangiana, and perhaps also Arachosia belonged to this area (note on 91,4). See H. P. Frankfurt, *CAH²* IV, pp. 165–93. The tribute seems excessive for such a poor region. Among these populations of Iranian stock the most important are the Sagartians: *Asagarta* in some Persian inscriptions; *Zikirtu* or *Zakruti* in Assyrian texts. The Sagartians did not support Cyrus against the Medians (I 125,4); the area rebelled in 521 (cf. Bis. inscr. §§33 and 52). For the Sagartians in Xerxes' army see VII 85,1.   *Σαραγγέων*...: cf. 117,1; VII 67,1. *Zranka* in the Persian lists: there are also *Δράγγοι, Δραγγιανή* (*-ιάνη*), and *Ζαραγγαῖοι* in Hellenistic Greek sources. The area corresponds to modern Sistan (Sakastan), between the eastern Iranian plateau and Pakistan; cf. G. Gnoli, *Ricerche storiche sul Sistan antico*, Rome 1967; W. Vogelsang, *IA* XX (1985), 69 ff. According to Strabo XI 10,1, Drangiana and Aria belonged to the same tributary district; according to Arrian, *Anab.* III 21,1, the Drangiani and the Arachosians were under the same satrap in 330 BC. On Prophthasia in Drangiana see Eratosthenes, in Strabo XI 8,9; XV 2,8; on the excavations at Dahan-i Ghulāman (perhaps a cult centre of the

Achaemenid period), cf. U. Scerrato, in *South-Asian Archaeology 1977*, Naples 1979, pp. 709–35.   Θαμαναίων: cf. 117,1. According to some they are the Arachosians.   Οὐτίων: cf. VII 68. Perhaps they should be identified with the *Yutiya*, who lived in a district of Persia that rebelled in 521; see Bis. inscr. §§40–4; cf. Dandamaev, pp. 184 f. They inhabited Carmania, where, in addition to the regular tribute, a tribute in kind was also paid (wood for building in *DSf*, l. 35 Kent; oil in Ctesias, *FGrHist* 68 F 38 Jacoby).   Μύκων: cf. VII 68. They are generally identified with the *Maka* or *Maciyā* of the Persian lists; they inhabited the modern Makran, a mountain strip along the Persian coast of the straits of Ormuz; cf. Hecataeus, *FGrHist* 1 F 289. Apparently Pura (perhaps Bampur) was a satrapal centre. There were other Makai in Oman and in the islands of the strait. See H. W. Bailey, *JRAS* (1982), 10–13; W. Eilers, *AMI* Ergänzungsband X (1983), 101–19; D. T. Potts, *The Arabian Gulf in Antiquity*, I, Oxford 1990, pp. 397–400.   τῶν ἐν τῆσι νήσοισι...: cf. VII 80. These are the islands of the strait of Ormuz, the largest of which is Qešm. The ones known in antiquity were Ὀάρακτα (Δώρακτα v.l. in Stephanus of Byzantium, s.v. Δῶρα), mentioned by Nearchus (*FGrHist* 133 F 28), and Kyrta, where Megabyzus was exiled; see Ctesias, *FGrHist* 688 F 14 (43); Stephanus of Byzantium, s.v. Κυρταία. The islands probably also functioned as a maritime connection on the route between the Persian Gulf and Egypt.   τοὺς ἀνασπάστους...: in the Persian penal code the 'uprooting' (cf. the Aramaic term, apparently official, *šrš* in Ezra 7:26; interpreted, however, in the more general sense of punishment by R. N. Frye, in Walser, p. 92) was one of the harshest punishments; it consisted in the deportation and forced internment of individuals or whole populations in foreign and distant lands, according to a practice already used on a much larger scale by the Assyrians (cf. B. Oded, *Mass-Deportations and Deportees in the Neo-Assyrian Empire*, Wiesbaden 1979) and by the neo-Babylonians. For ἀνασπάστους ποέειν cf. IV 204; V 12,1; 106,4; VI 9,4 and 32. On the Persian deportations in Herodotus cf. also III 149 with note. See R. Kulesza, *Eos*, LXXXII (1994), 221–50.   κατοικίζει: 'establish', 'settle', 'send to live'; cf. B. Virgilio, *AAT* CVI (1971–2), 374–6; Casevitz, pp. 165–73.

3. Σάκαι: according to Herodotus, Σάκαι is the Persian equivalent of the Greek Σκύθαι (VII 64,2); for the etymology of σάκος, a type of shield, see Stephanus of Byzantium, s.v. The name in the Persian lists is *Sakā*; *gi-mir(r)-ri* (Cimmerians) in Accadian. Some Persian lists distinguish the *Sakā haumavargā* (perhaps drinkers or makers of the beverage *haoma*; cf. the Greek forms in VII 64,2; Hecataeus, *FGrHist* 1 F 190; Hellanicus, *ibid.* 4 F 65; Ctesias, *ibid.*, 688 F 9 (3)) from the *Sakā tigrakhaudā*, 'of the pointed hood' (cf. note on 92,1), well known from the Bisitun inscription (§ 74) and from their leader Skunkha depicted on the bas-relief wearing his typical pointed hood. The *Sakā haumavargā* are very hypothetically located between lake Drangiana (Daryācheh-ye Sistan) and the Helmand, in what is today south-west Afghanistan; the modern name Sistan probably dates back to the Parthian period; see P. Daffinà, *L'immigrazione dei Saka nella Drangiana*, Roma 1967. The *tigrakhaudā* are localized by some beyond the Jaxartes (Syr Daria); whereas others identify them with the Massagetae of Herodotus (I 201

with note), or with the 'Sakā from beyond Sogdiana' who are indicated in some of Darius' lists as located on the northern border of the empire (*DPh, DH* Kent, see also *Iran* V (1967), 7). It is disputed whether Darius' campaign against the *tigrakhaudā* (see Bis. inscr. §74) is the one described in Book IV, or a previous campaign beyond the Jaxartes; see G. G. Cameron, *AI* IV (1975), 77–88; J. Harmatta, *AAnt Hung* XXIV (1976), 15–24; Briant, *État et pasteurs*, pp. 181–234; J. R. Gardiner-Garden, *Klio*, LXIX (1987), 326–450. On the Sakai at Marathon, cf. VI 113, 1; on the Sakai in the army of Xerxes and Mardonius, cf. VII 96,1; 184,2; VIII 113,2; IX 31,4–5; 71,1. On the 'allied' Sakai in the 4th cent. BC see Arrian, *Anab.* III 8,8.   Κάσπιοι: the oriental Caspians (cf. VII 67,1; 86,1), apparently different from the Caspians of the Armenian area (92,2). Some identify them with the inhabitants of Kaspatyros (102,1); others locate them on the south-eastern coast of the Caspian Sea.   Πάρθοι...: famous and important peoples of the Iranian north-east, between the Caspian and Bactria, as far as the Jaxartes (Syr Daria). Herodotus unites them all under the same νομός; however, in a later period Parthia and Aria were two different satrapies (Arrian, *Anab.* III 8,4). They were mainly nomadic peoples, but had agricultural settlements in oases and irrigated areas. To the four peoples listed here by Herodotus should be added the Hyrcanians (see 117,1 with note) and the Margians, whom Herodotus does not mention. The Parthians (*Parthava* in the Persian lists) occupied the area to the south-east of the Caspian Sea as far as the modern border between Iran and Afghanistan. They were a large Scythian-Iranian tribe, who rebelled in 522/1; see Bis. inscr. §§21 and 35. Around 250 BC they established. an autonomous kingdom under the dynasty of the Arsacids, which remained in power until AD 224; they were then incorporated in the empire of the Sassanids. According to some the satrapal seat was near modern Shahrud, according to others, near Qomis. On the Parthians see also 117,1; on their presence in Xerxes' army see VII 66.   Χοράσμιοι: cf. 117,1; VII 66. They appear as *Uvārazmīy/-iš* in the Persian lists; *Khwārizm* in Arabic. They lived north-east of Parthia along the lower Oxus (Amu Daria), between the desert area of Pesky Karakumy of Turkmen and Bukhara. In this area there are characteristic works of canalization and fortifications from the Achaemenid period. The topography and flora of the region were known to Hecataeus, who also mentioned a 'city' of the same name (*FGrHist* 1 F 292–3; cf. I. V. Pyankov, *VDI* (1972), 3–21). On Alexander and the king of the Chorasmians see Arrian, *Anab.* IV 15,4. On the excavations and the civilization of the Chorasmians see S. P. Tolstov, *Auf den Spuren der altchoresmischen Kultur*, Berlin 1953; M. Gibellino-Krasceninnikova, *EAA* II 1959, pp. 563–8; on Latin sources, P. Aalto and T. Pekkanen, *Latin Sources on North-Eastern Eurasia*, Pt. I, Wiesbaden 1975, pp. 151–3.   Σόγδοι: cf. VII 66. They appear as *Suguda* or *Sugda* in the Persian lists. Sogdiana was the intermediate area between Bactria–Chorasmia and the Massagetae, in other words, between the Oxus and the Jaxartes; it corresponds today to part of Uzbekistan and Tajikistan. Maracanda (Samarkand) became the capital of the sartapy of Sogdiana-Bactria under Alexander. On the civilization of this people see D. Mazzeo, *EAA* VII 1966, pp. 390–6.   Ἄρειοι: cf. VII 66,1

(Ἄριοι). It was also an ethnic of the Medians; see VII 62,1; cf. Paus. II 3,8. For κομμὸν Ἄριον cf. Aesch. *Choeph.* 423; Ἀρία, 'Persian land' in Hellanicus, *FGrHist* 4 F 179. It corresponds to *Haraiva* in the Persian lists, the region of Herat on the river Harī Rūd (Areios), in western Afghanistan. Cf. Strabo XI 10,1; Arrian, *Anab.* III 25,5, with the commentary of Bosworth, pp. 354 ff.

94,1. Παρικάνιοι: cf. VII 68; 86,2. They are different from their homonyms of 92,1 (with note): they are perhaps inhabitants of Baluchistan, east of the Mykoi (93,2). It was a torrid area, known in antiquity as Gedrosia and explored by Nearchus; on the Ichthyophagi in Gedrosia, cf. note on 19,1; Nearchus, *FGrHist* 133 F 1 (28–9) and 1b.   Αἰθίοπες οἱ ἐκ τῆς Ἀσίης: cf. VII 70. On the 'eastern' and 'western' Ethiopians see note on 17–25.   Ματιηνοῖσι: cf. I 189,1; 202,3; V 49,6; 52,4; they have to be distinguished from the Matieni of Asia Minor (see I 72,2 with note). It is uncertain whether they are the *Mitanni* or *Mannai* of Assyrian texts. Herodotus, for their localization, thinks of the basin of lake Urmia (cf. Strabo XI 14,8) and to the south of this basin as far as the Tigris. The area was inhabited around 400 BC by the Kardouchoi (perhaps the Kurds): see Xen. *Anab.* III 5,15–16. The Matieni of this area are not found in Xerxes' army. On Matiane in Media see Strabo II 1,14; XI 7,2. On the 'Matienian tombs', H. von Gall, *AA* (1966), 19–43; on Xerxes' trilingual inscription at Van see *XV* Kent; cf. P. R. Helm, 'Greeks' in the Neo-Assyrian Levant and 'Assyria' in Early Greek Writers', Diss. Pennsylvania 1980, pp. 327–32.   Σάσπειροι: they lived to the north of the Matieni, between Media and Colchis; cf. I 104,1; 110,2; IV 37; 40,1. For their presence in Xerxes' army see VII 79. They were also called Σάπειρες or Σάβειρες.   Ἀλαροδίοισι: cf. VII 79. The ethnic recalls the biblical Ararat (Urartu). Cf. Müller II, p. 92.

2. Μόσχοισι...: cf. VII 78–9. Populations of the coast of Pontus between the Thermodon (Sagmatas) and the Phasis in Colchis, bordered on the west by the Paphlagonians, and on the east by the Colchians (non-tributary; see 97,4) and the Euphrates. The Chalybes are not mentioned in Herodotus (I 28; cf. Hecataeus, *FGrHist* 1 F 202–3). These populations are found in several ancient lists: see Jacoby's commentary on Hecateus, *FGrHist* 1 F 202–8. On the coast there were several Greek cities, among them the so-called colonies of Sinope (Cotyora, Cerasus and Trapezus). Around 400 BC these peoples had become practically autonomous. The Moschi recall the *Muskana* of Assyrian texts and the *Mešekh* of Ezek. 27:13 and 32:26, and the modern district Meshkheti; cf. Müller II, pp. 180–2.   Τιβαρηνοῖσι: they lived near Cotyora; they recall the Hittite *Tapala*, the *Tabali* of the Assyrians, and the *Tuval* of Ezek. 27: 13 and 32: 26; cf. Müller II, p. 224.   Μάκρωσι: they were circumcised, like the Colchians and the Cappadocian Syrians; see II 104,3 and cf. Lloyd's note and *Commentary 99–182*, pp. 21 f.; Xen. *Anab.* IV 8,1 ff.; [Scylax], 85; Strabo XII 3,18; scholium to Apollonius of Rhodes II 392 ff. For the name cf. the modern Makhur Dagh; cf. Müller II, p. 176.   Μοσσυνοίκοισι: their name derives from μόσσυν, 'wooden tower', according to Xenophon, *Anab.* V 4,26. On the Mossynoeci in Xerxes' army see VII 78. They are said by Greek authors to be a warlike and extremely uncivilized people: see P. Brulé, in P. Briant (ed.), *Dans les pas des Dix-Mille*, Toulouse 1995, pp. 16–18; B. Tripodi, ibid., pp. 48–9. Cf. Müller II, p. 182.   Μαροί: they may correspond to the *Marassa* of the Hittites and to the *Mariannu* of the Assyrians; cf. the modern district Imerethia. Cf. Müller II, pp. 176–7.   'Ινδῶν: *Hiduš* in the Persian lists, *Sindhu* in Sanskrit, *Hdw* in Hebrew. Herodotus refers to the area of the lower Indus, between Multan and Karachi, bordered on the west by Baluchistan, on the east by the Indian desert, and on the north-east by Gandhara and Sattagydia (91,4). The area today belongs to Pakistan. It was conquered by Darius after its exploration by Scylax (IV 44) and became tributary (cf. 102,1); see T. C. Young, *CAH*[2] IV, pp. 66 f. Understood in this sense, India defined the eastern limit of the Persian empire, 'from Hiduš to Sparda', *DPh* ll. 7–8 Kent (cf. note on 90,1; 'from Hellespont to the Indus' in Arist. *De Mundo* 398a; 'from *Hdw* up to *Kuš*' in Esther 1: 1); on the Greeks and the Indians as the 'furthermost' peoples, cf. note on 38,3. On India in Herodotus, cf. chs. 98–106 with notes. On the Indians in the armies of Xerxes and Mardonius, cf. VII 65; 70; 86,1; VIII 113,2; IX 31,3,4. See in general A. D. H. Bivar, *CAH*[2] IV, pp. 194–210.   πλῆθός ... ἀνθρώπων: in Herodotus the Indians and the Thracians are the most numerous peoples in the world (cf. V 3,1); in both cases they are complex ethnics, comprising numerous tribes; cf. Ctesias, *FGrHist* 688 F 45 (2). According to Thucydides the most numerous people are the Scythians (II 97,5–6). Herodotus' ideas on the number of the Indians might have been formed by the exorbitant size of their tribute or perhaps related to the mass (infinite, in his view) of non-tributary Indians of the southern subcontinent.   τῶν ἡμεῖς ἴδμεν: cf. 60,4 with note.   πρὸς πάντας τοὺς ἄλλους: a clear exaggeration (unless we understand it in the sense of 'compared to any other νομός'). ἑξήκοντα ... ψήγματος: on the gold of India see 98,1–2; 102; 104–6. On the 'mystic' number 360 see note on 90,3; for the relation between gold and silver see 95,1 with note. The sum is symbolically excessive and imaginary. Some scholars believe that the sum refers to the total amount of gold in the entire empire, or to the equivalent in gold of 360 talents of silver. Ivory also came from India; see *DSf* l. 44 Kent.

95,1. τὸ μὲν δὴ ἀργύριον ...: using the exchange rate of 70:60 for the Babylonian talent in respect of the Euboean (Attic) talent (the exchange rate already mentioned by Herodotus, 89,2), the total of nineteen νομοί paying in silver is 7,600 Babylonian talents (excluding the 140 Cilician talents, see 90,3), equal to 8,866 Euboean talents (not 9,540 as Herodotus claims). Moreover, the sum of the two totals referred to in Herodotus, 9,540 and 4,680, is not 14,560, but 14,220. There have been various attempts to explain these mistakes. The simplest would be to suppose one or more mistakes in the manuscript tradition, and to correct in the text the two wrong totals: on such errors in Herodotus mss see R. Develin, *Phoenix*, CLIV (1990), 3–7. More subtle is the adjustment of the exchange rate: using 78:60 (instead of 70:60) the 7,600 Babylonian talents become 9,880 Euboean talents which, added to the 4,680 of India, result in Herodotus' total: 14,560. It is also very sensible to come near to the total by including the 140

Cilician talents (despite Herodotus' explicit statement to the contrary) and supposing that the 4,680 talents from India are Babylonian, and not Euboean (cf. the note of Rosén, ad loc.). In this way the two sums would be 9,030 and 5,460 Euboean talents, while the total of 14,490 would be inferior by only 70 talents to the 14,560 of Herodotus. It is easier to 'correct' mistakes than to explain their origin. They have been attributed to the use of the abacus, or to the possibility that Herodotus also included in his total sum monetary equivalents of the tributes in kind mentioned in the catalogue. Preferable perhaps is a hypothesis that some sort of confusion between monetary talent and weight talent occurred in calculating the exchange rate, supposing that the coins in the original list (cf. note on chs. 89–96) were Persian coins (gold darics and silver shekels; on Persian coinage from Darius onwards see M. J. Price, *REA* XCV (1989), 9–14, and R. Descat, ibid. 15–31) and in metal weights (1 daric: 8,4 grams; 1 shekel: 5,4 grams). See in this sense R. Descat, *REA* LXXXVII (1985), 97–112; P. Keyser, *CJ* LXXXI (1986), 238–42. The credibility of these sums has repeatedly been doubted, whether because of the mistakes in calculation, or the frequency of 'mystical' numbers, or the improbability of some of the figures. Radically sceptical is the hypothesis that the original source described a fixed tribute of 360 Babylonian talents for each of the twenty satrapies; according to this theory, the total (in silver) would have been 7,200 Babylonian talents which, added to the 140 Cilician talents, would result in 7,340 Babylonian talents corresponding to 9,540 Euboean talents (see A. G. Laird, *CPh* XVI (1921), 325 f.). According to others Herodotus' starting-point would have been the total sum, which he then divided more or less arbitrarily between the twenty satrapies (see P. Calmeyer, *AH* II (1987), 17 ff.).

96,1. *καὶ ἀπὸ νήσων*: the islands of the eastern Aegean, starting with Samos (see chs. 144–9). Their inhabitants probably correspond to the *Yaunā tyaiy drayahiyā* ('Ionians of the sea') of some Persian lists; cf. the *'yy ha-yam*, 'isles of the sea', that are defined as tributary in Esther 10: 1. On Cyrus and the islands see I 169,2 with note.   *καὶ τῶν ἐν τῇ Εὐρώπῃ*: cf. VII 108,1. Herodotus alludes to the parts of Thrace that were organized into military and fiscal governorships (with bases at Sestos, Byzantium, Doriscus, Eion), if not into a proper satrapy, and to the vassal-kingdom of Macedon. The area was conquered by Megabyzus during Darius' Scythian campaign and after it, then again by Mardonius in 492; after 479 the Persians evacuated it. It is disputed whether this area ought to include the *Skudrā* of some Persian lists and of the Persepolis tablets (related to *Skydra* in Macedon? See Olmstead, pp. 157–8; P. Lecoq, *Les Inscriptions de la Perse achéménide*, Paris 1997, p. 149), the *Sakā tyaiy paradraya* ('Scythians beyond the seas'), the *Yaunā tyaiy paradraya* ('Ionians beyond the seas') and the *Yaunā takabarā* ('Ionians with broad-brimmed hats' or *petasoi*): see *DPe* ll. 13 ff.; *DNa* ll. 28 f.; *XPh* ll. 24 ff.; *A?P* ll. 24 ff. Kent. See N. G. L. Hammond, *Chiron*, X (1980), 53–61; W. Pajakowski, *Maeander*, XXXVI (1981), 75–80; *Eos*, LXXI (1983), 243–55; J. M. Balcer, *Historia*, XXXVII (1988), 1–21; A. Fol and N. G. L. Hammond, *CAH²* IV, pp. 234–53, 493–6; E. N. Borza, *In the Shadow of Olympus*, Princeton 1990, p. 293.

2. θησαυρίζει: the bars or metal coins were first cut or indented in order to detect forgeries (cf. 56,2), and then partly melted; cf. the round castings of molten silver that Croesus dedicated at Delphi (I 51,5), and the forged ones of the treasure of Oroetes in Sardis (III 123,2). Herodotus here describes a stage of the hoarding process which regularly took place in the *ganzaka* (Aramaic *gnzkʾ*; cf. γάζα), or royal treasury. In addition to the treasury in Susa (cf. Diod. XVII 66,1–2), there were others also at Pasargadae, Persepolis, Ecbatana, and in the satrapal capitals (cf. 123,2 with note). In the Achaemenid period only a small part of the hoarded metal was coined; cf. Polycleitus of Larissa, *FGrHist* 128 F 3a; on the reversibility of the process of melting and on recoining, with reference to fr. 90 DK of Heraclitus, see P. Vannicelli, *RFIC* CXIII (1985), 397–404. Various data on the operation of the Persepolis treasury between 509 and 458 BC are provided by the numerous Elamite treasury tablets (*Persepolis Treasury Tablets*, ed. G. G. Cameron, Chicago 1948) and the fortification tablets (*PFT*), which register the payment orders, made by the treasury, of monthly or daily allowances for services and works carried out by clerks, craftsmen, workmen, messengers, couriers, etc. The treasury of Persepolis, which also controlled the other regional treasuries of Persis, was administered by a hierarchical bureaucracy of 'treasurers' of various ranks, in addition to attendants, agents, group leaders, scribes, etc., all under the *ganzabara* (*kanzabara* or *kapnuškira* in Elamite; γαζοφύλαξ) = 'he who is in charge of the treasury', a high office that under Darius was held by Pharnaces (possibly the father of Artabazus, mentioned in VII 66,2). Cf. Young, *CAH*² IV, pp. 83 ff. On the techniques of hoarding in the ancient East, cf. A. L. Oppenheim, *JNES* IV (1947), 116–20; M. A. Dandamaev, in Walser, pp. 45 ff., and in *SS* VII (1985), 96 f.; Dandamaev–Lukonin, pp. 195–209.

97,1. Περσὶς...χώρην: *Pārsa* (modern Fars) with its capitals, Pasargadae and Persepolis, was the heart of the Persian empire; it heads the list of the peoples governed by Darius in the Bisitun inscription (§6) and in *DPd* l. 6 Kent. It was excluded from the list of subject peoples.

2. Αἰθίοπες...: at VII 69,2 the Ethiopians of Nubia are represented as normal subjects, but those from Nysa did not pay tribute. In the Persian lists they appeared with the names of *Kūša* and *Kūšiyā*, and constituted the southern border of the empire; see *DPh* l. 6 Kent; Esther 1: 1. On the Ethiopians see chs. 17–25 and notes.   περί...Νύσην τὴν ἱρὴν: cf. II 146,2 with note. In the aetiological Greek legend found already in Homer (*Il.* VI 132 f.) and the *Homeric Hymn* to Dionysus (I 8 ff.; XXVI 1 ff.), Zeus carried the foetus of Dionysus sewn into his thigh and gave birth to him on Mt. Nysa, named thus in some versions after his nurse. The mountain, or the city near the mountain, was variously localized in Thrace, in India, in Arabia, in Ethiopia, and also in some Greek islands, especially those that produced wine. The Nysa in India was near a mountain called Meros ('thigh'): Arrian, *Anab.* V 1,5. Perhaps the localization in Ethiopia, at Meroe, of the cult of Zeus and Dionysus (II 29,6–7) has a similar aetiological origin. According to the most widely held opinion, the 'Ethiopians of Nysa' correspond to the people of Napata; however, the variant reading νῆσσον τὴν ἱρὴν (see

apparatus criticus) has suggested the 'sacred island' of Meroe. For this theory, and for a debatable connection between Nysa, the area of Τηνεσσίς (Strabo XVI 4,8) and *Ta-nehesi* (Nubia, in late Egyptian), see Desanges, *Recherches, p. 233, n. 93.*   οὗτοι...κατάγαια: some believe that the phrase is interpolated, since what is said about sperm does not concern only the Callantiae (cf. 100; 101,1) and the underground houses cannot refer to Ethiopia, but possibly to the troglodyte Ethiopians of Libya (IV 183,4). In any event the passage seems lacunose.   σπέρματι: cf. in the same sense VI 68,3; γονή means 'sperm' at 101,2; 109,1.   Καλλαντίαι: cf. 38,4.

3. οὗτοι συναμφότεροι: the obscurity of the earlier passage makes it uncertain whether these two people are the Ethiopians and the Callantiae, or the Ethiopians who bordered on Egypt and their neighbours.   ἀπύρου...: unmelted gold, crude, in dust, different from ἄπεφθος gold (pure; cf. I 50,2–3; II 44,2). On the χοῖνιξ as unit of measure (about a litre), cf. I 192,3; VI 57,3; VII 187,2. On the gold of Ethiopia, cf. III 23,4 with note; III 114; on that of India cf. 98,1; 102; 104–6.   φάλαγγας: the word occurs only here in Herodotus, who never uses it in the common sense of 'phalanx'.   ἐβένου: cf. 114. The word is of Egyptian origin (*nbny*); see B. Hemmerdinger, *Glotta*, XLVI (1968), 242; A. G. McGready, ibid., 249.

4. Κόλχοι: they lived north of the Saspirians (I 104,1; IV 37; 40,1), and according to Herodotus were related to the Egyptians (II 104–5); for the Colchians in Xerxes' army see VII 79; on the autonomous Colchians, south-east of Trapezus, see Xen. *Anab.* IV 8,8–9; V 2,1. Colchis corresponds in part to the modern Georgia and had at its centre the plain of the Phasis (Rhion). It is the legendary home of Medea, the destination of the Argonauts and of Greek colonists in historic times. The Greeks knew of many Colchian and related tribes: cf. Strabo XI 2,16–19 (an ancestor of Strabo was governor in Colchis under Mithridates). Colchis does not have corresponding names in the Persian lists; the old identification of the *Karkā* (note on 90,1) with the Colchians has now been abandoned. On the civilization of Colchis see O. D. Lordkipanidze, *Das alte Kolchis*, Konstanz 1985; Braund; on Herodotus and the Colchians, A. Boltunova, in *Actes XIV Conférence Internationale Eirene*, Jerevan 1979, I, pp. 51–5 (in Russian).

5. Ἀράβιοι: cf. 4,3; 5,2; 8,1 with note; 9; 88; 107–13 (Arabia).   λιβανωτοῦ: cf. 107,1 with note.

98–106. This somewhat chaotic *excursus* on India deals with the subject of the extraction of the gold which the Indians of the twentieth νομός paid to the Great King (94,2). That this must be the central subject of the *excursus* is clear from the introductory sentence of 98,1; Herodotus only treats this subject in chs. 102 and 105, with a brief link in 104,1, and a final hint in 106,2. The rest is a series of sub-digressions suggested by conventional subjects of Greek ethnographic literature since Hecataeus: geography and climate, flora and fauna, populations and customs. History is missing, either because it was an unusual subject in this type of literature, or because the Indians, like other exotic people who lived in the extreme regions of the world, seemed to the Greeks a happy people without history. But there is an abundance of curiosities and *mirabilia*, most notably the famous description of the giant, gold-digging ants (102,2) and the anatomical information on the camel (103). Herodotus describes very vaguely and generically the part of India beyond the Persian border; in fact, before the 3rd cent. BC the Greeks knew nothing about the southern subcontinent and the Ganges basin. The entire excursus has the rather marginal function of inserting into the geo-ethnographic description of the Persian empire some complementary information on its eastern periphery; in fact it links the description of the empire (chs. 89–96) to the chapters dedicated to the outermost regions of the world (107–16). For further information in Herodotus on the Indians and India see III 38,3–4 and IV 44. Herodotus cites 'the Persians' (105,1) as his source for the information about the extraction of gold. Otherwise he uses the anonymous 'it is said' (98,2; 99,1), interpreted by many as an allusion to written sources: e.g. Hecataeus, who may have read the *Periplous* of Scylax of Caryanda; Scylax had explored around 510 BC the Indus from Kaspatyrus (102,1 with note) down to the mouth of the river (IV 44; fragments of the *Periplous* in *FGrHist* 709). In general the *excursus* is useful evidence of the fanciful ideas about India entertained by 5th-cent. Greeks, and of the details of the Indian myth which Herodotus helped to spread, and which were later developed and completely reconstructed by the many Greek writers of *Indika*: from Ctesias (*FGrHist* 688 F 45–52) to the Alexander historians (Nearchus, Androsthenes) and Megasthenes (*FGrHist* 715). Among later writers the most important is Arrian, who lived in the 2nd cent. AD. On Greek notions on India, from their origins to Alexander, Reese, *passim* (on Herodotus see pp. 3–6 and 57–71), is still fundamental; cf. the more recent I. Puskás, *Oikoumene*, IV (1983), 201–7; A. Dihle, in *Entretiens Fondation Hardt*, XXXV, 1988; K. Karttunen, *India in Early Greek Literature*, Helsinki 1989; D. Lenfant, *Τόποι*, V (1995), 307–36. See also the bibl. cited in the note on chs. 89–96. On Megasthenes' *Indika*, and on the previous traditions see A. Zambrini, *ASNP* XII (1982), 71–149; XV (1985), 781–853; on the *Indika* of Arrian see *ASNP* XVIII (1987), 139–54. On India in the ancient world see G. Pollet (ed.), *India and the Ancient World*, Louvain 1987.

98,2. τῶν γὰρ ἡμεῖς ἴδμεν: cf. 60,4 with note.   ἀτρεκές: cf. 4,2.   ἐρημίη: Herodotus refers to the great Indian desert east of the Indus. For the relation between ἐρημίη and the uncertain in Herodotus, cf. H. Edelman, *Klio*, LII (1970), 79–86.
3. νομάδες: cf. 99,1. The tribes beyond the border, discussed in chs. 98–100, display elements characteristic of lack of civilization typical of Herodotus' way of thinking: they are nomadic and they copulate in public; some eat meat, others are vegetarian. Aeschylus (*Suppl.* 284 ff.) knew of nomadic Indians who shared a border with the Ethiopians.   ἕλεσι: some see in this word the Greek equivalent of *Sarasvatī*, 'the swampy', name of a small river south of Kashmir.   τοῦ ποταμοῦ: the Indus, strangely mentioned by name only at IV 44,1.   ἰχθύας: on the Ichthyophagi, cf. 19,1 with note. In Herodotus not only savages eat raw meat (I 202,3; III 99,1), but also the very civilized Egyptians (II 77,4).   καλαμίνων: the cane reed, also known as 'Indian cane' (Ctesias, *FGrHist* 688 F 45b (14); Strabo XVII 3,5) or bamboo.

99,1. *Παδαῖοι*: cf. [Tibullus], *Panegyricus Messallae* 144 f. Some see in the ethnic the Sanskrit *padja*, 'evil'; others the Dravidic population of the *Paṇḍyas* of southern India.   *νομαίοισι*: cf. 38,1 with note.   *ὃς ἂν κάμῃ τῶν ἀστῶν...*: on this and other forms of cannibalism, cf. note on 38,4.   *τηκόμενον τῇ νούσῳ*: this appears to be a rationalization by Herodotus.   *ὁ δὲ ἄπαρνός ἐστι*: cf. VI 69,2: a sort of 'judicial' debate, not without some irony.

100. *οὔτε τι σπείρουσι...*: the hypothesis that Herodotus refers here to the Brahmins, the Garmanes, or the Pramni, ascetic sects known to the Greeks and idealized by them only after Alexander, has no basis; see Nearchus, *FGrHist* 133 F 33; Onesicritus, ibid. 134 F 17a–b; Aristobulus, ibid. 139 F 41; Megasthenes, ibid. 715 F 33. Vegetarianism was widespread in India, especially among the Buddhists.   *φροντίζει δὲ οὐδείς...*: the Babylonians behaved differently (I 197).

101,1. *μεῖξις*: copulation in public, even with courtesans, was considered indecent by the Greeks; see e.g. Xenophon, *Anab.* V 4,33; *Dissoi Logoi* II 4 Robinson; Plato, *Hipp. Ma.* 299a; [Demosthenes] 59,33.

2. *ἡ γονὴ*: cf. 109,1 and note on 97,2. This belief was criticized by Aristotle, *Hist. An.* 523a18; *De Gen. Animal.* 736a19.   *θορήν*: cf. Alcman 24 [14] B 3 DK; for *θορός*, 'fish milk', see Herod. II 93,1.

102,1. *Κασπατύρῳ ... πρόσουροι*: north Indians belonging to the twentieth *νομός* of the Persian empire (94,2). Kaspatyrus (cf. IV 44,2), already known to Hecataeus (*Κασπάπ-*: *FGrHist* 1 F 295; on this disputed fragment see Jacoby's commentary), was the point of departure of the famous voyage of Scylax, whose initial report was probably the source of Hecataeus and in turn of Herodotus (see note on chs. 98–106). It has been variously located: at Puškalāvatī, Peshawar, or Multan; see G. Tucci, *East & West*, XXVII (1977), 16 f.; P. Daffinà, *AAntHung* XXVIII (1980), 1–8. The *Πακτυϊκή* of India (cf. IV 44,2; not to be confused with that of III 93,1), inhabited by the Pactyes (VII 67,2; 68; cf. 85,1), would correspond to the upper Indus, between the Hindu Kush and Multan (modern northern Pakistan). On the ethnical *pakhtun* in Gandhara see I. Puskás, *AUB* V–VI (1977–8), 77; on Vedic *Paktah* see Daffinà, op. cit.   *οἱ Βακτρίοισι...*: northern Indians, related to the Bactrians, called Derdaoi by Megasthenes, *FGrHist* 715 F 23b; cf. Pliny, *NH* XI 111; the area occupied by them probably corresponds to modern Dardistan.   *ἐρημίη διὰ τὴν ψάμμον*: cf. note on 98,2. The modern gold-fields of northern Pakistan are not located in the desert areas.

2. *μύρμηκες...*: see also 104,1 and 105. One of the most famous Herodotean *mirabilia*; modified and enlarged, the story enjoyed great success in antiquity until the late Roman period, starting perhaps with Sophocles who, it seems, placed the ants in Ethiopia (fr. 29 Radt); cf. Nearchus, *FGrHist* 133 F 8; Megasthenes, ibid. 715 F 23a–b; it was taken up again in the Middle Ages (e.g. in the epistle of 'Prester John' to Frederick II). Herodotus follows a motif centred on the theme of a treasure guarded by fabulous animals and the dangers that its theft involves. The Greeks usually set such legends in the furthest regions of the known world, which they believed to be extremely rich in precious materials: cf. e.g. the spices and birds of Arabia (chs. 107; 110–11), the gold and the griffins in the land of the Arimaspeans (116,1). Borrowed from Herodotus, griffins, Arimaspeans, and huge ants were joined in a famous passage of Goethe's *Faust* (7093–111). Similar motifs also existed in other literatures or folk-tales of the ancient world: the *Mahābhārata*, for instance, mentions the *pipīllika* ('gold of the ants': cf. χρυσὸν τὸν μυρμηκίαν in Heliodorus, *Aethiopica* X 26) precisely in relation to northern India. Some scholars think that the description of Herodotus reflects real animals: e.g. marmots (numerous in the auriferous areas of Dardistan), badgers, pangolins, anteaters; or even human beings: miners who can easily be compared to ants; on the subject cf. e.g. Theogenes, *FGrHist* 300 F 1; Strabo VIII 6,16. See Aly, p. 108; R. Hennig, *RhM* LXXIX (1930), 326–32; G. W. Regenos, *CJ* XXXIV (1938–9), 425–6; E. S. McCartney, *CJ* XLIX (1953–4), 234; G. Karsay, *AUB* V–VI (1977–8), 61–72; I. Puskás, ibid. 73–87.

3. παρέλκειν: to pull on either side of the female; or to help, from both sides, to carry the load of gold (cf. 105,2).

103. ἐπισταμένοισι...: Herodotus does not want to treat what the Greeks already knew. Camels were known to the Greeks since archaic times; for camels in Lydia in 546 BC see I 80,2–5; on Arabian camels see III 9,1; VII 86,2; 87; 184,4; on camels in the army of Xerxes and Mardonius see VII 83,2; 125; IX 81,2. The Greeks knew better the Arabian racing dromedaries (δρομὰς κάμηλος) with only one hump; the 'Bactrian' variety with two humps is depicted in the bas-reliefs of Persepolis. τέσσαρας...: double femoral bones and double knees in each of the back legs. The mistake, which Aristotle, *Hist. An.* 499a20, exposes well, probably derived from the false impression created by the camel when bending on its knees to enable loading.

104,2. θερμότατος...: Herodotus argues, on the assumption that the earth is flat and India is in the extreme east, that it must be the country closest to the rising sun; he therefore concludes that the maximal heat must be at dawn, the medial at midday, and the minimal at sunset; the opposite would occur in the west: cf. IV 181,3–4. This does not exclude the possibility that genuine information on the climate of India could have reached the Greek world; see M. Cary, *CR* XXXIII (1919), 148 f. For a completely different notion see Ctesias, *FGrHist* 688 F 45 (18). οὐ μεσαμβρίης...: although Herodotus was well aware of the astronomical division of the day (from dawn to dusk) into twelve hours— a division that he believed the Greeks learned from the Babylonians, together with the sundial (II 109,3)—he uses here the division into four parts in everyday use in Greece at the time: early morning (ὁ ἐωθινός), late morning (οὗ ἀγορῆς διαλύσιος)—about eleven o'clock, in any event before the midday heat—midday (μεσαμβρίη, and cf. μεσοῦσα δὲ ἡ ἡμέρη), and afternoon (ἀποκλινομένης δὲ τῆς μεσαμβρίης). Cf. IV 181,3–4, where the word used for early morning is ὄρθρος, 'dawn', and for the peak hours of the market (from about 9 until 11 a.m.) ἀγορῆς πληθούσης (cf. II 173,1; VII 223,1). Elsewhere Herodotus

uses the Homeric word δείλη (*Il.* XXI 111, etc.) for 'afternoon', which he divides
into 'first' (πρωίη, VIII 6,1) and 'late' (ὀψίη, VII 167,1; VIII 9).

105,1. ὑπὸ Περσέων: cf. para. 2. According to Fehling's well-known 'rule', p. 101,
Herodotus, when dealing with peoples from the outer 'ring', usually quotes as a
source a people of the inner 'ring'; e.g. when talking about the populations
beyond the Danube, he quotes the Thracians as a source.

106,1. αἱ δ' ἐσχατιαί: see chs. 114–16; on Ethiopia as an extremity of the world cf.
25,1; for ἐσχατιαί in the more common sense of the peripheral area of the
territory of a *polis* or a district see VI 127,2. See M. Casevitz, in A. Rousselle
(ed.), *Frontières terrestres, frontières célestes dans l'antiquité*, Perpignan–Paris
1995, pp. 19–30.   κάλλιστα ... ἔλαχε: there must exist in this world an equal
distribution of good and evil; Greece is poor (VII 102,1) but has an ideal climate
(for Ionia see I 142,1). It is a first hint at 'divine providence' (cf. 108,2).
2. Νησαίων ...: big and famous horses used by Persian kings and nobles, especially in cult processions. They were bred in Media, in the plain of Nisaea (cf. Bis.
inscr. §13), situated by Hellenistic sources to the south of Ecbatana (see e.g. Diod.
XVII 110,6; Strabo XI 13,7; Arrian VII 13,1). Νῖσος was said to be the
Greek translation of the original toponym Καταστιγώνα (Suidas, s.v.
ἵππος Νισαῖος); cf. R. Hanslik, *RE* XVII 1, 1936, coll. 712–13.   χρυσὸς
ἄπλητος: in fact India is not rich in gold.
3. εἴρια: cf. 47,2 with note; flax is a herbaceous plant, not a 'tree'.

107–13. The second digression on the Arabs and Arabia (the first is in ch. 8) is
essentially dedicated to the harvesting of spices and is linked with the *excursus* on
India through the motif of the fabulous treasures of the extreme regions of the
world. Spices are the treasure of Arabia, and are also guarded by strange and
dangerous animals; according to Pliny, *NH* XII 85, such stories had been invented
in order to raise the price of spices. The Arabian *excursus* is similar to the Indian
in its structure: from its main theme branch out, through association of ideas,
several sub-digressions on natural history not devoid of interest. On the Arabian
spices see Agatharchides of Cnidos, *On the Erythraean Sea* (ed. S. M. Burstein),
London 1989; for a structuralist analysis of the perfumes of Arabia cf.
M. Detienne, *Les Jardins d' Adonis*, Paris 1972, pp. 19–68.

107,1. λιβανωτός ...: the five main spices of Arabia (θυμιήματα, 'incenses', or
θυώματα, 'perfumes': cf. 113,1); almost all of them were unknown to Greek
writers before Herodotus; they came especially from southern Arabia, along the
caravan routes to the Mediterranean coast of Sinai (cf. ch. 5). Other spices came
also from Ethiopia, Syria, and India; therefore μούνη χωρέων πασέων is incorrect.
Among other important spices not mentioned by Herodotus in this chapter are
nard, ginger, and mastic. Cf. Theophrastus, *Hist. Plant.* IV 4,14; IX 4,1–10; 5,13;
and Pliny, *NH* XII 51 ff. The Greeks were acquainted with these spices through
the Phoenicians, and knew that their names were of eastern origin (111,2; 112).
The λιβανωτός (*lbnh* in Royal Aramaic and Hebrew; *lbnt* in Punic) is olibanum or

incense, an aromatic resin produced from plants of the same name (cf. the *v.l.* at IV 75,3) that grow in Arabia and eastern Africa. In antiquity it was used for cult purposes (see I 183,2; II 40,3; VI 97,2), for embalming (II 86,5), or as an unguent (IV 75,3). It was introduced to Christian cult under Constantine.   σμύρνη: *mr* Hebrew; myrrh, a resin that oozes from small trees that grow on the African coast of the Red Sea. It was used as perfumed unguent, for cult purposes, for embalming (II 40,3; 86,5 with note; cf. 73,3–4), and as a medicament (VII 181,2). See G. van Beek, *Biblical Archaeologist*, XXIII (1960), 70–95.   κασίη: *kesia* neo-Babylonian, *qṣy'h* (?) Hebrew; cassia, a leguminous aromatic plant with several species; some of them produce the Egyptian senna; it was also used for embalming (II 86,5).   κινάμωμον: cf. 111,2; *knmn* Hebrew; the cinnamon-tree is an aromatic plant from the bark of which various types of cinnamon and of camphor are obtained; see, however, R. Henning, *Klio*, XXXII (1939), 325–30, against the identification of the Herodotean cinnamon-tree with cinnamon. Ethiopia, together with Arabia, was considered in Hellenistic times the 'cinnamophorous' country par excellence; cf. the passages in *FGrHist* 673 (*Anhang*) F 95, 124, 155c–d. For the different notions of the ancients on the origin of cassia and cinnamon see L. Casson, *Ancient Trade and Society*, Detroit 1984, pp. 225–46, and *Periplus Maris Erythraei* (ed. L. Casson), Princeton 1989, pp. 122–4.   λήδανον: cf. ch. 112; an aromatic resin-gum that oozes from rock rose, a branchy bush of the cistus family (*Cistus salvifolius*).

2. ὄφιες ὑπόπτεροι: cf. 108,1; 109; poisonous but non-winged snakes that can be found where the cinnamon plant grows, according to Theophrastus, *Hist. Plant.* IX 5,2. Herodotus had already said that he had seen the spines and the vertebrae of the winged snakes of Arabia, killed by the ibises during spring invasions into Egypt; see II 75–6 with notes; on snake invasions also in Scythia, cf. IV 105,1. Fabulous winged snakes with multiple heads, which grow back when cut off, are found in all ancient mythologies; there is, however, a theory that Herodotus' winged snakes are locusts, which sometimes invade Egypt and Sinai in springtime; see R. W. Hutchinson, *CQ* NS VIII (1958), 100 f.

108,1. λέγουσι δὲ καὶ τόδε Ἀράβιοι: Herodotus attributes to a non-Greek oral source Greek ideas, and specifically his own ideas, on the finality of nature. ἐχίδνας: cf. 109,3; on the mummies of poisonous vipers in the Arabian steppes see Paus. IX 28,3–4.

2. τοῦ θείου ἡ προνοίη: the geo-biological equilibrium is maintained thanks to the 'wisdom' of divine providence—a typical Herodotean compromise between transcendental and immanent teleology, perhaps on the lines already traced by Xenophanes (21[11] B 24–5 DK) and Anaxagoras (59 [46] B 12 DK). Cf. Plato, *Prot.* 321b–c.

3. ἐπικυΐσκεται: on superfetation, not a very common phenomenon as Herodotus claims, cf. Aristotle, *De Gen. Animal.* IV 733a.

4. ἅπαξ ἐν τῷ βίῳ: cf. I 199,1. According to Aristotle, *Hist. An.* 579a2, this is a 'stupid tale', invented in order to explain the scarcity of lions; a lioness actually normally gives birth three times, once a year.

109,1. ἐκποιήσι: the act of procreation, rather than the *emissio seminis.*

2. τὰ τέκνα...: the mother's death at childbirth was seen by some Christian writers as Eve's punishment for letting herself be seduced by the serpent; see K. Smolak, *GB* IX (1980), 181–8.

110. τὴν δὲ κασίην: see 107,1 and note.   **θηρία πτερωτά:** cf. Theophrastus, *Hist. Plant.* IX 5; Pliny, *NH* XII 95–8.

111,1. κινάμωμον: cf. 107; see also the descriptions of Theophrastus, *Hist. Plant.* IX 5, and of Pliny, *NH* XII 85–94.   **ὁ Διόνυσος ἐτράφη:** in Arabia according to the Arabs (cf. 8,1 and 3 with note); at Nysa in Ethiopia, according to the version preferred by Herodotus (97,2 with note).

2. τὰ κάρφεα...: 'twigs', 'wood-shavings', 'sticks', with which the birds built their nests; cf. Aristophanes, *Av.* 642 f.; the form κάρφει (*v.l.* σκάρφει) occurs for the first time in a fragment of Aeschylus' *Bassarai* (24 *TGF*). Herodotus knows that the Greek language does not have an exact equivalent for what the Phoenicians call cinnamon. It is, however, possible that also κάρφος is a word of semitic origin (*qirfah* = cinnamon in Arabic). For the theory that in Mycenean times the word indicated a perfume see A. Sacconi, *Kadmos*, XI (1972), 22–6.

3. σοφίζεσθαι: cf. note on 4,2.

112. λήδανον: see note on 107,1.   **μύρων:** cf. 20,1 and 22,3. The word is of Semitic origin: *mu-ur-ra* Canaanean, *mr* Ugaritic; cf. σμύρνη, 107,1

113,1. θεσπέσιον: a Homerism; cf. e.g. *Od.* IX 210 f. See A. Lallemand, in *Peuples et pays mythiques*, Paris 1988, pp. 78 ff. (esp. pp. 81–2 and 89, n. 63). For the fabulous smell of *Arabia Felix* cf. Diod. III 46,1; Pliny, *NH* XII 86 (with criticism); Lucian, *Ver. Hist.* II 5 (who cites Herodotus).   **ὀΐων:** the different kinds of sheep, with carts to support their tails, are documented in late antique, medieval, and modern sources in various Eastern countries; see C. H. Benedict, *CJ* XXXVI (1940–1), 168 f.; H. C. Montgomery, ibid. 424; L. Keimer, *BIE* XXXVI (1953–4), 466–76, with illustrations.   **ἐπέλκειν, ἕλκεα:** a pun; cf. Pindar, *Pyth.* 2,167–9.

114–17. One has the impression that in these chapters Herodotus wanted to collect notes, glosses, and observations on the outermost regions of the world: two sentences on the south-western extremity (ch. 114, perhaps better placed in the Ethiopian *logos* at 17–25); some sceptical and polemical observations on Europe (115–16); and finally a description of the water problems of the northern Persian empire in Asia (117).

114. ἄνδρας...μακροβιωτάτους: cf. 17,1; 20,1.

115,1. ἐσχατιαί: the European outermost regions, almost unknown to 5th-cent. Greeks; cf. II 33,3; IV 45,1; 49,3.   **Ἠριδανόν...:** Herodotus argues against the theory that a river called Eridanus by the local barbarians flowed into the northern sea: he denies the existence of the river and the sea. On the sarcasm of the argumentation, cf. IV 45. In Hesiod (*Theog.* 338; fr. 150,23 Merkelbach–West) the Eridanus is a mythical river; Aeschylus places it in Iberia (fr. 73a *FTG*), perhaps confusing it with the Rhône, although Aeschylus himself probably localized the myth of Phaethon with reference to the Adriatic; see E. Culasso Gastaldi, in *I tragici greci e l' occidente*, Bologna 1979, pp. 49–56. The Eridanus was mentioned by Pherecydes, *FGrHist* 3 F 74; Ion of Samos placed it in Achaea and Choerilus of Samos in Germany (ibid., 696 F 34 f.); in Euripides (*Hyp.* 732 ff.) the connection with the Po seems evident: see L. Burelli, in *I tragici greci e l'occidente*, pp. 131–40. It cannot be excluded that the mythographers or the geographers criticized by Herodotus identified the Eridanus with the Po, and that they linked the Adriatic Sea with the northern sea or with the Baltic. Cf. the criticism of Strabo V 1,9. For the modern identification of the Eridanus with the Elbe see R. Henning, *Von rätselhaften Ländern*, Munich 1925, pp. 82–94.   τὸ ἤλεκτρον: the amber known to Homer and Hesiod; the Greek word can also indicate an alloy of gold and silver. Amber is a resin of underground fossilized plants, with deposits near the Baltic coast and in other places in central-northern Europe; it could be collected on the beaches, where the waves uncovered the clots; from Mycenean times amber (especially succinite of a clear yellow colour) reached the Aegean area by river and caravan routes; the trade flourished in the Archaic age and again in the Roman period. The main amber artefacts were of ornamental character: necklaces, amulets, figurines, and even statues. A renowned local amber craft flourished in the 6th cent. BC in Picenum, which does not have amber deposits of its own; perhaps there is a connection between this craft and the legend that amber was formed on the river Eridanus from the tears of the Heliadae, the sisters of Phaethon, who were transformed into poplars (the legend reflects a theory of the vegetable origin of amber); or else amber was carried by the river to the mythical 'Electrides islands' in the Adriatic. See A. Grilli, *Studi e ricerche sulla problematica dell' ambra*, Rome 1975, esp. pp. 279 ff.; L. Braccesi, *Grecità adriatica*, Bologna 1977², pp. 30–55; see also S. Ruscagni, *QUCC* XII (1982), 101–4, nn. 1–9.   οὔτε νήσους: Herodotus also denies the existence of 'the tin route', considering as mythical the 'Kassiterides islands' that various ancient geographers and historians identified with the small isles of the English Channel (Scilly, Wight) or with Cornwall and the British Isles. The explorations of Pytheas (4th cent. BC) helped to clarify views on the origin of tin (texts and analysis: R. Hennig, *Terrae Incognitae*, I, Leiden 1944², pp. 155–82; *Pitea di Massalia, L'Oceano*, ed. S. Bianchetti, Pisa–Rome 1998; B. W. Cunliffe, *The Extraordinary Voyage of Pytheas the Greek*, London 2001). See esp. Timaeus, *FGrHist* 566 F 74 and 164; (*Anhang*), 22,1–4.   κασσίτερος: Homer believed it to be a precious metal like gold and silver; see *Il.* XI 25; XVIII 474, 565, 574; XXIII 503, 561. According to some the word is of Sanskrit origin (*kaštira*; cf. Dionysius Periegetes, quoted by Stephanus of Byzantium, s.v. Κασσίτερα, who placed the island near India); according to others it is of Celtic origin (*kass*, 'far away'); see R. Hennig, *RhM* LXXXIII (1934), 162–70; R. Dion, *Latomus*, XI (1952), 306–14; J. Ramin, *Le Problème des Cassitérides*, Paris 1965; S. Lewuillon, *DHA* VI (1980), 235–66.

2. αὐτὸ κατηγορέει...: cf. IV 189,2. An obvious Greek element is the epic adverb ἦρι ('early in the morning'), common in composite names such as Erigonus, Erichthonius, Eriphilus; cf. the arguments concerning the names of

the continents in IV 45,2–5. Herodotus probably knew also the Eridanus of Attica; see Paus. I 19,5.   ὑπὸ ποιητέω... ποιηθέν: Ἠριδᾰνὸς fits perfectly in dactylic verse. Herodotus, despite the not very respectful τινος, is not arguing here against the poets, but against the historians and geographers who rationalize the myths of the poets. On Herodotus and the poets see H. Verdin, in *Historiographia antiqua. Festschrift W. Peremans*, Louvain 1977, pp. 53–76.   οὐδενὸς αὐτόπτεω: cf. IV 16,1. When there is no autopsy, Herodotus is incredulous; ἀκοή is not enough (cf. II 29,1). However such a rigid approach can sometimes result in erroneous conclusions, as in this case. On Herodotus and direct knowledge see General Introduction, pp. 15 ff.   τοῦτο μελετῶν: on Herodotus' efforts to obtain information, cf. II 44,1; on this motif in ancient historiography see Marincola, pp. 148–58.   ἐξ ἐσχάτης: exotic materials must by definition come from the outermost regions of the world.

116,1. πρὸς δὲ ἄρκτου τῆς Εὐρώπης: auriferous areas are found in north-central Asia, between the Urals and Siberia, north of the Altai mountains. However, it is unlikely that Herodotus included these areas in his conception of Europe (cf. IV 42,1), or that he could know anything about their gold deposits. But see R. Hennig, *RhM* LXXIX (1930), 326–30; B. Hemmerdinger, *QS* XVII (1983), 186 f.   γρυπῶν: the etymology is unknown and probably non-Greek. The griffin is a mythical animal, usually represented with a lion's body and an eagle's head and wings. Of very ancient Middle Eastern origin, it entered the repertoire of Assyrian, Egyptian, Hittite, Creto-Mycenean, archaic and orientalizing Greek (cf. IV 152,4), Persian, and especially Scytho-Dacian art; cf. IV 79,2; see A. Pasquier, *CRAI* (1975), 454–66. It then passed to Etruria, Rome, and barbaric and Romanesque art. It was a symbol of royalty, as divine animal or as a purely heraldic and ornamental device. In Persian art the motif of the struggle between king and griffin is frequent. The griffin as guardian of the Sun's gold also had a role in Mithraic cult; *gryphus* in fact was one of the titles of the initiated into the mysteries of Mithras in the Roman age. The legend of the battles between griffins and Arimaspians was one of the themes of the *Arimaspeia* of Aristeas of Proconnessus; see IV 13,1; 27; cf. J. D. P. Bolton, *Aristeas of Proconnesos*, Oxford 1962, esp. pp. 62 ff., 85–93; on the date see also G. Huxley, *GRBS* XXVII (1986), 151–5. The theme is found in classical literature, beginning with Aeschylus, *Prom.* 802–6. Ctesias transfers the griffins to India: they are birds as big as wolves, have lion paws, and hinder the extraction of gold (*FGrHist* 688 F 45 and 45h), with an obvious fusion or confusion of all the legendary animals that Herodotus describes in these chapters. See in general M. G. Matunti *et al.*, *EAA* III 1960, pp. 1056–63; C. Delplace *Le Griffon de l'archaïsme à l'époque impériale*, Brussels 1980; H. Brandenburg, *RAC* XII 1983, coll. 951–95; in ancient oriental art, A. M. Bisi, *Il grifone. Storia di un motivo iconografico nell' antico oriente mediterraneo*, Rome 1965; in Greek orientalizing art, A. Dierichs, 'Das Bild des Greifen in der frühgriechischen Flächenkunst', Diss. Regensburg 1981; *Boreas*, VIII (1985), 5–32; M. Leventopoulou, *LIMC* VIII 1, 1997, pp. 609–11; on the similar legend in the Book of Enoch, P. Grelot, *Vetus Testamentum*, XI (1961),

30–8.   Ἀριμασποὺς: cf. IV 13; 27. in this last passage Herodotus offers a Scythian etymology; but it is probably an Iranian ethnic, a compound of *aspa-*, 'horse'; see L. Vlad Borrelli, *EAA* I 1958, p. 637; X. Garbounova, *LIMC* VIII 1 1997, pp. 529–34. For Latin sources on the Arimaspians see P. Aalto and T. Pekkanen, *Latin Sources on North-Eastern Eurasia*, Pt. I, Wiesbaden 1975, pp. 58–61.   μουνοφθάλμους: according to Strabo I 2,10, Homer modelled his Cyclopes on the Scythian legend. The myth, which Herodotus rejects, was rationalized by others: the profession of archery could cause the atrophy of an eye (see e.g. Eustathius, *Comm. Dion. Perieg.* 31, mentioning anonymous 'ancient' writers who offered this explanation).   πείθομαι δὲ οὐδὲ: cf. the expressions of scepticism in IV 25,1; 105,2; 191,4.

3. ἐσχατιαί...: the concluding sentence refers back to 106,1; for the 'ring composition' technique in Herodotus see Beck.   περικληίουσαι: cf. περικεκλημένον immediately following at 117,1; according to J. E. Powell, *CR* LI (1937), 104 f., this is a pun.

117,1. ἔστι δὲ πεδίον...: this interesting chapter on the Persian water-control policy in Chorasmia seems to have been inserted here in order to recall the reader from the fabulous boundaries of the world to the administrative realities of the Persian empire and the story of Darius, which will resume at ch. 118. The area described by Herodotus was an integral part of the empire, but it also had its *mirabilia*. It is a historical fact that the Achaemenids, like their great Middle Eastern predecessors, monopolized water resources and distinguished themselves by their works of canalization, reservoirs, dams, irrigation, and water taxation. In its details Herodotus' description is semi-fantastic; in some aspects it recalls the description of the Thessalian alluvial plains (VII 129), although in this case it seems that Herodotus used oral sources (para. 6). The Persian water policy is presented as an example of oppressive taxation, worthy of Darius the 'shop-keeper' (89,3 with note), who is, however, not explicitly named. Herodotus says nothing about the interest which the Achaemenids undoubtedly had in the improvement and cultivation of land. On Herodotean hydrography, O. Longo, *QS* XXIV (1986), 23–53.   Χορασμίων: cf. 93,3 with note. This must be the area east of the Caspian Sea (sixteenth νομός), but further identification is impossible. The Hyrcanians (cf. VII 62,2) lived between the south-east coast of the Caspian Sea and Parthia; the Sarangaeans and the Thamanaeans (93,2) lived about 700 to 900 km. south-east, in Drangiana; they did not, therefore, border on the area described by Herodotus. Maybe he alludes to the area of Elburz, south-east of the Caspian Sea, where there were Persian works of canalization known to Polybius (X 28,2–4).

2. Ἄκης: cf. Hesychius, s.v. Ἄκις. It has been identified with the Oxus or, better, with the modern Atrak, which marks the border between Turkmenistan and the area of Iran to the east of the Caspian Sea. It must be the Ochos of Apollodorus of Artemita (*FGrHist* 779 F 4) and of Strabo (XI 7,3; 11,5); see I. N. Khlopin, *Orientalia Lovaniensia Periodica*, II (1971), 137–52. Some consider the Aces an imaginary river.   πενταχοῦ: the reading accepted by most editors, which

creates a fictitious correspondence between the five branches of the river and the five peoples; cf. the five Thessalian rivers at VII 129,1; πανταχοῦ is preferable. In Herodotus five is a 'typical' number; see e.g. III 25,4; 59,2; 80,1; Fehling, pp. 224–5.

3. πέλαγος: the artificial lake created by the inundation; cf. II 97,1; VII 129,3; for the reservoir of Nitocris see I 185,4–5.

4. ὁ θεός: Herodotus alludes here to Zeus, the god of rain (cf. 125,4), not to a divinity in a general sense.

5. κατὰ τὰς θύρας τοῦ βασιλέος: 'king's gate' is an oriental expression (cf. *bāb šarri* Accadian, s'r hmlk in Esther 2: 19, etc.); see O. Loretz, *Die Welt des Orient*, IV (1967–8), 104–8. Herodotus is thinking of the palace of Susa; cf. 77,1; 119,3; 120,2. For a similar scene in Samos see 42,1.   ἀνοίγειν...: there is a reminiscence of this passage in Lucian, *Icaromenippus* 25–6; see G. Anderson, *Philologus*, CXXIV (1980), 159–61.

6. χρήματα...φόρου: a clear reference to the catalogue of tributes (chs. 89–96), to the 'gifts' πάρεξ τοῦ φόρου (97,5), and to Darius' fiscal policy (89,3). With this reference Herodotus concludes the series of *excursus* started in ch. 89, and returns to the main narrative of the reign of Darius.

118–19. The story of Darius' reign, interrupted in ch. 88, is resumed with the pathetic episode of the death of Intaphernes. What emerges is the figure of an authoritarian yet humane monarch. The episode owes its fame to the words of Intaphernes' wife and to her tragic choice (119,6). The historical background is probably the period of turbulence of Darius' 'first year' (see note on 88,1). We know from the Bisitun inscription that Intaphernes was entrusted with the task of repressing the Babylonian revolt of the autumn of 521 (see note on chs. 150–60); therefore his eventual fall could be dated at least a year later than the death of Bardiya, and directly after the conspiracy of the seven as Herodotus claims. See the bibl. in note on chs. 61–88.

118,2. ἀγγελιηφόρος: cf. the v.l. at 126,2, and note to 34,1.

119,1. οἱ ἕξ: after the withdrawal of Otanes, the 'six' became five.

2. καὶ τοὺς παῖδας αὐτοῦ...: the capital punishment of an entire family is documented in all ancient civilizations, including archaic Greece; cf. IX 113,2; Ctesias, *FGrHist* 688 F 15 (56); Esther 9: 6–10.

6. ἀνὴρ μέν...: a famous argument echoed in Sophocles *Ant.* 905–12, although the authenticity of verses 905–12 has been disputed; cf. the similar choices or answers in Apollodorus II 6,4; Lucian, *Tox.* 61; *De Dea Syria* 18. It is senseless to contemplate what Darius would have done had the wife chosen her husband; it is a novelistic folk-tale motif (Aly, p. 109), found in many cultures, including Indian tales and the Persian *Mazbān-nameh*; cf. Th. Nöldeke, *Hermes*, XXIX (1894), 155–6. Some have held that tales of this type, in their original form, reflect an 'avuncular' system centring on the brother's priority over the husband; there are traces of such a system in the Ancient East and in Europe (Tacitus, *Germ.* 20,3). But tales of this kind could also reflect the juridical reality of certain forms of

pardon 'by choice' in cases of collective punishment. See H. Schmeja, *Gymnasium*, LXXII (1965), 203–7; G. Germain, *REG* LXXX (1967), 106–12; F. Gabrieli, *RSO* XVII (1937), 111–13, and in *Letterature comparate. Studi in onore di E. Paratore*, I, Bologna 1981, pp. 139–41; Erbse, pp. 143–4; R. S. P. Beekers, *Mnemosyne*, XXXIX (1986), 225–9; S. Murnaghan, *AJP* CVII (1986), 192–239; C. Shaw Hardy, *TAPA* CXXVI (1996), 101–9. Polycrates' daughter would choose her father, who is irreplaceable, over an eventual husband (124,2). For the scale of human affections, cf. note on 14,1.

7. ἡσθείς: cf. note on 32,2.

120–8. The double *logos* of the deaths of Polycrates and Oroetes, intimately connected internally as well as linked with the series of Samian *logoi* (chs. 39–60 and 139–49) and the story of the reign of Darius, unfolds through a theological-moral chain of 'offences' or 'faults' (αἰτίαι) and of 'revenges' (τίσεις). The first episode should be dated to the period of Cambyses' illness (120,1), around 523 BC; the second to the period that extends from Cambyses' death to the beginning of the reign of Darius (including the seven months of the Magus: 126,1), thus between the beginning of the spring and the autumn of 522 (see note on 67,2). It is a period of insurrections, in which the story of Oroetes would fit well (see Balcer, pp. 146 ff.); the story is not mentioned in the Bisitun inscription (but see what Darius says in §58). The sources of Herodotus on the two episodes are substantially Samian and above all oral. For the bibl., L. Boffo, *RAL* XXXIV (1979), 85–104; A. Abramenko, *Klio*, LXXVII (1995), 35–54.

120,1. Σαρδίων ὕπαρχος: cf. 90,1. In Herodotus ὕπαρχος indicates 'the governor'. The term can refer to a satrap (e.g. III 70,3; 126,2; IV 166,1; V 25,1; 73,2; 123; VI 1,1; 30,1; 33,3; 42,1; VII 6,1; IX 113,2); to a subordinate governor (V 27,1; VII 33; 105; 194,1; IX 116,1); to the vassal-king of Macedonia (V 20,4); to military commanders (VII 26,2; 106,1).   'Οροίτης: a successor of Tabalus, the first satrap of Sardis (I 153,3).   οὐκ ὁσίου: cf. 16,2. Oroetes' impiety consists of having plotted the killing of Polycrates without a motive of personal grudge. Herodotus does not consider as motives political reasons such as Polycrates' support of Cambyses; cf. 44,1–2.   ὡς μὲν οἱ πλεῦνες...: Herodotus prefers the version of the majority, which he compares to that of a minority (121,1). The version of the majority was Samian, patriotic, and sympathetic to the tyrant, who had fallen victim of the conflict between Greeks and Persians.

2. Μιτροβάτεα: perhaps *Mithrapatā* in Persian.   ἐν Δασκυλείῳ: cf. 90,2 with note. Dascyleum is today confidently located on the southern coast of lake Manyas, about 100 km. west of Bursa. The remains of a satrapal palace have been excavated, as well as seals and a stele of Graeco-Persian art. A famous 'paradise' was joined to the palace. See Lewis, pp. 51 f.; T. H. Corsten, *Epigraphica Anatolica*, XII (1988), 53–76; T. Bakin in P. Briant (ed.), *Dans les pas des Dix-Mille*, Toulouse 1995, pp. 269–85; Müller II, pp. 811–15.   κρινομένων δὲ περὶ ἀρετῆς: cf. Pindar, *Nem.* 7,10. The Athenian audience will have loved the allusion to sophistic disputes on 'virtue'.

3. νῆσον Σάμον...: Herodotus assumes that before the reforms of Darius, Ionia depended on the satrapy of Sardis.

121,1. οἱ δὲ ἐλάσσονες: another Samian version, but hostile to the tyrant; cf. Diod. X 16,4.   ἐν ἀνδρεῶνι: cf. 77,3 with note.   Ἀνακρέοντα: the famous lyric poet, who emigrated to Abdera in Thrace when his homeland, Teos, fell into the hands of the Persians around 540 (cf. I 168 with note). His *floruit* is dated approximately by that of Polycrates (532 BC), at whose court he resided (for sexual relations see Alexis of Samos, *FGrHist* 539 F 2). See A. A. Mosshammer, *The Chronicle of Eusebius and Greek Chronographic Tradition*, Lewisburg–London 1979, pp. 290–304. It is said that in his poetry Anacreon referred much to Polycrates and praised him; some think that the anecdote of this chapter also derives precisely from one of his poems. After Polycrates' death Anacreon joined the court of Hipparchus in Athens, where he died, probably at a very advanced age. See B. Gentili, *Anacreon*, Rome 1958. On Polycrates as patron of the arts see Berve II, pp. 585 f.; F. Sisti, *QUCC* II (1966), 91–102; Y. Hägg, *Eranos*, LXXXIII (1985), 92–102.

122,1. πάρεστι...αὐτέων: when presented with two versions, the choice is left to the reader.   ἐν Μαγνησίῃ: cf. 90,1 with note; 125,2. Μύρσον τὸν Γύγεω: the two names recur in the Lydian dynasty of the Mermnads (I 7,1). This Myrsus died in Caria during the Ionian revolt (V 121).

2. πρῶτος τῶν ἡμεῖς ἴδμεν: cf. 60,4 with note.   πάρεξ Μίνω...ἄρξειν: this is a clear polemical distinction between mythical age and historical age; see General Introduction, p. 30. Herodotus did not doubt the 'historicity' of Minos (see I 171,2–3; 173,2–3; VII 169,2 f.; 171,1): however, here he relegates him to the heroic age, about which nothing can be known for certain. Thucydides also had his doubts about Minos (I 4). On the myth of the thalassocracy of Minos see Ch. G. Starr, *Historia*, III (1955), 282–91. Samos is not the first historical thalassocracy registered by Greek chronographers: Rhodes, Miletus, Lesbos, and Phocaea precede her; see Diod. VII 11. Herodotus himself dated the thalassocracy of Aegina to *c*.600 BC (V 83,2); but here he is referring to a Samian patriotic tradition. For the topicality of the problem in the age of Herodotus see K. A. Raaflaub, *Arethusa*, XX (1987), 221 ff., 243 f. Cf. also the notes on 39,3 and 44,2.
3. Ὀροίτης...: for the epistolary form, cf. 40,1. The form and content of the letter, which is naturally fictitious, serve the story's moralizing purpose: cupidity blinds and leads to catastrophe.

123,1. ἱμείρετο: an implicit moral condemnation; cf. the desire (ἵμερος) for land (I 73,1; VI 137,2) and conquest (IX 3,1).   Μαιάνδριον...: on this person see 140,5–148, with related notes.   γραμματιστής: Polycrates has a secretary, just as the satraps; see 128,3.   τὸν κόσμον...: the secretary Maeandrius, who goes to inspect the treasures of Oroetes and indirectly contributes to the death of his master, finally dedicates the treasure of the latter to the city goddess of Samos (41,1). On the Heraion see 60,4 with note.
2. ἐποίεε τοιάδε: the stratagem of Oroetes delighted Herodotus, who also wished to underline the dangers of naive credulity. The similar stratagems of the Sege-

stans (Thuc. VI 6,3; 46,3–4) and of Hannibal (Nepos, *Hann.* 9) are also famous.   ὀκτὼ: the number seems invented to give the information more credit. For the methods of hoarding in the Persian empire see 96,2 with note.

124,1. θυγατρὸς: the story becomes dramatic with the entry on the scene of Polycrates' daughter. This child or girl, anonymous also in Lucian (*De Salt.* 54), is the heroine of the Hellenistic novel *Metiochus and Parthenope*, which has been partly reconstructed on the basis of papyrus fragments and a medieval Persian version; see H. Maehler, *ZPE* XXIII (1976), 1–20; T. Hägg, *Eranos*, LXXXIII (1985), 92–102; *SO* LIX (1984), 74 ff.; LXI (1986), 99–131. The name Parthenope is taken from the dialogue referred to in para. 2 of this chapter. Here the girl represents filial love: she fears for her father's fate; cf. the figure of the Spartan Gorgo in V 51.   ὄψιν ἐνυπνίου: a typical premonitory 'death dream', fulfilled and interpreted *ex eventu* (125,4).

125,2. διεφθάρη ... συμβληθῆναι: this final evaluation of Polycrates (cf. 39,3–4; 122,2) is undoubtedly of Samian, patriotic, and anti-Persian inspiration. The comparison with the great tyrants of Syracuse (Gelon and Hieron) probably dates back to the years 479–474 BC, when comparisons began to be made between the battles fought by Greeks against barbarians of the East and West (cf. VII 166). In fact Polycrates imitated more the Persian satraps than the Greek tyrants of his age (Periander and Pisistratus).

3. ἀνεσταύρωσε: see also Stesimbrotus of Thasos, *FGrHist* 107 F 29 ('Unechtes', Jacoby). Oroetes ordered his corpse impaled; cf. VII 238,1; IX 78,3; Esther 9: 13–14. The word refers to a living person in Herod. VII 194,1–2; cf. Esther 7: 9–10. In the Bisitun inscription Darius says *uzmayāpatiy akunavam* (II ll. 76; 91; III ll. 52; 92 Kent), 'I made him (to be put) on the stake'; but the Babylonian version of III l. 52 has ṣlbt, 'he crucified': again the verb *thlh* of Esther loc. cit., is understood in the *Midraš* (1: 12) as *nṣlb*, 'crucified'. Such penalties repelled the Greeks, though not always (IX 78,3–79,2; 120,4); to impale an enemy's head is already a Homeric custom; see *Il.* XVIII 176 f.   ἐλευθέρους: free from captivity, not from tyranny.

4. Πολυκράτεος ...: this is the final moral of the two *logoi* of Polycrates (chs. 39–60; 120–5), with a reference to his great εὐτυχίη (e.g. 40,1) and to the prophecy of Amasis (43,1).

126,1. τίσιες μετῆλθον: a key phrase; it connects Oroetes' crime with his final punishment, and also opens and concludes (128,5) the actual *logos* of Oroetes.   μετὰ ... βασιληίην: cf. note on 67,2.   μένων ... τὴν ἀρχήν: Herodotus probably means that Oroetes would not have supported the seven in their conspiracy against the Magi, identified with the Medesh (65,6 with note). Some think that the passage refers to the rebellion of the Mede Phraortes/Fravartiš (Bis. inscr. §§24–5, 31–2), which took place after Darius' ascent to the throne, a rebellion about which Herodotus undoubtedly had some information (I 130,2). In fact καὶ τῶν μάγων τὴν βασιληίην means 'and (after) the reign of the Magi'. Cf. the notes on 65,6 and 127,1 and see A. Poebel, *AJSL* LV (1938), 159 f.

2. ἐν ταύτῃ τῇ ταραχῇ: the disorders of the reign of the Magus; however, see note on 127,1. **Κρανάσπην**: anthroponymic compound of *aspa-*, 'horse'; *Karnapaka* in Hittite. Some suppose a mistake for Φαρνάσπην (cf. 68,1). ἀγγαρήιον: cf. ἄγγαρος in Aesch. *Ag.* 282; Xen. *Cyr.* VIII 6,17; Theopompus, *FGrHist* 115 F 109. For the alternative reading ἀγγειλιηφόρον cf. 118,2 with note. He is the mounted courier who delivers the king's letters and dispatches to satraps, military commanders, etc.; cf. 61,3 ff. and the *rṣim* of Esther 3: 13–15 (trans. τοὺς ἀγγάρους by Josephus, *Ant. Iud.* XX 203), 8: 10. It is used in the sense of 'courier service' at VIII 98, from which derives ἀγγάρεια, *angaria*, 'hard labour', 'slavery', 'requisition', and specifically for the Roman imperial *cursus publicus*. From Susa the courier arrived at Sardis by the 'Royal Road' (V 52–3). A Graecized term ἀστάνδης, (ἀσγ −, ἀσκ−) of probable Iranian etymology, is a synonym; see M. Rostowzew, *Klio*, VI (1906), 249–58; H. Happ, *Klio*, XL (1962), 198–201. κτείνει...: cf. 127,3. For a similar case see V 20,5–21,2.

127,1. οἰδεόντων ἔτι τῶν πρηγμάτων: cf. 76,2. Herodotus means that, since Darius had seized power only recently, the situation was still in turmoil; a bland phrase which reveals that he is not very well informed about the rebellions of 522/1. He knew about a Median rebellion (I 130,2) and the Babylonian one (III 150–60); however, it cannot be stated with certainty how extensive was his knowledge of all the other revolts listed in the Bisitun inscription. See the bibl. quoted in the note on chs. 61–88, and cf. notes on 65,6 and 126,1. μεγάλην τὴν ἰσχὺν...: Oroetes governed all of Asia Minor, with the exception of Cilicia; for the three νομοί here mentioned, cf. 90,1–2. Oroetes' position in 522/1 has been compared to that of Cyrus the younger, κάρανος of the Persian forces in Asia Minor and satrap of Lydia, Phrygia, and Cappadocia (Xen. *Hell.* I 4,3; *Anab.* I 9,7); see H. T. Wallinga, *AH* I (1987), 60 f.
2. τίς...ὁμίλῳ: a Homeric reminiscence; cf. *Il.* X 303 f. Darius reappears with a speech characteristic of his personality (cf. 72,2–5; 84,3 ff.). ἔνθα γὰρ...: perhaps a popular proverb. On 'practical wisdom' in Herodotus, cf. note on 4,2.

128,1. τριήκοντα...πάλλεσθαι: cf. Homer, *Il.* III 316; VII 161–83. **Βαγαῖος ὁ Ἀρτόντεω**: for another Artontes, IX 84,1; on Bagaios' son, Mardontes see VII 80; VIII 130,2.
2. σφηγῖδα: cf. 41,1 with note; for the Great King's seal or ring cf. Thuc. I 129,1 with the scholium; Xen. *He U.* I 4,3; Esther 3: 12; and esp. 8: 8. Hellanicus attributed to Atossa the invention of royal correspondence through epistles (*FGrHist* 4 F 178a).
3. περιαιρεόμενος: the most likely sense is that Bagaios takes off the sheath, or the string, that envelops every scroll before handing it to the scribe. For περιαιρέω in a similar sense cf. 41,2; 96,2; 159,1; VI 46,1. τῷ γραμματιστῇ τῷ βασιληίῳ: the secretary, the royal scribe, perhaps appointed directly by the king but in the service of the satrap. His functions were of a purely technical nature: in the first place, to read and write documents (cf. VII 100,1; VIII 90,4). Xenophon calls him

φοινικιστὴς βασίλειος (*Anab.* I 2,20): see Virgilio, pp. 83 f. The assumption of the entire scene is that the only person capable of reading is the specialist, the royal scribe: all the others, including the satrap, inspect the scrolls with the king's seals, and then listen to the reading.

4. μετῆκάν οἱ τὰς αἰχμάς: the deposition of the spears is a gesture directed at Oroetes, not at Bagaios; a gesture of deference would have been the lowering of the spear-points to the ground, as at VII 40,2.

129–38. The novelistic story of the physician Democedes, connected to those of Polycrates and Oroetes (cf. 125,1), ends with a 'comparative' chapter about another exile from Magna Graecia, Gillus (138). The story is well incorporated, using a chronological and aetiological link (ch. 129), into the stories of Polycrates and Oroetes and that of the Persian conquest of Samos (139–49). The period is around 520 BC, the disorders have passed, the empire is at peace, the king is free to plan new conquests (134). Herodotus presents a chain of chance events and futile pretexts; this is a concatenation typical of the novel, limited only to the actions and reactions of the characters. However, Herodotus shows himself perfectly capable of understanding the direct relation between political exile and foreign military intervention, and thus expressing the story's final denouement: 'these were the first Persians who came from Asia to Greece' (138,4). It is a concluding sentence, and at the same time an implicit reminder of the programmatic subject of the entire work: the 'cause' of the great conflict between Greeks and Persians. Elements of the oriental novel set in the palace and the harem, with the usual reversal of fate from prison to the king's court, from extreme misery to riches and fabulous power (well-known elements, e.g. in the biblical novels of Joseph, Esther, Daniel, and in the story of Aḥiqar), are joined with biographical data and other elements collected in Asia Minor and in Magna Graecia. Some have thought that the descendants of Democedes and other Crotoniates could have been oral informants of Herodotus: they could have met Herodotus in Thurii. The career of Democedes in Greece, in Ionia, and in Persia is nevertheless historically acceptable: he would probably be the first, but not the only, Greek physician at the Persian court, later followed by Apollonides of Cos and Ctesias of Cnidus, to mention only the most famous. The Greek presence in Persia during Darius' reign is a historical fact amply documented by archaeology and epigraphy. For other ancient sources on Democedes see 19 [9] DK; M. T. Cardini, *Pitagorici. Testimonianze e frammenti*, Florence 1958, pp. 106 ff. Cf. in general V. Pedicino, *Pagine di storia della medicina*, V (1961), 25–36; M. Michler, *Gesnerus*, XXIII (1966), 213–29; G. Walser, in *Festgabe Hans von Greyenz*, Bern 1967, pp. 196–8; Hofstetter, no. 79; W. R. Dawson, *BICS* XXXIII (1986), 88–90; A. Griffiths, *AH* II (1987), 37–51. A. Swerr, *Artz der Tyrannen*, Munich 1961, is a novel. On medical matters in Herodotus see note on 1,1.

129,1. χρόνῳ οὐ πολλῷ ὕστερον: an approximate synchronism between Oroetes' death and the accident that befell Darius.   στραφῆναι: from the cure described (para. 2; 130,3), it must have been a dislocation.

2. στρεβλοῦντες: Isocrates is less critical of Egyptian methods (11,22). On physicians and medicine in Egypt see note on 1,1.

3. ἑπτά...: 'typical' number in the art of storytelling of every time and place.   παρακούσας: cf. the similar situation in the story of Joseph in Gen. 41: 9–14.   πέδας: cf. 130,4. For the fanciful hypothesis that the shackles and the iron chains found in the sanctuary of Vigna Nuova, near Croton, are Democedes' dedication made after his return, see *Atti del XXIII Convegno sulla Magna Grecia*, Taranto 1984, pp. 328 f. Joseph shaved his beard and changed his clothes before his audience with Pharaoh; see Gen. 41: 14.

130,1. ἀρρωδέων: cf. 1,2; for the fate of the Egyptian physician at the court of Cambyses see 1,1.

4. πεδέων χρυσέων: cf. 23,4; perhaps the gift had to be understood also in a metaphorical sense.   ἡσθείς: cf. note on 32,2.   τῷ ἔπεϊ: cf. 1,5.

5. ὑποτύπτουσα...: see the apparatus criticus of Rosén. The precise sense of this passage (discussed already by Palmerius, *Exercitationes ad Herodotum*, 1688, p. 20) seems to be: 'when each of the women dipped with a saucer into the chest of gold...'   στατῆρας: we would expect gold-dust (94,2; 95,1; 98,1), as in the story of Alcmaeon and Croesus (VI 125,2–4), and not coins. The Persian staters are the darics (VII 28,2; 29,2), well known throughout the 5th cent.   ὁ οἰκέτης: he was an ex-slave of Democedes. Sciton is an Attic name; it means 'wretch', 'worthless'; it was also a stock character in ancient comedy. Herodotus uses the name humorously while, at the same time, aiming to add credibility to his story by exhibiting a false pedantic attitude.

131,1. ἐκ Κρότωνος: Croton, an Achaean colony (VIII 47), founded traditionally by Myscellus of Rhypae *c.*710 BC, north of the promontory of Lacinium (Capo Colonna, where the remains of the sanctuary of Hera Lacinia are still visible). In the 6th cent. it was a densely populated city, the metropolis of colonies on the coast of Calabria (Caulonia, Terina), famous for its physicians and athletes, and the main centre of Pythagoreanism in Magna Graecia. Herodotus knew about the wars of Croton against the rival city of Sybaris and about the destruction of the latter by the Crotoniates around 510 BC (V 44–7; VI 21,1). According to Herodotus, Croton was the only city of the Greek West that participated (with one ship, financed by the athlete Phayllos) in the battle of Salamis (VIII 47). The internal struggles of the 5th cent. the Syracusan occupation (379 BC), the wars against the Lucanians and the Brutti, and finally the campaigns of Pyrrhus and Hannibal in the 3rd cent. caused the city's decline. In 194 BC a Roman colony was founded in Croton. See the *Atti del XXIII Convegno sulla Magna Grecia.*; G. De Sensi Sestito, in *Storia della Calabria antica*, I, Rome–Reggio Calabria 1988, pp. 237 ff.; C. Morgan and J. Hall, in M. H. Hansen (ed.), *Introduction to an Inventory of Poleis*, Copenhagen 1996, pp. 205–8.   πατρί: his name was Calliphon and he had been a priest of Asclepius in Cnidos; see A. Griffiths, *AH* II (1987), 47 ff.   Αἴγιναν: according to Suidas, s.v. Δημοκήδης, the physician married on Aegina; on the marriage of Democedes see 137,5.

2. δημοσίῃ μισθοῦνται: Herodotus apparently has no problem in attributing to the late 6th cent. the system of the 'public physician' financed by the *polis*, well known at Athens from the 5th cent. onwards; see L. Cohn-Haft, *The Public Physicians of Ancient Greece*, Northampton, Mass. 1956, pp. 8 ff.; F. Kudlien, in H. Kloft (ed.), *Sozialmassnahmen und Fürsorge. Zum Eigenart antiker Sozialpolitik*, Graz–Horn 1988, pp. 75–102.   Ἀθηναῖοι...Πολυκράτης: although Athens was also at the time governed by tyrants, Herodotus here uses the ethnic typical of the free *polis*.   δυῶν ταλάντων: Suidas, s.v. Δημοκήδης, interpreted the passage to mean that Democedes cured the tyrant for the price of 2 gold talents (i.e. gold to the weight of 2 silver talents = more than 50 kg.).

3. ἐγένετο...πρῶτοι: a parenthetic sentence inserting the author's explanation; see Rosén, ad loc.   πρῶτοι μέν...: Croton's salubrity became proverbial thanks to its medical school, the Pythagorean diet, and its famous athletes; cf. 137,5. It was contrasted with the wealth and fabulous effeminacy of its neighbour and rival Sybaris.   Κυρηναῖοι...: cf. Pindar, *Pyth.* 5,85 f.; Chamoux, pp. 367 f.   Ἀργεῖοι: Sacadas is the most famous Argive musician of the archaic age, but belongs to the early 6th cent. Lasus of Hermione (VII 6,3), from the Argolid but not strictly an Argive, was a contemporary of Democedes.

132,1. ὁμοτράπεζος: cf. IX 16,2; Xen. *Anab.* I 8,25; σύσσιτος in Herod. V 24,4.

2. παραιτησάμενος: a fine example of solidarity between colleagues; cf. Dan. 2: 24. *Exempla* of solidarity between philosophers are especially numerous in Greek literature.   μάντιν Ἠλεῖον: Elean soothsayers were famous, especially those of the clan of the Iamidae (IX 33,1). It has been suggested that the soothsayer of this passage is the Iamid Callias, who lived in Croton around 510 (V 44,2; 45,2); but, if this were the case, the fact that he is not mentioned by name also in this passage would be inexplicable.

133,1. Ἄτοσσῃ: see 88,2 with note.   φῦμα: an inflammatory or apostemic tumor, but certainly benign; breast cancer should be excluded. Others have suggested acute superficial mastitis with suppuration and cellulite. See A. T. Sandison, *Medical History*, III (1959), 319–21; M. Michler, *Gesnerus*, XXIII (1966), 225 ff. In any case Atossa recovered, lived many years longer, and had children.

2. ἐς αἰσχύνην: the ethical problem of the doctor–patient relation, formulated in the time of Herodotus by the Hippocratic school.

134,1. ὦ βασιλεῦ...: Atossa expounds the doctrine that a king's virility is in the first place manifested in his martial enterprises (cf. 120,2), that every Persian king has the duty to extend the borders of the empire (cf. e.g. VII 8a,1 ff.), and that the people's inactivity endangers the ruler (this last one is a commonplace of Greek political wisdom; cf. e.g. Arist. *Pol.* 1313b28). Implicit in Atossa's words is a comparison with Cyrus and Cambyses. Darius agrees in principle: the problem is whether to conquer Scythia or Greece first. The dialogue may be defined as 'aetiological' (Heni, pp. 113 f.; cf. K. H. Waters, *Historia*, XV (1966), 162–4), in the sense that it aims to explain the 'cause' of the Persian campaigns against Greece, and, more generally, the reasons behind Persian expansionism. Modelled on Helen, the 'cause' of the Trojan war, Atossa becomes in Herodotus a 'cause' of the Persian wars; cf. Shimron, p. 65; G. Huxley, *Herodotus and the Epic*, Athens 1989, *passim*.

3. αὐξομένῳ ... ἀπαμβλύνονται: cf. Stobaeus, *Flor.* IV 116,81, where the motto is ascribed to Democedes (Δημοκήδου Zeller, DK; Δημοκρίτου *codd.*), and the well-known verses of Lucretius III 445–6. The comparison between the vigour of youth and the weakness of old age is as ancient as Homer, Mimnermus, and Solon. Here in Atossa's motto there reappears the notion of the physiological relation between physical and mental senility. The Pythagorean doctrine of the ἁρμονία between body and soul in their development was perhaps accepted by the medical schools of Magna Graecia.

4. ζεύξας γέφυραν: for Darius' bridge over the Thracian Bosphorus see IV 83,1; 85,1; 87,1; 88; 89,3. For Xerxes' bridge on the Hellespont cf. VII 10β,2; 33–6; 54–5. To join two continents separated by nature is for Herodotus an act of ὕβρις; see General Introduction, p. 38.

5. ἐπεὰν σὺ βούλῃ: the expression was sarcastic in one who knew (II 110,2) the failure of the Scythian campaign. Herodotus also stresses the fallacious prejudices of imperialistic states on 'primitive' peoples; see General Introduction, p. 43.   Λακαίνας: Herodotus seems to ignore that, before the exploratory expedition, Atossa could not have had such a great knowledge of Greek women. In later sources the whim of Atossa is presented as the 'cause' of the Persian wars (Aelian, *Nat. An.* XI 27).

6. κατασκόπους: cf. 19,1. Besides espionage Darius was undoubtedly interested in geographic explorations (IV 44), although always with an expansionistic aim; but it is Herodotus the traveller who projects on the Persian king his own desire for knowledge: see M. Rener, 'Historie und Theorie als Elemente der Personendarstellung bei Herodot', Diss. Göttingen 1973, pp. 28–32.

135,1. μὴ διαδρήσεται σφεας: years later Darius will have the chance to compare the moral behaviour of his Greek guests (VI 24); cf. the comparison between Scythes and Democedes in Aelian, *Var. Hist.* VIII 17.

2. δῶρα ...: cf. the story of the pharaoh and Joseph in Gen. 45: 19, 23.

3. ἀπ' οὐδενὸς δολεροῦ: Herodotus seems to disapprove of Democedes' behaviour, although he understands his desire for freedom.

136,1. τριήρεας: cf. note on 44,2.   γαῦλον: cf. 137,4; VI 17; VIII 97,1. The type of boat just called ὁλκάς (135, 2–3). It was a Phoenician merchant vessel with a round shape (Ugaritic 'gl = rounded ?), as defined in the lexica, that sometimes distinguish between γαῦλος and γαυλός, 'bucket' (VI 119,3; cf. Homer, *Od.* IX 223). It was already known as a Phoenician vessel to Epicharmus, fr. 54 Kaibel. The same kind of vessel was perhaps also called 'Sidonian'; cf. VII 100,2; 128,2; VIII 92,1; Callimachus, fr. 384,50 Pfeiffer. The general term used by Herodotus for a merchant ship is στρογγύλη νηῦς, 'round boat'; cf. I 163,2.

2. ἐκ ῥηϊστώνης τῆς: a textual crux, see *apparatus criticus*. The reading ἐκ ῥηϊστώνης would be a *hapax* in Herodotus. The Attic form ῥᾳστώνη has the meaning (especially in Plato) of 'facility', 'easiness', 'opportunity', but also of 'ease',

'comfort', etc. Most scholars think that what is actually meant here is that Aristophilides acted 'in favour' of Democedes; the meaning could also be: 'to the advantage' of Democedes (cf. ῥᾳστώνην φυγῆς in Plutarch, *Cam.* 20,2), or 'to the comfort' of the exile. See H. Erbse, *Glotta*, XXXIX (1960–1), 222–4, and note on I 57,3.   βασιλεύς: in this case it equals 'tyrant': Aristophilides has full powers, and the reference to the Tarentines in 138,3 does not have much force as an argument to the contrary. He can be neither a yearly magistrate nor a king for life, as at Sparta (the mother city of Tarentum), where there were two kings. See P. Carlier, *La Royauté en Grèce avant Alexandre*, Strasbourg 1984, pp. 471 f.; A. Jacquemin, *Ktema*, XVIII (1993), 21, n. 24. The source of the entire episode is surely Magna Graecia. On βασιλεύς and τύραννος in Herodotus see note on 42,2. On Tarentum see *Atti del X Convegno sulla Magna Grecia*, Naples 1971. εἶρξε...: the behaviour of the Ethiopian king towards Cambyses' spies was very different; see 21,2 ff.

137,1. διώκοντες: it is incomprehensible how the Persians arrived at Croton without a guide, and how they knew that Democedes was there.

2. οἱ μὲν...οἱ δὲ...: this is not a case of a pro-Persian and an anti-Persian faction, but rather of the political friends and enemies of Democedes, who in Iamblichus, *De Vita Pyth.* 257, is remembered as one of the leaders of the most intransigent oligarchic faction at Croton.   σκυτάλοισι: cf. σκυταλίς at IV 60,2. The form σκυτάλη is more common, especially for the Spartan *skytale*, a dispatch written on a strip of leather wrapped around a stick. On the brawl here described, cf. Athenaeus XII 522b–c, who against Timaeus (*FGrHist* 566 F 44) cites an aetiological local tradition on the origin of the Persian cloak, worn at Croton by the attendant of the *prytanis* during certain ceremonies; embedded in this tradition is the knowledge of following ages of the first Iranian influences in Magna Graecia; cf. e.g. the 'mantle of Alcisthenes', on which see P. Jacobstal, *JHS* LVIII (1938), 205 ff. and cf. note on 138,4.   ἔπεα τάδε: on this occasion Herodotus does not see the problem of the difference in languages and, therefore, of the need for interpreters.

3. προτέρην...προτέρην...: sentences written by one who knew from later events which was the first Greek city that Darius ordered the Persians to attack.

5. Μίλωνος: Milon is the most famous athlete of the archaic Greek world; he was wrestling champion six times at the Olympic Games, six times at the Pythian Games, and ten times at the Isthmian and Nemean Games. He was *strategos* of the Crotoniates in their final attack on Sybaris around 510. The numerous anecdotes about his extraordinary physical strength and his self-discipline transformed him into a semi-mythical hero, an incarnation of Achilles and Heracles, a symbol of Croton's healthiness and of the aristocratic 'agonistic man' of the archaic age. His house in Croton, the gathering of the Pythagorean 'synhedrion', was apparently burned down, perhaps during a popular revolt against the sect. On Milo see A. Mordze, *RE* XV 2, 1932, coll. 1672–6: A. Mele, in *Atti del XXIII Convegno sulla Magna Grecia*, Taranto 1984, esp. pp. 44 ff.; on Milo's gastronomy, M. Detienne, *Les Jardins d' Adonis*, Paris 1972, pp. 82 ff.; on Herodotus and the athletes, T. S.

Brown, *AncW* VII (1983), 17–29.   οὔνομα πολλὸν: Herodotus cannot imagine that Milon was not known even in Persia.   κατὰ δὲ τοῦτο: cf. 109,3. A
view not favourable to Democedes. It was related that afterwards the physician
was exiled with the other Pythagoreans by the rebel democrats, and that he retired
to an unknown site (see K. Scherling, *RE* XX 2, 1950, col. 2339), probably in the
indigenous hinterland of Croton; a price having been set on his head, he was
finally defeated in battle by the democratic leader Theages; see Iamblichus, *De
Vita Pyth.* 257 and 261.

138,1. Ἰηπυγίην: Herodotus' Iapygia extended east of Tarentum up to Brindisi
and included the whole of the Salento 'promontory' (IV 99,5), also inhabited by
other people related to the Iapygians and the Messapians (VII 170,2). In Hellanicus, Iapygia is the name of a city (*FGrHist* 4 F 86); according to Antiochus of
Syracuse (ibid. 555 F 3 and 13) the border between 'Iapygia' and 'Italia' passed
through the territory of Metapontum. Ephorus placed the Iapygians in the
neighbourhood of Croton (ibid., 70 F 140). In the 5th cent. Tarentum had to
fight strenuously against the Iapygians: on the catastrophe around 473 BC see
VII 170,3. Also the story of Gillus, set in the late 6th cent., assumes hostile
relations between the Iapygians and the ruling party in Tarentum. On the
Iapygians and the populations related to them see E. G. Salmon, *CAH*[2] IV,
pp. 676 ff. with a full bibl.; E. De Iuliis, *Gli Iapygi*, Florence 1988.   Γίλλος: a
very rare name. Herodotus, who certainly heard about this episode in
Magna Graecia, did not find it strange that a rich Tarentine could find refuge
among the indigenous populations and retain in exile the financial means
to ransom the Persians. In the version known to Apuleius (*Flor.* 15,56),
Gillus is a Crotoniate *princeps* who redeems Pythagoras from imprisonment by
Cambyses.

2. κάτοδον: in the sense of 'return' from exile, cf. I 60,3; 61,4; IV 163,1; V 62,2; IX
26,4. The expression φυγάδων κάθοδος became, from the 4th cent., a revolutionary
slogan and a rhetorical formula for referring to the 'return of the exiles' by force
and with the help of others. Cf. Introduction, p. 390.   ἵνα δὲ μὴ συνταράξῃ: a
scruple of panhellenic patriotism which Democedes did not have. The moralizing
purpose of this 'comparative' chapter is evident.   Κνιδίους: Spartan colonists
(I 174,1) like the Tarentines; cf. the links between Cnidos, Cyrene, and Thera
(IV 164,2), all colonies traditionally of Spartan origin. Through Lipari, a Cnidian
colony, Cnidos had direct interests in the West; see I. Malkin, *Myth and Territory
in the Spartan Mediterranean*, Cambridge 1994.   μάλιστα: compared to any
other Greek city subjected to Darius.

3. πειθόμενοι ... οὐκ ἂν ἔπειθον: a pun (J. E. Powell, *CR* LI (1937), 105) not
devoid of irony: the Cnidians were persuaded by an order of the king, whereas
the Tarentines (i.e. their tyrant: see note on 136,2) were not persuaded by the
words of their 'friends'.   ἀδύνατοι: in theory, the Cnidians declared themselves ready to use even force; cf. the more dignified argument used by the
Phoenicians in 19,2.

4. πρῶτοι ἐκ τῆς Ἀσίης...: cf. the note on chs. 129–38. On the first contacts between Persia and the Greek West see E. Ciaceri, *Studi storici per l' antichità classica*, V (1912), 1–42.

139–49. In this third and last Samian *logos* (for the first two see chs. 39–60 and 120–5) the story of Syloson, Polycrates' brother, and his return to power with Persian support is narrated (139–41 and 149); inserted in it is a very important digression on the government of the regent Maeandrius. The *logos* is chronologically connected to the story of Democedes (139,1) and to the account of the following Babylonian revolt (150,1): Darius has only just seized power (140,1). There also is a thematic link: like Democedes and Gillus, Syloson is a Greek exile who tries to return home with Persian help. The 'cause' of the Persian conquest of Samos (139,1) is attributed to the personal relations between Syloson and Darius; however, these relations were neither the result of pure chance nor of the simple will of the two protagonists: 'divine fate' must be the determining factor (139,3). The names and the episodes of this *logos* are clearly drawn from Samian sources, probably oral; in these the events had already been related tendentiously and favourably to Syloson, Darius, and Otanes; there is no lack of benevolent sympathy also for certain aspects of Maeandrius' policy; on the other hand there is hostility towards the Samian wealthy class and the brothers of Maeandrius, insofar as they represent two politically extreme positions. Around the historical nucleus, whose veracity there is no reason to doubt, Herodotus created an essentially anecdotal story, with unexpected changes of scene, dialogues, political speeches, and a series of ironically paradoxical events: Syloson asks Darius to restore Samos undamaged, but he receives it deserted after a massacre and a mass deportation; the regent-tyrant offers freedom, the people refuse it and Maeandrius, in order to save the island from the tyranny of another, becomes himself a tyrant; his half-crazy brother wants to resist the invaders by force; Otanes, the supporter of 'democracy' (80), restores monarchy in Samos; finally, in Sparta the encounter of two 'very just' men takes place, the just but unsuccessful Maeandrius and the uncorrupted Cleomenes, who deprives the exile of the hospitality and support of the Spartans. In addition to the bibl. mentioned in the note on chs. 39–60 see V. La Bua, *MGR* IV (1975), 41–102; J. Roisman, *Historia*, XXXIV (1985), 257–77; J. Labarbe, *Civiltà classica e cristiana*, VII (1986), 7–27; J. E. Van der Veen, *Mnemosyne*, XLVIII (1995), 129–45.

139,1. πρώτην: 'first' in a chronological sense: Samos is not the greatest or most famous city of the Greek and barbarian world, but it is the first city conquered by Darius beyond the borders of the Persian empire.　κατ' ἐμπορίην: as already in the time of Psammetichus (II 154) and Amasis (II 178).　θεηταί: cf. IV 85,1; VII 43,1.
2. εὐτυχίη: cf. note on 39,3.　χλανίδα: cf. Suidas, s.v., who defines it ἱμάτιον στρατιωτικόν, 'military mantle'; on this famous anecdote cf. Strabo XIV 1,8; Aelian, *Var. Hist.* IV 5; Julian, *Or.* 3,117b. The proverb Συλοσῶντος χλαμύς, meaning an amulet or the display of clothes is famous (Diogenianus V 14,

and Apostolius XVIII 27 Leutsch-Schneidewin; Suidas, s.v. χλαμύς). The exchange of a cloak for a kingdom reminded ancient scholars of the exchange of bronze for gold (χρύσεα χαλκείων) between Glaucus and Diomedes in the *Iliad* (VI 234–6; cf. Aelian, *Var. Hist.* IV 5). For another proverb connected with Syloson see note on 149.   δορυφόρος: Herodotus here cannot mean a simple bodyguard as e.g. at 128,3. Some understand it as 'spear-bearer', *arštibara*, one of the most important dignitaries of the Great King.

3. θείη τύχη: cf. I 126,6; IV 8,3; and the θείου προνοίη of III 108,2. A theological reflection of Herodotus without any relation to the Iranian idea of *khvarenah* (P. Calmeyer, *JDAI* XCIV (1979), 347–65).

140,1. ἀναβὰς δὲ ἐς τὰ Σοῦσα: cf. 30,3 with note.   ἵζετο...: see 117,5; 119,3; 120,2. Cf. the meeting of Zerubbabel and Darius in Josephus, *Ant. Iud.* XI 32 ff.   εὐεργέτης: from VIII 85,3 it emerges that the 'benefactors' of the Great King were called in Persian ὀροσάγγαι (*huvarzaka?, varusna?*), a term also known to Sophocles (fr. 183, 634 *TGF*), but which is interpreted by the lexicographers as 'bodyguards' (Hesychius and Photius, s.v.). There was an official list of 'benefactors', who sat on thrones in audiences (Diod. XVII 14,2), dined at the king's table (see 132,1), and even received lands as gifts; cf. J. Wiesehöfer, *Studia Iranica*, IX (1980), 7–21; Dandamaev–Lukonin, p. 138.

2. ὁ πυλουρὸς: cf. 72,5. Here the usher introduces the stranger into the audience hall.   ἔχω δὲ χρέος...: shortly afterwards Darius will need the Greek Democedes.

3. ἐς μέσον: cf. 62,1.   οἱ ἑρμηνέες: cf. 38,4. The dialogue, in view of its consequences, can be defined as 'aetiological'; cf. Heni, pp. 113 f.

5. μήτε χρυσόν...: a Samian tradition favourable to Syloson.   δοῦλος: Maeandrius is defined, in 123,1, ἄνδρα τῶν ἀστῶν: he was, in other words, a free man, though a subject of Polycrates like all Samians and despised by Telesarchus (142,5). Herodotus, who did not think it strange that an ex-slave could become 'regent' after his master's death (cf. VII 170,4), attributes to Syloson a term more suitable to a dialogue with the king of Persia, whose ministers, vicars, governors were all δοῦλοι, 'slaves'. Cf. e.g. I 114,5; VII 8β,3; 39,1; 96,2; VIII 102,2–3 (*badakā* is the usual term in the Bisitun inscription for 'subjects', 'vassals', the 'men loyal' to the Great King: cf. Aeschylus, *I Persiani*, ed. L. Belloni, Milan 1988, pp. xviii–xix).

141. καταβὰς: cf. note on 30,3.

142,1. Μαιάνδριος: the name, derived from the river Maeandrus, is common in Ionia and Samos; see Shipley, p. 105.   ἐπιτροπαίην...: according to a hostile version, known to Lucian, *Charon* 14, and accepted by some modern scholars, Maeandrius handed Polycrates over to Oroetes in order to seize power.   τῷ δικαιοτάτῳ...οὐκ ἐξεγένετο: clearly an ironical phrase which might, however, conceal a serious evaluation of Maeandrius: the tragic hero, full of good intentions, but overwhelmed by political reality. On Herodtus' characterization of Maeandrius see Ubsdell I, pp. 19–24. For Herodotus, the renunciation of tyranny is a very rare act of exemplary 'justice'; cf. the case of Cadmus of Cos in VII 164,1; for the contempt for tyranny see Archilochus, fr. 19 *IEG*, which Herodotus knew (I 12,2). The entire episode belongs to the anti-tyrannical Greek rhetorical tradition; cf. K. A. Raaflaub, *Arethusa*, XX (1987), 225 f.; C. Coulet, *REG* CV (1992), 371–84. Other Herodotean 'δικαιότατοι' are Cleomenes (148,2), Scythes (VI 24,1), and Aristides (VIII 79,1).

2. Διὸς 'Ελευθερίου βωμὸν: this extra-urban sanctuary, perhaps in the coastal suburb to the west of the city (see note on 54,1), was still visible in the time of Herodotus, who could have gathered information from local attendants. Perhaps in the same area there was also a gymnasium with a cult of Eros and with 'Eleutheria' festivals (Erxias, *FGrHist* 449 F 1). Herodotus viewed the Samian cult of Zeus Eleutherios as related to the ἐλευθερίη, the 'freedom' from tyranny offered by Maeandrius immediately after Polycrates' death; Maeandrius' dedication of the tyrant's furniture to the Heraion (123,1) was part of the same propaganda. The cult of Zeus Eleutherios had identical importance in Sicily, after the fall of the tyrannies in the years 472–461 BC; see Pindar, *Ol.* 12,1, which is now being dated to around 466. For this meaning of ἐλεύθερος and ἐλευθερίη in Herodotus cf. I 62,1; V 55; 64,2; 91,1; VI 5,1; VII 103,3; 104,4. On the other hand the famous cult of Zeus Eleutherios established at Plataea after the battle of 479 (Thuc. II 71,1; Paus. IX 2,5), and shortly afterwards probably also at Athens, celebrated 'freedom' from foreign control; however, since the Persian control of Greek cities was as a rule based on tyrannical regimes and since the danger of the restoration of the Pisistratids was still real at Athens, a clear-cut distinction between 'internal' and 'external' freedom is not possible. In antiquity the epithet Eleutherios was also used in relation to the manumission of slaves ('Zeus protector of freedmen'), hence in relation to the notion of personal judicial freedom. For the cult of Zeus Eleutherios see H. Schwabl, *RE* Suppl. XV 1978, coll. 1452–4; on the cult at Samos, Raaflaub, pp. 139 f. (who sees in the story of the institution of the cult 'eine historisierende Fiktion'); on the cult at Athens, V. J. Rosivach, *PP* XXXIII (1978), 32–47; XLII (1987), 262–85.   ἰδρύσατο: on the verb ἰδρύω and the consecration of sanctuaries, Malkin, pp. 139 ff.   ἐκκλησίην: a *hapax* in Herodotus and not attested in previous writers. Despite the Attic use of the word in the sense of popular assembly, here Herodotus is obviously thinking about a restricted council of nobles, the same who could be arrested, one by one, when making their way to the Acropolis on Maeandrius' invitation (143,1).

3. σκῆπτρον: cf. VII 52,2 in the sense of royal 'sceptre'; in the sense of 'stick' see I 195,2; VI 75,1. Cf. C. C. Chiasson, *Phoenix*, XXXVI (1982), 159 f.   δεσπόζων ἀνδρῶν ὁμοίων: the government of one man over equals is contrasted with the isonomic government of equals.   ἐς μέσον: cf. 80,2.   ἰσονομίην: cf. note on 80,6. Here isonomy indicates a free republican regime. It is a passage of great interest for the study of 5th-cent. anti-tyrannical Greek rhetoric.

4. ἐξαίρετα: cf. 84,1.   ἱερωσύνην...: cf. the cases of the king of Cyrene (IV 161,3) and of the descendants of Telines at Gela (VII 153,3). The founder or restorer of a cult was as a rule its first priest for life; the honour and the position were then inherited by his descendants. Since Maeandrius' reform had no followers, and since Samos returned to tyranny for about forty years (Syloson

around 519–515 and Aiax II around 514–480), it is not very likely that the cult remained in the family of the Maeandridae without interruption.

5. ἀλλ᾽ οὐδ᾽ ἄξιος ...: Maeandrius, however, has not offered himself as a candidate for power; on the contrary he asked to distance himself from it. It is worth noticing that Telesarchus does not oppose tyranny in principle: he denounces only the ineligibility of a candidate who is a 'pest' and of low origins, implicitly suggesting that he thought himself suitable, as indeed Maeandrius also perceived (143,1). For the abusive term ὄλεθρος, cf. J. Hornblower, *Hieronymus of Cardia*, Oxford 1981, pp. 157–8.   λόγον δώσεις: Telesarchus is not asking for the rendering of accounts (εὔθυνα) of a magistrate (see note on 80,3), but the account that the tutor (ἐπίτροπος, cf. ἐπιτροπαίην ... ἀρχήν, in 142,1) or the regent has to present at the end of his mandate; on the famous case of Micythus of Rhegium (VII 170,4), cf. Diod. XI 66,1–3.

143,1. νόῳ λαβὼν ... ἐν νόῳ εἶχε: with these words the tradition sympathetic to Maeandrius justifies his actions. Maeandrius' tyranny was short-lived. His regime was not different from that of Polycrates; the aristocracy was persecuted; those who remained became subject courtiers. Maeandrius continued Polycrates' autonomous and pragmatic policy towards Persia: a middle way between Syloson's unconditional Medism (perhaps also that of Lycaretus) and Charilaus' armed anti-Persian resistance (145,1). On the political significance of Maeandrius' escape to Sparta see note on 148,1.   ἐς τὴν ἀκρόπολιν: on the acropolis of Samos, cf. 54,1; 144; 146,2 and 4; 147,2.

2. Λυκάρητος: he was appointed governor of Lemnos by Otanes around 511 (V 27).   οὐ γὰρ ... ἐλεύθεροι: unless there is a lacuna, the sentence seems to refer to the prisoners: they would have preferred death to gaining personal freedom at the cost of collaborating with the new tyrant. However, many understand the sentence as an ironic concluding observation on the Samians in general during the government of Maeandrius.

145,1. ἐν γοργύρῃ: a cave or an underground prison with openings through which the approaches to the acropolis could be seen; not far from the citadel, from which it was also possible to hear the prisoners' screams. The word, or toponym, appears as early as Alcman, fr. 130 *PMG*: γεργύρα. If, as has been supposed, the original meaning of the word is 'drainage channel', it is possible that the cave was a branch of the tunnel of Eupalinus (see 60,1–3). For the Samian cult of Dionysus Γοργυρεύς, cf. e.g. Duris of Samos, *FGrHist* 76 F 61.

2. κάκιστε ἀνδρῶν: cf. II 115,4; III 29,2; VII 39,1. See Dickey, pp. 165–74; 289.

146,1. οὐκ ἐς τοῦτο ἀφροσύνης: Herodotus opposes a version hostile to Maeandrius; however, from his own account, Maeandrius appears to share responsibility for the massacre.

2. κρυπτὴ διῶρυξ: a sort of emergency exit, perhaps from Eupalinus' tunnel, which led outside the walls.

3. πάντα συμβεβάναι: *convenisse omnia*, according to Stein; but see J. E. Powell, *CQ* XXIX (1935), 154 f.   διφροφορευμένους: the Persian dignitaries who sat on thrones (cf. 144), and not, generally, 'the ones with a right to the throne'. The

διφροφόρος, carried the throne or the footstool on which the dignitary or the king himself sat or rested his foot when descending from his carriage; see Dinon, *FGrHist* 690 F 26; Suidas, s.v. διφροφόροι. In Athens the διφροφόροι were the assistants to the basket-carriers in processions; for Rome see Cassius Dio XLVII 10,3; LX 2,3.

147,2. ἐν τε ἱρῷ: the first sacrilege committed in Greek temples outside continental Asia Minor by the Persians.

148,1. ἐς Λακεδαίμονα: the Samian nobles were on good terms with Sparta (cf. 55,2); but, whereas in 525 Samian exiles obtained Spartan support against Polycrates (46,2), Maeandrius' attempt was unsuccessful. Sparta probably did not want to repeat its failed adventure in the eastern Aegean, engaged as it was in consolidating its supremacy in the Peloponnese. The anecdote underlines once again the cultural and moral contrast between Sparta and Ionia (cf. 46,1), anticipating the famous encounter between Cleomenes and Aristagoras of Miletus (V 49–51). The episode is repeated in Plutarch, *Mor.* 224a–b.   **Κλεομένεϊ:** Herodotus discusses Cleomenes, famous Spartan king (*c.*519–490), extensively in Books V–VI. Here the beginning of his reign poses an important chronological problem (cf. L. H. Jeffery, *CAH²* IV, pp. 356 f.). From this chapter it is possible to deduce that Cleomenes was already king when Maeandrius arrived, in other words in the year of the Persian conquest of Samos (520/519 BC); this agrees with the information given by Thuc. III 68,3. The attempt to raise the date of the beginning of Cleomenes' reign to 526/5 is unconvincing; cf. note on 46,1.

2. δικαιότατος ἀνδρῶν: an obvious ironic reference to what has already been said about Maeandrius (142,1) and to what will be said about Cleomenes himself (VI 65–6; 75; 84). Cf. 142,1 with note.   **ἐκ τῆς Πελοποννήσου:** from the entire territory of the Peloponnesian league. We know nothing of what happened to Maeandrius afterwards. Aelian alludes to a quarrel between Maeandrius and the Athenians which he considered the 'cause' of the Persian wars (*Var. Hist.* XII 53, probably a confusion with Aristagoras).

149. σαγηνεύσαντες: from σαγήνη, 'net' used for fishing and hunting. See the description of the Persian 'netting' technique at VI 31 (with Nenci's note); on the technique C. G. Whittick, *AC* XXII (1953), 27–31. For the hypothesis that it was originally an Eastern hunting practice see K. Meuli, *Gesammelte Schriften*, Basel 1975, pp. 699–729; cf. Briant, *Histoire*, pp. 310–11 = ET pp. 298–9. Samos would be the first case of mass deportation of Greeks in the reign of Darius. We do not know where the Samians were interned: perhaps in Asia Minor, and only for a short time if the repopulation of the island desired by Otanes envisaged the return of the deported. Under Darius followed the deportations of the Paeonians from Thrace to Phrygia (V 14–15; 17,1; 23,1; 98), of the Barcaei from Cyrenaica to Bactria (IV 204), of the Milesians to Ampe on the Persian Gulf (VI 18–20), of the Eretrians to Cissia (VI 119). On the motif of deportation in Herodotus see D. Ambaglio, *RIL* CIX (1975), 378–83; on the expression ἀναστάστους ποιεῖν, cf. note on 93,2. See also the notes to 14,1; 25,3; 59. Samos was deprived of its

inhabitants also by Greeks: by Lysander in 404/3 and by the Athenians in
365 BC.   παρέδοσαν Συλοσῶντι: Syloson is the first Greek tyrant imposed by
Darius. The Persian government made this system, which was initiated under
Cyrus (see V. La Bua, *MGR* IV (1975), 70 ff.), the pivot of its policy in the
subjected Greek territories until the Ionian revolt; cf. D. F. Graf, in *The Craft of
the Ancient Historian: Essays in Honor of Ch. G. Starr*, Lanham, Md. 1985,
pp. 79–123.   ἔρημον: Samos' ἐρημία under Syloson became proverbial:
ἔκητι Συλοσῶντος εὐρυχωρίη, 'thanks to Syloson there is much space'; see
Aristotle, fr. 574 Rose = Heraclides Lembus 34 Dilts; Strabo XIV 1,8; Zenobius
III 90 Leutsch–Schneidewin; Eustathius, *Comm. Dion. Perieg.* 533. The proverb
was understood in a sense openly hostile to the tyrant, who was accused (like
Syloson) of having caused the mass emigration of the citizens; Herodotus,
however, blames the Persians for the depopulation.   συγκατοίκισε: cf. Thuc.
VI 79,2; see Casevitz, p. 218. Herodotus (VI 8,2) knew that Samos contributed
sixty ships to the battle of Lade in 494. Thus he had to explain how the island
became repopulated before the Ionian revolt. Otanes probably brought back the
deported. Aristotle's evidence, fr. 575 Rose, on the sale of the Samian ἰσοπολιτεία
('equality of rights') to slaves for remedying the problem of depopulation refers
to a period of restored freedom after the fall of tyranny, e.g. after
479.   ἔκ τε ὄψιος ὀνείρου...: Herodotus supposes that the dream and the
disease had been interpreted for Otanes by the court Magi or by an oracle. On
the function of dreams in Herodotus, cf. General Introduction, pp. 42 ff. On the
sexual disease of Otanes as a punishment see W. H. Friedrich, *A&A* XVIII (1973),
113–16; P. Huyse, *AncSoc* XXI (1990), 147. The 'fault' of Otanes appears to be, at
first sight, the massacre and the netting of the Samians against Darius' orders
(147,1); cf. Mazares' disease after enslaving the Prieneans (I 161). However, since
he is punished by a god and not by Darius, it is possible that Herodotus was
thinking about a sacral, religious, or moral 'fault': e.g. the profanation of the
temples during the massacre (147,2). Cf. the sexual disease of the Scythians after
the profanation of the temple of Aphrodite at Ascalon (I 105,4).

150–60. These chapters form part of the so called 'Assyrian *logoi*' (see I 184 with
note). They narrate the story of the revolt and of the siege of Babylon, which is
linked chronologically (150,1) and thematically to the story of the Persian
conquest of Samos: Samos musters the fleet, Babylon the land forces (150,1;
151,1). The reasons for the revolt are not made clear; Herodotus only relates a
series of incredible and gory episodes; among them, at the centre of the entire
logos, is the famous story of the self-mutilation of Zopyrus (153–9). Herodotus'
sources are on the whole based on oral information collected in the East; the
hypothesis that Herodotus met Zopyrus the younger in Athens has no proof
(160,2 with note). The Bisitun inscription records two Babylonian revolts, one at
the beginning and the other at the end of the memorable year 522/1. The first one,
led by a certain Nidintu-Bel, erupted according to Babylonian tablets shortly
before 3 October 522 and was suppressed after two battles, fought on 13 and
18 November of the same year (§§16–20). The second one, led by the Armenian

Arkha, erupted according to Babylonian tablets before 25 August 521 and
ended on 27 November of the same year (§§49–50). The two rebels presented
themselves to the people with the name 'Nebuchadnezzar son of Nabonidos'
(Nebuchadnezzar III and IV in modern terminology); they are both depicted
(second and seventh in line) on the bas-relief of Bisitun among the other 'false
kings'; both were executed. In the period of time between the two rebellions
(December 522–August 521) it seems that Darius was the recognized king of
Babylon, at least to judge from the tablets dated by his name. The total period
which elapsed from the beginning of the first rebellion to the end of the second
roughly coincides with the year in which Darius suppressed all the revolts in
nineteen battles (cf. note on 88,1). Herodotus describes only one long siege which
lasted for nineteen months. His other information does not correspond with the
data provided by the Bisitun inscription or by archaeology. Ctesias ascribes the
siege to Xerxes and substitutes Zopyrus with Megabyzus (*FGrHist* 688 F 13);
some modern scholars prefer Ctesias' version to that of Herodotus; see on this
matter F. M. Th. de Liagre Böhl, *Bibliotheca Orientalis*, XIX (1962), 110–14; XXV
(1968), 150–3. For the bibl. see note on 88,1; esp. Balcer, pp. 125–30, and
A. Kuhrt, *CAH*² IV, p. 129 ff. On the chronology, Parker–Dubberstein,
pp. 15–17; on the topography of Babylon see the bibl. in note to I 177–200.

151,1. προμαχεῶνας: these are probably the dwellings (οἰκήματα) on the top of
the city walls (see I 98,4 with note; cf. I 164,1); here, however, the topographical
description is far less precise than the description of Babylon in Book
I.   **τοῦτο τὸ ἔπος**: cf. note on 1,5.

2. ἐπεὰν ἡμίονοι τέκωσι: an expression meaning 'never'; cf. *cum mula pepererit* in
Suetonius, *Galb.* 4,2; for similar oath formulas in Herodotus cf. I 165,3; VI 139,4.
See Aly, pp. 111 f. Herodotus, however, interprets the words of the Babylonian as
a prophecy (153; see Huber, pp. 20 f.). In Greece of the time of Herodotus a mule
giving birth was considered a supernatural phenomenon or a marvel; cf. VII 57,1.
Empedocles (31 B 92 DK), however, studied the problem from a rational point of
view; Aristotle knew of exceptional cases of fertile mules (*De Gen. Animal.*
747a25; b25; *Hist. An.* 577b23).

152. Κῦρος: cf. I 191; on the conquest of Babylon by Cyrus, see note to I 188–91;
T. C. Young, *CAH*² IV, pp. 36–41.

153–8. The episode of Zopyrus, narrated in a typically novelistic form with
dialogues rich in rhetorical formulations, presents the figure of the false deserter
who by a cunning stratagem manages to obtain the unconditional devotion of the
besieged and to open the gates to the enemy. The motif goes back to epic. In the
Odyssey Helen tells how Odysseus managed to enter Troy with his body lacerated
and dressed like a beggar (IV 242 ff., with the comment of S. West, in A. Heubeck
et al., *A Commentary on Homer's Odyssey*, I, Oxford 1988, pp. 208–9). Sinon, hero
of the *Ilias Parva* and of various tragedies (including one by Sophocles, fr. 542–4
TGF), enters Troy mutilated, convinces the besieged to introduce the wooden
horse, and gives the signal to the Achaean fleet; cf. the late epic versions of

Quintus Smyrnaeus (XII 243–59 Vian, with the commentary of M. Campbell, Leiden 1981, pp. 119–26; XIII 21–33; XIV 107–14 Vian) and of Tryphiodorus (219–29, 258–305, 510–1), with the observations of F. Vian, *Recherches sur les Posthomerica de Quintus de Smyrne*, Paris 1959, pp. 63–4, 89–90, 97. In Herodotus, Zopyrus' self-mutilation recalls in certain aspects that of Pisistratus (I 59,4). Here, however, Herodotus has introduced some innovations, using names and anecdotes collected in the East and adapting them to Greek epic models. The Herodotean story might itself have influenced, even if indirectly, both Roman historiography (e.g. the story of Sextus Tarquinius at the siege of Gabii: Livy I 53,5 ff.; Frontinus III 3,3, where the *exemplum* precedes that of Zopyrus; Dionysius of Halicarnassus, *Ant. Rom.* IV 55–8), and late Greek epic. See J. W. Jones, *CJ* LXI (1965), 122–8; J. ter Vrugt-Lentz, *Mnemosyne*, XX (1967), 168–71; T. Köves-Zulauf, *Würzburger Jahrb. für die Altertumswissenschaft*, XIII (1987), 121–2, 143, n. 153. The hypothesis of Herodotus' influence on Aristophanes' *Babylonians* is still very doubtful (D. Welsh, *GRBS* XXIV (1983), 137–50). On the possible source of Herodotus for this episode cf. note on 160,2. The proverb Ζωπύρου τάλαντα, 'Zopyrus' misfortunes', quoted by Cratinus in his comedy *Pylaia* (fr. 187 K–A), dated *c.*435–430 BC, is interesting; its meaning was discussed already in antiquity. Theopompus (*FGrHist* 115 F 66) included Zopyrus' story in his eighth book, dedicated to *mirabilia*, substantially following Herodotus. On Ctesias' version cf. note on chs. 150–60. Among the various late sources see Plutarch, *Mor.* 173a; Justin I 10,15–22. Polyaenus VII 12–3 (stratagem of Sirakes imitated by Zopyrus), and Frontinus III 3,4 (Cyrus mutilates Zopyrus and sends him to Babylon) both follow Herodotus.

153,1. Ζωπύρῳ: a good Greek name, not especially rare; it means 'he who inflames' or 'who is in flames'. Some have seen it as a Graecized form of *Šāpōr*, or *Šahpūre* in Pahlavi, or of *Zupari*, *Zaparašta* in Hittite. See K. Ziegler, *RE* X A, 1972, col. 765; O. K. Armayor, *AncW* I (1978), 149 with bibl. In Justin (I 10,15) Zopyrus is one of the seven conspirators; Diodorus (X 19, 2), contaminating two different traditions, writes Μεγάβυζος ὁ καὶ Ζώπυρος.   βρέφος: cf. I 111,5 a Homerism; see *Il.* XXIII 266; cf. *Anecdota Graeca* I, p. 84 Bekker.

2. καὶ οἱ πρὸς . . .: see 151,1. Cf. the prophecy on the capture of Veii in Livy V 15; Cicero, *Div.* I 100 and II 69; Dionysius of Halicarnassus, *Ant. Rom.* XII 11–14.

154,1. μόρσιμον: a famous Homerism; see e.g. μόρσιμον ἦμαρ; τὸ μόρσιμον is 'destiny' also in Pindar (*Pyth.* 12,53) and Aeschylus (*Th.* 263; 282). κάρτα . . . τιμῶνται: a parenthetic sentence of ethnographic content. ἀγαθοεργίαι: cf. 160,1.   ἐς τὸ πρόσω μεγάθεος: cf. Esther 6:3; see J. E. Powell, *CQ* XXIX (1935), 155.

2. ἀποταμὼν . . .: Zopyrus mutilates himself according to the Persian penal custom; cf. note on 69,5. According to Justin (I 10,15), he also cut off his lips (cf. the mutilation of Masistes' wife at IX 112).

155,1. ἀνέβωσε: cf. 14,9; the dialogue between Zopyrus and Darius begins with this gesture of 'non verbal communication' (D. Lateiner, *Arethusa*, XX (1987),

83–119). The dialogue characterizes the figure of a subject absolutely devoted to his king and prepares the reader for the narration of the following events. Cf. Heni, pp. 115 f.

2. οὐκ ἔστι οὗτος ἀνήρ: a Homerism already noticed by Eustathius (*ad Od.* VI 201).   Ἀσσυρίους: cf. 92,1 with note; Justin I 10,15.

5. σὺ δέ...: the project described by Zopyrus is novelistic, with fictitious numbers of days and troops; here are listed the five most famous gates of Babylon.   Σεμιράμιος...πύλας: the 'gate of Semiramis' is commonly identified with the great gate of Ishtar, along the walls on the north-west side of the city (cf. I 180,2 with note). Of the other gates here mentioned, one probably faced north ('gate of Nineveh'), two south ('Chaldean gate' or of Enlil and 'gate of Belis' or of Bel), and one east ('Cissian gate'). The western side is totally ignored ('the wall of Nabonidus' on the eastern bank of the Euphrates and the quarters west of the river), so as not to repeat the stratagem of Cyrus, already unsuccessfully attempted by Darius (ch. 152). On the gates of Babylon see E. Unger, *RLA* I 1928, pp. 339–42; J. MacGinnis, *BICS* XXXIII (1986), 70; see also the bibl. quoted in the note to I 177–200.

6. μετὰ δὲ τὴν εἰκοστὴν ἡμέρην: after the (τὴν) twentieth day, when the 4,000 men will have been already killed.   Πέρσας: the chosen troops reserved especially for the final attack.   Βηλίδας: Herodotus probably means the gate south of the sacred area of the 'temple of Bel' (Marduk), that contained the *ziqqurat* called *Etemenanki* and the *Esagila* (see I 181,2 with note). Κισσίας: identified with the 'Zababa gate', on the south-east corner, along the road to Cissia (see note on 91,4).   μεγάλα ἔργα ἀποδεξαμένου: cf. the formula of the proemium of the *Histories*: here the μεγάλα ἔργα are great military deeds.   βαλανάγρας: 'keys'; actually hooks used to 'grasp' or to 'fish' (ἀγρεύειν) the catch or the iron bar (βάλανος) inserted deeply inside the crossbar (μοχλός) fitted into the doorposts. The crossbar could then be removed only after the catch had been 'fished out' by the hooks. See the scholia to this passage (pp. 202–3) and esp. Thuc. II 4,3 and the scholia ad loc.; cf. LSJ, s.v. βάλανος and the note of M. Cagnetta, *Tucidide. La guerra del Peloponneso. Libri Secondo e Terzo*, Bari 1984, p. 27. Cf. also *Anecdota Graeca* I. 220 Bekker. For βαλανάγραι, true or false, see also Xen. *Hist. Gr.* V 2,29; Aeneas Tacticus XVIII 9, with commentaries of A.-M. Bon, *Énée le Tacticien, Poliorcétique*, Paris 1967, pp. 105–13, M. Betalli, *Enea Tattico, La difesa di una città assediata*, Pisa 1990, pp. 272–6, and D. Whitehead, *Aineas the Tactician: How to Survive Under Siege*, Oxford 1990, p. 147; Polybius VII 16,5 with Walbank's commentary, pp. 64–5; Polyaenus I 36,1 and II 36. For the archaeological documentation see H. Diels, *Antike Technik*, Leipzig–Berlin 1924³, pp. 40–56; see also S. A. Handford, *JHS* XLVI (1926), 181–4. Herodotus naturally had in mind the mechanisms of the gates of the Greek cities of his time. To hold the 'keys' of the city was a sign of supreme authority and maximum trust.

156,2. ἐπὶ τὰ κοινά...: the council, or rather the general assembly of the citizens, as in a Greek *polis*. During the revolts of 522/1 a false Nebuchadnezzar had the command at Babylon; see note on chs. 150–60.

157,1. οἱ δὲ Βαβυλώνιοι...: Herodotus stresses the ease with which Zopyrus plays his trick, especially since he is dealing with a popular assembly; cf. I 59,4–5; V 97.   ἀληθέα: for truth and falsehood in Book III see Introduction, pp. 391 ff.

3. περιχαρέες: cf. 35,3 with note.

4. στρατάρχης: a poetic term, used by mythological characters: cf. e.g. Pindar, *Pyth.* 6,31; *Isth.* 5,40; and VIII 44,2. It is seldom used by other Greek historians; on Josephus' usage (in a Roman context) see G. T. Tully, *ZPE* CXX (1998), 226–32.

158,2. Διὸς τοῦ Βήλου τὸ ἱρόν: the temple was north of the gate of Bel opened by Zopyrus; cf. note on 155,6.

159,1. τὸ δεύτερον: the first Persian conquest of Babylon (τὸ πρῶτον: I 191,6) was that of Cyrus in 539; on Xerxes in Babylon see I 183,3 with note to 183,2. See also above, note on 56,2.   τὸ τεῖχος περιεῖλε: Berossus, *FGrHist* 680 F 9a (152), ascribed to Cyrus the destruction of the outer walls. However, though they were dismantled more than once, the walls of Babylon were never razed to the ground (περιεῖλε); Herodotus himself had probably seen them, and some stretches of them are still visible.   κορυφαίους: cf. note on 82,3.   ἐς τρισχιλίους: according to the Bisitun inscription (§50) Darius ordered the rebel leader and his followers impaled; the Babylonian version of the inscription adds that the whole of the rebel army, including the dead and the survivors, numbered 2,497 men (§37 Voigtlander). See App. I, p. 535.

2. προιδών...προορῶντες: Darius was concerned about population, whereas the Babylonians were concerned about food; cf. J. E. Powell, *CQ* LI (1937), 104.   πέντε μυριάδων: a 'typical' number. The information serves to explain in a convincing manner how the population survived despite the killing of all the women (150,2); cf. what Herodotus says about the population of Xanthos at I 176,3.

160,1. παρὰ Δαρείῳ κριτῇ: this is in fact the judgement of Herodotus, who knew something also about the 'Persians who came after'.   μὴ Κῦρος μοῦνος: cf. note on 34,4.   ὡς βούλοιτο...: cf. Plutarch, *Mor.* 173a, and the words of Darius on Megabazus in IV 143,2.   εἴκοσι: by 'twenty' Herodotus means 'many'; however, it is possibly a reference to the twenty months of the siege; the Babylonians in Plutarch's version number 100.

2. δῶρα...: cf. the annual gifts to Otanes (84,1). According to Ctesias, *FGrHist* 688 F 13 (26), the largest gift was a lump of gold weighing 6 talents.   τὴν Βαβυλῶνα...: in other words Zopyrus had the right of residence in Babylon for life, with exemption from tribute; Herodotus does not say that he was appointed satrap. According to Ctesias, Zopyrus is the name of the Persian commander of Babylon killed by the rebels before the siege (of Xerxes: see note to chs. 150–60): if he had been appointed by Darius he would have governed for more than thirty years; however the versions of Herodotus and Ctesias of the whole Zopyrus episode are incompatible, and should not be combined. **Μεγάβυζος:** a homonym of his grandfather the conspirator (see note on 70,1), son-in-law of Xerxes according to Ctesias, *FGrHist* 688 F 13 (32), and Dinon, ibid. 690 F 1, and one of the great generals during the campaign in Greece of 480 (VII 82; 121,3). According to Ctesias, *FGrHist* 688 F 13 (31), he refused to sack Delphi. After the Egyptian campaign he was governor of Syria; around 448 he rebelled against King Artaxerxes, was then reconciled with him, was exiled to the Persian Gulf (cf. 93,2), and finally pardoned. He lived at the court of the Great King until the age of 76. See W. Kroll, *RE* XV 1, 1931, coll. 122–3. Zopyrus also had a daughter, raped by Sataspes, the circumnavigator of Africa (IV 43,2). **ἐν Αἰγύπτῳ:** cf. 12,4. On Megabyzus in Egypt, cf. Thuc. I 109,3–4; Ctesias, *FGrHist* 688 F 14 (37–8), with details unknown from other sources. **Ζώπυρος, ὃς ἐς Ἀθήνας…:** according to Ctesias, *FGrHist* 688 F 14 (40 and 45), Zopyrus the younger had fought with his father during the revolt against Artaxerxes; after the father's death he fled to Athens, with which his parents had good relations; he was apparently killed in unclear circumstances during an attempt to seize the Carian city of Caunos. The chronology of these events, unknown from other sources, is uncertain: they took place approximately in the years 440–430 BC; see Meiggs, p. 436 f. Chronological uncertainty prevents us from giving much weight to the hypothesis that Herodotus had met Zopyrus in Athens and had obtained from Zopyrus himself the hagiographic version, handed on in the family of Megabyzus, of the conspiracy of the seven, the deeds of the grandfather at Babylon, and other court events; for this famous hypothesis see J. Wells, *JHS* XXVII (1907), 37–47 (= Wells, pp. 95–111), with the well-grounded reservations of D. Hegyi, *AAntHung* XXI (1973), 82 f. The same doubts remain also in relation to Thucydides; see R. A. Gimadejev, *VDI* CLXIII (1983), 106–11. **ηὐτομόλησε ἐκ Περσέων:** the grandson imitates the grandfather by really deserting without mutilating himself.

THE INSCRIPTION OF DARIUS
AT BISITUN

This great trilingual inscription is carved on the rock of a hill near the village of Bisitun, locality known to the Greeks in antiquity by the name of Bagastana (Ctesias, *FGrHist* 688 F 1 [13,1–2]; Diodorus XVII 110,5; Isidorus of Charax, *FGrHist* 781 F 2(5); Stephanus of Byzantium, s.v. Βαγίστανα; from *Bagastana*, 'seat of the gods' or 'of god'), about 33 km. east of Kermanšah in Media, on the road to Ecbatana. The inscription was discovered in 1836 by H. C. Rawlinson, a British officer, copied, and then published by Rawlinson himself and E. Norris between 1846 and 1855. It was immediately recognized as one of the most important historical documents of the ancient East. Its value for the study of Mesopotamian and Iranian cultures can be compared to that of the trilingual Rosetta Stone for the study of ancient Egypt: in fact the inscription of Bisitun enabled the definitive decipherment of cuneiform writing, thus opening a new era in the history of linguistic, historical, and cultural studies of the ancient East.

The inscription is engraved on the sides of and underneath a large bas-relief (3×5.5 metres) which represents King Darius resting his foot on the Magus Gaumata and raising his right hand towards a winged figure (perhaps Ahura Mazda); opposite Darius are lined up the other eight rebels of the year 522/1 (all identified by name and ethnic in trilingual inscriptions placed apposite) with a rope round their necks; at the end stands the leader of the 'Sakā with the pointed hood', Skunkha, captured either in 520 or in 519 (see §74); behind Darius stand the spear-bearer and the bow-bearer of the king. On the right of the bas-relief the Elamite text of the inscription stretches over four columns (E I), on the left is the Babylonian version (B), not a literal translation of the Elamite text, containing many important additions (e.g. the number of the enemies killed and taken prisoners). Under-neath the Babylonian version is a copy of the Elamite text (E II) which was engraved when the first text began to be erased in order to make space for the sculpture of Skunkha. On the right of the Elamite version, in four columns and part of a fifth, is the Old Persian (OP) text; from the fifth column the Babylonian and the Elamite versions are missing (the Babylonian version is also missing from §70 to the end of the fourth column). The bas-relief and the first Elamite text form the oldest stage of the monument, probably dating back to 520; the figure of Skunkha, the fifth Persian column, and the Elamite copy are the latest part, datable to around 518. It has been supposed that the Persian text is a retroversion of the Elamite text into the original language probably dictated by Darius in person to the scribes. Some passages of the text have also survived thanks to two epigraphic fragments of the Babylonian version found in Babylon itself, and to an important Aramaic papyrus of the late 5th cent. BC, discovered in Elephantine (Upper Egypt) at the beginning of the 20th cent. and published by E. Sachau in 1911. The papyrus contains an Aramaic version of §§24–31 and 37–48 of the Old Persian text, but is much closer to the Babylonian version (§§22–5 and 30–8 Voigtlander). These fragments prove that the document was actually widespread in different languages in the provinces of the empire, as Darius explicitly states at §70. The text, monotonous and repetitive, using an extremely poor vocabulary and written in a formulaic and paratactic style, echoes the stylized epic style

typical of the *indices rerum gestarum* of ancient monarchs of the East and West. It is divided
into paragraphs which begin with the opening formula: 'Darius the king says' (seventy-six
paragraphs in the Old Persian version).

On the bas-relief and the stages and the chronology of the document see L. Trümpelmann, *AA*
LXXXII (1967), 281–98; H. Luschey, *AMI* I (1968), 63–94; W. Hinz, ibid. 95–8, and in
Neue Wege in Altpersischen, Wiesbaden 1973, pp. 15–19; H. Luschey, *AA* LXXXIX (1974),
114–19; R. Borger, *Nachrichten der Akademie der Wissenschaften in Göttingen* (1982), 103–32.
On the meaning of the winged symbol (Ahura Mazda, Achaemenes, or the 'genius' of
Darius) see A. S. Shahbazi, *AMI* VII (1974), 135–44; XIII (1980), 119–47; J. Duchesne-
Guillemin, in *Kunst, Kultur und Geschichte der Achämenidenzeit und ihr Fortleben*, *AMI*
Ergänzungsband X, Berlin 1983, pp. 135–6.

The first trilingual edition of the inscription is that of L. M. King and R. C. Thompson, *The
Sculptures and Inscription of Darius the Great on the Rock of Bisitun in Persia*, London 1907;
this is the basis of the edition of F. H. Weissbach, *Die Keilinschriften der Achämeniden*,
Leipzig 1911 (repr. 1968). For the Old Persian text with French translation and comment
see J. Oppert, *Les Inscriptions des Achéménides*, Paris 1851, pp. 8–202; text with an English
translation, Kent, pp. 116–35, and R. Schmitt, *Corpus Inscriptionum Iranicarum* I, 1,
London 1991; for English translation only, see Frye, pp. 363–8. For the Elamite text see
the French edition, with translation and notes, by F. Grillot-Susini *et al.*, *JA* CCLXXXI
(1993), 19–59; for a German translation see W. Hinz, *AMI* VII (1974), 121–34. For the
Babylonian text with English translation see Voigtlander, with the fragments discovered at
Babylon on pp. 63–6, and the critical notes of R. Schmitt, *Archiv für Orientforschung*,
XXVII (1980), 106–26; F. Malbran-Labrat, *La Version akkadienne de l'inscription trilingue
de Darius à Behistun*, Rome 1994. Aramaic text with English translation in Cowley,
pp. 248–71; J. C. Greenfield and B. Porten, *The Bisitun Inscription of Darius the Great:
Aramaic Version* (Corpus Inscriptionum Iranicarum I, vol. V), London 1982; B. Porten and
A. Yardeni, *Textbook of Aramaic Documents from Ancient Egypt* III 1, Jerusalem 1993,
pp. 60–71; III 2, foldouts 25–8.

David Asheri

THE INSCRIPTION TRANSLATED
BY MARIA BROSIUS

Column I

§1. I (am) Darius, the Great King, king of kings, king in Persia, king of the lands, the son
of Hystaspes (OP *Vištaspa*, Elam. *Mištašpa*), the grandson of Arsames, an Achaemenid.

§2. Darius the king says: 'My father (is) Hystaspes; the father of Hystaspes (is)
Arsames; the father of Arsames (is) Ariaramnes; the father of Ariaramnes (is) Teispes
(OP *Cišpiš*, Elam. *Zišpiš*), the father of Teispes (is) Achaemenes (OP *Haxāmaniš*, Elam.
Hakkamannuš).'

§3. Darius the king says: 'For that reason we are called Achaemenids. From ancient times
we are noble men. From ancient times our family has been royal.'

§4. Darius the king says: '(There are) eight in my family who formerly have been kings. I
(am) the ninth (king). Thus we are nine kings in succession.'

§5. Darius the king says : 'By the favour of Ahura Mazda I am king. Ahura Mazda
bestowed kingship upon me.'

§6. Darius the king says: 'These (are) the countries which belong to me. By the favour of Ahura Mazda I was their king: Persia, Elam, Babylonia, Assyria, Arabia, Egypt, (the People)-by-the-Sea, Lydia, Ionia, Media, Armenia, Cappadocia, Parthia, Drangiana, Aria, Chorasmia, Bactria, Sogdiana, Gandara, Scythia, Sattagydia, Arachosia, (and) Maka, altogether twenty-three countries.'

§7. Darius the king says: 'These (are) the countries which belong to me. By the favour of Ahura Mazda they were my subjects; they brought tribute (OP *bāji*, Elam. *baziš*) to me. What I said to them, either by night or by day, that they used to do.'

§8. Darius the king says: 'In these countries, the man who was loyal, I treated well, who was disloyal, I punished severely. By the favour of Ahura Mazda, these countries obeyed my law. As I said to them, thus they used to do.'

§9. Darius the king says: 'Ahura Mazda bestowed this kingdom upon me. Ahura Mazda brought me aid until I had held together this kingdom. By the favour of Ahura Mazda I hold this kingship.'

§10 Cambyses had a brother, Bardiya by name, of the same mother and the same father as Cambyses. Afterwards Cambyses slew Bardiya. When Cambyses had slain Bardiya, it did not become known to the people that Bardiya had been slain. Afterwards Cambyses went to Egypt. When Cambyses had set out for Egypt, the people became disloyal. The Lie grew greatly in the land, in Persia, Media, and the other countries.'

§11. Darius the king says: 'Afterwards there was one man, a Magus, Gaumata by name. He rose up from Paishiyauvada—from a mountain called Arakadri. In the month Viyaxna (Bab. *Addaru*) fourteen days had passed when he rose up (*11 March 522*). He lied to the people thus: "I am Bardiya the son of Cyrus, the brother of Cambyses." Afterwards all the people rebelled against Cambyses and went over to him, both Persia and Media, and the other countries. He seized the kingship. In the month Garmapada (Bab. *Du'zu*) nine days had passed (*1 July 522*), and then he seized the kingship. Afterwards Cambyses died his own death.'

§12. Darius the king says: 'The kingship, which Gaumata the Magus had seized from Cambyses, had from ancient times belonged to our family. Then Gaumata the Magus took from Cambyses both Persia and Media and the other countries. He took (them) and made them his own property. He became king.'

§13. Darius the king says: 'There was no man, neither a Persian nor a Mede nor anyone of our family, who might have taken the kingship from that Gaumata the Magus. The people feared him greatly, since he used to slay in great number the people who previously had known Bardiya. For this reason he used to slay the people: "That they may not know me, that I am not Bardiya, the son of Cyrus." No one dared say anything about Gaumata the Magus until I came. Afterwards I prayed to Ahura Mazda. Ahura Mazda brought me aid. In the month Bagayadiš (Bab. *Tašritu*) ten days had passed (*29 September 522*), then I with a few men slew Gaumata the Magus and the men who were his foremost followers. A fortress Sikayuvatiš by name and a district Nisaya by name, in Media—there I slew him. I took the kingship from him. By the favour of Ahura Mazda I became king. Ahura Mazda bestowed the kingship upon me.'

§14. Darius the king says: 'I restored the kingship, which had been taken away from our family, that I restored. I reinstalled it in its proper place. Just as they had been previously, so I restored the sanctuaries which Gaumata the Magus had destroyed. I restored to the people the farmsteads, the livestock, the servants, and the houses which Gaumata the Magus had taken away from them. I reinstalled the people in their proper places. I restored to Persia, Media, and the other lands what had been taken away, just as they were previously. By the favour of Ahura Mazda I did this. I strove until I had restored our royal house to its proper place, as it was previously. So I strove by the favour of Ahura Mazda, so that Gaumata the Magus did not take away our royal house.'

§15. Darius the king says: 'This (is) what I have done after becoming king.'

§16. Darius the king says: 'When I had slain Gaumata the Magus (there was) one man, Açina by name, the son of Upadarama; he rose up in Elam. He said to the people: "I am king in Elam." Afterwards the Elamites became rebellious (and) went (over) to Açina. He became king in Elam. And there was one man, a Babylonian, Nidintu-Bel by name, the son of Ainaira. He rose up in Babylonia. He lied to the people thus: "I am Nebuchadnezzar son of Nabonidus." Afterwards all the Babylonian people went (over) to Nidintu-Bel. Babylonia became rebellious, (and) he seized the kingship in Babylonia.'

§17. Darius the king says: 'Afterwards I sent (a messenger) to Elam. Açina was led to me bound. I slew him.'

§18. Darius the king says: 'Afterwards I went to Babylonia against Nidintu-Bel who called himself Nebuchadnezzar. The army of Nidintu-Bel held (the bank of) the Tigris. There it took its stand, and because of the waters (the river) was unpassable. Afterwards I embarked (part of) my army upon (rafts of) skin, another (part) I made ride on camels, and for another part I brought up horses. Ahura Mazda brought me aid. By the favour of Ahura Mazda we crossed the Tigris. There I defeated that army of Nidintu-Bel utterly; in the month Açiyadiya (Bab. *Kislimu*), twenty-six days had passed (*13 December 522*), then we fought the battle.'

§19. Darius the king says: 'Afterwards I went to Babylon. When I had not yet reached Babylon—(there is) a place, Zazana by name, on the Euphrates—there that Nidintu-Bel who called himself Nebuchadnezzar came with an army against me to fight a battle. Afterwards we fought the battle. Ahura Mazda brought me aid. By the favour of Ahura Mazda I defeated the army of Nidintu-Bel utterly. The rest (of the army) was thrown into the water, (and) the water carried it away. In the month Anamaka (Bab. *Tebetu*) two days had passed (*18 December 522*), then we fought the battle.'

Column II

§20. Darius the king says: 'Afterwards Nidintu-Bel fled with a few horsemen (and) went to Babylon. After that I went to Babylon. By the favour of Ahura Mazda I seized Babylon and captured Nidintu-Bel. Afterwards I slew that Nidintu-Bel in Babylon (*Babylonian text continues* [thereafter: *Bab. cont.*] and the nobles who were with him. I executed forty-nine. This is what I did in Babylon.).'

§21. Darius the king says: 'While I was in Babylon, these (are) the countries which became rebellious from me: Persia, Elam, Media, Assyria, Egypt, Parthia, Margiana, Sattagydia, (and) Scythia.'

§22. Darius the king says: '(There was) one man, Martiya by name, the son of Cincakhri, (and there is) a place Kuganaka by name, in Persia—there he lived. He rose up in Elam. He said to the people thus: "I am Imaniš, king of Elam." '

§23. Darius the king says: 'At that time I was near to Elam; afterwards the Elamites were afraid of me. They captured that Martiya who was their chief and slew him.'

§24. Darius the king says: '(There was) one man, Phraortes by name, a Mede, who rose up in Media. He said to the people thus: "I am Khšathrita, of the family of Cyaxares." After that the Median army that was in the palace, that became rebellious against me (and) went (over) to Phraortes. He became king in Media.'

§25. Darius the king says: 'The Persian and Median army which was under my control was a small force. After that I sent forth an army. (There was) a Persian, Hydarnes (OP *Vidarna*,

Elam. *Mitarna*) by name, my subject—him I made their chief. I said to them: "Go forth, defeat that Median army which does not call itself mine!" Afterwards Hydarnes marched off with the army. When he had come to Media, there is a place, Maru by name, in Media—there he fought a battle with the Medes. He who was chief among the Medes was not there at the time. Ahura Mazda brought me aid. By the favour of Ahura Mazda my army defeated that rebellious army utterly. In the month Anamaka twenty-seven days had passed (*12 January 521*), then the battle was fought by them. (*Bab. cont.*: They killed ⌈3,827?⌉ among them and took prisoner 4,329. Then Hydarnes did not undertake another campaign against Media.) Afterwards that army of mine waited for me in a district of Media called Kampanda until I came to Media. (*Bab. cont.*: Then they came to me at Ecbatana.)'

§26. Darius the king says: 'I sent an Armenian subject of mine, Dadaršiš by name, to Armenia. I said to him: "Go forth, defeat the rebellious army which does not call itself mine—defeat that!" Afterwards Dadaršiš marched off. When he arrived in Armenia, the rebels assembled (and) went forth to fight a battle against Dadaršiš. (There is) a village, Zuzahya by name, in Armenia—there they fought the battle. Ahura Mazda brought me aid. By the favour of Ahura Mazda my army defeated that rebellious army utterly. In the month Thuravahara (Bab. *Ayyaru*) eight days had passed (*20 May 521*), then the battle was fought by them.'

§27. Darius the king says: 'For the second time the rebels assembled and went forth to fight a battle against Dadaršiš. (There is) a fortress, Tigra by name, in Armenia—there they fought the battle. Ahura Mazda brought me aid. By the favour of Ahura Mazda my army defeated the rebellious army utterly. In the month Thuravahara eighteen days had passed (*30 May 521*), then the battle was fought by them. (*Bab. cont.*: They killed 546 among them and took prisoner 520.)'

§28. Darius the king says: 'For the third time the rebels assembled (and) went forth to fight a battle against Dadaršiš. (There is) a fortress, Uyava by name, in Armenia—there they fought the battle. Ahura Mazda brought me aid. By the favour of Ahura Mazda my army defeated that rebellious army utterly. In the month Thaigraciš (Bab. *Simannu*) nine days had passed (*20 June 521*), then the battle was fought by them. (*Bab. cont.*: They killed 472 of them and took prisoner 525(?) Then Dadaršiš did not undertake another expedition.) After that Dadaršiš waited for me until I came to Media.'

§29. Darius the king proclaims: '(There is) a Persian, Omises (OP *Vaumisa*, Elam. *Maumišša*) by name, my subject—him I sent to Armenia. Thus I said to him: "Go forth, there is an army which is rebellious and does not call itself mine—defeat it!" Afterwards Omises marched off. When he had come to Armenia, the rebels assembled (and) went forth to fight a battle against Omises. (There is) a district, Izala by name, in Assyria—there they fought the battle. Ahura Mazda brought me aid. By the favour of Ahura Mazda my army defeated that rebellious army utterly. In the month Anamaka fifteen days had passed (*31 December 522*), then the battle was fought by them. (*Bab. cont.*: They killed 2,034 of them.)'

§30. Darius the king says: 'For the second time the rebels assembled (and) went forth to fight a battle against Omises. (There is) a district Autiyara by name, in Armenia—there they fought the battle. Ahura Mazda brought me aid. By the favour of Ahura Mazda my army defeated that rebellious army utterly. In the month Thuravahara, on the last day (*11 June 521*), the battle was fought by them. (*Bab. cont.*: They killed 2,045 among them and took prisoner 1,558. Then Omises did not undertake another expedition.) After that Omises waited for me in Armenia, until I came to Media.'

§31. Darius the king says: 'Afterwards I went away from Babylon (and) went to Media. When I had come to Media, (there is) a place, Kunduru by name, in Media—there that

Phraortes who called himself king in Media came with an army to fight a battle against me. Afterwards we fought the battle. Ahura Mazda brought me aid. By the favour of Ahura Mazda I defeated the army of Phraortes utterly. In the month Adukani twenty-five days had passed (*8 May 521*), then we fought the battle. (*Bab. cont.*: We killed ⌜34,425?⌝ of them and took prisoner (...).)'

§32. Darius the king says: 'Afterwards that Phraortes fled with a few horsemen. (There is) a district in Media, Raga by name, there he went. After that I sent an army in pursuit. Phraortes was seized (and) led to me. I cut off his nose, ears, and tongue, and I put out one of his eyes. At my gate he was kept bound (and) all the people looked at him. After that I impaled him at Ecbatana. And in the fortress at Ecbatana I hanged the men who were his foremost followers. (*Bab. cont.*: I executed his nobles, a total of ⌜47⌝. I hung their heads inside Ecbatana from the battlements of the fortress.)'

§33. Darius the king says: '(There was) one man, Tritantaechmes (OP *Ciçantaxma*, Elam. *Zissantakma*) by name, a Sagartian, who became rebellious against me. He said to the people thus: "I am king of Sagartia, of the family of Cyaxares." After that I sent forth a Persian and Median army. (There was) a Mede, Takhmaspada by name, my subject—him I made their chief. I said to them: "Go forth, defeat the rebellious army which will not call itself mine!" Afterwards Takhmaspada marched off with the army, and he fought a battle with Tritantaechmes. Ahura Mazda brought me aid. By the favour of Ahura Mazda my army defeated the rebellious army and it captured Tritrantaechmes (and) led (him) to me. After that I cut off his nose and ears, and I put out one of his eyes. At my gate he was kept bound (and) all the people looked at him. Afterwards I impaled him at Arbela. (*Bab. cont.*: The total dead and surviving of the rebel force was ⌜447?⌝.)'

§34. Darius the king says: 'This (is) what I have done in Media.'

§35. Darius the king says: 'Parthia and Hyrcania rebelled against me. They called themselves supporters of Phraortes. My father Hystaspes was in Parthia—the people had abandoned him; they had become rebellious. After that Hystaspes marched off with the army which was faithful to him. (There is) a place, Vishpauzatiš by name, in Parthia—there he fought a battle with the Parthians. Ahura Mazda brought me aid. By the favour of Ahura Mazda Hystaspes defeated that rebellious army utterly. In the month Viyaxna twenty-two days had passed (*8 March 521*), then the battle was fought by them. (*Bab. cont.*: They killed ⌜6,346⌝ of them and took prisoner ⌜4,346?⌝.)'

Column III

§36. Darius the king says: 'Afterwards I sent forth a Persian army to Hystapses from Raga. When that army had reached Hystaspes, he took it (under his command and) marched off. (There is) a place, Patigrabana by name, in Parthia—there he fought a battle with the rebels. Ahura Mazda brought me aid. By the favour of Ahura Mazda Hystaspes defeated the rebellious army utterly. In the month Garmapada one day had passed (*11 July 521*), then the battle was fought by them. (*Bab. cont.*: They killed 6,570 of them and took prisoner 4,192. Then he executed their leader and the nobles who were with him, a total of 80.)'

§37. Darius the king says: 'After that the country became mine. This (is) what I have done in Parthia.'

§38. Darius the king says:'(There is) a country, Margiana by name, that rebelled against me. There was one man, Frada by name, a Margian—they made him their chief. After that I sent a Persian, Dadaršiš by name, my subject, satrap of Bactria, against him. I said to him: "Go forth, defeat the army which does not call itself mine!" Afterwards Dadaršiš with the army marched off, and he fought a battle with the Margians. Ahura Mazda brought me aid.

By the favour of Ahura Mazda my army defeated that rebellious army utterly. In the month Açiyadiya twenty-three days had passed (*28 December 521*), then the battle was fought by them. (*Bab. cont.*: He executed Frada and the nobles who were with him, a total of ⌈46?⌉. He killed ⌈55,2××?⌉ and took prisoner 6,572.)'

§39. Darius the king says: 'After that the country became mine. This (is) what I have done by me in Bactria.'

§40. Darius the king says: '(There was) one man, Vahyazdata by name, and (at) a place, Tarava by name, (and) a district, Yutiya by name, in Persia—there he lived. He rose up in Persia a second time. He said to the people: "I am Bardiya son of Cyrus." After that the Persian army, which was in the palace, (and which had come up) from Anshan previously, rebelled against me (and) went (over) to that Vahyazdata. He became king in Persia.'

§41. Darius the king says: 'Afterwards I sent forth the Persian and Median army which was under (my control). (There was) a Persian, Artavardiya by name, my subject—I made him their commander. The rest of the Persian army went after me to Media. Afterwards Artavardiya went with the army to Persia. When he arrived in Persia—there is a place named Rakha, in Persia—there that Vahyazdata who called himself Bardiya came with an army to fight a battle against Artavardiya. Afterwards they fought the battle. Ahura Mazda brought me aid. By the favour of Ahura Mazda my army defeated that army of Vahyazdata utterly. In the month Thuravahara twelve days had passed (*24 May 521*), then the battle was fought by them. (*Bab. cont.*: They killed 4,404 of them and took prisoner [...].)'

§42. Darius the king says: 'Afterwards Vahyazdata fled with a few horsemen (and) went to Paišiyauvada. From there he took an army to himself. Once more he marched to fight a battle against Artavardiya. There is a mountain, Parga by name—there they fought the battle. Ahura Mazda brought me aid. By the favour of Ahura Mazda my army defeated that army of Vahyazdata utterly. In the month Garmapada five days had passed (*15 July 521*), then the battle was fought by them. (*Bab. cont.*: They killed ⌈6,246⌉ of them and took prisoner ⌈4,464?⌉.) And (my army) captured Vahyazdata, and they captured the men who were his foremost followers.'

§43. Darius the king says: 'Afterwards I (impaled) Vahyazdata and the men who were his foremost followers—(there is) a place, Uvadaicaya by name, in Persia—there I impaled them.'

§44. Darius the king says: 'This (is) what I have done in Persia.'

§45. Darius the king says: 'That Vahyazdata who called himself Bardiya had sent forth an army to Arachosia against a Persian, Vivana by name, my subject, satrap of Arachosia, and he (*Vahyazdata*) had made one man their commander. He (*Vahyazdata*) had said to them: "Go forth and defeat Vivana and the army which calls itself (that) of Darius the king!" Afterwards the army which Vahyazdata had sent forth against Vivana marched off to fight a battle. (There is) a fortress, Kapišakaniš by name—there they fought the battle. Ahura Mazda brought me aid. By the favour of Ahura Mazda my army defeated that rebellious army utterly. In the month Anamaka thirteen days had passed (*22 December 522*), then the battle was fought by them. (*Bab. cont.*: The total dead and surviving of the troops whom Vahyazdata had sent was [...].)'

§46. Darius the king says: 'Once more the rebels assembled and went forth to fight a battle against Vivana. (There is) a district, Gandutava by name—there they fought the battle. Ahura Mazda brought me aid. By the favour of Ahura Mazda my army defeated that rebellious army utterly. In the month Viyaxna seven days had passed (*21 February 521*), then the battle was fought by them. (*Bab. cont.*: The total dead and surviving of the troops whom Vahyazdata had sent was 4,579.)'

§47. Darius the king says: 'Afterwards the commander of the army which Vahyazdata had sent forth against Vivana fled with a few horsemen and went off. (There is) a fortress,

Aršada by name, in Arachosia—past that he went. Afterwards Vivana marched off with the army in pursuit of them. There he captured him, and he slew the men who were his foremost followers. (*Bab. cont.*: The total dead and surviving of the troops of Vivana was [. . .].)'

§48. Darius the king says: 'After that the country became mine. This (is) what I have done in Arachosia.'

§49. Darius the king says: 'Whilst I was in Persia and Media, for the second time the Babylonians rebelled against me. (There was) one man, Arakha by name, an Armenian, the son of Haldita, who rose up in Babylonia—from a district called Dubala. He lied to the people thus: "I am Nebuchadnezzar son of Nabonidus." Afterwards the Babylonian people rebelled against me (and) went (over) to that Arakha. He seized Babylon. He became king in Babylon.'

§50. Darius the king says: 'Afterwards I sent forth an army to Babylon. (There was) a Persian, Intaphernes (OP *Vindafarna*, Elam. *Mindaparna*) by name, my subject—him I made their chief. I said to them: "Go forth, defeat that Babylonian army which will not call itself mine!" Afterwards Intaphernes went to Babylon with the army. Ahura Mazda brought me aid. By the favour of Ahura Mazda Intaphernes slew the Babylonians and led (them) in fetters. In the month Varkazana twenty-two days had passed (*27 November 521*), then he captured that Arakha who falsely called himself Nebuchadnezzar, and the men who were his foremost followers. I gave orders that Arakha and the men who were his foremost followers should be impaled at Babylon. (*Bab. cont.*: The total dead and surviving of the army of Arakha was 2,497.)'

Column IV

§51. Darius the king says: 'This (is) what I have done in Babylon.'

§52. Darius the king says: 'This (is) what I have done by the favour of Ahura Mazda in one and the same year, after I became king: I have fought nineteen battles. By the favour of Ahura Mazda I defeated them and captured nine kings. One (was) a Magus, Gaumata by name; he lied, saying: "I am Bardiya, the son of Cyrus." He made Persia rebellious. One (was) an Elamite, Açina by name, he lied, saying: "I am king in Elam." He made Elam rebellious. One (was) a Babylonian, Nidintu-Bel by name. He lied, saying: "I am Nebuchadnezzar son of Nabonidus." He made Babylonia rebellious. One (was) a Persian, Martiya by name. He lied, saying: "I am Imaniš, king in Elam." He made Elam rebellious. One (was) a Mede, Phraortes by name; he lied, saying: "I am Khšathrita, of the family of Cyaxares." He made Media rebellious. One (was) a Sagartian, Tritantaechmes by name. He lied, saying: "I am king in Sagartia, of the family of Cyaxares." He made Sagartia rebellious. One (was) a Margian, Frada by name. He lied, saying: "I am king in Margiana." He made Margiana rebellious. One (was) an Persian, Vahyazdata by name. He lied, saying: "I am Bardiya son of Cyrus." He made Persia rebellious. One (was) an Armenian, Arakha by name. He lied, saying: "I am Nebuchadnezzar son of Nabonidus." He made Babylonia rebellious.'

§53. Darius the king says: 'These (are) the nine kings whom I have captured in these battles.'

§54. Darius the king says: 'These (are) the countries which became rebellious. The Lie made them rebellious, because these men lied to the people. Afterwards Ahura Mazda gave them into my hand. As (was) my desire, so I treated them.'

§55. Darius the king says: 'You who shall be king hereafter, protect yourself vigorously from the Lie. The man who follows the Lie, punish him severely, if you shall think thus: "Let my country be secure!"'

§56. Darius the king says: 'This is what I did. By the favour of Ahura Mazda in one and the same year I have done it. You who shall read this inscription hereafter, let what (has been) done by me convince you, do not consider it a lie.'

§57. Darius the king says: 'I will take Ahura Mazda's anger upon myself that I did this truly, and not falsely, in one and the same year.'

§58. Darius the king says: 'By the favour of Ahura Mazda also I have done much more that (has) not (been) written down in this inscription; for this reason (it has) not (been) written down, lest what I have done should seem (too) much to him who will read this inscription hereafter, (and) this should not convince him, (but) he regard it (as) false.'

§59. Darius the king says: 'In their entire lives, previous kings have not done so much as I, by the favour of Ahura Mazda, have done in one and the same year.'

§60. Darius the king says: 'Now let what I have done convince you! Thus make (it) known to the people, do not conceal (it)! If you shall not conceal this record, (but) make (it) known to the people, may Ahura Mazda be a friend to you. May your offspring be numerous, and may you live long!'

§61. Darius the king says: 'If you shall conceal this record (and) not make (it) known to the people, may Ahura Mazda be your destroyer and may you have no offspring!'

§62. Darius the king says: 'I did this what I did in one and the same year. By the favour of Ahura Mazda I did (it). Ahura Mazda and the other gods who are brought me aid.'

§63. Darius the king says: 'For this reason Ahura Mazda and the other gods who are brought me aid because I was not disloyal, I was not a follower of the Lie. I was no evildoer, neither I nor my family, (but) I acted according to righteousness. Neither to the powerless nor to the powerful did I do wrong, and the man who supported my (royal) house, him I treated well, the man who did it harm, him I punished severely.'

§64. Darius the king says: 'You who shall be king hereafter—the man who shall be a follower of the Lie, or (the man) who shall be an evildoer, may you not be his friend, (but) punish him severely.'

§65. Darius the king says: 'You who shall hereafter look at this inscription which I have written down, and these sculptures, do not destroy (them). As long as you have strength, protect them!'

§66. Darius the king says: 'If you look at this inscription or these sculptures (and) do not destroy them and, as long as there is strength in you, protect them, may Ahura Mazda be your friend, and may your offspring be numerous, and may you live long! And may Ahura Mazda make what you shall do successful for you!'

§67. Darius the king says: 'If you look at this inscription or these sculptures (and) destroy them and do not, as long as there is strength in you, protect them, may Ahura Mazda be your destroyer, and may you have no offspring! And may Ahura Mazda let what you shall do go wrong for you!'

§68. Darius the king says: 'These (are) the men who at that time were there, when I slew Gaumata the Magus who called himself Bardiya. At that time these men cooperated as my followers: Intaphernes by name, the son of Vahyasparuva, a Persian; Otanes (OP *Utana*, Elam. *Huttana*) by name, son of Thukhra (Elam. *Tukkura*), a Persian; Gobryas (OP *Gaubaruva*, Elam. *Kambarna*) by name, the son of Mardonius (OP *Marduniya*, Elam. *Marduniya*), a Persian; Hydarnes (OP *Vidarna*, Elam. *Mitarna*) by name, the son of Bagabigna, a Persian; Megabyxus (OP, Elam. *Bagabuxša*) by name, the son of Datavahya (Elam. *Daddumaniya*), a Persian; Ardumaniš (Elam. *Hardumannuš*) by name, the son of Vahuka (Elam. *Maukka* (Gr. *Ochus*)), a Persian.'

§69. Darius the king says: 'You who shall be king hereafter, protect well the offspring of these men!'

§70. Darius the king says: 'By the favour of Ahura Mazda this (is) the inscription which I have made besides in Aryan. It has been written both on clay tablets and on parchment. I also wrote down my name and my lineage, and it was written down and was read (aloud) before me. Afterwards I have sent this inscription in all directions among the lands. The people strove (to use it).'

Column V

§71. Darius the king says: 'This (is) what I did in the second and the third year, after I became king. (There is) a country called Elam that became rebellious. (There was) one man, Athamaita by name, an Elamite. They made him (their) chief. After that I sent forth an army. (There was) one man, Gobryas by name, a Persian, my subject—I made him their chief. Afterwards Gobryas with the army went to Elam and fought a battle with the Elamites. Afterwards Gobryas defeated the Elamites and crushed (them); he captured their chief and led him to me. After that I slew him. After that the country became mine.'

§72. Darius the king says: 'Those Elamites were disloyal, and Ahura Mazda was not worshipped by them. I worshipped Ahura Mazda. By the favour of Ahura Mazda, as (was) my desire, so I treated them.'

§73. Darius the king says: 'He who worships Ahura Mazda, his shall be the (fulfilment of his) prayer, both (while he is) living and (when he is) dead.'

§74. Darius the king says: 'Afterwards I went with an army against Scythia. After that the Scythians who wear the pointed cap came against me, when I arrived at the sea. By means of rafts (*of skin*) I crossed it with the whole army. Afterwards I defeated those Scythians utterly. They (*the army*) captured another part of them (*Scythians*); that (part) was led to me bound. And they captured their chief, Skunkha by name, (and) led him to me bound. There I made another (their) chief, as was my desire. After that the country became mine.'

§75. Darius the king says: 'Those Scythians were disloyal, and Ahura Mazda was not worshipped by them. I, however, worshipped Ahura Mazda. By the favour of Ahura Mazda, as (was) my desire, so I treated them.'

§76. Darius the king says: 'He who worships Ahura Mazda, his shall be the (fulfilment of his) prayer, both (while he is) living and (when he is) dead.'

LIST OF SATRAPIES AND PEOPLES IN HERODOTUS AND IN THE PERSIAN INSCRIPTIONS

The two great Herodotean 'catalogues' of the Persian empire are respectively the list of νομοί and tributes in Book III (chs. 90–4), and the list of ethnic contingents of Xerxes' army in Book VII (chs. 62–95). We also have lists of *dahyāva* (peoples, lands, lands inhabited by peoples; cf. note on 89–96) in the following Persian royal inscriptions:

1. *DB* I §6 Kent: trilingual inscription of Darius at Bisitun (see Appendix I), with twenty-three names (including *Parsa*);
2. *DPe* Kent: inscription of Darius at Persepolis (Old Persian text), with twenty-six names;
3. *DSe* Kent: trilingual inscription of Darius at Susa (the Old Persian text is very mutilated), with thirty names;
4. Posener, nos. 8 and 9: hieroglyphic Egyptian stele of Darius near the Suez Canal; both texts are very fragmentary, with twenty-four names; the same names also appear in the following inscription;
5. *DSab*: base of a statue of Darius discovered in Susa; with twenty-four cartouches and ethnics in hieroglyphics (see J. Yoyotte, *JA* CCLX (1972), 253–66; *Cahiers de la Délégation Archéologique Française en Iran*, IV (1974), 181–3; M. Roaf, ibid. 73–160); P. Calmeyer, *AH* VI (1991), 285–303;
6. *DSm* Kent: trilingual inscription of Darius at Susa (very fragmentary);
7. *DNa* Kent: trilingual inscription of the tomb-monument of Darius at Naqš-i Rustam, north of Persepolis, with twenty-nine names;
8. *XPh* Kent: trilingual inscription of Xerxes at Persepolis, with thirty-two names.

The following comparative table contains the two catalogues of Herodotus and the Persian equivalents readable in the complete texts (nos. 1, 2, 5, 7, and 8 of the list above). In addition to the inscriptions, there are also three well-known series of bas-reliefs representing the peoples of the empire: in these series the ethnic is not indicated, and their identification is sometimes obvious but usually debated:

1. twenty-three 'delegations' of men bearing gifts or offerings to the Great King engraved on the sides and along the stairs of the *Apadana* of Persepolis;
2. twenty-eight canopy-bearers in the tripylon and in the 'Hall of a Hundred Columns' at Persepolis;
3. thirty canopy-bearers on the tomb-monument of Darius at Naqš-i Rustam.

For the essential bibliography see the comparative table of A. J. Toynbee, *A Study of History*, V, Oxford 1954, revised, simplified, and reproduced in *CAH*[2] IV, pp. 88–9, and Plates to

Vol. IV (1988), p. 44; for other tables see Herzfeld, pp. 357–60; C. Herrenschmidt, *Studia Iranica*, V (1976), 55. On the Persian lists see esp. P. J. Junge, *Klio* XXXIV (1942), 1–55; R. G. Kent, *JNES* II (1943), 302–36; Herzfeld, pp. 288 ff.; G. G. Cameron, *JNES* XXXII (1973), 47 ff.; P. Goukowski, *Essai sur les origines du mythe d' Alexandre*, Nancy 1978, pp. 222–4; P. Calmeyer, *Iran* XVIII (1980), 55–63; *AMI* XV (1982), 105–87; XVI (1983), 143–222; and in *Kunst, Kultur und Geschichte der Achämenidenzeit und ihr Fortleben*, *AMI* Ergänzungsband X, Berlin 1983, pp. 153–67; B. Jacobs, *Die Satrapien-Verwaltung im Perserreich zur Zeit Darius' III*, Wiesbaden 1994; Briant, *Histoire*, pp. 402–6, 956 f. = ET 390–4, 931 f. The fundamental study of the bas-reliefs is Walser, *Völkerschaften*; see also Herzfeld, pp. 350–6; W. Hinz, *Altpersische Funde und Forschungen*, Berlin 1969, ch. 5 (pp. 95–113); B. Jacobs, *Acta Praehistorica et Archaeologica*, XIII–XIV (1982), 75–84.

	Hdt. III 90–4 *nomoi*/tribute (in talents)	Hdt. VII 62–95 Ethnic contingents	DB I: §6	DPe	DSab	DNa	XPh
I	Ionians 400	100 ships	Yauna	Yauna tyaiy uškayā (Ionians on the mainland)	—	Yauna	Yauna (by the sea and across the sea)
	Magnesians	—		—	—	—	
	Aeolians	60 ships		—	—	—	
	Carians	70 ships		—	—	Karka	Karka
	Lycians	50 ships		—	—	—	—
	Milyans	30 ships		—	—	—	
	Pamphylians	—		—	—	—	
	—	Dorians 30 ships					
II	Mysians 500	Mysians	—	—	—	—	—
	Lydians	Lydians	Sparda	Sparda	Sparda	Sparda	Sparda
	Lasonians	Cabalians/Lasonians	—	—	—	—	—
	Cabalians						
	Hytennians	—					
III	Hellespontians 360	100 ships	—	—	—	—	—
	Phrygians	Phrygians					
	Thracians of Asia	Thracians (Bithynians)					
	Paphlagonians	Paphlagonians					
	—	Ligyans					
	Mariandynians	Mariandynians					
	Syrians (Cappadocians)	Syrians-Cappadocians	Katpatuka	Katpatuka	Katpatuka	Katpatuka	Katpatuka
		Matieni					
IV	Cilicians 500	100 ships	—	—	—	—	—
V	Phoenicia 350	300 ships	Athurā	Athurā	Athurā/Ešhur	Athurā	Athurā
	Syria-Palestine		—	—	—	—	—
	Cyprus	150 ships				—	
	Arabians (not paying tribute)	Arabians (with camels)	Arabāya	Arabāya	Arabāya	Arabāya	Arabāya

		200 ships Libyans (infantry and cavalry)	Mudrāya	Mudrāya	Kemt Tjemhou/Puti	Mudrāya Putāya	Mudrāya
VI	Egypt 700 neighbouring Libya	200 ships Libyans (infantry and cavalry)	Mudrāya	Mudrāya	—	Mudrāya Putāya	Mudrāya
	Cyrene, Barca lake Moeris	—	—	—	—	—	—
		Cyrene, Barca lake Moeris					
VII	Sattagydians 170	—	Thataguš	Thataguš	sdgwd	Thataguš	Thataguš
	Gandarians	Gandarians	Gadāra	Gadāra		Gadāra	Gadāra
	Dadicans	Dadicans	—	—	—	—	—
	Aparytians	—	—	—	—	—	—
VIII	Susa 300	—	Ūvja	Ūvja	ꜣ[rm?]	Ūvja	Ūvja
	Cissians	Cissians					
IX	Babylonia 1000	—	Bābiruš	Bābiruš	bbr	Bābiruš	Bābiruš
	Assyria	Assyria	—	—	—	—	—
X	Ecbatana 450	—	Māda	Māda	m[dj]	Māda	Māda
	Media	—	—	—	—	—	—
	Paricanians	—					
	Orthocory-Bantians	—					
XI	Caspians 200	Caspians	—	—	—	—	—
	Pausicae	—	—	—	—	—	—
	Pantimathi	—	—	—	—	—	—
	Daritae	—		Ūvja			
XII	Bactrians 360	Bactrians	Bākhtriš	bhtr	Bākhtriš	Bākhtriš	Bākhtriš
	Aeglians	—	—	—	—	—	—
XIII	Pactyicia 400	—	Armina	Armina	rmjn	Armina	Armina
	Armenia	Armenians	—	—	—	—	—
	adjoining lands as far as the Black Sea	—					
XIV	Sagartians 600	Sagartians	*DB IV:* Asagarta	Asagarta	srng	—	—
	Sarangians	Sarangians	Zraka	Zraka		Zraka	Zraka
	Thamanaeians						
	Utians	Utians	*DB III:* Yautiyā	—	—	—	—

(Continued)

Table (*Continued*)

	Hdt. III 90–4 νομοί/tribute (in talents)	Hdt. VII 62–95 Ethnic contingents	DB I: §6	DPe	DSab	DNa	XPh
XV	Mycians island dwellers (Red Sea)	Mycians island dwellers (Red Sea)	Maka	Maka	mg	Maciyā	Maciyā
	Saka 250	Sa-ka (on ships)	Sakā (*DB* V: Sakā tyaiy khaudām tigrām baratiy)	— / Sakā	— / skpt skt3	Sakā haumavargā, Sakā tigrakhaudā	Sakā haumavargā / Sakā tigrakhaudā
	Caspians	—	—	—	—	—	—
XVI	Parthians 300	Parthians	Parthava	Parthava	Prtw	Parthava	Parthava
	Chorasmians	Chorasmians	Uvārazmiya	Uvārazmiya	[hr]sm	Uvārazmiš	Uvārazmiš
	Sogdians	Sogdians	Suguda	Suguda	sgdj	Suguda	Sugda
	Arians	Arians	Haraiva	Haraiva	hrw	Haraiva	Haraiva
XVII	Paricanians 400	Paricanians	—	—	—	—	—
	Ethiopians of Asia	Ethiopians of the Orient	—	—	—	—	—
XVIII	Matienians 100	—					
	Saspirians	Saspirians					
	Alarodians	Alarodians					
XIX	Moschians 300	Moschians					
	Tibarenians	Tibarenians					
	Macrones	Macrones					
	Mossynoecians	Mossynoecians					
	Mares	Mares					
XX	Indians 360 (in gold)	—	—	Hiduš	Hndwj	Hiduš	Hiduš

TOTAL (in talents) 7,640
(+ 360 in gold)

BOOK IV

Aldo Corcella

INTRODUCTION TO BOOK IV

I

Book IV of the *Histories* begins with Darius' decision to march against the Scythians, which Herodotus places 'after the conquest of Babylon' described at the end of Book III. This vague dating has caused much discussion: it is difficult to establish when the expedition actually took place.[1] It must be acknowledged, in any case, that Herodotus' dating fits the 'logical time' of the narrative: he tells us that the expedition took place after the conquest of Babylon because he has decided to recount the two events in sequence. The actual lapse of time between them remains unspecified, hidden in the apparent continuity of the narrative, as so often in epic poetry.[2] While Darius' expedition is in its last stages (145,1) the Persians attack Libya: the whole of Book IV is centred on these two events which, though almost simultaneous, are told in succession.[3]

After announcing the Scythian expedition, Herodotus tells us what caused it. As usual in the *Histories*, the general economic explanation (Asia is rich, Darius wants to expand his territory) is accompanied by a particular cause: revenge. The motif of revenge takes us back to the invasion of Asia on the part of the Scythians narrated in Book I, 103–6. This flashback serves as a pretext to introduce a story about the return of the Scythians from Asia (1,3–4); and this excursus contains in turn another one about the way their slaves prepare milk (2). In ch. 4 the digression ends with a typical connective formula which takes us back to the expedition led by Darius, the topic introduced in ch. 1: 'this is how the Scythians came to rule over Asia, and . . . they went back to Scythia in the way I said. For this reason Darius wanted to take revenge on them and assembled an army.'

We would now expect to be told about the expedition. However, the narrative concerning Darius' attack begins only at ch. 83; chs. 5–82 are devoted to a long excursus about Scythia and the Scythians.

---

[1] It is more likely that it took place between 515 and 510 BC, rather than earlier: see notes on 1,1 and 166,1.

[2] On this issue see the excellent study by L. Huber, 'Herodots Homerverständnis', in *Synusia. Festgabe für W. Schadewaldt*, Pfullingen 1965, pp. 29–52, who quotes as an example precisely the opening of Book IV (p. 45). More generally, see L. Canfora, *Totalità e selezione nella storiografia classica*, Bari 1972. Sometimes Herodotus says in passing that he knows of some event that he has left out of the main narrative: at IV 44, for example, he mentions the conquest of India, which happened before Darius' great reform (cf. III 94,2) and could therefore have been included in Book III.

[3] αὐτοῦ at IV 1,1 suggests that Herodotus has in mind the overall structure of the narrative from the start: after the capture of Babylon the first historical event concerning the Persians, whose principal character is Darius, is the Scythian expedition; though there is another event that happens at the same time, but that does not involve Darius and will therefore be told later.

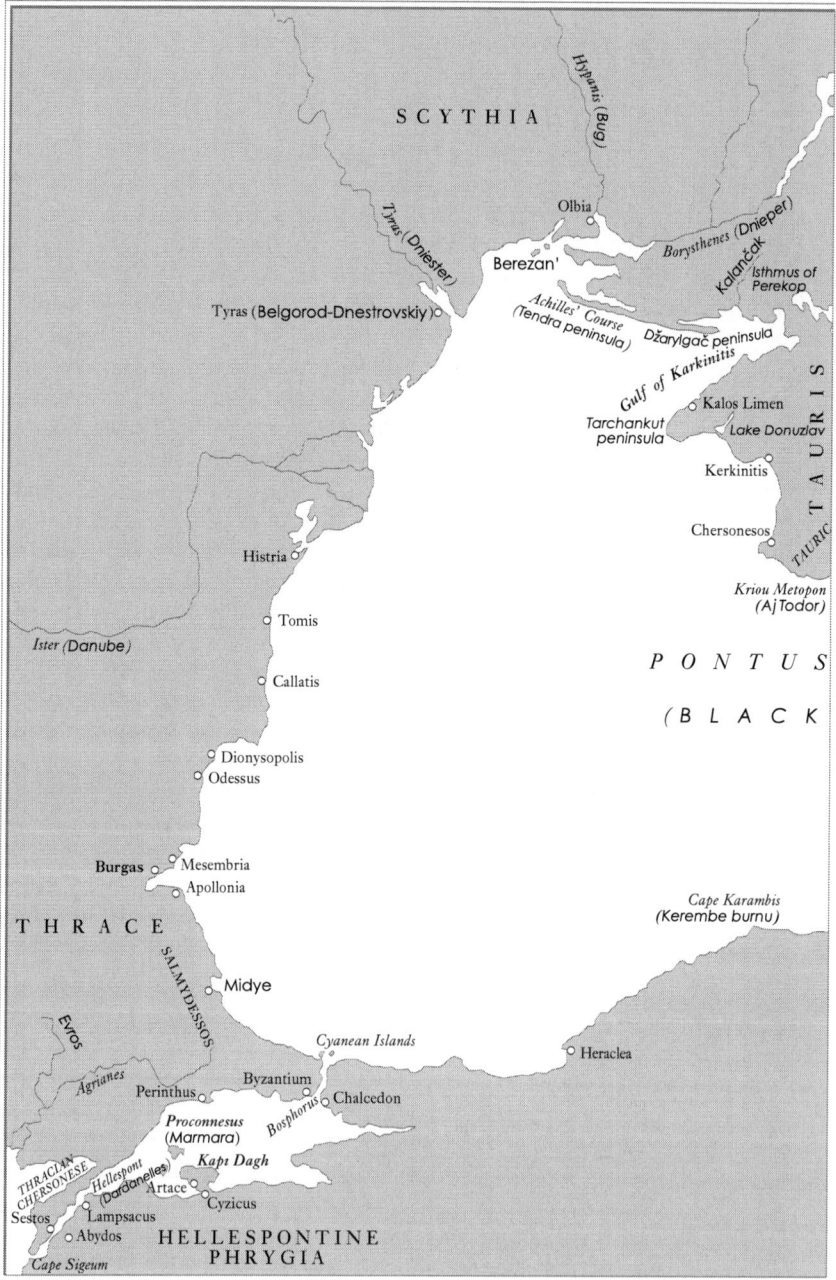

Map 34. The Black Sea

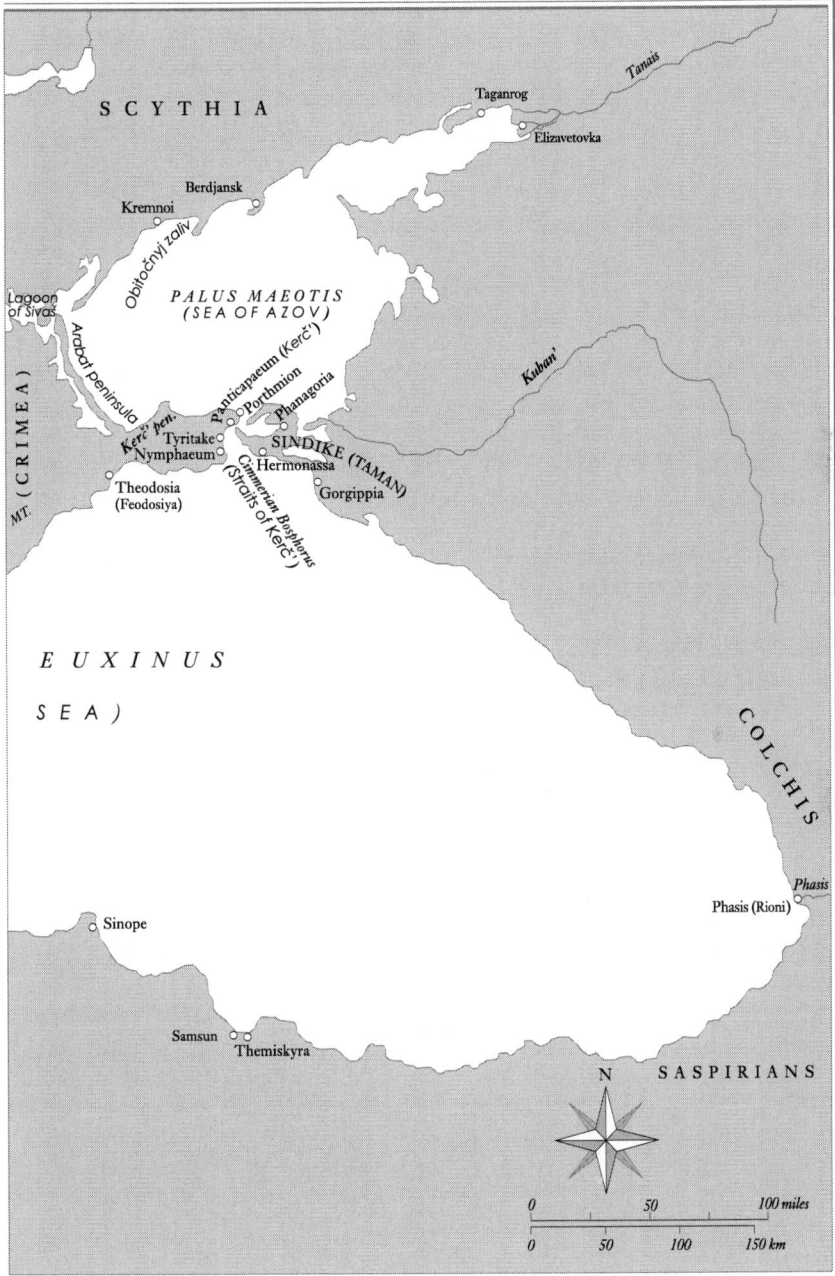

SCYTHIA

Tanais

Taganrog
Elizavetovka

Berdjansk
Kremnoi

Obitočnyj zaliv

PALUS MAEOTIS
(SEA OF AZOV)

Kuban'

Lagoon
of Sivaš

Arabat peninsula

(CRIMEA)

Kerč' pen.

Panticapaeum (Kerč')

Porthmion

Phanagoria

Tyritake
Nymphaeum

SINDIKE (TAMAN)

Hermonassa

Gorgippia

Cimmerian Bosphorus
(Straits of Kerč')

MT.

Theodosia
(Feodosiya)

EUXINUS

SEA)

COLCHIS

Phasis

Phasis (Rioni)

Sinope

Samsun
Themiskyra

N

SASPIRIANS

0		50		100 miles
0	50	100	150 km	

II

The digression about the Scythians has much in common with the Egyptian *logos* of Book II.⁴ The close resemblance between these two parts of the work stems from the similarity in Herodotus' attitude, and the consistent character of his research. While the Egyptian *logos* opens with the statement that the Egyptians are the most ancient, or almost the most ancient, of peoples (II 2), the Scythian excursus is introduced by the claim that the Scythians are the youngest one (IV 5); in both cases, the opening statements are defended in a section where the local traditions of the people in question are analysed and compared with Greek tales. The problem of the people's origin is then discussed in connection with the extension of their territory and with its boundaries. In the case of Egypt, Herodotus discusses the fact that it is a 'gift of the Nile' and its position between Asia and Libya, and gives an account of the regions in the far south towards the sources of the Nile (II 6–34); in the Scythian *logos*, he discusses the regions in the far north (IV 16–36).

Herodotus thus explores the boundaries of the *spatium historicum* as well as those of geographical space. His research leads him to criticize his predecessors: the mythical/historical narratives of the Greeks are refuted by the local traditions he records, while Ionian geography proves to be too schematic in comparison with the real world. The excursus on the parts of the world at IV 36,2–45 is not just an idle digression. By describing Scythia Herodotus has checked the data already known to the Greeks, which had been summarized in their geographical treatises and maps; the beginning of Book II was inspired by the same intention (as were the thoughts about the edges of the world at III 106–16). At IV 36,2–45 Herodotus is finally able to draw from this long enquiry some more general conclusions.

The apparently chaotic structure of the Scythian *logos* can be understood only if the above considerations are borne in mind. In the first place, Herodotus must confront earlier Greek authors. The origins of the Scythians and of the peoples who lived further north at 'the edges of the world' had already been discussed by a curious poet: Aristeas of Proconnesus, in an equally curious poem called *Arimaspea* (14–15). Aristeas, however, was one of those mysterious characters found in many a story about reincarnation, sudden disappearances, and ubiquity circulating in archaic and classical Greece; he cannot, as such, have appealed to Herodotus. In the opening of his poem he declared himself to have visited the Issedones 'due to the inspiration of Apollo'—a claim which may be compared to those of medieval Arab mystics always ready to leave their native Spain for a mysterious 'Orient'. Aristeas must have described a magic flight; he certainly talked about the Hyperboreans, the well-known mythical people devoted to Apollo. The subject of his poem was bound to meet with Herodotus' scepticism: the historian is explicit in his disbelief concerning Aristeas' journey. His doubts are shared by modern scholars. They hesitate to locate him chronologically, and

---

⁴ On the connection between the two *logoi*, see above all Trüdinger, pp. 14–34.

cannot decide whether he was a sublime charlatan who included in his 'journey of the soul' geographical, ethnographic, and mythical elements of different origins, or whether he did actually travel beyond the Propontis to the Greek settlements in the far north and the Euroasiatic steppe, where shamans and shamanic legends may have reinforced the Apollonian vocation which was widespread in all the Milesian colonies of the Pontic area.[5]

Herodotus, on his part, stimulated by his characteristic 'methodic doubt', begins in ch. 16 a scrupulous examination of the geographical and ethnographic data provided by Aristeas.[6] He starts with a statement of method concerning the sources of the poem: beyond Scythia, Aristeas claims to have first-hand knowledge only as far as the Issedones; for his knowledge of what was beyond (the Arimaspi, griffins, the Hyperboreans) he relied not on his own experience but on the accounts of the Issedones themselves. Herodotus is probably underlining a distinction which may have been implicit in Aristeas' work: the difference between direct knowledge and second-hand reports is very important in Herodotus and remains fundamental in all ancient historiography.[7] This preliminary distinction concerning Aristeas' sources soon proves to be rather malicious: at the end of his analysis Herodotus raises the suspicion that Aristeas did not even visit the Issedones (27; 32). It follows that the peoples in the far north mentioned by Aristeas, particularly the Hyperboreans, are poetic fictions, like the Eridanus mentioned at III 115.

Herodotus reaches his conclusion after a description of the geography of north-east Europe based on alternative sources; but, we may ask, what sources? He claims more than once to have had direct personal contact with the Scythians, and this is not at all implausible. The Greeks became acquainted with the nomads in the steppe north of the Black Sea already in very ancient times. Homer knew of the 'noble milkers of mares, who feed on milk, and the Ἄβιοι, the most just of men' (*Il.* XIII 5–6). These 'milkers of mares' are called 'Scythians' in a fragment ascribed to Hesiod (fr. 150 Merkelbach–West); another fragment describes 'those who feed on milk' as nomads who live on their own carts (fr. 151 Merkelbach–West). From the seventh century onwards, if not before, the Greeks were present in the Black Sea area.[8] The Milesians, in particular, founded a

---

[5] As examples of the two opposing views see Bolton and his reviewer W. Burkert, *Gnomon*, XXXV (1963), 235–40; cf. notes on chs. 14–15. Contact between Propontis and Olbia in the 6th cent. is attested, see Ju. G. Vinogradov, in *Acta Centri Historiae Terra Antiqua Balcanica*, II, Trinovi 1987, p. 23. On the cult of Apollo in the Pontic region, probably centred around Didyma, see Ehrhardt, pp. 130–47; A. S. Rusjaeva, *VDI* CLXXVII (1986), 25–64.

[6] It is generally assumed that Aristeas' statements had been taken up by Hecataeus in his work. Herodotus' criticism, however, indicates that he had direct access to the poem. Moreover, if we can take Aelian *Nat. An.* XI 1 (cf. *FGr Hist* 264 F 12) literally, Hecataeus did not mention the Hyperboreans at all. Cf., among others, Norden, p. 21; G. Nenci, *SCO* III (1955), 14–46; Schepens.

[7] Cf., among others, Norden, p. 21; G. Nenci, *SCO* III (1955), 14–46; Schepens.

[8] On the dating of the first settlements see most recently R. Drews, *JHS* XCVI (1976), 18–31; P. Alexandrescu, in *Mélanges P. Lévêque*, V, Paris 1990, pp. 1–8; G. R. Tsetskhladze, in Tsetskhladze–De Angelis, pp. 111–36, and the bibliography quoted in the next footnote.

BELARUS

Dnieper

Pripet

Styr

Desna   Seym

Kiev

Velikie Budki

U K R A I N E   Bel'sk

Sula

Psël

Makeevka

Žurovka   Vorskla

Čornyj Tikič

P O D O L A   Melgunov

Nemirov   Sinjucha

Alexandropol'

Ingulec   Bazavluk   Tolstaja Mogila

Černyj Tašlyk

Pervomajsk   Zeltokamenka
                              Kamenka   Nikopol'
                         Ordžonikidze
Prut   Voznesensk   Raskopana Mogila   Solocha

Dniestr   Cimbalka

C A R P A T H I A N   Tiligul   Bug   Malaja Lepaticha   Gajmanova Mogila

M O L D A V I A   Ingul   Kozel
                                                      Lake Kachovka   Oguz
                    Olbia
Siret   Nikolaev   Mordvinov I–II

Odessa

Džarylgač peninsula

Belgorod Dnestrovskij

Tendra peninsula

M O U N T A I N S   Gulf of Karkinitis

Reni   Ak-Mečet'
Galați   Lake Donuzlav
            Orlovka

Danube   Isaccea   Evpatorija
                    Tulcea
                                        TAURIC

D O B R U G I A   Kulakovskij

B   L   A   C   K

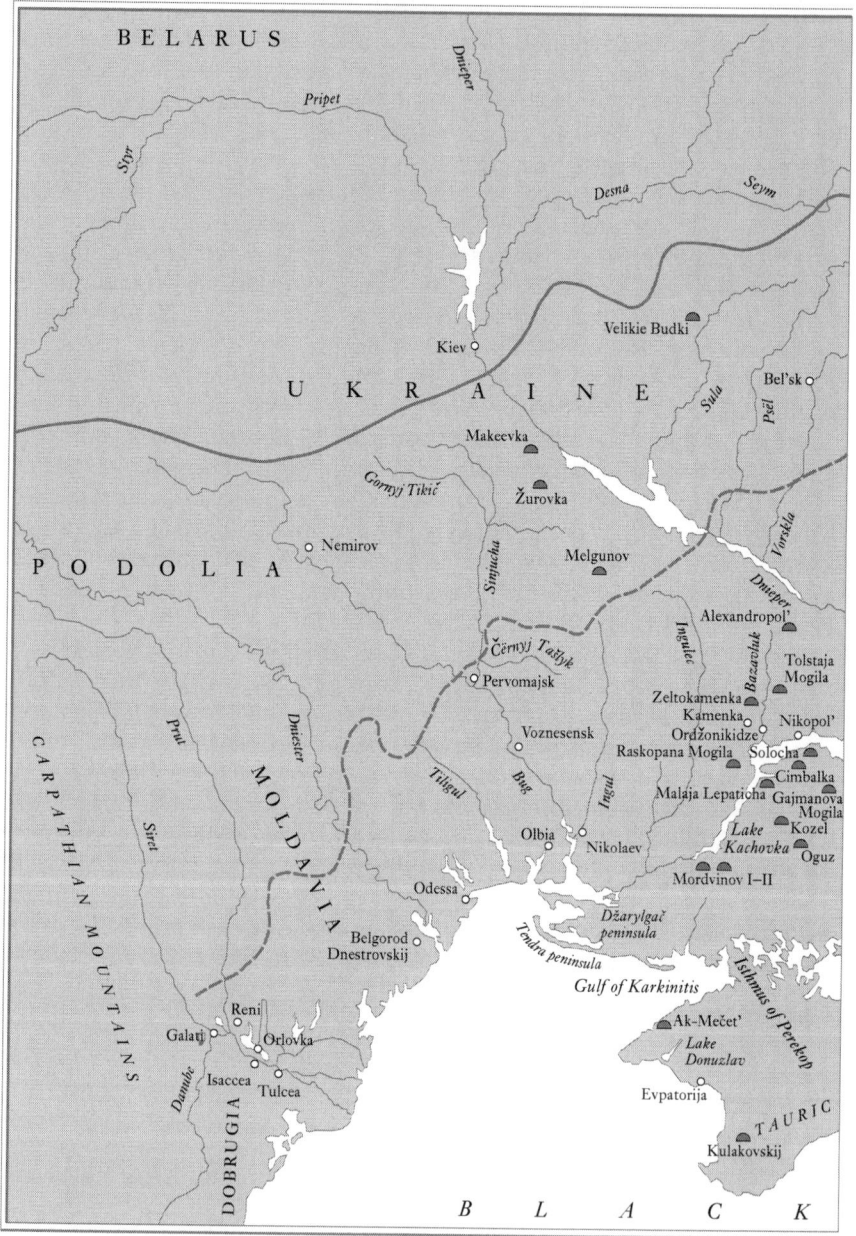

Map 35. The Scythian Steppe

FOREST-STEPPE BOUNDARY

STEPPE BOUNDARY

kurgan

N

Don

Voronež

0   50   100   150 *miles*

0   50   100   150   200   250 *km*

Don

Char'kov

U K R A I N E

Donets

Dniepropetrovsk

Bašmačka

Geremesov

Krasnokutsk

Zaprož'e

Mius

Konka

Berda

Don

Five Brothers

Taganrog

Chochlač

Veselyj

Elizavetovka

Molochnaja

Korsak

Obitočnaja

Berdjansk

Melitopol

Obitočnyj zaliv

S E A   O F

A Z O V

Kuban'

Akmonajskij val

Kul'-Oba

Ak-Burun

Elizavetinskaja Stantica

M T S

Seven Brothers

Ul'skij Aul

Kelermes

Karegodeuasch

Kurdžips

Majkop

S   E   A

Kostromskaja Stanica

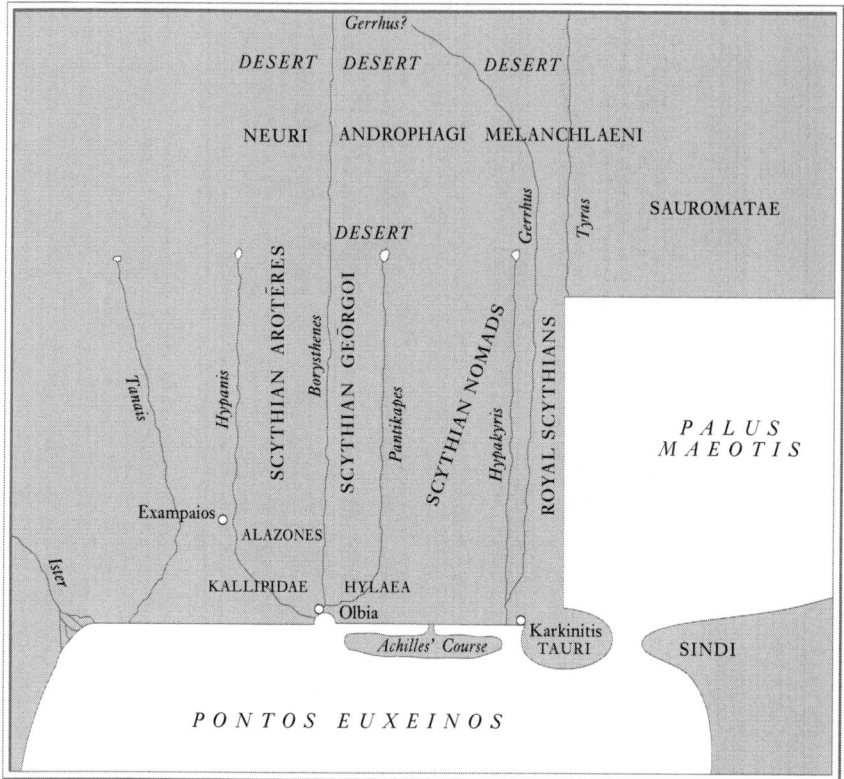

Gerrhus?

DESERT   DESERT   DESERT

NEURI   ANDROPHAGI   MELANCHLAENI

DESERT

SAUROMATAE

Tanais   *Hypanis*   *Borysthenes*   SCYTHIAN AROTERES   SCYTHIAN GEORGOI   *Pantikapes*   SCYTHIAN NOMADS   *Hypakyris*   *Gerrhus*   *Tyras*   ROYAL SCYTHIANS

PALUS MAEOTIS

Exampaios   ALAZONES

Ister   KALLIPIDAE   HYLAEA   Olbia

Achilles' Course   Karkinitis   TAURI   SINDI

PONTOS EUXEINOS

Map 36. Scythia according to Herodotus

number of colonies there.[9] Aristeas' experiences, whether real or imagined, stem from this context: he was born in the Propontis. Between the sixth and the fifth centuries the north shore of the Pontus had become an organic part of the Greek world. The relationship between the Greek colonists and the nomads living in the hinterland was varied: commercial exchange was intense and gave rise to the great Graeco-Scythian art, famous above all for its gold objects.[10] When the Scythian

[9] Among the most recent overall accounts, see D. B. Šelov, in H. Heinen (ed.), *Die Geschichte des Altertums im Spiegel der sowjetischen Forschung*, Darmstadt 1980, pp. 341–402; Ehrhardt; Ju. G. Vinogradov, in E. C. Golubcova (ed.), *Antičnaia Grecija. Problemy razvitija polisa*, I, Moscow 1983, pp. 366–420; G. R. Tsetskhladze (ed.), *The Greek Colonization of the Black Sea Area: Historical Interpretation of Archaeology*, Stuttgart 1998; Boardman, *Greeks Overseas*, pp. 238–66.

[10] For evidence and reproductions, the catalogues of the main exhibitions in recent years are essential after the work of E. H. Minns and M. I. Rostovtzeff; in particular, M. I. Artamonov, *Treasures from Scythian Tombs in the Hermitage Museum, Leningrad*, London 1969; *Gold der Skythen*; *Gold der Steppe*; Reeder. On the art of Euroasiatic nomads and the 'animal style' see also Jettmar; G. Charrière, *L'Art barbare scythe*, Paris 1971; B. Brentjes, *Der Tierstil in Eurasien*, Leipzig 1982; L. Galanina *et al.*, *Skythika*, Munich 1987; V. Schiltz, *Les Scythes et les nomades des steppes*, Paris 1994; E. Jacobson, *The*

state became a more organized entity, the Greek cities on the coast were probably forced to become a protectorate of the Scythians; whereas perhaps already by the mid-fifth century Olbia, the Milesian colony at the estuary of the Dnieper and of the Southern Bug, became part of the Athenian empire. Athens was extremely interested in the wheat produced in the hinterland and, as both Aristophanes and a number of vases show us, Scythian slaves were used in Athens as a police force.[11]

In this situation, it is not at all implausible that a traveller full of curiosity like Herodotus should have gone to the Pontic area. He declares himself to have sailed the routes of the Black Sea and to have personally measured their length (IV 85–6); he claims to have seen with his own eyes the big crater kept in Exampaeus, north of Olbia on the Southern Bug (IV 81), and to have visited Colchis (II 104). These statements have often been doubted; however, the seemingly implausible aspects of his descriptions are better explained as mistakes than as signs of bad faith.[12] In fact, most of the claims made by Herodotus about the ethnography of the Scythians turn out to be, by and large, correct: there are some unqualified generalizations, simplifications, misunderstandings, but archaeology often confirms even the tiniest details.[13]

Those who want to deny that the historian visited the Pontus must postulate another Herodotus before Herodotus, and claim that our historian, in using the earlier one as a source, added his mistakes to the original testimony. Some scholars have maintained this view and identified Herodotus' source with Hecataeus.[14] Indeed, it is likely that Hecataeus lurks somewhere in the background of Herodotus' *logos*. The whole structure of the geographical description recalls Hecataeus: Herodotus divides the area into strips between the rivers whose course he follows from the sea towards the sources. Moreover, a comparison with the tradition based on Ephorus (above all pseudo-Scymnus, 841ff., *GGM* I, pp. 231 ff.), with Pomponius Mela and with Pliny suggests that they all go back to a common Ionian source, most easily identified with Hecataeus.[15]

More particularly, the few extant fragments of Hecataeus concerning Scythia allow us to see that Herodotus is taking issue with him. When quoting Hecataeus,

---

Art of the Scythians, Leiden–New York–Cologne 1995. Two recent outlines of Scythian civilization are accompanied by excellent illustrations: A. I. Alexeev *et al.*, *Nomades des steppes. Les Scythes, VIIe–IIIe siècle av. J.-C.*, Paris 2001; I. Lebedynsky, *Les Scythes. La civilisation des steppes (VIIe–IIIe siècles av. J.-C.)*, Paris 2001.

[11] On the history of Olbia see above all Wąsowicz; S. D. Kryžickij, *Ol'vija. Istoriografičeskoe issledovanie architekturno-stroitel'nych kompleksov*, Kiev 1985; Vinogradov; Vinogradov–Kryžickij. On vase representations of Scythians see Vos. Scythians in Greece: Bäbler, pp. 163–81.

[12] The doubts concerning Herodotus' visit to the Pontus have been summarized by O. K. Armayor, *HSCPh* LXXXII (1978) 45–68; for the opposite view, see the notes on 85,2–4 and 86,4: the mistake in the measurements is due to the method used, and on 81,3–4 the dimensions of the crater have been estimated by sight; cf. the comparable size of the Delphic crater at I 51: are we to conclude that Herodotus has not visited Delphi either? See also Lloyd, note on II 104,6–7: Herodotus does not say that the Colchians are 'blacks', but that they are olive-skinned.

[13] See chs. 59–82 with the notes ad loc.; see also below, p. 560. A more sceptical view in S. West, in Bakker, pp. 437–56.

[14] The echoes between IV 86, 1 and Hecataeus, *FGrHist* 1 F 196 do not prove much: see notes on 85,2–4 and 86,4.

[15] For bibliography see note on chs. 16–31.

Stephanus of Byzantium calls the Melanchlaeni and the Issedones 'Scythian peoples' (*FGrHist* 1 F 185, 193). Strictly speaking, it is not certain that he is quoting Hecataeus verbatim, but in chs. 25–7 Herodotus distinguishes the Issedones from the Scythians, and at 20,2 he emphatically claims that the Melanchlaeni are 'a different people, not Scythians', although he ascribes to them Scythian customs (107). Herodotus makes similar claims about the Androphagi (18) whom pseudo-Scymnus again calls 'Scythians' at 848 (*GGM* I, p. 231; cf. also I 201 and 216 on the Massagetae). We thus have good grounds for concluding that Herodotus is criticizing a view which, given Stephanus' statements, must be that of Hecataeus. The focus of this ancient debate is the denomination 'Scythians', which was often used by the Greeks as a general term to indicate the nomads of the north-east (see e.g. *De Aeribus Aquis Locis*, 17 ff., and Strabo XI 6,2).[16] A similar way of life is indeed ultimately responsible for a 'family air' common to all the various peoples living in the steppe, regardless of their origin: the Persians too used a general term (*Sakā*) to indicate the whole of them. In fact, the history of the steppe has always featured waves of new invaders who eventually come to be assimilated, to a greater or lesser extent, to the previous people;[17] hence the name 'royal Scythians' for the dominant tribe, and the confusion about the total number of Scythians mentioned at ch. 81. Herodotus, on his part, wants to be more rigorous and uses the name 'Scythians' in a strict sense, though it is unclear whether he applies it to an 'ethnic' group or to a political entity which eventually emerged during the rule of the 'royal Scythians'.[18] In using the term strictly, he takes issue with Hecataeus.

The existence of a reference work which Herodotus occasionally corrects also serves to explain why the Neuri are placed north of the Scythian ἀροτῆρες at 17,2, but are said to have moved to a different area at 105: in the first passage Herodotus follows Hecataeus' *periegesis*, whereas in the second one he

---

[16] The name Σκύθαι may have been derived from an Eastern language (cf. the Assyrian *Aškuzai/Iškuzai*), but its remote origin is far from clear; see note on 6,2 and bibliography ad loc. The classicism of our sources in the Roman, late antique, and Byzantine periods is reflected in the usage of the term to indicate the various nomad peoples who succeeded the Scythians in ruling over the steppes north of the Black Sea, e.g. the Huns, the Pechenegs, and Cumans; Gibbon still used the terms 'Scythians' and 'Tartars' as synonyms in this general sense.

[17] On the overall uniformity of lifestyle among the peoples of the steppe see e.g. Chazanov; also A. M. Khazanov, *Nomads and the Outside World*, Cambridge 1982. It is for this reason that, on occasion, modern scholars still use the term 'Scythian' in its broadest sense, to indicate a *koine* of nomads from the Danube to the Altai, as well as expressions such as the 'Scythian-Siberian' world: see e.g. Martynov–Alekseev. Conversely, scholars debate whether the peoples living in the forest steppe further north and not just those in the southern steppe should be called 'Scythian' in the strict sense. For bibliography see note on chs. 16–31.

[18] The issue has been widely debated within Soviet historiography: for a review of the various positions see Nejchardt, pp. 78–84. As is usual in such matters, the 'ethnic' origin of the ancient Scythians has often been investigated in connection with the Scythian language(s), the character of which, as far as it could be reconstructed from the few remains, was the object of a long debate: after the studies by K. Müllenhoff and M. Vasmer, the comparison with the language of the Ossetes (a Caucasian people descended from the Alans) in the pioneering work of Vs. Miller, and then work by G. Dumézil and V. I. Abaev, has demonstrated that the 'Scythians', or some of them at least, spoke an Iranian language. An overview in Schmitt, pp. 92–4; see now S. R. Tochtas'ev, in V. Cojocaru (ed.), *Ethnic Contacts and Cultural Exchanges North and West of the Black Sea from the Greek Colonization to the Ottoman Conquest*, Jassy 2005, pp. 59–108.

corrects it.[19] Hecataeus, or in any case the earlier sources, are probably alluded to by the 'Greeks' who are criticized at 109,1 for identifying the Budini with the Geloni. The discussion about the Scythian γεωργοί who were called Borysthenites by the Olbians may also be a correction of Hecataeus, who probably followed the traditional dichotomy ἀροτῆρες/νομάδες without referring to γεωργοί.[20] The extant fragments of Hecataeus, moreover, show that Herodotus' description of Scythia was not as detailed as that of his predecessor; Hecataeus mentioned a number of names not quoted in the *Histories*. Of course, Herodotus did not want to write a new *periegesis*; he only wanted to give a general outline which would allow us to evaluate the credibility of Aristeas, and wished to describe the setting for the events he tells. While doing so, he modified this general outline in view of his newly acquired personal knowledge.

His personal knowledge covers in the first place the area around Olbia. From Olbia, Herodotus probably reached Exampaeus (81), while in Olbia itself he presumably had a chance to talk with Tymnes (76,6). He may also have talked to Scythian and Greek merchants who travelled a great trading route leading into Eurasia, a sort of ancient silk route (24). The description of Olbia is fairly accurate in its details (e.g. the promontory of Hippolaus with the temple of Demeter, 53,6); Herodotus sometimes quotes Olbians as sources (besides ch. 24, see 18,1 and 78,3). On the contrary, his knowledge of the coast east of Olbia is much vaguer: at most, he may have sailed along the Crimean coast and crossed the straits of Kerč, but he cannot have stayed on land for long periods nor have reached the sea of Azov.[21]

Information about Scythia could of course also be obtained from Scythian slaves in Greece (though one can harly imagine Herodotus relying on slaves rather than the priests and aristocrats he usually consults) or, more plausibly, from Greek merchants anywhere in the world. However, Herodotus is likely to have acquired the knowledge that he used to refute Aristeas' stories and correct Hecataeus' account in Olbia, where he could carefully compare his sources with the more reliable information obtained from Scythians and merchants. The conclusion that Herodotus' main concern at Olbia was to research the geography and ethnography of Scythia and, as in the case of Egypt, to verify the notions of the Greeks concerning the furthest regions of the *oikoumene*, is well grounded, and could be supported by further arguments.

III

Herodotus' observations on the geography of Scythia are not confined to the section which culminates in the digression on the parts of the world at 36,2–45. This latter can be considered as an appendix to the discussion of Aristeas' data.

[19] For a similar case in ch. 173 concerning Libya, see below pp. 568–9.
[20] See A. Corcella, *QS* XXXV (1992), 49–60.
[21] For a general discussion see H. Matzat, *Hermes*, VI (1872), 412–18; v. Fritz, *Griechische Geschichtsschreibung* I. *Text*, pp. 128–30. It seems arbitrary to interpret Herodotus' silence over the colonies in the Cimmerian Bosporus as politically significant (T. V. Blavatskaja, *Očerki političeskoj istorii Bospora v V–IV vv. do n.e.*, Moscow 1959, pp. 58–62).

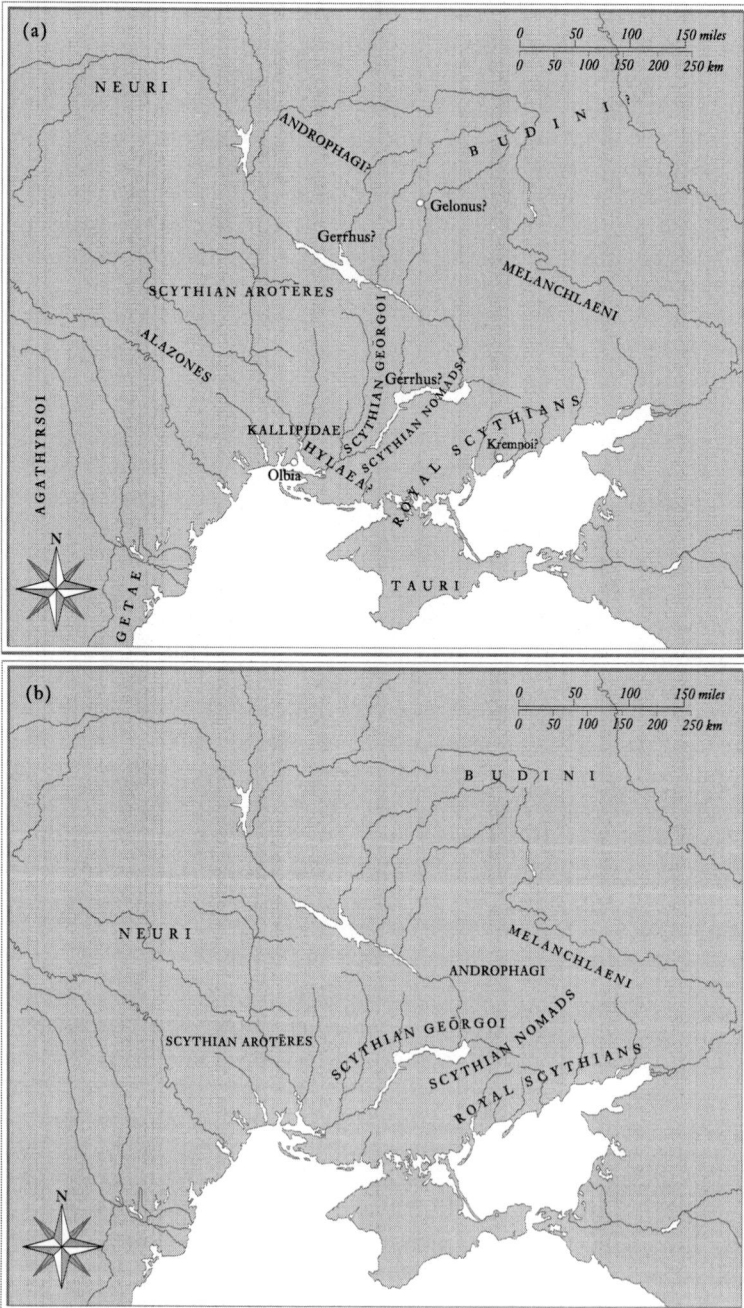

Map 37. Different reconstructions of Scythian ethnography.
(a): Hypothesis (see Commentary); (b): Reconstruction by B. N. Grakov;

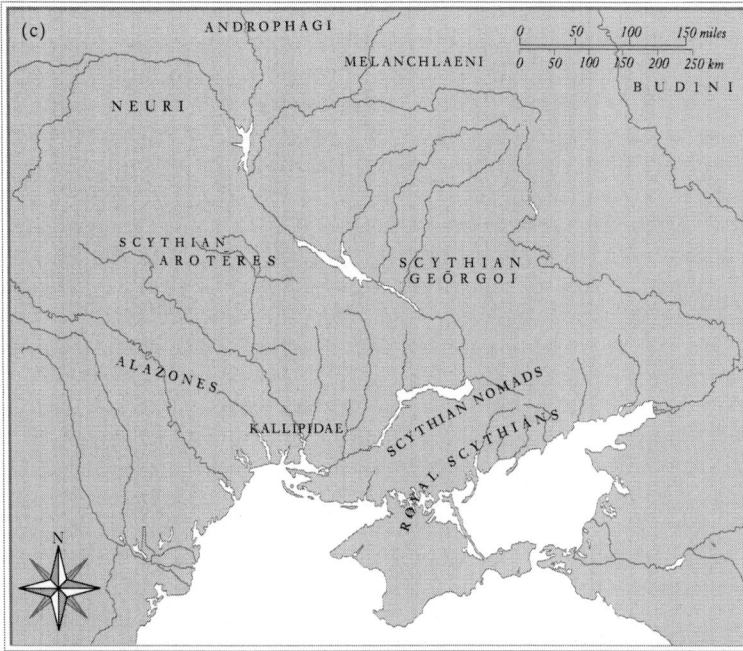

(c): Reconstruction by V. A. Il'inskaya and A. I. Terenožkin;
(d): Reconstruction by B. A. Rybakov.

Book IV

Herodotus has used local sources in order to reach 'the most distant regions' (ἐπὶ μακρότατον, 16,2), of which the Issedones mark the furthest limit. Once he has reached the limit, he allows himself a digression on the climate of the entire region and, at 31,2 he concludes in ring composition: 'I have reported what is being told about the most distant regions (μακρότατα)'. As for the Hyperboreans, their existence, stated by Aristeas and the Greeks, cannot be verified on the basis of Scythian sources and is therefore made the subject of a special discussion (32–6,1). Then Herodotus smoothly moves on to make his observations about the Ionian division of the world into three regions.

At this point, Herodotus announces the beginning of the ethnographic section (46–7). However, the narrative digresses somewhat artificially into a discussion of the main rivers of Scythia, most of which have already been mentioned in 16–21. The description of the customs of the Scythians will in fact only begin at ch. 59, and then extend up to ch. 82. In the geographical section (16–27) it is remarkable that only some of the non-Scythian peoples and their ethnography are discussed in any detail, others are mentioned by name alone (Neuri, Androphagi, Melanchlaeni, Sauromatae, Budini). The reason behind this choice becomes clear when Herodotus begins to report Darius' attack: the Scythians ask these peoples, who have been mentioned only by name, as well as the Tauri and the Agathyrsi, to make an alliance; this detail allows Herodotus to add another excursus on the ethnography of these peoples (102–17). Before this excursus, and before Darius' invasion of Scythia, Herodotus adds, at the last minute, the overall size and description of the region (99–101). In the Egyptian *logos* an analogous general account is placed, more naturally, at the beginning (II 6–8).

The Scythian *logos* on the whole appears rather chaotic. The real or apparent contradictions between individual sections have been explained analytically: Herodotus is supposed to have relied on a number of different sources.[22] To some extent at least, this explanation is undoubtedly correct, in that Herodotus is modifying a pre-existing picture. This is the reason why the place of the Neuri 'on the map' is north of the Scythian ἀροτῆρες on the Scythian border (17; 51; 102), while in ch. 105 we are told that they no longer live there. Similarly, the size of Scythia (a twenty-day walk east to west and again north to south) established in chs. 99–101 can hardly be reconciled with the information given in chs. 17 ff., where we are told that the land occupied by the nomad Scythians alone extended fourteen days from west to east (19). It is possible that there is a mistake in the manuscript tradition, but measuring distances in days would in any case lead to inconsistency: Herodotus may have been prepared to tolerate it.[23] The river Borysthenes poses a similar problem: Herodotus says that it extends for forty days sailing to the north. Some have tried to explain this statement too as an error in the manuscript tradition, but it may result from, *inter alia*, a measurement that took bends and meanders into account. The discrepancy between the ten days assigned to the land of the Scythian γεωργοί in 53,4 and the eleven days recorded in 18 is of no consequence; while the failure to mention the Androphagi can

---

[22] For this approach see above all Windberg, pp. 5–47.   [23] Cf. notes on 19,1 and 53–6.

perhaps be explained by the hypothesis that they lived north-east of the river which, in this case, did not cross their territory.[24]

In general, Herodotus' understanding of the hydrography of Scythia is very approximate.[25] His view of the region therefore contains some contradictions, which are due also to the different sources that he used (the narrative on Darius' expedition is evidence of this). However, we should not conclude that Herodotus mechanically reproduced different sources in different parts of Book IV without trying to harmonize them. Rather, the chaotic nature of the exposition mentioned before leads to a different conclusion:[26] Herodotus probably divided up and restructured material which, though not completely self-consistent, originally belonged to a unified treatise, a better organized ethnographic *logos*, like that on Egypt.

The method which can be seen to underlie the apparent chaos confirms this view. Though the section which begins with ch. 17 is mainly devoted to checking the data found in Aristeas' poem, Herodotus does not in fact restrain himself from telling us all he knows from the Pontic coast onwards. Yet, since he knows that there will be occasion to treat some of the peoples in the area later in the book, he does not linger on them in this section; he thus speeds towards his ultimate aim: the discussion of the Issedones and the Hyperboreans. He likewise only mentions the rivers that mark borders between different peoples (leaving out, for example, the Hypacyris) and does not describe them in detail. It is for this reason that he will contrive another occasion to talk about them (47). The introduction of the excursus on the shape and size of Scythia in chs. 99–101 is also rather artificial: some contradictions with the section devoted to Darius' expedition, and the formula which introduces it, clearly show that it was originally a self-contained treatise.[27]

In organizing his narrative, Herodotus is following well-defined criteria: given that, within the work as a whole, he has the opportunity to cover some Scythian material elsewhere, he begins by focusing on Aristeas' account, and accordingly divides into various sections a collection of material which can be easily imagined as having formed a unified treatise. Hence the chaotic nature of his treatment, which is not the product of chance. Moreover, the hypothesis that Herodotus included in his work one or more earlier treatises may explain some puzzling repetitions such as those concerning Hylaea and Exampaeus.[28] We can thus catch glimpses of Herodotus' activity before he composed the final version of his work, and perceive the sometimes difficult amalgamation of different stages. This view of the genesis of Herodotus' work is confirmed by other evidence.[29]

[24] See note on 53,4.

[25] This holds also for the course of the lower Danube: for a general discussion see notes on chs. 46–58.

[26] See above all Trüdinger, pp. 18–22.

[27] The first word is 'Scythia': see note on 99,1.

[28] See notes on 76,4 and 81,2.

[29] B. Bravo, *ASNP* s. IV, V (2000), 21–112 now explains most inconsistencies in Book IV by postulating massive interpolation: he brackets, fully or in part, chs. 2; 7,3–8,1; 10,3; 20,1; 25,2;

IV

The ethnographic section in the stricter sense (46–82, excluding the section on rivers) has often been quoted as an example of the structure of ethnographic monographs of the archaic and classical period. The organization of the material according to headings is one of their characteristic features.[30] It has already been said that archaeological finds and Graeco-Scythian art of the fifth and fourth centuries confirm the information given by Herodotus. His detailed descriptions are in some way linked to his scrupulous interest in discriminating between the real 'Scythians' and other Euroasiatic peoples. In this respect too, Herodotus distinguishes himself from the vaguer and more generalizing tradition current in his time. This tradition, which presented the peoples of the north as the archetypal 'just men', was as old as Homer. After Herodotus, and especially due to the Cynics, the 'Scythian mirage' became a constant feature of theories about 'the noble primitives' uncorrupted by civilization.[31] On the other hand, the Scythians were seen as savage and cruel barbarians. Strabo tells us at VII 3,7–9 that Ephorus tried to distinguish and mediate between these two different sides of their presentation.[32]

Herodotus is acquainted with legends about the superior wisdom of the Scythian Anacharsis, but he discusses this figure with detachment, if not outright irony (76–9). He knows that the Argippaei practice non-violence (23,5) and that the Issedones are just (26,2); within Thrace, he considers the Getae 'most just' (93), but his description of the Scythians proper is not idealizing in the least. On the other hand, though he sometimes indulges in negative descriptions, he does not over-emphasize them. As always, his description is shaped by an explicit or implicit comparison with Greek customs. His effort to translate a foreign culture into terms comprehensible to the Greeks generates some distortions; but the ideological elements which characterized the Greek image of the Scythians at this time, though somewhat more prominent in the account of the war, are largely absent from his ethnographic section.[33]

28–31; 36,1; 46,3; 61,1–2; 63; 76,1; 78,3; 79,2; 81; 82; 85,2–86; 99–101; 103,2; 105,1; 125,5–6. Some of these passages may indeed be corrupted, occasionally as a consequence of the addition of clumsy glosses or parallel texts (also cf. chs. 6,2; 33; 64; 106–7; 149,2; 156,3; etc.). Yet I cannot persuade myself that one and the same 'editor-forger' systematically interpolated Herodotus' work: many incongruencies—in the style, too—are to be explained, in my opinion, as a consequence of the complex 'prehistory' of the text.

[30] See above all Trüdinger, pp. 14–34, and note on chs. 59–82, with further bibliography.
[31] See e.g. E. Lévy, *Ktema*, VI (1981), 57–68.
[32] See *FGrHist* 70 F 42. On Ephorus and the Scythians see J. R. Gardiner-Garden, *Greek Conceptions of Inner Asian Geography and Ethnography from Ephoros to Eratosthenes*, Bloomington, Ind. 1987, pp. 1–11. On the Scythians in the *Corpus Hippocraticum*: S. West, *Eirene*, XXXV (1999), 14–32.
[33] Hartog often exaggerates in characterizing Herodotus' approach in terms of 'rhetoric of otherness'; see Pritchett, pp. 191–226. On the 'otherness' and 'sameness' of Herodotus' Scythians, see now Vignolo Munson, pp. 107–132.

V

Conversely, the narrative concerning Darius' expedition (which extends, through a series of digressions, from 83 to 144) has serious shortcomings. The march which leads to the Ister/Danube and the building of the bridge across the river are described with greater accuracy than the rest of the expedition, although the narrative focuses too narrowly on building activities. Herodotus must have had access to sources from within the army (Persians, or perhaps natives of the Hellespont and Ionians) which described the expedition. The Ionian tyrants who are left to guard the bridge assume an important role, and Herodotus considers himself able to quote their names and describe their position at the crucial moment when Darius returns from Scythia (137–9). The vividness with which this return is described (140–1) owes much to Herodotus' literary skill, but it also reinforces the impression that he is using an Ionian source speaking from within the camp.

As soon as Darius leaves the Ionians and penetrates into Scythian territory, we enter into legend. The main weakness of Herodotus' narrative consists in the account of the march of the army, which testifies to his lack of familiarity with tactics and logistics. Before leaving the Ister, Darius tells the Ionians to wait for him for no more than sixty days. The Scythians do not engage in an open conflict, and force on Darius a long march across the steppe. First, he travels eastward up to the Tanaïs/Don and enters the country of the Sauromatae; he then turns north towards the land of the Budini, where he finds time to destroy the wooden fortifications of Gelonus; he subsequently marches for seven days across an uninhabited region up to the mysterious river Oarus; then, after building some fortifications, he turns westwards, crossing the lands of the Melanchlaeni, the Androphagi and the Neuri up to the border with the Agathyrsi (in the north-western margins of Scythia); he eventually returns to Scythia proper, marching close to his route on the way in. At this point the Scythians decide to send a squad to the bridge guarded by the Ionians: the dialogue which ensues (133) shows that the sixty days are not yet supposed to be over.[34]

Not only is it impossible that Darius covered such an enormous distance and managed to cross the great rivers of the region, but there are even contradictions between this account and Herodotus' own image of Scythia: the Ister and the Tanaïs are twenty days apart (99–101); the land of the Sauromatae extends for fifteen days and the uninhabited region for seven (21–2; and between them, in any case, are the Budini); the return route along the northern border also takes twenty days (99–101); one must add, moreover, the time to destroy Gelonus and to build camps, as well as the time the Scythians took to reach the Ister, and so on.

---

[34] Bornitz, pp. 113–36 acutely defended some parts of Herodotus' narrative from unfounded criticism (see, above all, the notes on 136,3–4 and 137,1–2). However, he is wrong when he maintains that the sixty-day limit poses no difficulty (pp. 119–20). According to the time of the narrative, Darius has *already* finished his tour and is back in Scythia when a part of the Scythians leaves to go to the bridge (133).

Herodotus may have assumed that the forced march of the army was much faster than the trading caravans and carts driven by oxen whose speed was presumably reflected in the measurements; he may also have imagined alternative routes; but it is evident that he has no clear idea of how the expedition proceded once it crossed the Ister. The reference to the river Oarus, otherwise unknown, is particularly puzzling. If it is the Dnieper, Herodotus may have heard from his source of a long march towards this river in the east, though the Greeks actually called it Borysthenes. If this is the case, he may not have been able to locate it on the basis of his knowledge of the geography of Scythia, and may therefore have placed it in the 'empty space' beyond the Tanais, thus expanding greatly Darius' sphere of action.[35]

It seems that Herodotus found himself in a similar situation to Voltaire who, in describing the march of Charles XII through the Ukraine, was forced to declare: 'It is impossible for the reader to follow the route taken by the Swedes in these regions. Several rivers crossed by them are not to be found on the maps. We must not suppose that geographers know these lands as we know Italy, France, and Germany. Of all the disciplines, geography still has the greatest need of improvement, and ambition has hitherto taken more pains to devastate the earth than to describe it.'[36] Herodotus' Greek contemporaries did not dream of devastating the earth, but their description of it was nonetheless incorrect.

The above considerations show how much the intellectual frame of Herodotus' enquiries into the geography of Scythia is, in fact, inconsistent with the plan of the *Histories* as a whole. During his journey in the Pontic area he carried out a number of investigations, but he does not seem to have bothered to visit the places linked to Darius' expedition, nor to have made enquires in order to define more precisely the geographical area where it took place (and how it happened). Similar observations apply to his journey to Egypt, thus making the conclusions drawn by Kurt von Fritz irresistible:[37] Herodotus' travels to Egypt and Scythia were not motivated by an interest in the history of the Persian empire, but by a wish to verify the data given by Ionian scientists, and Hecataeus above all. Herodotus wanted to advance the knowledge of ethnography and check the available accounts, especially those concerning the most distant parts of the world, the origins of various peoples, and the *spatium historicum*. The Egyptian and Scythian *logoi* prove to be similar in their intent, though they are apportioned and adapted to the main narrative in different ways. It is possible that they were originally conceived as parallel narratives: apart from the many thematic correspondences,[38] it is remarkable how the phrase 'they *too* are determined in their refusal to adopt foreign customs' at IV 76,1 refers without further

[35] See also the notes on chs. 21, 108–9, and 122–4, with the bibliography quoted there (above all, Schramm, pp. 113–15).

[36] Voltaire, *Russia Under Peter the Great*, trans. M. F. O. Jenkins, Cranbury–London–Mississauga 1983, pp. 135 f.

[37] v. Fritz I, pp. 128–57.

[38] A. Bauer, *Die Entstehung des herodotischen Geschichtswerkes*, Vienna 1878, pp. 56–60, is still useful in places.

explanation to II 91,1. The suspect ἀλλήλων, 'mutually', which follows directly afterwards in the codices should perhaps be emended, but it may possibly be the trace of a phase in which the two *logoi* formed a unity.

VI

The problems outlined above are compatible with the hypothesis that Herodotus collected some information about Darius' expedition when he was in Scythia: he simply did not check it by making more detailed enquiries. If we speculate on the identity of the source which referred to the river Oarus and gave other factual information such as the existence of ruins of Darius' camps, we must conclude that it is unlikely to be a Persian source, though Herodotus must have gathered some information from the Persians. His knowledge of the names of the Scythian kings and their strategies, the epic tone of the account, some realistic details about the folklore, and the general point of view assumed in the narrative suggest that it is largely based on Scythian sources, perhaps mediated by the Greeks in Olbia.[39]

Herodotus presumably worked with somewhat partial material and must have tried to elaborate it so as to obtain a plausible account. He talks about the discomfiture of the king forced to cross a never-ending steppe and chase the Scythians, who suddenly appeared in swarms only to disappear again; and about the intelligence displayed by the Scythians themselves in leading the king around the borders of their land, thus exhausting his troops. It is no coincidence that in the narrative of the expedition the Scythians are portrayed in a more stereotypical fashion than in the previous chapters; and that the farming populations of chs. 17–18 do not appear at all.[40] Herodotus' Scythians thus become the archetype of the invincible warriors that dominate the annals and the imagination of all sedentary communities who have to deal with Euroasiatic nomads: Priscus' Huns, the Kumans or Pólovtsy in the *Slovo o pŭlku Igorevě* (*The song of Igor's Campaign*), the ghastly Pechenegs in Theophylactos of Bulgaria, the diabolical Tartars in the terrified Western sources.[41]

Unlike these later sources, Herodotus does not depict the Scythians as violent attackers and cruel pillagers. His view of the Scythians is constantly shaped by the model of the 'primitive enemy' who does not want to expand its domain but reacts with valour when attacked by a powerful nation.[42] Exactly as the Massagetae repel Cyrus and the Ethiopians Cambyses, the Scythians manage to stall the mighty Darius: the parallel will be made explicit by the wise adviser Artabanus at VII 18. In Herodotus' narrative, Artabanus also discourages Darius from launching the expedition against the Scythians (IV 83); and quotes this expedition when discussing the inherent weakness of great empires (VII 10γ).

[39] See note on chs. 102–42, with bibliography.

[40] The perspective adopted in the Herodotean narrative does not allow us to infer that these farming communities did not yet exist at the time of Darius' expedition, though some scholars have tried to do so. On Herodotus' different attitudes in descriptive and narrative sections, see now Dorati.

[41] Hartog has written some excellent pages on this topic, esp. pp. 63–8 = ET, pp. 44–50.

[42] See, above all, Hellmann, pp. 80 ff.; Cobet, pp. 104–20.

The campaign against the Scythians assumes in Herodotus the status of an example. The motives behind the expedition are not only Darius' desire for revenge, but also his awareness of his own might (1,1). The Scythians claim that he wants to impose his rule over all the peoples he meets, whether guilty or innocent (118,2–5): the peoples bordering with the Scythians refuse to adopt this view, but they will have to realize that Darius does not just threaten the Scythians. The discussion between the Scythian representatives and the kings of these peoples (118–19) becomes a paradigmatic debate not unlike those to be found in Thucydides' narrative of the Peloponnesian war. Confident in his own might, Darius advances scornful of danger, but he will soon change his mind. His contemptuous confidence, eventually humiliated, closely resembles that of Xerxes when he marches against Greece.

When Artabanus tries to dissuade Xerxes from attacking Greece and quotes the Scythian precedent (VII 10γ; cf. also VII 50,4 and 52,1), the connection between the two episodes becomes explicit; but it is present in Herodotus' narrative in a number of passages: in each case, Artabanus gives advice (IV 83, cf. VII 10); both expeditions aim at total subjugation (IV 118, cf. VII 8γ; 138,1); the episode concerning Oeobazus parallels that concerning Pythius (IV 84, cf. VII 38); Darius' 'touristic tour' at IV 85–6 is echoed by that of Xerxes at VII 44; and so on. In general, the theme of unity vacillating under the aggressor will be central also in the narrative of Xerxes' expedition; and the Athenians abandoning their city somehow parallel the Scythians laying waste the land behind them.[43]

Herodotus, however, is never schematic. While the contrast between the independent Scythians and the tyrannical Darius is certainly emphasized, it has to be said that the king manages to elude the Scythian trap. In the last part of the story Herodotus seems to enjoy reversing the outcome of the conflict; he shows the other side of the Scythians' 'simplicity': they are proud and free but also naive and without malice (cf. also 46). Darius and the Ionians are therefore able to trick them. The tyrant's cunning seems to win in the end. It is significant that the Ionian tyrants play such an important role, and that the sentence which effectively closes the narrative (142), before the appendix on Megabazus, is devoted to them: in the context of the opposition between freedom and slavery, the free Scythians see them merely as slaves faithful to their master. In view of the negative portrayal of the Ionian tyrants in the next two books, it cannot be pure chance that Herodotus wrote such a sentence in this emphatic position.

VII

We may suppose that Herodotus composed his narrative about Darius' expedition on the basis of the scarce (and biased) material he possessed, and of some basic principles which underlie all his historiography. He built the story around some problems (aggression, solidarity of those under attack, freedom,

---

[43] Cf. above all, Ph. E. Legrand, *REA* XLII (1940), p. 219–26; Bornitz, pp. 125–35. More generally see now Payen.

etc.) that had been of central importance in the Persian wars and were still hotly debated in the second half of the fifth century. It is thus difficult to evaluate the historical reliability of his reconstruction of events. The length of Darius' march is certainly exaggerated. Given that we cannot establish the actual range of his action with any certainty, any definition of the king's real motives becomes arbitrary: we cannot know whether he really wanted to subject all the nomads north of his empire or whether, as some have suggested, he just planned a demonstrative action in order to consolidate the borders of the empire and his new conquests in Thrace. The latter hypothesis indeed makes better sense of his decision to leave the fleet on the Danube.

Perhaps Darius was planning a *Blitzkrieg*, to be settled quickly with a pitched battle and without the support of the fleet, but the strategy adopted by the Scythians forced him to advance slowly and painfully, it weakened his troops and led him to face the beginning of the bad season, like Napoleon centuries later. We must in any case assume that his march was not as long as stated; Ctesias (*FGrHist* 688 F 13, para. 21) and Strabo (VII 3, 14) actually describe a smaller expedition, though it is difficult to establish whether they use ancient sources or simply want to contradict or rationalize Herodotus' account.[44] Herodotus himself knew that the Ionians had accompanied Darius up to the Ister, that the king had then entered the steppe and come back over two months later, and that, in the meantime, he had travelled and met more than once the elusive and mysterious knights of the steppe. In order to reconstruct this stage he must have relied on generalizations and perhaps pure fantasy. However, if we do not follow his work, we may end up offering an even more hypothetical reconstruction. We must thus accept some elements of his narrative while rejecting others, though this approach presents some methodological difficulties.

We know very little about what really happened; but we must in any case define the salient features of our main source before we can formulate or evaluate any hypothesis.[45]

VIII

On his return to Asia, Darius leaves Megabazus in Europe with the order to subject the Hellespont in its entirety. Megabazus is introduced with no more than two anecdotes (143–4): his operations will be described in Book V. At this point, Herodotus announces that he will move on to the Persian expedition in

---

[44] Strabo's information is now regarded as coming from a trustworthy source (Duris of Samos or Agatharchides of Cnidus) by P. Georges, *AJAH* XII (1987) [1995], 97–147 (esp. pp. 124–32), who follows Bury in identifying the Oaros with the Araros, cited by Hdt. IV 48 as a tributary of the Danube; see notes to chs. 102–42 and 122–4.

[45] For the various views and hypotheses see the commentary, and esp. notes on 1,1 and 102–42. After the phase of critical revision, the results of which can be read, for example, in the commentaries by How–Wells and Macan, some Soviet scholars have shown a tendency to accept, perhaps too hastily, Herodotus' account and especially some data, such as measurements and distances; see e.g. Rybakov and Černenko. A brief overview in Briant, *Histoire*, pp. 154–6, 931 = ET, pp. 141–3, 904.

Libya, which happened at the same time as the Scythian expedition.[46] In this case too the narrative is delayed: Herodotus first examines the reason for the expedition, that is, the deposition of Arcesilaus III in Cyrene; he is then tempted into summarizing the history of Greek colonization in that area, beginning with the foundation of Thera, the mother city of Cyrene. When the Persian army finally leaves Egypt for the Cyrenaica (167), Herodotus declares that the real aim of the expedition was to subjugate the Libyans, and digresses into a well-arranged description of the peoples of Libya (168–99); after these delays, the description of the expedition proper proves to be rather brief and disjointed (200–5).

In Book II, at ch. 161, Herodotus promised to tell in greater detail (μεζόνως) 'in the Libyan *logoi*' (ἐν τοῖσι Λιβυκοῖσι λόγοισι) the reasons for the end of the pharaoh Apries, limiting himself for the time being to a shorter account (μετρίως): 'Apries sent a large army against the people of Cyrene and was badly defeated; the Egyptians blamed him and rebelled against him...' Herodotus refers again to the downfall of Apries in IV 159: the Libyans in the region around Cyrene ask Apries to help them against the Cyrenaeans; but the Egyptian soldiers underestimate the Greeks, whose strength they had not previously experienced, and are defeated at Irasa, near the spring Theste; few of them survive and the rebellion against the pharaoh ensues. It is plausible to assume that when Herodotus mentioned the Λιβυκοὶ λόγοι, he had already a clear idea of the content of IV 146–205: the various sections into which this part of the book is divided justify the plural *logoi*. Some readers, however, have doubted whether this account of the reasons for the end of Apries can really be considered 'more ample', as Herodotus promised at II 161. In Book IV Herodotus clearly gives reasons for the expedition against Cyrene and adds some details; but we may still have the impression that when he made his announcement at II 161, he was planning a fuller discussion.

All the 'Libyan *logoi*' show signs of compression, and their composition is sometimes less than successful. In the narrative about Thera and Cyrene, the reference to the Aegidae in Thera at 149,2 is rather obscure: this may be due to a lacuna in the tradition, but it may also be a feature of an imperfect summary. The equation between Cyrene and Platea at 156,3 is certainly too brief. In general, Herodotus does not succeed in distinguishing clearly between different accounts.[47] In the second half, which is devoted to the peoples of Libya, Herodotus suddenly remembers that he 'ought to say something' about the geography of Libya after having written a sentence which ought to mark the transition to the expedition proper (197,1); he is clearly making a mechanical addition (197,2–199). The account of the war is rather puzzling: although Herodotus declares that the Persians wanted to subjugate all the Libyans, he

---

[46] One is immediately tempted to ask how Herodotus knew that the two expeditions were contemporary: it may be a narrative ploy, or perhaps he deduced that the events were contemporaneous on the grounds that Darius did not himself lead the Libyan expedition (cf. above, p. 545, n. 3). It is also possible that he actually knew in what year of Darius' reign the two expeditions took place and that the chronology is therefore historically reliable).

[47] See notes on chs. 145–67 and 157, 2.

only gives some brief account of the operations at Barca and Cyrene, though in the end (204) he refers to the beginning and says that the expedition went as far as Euesperides, west of Barca.

There is no proper account of the expedition, not even something equivalent to what we get for Scythia; the balance between the main narrative about the wars led by the Persians and the excursus on the Libyans is certainly tipped in favour of the latter. In this case too, Herodotus has included within his overall work a lot of material which was not originally intended to illustrate the history of Persian expansion.

IX

In the first part of the Libyan *logoi* Herodotus gives ample information about his sources, and tries to make careful distinctions between them.[48] The information he preserves is extremely interesting, because it allows us to get an impression of the traditions about the foundation of colonies current in the fifth century. They range from 'foundation myths' in the purest form, full of fantastic details (the first part of the Cyrenean version, 154–6), to mythical/historical accounts which exalt the origins of the oikists and present them as descendants of mythical characters such as the Argonauts (the tradition concerning Thera, 145–9), to historical or almost historical narratives (the Theran story about Cyrene, 150–3). Behind the genealogical traditions, specific biases can be discerned: the Cyrenaeans want to minimize the role of Thera, while the Therans insist on it; the Cyreneans, moreover, need to establish a link with the great Sparta or with Crete. The fact that the names of the main characters recur in Thera and Cyrene from the archaic period down to the Hellenistic era suggests that the local aristocratic families were to some degree responsible for the creation and diffusion of these foundation stories.

A comparison between the Cyrenean account in Herodotus and Pindar's Pythian Odes 4–5 (composed for Arcesilaus IV) and 9 shows that Herodotus based his narrative on a source that was somehow influenced by the Battiad dynasty, although it was no longer in power in Herodotus' day (he does not, however, report the more mythical elements found in Pindar, for example, Apollo's love for the nymph Cyrene, and the encounter between the argonaut Euphemus and the 'old man of the sea' who offers him the rule of Libya). Although Herodotus is using sources that reflected Battiad propaganda, he does not engage in propaganda himself; in fact, he seems to be acquainted with alternative versions.[49] In general, his portrayal of Cyrene reflects the conflict between the dynasty and the aristocracy which characterized the history of the city up to the fall of the Battiadae: Herodotus' informers should be identified, as usual, with the local aristocrats.[50]

---

[48] This is one of the cases in which Herodotus' excessive accuracy makes Fehling suspicious, cf. pp. 91–2.

[49] See, above all, ch. 179.

[50] See now S. De Vido, *AAT* CXXXII (1998), 1–42.

The Cyreneans appear as a probable or certain source also in the remaining part of the Libyan *logoi*. It is not certain that Herodotus went to Cyrene: he does not state it explicitly anywhere in the work. An apparent familiarity with the topography of the city, some accurate descriptions, and the inclusion of a number of details have led some scholars to believe that Herodotus did visit the city, perhaps in connection with his journey to Egypt; but the evidence is not conclusive: he may have obtained his information from important citizens of Cyrene met abroad, for example in Samos, which had close links with Cyrene (152,5). It is less likely that he used written sources.[51]

X

As in the case of Scythia, the geography and ethnography of Libya also seem to be influenced by Hecataeus: according to Felix Jacoby, chs. 168–99 of Book IV could in fact be included among the Hecataeus fragments, 'in that they constitute a summary of Hecataeus, with few changes, additions, or omissions'.[52]

It is possible that Jacoby's statement is excessive: the agreement between Herodotus, Hecataeus, and later sources, especially the periplus known under the name of Scylax, may be due to the fact that they describe correctly the same geographical area. Some passages clearly show that in the description of Libya, as in that of Scythia, Herodotus makes changes to the model he is following. The Psylli are an example: Herodotus first declares, as if he was writing a periplus, that they border on the Nasamones, but he then immediately adds that they are extinct (173). As in the case of the Neuri in Scythia, Herodotus follows the structure of his source, but he adds a new piece of information which, in this case, he claims to have obtained from the Libyans themselves. The fact that Hecataeus mentioned the 'gulf of the Psylli' (*FGrHist* 1 F 303), suggests that he should be identified as Herodotus' source. Hecataeus is probably also responsible for dividing the Libyans into farming and nomad communities (cf. the distinction made in the Scythian account)[53] and for arranging the geographical area into strips (once again paralleled in the presentation of Scythia).

The schematic division of Libya into strips leads to some distortion, especially in the western area. This area was less well known, because it was controlled by the Carthaginians. Herodotus seems to have formed a rather obscure picture of the area from their testimony (195–6). His information about the Libyans in the east, on the other hand, is often correct. The discovery of paintings and engravings on rock in the Sahara, the identification of the ancient kingdom of the

---

[51] On Herodotus' visit to Cyrene see above all Chamoux, pp. 153–6; and Lloyd, *Commentary 99–182*, p. 234. Chamoux is still the standard work on Cyrene; see now Bonacasa–Ensoli and Luni, where more recent literature is quoted. The fragments of the Greek authors of *Libyka* are now collected and commented in Ottone.

[52] *FGrHist* I a, 2nd edn., p. 371.

[53] On the possibility that Herodotus engaged in criticism also on this point see A. Grosskinsky, *Hermes*, LXVI (1931), 362–7; and the note on chs. 186–90.

Garamantes, the comparison with Egyptian texts and paintings, and also with the customs of the modern Berbers, who descend from the ancient Libyans, have on the whole confirmed Herodotus' account.[54]

This accuracy may be partially due to Hecataeus and to Herodotus' other sources, but he must have been able to collect a vast amount of evidence. For example, he made a specific enquiry into the local fauna ($\iota\sigma\tau o\rho\acute{e}o\nu\tau\epsilon\varsigma$, 192,3). In three cases, he distances himself from rather incredible reports: he attributes them to the Libyans, who must take responsibility (173; 187,3; 191,4). Cyrenean sources may occasionally have functioned as intermediaries, but Egyptian sources must have played an important role. Some of the interests displayed by Herodotus in his Egyptian enquiries are present also in some of his statements about Libya, as when he traces the origins of some Greek customs to the Libyans: for example, the way four horses are harnessed to a chariot, and the clothes of Pallas Athene (see above all 180 and 189; cf. II 50,2–3). The ethnography of Libya also shows traces of Herodotus' activities before he conceived the final version of his work. These activities explain the large space devoted to the excursus on Libya in comparison with the very slender main narrative about the Persian expedition against Barca.

XI

It has already been mentioned that Herodotus' treatment of the Persian expedition is extremely brief. It is possible that he had more material at his disposal, but that he decided to summarize it because, after so many digressions, he wanted to go through the main narrative quickly and, after the story of Megabazus, get to the Ionian revolt. It is also possible that, as in the case of the Scythian expedition, he did not know very much about the war between Barca and the Persians, because he had not made detailed enquiries.

The little he knows clearly derives from Cyrene: at the cost of making the events quite obscure, his source declared that Cyrene was completely innocent of the crimes perpetrated by the Battiad Pheretime together with the Persian army, and denied that the city took part in the war. We thus receive further confirmation that Herodotus obtained some information from the circle of Cyrenean aristocrats who were opposed to the tyrants and therefore fought against the Battiadae and the Persians at Cyrene. These aristocrats painted Pheretime in dark colours as a bloodthirsty monster, and were happy to consider her death as the just punishment for her tyrannical excesses.

This aristocratic stance suited Herodotus' mentality: of the whole conflict between Barca, Cyrene, and Libya, he remembers almost only the story of Pheretime and her exemplary death. On the other hand, one must admit that, though the Libyan expedition entailed the first confrontation between Persians and Greeks, it remained

---

[54] See above all the works by O. Bates, S. Gsell, P. Graziosi, H. Lhote, G. Camps, J. Desanges, R. Rebuffat, and F. Colin cited in the commentary.

a minor event and did not lend itself to wide-ranging considerations on Persian expansionism, or to predictions about the wars against the Greeks. The expedition against Barca thus becomes little more than a pretext to include in the overall work a different sort of material, which had been collected by Herodotus in the course of earlier research. The very statement that the Persians did not just want to punish Barca, but also to subdue the Libyans, though consistent with Herodotus' ideology and perhaps not completely false, is in the first place a device used to introduce the ethnographic excursus.[55]

XII

The structure of Book IV can be taken as a paradigm for Herodotus' approach. As in other parts of the work, and sometimes more so, Herodotus has included within the structure based on the military campaigns of the Persian kings a series of earlier treatises or, at least, information of a different kind; and has tried to organize the overall result as coherently as possible.

His efforts are not always completely successful: some links remain rather artificial. It is significant that precisely in the course of Book IV Herodotus declares, with pained resignation, that his narrative proceeds from one excursus to the next (30,1). He must also resort to formulas such as 'a reason that I shall explain after I have gone through what follows...' (145,1); and is often forced to make corrections as he goes along (see e.g. 63 and 198–9). As R. Lattimore pointed out,[56] it seems that Herodotus writes or dictates straight off; he thus takes up again earlier material and sorts it out into different parts of the narrative, promising to give some information later, and sometimes referring back to a previous passage in order to add a detail he had forgotten. It is not surprising that some inconsistencies remain. We should rather admire Herodotus' consistency: in his struggle with his own material, he manages to impose a structure and he is always aware of what will come afterwards. He never loses sight of the main narrative during his digressions. It is telling that, at ch. 46, when he is about to open the section about the ethnography of Scythia, he feels the need to refer back to Darius' expedition, which is still pending. Likewise, when he takes it up again at ch. 82, he declares: 'I shall now come back to the story I told in the beginning.'

This awareness of the main narrative thread, which is often bracketed but never interrupted altogether, can be seen also at a more general level. It has already been noted that the Scythian episode foreshadows some themes that will remain crucial in the work and will be taken up again later. Similarly, the role assigned to the Ionian tyrants constitutes an excellent introduction to the Ionian revolt, the narrative of which begins in the following book and focuses on the ambiguous and individualistic tyrants. Above all, the announcement made in chs. 131–8 of Book III, that the Greeks will soon be attacked, reminds us that Darius'

---

[55] See above all the note on 167,3.   [56] *CPh* LIII (1958), 9–21.

expedition against Scythia is a fundamental step in the Persian aggression against Europe. His attack will culminate in the great wars against the Greeks. At the same time, we are reminded that, in their wish to expand their enormous empire, the Persians have to face free and brave enemies, not at all inclined to submission and more dangerous than they appear to be. The Libyan expedition is a minor event, but it contains the first attack against a Greek community, and confirms that the Persians want to conquer large territories towards the west.[57]

Despite the apparent confusion, Herodotus continues to fulfil brilliantly the task he has set himself at the beginning of his work. While he takes every opportunity to recount the wondrous 'deeds of men' that he has investigated in years of research, he continues to assemble elements which can lead to a deeper understanding of the 'cause' of the war between Greeks and Persians.

Summary of Book IV

1–144	*Darius' Scythian expedition*
1–4	Causes and precedents.
5–82	*Excursus on the geography and ethnography of Scythia.*
5–45	Origins and geographical limits of the Scythians.
5–15	The different theories in play: the Scythian version (5–7); the Greek version (8–10); the opinions common to Scythians and Greeks (11–12); the version of Aristeas, his work and character (13–15).
16–45	Discussion of the boundaries of Scythia and testing of the information of Aristeas; with an appendix on the Hyperboreans (32–6,1) and on the Ionian world map (36–45).
46–82	*Scythian customs*
46–7,1	Nomadism.
47,2–58	Excursus on the rivers of Scythia.
59	The Scythian pantheon.
60–3	Sacrifices.
64–6	Customs of war.
67–9	Divination.
70	Oath-taking.
71–5	Funeral customs.
76–80	Attitudes towards foreign customs: Anacharsis and Scyles.
81	Scythian population numbers.
82	Wonders.
83–98	The advance of Darius from Asia to the Ister.
99–101	The shape of Scythia.
102–21	The strategy of the Scythians.
103–17	Ethnography of the peoples bordering on Scythia.
122–42	Darius' advance into Scythia, operations of war, and retreat.
143–4	Megabazus in Thrace.

[57] See Immerwahr, pp. 106–13; and Wood, p. 93.

COMMENTARY

1,1. *Μετὰ δὲ τὴν Βαβυλῶνος αἵρεσιν*: the precise date of the expedition is uncertain. The Bisitun inscription (V. 74; for English text see Book III, App. I) ascribes to the third year of Darius' reign (519/518 BC: see e.g. Dandamaev, pp. 69–71) a campaign against the Sakā (a Persian term covering all Scythians, both European and Asiatic) 'who wear the pointed cap' (*tyaiy xaudām tigrām barantiy*). According to some this is the expedition recounted by Herodotus: since J. M. Balcer, *HSCPh* LXXVI (1972), 99–132, see more recently Th. Petit, *AC* LIII (1984), 35–46; *EC* LV (1987), 175–9 with bibl. But this seems unlikely (see Cook, p. 239, n. 8), mainly because the Bisitun Sakā can hardly be different from those *Sakā tigraxauda* who in the Naqš-i Rustam inscription appear among the eastern peoples (probably the Massagetae: see Junge, pp. 70–1). The expedition attested in the Bisitun inscription cannot, therefore, be the one narrated by Herodotus, which must then be dated to the years between 515 and 510. The unreliable *Tabula Capitolina* (*IG* XIV 1297, col. II, ll. 22–5) seems to refer to the year 514/513 (see, among others, J. Harmatta, *AAntHung* XXIV (1976), 15–24; A. Shahbazi, *AMI* XV (1982), 189–235; Černenko, pp. 7–11; J. R. Gardiner-Garden, *Klio*, LXIX (1987), 326–30); while C. Masetti, *VDI* CLXI (1982), 106–10, suggests the year 515 on the basis of the Babylonian text edited by A. K. Grayson, *Babylonian Historical-Literary Texts*, Toronto–Buffalo 1975, pp. 28–37. The Herodotean dating 'after the capture of Babylon' (521) is rather vague: some have postulated a confusion with the expedition against the Sakā mentioned in the Bisitun inscription (e.g. M. Miller, *Klio*, XXXVII (1959), 34, 45, and A. Shahbazi, *AMI* XV (1982), 231–2); but see Introduction, p. 545.   *αὐτοῦ*: Herodotus will later discuss 'the other great expedition', led by Aryandes against Libya (145,1; see Introduction, p. 545, n. 3). The term *αὐτοῦ*, which has roused suspicion, might be a reminiscence of the Persian official custom, attested for instance at Bisitun, of distinguishing carefully between expeditions entrusted to generals and expeditions led by the king himself.   *ἀνθεύσης...Ἀσίης*: Herodotus had already spoken of the wealth of Asia in Book III; on the Scythians and the Cimmerians in Asia see I 15 and 103 ff., and the notes to IV 11,1; 12,1. The pattern of causality is typically Herodotean: revenge for a suffered wrong is the official motive (see IV 118) that directs an imperialistic will based on power (cf. I 29; 66,1; V 28–9), as had become clear already at III 134,1–2 (cf. Bornitz, pp. 115–16). The expedition was part of Darius' general expansionistic thrust; however, uncertainty on its true geographical extent (see note to chs. 102–42) makes it difficult to establish whether the aim of the operation was, consistently with the actions against the north-eastern Sakā, to ease nomadic pressure on the northern frontiers of the empire (e.g. Nenci, *Introduzione*, pp. 149–50; Černenko, pp. 11–15) and to reduce the Black Sea to a 'Persian lake' (M. A. Levi, *RFIC* LXI (1933), 58–70; cf. J. R. Gardiner-Garden, *Klio* LXIX (1987), 342–5 on the role of the Ionians), or if it was rather a preparation for expansion westward, with a marked interest for

Thrace (e.g. Rostovtzeff, p. 84; some have also suggested interest in the gold of the
Carpathians, see J. B. Bury, *CR* XI (1897), 277–82; cf. now P. Georges, *AJAH* XII
(1987), 97–147). See Introduction, pp. 564–5.   ἐπεθύμησε: this sounds already
like a presage of misfortune; cf. I 201; IV 79,1; Montgomery, pp. 24–5, 208–17.

3. τοὺς δὲ Σκύθας ... δούλους: from here to ch. 4 we have an aetiological tale (see
Aly, p. 112) on the origin of the trench that existed in Crimea. The theme of the
union of slaves and women during the absence of men, and of the struggle against
illegitimate children, is well attested in Greece (Antiochus, *FGrHist* 555 F 13;
Polybius XII 5–10; cf. D. Briquel, *MEFRA* LXXXVI (1974), 673–705). Also Greek
is the exploitative ideology of slavery in the episode (which recurs with variants in
Justin II 5,1–7; Domitius Callistratus, *FGrHist* 433 F 4; Ammianus Marcellinus
XXII 8,41). Cf. e.g. Myron of Priene, *FGrHist* 106 F 2, on the regular beating of
the Spartan helots 'so that they might never forget that they are slaves';
M. I. Finley, *Ancient Slavery and Modern Ideology*, London 1980, pp. 118–19.
The tale may have originated in the Greek cities of the Black Sea and may have
derived from reports of the struggles between the Scythians and pre-existing
populations (H. Kothe, in *Das Verhältnis von Bodenbauern und Viehzüchtern
in historischer Sicht*, Berlin 1968, pp. 103 ff., suggests the Cimmerians, who are
'dark' in *Od.* XI 14–16; see chs. 11–12; for a possible representation, see
E. V. Chernenko, *AncCiv* I (1994), 51–2). An aside (ch. 2) is included on the
blinding of all captured slaves; this information, which is isolated in Herodotus,
has been thought incredible and the result of a misunderstanding. Bibl. in
Narody, pp. 203–4, and C. Saerens, *Euphrosyne*, XVII (1989), 242–4. According
to T. Pekkanen, *QUCC* XI (1971), 57–8, the Scythians called subject peoples
'blind, dark' (*anda-*, from which Ἄνται/*Antes* in late ancient sources); see recently
V. Ju. Zuev, *VDI* CCXIII (1995), 175–82 (discussed by B. Bravo *ASNP* s. IV, V
(2000), 59–64, who regards ch. 2 as spurious); A. Griffiths, in Luraghi, pp. 168–73.

2,1. ποιεῦντες ὧδε: sexual stimulation in milking is paralleled among the Kalmuk
and the Jakut as well as among several African and Arab pastoral peoples,
including the Dinka (see *Narody*, p. 204). The processing of milk is better
described in Hippocrates, *De Morbis* IV 51,4, perhaps from a common source
(Hecataeus? Cf. also *De Aeribus Aquis Locis* 18; Pliny, *NH* XXVIII 133–4. See
I. M. Lonie, *The Hippocratic Treatises 'On Generation', 'On the Nature of the Child',
'Diseases IV': A Commentary*, Berlin–New York 1981, pp. 339–40; Thomas,
Herodotus, pp. 59–60). The Scythians separated by 'centrifuge' the most precious
buttery part, the whey, and the *hippake* (cheese). Just like the *qïmïz* for the
Mongolians, horse milk and its by-products were important in the diet of the
Scythians, termed ἱππημολγοί in Hesiod, fr. 150,15 Merkelbach–West (cf. *Il.* XIII
5). See N. A. Gavriljuk, *SA* (1987), 1, pp. 28–9; *Gold der Steppe*, pp. 94–5.
D. Braund, in Tsetskhladze, *Ancient Greeks*, pp. 521–30; S. West, *MH* LVI
(1999), 76–86.   φυσητῆρας ... ὀστεΐνους: cf. Aristophanes, *Ach.* 863 for bone
auloi. Bone pipes whose use is uncertain have been found in the *gorodišče* at
Bel'sk: B. A. Šramko, in *Archeologičeskie otkrytija 1969*, Moscow 1970, p. 243.

2. κοῖλα: 'deeply hollow' like churns. See C. Saerens, in *Studia varia Bruxellensia ad orbem Graeco-Latinum pertinentia*, Leuven 1987, pp. 95–102. For the finds of wooden vessels in tombs, see Rolle, *Totenkult* I 1, p. 180; *Narody*, p. 204. περιστίξαντες: Dobree's emendation, πέριξ στήσαντες, should not be overlooked (περιστείξαντες = making turn around, suggested by C. Saerens, *Euphrosyne*, XVII (1989), 235–44, has no parallels). The slaves are 'set around' the vessels and 'turn' the milk, while all the other tasks must be performed by the Scythians themselves.   τούτων... νομάδες: it is cynically implied that the Scythians only needed the slaves as a motive-power to 'centrifuge' the milk and not—as the Greeks did—for more complex agricultural tasks, and this made it feasible to blind them.

3,2. τάφρον: 20,1 seems to suggest that the trench ran north–south in order to stop the Scythians coming in from the Kerč' Strait (along a well-known route, cf. 28,1 and M. Ju. Vachtina *et al.*, *VDI* CLIV (1980), 155–61). Among the several remains of fortifications attested in the Kerč' Peninsula, the Akmonajskij val, which has been described by ancient travellers but is no longer traceable (cf. also B. Hemmerdinger, *Boll. dei Classici. Acc. Nazionale dei Lincei*, IX (1988), 54–6), fits the description better than the ramparts further east at Uzunlar and Tyritake. From Theodosia the Akmonajskij val must have reached to the base of the Arabat: if Dobree's conjecture of τῇ περ is accepted, this terminal point must have been viewed as the furthest from the 'bottom' of the Azov Sea, i.e. the mouth of the Don (see V. S. Ol'chovskij, *SA* (1981), 3, pp. 60–1; A. A. Maslennikov, *SA* (1983), 3, pp. 14–22); but Herodotus probably included in the trench also the lagoon of Sivaš (Stein, ad loc.). The transmitted text (ἥπερ ἔστι μεγίστη) seems instead hardly defensible, unless it does not mean '[the trench] which is the largest of all', and Herodotus tacitly assumes knowledge of the other trenches (for the linguistic usage, cf. e.g. Strabo VI 2,1).

4. νῦν... αὐτῶν: the spear and the bow were the most common Scythian weapons; see Meljukova, *Vooruženie*, pp. 14–45. Whips are also well attested in the archaeological record (see e.g. Talbot Rice, p. 130; *Narody*, p. 206).

4. οὕτως... στράτευμα: picks up 1,1 in ring composition. Then the long *excursus* on the Scythians begins, and the theme of Darius' expedition will not be taken up again until 83,1.

5–7. Herodotus opens with a fragment of Scythian 'folklore': see Norden, pp. 42 ff., 115 ff.; Aly, pp. 115–20; Raevskij, pp. 19 ff.; F. Thordarson, *SO* LXXI (1996), 42–58; LXXII (1997), 91–101; a variant in Diod. II 43. The theme of the first man and of his three sons has various parallels throughout the Indo-European world, and is probably connected with the Indo-Iranian division into the three functions of priest-king, warrior, and economic operator: see A. Christensen, *Les Types du premier homme et du premier roi dans l'histoire légendaire des Iraniens*, Leiden–Uppsala 1917–34; Dumézil, *Romans des Scythes*, pp. 169–211; Dumézil, *Mythe*, pp. 446–52 with bibl.; G. Holzer, *AAW* CXXV (1988), 193–213; the origin of the Germanic race is described in similar terms by Tacitus, *Germ.* 2–4 (see R. Wenskus, *Stammesbildung und Verfassung. Das Werden der frühmittelalterlichen gentes*, Cologne–Vienna 1977², pp. 147 ff.). But it is also found elsewhere: see e.g. H. Usener, *RhM* LVIII (1903), 6 ff.; Alföldi, pp. 42–68. Also the fall of incandescent objects from the sky has many parallels: see Dumézil and Alföldi, locc. citt.; K. Meuli, *Hermes*, LXX (1935), 160–1; R. Merkelbach, *Studien zur antiken Sozialgeschichte. Festschrift F. Vittinghoff*, Cologne 1980, pp. 93–4. Perhaps the objects are connected with the role of fire in Iranic royal ideology: M. L. Carter, *AI* I (1974), 171–202; Raevskij, pp. 87 ff.; cf. D. Briquel, *L'Épopée gréco-latine et ses prolongements européens*, Paris 1981, pp. 7–31. They are in fact used in the investiture of the youngest son, a typical folkloric theme (see also VIII 137), which here is perhaps linked to a law of succession of the youngest, characteristic of nomadic societies (cf. Alföldi, p. 50; Chazanov, pp. 94–8; F. Schlette, *EAZ* XXVIII (1987), 246). It is uncertain whether there is a relation between these first three clans and the geographical division of the Scythians into farmers, nomads, and 'royals' in chs. 16 ff. (E. Benveniste, *JA* CCXXX (1938), 534–7; for the opposite view, Dumézil). The only actual division of territory is that between the three sons of Colaxais, and produces the 'three kingdoms' of chs. 120 ff. (a division typical among nomadic societies; see Merkelbach, op. cit., pp. 89–90; Chazanov, pp. 127–30 and *passim*). Perhaps the original trifunctional legend was adapted when the 'royal' Scythians reached the region in a resettlement along the Dnieper which confirmed the subjugation of the pre-existing communities. See most recently Chazanov, pp. 36–54; A. M. Khazanov, *IA* XVII (1982), 49–63; esp. A. I. Ivantchik, *REG* CXII (1999), 141–92; less verifiable conjectures in W. Brandenstein, *Wiener Zeitschrift für die Kunde des Morgenlandes*, LII (1953–5), 183–211.

5,1. νεώτατον: see 7,1 and cf. II 2,1. According to Justin II,1 the Scythians are the most ancient people.   **Ταργίταον**: explained with the Iranic **darga-tava-*, 'which has great might', by V. I. Abaev, *Osetinskij jazyk i fol'klor*, I, Moscow 1949, p. 163. The connection with Τιργαταώ in Polyaenus VIII 55 and with *Tirgutawija* in a Mitannic text (O. N. Trubačëv, *VopJaz* (1976), 4, p. 60) is uncertain: cf. E. A. Grantovskij and D. S. Raevskij, in *Etnogenez*, p. 52; *Narody*, pp. 207–8.   **Δία...θυγατέρα**: Zeus is the Papaeus mentioned at 59,2. The worship of Borysthenes = Dnieper is already attested in an Olbian inscription of the 6th cent.: see A. S. Rusjaeva and Ju. G. Vinogradov, in *Gold der Steppe*, pp. 201–2; cf. Vinogradov, *Olbia*, Constance 1981, p. 15, and *SEG* XXX 913 = *IGDOP* 82. The daughter of Borysthenes can be linked with Api, goddess of earth and water and wife of Papaeus according to ch. 59, and also with the snake-woman of chs. 8–10; cf. Raevskij, pp. 46 ff.

2. Λιπόξαϊν...Κολάξαϊν: the Iranic form *xšāy-*, 'to be sovereign', is discernible in the second element of the names, while the first element is unclear. Cf. Dumézil, *Romans des Scythes*, pp. 191–2 with bibl. F. Cornillot, *Studia Iranica*, X (1981), 7–52; A. I. Ivantchik, *REG* CXII (1999), 141–92. Alcman (fr. 1,59 Davies) speaks of a horse Κολαξαῖος which is probably Scythian (G. Devereux, *CQ* LIX (1965), 176–84).

3. ἄροτρόν τε...φιάλην: cf. Curtius Rufus VII 8, 17–18: plough, yoke, cup = *patera*, spear, and arrow are related to the working of the land, worship, and war. Plough and yoke constitute a unit (E. Benveniste, *JA* CCXXX (1938), 532–4). War axes, which were used also by the Asiatic Sakā (see VII 61), are well represented in Scythian funerary contexts (cf. Meljukova, *Vooruženie*, pp. 65–8). Libations made with a cup (but the φιάλη = *patera* is a bowl; see H. Luschey, *Die Phiale*, Munich 1939; F. Brommer, *Hermes* CXV (1987), 8, 11; cf. 10,3) have retained a sacred and honorific value among several nomadic peoples; see A. Alföldi, *Folia Archaeologica*, III–IV (1941), 166–8; cf. 62,3; 66; 70.

6,1. ἀπὸ μὲν ... Παραλάται: Pliny, *NH* IV 48, VI 22 and 50, mentions the *Auchatae* and the *Cotieri* in his muddled lists of peoples; but they are rather 'castes' or 'classes'; see Dumézil, *Romans des Scythes*, pp. 172–83. Παραλάται recalls the Avestic *Paraδāta*, 'placed before', the epithet of a priest-king; and Τράσπιες can be related to the Avestic *Drvāspā*, 'of the mighty horses', while the rest of the names are more obscure: cf. Dumézil, *Romans des Scythes*, pp. 181–3; A. I. Ivantchik, *REG* CXII (1999), 148–55 (less certain combinations in H. Kothe, *Klio*, XLVIII (1967), 61–79; LI (1969), 15–88).

2. σύμπασι ... ὠνόμασαν: Σκόλοτοι (cf. Σκύλης; *Scolopitus* in Justin II 4) appears to be the Scythian variant of a form **skuδa-* (perhaps from the root *sku = 'to make move': 'the archers' or 'the nimble ones'), which is also the root of Σκύθαι and of the *Aškuzai/Iškuzai* found in Assyrian inscriptions. See Szemerényi, with bibl.; I. M. Diakonoff, *AI* XXI (1981), 137–8 (for different hypotheses see also F. Cornillot, *Indo-Iranian J.*, XXIII (1981), 29–39; A. V. Nazarenko, *Drevnejšie gosudarstva na territorii SSSR. 1987 g.*, Moscow 1989, pp. 233–7).

τοῦ βασιλέος ἐπωνυμίην: the transmitted text ('from the name *of the* king') presents some difficulties, unless Herodotus linked Σκόλοτοι to Κολάξαις; Greek ethnography normally traced names of peoples back to mythical eponymous kings (cf. Norden, pp. 324–6). S. Medaglia emends to τευ βασιλέος ἐπωνυμίην ('from the name of *a* king'); if the three words are not a gloss, they could be transposed after ὠνόμασαν so as to refer to the name Σκύθης (Th. Reinach, *REG* XXXIX (1916), 11–13).

7,1. χιλίων: a typical number; cf. Bessonova, p. 12; M. V. Skržinskaja, *VDI* CXCI (1989), pp. 79–81.

1–2. τὸν δὲ χρυσὸν ... αὐτός: the 'watch' appears to be an ordeal to test the priest-king's magic powers of protection of the community: see O. Glaser, *Archiv für Religionswissenschaft*, XXXIV (1937), 277–93; E. Norden, *Aus altrömischen Priesternbüchern*, Lund 1939, pp. 153–7; Alföldi, pp. 52, 188–94). An Ossetian parallel in Dumézil, *Le Livre*, pp. 24 ff. The concession of a piece of land must be interpreted as a means to isolate and confine the man who is predestined to die (οἱ = the one who has fallen asleep; cf. Paus. VIII 38,6); not as a reward for the king who completes the trial successfully.

3. τὰ δὲ ... ὄψιν: in the mythical narrative of the Scythians the original division of land ended with a mention of the northern borders, which Herodotus will discuss at ch. 31.

8–10. The legend is perhaps epic in origin, rather than local (cf. Fehling, pp. 45–6; Heracles already appears as forefather of the Scythians in Hesiod, fr. 150, 15–16

Merkelbach–West; a variant in the *Tabula Albani*, *IG* XIV 1293 A 93 ff., cf. Diod. II
43 and Val. Flacc. VI 48 ff.). Its aim is to assimilate the origins of the barbarian
people to Greek mythology: see E. J. Bickerman, *CPh* XLVII (1952), 65–81. As the
travelling hero par excellence (see L. Lacroix, *BAB* LX (1974), 34–60), Heracles was
the subject of many such 'myths of precedence': for a list, F. Brommer, *Herakles
II. Die unkanonische Taten des Helden*, Darmstadt 1984, pp. 142–3. Moreover, the
bow and the belt which were his traditional attributes (see A. Furtwängler, in
Roscher, *Lexikon* I, col. 2147; A. Violante, *Acme*, XXXVI (1983), 191–3), as well as
the recurrence of the golden cup of the Sun in the myth of Geryon (see Lacroix, art.
cit., pp. 53 ff.; Brommer, op. cit., pp. 105–6), made him an appropriate ancestor for
the Scythians. Heracles was especially worshipped in the region and seems to have
been the *interpretatio Graeca* of a Scythian hero, possibly Targitaus (see note to
59,1), while the legend as a whole appears to be an elaboration of local elements
into a Greek framework. Cf. Dumézil, *La Courtisane*, pp. 78–89, correcting
Raevskij, pp. 19–86 (who fails to convince in his attempt to relate to this legend
the scenes represented on the vases from Kul' Oba and Voronež (Hermitage inv.
KO 11; Kiev MIDU inv. AZS-2358); cf. *SA* (1970), 3, pp. 90–101 and I. Marazov,
VDI CLXXXVII (1988), 103–9. See now M. Visintin, *MD* XLV (2000), 43–81;
A. M. Ivantchik, in V. Fromentin and S. Gotteland (eds.), *Origines gentium*,
Bordeaux 2001, pp. 207–20.

8,1–2. Ἡρακλέα... ἀποδεικνῦσι: the myth of Geryon had been told by Hesiod,
Theog. 287 ff., 979 ff., and subsequently by Stesichorus, Peisander, Panyassis,
and Pherecydes; it was also very popular in figurative art (see A. Rumpf, *EAA*
III 1960, pp. 845–6, s.v. 'Gerione'; *LIMC* IV 1, pp. 186–90; V 1, pp. 73–85). Unlike
Hecataeus (*FGrHist* 1 F 26; cf. V. Ehrenberg, *Klio* XVI (1919), 327–31), Herodotus locates the mythical island of Erythia near Gadeira = Cadiz (on the dispute
over Ocean, see 36,2). On his return journey Heracles was said to have gone
through the most diverse regions (see O. Gruppe, *RE* Suppl. III 1918, coll.
1061 ff.). The form Γηρυόναο βόας found in some of the mss, though not Ionic,
could be accepted as an epic reminiscence.

3. ἵππους: we would expect a theft of cattle as in analogous myths (see Aly, pp.
120–2); the mares and the chariot give a more 'Scythian' touch.

9,1. μεξοπάρθενόν... διφυέα: Hesiod, *Theog.* 295 ff., had spoken of a serpent-
woman, Ἔχιδνα (a proper name in the *Tabula Albani*; cf. *LIMC* V 1, p. 115).
Here, in the Greek rendition, she is a manifestation of the 'great goddess' of
fertility and nature, of whom there are several representations in the Scythian
region: see M. I. Rostovtzeff, *REG* XXXII (1919), 462–81; G. Azarpay Laws, *AJA*
LXV (1961), 31–5; V. P. Petrov and M. L. Makarevič, *SA* (1963), 1, pp. 23–31;
Bessonova, pp. 93–8; F. Schlette, *EAZ* XXVIII (1987), 244–5 (cf. ch. 59 (ill. 35–6)).
The chthonic element of the cavern (also in Hesiod) must be purely mythical: in
the region caves are found only around the Moločnaja, but the region called
Hylaea (for which see note on 18,1) would not have reached that far.

4–5. τούτους... ποιήσεις: the trial which the sons must undergo on coming of age to prove themselves worthy of their father recalls the saga of Theseus, who when he has come of age takes possession of the sword and of the sandals purposely left him by his father Aegeus (cf. Plutarch, *Thes.* 3 ff.; D. Briquel, *RHR* CC (1983), 67–74). But while Theseus reaches his father, Scythes remains in possession of his mother's land.   ὧδε: the Scythians bent their bows in a special way, by drawing the bowstring to the shoulder, cf. Plato, *Leg.* VII 795a, and the scholia on *Il.* IV 122–3 and VIII 325. The Scythian bow had a double curvature; see Meljukova, *Vooruženie*, pp. 14–34; E. V. Černenko, *Skifskie lučniki*, Kiev 1982; H. Eckhardt, in *Gold der Steppe*, pp. 143–6; cf. the scenes on the vase from Kul' Oba (Hermitage inv. KO 11).

10,1. δύο...Ἡρακλέα: Herodotus wants to explain how Heracles continued thereafter to possess a bow.   Ἀγάθυρσον...Γελωνόν: eponyms of other peoples of the region; see the notes on 48,4 and 108–9.

3. ἀπό μὲν... Σκύθῃ: bowls (cf.5,3) hanging from belts are attested among Eurasian nomads in later times. See e.g. Gy. László and I. Rácz, *Der Goldschatz von Nagyszentmiklós*, Budapest–Vienna–Munich 1983, pp. 159–69; cf. Gy. László, *Études archéologiques sur l'histoire de la société des Avars*, Budapest 1955, pp. 158–85. There is, however, no iconographic confirmation for the Scythians, with whom the *rhyton* is often associated (cf. I. G. Elagina, *SA* (1959), 2, pp. 195–6; Bessonova, pp. 103–7; V. A. Rjabova, in *Gold der Steppe*, pp. 153–6); but the golden bowls found at Bratoljubovka and Kul'Oba, for instance, dating respectively from the 5th and the 4th cent. BC, have some hooks from which they could be hung, possibly from a belt (*Gold der Steppe*, cat. no. 120e, cf. A. I. Kubyšev, *Hamburger Beitr. zur Archäologie*, XVIII (1991), 131–40; Hermitage, inv. KO 31; T. M. Kuznecova, in *Kul'tura i iskusstvo narodov Vostoka*, Moscow 1987, pp. 57–9 wants to regard the 'Kelermes mirror', Hermitage, inv. 1904 1/27, as a φιάλη). Might the presence of a cup (φιάλη in Panyassis, according to Athenaeus XI 469c) in the myth of Geryon have had some influence? On the bulky Scythian belts see E. V. Černenko, *Skifskij dospech*, Kiev 1968, pp. 57–73, 148–50; on the likewise symbolic importance of belts in ancient Iranian societies, G. Widengren, *Der Feudalismus im alten Iran*, Cologne–Opladen 1969, pp. 21–30; A. M. Ivantchik, *REG* CXII (1999), 184–9. The last sentence seems corrupt: a suggestion might be φορέειν Σκύθας, τῇ δὴ μοῦνον μηχανᾶσθαι (τὸν) Σκύθην, 'the Scythians bear cups in the manner in which Scythes alone was able to arrange his'.

11–12. The arrival of the Scythians from the east, under the pressure of other peoples, has seemed plausible also to many modern scholars, given the instability of Eurasian nomads at the beginning of the 1st millennium (see e.g Talbot Rice, pp. 36–8; A. V. Matveev, in *Skifskaja epocha Altaja*, Barnaul 1986, pp. 85–8), and also on account of the parallel with nomadic waves which came from Asia in other historical periods. However, there is no archaeological record for a large-scale migration on the northern coast of the Black Sea in the 8th cent. (i.e. just before Cimmerian and Scythian penetration into Media), while the 'classical'

Scythian civilization does not develop until the end of the 7th cent. (with the return from Media). Anthropological data indicate a substantial continuity between the civilization of the bronze age (the so-called *srubnaja*) and Scythian civilization: see e.g. Martynov–Alekseev, pp. 38–60; bibl. in A. Häusler, *Altertum*, XXVII (1981), 49–54 and *Narody*, pp. 215–16. If the hypothesis of the arrival from Asia is not to be entirely abandoned in favour of the autochtonous origin of which the legends speak, then it must be supposed that Herodotus has compressed the chronology of events, and that the arrival of the Scythians corresponds to the penetration by the *srubnaja* civilization from the Volga and the Don during the second half of the 2nd millenium (see e.g. T. Sulimirski, *Bull. Inst. Archaeology of London*, XI (1959), 46–57; *CHI* II, pp. 165–73). Or else the arrival of the 'Scythians' during the 8th cent. must be held to have left little trace because they were nomads (cf. τοὺς νομάδας at 11,1) and blended into a very similar ethnic, cultural, and perhaps also linguistic (discussion in N. L. Členova, in *Etnogenez*, pp. 259–67) substratum, until (owing to Near Eastern influence) their culture presents a sharper picture after their stay in Media: see e.g. R. Rolle, *Saeculum*, XXVIII (1977), 307 ff.; A. M. Khazanov, *IA* XVII (1982), 57–63. Hence the composite character of the Scythian dominions, where farming peoples existed side by side with nomads (chs. 16 ff.). A recent overview in V. Yu. Murzin and S. A. Skory, *Il Mar Nero* I (1994), 55–98.

11,1. Σκύθας...Κιμμερίην: it seems here that the Volga lies behind the confused notion of 'Araxes' (cf. 40,1). The Massagetae (cf. I 201 ff.) must be located to the east of the Aral or between the Aral and the Caspian: see I. P. P'jankov, *VDI* CXXXII (1975), 46–70; Th. David, *DHA* II (1976), 133–8; *Narody*, pp. 181–3, n. 37.   **Κιμμερίων**: the 'Cimmerians' are already mentioned in the *Odyssey* (XI 14–16). Various Greek authors recount their deeds in Libya and Phrygia (cf. I 15), while the Eastern sources speak of the land of *Gāmīr* to the north-east of Armenia at the end of the 8th cent. BC, and of the presence of the *Gimirrāi* in Anatolia (see F. Lehmann-Haupt, *RE* XI 1921, coll. 397–434; I. M. Diakonoff, *AI* XXI (1981), 103–22). Herodotus wants to prove that they originally dwelt by the Black Sea on the basis of place-names: the concentration of these in the area of the straits (cf. Strabo XI 2,5) might be an indication that there the Greeks met the last remaining Cimmerians (see e.g. Gajdukevič, pp. 36 ff.; A. A. Maslennikov, *SA* (1980), 1, pp. 5–17; *VDI* CLV (1981), 150–62). But the names might have been suggested only by the reminiscence of an ancient presence no longer to be encountered: hence also the designation of 'Cimmerian tombs' for what must have been monuments of unknown origin on the Tyres = Dniester. In fact, attempts to identify the Cimmerians with an archaeological civilization (such as the civilization of the catacombs which preceded the *srubnaja*, e.g. Artamonov, *Kimmerijcy*; or the *srubnaja* itself, e.g. Terenožkin; see the doxography in *Narody*, pp. 169–73; Nejchardt, pp. 66–78) are not entirely convincing, to the extent that it has been supposed that this location is purely legendary (Cozzoli), or that it refers only to the period which followed the stay in Asia (A. K. G. Kristensen, *Who Were the Cimmerians, and Where Did They Come From? Sargon II, the Cimmerians,* *and Rusa I*, Copenhagen 1988). According to A. I. Ivančik, *Antičnaja Balkanistika*, Moscow 1987, pp. 48–55, the report of a clash between the Scythians and the Cimmerians, drawn from Aristeas (see ch. 13), referred in fact to Asia Minor. It is more likely that the Cimmerians were nomads who reached the Pontus at the same time as the Scythians, or shortly before them, and thence made their way into Asia—probably without women or children: cf. chs. 1–4—where they merged with the local peoples: cf. I. M. Diakonoff, *AI* XXI (1981), 122–40 (explaining the name through the Iranic *gām-īra-* = 'mobile unit'); I. V. Kuklina, *VDI* CLVI (1981), 162–73. See now G. B. Lanfranchi, *I Cimmeri. Emergenza delle élites militari iraniche nel Vicino Oriente (VIII–VII sec. a.C.)*, Padua 1990; A. I. Ivantchik, *Les Cimmeriens au Proche Orient*, Fribourg 1993 (rev. Russian edn.: A. I. Ivančik, *Kimmerijcy. Drevnevostočnye civilizacii i stepnye kočevniki v VIII–VII vekach do n.e.*, Moscow 1996).

2–4. τοὺς δὲ...χώρην: some have supposed a reminiscence of ritual fights between kings invested with priestly functions (see L. A. El'nickij, *Znanija drevnich o severnich stranach*, Moscow 1961, pp. 99 ff.), but the chieftains' noble choice to die has a faint parallel in Ossetian epic (cf. Dumézil, *Romans des Scythes*, pp. 277–81). The legend—coherent with the *topos* according to which barbarians prefer suicide to captivity (see Strabo III 4,17)—is employed to explain the existence of ancient tombs on the Dniester (Aly, pp. 122–3), for which, however, there is no archaeological evidence.   δεόμενον: a form of impersonal δεῖσθαι = δεῖν infrequently attested (F. Solmsen, *Glotta*, II (1910), 301–5), or else to be taken in agreement with πρῆγμα (Lat. *res poscit*: see J. Schweighäuser, *Lexicon Herodoteum*, London 1830², p. 80). But alternative readings in the manuscript tradition suggest that the text is corrupt (Reiske conjectured δεομένων, Buttman δέοι μένοντας).

12,1. καὶ νῦν...καλεόμενος: 'Cimmerian Bosphorus' was the Greek name current for the Strait of Kerč' (the local name was perhaps *Pantikapa*, cf. ch. 54); while the 'Cimmerian paths' (cf. 45,2) corresponded to the northern part, the Strait of Enikale, where the crossing was easier and the village of Πορθμίον was situated (see *PECS*, pp. 729–30; *Archeologija SSSR*, pp. 69–70): cf. S. R. Tochtas'ev, in *Etnogenez*, pp. 143–4. 'Cimmeria' must signify the eastern extremity of Tauris (ibid., p. 144) or else the north-western part of the Taman' Peninsula (Stein, ad loc.); while in Herodotean usage (cf. VII 108,2 and 112) and in the tradition of the *periploi* (see Peretti, p. 96) Κιμμέρια τείχεα can indicate a series of fortified coastal towns (cf. the *oppida Cimmeria* in Pomponius Mela II 3; on the ramparts and trenches of eastern Crimea see A. A. Maslennikov, *SA* (1983), 3, pp. 14–22). On the history of the region see F. V. Šelov-Kovedjaev, in *Drevnejšie gosudarstva na territorii SSSR. 1984 g.*, Moscow 1985, pp. 5–187. On the settlements on the Cimmerian Bosphorus see now G. Tsetskhladze, in Nielsen, pp. 39–81.

2–3. φαίνονται...τραφθέντες: the course along the narrow and densely wooded eastern coast of the Black Sea is highly unlikely (Herodotus cannot have had first-hand knowledge of the area; see H. Matzat, *Hermes*, VI (1872), 417). A crossing of the Caucasus has been suggested (e.g. I. M. Diakonoff, *AI* XXI (1981), 135–6; bibl. in *Narody*, pp. 218–19); while the passage of the Scythians through the

Derbent route might be accounted for by the need to avoid the Caucasian and Urartu peoples (V. B. Vinogradov, *Central'nij i Severo-Vostočnij Kavkaz v skifskoe vremja (VII–IV vv. do n.e.)*, Groznyj 1972, pp. 11 ff.). Traces of a Scythian kingdom can be detected in Azerbajdžan (Diakonoff, art. cit., pp. 119–21; for the opposite view, e.g. M. N. Pogrebova, *DHA* X (1984), 269–84).   Σινώπη: on the Cimmerians in Paphlagonia (cf. Strabo XII 3,8; Pseudo-Scymnus 948 ff., *GGM* I, p. 236) as well as in Bithynia and in the Troad see Cozzoli, pp. 100–2; Diakonoff, art. cit., pp. 104–11 (who discusses the Armenian *Gamirk'* = Cappadocia). The Greek colonization of Sinope does not seem datable to before the 7th cent. (G. R. Tsetskhladze, in Tsetskhladze–De Angelis, pp. 115–16; Boardman, *Greeks Overseas*, pp. 240–2; see, however, R. Drews, *JHS* XCVI (1976), 18–31). On the etymology, which can be linked to the Scythian word for 'wine', see Dumézil, *Romans des Scythes*, pp. 241–6; *Le Manuscrit de Roman Ghirsman: Les Cimmériens et leur Amazones*, ed. Th. de Sonneville-David, Paris 1983, pp. 38–9 and *passim*.   ξυνὸς Ἑλλήνων τε καὶ βαρβάρων: Herodotus must have heard the story from a Greek who drew it from a local source (see Aly, p. 122 and n. 2, who suggests Hecataeus).

13,1. Ἀριστέης ... Προκοννήσιος: evidence and fragments in *PEG* I, pp. 144–54; *EGF*, pp. 243–7. The dating of Aristeas is uncertain; 15,1 seems to suggest a fairly early date (8th or 7th cent.); in this case Aristeas would have been one of the first colonizers of Proconnesus, the modern-day island of Marmara (but perhaps the first colony was on one of the nearby islands: see G. Huxley, *GRBS* XXVII (1986), 153–5; Ehrhardt, pp. 38–40 with bibl.; Müller II, pp. 909–12): cf. Bolton, pp. 1–73. *Suidas* s.v. (α 3900 A.), dates him instead to the 6th cent., while stylistic analysis of the surviving fragments suggests a late date: see now A. I. Ivančik, *VDI* CLXXXIX (1989), 29–49; *AC* LXI (1993), 35–67. The mystical character of Aristeas' poem and his magical disappearances had caused him to be mythologized in Pythagorean circles (cf. Bolton, pp. 142–75), therefore Herodotus could offer no more than conjectures.   Καϋστροβίου: this name is modelled on that of the river Caystrus in Ionia; the second element is perhaps Anatolian in origin: see Huxley, art. cit., p. 154, n. 9.   φοιβόλαμπτος γενόμενος: in his poem (ποιέων ἔπεα) Aristeas declared that he had travelled as far as the Issedones 'possessed by Apollo': Herodotus' phrase might summarize a proem which described a shamanic flight: cf. Maximus of Tyre 38,3c; W. Burkert, *Gnomon*, XXXV (1963), 238–40; K. Dowden, *REG* XCIII (1980), 491. According to Bolton, pp. 134–41, this simply refers to the frenzied inspiration needed to make a journey to the 'Apollinean' northern regions; cf. N. Himmelmann-Wildschütz, ΘΕΟΛΗ ΠΤΟΣ, Marburg–Lahn 1957; W. R. Connor, *Class Ant* VII (1988), 155–89; Introduction, pp. 548–53. Apollo was greatly worshipped at Proconnesus; see Ehrhardt, pp. 40, 134–5.

1–2. Ἰσσεδόνων ... Σκύθῃσι: Aristeas too had spoken of the arrival of the Scythians from the East, spurred on by other peoples; but these peoples, aside from the Issedones, seemed to Herodotus to be legendary rather than real (cf. III 116,1–2). On the Issedones see chs. 25–6. On the Arimaspeans, ch. 27. On the

Hyperboreans, chs. 32–5: their uninvolvement in the chain of aggressions is evidence that they were idealized as a peaceful people already by Aristeas; the 'sea' beside which they dwell is the northern Ocean, in contrast with the 'southern sea', which is here the Black Sea; cf. ch. 37.

14,1–3. *Ἀριστέην...τὸ δεύτερον:* Aristeas shares the ability to disappear and reappear, and to be simultaneously in two places, with other 'wizard' figures (*γόητες:* see W. Burkert, *RhM* CV (1962), 36–55) such as e.g. Hermotimus of Clazomenae: see among others Rohde, p. 300; Burkert, pp. 120–65. A link with the shamanism of Central Asia (see e.g. K. Meuli, *Hermes*, LXX (1935), 137–76; Dodds, pp. 135 ff.; Levi, pp. 108–32) is doubted by J. Bremmer, *The Early Greek Concept of the Soul*, Princeton 1983, pp. 24–53. In the story told by Herodotus we have, not a journey of the soul such as that of Hermotimus (Pliny, *NH* VII 174), but rather a magic volatilization also of the body, as was the case e.g. with Cleomedes of Astypaleia (see Plutarch, *Rom.* 28; A. S. Pease, *HSCPh* LIII (1942), 1–36; L. Lacroix, in *Mélanges P. Lévêque*, I, Paris 1988, pp. 183–98). *κναφήιον:* the fuller's shop might symbolize purification and regeneration (cf. e.g. the ritual washing of the Pythagoreans, Diog. Laert. VIII 33; or the *βάπται* = "those who immerse" at Athens, see *PCG* V, pp. 331 ff.). *συντυχεῖν:* the meeting would have taken place at Artace (modern-day Erdek: see Erhardt, p. 38; Müller II, pp. 785–7, 864–7), which was the landing-point on the route to Cyzicus: this is why the place is mentioned. In order for the man from Cyzicus to arrive at Proconnesus in time (cf. Bolton, p. 133; Huxley, *GRBS* XXVII (1986), 151–3) we must suppose that the fuller's shop was imagined as being outside the town, near a spring. *Ἀριμάσπεα:* the title (not the original one according to Herodotus, see Bolton, pp. 20–38) described the subject-matter, namely the myths about the Arimaspeans which were told by the Issedones. A similar title is *Κύπρια*; see *PEG* I, p. 38.

15,1. *τάδε δὲ...εὕρισκον:* in the Pythagorean circles of Metapontum the Apollinean poet must have been transformed into a hero capable of metempsychosis: see Bolton, pp. 174–5. It is uncertain whether there occurred contamination with the mythical hero and son of Apollo, Aristeus (Diod. IV 82): see A. I. Ivančik, *VDI* CLXXXIX (1989), 45–8 with bibl. The 240 years counted back from an event which is not immediately contemporaneous with Herodotus (cf. *νῦν* below) bring us to a date which is perhaps too early for the events at Proconnesus (see Rohde, pp. 329–30, n. 110); but it is not possible to emend *συγκυρήσαντα* to *συγκυρήσας* (E. Schwyzer, *PhW* (1922), col. 528) in order to start counting back from Herodotus' time: see Bolton, p. 131. Perhaps the 'Aristeas' who appeared at Metapontum spoke of seven generations (number sacred to Apollo, cf. Roscher, *AGWL*, p. 7) from which Herodotus calculated, with some adjustements on the basis of the facts of Proconnesus, 240 years (the variant of 340 is rendered unreliable by the indirect tradition).

2. *κόραξ:* according to Pliny, *NH* VII 174, in Proconnesus Aristeas' soul flew away in the form of a crow. The bird as image of the soul (cf. e.g. Antoninus Liberalis I 6) recalls the world of the shamans: see e.g. K. Meuli, *Hermes*, LXX (1935), 157–8;

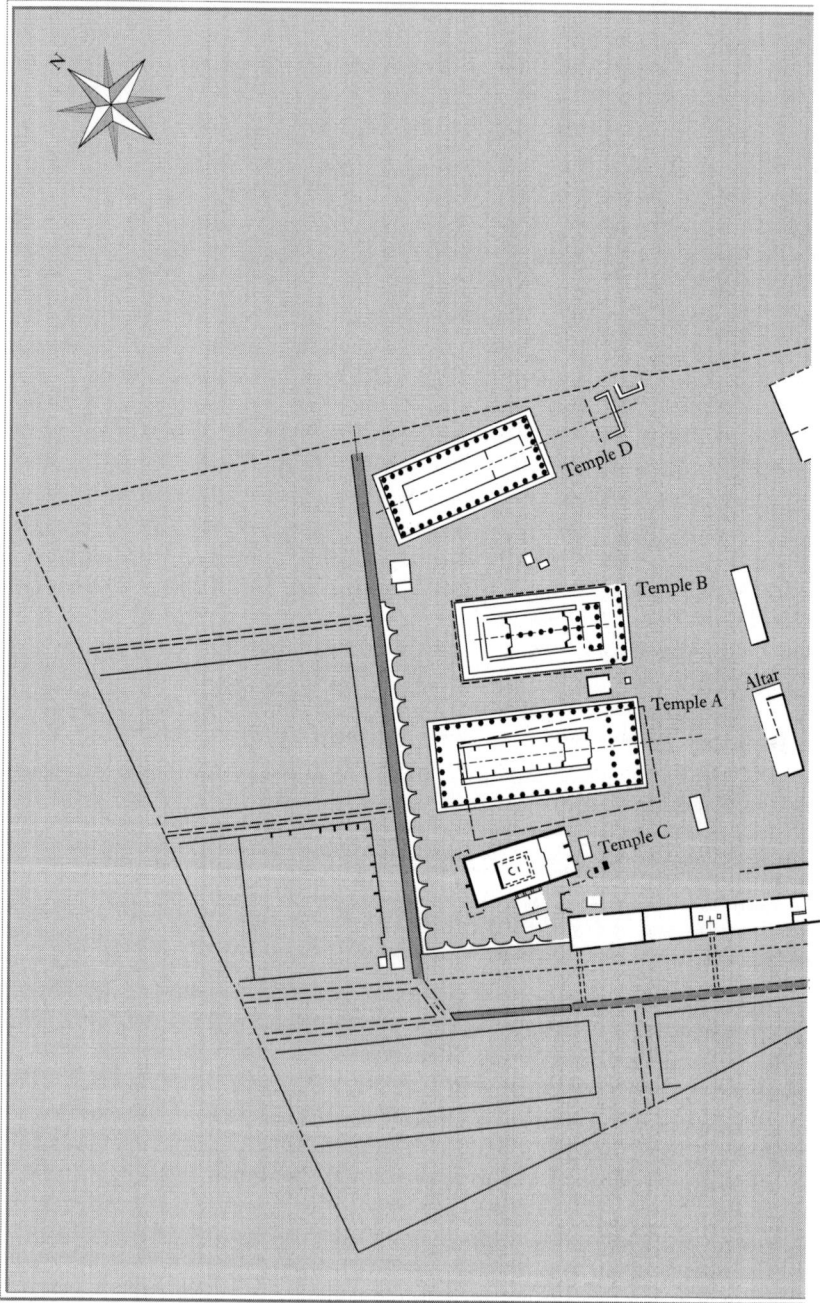

Map 38. Metapontum

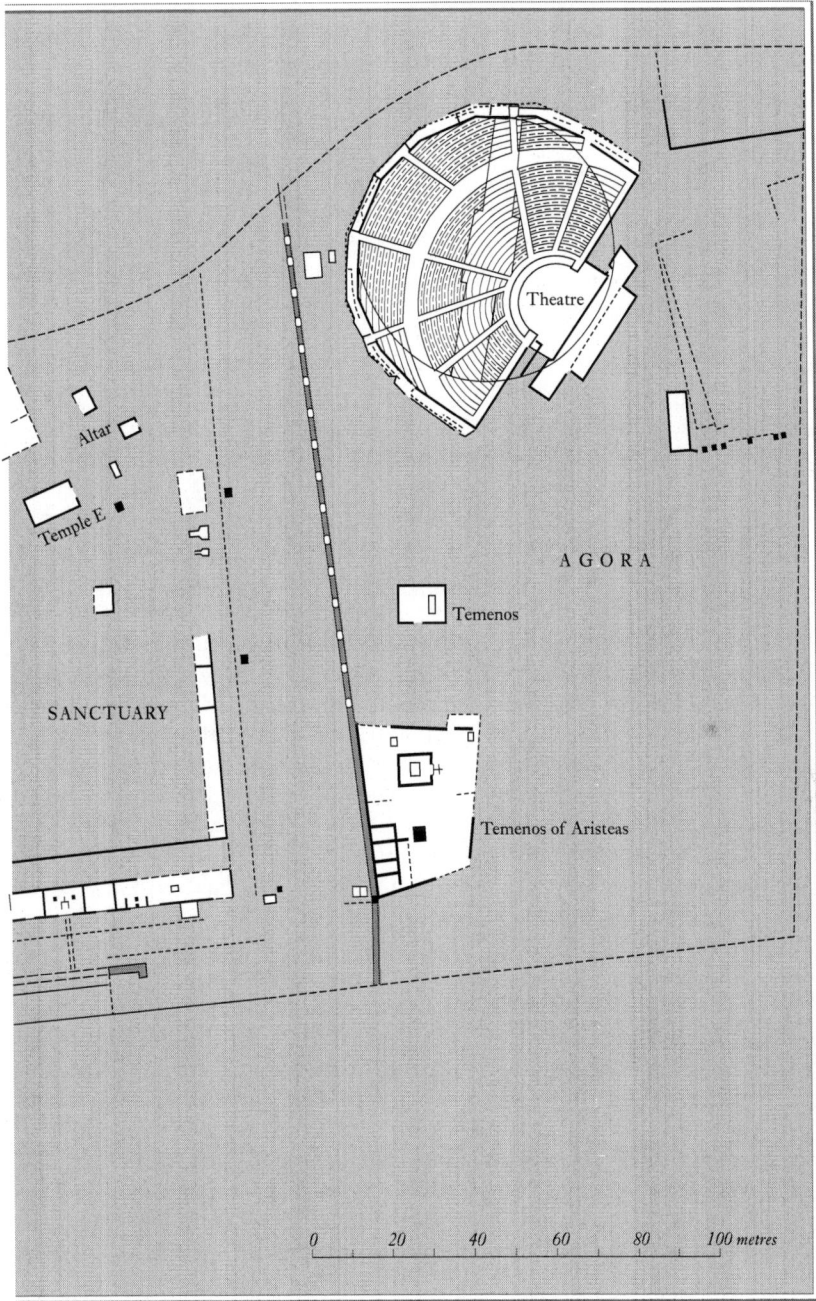

Theatre

AGORA

Altar

Temple E

Temenos

SANCTUARY

Temenos of Aristeas

0   20   40   60   80   100 metres

Testi dello sciamanesimo, pp. 118 and n. 1, 162–3; objections in Bremmer, op.cit., pp. 35–6. The crow was especially associated with Apollo: see O. Keel, *Vögel als Boten*, Freiburg–Göttingen 1977, pp. 79–91; Lindegger, p. 102, n. 2.

3. ἐς Δελφοὺς ... ἐπιτελέα: it was normal to consult the oracle at Delphi for such prodigies; see e.g. Paus. I 32,5, VI 9,6; Phlegon of Tralles, *Miracula* 3,5–6. On the formulaic ἄμεινον συνοίσεσθαι, cf. IV 156,2, V 82,1; 114,2.

4. καί νῦν ... ἵδρυται: the statue of Apollo with a laurel tree (of bronze according to Theopompus, *FGrHist* 115 F 248) may be depicted on some coins from Metapontum of the middle of the 5th cent. BC: see A. Stazio, in *Metaponto. Atti del XIII Convegno di Studi sulla Magna Grecia*, Naples 1974, pp. 82–4; S. P. Noe, *The Coinage of Metapontum*, New York 1984², pp. 56–7, nos. 314–20; cf. *LIMC* II 1, p. 217, no. 278, 'Apollon'. Its location in the *agora* (cf. E. Greco, *Magna Grecia*, Rome–Bari 1980, pp. 150–5; D. Mertens, *AA* (1985), 645–71) is now confirmed by findings of bronze leaves within a *temenos* of the 5th cent., which borders on the sanctuary area: Bottini, pp. 92–7; A. De Siena, in *Siritide e Metapontino. Storie di due territori coloniali*, Naples–Paestum 1998, pp. 156–9.

16–31. The information on the peoples beyond Scythia provided by Aristeas and by the legends is verified by Herodotus, so far as possible (ἐπὶ μακρότατον at 16,2 picked up by μακρότατα at 31,2 in ring composition), using the information drawn from local merchants (cf. ch. 24). The first step in such verification is the definition of the sources used by Aristeas, who had declared that he had first-hand knowledge only as far as the Issedones (cf. chs. 27 and 32; Introduction, pp. 548–9). This is followed by a list of the peoples who inhabit Scythia and the lands beyond Scythia that proceeds by longitudinal parallel 'strips', each defined by rivers: one after the other, these 'strips' are described beginning from the coast and reaching to the inner, unknown areas which are termed 'deserted'; see Jacoby, commentary to *FGrHist* I F 186–90; Harmatta, *Quellenstudien*; H. Edelmann, *Klio*, LII (1970), 79–86; on deserts see also J. Kolendo, *DHA* XVII (1991), 35–60. Herodotus borrows this system from a predecessor, probably Hecataeus (see Introduction); the indications of the days of travel probably originate in accounts of trade-routes. A day's journey by land equals 200 stades (between 35 and 42 km.) according to IV 100,1; while one day of navigation by river upstream can be computed as corresponding to a distance of between 24 and 36 km. (so Rybakov, pp. 28–9 and *passim*). However, the system of 'strips' distorted and simplified reality; and the numbers supplied by Herodotus, assuming that they are always realistic (cf. M. V. Skržinskaja, *VDI* CXCI (1989), 87–90), are not helpful for an accurate reconstruction of the geo-ethnographic situation of Scythia, among other reasons because of our ignorance of actual routes and travel conditions, as well as on account of the nomadic character of some peoples (L. A. Gindin, in *Etnogenez*, pp. 36–42, sees in the alternation of the verbs οἰκεῖν and νέμεσθαι a reference to the sedentary or nomadic nature of different peoples; but this represents more probably a stylistic variation modelled on the Homeric Catalogue of Ships: cf. schol. b on *Il.* II 494–877, p. 289.12–4 Erbse). Since at least the 18th cent. attempts have been made to locate the peoples mentioned by

Herodotus: this problem is closely linked to the identification of the rivers (see 47,2–58). The research by W. Tomaschek (*SAWW* CXVI (1888), 715–80; CXVII (1889), 1–70), F. Westberg (*Klio*, IV (1904), 182–92), and A. Herrmann (author of several entries in *RE*) has proved fundamental: cf. Minns, pp. 26–34, 101–14; K. Kretschmer, *RE* II A 1921, coll. 928 ff. During the last decades archaeology has supplied new material: see Il'inskaja–Terenožkin; *Archeologija Ukrainskoj SSR* II, Kiev 1986; *Stepi*, pp. 48–91; *Gold der Steppe, passim*. However, the identification of archaeological cultures (often difficult to differentiate from each other) with the peoples mentioned by Herodotus is by no means an easy task: see esp. Artamonov, *Etnogeografija*, and *Kimmerijcy*; I. V. Fabricius, *Archeologija*, V (1951), 50–80; Rybakov; Grakow, pp. 4 ff., 112 ff.; V. P. Jajlenko, *Sovetskaja Etnografija* (1983), 1, pp. 54–65. Brief overviews in *Narody*, pp. 222 ff.; Nejchardt, pp. 61–162; T. Sulimirski, in *CHI* II, pp. 149–53, 173 ff.; *Stepi*, pp. 40–8. Among other sources, Ephorus (*FGrHist* 70 F 158) agrees only in part with Herodotus and might be drawing on Hecataeus, as do perhaps also Pomponius Mela and Pliny: see Rostowzew, pp. 1–139; Harmatta, op. cit.; M. Plezia, *Eos*, L (1959–60), 27–42; P. Aalto and T. Pekkanen, *Latin Sources on North-Eastern Eurasia*, Wiesbaden 1975–80; Kuklina; J. R. Gardiner-Garden, *Historia*, XXXV (1986), 192–225; id., *Herodotos' Contemporaries on Scythian Geography and Ethnography*, Bloomington, Ind. 1987; id., *Ktesias on Early Central Asian History*, Bloomington, Ind. 1987; id., *Greek Conceptions of Inner Asian Geography and Ethnography from Ephoros to Eratosthenes*, Bloomington, Ind. 1987.

17,1. ἀπὸ τοῦ... Σκυθίης: the first 'strip' reaches along the Hypanis (the Southern Bug) while keeping to the west of the Borysthenes (the Dnieper, but see note to chs. 53–6). Its description begins with the southern edge, the coast, and with the central point represented by Olbia/Borysthenes (cf. ch. 101). The city stood on the right bank of the estuary of the Bug, which flows into the larger estuary of the Dnieper (cf. ch. 53). Βορυσθενεϊτέων ἐμπορίου: cf. ch. 24; it might indicate, not the urban centre in general (cf. ἄστυ at 78,3; πόλις at 79,2), but rather a dock, probably the present-day island of Berezan', where Milesian colonists planted their first settlement during the 7th cent., before spreading further along the coast: see Ju. G. Vinogradov, in *Chudožestvennaja kul'tura i archeologija antičnogo mira*, Moscow 1976, pp. 75–84; but in favour of a complete equivalence with the city of Olbia see J. Hind, in Nielsen, pp. 108–11. On Olbia and its history see among others E. Belin de Ballu, *Olbia. Cité antique du littoral Nord de la Mer Noire*, Leiden 1972; Wąsowicz; Ehrhardt, pp. 74–9; Vinogradov; Vinogradov–Križickij, with bibl. On Berezan' see now Solovyov. Καλλιππίδαι: the Callippidae (the name is probably Greek, 'of the beautiful horses') must have been Scythians who were to some extent hellenized. Ἕλληνες Σκύθαι: (the variant reading Ἑλληνοσκύθαι should be disregarded because it points to a later linguistic use) must be understood as 'Scythians (who are) Greeks'; cf. Ἑλλήνων Θρηίκων in Hecataeus, *FGrHist* I F 146 and Jacoby's note ad loc. Less likely is the possibility that such an expression defines a mixed ethnic group like the μιξέλληνες in *IOSPE* I 32 (see I. V. Šafranskaja, *VDI* LXVII (1956), 37–48; R. Hošek, *Listy Filologické*, CVI

(1983), 155–9). It is uncertain whether the Callippidae should be identified with the rural population of the Olbian *chora*, which dwelt along the estuary of the Bug in settlements that were Greek in nature but which had barbarian elements (cf. K. K. Marčenko, *SA* (1983), 1, pp. 67–79), or whether they were semi-nomads who dwelt in the steppes immediately to the north (A. S. Rusjaeva and M. V. Skržinkaja, *VDI* CL (1979), 25–36; V. M. Otreško, *SA* (1981), 1, pp. 26–41): see *Narody*, pp. 224–6; Nejchardt, pp. 96–101; *Stepi*, p. 45. Their territory reached westward as far as the river *Asiaces* (perhaps modern-day Tiligul) according to Pomponius Mela II 7; the Καρπίδες in Ephorus, *FGrHist* 70 F 158, settled along the Ister, sound like a distorted echo.   Ἀλιζῶνες: I prefer the reading Ἀλαζῶνες, which also appears in the grammatical tradition that goes back to Herodianus (see *Grammatici Graeci* III 1, pp. 27–8 Lentz; in Strabo XII 3,21 the text clearly needs to be amended); the reading ’Αλαζόνες, also attested in Pausanias at I 32,1, seems to me a banal rendition, while ’Αλιζῶνες is influenced by *Il.* II 856: cf. A. Corcella, *Boll. dei Classici Accademia Nazionale dei Lincei*, XV (1994), 91–9. They were beekeepers, according to Paus. I 32,1; according to Herodotus they inhabited a region where the Dniester and the Bug flow closer to each other and the Exampaeus was their northern border (see 52,3–4). This suggests that they were located in Podolia; however, some attribute to a group of their more southerly members the burials in pear-shaped graves, with Scythian-type funerary deposits, found near Nikolaev; these are, on the other hand, attributed to the Callippidae by Rusjaeva and Skržinskaja, art cit., pp. 25–36; bibl. in *Narody*, p. 226; Nejchardt, pp. 101–3; *Stepi*, p. 45.   σῖτον … κέγχρους: in the 5th cent. σῖτος denotes wheat as well as barley (see L. Gallo, *Alimentazione e demografia della Grecia antica*, Salerno 1984, p. 30); both were widely cultivated between Crimea and the wooded steppe to the north, and seeds and models have been found as votive offerings: see Blavatskij, pp. 74–83; Ch. Danoff, *RE* Suppl. IX 1962, coll. 995–8; B. A. Šramko, *Slovenská Archeológia*, XXI (1973), 147–66; Z. V. Janušević, *Arch.* XV (1981), 87–90; *Narody*, p. 227. Millet had been grown in southern Eurasia since the earliest times. It was used by the Scythians in the preparation of drinks (Glaucus, *FGrHist* 806 F I) and was the basic ingredient in the diet of the Sarmatians according to Pliny, *NH* XVIII 100; it retained a key role in the diet of Slavic peoples: cf. S. B. Ochotnikov, in *Pamjatniki drevnich kul'tur Severnogo Pričernomor'ja*, Kiev 1979, p. 59; Janušević, art cit., pp. 87–90; *Narody*, p. 228. The seeds (and models of seeds) of lentils, peas, chickpeas, and other pulses have been found at several sites (at the site of ancient Tyritake; in the neighbourhood of Char'kov, etc.). See Blavatskij, p. 78; Šramko, art cit., pp. 153–7; Janušević, art cit., pp. 90 ff.

2. ὑπέρ … πρήσι: the sale of cereal must have supplied the export from the Black Sea to the Aegean: on the subject see T. S. Noonan, *AJPh* XCIV (1973), 231–42; A. Ščeglov is more sceptical in *Le Pont-Euxin vu par les Grecs*, Paris 1990, pp. 141–59. The archaeological record testifies to a large volume of exchange during the 6th and 5th cents. between Greeks and barbarians on the middle course of the Bug and on the Sinjucha, as far as the Dnepr: cf. N. A. Onajko, *Antičnyj import v Pridneprov'e i Pobuž'e v VII–V vv. do n.e.*, Moscow 1966;

Ja. V. Domanskij, *ASGE* XII (1970), 47–53; P. Alexandrescu, *RA* (1975), 63–72; O. Ostroverchov, *Drevnosti*, pp. 84–94. Herodotus locates the ἀροτῆρες Scythians precisely in this territory, mostly wooded steppe intensely cultivated in antiquity: see P. D. Liberov, *VDI* XLVIII (1951), 178–85; *Narody*, pp. 228–30; Nejchardt, pp. 103–7; *Stepi*, pp. 45–6. It is less certain whether they extended to the west of the Bug as far as western Podolia and the Dniester (where they are located by e.g. Artamonov, *Etnogeografija*, p. 155; Grakow, p. 14). On their relationship with the γεωργοί Scythians, see ch. 18. **Νευροί**: Herodotus will speak again of the Neuri in ch. 105 (see Introduction, pp. 558). By his day they had shifted to join the Budini, but here their ancient location is given. The southern border with the ἀροτῆρες Scythians is, according to Herodotus, the source of the Tyras = Dniester (see ch. 51). The Neuri are mostly identified with the bearers of the Milograd culture in the wooded regions between Ukraine and Bielorussia, along the Pripjat' and the upper Dnieper. This area exhibits ancient Baltic place-names (T. Sulimirski, *Acta Baltico-Slavica*, V (1967), 12–15, *CHI* II, p. 184); but scholars believe the Neuri to be pre-Slavic: cf. Rybakov, pp. 145–8; *Narody*, pp. 231–2; Nejchardt, pp. 118–20; *Stepi*, pp. 46–7 (for a Celtic hypothesis, O. N. Trubačëv, *Etnogenez i kul'tura drevnejšich Slavjan*, Moscow 1991, pp. 43–5, 219). For a synthesis of the debate and a hypothesis on the name ('those who speak in a nasal way') see P. U. Dini, *Baltistica*, XXXI (1996), pp. 39–44.

18,1. ἡ Ὑλαίη: the second 'strip' begins with a wooded region, Hylaea = forested (area) (cf. 76,4); according to Alexander Polyhistor, *FGrHist* 273 F 16, its local name was Ἀβική (perhaps related to the snake-goddess Api, cf. chs. 8 and 59? For a connection with the Latin *abies*, see A. Mayer, *Zeitschrift für vergleichende Sprachforschung*, LXVI (1939), 96–9). Hylaea is mentioned already in the 6th-cent. inscription edited by A. S. Rusjaeva and Ju. G. Vinogradov, in *Gold der Steppe*, pp. 201–2 (*SEG* XLII 710; *IGDOP* 24; B. Bravo, in *Problemi*, pp. 254–64); cf. also *IOSPE* I² 34; Mela II 5; Pliny, *NH* IV 83. In present times the region to the east of the lower Dnepr, apart from rare trees, is covered by steppes and sand; however, at the beginning of the modern era forests still survived: several travel-lers mention oaks, birches, and other trees (see F. Brun, *Černomor'e*, II, Odessa 1880, pp. 11 ff.); while paleobotany allows us to reconstruct the presence of elms, peach-trees, pines, etc. (see N. I. Sokol'skij, *MIA* CLXXVIII (1971), 15–18; Kocybala, p. 51; *Narody*, pp. 232–3). Hylaea is crossed by the Panticapes and is bordered to the east by the Hypacyris: see chs. 54–5. ἄνω: defending the transmitted ἄνθρωποι see C. Saerens, in *Studia varia Bruxellensia IV. In honorem A. Gerlo*, Leuwen 1997, pp. 235–45.

1–2. ἀπὸ δὲ . . . ἕνδεκα: γεωργοί, a generic term for 'farmers'; it cannot signify, as suggested by W. Vogel (in *Festschrift E. Hahn*, Stuttgart 1917, pp. 150–66), 'farmers who use the mattock' in contrast with ἀροτῆρες: this latter term does not mean 'farmers who use the plough', but rather it denotes, in the language of Ionic ethnography, farmers in general as opposed to nomads (cf. Hecataeus, *FGrHist* I F 335; Herod. I 125,4; IV 152,3, 191; VII 50,4). It has been argued that one or both terms is a phonetic adaptation of non-Greek words (see H. Kothe,

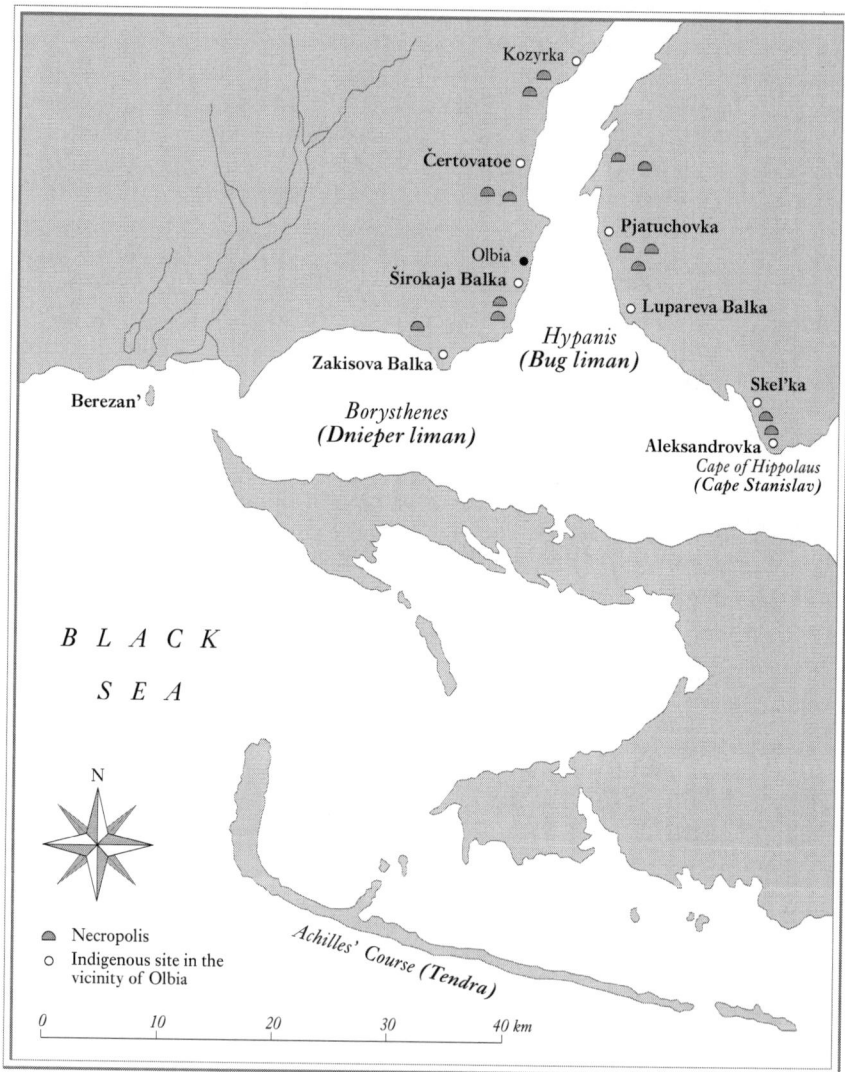

Map 39. The region of Olbia

Klio, LI (1969), 41 ff. with bibl.; V. I. Abaev, *VopJaz* (1981), 2, pp. 74–6; G. Holzer, *AAW* CXXV (1988), 197–8). It is more likely that Herodotus calls the Scythians east of the Borysthenes γεωργοί to distinguish them from the ἀροτῆρες, since he rejects the term Βορυσθενεῖται which was used by the inhabitants of Olbia and which he instead reserves for the Olbians themselves (cf. also Stephanus of Byzantium, s.v. Βορυσθένης). In the official documents of Olbia the name for

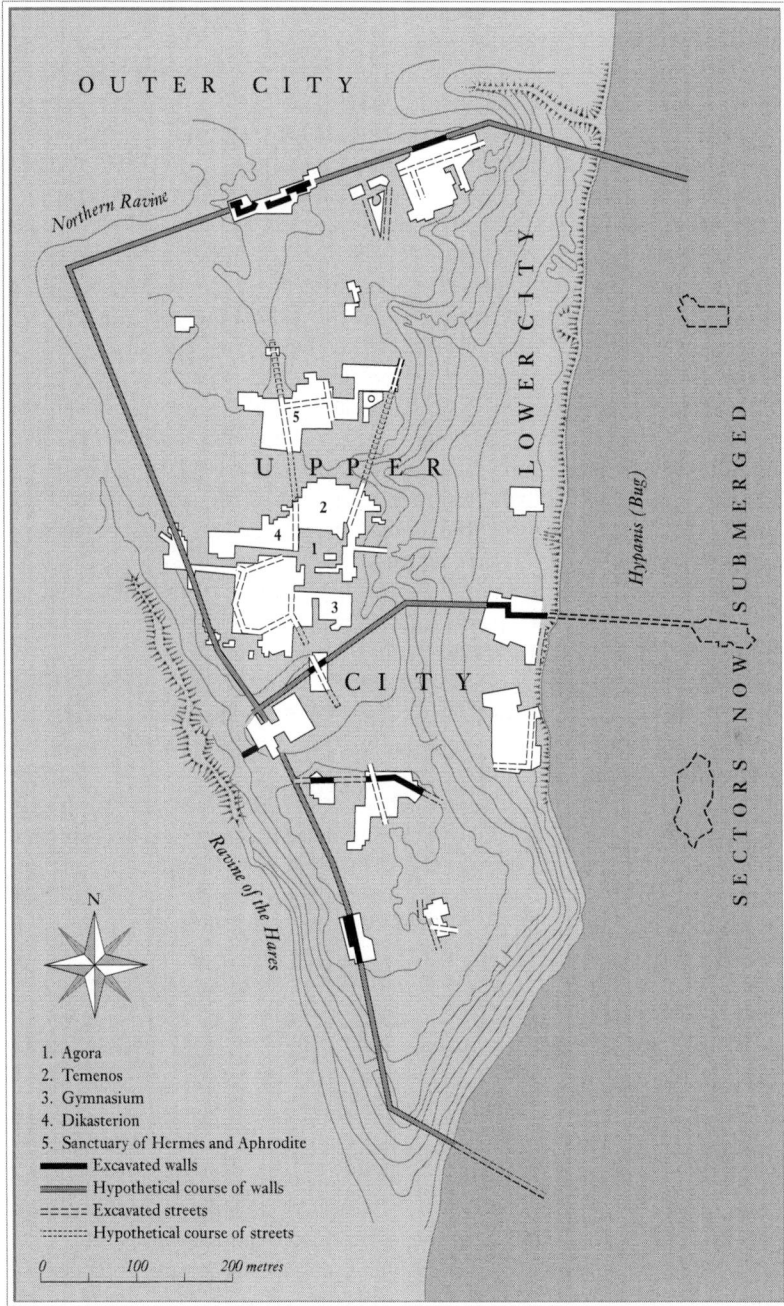

OUTER CITY

Northern Ravine

LOWER CITY

UPPER

5

2

4

1

3

CITY

Hypanis (Bug)

SECTORS NOW SUBMERGED

N

Ravine of the Hares

1. Agora
2. Temenos
3. Gymnasium
4. Dikasterion
5. Sanctuary of Hermes and Aphrodite
▬▬▬ Excavated walls
▬▬▬ Hypothetical course of walls
===== Excavated streets
:::::: Hypothetical course of streets

0   100   200 metres

Map 40. Olbia

the community is in fact οἱ ’Ολβιοπολῖται, from ’Ολβίη πόλις ('blessed city', an honorific term which might derive from an oracle; cf. M. V. Skržinskaja, *VDI* CLVII (1981), 142–7; Vinogradov, pp. 78–80); whereas the barbarian name Βορυσθένης, which perhaps originally indicated the estuary of Bug and Dnieper (discussion in Schramm, pp. 99–113), is often used for the city in literary sources (see Ehrhardt, p. 75; Vinogradov, pp. 25–31). Maybe the inhabitants of Olbia, who insisted on their Milesian character (see 78,2), wanted to banish all traces of 'barbarism' associated with them; Herodotus, however, does not take their cue: see A. Corcella, *QS* XXXV (1992), 49–60. The 11 days' stretch along the Borysthenes (but cf. 53.4) suggests that the γεωργοί Scythians were located along the left bank of the lower Dnepr, at least as far as the rapids. However, the eastern border at the river Panticapes presents difficulties (see ch. 54); and on the basis of archaeological similarities their territory is by some scholars made to include also the right bank (e.g. Jacenko, pp. 93 ff.); the wooded northern steppe, in the area of the rivers Sula, Psël, and northern Donec (e.g. V. A. Illins'ka, *Archeologija*, XXIII (1970), pp. 23–39); and the region further north, as far as Kiev (A. A. Moruženko, *SA* (1989), 4, pp. 37–8). Furthermore, if Herodotus' Borysthenes does not correspond entirely to the Dnepr, but is the Dnepr plus the Ingulec (see note on chs. 53–6), then the γεωργοί must be placed also between the Ingulec and the Dnepr; and, notwithstanding their different names, they can be thought in substance to be one with the ἀροτῆρες (Macan, ad loc.; Rybakov, pp. 143 ff.). Bibl. in *Narody*, pp. 233–5; Nejchardt, pp. 108–11; T. Sulimirski, *CHI* II, p. 183; *Stepi*, p. 46.   Ἀνδροφάγοι: on the Androphagi, 'man-eaters', cf. ch. 106. They are emphatically qualified as 'not Scythians', probably in polemical reply to Hecataeus (see Pseudo-Scymnus 848, *GGM* I, p. 231; cf. Strabo VII 3,6; Introduction, pp. 553–4); they are in fact included among the peoples who enclose Scythia to the north before the 'deserted' area: see ch. 102. Comparison with ch. 53 suggests that Herodotus does not place them immediately on the Borysthenes, and they must perhaps be sought to the north-east of the Dnieper. On the river Sula, a left tributary of the Dnieper, human remains are attested among cooking waste (T. Sulimirski, in *CHI* II, pp. 185–6); but scholars who locate there other peoples (γεωργοί Scythians, Budini, etc.) suggest for the Androphagi a location in the regions further north, as far as the river Pripjat' (Rybakov, pp. 96–7, 149 ff.) or Sejm (Moruženko, art. cit., p. 38: the area to the north of Kiev, where there have been no findings, would correspond to the first 'deserted' stretch). More suggestions in *Narody*, pp. 237–8; Nejchardt, pp. 131–3; *Stepi*, p. 47.

19. νομάδες ... Σκύθαι: in contrast with the previous groups of farming Scythians, for the nomadic Scythians a formula is used ('they neither sow nor plough') which echoes the Homeric Cyclopes (*Od.* IX 108–9). According to Herodotus they live in the steppe, but it is difficult to define their position, given the uncertainty regarding the rivers Panticapes and Gerrhus (see note to chs. 53–6). They can be roughly located between the lower Dnieper and the Moločnaja: cf. *Narody*, pp. 238–9; Nejchardt, pp. 111–13; *Stepi*, p. 46. τεσσέρων καὶ δέκα: the figure seems exaggerated (in ch. 101 the distance between the Borysthenes and the Palus Maeotis is of only 10 days). The original reading might have been τεσσέρων (cf. Rennell I, pp. 86–94); the figure $Δ = 4$ could have been interpreted as $Δ = 10$ (according the Attic system of numeration) and subsequently the two readings τεσσέρων and δέκα been combined: cf. Hemmerdinger, p. 168. See in any case the note to chs. 53–6.

20,1. πέρην ... εἶναι: τὰ βασιλήϊα are the 'royal ... territories', divided into three parts according to chs. 7 and 120 (in *IOSPE* I² 352, from the 2nd cent. BC, the expression designates the fortresses of kings). Here lived the 'royal' Scythians (βασιλήϊοι in para. 2 and at 71,2; 'free' at 110,2). Clearly these were a group, which included the royal family, that had gained supremacy over the other Scythians, farmers and nomads, and exacted tribute: cf. note to chs. 11–12, and the subdivision of the Persians at I 125 (cf. Gallotta, pp. 34 ff.). A similar system is found in the east for the Sakā (see Altheim–Stiehl, *Geschichte*, pp. 634–9) and among various nomad empires in later times: see Chazanov, pp. 154–64, 203 ff.; A. M. Khazanov, in *Terre et paysans dépendants dans les sociétés antiques*, Paris 1979, pp. 229–47; Gabain, pp. 5–6; G. Holzer, *AAW* CXXV (1988), 198–213; Priscus of Panopolis, *passim*, adopts the expression 'royal Scythians' to designate the Huns. According to Herodotus the territory of the royal Scythians extends to Crimea, north of the Tauric mountains, and along the coast of the *palus Maeotis* = Azov Sea (which to his mind runs on a north–south axis, see chs. 99–101), as well as along the Tanais = Don; cf. *Narody*, pp. 240–2; Nejchardt, pp. 113–18; T. Sulimirski, *CHI* II, pp. 174–9. Given also the uncertainty in the identification of the Gerrhus (see note to chs. 53–6), it is difficult to distinguish the 'royal' Scythians from the 'nomadic' Scythians; on the meaning of 'Scythians' in Herodotus, cf. Introduction, pp. 553–4. **τάφρον:** cf. chs. 3 and 28. B. Bravo, *ASNP* s. IV, V (2000), 67–71, proposes to interpret Τάφρος (or Τάφρη, varia lectio) as a place-name in this passage as well as at ch. 28 (both of which he regards as spurious). **Κρημνοί:** the *emporion* of Cremni (cf. 110,2) must be located between the Crimea and the northern coast of the Azov Sea (also cf. Ptolemy, *Geog.* V 3,4). However, according to Strabo VII 4,5 the entire area was deserted and, in the absence of precise archaeological evidence, its identification is disputed: see Ju. B. Boltrik and E. E. Fialko, *Skify severnogo pričernomor'ja*, Kiev 1987, pp. 40–8, who locate it on the mouth of the river Korsak, near Botevo. The coast of the Obotočnyj zaliv does, in fact, present some conspicuous crags which might account for the name Κρημνοί = 'cliffs' (see *Portolano del Mediterraneo* 5, Genoa 1983, p. 310). In the whole region there was early trade contact between Greeks and Scythians; there must have been a settlement in the vicinity of Taganrog, while on the delta of the Don, at Elizavetovka, an *emporion* was operating as early as the 5th cent. BC: see Gajdukevič, pp. 243–7; Y. Garlan, *DHA* VIII (1982), 142–52; F. Bosi, *RAL* XXXIX (1984), 79–99; I. B. Brašinskij and K. K. Marčenko, *Elizavetovskoje. Skythische Stadt im Don-Delta*, Munich 1984; M. Yu. Treister, *AncCiv* I (1994), 28–33. The proposal to identify Kremnoi with Panticapaeum (by J. Hind, in Nielsen, pp. 111–15) is attractive, but not altogether convincing.

2. **Μελάγχλαινοι**: on the Melanchlaeni, cf. ch. 107, where they are said to have
Scythian customs. Nevertheless they are here termed 'not Scythian' in polemic
reply to Hecataeus, *FGrHist* 1 F 185 (see Introduction, pp. 553–4). Their Greek
name means 'of the black cloaks'. The Iranic name for the Sauromatae seems to
have the same meaning (Dumézil, *Romans des Scythes*, p. 7; but see the various
opinions in R. Schmitt, in *ΛΗΝΑΙΚΑ. Festschrift für C. W. Müller*, Stuttgart–
Leipzig 1996, pp. 90–1), as also does the name *Σανδαράται*, attested in the 3rd
cent. BC for a group in the vicinity of Olbia (*IOSPE* I² 32 B 9); while other sources
mention some Melanchlaeni near the Colchians (Scylax, 79, *GGM* I, p. 61; Mela,
I 110; Pliny, *NH* VI 15), Herodotus locates them further north (cf. also ch. 100):
migrations have been suggested or else a misunderstanding on the part of
Herodotus (see e.g. L. A. El'nickij, *Znanija drevnich o severnych stranach*, Moscow
1961, pp. 71 ff.; cf. the case of the Boudini); but perhaps it is simpler to think of
several homonymous groups (cf. Minns, p. 104; e.g. the inhabitants of the
Cassiterides Islands are *μελάγχλαινοι* according to Strabo III 5, 11). As for the
locations suggested for the neighbouring peoples, some scholars locate them in
the area of the upper Donec: see e.g. B. A. Šramko, *Drevnosti Severskogo Donca*,
Char'kov 1964, pp. 233 ff. (objections in P. D. Liberov, *MIA* CXIII (1962), 76);
while other scholars identify them with the bearers of the Juchnov culture, further
to the north, between the rivers Desna and Sejm (see e.g. *Archeologija Ukrainskoj
SSR* II, Kiev 1986, pp. 46–7; Rybakov, pp. 152–66 ascribes the same culture to the
Budinoi). Bibl. in *Narody*, pp. 350–2; Nejchardt, pp. 133–6; T. Sulimirski, *CHI* II,
pp. 186–7; *Stepi*, p. 47. See the review in S. E. Rassadin, *Eurasia Antiqua*, III
(1997), 507–12, with justified doubts on the possibility of an archaeological
identification.

21. **Σαυρομ ατέων**: on the origin and the culture of the Sauromatians see chs.
110 ff. The archaeological record enables us to discern an area of 'Sauromatian'
culture in the steppes to the east of the Don as far as the Volga and the Ural, from
the Azov Sea up to the level of Saratov: see esp. Smirnov; id., *DHA* VI (1980),
139–53; Th. David, *DHA* VI (1980), 155–76; cf. *Narody*, pp. 363–5; Nejchardt,
pp. 143–7. The 15 days' journey from the mouth of the Don would bring one
approximately as far as the great curve of the Don (Lindegger, pp. 76–7;
cf. following note). As early as the 5th cent. BC groups of Sauromatians moved
to the west of the Don (K. F. Smirnov, *MIA* CLXXVII (1971), 191–6); but this
does not seem to offer sufficient justification for placing Herodotus' Sauromatians to the east of the Donec and understanding the latter, rather than the Don,
to be the upper part of the Tanais (Rybakov, pp. 50–5; cf. ch. 57). On the Tanais as
the border of Scythia, cf. 100,1.   **Βουδῖνοι**: cf. chs. 108–9 and 122–3; the
Boudini are nomads who inhabit a wooded area together with the Geloni, who
are farmers of Greek origin; in this area is the fort of Gelonus, built of wood,
which Darius reached and destroyed. The location of the Geloni-Boudini is very
controversial: cf. *Narody*, pp. 352 ff.; Nejchardt, pp. 120–31; *Stepi*, pp. 47–8. Some
scholars would place them in the Caucasus, positing a confusion on the part of
Herodotus (see note to 109,1; and cf. the Melanchlaeni). But according to the

indications given in ch. 21 (cf. Mela I 116) they must be sought to the north of the Sauromatae: a likely location seems to be the middle course of the Don, in the region between Voronež and the Volga, where early contacts with the Greeks are attested (e.g. see P. D. Liberov, *MIA* CLI (1969), 5–26). On the other hand several scholars identify the city of Gelonus with Bel'sk, a settlement on the Vorskla, a long way west of the Don: see Šramko, and objections by V. A. Il'inskaja in *Skify i sarmaty*, Kiev 1977, pp. 73–95; Rolle, *Skythen*, pp. 124–35; P. Georges, *AJAH* XII (1987), 136–7 (other scholars place in this region the Androphagi, the Melan-chlaeni, or the γεωργοί Scythians, see the preceding notes). When speaking of a 15 days' journey through the Sauromatae in order to reach the Boudini, Herod-otus seems to be referring to a specific trade route which probably followed the Don from its mouth (from Cremni? Cf. ch. 24); this reliance on an itinerary renders his localization credible; however, we do not know whether this route made some deviations to the winding course of the Don which Herodotus did not take into account (along the Donec according to Rybakov: see previous note). In any case it is unlikely that Darius, if he ever reached Gelonus, went much further than the Dnieper (see note to chs. 97 ff.; Introduction, pp. 561–2); and ch. 105 suggests that the Neuri and the Boudini were rather close to each other (see note to 105,1); a location to the west of the Geloni-Boudini does not seem improbable. It might then be correct to hold that the Geloni-Boudini, a composite people and 'large and numerous' (108,1), occupied a large area between the Volga, the Don, and the Dnieper (see e.g. Minns, p. 103; Grakow, pp. 122–3; B. A. Šramko, *Skifskij mir*, Kiev 1975, p. 122); or that the Boudini roamed between the Dnieper and the region further east: those who travelled up the Don met them in the wooded steppe between Voronež and Saratov, while Darius was able to reach them in the Bel'sk region or at any rate not much further than the Dnieper.

22–7. From the Boudini onwards it becomes difficult to follow the trade route which advanced into Eurasia. Herodotus speaks at first of a northward direction, then turns more and more eastward, but to his mind the coast from Crimea to the mouth of the Tanais runs on a north–south axis (cf. chs. 99–101) so that his indications cannot be projected just as they are onto a map. The elements of physical geography seem to be of greater relevance (cf. most of all Bolton, pp. 104–18; Lindegger, pp. 71–93). Past the region of woods, or wooden steppe, of the Geloni-Boudini, the 7 days through a deserted area might correspond to the steppe along the Volga to the north of Syzran (see also E. D. Phillips, *Artibus Asiae*, XVIII (1955), 166); at any rate the region rich in trees inhabited by the Thyssagetae and the Iyrcae must be sought between the Oka and the Ural, whereas there is some controversy surrounding the identification of the 'stony and rough' region (23,1) which follows the 'detached' Scythians, and the 'tall mountains' at the foot of which live the Argippaei. The mention of Arimaspians and griffins suggests an auriferous region (cf. III 116): important veins, which were exploited as early as prehistoric times, are to be found on the Urals as well as on the massifs of Central Asia, especially on the Altai (cf. Rolle, *Scythians*, pp. 52–3; N.L. Členova, *SA* (1983), 1, pp. 56–7), and there has been much discussion on whether the route passed near the former or the latter. See, together with the abundant earlier bibl., in Bolton, *passim*; Lindegger; H. W. Haussig, *AAntHung* XVIII (1980), 9–24; id., *Geschichte vorislamischer Zeit*; N. L. Členova, *SA* (1983), 1, pp. 47–66. A location on the Urals, for the Argippaei at least, seems more prudent: see notes to ch. 23.

22,1–2. μετὰ δὲ ... ἔχεται: the hunting practices of the Thyssagetae and Iyrcae suggest a location in the wooded steppe or in the forest; according to Pomponius Mela I 116, these two peoples inhabit 'great forests' (cf. Pliny, *NH* VI 19; the form *Turcae/Tyrcae* here attested is simply a mistake: cf. A. Salač, *Eunomia*, I (1957), 50–5). Rybakov, p. 192, identifies the Thyssagetae with the Gorodec culture between the Oka and the Volga and the Iyrcae with the D'jakovo culture to the north-west (cf. K. A. Smirnov, *SA* (1987), 4, pp. 40–3); but with regard to the Iyrcae, some have also pointed to the Anan'ino culture, between the Kama and the Urals (e.g. A. P. Smirnov, *Skify*, Moscow 1966, p. 102; cf. Jettmar, pp. 53–7); or, further to the south-east, to the region between the Ural and the Tobol (e.g. Sulimirski, *Sarmatians*, p. 61; id., *Prehistoric Russia*, pp. 310 ff.). See Th. David, *DHA* III (1979), 147–52; *Narody*, pp. 244–8; Nejchardt, pp. 136–7; *Stepi*, p. 47. The name of the river Ugra, on the border between the Juchnov and the D'jakovo cultures, may be reminiscent of the Iyrcae: cf. M. I. Pogrebova and D. S. Raevskij, *VDI* CLXXXVIII (1989), 49, n. 38. Among the 'Siberian gold' discovered in the 18th cent. between the rivers Tobol and Enisej (see Jettmar, pp. 9 ff., 197–218) there are two plaques which represent a hunting scene similar to the one described by Herodotus.

3. Σκύθαι ... ἀποστάντες: on the basis of the information furnished by Herodotus the 'detached' Scythians must not be located in the area of Voronež, as Rybakov suggests, pp. 118 ff., but to the east of the Thyssagetae and the Iyrcae. Pogrebova and Raevskij, art. cit., pp. 40–65, place them on the south-western limit of the Anan'ino culture, more or less in the Kazan' area, where contact with the Scythian cultures of the Caucasus is attested (cf. Jettmar, pp. 55–6); the detachment from the royal Scythians would have taken place before these reached the Black Sea (cf. chs. 11–12). Other scholars, who extend the trade route beyond the Urals, locate the 'detached' Scythians in the region of Orenburg or further east; L. A. El'nickij, *Skifija evrazijskich stepej*, Novosibirsk 1977, pp. 114, 201, identifies them with the Sakā of Kazakhstan (cf. Choerilus, fr. 5 Bernabé): see *Narody*, p. 248; Nejchardt, pp. 138–9. According to some later sources (esp. Justin XLI 1,1; Arrian, *FGrHist* 156 F 30) the Parthians were Scythian exiles. Haussig, *AAntHung* XVIII (1980), p. 16, suggests identifying the 'detached' Scythians with the Parthians themselves, who perhaps at this time were settled further north, in Kazakhstan (B. Ph. Lozinski, *The Original Homeland of the Parthians,* 'sGravenhage 1959); according to J. R. Gardiner-Garden, *Apollodoros of Artemita and the Central Asian Skythians*, Bloomington, Ind. 1987, pp. 10–17, these traditions preserve the memory of 'colonizations' made by groups of young Scythians, similar to the Latin *ver sacrum* (cf. chs. 110 ff.).

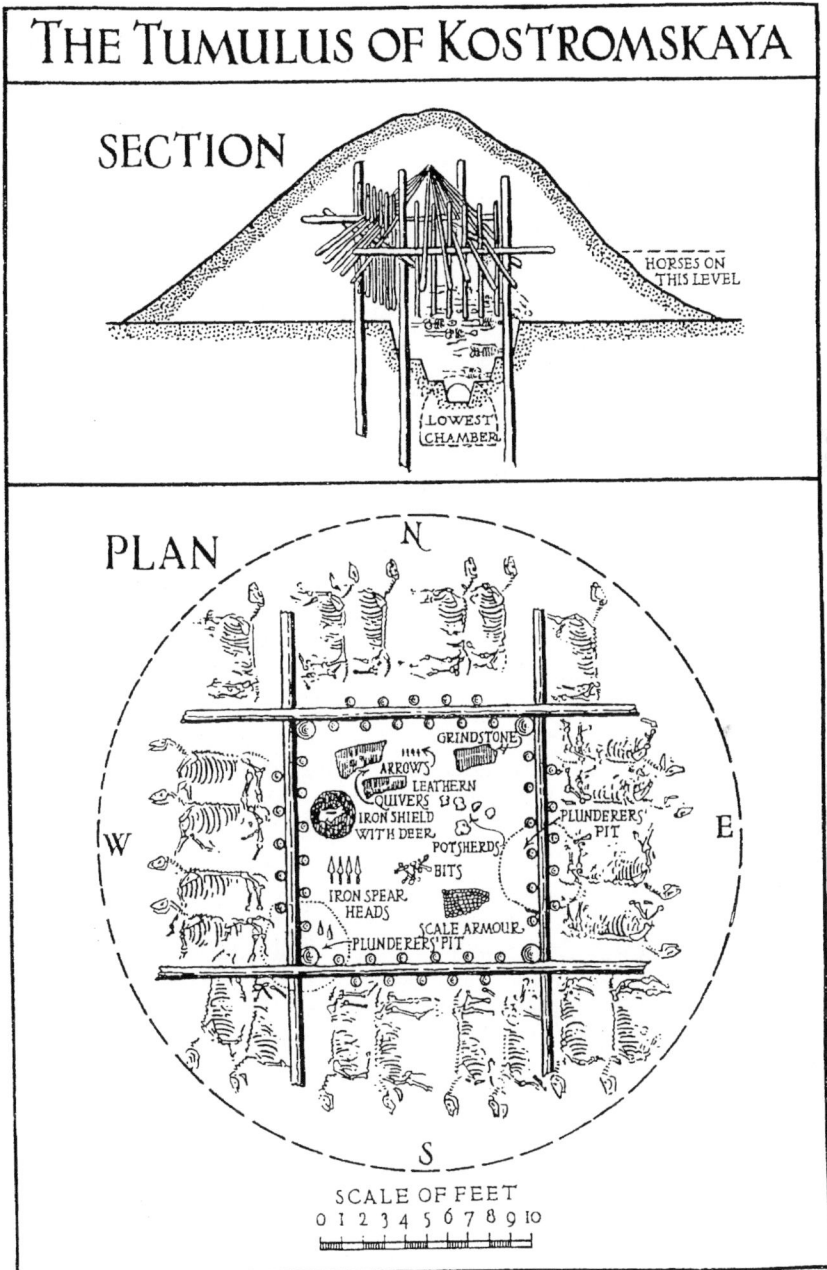

THE TUMULUS OF KOSTROMSKAYA

SECTION

HORSES ON THIS LEVEL

LOWEST CHAMBER

PLAN

N

GRINDSTONE

ARROWS
LEATHERN QUIVERS
IRON SHIELD WITH DEER
POTSHERDS
BITS
IRON SPEAR HEADS
SCALE ARMOUR
PLUNDERERS' PIT

PLUNDERERS' PIT

W

E

S

SCALE OF FEET
0 1 2 3 4 5 6 7 8 9 10

Map 41. The Kurgan of Kostromskaja Stanica (Kuban' VII–VI century) after Rostovtzeff; see Herod. IV 71–5

23,1. μέχρι ... τρηχέα: the description of the long 'stony and rough' stretch of land which leads up to the 'tall mountains' ('which no one crosses', see 25,1) may lend itself to the different appearance which, after the wooded steppe, characterizes the elevation of the Turgaj and the Kirgiz steppe as far as the Kara Tau or, in the north-east, the mountains of Kazakhstan, and the large ranges of Central Asia: see e.g. Lindegger, pp. 78–9, who suggests a route along the oases to the north-east of the Syr Dar'ja. See also the description by William of Rubruck, *Itinerarium* XXII (in *Mongol Mission*, pp. 133–4). On the other hand, other scholars identify the 'stony and rough' region with the foothills of the Urals, and the 'tall mountains' with the Urals themselves: see among others A. Herrmann, *RE* IX 2, 1916, cols. 2235 ff.; R. Henning, *RhM* LXXIX (1930), 326–33; *Klio*, XXVIII (1935), 242–54; N. L. Členova, *SA* (1983), 1, pp. 54 ff. This hypothesis cautiously reduces the dimensions of the trade route; the Urals are not especially high, and they are certainly not impossible to cross, but we would need to imagine a mythical transfiguration (see e.g. A. V. Matveev, *Skifskaja epocha Altaja*, Barnaul 1986, pp. 85–8).

2–5. διεξελθόντι ... Ἀργιππαῖοι: the physical traits of the Argippaei are clearly Mongolian: see E. D. Phillips, *Artibus Asiae*, XVIII (1955), 168 ff.; XX (1957), 162; XXIII (1960), 126 with bibl. Mongolian elements had early on filtered into the west, especially into the Anan'ino culture west of the Urals (Jettmar, pp. 54, 57); and if the identification of the 'tall mountains' with the Urals is accepted, then the Argippaei can be located in Bashkiria, between the Belaja and the Urals (and perhaps even identified with the Anan'ino culture?). In this area and to the east of the Urals there grows the wild cherry tree (*Pronus padus*), which might correspond to the ποντικόν and which to this day the Bashkirs use like the Argippaei (see *Narody*, pp. 250–1; H. Mühlenstein, in *O-o-pe-ro-si. Festschrift für E. Risch zum 75. Geburtstag*, Berlin 1986, pp. 561–4). Ποντικόν at 23,3 might be an Iranian word (see Herzfeld, pp. 254, n. 3, 283, n. 1), while ἄσχυ finds a parallel in the Tatar word *ačy, eče*, and in the Bashkir *asy, ese*, names of the same drink (lit. 'bitter, sharp': see N. L. Členova, *SA* (1983), 1, p. 55; cf. the testimony of Onesicritus, *FGrHist* 134 F 3, on the trees called *occhi* in Hyrcania). The hut made of waterproof felt (to protect against water, snow, and wind: cf. *De Aeribus Aquis Locis* 18) is a primitive form of the nomadic *jurta* (or *čum*): see Phillips, *Artibus Asiae*, XXIII (1960), 126; *Narody*, p. 251 (in general T. Faegre, *Tents, Architecture of the Nomads*, New York 1979; on felt see Haussig, *Geschichte islamischer Zeit*, pp. 247–8; N. V. Polosmak, *AncCiv* I (1994), 346–54). But if the Argippaei really lived under the trees without any protection during the summer, then we must assume that they lived, or at least roamed, further south: scholars who take the 'tall mountains' to be the ranges of Central Asia place them e.g. to the south of the Tarbagataj (Junge, pp. 36–40); at the foot of the Altai, in the neighbourhood of Pazyryk (Minns, pp. 108–9; Bolton, p. 115; Sulimirski, *Prehistoric Russia*, pp. 310–13; Rolle, *Scythians*, pp. 56–7); near the Kara Tau (Lindegger, p. 79); in the Ili valley (Haussig, *AAntHung* XVIII (1980), 16); etc. Their name ('Ὀργιμπαῖοι and other variants are attested, also in Mela II 117 and Pliny, *NH* VI 35) can be connected to that of the goddess Ἀργίμπασα (59,2); the 'sacred neutrality' of which Herodotus speaks suggests a special relationship with the goddess and a priestly function (in Greece, Elis was neutral because it was sacred to Zeus, according to Ephorus, *FGrHist* 70 F 115). In a representation from Pazyryk a knight is shown in the act of paying homage to an apparently bald divine figure (cf. Phillips, *Artibus Asiae* XXIII, pp. 126–8): also on the Altai the 'sacred' people may have been known, and its neutrality rendered it an excellent intermediary for trade between the Black Sea and Asia.

24. καὶ γὰρ...διαπρήσσονται: the existence of the trade route is confirmed by findings of artefacts of Greek-Scythian craft (especially mirrors) along the Don, the Volga, and in the region of the Urals: see B. N. Grakov, *Archeologija*, I (1947), 23–38; N. L. Členova, *SA* (1983), 1, pp. 47–66. The area of the Urals had been involved since prehistoric times in exchanges with the Orient and China (see Lindegger, pp. 80–2; H. W. Haussig, *AAntHung* XVIII (1980), 10–15); traces of Greek–Scythian trade beyond the Urals are less frequent (on the findings of Olbian coins dating from the 4th cent. BC in Zungaria, see R. Hennig, *Klio*, XXVIII (1935), 247; Haussig, art. cit., p. 16). The region of the Argippaei constituted a caravan junction: Scythians and Greeks could buy the gold of the Arimaspians, and probably also Chinese silk, which is attested as early as the 5th cent. in Kerč' and Athens (see H. Hundt, *JRGZ* XVI (1969), 65–71; M. C. Miller, *Athens and Persia in the Fifth Century B.C.: A Study in Cultural Receptivity*, Cambridge 1997, pp. 77–79 with bibl.) and the furs imported from the north (R. Hennig, *Vierteljahrsschrift für Sozial- und Wirtschaftsgeschichte*, XXIII (1930), 1–25). In return the Greeks could offer e.g. salt and wine (cf. 53,3 and 66), as well as artefacts. A branch of the trade route must have begun at Olbia and then joined the sections which came from 'other emporia', especially from mouth of the Don (cf. ch. 21): see N. A. Onajko, *Antičnyj import v Pridneprov'e i Pobuž'e v VII–V vv. do n.e.*, Moscow 1966, p. 50; O. S. Ostroverchov, in *Drevnosti*, pp. 89–92; R. Rolle, in *Untersuchungen zu Handel und Verkehr der vor- und frühgeschichtlichen Zeit in Mittel- und Nordeuropa* I, Göttingen 1985, pp. 460–90; J. Hind, *Il Mar Nero*, II (1995/6), 113–26. The figure 'seven' for the languages and interpreters corresponds to the peoples mentioned from ch. 21 onwards, if it is assumed that the 'detached' Scythians spoke a dialect of their own, and if the Boudini are distinguished from the Geloni; but Herodotus must have reckoned also a Greek–Scythian translator, always assuming that this is not an approximate or merely symbolic figure (cf. Fehling, p. 76; M. V. Skržinskaja, *VDI* CXCI (1989), 90).

25,1. οἱ δὲ...ἀρχήν: the 'men with goat's feet', if they are not mythical figures, are a transfiguration of the mountain peoples clothed in furs. Other ancient sources (Dionysus Periegetes 310, *GGM* II, p. 120; Mela III 56; Pliny, *NH* IV 95) placed in the northern regions men with horses' feet, and medieval sources men with the feet of oxen; see P. Daffinà, *Giovanni di Pian di Carpine, Storia dei Mongoli*, Spoleto 1989, pp. 455–6, n. 56. On monsters in ancient geography: E. Bianchi, *Acme*, XXXIV (1981), 227–49. The night which lasts six months might be a reference to polar nights (καθεύδουσι does not mean 'they sleep' but rather 'they spend the night', cf. Aeschylus Agamemnon, II, ed. E. Fraenkel, Oxford 1950, p. 3). Northern 'kingdoms of darkness' appear already in the Odyssey (IX 13 ff.) and in a Babylonian map of the world of Persian times (E. Unger, Antiquity, IX (1935), 314); on medieval times, cf. P. Pelliot, Notes on Marco Polo, II, Paris 1963, pp. 616–24. The indication of six months is perhaps owing to a generalization of empirical data: cf. Diog. Laert. IV 58 (on Bion of Abdera); Stephanus of Byzantium, s.v. Γέρμαρα; Berger, p. 126; A. Szabó, ACD XXVI (1990), 19–22. ἐμοὶ μέν: the μέν solitarium (Denniston, Greek Particles, pp. 381–2) implies a contrast with other, more gullible, individuals: cf. IV 42,4 and V 86,3.

2. 'Ισσηδόνων: the Issedones, not directly touched by the trade route, were not necessarily bordering on the Argippaei: Greek and Scythian merchants may have met some of their agents in the markets of the Argippaei (cf. H.W. Haussig, AAntHung XVIII (1980), 17). Their existence was well known to the Greeks: as well as Aristeas (fr. 4 Bernabé: 'Ισσηδοί), Alcman also spoke of them (fr. 156 Davies:'Εσσηδόνες/'Ασσηδόνες; on the forms of their name, cf. Mela II 2,9, and 13; Pliny, NH IV 88; Bolton, p. 184; W. Burkert, Gnomon, XXXV (1963), 35–6). According to Hecataeus, FGrHist 1 F 193, they were a 'Scythian' people (see Introduction, pp. 553–4). Ptolemy (Geog. IV 13,3; VI 15,4; 16,5 and 7) locates them in eastern Turkestan and in the Tarim valley, but he could be reflecting a later situation (discussion in A. Herrmann, RE IX 2, 1916, cols. 2235 ff.; A. Berthelot, L'Asie ancienne Centrale et Sud-Orientale d'après Ptolémée, Paris 1930; H. W. Haussig, ZDMG CIX (1959), 148–90; A. Silberman, RPh LXIV (1990), 99–110); in I 201 Herodotus locates them opposite the Massagetae, i.e. beyond the Syr-Dar'ja. The characters of their culture link them to several groups between the Don and Central Asia (see note to 26,1), and there is no certainty on their exact location: on the eastern slopes of the Urals (where a tributary of the Tobol bears the name of Iset': see K. F. Smirnov, DHA VI (1980), 143–5; N. L. Členova, SA (1983), 1, pp. 54 ff.); near the Issyk-Kul (e.g. S. I. Rudenko, Kul'tura naselenija Central'nogo Altaja v skifskoe vremja, Moscow–Leningrad 1960, pp. 173 ff.; Lindegger, pp. 82–92); also in Tibet (W. Tomaschek, SAWW CXVI (1886), 734 ff.) or in the Tarim valley (Haussig, ZDMG CIX, pp. 148–90; AAntHung XVIII, pp. 17–18). Th. David, DHA II (1976), 138–40; III (1977), 115–96; VI (1980), 160–4 (with bibl.) identifies them with the Tasmola culture, settled in central Kazakhstan from the 7th cent. BC. Haussig, Geschichte islamischer Zeit, p. 10, interprets their name as meaning 'the silk people'; A. von Blumenthal, Zeitschrift für Namenforschung, XIV (1938), 301, thought of a connection with the Celtic word essedum = 'chariot'. Identification with the Wu-sun of Chinese sources is very uncertain: see Lindegger, pp. 88–92; Levi, pp. 62–81.

26,1. ἐπεὰν ἀνδρὶ... προτίθενται: endocannibalism is common to the Issedones and to the Massagetae (I 216, cf. III 38 and 99): see Bolton, pp. 76–7; P. Daffinà, Il nomadismo centroasiatico, I, Rome 1982, pp. 19–23; Mora, pp. 159–64. From the mummified bodies at Pazyryk, in the Altai, some muscle parts were removed, perhaps to be eaten: see e.g. Jettmar, p. 111; Rudenko, p. 283; E. M. Murphey and

J. P. Mallory, *Antiquity* LXXIV (2000), 388–94. William of Rubruck, *Itinerarium* XXVI (= *Mongol Mission*, pp. 141–5; cf. John of Pian di Carpini, V 14 = *Mongol Mission*, p. 21) attributes to the peoples of Tibet both endocannibalism and the use of skulls as cups (cf. B. Laufer, *Use of Human Skulls and Bones in Tibet*, Chicago 1923). The latter custom had a magic significance (cf. ch. 65): for evidence from Bijsk, in the Altai, and several parallels, see A. Rieth, *AW* II (1971), 47–51; cf. Bolton, pp. 77–9; Burkert, *Homo Necans*, p. 224, n. 39; M. J. Becker, *PP* XLI (1986), 41–8.

2. γενέσια: 'anniversaries of the dead', celebrated on the day of the death of an ancestor, according to Ammonius, *De Adfin. Vocab. Diff.* 116 Nickau; cf. F. Jacoby, *CQ* XXXVIII (1944), 65–75; R. Garland, *The Greek Way of Death*, Ithaca, NY 1985, pp. 104 ff.   καὶ οὗτοι: like the Argippaei; the connection between justice and equality among the sexes is far from obvious for that time, cf. Giraudeau, p. 125. ἰσοκρατέες ... αἱ γυναῖκες: the equal status of women is attested also for the Sauromatians; see note to chs. 110–17.

27. τοὺς μουνοφθάλμους ... ὀφθαλμόν): on the Arimaspians and the griffins see note to III 116,3 and 3–4, with bibl.; Romm, pp. 67–77; *LIMC* VIII 1 pp. 529–34, 609–11. The griffins, often pictured in the art of the steppes, recall legendary figures of the folklore of Central Asia, China, India, etc: A. Alföldi, *Gnomon*, IX (1933), 517; K. Meuli, *Hermes*, LXX (1935), 155–7; Bolton, pp. 80 ff.; Potratz, p. 167; Albaum–Brentjes, pp. 220–3. The single eye of the Arimaspi is a mark of inferiority (Lindegger, p. 87), or it is mythically linked to their activity of producing metals (cf. G. Camassa, *L'occhio e il metallo*, Genoa 1983, with bibl.). The legend may have contributed to hide the real origin of the gold sold by the Issedones (cf. W. C. Brice, *Antiquity*, CIX (1954), 78–84); in this case, the true correspondents of the Arimaspians and the griffins may have been on the Altai, near the upper Irtyš (see R. Dyer, *Lexicon des frühgriechischen Epos*, I, Göttingen 1979, col. 1275; *Narody*, p. 256; for a location in the Urals see e.g. N. L. Členova, *SA* (1983), 1, pp. 54 ff.). In the wake of Aristeas (frs. 5 and 6 Bernabé; cf. Aeschylus, *Prom.* 803 ff.; Pliny, *NH* VII 10) Damastes of Sigeum (*FGrHist* 5 F 1) also located them beyond the Issedones, and between them and the Hyperboreans he placed the Rhipaean mountains, the sources of the wind Boreas (perhaps an echo of the Central Asian 'mountains of the wind'; Bolton, pp. 93–8; on the Urals see Členova, art. cit., pp. 54 ff.). Herodotus refuses to speak of the Rhipaean mountains (cf. note to 47–58), shows himself sceptical about griffins and Arimaspians (cf. III 116), and believes that the existence of the Hyperboreans cannot be verified (chs. 32 ff.); upholding a Scythian derivation for the name Ἀριμασποί, he casts doubt on the fact that Aristeas had drawn his information from the Issedones and that he had really reached them: cf. chs. 16 and 32; Introduction, p. 549. However, his Scythian interpretation does not find certain confirmation in Iranic roots: Ἀριμασποί seems rather to be a compound of *aspa-* = 'horse'; discussion in H. H. Schaeder, *Iranica*, I, Berlin 1934; see now E. Pirart, *Boletín de la Asociación Española de Orientalística*, XXXIV (1998), 239–60. It is hard to tell whether Herodotus misunderstood his informants or whether the dispute with Aristeas induced him to tell a deliberate lie.

28–31. Herodotus has reached the farthest point of verifiable knowledge: to the Hyperboreans, to his mind more mythical than real, he will devote an appendix in chs. 32–6. At this point he can give an outline of the climate of the entire region. In accord with the *De Aeribus Aquis Locis* 18 and Strabo VII 3,18, Herodotus speaks of an extremely cold climate, even during the summer, and he describes Scythia as an 'inverted' world compared to the Mediterranean world, at the cost of a certain amount of exaggeration (cf. Ovid's hyperbolas, *Trist.* III 10 and *passim*; *Pont.* III 1,11 ff. and *passim*; see Trüdinger, pp. 34 ff.; Ch. Danoff, *RE* Suppl. IX 1962, coll. 938–49; Hartog, pp. 46–8 = ET pp. 28–30.; the 'inversion' is all the more evident in that Greece, by contrast, was considered to have a 'winter' of four months and a 'summer' of eight: see O. Longo, *QS* XIV (1988), 27–50). However, the climate of Ukraine must actually have been harsher in antiquity due to the presence of larger forests (cf. T. Sulimirski, *Archeologia*, XII (1961), 1–18); and Herodotus is speaking not only of the Pontic regions, where the climate was milder, but of the entire area as far as the mountains of the Argippaei and the Issedones. Cf. Neumann, *Die Hellenen*, pp. 58–73; Ebert, pp. 8–10; *Narody*, pp. 258–9. This whole section is regarded as spurious by B. Bravo, *ASNP* s. IV, V (2000), 72–9, who notes some singularities in the style.

28,1. ἡ δὲ θάλασσα...Κιμμέριος: in present times, between December and March there is ice and even a complete freezing over at the estuaries of rivers and in the area of Odessa, as well as in the Azov Sea (*Narody*, p. 259; *Portolano del Mediterraneo*, V, Genoa 1983, pp. 169, 173, 182–3, 191, 216–17, 308–9, 316, 319, 322, 327–8). On the freezing over of the Kerč' Strait, not infrequent today (ibid., p. 276), cf. Strabo II 1,16 and VII 3,18; Mela I 115; Pliny, *NH* IV 87; Gellius XVII 8,16; Macrobius, *Sat.* VII 12,31 ff.   καὶ ἐπὶ...Σίνδους: the royal Scythians could cross over the frozen strait 'to this side (west) of the trench' (cf. chs. 3 and 20; Ph. E. Legrand, *REA* XL (1938), 230, suggested reading ἐκτὸς τάφρου, 'on the other side of the trench', thinking of the Scythians of the Kerč' peninsula, but it does not seem as though Herodotus pictured a great distance between the strait and the trench). This must have been a case of winter transhumance which assumed the character of actual invasions, to the extent of prompting the defensive reinforcement of the Greek cities on the strait: see Gajdukevič, pp. 40–2; M. Ju. Vachtina, *et al.*, *VDI* CLIV (1980), 155–61; Ju. G. Vinogradov, *Chiron*, X (1980), 74–6; id., in E. C. Golubcova (ed.), *Antičnaja Grecija*, I, Moscow 1983, p. 402; A. M. Khazanov, *DHA* VIII (1982), 17–18; F. V. Šelov-Kovedjaev, *Drevnejšie gosudarstva na territorii SSSR. 1984 g.*, Moscow 1985, pp. 66–7; J. R. Gardiner-Garden, *Historia*, XXXV (1986), 209 ff. The Sindi had settled in the Taman' peninsula: Ju. S. Kruškol, in *Studien zur Geschichte und Philosophie des Altertums*, Budapest 1986, pp. 293–9; D. B. Šelov, *Demografičeskaja*, pp. 232–47; F. V. Šelov-Kovedjaev, *Klio*, LXXI (1989), 216–25.

2–3. κεχώρισται...[νενόμισται]: Herodotus correctly describes the increased rainfall during the hot months and the scarcity of thunderstorms during the winter which characterize the northern regions in comparison with the Aegean; however, he exaggerates in speaking of uninterrupted rain during the summer:

cf. *Narody*, p. 261. On the other hand it is not true that the region to the north of the Black Sea is little subject to seismic activity (cf. *Narody*, pp. 261–2). The Greeks perceived thunder and earthquakes as similar phenomena (cf. *Euripides, Hippolytus*, ed. W. S. Barrett, Oxford 1966², pp. 384–5; in Byzantine times this gave birth to a special literary genre, the *seismobrontologia*); and ancient science included earthquakes in the sphere of meteorology, linking them with the seasons: according to Pliny (*NH* II 195), for instance, seismic disturbances are more common during the autumn, like lightning, and Gaul and Egypt are exempt from them on account of extreme cold and heat (cf. Hesiod, *Th.* 706–7; Anaximander, 12 A28 DK; Anaximenes, 13 A24 DK; Arist. *Meteor.* II 8–9; Seneca, *Quaest. Nat.* II 1,3; see Berger, pp. 153–6).

4. ἵπποι... ἀνέχονται: osteological finds attest the presence of donkeys and mules only near the Greek cities, where they were imported by the colonists: see V. I. Calkin, *MIA* LIII (1960), 35–50; CLIV (1969), 283; *Narody*, p. 263 (on the horses reared in Scythia, see R. Rolle, in *Festschrift für R. Pittioni*, I, Vienna 1976, pp. 756–76). Cf. ch. 129; Arist. *De Gen. Animal.* 748a22 ff.; *Hist. An.* 605a20 ff.; Strabo VII 3,18; Pliny, *NH* VIII 43.

29. δοκέει δέ...μόγις: species of cattle without horns or with short horns are well attested by osteological finds; cf. V. I. Calkin, *MIA* LIII (1960), 10–35; *Narody*, pp. 263–4. But species with horns are also attested; and the reason adduced by Herodotus is erroneous, despite the 'proof' of *Od.* IV 85: see already Aelian, *Nat. An.* II 53. This kind of explanation is parallel to Democritus' aetiologies: see Diller, p. 45, n. 78. Also cf. *De Aeribus Aquis Locis* 18; Arist. *Hist. An.* 606b18 ff.; Strabo VII 3,18; Tacitus, *Germ.* 5,1 (on Germany).

30,1. θωμάζω δέ...οὐδενός: we have here a brief excursus, prompted by the similarity in subject-matter, which Herodotus explicitly describes as such (προσθήκη = 'addition') and which he justifies by his general tendency to make such excursuses; ὁ λόγος refers to the Scythian narrative begun with Book IV (cf. ὅδε ὁ λόγος in 16,1) rather than the work as a whole. See Cobet, pp. 45–59; Introduction, p. 570.   ἐκ κατάρης τευ: Herodotus, sceptical as usual in such matters (cf. e.g. ch. 36), merely alludes to a legend known to us from Plutarch, *Mor.* 303b (cf. Antigonus of Carystus 13; Paus. V 5,1) and according to which Oenomaus set a curse on mules because of his love for horses. See H. Verdin, *Gisteren en morgen voorbij*, Leuven 1987, pp. 77–85.

31,1–2. περὶ δὲ τῶν πτερῶν... εἴρηται: after he has spoken of the harsh climate of Scythia, Herodotus is able to furnish an effective explanation of the 'feathers' in the Scythian legend (7,3; Pliny, *NH* IV 88): the Scythians, drawing from their northern neighbours (cf. 7,3), compare the incessant snow of the far north to feathers (cf. e.g. Leucippus, 67 A1 DK; examples of the same comparison are found in Aly, pp. 118–19). According to Herodotus, the Scythians and their neighbours, who certainly were well acquainted with snow, intentionally made use of a metaphor, which could be translated into real terms (like e.g. in II 54–7; Corcella, pp. 83, 94–6). This is implied in the use of εἰκάζειν with the meaning 'to compare' (A. Rivier, *Un emploi archaïque de l'analogie chez Héraclite et Thucydide*,

Lausanne 1952, pp. 41–63); τὰ ... πτερὰ, dependent on λέγειν, has the article because it is an actual quote from the Scythian tale, while τὴν χίονα is dependent on εἰκάζοντας (a different interpretation is now proposed by B. Bravo, *ASNP* s. IV, V (2000), 77; for εἰκάζειν with the simple accusative, cf. IV 133,1). However, some scholars do not agree with this Herodotean rationalization and think that the legend alluded to the feathers of swans. Cf. most recently Lindegger, p. 63, n. 13: feathers of birds in the extreme north are imagined e.g. by the Ciukci, cf. E. Lot-Falck, *Il tamburo dello sciamano. Miti e racconti eschimesi*, Milan 1989, p. 153 and n. 2. Dumézil, *Romans des Scythes*, pp. 339–51, establishes a parallel with the mythical 'cotton-wool snow' of some Abkhazian legends. Cf. V 10.

32–5. Finally the question of the Hyperboreans is tackled: see O. Crusius and M. Mayer, in Roscher, *Lexicon* I, coll. 2805–41; H. Daebritz, *RE* IX 1 1914, coll. 258–79; Romm, pp. 60–7; K. Fabian, *Die Hyperboreer*, Frankfurt am Main 1997. According to Herodotus (cf. Pindar, *Ol.* 3,31) Ὑπερβόρεοι means 'beyond the northern wind' (cf. 36,1); from Aristeas onwards this people was variously located and idealized: see Dion, pp. 260–70. For the most part modern scholars explain the name as 'beyond' or 'above the mountains' (O. Schroeder, *Archiv für Religionswissenschaft*, VIII (1905), 69–84), referring it to Thrace (to which points also 33,5: see L. Weber, *RhM* LXXXII (1933), 165–229; J. Wiesner, *Die Thraker*, Stuttgart 1963, pp. 59–61; H. Kothe, *Klio*, LII (1970), 205–30); while J. Harmatta, *AAntHung* III (1955), 57–66, thinks of the north-western Balkans. Through this route must have come 'northern' elements (see A. H. Krappe, *CPh* XXXVII (1942), 353–70; F. M. Ahl, *AJPh* CIII (1982), 373–411; cf. 36,1 on Abaris) of the cult of Apollo and Artemis, to which was associated in Delos the 'chthonic' cult (cf. W. Burkert, *Greek Religion*, Oxford 1985, p. 202) of two tombs of the 2nd millennium, which had probably been cult centres for some time (different views in H. Gallet de Santerre, *Délos primitive et archaïque*, Paris 1958, pp. 113–99; Ph. Bruneau, *Recherches sur les cultes de Délos*, Paris 1970, pp. 45–8). As for the offerings, their arrival in Delos is attested in inscriptions of the 4th cent. BC: see J. Tréheux, in *Studies Presented to D. M. Robinson*, II, St Louis 1953, pp. 762–3. Unless this is a case of ritual simulation (L. A. El'nickij, *MASP* IV (1962), 209–12), they may have come from communities of Greek origin in the Balkans (C. T. Seltman, *CQ* XXII (1928), 155–9; A. D. Nock, *CR* XLIII (1929), 126) or even just from Epirus (R. L. Beaumont, *JHS* LVI (1936), 198–9); it is less likely that they came from the Baltic along the 'amber route' (R. Harris, *JHS* XLV (1925), 229–42).

32. Ὑπερβορέων ... λέγουσι: here more explicitly than at ch. 27 Herodotus disbelieves that Aristeas actually drew from the tales of the Issedones. As a matter of fact, Aristeas could believe that he was identifying in the northern peoples (if not in the Chinese: see Bolton, pp. 98–101) the Hyperboreans of myth. Their name, which is Greek, was of course unknown to the Scythians whom Herodotus questioned, in contrast with the 'Scythian' name of the Arimaspians (see Introduction, pp. 548 ff.).   'Ησιόδῳ: cf. fr. 150 Merkelbach–West (Hyperboreans 'rich in horses', in a series of remote peoples).   'Ομήρῳ ... ἐποίησε: fr. 2 Bernabé = 2 Davies. The *Epigoni*, followed by the *Thebais*, was attributed also to Antimachus of Teos (*Test.* 1 and 2 Bernabé); on the doubt, cf. II 117; H. Diels, *Neue Jahrb. für das klassische Altertum* (1910), 24–5; H. Verdin, *Historiographia antiqua*, Leuven 1977, p. 59.

33,1. ἱρά: the nature of the offerings was secret according to Pausanias I 31,2; in Callimachus, *Del.* 283–4 they appear to be ears of corn, which seems likely: see Tréheux, in op. cit., pp. 765–6; Bruneau, op. cit., p. 40; W. H. Mineur, *Callimachus, Hymn to Delos, Introduction and Commentary*, Leiden 1984, p. 226.

1–2. ἐξ Ὑπερβορέων ... Δῆλον: the itinerary, vague at first, can be more easily recognized beginning with the Adriatic and Dodona: see G. B. Biancucci, *RFIC* CI (1973), 207–20. The route is not dissimilar in Callimachus *Del.* 275 ff. and *Aet.* fr. 186 Pfeiffer = 97 Massimilla, while Paus. I 31,2, reflects an 'Athenian' version, cf. Tréheux, op. cit., pp. 766–70; Bruneau, op. cit., pp. 40–4. It is not to be ruled out (see e.g. U. von Wilamowitz-Moellendorf, *Der Glaube der Hellenen*, I, Basel 1955², pp. 100–1) that the offerings were sent out from the sanctuary at Dodona, and that the rest was a legend (with 'Scythians' used generally for the peoples of the north). The reason why Andros was omitted is unknown, see Biancucci, art. cit., p. 216 (cf. Tréheux, in op. cit., pp. 770 ff.).

3. Ὑπερόχην τε καὶ Λαοδίκην: on the variants of the names, and the possibility of reading Λαοδόκην, see L. Weber, *RhM* LXXXII (1933), 201, n. 1; L. Radermacher, *RhM* XCIII (1950), 325, n. 1.   **Περφερέες:** perhaps Πέρφερες must be read (cf. Hesychius, p. 2010 Schmitt), an Aeolic form which can be explained as 'the ones who carry around' (Weber, art. cit., pp. 225–7). The Herodotean text suggests that there was in Delos a priestly college in charge of processions which found its mythical archetype in the Hyperborean escorts.

4. τοῖσι πλησιοχώροισι: Wesseling's emendation for τοὺς πλησιοχώρους of the mss. The word may perhaps be expunged as a gloss to τοὺς οὔρους suggested by 33,1.

5. οἶδα δὲ ... τὰ ἱρά: 'Queen Artemis' (cf. V 7; *Diana regina* appears in Thracian inscriptions of the Roman period; see G. Kazarow, *RE* VI A 1 1936, coll. 505–9) must be identified with the Thracian 'great goddess' Bendis: see A. Fol and I. Marazov, *Thrace and the Thracians*, London 1977, p. 22; Z. Gočeva, *Klio*, LXVIII (1986), 85–6. Are perhaps the doubtful readings of the tradition, ἐχούσας and θυούσας, both glosses to be expunged, and τὰς ... γυναῖκας a proleptical subject, with τὰ ἱρά governed by θύωσι? On the Paeonians see note to 49,1; on the type of argument, cf. ch. 195.

34,1–2. καὶ ταῦτα ... τὸ σῆμα: the cutting of hair on a tomb has several parallels: cf. Paus. I 43,4 (Iphinoe); Euripides, *Hipp.* 1423 ff.; Paus. II 32,1–4; Lucian, *De Syria Dea* 60 (Hippolytus); see S. Eitrem, *Opferritus und Voropfer der Griechen und Römer*, Kristiania 1915, pp. 363–6; Burkert, *Homo Necans*, p. 231, n. 4. It is a rite of passage (see K. Dowden, *Death and the Maiden*, London–New York 1989, pp. 1–3 and *passim*), not without agricultural elements: see e.g. Nilsson,

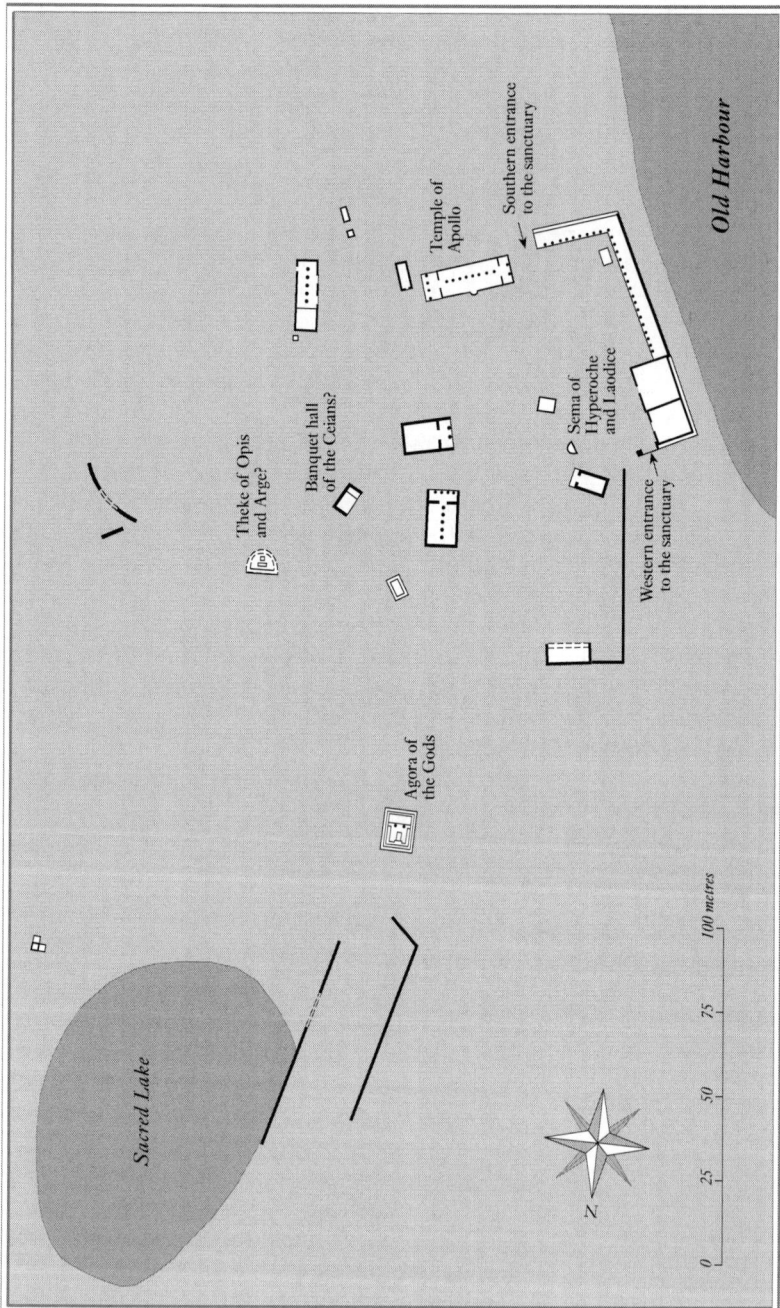

Map 42. Delos: the sanctuary of Apollo at the start of the fifth century

Griechische Feste, p. 208. The tomb must be identified with a semicircular trench near Artemisium, which contained Mycenean pottery (Bruneau–Ducat, pp. 149–50, no. 41). On the olive tree see Gallet de Santerre, op. cit., pp. 193–5.

35,1. τὴν Ἄργην τε καὶ τὴν Ὦπιν: the name Ὦπις (Οὖπις in other sources) is attested as epithet of Artemis (see O. Höfer, 'Opis', in Roscher, *Lexikon* III, coll. 927–30; G. Radke, *RE* IX A 1 1961, coll. 926–9) and is perhaps of Asian origin (W. Fauth, *BzN* IV (1969), 148–71). Instead of Ἄργη other sources cite Ἑκαέργη, which corresponds to Ἑκάεργος of Apollo (see Höfer, op. cit., coll. 928–9; L. Radermacher, *RhM* XCII (1950), 325–9): it might be a hypostasis of Artemis, or of ancient Aegean goddesses which were absorbed into her cult.

2. τῇ Εἰλειθυίῃ: cf. *Hymn. Hom. Ap.* 97 ff., 'Eileithyia who induces women's labour'. On her cult, Bruneau, *Recherches sur les cultes de Délos*, pp. 212–19.

ἅμα αὐτοῖσι τοῖσι θεοῖσι: did Arge and Opis come with Artemis and Apollo? Postulating a tradition according to which Apollo and Artemis were not born on Delos, but came there later (thus e.g. W. Sale, *HThR* LIV (1961), 75–89; an arrival of Apollo with two Hyperboreans is depicted on a Melian vase dating from the 7th cent. BC, *LIMC* II 1, p. 304, *Apollon* no. 1005; see e.g. E. Simon, *Die Götter der Griechen*, Munich 1980², p. 127) would, however, imply incoherence on Herodotus' part. ἅμα αὐτοῖσι τοῖσι θεοῖσι <γενομένοισι> may perhaps be integrated. If, on the other hand, we are to understand by 'the divinities' the cortège of goddesses present at the birth, then Ph.-E. Legrand's αὐτῇσι τῇσι θεοῖσι (*REA* XL (1938), 230–1) is preferable.

3. Ὤλην ἀνὴρ Λύκιος: a semi-mythical Lycian or Hyperborean poet, to whom several hymns were attributed: for other attestations see P. Maas, *RE* XVII 2 1937, coll. 2432–3. The hymns of Olen, which were sung at the great religious meetings of Ionians and islanders (cf. Thuc. III 104,3), seem to be alluded to in *Hymn. Hom. Ap.* 146–64.

4. τῶν μηρίων ... ἐπιβαλλομένον: these must be the sacrifices on the altar of Artemis: the bones of the lower limbs, μηρία, were the portion reserved for the gods; see e.g. K. Meuli, *Phyllobolia für P. von der Mühll*, Basel 1946, pp. 215 ff. For the scattering of the ash resulting from a sacrifice, some parallels in Nilsson, *GgrR*, pp. 86–8. ἡ δὲ θήκη ... ἱστιητορίου: the identification with a tomb on the south side of the portico of Antigonus, which contains pottery dating from Late Helladic I and III, is contested but likely (F. Courby, *Exploration archéologique de Délos*, V, Paris 1912, pp. 63–74). On Herodotus' topographic evidence in connection with procession routes see Bruneau–Ducat, pp. 144–5, no. 32; A. Papageorgiu-Venetas, *Délos. Recherches sur une ville antique*, Munich 1981, pp. 42–51. The location of the 'banquet hall of the Ceans' is uncertain (perhaps Bruneau–Ducat, n. 19): cf. G. Roux, *Études déliennes*, Paris 1973, pp. 525–54; L. Gernet, *The Anthropology of Ancient Greece*, Baltimore 1981, pp. 35–6, n. 2.

36,1. Ἀβάριος: ascetic and healer, follower of Apollo, of uncertain dating: sources in E. Bethe, *RE* I 1 1893, coll. 16–17. His reputation spread in Pythagorean contexts (see Bolton, pp. 157–8; pp. 149–50) on account of his shamanic qualities: the arrow is symbolic of flight, and according to some traditions Abaris flew on it (cf. P. Wolters, *SBAW* (1926), 3–18; L. P. Potapov, *Sovetskaja Etnografija* (1934), 64–76). These characteristics suggest contact with central and northern Eurasia: see K. Meuli, *Hermes*, LXX (1935), 159–63; Dodds, pp. 140–1; H. W. Haussig, *Byzantinoslavica*, XXXIV (1973), 188, connects the name with that of the Avars (reservations in J. Bremmer, *The Early Greek Concept of Soul*, Princeton 1983, pp. 43–6). The qualification of 'Hyperborean' stems from here.   οὐ λέγω ... σιτεόμενος: the transmitted text can, with a quibble (cf. VII 137,1), be understood as 'I shall not expound in detail..., confining myself to saying that...'. Reiske expunged λέγων; in this case, οὐ might be expunged as well (dittographic or the remnant of a correction): cf. 99,5, and Kühner–Gerth, *Gr. Grammatik* II, pp. 99–100, and 583. Rosén brackets the whole sentence λέγων ... σιτεόμενος (cf. B. Bravo, *ASNP* s. IV, V (2000), 79–80). οὐ λέγω γέλων is now proposed by C. Saerens, in *Studia varia Bruxellensia*, III, Leuven 1994, pp. 145–58 (with full discussion).   εἰ δέ ... ἄλλοι: Herodotus argues against the artificial character of the (wholly Greek) name of a people which means 'beyond the north wind' (cf. the analogous contention in III 115,2) by ironically taking the geometrical and symmetrical viewpoint of Ionian geographers. If these postulate a people who are defined by its northernness, then why don't they also postulate a southern one? The argument was misunderstood by Eratosthenes, I B 21 Berger = Strabo I 3,22; see Ph.-E. Legrand, *REA* XL (1938), 231–2 (a contrasting view in J. Romm, *TAPhA* CXIX (1989), 97–113).

2. γελῶ: from the preceding consideration on geographical symmetry springs the vast polemical argument, which lasts until ch. 45, against the artificial character-istics of Ionic maps (cf. II 21 ff.; IV 8,2). The circular image of the earth was current among ancient cartographers (see Agathemerus I 1, *GGM* II, p. 471; Anaximander, 13 A10, B5 DK; cf. Berger, pp. 31–9); while the idea of Ocean surrounding the *oikumene*, derived from myth and epic, was held as true by many 'physicists' (38 B1 DK) and by Hecataeus (*FGrHist* 1 F 18, F 36, F 302; cf. Berger, pp. 39–77). The equivalence between Asia and Europe followed from the inscrib-ing of the *oikumene* in a circle (see Heidel). To the 'scientific' speculation of the Ionians (cf. Janni, p. 30 and *passim*), Herodotus opposes a more empirical approach. His scheme begins with a description of Asia (chs. 37–41) from which emerges the specific situation of Libya, by Herodotus' time considered a third part of the world (cf. II 16) in contrast with the older twofold conception mentioned in 36,2 (cf. Berger, pp. 77–100; Zimmermann, pp. 23–133). However, this threefold division threw out of balance the relation between a boundless Europe, whose northern border with the Ocean was not quite clear (cf. III 115,2), and an Asia and Libya which taken together were the same in length as Europe alone (to which all the regions north of the Phasis, Caspian, and Araxes were attributed: 40,1), and in width were more limited, since they had been circum-navigated (42–5,1). Originally, the idea of an Ocean surrounding the earth and source of the Nile and the Phasis/Tanais was meant to furnish natural borders for the sectors of the earth, which were thought of as 'islands' (cf. Strabo I 4,7). According to Herodotus, these borders reveal themselves as purely conventio-nal (39,1; cf. II 16), and the division into uneven sectors appears therefore

irrational (42,1; 45,2): cf. Scheliha; Thomas, *Herodotus*, pp. 75–101; Bichler, pp. 15–21. On Herodotus' Europe see now Sieberer; on Libya, Zimmermann, *passim.* γῆς περιόδους: περίοδος τῆς γῆς is here, as in V 49,1, the 'map': cf. Ar. *Nub.* 206; Diog. Laert. V 51; Arrian, *Ind.* III 1; Aelian, *Var. Hist.* III 28; Aristotle, *Meteor.* 362b12 ff., seems to be echoing the Herodotean passage. Maps were the object of explanatory commentaries (see ἐξηγησόμενον here) which could be put into writing (Peretti, p. 21, n. 18; F. Prontera, *Strabone. Contributi allo studio della personalità e dell'opera*, I, Perugia 1984, pp. 239–40). γῆς περίοδοι are attested, before Herodotus, for Anaximander (12 A2 DK), Scylax (Suidas, s.v. [σ. 710 A.]; see Peretti, pp. 69–80), Hecataeus (*FGrHist* 1 F 125; see Jacoby, *RE* VII 2 1912, col. 2672; G. Nenci, *Hecataei Milesii Fragmenta*, Florence 1954, pp. xv–xvi). κυκλοτερέα ὡς ἀπὸ τόρνου: strongly ironical; cf. Plato, *Tim.* 33b; Strabo I 3,3; II 5,5; Berger, p. 35, n. 4.

37–41. Without consideration for abstract divisions between the parts of the world, Herodotus reviews the *oikumene* proceeding by peoples (cf. II 17,1). The starting-point are the Persians, who are located in the southern portion of the continental strip, between the Black Sea and the Erythraean Sea. All that lies to the west is grouped into two 'peninsulae', of which the first is Asia Minor; the second, dilated to include Libya (which is in any case rather narrow in Herodotus' mind: see notes ff.), may seem artificial. As a matter of fact Herodotus is adopting the viewpoint according to which Persia is at the centre of the world, probably on the basis of a Persian map, perhaps one linked with the activities of Scylax (see J. L. Myres, *Geographical J.*, VI (1896), 606–31; Myres, pp. 37–40; P. Calmeyer, *AMI* XV (1982), 176–8). The exposition by 'peninsulae' is connected in part to the geographical placement of peoples in the royal lists (Heidel, pp. 52–3), but for the most part it is a polemic expedient against the Ionic threefold division: in place of geometrical space, a more 'dynamic' space is put forward, following the course of a *periplus* (see Janni, p. 16, n. 2). Hence the emphatic *exordium*, with Πέρσαι in asyndeton.

37. Πέρσαι... ἐκδιδοῖ: 'south sea' and 'north sea' (here the Indian Ocean and the Black Sea) are designations relative to the continental strip between Persians and Colchians (see A. I. Dovatur, *VDI* CLXI (1982), 110–13). The name of the Erythraean ('red') Sea could be of Persian origin; see R. Schmitt, *Sprachwissenschaftliche Forschungen. Festschrift für J. Knobloch*, Innsbruck 1985, pp. 411–12; id., in *Hellas und der griechische Osten. Festschrift für P.R. Franke*, Saarbrücken 1996, pp. 219–24. Μῆδοι... Σάσπειρες: the Saspeiri must be located in the Çoruh valley (see III 94,1; Müller II, pp. 216–17); by 'Medians', then, the great historic Media must be meant; see Herzfeld, p. 287; P. Briant, *L'Asie centrale et les royaumes proche-orientaux du premier millénaire*, Paris 1984, pp. 35–43. Cf. I 104,1. Κόλχοι: in the valley of the Phasis, modern-day Rion; see O. Lordkipanidze, *Das alte Kolchis und seine Beziehungen zur griechischen Welt vom 6. zum 4. Jh. v. Chr.*, Konstanz 1985; *Das alte Georgien*, Weinheim 1990; *AncCiv* I (1994), 127–68; Braund. ἐς τὴν... ἐκδιδοῖ: the Phasis is mentioned because it is the northern border of Asia (see 45,2).

38,2. Ἑλλήσποντον: including, as often in 5th-cent. usage, the Propontis; see How–Wells, ad loc.; Müller II, p. 838.   Σιγείου τοῦ Τρωικοῦ: town and promontory (Yenişehir Burnu) on the south-western end of the Dardanelles; Müller II, pp. 932–5.   Μυριανδικοῦ κόλπου: the gulf of Alexandretta, if not a bay on its southern end (S. Smith, *Mélanges syriens offerts à R. Dussaud*, I, Paris 1939, pp. 27–31). Cf. D. Asheri, *Quaderni storici*, LXXVI (1991), 40; Müller II, pp. 183–4.   Τριοπίου ἄκρης: the Deve Boynu Burnu, the extremity of the Cnidus peninsula (Reşadiye): see Müller II, pp. 390–5.   τριήκοντα: the lists in III 90 ff. and VII 72 ff. have in common, for the region in question, twenty-four to twenty-six names (excluding the Colchians, whom Herodotus, however, could have reckoned): Moschi, Tibareni, Macrones, Mossynoeci, Mares, Alarodi, Armenians, Syrians = Cappadocians, Matieni, Paphlagonians, Mariandyni, Thracians of Asia, Hellespontians, Aeolians, Ionians, Mysians, Lydians, Carians, Lycians, Milyans, Phrygians, Pamphylians, Cilicians; the Cabali/Cabelei and the Lasoni are two different peoples in III 90,1, the same people in VII 77; and from the second list a name has been lost in VII 76. Moreover, the names of the Magnesians and of the Hytennians are to be found in the first list, of the Dorians and the Ligyans in the second. In I 28 the 'Thracians of Asia' are further divided into Bithynians (cf. VII 75,2) and Thynians, and the Chalybes (who might belong to the peoples between Armenia and the Euxine mentioned in III 93,1) also figure, whereas other peoples, like the Caunians, are mentioned elsewhere. The figure 'thirty' might be a round one, or it might result from taking larger clusters and subdivisions into account.

39,1. ἥ τε Περσική: indicated as the starting-point, even though it has already been included among the continental peoples at ch. 37.   νόμῳ: 'by convention' (cf. F. Heinimann, *Nomos und Physis*, Basel 1945, pp. 82–3), without a natural border (not φυσικῶς, as e.g. Strabo I 2,28 says) because Libya is a continuation of it.   τὸν κόλπον τὸν Ἀράβιον: the Red Sea.   ἐς τὸν... ἐσήγαγε: see II 158,1; and C. Tuplin, *AH* VI (1991), 237–83. The mention of the canal matches the mention of the Phasis at ch. 37, as if to signal a possible—though not natural—border.
2. μέχρι... μοῦνα: Persia and Phoenicia (linked with the continental strip as part of the 'large flat space', cf. Ph. Legrand, *REA* XL (1938), 233–4) are only the starting-point of the 'peninsula': the three 'peoples' must be Assyrians, Arabs, and Palestinian Syrians.   τῆσδε τῆς θαλάσσης: the Mediterranean Sea (cf. V. Burr, *Nostrum mare*, Stuttgart 1932, pp. 109 ff.).   Συρίην τὴν Παλαιστίνην: the coastal strip between Egypt and Phoenicia; see I 105,1.

40,1. ὁ Ἀράξης... ἀνίσχοντα: there is here a confused notion of the Amu-Dar'ja or the Syr Dar'ja; cf. I 202,1: the name Ἀράξης must have been used of several rivers (see Altheim–Stiehl, *Geschichte*, pp. 125–6), hence the contamination in Herodotus. Cf. 45,2: by adopting a longitudinal border, Herodotus obtains a Europe which is 'longer' than Asia and Libya put together.
2. Ἰνδικῆς: the *Hinduš* of Persian sources, i.e. the Indus valley; see III 98–105.   ἔρημος: the Thar desert, see III 98,2.

41. ἀπὸ... ἐκδέκεται: the idea of a continuity as far as Libya was aided by the fact that the Persian empire extended as far as Cyrene and Barca. As in II 17,1, Egypt cannot be attributed either to Asia or Libya.   δέκα... στάδιοι: cf. II 158,4 (and Strabo XVII 1,21). The figure (at least 179 km.) is excessive against the actual 115 km.

42,2. Νεκῶ... κόλπον: on Necho (610–595 BC) and his canal see II 158–9. Cf. note to II 158,2–3.

2–4. ἀπέπεμψε... δεξιά: already Posidonius (see Strabo II 3,4–5; cf. I 2,26; other sources in Gsell, *Hérodote*, pp. 229–30), followed by many modern scholars, cast doubt on the enterprise. At any rate, the length of time indicated is realistic, and the winds and currents favourable (see already Rennell II, pp. 375–408), while the detail that the Phoenicians 'had the sun on their right' (seafaring expression; cf. Homer, *Od.* V 273–7, and Peretti, p. 92 and n. 101), as would, in fact, have been the case for one who travelled (south-) westwards while keeping to the south of the line of the apparent course of the sun, seems a guarantee of truth: see further below. But the enterprise is absolutely exceptional for the time, and might be merely a 'saga' invented by the Egyptians to contrast a successful expedition to the failed expedition of Xerxes, or by the Greeks as a legendary 'Pharaoh's exploit' (A. B. Lloyd, *JEA* LXIII (1977), 148–55). Necho's interests in the Red Sea and the southern regions are, in any case, well attested: the extraordinary enterprise could arise from these, even though it might not have been 'planned' to the extent that Herodotus states: see H. T. Wallinga, *Achaemenid History I. Sources, Structures and Synthesis*, Leiden 1987, pp. 55–9; Zimmermann, pp. 99–102, 116–19. Φοίνικας: close relations between Phoenicians and Egyptians (cf. II 112) are well attested from the Late Period: cf. E. Bresciani, *Egitto e Vicino Oriente*, X (1987), 69–78; S. F. Bondì, in *Hérodote et les peuples non grecs*, pp. 267–72. ὁρμηθέντες... Αἴγυπτον: the Phoenicians would have doubled Cape Guardafui in autumn, sailed on taking advantage of the northern monsoon, and reached the height of the Tropic of Capricorn by January–February. In the Mozambique Channel, when the coastline faced south-west, the midday sun must have at one point appeared to the north, i.e. 'to the right', then more and more distinctly to the right as winter approached the southern hemisphere while they navigated westwards along the south African coasts, until the first stop (see Gsell, *Hérodote*, p. 228). The Agulhas current, the south-easterly trade winds, and the Benguela current would then have aided the rest of their journey in the Atlantic. φθινόπωρον: 'sowing season', different in the two hemispheres. A first stop must have taken place at the southern extremity of Africa, another one in its north-western part (Gsell, *Hérodote*, pp. 226–7). The recourse to sowing has few parallels in ancient seafaring (ibid., pp. 235–6; Lloyd, art. cit., pp. 148–55); but this very fact might be proof that the tale is not made up.   ἐμοὶ... τεῳ: this ironic expression (also in V 86,3, without δή) must imply a polemic with the source (known to the public?). Herodotus, though he has some notion of the apparent motion of the sun (cf. II 25–6), finds 'the sun on the right' unbelievable, perhaps solely on account of an incoherent understanding of astronomical phenomena (thus Berger, p. 68; other hypotheses in Desanges, *Recherches*, 9–16); but more probably because he supposes that the navigation took place during the austral summer, while the sun was above Libya, and that since the latter is not 'wide' (42,1; cf. III 17,1, and 114, on the extreme location of the Ethiopians) it does not reach beyond the Tropic.

43,1. *Καρχηδόνιοί εἰσι... λέγοντες*: in Herodotus' time Carthaginian supremacy over western Libya precluded Greek access to the area, and the last non-Carthaginian to have entered the area, Sataspes, had not solved the matter. The Carthaginians must have spoken not so much of other circumnavigations which had been carried out, but rather of the feasibility of circumnavigations (cf. *ἐοῦσα περίρρυτος* at 42,2, which concept must be understood also with *ἐγνώσθη*, and with *ἐξευρέθη* at 44,1; see 44,3; 45,1 and 4). A reference to the explorations of Hanno (cf. ch. 196) is doubtful, see Gsell, *Hérodote*, pp. 231–3; Desanges, *Recherches*, pp. 35–7; Zimmermann, pp. 98–132; cf. chs. 195–6.   ***Σατάσπης***: the expedition of Sataspes (**Satāspa*, Elam. *ša-da-aš-ba*; see W. Brandenstein, *BzN* IV (1953), 288, and Mayrhofer, p. 229; son of one *Čišpiš*), which must have been reported to Herodotus in Samos (43, 7), need not be doubted: see A. Klotz, *Klio*, XXX (1987), 343–6; F. Colin, *ZPE* LXXXII (1990), 287–98. However, it is difficult to determine its date and extent. According to v. Fritz I, p. 6, n. 14, it took place before the expedition in Greece; according to H. Swoboda, *RE* II A 1 1921, col 61, between 475 and 467 BC. The 'Pygmies' may suggest the inhabitants of Cameroon (Klotz, art. cit., p. 346), but in antiquity these dwelt further north (cf. II 32,6, and Lloyd, *Commentary 1–98*, pp. 138–9; Lloyd, note to II 32,28). Peoples of short stature such as the Gagu are still attested today on the Ivory Coast (see Gsell, *Histoire* I, pp. 511–12; Desanges, *Recherches*, pp. 29–33).

2. *Ζωπύρου τοῦ Μεγαβύζου*: cf. III 153,1.

4. *Σολόεις*: cf. Hanno, *Periplus* 3, *GGM* I, p. 3. Mostly identified with Cap Cantin, or Cap Spartel (see e.g. Goebel, pp. 57–8; J. Carcopino, *Le Maroc antique*, Paris 1943, pp. 91–2), it is said to lie west of the Pillars of Heracles and at the west end of Libya 'by the northern sea' (II 32,4), which, in the strict sense, would prove contradictory to IV 42,2, where the same 'northern sea' appears to be on this side of the Pillars, but can be accepted, as a loose statement, if Herodotus located it not too far from these latter (which is one of the arguments against the identification of Herodotus' Pillars of Heracles with the Sicily Channel now proposed in a whimsical and sometimes uncritical, yet stimulating book: S. Frau, *Le colonne d'Ercole*, Rome 2002).

5. *ὄρεα*: Mt Cameroon and the slopes of the highlands; or the slopes of Fouta-Djalon, Loma, and Nimba, if the 'Pygmies' are to be located between Guinea and the Ivory Coast.   ***ἀδικέειν οὐδέν***: on the contrary, violence was habitual on such expeditions; see *Od.* IX 40–2; Mimnermus, fr. 3 Gentili–Prato.   ***πρόβατα***: in favour of the reading *βρωτά* (as opposed to *πρόβατα*='flocks', which is also closer to the above-mentioned passage from the *Odyssey*) see e.g. Desanges, *Recherches*, p. 29, n. 2: they would not have been herdsmen.

6. τοῦ δὲ... ἐνίσχεσθαι: Herodotus seems to think that this is an excuse: in 43,4 he had adduced as the cause dismay for the difficulty of the enterprise. According to F. Colin, *ZPE* LXXXII (1990), 287–98, Sataspes invented the pretext basing himself on Egyptian tales (cf. II 102). However, Sataspes might truly have been obstructed by winds and currents, which are unfavourable off the coast of Sierra Leone as well as of Cameroon (see already Rennell II, pp. 405–6). ἀνεσκολόπισε: this is the typical punishment, and the anecdote is of interest to Herodotus also because it illustrates the king's criteria of justice: cf. I 137,1; VII 194,2; O. Bucci, *RIDA* XXV (1978), 20–3; Briant, *Histoire*, p. 348 = ET, p. 336.

7. τούτου... ἐπιλήθομαι: thus Herodotus, while alluding to the source, withholds the name of the Samian character involved in order to avoid compromising him: cf. I 51,4; II 123,2 (the opposite in VII 214,3).

44,1. κροκοδείλους: the *Crocodilus palustris*. The Indus is the 'second' after the Nile; cf. Arrian, *Anab.* VI 1,2, and E. A. Schwanbeck, *Megasthenis Indica*, Bonn 1846, pp. 2–5. Σκύλακα... Καρυανδέα: Scylax, born in Caryanda, a Carian city close to Myndus and Cos, left a report of the voyage of exploration he undertook on behalf of Darius (*FGrHist* 709 F 1–7; on the date cf. note to 44,2), and was also the author of a Γῆς περίοδος and of a biography of Heraclides of Mylasa: see Peretti, pp. 57–83; G. Schepens, *FGrHist* (continued) 1000. On the Persian kings' use of Carian sailors see Herzfeld, pp. 43–4, 275–87.

2. ἐκ Κασπατύρου... γῆς: cf. III 102, 1; the indication of both the region and its capital might follow a Persian model; see Herzfeld, p. 338, n. 4. Hecataeus (*FGrHist* 1 F 295) locates Κασπάπυρος (perhaps the more correct form; cf. the Indian *pura* = 'city') in the Gandhāra; variously identified, it is perhaps Pešāvar, while Πακτυϊκή (cf. the Vedic *Paktah*) might be related to *pashtō*, the language spoken in modern-day Afghanistan; bibl. in P. Daffinà, *AAntHung* XXVIII (1980), 1–4; note to III 102,1–2. On the various hypotheses advanced see, however, the objections of K. Karttunen, *India in Early Greek Literature*, Helsinki 1989, pp. 41–8, 65–8. πρὸς... ἀνατολὰς: the mistake (the Indus flows south-westwards) might stem from attributing to the Indus the direction of the Kābul, from whose lower course (the only navigable stretch) Scylax had set out. τριηκοστῷ: the figure seems excessive; unless it is conventional, or modelled on the Phoenician circumnavigation of Africa (Herzfeld, p. 282), then they must have made several stops (Peretti, p. 57). πρότερον: see 42,2–3.

3. μετὰ... ἐχρᾶτο: Darius must have aimed, as well as at the subjugation of Pañjāb and Sindh, at the establishment of a great sea-path, in connection with the works on the Nile canal–Red Sea; on Achaemenid interest in the Indian Ocean see F. Miltner, *Saeculum*, III (1952), 522–55. The Kabret stele (Posener, pp. 76–7, 180–1) mentions the voyage of a fleet burdened with Egyptian tributes to Persia (see A. V. Edakov, *VDI* CLII (1980), 113); this sea-path was at any rate soon abandoned, see J. F. Salles *Achaemenid History, IV. Centre and Periphery*, Leiden 1990, pp. 117–18. The date is uncertain: perhaps exploration and conquest proceeded hand in hand (H. Schiwek, *Bonner Jahrb.*, CLXII (1962), 8–19), while the region of Hinduš does not appear in the Bisitun list (518BC) but is

present in one of the inscriptions of Tell el-Markhūta and on the plinth of the statue of Darius at Susa, dating from the first years of the 5th cent.: see F. Gisinger, *RE* III A 1 1927, coll. 620–1; Daffinà, art. cit., p. 2; Frye, p. 104; A. D. H. Bivar, in *CAH* IV, pp. 194–210; Briant, *Histoire*, pp. 152–3, 494–5 = ET, pp. 139–40,477 (cf. Introduction, p. 545, n. 2).

45,2. ἐπ᾽ ὅτευ... γυναικῶν: the division into three is attributed to the 'Ionians' in II 16. The derivation of the name Εὐρώπη, which denotes solely continental Greece as opposed to the Peloponnese and the islands in *Hymn. Hom. Ap.* 251, is uncertain: a Semitic origin ('land of the west') is no longer accepted, and some have suggested a connection with εὐρύς ('spacious land'? See Dombrowski; C. Milani, in *L'Europa nel mondo antico*, Milan 1986, pp. 3–11). The name Ἀσία, which at first must have indicated a part of Lydia (cf. Ἀσίω ἐν λειμῶνι in *Il.* II. 461), probably derives from the Hittite toponym *Assuwa* ('good land', from the Hittite *assus*, equivalent to the Greek ἐΰς; see D. J. Georgacas, *Names*, XVII (1969), 1–90) through the determinative *ἈσϜία = Mycenean *a-si-wi-ja*. Λιβύη/Λίβυες is the Greek rendition of the Egyptian *rbw*, attested since Ramessid times as the name of a people west of the Delta (see J. Osing, in *LdÄ* III 1980, coll. 1015–33; Zimmermann, pp. 6–21; note to chs. 168–99). As for the female characters, Libya, not attested earlier than Pindar, *Pyth.* 9,55 and Aeschylus, *Supp.* 316, is an artificial eponym (cf. E. Catani, *QAL* XII (1988), 385–400); while Asia and Europa were already known with a precise identity to Homer and Hesiod (see notes on 45,3 and 4), and especially in the case of the latter the coincidence of name and toponym might be the result of a mere convergence, so that the attempt to connect geographical names with myths might have appeared controversial and strained. Cf. *LIMC* II 1, pp. 857–8, IV 1, pp. 92–3, VI 1, pp. 284–6.   (οἱ δὲ... λέγουσι): cf. Agathemerus I 3, *GGM* II, p. 472; Aristides 36,87 Keil. The Phasis is indicated as a border in Aeschylus, fr. 191 Radt. The line Tanais–Palus Maeotis–'Cimmerian routes' (see 12,1), perhaps already mentioned by Hecataeus (see Jacoby's commentary to *FGrHist* 1 F 195: it is not certain whether the Tanais mentioned by Hecataeus is the Don), is presupposed in *De Aeribus Aquis Locis* 13, and generally adopted by subsequent geographers (e.g. Strabo VII 4,5).

3. γυναικὸς: the Oceanid Asia (Hesiod, *Theog.* 359) is Prometheus' wife also according to Stephanus of Byzantium, s.v. Ἀσία; according to Apollodoros I 2, 2–3 she is his mother.   ἐπὶ Ἀσίεω: see also Dionysus of Halicarnassus, *Ant. Rom.* I 27; other sources in Roscher, *Lexikon* I, col. 609. The name Ἀσίας might have originated from Ἀσίω in *Il.* II 461, taken as genitive Ἀσίω (J. Wackernagel, *Sprachliche Untersuchungen zu Homer*, Göttingen 1916, p. 86, n. 1). The Lydians in Herodotus might then conceal some Λυδιακά (Xanthus?). In fact, the Homeric expression, and perhaps also the name of the tribe Ἀσιάς of Sardis (also known from inscriptions: cf. *SEG* XIX 713–14; P. Herrmann, *Chiron* XXIII (1993), 233–48), are reminiscences of Assuwa.

4. Εὐρώπης: according to Herodotus, Europa, presumably Agenor's daughter (IV 147,4), was abducted by Cretans (I 2,1) and went to Lycia with her son

Sarpedon (cf. I 173,2). For the different versions of the myth, starting from *Il.* XIV 321–2, and Hesiod, fr. 141 Merkelbach–West, see W. Bühler, *Europa. Ein Überblick über die Zeugnisse des Mythos in der antiken Literatur und Kunst,* Munich 1968. To overcome the difficulty, Antimachus, fr. 3 Wyss, has Europa reach Boeotia (see L. Prandi, in *L'Europa,* op. cit., p. 38, n. 5); while Hippias (*FGrHist* 6 F 3; see also the scholium to Euripides, *Rh.* 28, pp. 327–8 Schwartz) turns to the Oceanid Europa, who appears together with Asia in Hesiod (*Theog.* 357 and 359); and Hegesippus (*FGrHist* 391 F 3) introduces into the myth a third, Thracian, Europa.

5. αὐτῶν: unless the text is corrupted, αὐτῶν, partitive, must pick up ταῦτα: 'those of these things which are common knowledge' (cf. Aristophanes, *Plut.* 1185). It is unlikely that it picks up τῶν διουρισάντων at 45,2 ('their doctrines', cf. II 17,2), or that it is equivalent to the περὶ αὐτῶν which recurs in the *locus similis* of Plato, *Phdr.* 230a (see Kühner–Gerth, *Gr. Grammatik* I, pp. 335–6; if so also αὐτέων could be defended).

46,1–2. ὁ δὲ Πόντος... ἄγαμαι: the more strictly ethnographic section begins here. With the phrase 'towards which Darius was marching', Herodotus points to the theme which he announced in ch. 1 and which he will not resume until ch. 83. The interest for the greater or lesser 'intelligence' of peoples and their customs (cf. I 136–7, and 196–9) is characteristic of the mind-frame of ancient ethnography, which sought after 'superlatives': see Trüdinger, pp. 27 ff.; Diller, pp. 83–8; Corcella, pp. 86–8. On Anacharsis see chs. 76–7. ἐντός: 'inside' coming from the coast, cf. ch. 173.

2–3. τὸ δὲ... προσμίσγειν: the mobility of nomads has always impressed sedentary peoples: see Briant, *État et pasteurs,* esp. pp. 12–25. In the case of the Scythians, the war with Darius had highlighted how it implied an advantageous 'impregnability' (cf. IV 83, 97, 127, 134; VII. 10α, 2; and see already Aeschylus, *Eum.* 700–3). It is for this reason that Herodotus here stresses the fact that the dominant Scythians were nomads, while neglecting the subject sedentary groups, and that he sees in this a strategic device, as will also Arrian, *FGrHist* 156 F 72. See Hartog, pp. 207–19 and *passim* = ET, pp. 193–206; Introduction, p. 563. φερέοικοι: this vivid expression had been used by Hesiod (*Op.* 571) to describe the snail, while in later authors it designates other animals: cf. *Hesiod, Works and Days,* ed. M. L. West, Oxford 1978, p. 302; I. Waern, Γῆς ὀστέα. *The Kenning in Prechristian Greek Poetry,* Uppsala 1951, pp. 38–46, 119–20. Here it alludes to the fact that the Scythians carry their homes (tents) on wagons, as is stated immediately afterwards: cf. chs. 28, 114, 121; Hesiod, fr. 151 Merkelbach–West; Pindar, fr. 105 Snell–Maehler; Aeschylus, *Prom,* 709 ff.; *De Aeribus Aquis Locis* 18; B. Bravo, *ASNP* s. IV, V (2000), 80–1 regards φερέοικοι ἐόντες as an interpolation, suggested by the οἰκοφόρα of Pseudo-Arrian's *Periplus Ponti Euxini* 49 (*GGM* I, p. 413). Scythian wagons are variously represented in Greek vase-painting (see Vos, pp. 6–12); fragments have been found in graves, as well as clay models which exhibit various superstructures: see Rolle, *Totenkult* I 1, pp. 74–5; 113–21; A. Häusler, *Altertum,* XXVIII (1982), 16–26; S. S. Bessonova, in *Drevnosti stepnoj,* pp. 102–17; *Narody,* p. 260; R. Rolle, in *Gold der Steppe*, pp. 85–92. Cf. note to 71,1.   ἱπποτοξόται: on the Scythians as archers on horseback see Thuc. II 96, 1; Aelian, *Tac.* II 13. The technique was developed by the nomads of the steppe as early as the end of the 2nd millennium; cf. A. Azzaroli, *An Early History of Horsemanship*, Leiden 1985, pp. 45–6, 66 ff.   ἀπὸ κτηνέων: on the diet based on meat and milk, cf. N. A. Gavriljuk, *SA* (1987), 1, pp. 21–34.

47–58. Herodotus cleverly relates the custom of nomadism to its environmental prerequisite: the existence of vast, well-watered flatlands able to provide pasture for the herds (cf. Briant, *État et pasteurs*, pp. 26–7). However, this connection serves him primarily to introduce a new *excursus* on the rivers of Scythia, which picks up on, and expounds, the information furnished at chs. 16 ff. (see Introduction, pp. 557 ff.). Τοῖσι μὲν δὴ ὀνομαστοῖσι..., at the beginning of ch. 58, picks up in ring composition ὅσοι δὲ ὀνομαστοί at 47,2 and closes the section (of which ch. 58 is only an appendix), while τὰ ... μέγιστα at the beginning of ch. 59 alludes to the device of nomadism, termed μέγιστον in ch. 46. These surveys of large rivers were of great interest to the Greek audience, which in its own land was accustomed only to torrent-like streams (see ch. 82); the parallel with the very different Egyptian canalization, described in II 108, is merely formal: cf. O. Longo, *QS* XXIV (1986), 30, 39–44. The Scythian hydrographic system traced by Herodotus creates several problems of identification. Geological surveys do not allow us to postulate very relevant modifications since Herodotus' times (L. Kádár, *Acta Geographica Debrecina*, XIV–XV (1975–6), 109–257, is not to be relied upon). First of all, it must be held in mind that rivers were known insomuch as they were used as lines of communication ('navigable from the sea') crossed by land routes; and, as is demonstrated by the case of the Ister, it was possible for different rivers along the same route to be considered one, or for different stretches of the same river to be considered different rivers. Hence the tendency to describe rivers as parallel lines perpendicular to the coast, which was the point of departure for penetration inland (cf. Janni, pp. 136–40). For this same reason Herodotus does not have an exact perception of the sources of rivers, which lay well away from the commercial routes: the hypothesis of the origin of all Scythian rivers from lakes might be linked to some notion of the marshy regions between Bielorussia and Ukraine, but it is in the first place the result of a general theory, opposed to the other theory which traced the origin of Scythian rivers in the Rhipaean mountains, which are not mentioned by Herodotus: see e.g. Aristotle, *Meteor.* I 13, 350b8–11; Berger, pp. 156–7. Extensive discussions in Schramm, *passim*; Rybakov, pp. 26–62; *Narody*, pp. 19–22, 271–93; *Stepi*, pp. 40–1.

47,2. πεντάστομος: by using this term Herodotus achieves an immediate effect of amplification. The Ister = Danube had five mouths also according to e.g. Ephorus, *FGrHist* 70 F 157; while other authors (e.g. Strabo VII 3,15) discerned seven mouths in the complex delta of the Danube, which at present has three main mouths: the sources in *Pomponii Melae de chorographia libri tres*, ed. P. Parroni, Rome 1984, p. 281; cf. N. Panin, *Dacia*, NS XXVII (1983), 175–84.

48–50. 'Ἴστρος was originally the name for the lower course alone of the Danube, known to the Greeks from the 7th cent. BC at least: see Schramm, p. 30, n. 46 and pp. 68–76; Pippidi; Boardman, *Greeks Overseas*, pp. 240–5, 247–50. For its upper course and its direction, Herodotus' information is for the most part incorrect (cf. II 33–4, IV 99–101; Arist. *Meteor.* I 13, 350b1 ff.): it allegedly originates in the area of the Pyrenees/Iberia (on Pyrene = Port Vendres, the Celts and the Cunesii/Cuneti see note on II 33,3) and bends south-east from northern Europe before flowing into Scythia from the west. Herodotus' Ister is in fact the transposition of a transcontinental route which initially ran up the Danube from its mouth but later, following the Sava and its tributaries, reached the plain of the Po (cf. Strabo IV 6,10, and VII 5,2, as well as the name of Istria) and thence western Europe: see R. Dion, *RPh* XLII (1968), 7–41. This enormous river becomes for Herodotus the European counterpart of the Nile (cf. II 26 and 33): like the Nile, it has a constant flow (this is not true, cf. *Narody*, pp. 272–3; but Herodotus is thinking of the more considerable variation in regimen of the rivers of the Aegean); and it is longer than the Nile only by virtue of its tributaries, which, unlike the ones of the upper Nile, were known to the Greeks because they were used by travellers and merchants.

48,2–3. διὰ μέν... Ἴστρον: the name Porata/Pyretus is preserved in that of the Prut, nowadays the border between Romania and the Moldavian Republic: see Schramm, pp. 49–55. According to some, the Tiarantus corresponds to the Siret, directly to the west (but there is no etymological connection: see Schramm, p. 218; for the opposite view, V. Pârvan, *Consideraţ iuni asupra unor nome de râuri daco-scitica*, Bucharest 1923). By postulating an imprecision in the text it is then possible to think, for the Ararus, the Naparis, and the Ordessus, of several tributaries of the Siret such as the Bistriţa, the Moldava, and the Trotuş (see most recently A. Vulpe, *StClas* XXIV (1986), 33–43); if, on the other hand, the Tiarantus does not correspond to the Siret, they might be the rivers which from the Transylvanian Alps flow down through Valachia toward the Danube: e.g. Tiarantus = Olt; Ordessus = Argeş; Naparis = Ialomiţa; Ararus = Siret (there might be a connection between the names Ὀρδησσός and Argeş; on the name Νάπαρις see Schramm, pp. 45 and 48; E. I. Solomonik, *Novye epigrafičeskie pamjatniki Chersonesa*, Kiev 1973, pp. 11–13). Discussion in A. I. Meljukova, *MIA* CL (1969), 61–2; *Narody*, pp. 273–5; Vulpe, art. cit., pp. 33–43; on Scythia's borders see chs. 99–101. The left tributaries of the lower Danube were intensely frequented by Greek merchants between the 6th and 5th cent.: cf. Pippidi, pp. 50–1; Isaac, pp. 269–70; B. Mitrea, *Numismatica e antichità classiche*, XII (1983), 119–33.

4. ἐκ δὲ Ἀγαθύρσων... Ἴστρῳ: the name of the Μάρις (Μάρισος in Strabo VII 3,13; cf. V. Georgiev, *BzN* XII (1961), 92) is preserved in that of the Mureş/Maros, which flows into the Tibiscus (Tisa), left tributary of the Danube, running from the Carpathians and Transylvania. Here (and perhaps also in Moldavia as far as the Dniester) lived the Agathyrsi (cf. ch. 104): see A. I. Meljukova, *MIA* LXIV (1958), 5–102; Rybakov, pp. 125–6; *Narody*, pp. 346–7; Ju. K. Kolosovskaja, *VDI*

CLXII (1982), 47–69; and in *Etnogenez*, pp. 181–93; Nejchardt, pp. 151–3; J. R. Gardiner-Garden, *Klio*, LXIX (1987), 336–8.

49,1. ἐκ δέ ... Ἴστρον: with these two groups of three rivers we seem to move on to the tributaries of the right bank. The Atlas (a Thracian name, see I. Duridanov, *Die Sprache der Thraker*, Neuried 1985, pp. 23–4), the Auras, and the Tibisis, in fact, flow from the Balkans: Mt Haemus (Thracian name for 'mountain ridge', see ibid., p. 30) corresponds to the Stara Planina, in which Herodotus seems to include also the western Balkans (see below; Müller II, pp. 822–5). The Athrys, the Noes, and the Artanes, on the other hand, flow from the territory of the Crobyzi, which Hecataeus, *FGrHist* 1 F 170 located south of the Ister (not far from the coast according to later sources: see M. Fluss, *RE* XI 2 1922, col. 1941; Danov, pp. 130–1). The names are not attested elsewhere, except for some loose quotations in Valerius Flaccus (*Argonautica* IV 719; VI 50, 100; cf. also the unknown locality on the Danube with the name of Τίβισκα in Ptolemy, *Geog.* III 10,12). Ἄθρυς is thought to be a variant of *Ieteros/Iantros*, modern-day Jantra, an important route towards the south (cf. T. Ivanov, *Klio*, XLVII (1966), 5–10; A. Fol, *La cultura e il patrimonio dei Traci*, Rome 1984, pp. 91–2; Duridanov, op. cit., p. 23); it is perhaps possible to draw a connection between Ἄυρας and *Abrit(t)us*, a Roman centre on the Beli Lom, near modern-day Razgrad; while it is unlikely that Νόης is linked with *Novae*, near modern-day Svištov (which is rather a Latin toponym, 'new coach stations'). All identifications remain hypothetical, and some have even thought that Herodotus has transposed to the south some tributaries of the left bank (the Τίβισις would then be the Tibiscus/Tisa): see most recently A. Vulpe, *StClas* XXIV (1986), 33–43; cf. *Narody*, pp. 275–6.

ἐκ δέ ... ἐς αὐτόν: the Σκίος is the Ὄσκιος of Thuc. II 96,4 and the *Oescus* of the Latin sources, modern day Iskǎr (on the name, which would mean 'water', see Duridanov, op. cit., pp. 36–7). It springs from the Rila mountains, which for Herodotus correspond to Mt Rhodope, and it flows towards the Danube, passing through the western and central Balkans, and offering an excellent communication route with the valleys of Nesta and Marica. On the Paeonians, who were settled in northern Macedonia, see V 1 ff.; I. L. Merker, *Balkan Studies*, VI 1 (1965), 35–54.

2. ἐξ Ἰλλυριῶν ... δέκεται: it is likely that the Βρόγγος is the Great Morava (Βάργος/Μάργος according to Strabo VII 5,12), in whose valley, to the south-east of Belgrade, had settled the Triballi, who later moved eastward (cf. Danov, pp. 100–3; F. Papazoglou, *The Central Balkan Tribes in Pre-Roman Times*, Amsterdam 1978, pp. 8–88). The Ἄγγρος might be the western Morava and/or the Ibar. Along these rivers there ran roads, which led, as well as to Illyria, to the valley of the Vardar and thence to the Aegean: cf. Danov, pp. 135–8; *Il crinale d'Europa. L'area illirico-danubiana nei suoi rapporti con il mondo classico*, Rome 1984.   **ἐκ δέ ... ἐς αὐτόν**: in the rivers Alpis and Carpis, not otherwise attested, some see a distorted echo of Alps and Carpathians. But Κάρπις might correspond to the *Colapis* in Pliny, *NH* III 148 (Κάλαπις in the codices of Strabo VII 5,2; cf. IV 6,10), i.e. to the Kupa, which springs from the heights of the Carsus

(Ἄλβιον) and flows into the Sava, linking the Danube with the Alpine and Transpadane area 'beyond the Umbrians' (who were then settled between Picenum and Po; cf. I 94 and D. Briquel, *MEFRA* LXXXV (1973), 357–93).

51. Τύρης: this is the Dniester: on the derivation from **tura-* = 'fast' cf. Schramm, pp. 85–93. By Τυρῖται Herodotus seems to mean all the Greeks who dwelt on its lower course in various settlements (see e.g. *Archeologija SSSR* IX, pp. 26–32). Among these, on the site of modern-day Belgorod Dnestrovskij, there was already by the 6th cent. the town of Tyras, a Milesian foundation according to pseudo-Scymnus 803, *GGM* I, p. 229, which was, however, of little importance in Herodotus' day (see most recently T. R. Samojlova, *Tira v VI–I vv. do n.e.*, Kiev 1988, with bibl.; M. Yu. Treister, *AncCiv* I (1994), 5–6).

52,1. Ὕπανις: the Hypanis, at whose mouth was Olbia, is the Southern Bug: on the name, perhaps connected to that of the Kuban', cf. Schramm, pp. 93–9. The colonists probably considered as its upper course the tributary Sinjucha, which flows through an area that was intensely frequented by Greek merchants: see K. K. Šilik, in *Problemy antičnoj istorii i kul'tury*, II, Erevan 1979, p. 454; Rybakov, pp. 31–6; on Greek trade see note to 17,2. The 'lake' from which the Hypanis is supposed to originate seems in this case not to be merely the result of a general theory (see note to chs. 47–58): it has a specific name, 'mother of the Hypanis', probably translated from Scythian (see ch. 86); and the wild horses, widespread in Ukraine up until the 19th cent. (see *Narody*, p. 279), are mentioned also in the Olbian inscription from the 6th cent. edited by A. S. Rusjaeva and Ju. G. Vinogradov, in *Gold der Steppe*, pp. 201–2 (*SEG* XLII 710; *IGDOP* 24; B. Bravo, in *Problemi*, pp. 254–64; cf. Vinogradov, *Olbia*, p. 18). According to Rybakov, p. 34, this is lake Tikič, from which originates the Gornij Tikič, which flows into the Sinjucha; other suggestions in *Narody*, p. 279.

3. Ἐξαμπαῖος: cf. ch. 81, which seems to attest a visit paid by Herodotus to the place. The name 'sacred ways' suggests a nexus of roads and trade activities: cf. O. S. Ostroverchov, in *Drevnosti*, pp. 86–7. Ἐξαμπῖος may be a version of **afsantai-*, with the same root of the Avestic *spənta-* = 'saint' (Dumézil, *Romans des Scythes*, p. 305; other hypotheses in E. A. Grantovskij and D. S. Raevskij, in *Etnogenez*, p. 57; cf. also the name ΙΓΔΑΜΠΑΙΗΣ in a graffito cited by Ju. G. Vinogradov, in *Demografičeskaja situacija*, p. 142). The identification of the 'bitter source' where the Exampaeus lay is very controversial: *Narody*, pp. 280–1. The lower Bug is in fact fairly salty already to the north of Nikolaev, but it is on account of the sea water which flows into it; some scholars would therefore locate the Exampaeus close to the sea (in accordance also with Mela II 7), e.g. identifying the source with the Gniloj Elanec, 25 km. to the north of Nikolaev (Šilik, op. cit., pp. 450 ff.). But Herodotus seems to have in mind a more northerly location: cf. Vitruvius VIII 3,11; other sources in *Pomponii Melae de chorographia libri tres*, ed. P. Parroni, Rome 1984, p. 279. Some have thought of the region of Pervomajsk, suggesting the Sinjucha or the Cërnyj Tašlyk (Rybakov, pp. 36–7); or of the area of Voznesensk, where flows the river Mertvovod, 'dead water' (cf. Ostroverchov, in op. cit., pp. 86–7).

4. συνάγουσι... τὰ τέρματα: lit. 'they make their winning-posts converge', a peculiar sporting metaphor (cf. H. Blümmer, *Jahrb. für klass. Philologie*, CXLIII (1891), 38).

53–6. The Borysthenes must be the Dnieper (cf. note to 18,1–2); but the identification of Panticapes, Hypacyris, and Gerrhus remains an unresolved problem. The Hypacyris flows into the sea 'in correspondence of the town of Carcinitis', leaving on its right the 'Achilles' course'. Καρκινῖτις (in this form already in Hecataeus, *FGrHist* 1 F 184) is a variant of Κερκινῖτις, the name of a colony in the vicinity of modern-day Evpatorija in western Crimea (see O. D. Daševskaja, *VDI* CXIV (1970), 121–8; V. S. Dračuk and V. A. Kutajsov, *VDI* CLXXII (1985), 82–6; Ju. G. Vinogradov, in *Acta Centri Historiae 'Terra Antiqua Balcanica'*, II, Trinovi 1987, p. 33; V. A. Kutajsov, *Antičnyj polis Kerkinitida*, Kiev 1990; G. Hedreen, *Hesperia*, LX (1991), 313–30). The 'Achilles' Course', which is along Hylaea (see 76, 4), is the sandy strip of land which today bears the name of Tendra Peninsula and which, stretching eastwards to form the Džarylgač peninsula, penetrates the Bay of Karkinit (according to a legend recounted by Pomponius Mela II 5, Achilles raced there: other sources and traditions in *Pomponii Melae de chorographia libri tres*, pp. 276–7; Achilles was very much worshipped in the Pontus: see most recently, pp. 221–66; J. Hupe (ed.), *Der Achilleus-Kult in nördlichen Schwarzmeerraum*, Rahden 2006; Heinin, pp. 59–66; M. Yu. Treister, *AncCiv* I (1994), 17–19; B. Bravo, in *Problemi*). The Hypacyris might therefore be identified with the Kalančak, which flows into the Gulf of Karkinit to the north-east of the eastern extremity of the Džarylgač peninsula; while the indication of the proximity with Carcinitis must be taken in a vague sense (perhaps the entire gulf was considered as the estuary of the Kalančak? But some also think of the lake Donuzlav: Daševskaja, art. cit., pp. 122–3; *Narody*, pp. 287–9). The Kalančak, however, is a river of very slight importance; and it is difficult to understand what the Gerrhus might be, which merges into it flowing from a homonymous locality on the Dnieper. The Panticapes is also mysterious. The name, which means 'rich in fish' (cf. V. I. Abaev, *Studia in honorem D. Dečev*, Sofia 1958, pp. 183–9), is reminiscent of the presumed Scythian name of the Strait of Kerč, where the city of Παντικάπαιον stood (repeated names of rivers are common in the Pontic area, probably in connection with the migration of peoples: see Schramm, *passim*; M. Ju. Vachtina *et al.*, *VDI* CLIV (1980), 160). If it is the Ingulec (see e.g. Minns, p. 29), Herodotus has made it a left tributary instead of a right one; moreover, the Dnieper only has left tributaries of any relevance from the area of the rapids onwards, whereas according to Herodotus the Panticapes flows through Hylaea, near the coast: cf. *Narody*, pp. 285–7. Undoubtedly Herodotus's information was indirect and confused, since he cannot have visited personally the regions to the east of Olbia (see v. Fritz, I, pp. 129–30; Introduction, p. 557). Deserving of notice is in any case the suggestion made by T. Struve, *RhM* XXIX (1874), 67–70: in his opinion the Borysthenes corresponds to a fluvial route which began in the lower Dnieper, but then ran up the Ingulec; while the Panticapes is the Dnieper upstream of the confluence with the Ingulec (including the right tributary Bazavluk). As a matter of fact, Greek trade between the 6th and 5th cents. BC followed rather the Ingulec than the Dnieper; the latter was navigable only as far as the rapids (in correspondence with Zaporož'e), whereas with the small boats attested in the archaeological record the Ingulec could be negotiated for a long way upstream: see N. A. Onajko, *Antičnij import v Pridneprov'e i Pobuž'e v VII–V vv. do n.e.*, Moscow 1966, pp. 39–40; O. S. Ostroverchov, in *Drevnosti*, pp. 84–8; A. Wąsowicz, *DHA* VI (1980), 31 ff. The Hypacyris might then be the Kalančak linked with the Konka, which seems at one time to have lengthened its course in parallel with the Dnieper, joined to it by a series of small canals that today have flown together to form the lake of Kachovka (see Rybakov, pp. 46–50). If, then, the locality Gerrhus is placed on the middle Dnieper (in correspondence with Sula according to V. A. Il'inskaja, *Skify Dneprovskogo lesostepnogo levoberež'ja*, Kiev 1968, pp. 178–80; cf. Rolle, *Totenkult* I 1, pp. 156–8; T. Sulimirski, in *CHI* II, pp. 180–1), it is possible to suppose that from the Ingulec, by way of a stretch on land, the route joined again with the Dnieper until it reached this region; while the river Gerrhus would correspond to the curve of the Dnieper, which thus would meet again with the Hypacyris = Konka. This would imply for the γεωργοί Scythians a location to the east of the Ingulec, on the right bank of the Dnieper (see note to 18, 1–2); while the 'nomadic' Scythians could have moved between the Gulf of Karkinit and the area of the rapids of the Dnieper (the 14 days' journey in ch. 19 must be understood along the axis south west–north east). The identification of the area of Gerrhus, mysterious site of the tombs of the Scythian kings (see chs. 71 ff.; 127), is, however, the subject of much discussion. Some have also suggested the region of Nikopol' and Kamenka, before the rapids, where large and rich tombs have in fact been found, but for the most part dating from the 4th cent. BC (but see B. N. Mozolevskij, *SA* (1986), 2, pp. 70–83, who identifies tombs dating from the 6th–5th cents. in the area). The river Gerrhus may then correspond to a route which, from the region of Nikopol', ran along the Moločnaja and, through the swamps of the north-western Azov Sea and the isthmus of Perekop, reached the gulf of Karkinit = Hypacyris. Discussion in *Narody*, pp. 290–2; Nejchardt, pp. 115 ff.

53,2–3. τῶν δὲ λοιπῶν... ἄξια: on the fertility of the steppe in the region of the Dnieper, cf. Neumann, *Die Hellenen*, pp. 14 ff.; Ebert, pp. 2–5; and notes to 17,1 and 2. The production of salt was still important at the time of Dio Chrysostom (*Or.* 36,3): cf. A. Wąsowicz, *Archeologia*, XVII (1966), 244–5; Wąsowicz, pp. 27–8; R. Baladié, *Il Mar Nero*, I (1994), 145–66 (with the testimonies of various travellers). Salt was used, among other things, to preserve fish (cf. I. G. Pidopličko, in *Ol'vija*, Kiev 1940, pp. 209–10); of these the ἀντακαῖοι are sturgeon (an etymological suggestion in O. Trubačëv, *Indogermanische Forschungen*, LXXXII (1977), 134–5: 'pointed body'; cf. M. I. Zolotarëv, *VDI* CLXXVII (1986), 88–93, on coins in the shape of sturgeon dating from the 6th–5th cents.). From the whole area of the Pontus valuable salted fish was exported (cf. τάριχος on the inscription from Carcinitis dating from the 5th–4th cents., ed. E. I. Solomonik, *VDI* CLXXXII

(1987), pp. 114–25): see Ch. Danoff, *RE* Suppl. IX 1962, coll. 955 ff.; Pippidi, pp. 51 and 238, n. 23.

4. μέχρι...νέμονται: the figure 'forty days' seems excessive compared to the twenty days of extension north–south of Scythia (see chs. 99–101), and to the ten days assigned to the territory of the γεωργοί Scythians, who are separated from the sea only by Hylaea according to ch. 18 (where, on the other hand, the figure mentioned is eleven days: the difference might be due to the inclusion of the estuary, see Ju. Vinogradov, *Chudožestvennaja kul'tura i archeologija antičnogo mira*, Moscow 1976, p. 79). An error is possible in the ms tradition, often amended to τεσσέρων καὶ δέκα, 'fourteen' (ten-eleven for the 'farmers' plus the stretch of Hylaea); the error must, however, be very old, since the figure 'forty days' appears also in pseudo-Scymnus, 816– 8, *GGM* I, p. 230; pseudo-Arrian, *Periplus Ponti Euxini* 59, *GGM* I, p. 417; Mela, II 6 (on the other hand, Strabo VII 3,17 gives too small a figure for the limit to which the Borysthenes is navigable, 600 stades: might he be referring to the Ingulec?). But perhaps the forty days, which correspond to the duration of funerary processions (see 73,1), are just a generic figure in tune with the mysterious character of the Gerrhus; bibl. in *Narody*, pp. 283–4. Perhaps the Androphagi of ch. 18 are not mentioned here because they were far away from the course of the river, towards the north-east; but some have also suggested that different sources were used, see Introduction, pp. 558–9.

6. τὸ δὲ μεταξὺ...κατοίκηνται: the Cape of Hippolaus, described as a 'wedge of land' (ἔμβολον: on the expression see L. Robert, *Opera Minora Selecta* IV, Paris 1979, pp. 350–1) also by Dio Chrysostom, *Or.* 36,2, is mostly identified with Cape Stanislav. No remains have been found of the temple, which was perhaps destroyed by the water (cf. Waṣowicz, *Olbia*, p. 82); but the cult of Demeter is well attested in Olbia by pottery, graffiti, and coins: see Rusjaeva, pp. 37 ff. For a different hypothesis (which takes the variant reading 'Mother' of the gods into account, cf. 76,3), see now B. Bravo, in *Problemi*, pp. 249–52.

57. Τάναϊς: this is the Don: from the root *danu-* = 'river', from which Danube, Dnestr and Dnieper also derive; see Schramm, pp. 33–4. The Ὕργις may be the Donec (see note to 123,3). According to Rybakov, pp. 50–5, the Tanais corresponds to the lower Don plus the Donec, and the Hyrgis to the middle Don: but see note to 21,1.

58. ἀνοιγομένοισι δὲ τοῖσι κτήνεσι: 'from the examination of open, dissected animals' (on the verb, cf. Aristotle, *Hist. An.* 497b17, 531a16, 594b27, 604a24). That same practice of dissection of animals is presupposed which, precisely in relation to the study of bile, Aristotle, *De Part. Animal.* IV 2,677a30 ff. attributed to certain 'ancient' scientists (probably Anaxagoras: see 677a5 ff. and M. Vegetti, *RIL* (1965), 193–213; cf. also the Democritus of the Hippocratic *Epistles* IX, p. 356 Littré = XVII 3, p. 78, ll. 3–5 Smith). According to Theophrastus, *Hist. Plant.* IX 17,4, the animals of the Pontus do not have bile because they eat absinth. There were diverse opinions on this issue, as appears from the parallel texts cited

in *Theophrastus of Eresos. Commentary vol. 5. Sources on Biology,* by R. W. Sharples, Leiden – New York – Cologne 1995, pp. 178–81; cf. Menander, *Samia* 416, where the attack of bile suffered by Demea (χολᾷ) is attributed to the insalubrity of Pontus.

59–82. After the digression on rivers, the ethnographic section can resume with a series of 'chapters', each one opening with a flag-word which announces its content: 'gods' (59); 'sacrifice' (60–3); 'customs of war' (64–6: linked with the cult of Ares described directly before); 'soothsayers' (67–9); 'oaths' (70); 'burials' (71–5); 'attitude towards foreign customs' (76–80); 'population' (81); 'wonders' (82). This method by 'headings' is typical of the ancient ethnographical tradition; and the subdivision and succession of topics finds some parallels in the ethnographic sections dedicated to Persia (I 131 ff.) and to Egypt: see Trüdinger, pp. 21–6; Norden, pp. 464–5; Müller, *Geschichte*, pp. 106–15; Dorati, pp. 53–90.

59,1. θεούς: Herodotus discerns in the Scythian pantheon the corresponding Greek gods in accordance with the practice of *interpretatio Graeca:* cf. Linforth, pp. 201–43; J. Vogt, *Orbis. Ausgewählte Schriften zur Geschichte des Altertums,* Freiburg 1960, pp. 11–46; W. Burkert, in *Hérodote et les peuples non grecs,* pp. 1–32; Harrison, pp. 208–22. Such transposition supplies an indication of the nature of the Scythian gods, but also runs the risk of distorting it: see H. J. Diesner, *RhM* CIV (1961), 202–12; M. I. Artamonov, *ASGE* II (1961), 51–81; V. I. Abaev, *Drevnij mir,* Moscow 1962, pp. 445–50; Mora, pp. 49–55, 81–101, 256–61. Drawing perhaps from the Scythians whom he met in Olbia (see S. A. Žebelev, *Severnoe Pričernomor'e,* Moscow–Leningrad 1953, pp. 29–31), Herodotus is also able to furnish the local names of the gods (cf. I 131; II 42,5; 144; 156,5; III 8; the absence of the Scythian counterparts to Heracles and Ares might be due to a lacuna between Ἀργίμπασα and Ποσειδέων at 59,2). Etymological interpretation of these names is rendered difficult also by the uncertainty on the faithfulness of the Greek version (a review in V. P. Petrov, *Archeologija,* XV (1963), 19–32); attempts to identify the various divinities in representations of Graeco-Scythian art have also given uncertain results. Cf. W. D. Blawatsky and G. A. Kochelenko, *Hommages à M. J. Vermaseren,* Leiden 1978, pp. 60–6; Bessonova; *Narody,* pp. 293–8; Nejchardt, pp. 185–213.

Ἱστίην: Hestia/Tabiti is called 'queen of the Scythians' at 127,4; and according to 68,2 the oath over the royal hearths (ἱστίαι) was the most solemn for the Scythians. Tabiti corresponds to the Greek goddess Hestia in that she is the divinity of the hearth; and her name, comparable to the *Tapatī* of the *Mahābhārata,* means 'she who warms': see among others W. Brandenstein, *Wiener Zeitschrift für die Kunde des Morgenlandes,* LII (1953–5), 191; E. A. Grantovskij and D. S. Raevskij, in *Etnogenez,* pp. 53–5; Dumézil, *Romans des Scythes,* pp. 123–68, with the Ossetian parallel of the daughter of the sun Acyrūxs (reservations in Dumézil, *La Courtisane,* pp. 124–5; on the hearth among the Ossetians see also Dumézil, *Le Livre,* pp. 13 f.). The great importance of Tabiti, in connection with royalty, has a parallel in the Iranic (and Vedic) cult of fire, which Nymphodorus (in Clement of Alexandria, *Protr.* IV 65,1) attests also for the Sauromatians (cf. A. Häusler, *ZArch* XVII (1983), 162–4): see J. Hertel, *Die arische Feuerlehre*, Leipzig 1925; J. H. Kramers, in *Analecta Orientalia*, Leiden 1952, pp. 343–63; J. Duchesne-Guillemin, *East & West*, NS XIII (1962), 198–206; D. Briquel, *L'Épopée gréco-latine et ses prolongements européens*, Paris 1981, pp. 10–13; C. Campe, in *Wörterbuch der Myth.* I 4, pp. 341–3 (*ātar-*, the Iranic principle of fire, is masculine, but Xenophon, *Cyr.* I 6,1, and VII 5,57 translates it as ʿ*Εστία*). In an Indo-European context the connection between fire/hearth and king is well attested also for the Roman Vesta (see Alföldi, pp. 188–94), while the Greek Hestia has, among other things, the role of 'centre of the world' (see J.-P. Vernant, *Mythe et pensée chez les Grecs*, Paris 1985², pp. 155–201); but also among the Altaic nomads the spirit of the hearth and of the family, the 'mother-fire', is the object of special veneration (J. P. Roux, *RHR* XVIII (1976), 67–101; *Testi dello sciamanesimo*, pp. 149–51). In the light of these parallels, the Scythian cult of fire/hearth might be described as the expression of the unity of the people in the house of the king: see Raevskij, pp. 87–109; Hartog, pp. 135–41 = ET, pp. 119–25; Bessonova, pp. 27–36. Raevskij, pp. 94–106, identifies as Tabiti the goddess seated in profile with a mirror in her hand which recurs in Graeco-Scythian art associated with a man with a cup, and he interprets the scene (usually defined as one of 'communion') as a sacred wedding between the king and the goddess (see e.g. the plaque from Čertomlyk, Hermitage inv. Dn 1863 1/172). Against such interpretation see e.g. Ju. G. Vinogradov, *Epigraphica*, XLIII (1981), 24; Bessonova, pp. 99–103: the iconography is reminiscent rather of Greek representations of Aphrodite, and suggests Argimpasa (see M. I. Rostovcev, *Izvestija archeologičeskoj komissi*, XLIX (1913), 1–62, 133–40; cf. note to 23,2–5). Tabiti might correspond instead to the figure represented frontally between a hearth or torch and a figure with a vase on a gold plaque from Čertomlyk (Hermitage inv. 1863 1/374a). But, there is much uncertainty: a discussion in Bessonova, pp. 93–117; Nejchardt, pp. 191–7.   *Δία...γυναῖκα*: Zeus/Papaeus features in the legend of the origins (chs. 5–7) as the father of Targitaus; the king Idanthyrsus calls him an 'ancestor' in 127,4. His Scythian name seems to Herodotus 'most appropriate' (cf. a similar judgement at 52,1) because it is fitting for his role of primal 'father' (cf. the Greek *πάππας*; the link with the exclamation of pain *παπαί*, suggested by A. Loma, *Živa Antika*, XXX (1980), p. 257–64, is unlikely). *Παπαῖος* might in fact have this derivation, unless it is to be related instead to the Iranic *pā(pa)-* = 'to defend, to protect': see Vasmer, p. 15; L. Zgusta, *AO* XXI (1953), 270–1; Grantovskij–Raevskij, in *Etnogenez*, p. 54 (for the appearance of the name in Pontic onomastics, see L. Zgusta, *Die Personennamen griechischer Städte der nördlichen Schwarzmeerküste*, Prague 1955, pp. 303–4). He can be interpreted as a divinity of the sky, cosmogonically united to the divinity of the earth, Api: see Bessonova, pp. 41–3; Nejchardt, pp. 197–9; if he is to be identified with the figure surmounted by a bird from Dnepropetrovsk (*Gold der Steppe*, cat. no. 121, ill. at pp. 363–4), he must have reminded the Greeks of the iconography of the bearded Zeus accompanied by the eagle. However, Api seems to correspond to a river goddess (the daughter of Borysthenes at 5,1), and her name can be linked to the Iranic *āp-* = "water" (see

Vasmer, p. 11; Brandenstein, art. cit., pp. 190–1; Grantovskij–Raevskij, in *Etnogenez,* p. 54; Zgusta, art. cit., pp. 270–1, thinks rather of a childish name for 'mother'). She may have been a 'great mother', associated to the Greek Gē on account of her traits of fertility, but also belonging to the world of water and vegetation (see in general V. Dini, *II potere delle antiche madri,* Turin 1980, pp. 11–30; cf. note to 18,1 on Ἀβική); and she was probably conceived as a snake-goddess (see note to 9,1). Discussion in Raevskij, pp. 44–9; Bessonova, pp. 36–7.   Ἀπόλλωνα: the Scythian counterpart of Apollo is uncertain even in its name; the Οἰτόσυρος of the codices might find a confirmation in Οἰτόσκυρος, the epithet of Apollo-Mithras in *IG* XIV 114*, but the inscription does not seem authentic; while the indirect tradition has Γοιτόσυρος (but some have discerned in the initial 'gamma' the mark of an original 'digamma'). The interpretation as **gaēθōsūra-* = 'rich in cattle' or 'master of the living world' (see Vasmer, p. 13) might suggest a parallel with the Iranic Mithras, often assimilated to Apollo; but other interpretations are possible: see G. Kazarow, *RE* XVII 2 1937, coll. 2300–1; *Narody,* p. 297; Bessonova, pp. 43–4; Dumézil, *La Courtisane,* pp. 121–2; Grantovskij–Raevskij, in *Etnogenez,* pp. 54–5; Mora, p. 51; A. Panaino, *Atti del Sodalizio Glottologico Milanese,* XXIX (1987/8), 159–65 (less reliable are the hypotheses by G. W. Elderkin, *AJPh* LVI (1935), 342–6). οὐρανίην Ἀφροδίτην: also in the case of the counterpart of Aphrodite the name is uncertain (Ἀργίμπασα, Ἀρίππασα; the variant Ἀρτίμπασα is attested by less significant mss, and the two inscriptions *IG* XIV 85* a and b, which would confirm it, are probably not authentic); all the more uncertain is the etymology: see Bessonova, p. 37; Grantovskij–Raevskij, in *Etnogenez,* pp. 55–6 (cf. note to 23,2–5 about the Argippaei). Aphrodite Urania was the Greek version of such divinities as the Syrian goddess from Ascalon (Aštart), with whom the Scythians did in fact have a connection (see I 105; IV 69; Mora, pp. 231–3); and a Greek cult of Aphrodite Urania or Apaturia is attested on the Cimmerian Bosporus since the 6th cent. BC (see L. P. Charko, *KSIIMK* XIII (1946), 137–41; S. R. Tochtas'ev, *VDI* CLXXVII (1986), 138–45). She must have been a goddess connected with sexuality and fertility, and it is difficult to distinguish her from Api (for possible representations, cf. preceding notes): see Bessonova, pp. 37–41.   Ἡρακλέα καὶ Ἄρεα: Heracles seems to be a 'translation' of Targitaus, given the analogy between the two characters in the legends on the origins at chs. 5–10 (see B. N. Grakov, *KSIIMK* XXXIV (1950), 7–18; Raevskij, pp. 54–61; Bessonova, pp. 44–5; cf. ch. 82). The equation Heracles–Targitaus may have developed during the time of the 'Scythian protectorate' over Olbia (cf. chs. 78–80), as shown by the Olbian coins dating from the 5th cent. which depict Heracles in the act of drawing the bow, and the foreign name EMINAKO: see P. O. Karyškovskij, *SA* (1960), 1, pp. 179–95, *Rannij železnyi vek Severo-Zapadnogo Pričernomor'ja,* Kiev 1984, pp. 78–89; Vinogradov, pp. 92–4. On Ares see note to 62,1.   οἱ δὲ ... θύουσι: the figure of Poseidon/Thagimasadas (the variant Θαγι- seems corroborated also by some onomastic parallels in Pontic inscriptions, see V. P. Petrov, *Archeologija,* XV (1963), 31–2; Mora, p. 52) is rather problematic. It is unlikely that the royal Scythians worshipped a sea-god (see, however, Dumézil, *La Courtisane,* pp. 125–6, who points to the Ossetian spirit called 'fish-head'; Dumézil,

p. 245, n. 14 for a suggestion on the etymology). It is more probably that Thagimasadas was associated with Poseidon because of his connection with horses, which were of great importance in the Scythian religious sphere (see E. E. Kuz'mina, *Skify i Sarmaty*, pp. 96–119): discussion in Bessonova, pp. 50–3. The name Thagimasadas, which to some appears Thracian (see e.g. D. Detschew, *Die thrakischen Sprachreste*, Vienna 1957, p. 409), can be compared to the Octamasades of ch. 80; Justi, p. 502, understood -μασάδας to mean 'great' by reference to Ossetian (E. Bazin-Foucher, *Bull. de l'École Française d'Extrême Orient*, XLIV (1947–50), 13–20 is unreliable).

2. ἀγάλματα . . . νομίζουσι: the absence of statues, altars, and temples marks the difference from Greek culture and religion (cf. I 131; II 4; IV 108; Plato, *Prot.* 322a; Hartog, p. 189 = ET, p. 175; Mora, pp. 55–6). In this sense the statement is fundamentally true. Although some traces of 'sanctuaries' can be discerned (M. I. Artamonov, *ASGE* II (1961), 83), and between the Danube and the Don rough anthropomorphic *cippi* are attested dating also from the 6th and 5th cent. (the *kamennye baby*: discussion in D. S. Raevskij, *Srednjaja Azija, Kavkaz i zarubežnyj vostok v drevnosti*, Moscow 1983, pp. 40–60; cf. also M. Ch. Bagaev and V. S. Ol'chovskij, *SA* (1989), 4, pp. 261–7; V. P. Belozov, in *Gold der Steppe*, pp. 161–4), there were no places reserved for sacrifices which displayed the cultic association typical in Greece.

60–1. Scythian sacrifice is described in contrast with the Greek model, as demonstrated by the note on the absence of fire, consecration, or libation: κατάρχεσθαι at 60,2 refers to the sprinkling of lustral water and scattering of barley-grains to consecrate the victim; on ἐπισπένδειν at 60,2, see note to 62,3 (cf. Hartog, pp. 187–201 = ET, pp. 173–88, with the reservations of Mora, pp. 56–7). The method of suffocation must have aimed at avoiding the shedding of blood, which was a taboo also for many Altaic peoples (see *The Travels of Marco Polo* (tr. R. Latham), London 1958, pp. 118, 130 f.; *Testi dello sciamanesimo*, p. 90); the same ritual was enacted for the burial of kings, see chs. 71 ff. Scythian tombs have yielded a large quantity of cauldrons of various shapes and often still containing remains of animals, including horses: see M. Ebert, *Prähistorische Zeitschrift*, IV (1912), 451–4; Talbot Rice, pp. 131–2; *Narody*, p. 299; N. A. Gavriljuk, *SA* (1987), 1, p. 24; and in *Gold der Steppe*, pp. 93–4 (we do not know exactly in what way 'Lesbian' cauldrons were singular; presumably they were fairly rounded). Bones do not burn easily (it is rather desiccated dung that has always been used in the steppes in the absence of wood): it is possible that the burning of bones and the cooking of meat in the entrails, explained rationalistically by Herodotus, constituted a special ritual, which finds some parallels in Mongolian customs: cf. John of Pian di Carpine III 2, 3, 12 (= *Mongol Mission*, p. 9); Neumann, *Die Hellenen*, pp. 258–64; Rudenko, pp. 61–2 (doubts on the authenticity of ch. 61, up to ἕκαστον, are now expressed by B. Bravo, *ASNP* s. IV, V (2000), 81–3). Sacrifices of horses, which were extremely rare in Greece, are attested for the Massagetae in I 216,4 and for the Sauromatians in Paus. I 21,6:

cf. in general W. Koppers, *Wiener Beiträge zur Kulturgeschichte und Linguistik*, IV (1936), 279–411; on the Altaic peoples, *Testi dello sciamanesimo*, pp. 55 ff.

62,1. Ἄρεϊ: the cult of Ares was closer to the Greek model; the heap could be viewed as a temple and the sword as a representation of the god, while the human sacrifice involved libation and the shedding of blood, like Greek sacrifice: see Hartog, p. 204 = ET p. 191; Mora, pp. 53–4 (cf. notes to 62,3 and 4). The Scythian cult of the *akinakes* (the short sword used also by the Persians, see VII 54,2) is also mentioned by Eudoxus, fr. 303 Lasserre; Mela II 15; Lucian, *Iupp. Trag.* 42; *Tox.* 38; *Scytha* 4; Priscus of Panopolis (frs. 8 and 10 Bornmann) says that a Scythian 'sword of Ares' was rediscovered in Attila's time (cf. R. Merkelbach, *Eranos-Jahrbuch*, XXXV (1966), 151–2; Dumézil, *Romans des Scythes*, pp. 78–83, 21 ff., is at times inexact). The same cult was practised by the Sauromatians according to Hicesius in Clement of Alexandria, *Protrept.* IV 64,5, and by the Alans according to Ammianus Marcellinus XXXI 3,21 (cf. XVII 12,21 on the Quadi). However, the worship of weapons is not exclusive to the Eurasian nomads; cf. e.g. Acusilaus, *FGrHist* 2 F 22; Aelian, *Nat. An.* XII 30. The *akinakes* was an idol of the god of war, but it may also have had the function of 'axis of the world'; and the ritual may have aimed at consecrating the military supremacy over the subjugated enemy and the conquered territories: D. S. Raevskij, *Altertum*, XXVII (1981), 21–2; Bessonova, pp. 45–50. The Scythian Ares may find a continuation in the warlike Batraz of the Ossetian epic, in whose legend the sword and the heap recur: Dumézil, *Romans des Scythes*, pp. 78–83, 21 ff. Archaeology has provided partial confirmations. Apart from the findings of weapons stuck in the ground in several burials (Rolle, *Totenkult* I 1, p. 125; *Stepi*, p. 121), and the representation of a sword on a late Scythian Crimean stele (cf. T. N. Vysotskaja *et al.*, in *Archeologičeskie otkrytija 1976*, Moscow 1977, pp. 280–9), an *akinakes* on the summit of a mound has been found at Nosaki, in the area of Zaporož'e (cf. Ju. Boltrik, *Archeologičeskie issledovanija na Ukraine v 1976–1977 gg*, Užgorod 1978, pp. 60–1; possible parallels in L. V. Subbotin and S. B. Ochotnikov, *Drevnosti*, pp. 108–11; V. V. Otroščenko, *Novye pamjatniki drevnej i srednevekovoj chudožestvennoj kul'tury*, Kiev 1982, pp. 15–16; A. M. Leskov, in *I tesori dei kurgani del Caucaso settentrionale*, Rome 1990, pp. 25–6). On the diffusion of short swords (mostly of bronze) in Scythia, see W. Ginters, *Das Schwert der Skythen und Sarmaten in Südrussland*, Berlin 1928; Meljukova, *Vooruženie*, pp. 46–64; E. V. Černenko, in *Skifija i Kavkaz*, Kiev 1980, pp. 7–30.   **κατὰ νομοὺς ... ἀρχέων**: the νομοί are districts governed by νομάρχαι = 'district chiefs' (ch. 66; an attempt at identification on archaological ground in A. I. Kubyšev, *Hamburger Beiträge zur Archäologie*, XVIII (1991), 131–40); this hints at the organization on a territorial basis of the Scythian kingdom, perhaps following on the subjugation of sedentary peoples: cf. J. Radet, *Mémorial Lagrange*, Paris 1940, pp. 21–6; Chazanov, pp. 111 ff. (with the reservations expressed by E. A. Grantovskij, *VDI* CLIV (1980), 133 ff.); Briant, *État et pasteurs*, p. 225. The ms tradition suggests the reading τῶν αρχηΐων: the ἀρχεῖα are generally the premises of the magistrates; in the case of the nomad Scythians, these might be conceived as specific places situated in the permanent settlements of the subject peoples or on the fixed routes of transhumance, where the nomarch periodically collected tributes and administered justice.   ὅσον . . . ἔλασσον: the improbable dimensions suggest a mythical transfiguration; see M. V. Skržinskaja, *VDI* CXCI (1989), 86.

3. οἶνον . . . ἀκινάκεος: on ἐπισπένδειν, the libation of wine see J. Casabona, *Recherches sur le vocabulaire des sacrifices en grec*, Aix-en-Provence 1966, p. 249 (on the wine, cf. ch. 66). Possible examples from the 4th cent. BC of the kind of vase to which Herodotus refers are indicated by T. M. Kuznecova, *KSIA* CXCIV (1988), 17–23; also in Greek sacrifices the blood of the victim was gathered in a vessel, the *sphageion*, before being sprinkled on the altar: cf. J. L. Durand, in M. Detienne and J.-P. Vernant (eds.), *The Cuisine of Sacrifice Among the Greeks*, Chicago 1989, pp. 119–28.

4. τῶν . . . νεκρός: the mutilation of the corpse (a Persian parallel in Plutarch, *Art.* 13) constitutes the ultimate humiliation for the vanquished and immolated enemy: see the Ossetian parallel in Dumézil, *Le Livre*, pp. 224–8, and Dumézil, *Romans des Scythes*, pp. 251–3; B. Lincoln, *Death, War and Sacrifice*, Chicago–London 1991, pp. 198–208 (cf. also Lucian, *Tox.* 10). In two mounds in the Republic of Mordvinia a finger-bone and a scrap of skin have been found (cf. note to 64,2–4), which have been interpreted as war trophies by P. D. Stepanov, *KSIA* CXXXVI (1973), 86–91.

63. Θυσίαι . . . θέλουσι: within the formula of transition, a 'note' is curiously inserted (which awakes suspicion in B. Bravo, *ASNP* s. IV, V (2000), 83): Herodotus seems to want to salvage a piece of information which perhaps he ought to have given at the end of ch. 61 (on such 'corrections in stride' see R. Lattimore, *CPh* LIII (1958), 9–21). Pigs, which are sedentary animals, were certainly not to be found among the nomadic Scythians (e.g. cf. I. B. Brašinskij and K. K. Marčenko, *Elizavetovskoje. Skythische Stadt im Don-Delta*, Munich 1984, p. 41); a small number of pig's bones have, however, been found in the vicinity of the agricultural settlements: see, among others, V. I. Calkin, *MIA* LIII (1960), 58–9; V. I. Bibikova, *Drevnosti vostočnogo Kryma*, Kiev 1970, p. 108.

64–6. Among all warrior nomadic aristocracies the criterion of *valentia* is in the first place success in raids (interesting parallels in S. Campetti and E. Borzatti von Löwenstern, *L'altra umanità*, Florence 1983, pp. 73–7). It is only by demonstrating that he has slain the foe that the warrior gains the right to a share in the booty; and each year the *valentia* is sanctioned during the communal banquet overseen by the nomarch (cf. ch. 62), the privileged place in the social organization of several peoples: see Chazanov, pp. 183–5.

64,1. ἐπεὰν . . . ἐμπίνει: drinking the blood of enemies serves the purpose of appropriating their strength: parallels in How–Wells, ad loc.; e.g. cf. Paulus Diaconus, *Historia Langobardorum* I 11.   ὅσους . . . οὔ: the scene of a warrior who is carrying the severed heads is represented on a cup (or a beret?) from the mounds of Kurdžips, near Majkop: see A. Rieth, *AW* II (1971), 47–8; for more iconographic evidence, cf. Haussig, *Archäologie*, pp. 34–5, and the plaque with the serpent-goddess from Kul' Oba (Ermitage inv. KO 70). Cf. also ch. 117, and Strabo XV 2, 14 (on the Carmani).

2–4. ἀποδείρει... περιφέρουσι: cf. *Dissoi logoi* II 13 (90 DK); the verb ἀποσκυθίζειν, compounded with the name of the Scythians, means 'to remove the scalp' (see Hartog, p. 173 = ET, pp. 158–9). On the verb σαρκίζειν, cf. T. H. Williams, *CR* XXVI (1912), 122–3; Sophocles, fr. 473 Radt, alludes to the Scythian χειρόμακτρον made with human skin; as for the βαίτη (64,3), it is a rustic cloak made of hides sown together: see e.g. the scholium to Aristophanes, *Vesp.* 1133. Pomponius Mela II 14 attributes the use of human skin to the Geloni; Pliny, *NH* VII 12 to the Anthropophagi; Ammianus Marcellinus XXXI 2,14, and 22 to the Vidini, Geloni, and Alani. On possible archaeological evidence of scraps of human skin preserved as trophies see P. D. Stepanov, *KSIA* CXXXVI (1973), 86–91; Rolle, *Totenkult* I 1, p. 86 and n. 133. One of the corpses from Pazyryk, in the Altai, appears to have been flayed; see Jettmar, p. 112; Rudenko, p. 221; Rolle, *Scythians*, pp. 90–4. For a possible echo in the Ossetian epic see Dumézil, *Le Livre*, pp. 81–3; Dumézil, *Romans des Scythes*, pp. 253–4. See most recently P. Riedlberger, *Klio*, LXXVIII (1996), 53–60.   φαρετρέων: the typical Scythian quiver, which hung from the belt, contained both arrows and the bow: see Meljukova, *Vooruženie*, pp. 32–4; W. Rätzel, *Bonner Jahrb.*, CLXXVIII (1978), 163–80; *Narody*, pp. 203–4; depictions in Vos, pp. 49–50.   ἦν ἄρα: the phrase means something like 'and so it was observed that...' in connection with a revealing experience: see Denniston, *Greek Particles*, pp. 36–7. But in this descriptive context the experience is not indicated (see Stein, ad loc.): perhaps Herodotus is recording the impression of the witness who said that he had seen the skin.

65,1. αὐτὰς... ποτηρίῳ: cf. *Dissoi logoi* II 13 (90 DK); Plato, *Euthd.* 299e; Strabo VII 3,7; Mela II 13. The custom of drinking from the skulls of enemies, probably in order to appropriate their strength, has various parallels from the early Paleolithic to the middle ages and later: see note to 26,1, and cf. Hartog, pp. 171 ff. = ET pp. 156 ff.; Mora, pp. 57–8. A specimen of a Scythian cup/skull coated on the inside with gold and with traces of leather on the outside, as in Herodotus' description, is published by A. Rieth, *AW* II (1971), 47–51 (who casts doubts on its authenticity).

2. ποιεῦσι... λέγοντες: it is strange that the Scythians should violate the bloodties that are fundamental in nomadic societies and exhibit such fierceness against relatives (for this is the meaning of οἰκήϊοι; discussion in Chazanov, pp. 102–4). Among the aristocracy and the royal family the sense of honour and the ambition for power must have occasioned fratricidal strife, resolved with combats/ordeals before the king (παρὰ τῷ βασιλέϊ); and perhaps Herodotus had in mind episodes such as that of Saulius and Anacharsis; see chs. 76–7.

66. τοῖσι δ' ἂν... τοῦτο: Aristotle, *Pol.* VII 2, 1324b17–18, mentions the custom of exclusion from the banquets as proof of the belligerent temperament of the Scythians, with parallels from other communities; cf. Mela II 13. In the Ossetian epic the Narts, gathered together at a banquet, recount their exploits before a magic cup, the *Nart-amongœ*, which confirms or denies them: see Dumézil,

Romans des Scythes, pp. 225–46 (cf. Lucian, *Tox.* 44–5). The wine must have been imported from Greece (for the 5th cent. BC the little evidence we have shows that it came mainly from Chios, and to a lesser extent from Thasos and Mende: see I. B. Brašinskij, *Metody issledovanija antičnoj torgovli*, Leningrad 1984, pp. 153–4). Among the Greeks the Scythians had the reputation of drinking pure wine and of being drunkards (cf. Hartog, pp. 183–4 = ET, pp. 169–70); but Herodotus does not, in his fourth book, appropriate this *topos* (which recurs, however, in VI 84).

67,1. *Μάντιες ... συντιθεῖσι*: the description is not entirely clear: ἐπὶ μίαν ἑκάστην seems to be an expression drawn from military language, 'in single file' (see Stein, ad loc.); the θεσπίζειν may have consisted in the invocation of spirits, until the one responsible for the evil was discerned; the prefix of the verb συντιθεῖσι is odd (Th. Gomperz, *SAWW* CIII (1883), 580, n. 1 suggested τιθεῖσι). Divination by means of willow wands was attributed in similar terms to the Alani by Ammianus Marcellinus XXXI 2,24 (cf. also Tacitus, *Germ.* 10,1 on the Germans); and is still practised by the Ossetians, see Dumézil, *Romans des Scythes*, pp. 212–13. The bundle of switches was also used by Persian Magi: cf. Strabo XV 3,14–15, Dinon, *FGrHist* 690 F 3; a possible representation of a Magus with wands appears in the 'treasure of the Oxus' (see O. M. Dalton, *The Treasure of the Oxus*, London 1964³, p. 19; E. V. Zejmal', *Amu-dar'inskij klad*, Leningrad 1979, pp. 51–3; doubts in R. Ghirshman, *Persia: From the Origins to Alexander the Great*, trans. S. Gilbert and J. Emmons, London 1964, p. 94). Among the burials of the Sauromatians on the river Ilek (cf. Th. David, *DHA* VI (1980), 164–9), the man interred in the kurgan of Mečet-saj held in his hand a bundle of wands (perhaps of poplar rather than willow): see *Narody*, pp. 304–5.

2. *οἱ δὲ 'Ενάριες ... δοῦναι*: on the 'Ενάριες and their relation to Aphrodite (Argimpasa), see note to I 105,13. The form ἀναριεῖς in *De Aeribus Aquis Locis* 22, is perhaps a better rendition of an original *a-nar-ya-*, formed by *nar* = 'man' and privative *a*: see K. Meuli, *Hermes*, LXX (1935), 131 and n. 5 with bibl. The 'feminine illness' of the Enarees can be explained in the light of the ritual transvestism of Siberian shamans, some of whom attain an actual psychological sex switch: see among others W. R. Halliday, *ABSA* XVII (1910–11), 95–102; Meuli, art. cit., pp. 127–37; Dumézil, *Romans des Scythes*, pp. 212–17. On the Siberian shamans see G. Bleibtreu-Ehrenberg, *Anthropos*, LXV (1970), 189–228; V. I. Basilov, *Glazami etnografa*, Moscow 1982, pp. 157–79; on a male burial of the Scythian period with cultic objects and items of female apparel on the river Bystovka, in the region of the Ob' see T. N. Tronckaja, *Skifo-sibirskij mir. Isskustvo i ideologija*, Novosibirsk 1987, pp. 59–63. Rostovtzeff, p. 105, saw the Enarees in the beardless figures depicted standing behind a goddess (Argimpasa?) on the tiara of Karagodeuašch (Ermitage inv. 2492/7; reservations in Bessonova, pp. 107–11); on an attempt to identify the central figures on the pectoral from Tolstaja Mogila as Enarees (*Gold der Steppe*, cat. no. 104, ill. at pp. 387–93), see D. A. Mačinskij, in *Kul'tura Vostoka. Drevnosti i rannee sredne-vekov'e*, Leningrad 1978, pp. 139–45. *φιλύρης ... χρᾷ*: Herodotus finds confirma-tion of the link between the Enarees and Aphrodite in the use of the bark of the lime-tree (very common to the north of the steppe). In Greece the lime-tree was in fact sacred to Aphrodite, as testified by Cornutus, *De Natura Deorum*, p. 46, 15–17 Lang, who links φιλύρα to φιλεῖν and mentions the use of the fibre of the lime-tree in the making of garlands (cf. Xenarchus, fr. 13 Kassel–Austin; Horace, *Carm.* I 38,2; Pliny, *NH* XVI 65; Aelius Dionysius φ 14 Erbse). The twining and unravelling of the bark of the lime-tree is reminiscent of a similar method of divination practised with a piece of cloth by Ossetian witches: see Dumézil, *Romans des Scythes*, pp. 217–18.

68,1. βασιλεὺς...κάμῃ: the illness of the king is caused by the perjury of a subject, which violates the royal hearth. Behind this there lies the conception, common among various 'primitive' peoples, that illness is the result of witchcraft or of an illicit action which must be discerned by means of divination and then punished: classic treatments in L. Lévy-Bruhl, *Primitives and the Supernatural*, London 1936; E. E. Evans-Pritchard *Witchcraft, Oracles and Magic Among the Azande*, Oxford 1937; cf. Chazanov, pp. 172–4. In order to offset the great power of the diviners (on their social role, cf. Chazanov, pp. 168–79), the king verifies their pronouncement by setting them one against the other and adopting a criterion of majority. Herodotus describes this in a rather obscure manner: he appears to imply that each group of diviners always expresses a unanimous opinion, and that the summoning of new diviners comes to a halt when a group agrees with the one preceding it.

2. βασιληίας ἱστίας: the Ossetians also swore oaths by the hearth (see Vs. Miller, *Osetinskie etjudy*, II, Moscow 1882, pp. 248–9). On the role of the royal hearth see note to 59,1; Hartog, pp. 129 ff. = ET, pp. 112 ff.

69,1. ἀπολλῦσι...τοιῷδε: the diviners who are caught in the wrong are sent to the stake so as to destroy them completely in the sacred fire (cf. Hartog, p. 147 = ET, pp. 131–2). Cremation may perhaps have been the special mode of burial reserved for priests; see Bessonova, p. 59.

2. φρυγάνων: part of the tradition has καμάρης φρυγάνων, which can be accepted (L. Weber, *PhW* LIV (1934), coll. 1068–71): καμάρη means 'covering, canopy' (cf. I 199,1), and the singular would here be used in a collective sense.

3. τοὺς δ' ἂν ἀδικέει: the custom is coherent with the fundamentally patrilinear character of the Scythian family: see Chazanov, p. 86 and *passim*; cf. chs. 114–15.

70. αἷμα συμμίσγουσι: the oath with the shedding of blood (cf. Mela II 12) is practised among many peoples (in Herodotus see I 74,6 and III 8,1). As shown also by Lucian, *Tox.* 37 and 63, the oath creates a 'blood kinship' among the chiefs who join into a faction, including their followers, to the detriment of their enemies. The curved dagger, arrows, the axe, and the javelin are in fact the offensive weapons more frequently attested in Scythian burials, together with the spear (see Meljukova, *Vooruženie*). Cf. Chazanov, pp. 107–11; Rolle, *Scythians*, pp. 69–71. A scene of two Scythians drinking from the same vessel (a *rhyton*) is depicted on plaques from Kul'Oba (Hermitage inv. KO 41), Solokha (Hermitage inv. Dn 1913 1/42) and Berdjansk (*Gold der Steppe*, cat. no. 100g), and on a diadem from Sakhnovka (Kiev, MIDU inv. DM-1639 = *Gold der Steppe*, cat. no. 99).   **ὑπέατι**: the Ionic form ὕπεας for ὄπεας = 'awl', has a parallel in Hesychius' ὕπεα (υ 267 Schmitt, cf. *Glossaria Latina* II, Paris 1926 (repr. Hildesheim 1965), p. 264; the form ὕπεας with a rough breathing is preferred by e.g. P. Chantraine, *Dictionnaire étymologique de la langue grecque. Histoire des mots*, III, Paris 1968, p. 807, s.v. ὄπεας, while ὕπεας with a smooth breathing is preferred by, among others, H. W. Smyth, *The Sounds and Inflections of the Greek Dialects: Ionic*, Oxford 1894, p. 331). The term may have occurred also in Hipponax, fr. 78,6 Degani, but on the papyrus the initial vowel cannot be read. On the term see now B. Vine, *Glotta*, LXXII (1994), 31–40. Awls—like knives—are frequently found in Scythian tombs and settlements: *Narody*, p. 306.

71–5. The magnificent funerals of the Scythian kings have several parallels among Eurasian nomads of every age, as well as in China and elsewhere: see esp., on the Altaic peoples, J. P. Roux, *La Mort chez les peuples altaïques anciens et médiévaux*, Paris 1963, pp. 135–74; on the Ossetians, Dumézil, *Romans des Scythes*, pp. 249–61. The ritual witnesses to the belief in an afterlife which the dead man must reach with his retinue and fully equipped: cf. among others Bessonova, pp. 61–2; F. Thordarson, in *A Green Leaf: Papers in Honour of Prof. J. P. Asmussen*, Leiden 1988, pp. 539–47. According to B. Lincoln, *Death, War and Sacrifice*, Chicago–London 1991, pp. 180–97, the king, as the fulcrum of the community, carried with him to the tomb what revolved around him. The description of the grave surmounted by a mound (Russian *kurgan*, Ukrainian *mogila*) is fundamentally correct, and many elements reported by Herodotus have found confirmation in several of the richest among the burials dating between the 7th and 4th cents. BC scattered in the steppe and in the pre-Caucasian region: since N. Kondakoff *et al.*, *Antiquités de la Russie méridionale*, Paris 1891, and Rostowzew, pp. 270–542, see now the analyses by V. S. Ol'chovskij, *SA* (1978), 83–97; Rolle, *Totenkult*, I; id., *Scythians*, pp. 19–53; *Narody*, pp. 307–15. More details have been confirmed by the frozen tombs of the Altai, belonging to a similar people, where also perishable goods have been preserved: Jettmar, pp. 80–150; Rudenko; M. Gryaznov, *South Siberia*, London 1969. No single tomb, however, mirrors precisely the grandiose picture depicted by Herodotus: the tombs which come closest to it are those in the region of the Kuban' dating from the 7th–6th cents. (see now L. K. Galanina, *Die Kurgane von Kelermes. 'Königsgräber' der frühskythischen Zeit*, Moscow 1997). Hence the uncertainty on the location of the Gerrhus and the of Gerrhi (cf. notes to chs. 53–6 and 71,3). We may suspect that Herodotus did not describe the funerals which belonged to his time, but a magnificent ancient funeral which was preserved in the collective memory, perhaps handed down through epic: see Minns, pp. 87–8; T. Sulimirski, *CHI* II, pp. 170–1; Raevskij, *Model' mira*, pp. 74–5.

71,1. κατακεκηρωμένον … ὀπίσω: the practice of embalming using vegetable substances is confirmed by similar burials in Pazyryk and other localities of the Altai (see e.g. Jettmar, pp. 111–13). The aim was in the first place practical: that of preserving the body during the long procession and until the feast celebrated a year later; secondly, it must have aimed at preserving the body intact for the afterlife. Wax protected from larvae and allowed the application of cosmetics, while the κύπερος (an aromatic species of nut sedge, the *Cyperus longus* or the *Cyperus rotundus*), θυμίημα ('perfumed essence for burning, incense'), celery, and anise, probably imported from the Mediterranean, emanated a pleasant smell. A long discussion in Rolle, *Totenkult* I 1, pp. 82–9; id. *Scythians*, p. 28.

κομίζουσι... ἔθνος: the 'last journey' of the dead man on a cart or other means of transport finds various ethnographic parallels: see e.g. M. Ebert, *Prähistorische Zeitschrift*, XI–XII (1919–20), 179–96; cf. Alexander the Great's funeral procession in Diod. XVIII 26–8. The chariots were subsequently taken apart and their parts placed in the tombs: for a survey see Rolle, *Totenkult* I 1, pp. 113–21 (an example has been reconstructed from kurgan 5 at Pazyryk).

2. οἳ δὲ... διαβυνέονται: the custom of wounding oneself in token of mourning for the king is attested among several Eurasian nomadic peoples (see *Narody*, p. 310): cf. e.g. Priscus of Panopolis, fr. 23 Bornmann, on the Huns; the scene is depicted in the wall- paintings of Pjandžikent (7th cent. AD; Gabain, pp. 51–3, 127–8). On the Ossetians, cf. Dumézil, *Romans des Scythes*, p. 251.

3. ἐπεὰν... ταφῇσι: on the Gerrhus and the Gerrhi see note to chs. 53–6. The difficulty in finding the royal tombs (cf. 127, 2–3) is linked to their 'extreme' location; 'untraceability' was a characteristic of the tombs of many great nomad kings, from Attila to Genghis Khan (see e.g. Gabain, p. 96): rather than an actual fact, the position of the Gerrhus and of the Gerrhi may be a mythical element, or at any rate a fact elaborated within an ideological scheme, see Hartog, pp. 148–70 = ET, pp. 133–56; Raevskij, *Model' mira*, pp. 74–5.

4. καὶ ἔπειτα... καταστεγάζουσι: both the pallets made with plants beneath the coffin and the wooden 'canopies' above it are to be found in many tombs; the mound at Ul'skij Aul (Kuban') is especially close to Herodotus' description: see Talbot Rice, pp. 96–8; *Narody*, pp. 310–1. ἐν δὲ... χρυσέας: the burial of servants, concubine, horses, and implements served the purpose of ensuring that the dead man could live fittingly in afterlife (parallels in P. Haider, *Kritische und vergleichende Studien zur Alten Geschichte und Universalgeschichte*, Innsbruck 1974, pp. 89–120; on the women, cf. F. Schlette, *EAZ* XXVIII (1987), 242–3; on the horses, L. Malten, *JDAI* XXIX (1914), 179–256; A. Azzaroli, *An Early History of Horsemanship*, Leiden 1985, *passim*). It is fairly common to find in burials some 'secondary' dead whose position betrays their specific function; e.g. in the tombs of Ordžonikidze a skeleton was found seated, like a guard, while another was found among the horses: Rolle, *Totenkult* I 1, pp. 89–96; on the ἀγγελιηφόρος, see E. A. Grantovskij and A. I. Ivančik, *VDI* CCXIII (1995), 162–9. As for the horses, they are often found in separate chambers; their numbers fluctuate between one or two in some tombs on the Dnieper to approximately 400 at Ul'skij Aul: see R. Rolle, *Festschrift für R. Pittioni*, Vienna 1976, pp. 756–76; id., *Totenkult* I 1, pp. 96–112. The death by suffocation was aimed at avoiding bloodshed (see note to chs. 60–1). The horses at Pazyryk were killed with a blow to the head; the skulls of the Ukrainian tombs show no traces of such a blow and must therefore have been truly suffocated, see Rolle, *Festschrift*, pp. 757 and 763.

ἀργύρῳ... χρέωνται: silver and bronze are in fact well attested in princely burials:

this report is effected by exaggeration and by the influence of a *topos* attested also, e.g., about the Ethiopians in III 23,4 (cf. note to III 23,14).

72,1. ἐνιαυτοῦ... τοιόνδε: the ghostly cavalcade set up outside the mound on the anniversary of the kings' death cannot be confirmed by the archaeological record. However, in some mounds (e.g. Ordžonikidze, Tolstaja Mogila, Želtokamenka) there have been found the remains of animals, all killed at the same time, situated in a higher layer than the original flooring of the funerary chamber; this suggests the consumption of funerary banquets some time after the burial of the deceased man; see V. I. Bibikova, *SA* (1973), 4, pp. 63–8; Rolle, *Totenkult* I 1, pp. 49–55; B. N. Mozolevskij, in *Drevnosti stepnoj*, p. 219; E. V. Chernenko, *AncCiv* I (1994), 46–8.   ἀργυρώνητοι... θεράποντες: the absence of slaves bought from outside, who are instead substituted by free men (perhaps impoverished), seemed odd to 5th-cent. Greeks, but is understandable in a nomad society: see Chazanov, pp. 131–64 (discussion in A. Häusler, *EAZ* XXV (1984), 438 ff.). Greek ethnography of subsequent ages also adopts the terms θεράπων and θεραπεύειν to denote analogous 'cortèges' of free men: see e.g. Polyb. II 17,12; Diod. V 29,2; Norden, pp. 124–5.

2–5. τούτων... ἀπελαύνουσι: stuffed horses were mounted on posts on the occasion of funerary rituals also e.g. among the Mongols, as remarked by John of Pian di Carpini, III 12 (in *Mongol Mission*, pp. 12–13; cf. William of Rubruck, *Itinerarium* XXV, ibid., p. 141). For a possible Ossetian reminiscence see Dumézil, *Le Livre*, p. 132–3; Dumézil, *Romans des Scythes*, pp. 255–8. This macabre representation was perhaps meant to evoke a horse-race to escort definitely the dead man to the afterlife: see Bessonova, pp. 61–2; Thordarson, in op. cit., pp. 545–7.

4. χαλινοὺς δὲ καὶ στόμια: for a review of Scythian bits, amply attested in tombs, see Potratz, pp. 39–84.

73,1. οὕτω... θάπτονται: for private citizens the procession is reproduced on a reduced scale. Forty (or thirty) is the number of days which, according to the beliefs of many Indo-European peoples, the soul needs in order to leave the body after death: see K. Ranke, *Indogermanische Totenverehrung* I. *Der dreissigste und vierzigste Tag im Totenkult der Indogermanen*, Helsinki 1951; cf. note to 73,2.

2. καθαίρονται: as is clear from chs. 74–5, in order to 'purify' themselves after funerals the Scythians inhaled the fumes of hemp. Herodotus defines this as a 'bathing' (see note to 25,2–3; it has even been supposed that the Slavic *kopati se*, 'to wash oneself', derives from the name of hemp with relation to this custom: see O. N. Trubačëv, *Etnogenez i kul'tura drevnejšich Slavjan*, Moscow 1991, pp. 75–6); but the prevailing element is that of the ecstatic experience, as made evident by the parallels in the use of drugs in Iranic religion: see e.g. C. J. Vooys, *Hermeneus*, XXVII (1956), 152–3; Eliade, *Shamanism*, pp. 394–5; on the Massagetae see I 202,1; on the Thracians, Mela II 21. K. Meuli, *Hermes*, LXX (1935), 121–7, remarked the analogous custom of Altaic shamans of purifying the tent from the soul of the deceased man forty days after his death (cf. *Testi dello sciamanesimo*, pp. 166–9; see Eliade, *Shamanism*, pp. 200–14 on the shaman *psychopompus*). However, here Herodotus is not speaking of shamans: if his description is

accurate, we must think of rituals practised by the heads of the family (cf. K. Dowden, *REG* XCIII (1980), 486–7). The presence of *Cannabis sativa* in Scythia (cf. also Hesychius κ 673 Latte) is confirmed by findings in the region of the Kuban', from Nemirov, etc.: see Blavatskij, pp. 82–3; Ch. Danoff, *RE* Suppl. IX 1962, coll. 1001–2; B. A. Šramko, *Slovenská Archeológia*, XXI (1973), 157–8; Z. V. Janušević, *ZArch* XV (1981), 90. But the most detailed confirmation of Herodotus' account has come from kurgan 2 at Pazyryk with the finding of two 'stoves' containing stones and seeds of hemp, the frame—consisting of six stakes—of a miniature tent with traces of the canvas, and a flask with more seeds; cf. Jettmar, pp. 113–14; Rudenko, pp. 284–5. The seeds had been left to burn in the tomb; but the equipment must have been an object of everyday use, and not reserved solely for purification after a funeral: see G. Ränk, *Festschrift M. Zender*, I, Bonn 1972, pp. 490–6; Rolle, *Skythen*, pp. 101–2; G. Wolf and F.M. Andraschko, in *Gold der Steppe*, pp. 157–60.

74. καὶ ἐξ αὐτῆς ... εἷμα: on hemp in Thrace (cf. Hesychius κ 673 Latte), see G. Kazarow, *Beiträge zur Kulturgeschichte der Thraker*, Sarajevo 1916, pp. 16 ff. Unlike linen (often associated with it; see e.g. Artemidoros, *On.* III 59), hemp was a novelty to the Greeks of the 5th cent.: cf. F. Orth, *RE* VII 2 1912, coll. 2313–16. The formula ὃς δὲ μὴ εἶδέ κω ... suggests first-hand knowledge; cf. chs. 81 and 99.

75,2. ἀγάμενοι ... ὠρύονται: 'howling' is a rather odd effect of joy: K. Meuli, *Hermes*, LXX (1935), 122 and 125 thinks rather of shouts to send away the soul of the deceased. But there is in the verb an animal metaphor which underlines the savageness of the funerary ritual as a whole; cf. Hartog, p. 166 = ET, p. 151.

3. τοῦτό ... λαμπραί: the scarce use of water for personal hygiene is typical of life in the steppes; see e.g. Neumann, *Die Hellenen*, p. 294. The 'beauty mask' of the women is also interpreted as a funerary ritual by Meuli, art. cit., pp. 126–7 (with ethnographic parallels; cf. II 85); but the use of precious woods, presumably imported, suggests an aesthetic practice of the women of the aristocracy (see F. Schlette, *EAZ* XXVIII (1987), 240–1; R. Rolle and G. Wolf, in *Gold der Steppe*, pp. 127–9). Herodotus introduces the information as an appendix to the section on funerals, playing on the concept of 'bathing' in strained connection with that of 'purification'.

76–80. Herodotus speaks of openness towards foreign customs also in relation to the Persians (I 135) and the Egyptians (II 91); καὶ οὗτοι at 76,1 especially underlines the similarity with the behaviour of the Egyptians, witnessing to the close link between the two *logoi* (see Introduction, pp. 548 ff. and 562–3; also the ἀλλήλων of the codices in the following line, 'between them', if retained, may be an allusion to the relation between Scythians and Egyptians; B. Bravo, *ASNP*s. IV, V (2000), 84–5 suspects interpolation). The stories of Anacharsis and Scyles, modelled along similar lines, contain manifest fictional elements (see Aly, pp. 127–8; M. V. Skržinskaja, *VDI* CLXII (1982), 87–103; T. M. Kuznecova, *KSIA* CLXXVIII (1984), 11–17; Vinogradov, pp. 98–100; on Scyles, see also Dumézil,

Romans des Scythes, pp. 352–9). The historicity of the Scyles episode is, at any rate, very likely, more so than that of the Anacharsis episode (see notes below); both witness to the uneasiness of the more traditionalist Scythians in the face of the increasing infiltration of Greek culture, which is well attested by the importation of artefacts between the 6th and the 5th cent.: see Chazanov, pp. 234–8; A. M. Khazanov, *DHA* VIII (1982), 15–17. However, it is remarkable that Herodotus should present as being typically Greek two cults (of the Mother of the Gods and of Dionysus) which are in some respects exotic and whose introduction into Greece had provoked, according to some traditions, negative reactions (see Hartog, pp. 81–102 = ET, pp. 61–84). Is perhaps Herodotus, who considers many Greek gods to have been imported, polemically targeting through these Scythian tales excessive defensiveness against foreign religions? See also Mora, pp. 225–39.

76–7. A rich body of anecdotes flourished around the figure of Anacharsis: see Kindstrand, with bibl. Some aspects of the 'legend' of Anacharsis must have been known to Herodotus already before he reached Scythia, where he was able to acquire only some details from Tymnes (see von der P. Mühll, *Festgabe für H. Blümner*, Zurich 1914, pp. 425–33). In the Peloponnesian version (ch. 77) Anacharsis appears in his more usual garb, as the barbarian endowed with a simple and healthy virtuousness; the image of an Anacharsis who is enthusiastic about Greek culture is less common in antiquity (see e.g. Diog. Laert. I 103, and cf. Kindstrand, pp. 26–30) but it is more congenial to Herodotus' 'diffusionistic' attitude. If, as Herodotus states, Anacharsis was truly the uncle of the Scythian king Idanthyrsus, he must have lived in the 6th cent. However, Herodotus emphasizes this detail as a novelty drawn from Tymnes and unknown to the majority, while he declares that he was unable to obtain information from the Scythians: this could give rise to the suspicion that Tymnes pandered to Herodotus' curiosity with some fabricated details, and that Anacharsis was merely a figure of the imagination (discussion and bibl. in Kindstrand, pp. 13–23; in any case the arguments to make of Anacharsis a 'shaman of the north' are flimsy). The name Ἀνάχαρσις may be authentically Iranian ('uninjured, pure'), but also Greek: a survey of opinions appears in R. Schmitt, in *ΛHNAIKA, Festschrift für C. W. Müller*, Stuttgart–Leipzig 1996, pp. 83–4; cf. note to 76,6.

76,2. θεωρήσας ... πολλὴν: on travel with the objective of seeing and acquiring knowledge (as with Solon I 30,1), see Drexler, pp. 25 ff.   ἀποδεξάμενος: from ἀποδεικνύναι = 'to show': cf. VII 23,3; Plato, *Hipparch.* 228b (the derivation from ἀποδέκεσθαι = 'to receive', advanced by Kindstrand, pp. 27–8, is impossible with σοφίην as object).
3. τῇ Μητρὶ τῶν θεῶν: Cyzicus and the nearby Mt Dindymus = Kapı Dagh, was the centre of an ancient cult of the Mother of the Gods (Cybele), held to have originated with the Argonauts: see among others Apollonius Rhodius I 1092 ff.; Neanthes of Cyzicus, *FGrHist* 84 F 39; M. J. Vermaseren, *Corpus Cultus Cybelae Attidisque*, I, Leiden 1987, pp. 91–7. The participants of the nocturnal feast (παννυχίς) carried the tambourine (τύμπανον: cf. e.g. *Hymn. Hom.* XIV 3; Pindar,

fr. 70b,9 Snell–Maehler; Euripides, *Bacch.* 59) and figurines of gods on their breast (ἀγάλματα called προστηθίδια and τύποι by Polybius XII 37,6; cf. Dionysius of Halicarnassus, *Ant. Rom.* II 19,4; Cornutus, *De Natura Deorum*, p. 6,11 Lang), as is confirmed also by representations: see H. Hepding, *Attis, seine Mythen und sein Kult*, Giessen 1903, pp. 127–9; M. J. Vermaseren, *Cybele and Attis: The Myth and the Cult*, London 1977, pp. 28–9 and 97; L. Robert, *Opera Minora Selecta*, V, Amsterdam 1989, p. 755. On oaths to the Mother of the Gods on setting out to sea, cf. Hartog, p. 88 = ET, pp. 68–9. Apart from the Anacharsis episode, the cult of the Mother of the Gods flourished at Olbia starting from the 6th cent.: see M. M. Kobylina, *Divinités orientales sur le littoral nord de la Mer Noire*, Leiden 1976, pp. 2–5; Rusjaeva, pp. 101–14; Vermaseren, *Corpus Cultus Cybelae Attidisque*, VI, Leiden 1989, pp. 147–55. The 6th-cent. inscription edited by A. S. Rusjaeva and Ju G. Vinogradov, in *Gold der Steppe*, pp. 201–2 (*SEG* XLII 710; *IGDOP* 24) seems to hint at altars in Hylaea to the Mother of the Gods, to Borysthenes and to Heracles 'recently destroyed' (by the Scythians? cf. Vinogradov, *Olbia*, pp. 16–18; B. Bravo, in *Problemi*, pp. 254–64).

4. ἡ δέ ἐστι... πλέη: after the several mentions of these two places (9,1; 18,1; 19; 54–5) the specification is remarkable; but, aside from the fact that Herodotus has probably re-elaborated previous material (see Introduction, p. 559), the tale stands, in some respects, as an autonomous *logos* (cf. A. Corcella, *ASNP* s. III, XV (1985), 382–5), and the mention of the wooded nature of Hylaea is appropriate in the context of the cult of the Mother of the Gods (cf. e.g. *Hymn. Hom.* XIV 5).

6. ὡς δὲ ἐγώ... Ἀνάχαρσιν: Tymnes was a 'henchman' of the Scythian king Ariapeithes (cf. ch. 78), and it is likely that Herodotus met him in Olbia, though this is not explicitly stated (see Vinogradov, pp. 103–4; J. R. Gardiner-Garden, *Klio*, LXIX (1987), 348–9). The name, well attested in Caria (see e.g. *Syll.* 46,25; 169,73, in Herodotus cf. V 37,1 and VII 98), might have been borne by a native of Olbia as a Milesian inheritance; the interpretation as a Scythian name is less likely (cf. Zgusta, pp. 153–4). Herodotus lists the genealogy of the Scythian kings rather emphatically, and he uses a phrase calculated to make an impression ('let him know that he was killed...'; an imitation in Paus. I 6,8): this belies pride in the discovery, in connection with a matter which was obviously unclear (cf. Kindstrand, p. 10). Among the names cited Σπαργαπείθες sounds authentically Iranian (it is the name of an Agathyrsian king in 78,2; cf. the Massagetan Σπαργαπίσης of I 211: see Justi, p. 506; Altheim–Stiehl, *Geschichte*, p. 128). The other names are less clear; see, however, Justi, pp. 116 and 292; Grantovskij–Raevskij, in *Etnogenez*, p. 56.

77,1. ὑπὸ Πελοποννησίων: according to the Peloponnesian tale, which is clearly propagandistic, Anacharsis, far from being a philhellene and a martyr of Greek culture, once he had returned to his homeland criticized the empty wisdom of the Greeks, and appreciated only the simple and wise 'laconicism' of the Spartans. For Anacharsis as upholder of σωφροσύνη and of conciseness see esp. Maximus of

Tyre 25,1; cf. Kindstrand, pp. 40–2, 127–8.   ἀσχόλους ... ἐς πᾶσαν σοφίην: it
has the meaning of 'occupied in every form of knowledgeable activity', with a
negative connotation which is reminiscent of the polemic against πολυμαθίη of
Heraclitus, DK 22 B 40, and above of all the ideological clash between Spartan
conservatism and Athenian πολυπραγμοσύνη in the 5th cent. (see V. Ehrenberg,
JHS LXVII (1947), 46–67). No parallels for this use of ἐς with ἄσχολος have been
found (περί and πρός are the norm), but the interpretation 'they have no spare
time for any wise activity' is impossible; see M. Hutton, *TAPhA* XLI (1910), 11–13.

78–80. In the episode of Scyles it is possible to discern a struggle for power which
led Octamasades to depose his brother at a time of marked expansion of the
Scythian kingdom. Scythian control seems in fact to reach as far as the Thracian
borders, and the story told by Herodotus suggests a protectorate over Olbia,
which Scyles could enter freely, having garrisoned the army below the walls: see
Ju. G. Vinogradov, *Chiron*, X (1980), 63–100; A. M. Khazanov, *DHA* VIII (1982),
17–21; Vinogradov, pp. 81–109. The historicity of King Scyles seems to be
confirmed by the finding of a ring bearing his name (ΣΚΥΛΕΩ) in the neighbourhood of Istria, the town of his mother (see, also on the genealogy of Scythian
kings, Ju. G. Vinogradov, *Epigraphica*, XLIII (1981), 9–37); coins with the legend
ΣΚ or ΣΚΥΛ are known from the region of the Dniester: cf. Vinogradov,
pp. 106–7 (Σκύλης, however, may have been the dynastic name of the kings;
cf. note to 6,2 and F. Cornillot, *Indo-Iranian J.*, XXIII (1981), 29–39). The
concomitance with the reign of Sitalces suggests a date for the episode of the
death of Scyles towards the middle of the 5th cent., shortly before Herodotus'
visit to Olbia: see Vinogradov, *Epigraphica*, XLIII, pp. 28–30.

78,2. Ἀριαπείθης ... παῖς: as in ch. 76, Herodotus takes pleasure in supplying
superfluous details to corroborate his information. Ἀριαπείθης is an Iranic name
formed like Σπαργαπείθης; see Mayrhofer, p. 139. He had at least three wives: a
Greek woman from Istria (south of the mouth of the Danube; cf. Pippidi,
pp. 37 ff.; Isaac, pp. 268–78, with archaeological confirmations of relations with
Scythia) by whom Scyles was born; a Scythian woman, subsequently inherited by
Scyles, Opoea (for a possible Iranic etymon, from *hu*- and *pā*-, 'well protected',
see Justi, p. 233), from whom was born Oricus (perhaps linked with Avest.
vairya- = 'worthy, to be chosen'; see Zgusta, p. 260); and a Thracian woman
(80,1), the daughter of King Teres. Polygamy, like the custom according to which
a son inherits his father's wives, is typical of Eurasian nomadic societies: see
Chazanov, pp. 77–82. On his Greek education by his mother, cf. VI 138,2;
S. G. Cole, *Reflections on Women in Antiquity*, New York 1981, pp. 219–45.
3. (οἱ δὲ ... Μιλησίους): the information underlines the Greek nature of Olbia
(cf. note to 18,1–2). The phrase used by Herodotus does not warrant the
assumption of the existence, already in the archaic and classical periods, of an
actual treaty of *isopolitia* between Miletus and Olbia such as there was in the
Hellenistic period (*Syll.* 286 = Tod II 195): bibl. and discussion in Ehrhardt,
pp. 235–7.   προαστίῳ: given the nomadic character of the Scythians,

Herodotus must mean by προάστιον the empty space around the city rather than the districts outside the walls (see in general G. Audring, *Klio*, LXIII (1981), 215–31). The identification of the προάστιον with the 5th-cent. suburb to the west of the citadel cannot, therefore, be well founded (Ju. I. Kozub, *Archeologija*, XXIX (1979), 3–34): see K. K. Marčenko, *VDI* CLXI (1982), 126–36.

4. τεῖχος: on the existence of walls at Olbia as early as the 5th cent., probably in reaction to Scythian pressure, see Wąsowicz, pp. 68–9; *Archeologija SSSR* IX, pp. 190–3; Vinogradov, pp. 82–3.   τὴν στολὴν... τὴν Σκυθικὴν: the typical Scythian dress, of leather, included close-fitting breeches and tunic, a belt, high boots, and a pointed cap: see e.g. Talbot Rice, pp. 57–63; L. S. Klocko, *Archeologija*, XLVII (1984), 57–68; ead., in *Gold der Steppe*, pp. 105–10.

79,1. ἐπείτε... γενέσθαι: for such statements, which anticipate a tragic outcome (like ἐπεθύμησε; cf. note to 1,1), see P. Hohti, *Arctos*, IX (1975), 31–7: violation of one's own *nomos* is a source of disaster.   Διονύσῳ Βακχείῳ: the cult of Dionysus is well attested in Olbia from the 6th cent. onwards by a series of graffiti: see Rusjaeva, pp. 72–91; Ehrhardt, pp. 167–70 (on the epiclesis Βακχεῖος, Milesian in origin). Herodotus' description, with the mention of the thiasos (79,5; for a parallel in Olbia from the 3rd cent. BC see A. Kocevalov, *Würzburg Jahrb.*, III (1984), 265), shows that this was not a state cult but that it took place in public and was accessible by initiation; see H. Jeanmaire, *Dionysos*, Paris 1951; M. L. West, *ZPE* XLV (1982), 17–29; Bottini, pp. 151–7.

2. τὴν... ἔστασαν: a marble statue of a griffin dating from the 5th cent. BC was found in Olbia at the beginning of the 20th cent.: see e.g. *Archeologija SSSR* IX, p. 213 and table XCVIII 1. The decoration seems inspired, rather than by the Scythian 'animalistic style', by oriental palaces, which were not unknown in the area of the Greek colonies.   ἐνέσκηψε βέλος: cf. e.g. VII 10ε. On lightning in the Orphic cult at Olbia see M. L. West, *ZPE* XLV (1982), 19; D. M. Cosi, *Museum Patavinum*, V (1987), 217–31: it cannot be ruled out that Herodotus has retold in a moralistic sense a story originally Orphic.

3. οὐ γάρ... ἀνθρώπους: it was probably Ionic rationalism which, through the Scythians, voiced such criticism against a Greek custom (see e.g. E. Lévy, *Ktema*, VI (1981), 62). For his part, Herodotus, who disagrees with the idea that Dionysus was 'invented' by the Greeks (see II 48–50), is perhaps rather aiming a polemic at the attitude of the Scythians; see note to 76–80.

4. διεπρήστευσε: the (δι)επρήστευσε of the mss is a *hapax* which can only have the meaning—strained, with πρός—of 'to inflame'. A verb is needed which denotes a stealthy movement (cf. Vinogradov, pp. 101–2): Stein's conjecture of διερπήστευε (from ἑρπηστής, ἕρπειν = 'to crawl') is not once attested.

80,1–2. ὡς δὲ... Θρηίκην: perhaps Scyles turns to Thrace in the hope of receiving military support (M. V. Skržinskaja, *VDI* CLXII (1982), 181), while Olbia must have been annexed immediately by Octamasades (Vinogradov, p. 105); the Thracian dynasty of the Odrysians, at any rate, shared Scyles' philhellenism (cf. J. R. Gardiner-Garden, *Klio*, LXIX (1987), 345–8). Following Darius' expedition, the Scythian and Thracian kingdoms, both of them in a phase of expansion, came in contact. The Thracian king Teres had stabilized the border on the Ister by the marriage of one of his daughters to Ariapeithes, while Sitalces had consolidated it by refusing to join battle with his nephew Octamasades; the name of the latter—now attested also on a cup dating from the 5th cent. BC from Hermonassa and among the Sindi in the 4th cent. (see now *SEG* XLIII 1993, no. 515; Ju. G. Vinogradov, *VDI* CCXLII (2002), 3–22; Heinen, pp. 19–28)—is by some considered Thracian (e.g V. Beševliev, *Untersuchungen über die Personennamen bei den Thraken*, Amsterdam 1971, pp. 12–14), while at the same time a Thracian prince by the name of Σκυθοδόκος is attested (see Z. Velkova, *Studia Thracica*, I (1975), 139–41): on the relation between Scythians and Thracians see Meljukova, *Skifija*, with the archaeological evidence. The chronology of events is not known. Teres' activity may date to the seventies or sixties of the 5th cent., Sitalces dies in 424; see e.g. Danov, pp. 282 ff. with bibl. (it is unlikely that Euripides, *Rh.*, 406 ff., is alluding to these events; see V. Iliescu, *Klio*, LVIII (1976), 367–76). The identity of Sitalces' brother, who lived in exile among the Scythians, is unknown: among the sons of Teres Sparadocus is known, who might have reigned before Sitalces (see Danov, pp. 292–3): if he did not die an untimely death, might Sitalces have usurped his kingdom and driven him to find refuge among the Scythians?

81,1. πλῆθος ... εἶναι: the Scythian population could be considered more or less numerous according to the extension given to the concept of 'Scythian': see Introduction, pp. 553–4. The most widespread idea was that they were a very numerous people, the most numerous according to Thuc. II 97,6 (cf. Xen. *Cyr.* I 1,4; while Herodotus gives first place to the Indians, followed by the Thracians; see V 3,1). It was said that they were 'few' only in a relative sense, 'considering that they are Scythians' (the sense of ὡς Σκύθας εἶναι is restrictive: cf. II 8,3; J. E. Powell, *Hermes*, LXVIII (1933), 124).

2. τοσόνδε ... ἀπέφαινόν μοι ἐς ὄψιν: S. West, *Scripta Classica Israeliana*, XIX (2000), 15–34, interprets 'they indicated thus much to me by way of illustration', and then reads ὥς ἐστι with a part of the mss, to the effect that Herodotus would not be saying that he saw the vessel, which would only have been mentioned to him as evidence; yet ἀπέφαινον λόγῳ would in this case be expected, while the statement 'to whom has not yet seen it, I will describe it' below seems to imply direct vision (cf. 99,5). The sentence, lit. 'they brought forward to my sight this much', is strange, however, and this, together with other incongruities, leads B. Bravo (*ASNP* s. IV, V (2000), 85–8) to the conclusion that the whole of ch. 81 is spurious.   ἐστι ... ποιέειν: despite pointing the reader to his previous treatment of the subject (ch. 52), Herodotus provides a summary without any apparent purpose. Is he perhaps summing up the more ample exposition given in a partial first draft, which has now lost its purpose since in the complete work the Exampaeus has already been treated? See Introduction, p. 559.

3–4. ἐν τούτῳ ... ἕξ: the bronze vessel is of such dimensions as to cast doubt on its feasibility on technical grounds: it must have contained up to 20,000 litres, with a thickness of 110–30 mm.; cf. K. K. Marčenko and O. M. Ščeglov, *Archeologija*, LXVII (1989), 117–21, who calculate its height to have been between

4 and 9½ m. and its weight more than 7 tons. This casts a shadow over Herodotus' claim to have seen the vessel (see O. Kimball Armayor, *HSCPh* LXXXII (1978), 48–57); but he probably furnished a rough estimate, which was exaggerated and based on sexagesimal numeration: see M. V. Skržinskaja, *VDI* CXCI (1989), 85–6. Upholding Herodotus' veracity see, however, Pritchett, pp. 245–52; p. 249 (with reference to the silver crater mentioned by Callixenus, *FGrHist* 627 F 2). According to I 51,1–2 the golden crater given to Delphi by Croesus was no smaller; but the comparison with Pausanias' crater in Byzantium was more fitting because it too was of bronze, as we learn from Nymphis, *FGrHist* 432 F 9. Nymphis accuses Pausanias of having passed off the crater as his personal offer and of inscribing on it a boastful dedication: Herodotus, in contrast, always gives a positive judgement of Pausanias; see e.g. Corcella, pp. 201–2.

4–6. τοῦτο ὦν ... τοῦτον: the typical arrow-points with three lobes are always present in Scythian burials (see Meljukova, *Vooruženie*, pp. 14–34; H. Eckhardt, in *Gold der Steppe*, pp. 144–7). Often they reveal themselves to be unsuited for military use, so that they must have had—as they probably had in this case—a symbolic function in that they represented the valour of the warrior; in the Greek colonies, coins in the shape of the point of an arrow were used: see B. N. Grakov, *Istorija, archeologija i etnografija Srednej Azii*, Moscow 1968, pp. 101–15; S. Sorda, *Annali dell'Istituto Italiano di Numismatica*, XXVI (1979), 185–206; C. Grottanelli and N. F. Parise, *Dialoghi di Archeologia*, IV (1986), 133–7. The great cauldron, which often for the peoples of the steppes is a tribal possession and an ensign of sovereignty, thus assumes the meaning of a symbol of the unity under the king of the warrior community: see F. Bosi, in *Mnemosynum. Studi in onore di A. Ghiselli*, Bologna 1989, pp. 65–74. A similar form of census in military expeditions is attributed to the Parthians by Procopius, *Bell. Parth.* I 18,52–3; other parallels in How–Wells, ad loc. (Malaysia); T. J. Brown, *Ancient History Bull.*, II (1988), 1, n. 2; Dumézil, *Romans des Scythes*, pp. 360–1 (Circassians). But, the episode seems legendary and can be compared to the first Roman census held by means of coins by Servius Tullius (Dionysius of Halicarnassus, *Ant. Rom.* IV 15,4–5). King Ariantas is otherwise unknown; his name is Iranic: see e.g. Justi, p. 23.

82. θωμασία ... ποταμόν: on the 'wonders' (almost entirely lacking also in Lydia, see I 93,1), cf. H. Barth, *Klio*, L (1968), 93–110; Müller, *Geschichte*, p. 115, n. 200; on the rivers see note to chs. 47–58. Like the 'footprints' attributed to Christ, saints, or paladins in Palestine and Europe, or the 'feet of Buddha' in the East, so too the 'footprint of Heracles' (cf. chs. 8–10 and 59) must have been a natural hollow in a rock (calcareous rocks prone to erosion surface in the middle Dnestr); at Agyrium, in Sicily, analogous 'imprints' of the cattle of Geryon were shown (Diod. IV 24), cf. K. M. D. Dunbabin, *J. Roman Archaeology*, III (1990), 85–109, and the parody by Lucian, *VH* I 7. Two cubits (approximately 90 cm.) was also the size of the sandal of Perseus in II 91, coherently with the idea that the ancients were larger; cf. I 68,3.   τοῦτο ... λόγον: resumes the account of Darius' expedition begun at the opening of the book; for similar formulae, see I 140,3 and VII 137,3; cf. A. Corcella, *ASNP* s. III, XV (1985), 348–9.

83,1. παρασκευαζομένον...Βόσπορον: the ships must have been supplied in the first place by Ionians, Aeolians, and Hellespontines (cf. 89,1), but perhaps—if it is true that 'all' subjects were involved (87,1)—also by Phoenicians, Egyptians, Cypriots, and other peoples of Asia Minor, as in the case of Xerxes' expedition against Greece (VII 89 ff.). On analogies between the two expeditions see note to chs. 102–42; Introduction, p. 564.   Ἀρτάβανος: Artabanus (*Rtaba-nuš, Elam. *Ir-da-ba-nu-iš*, see Mayrhofer, p. 163 with bibl.), brother of Darius, plays here the role of the unheeded 'wise adviser' (cf. R. Lattimore, *CPh* XXXIV (1939), 24–35). In Book VII he will play the same part with his nephew Xerxes and will recall, among other things, the Scythian expedition (VII 10α–γ). On the 'impregnability of the Scythians' see note to 46,2–3.

84,1–2. Οἰόβαζος...ἐλίποντο: the episode has a parallel in the story of Pythius in VII 38–9, and aims at highlighting the reluctance of the subjects (cf. VII 13,3; *De Aeribus Aquis Locis* 16). In Οἰόβαζος there is *bāzu-/bādu-* = 'arm' (or *vazdah-* = 'supporter': R. Schmitt, *ZDMG* CXVII (1967), 128, 132, n. 97); if the first part is *vahyah-* = 'better' (Justi, p. 232; R. Schmitt, *ZDMG* CXVII (1967), 134 and n. 121) might there be a connection with Elam. *Man-ya-ba-du-iš* (Mayrhofer, p. 189)?

85,1–2. Δαρεῖος...θωμασιώτατος: Darius' excursion is mostly a narrative artifice to open an *excursus* on the Pontus, as in the case of Xerxes at VII 128–30 (cf. e.g. V 51,3; VI 137–40); it may have been invented for this purpose: see Fehling, p. 134 (therefore, the deletion of 85,2–86 proposed by B. Bravo, *ASNP* s. IV, V (2000), 88–92 can hardly be accepted). On the Pontic area and the straits in Herodotus see now Müller II, pp. 199–204, 792–9 (Bosphorus), 800–2 (Byzantium), 812–14 (Propontis), 829–40 (Hellespont), 850–2 (Chalcedon), 859–63 (Cyanean islands). Chalcedon was situated on the southern extremity of the Bosporus, on the Asian bank, in the vicinity of modern-day Kadıköy (*PECS*, p. 216). The Cyanean islands ('deep blue') must be identified with the rocks and the shallows by Cape Anadolu and Rumeli (cf. *Portolano del Mediterraneo*, V, Genoa 1983, pp. 92–3). The term 'wandering' (πλαγκταί is used of Scylla and Charybdis in the *Odyssey*; cf. e.g. Arrian, *Periplus Ponti Euxini* 25, p. 128 Roos) or 'clashing' (συμπλήγαδες) was connected to the myth of the Argonauts: it was in fact recounted that, in order to enter the Pontus, they had to sail through two mobile rocks which continuously opened up and closed in again (cf. K. Meuli, *Odyssee und Argonauktika*, Berlin 1921, pp. 87–9). In the end it was perhaps an optical illusion (cf. W. F. Pickard, *G&R* XXXIV (1987), 1–6). As usual, Herodotus grants little credibility to the mythical report.

2–4. τὸ μὲν μῆκος...καλέεται: the measurements given in this and in the following chapters are not in all cases exact, however we might calculate the stade (whose regional variants fluctuate between 177 and 213 m.; the fathom is one-hundredth of a stade): see the tables in Rawlinson III[4], p. 76; *Narody*, p. 325; Ch. Danoff, *RE* Suppl. IX 1962, coll. 868–71. The margin of error diminishes for the smaller measures: the Bosporus is approximately 780 m. wide at its narrowest point, against the 710–840 given by Herodotus, and approximately 30 km. long, against the 21–5 of Herodotus; the Sea of Marmara is approximately 80 km. wide, against the 90–100 given by Herodotus, and approximately 280 km. long, against the 250–300 of Herodotus; the Strait of the Dardanelles measures about 1.3 km. at its narrowest point, against the 1.2–1.5 km. given by Herodotus, and it is about 120 km. long, against the 71–84 of Herodotus. The error is much greater in the case of the Black Sea: from the Bosporus to the Phasis = Rion, even hugging the coast, the distance is not much greater than 1,200 km., whereas Herodotus reckoned 2,000–2,300 km., while from Themiscyra on the Thermodon river (modern-day Terme Çayi, about 60 km. east of Samsun: see *PECS*, p. 907; Müller II, pp. 222–3) to the Sindica (and the Kerč' Strait: cf. ch. 28) the distance is about 400 km., against the 600–700 given by Herodotus. The unreliable system of conversion of days (and nights) of navigation into linear measures accounts for the errors, which are inevitably greater the greater the distances: the particular navigation measured by Herodotus may have been hindered by winds and accidents of various kinds, but the sailors tended to overestimate the speed of the vessel (Scylax 69, *GGM* I, p. 58, reckons 500, not 700 stades for a day's navigation; nor is it possible, after a long—summer's—day of sailing, to have also a long night). In Strabo II 5,22–3, and Pliny, *NH* IV 86–7 and VI 2–3, the errors are smaller; but even William of Rubruck, trusting in merchants, reports for the Black Sea the disproportionate length of 1,400 miles (*Itinerarium* I = *Mongol Mission*, p. 89). In short, Herodotus must undoubtedly have misunderstood the information, itself exaggerated, supplied to him by the sailors who offered him the passage; however, it is not necessary to suppose that he did not make the voyage himself (O. K. Armayor, *HSCPh* LXXXII (1978), 45–9; cf. S. West, *Scripta Classica Israelica*, XIX (2000), 27–8), and that he reported 'typical' figures (Fehling, pp. 166–7): see Pritchett, pp. 234–42 and the data for comparison in Mele, pp. 53–5. On Herodotus' navigations on the Black Sea, cf. H. Matzat, *Hermes*, VI (1872), 412–8; v. Fritz I, pp. 128–30 (the journey along the northern coast postulated by Rybakov, pp. 81–6, is improbable). The route from the Bosporus to Colchis was aided by the currents; while the crossing of the Black Sea from south to north was made also along a shorter route (from Cape Karambis = Kerempe burnu to the Kriou Metopon = Aj Todor), as demonstrated by the relations between Heraclea and Chersonesus: see V. F. Gajducevič, *KSIA* CXVI (1969), 16–19; M. Zolotarëv, in *Demografičeskaja situacija*, pp. 94–100; Ju. Vinogradov and M. Zolotarëv, *Le Pont-Euxin vu par les Grecs*, Paris 1990, pp. 98–9 (against the doubts expressed by M. I. Maximowa, *Klio*, XXXVII (1959), 101–18, see v. Fritz I, p. 92, n. 12).

86,4. μοι μεμετρέαται: the *Epimerismi Homerici* (J. A. Cramer, *Anecdota Graeca* I, p. 287) attribute to Hecataeus the following fragment (*FGrHist* 1 F 196): ὁ μὲν οὖν Βόσπορος καὶ ὁ Πόντος οὕτω καὶ ὁ Ἑλλήσποντος κατὰ ταὐτά μοι μεμετρέαται. The author of the *Epimerismi* may have made a mistake (cf. the attribution to Hipponax in *Etymologicum Magnum* 578,41–4 and in Zonaras 1352), and in any case it is not necessary to think of plagiarism or of a Herodotean allusion (Armayor, art. cit., pp. 45–9; B. Bravo, *ASNP* s. IV, V (2000), 89–90): Herodotus

644 *Commentary*

and Hecataeus may have both made the calculation independently, and described it with a typical formula. παρέχεται... τοῦ Πόντου: in ancient texts the dimensions of the *Palus Maeotis*, i.e. the Azov Sea (which in present times amounts to about 1/13 of the Black Sea), are often exaggerated. According to Scylax 69, *GGM* I, 58, it was half the size of the Pontus, while according to Strabo II 5,22–3 it was about a third; William of Rubruck (*Itinerarium* I) still spoke of 700 miles in length and in width. According to Polybius IV 40 it was becoming progressively smaller with time, but geological analysis refutes this hypothesis (bibl. in *Narody*, p. 328): rather, its shallow waters prevented fast navigation, thus causing the distances to be overestimated. Μαιῆτις, feminine of Μαιήτης, 'Maeotian' (cf. ch. 123) is the Ionic form for Μαιῶτις: the name is treated like an adjectival formation of the kind of Ἰταλιώτης/Ἰταλιήτης (see Schramm, pp. 184–5). In Greek Μαῖα means 'nurse': Μαιῆτις might then have had the force of 'mother of the Pontus'. The latter was the local name (cf. 52,1), as shown by Pliny, *NH* VI 20, who reports the Scythian form *temarunda(m)*; for an explanation of *temarun-d(h)a-* = 'which generates the black sea' (not a strictly Scythian form, but from an 'Indo-Aryan' substratum), see O. N. Trubačëv, *Antičnaja Balkanistika 2. Predvaritel'nye materialy*, Moscow 1975, pp. 38–47.

87,1. στήλας: the stele with an inscription in 'Assyrian' characters (probably the cuneiform script of the Achaemenid inscriptions; see, however, C. Nylander, *OA* VIII (1968), 119–36; R. Schmitt, in *Zum Umgang mit fremden Sprachen in der griechisch-römischen Antike*, Stuttgart 1992, pp. 21–35) and one in the local language, finds parallels in the Egyptian inscriptions in ancient Persian, Elamite, and Egyptian: see S. West, *CQ* XXXV (1985), 281–2; Pritchett, pp. 148–9. They must have stood on the European side of the strait, given that they were reused by the Byzantines. τούτων... συνελέχθησαν: the figure of 700,000 men (also in Justin II 10,18; Ctesias, *FGrHist* 688 F 13, para. 21, speaks of 800,000) is clearly exaggerated, like all the numbers referring to Persian contingents in Herodotus: it is a folkloric rather than a true report (see M. V. Skržinskaja, *VDI* CXCI (1989), 84–5; on the reckoning by tens of thousands, C. Hignett, *Xerxes' Invasion of Greece*, Oxford 1963, pp. 350–5). Also the 600 seem like a conventional figure, recurrent for the Persian fleets (cf. ibid., pp. 347–8). See in general Černenko, pp. 18–20; A. Fol and N. G. L. Hammond, in *CAH* IV, p. 238. In any case, Herodotus does not state that he drew on the inscription for these figures, of which he gives notice as an aside.

2. τῆς Ὀρθωσίης Ἀρτέμιδος: the cult of Artemis Orthosia had probably reached Byzantium from its motherland of Megara; on the cults of Artemis and Dionysus in Byzantium, which are attested by the names of the months, numismatics, etc., see K. Hanell, *Megarische Studien*, Lund 1934, pp. 181 ff., 211–12; Isaac, pp. 215–37, esp. pp. 235–6 with bibl. τοῦ δὲ Βοσπόρου... ἱροῦ: on the northern mouth of the Bosporus, the 'temple' par excellence was that of Zeus Ourios on the Asiatic bank, not far from Anadoulu-Kavaği (cf. C. J. Brandis, *RE* III 1 1897, coll. 752–3); but there was another temple opposite this one, on the European bank (e.g. see Strabo VII 6,1). Herodotus believes that the bridge was

built over the middle of the Bosporus, probably because that was the narrowest part (cf. Polybius IV 43,2, Dionysius of Byzantium 57 Güngerich), i.e. the stretch of sea between Rumeli Hissar and Anadolu Hissar (see already D. F. Kruse, *Über Herodots Ausmessung des Pontus Euxinus*, Breslau 1818, p. 109).

88,1. πᾶσι δέκα: lit. 'ten of each kind', an idiomatic expression meaning 'abundantly': cf. Pindar, fr. 170 Snell–Maehler; Herod. I 50,1; III. 74,2; VI 57,3; IX 81,2; Theopompus, *FGrHist* 115 F 179; Andriscus, ibid. 500 F 1; Porphyry, *De Abst.* II 60.   **γραψάμενος:** Herodotus was able to see the picture dedicated by Mandrocles (a theophoric name from Asia Minor; see Zgusta, p. 287), in the Heraion of Samos, which by the time of Strabo (XIV 1,14) had become a 'gallery'. On Herodotus and Samos, see, note to 39–60, with bibl.; cf. III note to III 60,12 on the Heraion, and *Griechenland. Lexikon*, pp. 262–4. It is impossible to tell solely on the basis of the verbal forms (middle γράφεσθαι against active ἐπιγράφειν) whether Mandrocles, having commissioned the picture, wrote the epigram himself or made someone else write it (the epigram is listed as anonymous in *Anthologia Palatina* VI 341 = D. L. Page, *Further Greek Epigrams*, Cambridge 1981, pp. 193–4): see G. Dunst, *Athenische Mitteilungen*, LXXXVI (1972), 123–4; S. West, *CQ* XXXV (1985), 282. The picture of Darius on the throne which Herodotus saw in Samos must have provided the inspiration for the analogous story of Xerxes (VII 44), as it perhaps inspired also the Samian Choerilus (fr. 5 Bernabé): see A. Barigazzi, *Hermes*, LXXXIV (1956), 180–1.

89–96. The march in Thracian territory is told briefly by Herodotus, who does no more than report some episodes connected with the building of monuments: see Danov, pp. 261–6; N. G. L. Hammond, *Chiron*, X (1980), 53–61; Černenko, pp. 57–64 (with a discussion of the doubtful archaeological traces of the passage of the Persians); A. Fol and N. G. L. Hammond, *CAH* IV, pp. 238–9, with bibl. While the fleet proceeded as far as the Ister, the army was forced to penetrate inland because the coast of European Turkey on the side of the Black Sea was rendered impracticable by the wooded declivities of the Istranca mountains; there are, however, uncertainties as to what course it followed. Darius met, at the springs of Tearus, the road which from Hieron, on the Sea of Marmara, led to Apollonia, on the Gulf of Burgas, by way of the Istranca mountains; he then reached the Artescus river, whose identification is controversial (see note to ch. 92) and, skirting the territories of the Scyrmiadae and Nipsaeans, between European Turkey and the Gulf of Burgas, he entered the region of the Getae, on the right bank of the lower Danube. According to some (see esp. Hammond, art. cit., pp. 53–61; J. M. Balcer, *Historia*, XXXVII (1988), 8–9), Darius marched westwards as far as the great road which from Aenus ran up the valley of the Hebrus/Maritza towards the Danube, with the aim of ensuring control over a larger portion of Thrace (cf. IV 118,1, and the placement of a garrison at Doriscus mentioned at VII 59,1). But the most natural hypothesis is that, from the springs of Tearus, Darius returned as soon as possible to the Pontic coast and continued in a northerly and north-easterly direction along the route from Hieron to

Apollonia: thus the mention in the text of this route finds fuller justification, and the submission of the Thracians inside Salmydessus is more easily understood. See the clarification in Müller II, pp. 809–10 and 955–8.

89,1. τὸ γὰρ δή ... Ἑλλησπόντιοι: the indication of Ionians, Aeolians, and Hellespontines as commanders of the fleet (without the mention of other participants; see note to 83,1) serves the purpose above all of introducing and justifying the important role played by local tyrants later on in the narrative; Introduction, p. 564. However, it is not entirely unlikely: the Ionians, especially the Milesians, were better acquainted than anyone else with the Pontic coasts, and they might find support in the colonies.

2. τὸν αὐχένα: according to Strabo VII 3,15, the bridge was built on the seaward part of the 'island' of Peuce, which was created from the complex ramifications of the river. Herodotus seems to be describing a point further upstream, not too far from Tulcea, perhaps between Orlovka on the left bank and Isaccea on the right, where some bridges were built by the Romans: see Černenko, pp. 61–2.

90–1. A. Jochmus, *J. Royal Geographical Soc.* (1854), 43–4, located the springs of the Tearus near the locality of Pinarhisar, on the Istranca, where he met with reports of a lost inscription, perhaps cuneiform, of which the probable base has been found (E. Unger, *AA* (1915), 3–17). Jochmus thought the Tearus (also mentioned by Pliny, *NH* IV 45) to be a fusion of the rivers Bunar and Semer, and the Contadesdus to be the Karistiran; according to V. Beševliev, *Studia Balcanica*, X (1975), 19–22, the Tearus is instead the Biükdere, and the Contadesdus the Koevska. In any case they must be streams which, from the Istranca mountains, flow into the Erginus = Ἀγριάνης, which in turn flows into the Hebrus/Maritza; see now Müller II, pp. 942–8 and 858 (Contadesdus = Poyrale Dere; cf. pp. 770–1 on the Agrianes and pp. 825–7 on the Eurus). On Aenus, modern-day Enez, see J. M. F. May, *Ainos, Its History and Coinage, 474–341 B.C.*, Oxford 1950; Isaac, pp. 140–57 with bibl.; Müller II, pp. 773–7.

90,2. ὁδός ... ἑκατέρη: the exact location of Heraeum (or *Heraion teichos*: the sources in Isaac, p. 203) is unknown, but the site was not far from Perinthus, modern-day Ereğli (see L. Robert, *StClas* XVI (1974), 61–9; Isaac, pp. 204–7 with bibl.; Müller II, pp. 841–3, 900–3; Hamdi Sayar). Therefore the journey from Heraeum to Milesian Apollonia, modern-day Sozopol on the Gulf of Burgas (see Ehrhardt, pp. 61–2; Isaac, pp. 241–7 with bibl.), must have taken more than 4 days: cf. Danov, p. 141.

91,1–2. ἡσθεὶς τῷ ποταμῷ ... ἐγράφη: the interest for the water of rivers is a typical Persian trait: see I 138,2; E. Gabba, *RIL* CXXV (1991), 309–11. The titles attributed to Darius are not implausible: cf. e.g. inscription B from Naqš-i Rustam, vv. 27–49; see J. Friederich, *Die Welt als Geschichte*, II (1936), 108; M. Hosu, *Latina & Graeca*, V (1974), 40–5; S. West, *CQ* XXXV (1985), 296.

92. Ἀρτησκός: there is much uncertainty about the location of the Artescus, and of the original seat of the Odrysians, who later became rulers of the whole of

Thrace. It is uncertain whether this is the same river as mentioned by Hesiod, *Theog.* 345, where the *codices* give Ἄλδησκος, Ἀρδησκός, Ἀρδισκός: the Thracian river-name (cf. I. Duridanov, *Die Sprache der Thraker*, Neuried 1985, pp. 22, 50–1) may have been widespread (Dionysius Periegetes, pp. 314–20, *GGM* II, 120–1, seems to locate a river of the same name to the north of the Danube). Some have thought (see esp. V. Velkov, *Geschichte und Kultur Thrakiens und Mösiens*, Amsterdam 1988, pp. 9–15) that the name is preserved in that of the Arda, thus limiting the region of the Odrysians to the valley of the Hebrus/Maritza and of the Tundža. But it is not certain that Darius penetrated so far west (see note to chs. 89–96): the Artescus could be another tributary of the Erginus, and the territory of the Odrysians could have reached as far as the Istranca; cf. Danov, pp. 119 ff., 264. Müller II, p. 788 has recently favoured the Teke Dere. On the Odrysians see now Z. H. Archibald, *The Odrysian Kingdom of Thrace: Orpheus Unmasked*, Oxford 1998.   ἐπὶ τοῦτον δὴ ... στρατίην: this is perhaps a local legend to explain the origin of two large heaps of stones (cf. ch. 81); for this kind of tradition (cf. e.g. in the Old Testament, Joshua 4) see Aly, p. 130. Cf. the return to the theme in 'Faustus of Byzantium' III 7 and Moses of Khoren II 12 (trans. R. W. Thomson, Cambridge, Mass. 1978, p. 148).

93,1. Γέτας: the Getae were settled between the Balkans and the lower Danube. According to Herodotus (V 3), they were different from the other Thracians, and Thuc. II. 92 defines them as similar to the Scythians. N. G. L. Hammond, *Chiron*, X (1980), 58–9, suggests an identification with the 'Sakā beyond the sea' of the Achaemenid inscriptions. Some scholars think of them as a group relatively distinct from the Thracians to the south of the Balkans, closer—also linguistically— to the Dacians: among others see D. Berciu, *Dacia*, V (1961), 163–84; H. Daicoviciu, *Thracia*, IV (1980), 5–14; N. Barbuta, *Latomus* XXXIX (1980), 386–92; V. I. Georgiev, *ANRW* II 29,2, pp. 1148–213. Herodotus idealizes their courage and sense of justice, as do also e.g. Strabo VII 3,8 and Horace, *Carm.* III 24,11 ff. (cf. Mela II 18; Introduction, p. 560): after Darius' withdrawal they probably regained their independence, since they are not listed among Xerxes' contingents.   Σαλμυδησσὸν: here Salmydessus denotes not the city (modern-day Midye), but—as in Strabo VII 6,1 for instance—the entire Pontic coast of European Turkey: sources and bibl. in Isaac, pp. 239–40; Müller II, pp. 919–24. The Skyrmiadae, if Σκυρμιάδαι is the correct reading, seem to correspond to the Skymniadae found in Eudoxus, fr. 304 Lasserre; as for the Nipsaei (vv. ll. Nypsaei, Mypsaei), Stephanus of Byzantium, s.v., mentions the town of Νίψα in Thrace, which name can be integrated into one of the Athenian tribute lists (cf. *The Athenian Tribute Lists*, I, Cambridge, Mass. 1939, pp. 357, 526). They should be located directly inland from the coast, as far as Mesembria, modern-day Nesebăr (cf. VI 33; Isaac, pp. 249–54 with bibl.; Müller II, pp. 881–2).

94–6. The Getae practised rites to become immortal (ἀθανατίζοντες): they believed that when they died they would join the δαίμων (intermediary between man and god) Salmoxis in a kind of paradise; every four years their relationship with Salmoxis was renewed by the sending of a messenger. For the other sources, not all of them coherent, and the interpretation of the cult, see esp. Rohde, pp. 263–6; I. M. Linforth, *CPh* XIII (1918), 23–33; Eliade, *Zalmoxis*, pp. 21–75; P. Alexandrescu, *DHA* VI (1980), 113–22; I. G. Coman, *RHR* CXCVIII (1981), 243–78; C. Marcaccini, *Sileno*, XXIV (1998), 135–58. Such faith in immortality, linked to the figure of a semi-divine hero founder in the context of an exclusive circle, reminded the Greeks of Pythagoreanism; and with a patriotic bias which Herodotus exposes in ch. 95, they believed that Salmoxis was just a cunning swindler who modelled himself on Pythagoras. Herodotus, on the contrary, though he states his intention not to take sides, describes the Greek rationalistic interpretation with a certain amount of irony, and proposes a chronologic argument (96,1) which is reminiscent of the polemic of II 123 on the originality of the Greeks: it was rather Pythagoras who might have drawn inspiration from Salmoxis.

94,1. παρὰ Σάλμοξιν... Γεβελέϊζιν: in other sources the name appears as Ζάλμοξις or Ζάμολξις: the form Σάλμοξις/Ζάλμοξις seems confirmed by the name of the Getan sovereign Zalmodegikos (cf. D. M. Pippidi, *Epigraphische Beiträge zur Geschichte Histrias in hellenistischer und römischer Zeit*, Berlin 1962, pp. 75–88; *SEG* XVIII 288); Ζάμολξις is simply a form with metathesis. The etymology is disputed (from *g'hem-ol* = 'land'?, from ζαλμός *kolmo-* = 'skin, protection'?), and has suggested both chthonic and solar interpretations (for further reading see note to chs. 94–6). As for the other name, Γεβελέϊζις (or Βελέϊζις), the tradition is too uncertain and does not offer sufficient bases for interpretation: C. Poghirc, *Thracia*, II (1974), 357–60, suggests emending to Νεβελέϊζις, from *nebhul-* = 'sky'. It unlikely that it is etymologically equivalent to Ζάμολξις (despite P. Kretschmer, *Glotta*, XXIV (1936), 44–8); it may, instead, be an attribute. Also uncertain is the connection with Zbelsurdos, Thracian god of the storm (to be associated with the Lithuanian *žyburỹs* = 'light, torch'; cf. G. Kazarow, *RE* VI A 1 1936, coll. 515–17; V. I. Georgiev, *ANRW* II 29,2 1983, p. 1171). See Eliade, *Zalmoxis*, pp. 51–5; S. Paliga, *DHA* XX 2 (1994), 137–50.

2–3. διὰ... ζῶντι: a ritual similar to this 'divine judgement' has been reconstructed on a Daunian stele by S. Ferri, *RAL* XXIX (1974), 230–6. The final remark, 'they give him instructions while he is still alive', sounds ironical, perhaps not involuntarily.

4. οὗτοι... σφέτερον: similar customs in I 172,2; IV 173, and 184,2; parallels in Rohde, p. 278, n. 63; Aly, p. 66; *Testi dello sciamanesimo*, p. 318. The ritual must have had an apotropaic function against the storm: cf. V. E. Orël, in *Problemy antičnogo* pp. 116–23, with Slavic parallels. In the eyes of the Greeks this seemed a lack of recognition of the god of the sky (for ὁ θεός in this sense see e.g. III 117,4; cf. Harrison, pp. 218–19). More strained is the interpretation as a positive cultic act of emulation of the god: Eliade, *Zalmoxis*, pp. 52–53; Mora, pp. 169–73.

95,1. δουλεῦσαι: Getan slaves were common in Greece, as demonstrated by the typical servile name of Γέτης (see V. I. Velkov, *VDI* CIV (1967), 70–80): thus Salmoxis was reduced to a more 'natural' condition in the eyes of a Greek.

2. ἅτε... Πυθαγόρῃ: the excessive insistence on the superiority of the wisdom of the Greeks and of Pythagoras smacks of irony: what Salmoxis learns from them is how to cheat the 'righteous' Getae (cf. I 60,3). In fact the tone of the entire tale is ironic (cf. esp. at 95,3 the very prosaic πανδοκεύοντα): see Hartog, pp. 102–25 = ET, pp. 84–109.

4–5. κατάγαιον... Σάλμοξις: the same story is also in Hellanicus, *FGrHist* 4 F 73. A similar trick was reported also about Pythagoras (Diog. Laert. VIII 41; on the antiquity of this tradition see Burkert, pp. 154–9). Sophocles, *El.* 62, speaks about 'wise men' who hide, pretending to be dead, as a well-known fact.

97–8. With the crossing of the Ister the account of the expedition becomes progressively more incredible. According to Herodotus, Darius' intention was to destroy the bridge once he had crossed it and to advance by land; Coes persuades him to preserve the bridge as an 'emergency exit' in case the Scythians should prove 'impossible to find'; Darius agrees, but assigns to the Ionians who are to guard the bridge a term of sixty days, after which they can return to their homes. This only makes sense if, after the sixty days, Darius intended to return by a different route, i.e. through the Caucasus, having subdued the Scythians (e.g. see Bornitz, pp. 116–17). But if this was his plan, it is odd that he should leave the fleet behind on the Ister (cf. ch. 141) rather than make it sail along the coast to support his advance (the hypothesis of Gallotta, pp. 62–6, according to which Darius was moved to this action by revolts among the Ionians, is not sufficiently grounded). In the logic of the narrative, the episode serves in the first place as an explanation of why the Ionians halted at the Ister, and also as a reminder of the theme of the 'impregnability' of the Scythians (see note to 46,2–3): fixing a symbolic terminus of sixty days (cf. note to 98,1), Darius signals his dangerous venture into an unknown land, like the sultan in the *Thousand and One Nights* ('The Fisherman and the Jinn') who, in his quest of a fabulous lake, asks his vizier to await him no longer than three days. Herodotus had probably obtained some information which was more detailed, but also elaborated with novelistic elements, on what had happened in the camp of the Ionians who had been left behind to guard the bridge, but—as the rest of the narrative shows—he had not been able to form a sufficient idea of the general strategy of Darius and of the actual conduct of operations (see note to chs. 102–42; Introduction, pp. 561 ff.).

97,1. Ἴωνας: including Aeolians and Hellespontines; see ch. 137.

2. Κώης: the name derives from that of the island of Cos: Zgusta, p. 262. Coes, who is here just a military leader, will become a tyrant (V 11). πυθόμενος... ἀποδείκνυσθαι: the whole of Coes' behaviour and speech is portrayed as being very wise: wisdom is not infrequent in the addresses to the Persian king by Herodotus' characters (cf. e.g. VII 10α,1, θ), and here it is especially fitting since it comes after the episode of Oeobazus.

6. σωθέντος...ἀμείψωμαι: on the gratitude of the king, see Briant, *Histoire*, pp. 315–16 = ET, pp. 303–4.

98,1. ἄμματα ἑξήκοντα: such a primitive method of counting may come as a surprise (parallels in M. P. Nilsson, *Primitive Time-reckoning*, Lund 1920, pp. 319–23): perhaps there is a touch of irony or at any rate a novelistic elaboration; see M. V. Skržinskaja, *VDI* CXCI (1989), 82–4.

99–101. Before the narrative of the expedition there is another geographical *excursus* on Scythia; though this is useful in providing a background to Darius' expedition, it is, in substance, autonomous: see Cobet, pp. 85–121. The image of Scythia projected in this *excursus* is very different from that of the preceding chapters: it is no longer an inhabited space crossed by rivers but rather a geometrical diagram devoid of any characterizing elements, a 'chess-board' open to the movements of the armies (Minns, p. 27). Some have supposed the use of different sources, also on the basis of some contradictions, while B. Bravo, ASNP s. IV, V (2000), 92–6 regards the whole as spurious (see Introduction, pp. 558 ff.); but above all there is a different approach to geographical space. This 'square Scythia' is the first attempt of which we know to construct a two-dimensional image of the little-known inner regions: in order to do this ancient geographers, as late as Eratosthenes (see Strabo II 1,22 ff.) and Ptolemy (*Geog.* I 2,4), had to start from linear measurements drawn from *peripli* and itineraries and convert them into the sides of a geometrical shape, thus inevitably neglecting meanderings and different orientations: see Berger, p. 104; Janni, pp. 47–9, 102. Thus Herodotus can construct his quadrangle by considering the two stretches of coast from the Danube to Evpatorija and from the peninsula of Kerč' to the Don as more or less straight lines that join, forming a considerable angle: see J. L. Myres, *Geographical J.*, VI (1896), 606–31; id., *Herodotus*, pp. 32 ff.; E. Lanzillotta, ΓΕΩΓΡΑΦΙΑ, *Atti del secondo convegno maceratese su Geografia e cartografia antica*, Rome 1988, pp. 93–103. The reconstruction is not very realistic and is carried out 'schematically' (τυπωδῶς as Strabo II 1,23 says); rather than assuming a map (Stein, ad loc.) it seems to substitute it with the verbal description. See most recently J. G. F. Hind, in Tsetskhladze, *North Pontic Archaeology*, pp. 25–31; id. in Tsetskhladze–Snodgrass, pp. 41–8.

99,1. τῆς δὲ Σκυθικῆς γῆς...πρόκειται: the opening shows the relative independence of the *excursus*: the first word, styled as a title (cf. e.g. the exordium of Pausanias' *Periegesis*), is 'Scythia', whereas there is no emphasis on Thrace, which was the subject of the previous chapters. The 'gulf' corresponds to the north-western coast of the Black Sea, which draws a curve. ὁ Ἴστρος... τετραμμένος: in II 33–4 Herodotus seemed to be stating that the Ister flowed from the north symmetrically with the Nile, but also ch. 48, in which its five tributaries are lined up from east to west, implies that in its last stretch the river flows toward the south-east; in fact the last stretch of the Danube, more or less starting from Galați and Reni, flows roughly south-eastwards (and this was even more so in antiquity if one of the mouths of the delta came closer to the city of Istria; cf. II 33,2; Pippidi, p. 39). The image Herodotus had of the Ister is therefore unclear; see How–Wells' clarifications, ad loc.; and A. Vulpe, *StCl* XXIV (1986), 38–40; on the tendency to overlook the meanderings of rivers see note to chs. 47–58; the peculiar statement that it flows into the sea in Scythia must be taken to mean that it skirts it (IV 49,3; unless Legrand's emendation to ἐς αὐτόν = 'in the gulf' is to be followed). The Ister marks the border of the Thracian kingdom also for Thuc. II 97,1: the statement is fundamentally true on the political plane, even though Thracian influences are evident as far as the Dniester, see A. I. Meljukova, *MIA* CL (1969), 61–80; ead., *Skifija*.

2. τὸ δὲ... μέτρησιν: the description will follow the course of an actual *periplus*, from west to east. Presumably, when sailing from Olbia to Carcinitis (Evpatorija: see note to chs. 53–6), ships made directly for Cape Tarchankut without entering the gulf of Karkinit, and this may have contributed to create the impression that the coast followed a straight line (cf. also the same note, on the Hypacyris).   ἀρχαίη Σκυθίη: the definition 'ancient Scythia' is a mystery. It is unlikely that it is related to ethnic stratification in the region (see e.g. H. Kothe, *Klio*, LI (1969), 37–9; O. N. Trubačëv, *VopJaz* (1979), 4, pp. 33–4; most recently, K. K. Marčenko and M. Ju. Vakhtina, *Hyperboreus*, III (1997), 179–85), given that according to Herodotus the original seat of the Scythians was elsewhere, in Asia (chs. 11–12; but the myths in chs. 5–10 portrayed the Scythians as having been born on the Borysthenes); and the hypothesis that, according to Herodotus, this was the first part of Scythia to become known to the Greeks is unsatisfactory (Macan, ad loc.). It is possible that Herodotus distinguished 'ancient Scythia' from the new Persian satrapy, or district, named *Skudra*, Thrace: cf. W. Pajākowski, *Eos*, LXXI (1983), 243–55; J. M. Balcer, *Historia*, XXXVII (1988), 1–21 (on the etymological relation between Σκυθία and *Skudra* see Szemerényi, pp. 23–6). According to Strabo VII 4,5 the region between the Dnieper and Crimea, remnant of the great Scythian kingdom of the 4th cent. BC, was once called 'little Scythia' (cf. Windberg, pp. 23–4): but by 'little Scythia' or 'Scythia minor' Dobrugia, to the south of the Danube, was usually meant. The name does not date back to earlier than the 4th cent., but Scythian penetration into Thrace occurred immediately after Darius' expedition (discussion in Pippidi, 49–50; cf. VI. 40): was perhaps 'ancient Scythia' contrasted with the larger Scythia which had come into being with expansion? Or is ἀρχαίη Σκυθίη a gloss, later incorporated into the text, by a reader of later times who knew of the existence of a 'new Scythia' this side of the Ister? (Cf. B. Bravo, *ASNP* s. IV, V (2000), 93–4.)

3. τὸ δὲ: Tauris, which to Herodotus is a promontory that occupies the southeastern corner of the Scythian quadrangle (cf. note to 103,1), corresponds roughly to southern Crimea: following the coast, it reaches from Evpatorija (Carcinitis) up to Theodosia and the base of the Kerč' peninsula (known as 'rocky peninsula' on account of its declivities). Herodotus describes it as entirely mountainous, overlooking the stretch of steppe between Evpatorija and Sevastopol'. Above all, its orientation is uncertain: the coast from Theodosia to the mouth of the Don is described as if it proceeded lineally more or less from

south to north, washed by an 'eastern sea' which—as 100,1 shows—comprises the Black Sea on the level of the Strait of Kerč' and the Azov Sea (for the Greeks this is a λίμνη, 'marsh, lake', but here θάλασσα is a generic term for 'expanse of water'; cf. e.g. Paus. II 30,7). The convention of the *peripli* according to which the coast was always described in linear progression made it in some ways difficult to understand how, after having left the region of the Scythians and having come to the Tauri, the Scythians could be encountered again (the 'royal' ones, see ch. 20): cf. e.g. Scylax 68, *GGM* I, p. 57. Hence the need for two *exempla ficta*, chosen from a range of possible ones, addressed to two sorts of audiences, one which has a greater familiarity with Attica, and one which has a greater familiarity with southern Italy (Herodotus must have known both of them: to reach Thurii he himself probably made the *periplus* of the Salentine peninsula which he here describes). The demes of Anaphlystus and Thoricus, respectively on the western and eastern coast of Attica, were conspicuous points for the traveller who coasted Sunium on account of the presence of fortifications which were clearly visible from the sea (see Scylax 57, *GGM*, p. 46; D. Whitehead, *The Demes of Attica*, Princeton 1986, pp. 402–3; cf. Peretti, p. 96, n. 109). On γοῦνος see Lanzillotta, op. cit., pp. 99–103: it is the hill whose summit—ἄκρη—reaches towards the sea (also cf. J. L. Myres, *G&R* XII (1943), 33–42). By 'Iapygia' Herodotus seems to mean not just the Salentine peninsula but the whole of Apulia, including the area to the north of the line Brindisi–Tarentum: discussion in G. Nenci, *ASNP* s. III, VIII (1978), 43–58; E. De Juliis, *Gli Iapigi. Storia e civiltá della Puglia preromana*, Milan 1988, pp. 14–15.

100,2–101,3. ἤδη ὦν ... τοσαύτη: it is unlikely that, in this context of objective statements, ὡς ἐούσης τετραγώνου at 101,1 means 'assuming that it is square' (Hartog, p. 352 = ET pp. 346–8): Herodotus seems to think that it actually is ('since it is square'), though with the inevitable approximations inherent in such statements. The southern side of the quadrangle must be reckoned from the mouth of the Danube along a road which reached Olbia and thence continued towards the isthmus of Perekop as far as the Kerč' peninsula. The sum of 20 days' walk (= 4,000 stades = 700–800 km.) is on the whole correct (on the trade routes between the Danube and the northern coast of the Black Sea see A. S. Ostroverchov, in *Drevnosti*, pp. 88–9; L. V. Subotin and I. T. Černjakov, *Archeologija*, XXXIX (1982), 15–23). The other sides are less clear: the eastern one, also washed by the sea, follows the western and northern coast of the Azov Sea, but it might in part run inland reaching the Melanchlaeni (see note to 20,2); the western side seems to follow the Ister for a stretch before turning away from it to reach the Agathyrsi in Transylvania (see note to 48,4). An exact transposition onto a map is difficult (see Minns, pp. 27–8): in order to find his bearings in the little-known interior Herodotus adopted as sides of the quadrangle the routes that penetrated it, even though their direction was not well definable geometrically.

102–42. The implausibilities in the narrative of the expedition in Scythia have been denounced several times: still useful are the analytical summaries by Macan, pp. 33–54; How–Wells I, pp. 429–34. Above all, the extensive wandering of Darius is incredible, even for Herodotus' geographic conceptions (see Introduction, pp. 561 ff.): in little less than sixty days the king, with a massive army and without the support of the fleet, reaches beyond the Don and turns northwards, stops to build some forts, and turns westward again to return to the starting-point, all of this while having to cross the great rivers of this vast region. The extensive wandering of Darius is the result of amplification on the part of the sources on the one hand, and of Herodotus' generalizations on the other. Clearly he knew that Darius had crossed the Ister and had returned to it some time later; but as to what happened in the meantime, he must have had scanty and not very accurate information, including perhaps some tales of Scythian origin which described the war in quasi-epic terms: cf. Dumézil, *Romans des Scythes*, pp. 327–38 (parallels for the various episodes); Raevskij, *Model' mira*, pp. 68–71 (Darius is made to go around the limits of Scythia anticlockwise); A. Fol and N. G. L. Hammond, *CAH* IV, pp. 2349–43 (on the Scythian viewpoint of the narrative); P. Georges, *AJAH* XII (1987), 119–23. Moreover, the vague and amplified reports of the sources offered the cue for a reconstruction of events coherent with some fundamental principles of Herodotean historiography. According to Herodotus, in fact, the 'impregnability' of the Scythians (cf. note to 46,2–3) is the consequence of the 'primitive' nomadic lifestyle which seems to characterize all Scythians in the narrative of the war, while he makes no mention here of the farming peoples; on the other hand the infantry of the Persians, who elsewhere are normally represented as archers and riders, is placed in relief, so as to highlight the contrast with the highly mobile and fugitive Scythians (cf. Hartog, pp. 53–79 = ET, pp. 34–60). Darius, who wanders for a long time on their tracks and is humiliated by the contemptuous replies of Idanthyrsus and by the superior indifference of the enemy, comes to represent the exemplary figure of the wealthy and powerful king defeated by a primitive and simple adversary, in accordance with a *topos* omnipresent in Herodotus' oeuvre (Cyrus and the Massagetae, Cambyses and the Ethiopians, etc.; see Cobet, pp. 104–20). More specifically, the Scythian war, in which the attacked party withdraws before the immense army of the king only later to put it to flight, becomes for Herodotus a prefiguration of Xerxes' war against the Greeks, as is shown by several detailed correspondances (see Ph.-E. Legrand, *REA* XLII (1940), 219–26; Bornitz, pp. 125–35: Fehling, pp. 144–5). Hence also the narrative structure of the story, with Darius who from his initial over-confidence comes to a sudden awareness of his weakness and turns to flight, and with a series of significant scenes of dialogue which underline the turning-points in the narrative: cf. Immerwahr, pp. 106–10; Bornitz, pp. 113–36; Hunter, pp. 176–225. Therefore the amplifications of the sources, as well as his own personal inclinations, led Herodotus to enlarge Darius' march; but the various geographical details of the story show that he believed himself to be describing it with a certain degree of exactitude and scruple. Herodotus probably tried to situate the reports of his sources into his own geographical scheme, but being unable to find an exact correspondence for some elements he was led by the emphasis of the sources and by his own criterion of reconstruction to locate too far east an episode which might have taken place little beyond the Dnieper. Strabo VII 3,14 even seems to be making Darius move on this side of the Dnestr, and it is impossible to tell whether he relies on an alternative source (cf. Pherecydes, *FGrHist* 3 F 174; Ctesias, ibid. 688 F 13,20–1) or is simply rationalizing the Herodotean narrative. J. B. Bury, *CR* XI (1897), 277–82, thought of an expedition in the area of the Carpathians; so now P. Georges, *AJAH* XII (1987), 97–147. Other scholars have suggested more or less extensive redimensioning (see most recently Černenko, pp. 65–99, who makes Darius reach the northern coast of the Azov Sea, resuming in part Rybakov's theses, pp. 169–84); or else they have postulated in Herodotus' narrative a confusion with an expedition against the Sakā in the Caucasian region (see note to 109,1 and 122–4; a review of opinions in *Narody*, pp. 368–71). Once doubt has been cast on the Herodotean account it is difficult to find bases for alternative reconstructions: see, however, the notes which follow and the Introduction, pp. 564–5.

102–19. Like all expeditions by Persian kings, also the one against Scythia proves itself, notwithstanding the motive of revenge (cf. note to 1,1–2), inspired by the will to conquest which overtakes 'the guilty and not guilty': see esp. VII 8γ3 and 138,1; cf. J. De Romilly, *REG* LXXXIV (1971), 314–37; Bornitz, pp. 115–17: Evans, *Explorer*, pp. 9–40. In the face of such an attack there is the need for as wide a coalition as possible. This theme will be fundamental in the narrative of the Greek war against Xerxes and reflects a fundamental preoccupation of Herodotus and of his time (see note to chs. 118–19). But it cannot be excluded that the Scythian kingdom, which at that time was in a phase of consolidation, was actually able to unite around itself other peoples in response to Darius' attack: Chazanov, pp. 225–38; A. M. Khazanov, *DHA* VIII (1982), 10–17; it may not be accidental that the Boudini-Geloni and Sauromatians took part in the alliance, since they had an interest in the trade route described at chs. 21 ff. The embassy of the Scythians to the neighbouring peoples supplies the opportunity to furnish the ethnographic information which had been postponed during the exposition of chs. 16 ff.: see Introduction, pp. 557–8.

103,1. Ταῦροι: the Tauri inhabited the homonymous mountains, but also the steppes of Crimea; they were known to Greek sailors, who were the victims of their attacks, as a savage people given to piracy, war, and human sacrifice (still attested in Tacitus, *Ann.* XII 17), but the archaeological record gives evidence also for settlements of a more peaceful nature: see A. M. Leskov, *Gornyj Krym v I tys. do n.e.*, Kiev 1965; id., *AW* XI 4 (1980), 39–53; A. N. Ščeglov, in *Demografičeskaja situacija*, pp. 204–18; *Narody*, pp. 343–5; Nejchardt, pp. 147–50; *Stepi*, pp. 80–3. **τῇ παρθένῳ:** the cult of the 'maiden' was very important in the Greek colony of Chersonesus (near Sevastopol'; among others cf. Strabo VII 4,3; *IOSPE* I² 184, 352; L. A. Pal'ceva, *Iz istorii antičnogo obščestva*, Gor'kij 1979, pp. 30–46); but it is not at all certain whether it was modelled on the local Tauric cult. The figure of the 'maiden' is in fact widespread in the Mediterranean (also at Halicarnassus, see *Syll.* 46,3), hence Herodotus can refer to the goddess as ἡ παρθένος without further specifications (against a direct identification with Artemis and other goddesses, see Ehrhardt, p. 149). On the other hand, in the human sacrifices of the Tauri and the virginal character of the goddess the Greeks found points of contact with the myth and cult of Iphigenia and Artemis, whose attribute ταυροπόλος lent itself to association with the Tauri (U. von Wilamowitz-Moellendorff, *Der Glaube der Hellenen*, Basel 1955², p. 177, n. 2). Beginning at least from Euripides' *Iphigenia in Tauris*, the Tauric goddess is identified with Artemis (cf. e.g. Diod. IV 44,7); Herodotus instead identifies her with Iphigenia, perhaps looking to the tradition according to which Iphigenia became a goddess, assimilated to Hecate (Hesiod, fr. 23 Merkelbach–West, cf. Paus. I 43, 1; Stesichorus, fr. 215 Davies). It is disconcerting that the identification with 'Iphigenia, daughter of Agamemnon' should go back to the Tauri: cf. e.g. the inscription with the name of Ulysses and Laertes in Germany mentioned by Tacitus, *Germ.* 3,2. We might postulate that the name of the Tauric divinity was assonant with that of 'Ιφιγένεια (does the ΒΟΦΙ in a graffiti from Chersonesus bear some relation?): see I. I. Tolstoj, *Grečeskie graffiti drevnich gorodov severnogo Pričernomor'ja,* Moscow–Leningrad 1953, p. 66, n. 96); according to Ammianus Marcellinus XXII 8,34 the local name of the goddess was Orsilochoe, which, however, is a Greek name: cf. Antoninus Liberalis 27; but this may be one of those instances in which Herodotus, or his informant, flaunts an imaginary source: see Fehling, pp. 38–9. Also cf. B. Bravo, *ASNP* s. iv, V (2000), 97–101, who expunges τὴν δὲ δαίμονα . . . εἶναι at 103,2.

2. τὸ ἱρόν: Euripides, in his *Iphigeneia in Tauris*, pictures it as an archaic Greek temple, but it is more likely that it was a sacred spot rather than a building: cf. M. V. Skržinskaja, *Drevnejšie gosudarstva na territorii SSSR, 1986 g.,* Moscow 1988, pp. 176–91. On the fruitless attempts at identification see O. Dombrovskij *et al.*, *Aju Dag—'svjataja' gora*, Simferopol' 1974, pp. 19–28.

3. ἀποταμὼν . . . ὑπεραιωρέεσθαι: the apotropaic use of the skull-trophy has various parallels: see Diod. V 29,4 and Strabo IV 4,5 (Celts); *Narody*, p. 346 (southern Russia); M. J. Becker, *PP* XLI (1986), 37.

104,1. Ἀγάθυρσοι: on the location of the Agathyrsi see note to 48,4 with the bibl. cited; the abundance of gold was due to the rich gold-mines of the Carpathians (O. N. Trubačev, in *Etnogenez*, p. 151, sees in the first part of the name the Dacian word for 'gold'). Their Thracian character does not exclude a possible mingling with Scythian peoples, which is confirmed by the Iranic name Σπαργαπείθης in 78,2 (bibl. and discussion in J. R. Gardiner-Garden, *Klio*, LXIX (1987), 336–8). Some similarities between the Transylvanian archaeological culture and the Scythian one (inhumation, grave goods, etc.) have led some to think of a migration of the Agathyrsi from the Pontic steppes, reflected perhaps in the legend at chs. 8–10 (cf. V. Vasiliev, *Sciții agatîrși pe teritoriul României*, Cluj–Napoca 1980; R. Hoddinott, *The Thracians*, London 1981, pp. 89–90; M. Oppermann, *Thraker zwischen Karpathenbogen und Ägäis*, Leipzig 1984, p. 117). The evaluation, in some respects positive, of the sharing in common of women is influenced by utopian reflections (M. Hadas, *CPh* XXX (1935), 120–1);

the report may derive from a Greek interpretation of a special system of classification of kinship (V. Andò, *Φιλίας χάριν. Miscellanea di studi classici in onore di
E. Manni*, I, Rome 1980, pp. 89–93).

105,1. Νευροί: on the location of the Neuri see note to 17,2. The fact that they
crossed the territory of the Boudini suggests that the latter were located not too
far from the upper Dnieper: cf. notes to chs. 21 and 122–4. At 125,3 Herodotus
says that the Scythians and Darius passed through Neuris (Νευρίς), which by
then must no longer have been inhabited by Neuri; but in the same context the
Neuri are mentioned among those who flee (from the territory of the Boudini?)
before the invader; cf. Introduction, pp. 553–8.   **ὑπὸ ὀφίων:** the invasion of
snakes is considered to be the transfiguration of an enemy invasion, perhaps by a
people who worshipped the serpent, whose cult is attested among Baltic peoples
(discussion in *Narody*, pp. 348–9); but e.g. Strabo III 2,6 mentions invasions by
snakes as a plausible reason for abandoning a country.

2. λύκος ... ἀποκατίσταται: as for lycanthropy (cf. Mela II 1,13), it is difficult
to establish whether it should be interpreted as a spontaneous individual phenomenon or as a collective ritual—perhaps of disguise—like the one practised in
the Arcadian *Lykaia*. The reference to annual recurrence may be understood also
in relation to the spontaneous transformations of lycanthropes, which, according
to Marcellus of Side, always occurred in February (see W. H. Roscher, *AGWL*
XVII (1897), 79–81). On the forms of lycanthropy in antiquity see L. Gernet, *The
Anthropology of Ancient Greece*, Baltimore 1981, pp. 125–39; C. Mainoldi, *L'Image
du loup et du chien dans la Grèce ancienne d'Homère à Platon*, Paris 1984,
pp. 11–35; T. Paroli, *Semiotica della novella latina*, Rome 1986, pp. 281–317;
R. Buxton, *Interpretations of Greek Mythology*, London–Sydney 1987, pp. 60–79. It
is not possible to use the element of lycanthropy to draw a connection between
Neuri and Slavs: lycanthropy is also well attested amongst the Baltic peoples
(J. Balỹs and H. Biezas, in *Wörterbuch der Myth.* I, 2, pp. 449–50) and in the
Germanic world (Paroli, op. cit., pp. 311 ff.); on the Dacians see Eliade, *Zalmoxis*,
pp. 10–20.

106,1. Ἀνδροφάγοι: cf. note to 18,3. The description is conventional: cf. the
Homeric Cyclops, *Od.*, IX 106 ff.; also the name Ἀνδροφάγοι, in place of the
normal Ἀνθρωποφάγοι, is influenced by poetic language cf. *Od.*, X 200). It was
perhaps a mythical people of cannibals sung by epic which was later located on
the limits of known geographical space. In fact the Androphagi were cut off from
the trade routes, and were not very well known, which circumstance may have
given rise to such rumours (cf. e.g. Strabo IV 5,4 on Ireland). Similar cursory
notes on 'nasty peoples' are to be found in Marco Polo, e.g. see *Divisament
dou monde* 166 = *Milione* 162; *The Travels of Marco Polo*, London 1958, p. 253;
a generally sceptical position on such reports in W. Arens, *The Man-eating Myth*,
New York 1979. The remark 'unique among these peoples' could be a polemic
against a tradition (probably in Hecataeus, see Introduction, p. 554) that attributed cannibalism to all the populations of this area: see note to 109,1.

107. **Μελάγχλαινοι:** if they were not just the result of misunderstanding (cf. note to 20,2), the Melanchlaeni must not have been very well known.

108–9. An ethnographic *logos* in miniature; cf. Müller, *Geschichte*, pp. 112–13. On the location of Boudini and Geloni see note to ch. 21. Herodotus states that the Geloni, who are of Greek origin, inhabit a town in the territory of the Boudini, but he does not accept the Greek position according to which 'Geloni' is also the name of the Boudini. This betrays a polemic (cf. Introduction, pp. 553–8): in the Greek legend on the origin of the Scythians (chs. 8–10) the Geloni, who were descendants of Heracles, were a very important people, almost on a par with the Scythians; but Herodotus reduces their role and, consequently, also that of the Greeks in Scythia. For a historical-ideological reading see T. V. Blavatskaja, *SA* (1986), 4, pp. 22–33: at bottom there would be an attempt at Greek settlement in the territory of the Boudini, which, however, did not succeed in achieving a real hellenization; also cf. A. D. Nock, *CR* XLIII (1929), 126; M. Cary, *CR* XLII (1929), 214. In fact the permanent presence of a group of Greeks in the wooded steppe or in the forest is not attested archaeologically; even those who identify the town of Gelonus with the settlement of Bel'sk on the Vorskla consider the report of the presence of Greeks to be false and founded on similarities between the cultures: see B. A. Šramko, *Bel'skoe gorodišče skifskoj epochi (gorod Gelon)*, Kiev 1987, with bibl. (cf. pp. 161–2, for a ring with the effigy of Dionysus, which, however, is a sporadic and late finding). The identification with Bel'sk is at all events doubtful, though the placement of Geloni and Boudini further west than stated by Herodotus is not impossible: see notes to 21; 105.1; 122–4.

108,1. **γλαυκόν τε ... πυρρόν:** this is the usual definition for the barbarians of the north: cf. Xenophanes, 21 B16 DK (Thracians); *De Aeribus Aquis Locis* 20 (Scythians); πυρρός refers rather to complexion than to hair-colour, see most recently M. M. Sassi, *RFIC* CX (1982), 391–3. The detail is not therefore a sufficient element to take the Boudini as a Baltic, pre-Slavic, or Finno-Ugric people: discussion in *Narody*, p. 354. **τοῦ δὲ τείχεος ... ἐστί:** the perimeter of Bel'sk, which is 25,000 × 995 m., corresponds roughly with this information: B. A. Šramko, *SA* (1975), 1, pp. 79–80.

109,1. **φθειροτραγέουσι:** Strabo XI 2,1; 14; 19, attests to the presence in the Caucasian region of the *Φθειροφάγοι*, 'lice-eaters', so called after their uncleanliness: cf. among others Mela I 110; Pliny, *NH* VI 14; Arrianus, *Periplus Ponti Euxini* 18, pp. 120–1 Roos. Some modern scholars explain the name instead as 'pine-seed eaters' (for φθείρ in the sense of 'fir-cone', cf. Theophrastus, *Hist. Plant.* II 2,6; Hesychius φ 378 and 383 Schmitt), accepting the Caucasian location—attested also for the Melachlaeni; see note to 20,2—and postulating a geographical confusion on the part of Herodotus: see among others G. F. Hudson, *CR* XXXVIII (1924), 158–62; V. F. Beljaev, *VDI* XCI (1964), 130–6; Kuklina, pp. 139–40; J. R. Gardiner-Garden, *Klio* LXIX (1987), 331–5; cf. note to chs. 122–4. The interpretation 'lice eaters' (cf. the Adymarchidae in 168,1) seems more natural, underlining the primitiveness of the Boudini in contrast to the customs of the Geloni: cf. e.g. John of Pian di Carpini, IV 7 (= *Mongol Mission*, p. 16); Lindegger, p. 64; but supporting the other hypothesis is perhaps the root τραγ-, 'to nibble' (thus A. Paradiso, *SCO* XLVII (2000), 479–83). The remark 'alone in this region' is probably polemic against the tradition of the 'Greeks' (probably Hecataeus, see Introduction, p. 554) on which more is said below: this tradition, drawing no distinction between Boudini and Geloni, may have attributed to a single nomadic people, named 'Geloni' after their city, the singular custom of eating lice (or pine-seeds), and Herodotus, bearing in mind this tradition, quickly alluded to it quoting a word (φθειροτραγέουσι) not fully clear in itself (or to us at least).   γῆς τε... κήπους: in addition to highlighting the contrast between the nomadic lifestyle and agriculture, mentioning the presence of orchards and gardens is the best way to underline the superior civilization of the Geloni: cf. e.g Strabo IV 5,2; Tacitus, *Germ.* 5 and 26. For the cultivation of cereal between the Dnieper and the Don see Z. V. Januševic, *ZArch* XV (1981), 93; on evidence for fruit-trees and horticultural products see Blavatskij, pp. 85–6; *Archeologija SSSR* IX, pp. 155–6. For agriculture and the gardens (of apple-trees) at Bel'sk, B. A. Šramko, *Slovenská Archeológia*, XXI (1973), 158; id., *Archeologija*, LVII (1987), 77–8.

2. ἐν δὲ ταύτῃ... ἄκεσιν: otters and beavers were, and still are, widespread on the Dnieper and on the Don and Volga: see V. I. Calkin, *MIA* LIII (1960), 78–9; *Narody*, pp. 361–2. The animals 'with a square muzzle' must be a furred species not too dissimilar in appearance from otters and beavers, maybe martens or minks (it is unlikely that they are elks, or the seals of the Caspian hypothesized by S. Casson, *CR* XXXIV (1920), 30–1). On the furs (σισύρναι/σίσυραι) of the Scythians cf. [Plato], *Eryxias* 400c; on the use Caspian peoples made of these same furs, Herod. VII,67. Beavers in particular (and only those from the Pontus, see Strabo III 4,15) provided the medication indicated here and are often mentioned in the gynaecological treatises of the Hippocratic corpus: see *De Nat. Mul.* 3, 26, 32; *Mul.* I 71, etc. (cf. M. Wellmann, *RE* III 1 1897, coll. 401–2).

110–17. On the location of the Sauromatians see note on 21,1. The continuity between Sauromatians and those Sarmatians who between the 3rd and 2nd cents. BC became masters of the steppes to the north of the Black Sea has at times been doubted (Rostovtzeff, p. 113; Harmatta, *Studies*, pp. 8–10), but today is for the most part recognized: from the 'Sauromatian phase' (6th–5th cents.), heir to the *srubnaja* and Andronovo cultures, to the 'late-Sarmatian phase' (until the 4th cent. AD) there is a continuous evolution; in general see K. F. Smirnov, *Savromaty*, Moscow 1964; Sulimirski, *Sarmatians*; *Stepi*, pp. 147–214; a review in A. Häusler, *ZArch* XVII (1983), 159–94. The western Sauromatian culture is in some respects similar to the Scythian one; and between the Black Sea and the Caspian many burials of women with weapons and traces of wounds have been found: see R. Rolle, in *Beiträge zur Archäologie Nordwestdeutschlands und Mitteleuropas. Festschrift K. Raddatz*, Hildesheim 1980, pp. 257–94; Rolle, *Scythians*, pp. 94–9; K. F. Smirnov, *DHA* VIII (1982), 121–41 (burials of this kind are also attested among the Scythians, but with less frequency). Also e.g. the *De Aeribus Aquis*

Locis 17 speaks of the warrior women of the Sauromatians, while according to Ephorus, *FGrHist* 70 F 160, they were a people governed by women (cf. e.g. Scylax 70, *GGM* I, p. 59; Mela I 116; Pliny, *NH* VI 19; in the whole region the memory of warlike queens was preserved: see Diod. II 43). Whether it is possible to speak of a residue of matriarchy is a moot point, and the Greeks might have exaggerated, taking as a starting point, for instance, the existence of associations of warrior-women: different points of view in B. N. Grakov, *VDI* XXI (1947), 100–21; Chazanov, pp. 83–6; Häusler, art. cit., pp. 164–8; F. Schlette, *EAZ* XXVIII (1987), 241–2; J. Davis-Kimball, *JIES* XXV (1997), 327–43. The impression made on the Greeks by such an unusual role for women is testified by the location among the Sauromatians of the Amazons, the mythical image for an 'inverted' relationship between man and woman: see Tyrrell. It must not be ruled out that the myth of the Amazons originated from early contact with the world of the nomads (a review of opinions in F. Witek, *RAC* Suppl. I, coll. 289–301; cf. note to 110,2); but the Herodotean tale, with its impertinent details, sounds like an aetiological legend to account for the role of women among the Sauromatians, which originated perhaps no earlier than the 6th cent., when Amazons dressed in the Scythian manner appear in vase-painting and there is even attested the name Skyleia for an Amazon: see D. von Bothmer, *Amazons in Greek Art*, Oxford 1957; H. A. Shapiro, *GRBS* XXIV (1983), 105–14; M. V. Skržinskaja, in *Problemy*, pp. 48–9. On a similar tale in medieval Bohemia see L. Leger, *Les Anciennes civilisations slaves*, Paris 1921, p. 76.

110,1. Οἰόρπατα: this does not seem to be an exact rendering: in the first part it is possible to discern the Iranic *vīra-* = 'male, man', but the second part is reminiscent rather of *pati-* = 'lord'. V. I. Abaev, *Osetinskij jazyk I fol'klor*, I, Moscow 1949, pp. 172, 176, 188, thinks of a form like *οἰρόματα = vīra-mār-ta- =* 'slayers of men'; cf. also L. Zgusta, *AION* I (1959), 151–6. Ἀμαζόνες, explained by the Greeks as 'without breasts', may have an Iranic root (*hama-zan-* = 'all women': B. Hemmerdinger, *SIFC* LXXXI (1988), 146–7), or an Illyrian or Thraco-Phrygian one (G. Bonfante, *RAL* XXVII (1983), 151–3; id., *SIFC* LXXXII (1989), 116); further reading in Witek, *RAC* Suppl. I, coll. 289–90.   **τοὺς Ἕλληνας:** to accomplish his ninth labour, Heracles, together with other heroes, had to take possession of the girdle of the queen of the Amazons; here it cannot be Heracles, but perhaps one of his companions.

2. Κρημνούς: see note to 20,1; the 'free' Scythians are the 'royal Scythians', who considered all others to be their slaves (20,1).

111,1. τὴν πρώτην ἡλικίην: Dietsch's correction; if we accept the transmitted text (τὴν αὐτὴν ἡλικίην), the meaning would be 'of the same age', i.e. all of them smooth-cheeked youths (cf. Ch. Ch. Charitonides, *Mnemosyne*, XXXVII (1909), 252–4).

113,3. ἐκτιλώσαντο: lit. 'they tamed'. For an anthropological reading, contrasting the regular Greek marriage, see F. S. Brown and W. B. Tyrrell, *CJ* LXXX (1985), 297–302; but it is more likely that it is just an ironic stroke.

114,3–4. "ἡμεῖς... συμφέρεσθαι: on the sedentary way of life of Scythian women, cf. also *De Aeribus Aquis Locis* 21; conditions are no different among many Eurasian nomads; see e.g. F. Schlette, *EAZ* XX–XXVII (1987), 235–6. The circumstance that men, instead of women, bring dowries and leave their paternal home constitutes, in the eyes of Greeks, a subversion of ordinary rules: see Tyrrell, pp. 41–3.

117. φωνῇ... Ἀμαζόνες: the fact that the Sauromatians/Sarmatians spoke an Iranic dialect similar to the Scythian one, but with characteristics of its own, seems to be true: for some attempts at isolating its distinctive traits, especially on the basis of personal names, see Zgusta, pp. 208–71; Harmatta, *Studies.* τά περὶ γάμων... ἐκπλῆσαι: cf. *De Aeribus Aquis Locis* 17; Nicolaus of Damascus, *FGrHist* 90 F 103; Diod. III 52 (Amazons in Libya). On the first slaying of a foe as rite of passage see also e.g. Tacitus, *Germ.* 31 (Chatti); cf. ch. 66.

118–19. The issue of creating a coalition against an attacker who aims at subjugating everyone will be of fundamental importance to the narrative of Xerxes' invasion (VII 138 ff.); and also the standpoints illustrated in this debate between Scythian messengers and the neighbouring kings find precise parallels there: see Ph.-E. Legrand, *REA* XLII (1940), 225–6. On the threat of leaving or coming to an agreement with the king, cf. VIII 62,2 and IX 11,1–2; on the assertion of the sole responsibility of the attacked party by those who refuse the alliance, cf. VIII 142. On the whole these are rhetorical arguments which must have been familiar to the audience in an age of great military coalitions and wars: cf. e.g. the *agon* in Thuc. VI 75–88.

118,1. καταστρεψάμενος Θρήικας: the statement, repeated in para. 5, is exaggerated: see note to chs. 89–96.

119,4. ἡμεῖς... οὐ πεισόμεθα: non-aggressiveness, counterbalanced, however, by vigour in meeting an attack, is a typical trait of 'primitive opponents' in Herodotus; cf. esp. III 21,2–3; but in this case the audience must have felt how such a position was senseless in the face of the attack. It is not necessary to amend the emphatic οὐ πεισόμεθα, 'we will not endure'; cf. e.g. Demosthenes 9,13; 24,149.

120,1. ὑπεξιόντες... διελόντες: the Scythians adopt the strategy of retreating in two groups and laying waste the land before Darius: cf. ch. 140 (the damaging of wells and springs does not make much sense in a land so rich in rivers, but Herodotus is drawing a conventional picture; see e.g. Aeneas Tacticus 8; V. D. Hanson, *Warfare and Agriculture in Classical Greece*, Pisa 1983, pp. 98–100). Herodotus explains their strategy as an intention to involve those who had refused to fight: he will ascribe a similar aim to Themistocles in Salamis (see VIII 80,1). In fact, they may have had no choice under the pressure of Darius' army (see Fol–Hammond, *CAH* IV, p. 240) though, in the event—as in the case of the Russian retreat before Napoleon—their move turned out to be the winning move. The hunter will become the hunted: on the language of hunting in the narrative see Hartog, pp. 59–63 = ET, pp. 40–4. On the division of

Scythia into three kingdoms, see ch. 7; on the βασιλήϊα, ch. 20. Of the three kings, the name *Τάξακις* may be connected to ancient Persian *taxš-* = 'to cut, to build' (cf. the Sanscrit proper name *Tákṣaka*); *Σκώπασις* and *'Ιδάνθυρσος* are more doubtful (in other sources *'Ινδάνθυρσος* is given, perhaps from the same root as the ancient Persian *vindat-* = 'to find, to obtain', cf. *'Ινταφέρνης?*): see K. Müllenhoff, *Deutsche Altertumskunde*, III, Berlin 1892, pp. 120–1; O. N. Trubačëv, in *Etnogenez*, p. 150, is less plausible.

121. τέκνα ... γυναῖκες: the sending of women and children away from the field of operations in the case of invasion was common in Greece; the instance of the evacuation of Athens on the arrival of Xerxes is significant (VIII 41, with parallel texts cited by L. Piccirilli, *Plutarco, Le vite di Temistocle e Camillo*, Milan 1983, pp. 245–6, note to *Themistocles* 10,19). For other instances see Hanson, op. cit., pp. 97–8. Once again the Scythians foreshadow the Greeks.

122–4. It has already been said that it is unlikely that Darius penetrated beyond the Don. Herodotus must have known of an eastward march, and for subsequent events must have had two items of information: the destruction of the wooden city of the Boudini (Gelonus, cf. chs. 108–9); and the construction of some forts on the river Oarus whose remains, it was thought, were still visible. The precise extension of the region of the Boudini is unclear (see notes to chs. 21 and 108–9). Those who locate it in the Caucasus think that Herodotus inserted in the narrative of the Scythian expedition an episode belonging to another Persian expedition which reached the Kuban' from the south-east. But the Boudini may have dwelt also to the west of the Don, and Gelonus may correspond to the citadel of Bel'sk on the Vorskla, left tributary of the Dnieper: Herodotus may have transposed to the east an event which occurred further to the west. Aside from general motivations (see note to chs. 102–42), a cause of this misplacement might have been the mention of the river Oarus on the part of Herodotus' source. It is in fact difficult to identify this river, which is otherwise unknown to the ancient sources. According to Herodotus it runs to the east of the Don but flows into the Azov Sea: these conditions cannot both be satisfied, and some have thought of the Volga or various other watercourses (the Kuban' according to G. F. Hudson, *CR* XXXVIII (1924), 159–62; the Korsak according to Rybakov, pp. 54–9; even a river of the area of the Carpathians according to J. B. Bury, *CR* XI (1897), 280). The name Oarus sounds Iranic (< *varu-* = 'wide'), and is reminiscent of the Var in Jordanes, *Getica* 269 and of the Βαρούχ in Constantinus Porphyrogenitus, *De Admin. Imp.* 38, l. 68 Moravcsik, to be identified with the Dnieper. It is conceivable that the Scythian tale of the war mentioned the river Oarus = Dnieper, but that Herodotus, being unable to find it on his map, located it in the empty space east of the Tanais, perhaps also due to a confusion of names: see Schramm, pp. 113–15; J. Harmatta, in *Hérodote et les peuples non grecs*, pp. 128–30. In this case, Darius may perhaps have crossed the Dnieper and reached the Boudini on the Vorskla (Bel'sk); in this region of wooded steppe fires and destruction are, in fact, attested in various localities at the end of the 6th cent., and they may perhaps be related to Darius' expedition: see esp. A. A. Moruženko, in *Skifskij mir*, p. 144 (but cf. Ju. G. Vinogradov, *Epigraphica*, XLIII (1981), 33, and Vinogradov, pp. 84–5, who relates the destruction to the subsequent phase of Scythian conquest). P. Georges, *AJAH* XII (1987), 124–32, who has Darius campaign in the regions of the Danube, proposes now to identify Darius' forts with the 'palace' mentioned in the Old Persian foundation inscription found at Gherla (Romanian Transylvania) and published by J. Harmatta, *AAntHung* II (1954), 1–14. Any reconstruction is of necessity hypothetical, see Introduction, pp. 564–5.

122,2. πρὸς ἠῶ τε καὶ τοῦ Τανάϊδος: the alternation of accusative and genitive should be interpreted more or less as 'moving eastward and to the side of the Tanais' (cf. II 121; IV 48,3); but there are no parallels for a preposition governing two different cases.

123,2–3. ἡ δὲ ἔρημος . . . οἰκέουσι: cf. 22,1.

3. Μαιητέων: name of the people settled between the mouth of the Don and of the Kuban', whose ethnic composition was in fact varied: see I. V. Amfimov, *Drevnie poselenija Prikuban'ja*, Krasnodar 1953; *Narody*, pp. 376–7; J. R. Gardiner-Garden, *Historia*, XXXV (1986), 192–225.   **Λύκος, Ὄαρος, Τάναϊς, Σύργις:** on the Oarus see note to chs. 122–4. If the Tanais is the Don, then the Syrgis, which must certainly correspond to the Hyrgis in ch. 57 (here the initial sigma can only be a dittographic error), is probably the Donec; according to Rybakov, pp. 53–4, the Tanais is the Donec and the Sirgis is the Don or the Čir, its tributary. The Lycus, mentioned also by Ptolemy, *Geog.* III 5,13 (but there were many rivers with this name), is mostly identified with one of the watercourses—which, however, are anything but 'large'—that flow into the northern coast of the Azov Sea, such as the Kal'mius or the Obitočnaja (Rybakov, pp. 54–9); Schramm, p. 186 suspects that the name Λύκος may be just a double of "Υργις (from the same root, *u̯elg-).

124,1. τείχεα: Herodotus' narrative seems to suggest that Darius' intention is to build a line of forts as a screen and base for attacks on the Scythians, but that when he sees that they are still fleeing he is forced to carry on chasing them. In fact, if Darius really built these forts, he may have done so with the aim of creating a frontier line (cf. Fol–Hammond, *CAH* IV, pp. 240–1). But the forts may simply have been ancient ruins (on the Dnieper?) fantastically ascribed to a famous historical character who had passed there by local traditions; cf. the Cimmerian tombs in 11,4.

125,1–4. ἐλαύνων δὲ . . . διαμαχήσονται: after the long and unrealistic peregrination, Darius and the Scythians return to within a small distance of the Ister. Here the narrative becomes more credible, and the theatre of operations is not too dissimilar from that of Strabo VII 3,14. In spite of the proud intentions of 119,4, Melanchlaeni, Androphagi, and Neuri turn to flight, and even the Agathyrsi do not join the Scythians: this is a decisive development which will induce the Scythians to change their plans (see note to 128–42). Worthy of notice is the *variatio* ὡς . . . ἐτάραξαν . . . ταραχθέντων . . . ταρασσομένων (para. 3); cf. Macan, ad loc.

6. οὐκέτι... ἀπικνέοντο: οὐκέτι is to be taken with ἀπικνέοντο ('they gave up going...'), as is shown by the οἱ δέ which follows and which also refers to the Scythians with adversative force (cf. A. Corcella, *ASNP* s. III, XV (1985), 418–20). B. Bravo, ASNP s. IV, V (2000), 102 expunges ἀπείπαντας, as well as Μελάγχλαινοι... τεταραγμένοι above.

126–7. The turning point in the development of events is signalled by a pair of speeches, as is usual in Herodotean narrative technique: cf. Hunter, pp. 193–6. On the one hand, the preceding events are summed up, stressing one last time the strategic importance of nomadism and of the 'impregnability' of the Scythians; on the other, the proud attachment of the Scythians to freedom is highlighted, a theme which will subsequently be of great importance, in contrast with the position of the Ionians.

126. γῆν τε καὶ ὕδωρ: on the concession of earth and water in token of recognition of Persian power (and in practice of 'slavery' as Aristotle will say, *Rhet.* II 23, 1399b11 ff.), see L. L. Orlin, in *Michigan Oriental Studies in Honor of G. C. Cameron*, Ann Arbor 1976, pp. 265–6; A. Kuhrt, *AH* III (1988), 87–99; A. Corcella, *Annali della Facoltà di Lettere e Filosofia dell' Università degli studi della Basilicata*, 1993–1994 [Potenza 1996], pp. 41–56; id., in *Scritti in ricordo di G. Bona*, Potenza 1999, pp. 73–90.

127,1–2. οὕτω... μάχην: Idanthyrsus provocatively exaggerates: the absence of a fixed seat enables him to wander for a long time, but, as Herodotus well knows, this is an intelligent strategic move (cf. 46,1–2 and 120–1) and not the usual practice (on the relatively limited character of nomadism in the steppe, which for the greater part was seasonal and along fixed routes, see Chazanov, pp. 5–14 and *passim*, with bibl.). Themistocles will be equally clever when, inverting the traditional Greek mind-frame, he will forgo defending Athens: see Introduction, p. 564.

2. τάφοι πατρώιοι: on the hiddenness and sacredness of the royal tombs see notes to chs. 53–6 and 71,3.

4. Δία... βασίλειαν: see ch. 59.   σοί... ἐλθεῖν: see chs. 131–2; a parallel situation (Cambyses and the Ethiopians) in III 21.   τοῦτό ἐστί... ῥῆσις": according to the paroemiographical tradition (see Diogen. V 11, *CPG* I 250, 14) the last words of Idanthyrsus, κλαίειν λέγω = 'a plague on you, the devil take you' (a not-uncommon expression in comedy; see e.g. Aristophanes, *Vesp.* 584), would have given origin to the saying ἡ ἀπὸ Σκυθέων ῥῆσις, 'the statement of the Scythians', used by several Greek authors to indicate an abrupt remark which leaves no hope: see e.g. Lucian, *Dial. Mar.* 10,4; Demetrius, *De Elocutione* 216, 297; Athenaeus XII. 524e; Aristaenetus II 20; Aelian, *Rust. Ep.* 14, etc. Diogenes Laertius I 101 instead refers the proverb to the laconic replies of Anacharsis (cf. Kindstrand, p. 54, n. 13). Some have suspected that τοῦτό ἐστι ἡ ἀπὸ Σκυθέων ῥῆσις in the Herodotean text may be a gloss by a reader who recognized in the words of Idanthyrsus the origin of the proverb. But it is rather the epigrammatic conclusion of the memorable speech (cf. Strabo VII 3,8), pronounced as the seal to what the ambassador is to report to Darius (see 128,1; cf. the use of ἀπὸ, 'from the Scythians', and I 152,3). The whole of Idanthyrsus' speech is punctuated by solemn formulae; an equally solemn phrase in the third person closes e.g. Ajax's speech in Sophocles, *Ai.* 864–5.

128–42. Since the attempt to involve the neutral peoples has failed, the Scythians alter their plan: before coming to the decisive conflict (cf. 120,4), they cut Darius' retreat towards the Ister by making contact with the Ionians, while in the meantime detaining him in Scythia and wearing down his resistance. Thus Darius was being trapped in the desert steppe (cf. ch. 130) while the bad season and 'general Winter' were approaching (cf. Bornitz, pp. 117–18; Fol–Hammond, *CAH* IV, pp. 241–2; Cernenko, pp. 100–11). Herodotus builds the whole of this last section on the contrast between the love of freedom of the Scythians and the subservience of the Ionians to Darius; he creates a ring composition: the Scythians initially appeal to the Ionians in outrage at the mere mention of slavery (128,1); their last words, placed as an epigraph to the episode of the war, amount to an accusation against the servile disposition of the Ionians (ch. 142).

128,3. ἡ μὲν δὴ ἵππος ... φοβεόμενοι: on this contrast between Scythian cavalry and Persian infantry, see Hartog, pp. 63–8 = ET pp. 44–50.

129,1. τῶν τε ὄνων ... καὶ τῶν ἡμιόνων: on the absence of donkeys and mules in Scythia see 28,4. The donkeys and mules in Darius' army must have served to carry provisions, since no logistical support was given from the fleet (which must have made the advance even slower). What is of interest to Herodotus is the θῶμα, the curious anecdote (cf. I 80), which offers the opportunity for a picturesque description of the frightened horses with cocked-up ears. But the mention of the donkeys and of the limited Persian success is also a discreet signal for the reversal which will occur at ch. 135; see Hunter, p. 198 note 30.

2. ὑβρίζοντες: when used of animals, the verb usually indicates restless behaviour, especially due to satiety and sexual stimulation: cf. e.g. Xen. *Cyr.*, VII 5,62; Aelian, *Nat. An.* X 10, XI 18; D. M. MacDowell, *G&R* XXIII (1976), 15–6. Here, of course, the reference is primarily to their braying.

3. τοῦ πολέμου: depends on ἐπί σμικρόν τι, which is advisable to interpret as having a temporal force: '(the Persians) obtained these positive results for a brief part of the war', until, that is, the horses became accustomed to donkeys and mules.

130. ἵνα παραμένοιεν: on the intention of detaining Darius see note to chs. 128–42: the Scythians are playing a cat-and-mouse game, leading Darius wherever they wish in anticipation of the finishing stroke.

131,1. δῶρα ... πέντε: when Darius no longer knows how to escape from the grip of the Scythians, then the kings can send him the 'gifts' promised in ch. 127, whose significance is precisely that Darius will not be able to escape the trap: as Herodotus had anticipated at 46,2, the Scythians don't let themselves get caught and neither do they allow those who attack them to get away (cf. Hartog, p. 78 = ET, pp. 59–60). The sending of a symbolic message is not at all implausible for an illiterate people, especially in the world of the steppes: a rich harvest of parallels, Chinese, Mongolian, Turkish, etc. in S. West, *JHS* CVIII (1988), 207–11; also cf. Mazzarino, *Il pensiero*, pp. 143–6; R. Merkelbach, *ZPE* XIX (1975), 203–7; Raevskij, *Model' mira*, pp. 64–8; D. Lateiner, *Arethusa*, XX (1987), 83–107 (esp. pp. 98–100). The same episode is told by Clement of Alexandria, *Strom.* V 8,44, p. 355, 13 ff. Stählin, as an example of 'symbolic' form (G. B. Vico, *Scienza Nuova Terza* II 2,4, will draw his inspiration from him); the source cited is one Pherecydes, it is not clear which one: see *FGrHist* 3 F 174; West, art. cit., p. 210. The story of Pherecydes is independent from that of Herodotus, as shown by several divergences: the episode takes place directly after the crossing of the Ister, the two interpretations are attributed to Orontopatas and Xiphodres, there is only one arrow, and a plough also appears (this not necessarily a marginal detail, cf. chs. 5–7). On the relationship between the two versions see A. Momigliano, *RFIC* X (1932), 346–51; G. De Sanctis, *In memoria lui Vasile Pârvan*, Bucharest 1934, pp. 110–11; West, art. cit., pp. 210–11: in the version of Pherecydes the references to a sedentary life are doubtful, but the location on the Danube and the names of the characters may be authentic, and Herodotus may have simplified. In Ctesias, *FGrHist* 688 F 13,21 there is instead an exchange of bows between the two kings, and the Scythian one is bigger (cf. Herod. III 21).

132,1. Δαρείου ... παραδιδοῦσι: Darius' interpretation is little more than wishful thinking: the novelistic framework required that the correct solution be preceded by an erroneous one (cf. e.g. VII 142–3); and in this way the king's unfounded confidence is highlighted one last time. Darius' explanation appears in any case strained, especially in the comparison between the bird and the horse, which in turn is clearly symbolic of the Scythians (a similar comparison in e.g. Homer, *Il.* II 764; on the arrows see note to 81,4–6; by μῦς, 'mouse', some rodent of the steppe must be understood, cf. V. I. Calkin, *MIA* LIII (1960), 79–80). In the version of Pherecydes the bird more logically represents the air: may Herodotus have intended to accentuate the weakness of the king's interpretation?

2–3. συνεστήκεε ... βαλλόμενοι: because of his past (III 70,2; 73; 78,4–5) Gobryas (*Gaubaru-*) was above suspicion of defeatism. His interpretation is, of course, the correct one in the logic of the narrative; but is it also actually closer to the mentality of the peoples of the steppes: in Russian folktales and epic animals are still frequently used to indicate rapid movement in the various elements; see e.g. *Slovo o pŭlku Igoreve* (*The Song of Igor's Campaign*, 13–18, 639–50, 659–66, 751–70). Cf. Mazzarino, *Il pensiero*, pp. 145–6 for a relation to the 'animalistic style' of Scythian art and the concept of the animal as a spirit; Benardete, pp. 117–18.

133,1–3. ἡ δὲ Σκυθέων ... ἠπείγοντο: when the other part of the army, which had been sent to meet the Ionians (cf. 120,2; 128,2), reaches the Ister, the sixty days (cf. ch. 98) have not yet expired, despite the lengthy wanderings: see note to chs. 102–42; Introduction, p. 561 and n. 34. The result of the meeting between

Scythians and Ionians is mentioned at this point with a skilful change of scene to create an effect of suspense: the Scythians offer freedom to the Ionians (cf. note to chs. 128–42), and the Ionians accept. Darius now seems doomed.

134,1. ἀντετάχθησαν οἱ . . . Σκύθαι: for a moment it appears that they are about to come to an armed collision, the final closing of the trap laid for Darius. But the Scythians, free and undisciplined, reveal themselves unfit for pitched battle, and the indifference they show towards Darius turns against them: the king at last abandons his swaggering confidence, becomes aware of his weakness, and entrusts himself to Gobryas' counsels, thus avoiding a definitive defeat. On this reversal of the situation, see Bornitz, p. 119; Hunter, pp. 199 ff.; Introduction, p. 564.   **πεζῷ καὶ ἵπποισι:** an infantry corps is attributed to the Scythians, who had so far been portrayed as horsemen. This is not entirely unrealistic (see V. D. Blavatskij, *Očerki voennogo dela v antičnych gosudarstvach severnogo pričernomor'ja*, Moscow 1954, p. 20; cf. Černenko, p. 103); but 'with infantry and cavalry' is above all a conventional element in the description of the preparations for a battle.   **λαγός:** hares are common in the steppes and constituted an important element in the diet of the Scythians (V. I. Calkin, *MIA* LIII (1960), 79; V. I. Bibikova, *Drevnosti vostocnogo Kryma*, Kiev 1970, p. 97). They are variously represented in Graeco-Scythian art (e.g. on the eighty-four small golden plaques now at the Ashmolean Museum in Oxford: see M. Vickers, *Scythian Treasures in Oxford*, Oxford 1979, pp. 36–7, with other references); at Kul' Oba was found the representation of a rider with spear who seems be aiming at a hare (Hermitage inv. KO 48). It cannot be excluded that in an original version of the story the scene of the hare had a religious or symbolic value: cf. VII 57,1 and the hare of the Britannic queen Boudicca in Cassius Dio LXII 6,1; for the hare as spirit, *Testi dello sciamanesimo*, pp. 84–5 and *passim*; in general, J. Layard, *The Lady of the Hare*, London 1944. See E. E. Kuz'mina, in *Skify i Sarmaty*, p. 109; ead., *Le plateau iranien et l'Asie Centrale dès origines à la conquête islamique*, Paris 1977, p. 211; Černenko, p. 103; Raevskij, *Model' mira*, pp. 60–4. But to Herodotus the hunt has only the value of a game, similar to the *buskashi* of more recent nomadic peoples: see Rolle, *Scythians*, pp. 106–7.

135,1. τοὺς μὲν καματηροὺς . . . ἐν τῷ στρατοπέδῳ: the cynical abandonment of the weakest and the sick (see also I 207,7; III 155,5) serves to conceal the trick, but also to make a speedier retreat, which in actual fact is a headlong flight: cf. the retreat of the Athenians in Sicily in Thuc. VII 75, or the evacuation of Camarina in Diod. XIII 111,4. However, the pretext of guarding the camp was a good one, since in the case of emergencies the task of watching was normally entrusted to the less able men; see e.g. Thuc. II 13,7; Diod. XV 65,2 and 83,3 (cf. also Isaeus, fr. 10 Roussel).

136,1–2. ἡμέρης . . . ἀπικόμενοι: the absence of regularly traced roads, with routes marked by landmarks such as mounds, and which only the nomads were able to easily identify, is characteristic of the steppes and has always made an impression on sedentary peoples: cf. e.g. the 'unprepared ways' of the *Slovo o pŭlku Igorevĕ* (*The Song of Igor's Campaign*, 127). The Scythians do not follow the tracks of the

Persians, but naively take the most direct route (cf. ch. 142): perhaps they wanted to make sure that the way across the Ister was cut, and lie in wait for them.

3–4. ἄνδρες Ἴωνες . . . χάριν: though the sixty days have expired the Ionians are still at the bridge, and this seems unfair to the Scythians, who reiterate their appeal to abandon it (cf. 133,3).

137,1–2. Μιλτιάδεω . . . Ἱστιαίου: the debate between the tyrants, and especially Miltiades' position, have often appeared unhistorical (cf. also Nepos, *Milt.* 3). Tyrant of the Thracian Chersonesus (the peninsula of Gallipolis; on the Philaids in this region, cf. VI 34 ff.; Berve, pp. 79–85, 564–9), and subsequently hero of the first Persian war, Miltiades would have spread this version of events; but in actual fact, having been compelled to take part in the expedition on account of the delicate geographical position of his territories (the only European except for Ariston of Byzantium), he always remained faithful to the king, so much so that he subsequently maintained his power (VI 40): thus especially according to H. Berve *Miltiades*, Berlin 1937, pp. 41–2 (it is difficult to believe Nepos, *Milt.* 3,6, who says he fled the Chersonesus after the expedition: see the discussion in K. Kinzl, *Miltiades-Forschungen*, Vienna 1968, pp. 81–96 with bibl., more sceptical, B. Shimron, *WS* C (1987), 32–4; E. Obst, *Klio*, IX (1909), 413–15, denied that Miltiades took part in the expedition, but it would then be difficult to explain how such a tradition arose). But see Bornitz, pp. 114–25: Miltiades did not act in opposition to Darius since the term of sixty days had expired and departure would not count as an offence against the king whose own order he was thus obeying (cf. 98,2; 133,3); on the other hand, the threatening presence of the Scythians fully justified abandoning the position (so much so that, in order to stay, the Ionians will have to resort to a trick: ch. 139). In sum, the acceptance of the proposal of the Scythians on the part of Miltiades—and, initially, of the other tyrants—was not a betrayal, and Darius would not necessarily take it as one; rather, it was Histiaeus, subsequently Darius' favourite (V 11 ff., but see already IV 141), who acted beyond the call of duty (cf. VII 10γ). At any rate, if the tradition of the council of Miltiades, whether it be true or false, was preserved and reached Herodotus, the reason for this was most probably that it was used in favour of the former tyrant, and amplified in an anti-Persian sense in the political debate of the nineties: see D. Viviers, *RFIC* CXV (1987), 288–313. On the tyrants of Asia Minor as 'vassals' or 'clients' put in place by the Persian king see Berve, pp. 85 ff., 569 ff.; P. Tozzi, *La rivolta ionica*, Pisa 1978, pp. 118 ff., with bibl.; D. F. Graf, *The Craft of the Ancient Historian: Essays in Honor of Ch. G. Starr*, Lanham 1985, pp. 79–123; N. Luraghi, *Klio*, LXXX (1988), 22–46; M. M. Austin, *CQ* XL (1990), 289–306; on the contrast between tyrant and democracy see V. J. Rosivach, *QUCC* NS XXX (1988), 43–57.

138,1–2. Ἑλλεσποντίων μὲν τύραννοι . . . Κυμαῖος: the catalogue, Homerically limited only to notable characters (cf. e.g. VII 96 ff.), testifies to the widespread diffusion of tyranny, under Persian protection, in Asia Minor and on the islands; 'Ionians' include also Hellespontines and Aeolians, cf. 83,1 and 89,1; Tozzi, op. cit., pp. 25–7 with bibl. With the exception of Histiaeus, the rest of the tyrants mentioned are little more than names (cf. Berve, pp. 86–7, 91, 96, 106–7, 115). Aeaces of Samos was the son of Syloson, brother of Polycrates, and bore the name of his grandfather; cf. VI 13–14, 22, 25. Strattis of Chios is mentioned again at V 38, VI 31, VIII 132; Aristagoras of Cumae at V 27–8. Of Hippoclus from Lampsachus the son is known, Aeantides, who married Archedice, daughter of Hippias (Thuc. VI 59,3–4). Abydos was near Nagara Point; Parius is modern-day Kemer (see Erhardt, pp. 32–3, 36–7); Lampsacus is Lâpseki to this date (*PECS*, p. 480; P. Frisch, *Die Inschriften von Lampsakos*, Bonn 1978).

139,1. οὗτοι ὦν ... προσθεῖναι: after Darius' trick, also the Ionians easily trick the Scythians, who in their simplicity do not seem to conceive of any guile: see Hunter, pp. 210–13; Introduction, p. 564.   **πειρῷατο ... γέφυραν:** we should perhaps understand πειρῷατο as absolute and meaning 'to attack' (Rosén).

140,1–2. αἴτιοι ... ἐσφάλησαν: once again the moves of the Scythians (cf. 120,1) turn out to their disadvantage, and Herodotus underlines it emphatically and stresses their naivety.
3. οἱ δὲ δὴ ... πόρον: the retreat of the Persians along their previous tracks implies that, after their extensive wanderings, they were able to find the way by which they had come (ch. 125). It would be easier to believe this if their wanderings had been briefer: is it yet another trace of the 'dilation' operated by Herodotus?
4. οἷα δὲ ... ἀπικόμενοι: the depiction of the arrival of the Persians on the Ister is artfully contrived: during the night, at first there is fear, then the call and Histiaeus' immediate response (cf. Macan, ad loc.).

141. Ἱστιαῖον: that Darius should summon, of all people, Histiaeus, who had a little earlier been depicted as his most faithful supporter, is a very effective touch; but it is not necessarily mere narrative invention, given that Miletus must have been the leading Ionian city in the fleet (cf. note to 89,4–5), also on account of its interests in the Pontus. Ever since the Homeric Stentor, a powerful voice was highly appreciated in the army: cf. VII 117,1.

142. τοῦτο μέν ... μάλιστα: the lapidary statement of the Scythians underlines in closing the contrast between their free spirit and the servility of the Ionians which is a fundamental element in the narrative: see note to chs. 128–42. Herodotus willingly acts as spokesman to the Scythians, given his generally unfavourable judgement of the Ionians: see Tozzi, op. cit., pp. 30–1 and *passim*; Hart, pp. 181–2; *Ippocrate, Arie Acque Luoghi*, ed. L. Bottin, Venice 1986, pp. 30–3. Cf. Introduction, pp. 564 and 570.

143,1. Δαρεῖος ... Ἀσίην: according to Ctesias, *FGrHist* 688 F 13,21, Darius went back by way of the Bosporus, and punished the rebellious Chalcedonians. In actual fact, perhaps a revolt of Chalcedon and Byzantium (cf. V 26), or of the Getae and the other Thracians on the Pontic coast, induced Darius to cross Thrace by the safer and more convenient route along the Hevros/Marica (see N. G. L. Hammond, *Chiron*, X (1980), 545; note to chs. 89–96) and then re-enter Asia by the Hellespont, which was controlled by Miltiades (Sestus was not far from modern-day Ece,bat, and it was thence that the crossing was made to

Abydus opposite: see Isaac, pp. 195–6; Müller II, pp. 927–32; also cf. Strabo XIII 1,22). See S. Dimitriu, *Dacia*, NS VIII (1964), 133–44 (fires at Istria attributable to the Scythians who pursued Darius? cf. also VI 40); P. Alexandrescu, *Studii și cercetări de istorie veche*, VII (1956), 319–42; Černenko, pp. 106–10. Μεγάβαζον: the activity of Megabazus (perhaps *Bagbādu-/ -bāzu, Elam. *Ba-ka-ba-du-iš*, but see the bibl. in Mayrhofer, pp. 134–5) on the Hellespont will be described in Book V. Here Herodotus limits himself to introducing the character by telling two anecdotes, then he moves on to the expedition in Libya.

2. ὁρμημένου... ὑπήκοον: the anecdote is reminiscent of Darius' statement about Zopyrus in III 160,1 (and to Zopyrus it is referred by Plut. *Mor.* 173a), but with a novelistic setting on which cf. e.g. III 32. The great number of seeds of the pomegranate, symbol of abundance and fertility in the folklore of many peoples (cf. e.g. I. Chirassi, *Elementi di culture precereali nei miti e riti greci*, Rome 1969, pp. 73–90), has given birth to analogous anecdotes in several other contexts: see Aly, pp. 132–3.

144,1–2. ὁ Μεγάβαζος εἶπας... τυφλοί: Megabazus' statement is by simplification ascribed to a foundation oracle by Strabo VII 6,2; Tacitus, *Ann.* XII 63; Stephanus of Byzantium, s.v. Βυζάντιον; Hesychius of Miletus, fr. 4,20 (*FHG* IV, p. 147); Eustathius, *Commentarii in Dionysii Periegetica* 803, *GGM* II, p. 357. The advantage of Byzantium's position was due its harbour and the currents which rendered communication easier and fishing more profitable (Strabo VII 6,2; Polybius IV 43–4). If Chalcedon was truly founded before Byzantium, the colonists looked more to the lands than to the advantages linked to the sea (discussion in Isaac, pp. 219–20; I. Malkin and N. Shmueli, *Mediterranean Historical Rev.*, III (1988), 21–36); at any rate, the foundation dates of the two Megarian colonies are uncertain (perhaps in the second half of the 7th cent.): sources, bibl., and discussion in K. Hanell, *Megarische Studien*, Lund 1934, pp. 123 ff.; Boardman, *Greeks Overseas*, pp. 241–2; Isaac, pp. 218–19).

145–67. Contemporaneously with Megabazus' activities in Thrace, another Persian expedition to Libya takes place (on the chronology and the objective see notes to 1,1 and 167,3; Introduction, pp. 565 ff.). But, in order to come to the expedition, which was related to the death of the king of Cyrene, Arcesilaus III, Herodotus furnishes a lengthy antecedent on Greek colonization in Cyrenaica. The long *excursus* (on which see also Cobet, pp. 137–9) is constructed by comparing accounts ascribed to different sources, evidently genealogies and 'foundation sagas' (*ktiseis*), at times reproduced with their characteristic legendary traits present already in the prototype, Homer, *Il.* II 653–70 (see F. Prinz, *Gründungsmythen und Sagenchronologie*, Munich 1979; Fehling, pp. 70–1, suspects an artificial construction, but this cannot be demonstrated). Cyrene was a colony of Thera, and Herodotus takes his cue from the colonization of Thera by Spartiates and Minyans (chs. 145–9): thus it would also be explained how and why Battus, the founder of Cyrene, was of Minyan descent (150,2). This is told on the basis of Spartan and Therean sources, which are in agreement (for attempts to isolate passages from the two sources see the bibl. in M. Nafissi, *AFLPer* XVIII 1 (1980–1), 192–3). The Therean tradition then continued by narrating how, after the command of the Pythia to colonize Libya, initially explorers, then two penteconters were sent to the island of Platea (chs. 150–3). But the Cyreneans, who, on the events which followed were in agreement with the Thereans, gave a different version of the preliminaries and of the vicissitudes of Battus (154,1): thus from ch. 154 Herodotus offers the divergent Cyrenean version, until it comes to coincide once again with the Therean one. The text does not make explicit at what point precisely this convergence takes place (after all, in this whole section Herodotus seems to have summed up his sources rather roughly, with excessive concision; see note to 149,1–2 and 156,3, and Introduction, pp. 566–7). A. J. Graham, *JHS* LXXX (1960), 96–7, noticing the similarity between the end of ch. 153 and 156,2, has seen in 156,2 the caesura; but even just the fact that in 156,3 the island of Platea is presented as if for the first time ('an island opposite Libya, which is called Platea') is evidence that Herodotus is here still giving the Cyrenean version, independent of the Therean one which had already dealt with Platea. F. Jacoby, *RE* Suppl. II 1913, col. 436, discerned more correctly in ch. 157 the point of convergence (see now M. Giangiulio, *ASNP* s. III, XI (1981), 4, n. 7). It can even be doubted whether the exact point should not be placed later (see note to 157,1); full discussion by C. Caserta, in *Erodoto e l'Occidente*, Rome 1999 (*Kokalos* Suppl. 15), pp. 67–109 (whose conclusions are not fully convincing).

Then there follow the events which lead up to the foundation of Cyrene, and a brief exposition of its history until the death of Arcesilaus III and the attack by the satrap Aryandes against the city of Barce. The first chunk of Thereo-Spartan tradition, though linking back to the myth of the Argonauts, ignores the legendary elements which characterize the story of the Argonaut Euphemus in Pindar, *Pyth.* 4 (cf. note to 150,2 and 179,1); Herodotus also passes over in complete silence, according to his normal practice, the myth of the love between Apollo and the nymph Cyrene already known to Pindar, *Pyth.* 9 (cf. note to 157,1–2): of great importance for an evaluation of these legends are the studies by Studniczka (on a presumed Peloponnesian tradition contrasted by a Battiad tradition); Malten (according to whom Herodotus is rationalizing the Peloponnesian legend of Euphemus, which had been appropriated by the Battiad tradition); Pasquali, *Quaestiones Callimacheae*, now in *Scritti*, pp. 240–92 (traditions of Thessalian origin in Cyrene); see further Chamoux, pp. 69–91; Haider, pp. 139–47. As for the Cyrenean and the Therean traditions, though they agree on the basic facts, they seem to have different aims. The Therean version tends to accentuate the role of the island in the foundation, limiting that of Battus; while the Cyrenean version, which finds confirmation in the Battiad traditions gathered by Pindar, *Pyth.* 4 and 5, is centred rather on Delphi than on Thera (to which it attributes instead an unpleasant behaviour towards the colonists), and gives greater relief to the figure of Battus, to whom it attributes heroic traits. Herodotus does not side with either version; the Cyrenean version has the ring of a fable in the passages which deal with Battus, but the refusal of the Thereans to welcome the colonists on their return may be authentic (cf. notes to 150,2; 153; 156,3; 157,1, *SEG* IX 3 = ML 5). The rise of two versions is probably due to the fact that the small Thera was trying to publicize its role as motherland, while the powerful Cyrene between the 6th and 5th cents. was seemingly more interested in entertaining closer relations with Sparta: in general see Malten, pp. 107 ff.; Aly, pp. 134–9; Chamoux, pp. 92–114; Nafissi, art. cit., pp. 183–213; id., in *Cyrenaica*, pp. 375–86; C. Calame, *Métamorphoses du mythe en Grèce antique*, Geneva 1988, pp. 105–25; id., *Approaches to Myth*, Baltimore 1988, pp. 277–341; id., *Mythe et histoire dans l'Antiquité grecque. La création symbolique d'une colonie*, Lausanne 1996; P. Vannicelli, *QUCC* NS XLI (1992), 55–73; id., *Erodoto e la storia dell'alto e medio arcaismo*, Rome 1993, pp. 123–48; M. Giangiulio, in Luraghi, pp. 116–37; I. Malkin, in Derow–Parker, pp. 153–70. In fact, the archaeological record shows several localities in Cyrenaica to have been reached in the 7th cent. by Greek colonists, perhaps not from Thera alone; therefore, of the three dates given by Eusebius for the foundation of Cyrene (1336, 761, 631 BC), the last one may be conventionally accepted: see among others Chamoux, pp. 70–3, 120–4; J. Boardman, *ABSA* LXI (1966), 149–56; id., *Greeks Overseas*, pp. 153–9; id., in Tsetskhladze–De Angelis, pp. 137–49; Haider, pp. 128–39. Although the Libyan coast may have been sporadically known previously, the arguments are still too weak for a pre-colonization in the 2nd millennium, as held by e.g. S. Marinatos, *Excavations at Thera*, VI, Athens 1974; S. Stucchi, *QAL* V (1967), 19–45; VIII (1976), 19–73; id., in *Le origini dei Greci. Dori e mondo egeo*, Rome 1985, pp. 341–7 with bibl.; see Haider, pp. 83–152.

The modalities of the process of foundation in the traditions known to Herodotus display various elements typical of Greek colonization, such as the role of Delphi (Schaefer, pp. 224–31; in general, cf. Malkin, pp. 17–91; P. Londex, *Greek Colonists and Native Populations*, Canberra–Oxford 1990, pp. 117–27) or the settlement first on an island and later on the mainland (as in the case of Pithecoussae-Cuma or of Berezan'-Olbia: other instances in B. Schmid, *Studien zu griechischen Ktisissagen*, Freiburg i.d. Schweiz 1947, pp. 172–3). The merely religious motive is accepted by G. L. Cawkell, *CQ* XLII (1992), 290–2. At any rate, the colony of Cyrene was primarily agricultural in character (see note to 199,1); therefore it is not implausible that the colonists emigrated from Thera because of a drought, in contrast with the theory of Menecles of Barce (*FGrHist* 270 F 6) who saw as the stimulus for colonization the political conflicts at Thera (followed in this by Mazzarino, *Il pensiero*, pp. 218–20; also cf. G. Pugliese Carratelli, *QAL* XII (1988), 25–7; a position which combines the two above in e.g. M. Colomba, *Archivio storico siciliano*, s. iv, VI (1980), pp. 45–80; Nafissi, art. cit., pp. 199–200; cf. note to 157,1–2).

145–9. In the colonization of Thera, modern-day Santorini, a part is played by the Minyans, the descendants of the Argonauts and forefathers of Battus, but above all by the family of the Aegeidae, which was related to the founder Theras. The Aegeidae, who were powerful in Sparta as well as in Thera (and maybe also in Cyrene, see note to 149,1–2), were perhaps responsible for the tradition according to which Thera was colonized by Sparta in very ancient times, soon after the return of the Heracleidae to the Peloponnese (see among others Kiechle, pp. 82–95; Nafissi, art. cit., pp. 183–213; id., op. cit., pp. 375–86). This early dating agrees with the dating of Thuc. V 112,2, for the colonization of Melos, the first stop along the route which reached from the Peloponnese to Dorian Crete by way of Thera. In reality, though, after the great flourishing of Minoan civilization on the island, the Doric city of Thera on the promontory of Mesavouno is not again attested in the archaeological record until the 8th or 7th cent. (see in general F. Hiller v. Gärtringen, *Thera*, I–IV, Berlin 1899–1909; S. Marinatos, *Excavations at Thera*, I–VII, Athens 1967–76; a summary and bibl. in *PECS*, pp. 908–9; Müller I, pp. 1047–52; *Griechenland. Lexikon*, pp. 667–71). Therefore the tendency is to move the date of the colonization of Thera to this time; see e.g. F. Hiller von Gärtringen, *Klio*, XXXIII (1940), 57–72; G. L. Huxley *Early Sparta*, London 1962, pp. 22–4; in general, D. Musti, in *Le origini dei Greci*, op. cit., p. 69, n. 20.

145,2. τῶν ... Λήμνου: when the Argonauts landed at Lemnos they found only the women, who had killed their fathers and husbands (cf. VI 138,4), and they lay with them, thus generating a large progeny: cf. among others Homer, *Il.* VII 467–9; Apollonius Rhodius I 607 ff; the myth was the subject of Aeschylus' *Hypsipyle* and Sophocles' *Lemniae*. For the arrival at Lemnos of the Pelasgi, who had been driven out of Athens, Herodotus cites two traditions in VI 137–40; here he is unhesitatingly adopting the Athenian version according to which the Pelasgi molested the women of Attica.   παίδων παῖδες: epic-sounding expression for 'descendants' (cf. *Il.* XX 308).   ἱζόμενοι ... ἀνέκαιον: lighting a fire may have implied the intention of settling permanently in a place (F. Prontera, *AFLPer* XVI–XVII 1 (1978–80), 157–66; Malkin, pp. 114–34); hence the worried reaction of the Spartans. The Taygetus is the massif between Laconia and Messenia.

3. Μινύαι: the Minyans were a Boeotian population settled in the area of Orchomenus (see e.g. I 146,1), and linked also to southern Thessaly, where the city of Minya was; but, at least beginning with Stesichorus, fr. 238 Davies, they were in various ways linked or identified with the Argonauts: cf. e.g. Apollonius Rhodius I 228–33; H. E. Stier, *RE* XV 2 1932, coll. 2017–20; F. Hiller von Gärtringen, *KP* III 1969, col. 1345; F. Vian, *Apollonios de Rhodes*, I, Paris 1974, pp. 10–12. The settling of the Minyans on the Taygetus has been interpreted as a memory of the presence of pre-Dorian populations, linked to Boeotia and to Thessaly, in Laconia (see e.g. Kiechle, pp. 25–39 with bibl.; on possible relations to the ancient site of Arkines on the Taygetus, H. Waterhouse and R. Hope Simpson, *ABSA* LVI (1961), 174 and n. 229). These ethnic interpretations leave some doubts (see Nafissi, p. 324 and n. 214); but in the myth it is possible to discern the memory of cultural bonds between the Peloponnese and Boeotia (and the eastern world, through the Cadmeians) in the Mycenean age. Cf. note to 148,1–3.

4. ἐς τοὺς πατέρας: among the Argonauts, the Dioscuri, sons of Tyndareus, had especially close links to Laconia, and Herodotus makes a clear reference to them: cf. para. 5. But also Euphemus, the ancestor of Battus (see note to 150,7), came from Cape Taenarum (see Pindar, *Pyth.* 4): cf. Prontera, art. cit., pp. 163–5.

5. δεξάμενοι... ἄλλοισι: the inclusion of foreigners into the civic body, difficult anywhere in Greece, was so especially in the Sparta of historic times (cf. IX 33–5): hence the need for Herodotus to recall the relation with the Dioscuri, who were much worshipped in Sparta. Aristotle, *Pol.* II 9, 1274a34 ff., and Ephorus, *FGrHist* 70 F 117, on the other hand, attribute to the days of the first kings a greater openness to external accretions (cf. Nafissi, p. 44, n. 49).   φυλὰς: the three Dorian tribes of the Hylleis, Pamphyli, and Dymanes; cf. D. Roussel, *Tribu et cité*, Paris 1976, pp. 233–45.

146,1. χρόνου δὲ... διελθόντος: Valerius Maximus IV 6, ext. 3, and the scholiast to Pindar, *Pyth.* 4,88, are probably dependent on Herodotus (also cf. Polyaenus VIII 71); Plutarch, *Mor.* 247 and 269b, and Polyaenus VII 49, speak instead of the Pelasgi and Tyrrheni, of whom they say that they colonized Melos and Crete.

2. νυκτός: the practice, probably inspired by a superstitious scruple of secrecy, is not otherwise attested. The execution of Agis, in the 2nd cent. BC, seems to take place late at night (Plutarch, *Agis* 19, with indications on the 'prison', ἑρκτή): cf. D. M. MacDowell, *Spartan Law*, Edinburgh 1986, pp. 145–6.

4. πᾶσαν... ἐσθῆτα: examples of stratagems founded on disguise are abundant in ancient and modern times (see e.g. V, 18–20; Plut. *Sol.* 8; Aly, p. 139; How–Wells, ad loc.). It is, therefore, not likely that the anecdote reflects a Spartan ritual (G. Dumézil, *Le Crime des Lémniennes*, Paris 1924, pp. 51 ff.); rather, the presence of a group of citizens of inferior status married to Spartan women at the origin of a colonization is reminiscent of the analogous tales on the Spartan colonies of Locri and Tarentum: cf. D. Briquel, *MEFRA* LXXXVI (1974), 673–705; M. Nafissi, *AFLPer* XVIII 1 (1980–1), 189–90; Nafissi, pp. 35–51 with bibl.

147,1. Θήρας: through Polynices, the son of Oedipus, the family of Theras (the Aegeidae, see 149,1) was related to the Cadmeans of Boeotia (cf. V,57–61; Paus. IX 5,10–15; R. B. Edwards, *Kadmos the Phoenician*, Amsterdam 1979). Among the family tombs of the Aegeidae at Sparta there was a *heroon* of Cadmus (Paus. III 15,8). According to F. Hiller von Gärtringen, *Klio* XXXIII (1940), 71–2, the Boeotian Minyans were the people guided by the 'Cadmean' Aegeidae: for Boeotian and Asiatic elements in Laconia see note to 145,3, and H. Erlenmeyer, *Kadmos*, V (1966), 49–57; for the diffusion of Cadmean themes in Laconian ceramics of the 6th cent., Nafissi, pp. 325–6. The name Theras (Θήρας) points to θῆρα, 'hunt', and perhaps to the locality of Therae, on the Taygetus (Paus. III 20,5; cf. Hiller von Gärtringen, art. cit., pp. 61–2).

2. τῆς μητρὸς ἀδελφεός: Theras' sister, who had been wedded to Aristodemus and had borne the first Spartan kings, was called Argeia according to VI 52,2; the regency on the part of the mother's brother testifies to the role played by kinship on the mother's side, which is variously attested in myth (e.g. Creon in Thebes) as well as in historical fact (see e.g. Lysias 32; J. Bremmer, *ZPE* L (1983), 173–86). The kinship with the royal family is evidence of the great prestige enjoyed by the Aegeidae (however, the hypothesis of G. Gilbert, *The Constitutional Antiquities of Sparta and Athens*, New York 1895, pp. 5–6, that they were a third royal family is not well founded; Nafissi, p. 323, n. 211). Parallel to this is the episode of Dorieus,

told in V 39–48, to which the Aegeidae are perhaps related: see Nafissi, art. cit.,
pp. 205–8.

4. ἦσαν...: cf. Paus. III 1,7–8; scholium to Pindar, *Pyth.* 4,11 (foundation of
temples at Thera on the part of Cadmus). Various traditions speak of ancient
Phoenician settlements in several locations on the Aegean: see G. Bunnens,
L'Expansion phénicienne en Méditerranée, Bruxelles 1979. Herodotus, who dated
the beginnings of Phoenician civilization to the 3rd millennium, had no difficulty
in relating these settlements to the figure of Cadmus, who belonged to the time a
few generations before the Trojan war, more or less in the 14th cent.; whereas
modern scholars do not discern a Phoenician *ethnos* before around 1200 BC:
cf. note to I 1,1; II. Reports of the Phoenicians in the 2nd millennium may be
generic allusions to contacts with the East (an assessment in D. Musti, *Storia
greca*, Rome–Bari 1989, pp. 65–6, 121–2); whilst beginning from the 10th cent.
Phoenician presence is, in actual fact, well documented in various sites in the
Aegean; cf. J. N. Coldstream, *Phönizier im Westen*, Mainz 1982, pp. 261–75;
H. G. Niemeyer, *JRGZ* XXXI (1984), 20–2, 62–72; S. F. Bondì, in *Hérodote et les
peuples non grecs*, pp. 273–8. Archaeological confirmation is lacking for Thera: the
memory of a Phoenician presence was above all a mythical precedent for
the claim of the 'Cadmean' Theras and of the Aegeidae (Malten, p. 184; F. Vian,
Les Origines de Thèbes, Cadmos et les Spartes, Paris 1963, p. 62).
Καλλίστη: cf. Pindar, *Pyth.* 4,258; Callimachus, fr. 716 Pfeiffer; Apollonius
Rhodius IV 1755–64 (and schol.); Strabo VIII 3,19 and XVII 3,21; Hesychius κ
489 Latte. The mention of several names for a geographical site is typical of the
poetic tradition; cf. Braswell, p. 356.   Μεμβλιάρεω: this does not seem a
Greek name, despite Studniczka, pp. 52 ff.; there is some similarity with *Memblis*,
the original name of Melos according to Pliny, *NH* IV 12: cf. Bunnens, op. cit.,
p. 259, who thinks of a connection with Biblos; these would be Carian names
according to A. Fick, *Vorgriechische Ortsnamen*, Göttingen 1905, p. 57. According
to Stephanus of Byzantium, s.v., Membliarus was also an alternative name for the
island of Anaphe, to the east of Thera, and owed its origin to the same figure. The
name Ποικίλης is reminiscent of ποικίλος, 'multicoloured': it may be an invented
name, related to the processing of murex and the use of dyes typical of the
Phoenicians, or it may be an adaptation of a non-Greek name.

5. ἐπὶ γενεάς...ὀκτὼ ἀνδρῶν: the detail was probably drawn from the Therean
source, and not calculated on the basis of the parallel line Cadmus–Theras,
where according to Herodotus there were nine generations (Cadmus–Poly-
dorus–Labdacus–Laius–Oedipus–Polynices–Thersander–Autesion–Theras: see
IV 147,1 and V 59–60): cf. H. Büsing, *Thiasos. Sieben archäologische Arbeiten*,
Amsterdam 1978, pp. 63–5. On such computations of generations in oral traditions see e.g. Gould, pp. 39–40; Thomas, *Oral Tradition*.

148,1–3. ἐπὶ τούτους δὴ...τινάς: in the Thereo-Spartan tradition, the role
played by the 'irregular' Minyans was preserved (and was essential to the genealogy of Battus; see 150,2), but it was prudently limited in favour of the 'authentic'
Spartans. The strictly organized manner in which the colonization is carried out,

according to tribes (cf. note to 145,5), may be an anachronism (Roussel, op. cit., p. 260); but see ch. 153.

4. οἱ γὰρ πλεῦνες ... ἐπόρθησαν: the towns of Lepreum, Macistus, Phrixae, Pyrgus, Epium, and Nudium were in Triphylia, the coastal region of the western Peloponnese which lies north of Messenia and west of Elis, and which is bounded to the north by the Alpheios and to the south by the Neda. *Lepreon* was on the river Neda, close to the modern-day city of the same name; *Phrixa(i)* on the hill of Palæophanarus, 7 km. east of Olympia; *Makistos/Makiston* (probably to be identified with *Samikon*) at the foot of the Kaiapha mountains not far from the coast; *Epion* (also *Aipyon*, *Aipion*) can be identified with the site of Kastro of Platianà on the north-eastern slopes of the same mountains; *Pyrgos* (*Pyrgoi*) stood perhaps on the hill of Hagios Helias, directly to the north of the Neda; *Noudion* is otherwise unknown (other sources, bibl., and discussion in Müller I, pp. 763–5, 795–800, 808, 832–3, 839–40; cf. *PECS*, pp. 498–9, 802; *Griechenland. Lexikon*, pp. 381–2, 401, 580). Strabo VIII 3,3 interpreted the name Triphylia as 'three tribes', in connection with the fact that the Epeii, Minyans, and Eleans mingled there. The presence of Minyans found validation in the name of the river Minyeius (Homer, *Il.* XI 722, cf. Strabo VIII 3,19): it is considered purely legendary by B. Niese, *Hermes*, XLII (1907), 457–62, but cf. F. Kiechle, *Historia*, IX (1960), 38–45. The Caucones, who are mentioned as a Peloponnesian people in *Od.* III 366, are considered in the post-Homeric tradition to be the remotest inhabitants of Triphylia and Elis, together with the Epeii (cf. Herod. I 147; Strabo VIII 3,11; 16–17; 30; Kiechle, art. cit., pp. 26–38); while 'Paroreatae' (lit. 'those along the mountains') was the geographical definition of the peoples settled on the slopes of the Minthi and Caiapha mountains, used by Herodotus (V 73,2) for the Minyans themselves, and still in use later (cf. Strabo VIII 3,18; Kiechle, art. cit., pp. 23–4). The Elean raid in Triphylia cannot be dated precisely: the devastation of the territory of Lepreum in 421 reported by Thuc. V 31,3, is too late to belong to Herodotus' chronological framework; but, from as early as the end of the third Messenian war (*c.*460 BC) and until the end of the 5th cent., Triphylia, except for Lepreum, was under the dominion of the Eleans; cf. Xen. *Hist. Gr.* III 2,22–31; Strabo VIII 3,30 and 33; Kiechle, art. cit., pp. 21–4.   τῇ δὲ ... ἐγένετο: on the *oikistes* as eponymous founder, see I. Malkin, *Athenaeum*, LXIII (1985), 114–30 (esp. p. 117). Theras, as founder, was the object of a cult at Thera; cf. Paus. III 1,8; 15,6; IV 7,8; Malkin, pp. 195–6.

149,1–2. ὁ δὲ ... γεγονόσι: as well as in Sparta, the Aegeidae were present in Thera (cf. also Pindar, *Pyth.* 5,75; M. Nafissi, *AFLPer* XVIII 1 (1980–1), 191; cf. note to 149,1 on personal names), and perhaps also in Cyrene (most recently, M. Corsano, *Cirene. Storia, mito, letteratura*, Urbino 1990, pp. 123–9): in general see Nafissi, pp. 322–7, 365–9, with sources and bibl.; P. Vannicelli, *QUCC* NS 41 (1992), 55–73; R. Ganci, in *Erodoto e l'Occidente*, Rome 1999 (*Kokalos* Suppl. 15), pp. 213–59. Herodotus' genealogy, with Aegeus giving his name to the clan but being born only after the departure for Thera, might then seem contradictory: the Therean aristocracy clearly wished to relate itself to the Spartan Aegeidae through a common ancestor, i.e. Theras, but they felt the need to preserve a name (Aegeidae) which was consecrated by the role played in the cult by Aegeus (see note to 149,1; A. Brelich, *Gli eroi greci*, Rome 1958, pp. 149–50; Nafissi, art. cit., pp. 191–9 with bibl.). May the obscure and perhaps lacunose sentence at the end of the chapter, which seems to point to a repetition at Thera of an event which had already taken place at Sparta, sum up a tale in which the descendants of Theras at Thera questioned an oracle and received a divine sanction of their relation to the Aegeidae of Sparta?

1. *Οἰόλυκος*: the formation of the name is not obvious (one would rather expect *Οἰλύκος*; on the *Οἰλυκίδαι* see *Bulletin Épigraphique* (1995), 337): should it perhaps rather be related to *οἶος* = 'alone', something to the effect of 'lone wolf'? Herodotus' tale is then just an aetiological anecdote similar e.g. to the biblical one in Judg. 6: 32 (on mythical 'talking' names, cf. M. Sulzberger, *REG* XXXIX (1926), 381–447). *Οἰόλυκος* is in any case a well-attested name in the Greek world, including Thera (*IG* XII 3 Suppl. 1549, 6); and *Αἰγεύς* is also found in Thera (*IG* XII 3, 606, 46; *IG* XII Suppl., p. 221, n. 694; cf. *IG* XII 3 Suppl. 1502). Two *heroa* were dedicated in Sparta to Oeolycus and Aegeus, built at the same time as the *heroa* of Cadmus and Amphilochus by the descendants of Aegeus (Paus. III 15,8).   *φυλή*: the term *φυλή*, which recurs also in the scholium to Pindar, *Isthm.* 7,18, seems inappropriate: at Sparta there were only the three Dorian 'tribes' (see note to 145,5). In other sources the Aegeidae are a 'phratry' (Aristotle, fr. 325 Rose; scholium to Pindar, *Pyth.* 5,101b): a confusion with the Attic tribe of Aegeis has been supposed (Malten, p. 186, n. 1), or a transposition to Sparta of what might have been true for Thera (Kiechle, p. 93, n. 1), or an ancient role of *phylobasileis* (G. L. Huxley, *Early Sparta*, London 1962, p. 104, n. 88); discussion in Nafissi, pp. 322–3.

2. *Ἐρινύων*: a person's 'Erinys' implied the curse cast by someone—especially a parent—who had been wronged (see already Homer, *Il.* XXI 412; *Od.* XI 279–80; XVII 475; on the Erinyes as the cause for lack of children, cf. e.g. *Il.* IX 453). The descendants of Oedipus were burdened by the curse he cast on his sons (see e.g Aesch. *Theb.* 70), and Oedipus' murder of Laius must have been the source of a further 'Erinys': according to Paus. IX 5,14, it was these 'Erinyes of Laius and Oedipus' which forced Autesion, father of Theras (cf. 147,1), to leave Thebes for the Peloponnese. In tradition, the lack of children is a common reason for consulting an oracle (examples in Fontenrose, p. 443); and also the advice to found a temple and a cult in order to appease the divinity belongs to a common type of oracular utterance: see e.g. I 167,2; V 82,1; Paus. II 3,6–7; Baton, *FGrHist* 268 F 3 (cf. the cult of the Eumenidae at Athens according to Aeschylus, *Eum.* 804 ff.; on the cult of the Erinyes in general, P. Robin, *Le Culte des Erinyes dans la Grèce classique*, Paris 1939).

150–3. The Therean version: see note to chs. 145–67.

150,2. *Γρῖννος ὁ Αἰσανίου*: the name, later attested in Thera in Hellenistic times as *Γρῖννος* (*IG* XII 3, 330, 3 and 82; 1032), does not seem Greek. *Αἰσάνιος*

(*Αἰσανίας*?) can be traced back to the Greek word *αἶσα* (for names with the same root in Thera and Cyrene, cf. *LGPN* I, p. 20; in general, F. Solmsen, *Beiträge zur griechischen Wortforschung*, I, Strassburg 1909, pp. 71–2), but does not seem to be otherwise attested, and perhaps is also not Greek. On the function of the 'king' at Thera (and at Cyrene), perhaps not properly monarchical, see R. Drews, *Basileus: The Evidence for Kingship in Geometric Greece*, New Haven–London 1983, pp. 121–8; in the narrative structure of the foundation saga the presence of a king was at any rate appropriate, whilst the 'covenant of the founders' (*SEG* IX 3 = ML 5) attributes to Thera at this time a popular assembly; cf. note to ch. 153.   *ἑκατόμβην*: on the hecatombs at Delphi, cf. *Hymn. Hom. Ap.* 289; Schaefer, p. 224, n. 1.   *Εὐφημίδης*: Paulmier's amendment (*Εὐθυμίδης* mss) is plausible: the Argonaut Euphemus appears in fact in Pindar's Battiadic saga, *Pyth.* 4, and the name is later attested in Cyrene (*SEG* XX 742, I 18); cf. Chamoux, pp. 83–91.

3. *χρεωμένῳ . . . Βάττον*: cf., in the Cyrenean version, at 155,3. According to the Thereans, Battus is not invested directly by the divinity, but by their king: thus the role of Thera as mediating party between Delphi and Cyrene was highlighted.

4. *μετὰ δὲ . . . ἀποικίην*: cf. 155,4. Herodotus is not aware of ancient relations between Thera and Libya; see note to chs. 145–67.

151,1. *ἑπτὰ . . . ἐξαυάνθη*: the Cyrenean version is more concise: see 156,1; cf. Justin XIII 7,4. A drought was a common reason for consulting oracles: examples in Fontenrose, p. 442. The legend hints at difficult economic conditions on the small and poor island, which were often a cause for colonization: see e.g. Chamoux, pp. 99, 113–14; Schaefer, pp. 223–4; Boardman, *Greeks Overseas*, pp. 153–5; C. Calame, *Métamorphoses du mythe en Grèce antique*, Geneva 1988, pp. 115–16; A. Jähne, *Klio*, LXX (1988), 145.

2. *πέμπουσι . . . Κορώβιος*: in the Cyrenean version Crete plays a greater role: see ch. 154. The Thereans had necessarily to appeal to Crete, which was located on the route to Libya and was an important commercial centre in the eastern Mediterranean; more especially, the town of Itanus, which was on the eastern extremity of the island (on the site of Erimoupolis, a little to the south of Cape Sideros) and was mythically linked to the Phoenician world, was in an excellent position for exchanges with Cyprus, Phoenicia, and thence Egypt and Libya (cf. note to 152,1–3): see *PECS*, pp. 420–1; Müller I, pp. 952–3; *Griechenland. Lexikon*, pp. 281–2. Herodotus does not assume contacts and regular routes between Crete and Libya: though it cannot be ruled out that there were contacts in Mycenean times, and that in archaic times some Cretan fishermen frequented the African coast (like the fishers of sponges in the Aegean until not long ago: Chamoux, pp. 102–3), Corobius is merely drawn fortuitously by northerly winds (but see V. Purcaro Pagano, *QAL* VIII (1976), 285, and cf. note to 179,2; more generally, A. Karetsou *et al.*, *Crete–Egypt: Three Thousand Years of Cultural Links*, Herakleion–Cairo 2001). It is difficult to explain the name *Κορώβιος* with Greek: the derivation from *κόρος* and *βίος*, 'satiety of life', and the identification with an 'old man of the sea' in P. Knapp, *Philologus*, XL VIII (1889), 498–504, is not

convincing; see Chamoux, pp. 100–1. Could it be a name in -βιος from Asia Minor (see E. Laroche, *Les noms des Hittites*, Paris 1966, pp. 317–19, and cf. Καϋστρόβιος in 13,1) or at any rate an eastern name, as Ἴτανος seems to be? Cf. J. Boardman, in Tsetskhladze–De Angelis, p. 143.   Πλατέαν νῆσον: the island of Platea (of the same size as Cyrene, according to 156,3, and 'flat' as the name suggests) is one of the islands of the Gulf of Bomba: cf. Scylax 108, *GGM* I, p. 83; *Stadiasmus Maris Magni* 41, *GGM* I, p. 442; Stephanus of Byzantium, s.vv. Πλαταιαί and Πλατεῖα. There are no archaeological confirmations, but the most probable identification is with Geziret Marakeb: cf. A. Fantoli, *Universo*, XXXVII (1957), 1051–66; Haider, pp. 130–1; further bibl. in Purcaro Pagano, art. cit., pp. 344–5.

152,1–3. μετὰ δέ... ἐκέρδησαν: the episode of Colaeus was, in all likelihood, told by the Therean source, and Herodotus only added the reference to Sostratus (against Chamoux, pp. 103–4, see e.g. M. Nafissi, *AFLPer* XVIII 1 (1980–1), 194, n. 131). On the figure of Colaeus, merchant and ναύκληρος ('captain of a ship'), see Mele, pp. 41, 44, 67, 80–1. Colaeus was blown out of course by north-easterly winds (ἀπηνείχθη), probably as he was sailing from Rhodes to Cyprus with the intention of hugging the coast of Phoenicia and 'Palestine Syria' until he reached Egypt (cf. II 182, and already *Od.* IV 81–9): in 1385 the pilgrim Lionardo Frescobaldi, for instance, was carried from the Gulf of Alexandretta to the vicinity of the coasts of 'Barberia' (*Viaggio in Egitto e in Terra Santa*, p. 185 Bartolini; cf. notes to 151,2, 164,2, and 179,2). It cannot be excluded that Colaeus already undertook the direct crossing from Rhodes to Egypt which was practised in Hellenistic times (Strabo II 5,24): in general see W. Helck, *MDAI(K)* XXXIX (1983), 81–92. Trade relations between Samos and Egypt as early as the 7th cent. BC are at any rate well attested by the Egyptian ivories and bronzes of the Heraion: B. Freyer-Schauenburg, *Elfenbeine aus dem samischen Heraion*, Hamburg 1966; U. Jantzen, *Ägyptische und orientalische Bronzen aus dem Heraion von Samos*, Bonn 1972; Boardman, *Greeks Overseas*, pp. 113–14; Haider, pp. 208–9; also cf. II 178, III 26, III 39. On Tartessus, the region at the mouth of the Guadalquivir, 'untouched' by the Greeks but already known to the Phoenicians, see note to I 163,6, with bibl.; and also M. Koch, *Tarschisch und Hispanien*, Berlin 1984; C. G. Wagner, *Rivista di studi fenici*, XIV (1986), 201–28; J. G. Chamorro, *AJA* XCI (1987), 197–232 (an identification with Sardinia is now proposed by S. Frau, *Le colonne d'Ercole. Un'inchiesta*, Rome 2002, cf. note to 43,4). The journey from Platea to Tartessus was in fact favoured by easterly and north-easterly winds, which, during the summer, are dominant along the coasts of Tunisia, Algeria, and Morocco (*Portolano del Mediterraneo* II B, Genoa 1987, pp. 45, 83, 175, 217; III, Genoa 1982, pp. 3, 12–13, etc.): the phrase 'escorted by a god', which is Homeric (cf. *Il.* VI 171; *Od.* V 32; Harrison, pp. 99–100), alludes to the ease of the journey, while Herodotus seems to ignore the small Syrtis, cf. note to chs. 186–90. Samian contact with Tartessus finds confirmation in some ivories of western Phoenician provenance in the Heraion (B. Freyer-Schauenburg, *Madrider Mitteilungen*, VII (1966), 89–108; M. E. Aubet-Semmler, *Hamburger Beitr. zur Archäologie*, IX

(1982), 15–56): perhaps it was more regular than the story of Colaeus gives us to understand. The consequent availability of Atlantic tin may perhaps have contributed to the flourishing of the Samian toreutics (see note to 152,3–4), but later it was mostly the Phoceans (cf. I 163) who travelled the route regularly: discussion in J. M. Alonso-Nuñez, *AC* LVI (1987), 246–8; cf. Shipley, pp. 54–65.

3. μετά γε... ἄλλον: the tendency to draft 'rankings' (cf. note to 46,1–2) induces Herodotus to mention Sostratus, who was clearly renowned for his success in trade. He is not mentioned in any other literary source, but during the excavations of the temple of Hera at Gravisca (Tarquinia) an anchor was found which dates from the end of the 6th cent. and which has a dedication to Apollo Aeginetes from a certain Sostratus, perhaps the same man as Herodotus': M. Torelli, *PP* XXVI (1971), 44–67; P. A. Gianfrotta, *PP* XXX (1975), 311–18; F. D. Harvey, *PP* XXXI (1976), 206–14. Also to this figure may be related the mark ΣΟ frequently found on vases in Etruria (A. W. Johnston, *PP* XXVII (1972), 416–23). Sostratus' great success must therefore be linked with activities in Etruria (certainly not in Tartessus: C. Tronchetti, *PP* XXX (1975), pp. 366–8). If the Sostratus and Leodamas who made dedications at Naucratis in Egypt are his grandfather and his father (as M. Torelli believes, *PP* XXXVII (1982), 317–18), we then have the evidence for a large aristocratic family (as the names show: B. Bravo, *DHA* X (1984), 120) dedicated to international trade.

4. οἱ δὲ Σάμιοι... ἐρηρεισμένους: for the tithe on trade profits, parallels in Bravo, art. cit., pp. 115–19. Herodotus seems to be drawing on the dedicatory inscription: see G. Dunst, *Athenische Mitteilungen*, LXXXVII (1972), 99–100. Bronze craters with griffin *protomai* were widespread in Greece, especially as luxury votive gifts for the great sanctuaries, throughout the archaic age, and many *protomai* have been found in Samos itself (U. Jantzen, *Griechische Greifenkessel*, Berlin 1955). The model is Eastern, but some were perhaps manufactured in the Peloponnese (whence may derive the definition 'Argolic crater'; as late as the 4th cent. BC. Antiphanes, fr. 233 Kassel–Austin, extols the Argive *lebes*, cf. *IG* II² 1425, 359, as does Claudian, *De Bell. Goth.* 611): see H. V. Herrmann, *Die Kessel der orientalisierenden Zeit*, I, Berlin 1966; II, Berlin 1979; F. Canciani, *Storia e civiltà dei Greci*, I 2, Milan 1978, pp. 488–91; M. Torelli, ibid., p. 656; most recently, A. Sakowski, *AM* CXII (1997), 1–24; ead., *BABesch* LXXIII (1998), 61–82 (who identifies the 'Argolic crater' with the *dinos*). The dimensions of crater and pedestal must have been enormous (4.50–4.80 m. in height) according to the indications furnished by Herodotus, but some colossal griffin *protomai* found at Samos and Olympia testify to the fact that such votive vases were in use in the 7th cent. (Jantzen, op. cit., pp. 67–9; Herrmann, op. cit. II, pp. 75 ff., 153; on their possible collocation in the Heraion, probably not far from the ships there dedicated, H. Walter, *Das griechische Heiligtum, dargestellt am Heraion von Samos*, Stuttgart 1990, pp. 88–9). Human figures often appeared as pedestals for stone basins, but there are no archaeological parallels for bronze craters (also Paus. III 18,7; IV 14,2, is somewhat different): see F. Studniczka, *Antike Plastik. W. Amelung zum 60. Geburtstag*, Berlin–Leipzig 1928, pp. 251–4; Herrmann, op. cit. II, p. 171.

5. *Κυρηναίοισι ... συνεκρήθησαν*: the bond between Cyrene and Samos was part of a more general network of commercial relations which also involved Sparta, and which is attested by the diffusion of Laconian pottery: an assessment in Nafissi, pp. 253–76; Applebaum, pp. 11–12, postulates the participation of a Samian contingent in the foundation of Cyrene. The events of the reign of Arcesilaus III confirm the existence of such bond (chs. 162–4), while it is doubtful whether the head of a lion on one side of some Cyrenean tetradrachms from the 6th cent. can be read as a symbol of Samos (Chamoux, pp. 240–1); Theochrestus, *FGrHist* 761 F 1, will make of Aristotle/Battus the descendant of a certain Samus, founder of Thera and himself descendant of Euphemus.

153. *εἴη ... ἐκτισμένη*: the presence of Corobius must have served as the guarantee that the 'colonisation' had taken place: cf. Casevitz, p. 34. *Θηραίοισι δὲ ἔαδε*: the decision of the Thereans is presented as a kind of decree. A Cyrenean inscription from the 4th cent. BC (*SEG* IX 3 = ML 5) does, in fact, report a 'covenant of the founders', i.e. the decree by which it was decided in Thera to send the colonists. The decree displays some points of contact with the Herodotean text (cf. also the notes to 156,3 and 157,1). It defines Battus as *ἀρχαγέταν τε καὶ βασιλέα*, corresponding to *ἡγεμόνα καὶ βασιλέα*, 'commander and king' (on these terms see Malkin, pp. 241–50 with bibl.), and talks of a levy for colonists on a family basis, one son of each family (but there is a lacuna in the inscription; however, the Herodotean text might also have a lacuna after *ἄνδρας*: suggestions in J. H. Oliver, *GRBS* VII (1966), 25–9; O. Hansen, *AJPh* CV (1984), 326–7). Its authenticity is doubtful: the evidently anachronistic elements can be explained as the effect of a formal revision of the ancient decree (thus e.g. A. J. Graham, *JHS* LXXX (1960), 94–111); while S. Dušanić (*Chiron*, VIII (1978), 55–76) thinks of a forgery originating in the context of the Platonic Academy. The problem of the relationship with the Herodotean text is connected to this: the inscription may have been cited by Herodotus' source, or else—if it is a forgery—it may depend on Herodotus or on a common Therean source (perhaps a written source: also cf. Chamoux, pp. 105–11; L. H. Jeffery, *Historia*, X (1961), 139–47; Seibert, pp. 9–71; A. Chaniotis, *Historie und Historiker in den griechischen Inschriften*, Stuttgart 1988, p. 238, 264; L. Criscuolo, *Simblos*, III (2001), 31–44).   *χώρων*: for the archaeological data on the political-geographical divisions of the Theran territory, see F. Hiller von Gärtringen, *RE* V A 2 1934, coll. 2280–1.   *δύο πεντηκοντέρους*: between 150 and 160 men could travel on two penteconters; this is already quite a significant number for the small Thera (Schaefer, p. 232; cf. Malkin, p. 62). The colonists counted on finding women on the site; cf. chs. 164, 168, 186.

154–6. The Cyrenean version (for its extent, see notes to chs. 145–67 and 157,1) clearly has the character of a fable (cf. Aly, pp. 137–8), with typical elements such as the evil stepmother, the heroine who escapes death (like Snow White or like Cyrus, Moses, Romulus), the clever trick which bypasses a condition by interpreting it literally (cf. e.g. 201,1–2, or Stobaeus III 28,21), the hero marked by an infirmity (cf. note to 155,1–2). A substratum of Battiad tendency can be discerned, filtered through aristocratic sources, as shown by comparison with *Pythians* 4 and 5 shows: see most recently P. Giannini, in *Cirene. Storia*, pp. 51–95; Introduction, p. 567.

154,1. ἔστι ... πόλις: typical *exordium* of narrative and fable, already found in Homer: cf. J. Wackernagel, *Philologus*, XCV (1941), 18; M. Nøjgaard, *Le Fable antique*, Copenhagen 1964, pp. 231–5; Ch. H. Kahn, *The Verb 'be' in Ancient Greek*, Dordrecht–Boston 1973, pp. 245–60; S. Fornaro, *Glauco e Diomede. Lettura di Iliade VI 119–236*, Venosa 1992, pp. 40–3. Oaxus (Ὄαξος/Ἄξος, different renderings of Ϝάξος, cf. *Inscriptiones Creticae*, II, ed. M. Guarducci, Rome 1939, pp. 42 ff.; A. C. Cassio, *ZPE* LXXXVII (1991), 47–52) corresponds to the modern village of Axos, about 30 km. south-west of Iraklion: Müller I, pp. 988–9; *Griechenland. Lexikon*, p. 473. Crete plays a part also in the Therean version (ch. 151), as well as, e.g. in the legendary tale of the nymph Cyrene in Agretas, *FGrHist* 762 F 1, or in the myth of Acacallis, daughter of Minos, in Libya in Apollonius Rhodius IV 1490 ff. At bottom there is the memory of the relations between Crete, Thera, and Libya, which are strengthened by the arrival of the Cretans at Cyrene under Battus II (cf. 161,3): see Pasquali, *Scritti*, p. 252; Schaefer, pp. 222–3; Giannini, op. cit., pp. 93–5; G. Ottone, *QAL* XVII (1995), 31–9 (Applebaum, pp. 11–12, thinks that a Cretan nucleus may have participated in the foundation of the town). Ἐτέαρχος and Φρονίμα are names well attested in historic times both at Crete and at Cyrene (*LGPN* I, pp. 168, 476); while the names Πολύμναστος (father of Battus also in the Therean version and in Pindar, *Pyth.* 4,59) and Θεμίσων are found from the 5th–4th cent. onwards in Cyrene (ibid., pp. 212, 379): perhaps the noble families of Cyrene, related to those of Crete, made their ancestors the protagonists of the foundation myth. On the aristocratic character of the merchant Themison, 'guest' of the king, see Mele, pp. 42, 73–4.

2. μαχλοσύνην: specific term for 'shamelessness' in women; cf. M. Detienne, *The Gardens of Adonis*, Princeton 1994², pp. 121 and 190, n. 104.   **ἔργον οὐκ ὅσιον ἐμηχανᾶτο:** analogous narrative formulae are used to announce murderous intentions in II 119,2 and III 120,1.

3. καταποντῶσαι: a punishment at whose origin there was perhaps an ordeal: G. Glotz, *Études sociales et juridiques sur l'antiquité grecque*, Paris 1906, pp. 86–8; C. Gallini, *SMSR* XXXIV (1963), 61–90.

155,1–2. χρόνου ... ἐν Λιβύῃ: already Pindar, *Pyth.* 5,87, and subsequently several other authors know of Aristotle as an alternative name for Battus. Battus might therefore really be a nickname meaning 'stutterer' (cf. βατταλίζειν), even though it is attested as a proper name throughout the Greek world: see O. Masson, *Glotta*, LIV (1976), 84–98; Dobias-Lalou, p. 285. Herodotus' hypothesis (cf. also the scholium to Pindar, *Pyth.* 4 inscr. b; Hesychius β 349 Latte) is much less convincing, despite the possible confirmation in *bity*, royal name in Lower Egypt (and cf. U. Pestalozza, *PP* IV (1950), 202–5): see e.g. Chamoux, pp. 95–8. It may be found surprising that the nickname was adopted as a proper name and passed on in the Battiad dynasty in alternation with Ἀρκεσίλας (already attested in archaic times in Crete, see A. Chaniotis, *ZPE* LXXVII (1989), 69; according to Schaefer, pp. 234–6, this name also alludes to royalty, something to the effect of 'who protects the people'). That this was possible is at any rate demonstrated by Herodotus himself at 149,1. In any case, the element of the stutter (cf. Pindar, *Pyth.* 4,63; Acesandrus, *FGrHist* 469 F 6), at times interpreted as a mark of anti-Battiadic spirit, belongs, on the contrary, to the 'heroic' picture of Battus, impaired like, e.g., the founder of Croton, Miscellus: see Pasquali, *Scritti*, pp. 252 ff.; A. Brelich, *Gli eroi greci*, Rome 1958, pp. 233–48 and *passim*; M. Giangiulio, *ASNP* s. III, XI (1981), 1–24; D. M. Cosi, *Le ragioni del silenzio*, Padua 1983, pp. 123–54.

3–4. ἐπείτε... Θήρην: in contrast with the Therean version, the Pythia directly invests Battus with the role of *oikistes*, and does so of her own initiative, ignoring the purpose for which Battus had come (cf. Pindar, *Pyth.* 4,3 ff., 63; *SEG* IX 3 = ML 5, 1. 24; in general, B. Schmid, *Studien zu griechischen Ktisissagen*, Freiburg i.d. Schweiz 1947, pp. 158, 179; H. W. Parke, *JHS* LXXXII (1962), 145–6; Braswell, op. cit., pp. 144–6). According to Paus. X 5,7 (cf. Pindar, *Pyth.* 5,57), Battus, once he reached Libya, was also cured of his stutter: perhaps in the original legend the Pythia also solved the problem about which Battus was consulting her. The oracle, like others cited in this context, is held to be an *a posteriori* invention, but, if the name Battus was not assumed in Lybia, it may be authentic (see e.g. Schmid, op. cit., pp. 148–53; Kirchberg, pp. 51–8; Fontenrose, pp. 120–3; Malkin, pp. 60 ff.; for other sources, P–W II, p. 18, no. 39; an extended version in Diod. VIII 29, on which see Fontenrose, pp. 174–5). On the idea that the Pythia was able to speak foreign languages, cf. VIII 133–5; on the unheeded oracle, cf., in the Therean version, 150,4.   μηλοτρόφον: see already *Od.* IV 85–9 and Pindar, *Pyth.* 9,62. The nomads of the mainland were to a large extent shepherds (cf. e.g. 172,1): see among others Chamoux, p. 234; B. Brentjes, *Altertum*, XXVI (1980), 69–76; Libyan herdsmen are depicted on sandstone reliefs on the outskirts of Cyrene: see S. Stucchi, *Da Batto Aristotele a Ibn el-' As*, Rome 1987, pp. 19–20.   οἰκιστῆρα: a Doric form, of a kind that appears also in the other oracles, perhaps some sort of official title in Dorian Cyrene: see G. Pasquali, *Glotta*, V (1914), pp. 197–202 (= *Scritti*, pp. 585–9); Dobias-Lalou, p. 235.

156,1. συνεφέρετο παλιγκότως: cf., in the Therean version, 151,1.

2. ἡ δὲ Πυθίη... πρήξειν: as in the Therean version (151,1), the second oracle is reported in indirect speech; the expression ἄμεινον πρήξειν is, however, typical of the language of oracles (cf. note to 15,3). The mention of the name of the colony, though it did not yet exist, is common in foundation oracles in connection with the idea that the god knows beforehand the land where he is sending the colonists (cf. 157,2; Malkin, p. 91). It is not necessarily a mark of forgery, since it may derive from visits or pre-colonizations (further examples in Schmid, op. cit., p. 158; the name of Cyrene appears also in the version of the first oracle in Diod. VIII 29 and in the 'covenant of the founders', *SEG* IX 3 = ML 5, 1. 25; cf. A. J. Graham, *JHS* LXXX (1960), 107; S. Dušanić, *Chiron*, VIII (1978), 58).

The name Κυρήνη is perhaps of Libyan origin ('the city of asphodels', from *kyra* attested in Dioscorides I 235): see V. Bertoldi, *Mélange Émile Boisacq*, I, Bruxelles 1937, pp. 47–63; Chamoux, pp. 126–7; Dobias-Lalou, pp. 256–8.

3. οἱ δὲ... ἐκέλευον: the 'covenant of the founders' (*SEG* IX 3 = ML 5, ll. 33–7) prescribes the option of returning to Thera only in the case of necessity. This clause (exceptionally mild according to e.g. R. Werner, *Chiron*, I (1971), 62–5) is a justification *post eventum* of the reception accorded to the colonists, according to Dušanić, art. cit., p. 61. On the impossibility of turning back from colonizations, cf. I 165,2–3; Plut. *Mor.* 293a–b (the Corcyreans and Eretria); Graham, pp. 53, 110–11; A. Burnett, *Class Ant* VII (1988), 152–3.   λέγεται... πόλι: does this enigmatic statement (marking the end of the Therean version, according to Aly, p. 138) aim at indicating the smallness of the island, which was barely sufficient to provide for the colonists (cf. 159,1), and thus at motivating the discomfort which is spoken of directly afterwards? Or perhaps in the source, badly summarized by Herodotus, the oracle furnished indications of the size of Cyrene, which the colonists initially believed they recognized in Platea, later to correct themselves? Or is it a glossa prompted by the name Πλατέα ('flat', but also 'wide')?

157,1. ἕνα αὐτῶν: like Corobius according to the Therean version (151,3). The occurrence of this double may lead one to suspect that the version common to Thera and Cyrene does not begin until later, perhaps in para. 3. The 'covenant of the founders' (*SEG* IX 3 = ML 5, 1.24 ff.) does not, in fact, mention Platea; but it is hard to believe that the Therean version made the colonists simply transit through Platea and arrive directly at Cyrene (and that perhaps the solely Cyrenean version carries on until ch. 158 inclusive, taking τὰ περὶ Βάττον at 154,1 to mean the whole of Battus' life: Malkin, p. 60). Against this is the emphasis with which the colonization of Platea is spoken of at ch. 153, in the middle of the Therean version. Herodotus himself must have encountered difficulties in comparing the two versions, to the extent of not being able to flag the precise point where the common version began, as would have been the natural course in his system of formulae of presentation and recapitulation.

1–2. ἀπικόμενοι δὲ... Λιβύην: when they find that they are no 'better' in Platea, as the oracle had promised, the colonists consult it once again. The Pythia voices Apollo's irony on the mistake of the colonists, and makes them understand how, by staying on the island, they have left untouched Libya 'proper' (αὐτήν), i.e. the continent (cf. also Plut. *Mor.* 408a; *Anth. Pal.* XIV 84). For an attempt to place at this stage the tale of Menecles of Barce (*FGrHist* 270 F 6), cf. H. W. Parke, *Hermathena*, XXVII (1938), pp. 56–78; H. H. Rohrbach, 'Kolonie und Orakel', Diss. Heidelberg 1960, pp. 38–40; objections in Chamoux, p. 112; cf. Malkin, pp. 66–7. The *incipit* of the oracle is Doric (αἰ τὺ), in accord with the *ethnos* of those consulting it (cf. note to 159,3); Apollo's claim that he knew Libya personally may be an allusion to the myth of Apollo and Cyrene told e.g. by Pindar, *Pyth.* 9.

3. Ἄζιρις: Callimachus, *Apoll.* 89 mentions an Ἄζιλις; Ptolemy, *Geog.* IV 5,2, an Ἄζαλις (on the substitution λ–ρ, cf. C. Dobias-Lalou, *QAL* XII (1988), 89; on the

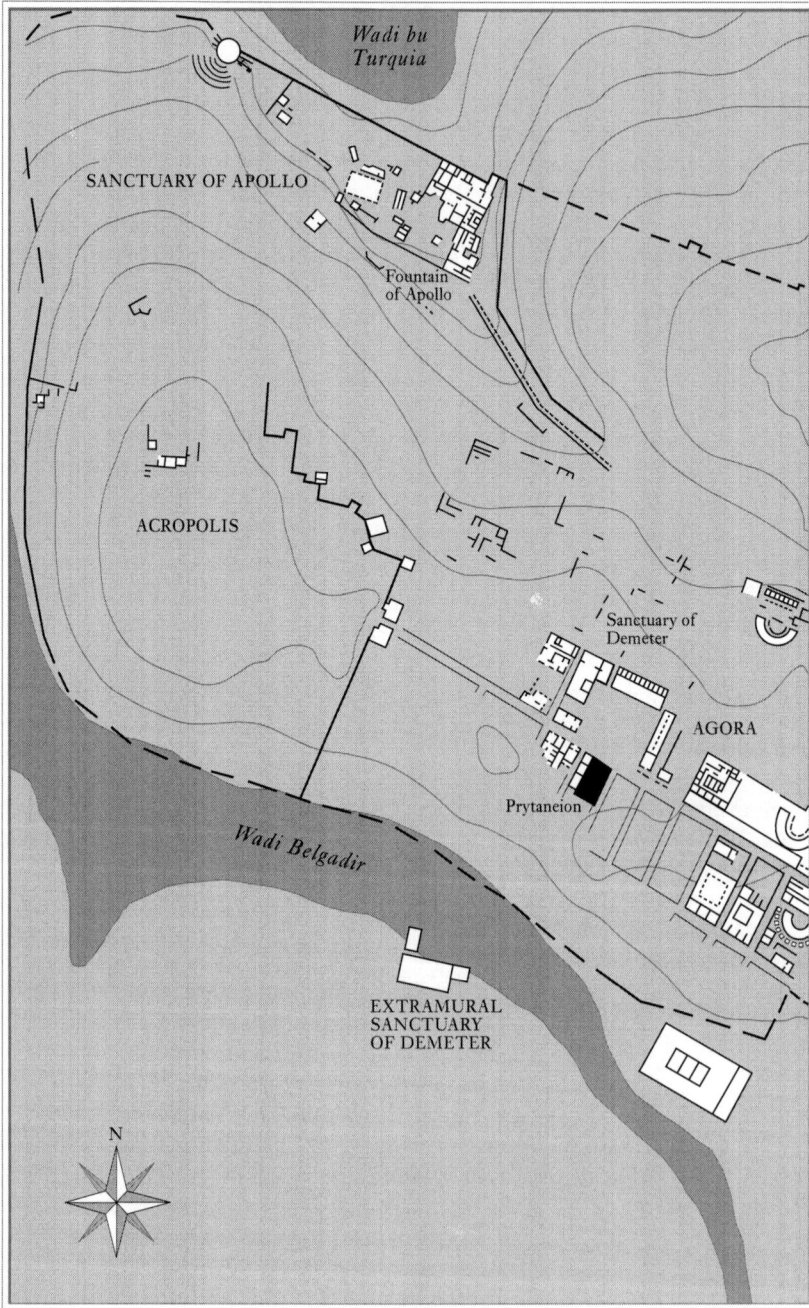

Map 43. Cyrene

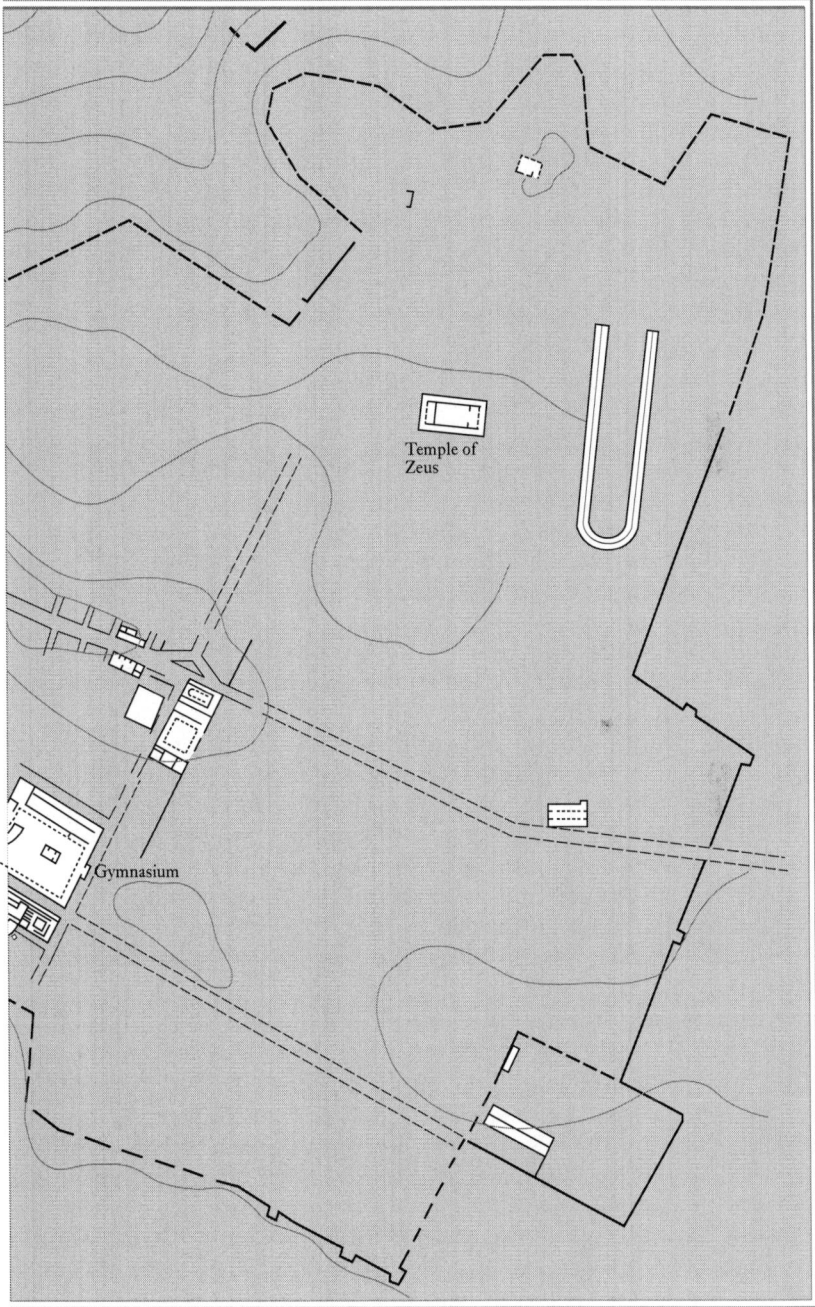

Temple of
Zeus

Gymnasium

etymon, A. M. Bisi Ingrassia, *QAL* IX (1977), 126–7); while the *Stadiasmus Maris Magni* 46–7, *GGM* I, p. 444, places the locality of Ἄζαρις (but the text is uncertain) 150 stades to the east of Darnis/Derna, and 100 stades to the west of Cape Chersonesus/Raset-Tin. This point corresponds to the mouth of the Wadi el-Khalig, where in fact a Greek settlement with pottery dating from the second half of the 7th cent. has been found (J. Boardman, *ABSA* LXI (1966), 150–2; V. Purcaro Pagano, *QAL* VIII (1976), 330, with other sources and bibl.; Haider, pp. 132–3). The indication 'opposite' Platea would then be incorrect (cf. on similar phenomena e.g. Janni, pp. 108–14, 128, n. 147); but, in favour of a location closer to the island (Wadi et-Tmimi) see e.g. Chamoux, pp. 118–20. However, it must have been a region rather than a locality; see also A. Jähne, *Klio*, LXX (1988), pp. 148–50.

158,1–2. ἑβδόμῳ... Ἴρασα: Irasa (cf. 159,5), also mentioned by Pindar, *Pyth.* 9,106, and by Pherecydes, *FGrHist* 3 F 75, has not been identified with certainty. It may correspond to the spring Ersen (Zā'wiya Umm er-Rzem, on the road from Derna to Bomba), but this would imply that Aziris was in the Gulf of Bomba: see Neumann, *Nordafrika*, pp. 15–18; Chamoux, p. 120; doubts in Goodchild, pp. 17–18, who thinks rather of Derna. It is not clear why the Libyans should lead the Greeks to a favourable place but conceal to them the beautiful location of Irasa: perhaps (Chamoux, p. 120) the local tribe (the Giligamae: ch. 169) is ridding itself of the Greeks by persuading them to move to the territory of the neighbouring tribe (the Asbystae: ch. 170). At the root of the tradition there may also be the aim of amicably involving the Libyans in the history of Cyrene (A. Jähne, *Klio*, LXX (1988), 152–3).

3. κρήνην... Ἀπόλλωνος: the spring of Apollo, known already to Pindar, *Pyth.* 4,294, and still active, surfaces on a natural terrace on the north-eastern slope of the acropolis, where the temple of the god was built: see e.g. Chamoux, p. 303; Goodchild, pp. 19–21, 109–12; Stucchi, pp. 581–96; Bonacasa–Ensoli p. 118.   ὁ οὐρανὸς τέτρηται: an allusion to the abundance of rain (cf. e.g. Pindar, *Pyth.* 4,52), which is due to the hill which rises to the south of the town: a geographical description in Chamoux, pp. 11–17. The image presupposes the idea of a solid celestial vault, for which cf. W. Vycichl, in *Wörterbuch der Myth.* 2, pp. 634–5.

159,1. ἐπὶ μέν νυν... ἐστάλησαν: the reigns of Battus I and of the little-known Arcesilaus I last until about 580 (Chamoux, pp. 128–34; on the development of Cyrene under Battus I and on his cult see also H. Büsing, *Thiasos. Sieben archäologische Arbeiten*, Amsterdam 1978, pp. 66–75; Malkin, pp. 204–16). It is difficult to take literally the statement that the number of colonists remained constant (see most recently Jähne, art. cit., p. 153): it is meant to underline the contrast with what follows.

2. Βάττου τοῦ εὐδαίμονος καλεομένου: the reign of Battus II 'the prosperous' (cf. also Plut. *Cor.* 15) lasted at least until 570BC, date of the battle of Irasa (see note to 159,4–5), but we do not know when he died (see note to 160,1). The summons for new colonists, which was perhaps intended to strengthen the power of the king against the aristocracy of Therean origin, led to territorial expansion, especially towards the east, and to the breakdown of the equilibrium with neighbouring peoples, who were being deprived of pasture-land: see Chamoux, pp. 134–6; Schaefer, pp. 237–45; Jähne, art. cit., pp. 154–8. Ἕλληνας πάντας: from ch. 161 it can be surmised that Peloponnesians, Cretans, and inhabitants of the islands came to Cyrene; the *Chronicle of Lindos* (*FGrHist* 532,17) mentions some colonists from Lindos who took part in the colonization of Cyrene with Battus: the episode is instead referred to this phase by Chamoux, pp. 124–5. Parallels for the arrival of new colonists (ἔποικοι) at a later stage e.g. in Schmid, op. cit., pp. 180–1 (Chios, Samos, etc.). γῆς ἀναδασμῷ: on the criteria for the distribution of land to new colonists see D. Asheri, *Distribuzioni di terre nell'antica Grecia*, Turin 1966, pp. 27–9 and *passim*; id., *Rivista di storia antica*, I (1971), 77–91; E. Lepore, *Problèmes de la terre en Grèce ancienne*, Paris–Le Haye 1973, pp. 15–47.

3. ὃς δέ... μελήσειν: the oracle (cf. *Anth. Pal.* XIV 85), it too with Doric traits, may contain an intentional ambiguity, depending on whether γᾶς ἀναδαιομένας is a comparative clause with ὕστερον, or a genitive absolute ('after the distribution of the land' or 'too late, when the distribution of land is already taking place'), so as to justify a possible unfortunate migration (B. A. van Groningen, *Mnemosyne*, IX (1956), 295); the oracle may therefore be historical.

4. Ἀδικράν: the name, not otherwise attested (but cf. the toponym *Idicra* in *Itinerarium Antoninum* 28,4), displays the termination -*an* typical of many Libyan names; cf. O. Masson, *AntAfr* X (1976), 52–3. It is most likely that the neighbouring Libyans were the Asbystae; see ch. 170.

4–6. πέμψαντες... ἀπ' αὐτοῦ: cf. II 161,4; Diod. I 68; II: the pharaoh sends in aid of the Libyans, who had long been tied to Egypt and under his dominion (cf. Chamoux, p. 135; Schaefer, pp. 240–1), the mercenaries called μάχιμοι, of Libyan origin. The Egyptian sources allow us to date the episode to 571/570 BC; for Irasa see note to 158,1–2 (the spring Theste is unknown, cf. the locality of Θεστίς in Stephanus of Byzantium, s.v.). The clash between the Cyreneans and the Libyans is depicted on a golden plaque from the Artemisium of Cyrene; see D. White, *QAL* XII (1988), 76 and n. 45. After the fall of Apries, his successor Amasis made an alliance with Cyrene, probably with Battus II himself: see II 181–2.

160,1. Ἀρκεσίλεως: Arcesilaus II, known as 'the cruel' (ὁ χαλεπός: Stephanus of Byzantium, s.v. Βάρκη), is probably the Arcesilaus depicted on the Laconic cup n. 194 Stibbe, with a representation of the weighing of silphium. His chronology is uncertain. Mazzarino, pp. 146–52, 301–5, has hypothesized that he reigned for no more than two years and was killed as early as 569 or 568; he identifies as Cyrene the town of Putujaman, indicated as allied to the pharaoh Amasis in an inscription by Nebuchadnezzar II of 568/567 (*ANET*[3], p. 308), and integrates the name Learchus in the...]*ku* in the same inscription, making him the king of Cyrene already for that year. It is likely that Putujaman is Cyrene, at this date an ally of Egypt (see note to 159,4–5; E. Edel, GM XXIX (1978), 13–20); but...]*ku* is

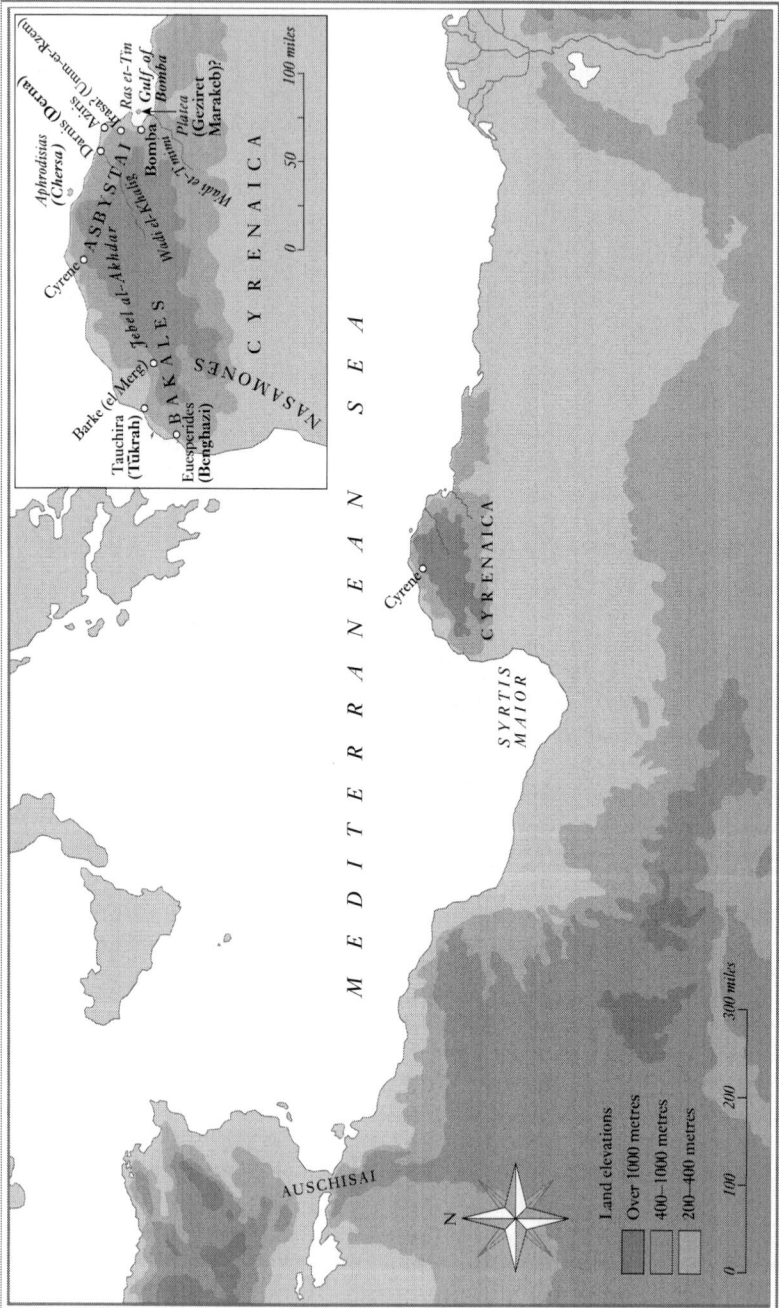

Map 44. Cyrenaica

not necessarily the name of its sovereign and the identification with Learchus is far from convincing (cf. Chamoux, pp. 142–3; Schaefer, p. 242, n. to 1 and 3): it is better to date the reign of Arcesilaus II between the sixties and the fifties of the century (c.566–560 according to Stibbe, pp. 195–201). Dynastic conflicts, not uncommon in tyrannies, were probably at the root of the strife with his brothers; the reforms later enacted by Demonax show that Arcesilaus' 'cruelty' must have implied also a despotic handling of the monarchy (cf. Diod. VIII 30,1; Plut. *Mor.* 260d–e; R. Drews, *Basileus: The Evidence for Kingship in Geometric Greece*, New Haven–London 1983, pp. 121–8), to the detriment of the aristocracy and the natives: see Chamoux, pp. 136–8; Schaefer, pp. 245–7. τοῖσι ἑωυτοῦ ἀδελφεοῖσι: Stephanus of Byzantium, s.v. Βάρκη, mentions as the founders of Barce four brothers, Perseus, Zacynthius, Aristomedon, and Lycus: according to Stephanus' source, Learchus is not one of the brothers (see note to 160,4), unless he had remained at Cyrene. ἔκτισαν ... Λίβυας: Barce stood on the highland to the west of Cyrene, on the site of modern-day el Merj; sporadic excavations have brought to light materials from the 5th cent.: cf. M. Vickers and A. Bazama, *Libya Antiqua*, VIII (1971), 69–84; V. Purcaro Pagano, *QAL* VIII (1976), 329–30 (other sources and bibl.); Boardman, *Greeks Overseas*, pp. 153–9; Laronde, pp. 49–52. The fusion of Greeks and Libyans (outside the city there were Auschisae and Bacales: ch. 171) is confirmed e.g. by the name of Alazir at 164,4 (cf. ch. 186); for the hypothesis that the brothers of Arcesilaus settled in a pre-existing native site see E. Fabbricotti, *QAL* XI (1980), 5–9.

2–3. μετὰ δὲ ... πεσεῖν: Leucon may be the Leucoe of Ptolemy, *Geog.* IV 5,28, to the eastern borders of Cyrenaica. The 7,000 fallen hoplites, if the figure is reliable, are a sign of the large size of Cyrene at the time; cf. Schaefer, p. 247.

4. μετὰ δὲ ...'Ερυξώ: the episode is told also by Nicolaus of Damascus, *FGrHist* 90 F 50, while according to Plutarch, *Mor.* 260d–261d, and Polyaenus VIII 41, Learchus (Laarchos) was a friend, not a brother, of Arcesilaus (thus also F. Jacoby, *Hermes*, LX (1925), 371–2, but it may be just a romanticized version; see e.g. Schaefer, p. 247, n. 4). G. P. Schaus, *AJA* LXXXVII (1983), 88–9, connects the name 'Ερυξώ to the 'Ορυξώ he reads on the above-mentioned 'cup of Arcesilaus'.

161,1–3. διεδέξατο ... τριφύλους ἐποίησέ σφεας: we know from Plutarch, *Mor.* 261b, that a regency preceded the ascent to the throne of Battus III 'the lame' (Schaefer, p. 248). At any rate, the monarchy had become weaker, to the extent that it was the Cyreneans as a body, and not the king, who consulted the oracle at Delphi (cf. G. Pugliese Carratelli, *QAL* XII (1988), 28). The nomination of a 'mediator' (καταρτιστήρ; διαιτητής in Diod. VIII 30,2; Demonax appears as the 'king of Mantinea' in Heraclides, *P Oxy* 1367, ll. 19 ff. = Hermippus, *FGrHist* 1026 F 3; cf. also Ephorus, *FGrHist* 70 F 54 and J. Bollansée, *Anc. Soc.* XXVII (1996), 289–300; his name recurs in Cyrene in the 4th cent.: *SEG* IX 50, 46 and 147) has parallels, for instance, in some Delphic responses to Sparta (P–W II, nos. 223, 224, 229). On the recourse to external mediators in the archaic period, and on the reputation of the Arcadians (eg. in Polybius VI 43), see Chamoux, p. 139.

Demonax's reform aimed at consolidating the civic body by integrating new arrivals and limiting the power of the king; Aristotle, *Pol.* VII 4, 1319b19 ff., compared it to Cleisthenes' reform in Athens and discerned in it, perhaps wrongly, some democratic traits: a discussion in Chamoux, pp. 138–42; Schaefer, pp. 248–52; A. Jähne, *Klio* LXX (1988), 158–61; K. J. Hölkeskamp, *Hermes*, CXXI (1993), 404–21; cf. also S. Stucchi, *L'agorà di Cirene*, I, Rome 1965, pp. 69 ff., on the restoration of the *agora* which probably ensued (see now Bonacasa–Ensoli, pp. 59–80). The distribution of the citizens into tribes according to the origin of the colonists finds some parallels in other colonies (e.g. in Thurii; reservations on their ethnic character are expressed by D. Roussel, *Tribu et cité*, Paris 1976, pp. 300–3). The number of three tribes (perhaps modelled on the Dorian ones?) is confirmed by epigraphic evidence of the 4th cent. (*SEG* IX 72, 134; *phylé* and phratry in *SEG* IX 3 = ML 5, 1. 15).

3. περιοίκων: it is not certain who the '*perioici*' were: perhaps the natives who had taken part in the colonization (e.g. Schaefer, p. 249; cf. 159,4), or perhaps rather the Greek 'clients', of Therean origin, of the aristocracy descended from the first colonists (Chamoux, pp. 221–4; Jähne, art. cit., p. 159; they were the Thereans who were not free men according to V. P. Jajlenko, *Grečeskaja kolonizacija VII–III vv. do n.e.*, Moscow 1982, p. 81; cf. O. Hansen, *AJPh* CV (1984), 326–7); in any case, the term περίοικοι without further specification cannot mean, in a Cyrenean context and following the mention of the Thereans, the *perioici* of Laconia, as G. Schaus, in *Cyrenaica*, pp. 395–403 would have it. Cf. most recently F. X. Ryan, *LibStud* XXXII (2001), 79–85.   τεμένεα . . . καὶ ἱερωσύνας: in Mycenean and Homeric Greek the τεμένη are allotments of land, estates, but the word soon acquired the meaning of 'sacred precinct' (discussion and further reading in Malkin, pp. 139–41). In his capacity of founder of the colony, Battus I must have distributed the land reserving some areas for cult (cf. *Od.* VI 9–10; Pindar, *Pyth.* 5,89 ff.). Given the context, it is likely that the τεμένεα which belonged to the king were not simply allotments in the Homeric sense but rather sacred areas (at any rate, the hero-worship of the founder of the colony gave a special status to the possessions inherited by his descendants). As in many other Greek cities (cf. Arist. *Pol.* III 14, 1295b16–17), 'the king' retains religious functions, while 'everything else' (the authority to govern, command of the army, in short, the 'offices', τιμαί, mentioned at ch. 162) passes into the hands of the community: cf. the case of Meandrius of Samos III 143; Drews, op. cit., pp. 121–8.

162–7. The tale of Arcesilaus III, though it is in an anecdotal form and tinged with tragic irony, affords a clear understanding of the actual facts: cf. Chamoux, pp. 144–59. The successor of Battus III attempts, with the aid of his mother, to restore his dynastic power by tyrannical opposition to the aristocracy which had benefited from the reforms. Failure causes the two to find refuge in Samos and in Cypriot Salamis: these towns must have had commercial relations with Cyrene (see notes to 151,2 and 152,5); above all, the presence of Polycrates and Euelthon was a guarantee of international solidarity among 'tyrants'. By the promise of land distribution (on this expedient of tyrants against the landed aristocracy see D. Asheri, *Distribuzioni di terre nell'antica Grecia*, Turin 1966, pp. 74 ff.), Arcesilaus raises an army and returns to his country; there follows a retaliation and an alliance with the king of Barce, where Arcesilaus probably based the military operations against his enemies (Noshy, pp. 66–71), until the anti-tyrannical party regains the upper hand and kills him. The Persians are then called to intervene, since Arcesilaus III had submitted himself to Cambyses after the latter had conquered Egypt. The conquest of Egypt took place in 525 (cf. III 1–38): Arcesilaus' exile in Samos has been dated to both before that date (around 530, after Polycrates' coup of 533: e.g. Chamoux, p. 146), and, with less likelihood, after it (B. M. Mitchell, *JHS* LXXXVI (1966), 99–113; discussion in Noshy, pp. 53–78). The date of his death is linked to that of Aryandes' expedition; see note to 167,3.

162,3. τῆς δὲ Σαλαμῖνος ... κεῖται: the city of Salamis on the island of Cyprus was on the east coast, about 6.5 km. from Famagosta: Euelthon (father of Syromus, grandfather of Chersis, great-grandfather of Gorgo and Onesilus: V 104,1) is known to us also through some coins in which he proclaims himself king of all the Cypriots, with the effigy of a ram and his name in syllabic writing, *E-u-we-le-to-to-se Ku* = Εὐϝέλθοντος Κυ(πρίων): see *PECS*, pp. 794–6 and Müller II, pp. 1001–8; V. Karageorghis, in *CAH* III, pp. 69–70; cf. the bibl. in H. Gesche, *Jahrb. für Numismatik und Geldgeschichte*, XX (1970), 161–216; C. M. Kraay, *Archaic and Classical Greek Coins*, London 1976, p. 301. On the thurible in the 'treasury of the Corinthians' at Delphi, see note to I 14,7.

3–5. ἀπικομένη ... στρατιῆ: the anecdote attracted Herodotus' interest on account of the unusual combative spirit in a woman and of the effective reply (cf. the tales on Artemisia at VII 99 and in Book VIII, or the mention of Eryxo at IV 160,4). On the one hand the assertive personality of Pheretime, who will subsequently play an important part, is highlighted; on the other hand, the manner in which she is silenced betrays the sarcastic bias of the source, which was probably Cyrenean (cf. note to 205.). The name Φερετίμα is attested in archaic times at Thera (*IG* XII 3,39; cf. Chamoux, p. 149, n. 2).

163,2–3. ἐπὶ μὲν ... καλλιστεύων: traces of hexameters can be discerned in the prose paraphrase of the response: for an attempt to reconstruct it, see P–W p. 31, no. 70. The indication of the end of the dynasty after eight generations reveals that it was composed *post eventum* (the dynasty ends around 440 BC with the Arcesilaus IV whom Pindar sang; see Chamoux, pp. 160–210). Herodotus reports analogous oracles for the Mermnadae (I 13,2) and Cypselidae (V 92ε,2) as evidence of the intrinsic instability of dynastic power. The second part of the response, which alludes to the events narrated in subsequent chapters, is not very clear: the 'bull' must be Alazir (for the comparison, cf. Homer, *Il.* II 480 ff.); ἀμφί(ρ)ρυτος, 'surrounded by water', may apply to Cyrene because it was bounded by two *widian* (Wadi bel Gadir and Wadi bu Turquia; according to Pindar, *Pyth.* 9,55 the city was on a hill 'surrounded by plains', ἀμφίπεδος), and to Barce perhaps because water stagnates around it during the rain season (Chamoux, pp. 133 and 146, n. 1).

164,2. τοὺς δέ... ἀπέστειλαν: Arcesilaus sends the prisoners to his mother and Euelthon at Cyprus; but the ship reaches Cnidus instead, perhaps due to the north-easterly winds (ἀπενειχθέντας: see notes to 151,2, 152,1–3, and 179,2). Cnidus too was a Spartan colony (I 174,2), and it had a relation of 'kinship' (συγγένεια: *IG* XII 3,322) with Thera; moreover the Cyreneans on board must have been aristocrats, descendants of the first Theraean colonists (Chamoux, pp. 148–9). **πύργον... ἰδιωτικὸν:** the 'tower' is described as 'private' to distinguish it from the city's fortifications: it must, however, be distinguished from toponyms proper, such as e.g. πύργος Εὐφράντα (Strabo XVII 3,20; Ptolemy, *Geog.* IV 3,4; unlike Chamoux, p. 221), and understood as a fortified element of a farmhouse: cf. J. H. Young, *Hesperia*, XXV (1956), 122–45; M. Nowicka, *Les Maisons à tour dans le monde grec*, Paris 1975, pp. 96 ff.; on towers in the Cyrenean *chora* see Stucchi, *passim*; Laronde, pp. 131, 257 ff. The name Ἀγλώμαχος is well attested in Cyrene in the 4th cent. (*SEG* IX 49, 31; 50, 38; cf. 46, 57). On the custom of setting fire to towers in which enemies are barricaded see e.g. Xenophon, *Hist. Gr.* VII 2,8; 2 Macc. 10: 36; *Testamentum Iudae* 5,5.

4. εἶχε... Ἀλάζειρ: the daughter of Alazir was related to Arcesilaus III because she was a descendant of the brothers of Arcesilaus II, who was his grandfather (160,1). However, the name Alazir is clearly Libyan, and can be compared to the ΑΛΑΤ(ΤΕΙΡ) on a coin from Barce (E. S. G. Robinson, *Catalogue of the Greek Coins in the British Museum: Cyrenaica*, London 1927, p. 105), and to the Cyrenean Ἀλαδδειρ, son of a Battus (*SGDI* 4859: 1st cent. AD): see O. Masson, *BCH* XCVIII (1974), 263–70; id., *AntAfr* X (1976), 53, 59–60; Dobias-Lalou, pp. 57–8. At Barce there had been a thorough integration between Greeks and Libyans; cf. 186,2. **εἴτε ἑκὼν εἴτε ἀέκων:** ironic expression: 'whether he wanted it or not (= though he did not wish it, though he had tried to avoid it), having misinterpreted the oracle (cf. I 71,1; IX 33,2), he fulfilled his destiny.' Cf. note to III 64,16–17; Harrison, p. 241.

165,1. ἡ δὲ μήτηρ... παρίζουσα: the energetic figure of Pheretime comes to the fore. On the presence of a 'council' at Cyrene (attested in the 4th cent. in *SEG* IX 1,16–19), and the other governing bodies, see Chamoux, pp. 213–19.

2–3. ἦσαν... τέθνηκε: cf. III 14,3–4. In the framework of Herodotus' narrative, a pro-Persian stance as cause of the death of Arcesilaus is adduced only as a pretext; see note to 167,3.

166,1. ὁ δὲ Ἀρυάνδης: Aryandes (*Aryavanda-?) must be identified with the anonymous satrap whom Darius entrusted with the task of restoring the ancient Egyptian legislation in the third year of his reign (519/518 BC): Spiegelberg, *Demotische Chronik* pp. 30–2; cf. note to III 91,7. After him, demotic documents attest as satrap in 492/492 Prndd/Prntt = Farnadāta-(W. Spiegelberg, *Sitzungsberichte der Preussischen Ak. der Wiss.* (1928), 604–22; but the date of the deposition of Aryandes, which Herodotus presents as not being close at hand at the time of the Libyan expedition, is uncertain. Polyaenus VII 11,7 speaks of a rebellion of the Egyptians against Aryandes and of a visit of Darius to Egypt (attested also by Herodotus, II 110): this visit is said to have been concurrent with the death of an Apis, and, consequently, can be dated to between 518 and 517 BC (cf. note to III 27–9): hence the hypothesis that Darius deposed Aryandes on this occasion (Hinz, pp. 190–2). If Aryandes was in fact deposed between 518 and 517, then the Herodotean synchrony of Libyan and Scythian expeditions is artificial (thus e.g. Noshy, pp. 53–78), or else the 'early' dating for the Scythian expedition must be accepted (e.g. Th. Petit, *AC* LIII (1984), 40–2; cf. note to I,1). However, Polyaenus' authority is weak: against the reality of this visit by Darius see e.g. Cook, p. 60; T. Cuyler Young Jr., in *CAH* IV, pp. 64–5; for a lower dating of the visit, C. Tuplin, *AH* VI (1991), 249–50, 264–7. In any case, it is only modern scholars, not Herodotus or Polyaenus, who establish a link between the king's visit and the deposition of the satrap, which may also have occurred in the first decade of the 5th cent.: see among others G. Busolt, *Griechische Geschichte bis zur Schlacht bei Chaeronea* II, Gotha 1895², pp. 532–6; Posener, p. 176; G. G. Cameron, *JNES* II (1943), 307–14; B. M. Mitchell, *JHS* XCIV (1974), 174–7; J. D. Ray, in *CAH* IV, p. 262. If the cause of the punishment was truly the minting of a coin which emulated that of Darius, then this would stand as confirmation of a later dating: for it is unlikely that the 'daric', the new coin with a gold content of no less than 980 parts to 1,000, and with the representation of the archer king, could have been put into circulation before 516/515 (cf. E. S. G. Robinson, *NC* XVIII (1958), 187–93; A. D. H. Bivar, in *CHI* II, pp. 617–18). Aryandes must have done this with an eye to prestige rather than to gain: against the hypothesis of J. G. Milne, *JEA* XXIV (1938), 245–6, according to whom Aryandes played on the rate of exchange between the silver siglus and the gold daric to acquire gold, see e.g. M. Giacchero, in *Studi di Storia Antica in memoria di L. de Regibus*, Genoa 1969, pp. 115–17. But in actual fact there is as yet no evidence for silver sigli coined or widely circulating in Egypt (A. D. H. Bivar, in *CHI* II, p. 619); bibl. and discussion, with conclusions in favour of the veracity of Herodotus, in C. Tuplin, *REA* XCI (1989), 61–83. Cf. now M. Alram, in *Encyclopaedia Iranica*, VII (1994), 36–40; R. Descat, *AIIN* XLII (1996), 9–20; Briant, *Histoire*, pp. 153, 421–2, 960 = ET, pp. 141, 408–9, 935; P. Vargyas, *IA* XXXV (2000), 33–46; more literature in P. Briant, *Bulletin d'histoire achéménide*, II, Paris 2001, pp. 129–31.

167,1. στρατηγὸν... γένος: Amasis, a Maraphian, is Persian (the Maraphians are a Persian tribe which has not been located: I 125,3); but he seems to bear an Egyptian name (see Lloyd, note on II 162, 1–2; P. Huyse, *Iranische Namen in den Griechischen Dokumenten Ägyptens*, Vienna 1990, pp. 30–1; in general, J. Boardman, in J. Paul Getty Center for the History of Art and the Humanities, *Papers on the Amasis Painter and his World*, Malibu 1987, pp. 141–52), which he may have assumed in Egypt (thus now Briant, *Histoire*, p. 498 = ET, p. 482); unless it is a Persian name, which has been distorted and assimilated to the better-known name of the pharaoh (there is, however, no reason to identify him with the Arsames in Polyaenus VII 28,1). Badres, a Pasargadian (cf. I 125,3), has a Persian name, comparable to the *Ha-ba-at-ra* at Persepolis (perhaps *Abadra, cf. the Avestic *hu-ba-δra-*, 'happy': see R. Schmitt, *ZDMG* XCVII (1967), 129;

Mayrhofer, p. 151); cf. also IV 203,2; VII 77. For the mention of the tribe by name, see Briant, *Histoire*, pp. 483–4 = ET, pp. 468–9.

2. πρὶν δὲ... ὑπ' αὐτοῦ: the sending of a herald must have aimed at having the responsible persons handed over and at a consequent submission. But the Barceans assume collective responsibility (cf. 200,1; for a similar situation see IX 86–8): this may be a trace of a patriotic, anti-tyrannical, and anti-Persian version by the Barcean aristocracy

3. αὕτη... οὐδέν: the sentence picks up the statement of 145,1. Herodotus puts forward as a personal opinion the idea that the true cause of the expedition was the will to subjugate the whole of Libya. This tallies with his general conception of Persian expansionism (cf. note to 1,1–2 and 102–19; Introduction, pp. 545 and 569–70), while, on the other hand, furnishing a pretext for opening, with a formula that links back to 197,1 by ring composition, the excursus on the peoples of Libya; but in the narrative of the expedition there will be no reference to actions purposefully intended against the Libyan tribes (although some aims which transcend the punishment of Barce seem to emerge in 203,3–4 and 204–1; cf. Noshy, pp. 57–9). In actual fact the Libyan peoples directly bordering with Egypt had submitted themselves immediately after the conquest of Egypt in 525 (see III 13,3–4; 91,2); but there is no mention of Libya either in the Bisitun inscription of 519 BC or in the inscription of Persepolis (c.513). The Libyans do, however, appear as *Tmḥw* = demotic *Pwd/Pjjt* = *Puti/Putāyā*, on the steles of Suez (Posener, nos. 8–9), on the statue of Darius from Susa (J. Yoyotte, *JA* CCLX (1972), 253–66; P. Calmeyer, *AH* VI (1991), 285–303), and at Naqš-i Rustam (*DNa* 29–30), all of which can be dated to the beginning of the 5th cent. Therefore Herodotus may be, to a certain extent, correct in supposing a Persian plan for expansion west of Egypt which was put into action, or even just propagandized, between 513 and the end of the century (see e.g. Cook, pp. 58, 64; J. Harmatta, *ACD* XXVII (1991), 3–7; objections in Noshy, pp. 56–60). Aryandes' expedition, if it must be dated to around 513 as contemporary with the last phase of the Scythian expedition (see note to 1,1; against an early dating, note to 166,1), may have brought the Persians into contact with the other Libyan tribes in Cyrenaica and offered the cue for the new expansionistic aims, though its immediate and main objective, and perhaps originally the only objective, was that of re-establishing in Cyrenaica a personal regime which would remain loyal (A. Laronde, in *Cirene. Storia*, pp. 35–41).

168–99. Λίβυες was the Greek name for all the peoples west of Egypt; it is the same as the Egyptian *rwb* (Lebu), name of a particular tribe attested from the XIXth Dynasty. The Greeks perhaps took the name from the Egyptians, as did the Jews (*Lubîm*), though the presence of the name LBY in a Punic context may lead to suppose that the Libyans themselves used the term with a generic meaning (to be connected perhaps with the place-name *Lepcis* and the tribe-name *Lebu* in Senegal?). As a generic term the Egyptians used *Tmḥw* (Temehu), while the Persians called the Libyans *Putāyā*, which name is perhaps related to that of Βουτώ (cf. II 59,3). Egyptian depictions show that they were peoples with fair skin and hair (this is confirmed by Greek sources; see e.g. Scylax 110, *GGM* I, p. 88), and this induces one to think of them as the ancestors of the modern-day Berbers (cf. note to 183,4). See among others Gsell, *Histoire* I and V; Bates; Chamoux, pp. 35–68; G. Camps, in *CHA* I, pp. 612–23; R. C. C. Law, in *CHA* II, pp. 87–147; J. Desanges, in *GHA* II, pp. 423–40; Camps, *Berbères*; Zimmermann, pp. 6–21. On the relationship between the Libyans and Egypt: G. Möller, *ZDMG* LXXVIII (1924), 30–70; Hölscher; H. Goedicke, *MDAI(K)* XVIII (1962), 26–49; T. Gostynski, *BIFAN* XXXVII (1975), 473–588; A. Spallinger, *J. Soc. of Egyptian Antiquity*, IX (1979), 125–62; J. Osing, in *LdÄ* III, coll. 1015–33; K. A. Kitchen, *Revue d'Égyptologie*, XXXVI (1985), 177–9; A. Nibbi, *Lapwings and Libyans in Ancient Egypt*, Oxford 1986; Leahy; Vittmann, pp. 1–20. Though with occasional confusions, the exposition on the Libyans is arranged around the distinction between nomadic groups, from Egypt to lake Tritonis, and farming groups, to the west; the nomads are listed from east to west in strips, first the coastal tribes, then—beyond the strip 'of the animals'—the line of oases on the limits of the Sahara. The picture which emerges (cf. II 32,4), though not disagreeing with reality (see note to chs. 181–5), suffers from the geometrization typical of ancient geography. In all probability Herodotus is modelling his account on Hecataeus', but he seems to be on the one hand summarizing the latter's information, on the other hand correcting it by drawing on different sources (cf. esp. chs. 173, 187, and 191): see Windberg, pp. 47–67; F. Jacoby, *RE* VII 2 1912, coll. 2727–34; Lloyd, *Commentary 1–98*, pp. 135–7; Introduction, pp. 568–9. More or less extended ethnographic notes are furnished for the various groups of Libyans, with a marked interest in the more peculiar oddities and in the differences and similarities in customs, at times with a diffusionistic attitude towards Egypt and Greece: cf. A. B. Lloyd, in *Hérodote et les peuples non grecs*, pp. 236–42. In spite of some unwarranted interpretations the resulting picture, when compared with reports by other authors and with the anthropological and ethnographical data for the modern Berber world, is fundamentally correct: see esp. Neumann, *Nordafrika*; Gsell, *Histoire* I; id., *Hérodote*; for the other ancient sources see Desanges, *Catalogue*; G. Abitino, *Memorie della Società Geografica Italiana*, XXXII (1979), 9–123; Desanges, *Pline*; N. Berti, *Geografia e storiografia nel mondo classico*, Milan 1988, pp. 145–65; Colin.

168,1. Ἀδυρμαχίδαι: the name of the Adyrmachidae has been related to that of the Temehu (G. Möller, *ZDMG* LXXVIII (1924), 48): but see the reservations of Hölscher, p. 50, who points instead to a relation with the name of the Berber group of the Ithermaken. On the possibility of a connection with the groups ADRMKDE/ADRMKDD which appear on some Meroitic inscriptions at Kawa see Desanges, *Pline*, pp. 420–1. Their territory stretched from the Plinthinetes Gulf = Arabic Gulf (cf. II 6) to the Gulf of Sollūm, where Plynus must be located (Πλυνός, 'the washing place', also called Κατάβαθμος μέγας, 'great slope': cf. Scylax 108, *GGM* I, p. 82; Lycophron, *Alexandra* 149; Strabo XVII 3,32; discussion in V. Purcaro Pagano, *QAL* VIII (1976), 337 and 345; Laronde, pp. 225–6). Cf. Gsell, *Hérodote*, pp. 120–1; Desanges, *Catalogue*, pp. 169–70 (with other sources). On their Egyptian customs, cf. Colin, pp. 139–59.

ἐσθῆτα... ῥίπτει: Libyan dress was characterized by the use of hides, mostly worn over the shoulders (cf. IV 189; VII 71): see Bates, pp. 118–33; Gsell, *Hérodote*, pp. 163–5; Hölscher, p. 33. The use of rings around the ankles was widespread, and still is among Berber women (Bates, p. 133; Gsell, *Hérodote*, pp. 165–6; cf. ch. 176). On the attention to hairstyle, cf. chs. 175, 180, 191; on lice, 109,1.

2. οὗτοι... διαπαρθενεύεται: the peculiar sexual customs of the Libyans attract Herodotus' attention also at chs. 172, 176, 180. The different systems of social and family organization of the Libyans, who, like many nomads, practised polygamy (cf. Bates, pp. 108–11; S. Campetti and E. Borzatti von Löwenstern, *L'altra umanità*, Florence 1983, pp. 57–62), are translated into rather simplistic and, at times, negative terms (Trüdinger, pp. 31–2; M. Rosellini and S. Saïd, *ASNP* s. III, VIII (1978), 944–1005; V. Andò, *Φιλίας χάριν. Miscellanea di studi classici in onore di E. Manni*, I, Rome 1980, pp. 85–102; Mora, pp. 64–72; G. Casadio, *Civiltà classica e mondo dei barbari. Due modelli a confronto*, Trento 1991, pp. 116–25), but much trustworthy information can be recovered (see F. Colin, in D. Mendel, and U. Claudi (eds.), *Ägypten im afro-orientalischen Kontext. Gedankenschrift P. Behrens*, Cologne 1991, pp. 55–72; Colin, pp. 19–36). The *ius primae noctis*, variously widespread in the world, does not lack parallels in northern Africa: see Gsell, *Hérodote*, pp. 196–7; id., *Histoire* V, p. 31.

169,1. Γιλιγάμαι: the Giligamae, whose probable correct name is restored from Stephanus of Byzantium, s.v., but who are otherwise unknown, occupied an area which was later inhabited by the Marmarydae, from the Gulf of Sollūm to the island of Aphrodisias, which must be identified with Chersa, a little to the west of Derna (cf. Scylax 108, *GGM* I, p. 83; *Stadiasmus Maris Magni* 41, *GGM* I, p. 442; Ptolemy, *Geog.* IV 4,7; Stephanus of Byzantium, s. v.; V. Purcaro Pagano, *QAL* VIII (1976), 327): see Gsell, *Hérodote*, pp. 121–2; Desanges, *Catalogue*, p. 163.   ἥ τε Πλατέα... Ἄζιρις: on Platea and Aziris see note to 151,2 and 157,3. The 'harbour of Menelaus' was so called in memory of the legend of the arrival of Menelaus in Libya, perhaps by distortion of a local name: cf. Homer, *Od.* IV 80 ff.; Herod. II 112–120; Haider, pp. 151, 211 ff.; Lloyd above, note on II 119. It was the site of Agesilaus' death, according to Nepos, *Ages.* 8. Reports of *peripli* (cf. Scylax 108, *GGM* I, p. 82; *Stadiasmus Maris Magni* 41, *GGM* I, p. 440; Strabo XVII 3,22; Ptolemy, *Geog.* IV 5,13) allow us to identify it with one of the inlets between Tobruk and the Gulf of Sollūm, probably Marsa Gabes (Stucchi, p. 385, n. 13; V. Purcaro Pagano, art. cit., pp. 295 and 340; W. Helck, *MDAI(K)* XXXIX (1983), 81–2, 90) or Marsa el-Aora (Laronde, pp. 224–5).

σίλφιον: silphium grew wild on the highland, in the sub-Saharan steppe between the Gulf of Bomba and the 'mouth' of the greater Syrtis off Bengasis (cf. also Scylax 108, *GGM* I, p. 83). Here it was gathered by the natives and sold to the kings of Cyrene, who probably held a monopoly (Aristotle, fr. 528 Rose): the 'cup of Arcesilaus' (see note to 160,1) shows Arcesilaus II supervising the weighing and storing of the roots of silphium, and the plant is often depicted on the coins of Cyrene. Cited already by Solon, fr. 33,1 Gentili–Prato, silphium was used in cookery, whilst the juice which was extracted from it (Latin *laserpicium* < *lac serpicium*, 'silphium milk') was highly appreciated in antiquity as a spice and as medication. But by Strabo's day it was becoming rare (see XVII 3,22), probably because of excessive cultivation and of the failing of nomadic economy. Today it is no longer possible to identify it with certainty, or to establish whether it has become extinct. The information from ancient sources (in the first place Theophrastus, *Hist. Plant.* VI 3,1–7 and Pliny, *NH* XIX 38–46) and the representations on coins suggest that it was an umbrelliferous, similar to the *Thapsia garganica* or the *Ferula narthex* (asafoetida), while some have thought of a papaveraceous plant. If some terracotta figures holding silphium are represented in scale (cf. P. Pensabene, *QAL* XII (1988), 124–34, nos. 21–36), the plant must have been between 20 and 30 cm. in height: cf. Chamoux, pp. 246–63 (with earlier literature); D. Roques, *REG* XCVII (1984), 218–31; F. Chamoux, *Bull. de la Société Nationale des Antiquaires de France* (1985), 54–9; id., in *Cyrenaica*, pp. 165–72; J. P. Bocquet, *Dossiers d'Archéologie*, CXXIII (1988), 88–91.

170. Ἀσβύσται: the Asbystae have sometimes been identified with the Isbet (*'Isbt*) of a document of Ramses III, and with the Isebeten cited by the Tuareg as their pagan predecessors: Bates, p. 47; W. Vycichl, *RSO* XXXI (1956), 211–20; J. Osing, in *LdÄ* III, col. 1017. The connection is anything but certain: cf. Desanges, *Catalogue*, pp. 147–9; id., *Pline*, pp. 374–5, with other sources and bibl. Inhabitants of the interior (μεσήπειροι) also according to Dionysius Periegetes 211, *GGM* II, p. 113, more than other Libyans they had contacts with Greek colonists, to some extent mingling with them (see note to 186,2). This set in motion a process of acculturation (cf. also Mela I 41), which is confirmed by, among other things, funerary architecture: see L. Bacchielli, *Africa*, XXXIII (1978), 605–22; id., *QAL* XII (1988), 459–88; M. Luni, *QAL* XII (1988), 415–58; Colin, pp. 127–59. Great skill in driving *quadrigae* as a characteristic of the Libyans finds confirmation at chs. 183, 189, 193 (also cf. VII 6 and 184, as well as Sophocles, *El.* 702; Diod. XX 38 and 64). It was perhaps on account of Libyan influence (cf. 189,3) that this skill was shared also by the Greeks of Cyrene, whose army included, in the 4th cent., a contingent of *quadrigae* (*SEG* IX 46, pp. 49–50; cf. Chamoux, pp. 236–7; M. L. Lazzarini, *QAL* XII (1988), 171–4).

171. Αὐσχίσαι: also the Auschisae live in the interior, and their territory is washed by the sea only along the western border (Ptolemy, *Geog.* IV 5,12, even places them near the oasis of Augila; cf. Stephanus of Byzantium, s.v. Αὐσχίται; Diod. III 49,1): see Gsell, *Hérodote*, p. 124; Desanges, *Catalogue*, p. 149. They must not be confused with the Αὔσιγδοι in Hecataeus, *FGrHist* 1 F 330; see F. Jacoby's commentary ad loc.   **Εὐεσπερίδας:** cf. chs. 198, 204; renamed Berenice in Ptolemaic times, it was about 3 km. north of Benghazi, where there have been findings dating from the first half of the 6th cent.: see among others R. G. Goodchild, *Benghazi: The Story of a City*, London 1963², pp. 1–7; J. Boardman, *ABSA* LXI (1966), 155–6; *PECS*, p. 320; J. A. Lloyd (ed.), *Excavations at Sidi Khrebish, Benghazi (Berenice)*, I, Tripolis 1982; *Cyrenaica* pp. 28–33; J. Lloyd, in ibid., pp. 49–66; M. Vickers and D. W. J. Gill, *LibStud*

XVII (1986), 97–108; Haider, pp. 137–8. The name (on the variants of which see Dobias-Lalou, p. 255) was related to the Libyan location of the myth of the Hesperides: Dion, pp. 141–5; S. Stucchi, *QAL* VIII (1976), 19–73; Haider, pp. 148–9. *Βάκαλες*: the variant *Βάκαλες* (against *Κάβαλες*) is confirmed by Callimachus, fr. 484 Pfeiffer; Agroetas, *FGrHist* 762 F 2; Nonnus XIII 376 (cf. also Ptolemy, *Geog.* IV 5,12); moreover, by the frequency of the proper name *Βάκαλ* in Cyrenaica (*SEG* IX 1,81; 64, 89, 92; 181,4; 348,152; it may be a slave name: L. Gasperini, *QAL* XII (1988), 412–13): cf. O. Masson, *AntAfr* X (1976), 59; id., *MH* XLI (1984), 139–42. A relation with *bqn* in Ramessid inscription is not implausible: see Bates, pp. 47–8; J. Osing, in *LdÄ* III, col. 1017. They were settled on the western side of the Jabal al-Akhdar: Tauchira, renamed Arsinoe in Ptolemaic times, corresponds to modern-day Tocra (Tūkrah); founded by Cyrene according to the scholium to Pindar, *Pyth.* 4,15, it has in fact revealed materials datable to as early as between 630 and 590 BC, which cast doubt over this report: see Boardman, opt. cit., pp. 153–5; id. and J. Hayes, *Excavations at Tocra 1963–1965*, I, London 1966; J. Boardman and J. Mayer, *Excavations at Tocra 1963–1965*, II, London 1973; *PECS*, p. 886; Haider, pp. 35–7; on the name, Dobias-Lalou, p. 285.

172,1. *Νασαμῶνες*: to the important Nasamonian people, already mentioned at II 32, Herodotus dedicates a small ethnographic treatise arranged by headings (cf. Trüdinger, p. 26; note to chs. 59–82). Attacked by Domitian in 85/86 and still reported in the *Tabula Peutingeriana*, the Nasamonians are present also in ancient poetical geography and in myth: the eponymous Nasamon is the son of Garamas according to Apollonius Rhodius IV 1492. The name may be linked to that of the god Ammon; see Desanges, *Pline*, pp. 369–71. They were nomads who roamed between the eastern and southern coasts of the greater Syrtis and the oasis of Augila (Awjlah, still full of palms today: Theophr., *Hist. Plant.* IV 3,1 and note on ch. 182). In the oasis they may have exacted a tribute in kind from local subject peoples (Gsell, *Hérodote*, pp. 124–6; Desanges, *Catalogue*, pp. 152–4). A possible allusion to the herds along the coast tended by isolated herdsmen in Apollonius Rhodius IV 1496–501; see E. Livrea, *QAL* XII (1988), 187. On transhumance in the region see Bates, pp. 91–2; D. L. Johnson, *The Nature of Nomadism*, Chicago 1969; A. Laronde, *LibyStud* XX (1989), 131; Colin, pp. 40–87.
ἀττελέβους: locusts are extremely frequent in northern Africa; according to Dioscorides II 52 they were part of the diet of the inhabitants of the region around Lepcis, as well as of the Acridophagi in Ethiopia, and are still included in the diet of various peoples of the Sahara: Gsell, *Hérodote*, pp. 176–7; id., *Histoire* I, pp. 135–7; Lhote, pp. 112 f.; Colin, pp. 85–7.
2. *γυναῖκας … ἐξ οἴκου*: the similarity to the Massagetae (I 216,1) consists in the sharing of women, and in the custom of indicating the intention to lie with a woman by planting an object, whether a quiver or a stick, in front of her dwelling (also cf. Strabo XIV 4,25 on Arabs). However, the system prescribed polygamous marriage, typical among nomadic peoples; the custom according to which the bride lies with several members of the community finds parallels in various

contexts (cf. Mela I 46; Diod. V 18; discussion in Gsell, *Hérodote*, pp. 194–6; S. Pembroke, *JWI* XXX (1967), 12–18; V. Andò, Φιλίας χάριν. *Miscellanea di studi classici in onore di E. Manni*, I, Rome 1980, pp. 94–5; see note to 168,2).

3. ὁρκίοισι... χρᾶται: the worship of ancestors and the custom of swearing by the tombs of illustrious men are still alive in the Berber world: see Gsell, *Hérodote*, pp. 183–4; Picard, pp. 18–21; Decret–Fantar, pp. 257–9; Camps, *Berbères*, pp. 233–42. Also the practice of divination by incubation in the tombs of ancient ancestors (cf. Heraclides Ponticus, fr. 134 Wehrli; Mela I 46; Pliny, *NH* V 45) is widespread among the Tuareg: see Bates, pp. 318–22; Gsell, *Hérodote*, pp. 184–5; Camps, *Aux origines*, pp. 191–3, 557–9; id., *SS* VII (1985), 55–8 (with archaeological evidence, on which cf. also M. Luni, *QAL* XII (1988), 454–6; Luni, pp. 193–200); Vycichl, in *Wörterbuch der Myth.* I 2, pp. 685–6.

4. πίστισι... λείχουσι: for a persistence of this custom in the 18th cent. see Gsell, *Hérodote*, p. 183, n. 5.

173. Ψύλλοι: Hecataeus spoke of a 'Gulf of the Psylli', meaning perhaps the greater Syrtis (*FGrHist* I F 303); and Herodotus follows his source in mentioning the Psylli though he considers them to have become extinct (cf. 17,2 and 105,1; Introduction, p. 568). As a matter of fact many later authors continue to mention the Psylli as still inhabiting the Syrtis or the interior (see e.g. Strabo XVII 3,23) and as being famous snake-charmers (e.g. Lucan IX 893 ff.; cf. Gsell, *Histoire* I, p. 133, n. 1). The legend told by Herodotus (cf. Gellius XVI 11,4–8) belongs to a series of tales about caravans, armies, or peoples swallowed up by the *ghibli*, and by sandstorms (cf. III 26 and note), and may conceal a conquest on the part of the Nasamonians (thus Pliny, *NH* VII 14) which left some survivors: see Gsell, *Hérodote*, pp. 126–8; Desanges, *Catalogue*, pp. 155–6. The idea of the war against the wind, reported with scepticism, may also be linked to the conception of the winds as divine forces attested by Mela I 8, which is still alive among the Berbers (cf. Bates, pp. 174–6; Vycichl, *Wörterbuch der Myth.* I 2, pp. 697–8). See now Colin, pp. 161–215.

174. Γαράμαντες: neither the position nor the characterization of this people matches those of the warlike Garamantes in ch. 183. Stephanus of Byzantium, s. v., and Eustathius, *Comm. in Dionysii Periegetica* 217, *GGM* II, pp. 254–5, also read Γαράμαντες; but Mela, I 47 and Pliny, *NH* V 45 refer the same information as reported by Herodotus to a people called *Gamphasantes*, so that it is not impossible that the Herodotean codices may have changed an original Γαμφάσαντες to a more obvious reading: see Bähr, ad loc.; Neumann, *Nordafrika*, pp. 21–3; Gsell, *Hérodote*, p. 128; Desanges, *Catalogue*, pp. 91–2 (Windberg, pp. 55–6, on the other hand, thought of a divergence in the sources). They are the only people whom Herodotus mentions in the region inhabited by beasts (see note to chs. 168–99), and they must be located south of the Syrtis (but see Desanges, *Catalogue*, 92 for a location in the neighbourhood of Ghadāmis). Their isolated and pacific character can be compared to that of the Argippaei (ch. 23), and the report may be influenced by elaboration in a utopian direction. At root there is perhaps the absence of relations with the neighbouring peoples, owing to the beasts which infested the region (cf. Desanges, *Pline*, pp. 473–4).

175,1. Μάκαι: the Macae (cf. V 42,3) inhabited the western coasts of the Syrtis: according to Scylax 109, *GGM* I, pp. 84–5, from its southernmost point (near the 'altars of the Phileni' close by Râs Lānūf) up to the river Cinyps near Neapolis/ Leptis Magna, which must be identified with wadi Khaam, between Khums and Zlitan (Gsell, *Hérodote*, pp. 89–91; cf. also IV 198,2 and V 42,2). In actual fact the wadi Khaam is longer than 200 stades (= 35–40 km.), so that it is difficult to locate the 'hill of the Charites' mentioned also by Callimachus, fr. 673 Pfeiffer. The Macae were transhumant nomads (Scylax 109, *GGM* I, p. 85), and are still mentioned at the beginning of the 6th cent. AD (*SEG* IX 356 and 414): see Gsell, *Hérodote*, p. 129; Desanges, *Catalogue*, pp. 106–7; id., *Pline*, pp. 375–6; for an archaeological reconnaissance, R. Rebuffat, *CRAI* (1982), 188–99. The toponym *Macomades* may be reminiscent of their name; see, however, A. M. Bisi Ingrassia, *QAL* IX (1977), 129–31.   **λόφους ... ἐν χροΐ:** the hairstyles of the Libyans attract the attention of Herodotus also at chs. 168, 180, and 191. Bas-reliefs on rock-faces and Egyptian depictions do, in fact, attribute to the Libyans various unusual hairstyles, which may have acted as tribal markers. In Tertullian's day some Numidians still grew a single crest on an otherwise shaven head (*De Pallio* 4; cf. also the Hermes in the Baths of Antoninus at Carthage), whilst parallels are not lacking among modern Berbers: see Neumann, p. 132; Bates, pp. 133–7; Gsell, *Hérodote*, pp. 162–3; S. Ferri, *Atti del III Congresso di Studi Coloniali*, Florence 1937, pp. 162–7.   **στρουθῶν ... δορὰς:** an example of shield made of the skin of an ostrich, probably of Saharan origin, is preserved at Lagos; see H. M. Currie, *RhM* CV (1962), 283–4 (S. Stucchi, *QAL* VIII (1976), 32–3, is not entirely convincing). On the presence of ostriches in the region see note to 192,2.

176. Γινδᾶνές: the Gindanes are otherwise known only to Stephanus of Byzantium, s.v., who associates them with the Lotophagi, directly following; they must be located in north-western Tripolitania (Gsell, *Hérodote*, p. 130; Desanges, *Catalogue*, p. 97). Can the name be related to the anthroponym Γιλδαν, from the Libyan-Berber root *GLD* = 'king' (cf. O. Masson, *AntAfr* X (1976), 56)? On the polyandry of the women among the Gindanes, perhaps to be referred only to the stage before marriage (cf. e.g. V 6,1), see Gsell, *Hérodote*, p. 197; Andò, op. cit., p. 97; cf., also on anklets, the notes to ch. 168.

177. Λωτοφάγοι: the *Odyssey* talked of a 'lotus-eating' people: Odysseus came among them having been blown off course by a northerly wind as he was rounding Cape Malea (cf. ch. 179). The 'lotus' ('lotus of Cyrene' at II 96,1) is usually identified with wild lotus, *Zizyphus lotus* (sources—esp. Polybius XII 2— and discussion in Gsell, *Hérodote*, pp. 94–6; A. Steier, *RE* XIII 2 1927, coll. 1515–32). However, this plant is widespread throughout the North African coast, and was often confused with various more or less similar species (cf. B. Herzhoff, *Hermes*, CXII (1984), 257–71). As a result, post-Homeric authors located the Lotophagi in the most disparate regions, from Morocco to Cyrenaica; it is not easy to determine where exactly Herodotus placed them. According to several authors (e.g. Polybius I 39,2 and XXXIV 3,12; Strabo III 4,3 and XVII 3,17), some Lotophagi lived on the island of Meninx, modern-day

Jerba, and the promontory mentioned by Herodotus might then be that of Zarzis. But these Lotophagi may instead correspond to the Machlyans of ch. 178, who also eat lotus; whilst, on the other hand, Scylax 110, *GGM* I, pp. 85–6, talks of the Lotophagi extending from the greater to the lesser Syrtis, so that a more eastern location cannot be excluded (directly east of Tripolis according to R. Carpenter, *AJA* LX (1956), 234). See Gsell, *Hérodote*, pp. 130–1; Desanges, *Catalogue*, pp. 103–5; Dion, pp. 22–6; Desanges, *Pline*, pp. 267–9; Peretti, pp. 138–9, 229–31, 303 ff.

178. Μάχλυες: the Machlyans are still mentioned by Nicolaus of Damascus, *FGrHist* 90 F 103q, and by Pliny, *NH* VII 15 (cf. Stephanus of Byzantium, s.v. *Μάζυες*); perhaps they are the same as the *Μάχρυες* in Ptolemy, *Geog.* IV 3,6; see Gsell, *Hérodote*, pp. 131–3; Desanges, *Catalogue*, pp. 107–8. Their name may derive from a root *MKR, MGR*, 'to be large' (O. Masson, *AntAfr* X (1976), 59). **Τρίτων ... Φλά:** like the Lotophagi, the river Triton and the Tritonis marsh, mythically linked to the adventures of the Argonauts, were variously located, from the Cyrenaica (e.g. Pherecydes, *FGrHist* 3 F 75; Strabo XVII 3,20), to the western extremity of Africa (Diod. III 53–5): as in the case of the Hesperides, of the Lotophagi, and of Atlas, the ancient legends were moved to different locations as more knowledge was acquired (see notes to chs. 171, 177 and 184,1). At any rate, Herodotus places the 'Tritonis marsh' in the neighbourhood of the lesser Syrtis (of which he is unaware, cf. note to chs. 186–90); the sheet of water cannot be the Chott al Jerid, which was never connected to the sea in historic times, but rather it is either the Gulf of Gabès (Gsell, *Hérodote*, pp. 77–84) or it must be more specifically identified with the Gulf of Bou Grara between Jerba and the mainland (e.g. Peretti, pp. 311–33): sources, bibl., and discussion in J. Peyras, and P. Trousset, *AntAfr* XXIV (1988), 149–204. Cf. now Coppola, pp. 121–38. The island of Phla, otherwise unknown (Stephanus of Byzantium, s.v. *Φίλα*, locates it in Egypt confusing it with island of Philes on the Nile), would then be Jerba; it is more difficult to locate the river Triton among the *widian* of the area (wadi bou Ahmed? wadi el Hallouf?). **ταύτην ... κτίσαι:** the report of the oracle may have been linked to the saga of the Argonauts (see note to 179,1), and perhaps to the enterprise of Dorieus (V 42); see A. von Stauffenberg, *Historia*, IX (1960), 185.

179,1. Ἰήσονα: with a certain amount of caution, introducing it as a tale narrated by others, Herodotus furnishes a version of the myth of the Argonauts in Libya. Another version is known from Pindar, *Pyth.* 4: a god in the form of Eurypylus entrusts to Euphemus (see note to 150,2) a clod of earth; from Euphemus, through Lemnos and Sparta, will spring the founder of Thera, Battus (cf. also Apollonius Rhodius IV 1223 ff.; Lycophron, *Alexandra* 877 ff.). In contrast with the Pindaric tradition, which, being located in Cyrenaica (cf. note to 178), aimed at justifying Therean colonization and the rights of the Battiadae, Herodotus sets the episode in the lesser Syrtis, dispenses with any reference to a previous colonization, and is perhaps not lacking in irony in mentioning the hiding of the tripod. It is difficult to tell whether he is drawing on an older tradition, not yet affected by Battiad propaganda, or whether he is reflecting new aims of the

Greeks in the West, to which also Dorieus' attempt testifies (see now P. Vannicelli, *QUCC* ns XLI (1992), 69–71, who highlights the role of Sparta; on the hypothesis that Epimenides was used as a model, G. L. Huxley, *Greek Epic Poetry from Eumelos to Panyassis*, London 1969, p. 81; cf. Dion, pp. 43–64). Moreover, some have suggested that this complex of legends may preserve the memory of Mycenean contacts; see, among others, Studniczka; Malten; Chamoux, pp. 83–9; Haider, pp. 145–9; Braswell, pp. 6–23, 89–117; cf. note to chs. 145–67. Triton may be the Greek translation of a local divinity; see note to 180, 2–5. ἄλλην τε...χάλκεον: cf. Diod. IV 56; on the hecatomb at Delphi see note to 150,2. The tripod (a typical offer in the treasuries, cf. 152,4) assumes the meaning of a symbol of possession, like the clod of earth in Pindar, *Pyth.* 4: see N. Strosetzki, *Hermes*, LXXXVI (1958), 1–17; L. Gernet, *The Anthropology of Ancient Greece*, Baltimore 1981, pp. 79–80, 89–90.

2. ὡς πλέοντα...Μαλέην: the storm at Cape Malea which blows ships out into the open sea and towards the coasts of Libya was a commonplace in the literature of the *nostoi* (cf. *Od.* III 287 ff., IV 514 ff., IX 80 ff., XIX 187 ff.; Herod. II 113,1; Euripides, *Cyc.* 18 ff.; Apollonius Rhodius IV 1232 ff.; A. Momigliano, *SIFC* VIII (1930), 318). In fact, the northerly and north-easterly winds, which are dominant during the summer in the Mediterranean (the 'etesiae'), could easily blow ships off their course and carry them to the African coasts, as several historical episodes testify (in Herodotus, as well as IV 151–2 and 164 see VII 168; also Thuc. VII 50,2; Plut. *Dio* 22–5; V. Purcaro Pagano, *QAL* VIII (1976), 258–9). Hence the proverb on the dangerousness of Cape Malea in Strabo VII 16,2; cf. Athenaeus II 36 f. βράχεσι: between the Gulf of Gabès, the island of Jerba, and the Gulf of Bou Grara there are various sandbanks (*Portolano del Mediterraneo* II B, Genoa 1987, pp. 251–60), and Jerba is called 'island of the shallows' (νῆσος ἧ ὄνομα Βραχείων) in Scylax 110, *GGM* I, p. 86 (cf. Polybius I 39,2–4). Sandbanks are not lacking also in the area of Bengazi, the other region where the myth was set (see note to ch. 178; *Portolano del Mediterraneo* III, Genoa 1982, p. 44).   καὶ οἱ ἀπορέοντι... ἀποστελέειν: Triton comes to represent the typical figure of the 'old man of the sea', who, like Proteus in *Od.* IV 382 ff., or Nereus in Pherecydes, *FGrHist* 3 F 16a, helps to overcome a difficulty by indicating a route and has prophetic powers: cf. M. Detienne and J.-P. Vernant, *Cunning Intelligence in Greek Culture and Society*, Chicago–London, 1991, pp. 107–30.

180,1. τούτων...τὰ ἔμπροσθε: the Auseans are otherwise known only to Stephanus of Byzantium, s.v.; the *Tabula Peutingeriana* reports a river *Ausere* a little further to the south-east, by Neffatia: see Desanges, *Catalogue*, p. 81; cf. notes to 175,1 and 191,1.

2–5. ὀρτῆ...θυγατέρα: the ritual fight (cf. Mela I 36) finds paralles at Caesarea in Mauretania in the age of Augustine (*De Doc. Christ.* IV 24,53), and subsequently among the Berbers (Gsell, *Hérodote*, pp. 191–2; Decret–Fantar, pp. 248–50). Especially close to it was the 'feast of salt' celebrated in Ghāt, in the Fezzan, until a few decades ago, which included a war-dance among women and an inspection of virginity (Camps, *Berbères*, pp. 207–8; id., *SS* VII (1985), 51–2).

The procession and the battle constituted perhaps a rite of initiation and purification, with the undertones of an ordeal: see S. Ribichini, *Studi storico-religiosi*, II (1978), 39–60; A. Mastrocinque, *Politica e religione nel primo scontro tra Roma e l'Oriente*, Milan 1982, pp. 61–4; Mora, p. 69; A. Brelich, *Guerre, agoni e culti nella Grecia arcaica*, Bonn 1961. Herodotus emphatically insists on the indigenous nature of the goddess celebrated, perhaps opposing a theory which posited a Greek origin. Clearly she was an armed virgin goddess linked to the world of the waters, similar to the Egyptian Neith or to the Punic Astarte, and could therefore be assimilated to Athena (cf. ch. 189; see, among others, Gsell, *Hérodote*, pp. 187–91; Vycichl, *Wörterbuch der Myth.* I, 2, pp. 607 and 655). The traditional epithet Τριτογένεια contributed in the linking of Athena with Triton and his lake (on the meaning of the epithet, very uncertain, bibl. in *Hesiod: Theogony*, ed. M. L. West, Oxford 1966, p. 404, and J. Taillardat, *RPh* LXIX (1995), 283–8; on Athena and Triton, Paus. IX 33, 7; Apollodorus III 12,3; C. Bearzot, op. cit., pp. 43–60). On their part, Triton and Poseidon must have been local divinities of the waters (cf. II 50,2–3; Polybius VII 9,2): the worship of waters is still widespread among the Berbers; cf. R. Basset, *RHR* (1910), 299–300; Picard, pp. 14–5; Vycichl, *Wörterbuch der Myth.* I 2, pp. 657–8, 661–2, 691–2; Decret–Fantar, pp. 243–7; M. Fantar, *L'Homme méditerranéen et la mer*, Tunis 1985, pp. 411–18; Beschaouch, ibid., pp. 419–24; S. Ben Baaziz, ibid., pp. 425–36.   πρὶν δὲ...

Ἔλληνας: the reasoning is not entirely clear. Perhaps Herodotus is stating that the girls carried in procession (to impersonate the goddess; cf. I 60) are made to wear weapons of Greek origin; and, in order not to weaken his theory on the indigenous origin of the cult, he is concerned to explain in an aside that the ritual already existed before the arrival of the Greeks, but the Libyans must evidently have made use of Egyptian weapons, which already existed at that time since they were the model for the Greek ones. Also Plato speaks of an Egyptian origin for Greek weapons, *Tim.* 24,8: in actual fact, the typical Egyptian shield, oblong in shape, was different from the circular Greek shield, which was of Eastern derivation, although the latter appears in Egypt as early as the 14th cent. BC with the 'peoples of the sea'; whilst the helms testify contacts with the Near East (cf. *Archaeologia Homerica*, I E, Göttingen 1977, pp. 9–10, 30–1, 57–74), and the 'Corinthian' helm, which was provided with protection for nose and cheeks, was typically Greek and linked to hoplite warfare (see E. Kunze, *VII. Bericht über die Ausgrabungen in Olympia*, Berlin 1961, pp. 56–128). At any rate, Herodotus' consideration is not necessarily contradictory with the idea that the apparel of the Greek statues of Athena was inspired by that of Libyan women (ch. 189); whether the Auseans and the Machlyans did actually buy weapons from Greek colonists (which would be easier to explain nearby Cyrenaica; see note to ch. 178 and S. Stucchi, *QAL* XII (1988), 204, n. 18), or whether Herodotus misunderstood a source which did no more than observe some similarities between the Greek and the Libyan cults, remains uncertain.

5–6. μεῖξιν ... νομίζεται: sexual promiscuity 'like beasts' (cf. I 203,2; III 101,1; Marco Polo, *Divisament dou monde* 62,12–13 = *Milione* 61,10–1; *The Travels of Marco Polo*, London 1958, p. 92) is not easily reconciled with the preservation of virginity presupposed in the feasts in honour of Athena, unless it is explained as the indication of a particular form of marriage organization (Gsell, *Hérodote*, pp. 193–4). This negative connotation (cf. note to 168,2) hides perhaps a system of polyandry (S. Pembroke, *JWI* XXX (1967), 10–11), or a system of kinship in which the wife of an individual has the value of a 'wife' for the group as a whole (Ribichini, art. cit., 42, n. 12). Patrilinear descent is in any case safeguarded by the criterion of physical resemblance (cf. Aristotle, *Pol.* II 4, 1262a14–24, who draws on this passage or a parallel passage; Mela I 45, and Pliny, *NH* V 45, on the Garamantes; Nicolaus of Damascus, *FGrHist* 90 F 103d, on the Libourni). Cf. note to 168,2.

181–5. Having reached the western border of the coastal region inhabited by nomads, Herodotus moves on to consider the interior. The division in three strips from the coast to the desert, already indicated in II 32, is schematic, but founded on reality (see e.g. Bunbury I, pp. 274–6; Neumann, *Nordafrika*, pp. 5–11; Lloyd, *Commentary 1–98*, pp. 135–7). Here, the desert is limited by a 'sand bank' which allegedly stretches from Thebes in Egypt to the Pillars of Heracles and beyond (185,1; Pritchett, pp. 129–32), punctuated at regular intervals of 10 days' walk by 'salt hills', listed one after the other with the typical formulaic language of the *periegesis*. These hills are nothing other than oases (cf. III 26): Herodotus' erroneous conception of them may derive from his awareness of the generally high salinity of the Saharan territories (cf. ch. 185) and of the salty quagmires (*sabkha*) in the inner parts of the coast, as well as perhaps of the presence of calcareous plaques in many oases; but it may also result from the preconception that water-springs normally flow from highlands (Neumann, pp. 5–9). Moreover, the regular disposition along a line which cuts the whole of northern Libya is the result of extrapolation and extension of known data, which becomes more arbitrary in the less well known westernmost section (cf. Windberg, pp. 86–7; Gsell, *Hérodote*, pp. 102–5). The image of the 'bank' (literally 'brow': cf. L. Robert, *Hellenica* II, Paris 1946, p. 138) to indicate the line of depressions to the southern border of Marmarica between Egypt and Augila is not inappropriate, and the actual existence of a Saharan caravan route which reached from Egypt to at least as far the Fezzan is credible: see, among others, Gsell, *Histoire* I, pp. 56–68; J. Leclant, *BIFAO* XLIX (1950), 193–253 (esp. pp. 240–3); R. Carpenter, *AJA* LX (1956), 231–42; R. Rebuffat, *Libya Antiqua* VI–VII (1969–70), 181–7; id., *Studi Magrebini*, III (1970), 1–20; M. Luni, *QAL* XI (1980), 130–7; A. Laronde, in *Cyrenaica*, pp. 199–206; M. Liverani, *JESHO* XLIII (2000), 496–520 (in general, on oases between Egypt and the Sahara in antiquity see P. Trousset, *L'Eau et les hommes en Méditerranée*, Paris 1987, pp. 25–41; L. L. Giddy, *Egyptian Oases: Baharyia, Dakhla, Farafra and Kharga During Pharaonic Times*, Warminster 1987; G. Wagner, *Les Oasis d'Egypte à l'époque greque, romaine et byzantine, d'après les documents grecs*, Cairo 1987).

181,3–4. ὕδωρ κρηναῖον … ἠλίου: the first oasis starting for Egypt is that of Siwa, the site of the famous temple of Ammon: see Lloyd, *Commentary 1–98*, pp. 195–8; note on II 42,5; note on III 26,2. But the town of Thebes (Karnak) is a lot more than 10 day's journey away (900 km. corresponding to about a month): the information is unrealistically schematic, but Θῆβαι may also be understood to mean Thebais, as in II 15,3, and we may think of a route which reached Sîwa from lower Egypt, perhaps by way of Baharîya (discussion in Leclant, art. cit., pp. 240–2). The spring of the Sun was well known in antiquity: cf., among others, Diod. XVII 50; Curtius Rufus IV 7,22; Arrian, *Anab.* III 4,2; Lucretius VI 841 ff.; Ovid, *Met.* XV 309–10; Mela I 39; Pliny, *NH* II 228. It must be identified with 'Ain el-ḥammām, a source still active which, by its constant temperature (29°C), creates the impression described by Herodotus by contrast with the variations of the external temperature: see Gsell, *Hérodote*, pp. 105–7; Vycichl, *Wörterbuch der Myth.* I 2, p. 678 (for similar phenomena, cf. also Pliny, *NH* V 36; Augustine, *De Civ. Dei* XXI 5). For the wholly paratactic syntax of the description, cf. Homer, *Il.* VI 148.

182. Αὔγιλα: the complex of oases which includes Augila (Awjilah) is in fact situated some 10 days west of Siwa, along a track which runs through Giarabub (Jaghbūb) and was used also in modern times. The locality was well known to the ancients (cf. Mela I 23 and 46; Pliny, *NH* V 26–7, 43, 45, somewhat confused; Ptolemy, *Geog.* IV 5,12–13; Gsell, *Hérodote*, pp. 146–7): see, among others, Neumann, *Nordafrika*; Leclant, art. cit., p. 242; on the name, W. Vycichl, *Muséon*, LXXXVI (1973), 175–8.

183,1. ἀπὸ δὲ ... ἰσχυρῶς: after some 10 days walk west of Awjilah (Pliny, *NH* V 26, speaks of 12 days), one comes to the oasis of Zallah, or to the neighbourhood of Waddan and Suknah. These last two localities are situated on a road, known also to Ptolemy (*Geog.* I 10,2), that runs from Tripolitania to the Fezzan bypassing the Hamadah al Hamra, and which perhaps corresponded to 30 days' track that led from the land of the Lotophagi to the Garamantes. The 'very large' people of the Garamantes of whom Herodotus speaks can thus be located in a vast territory including the oases of the Fezzan, but whose north-eastern extremity was the area of Zallah linked with Awjilah: see Gsell, *Hérodote*, pp. 147–50; R. Rebuffat, *Libya Antiqua*, VI–VII (1969–70), 181–7; id., *Studi Magrebini*, III (1970), 1–20. The Garamantes, for whom a descent from a Garamas, son of Acacallis, daughter of Minos (Apollonius Rhodius IV 1489–94) was imagined, are known throughout antiquity as the inhabitants of the Fezzan and of the neighbouring areas, whence they probably controlled the trade with the interior of Africa. In Pliny's day (*NH* V 26) and in Ptolemy's (*Geog.* IV 16,2), their capital was Garama, modern-day Jarmah, where excavations have demonstrated occupation from the 5th–4th cents. BC: see, among others, Gsell, *Hérodote*, pp. 150–1; Desanges, *Catalogue*, p. 93–6; Ch. Daniels, *The Garamantes of Southern Libya*, Stoughton 1970; G. Caputo, in Φιλίας χάριν. *Miscellanea di studi classici in onore di E. Manni*, II, Rome 1980, pp. 377–94; E. M. Ruprechtsberger, *Die Garamanten*, Zurich 1989 (supplement to *AW* XX (1989)); Ch. Daniels, *LibyStud* XX (1989), 45–61; D. J. Mattingly *et al.*, *Libya Antiqua*, NS III (1997), 175–99; IV (1998), 219–49. **ἐπὶ τὸν ἅλα ... σπείρουσι:** the Garamantes probably covered the dry saline land with humid soil taken from the bottom of the *widian*, as was customary for a long time in the Fezzan (cf. e.g. G. F. Lyon, *Narrative of Travels in Northern Africa*, London 1821, p. 271): Gsell, *Hérodote*, p. 172; R. Carpenter, *AJA* LX (1956), 235.

2. οἱ ὀπισθονόμοι βόες: for other sources, see *Pomponii Melae de chorographia libri tres*, ed. P. Parroni, Rome 1984, pp. 214–15. In partial confirmation of this singular report can be cited the rock-face paintings of the Tassili n'Ajjer, where there appear various figures of oxen with horns pointing frontward or even downward, parallel to the muzzle. When grazing, they must really have moved backwards; or perhaps the representations (no doubt more ancient than the 5th cent. BC) gave rise to the legend: cf. Carpenter, art. cit., p. 235; G. Camps, *SS* VII (1985), 44–5.

4. οἱ Γαράμαντες ... ἀκούομεν: the use of bigae and quadrigae on the part of the peoples of the Sahara has received impressive confirmations from various paintings and rock-face incisions of the so-called 'Equidian' culture, widespread in particular in the Tassili n'Ajjer and in the Fezzan: see, above all, Graziosi; G. Camps and M. Gast, *Les Chars préhistoriques du Sahara. Archéologie et techniques d'attelage*, Aix-en-Provence 1982; H. Lhote, *Les Chars rupestres sahariens*, Toulouse 1982; H. Hayen, *Achse, Rad und Wagen. 5000 Jahre Kultur- und Technikgeschichte*, Göttingen 1986, pp. 80–4; G. Camps, *AntAfr* XXV (1989), 11–40. Imported perhaps from Egypt, chariots were used by the dominant Libyans, Europoids of Mediterranean origin and ancestors of the Berbers, who in the 2nd millennium imposed themselves on a substratum of melanodermic populations (see J. Desanges, *GHA* II, pp. 432–3; Camps, *Berbères*, pp. 56–72; id., *Mélanges E. Delebecque*, Aix-en-Provence 1983, pp. 43–59; cf. note to chs. 168–99). Analysis of osteological finds in the Fezzan has in fact revealed how, already in antiquity, there was coexistence between different ethnic groups (G. Sergi, *Monumenti dell' Accademia dei Lincei*, XLI (1951), coll. 443–556). The 'Ethiopian' (i.e. black or negroid, see note to 197,2) τρωγοδύται represent a subjugated ethnic group, to be identified perhaps with the ancestors of the modern melanodermic farmers of the oases and of the Tebu of the Tibesti, who to this day are famously good runners (a general picture in P. Fuchs, *Sahara: 10.000 Jahre zwischen Weide und Wüste*, Cologne 1978, pp. 136–7 and in J. Chapelle, *Nomades Noirs du Sahara*, Paris 1982, pp. 33–7): see Gsell, *Hérodote*, pp. 151–4; Desanges, *Catalogue*, pp. 139–40 (with the other ancient sources); Desanges, *Pline*, pp. 470–1; on the frequency of running-scenes in the representations on rock-faces, J. Tschudi, *Pitture rupestri del Tasili degli Azger (Sahara Algerino)*, Florence 1955, p. 31. The variant τρωγλοδύται, 'who enter into holes', though it is appropriate for a reptile-hunting people, is suspect and probably due to popular etymology, and Herodotus does not say explicitly that they were 'troglodytes': on troglodytic architecture in the whole of northern Africa see, however, Decret–Fantar, pp. 40–2.   σιτέονται ... ἑρπετῶν: a diet based on reptiles is anything but rare in the Sahara; see Lhote; cf. chs. 191–2.

γλῶσσαν ... νυκτερίδες: the comparison of their voices with the squeaking of bats can find a confirmation in the unusual sounds of the language of the Tebu, but is to some extent conventional: the Greeks normally likened foreign languages to the sounds of birds (cf. II 57; *Aeschylus Agamemnon* II, ed. E. Fraenkel, Oxford 1950, p. 447), and the expression is modelled on Homer, *Od.* XXIV 6–7 (cf. also III 110; Aly, p. 134; on τρίζω, M. Bettini, *Antropologia e cultura romana*, Rome 1986, pp. 228–35; also πόδας τάχιστοι betrays the influence of the Homeric πόδας ταχύς).

184,1. ἀπὸ δὲ Γαραμάντων: after the Fezzan, the subsequent stops of the caravan route are more obscure (cf. Neumann, *Nordafrika*, pp. 114–23; Fehling, p. 162). Following a more or less westerly direction, the first group of Atlantes (or Atarantes) may be located in the region of Ghadhāmis (Gsell, *Hérodote*, p. 155, n. 4) or in the Tassili n'Ajjer (e.g. H. Lhote, *Revue Africaine*, XCVIII (1954), 62–4). The report of a Mt. Atlas of which the peak is never visible created problems already for the ancients (see Paus. I 32,5), and is influenced by the legend of the 'pillars of the sky'. Herodotus may perhaps be correct in attributing this legend to the local inhabitants (cf. Mela III 95; Pliny, *NH* V 7; Maximus of Tyre VIII 7; Martianus Capella, *De nuptiis Merc. et Phil.* VI 667; R. Basset, *RHR* (1910), 291–5; Vycichl, *Wörterbuch der Myth.* I 11, pp. 667, 693–4; Desanges, *Pline*, pp. 101–3); but it was widespread also in the east (cf. e.g. the itinerary of Sargon: Herzfeld, pp. 226–7), and, in connection with the figure of the giant Atlas, in Greece (see esp. *Od.* I 52–4; Hesiod, *Theog.*, 517–19). The pillar, or pillars, were soon located in the extreme west, as in the cases of the Hesperides, of the Lotophagi, and of Triton (see U. von Wilamowitz-Moellendorff, *Euripides Herakles*, III, Darmastadt 1959³, pp. 94–100; Haider, pp. 147–52); and like these (see notes to chs. 171, 177, and 178), they too were probably moved to different locations as more knowledge was acquired (cf. Frau, and note to 43,4). Thus Herodotus' indication, though it may be founded on some true facts, is, at least in part, a rationalization of the legend. Herodotus' Mt Atlas is in any case located further east than the mountain which still today is called Atlas and the 'Atlantic Sea' of which he speaks in I 202,4 (on the diffusion of the name 'Atlas' and its derivatives, especially in Diod. III 56–61, see F. Chamoux, *QAL* XII (1988), 57–65). It is possible to think that Herodotus heard reports of some oasis in the Hoggar whose name was reminiscent of that of the Atlas, and that he described this massif in the terms of the legend (cf. Pritchett, p. 50); R. Carpenter, *AJA* LX (1956), 236–7, has suggested that Herodotus may have inserted in his framework, with a 'bank' running east–west, a caravan route which in actual fact turned southwards past the Fezzan and, touching the Tibesti, passed along the peak of Toussidé in the massif of Tarsus (north-western Chad), which is to be identified with the Atlas itself. Other sources and discussion in Gsell, *Hérodote*, pp. 107–10, 154–5; Desanges, *Catalogue*, pp. 253–4; id., *Pline*, pp. 466–9.   τοῖσι οὔνομά ἐστι Ἀτάραντες: Ἄτλαντες mss, and the name *Atlantes* is found also in Mela I 43, who confuses under the name the traits of this people and of the following one; but it is unlikely that the two groups were homonymous, and the emendation Ἀτάραντες suggested by Salmasius is rendered convincing by the comparison with Stephanus of Byzantium, s.v. Ἄτλαντες (which distinguishes between Ἄτλαντες and Ἀτάραντες: but the text is confused; cf. Rhianus, *FGrHist* 265 F 2, with

F. Jacoby's commentary), and with Nicolaus of Damascus *FGrHist* 90 F 103u (where the ms tradition offers corrupt readings which, however, point rather to Ἀτάραντες than to Ἄτλαντες). The name has been connected to the Berber *adrar* = 'mountain': Adrar is also the name of the Tuareg in southern Algeria; for a derivation from *ataram* = 'west' see, however, F. Beguinot, *Mémorial H. Basset*, Paris 1928, pp. 20–42. The report of the absence of personal names might stem from a reluctance to make known one's name in order to avoid falling victim to spells (Gsell, *Hérodote*, 192–3), or else to the existence of a taboo on the name of the head of the family on the part of its members, attested among the Tebu and in western Algeria (Carpenter, art. cit., p. 237). The curse against the sun when it rises high above their heads (this interpretation of ὑπερβάλλοντι is perhaps preferable to the meaning 'excessive'; cf. Nicolaus of Damascus *FGrHist* 90 F 103u; Strabo XVII 2,3; Diod. III 9,2; according to Mela I 43, and Pliny, *NH* V 44, the sun was cursed also when it set) are understandable in the climatic conditions of the Sahara, but Herodotus wants above all to report a curious anecdote, perhaps as a source of hilarity (see *Ippocrate, Arie Acque Luoghi*, ed. Bottin, Venice 1986, p. 14); cf. ch. 173. See now Vanhaegendoren.

4. καλέονται γὰρ δὴ Ἄτλαντες: also Ἄτλας and Ἄτλαντες may be hellenizations of a form close to *adrar* (cf. Δύρις in Strabo XVII 2,3; W. Steinhauser, *Glotta*, XXV (1936), 229–38; reservations in W. Vycichl, *RSO* XXXI (1956), 211–20). In any case, it is possible that a local name offered the cue for a connection with the legend of Atlas and of the pillars of the sky. The vegetarian diet of the Atlantes may correspond to the diet of the oases, which is based mainly on dates (Neumann, *Nordafrika*, pp. 122–3). The report of the absence of dreams is legendary, and perhaps linked to the unusual diet: on the relation between diet and dreams, already postulated by the Pythagoreans, cf. e.g. Plato, *Resp.* IX 571c–572b; Aristotle, *De Som. et Vig. et Div. Per Somt.*; Plutarch, *Quaes. Conv.* 686a–b; Tertullian, *De Anima* 48; G. Guidorizzi, in O. Longo and P. Scarpi (eds.), *Homo edens*, Milan 1989, pp. 169–76. Thus Herodotus' Atlantes belong in the world of utopia, see Bichler, p. 41 and n. 96.

185,1–3. μέχρι μὲν ... οὐδέν: Herodotus indicates the limits of his knowledge, but shows himself convinced that the 'bank' continues beyond the Pillars of Heracles: this is an eloquent proof of the element of generalization which is implicit in his description. Herodotus speaks once more of the 'bank' as a whole because this allows him to introduce the report of the houses made of salt, which is placed here because it has a comprehensive sense (thus e.g. Gsell, *Hérodote*, pp. 103–5, unlike most commentators, who see in it the indication of a another oasis beyond the Atlas): for the phrase διήκει ... οἰκέοντες picks up the statements at 181,2, and also the article in τῶν ἁλίνων χόνδρων must be explained as a reference to that chapter. The rocks of a large portion of the Sahara are generally saline, and actual salt-mines can be found in various localities, Siwa among them (the colour depends on the varying degree of purity). The use of salt as a building material, remarked also by Pliny, *NH* V 34, with its consequent dissolution on the rare occasions when it rains, finds parallels in modern times, cf. Neumann, pp. 88–91;

Gsell, *Hérodote*, p. 180; How–Wells, ad loc.; R. Carpenter, *AJA* LX (1956), 240–1; LXI (1957), 176–7 (Dancalian Desert); Lhote (In Salah, Agorgott, Taouden); Desanges, *Pline*, pp. 378–80. The description of the Sahara desert is perhaps a little too emphatic, but it confirms the fact that in the 5th cent. BC the desertification was complete: see in general *Sahara: 10.000 Jahre zwischen Weide und Wüste*, Cologne 1978.

186–90. Linking back to ch. 180, Herodotus sets out to tell of the peoples settled along the coast to the west of lake Triton, and of the Auseans: he relies on the linear description of a *periplus* and therefore he ignores the sinuosity of the lesser Syrtis and imagines the coast to be a straight line (on this tendency, cf. Janni, pp. 141–2). The river Triton is for him the line of demarcation between the nomadic Libyans to the east and the farming Libyans to the west. This distinction is normal in ancient geography (cf. chs. 18–19), and was already present in Hecataeus, *FGrHist* 1 F 335, who indicated as the boundary the otherwise unknown city of Megasa; but Herodotus is perhaps correcting Hecateus if the Μάζυες, who the latter terms as still nomads (*FGrHist* 1 F 334), correspond to the farming Μάξυες of ch. 191: see A. Grosskinsky, *Hermes*, LXVI (1931), 326–7. At any rate, the distinction between nomads and farmers, though a little strained, corresponds on the whole to reality. The absence of traces of settlements in the Libyan desert from the 4th millennium until Roman times is a proof of the nomadic nature of the peoples who lived there (see R. Rebuffat, *CRAI* (1982), 188–99); on the other hand, in the Maghreb a plough is still in use which does not derive from the Phoenicians or the Romans but whose origin must perhaps be attributed to the ancient Libyan farmers, while the proto-historic burials have yielded pottery, the mark of a sedentary style of life (G. Camps, *SS* VII (1985), 41–2). On the fortune of the term νομάδες, whence later came *Numidae*, see A. Luisi, *Conoscenze etniche e rapporti di convivenza nell'antichità*, Milan 1979, pp. 57–74. But before listing the farming peoples Herodotus devotes a brief *excursus* to the ethnography of the nomadic Lybians, describing with his customary method by headings (cf. note to chs. 59–82) those characters, common to all tribes, which required a general treatment: cf. Windberg, p. 61; F. Jacoby, *RE* VII 2 1912, col. 2728.

186,1. θηλέων... τρέφοντες: the breeding of pigs was incompatible with the nomadic lifestyle (cf. ch. 63), while the Greeks were accustomed to sacrificing and eating them (cf. note on II 47). On the other hand, abstention from cow's meat on the part of the Libyans was reminiscent of the Egyptian cult of Isis (see II 41). Although Herodotus does not say so explicitly, it is likely that the Libyans practised the cult of Isis, which they passed on to the women of Cyrene and Barce: perhaps they drew it from Egypt, but it cannot be excluded that the cult of a goddess-cow was in origin a common one to both Libyans and Egyptians. Hathor, the cow of Isis, does in fact display connections with the west and Libya; see J. Osing, *LdÄ* III, col. 1023; on the popularity of the cult of Isis in northern Africa in Carthaginian and Roman times, Decret–Fantar, pp. 43–4, 272–3.

2. βοῶν ... γεύονται: the existence of similar cult practices among the Libyans and the women of Barce and Cyrene is a further proof of the Libyan origin of the women married by the colonists (cf. chs. 153, 164, 168): also Pindar, *Pyth.* 9,105 ff. and Callimachus, *Apoll.* 85–7, allude to these mixed marriages, which are mentioned in the 4th cent. BC in *SEG* IX 1,2 ff., and the Libyan-Greek personal names to be found in both cities constitute a further confirmation (O. Masson, *AntAfr* X (1976), 52; R. C. C. Law, *CHA* II, pp. 114–16; L. Gasperini, *QAL* XII (1988), 404–5; Colin, pp. 128–39, with some nuances). Monthly fasts in honour of Isis 'of the ten thousand names' are mentioned in the Cyrenean sacred law of the 1st/2nd century AD edited by G. Oliverio, *QAL* IV (1961), 30, n. 10 (= *SEG* XX 721; cf. also *SEG* IX 192); and Isis is recognizable in some representations of goddesses dressed in Libyan fashion from Barce and Cyrene (see E. Fabbricotti, *QAL* XII (1988), 221–44, esp. p. 235; L. Bacchielli, ibid., pp. 482–7; the cult interfered in some way with that of Demeter; cf. II 59; D. White, ibid., pp. 79–84). That the women of Cyrene, in contrast with those of Barce (who were more markedly Libyan: see 160,1; 164,4), did not abstain from pork is confirmed by the remains of pig sacrifices in the extramural sanctuary of Demeter; cf. M. Luni, ibid., pp. 450–4; S. Ensoli Vittozzi, in *L'Africa romana*, X, Sassari 1992, pp. 167–250; Bonacasa–Ensoli, pp. 55–7 and 180; Luni, pp. 196–7. See now S. De Vido, in Grottanelli–Milano, pp. 91–113.

187,1. οὐκέτι ... ποιέειν: the emphatic negation is perhaps in polemic reply to different theories; see note to chs. 186–90.

2–3. οἱ γὰρ δὴ ... Λίβυες: the good health of the North African nomads (cf. II 77,3; Sallust, *Iug.* 17,6; the opposite view in *De Morbo Sacro* 1) is a fact and is consequent on the harsh selection operated during childhood by the difficult living conditions, the dry climate, and the basic diet (see e.g. Neumann, *Nordafrika*, pp. 126–7; Gsell, *Hérodote*, pp. 156–7). The use of cauterization is still attested in modern times in the whole of Africa (see e.g. Bates, p. 113). The practice had perhaps more of a magic-ritual value than a therapeutic one, and undoubtedly magical in character was the libation of the urine of a he-goat in case of spasms (cf. É. Benveniste, *Indo-European Language and Society*, London 1973, p. 473); but Greek medicine, which generally believed in the practice of cauterization (cf. V. Di Benedetto, *Il medico e la malattia. La scienza di Ippocrate*, Turin 1986, pp. 167–76), tended to consider as therapeutic, also among other peoples, those practices which entailed burning: cf. e.g. *De Aeribus Aquis Locis* 20, on the Scythians. In fact, the description in terms of the flow of φλέγμα from the head is affected by elaboration of the ethnographic data in the light of Greek medical science, see esp. *De Aer. Aqu. Loc.* 3 and 10; *De Morbo Sacro* 5–6; *De Morbis* I, II, and IV; *De Affect.*; cf. I. M. Lonie, *The Hippocratic Treatises 'On Generation', 'On the Nature of the Child', 'Diseases IV': A Commentary*, Berlin–New York 1981, pp. 277–9. It is possible to think of a mediation on the part of a

Greek source (Hecataeus?), which Herodotus reads with scepticism because he prefers the climatic-type explanation expounded at II 77,3. Cf. Diller, p. 69, n. 107; F. Heinimann, *Nomos und Physis*, Basel 1945, pp. 179–80; G. Wöhrle, *Studien zur Thema der antiken Gesundheit*, Stuttgart 1990, pp. 33–5; Pritchett, p. 88; Thomas, *Herodotus*, pp. 75–101.

188. θυσίαι... αὐτοῦ: parallels for this sacrificial ritual, which must be taken as authentically indigenous and inspired by the need to protect the house, are not known: Neumann, p. 136; Gsell, *Hérodote*, p. 191; Decret–Fantar, p. 260. θύουσι δὲ... Ποσειδέωνι: on Athena, Triton, and Poseidon see note to 180, 1–5. The cult of the sun and moon is testified by Ibn Khaldūn (*Kitāb el-'Ibar* VI 89) for the Berbers of the 14th cent. AD, and is still alive in modern times; as for antiquity, inscriptions with sun and moon symbols on rock-faces in Algeria and Tunisia, Latin inscriptions with dedications to the god *Sol* and to *Diana Augusta Maurorum* (*CIL* VIII 8436), the figures of *Caelestis* and *Versutina*, and various other sources, testify to the flourishing of these cults, which are also close to the corresponding Egyptian (especially Amon in the form of ram) and Punic cults (Baal Hammon and Tanit): see among others Bates, pp. 187–200; R. Basset, *RHR* (1910), 301–5; Gsell, *Hérodote*, p. 185; id., *Histoire* I, pp. 248–53; Picard, pp. 21–5; Vycichl, *Wörterbuch der Myth.* I 2, pp. 648–9, 677–8; Desanges, *Pline*, pp. 467–8; Decret–Fantar, pp. 253–5, 259–61; Camps, *Berbères*, pp. 215–20; E. Fabbricotti, *QAL* XII (1988), 231–3.

189,1–2. τὴν δὲ ἄρα ἐσθῆτα... μετωνόμασαν: on the cult of the Libyan 'Athena' see note to 180, 1–5. In the context of the similarities between the Greek and the Libyan cult, the constant presence of the aegis in traditional depictions of Pallas Athena was an excellent cue for the diffusionistic theories dear to Herodotus. The αἰγίς of Athena was a kind of cloak with fringes, corresponding to the snakes of the Gorgon's head; the root of the term is uncertain, but the derivation from αἴξ = 'goat' soon became prevalent, and may be correct if the aegis was originally a primitive protection made from hides (bibl. and discussion in *Archaeologia Homerica*, I E, Göttingen 1977, pp. 53–6; L. Bodson, *Mélanges P. Lévêque*, IV, Paris 1990, pp. 50–60). The leather garments of the Libyan women ('clad in goat-skins from the upper neck to the back and hips' according to Apollonius Rhodius IV 1348–9) were a sort of small mantle worn on the shoulders and longer at the back: some fragments have been found in Saharan tombs of proto-historic age (Camps, *Aux origines*, pp. 472–6; H. Lhote, *Bull. d'Archéologie Marocaine*, XII (1979–80), 323–54), and leather cloaks appear in some Hellenistic representations from Cyrene (Fabbricotti, art. cit., pp. 221–44, esp. pp. 221–2). The custom of dyeing the skins red using olizarine extracted from madder (*Rubia tinctorum*, abundantly present in the region) is continued by the Berbers; Gsell, *Hérodote*, p. 165.

3. δοκέει δὲ... καλῶς: the ὀλολυγή was the typical cry of Greek women when they invoked a divinity (Athena in Homer, *Il.* VI 301) and at other cultic occasions: see J. Rudhardt, *Notions fondamentales de la pensée religieuse et actes constitutifs du culte dans la Grèce classique*, Geneva 1958, pp. 176–80; L. Deubner, *Kleine Schriften zur classischen Altertumskunde*, Königstein 1981, pp. 607–34. To this day, on the same occasions, Berber women customarily intone a cry, the *you-you* (Gsell, *Hérodote*, p. 160; L. Gernet, *Les Grecs sans miracle*, Paris 1983, pp. 247–57): in connection with the cult of Athena, the idea of a transmission from Libya to the Greeks was easily conceived.   καὶ τέσσερας ... μεμαθήκασι: on the use of quadrigae on the part of the Libyans, cf. chs. 170, 183, 193; on the manner of yoking them, entirely original with respect to the eastern one, J. Spruytte, *AntAfr* XXII (1986), 29–55. The tradition of quadrigae at Cyrene may be influenced by the Libyan model (see note to 170,1), but in a Greek context the quadriga is already known to Homer, and is present in late geometric representations of the 8th cent. (*Archaeologia Homerica*, I F, Göttingen 1968, pp. 22–3, 64–8, 99). The Libyan derivation can be accepted only if relations between Greeks and Libyans are postulated already before the colonization of Cyrenaica (see note to chs. 145–67; G. Camps, *SS* VII (1985), 47–50).

190. θάπτουσι ... ἀποθανέεται: this statement is not entirely correct: in fact, whilst the Greeks buried their dead lying stretched, in the whole of northern Africa palaeo-Berber tombs have yielded bodies which had been laid to rest with legs more or less bent, and in Tripolitania the seated position is still attested in Muslim times; see Gsell, *Hérodote*, pp. 181–3; Camps, *Aux origines*, esp. pp. 467–9; Vycichl, *Wörterbuch der Myth.* I 2, pp. 628–9. At the root of this custom, widespread among various peoples, there is perhaps the fear that the departed may return. Perhaps Herodotus' sources omitted mentioning the bending of the legs in connection with other tribes, whereas they reported it in the case of the Nasamonians, probably because among this tribe the dead were the object of special worship; see ch. 172.   οἰκήματα ... χρέωνται: cf. Hellanicus, *FGrHist* 4 F 67. The parallel which best fits these nomadic dwellings is the tent of the Tebu or of the Tuareg of the Air and of the region of Agadir, which is made of woven mats bound to light wooden structures and easily transported on beasts of burden, whilst the *mapalia* of the Latin sources were heavier structures: after Gsell, *Hérodote*, pp. 177–9, see Camps, art. cit., pp. 53–4 with bibl.

191,1. *Μάξυες*: it is not certain whether the farming *Μάξυες* of Herodotus correspond to the nomadic *Μάζυες* of Hecataeus, *FGrHist* 1 F 334. Their name is reminiscent rather of the *Maxitani* in Justin XVIII 6,1, or of the colony *Maxula* in Pliny, *NH* V 24. All these names, and other similar ones, like the Libyan *Mazaces/ Mazices* and the Berber *Imazigen*, may however be traced back to a common root *MZG*, with a meaning akin to 'to be noble': see Bates, pp. 42–3; Gsell, *Hérodote*, pp. 133–5; Desanges, *Catalogue*, pp. 111–13. More specifically, the personal name *Μάσκυξ* may be traced back to the ethnic *Μάξυες* (O. Masson, *AntAfr* X (1976), 52); it is less certain whether they must be identified with the *mšwš* (Meshwesh) which the Egyptian sources place west of Nubia (J. Osing, *LdÄ* III, col. 1016; reservations in e.g. Gsell, *Histoire* I, p. 354; Chamoux, pp. 55–6; cf. now G. Vittmann, *Enchoria*, XXV (1999), 123–4; Vittmann, pp. 17 and 251, n. 72). οἳ τὰ ἐπὶ δεξιὰ ... χρίονται: the peculiar hairstyle of the Maxyes may be reminiscent of the thick side-plaits of some Libyans in the Egyptian representations (see note to 175,1); whilst the custom, also shared by the neighbouring peoples (ch. 194), of painting themselves with ochre has left traces on the bones of the dead of various tombs in Tunisian and Algerian territory from the palaeolithic onwards (Gsell, *Hérodote*, pp. 160–2; Camps, art. cit., pp. 54–5). φασὶ... ἐκ Τροίης ἀνδρῶν: the theory of a Trojan origin can be compared to analogous traditions concerning e.g. the Elymi (Thuc. VI 2,3) or the Veneti (Strabo XIII 1,53), while according to Lysimachus of Alexandria the Antenoridae came to the Libyan king Amnacus in Cyrenaica (*FGrHist* 382 F 6; cf. Pindar, *Pyth.* 5,82–5). These are, for the most part, propagandistic traditions risen in a colonial context (most recently L. Braccesi, *QAL* XII (1988), 7–14; Pritchett, pp. 39–41; Coppola, pp. 121–38). But it cannot be excluded that in the case of the Maxyes a memory was preserved of the relations between the Meshwesh and the 'peoples of the sea' testified by Egyptian sources for the 2nd millennium (a refinement in Haider, pp. 118–27; cf. also Sallust, *Iug.* 17; Camps, *Berbères*, pp. 19–28; Decret–Fantar, pp. 28–38).

2. ἡ δὲ χώρη αὕτη: some essentially correct considerations on the differing nature of the territory east of the river Triton lead to an *excursus* on the fauna of the region which lasts until ch. 192 and which is followed by a treatment of the fauna of the region of the nomadic Libyans to the east. Leaving aside the excessively schematic division in two areas, and some isolated mistakes, the description is correct: other literary sources, representations, and finds attest that in ancient times there still lived in northern Africa many species which have subsequently become extinct. Cf., on all that follows, Neumann, pp. 152–65; Gsell, *Hérodote*, pp. 96–9; id., *Histoire* I, pp. 100–37; G. Camps, *Bull. Arch. du Comité de Travaux Historiques (B)*, XX–XXI (1984–5), 17–27; id., *SS* VII (1985), 42–5; id., *CRAI* (1990), 35–57.

4. ὄφιες οἱ ὑπερμεγάθεες: on large snakes (pythonids) in the region cf. e.g. Strabo XVII 3,5; Valerius Maximus I 8 ext. 19; Pliny, *NH* VIII 37; Gellius VII 3. λέοντες: lions were present in Algeria, Tunisia, and Morocco as late as the 19th cent.   ἐλέφαντες: cf. among others Aristotle, *Cael.* II 14,298a13; Polybius XII 3,5; Strabo XVII 3,7–8; Gsell, *Histoire* I, pp. 74–81; Desanges, *Pline*, p. 97.   ἄρκτοι: the bears of Numidia were imported to Rome according to Pliny, *NH* VIII 131, (cf. L. Keimer, *BIE* XXXVI (1952–4), 455–8). ἀσπίδες: various species of vipers are omnipresent in the Maghreb; cf. Vitruvius VIII 3,24; note to 192,2.   ὄνοι... ἔχοντες: undoubtedly a variety of antelope of the subfamily *Orycinae*, which is the closest to equines. οἱ κυνοκέφαλοι... ἀκατάψευστα: the ἀκατάψευστα, 'not invented', of the most authoritative codices seems to be contrasting the other animals with those just mentioned; or else, if it refers to animals of the same kind, it is ironic, given the care with which Herodotus attributes to the Libyans the responsibility for the reports on these monstrous animals (the variant ἀκατάψαυστα, 'which cannot be touched' pleased B. de Montfaucon, *Mémoires de l'Académie des Inscriptions et Belles Lettres*, XII (1740), *Histoire*, pp. 170–5; it is transmitted by the codex T and is not otherwise attested in Greek). The 'dog-heads' and the 'headless' have sometimes been understood as being monkeys, and the same can go for the 'wild men and women' (cf. also Hanno, *Periplus* 18, *GGM* I, 13–14; Paus. II 21,6).

In northern Africa there were, however, only macaques (cf. ch. 194): may the Libyans have had vague reports of the larger primates of the southern regions? It is also possible to think that by these terms they referred to peoples which to their eyes were more primitive (the *cynocephali* were masked men according to Vycichl, *Wörterbuch der Myth.* I 2, p. 637; while the *acephali*, already identified as the *Blemyes* of Nubia by Mela I 48 and Pliny, *NH* V 46, were men who wore a wide *burnus* according to J. Desanges, *GHA* II, p. 435). But they may also be just monsters conjured up by the imagination: the 'headless' were already known as στερνόφθαλμοι to Aeschylus, fr. 441 Radt; while Ctesias locates the 'dog-heads' in India, and Pliny, *NH* V 46, lists an impressive collection of monsters, whose memory will remain alive throughout antiquity and the Middle Ages (cf. G. Knaak, *Hermes*, XXV (1890), 457–60; M. Fenikowski, *Eos*, XXXIX (1938), 183–90; R. Shafer, *Historia*, XIII (1964), 499–503; Desanges, *Pline*, pp. 475–8; K. Karttunen, *Arctos*, XVIII (1984), 31–6; P. Daffinà, in *Giovanni di Pian di Carpine, Storie dei Mongoli*, Spoleto 1989, pp. 437–9; Romm, pp. 77–80).

192,1. πύγαργοι ... βουβάλιες: various species of Antilopines: probably the *Gazella dama*, the common gazelle (*Gazella dorcas*), and the bubal (*Bubalis mauretanica*).   ὄνοι ... πίνουσι: wild asses (onagers) were widespread, and widely employed as beasts of burden before the introduction of the camel; their resistance to thirst could be appreciated along the Saharan caravan routes; cf. B. B. Shaw, *BIFAN* XLI (1979), 706.   ὄρυες ... ἐστι: these animals with long horns are undoubtedly antelopes, identical to the *oryx* in Pliny, *NH* X 201: perhaps a species of *Oryx*, provided with long horns with a single curvature, or the *Addax nasomaculatus*, with horns curved several times (see Pliny, *NH* XI 124). The horns were used as arms (πήχεες) in the making of lyres or citherns, but the sentence is not entirely clear (on the syntax, cf. III 98,3): it can be read both with τοῖσι Φοίνιξι = 'by the Phoenicians', or τοῖσι φοίνιξι = 'for the *phoinikes*', the name of a stringed instrument according to Aristotle, *Prob.* 918b8 and Athenaeus XIV 636b, 637a–b (who cites Ephorus and Scammon in support of its Phoenician origin). The second interpretation has perhaps the advantage of making explicit the fact that a musical instrument is what is being talked about, given that πήχεες, whose primary meaning is 'elbows, lower arms', is not of itself univocal. In the Phoenician sphere a kind of cithern whose arms have the appearance of single-curved horns is depicted as early as the 13th–12th cent. BC on an ivory from Megiddo (cf. e.g. *I Fenici*, ed. S. Moscati, Milan 1988, pp. 36–7); but there are various kinds of 'Syrian' and Phoenician cithers; see, in general, M. Guillemin and J. Duchesne, *AC* IV (1935), 117–24; M. Wegner, *Die Musikinstrumenten des Alten Orient*, Münster 1950, pp. 34–7; S. Michaelides, *The Music of Ancient Greece: An Encyclopaedia*, London 1978, p. 250; M. Maas and J. M. Snyder, *Stringed Instruments of Ancient Greece*, New Haven–London 1989, pp. 145–7, 232, n. 98 (cf. also Lucian, *Dial. Mar.* I 4).

2. βασσάρια: 'small foxes', according to Hesychius β 306 Latte: it is the desert fox, the *fennec*. According to Hesychius it is a Libyan word, but similar terms appear in various Greek dialects, so that the statement may be an autoschediasm

(C. Dobias-Lalou, *QAL* XII (1988), 90; Dobias-Lalou, pp. 281 and 284). ὕαιναι...ἄγρυοι: hyenas and porcupines were widespread in the region and are represented on mosaics from Roman times; the 'wild goats' were probably mouflons. δίκτυες...βόρυες: what the δίκτυες and βόρυες might be is far from clear: according to Hesychius δ 1839 Latte, δίκτυς is the Laconic word for ἰκτῖνος, 'kite' (is Herodotus drawing from the Dorian Cyreneans? The kite migrates to North Africa during the winter). Jackals (the 'wolves' of other ancient sources) and large felines (panthers, but also cheetahs) were at that time abundant in North Africa. κροκόδειλοι...ἐμφερέστατοι: the varan of the desert (*Varanus arenarius*); cf. II 69,3. στρουθοὶ κατάγαιοι: still Synesius, *Epis.* 133,67 Casini, attests the presence in Cyrenaica of ostriches, which have disappeared from northern Africa only in recent times: see H. Camps-Fabrier, *La disparition de l'autruche en Afrique du Nord*, Algiers 1963, esp. pp. 23–7 (cf. ch. 175). The adjective κατάγαιος, 'terrestrial', serves to distinguish the ostrich from the στρουθός = 'sparrow'. ὄφιες...ἔχοντες: not the horned viper (*Cerastes cornutus*) which has two horns (cf. II 74), but rather the puff adder (*Bitis arietans*): cf. G. Camps, *CRAI* (1990), 51. πλὴν...οὔκ ἐστι: the statement (repeated by Aristotle, *Hist. An.* VIII 28, 606a6–7; Pliny, *NH* VII 120 and 228; Helianus, *Nat. An.* XVII 10) is incorrect; see Gsell, *Histoire* I, pp. 115–18.

3. μυῶν...ἐχινέες: cf. Aristotle, *De Mir. Ausc.* 27. The name ἐχινέες is similar to ἐχῖνοι, 'hedgehogs', described in Cyrenaica by Aelian, *Nat. An.* XV 26. δίποδες is also a Greek name ('bipeds') which makes it possible to recognize the 'jumping mouse' of the desert, or jerboa (*Iaculus iaculus*), widespread in Tripolitania and Cyrenaica. The Libyan name ζεγέριες may be preserved in the Berber of Awjilah *éqzer*, 'mouse' (U. Paradisi, *PP* XVII (1962), 201–5; id., *RSO* XXXVIII (1963), 61–5). Moreover, the word *azgar* is attested in Berber, with the meaning 'country, highland', whence might have originated the equivalence with βουνός = 'hill'. But it is also possible to suppose a connection with the root ZGR, 'red': it would then be a 'red mouse' (G. Camps, *SS* VII (1985), 43–4; Gsell, *Hérodote*, p. 66, pointed to the plant called ζίγαρ in Punic and βουνίον in Greek, 'belonging to the hill', according to Dioscorides IV 123). Might then the characteristic red colour of the highland in the region of Cyrene justify a connection between ZGR = 'red' and βουνός = 'hill'? (Cf. 199,1; by 'Greeks' we must here understand the Cyreneans; see Aly, p. 133). See now Dobias-Lalou, pp. 287–8. At any rate, the animal must in all likelihood be identified with the gundi (*Ctenodactylus gundi*), a tawny-coloured rodent common on the craggy hills of the desert; see Z. Kadar, *ACD* VIII (1972), 16. εἰσὶ δὲ...ὁμοιότατοι: Strabo XVII 3,4 speaks of a γαλῆ in what is now Morocco, probably intending the genet, widespread in northern Africa as well as in Spain. Specimens of the Spanish genet, or a similar species, had perhaps been imported to Greece from Tartessus, so that Herodotus could allude to them as to a well-known animal (J. M. Alonso-Nuñez, *AC* LXI (1987), 248; 'the Tartessian weasel' is cited also by Aelian, *Var. Hist.* XIV 4; Aristophanes, *Ran.* 475; Suidas γ 29a.): in fact, the Greeks normally used weasels and such animals to hunt mice. ὅσον...ἐξικέσθαι: cf. I 171,2; II 34,1; IV 16,2. The essential truthfulness of this information confirms the depth of the research, which is founded on

an inquiry among Cyreneans and Libyans; and the sentence proudly seals a list which, bunching together as it does one after another the names of the most diverse animals, must have been greatly effective.

193. Ζαύηκες: the Zaueces were cited already by Hecataeus, *FGrHist* 1 F 336, but they do not appear again in later authors. Their exact location is uncertain, in relation to that of the following peoples: see Desanges, *Catalogue*, pp. 142–3, and note to ch. 194, cf. chs. 170, 180, 183, 189.

194. Γύζαντες: the decision between the variants Γύζαντες and Ζύγαντες is not an easy one. Hecataeus, *FGrHist* 1 F 337, mentions a place called Ζυγαντίς. The source is Stephanus of Byzantium, s.v., who adds that its inhabitants, the Ζύγαντες, were producers of honey, citing on the matter Eudoxus of Cnidus; but Apollonius, *Historia Mirabilis* 38, cites the same text of Eudoxus (fr. 323 Lasserre) and attributes to it the reading Γύζαντες; also Γύζαντες is the Herodotean reading according to Stephanus of Byzantium, s.v., who, on the other hand, declares that the more correct form is Βύζαντες (cf. also Eustathius, *Comm. in Dionysii Periegetica* 803, *GGM* II, p. 357). Perhaps also Eudoxus read Γύζαντες (and Stephanus of Byzantium, s.v., Ζυγαντίς, may have wrongly assimilated it to the toponym in Hecataeus). At any rate, Ζυγαντίς/Ζύγαντες can be associated with a *Ziguensis mons*, the Djebel Zaghouan, and with *Zeugitana*, which, in Roman times, was the name of the region corresponding to northern Tunisia; whilst southern Tunisia, from the Gulf of Hammamet to the Gulf of Gabès, was called *Byzacium* or *Byzacena* (hence the Βύζαντες of Stephanus of Byzantium). Moreover, the root Ζυγαντίς, *Ziguensis*, and *Zeugitana* (perhaps *ZWG* = 'to be red': Camps, *Berbères*, pp. 88–90; or *ZG* = 'forest': J. Peyras and P. Trousset, *AntAfr* XXIV (1988), 187–8), may be preserved in the Herodotean Ζαύηκες: whilst Γύζαντες can be associated with the *pagus Gunzuzi* in the plain of Fahs (G. Picard *et al.*, *CRAI* (1963), 124–30; for a connection with the name of the Libyan god *Gurzil* and the toponym Γύρζα/Γούρζα see Ch. Daniels, *The Garamantes of Southern Libya*, Stoughton 1970, p. 33) for which Βύζαντες/ *Byzacium* may be an alternative phonetic rendering. In sum, Zaueces and Gyzantes, together with the Maxyans with whom they share the use of ochre (191,1), lived on the eastern coast of Tunisia, though it is difficult to determine precisely their respective territories: discussion in Neumann, *Nordafrika*, pp. 61–4; Gsell, *Hérodote*, pp. 135–9; Desanges, *Catalogue*, pp. 97–8. ἐν τοῖσι ... ποιέειν: on African melliferous bees, cf. Pliny, *NH* XI 33; while, to this day, the inhabitants of Djebel Ousselat, north of Kairouan, are renowned producers of artificial honey (G. Camps, *SS* VII (1985), 54; cf. also VII 31). ἐν τοῖσι ὄρεσι: the mountains populated with monkeys correspond to the Zeugitana ridge, with the Djebel Zaghouan on its north-eastern margin: on the presence of monkeys in Tunisia at the time see Gsell, *Histoire* I, p. 109.

195–6. As early as the 6th cent. BC Carthaginian supremacy prevented the Greeks from collecting first-hand information on the north-western coast of Africa (see note to 43,1). What little Herodotus knows about it is drawn from the Carthaginians and is vague and confused.

195,1–2. κατὰ τούτους...χρυσοῦ: the Island of Cyrauis is subsequently mentioned only by Stephanus of Byzantium, who, though with a minimal graphic variant, follows Herodotus (s.v. Κύραυνις). The position and the description of the island (a perimeter of approximately 35 km.; cf. also Pliny, *NH* V 41) suggest an identification with Chergui, the largest among the Kerkenah islands, opposite Sphax, whose ancient name is generally Kerkina. However, this island is a fair distance away from the coast: διαβατόν would then have to be understood as meaning 'that can be easily reached by sea'; if on the other hand, as is more natural, it means 'that can be reached by wading', then we must think of a confusion with Jerba (Gsell, *Hérodote*, pp. 85–7), or that the level of the Mediterranean Sea was lower at that time (Camps, *SS* p. 39, n. 6). The cultivation of olives and vines may also find confirmation in Jerba; at any rate, the oleaster is present in northern Africa from the early palaeolithic, and the cultivated form was perhaps introduced in Tunisia by the Carthaginians (H. Camps-Fabrier, *L'olivier et l'huile dans l'Afrique romaine*, Algiers 1953, pp. 11–13). The Carthaginians may also be responsible for the implantation of the cultivated vine, which probably came from Egypt (E. Catani, in *Cyrenaica*, pp. 145–6). While there are some salty quagmires (*sabkha*) on the island of Chergui, it is geologically improbable that there ever was gold; and already in Niebuhr's day it was hypothesized that Herodotus (or his Carthaginian sources, in order to disorientate the Greeks) confused Chergui with an island positioned on the Atlantic gold route to which Herodotus seems to be alluding in ch. 196 (perhaps the Kerne of Scylax 112, *GGM* I, p. 93): see e.g. Neumann, *Nordafrika*, pp. 64–71. Cf. also Achilles Tatius II 14, 9–10.

2–4. ταῦτα...ἀληθείῃ: in response to a report which is hard to believe, the mechanism of analogy with an acknowledged fact springs in to action (cf. F. Haible, 'Herodot und die Wahrheit', Diss. Tübingen 1962, pp. 115–18; C. Darbo-Peschanski, *Le Discours du particulier. Essai sur l'enquête hérodotéenne*, Paris 1987, pp. 150–1). In fact, the analogy is here rather superficial and aimed only at demonstrating that everything is possible; purely superficial is also the comparison, often cited by commentators, with the vessels made of feathers which between the 18th and 19th cents. the explorer Mungo Park saw still in use in various African auriferous regions for the transport of extracted gold. The 'lake of tar' in the Ionic island of Zacynthus was a famous wonder, mentioned by several ancient sources (cf. Ctesias, *FGrHist* 668 F 45, 20; Eudoxus, fr. 368 Lasserre = Antigonus, *Mirabilia* 169; Vitruvius VIII 3,8; Pliny, *NH* XXXV 178; Aelian, *Var. Hist.* XIII 16; Dioscorides I 73), and a stop not to be missed by tourists of the past centuries, who confirm that still in modern times bitumen was sometimes extracted in the manner described by Herodotus (cf., among others, E. Dodwell, *Classical and Topographical Tour Through Greece*, London 1819, pp. 81–2). It is the lake of Kerí, on the western extremity of the Gulf of Laganá, which to this date produces bitumen; and at a small distance from the coast two springs leave oily patches on the surface of the sea: see Müller I, pp. 915–18.   Πιερικῆς πίσσης: the pitch of Pieria (a coastal region of Macedonia) was produced with tar extracted from the forests of

Mt Olympus, and was the best in Greece according to Pliny, *NH* XIV 128; cf. *Geoponica* VI 5,1.

196,1. χρυσὸν: the exact location on the north-western coast of Africa where the Carthaginians gathered their gold is uncertain. Gold is found already in southern Morocco: E. Goebel, *Die Westküste Afrikas im Altertum*, Leipzig 1887, p. 72; for the findings of Ionic-Attic amphorae from the 7th cent. BC in the area of Mogador/Essaouira see H.G. Niemeyer, *JRGZ* XXXI (1984), 29–30. But some have thought also of the Rio de Oro (the coastal region of the western Sahara) or of the region of Nouadhibou (northern Mauretania), or of Senegambia. Moreover, the connection between such trade and the expedition of Hanno is uncertain, the latter being the founder of a series of colonies beyond the Pillars of Heracles as far as the island of Kerne, indicated as an auriferous area by Palephatus, *Incredibilia* 31 (variously identified, it must perhaps be located in the proximity of Saquia al Hamra, in the northern part of the western Sahara; cf. Scylax 112, *GGM* I, pp. 93–4): various points of view in Gsell, *Histoire* I, pp. 468–523; id., *Hérodote*, pp. 239–40; J. Carcopino, *Le Maroc antique*, Paris 1943, pp. 73–163; Desanges, *Recherches*, pp. 39–86; Peretti, pp. 373–417. 'Silent barter' was universally diffused in frontier areas, where verbal communication was impossible and diffidence towards newcomers rendered direct contact difficult: cf. e.g. Mela III 60; Pliny, *NH* VI 88; *Periplus Maris Erythraei* 65, *GGM* I, pp. 304–5 = pp. 21–2 Casson; Philostratus, *Vita Apollonii* 6,2; Ammianus Marcellinus XXIII 6,68; Solinus 50,2 ff.; Cosmas Indicopleustes II 51 ff. and 139. See in general P. J. H. Grierson, *The Silent Trade*, Edinburgh 1903; and—against the hypercritical doubts of P. F. de Moraes Farias, *History in Africa*, I (1974), 9–24, and correcting the exclusively economic interpretation of M. Giacchero, *Studi di Storia Antica in memoria di L. de Regibus*, Genoa 1969, pp. 93–8—cf. the notations in terms of initial exchange of gifts of N. F. Parise, *QAL* VIII (1976), 75–80; A. Giardina, *Studi storici*, II (1986), 277–302; R. Danieli, *Aevum*, LXV (1991), 25–8.

197–9. The formula 'they did not care about the king of the Medes', linking back to 167,3 by ring composition, ought to mark the resumption of the narrative of the Persian expedition; but Herodotus remembers that he has still (ἔτι) something to say on Libya, and he adds, in a rather mechanical manner, one last aside: the impression given is that of a correction to the work in progress (cf. ch. 63; Introduction, p. 570).

197,2. τοσόνδε … ἐπήλυδες: cf. II 32,4. Αἰθίοπες, 'burnt faces', is, like the Arabic *Sūdān*, a generic name for the dark-skinned populations of the south, as opposed to the Europoid Libyans (see J. D. Georgacas, *Siculorum Gymnasium*, XXXI (1978), 309–11; note to III 17–25). The Old Testament makes the analogous distinction between *Lubîm* and *Kūsh* (2 Chron. 16: 8).

198,1. Κίνυπος: the region which took its name from the Cinyps = wadi Khaam (cf. ch. 175) was in fact better irrigated and more favourable to agriculture than the rest of Tripolitania (where the land was not 'black' but reddish and sandy; cf. II 12), as demonstrated, among other things, by the efforts made by the Romans to further improve it with hydraulic works; but the picture delineated by Herodotus (cf. Scylax 109, *GGM* I, pp. 84–5; Ovid, *Pont.* II 7,25; Mela I 37; Claudian, *In Eutr.* I 405) seems exaggerated, perhaps due to an idealization connected with Greek colonial ambitions (cf. chs. 178–9; V 42): see Gsell, *Hérodote*, pp. 89–91; id., *Histoire* I, pp. 69–70; Desanges, *Pline*, pp. 257–9; O. Longo, *QS* XXIV (1986), 24–5. Also the description of the region of Euesperides/Benghazi is not untrue but rather emphatic: see Chamoux, pp. 226–7, 230. On the fertility of the Babylonian territory see I 193.

199,1. ἔχει... τρεῖς ὥρας: the three levels of the Cyrenean territory are well described: after the narrow coastal strip, the Jabal al-Akhdar rises on two steps, the one with a height of 200–300 m., the other of about 600 m., and the lower step is furrowed by *widian*, creating the impression of different hills (βουνοί: see following note); cf. Chamoux, pp. 14–15; Laronde, p. 459. The varying altitude made the fruits ripen at different times, making it possible to use the same workforce for several harvests: see Chamoux, pp. 230–1; D. L. Johnson, *Jabal al Akhdar, Cyrenaica*, Chicago 1973; Applebaum, pp. 74–129; A. Laronde, in *Cyrenaica*, pp. 183–91; on agriculture in Cyrene in general, Ch. H. Coster, *Studies in Roman Economic and Social History in Honor of Alan Chester Johnson*, Princeton 1951, pp. 3–26; A. Laronde, *LibStud* XX (1989), 127–34; id., *CRAI* XCVI (1996), 503–27; A. Jähne, *Klio*, LXX (1988), 145–66 (cf. also D. White, *QAL* XII (1988), 67–84; C. Trombetti, *Siris* VI (2005), 37–61; and Luni, pp. 127–32 and 147–70 on the cult of Demeter; and note to 164,2).   τὰ βουνοὺς καλέουσι: despite the statement by Aelius Dionysius β 17 Erbse, that βουνός is a 'barbarian' word, here it appears in 192,3 as the Greek translation of a Libyan term. It can, therefore, be supposed that it was a Cyrenean, or at any rate Doric, word which was soon absorbed by the other dialects (already Aeschylus, *Supp.* 117 and 776, uses the word βουνίς, which derives from it: a discussion in P. Chantraine, *Dictionnaire étymologique de la langue grecque. Histoire des mots* I, Paris 1983³, p. 190); but it is difficult to think of it as a Libyan term (or an Egyptian one: Bernal, p. 456, n. 82). However, by indicating the denomination βουνοί as Cyrenean, Herodotus perhaps wanted not so much to furnish a gloss exclusively belonging to one particular dialect as to indicate the idiosyncratic way in which the Cyreneans designated a singular geographical phenomenon such as the step furrowed by *widian*, which lacked a specific name in Greek, with a more general term ('hills') (thus now Dobias-Lalou, pp. 288–9); on this particular type of 'gloss' see Aristotle, *Poet.* 25, 1461a10 ff.; H. Diels, *Neue Jahrb. für klassische Philologie*, XXV (1910), 14; K. Latte, *Philologus*, LXXX (1925), 157.

200,1. οἱ δὲ... Βάρκην: on the communication routes between Egypt and Cyrene see M. Luni, *QAL* XI (1980), 130–7.   ἐπαγγελλόμενοι... λόγους: cf. 167,2.

2–3. ἐνθαῦτα... Βαρκαῖοι: the digging of galleries by those besieging a city, and of counter-galleries by those defending it, was a common expedient throughout antiquity: see the full treatment given by Aeneas Tacticus 37 (who also cites the Herodotean passage), and the discussion by M. Bettalli, *Enea Tattico, La difesa di* *una città assediata*, Pisa 1990, pp. 327–9. For the episode of the shield see also Polybius XXI 28,7–8; Vitruvius X 16.

201,1. ποιέει τοιάδε: cf. Polyaenus VII 34. For verbal tricks of this kind, which are typical of popular tales (Aly, p. 135), cf. ch. 156 (as a stratagem of war, e.g. Thuc. III 34,3; Polyaenus VI 22); the formulae of impossibility common in oaths lent themselves easily to such misunderstandings; see note on III 151,2. On Herodotus' interest in the theme of deception see J. S. Catlin, 'The Concept of Deception and Related Motifs in the "Histories" of Herodotus', Diss., Chapel Hill 1969, esp. p. 11; M. Dorati, *QS* XXXVIII (1993), 65–84.

2. ἀξίην: the tribute, payment of which had evidently ceased with the death of the king loyal to Darius (ὑποτελέειν is a technical term): cf. note to 167,3.

202,1. τοὺς μέν … τεῖχος: impalement is a typical Persian punishment (see note to 43,6), and also the display of mutilated parts must have seemed barbarous to the Greeks (cf. IX 78–9): note on III 125,10. Thus, Pheretime assumes cruel, witchlike traits (Aly, p. 135), in anticipation of the bad end to which she will come.

2. ὅσοι … Φερετίμη: on the Battiads in Barce see ch. 160.

203,1–3. τοὺς ὧν δή … Αἴγυπτον: according to Menecles of Barce, *FGrHist* 270 F 5, and Polyaenus VIII 47, Pheretime and the Persians took possession of Cyrene, but this may be simply a generic and inexact version (differently F. Jacoby in the commentary to the fragment of Menecles). In fact, it is not impossible that the Persians attempted to remain in the territory of Cyrene, perhaps with the aim of subjugating the Libyan tribes, and that this created frictions with the city (Noshy, p. 58; cf. note to 167,3): some have related to these Persian activities the burial of some beheaded statues of the end of the 6th cent., which may have resulted from Persian acts of vandalism (R. G. Goodchild, *Libya Antiqua*, III–IV (1966–7), 190–7). However, the position of Cyrene in the Herodotean narrative is not entirely clear and is perhaps affected by the wish to deny any compromise with Pheretime and the Persians, while, in actual fact, the restoration of the Battiads in the city with Battus IV is an indication that Cyrene did not remain wholly detached (cf. B. M. Mitchell, *JHS* LXXXVI (1966), 103–5; see note to 205; Introduction, p. 569). To the anti-tyrannical and anti-Persian tendency of Herodotus' Cyrenean sources must then be ascribed the reference to the oracle which prescribed that the city gates should be opened, which concession was, however, counterbalanced by the subsequent refusal, and the reference to the god-sent panic which seized the Persians (cf. VII 10ε; 43,2; VIII 38; on the panic factor in the ancient armies, cf. Aeneas Tacticus 27; Bettalli, op. cit., pp. 292–4). On the contrary, the concession of transit through the territory and of viaticum, could be mentioned without scruple, since it was not considered compromising by the Greeks of the 5th cent.; D. J. Mosley, *RIDA* XX (1973), 161–9; V. Alonso Troncoso, *Neutralidad y Neutralismo en la Guerra del Peloponeso (431–404 a.C.)*, Madrid 1987, pp. 79–115.　　**Διὸς Λυκαίου ὄχθον:** the cult was of Arcadian origin, perhaps connected to the arrival of new colonists under Battus II (ch. 159) or to the activity of Demonax (ch. 161); the hill is probably the one to the east of the ancient city where stand the remains of the great temple of Zeus: see Chamoux, pp. 320–39; Goodchild, pp. 149–55; Stucchi, *passim*.

4. παραλαβόντες . . . ἀπίκοντο: here emerges the contrast with the Libyans which was implied but never until now made explicit in the narrative: see note to 167,3.

204. οὗτος . . . ἦλθε: Herodotus takes one step back, in demonstration of how the narrative is fragmented (see Introduction, pp. 560 ff.). The Persians must have gone as far as Euesperides during or after the siege of Barce, and this appears to imply that their aims went beyond the capture of the city; see note to 167,3. For possible archaeological traces of the passage of the Persians, B. Jones, in *Cyrenaica*, p. 32; J. Lloyd, ibid., p. 53. τοὺς δὲ . . . Βακτρίη: deportation following conquest was a favoured tool of Eastern monarchs. On the deportations by the Persian kings (cf. e.g. III 149; V 14–15; 17,1; 23,1; 98; VI 18–20; 119; Ctesias, *FGrHist* 688 F 13,10; Diod. XVII 110,4), see D. Ambaglio, *RIL* CIX (1975), 378–83; J. M. Cook, *CHI* II, pp. 285–6; note to III 93,6 and note to 149,1; R. Kulesza, *Eos*, LXXXII (1994), 221–50; Briant, *Histoire*, pp. 446–7, 521–2, 771–2 = ET pp. 433–4, 505–6, 751–2. The locality of Barce in Bactria is otherwise unknown.

205. οὐ μὴν οὐδὲ . . . γίνονται: why Pheretime, having won, should immediately return to Egypt (thus also Menecles of Barce, *FGrHist* 270 F 5, and Polyaenus VIII 47), is far from clear. The reactions which must have ensued on the cruel punishment of Barce may have made it advisable for Pheretime to abandon the scene, leaving the sovereignty to the less compromised nephew Battus IV and retiring to private life among the Persians; but the doubt remains that it might have been the Cyreneans who kept silent on a possible permanence of Pheretime in Cyrene, alleging that she died an exemplary and miserable death on foreign soil (cf. Introduction, p. 569). Pheretime pays for her excesses by virtue of the same criterion which, according to Herodotus, spelt the downfall of Troy (II 120,5): it is an application of the principle of divine φθόνος (see General Introduction, pp. 38 f.; Harrison, pp. 102–21), but with a moral connotation which is highlighted by the manner of her death. 'Phthiriasis' can, in fact, be considered a true illness, a form of scabies or at any rate an infection caused by the larvae of mites (and not by 'lice'), but starting with this Herodotean passage, ancient historians will turn it—at times with scarce regard for truth—into a *topos* for the repugnant death of a negative character: see A. Keaveney and J. A. Madden, *SO* LVII (1982), 87–99, and, more fully, Th. Africa, *Class Ant* I (1982), 1–17. ἡ μὲν δὴ . . . ἐς Βαρκαίους: in solemn summarizing formulae, the mention of the full name of the character, including the patronymic, is common and effective (cf. e.g. I 45,3; III 66,2; 88,1; VI 71,1; VII 186,2; VIII 140α,1). Also in this instance it has been suggested that Βάττου may be a patronymic, hypothesizing that Pheretime was daughter of Battus II (for marriages to blood-relations among the Battiads see 164,4); but it is more naturally a genitive of possession indicating her husband (Battus III): cf. e.g. Euripides, *Or.* 1686–7; Aristophanes, *Eq.* 449; *Eccl.* 46, 49, 51; *Lys.* 270; in Latin, Virgil, *Aen.* III 319; Tacitus, *Ann.* IV 11,2, etc.